What the customer wants:

I want a car that's built right.

I want dealer service that is fair, reliable, and pleasant.

I want some career skills that I can sell so I can afford to buy a car!

Building a quality car and having it serviced well are the essence of operations management (OM). Providing you with OM concepts that can help you in your career is the essence of this book.

American industry has entered this decade with a dramatically changed view of manufacturing and service operations' role in attaining competitive advantage. In the 70s and 80s, many domestic companies saw their market share decline due to their inability to compete with foreign firms in terms of product design, cost, or quality. Theories to explain this development span cultural differences, government macroeconomic policies, merger mania, neglect of human resources, insufficient investment in technology and R&D, and an excess of lawyers and/or MBAs. Whatever the cause, most experts now agree that world-class performance by operations in delivering high-quality, cost-competitive products and services is essential to survival in today's global economy.

3

Helping students understand the fundamental concepts and techniques necessary for attaining world-class performance in manufacturing and service operations is the main objective of this book. Besides its importance to corporate competitiveness, reasons for studying this field are

1. *A business education is incomplete without an understanding of modern approaches to managing operations.* Every organization produces some product or service so students must be exposed to modern approaches for doing this effectively. Moreover, hiring organizations now expect business graduates to speak knowledgeably about many issues in the field. While this has long been true in manufacturing, it is becoming equally important in services, both public and private. For example, "reinventing government" initiatives draw heavily on total quality management, business process reengineering, and just-in-time delivery—concepts that fall under the OM umbrella.

2. *Operations management provides a systematic way of looking at organizational processes.* OM uses analytical thinking to deal with real world problems. It sharpens our understanding of the world around us, whether we are talking about how to compete with Japan or how many lines to have at the bank teller's window.

3. *Operations management presents interesting career opportunities.* These can be in direct supervision of operations or in staff positions in OM specialties such as materials management and quality assurance. In addition, consulting firms regularly recruit individuals with strong OM capabilities to work in such areas as process reengineering and computer-based inventory systems.

4. *The concepts and tools of OM are widely used in managing other functions of a business.* All managers have to plan work, control quality, and ensure productivity of individuals under their supervision. Other employees must know how operations work to effectively perform their jobs. (See insert, "OM and Other Business Specialties.")

OM and Other Business Specialties

Accountants need to understand the basics of inventory management, capacity utilization, and labor standards to develop accurate cost data, perform audits, and prepare financial reports. Cost accountants in particular must be aware of how just-in-time (JIT) and computer-integrated manufacturing (CIM) work.

Financial managers can use inventory and capacity concepts to judge the need for capital investments, to forecast cash flow, and to manage current assets. Further, there is a mutual concern between OM and finance in specific decisions such as make-or-buy and plant expansion and/or relocation.

Marketing specialists need to understand what operations can do relative to meeting customer due dates, product customization, and new product introduction. In service industries, marketing and production often take place simultaneously, so marketing and OM have overlapping interests.

Personnel specialists must know how jobs are designed, the relationship between standards and incentive plans, and the types of production skills required of the direct workforce.

MIS specialists often install operations information systems that they themselves design or that are developed as off-the-shelf software by computer companies. A major business application of computers is in production control.

Entrepreneurs often fail because they run out of working capital due to poor production planning and inventory management. (Need we say more?)

PRODUCTION AND OPERATIONS MANAGEMENT

Manufacturing and Services

PRODUCTION AND OPERATIONS MANAGEMENT
Manufacturing and Services

Seventh Edition

Richard B. Chase
University of Southern California

Nicholas J. Aquilano
University of Arizona

IRWIN
Chicago • Bogotá • Boston • Buenos Aires • Caracas
London • Madrid • Mexico City • Sydney • Toronto

©RICHARD D. IRWIN, INC., 1973, 1977, 1981, 1985, 1989, 1992, and 1995.

Senior sponsoring editor: Richard T. Hercher, Jr.
Developmental editor: Gail Korosa
Marketing manager: Brian Kibby
Project editor: Stephanie M. Britt
Production supervisor: Bob Lange
Designer: Mercedes Santos/Maureen McCutcheon
Cover designer: Katherine Farmer
Cover illustration: Carlos Alejandro
Graphics supervisor: Heather Burbridge
Compositor: The Clarinda Co.
Typeface: 10/12 Times Roman
Printer: Von Hoffmann Press, Inc.

Library of Congress Cataloging-in-Publication Data

Chase, Richard B.
    Production and operations management : manufacturing services /
Richard B. Chase, Nicholas J. Aquilano.—7th ed.
        p.   cm.
    Includes index.
    ISBN 0-256-14023-5 ISBN 0-256-16728-1 (instructor's ed.) ISBN
    0-256-16546-7 (int'l. student's ed.)
    1. Production management.   I. Aquilano, Nicholas J.   II. Title.
TS155.C424   1995
    658.5—dc20   94–31409

To our wives
Harriet and Nina
and to our children
Laurie, Andy, Glenn, and Rob
Don, Kara, and Mark

Preface

Operations management (OM) has seen a revolution in recent years, becoming a topic of critical importance in business today. Demands for quality, time-based competition, and international production have demonstrated that superior management of the operations function is vital to the survival of the firm. An understanding of OM strategy and its function is a necessary part of any good business education.

The field of operations management ranges from high-tech manufacturing to high-touch services so we have tried to balance the treatment of the manufacturing and service aspects. To emphasize the importance of services, a logo appears in the text margin next to service discussions. Our aim is to cover the latest and most important issues facing OM managers as well as the basic tools and techniques, and to provide examples of leading-edge companies and practices. We have done our best to make the book interesting reading. We hope you enjoy it.

ACKNOWLEDGMENTS

Several very talented scholars have made major contributions to specific chapters in the book. We are pleased to thank

Ravi Behara of Stephen F. Austin State University (Business Process Reengineering, Facility Location, and Strategic Capacity Planning).

Louis R. Chase, editor extraordinair and Shakespeare expert (several chapters).

Marilyn Helms of the University of Tennessee at Chattanooga (Operations Strategy and Competitiveness, and Just-in-Time Systems).

Michael J. Maggard of Northeastern University (Service Design).

David O'Donnell of the University of Southern California (Project Management).

"Raj" Rajagopalan of the University of Southern California (Technology Management).

Alex Zhang of the University of Southern California (Simulation).

Special thanks to Ross L. Fink of Bradley University and Jack Yurkiewicz of Pace University, who each solved all of the examples and problems and checked our answers for accuracy, and also colleagues at USC Warren Erikson, Richard D. McBride, and K. Ravi Kumar.

Thomas Foster of Boise State University prepared the Instructor's Manual. Phillip Fry, also of Boise State University, prepared the Test Bank. Marilyn Helms of the University of Tennessee at Chattanooga revised the Study Guide. These supplements are a great deal of work to write and we appreciate their efforts, which make teaching the course easier for everyone who uses the text.

We also thank the following reviewers for their many thoughtful suggestions for this edition: Joseph Blackburn, Vanderbilt University; James Blocher, Indiana University; Jim Browne, New York University; Farzaneh Fazel, Illinois State University; Lissa Galbraith, Florida State University; Dennis Geyer, Golden Gate University; Stephen Huxley, University of San Francisco; Yunus Kathawala, Eastern Illinois University; Doan Modianos, Bradley University; Winter Nie, Colorado State University; Roderick Reasor, Virginia Polytechnic Institute and State University; Powell Robinson, Texas A&M University; and Jerry Wei, University of Notre Dame.

We once again thank those individuals whose input over the past editions has helped the book evolve to its present form: Wayne Cunningham, University of Scranton; Edward Gillenwater, University of Mississippi; Satish Mehra, Memphis State University; Graham Morbey, University of Massachusetts at Amherst; R. Natarajan, Tennessee Technological University; Fred Raafat, San Diego State University; Edward Rosenthal, Temple University; David Booth, Kent State University; Thomas Cywood, University of Chicago; Mike Martin, Dalhousie University; James Perry, George Washington University; Dan Rinks, Louisiana State University; Raj Srivastavo, Marquette University; Robert Trend, University of Virginia; Everette Adam, University of Missouri–Columbia; Lawrence Bennigson, Harvard University; John G. Carlson, University of Southern California; Amiya K. Chakravarty, University of Wisconsin–Milwaukee; Joel Corman, Suffolk University; Robert B. Fetter, Yale University; William A. Fischer, University of North Carolina; Dale R. Flowers, Case Western University; Carter Franklin III, Houston Baptist University; Oliver Galbraith III, California State University–San Diego; Stanley J. Garstka, University of Chicago; Michael Hotenstein, Penn State University; Gordon Johnson, California State University–Northridge; Frank L. Kaufman, California State University–Sacramento; Lee Krajewski, Ohio State University; Hugh V. Leach, Washburn University; John D. Longhill, East Carolina University; John R. Matthews, University of Wisconsin; Brooke Saladin, University of Georgia; Ted Stafford, University of Alabama–Huntsville; Trevor Sainsbury, University of Pittsburgh; Chuck Baron Shook, University of Hawaii at Manoa; John E. Stevens, Lehigh University; and Jesse S. Tarleton, College of William and Mary.

We also thank University of Southern California doctoral students Andreas Soteriou, Steven Yu, and Sukanta Mishra for their help in digging out late-breaking ideas and developing new problems for the book. Much thanks to Danie Mann, program manager at the Center for Operations Management, for her help and care in all aspects of manuscript production.

We indeed appreciate the enthusiastic support and innovativeness of Dick Hercher, our long-time editor at Richard D. Irwin, whose help in coordinating all of the resources behind the scenes has been terrific.

There are two people we want to single out for very special acknowledgments and thanks. U.S.C. doctoral student Doug Stewart contributed his considerable technical and writing skills in many chapters. He has been our right-hand man throughout the revision process. His help has been invaluable. To Gail Korosa (our developmental editor at Irwin), what can we say? Your dedication (obsession?) to helping us make this our best edition ever cannot be overstated.

Last, but certainly not least, we thank our families who for the seventh time let the life cycle of the book disrupt theirs.

Richard B. Chase
Nicholas J. Aquilano

Preface for the Student
(by a Student)

Operations management lies at the heart of the great changes sweeping through today's business environment. The competitive pressures for higher quality, quicker response time, superior service, and total customization can only be met through more intelligently run business operations. Even the recent enthusiasm for corporate reengineering is fundamentally about better managing operations.

I have found operations management to be the most relevant and enjoyable part of my business studies. This subject is about the fundamental essence of the firm—how its products are made, and how its services are delivered to customers. It involves everything from strategic concerns such as aggregate planning, plant location, and service capacity expansion, to tactical issues such as daily order scheduling, statistical quality control, and inventory control. Studying such a broad range of topics has helped me achieve a balance between skill with the necessary analytical tools, and an understanding of the underlying conceptual issues.

Dr. Chase and Dr. Aquilano have written a clear text addressing important current issues such as service management, just-in-time production, total quality management, and reengineering, while still covering such fundamental operations management topics as layout, job design, and forecasting. Box inserts throughout the book provide insights into some of the best current operations management practices. In addition, the authors have used their extensive experience to seek out examples of companies that have found radical new ways to run their operations—ways that may reflect how all such businesses will be operating in the future. They call these examples "Breakthroughs." Several chapters also have special supplements devoted to more technical topics, such as technology management, linear programming, and waiting line theory. The supplements allow these topics to be clearly addressed without confusing the issues presented in the chapters. I am sure that as you read this book, you will appreciate the importance of operations management as a central part of any good business education, and I hope that you will become as fascinated with the field as I am.

Richard D. Bergin
Student, School of Business Administration
University of Southern California

Contents in Brief

Contents

Chapter 7
Forecasting
262

Chapter 8
Strategic Capacity Planning
316

Supplement 8
Linear Programming
341

C h a p t e r 15

Inventory Systems for Dependent Demand: MRP-Type Systems
586

C h a p t e r 16

Operations Scheduling
634

I

NATURE AND CONTEXT OF OPERATIONS MANAGEMENT

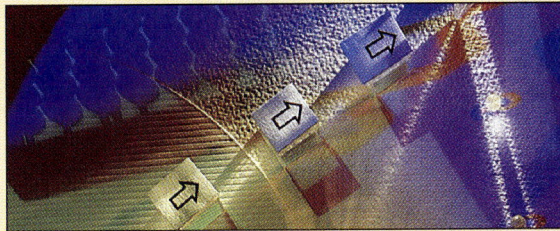

How we manage productive resources is critical to strategic growth and competitiveness. Operations management is the managing of these productive resources. It entails the design and control of systems responsible for the productive use of raw materials, human resources, equipment, and facilities in the development of a product or service. This section addresses the issues of operations strategy and competitiveness and how the field of operations management can provide direction in gaining and maintaining competitive advantage.

C h a p t e r

1

Introduction to the Field

C H A P T E R   O U T L I N E

K E Y   T E R M S

The Customer

Operations Management (OM)

Service Operations

Corporate Strategy

Operations Strategy

Production System

Five P's of Operations Management

Core Services

Value-Added Services

Scientific Management

Materials Requirements Planning (MRP)

Just-In-Time (JIT)

Total Quality Control (TQC)

Computer-Integrated Manufacturing (CIM)

Flexible Manufacturing System (FMS)

Factory of the Future (FOF)

ISO 9000

Business Process Reengineering (BPR)

Mass Customization

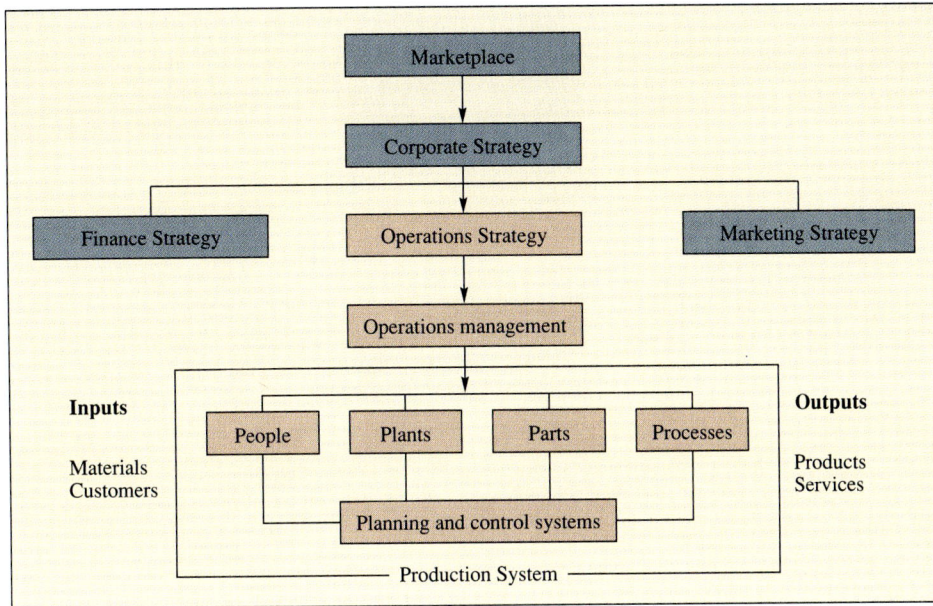

1.1 THE FIELD OF OPERATIONS MANAGEMENT

Operations management may be defined as the design, operation, and improvement of the production systems that create the firm's primary products or services. Like marketing and finance, OM is a functional field of business with clear line management responsibilities. This point is important because operations management is frequently confused with operations research and management science (OR/MS) and industrial engineering (IE). The essential difference is that OM is a field of management, while OR/MS is the application of quantitative methods to decision making in all fields, and IE is an engineering discipline. Thus, while operations managers use the decision-making tools of OR/MS (such as linear programming) and are concerned with many of the same issues as IE (such as factory automation), OM's distinct management role distinguishes it from these other disciplines.

Operations decisions are made in the context of the firm as a whole. Starting at the top of Exhibit 1.1, the marketplace (the firm's customers for its products or services) shapes the firm's **corporate strategy.** This strategy is based on the corporate mission, and in essence reflects how the firm plans to use all its resources and functions (marketing, finance, and operations) to gain competitive advantage. The **operations strategy** specifies how the firm will employ its production capabilities to support its corporate strategy. (Similarly, the marketing strategy addresses how the firm will sell and distribute its goods and services, while the finance strategy identifies how best to utilize the firm's financial resources.)

Within the operations function, management decisions can be divided into three broad areas:

Strategic (long-term) decisions.

Tactical (intermediate-term) decisions.

Operational planning and control (short-term) decisions.

Operations Management Defined

Operations Decisions

Ben and Jerry's mission statement impacts decisions such as where to locate and how to make the product. The company believes its social mission is to improve the quality of life in its local, national, and international communities. Its success, however, is based upon producing a great ice cream (with large chunks of chocolate in each quart of Cherry Garcia).

The strategic issues are usually very broad in nature, addressing such questions as: How will we make the product? Where do we locate the facility or facilities? How much capacity do we need? When should we add more capacity? Thus, by necessity, the time frame for strategic decisions is typically very long—usually several years or more, depending on the specific industry. (Chapter 2 discusses operations strategy in depth.)

Operations management decisions at the strategic level impact the company's long-range effectiveness in terms of how it can address its customers' needs. Thus, for the firm to succeed, these decisions must be in alignment with the corporate strategy. Decisions made at the strategic level become the fixed conditions or operating constraints under which the firm must operate in both the intermediate and short term.

At the next level in the decision-making process, tactical planning primarily addresses how to efficiently schedule material and labor within the constraints of previously made strategic decisions. Issues that OM concentrates at this level are: How many workers do we need? When do we need them? Should we work overtime or put on a second shift? When should we have material delivered? Should we have a finished goods inventory? These tactical decisions, in turn, become the operating constraints under which operational planning and control decisions are made.

Management decisions with respect to operational planning and control are narrow and short-term by comparison. Issues at this level include: What jobs do we work on today or this week? Who do we assign to what tasks? What jobs have priority?

Production Systems

The heart of OM is the management of production systems. A **production system** uses operations resources to transform inputs into some desired output. An input may be a raw material, a customer, or a finished product from another system. As indicated in the bottom of Exhibit 1.1, operations resources consist of what we term the **five P's of operations management:** people, plants, parts, processes, and planning and control systems. *People* are the direct and indirect workforce. *Plants* include the factories or service branches where production is carried out. *Parts* include the materials (or, in the case of services, the supplies) that go through the system. *Processes* include the equipment and steps by which production is accomplished. *Planning and control systems* are the procedures and information management uses to operate the system.

System	Primary Inputs	Resources	Primary Transformation Function(s)	Typical Desired Output
Hospital	Patients	MDs, nurses, medical supplies, equipment	Health care (physiological)	Healthy individuals
Restaurant	Hungry customers	Food, chef, wait-staff, environment	Well-prepared, well-served food; agreeable environment (physical and exchange)	Satisfied customers
Automobile factory	Sheet steel, engine parts	Tools, equipment, workers	Fabrication and assembly of cars (physical)	High-quality cars
College or university	High school graduates	Teachers, books, classrooms	Imparting knowledge and skills (informational)	Educated individuals
Department store	Shoppers	Displays, stock of goods, sales clerks	Attract shoppers, promote products, fill orders (exchange)	Sales to satisfied customers
Distribution center	Stockkeeping units (SKUs)	Storage bins, stockpickers	Storage and redistribution	Fast delivery, availability of SKUs

E X H I B I T 1.2
Input–Transformation–Output Relationships for Typical Systems

Transformations that take place include

Physical, as in manufacturing.

Location, as in transportation.

Exchange, as in retailing.

Storage, as in warehousing.

Physiological, as in health care.

Informational, as in telecommunications.

These transformations, of course, are not mutually exclusive. For example, a department store can (1) allow shoppers to compare prices and quality (informational), (2) hold items in inventory until needed (storage), and (3) sell goods (exchange). Exhibit 1.2 presents sample input–transformation–output relationships for a variety of systems. Note that only the direct resources are listed. A more complete system description would, of course, also include managerial and support functions.

At the most basic level, the difference between a good and a service is that a service is something that "if you drop it on your foot, it won't hurt you." More formally, the essential difference between the two is that service is an intangible process, while a good is the physical output of a process. Further, other differences are that in services, location of the service facility and direct customer involvement in creating the output are often essential factors; in goods production, they usually are not. There are many shades of gray here. Manufacturers provide many services as part of their product, and many services often manufacture the physical products that they deliver to their customers or consume goods in creating the service. (See Exhibit 1.3 for the classic depiction of the goods/service content of different service businesses.) McDonald's manufactures a tangible product, but because it is designed to have some contact with the customer to complete the service production process, the firm is in the service category.

Differences between Services and Goods Production

EXHIBIT 1.3

Comparison of Goods and Services Content for Different Service Businesses

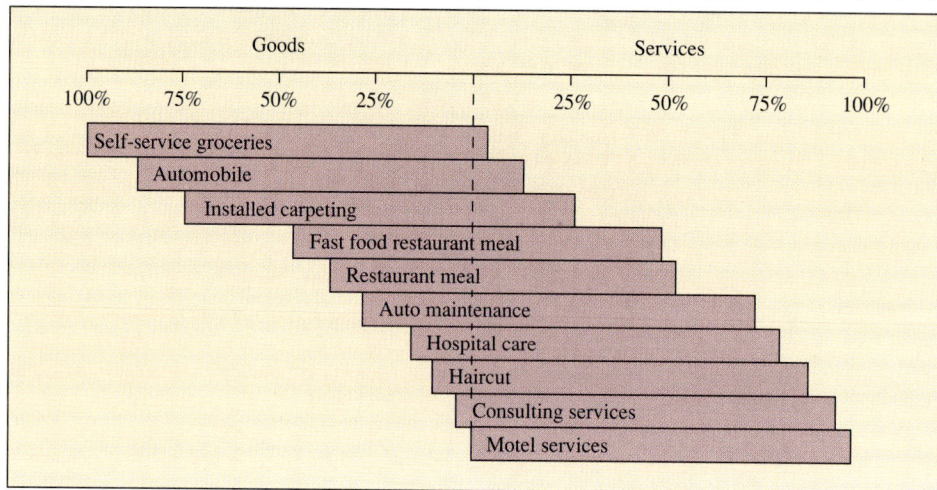

Source: W. Earl Sasser, R. Paul Olsen, and D. Daryl Wyckoff, *Management of Service Operations: Text, Cases, and Readings* (Boston: Allyn & Bacon, 1978), p. 11.

Also, from an operations perspective, customers are on the "shop floor" when consuming many services. The shop floor may be called the front office, dining area, operating room, or passenger cabin, depending on the industry. There are also many behind-the-scenes activities with tangible inputs and outputs. For example, major airlines, banks, and insurance companies have large back offices that support customer contact operations. As the service design chapter relates, such back-office operations process things and information (e.g., tickets, checks, and claims) and so can be run much like a factory.

OM in the Organizational Chart

Exhibit 1.4 locates operations activities within a manufacturing organization and a service organization. Aside from differences in terminology, the service organization also differs from the manufacturing firm in structure. The manufacturing company typically groups operations activities to produce its products in one department. Service firms scatter operations activities throughout the organization. For example, reservations scheduling in an airline is part of the production process for airline travel, even though it is carried out by a non-operations department. This is seen even more clearly in banking where there is often a retail operations department and a check processing operations department. Note that in manufacturing the plant manager's position is used to administer the various support activities required for production. Note also that in both types of organizations, it is typical for operations activities to account for the lion's share of capital investment and workforce. Exhibit 1.5 lists some line and staff jobs that are frequently viewed as relating to the operations function.

1.2   CLOSED VERSUS OPEN SYSTEMS VIEWS OF OPERATIONS

The manufacturing organization chart in Exhibit 1.4 shows reporting arrangements and typical operations responsibilities. It does not really convey how the manufacturing organization, particularly the factory itself, relates to its external and internal environments. Contrasting open and closed system views of manufacturing gives us a perspective on these relationships.

E X H I B I T 1.4   *OM in the Organization Chart*

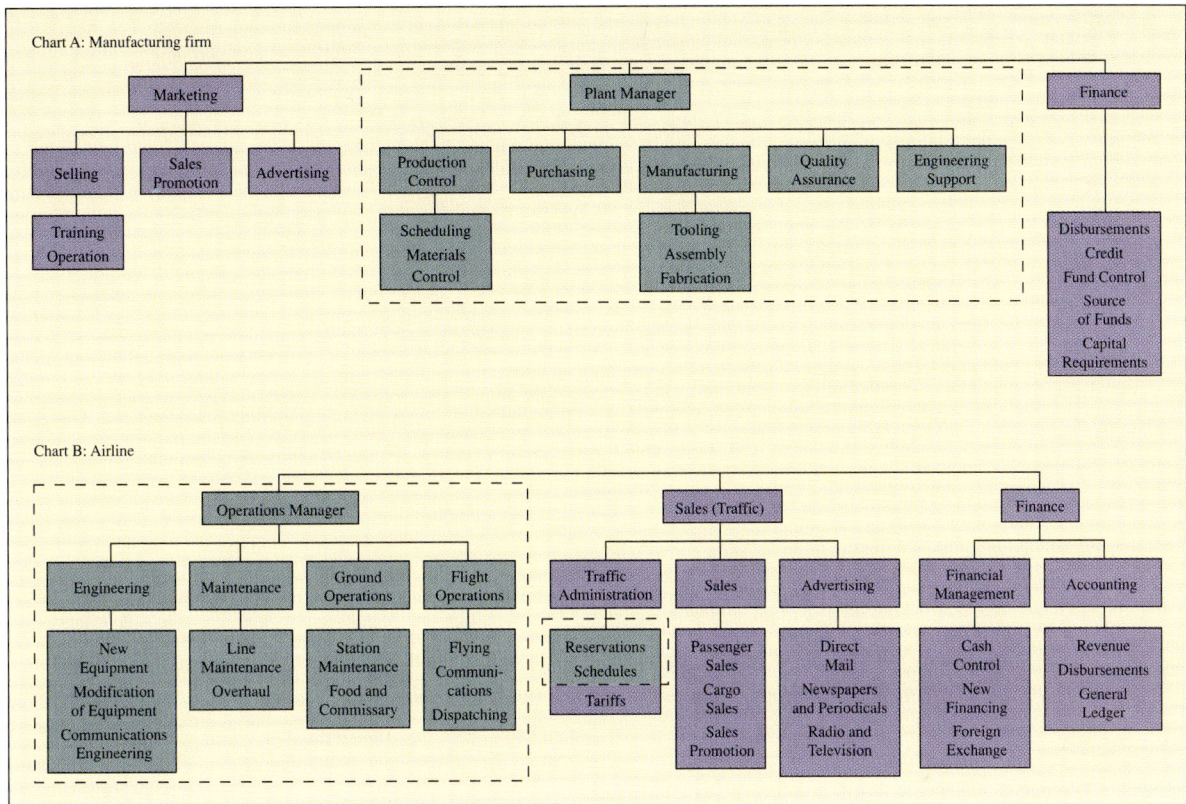

Chart A: Manufacturing firm

```
                    Marketing            Plant Manager                           Finance

        Selling    Sales       Advertising   Production  Purchasing  Manufacturing  Quality    Engineering      Disbursements
                   Promotion                 Control                               Assurance   Support          Credit

        Training                             Scheduling              Tooling                                    Fund Control
        Operation                            Materials               Assembly                                   Source
                                             Control                 Fabrication                                of Funds
                                                                                                                Capital
                                                                                                                Requirements
```

Chart B: Airline

```
                Operations Manager                        Sales (Traffic)                      Finance

    Engineering  Maintenance  Ground      Flight      Traffic        Sales    Advertising   Financial    Accounting
                              Operations  Operations  Administration                        Management

    New          Line         Station     Flying      Reservations   Passenger  Direct       Cash         Revenue
    Equipment    Maintenance  Maintenance Communi-    Schedules      Sales      Mail         Control      Disbursements
    Modification Overhaul     Food and    cations                    Cargo      Newspapers   New          General
    of Equipment              Commissary  Dispatching Tariffs        Sales      and Periodicals Financing  Ledger
    Communications                                                   Sales      Radio and    Foreign
    Engineering                                                      Promotion  Television    Exchange
```

E X H I B I T 1.5

Line and Staff Jobs in Operations Management

Organizational Level	Manufacturing Industries	Service Industries
Upper	Vice president of manufacturing Regional manager of manufacturing	Vice president of operations (airline) Chief administrator (hospital)
Middle	Plant manager Program manager	Store manager (department store) Facilities manager (wholesale distributor)
Lower	Department supervisor Foreperson Crew chief	Branch manager (bank) Department supervisor (insurance company) Assistant manager (hotel)
Staff	Production controller Materials manager Quality manager Purchasing agent Work methods analyst Process engineer	Systems and procedures analyst Purchasing agent Inspector Dietician (hospital) Customer service manager

Traditionally, manufacturing managers have sought to protect their factory operations from outside disturbances through the use of buffers between the plant and its customers. These buffers can be physical (such as inventories) or organizational (such as the other functions shown surrounding the "factory" in Exhibit 1.6). Note that with the exception of the purchasing function—which is often part of the manufacturing

E X H I B I T 1.6
Closed versus Open Systems Views of Manufacturing Operations

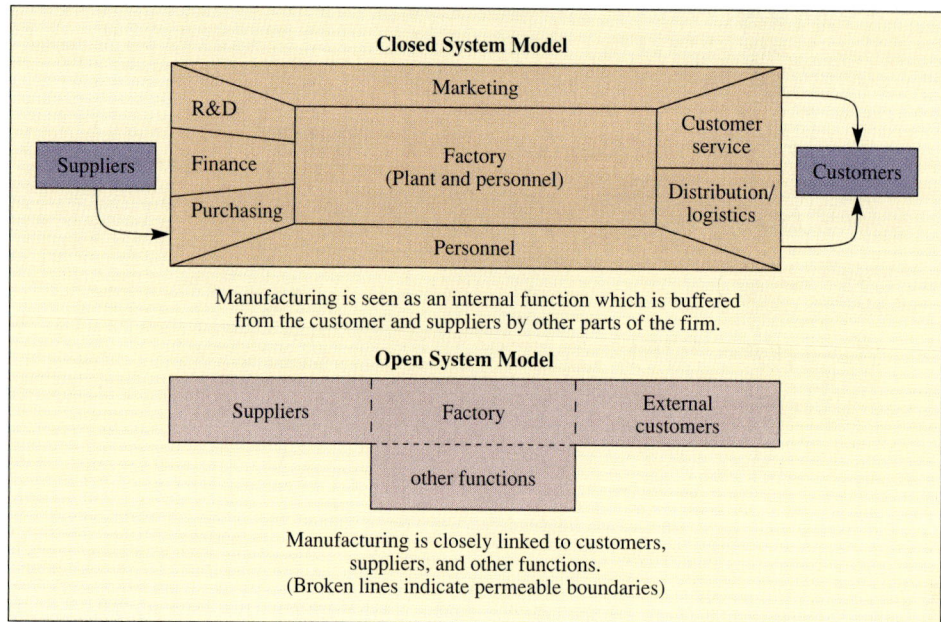

Closed System Model

Manufacturing is seen as an internal function which is buffered from the customer and suppliers by other parts of the firm.

Open System Model

Manufacturing is closely linked to customers, suppliers, and other functions.
(Broken lines indicate permeable boundaries)

organization—manufacturing has few formal direct links with the outside environment. (Purchasing itself, under this model, deals only with suppliers.)

This **closed system** view, with its reliance on buffering, has been perceived as desirable for three reasons. (1) Interaction with customers, vendors, and salespeople can be a disturbing influence on production. (2) The production transformation process is often more efficient than the processes for obtaining inputs and disposing of finished goods. (3) With certain processes (for example, auto assembly lines and continuous flow processes such as petroleum refining), productivity can be maximized only by operating at a continuous rate which is often different from the market-demanded rate.

The inherent drawbacks of the closed system model are now becoming readily apparent, however. One drawback is lack of flexibility due to information lags between the factory and the so-called boundary functions. Another is an "us versus them" attitude (for example, "People in the factory don't understand the business," "People in marketing don't know our problems."). Finally, lack of interaction with the customer (discussed shortly) loses some competitive opportunities for the business.

The **open system** model of factory operations is obviously quite different. Here, the factory is open to communication and interaction with its customers and suppliers, and it develops means to eliminate procedural and personal barriers between itself and other functions. This calls for a service orientation on the part of manufacturing operations.

1.3   MANUFACTURING OPERATIONS AS SERVICE

The emerging model in industry is that every organization is in the service business. This is true whether the organization makes big planes or Big Macs. From this we must recognize that manufacturing operations, as well as every other part of the organization, are also in the service business even if the customer is an internal one. In manufacturing,

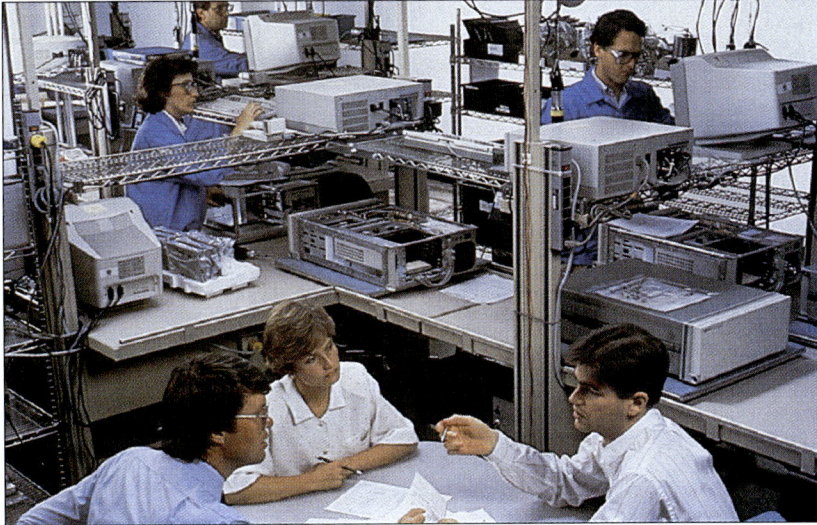

such services can be divided into core and value-added services provided to internal and external customers of the factory.

The **core services** customers want from the factory are products that are made correctly, are customized to their needs, are delivered on time, and are priced competitively. These are commonly summarized as the classic performance objectives of the operations function: *quality, flexibility, speed,* and *price* (or cost of production). Achieving these services is the focus of this book, and is discussed in detail in Chapter 3.

Value-added services are services that simply make the external customer's life easier or, in the case of internal customers, help them to better carry out their particular function. Chase and Garvin (1992) suggest that value-added factory services can be classified into four broad categories: information, problem solving, sales support, and field support.

1. **Information** is the ability to furnish critical data on product performance, process parameters, and cost to internal groups (such as R&D) and to external customers, who then use the data to improve their own operations or products. For example, Hewlett-Packard's Fort Collins quality department provides quality data sheets and videotapes documenting actual product testing and field quality performance to field sales and service personnel.

2. **Problem solving** is the ability to help internal and external groups to solve problems, especially in quality. For example, Raritan Corporation, a metal rod fabricator, sends factory workers out with salespeople to troubleshoot quality problems. Those factory workers then return to the factory and join with shop floor personnel on remedial efforts.

3. **Sales support** is the ability to enhance sales and marketing efforts by demonstrating the technology, equipment, or production systems the company is trying to sell. In part Digital Equipment Corporation sells its CIM (computer-integrated manufacturing) system by showcasing it on its own factory floor. Sometimes sales are enhanced by the factory showing off its workforce's skills. For example, to demonstrate its products' quality, Sara Lee has visitors observe the artistic skills of its "meringue fluffers" on its pie line.

<table>
<tr><td>

*Linking the
Shop-Floor
Worker to the
Customer*

</td><td>

Tektronix, a manufacturer of electronic equipment, has pioneered direct communication between customers and shop-floor employees. Into the shipping carton of every oscilloscope it sells, the company inserts a postcard listing the names of the workers who built the scope along with an "800" number to a phone on the shop floor. Every day the factory gets several calls from customers; the six people working in the repair area who answer them have all received telephone training.

Customers call for various reasons: to ask questions about the use of their oscilloscopes, to request information about other Tektronix products, and to see if "they can really talk to the person who made their product." Workers and managers meet daily to discuss these calls; if necessary, further conversations with the customer follow up the meetings. In some cases, workers will call customers six months after delivery to find out how well their products are performing.

Source: R. B. Chase and D. A. Garvin, "The Service Factory," *Harvard Business Review,* July-August 1989, pp. 65–66.

</td></tr>
</table>

4. **Field support** is the ability to replace defective parts quickly (for example, Caterpillar promises to make repair parts available anywhere in the world within 48 hours) or to replenish stocks quickly to avoid downtime or stockouts (for example, The Limited, a retail chain, is linked to its Hong Kong textile mills via a sophisticated computer system that signals factories to begin producing fast-selling items as soon as weekly sales figures are collected).

Value-added services provided to external customers yield two benefits. First, they differentiate the organization from the competition. Indeed, in many cases it is easier to copy a firm's product than it is to create the value-added service infrastructure to support it. Second, they build relationships that bind customers to the organization in a positive way, as the sidebar, "Linking the Shop-Floor Worker to the Customer," relates.

1.4   PLAN OF THIS BOOK

This book is organized around the stages that a production system goes through in its birth-to-maturity **life cycle.** We have chosen this structure because it mirrors system development in the real world. The text starts by analyzing the competitive strategy under which the system is to operate. It then looks at product design and process choices that set the foundation for the system per se. Next, it considers the design of the various parts of the production system—getting the five P's of OM into alignment to achieve efficient production. The book then presents tools to help plan and control the system's start-up. The text then deals extensively with the system in steady state, focusing on day-to-day operations. The book concludes with revising the system to achieve major improvements in performance. Exhibit 1.7 identifies key issues in each stage of system operation.

Note that the text is not built around the life cycle of any one system. On the contrary, we have intentionally chosen examples from a variety of manufacturing and service operations to emphasize that good operations management is essential in such diverse systems as hospitals, banks, universities, and, of course, factories.

1.5   HISTORICAL DEVELOPMENT OF OM

Exhibit 1.8 gives a timeline of OM's history. We now highlight some of its major concepts and their developers.

Stages	Key Issue	
Birth of the system	What are the goals of the firm?	Chapters 1, 2
	How does OM strategy relate to the goals?	Chapters 1, 2
	What product or service will be offered?	
Product design and process selection	What is the form of the manufactured product?	Chapter 3
	How is it developed?	
	How do you manage information technology to make the product or service?	S-3
Design of the system	How do you design a service?	Chapter 4, S4
	How do you achieve high quality?	Chapter 5
	How do you design for just-in-time production?	Chapter 6
	How do you determine demand for the product or service?	Chapter 7
	What capacity do you need?	Chapter 8, S8
	Where should the facility be located?	Chapter 9
	What physical arrangement is best to use?	Chapter 10
	How will the job be performed and measured?	Chapter 11
	How will workers be compensated?	Chapter 11
	How do you measure learning?	Chapter 11
Start-up of the system	How do you manage start-up projects?	Chapter 12
The system in steady state	How do you manage day-to-day activities of production planning, scheduling, and inventories?	Chapters 14–16, S-16
	How do you manage suppliers and purchasing?	Chapter 17
Improving the system	How do you make major improvements in system performance using business process reengineering?	Chapter 18
	How do you reconceptualize the system using the theory of constraints?	Chapter 19
	How do the pros in OM consulting analyze manufacturing strategy?	Epilogue

Scientific Management

Although operations management has existed since people started to produce, the advent of **scientific management** around the turn of the century is probably the major historical landmark for the field. This concept was developed by Frederick W. Taylor, an imaginative engineer and insightful observer of organizational activities.

The essence of Taylor's philosophy was that (1) scientific laws govern how much a worker can produce per day, (2) it is the function of management to discover and use these laws in the operation of productive systems, and (3) it is the function of the worker to carry out management's wishes without question. Taylor's philosophy was not greeted with approval by all his contemporaries. On the contrary, some unions resented or feared scientific management—with some justification. In too many instances, managers of the day were quick to embrace the mechanisms of Taylor's philosophy—time study, incentive plans, and so forth—but ignored their responsibility to organize and standardize the work to be done. Hence, there were numerous cases of rate cutting (reducing the payment per piece if the production rate was deemed too high), overwork of labor, and poorly designed work methods. The overreaction to such abuses led to the introduction of a bill in Congress in 1913 to prohibit the use of time study and incentive plans in federal government operations. The unions advocating the legislation claimed that Taylor's subject in several of his time-study experiments, a steelworker called Schmidt, had died from overwork as a result of following Taylor's methods. (As evidence they even distributed pictures of

E X H I B I T 1.8

Historical Summary of OM

Year	Concept or Tool	Originator or Developer
1911	*Principles of Scientific Management;* formalized time-study and work-study concepts.	Frederick W. Taylor (United States)
1911	Motion study; basic concepts of industrialized psychology.	Frank and Lillian Gilbreth (United States)
1913	Moving assembly line.	Henry Ford (United States)
1914	Activity scheduling chart.	Henry L. Gantt (United States)
1917	Application of economic lot size model for inventory control.	F. W. Harris (United States)
1931	Sampling inspection and statistical tables for quality control.	Walter Shewhart, H. F. Dodge, and H. G. Romig (United States)
1927–33	Hawthorne studies of worker motivation.	Elton Mayo (United States)
1934	Activity sampling for work analysis.	L. H. C. Tippett (England)
1940	Multidisciplinary team approaches to complex system problems.	Operations research groups (England)
1947	Simplex method of linear programming.	George B. Dantzig (United States)
1950s–60s	Extensive development of OR tools of simulation, waiting line theory, decision theory, mathematical programming, computer hardware and software, project scheduling techniques of PERT and CPM.	United States and Western Europe
1970s	Development of a variety of computer software packages to deal with routine problems of shop scheduling, inventory, layout, forecasting, and project management; rapid growth of MRP. Service quality and productivity; introduction of mass production in the service sector.	Computer manufacturers, researchers, and users in the United States and Western Europe Joseph Orlicky and Oliver Wight (United States) McDonald's restaurants
1980s	Manufacturing strategy paradigm for using manufacturing as a competitive weapon Extensive use of JIT, TQC, and factory automation (CIM, FMS, CAD/CAM robots, etc.).	Harvard Business School faculty Tai-ichi Ohno of Toyota Motors (Japan), W. E. Deming and J. M. Juran (United States), and engineering disciplines
1990s	TQM becomes pervasive; Baldrige Quality Award and ISO 9000 used as certification for quality excellence. Business process reengineering used to make radical changes in production (and other) processes.	Quality gurus, American Society of Quality Control, and International Organization for Standardization Michael Hammer and major consulting firms

Schmidt's "grave.") It was later discovered that Schmidt (whose real name was Henry Nolle) was alive and well and working as a teamster.[1] Ultimately, the bill was defeated.

Note that Taylor's ideas were widely accepted in contemporary Japan. A Japanese translation of Taylor's book, *Principles of Scientific Management* (titled *The Secret of Saving Lost Motion*), sold more than 2 million copies. To this day, there is a strong legacy of Taylorism in Japanese approaches to manufacturing management.[2]

---

[1]Milton J. Nadworny, "Schmidt and Stakhanov: Work Heroes in Two Systems," *California Management Review* 6, no. 4 (Summer 1964), pp. 69–76.

[2]Charles J. McMillan, "Production Planning in Japan," *Journal of General Management* 8, no. 4, pp. 44–71.

Notable coworkers of Taylor were Frank and Lillian Gilbreth (motion study, industrial psychology) and Henry L. Gantt (scheduling, wage payment plans). Their work is well known to management scholars. However, it is probably not well known that Taylor, a devout Quaker, requested "cussing lessons" from an earthy foreman to help him communicate with workers; that Frank Gilbreth defeated younger champion bricklayers in bricklaying contests by using his own principles of motion economy; or that Gantt won a presidential citation for his application of the Gantt chart to shipbuilding and refitting during World War I.

Moving Assembly Line

The year 1913 saw the introduction of one of the machine age's greatest technological innovations—the moving assembly line for the manufacture of Ford cars.[3] Before the line was introduced, in August of that year, each auto chassis was assembled by one worker in about 12½ hours. Eight months later, when the line was in its final form, with each worker performing a small unit of work and the chassis being moved mechanically, the average labor time per chassis was 93 minutes. This technological breakthrough, coupled with concepts of scientific management, represents the classic application of labor specialization and is still common today.

Hawthorne Studies

Mathematical and statistical developments dominated the evolution of operations management from Taylor's time up to around the 1940s. An exception was the Hawthorne studies, conducted in the 1930s by a research team from the Harvard Graduate School of Business Administration and supervised by sociologist Elton Mayo. These experiments were designed to study the effects of certain environmental changes on assembly workers' output at the Western Electric plant in Hawthorne, Illinois. The unexpected findings, reported in *Management and the Worker* (1939) by F. J. Roethlisberger and W. J. Dickson, intrigued sociologists and students of "traditional" scientific management alike. To the surprise of the researchers, changing the level of illumination, for example, had much less effect on output than the way in which the changes were introduced to the workers. That is, reductions in illumination in some instances led to increased output because workers felt an obligation to their group to keep output high. Discoveries such as these had tremendous implications for work design and motivation and ultimately led many organizations to establish personnel management and human relations departments.

Operations Research

World War II, with its complex problems of logistics control and weapons systems design, provided the impetus for the development of the interdisciplinary, mathematically oriented field of operations research. Operations research (OR) brings together practitioners in such diverse fields as mathematics, psychology, and economics. Specialists in these disciplines form a team to structure and analyze a problem in quantitative terms so they can obtain a mathematically optimal solution. As mentioned earlier, operations research, or its approximate synonym *management science,* now provides many of the quantitative tools used in operations management as well as other business disciplines.

OM's Emergence as a Field

In the late 1950s and early 1960s, scholars began to deal specifically with operations management as opposed to industrial engineering or operations research. Writers such as Edward Bowman and Robert Fetter (*Analysis for Production and Operations Management* [1957]) and Elwood S. Buffa (*Modern Production Management* [1961]) noted the

---

[3]Ford is said to have gotten the idea for an assembly line from observing a Swiss watch manufacturer's use of the technology. Incidentally, all Model-T Fords were painted black. Why? Because black paint dried fastest.

Japan's Personalized Bike Production

Does your bike fit you to a "t"? Would you like one that does? If you are willing to pay 20 to 30 percent more than you would pay for a mass-produced bike, you can get a Panasonic bike manufactured to exactly match your size, weight, and color preference. You can even get your bike within three weeks of your order (only two weeks if you visit Japan). This is accomplished via a process called the Panasonic Individual Customer System (PICS), which skillfully employs computers, robots, and a small factory workforce to make one-of-a-kind models at the National Bicycle Industrial Company factory in Kokubu, Japan.

The National Bicycle Industrial Company (NBIC), a subsidiary of electronics giant Matsushita, began making the bikes under the Panasonic brand in 1987. With the introduction of its personalized order system (POS) for the Japanese market (PICS was developed for overseas sales), the firm gained international attention as a classic example of **mass customization**—producing products to order in lot sizes of one.

The factory itself has 21 employees and a computer-aided design system, and is capable of producing any of 8 million variations on 18 models of racing, road, and mountain bikes in 199 color patterns for virtually any size person.

The PIC system works in the following way. A customer visits a local Panasonic bicycle store and is mea-

sured on a special frame. The storeowner then faxes the specifications to the master control room at the factory. There an operator punches the specs into a minicomputer, which automatically creates a unique blueprint and produces a bar code. (The CAD blueprint takes about three minutes as opposed to three hours required by company draftspeople prior to computerization.) The bar code is then attached to metal tubes and gears that ultimately become the customer's personal bike. At various stages in the process, line workers access the customer's requirement using the bar code label and a scanner. This information, displayed on a CRT terminal at each station, is fed directly to the computer-controlled machines that are part of a local area computer network. At each step of production, a computer reading the code knows that each part belongs to a specific bike, and tells a robot where to weld or tells a painter which pattern to follow.

Despite the use of computers and robots, the process is not highly automated. Gears are hand-wired, assembly is manual, and the customer's name is silk-screened by hand with the touch of an artisan. The entire manufacturing and assembly time required to complete a single bike is 150 minutes, and the factory can make about 60 a day. NBIC's mass-production factory (which makes 90 percent of its annual production) can make a standard model in 90 minutes. One might ask why a customer must wait two to three weeks given that it takes less than three

---

commonality of problems faced by all productive systems and emphasized the importance of viewing production operations as a system. They also stressed the useful applications of waiting line theory, simulation, and linear programming, which are now standard topics in the field. In 1973, Chase and Aquilano's first edition of this book stressed the need "to put the management back into operations management" and suggested the life cycle as a means of organizing the subject.

Computers and the MRP Crusade

The major development of the 1970s was the broad use of computers in operations problems. For manufacturers, the big breakthrough was the application of **materials requirements planning (MRP)** to production control. This approach ties together in a computer program all the parts that go into complicated products. This program then enables production planners to quickly adjust production schedules and inventory purchases to meet changing demands for final products. Clearly, the massive data manipulation required for changing schedules on products with thousands of parts would be impossible without such programs and the computer capacity to run them. The promotion of this approach (pioneered by Joseph Orlicky of IBM and consultant Oliver Wight) by the American Production and Inventory Control Society (APICS) has been termed *the MRP Crusade*.

hours to make a custom model. According to the general manager of sales, "We could have made the time shorter, but we want people to feel excited about waiting for something special."

To provide a more personal touch to mass customization, the factory is given the responsibility to communicate directly with the customer. Immediately after the factory receives the customer's order, a personalized computer-generated drawing of the bicycle is mailed with a note thanking the customer for choosing the bike. This is followed up with a second personal note, three months

later, inquiring about the customer's satisfaction with the bicycle. Finally, a "bicycle birthday card" is sent to commemorate the first anniversary of the bicycle.

NBIC is now contemplating extending the Panasonic system to all of its bicycle production, while Matsushita is considering applying the concept to industrial machinery.

Source: Surech Kotha, "The National Bicycle Industrial Company: Implementing a Strategy of Mass-Customization," case study form the International University of Japan, 1993; and Susan Moffat, "Japan's New Personalized Production," *Fortune*, October 22, 1990, pp. 132–35.

Despite computers and robots, the gears are hand wired, assembly is manual, and the customer's name is silk-screened by hand.

At various stages in the process, line workers access the customer's requirements using the bar code label and a scanner.

JIT, TQC, and Factory Automation

The 1980s saw a revolution in the management philosophies and the technologies by which production is carried out. **Just-in-time (JIT)** production is the major breakthrough in manufacturing philosophy. Pioneered by the Japanese, JIT is an integrated set of activities designed to achieve high-volume production using minimal inventories of parts that arrive at the workstation just in time. This philosophy—coupled with **total quality control (TQC),** which aggressively seeks to eliminate causes of production defects—is now a cornerstone in many manufacturers' production practices.

As profound as JIT's impact has been, factory automation in its various forms promises to have even greater impact on operations management in coming decades. Such terms as **computer-integrated manufacturing (CIM), flexible manufacturing systems (FMS),** and **factory of the future (FOF)** are already familiar to many readers of this book and are becoming everyday concepts to OM practitioners.

Manufacturing Strategy Paradigm

The late 1970s and early 1980s saw the development of the Manufacturing Strategy Paradigm by researchers at the Harvard Business School. This work by professors William Abernathy, Kim Clark, Robert Hayes, and Steven Wheelwright (built on earlier efforts by Wickham Skinner) emphasized how manufacturing executives could use their factories' capabilities as strategic competitive weapons. The paradigm itself identified how what we call the five P's of production management can be analyzed as strategic and tactical decision variables. Central to their thinking was the notion of factory focus and manufacturing trade-offs. They argued that because a factory cannot excel on all performance measures, its management must derive a focused strategy, creating a focused factory that does a limited set of tasks extremely well. This raised the need for making trade-offs among such performance measures as low cost, high quality, and high flexibility in designing and managing factories.

Service Quality and Productivity

The great diversity of service industries—ranging from airlines to zoos, with about 2,000 different types in between—precludes identifying any single pioneer or developer that has made a major impact across the board in these areas. However, one service company's unique approach to quality and productivity has been so successful that it stands as a reference point in thinking about how to deliver high-volume standardized services. In fact, McDonald's operating system is so successful that the president of Chaparral Steel used it as a model in planning the company's highly efficient mini-mills.

Total Quality Management and Quality Certification

The unquestioned major development in the field of operations management, as well as in management practice in general, is total quality management (TQM). Though practiced by many companies in the 1980s, it become truly pervasive in the 1990s. All operations executives are aware of the quality message put forth by the so-called quality gurus—W. Edwards Deming, Joseph M. Juran, and Philip Crosby. Helping the quality movement along is the Baldrige National Quality Award started in 1986 under the direction of the American Institute of Quality Control and the National Institute of Standards and Technology. The Baldrige Award recognizes up to five companies a year for outstanding quality management systems.

The **ISO 9000** certification standards put forth by the International Organization for Standardization now play a major role in setting quality standards for global manufacturers in particular. Many European companies require that their vendors meet these standards as a condition for obtaining contracts.

Business Process Reengineering

The need to become lean to remain competitive in the global economic recession in the 1990s pushed companies to seek major innovations in the processes by which they run their operations. The flavor of **business process reengineering (BPR)** is conveyed in the title of Michael Hammer's influential article "Reengineering Work: Don't Automate, Obliterate." The approach seeks to make revolutionary changes as opposed to evolutionary changes (which are commonly advocated in TQM). It does this by taking a fresh look at what the organization is trying to do in all its business processes, and then eliminating nonvalue-added steps and computerizing the remaining ones to achieve the desired outcome.

1.6   CONCLUSION

We conclude our introductory chapter with a summary of current issues facing OM executives. These interrelated issues will be addressed as we move through the system life cycle.

1. *Speeding up the time it takes to get new products into production.* This calls for coordination between product designers, process engineers, and production. To be effec-

tive, such specialties must work as a team to avoid the common "silo effect" where each group worries only about its particular function.[4]

2. *Developing flexible production systems to enable mass customization of products and services.* In virtually every industry, there is a broadening of product lines to provide the variety of choices that customers want (or at least, that marketers say they want). This is seen in cars, where Buick has a suspension system that lets a driver choose between a soft or a sport ride; in computers, where Toshiba alone produced more than 30 varieties of laptop computers between 1986 and 1990; and even in diapers where Procter & Gamble Pampers Phases line has 13 different product designs (not just sizes) that reflect changes in infants as they grow to toddlers.[5]

3. *Managing global production networks.* This issue has three aspects. One is assuring that components produced outside of the United States meet design and quality requirements. This entails careful selection of suppliers and anticipating local labor and government actions. The second is managing the logistics of shipping and receiving parts. The third is developing the information system to track and monitor the first two. (Note that foreign transplants to the United States confront the same three issues!)

4. *Developing and integrating new process technologies into existing production systems.* Technology is abundant, but applying it effectively is often difficult. Sometimes the problem lies in the complexity of linking computer-based systems. Other times it involves cost accounting measures that force high utilization of expensive equipment, even if some less expensive machine could perform the task just as well. (A common example here is dedicating costly flexible manufacturing machinery to making long runs of a single product model rather than using cheaper inflexible equipment.)

5. *Achieving high quality quickly and keeping it up in the face of restructuring.* TQM is here to stay, but companies do not have the luxury of the long development periods to achieve quality parity with the competition. Likewise, it is hard to maintain workforce enthusiasm for quality when their jobs are at risk.

6. *Managing a diverse workforce.* Multiple languages and multiple cultures are common on U.S. shop floors as well as in other developed countries. For example, 26 different cultures are represented among the 420 workers at Toyota Autobody of California's truck bed assembly plant in Long Beach. (Only four of these workers are Japanese, and they are staff advisers on assignment from Japan.)

7. *Conforming to environmental constraints, ethical standards, and government regulations.* Issues of social responsibility affect all parts of the organization, but operations is often the focal point because it is the prime user of physical resources that may lead to pollution and other safety hazards. Companies are now developing so-called *green* strategies as part of their corporate planning.

1.7   REVIEW AND DISCUSSION QUESTIONS

1. What is the difference between OM and OR/MS? Between OM and IE?
2. How would you distinguish OM from management and organizational behavior as taught at your university?

---

[4] The pressure to introduce new products quickly was brought home to one of the authors as he jogged on a treadmill in a health club in a Singapore hotel. An executive (who was running significantly faster, incidentally) on another treadmill reported that the computer peripherals company he works for has to introduce an average of one new product a month to keep its market position. He was in Singapore to work out some production details with a local supplier. (The author was doing research on services—theme parks, to be exact.)

[5] These examples are taken from B. Joseph Pine II, *Mass Customization: The New Frontier in Business Competition* (Boston: Harvard Business School Press, 1993), pp. 33–39.

3. Business writer Tom Peters proposed a new concept for an organization chart—a circle with the heading "OK, everybody come inside." How might this relate to the open systems view of operations?

4. Look at the want ads in *The Wall Street Journal* and evaluate the opportunities for an OM major with several years of experience.

5. What factors account for the resurgence of interest in OM today?

6. Using Exhibit 1.2 as a model, describe the input–transformation–output relationships in the following systems:

    a. An airline.
    b. A state penitentiary.
    c. A branch bank.
    d. The home office of a major banking firm.

7. Sketch the production-delivery system used by the National Bicycle Industrial Company in providing the Panasonic bicycle. How do the five P's work together to satisfy the "sixth P," the purchaser? Could this approach be applied to other consumer goods? Give examples.

8. What is the life cycle approach to production/operations management? Does it make sense to you? Could it be applied to any other fields you are studying?

9. What are the implications for marketing of Tektronix's "hot-line" to the shop-floor worker?

10. Suppose that *Variety,* the Hollywood trade paper noted for its colorful jargon, presented the following headlines relating to OM. What particular historical events or individuals would they refer to?

    FRED RISKS X-RATING TO GET ACROSS PRINCIPLES
    HAWTHORNE WORKERS DO IT FASTER IN THE DARK
    STEEL KING VISITS GOLDEN ARCHES
    MATERIALS MANAGEMENT MAVENS GET WITH THE PROGRAM
    INVENTORY—OH NO!
    FRANKY BURIES YOUNG STUDS AT BRICKOFF
    CLOCKWISE HENRY BECOMES MARVEL OF MOTOWN
    P.S.M. TOPS CHARTS IN GINZA
    HERO MEDAL FOR HANK AS BOAT BIZ BOOMS
    CRIMSON GANG SEEKS COMPROMISE ON SHOP FLOOR
    EXECS FOLLOW GURU'S RECIPE FOR BIG Q STEW

1.8   SELECTED BIBLIOGRAPHY

Apte, Uday. "Operations Management Course Notes." Southern Methodist University, 1993.

Bowman, Edward, and Robert Fetter. *Analysis for Production and Operations Management.* Homewood, IL: Richard D. Irwin, 1957.

Buffa, Elwood S. *Modern Production Management.* New York: John Wiley & Sons, 1961.

Chase, Richard B., and David A. Garvin. "The Service Factory." *Harvard Business Review* 67, no. 4 (July-August 1989), pp. 61–69.

———. "The Service Factory: A Future Vision." *Quality in Services Conference 2.* Eberhard E. Scheving, Evert Gummesson, and Charles H. Little, eds. St. Johns University Service Research Center, 1992, pp. 91–100.

Chase, Richard B., and Eric L. Prentis. "Operations Management: A Field Rediscovered." *Journal of Management* 13, no. 2 (October 1987), pp. 351–66.

Cole, Robert E. "The Quality Revolution." *Production and Operations Management* 1, no. 1 (Winter 1992).

Davidow, W. H., and M. S. Malone. *The Virtual Corporation.* New York: HarperCollins, 1993.

Deming, W. Edwards. *Out of the Crisis.* Cambridge, MA: Massachusetts Institute of Technology, Center for Advanced Engineering Study, 1986.

Drucker, Peter F. "The Emerging Theory of Manufacturing." *Harvard Business Review,* May-June 1990, pp. 94–102.

Giffi, Craig, Aleda V. Roth, and Gregory M. Seal, eds. *Competing in World-Class Manufacturing: America's 21st Century Challenge.* Homewood, IL: Business One Irwin, 1990.

Hammer, Michael. "Reengineering Work: Don't Automate, Obliterate." *Harvard Business Review,* July-August 1990, pp. 104–12.

Hayes, Robert H., Steven C. Wheelwright, and Kim B. Clark. *Dynamic Manufacturing.* New York: Free Press, 1988.

Osborn, D. *Reinventing Government.* New York: Plume, 1993.

Quinn, James Brian. *Intelligent Enterprise.* New York: Free Press, 1992.

Schonberger, Richard J. *World Class Manufacturing: The Lessons of Simplicity Applied.* New York: Free Press, 1986.

Skinner, Wickham. "Manufacturing—Missing Link in Corporate Strategy." *Harvard Business Review,* May-June 1969, pp. 136–45.

_____. "The Focused Factory." *Harvard Business Review,* May-June 1974, pp. 113–21.

Stalk, Jr., George, and Thomas M. Hout. *Competing against Time.* New York: Free Press, 1990.

Vargas, Gustavo A., and Thomas W. Johnson. "An Analysis of Operational Experience in the US/Mexico Production Sharing (Maquiladora) Program." *Journal of Operations Management* 11 (1993), pp. 17–34.

Womak, James P., Daniel T. Jones, and Daniel Roos. *The Machine That Changed the World.* New York: Rawson Associates, 1990.

Chapter

2

Operations Strategy and Competitiveness

CHAPTER OUTLINE

KEY TERMS

Four Basic Operations Stategies
Plant-Within-a-Plant (PWP)
Operations Priorities
Qualifier
Order Winner
Operations Capabilities
Core Enterprise
Keiretsu
Order Fulfillment Cycle
Competitiveness
Productivity

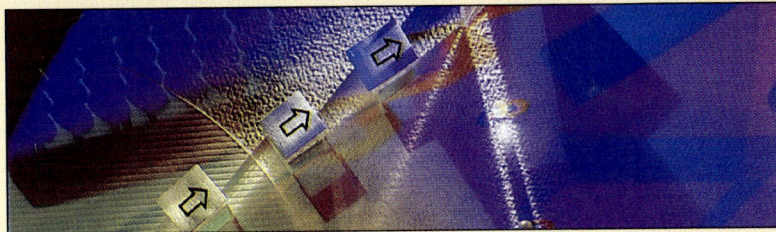

Should anyone doubt the contribution of manufacturing operations to competitive success, consider the dominant companies (mainly Japanese) in industries such as motorcycles, domestic appliances, automobiles, and consumer electronics. At one time all of these industries were seen as making products that were mature, were manufactured in high volume, and had typical cash flows. Their manufacturing operations were considered capable of only marginal change. Developed markets existed with established market leaders. It was assumed that competition would be a matter of advertising, image, and occasional product development. Manufacturing had little to do except control costs, maintain scheduled delivery, and keep quality levels acceptable. The real initiative lay elsewhere—with marketing, strategy, and finance. Yet the companies that are now market leaders did succeed in transforming their industries—partly, it is true, because of their marketing skills and financial environment, but primarily because they saw the overwhelming advantage to be gained from a sharper manufacturing regime.

Source: Nigel Slack, *The Manufacturing Advantage* (London: Management Books 2000 Ltd., 1991).

A company that is considered to be world class recognizes that its ability to compete in the marketplace depends on developing an operations strategy that is properly aligned with its mission of serving the customer. A company's competitiveness refers to its relative position in comparison to other firms in the local or global marketplace. In this chapter, we address operations strategy in manufacturing and services, how the United States is faring in industrial competitiveness, and how operations performance is measured.

2.1   OPERATIONS STRATEGY

What Is Operations Strategy?

Operations strategy is concerned with setting broad policies and plans for using the production resources of the firm to best support the firm's long-term competitive strategy. As mentioned in Chapter 1, typical operations strategy issues include

Capacity requirements: amount, timing, type.

Facilities: size, location, specialization.

Technology: equipment, automation, linkages.

Vertical integration: extent of use of outside suppliers.

Workforce: skill level, wage policies, employment security.

Quality: defect prevention, monitoring, intervention.

Production planning/materials control: sourcing policies, centralization, decision rules.

Organization: structure, control/reward systems, role of staff groups.

Each of these issues is discussed in detail in later chapters.

Looking at operations strategy from an historical perspective, U.S. companies in the post–World War II era experienced tremendous consumer demand, which had been pent up during the war. As a result, manufacturing in this country emphasized turning out high volumes of products to satisfy this demand.

During this period, corporate strategy was usually developed by the marketing and finance functions. The manufacturing or operations function would then be told to produce the required products at minimum cost without having any understanding or input into the overall goals of the company. Within this framework, the production function in an organization concentrated primarily on obtaining low-cost, unskilled labor and constructing highly automated facilities, both with the intent of minimizing production costs.

The Emergence of Operations Strategy

The role of the operations management function (i.e., to minimize production costs) remained virtually unchanged throughout the 1950s and early 1960s. By the late 1960s, at the Harvard Business School, C. Wickham Skinner (who is often called the grandfather of operations strategy) recognized this weakness among U.S. manufacturers and suggested the need for an operations strategy to complement existing marketing and finance strategies. In one of his initial articles on the subject, Skinner referred to manufacturing as the missing link in corporate strategy.[1]

Subsequent work in this area by Harvard Business School researchers (including William Abernathy, Kim Clark, Robert Hayes, and Steven Wheelwright) continued to emphasize the importance of using the strengths of a firm's manufacturing facilities as a competitive weapon in the marketplace. They also argued that a firm could not be com-

---

[1]C. Wickham Skinner, "Manufacturing—The Missing Link in Corporate Strategy," *Harvard Business Review* 47, no. 3 (May–June 1969), pp. 136–45.

petitive in the long run if manufactur ing's strategic role was limited to stage 1 or 2, as described in Exhibit 2.1.

From the work of Skinner and others, **four basic operations strategies** were identified: **cost, quality, speed of delivery,** and **flexibility.** These four strategies translate directly into characteristics used to direct and measure manufacturing performance.

Types of Operations Strategies

Cost   Within every industry, there is usually a segment of the market that buys strictly on the basis of low cost. To successfully compete in this niche, a firm must be the low-cost producer. But even doing this does not always guarantee profitability and success.

Products sold strictly on the basis of cost are typically commoditylike in nature. In other words, customers cannot distinguish the products of one firm from those of another. As a result, customers use cost as the primary determinant for making a purchase.

However, this segment of the market is frequently very large and many companies are lured by the potential for significant profits, which they associate with the large unit volumes of product. As a consequence, competition in this segment is fierce—and so is the failure rate. After all, there can only be one low-cost producer, which usually establishes the selling price in the market.

Quality   Quality can be divided into two categories: **product quality** and **process quality**. The level of quality in a product's design will vary as to the market segment it is aimed for. Obviously, a child's first two-wheel bicycle is of significantly different quality than the bicycle of a world-class cyclist. The use of thicker sheetmetal and the

Stage 1	Minimize manufacturing's negative potential: "Internally neutral." (Don't screw up.)	Outside experts are called in to make decisions about strategic manufacturing issues. Internal, detailed management control systems are the primary means for monitoring manufacturing performance. Manufacturing is kept flexible and reactive.
Stage 2	Achieve parity with competitors: "externally neutral." (Be as good or as bad as the next guy.)	"Industry practice" is followed. The planning horizon for manufacturing investment decisions is extended to incorporate a single business cycle. Capital investment is the primary means for catching up with competition or achieving a competitive edge.
Stage 3	Provide credible support to the business strategy: "internally supportive." (Be consistent with corporate strategy.)	Manufacturing investments are screened for consistency with the business strategy. A manufacturing strategy is formulated and pursued. Longer-term manufacturing developments and trends are addressed systematically.
Stage 4	Pursue a manufacturing-based competitive advantage: "externally supportive." (Be a full partner in the company.)	Efforts are made to anticipate the potential of new manufacturing practices and technologies. Manufacturing is involved "up front" in major marketing and engineering decisions (and vice versa). Long-range programs are pursued in order to acquire capabilities in advance of needs.

E X H I B I T 2.1
Stages in Manufacturing Operations Strategic Role

Source: Reprinted by permission of the *Harvard Business Review.* An exhibit from "Competing through Manufacturing" by Steven C. Wheelwright and Robert H. Hayes (January/February 1985). Copyright © 1985 by the President and Fellows of Harvard College; All Rights Reserved. Comments in parentheses from D. Clay Whybark, "Strategic Manufacturing Management," IRMIS Working Paper #W601, School of Business, Indiana University, February 1986.

application of extra coats of paint are some of the product quality characteristics that differentiate a Mercedes-Benz from a Hyundai. One advantage of offering higher-quality products is that they command higher prices in the marketplace.

The goal in establishing the proper level of product quality is to focus on the requirements of the customer. Overdesigned products with too much quality will be viewed as being prohibitively expensive. Underdesigned products, on the other hand, will lose customers to products that cost a little more but are perceived by the customers as offering much greater benefits.

Process quality is critical in every market segment. Regardless of whether the product is a child's first two-wheeler or a bicycle for an international cyclist, or whether it is a Mercedes-Benz or a Hyundai, customers want products without defects. Thus, the goal of process quality is to produce error-free products through total quality management.

Speed of Delivery   Another market niche considers speed of delivery to be an important determinant in its purchasing decision. Here, the ability of a firm to provide dependable and fast delivery allows it to charge a premium price for its products.

Flexibility   Flexibility, from a strategic perspective, refers to the ability of a company to offer a wide variety of products to its customers. Flexibility is also a measure of how fast a company can convert its process(es) from making an old line of products to producing a new product line. Product variety is often perceived by the customer to be a dimension of speed of delivery.

Factory Focus and Trade-offs

Central to the concept of operations strategy, during the late 1960s and early 1970s, was the notion of factory focus and trade-offs. The underlying logic was that a factory could not excel simultaneously on all four performance measures. Consequently, management had to decide which parameters of performance were critical to the firm's success, and then concentrate or focus the resources of the firm on those particular characteristics.

For example, if a company wanted to focus on speed of delivery, then it could not be very flexible in terms of its ability to offer a wide range of products. Similarly, a low-cost strategy was not compatible with either speed of delivery or flexibility. High quality was also viewed as a trade-off to low cost. For those firms with very large, existing manufacturing facilities, Skinner even suggested the creation of a **plant-within-a-plant (PWP)** concept, in which different locations within the facility would be allocated to different product lines, each with their own operations strategy. Under the PWP concept, even the workers would be separated to minimize the confusion associated with shifting from one type of strategy to another.[2]

The concepts of factory focus and PWPs are still widely employed today. However, as discussed next, the notion of trade-offs has given way to the need to do everything well and the issue has instead become determining priorities.

Establishing Priorities

Beginning in the mid-1960s, competition became more intense as more and more foreign goods started to invade markets that were predominantly controlled by U.S. firms. This trend toward a more global perspective in terms of market competition continues to this day. In the mid-1960s, for example, only 7 percent of the U.S. economy was exposed to international competition. However, by the 1980s, this figure exceeded 70 percent and it is still growing.[3]

As a one-world economy (or global village) evolves, there has emerged a group of companies that have adopted an international perspective toward both manufacturing and marketing. Within this global area, competition is significantly more intense due to both the greater number of "players" and the tremendous opportunities that exist.

Those companies that have excelled on the international level have often been called **world-class manufacturers.** Events in the world marketplace during the 1970s and 1980s, in terms of the growing intensity in competition, forced these companies to reexamine the concept of operations strategy, especially in terms of the so-called necessary trade-offs.

Managers began to recognize that they did not really have to make trade-offs between these different strategies. What emerged instead was a realization for the need to establish priorities among the four strategies as dictated by the marketplace.

In the late 1960s and early 1970s, cost was the primary concern (a holdover from the 1950s philosophy that manufacturing's only objective was to minimize production costs). But as more and more companies began to produce low-cost products, it became apparent that they had to develop other ways to differentiate themselves from their competitors. The priority thus shifted to quality. Companies at this time obtained a competitive advantage by producing high-quality products, which allowed them to charge more—although price still was a factor in the consumer's buying decision. But competition soon caught up again, and many competitors were offering high-quality products that were reasonably priced.

In seeking another competitive advantage in the marketplace, companies turned to speed of delivery as a means of differentiating themselves from the rest of the pack. Now the ante into the game was high-quality products that were reasonably priced and could be quickly delivered to the customer. Sometimes this ante is termed a **qualifier** (to enter the market). It is often used in contrast to an **order winner**—the feature that leads customers to choose your product over competitors'.

In recent years, George Stalk, Jr., a leading management consultant, has identified speed of delivery as a major factor in determining the success of a company, stating that there is a very high correlation between both profit and growth in market share, and the

---

[2]C. Wickham Skinner, "The Focused Factory," *Harvard Business Review* 52, no. 3 (May–June 1974), pp. 113–22.

[3]S. C. Gwynne, "The Long Haul," *Time*, September 28, 1992.

speed with which a firm can deliver its products.[4] Companies are therefore concentrating their resources on reducing product lead times with dramatic results. Products that once took weeks or months to deliver are now being shipped within hours or days of the receipt of an order.

Eventually, the competition again caught up and the more aggressive firms looked for another means to obtain a competitive advantage. This time flexibility was selected, as reflected by the firm's ability to produce customized products. Now the marketplace dictated that for firms to succeed, they had to produce reasonably priced, customized products of high quality that could be quickly delivered to the customer.

A good example of a firm that has accomplished this is the National Bicycle Company in Japan (discussed in Chapter 1). The total cycle time to produce the bike is three hours, although the actual delivery is about two weeks. (Market surveys have suggested that this is the "optimum" delivery time in terms of customer satisfaction.)[5]

As the "rules" for operations strategy shifted from that of primarily reducing manufacturing costs to that of including quality, speed of delivery, and flexibility, the paradigm for the operations management function has also shifted. The paradigm of minimizing production costs has been replaced with that of providing full service to the customer.

The Information Age

Today, world-class manufacturing companies are again looking for a breakthrough that will provide them with another competitive advantage in the marketplace. The 1993 annual meeting of the Operations Management Association (OMA) focused on the topic of service breakthroughs, with several presentations suggesting that service (in particular, postpurchase service) is the approach by which companies will differentiate themselves in the near future. Cadillac, Lexus, and Nissan, for example, now offer extensive warranty packages that include such things as road service, travel planning, and the use of loaner vehicles during the warranty period.

Warranty packages such as these will permit companies to capture all the data pertaining to product defects and malfunctions (at least those that occur during the warranty period). Such information can then be fed back into the product design process to further refine the product.

By incorporating such consumer information into the operations process, companies will officially make the transition from the Manufacturing Age into the Information Age. Previously, a company achieved competitive advantage through its operations processing capability. Now competitive advantage is achieved primarily by using information from the marketplace.

2.2   A FRAMEWORK FOR OPERATIONS STRATEGY IN MANUFACTURING

Operations strategy cannot be done in a vacuum. It must be linked vertically to the customer and horizontally to other parts of the enterprise. Exhibit 2.2 shows these linkages between customer needs, their performance priorities and requirements for manufacturing operations, and the operations and related enterprise resource capabilities to satisfy those needs. Overlying this framework is senior management's strategic vision of the firm. The vision identifies, in general terms, the target market, the firm's product line, and its **core enterprise** and **operations capabilities**.

---

[4]George Stalk, Jr., "Time—The Next Source of Competitive Advantage," *Harvard Business Review,* July–August 1988, pp. 41–51.
[5]Susan Moffatt, "Japan's New Personalized Production," *Fortune,* October 22, 1990.

The choice of a target market can be difficult, but it must be made. Indeed, it may lead to turning away business—ruling out a customer segment that would simply be unprofitable or too hard to serve given the firm's capabilities. Examples here are U.S. car companies not producing right-hand drive cars for the Japanese and British markets as well as clothing manufacturers not making half-sizes in their dress lines. **Core capabilities** (or competencies) are those skills that differentiate the manufacturing (or service firm) from its competitors.

The general process is that customer-based new-product or current-product requirements give rise to performance priorities that then become the required priorities for operations. Exhibit 2.2 shows these priorities linking into an enterprise capabilities "barrel" since operations cannot satisfy customer needs without the involvement of R&D and distribution and without direct or indirect support of financial management, human resource management, and information management. Given its performance requirements, an operations division uses its capabilities (as well as those of its suppliers) to achieve those requirements—that is, to win orders. These capabilities include technology, systems, and people (i.e., the five Ps restated at a broader level). CIM (computer-integrated manufacturing), JIT (just-in-time), and TQM (total quality management) represent fundamental

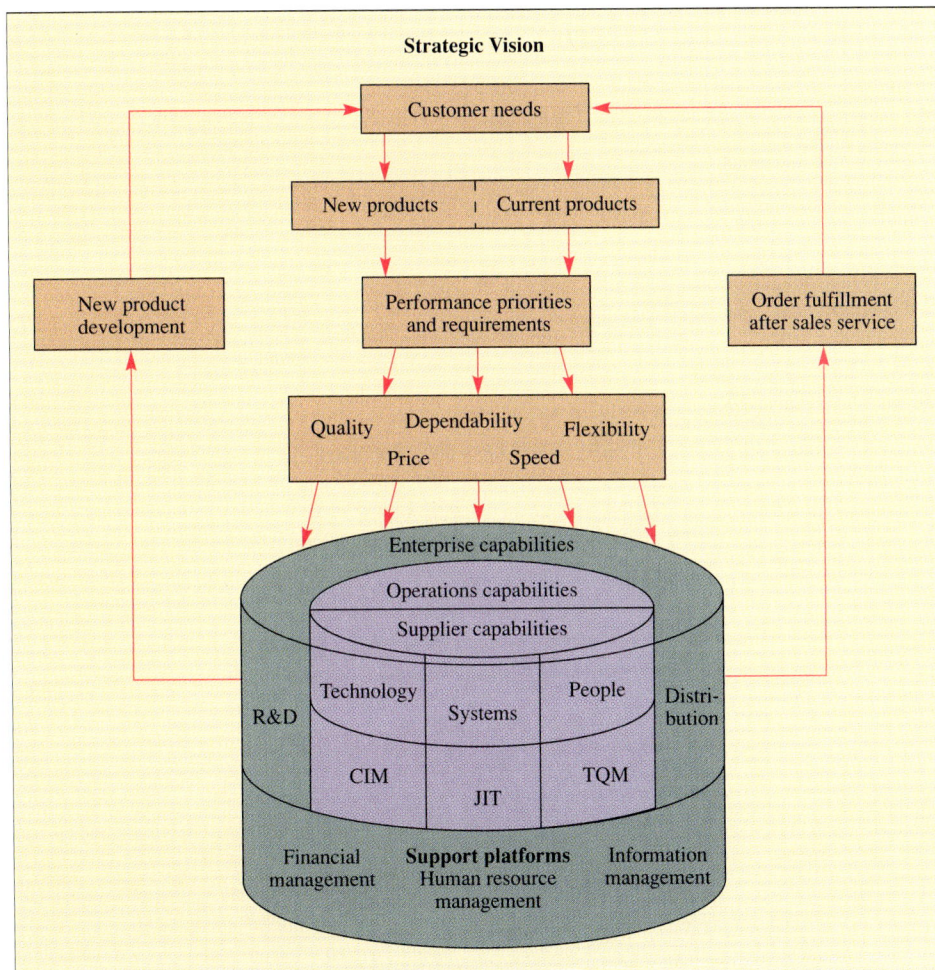

E X H I B I T 2.2
Operations Strategy Framework: From Customer Needs to Order Fulfillment

Break*through*

Strategy as Capability Building: Toshiba's T-3100 Laptop

Much of manufacturing strategy involves the building and leveraging of production function capabilities. While the exact contents of a manufacturing strategy will vary from industry to industry and company to company, manufacturing strategy as a pattern of choices should be linked to the business strategy that must be accomplished to win orders.

Toshiba successfully deployed a manufacturing strategy to produce the breakthrough T-3100 laptop personal computer. Toshiba first introduced the T-3100 laptop computer at a trade show in London in January 1986. Since that time, Toshiba has been the market leader of laptop computers in the United States, Europe, and Japan. The stages in Toshiba's customer-driven manufacturing strategy development are given below, defined by business, marketing, and manufacturing strategies.

Business Strategy

Toshiba's strategic intent was to penetrate the desktop computer market at a time when the IBM PC dominated. As a late entry, it sought to develop a highly differentiated product from the IBM desktop, yet maintain IBM operating standards. The initial business strategy was to develop a computer that would compete on price and performance. The specifics of the product features were left to marketing, engineering, and manufacturing.

The actual laptop design evolved from the business unit differentiation strategy.

Marketing Strategy

  Customer Requirements. Extensive market research of the personal computer market in the United States was conducted through the joint efforts of a U.S. consulting firm and Toshiba's marketing and engineering personnel. Personal computer dealers were the prime target for focused interviews concerning the new product. The results showed a distinct need for a significantly smaller personal computer that performed exactly the same as a desktop model.

  Product Concept. The product that was conceived based on customer requirements was a desktop computer that could be used on any desk and perform exactly as a conventional desktop computer would.

  Product Design. The design of the product was to match the needs of the end users, who liked the look and convenience of flat displays. This concept led to the laptop style.

  Target Pricing. To set the sales price, Toshiba carefully determined what sales price would be accepted by consumers for significant market penetration. A target sales price was established and, after deducting a desirable profit, a target cost was introduced. Prior to the T-3100, Toshiba made pricing decisions on a cost-plus

concepts and tools used in each of the three areas. We have shown suppliers in the operations capabilities barrel to reflect the fact that suppliers do not become suppliers unless their capabilities in technology, systems, and people management pass certification tests. In addition, virtually every operations capability is now subjected to a "make-or-buy" decision. It is current practice among world-class manufacturers to subject each part of a manufacturing operation to the question, If we are not among the best in the world at, say, metal forming, should we be doing this at all, or should we subcontract to someone who is? In the computer industry, for example, the majority of manufacturers outsource fabrication of component parts, leaving just assembly and testing to be done in-house (or, as is becoming quite common, at the customer's facility, since that is where the product must function properly).

As a final comment, we should emphasize that the mark of a good operations strategy is that it sees capabilities as supporting what Hayes and Pisano term the intended direction of the firm, not just its current situation.[6] Warren Bennis, an expert in leadership,

---

[6]Robert H. Hayes and Gary Pisano, "Beyond World Class: The New Manufacturing Strategy," *Harvard Business Review,* January–February 1994, pp. 77–85.

basis. The target costing method set the standard for joint product and process development and, subsequently, for the evolution of the Toshiba manufacturing strategy.

Manufacturing Strategy

Integration Choices. Having established a target cost, Toshiba worked on an integrated approach to the development of detailed product design and production processes. Key elements of the manufacturing strategy were the use of value analysis and computer-aided design. It was clear to the Toshiba team that since the product concept was so new, they would have to introduce innovative parts and manufacturing technologies.

Since no currently available hard disk drive was small enough to install in the T-3100, an entirely new component had to be developed. The printed circuit boards also had to be redesigned. To minimize the size and thickness of the printed circuit boards, the Toshiba development team worked with the company's LSI (large scale integration) division to produce a super-integrated LSI chip. Simultaneously, the Toshiba Manufacturing Engineering Laboratory was involved in the development of a special surface-mount technology that would ensure that the LSI chips were soldered flatly on the boards. A special soldering machine was engineered for this process.

Along with internal integration, supplier integration efforts with Matsushita Electronics Devices were initiated for the production of the plasma display. Toshiba asked Matsushita to develop and introduce specially designed plasma displays. Toshiba also advised Matsushita on the introduction of a robotic manufacturing system for the special plasma displays that would be required for the T-3100.

Structural and Infrastructural Choices. To produce the T-3100, Toshiba employed JIT, TQC teams, advanced manufacturing technology including CIM, and robotics. These manufacturing strategy choices were useful for continuous improvement of product and processes and provided the necessary capacity to meet demand. Toshiba's business strategy dictated a global playing field. Consequently, new production facilities were established in the United States and West Germany.

Toshiba's manufacturing strategy had been engineered to use all the company's capabilities as a comprehensive electronics manufacturer. It required extensive use of boundary management to enable the product design to meet the size, weight, and performance attributes required by customers and to enable the production processes to meet specifications at relatively low cost. Toshiba's manufacturing processes supported its corporate strategy, making the company a global market leader in laptop computers.

Source: Craig A. Giffy, Aleda V. Roth, and Gregory M. Seal, eds., *Competing in World-Class Manufacturing*, National Center for Manufacturing Sciences, Business One Irwin, 1990.

---

calls such looking ahead "the Gretsky Factor—imagining not where the puck is, but where it is going to be."[7]

For an example of how one company put these elements together, see "Strategy as Capability Building: Toshiba's T-3100 Laptop."

The main objectives of manufacturing strategy development are (*a*) to translate required priorities (typically obtained from marketing) into specific performance requirements for operations, and (*b*) to make the necessary plans to assure that operations (and enterprise) capabilities are sufficient to accomplish them. The steps for developing priorities are

Developing a Manufacturing Strategy

1. Segment the market according to the product group.
2. Identify the product requirements, demand patterns, and profit margins of each group.
3. Determine the order winners and qualifiers for each group.
4. Convert order winners into specific performance requirements.

---

[7]Warren Bennis, speech before the 1992 Leadership Conference, University of Southern California.

Manufacturing Strategy and Focus

The process of achieving a satisfactory manufacturing segmentation that maintains focus is often a matter of deciding which products or product groups fit together in the sense that they have similar market performance characteristics and/or they place similar demands on the manufacturing system. For example the accompanying table shows how two product groups manufactured by one instrument manufacturer differ in their manufacturing requirements. The first product group is a range of standard electronic medical equipment that was sold "off the shelf" direct to hospitals and clinics. The second product group is a wider range of measuring devices that were sold to original equipment manufacturers and often had to be customized to individual customer requirements. The analysis of the two product groups in the table shows that they have very different market competitive characteristics. Therefore, very different external performance objectives are required from the manufacturing operation. Each product group also has different priorities for its internal performance objectives. Product group 1 needs to concentrate on cost and quality performance. All other internal performance objectives should be bent to achieving this. Product group 2 needs the flexibility to cope with a wide product range and with considerable design turbulence.

Such very different competitive needs will almost certainly require two separate focused units, each devoted to providing the things that are important in their separate markets. [Further analysis is required to determine the specific capabilities of these focused units.]

Manufacturing Requirements Differences	Product Group 1	Product Group 2
Products	Standard medical equipment	Electronic measuring devices
Customers	Hospitals/clinics	Medical and other OEMs
Product specs	Not high tech but periodic updates	Varies, some high specs; others less so
Product range	Narrow—4 variants	Wide, many types and variants, some customisation
Design changes	Infrequent	Continuous process
Delivery	Customer lead-time important—ship directly from stock on hand	On time delivery important
Quality	Conformance/reliability	Performance/conformance
Demand variation	Financial year related but predictable	Lumpy and unpredictable
Volume/line	High	Medium to low
Margins	Low	Low to very high

External Performance Priorities	↓	↓
Order winners	Price Product reliability	Product specification Product range
Qualifiers	Delivery lead-time Product specification Quality conformance	Delivery dependability Delivery lead-time Price

	↓	↓
Main Internal Performance Requirements	Cost Quality	New product flexibility Range flexibility Dependability

Source: Nigel Slack, *The Manufacturing Advantage,* Management Books 2000 Ltd., London, 1992, pps. 14–15.

At Citicorp, order winners include branches with tellers available from 8 A.M. to 6 P.M. and retrained to handle more than cash transactions. Each branch tripled the number of automated teller machines, and personal bankers can access records of any customer who needs more help.

An example of this process, along with a discussion of focus, is presented in "Manufacturing Strategy and Focus."

2.3   OPERATIONS STRATEGY IN SERVICES

Operations strategy in service firms is generally inseparable from the corporate strategy. For most services, the service delivery system is the business and hence any strategic decision must include operations considerations. However, operations executives do not always have a voice equal to other functions of the firm. A marketing decision to add a new route for an airline, or add new in-flight services, may be made despite operations' protests about feasibility.

Although we will discuss service strategy in Chapter 4, we should note that many of the strategy concepts discussed relative to manufacturing also apply to services. For example, service firms may use the plant-within-a-plant (PWP) structure to achieve focus. Hospitals using the PWP focus may have separate units for distinct patient services such as cardiac units, oncology units, labor and delivery units, and rehabilitation units. Major department stores group products and services into separate units or "departments," with a separate customer focus, ordering, product arrangement, flow, and strategy. Each department—women's sportswear, customer service, children's apparel, housewares, and men's clothing—focuses on specific customer niches with unique needs, particularly if the organization serves a variety of customers and markets with distinct needs. Likewise, order winners and qualifiers have service applications. For a bank, qualifiers might be a good location, availability of tellers and loan officers, and ATMs. Order winners might be relationship banking and customer-oriented banking hours.

The nature of operations role in achieving corporate-wide competitiveness in services is shown in the four-stage model in Exhibit 2.3. The first column of the exhibit lists four proposed stages of service firm competitiveness. Across the top are the major service dimensions that operations executives must address in strategy development. The entries in the table reflect our interpretation of the views held by senior management of companies that fit into each stage.

E X H I B I T 2.3   *Four Stages of Service Firm Competitiveness*

		Important Performance Dimensions			
Stage	**Characteristics**	**Service Quality**	**New Technology**	**Workforce**	**First Line Management**
I. Available for service	Customers patronize service firm for reasons other than performance. Operations is reactive at best.	Subsidiary to cost; highly variable.	When necessary for survival, under duress.	Negative constraint.	Controls workers.
II. Journeyman	Customers neither seek out nor avoid the firm. Operations functions in a mediocre, uninspired fashion.	Meets some customer expectations; consistent on one or two key dimensions.	When justified by cost savings.	An efficient resource; disciplined; follows procedures.	Controls the process.
III. Distinctive competence achieved	Customers seek out the firm based on its sustained reputation for meeting customer expectations. Operations continually excels, reinforced by personnel management and systems that support an intense customer focus.	Exceeds customer expectations; consistent on multiple dimensions.	When it promises to enhance service.	Permitted to elect among alternative procedures.	Listens to customers; coaches and facilitates workers.
IV. World-class service delivery	The name of the company is synonymous with service excellence. Its service does not just satisfy customers; it delights them, and thereby expands customer expectations to levels its competitors cannot fill. Operations is a quick learner and fast innovator; it masters every step of the service delivery process and provides capabilities that are superior to competitors' capabilities.	Raises customer expectations; seeks challenges; improves continuously.	Source of first-mover advantages, creating ability to do things competitors cannot do.	Innovative; creates procedures.	Is listened to by top management as a source of new ideas. Mentors workers to enhance their career growth.

Here are some additional comments about the framework: First, the stage attained by any given firm is a composite. Every service delivery system embodies a unique set of choices about service quality, workforce policies, and so forth. A company may be at a different stage for a given dimension, or have service units that are further or less advanced than others. Second, a firm can be very competitive (Stage III or even Stage IV) even if it is not outstanding on all dimensions. This could happen when it is doing an exceptional job on its critical success factors. Third, it is difficult or impossible to skip a stage in moving up the ladder. A company obviously must achieve journeyman performance before distinctive competence, and must attain distinctive competence before becoming world class. (However, a firm can move through the stages relatively rapidly. For example, Scandinavian Airlines System (SAS) instituted some 120 service improvements that moved it from Stage I to Stage III within a year and a half. ValuJet seems to be there already, as the Breakthrough box on ValuJet relates. Finally, it is all too easy to slip back a stage. The Los Angeles Police Department (LAPD), for example, was viewed as being equivalent to a Stage III law enforcement organization before the Rodney King incident was made public.[8]

2.4   U.S. COMPETITIVENESS

The wealth and power of the United States depends upon maintaining mastery and control of production.

> Stephen S. Cohen and John Zysman, *Why Manufacturing Matters: The Myth of the Post-Industrial Economy* (New York: Basic Books, 1987)

In the next century, the United States will be our farm and Western Europe our boutique.

> Attributed to a Japanese minister of trade in Gore Vidal, "Rebirth of a Nation: Why Italy Works," *Los Angeles Times,* May 1, 1988

Competitiveness for a nation is the degree to which it can, under free and fair market conditions, produce goods and services that meet the test of international markets while simultaneously maintaining and expanding the real incomes of its citizens.

> The President's Council on Industrial Competitiveness, 1985

For most of the past 15 years, the United States has had a serious manufacturing competitiveness problem as measured by productivity growth and market share loss. Some experts claim—with justification—that manufacturing lacks the government support that foreign nations provide to its competitors. Also, a large portion of the blame is frequently put on the relative strength of the dollar against foreign currencies. However, the U.S. trade deficit increased during the 1970s when the dollar *depreciated* by 15 percent. A similar phenomenon occurred in the 1980s.

Some say that our reliance on manufacturing is outdated and, given our shift to services, there is no problem. (See the box "The Final Frontier.") And, indeed, exported services have produced a surplus in the trade balance equation. However, people who see a shift to the service economy as a salvation miss two crucial points. First, service and manufacturing are closely linked. Many services are purchased by manufacturing firms (for example, advertising, legal, health care, and accounting services). The United States cannot be supported only by a strong service sector. Second, although foreign purchases of services are high at the present time, it is naive to believe that foreign manufacturers and their developing societies will forever be dependent on U.S. services. Japan is building a strong financial base that is already competing with and even surpassing the United States in both the world and domestic marketplaces.

Another rationalization for the past disappointing performance of the United States in the global marketplace is that the poor performers are just isolated industries and that

---

[8]One of the authors of this book had the unique experience of lecturing on service quality to 100 of the LAPD's senior staff (including the chief) during the height of the King controversy.

Brea**k***through*

ValueJet

Seemingly overnight, tiny ValuJet Airlines Inc. has demonstrated a knack for getting noticed—and for getting under the skin of its giant Atlanta-based neighbor, Delta Air Lines.

A recent entry in the expanding field of low-cost, no-frills carriers, ValuJet began flying in October and now serves 12 Southern cities with short-haul flights from Atlanta. One-way fares range from $39 to $149.

Besides reaching more cities with scheduled service than other discount airlines operating out of Atlanta, ValuJet has used clever marketing that has drawn attention from far beyond its relatively limited service area.

ValuJet's logo—a looping, smiling cartoon airplane known as "The Critter"—is plastered on jets, bumper stickers and billboards. The carrier's promotions include a contest in which travelers choose ValuJet's next new destination.

"Travel today has become a hassle. Our marketing has been fun. We don't take ourselves too seriously," ValuJet President Lewis Jordan said. "It's all cartoons and fun, and centered around families and children."

Passengers can play in-flight games. A passenger who guesses the age of a flight attendant, for example, wins a T-shirt.

But behind ValuJet's rapid success are rock-bottom operating costs.

Like other low-cost carriers modeled after Dallas-based Southwest Airlines, ValuJet favors informal dress for its staff and peanuts instead of meals on board.

Instead of paper tickets, ValuJet gives passengers only a confirmation number when a reservation is made, and it won't transfer luggage to another carrier.

The airline boasts that it pays employees far less than the industry standard, yet it has been able to attract experienced personnel who lost jobs with financially strapped or failed carriers.

The upstart airline filled 80 percent of its seats in its first full month of business, though that figure has since dropped to 56 percent.

It's such numbers, not the promotional antics, that worry Delta, which has been grappling with low-price competition elsewhere as it struggles to return to profitability.

ValuJet put Delta on the defensive by forcing the larger airline to match low fares on its home turf. ValuJet lodged predatory-pricing complaints with federal regulators when Delta fought back.

Last week, the Department of Transportation said it had dropped a probe of whether Delta was trying to drive its smaller competitor out of business.

"Are we trying to put them out of business? Let's turn that question around to 'Is ValuJet's goal to put Delta out of business?' " Delta spokesman Bill Berry said. "We're simply competing on the open market, and the open market is not a kind and friendly place."

Delta says it has no choice but to hit ValuJet head-on.

"By itself, they are extremely small and minute, but there are dozens of 'ValuJets' in our system," Berry said. "To fail to be price-competitive is to give up an important segment of the marketplace."

Valujet airlines at a glance

- **Headquarters:** Atlanta
- **Cities served: Florida:** Fort Lauderdale, Jacksonville, Orlando, Tampa, West Palm Beach, and Fort Myers; **Tennessee:** Memphis and Nashville; **Kentucky:** Louisville; **Louisiana:** New Orleans; **Georgia:** Atlanta and Savannah; Washington, D.C. (Dulles)
- **Fares:** One-way tickets from Atlanta to most destinations range from $49 during off-peak hours and with 21-day advance purchase, to $149 for a walk-up ticket during peak hours.
- **Fleet:** Owns and operates seven DC-9 jets, formerly owned by Delta Air Lines.
- **Financing:** Founders invested $3.4 million of own money to start company. A $14 million private sale of equity was completed in December.
- **Salaries:** Lower than industry standard. For example, a captain at ValuJet makes $42,000 a year. Industry-wide, captains of DC-9s earn from $75,000 to $138,000, according to Future Aviation Professionals of America.

Source: Marc Rice, "Little Airline Flies High,"*Orange County Register,* February 26, 1994. Reprinted by permission of The Associated Press

The Final Frontier

S

The industrial economies should be renamed the service economies: they employ twice as many workers in services as in industry. The growth of services is nothing new. As early as 1900 America and Britain both had more jobs in services than in industry. By 1950 services employed half of all American workers. Last year the figure hit 76%.

America has by far the biggest service sector, accounting for 72% of its GDP. At the rich world's other extreme, Germany's still provides only 57% of its GDP, thanks partly to a multitude of restrictive practices which have choked expansion.

Meanwhile, the share of manufacturing has fallen in all the big economies. It now accounts for only 23% of America's GDP (and an even smaller 18% of jobs). In Britain and Canada manufacturing has tumbled to less than 20% of total output. Even in Japan and Germany, the strongholds of industry, manufacturing is now no more than 30% of GDP.

Services are also the fastest-growing part of international trade, accounting for 20% of total world trade and 30% of American exports. This excludes those services that are not traded, but are delivered by subsidiaries set up in foreign markets. Services account for about 40% of the stock of foreign direct investment by the five big "industrial economies."

Sales of services by the foreign affiliates of American companies were worth $119 billion in 1990 (the latest figures available), not far behind America's $138 billion-worth of cross-border sales of private services. These sales do not contribute directly to output or jobs in America, but the economy does benefit when the profits from American company operations abroad are brought home. As governments open their borders to foreign companies, the scope for future expansion of trade and foreign direct investment in services is huge.

Policemen and prostitutes, bankers and butchers are all lumped together in the service sector, but not all have grown at the same rate. Top of the league are legal and business services, which grew by 106% and 67% respectively, followed closely by health (59%) and recreation (53%). Jobs in older services grew more slowly. Employment in transport and communication, for instance, grew by only 13%.

Some economists argue that the boom in services is caused mainly by firms contracting out jobs they used to do for themselves, such as catering, advertising, and data-processing. But studies in America and Britain suggest that this explains only a fraction of the increase.

If anything, official figures may understate the true importance of services in both output and jobs, as many activities in manufacturing firms are really services. Government number-crunchers stick *The Economist,* along with all newspapers, in the manufacturing sector, even though few employees actually make anything. The work of a freelance journalist, by contrast, is counted in the service sector. The division between services and manufacturing is becoming steadily less useful.

As a recent OECD report* points out, services and manufacturing have become increasingly interconnected, as manufacturers buy more inputs from service firms and vice versa. Higher spending on advertising, financial management, and a speedier delivery system mean that more service value is added to each unit of manufacturing output.

Take General Motors, the archetypal manufacturer. Its biggest single supplier is not a steel or glass firm, but a health care provider, Blue Cross–Blue Shield. In terms of output, one of GM's biggest "products" is financial and insurance services, which together with EDS, its computing-services arm, account for a fifth of total revenue.

But few manufacturers will admit how much they rely on services. Sony's chairman, Akio Morita, proclaimed in a speech at this year's meeting of the World Economic Forum in Davos that "an increased focus on manufacturing will help us to re-lay the foundation of our economy. Only manufacturing can provide employment opportunities of quality, scope and number . . . The service sector can only survive if there is a productive manufacturing sector to serve." Yet look closer at Sony: as much as a fifth of its revenues now come from its film and music businesses. Add in design, marketing, finance, and after-sales support, and service activities probably account for at least half of Sony's business.

---

*The Final
Frontier
(continued)*

Those who call for an industrial policy to help manufacturing are missing the point. If services account for half of the sales price of goods, then improving efficiency there may be a better way to trim the cost of the final product, and thus to become more competitive, than tinkering with the production process.

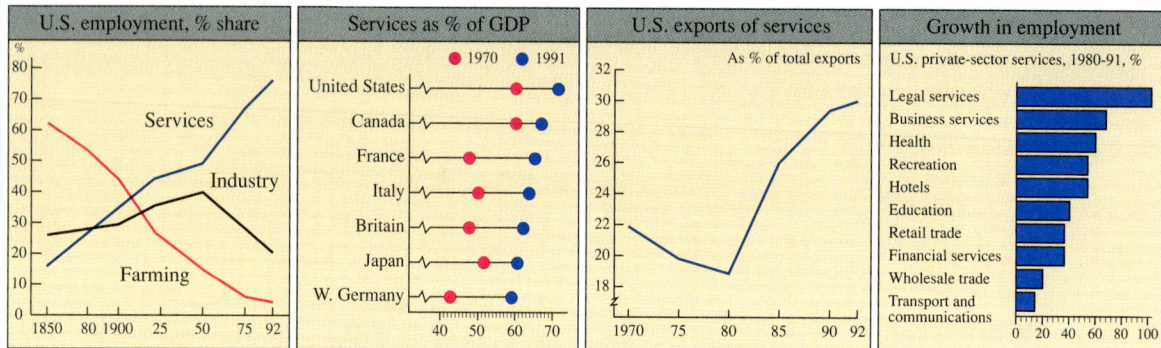

| U.S. employment, % share | Services as % of GDP | U.S. exports of services | Growth in employment |

*"Structural Shifts in Major OECD Countries," *Industrial Policy in OECD Countries: Annual Review, 1992,* published by the OECD.

Source: "The Final Frontier," *The Economist,* February 20, 1993. © 1993 The Economist Newspaper Group, Inc. Reprinted with permission.

---

overall performance is what really matters. This might be true—a dollar's worth of exported wheat has the same value as a dollar's worth of electronics. Unfortunately, the poor performance is not isolated to just a few industries. Portfolio theory has taught us the benefit of diversification. The United States needs a more diversified portfolio in exports.

2.5   MEETING THE COMPETITIVE CHALLENGE

In 1985, the MIT Commission on Industrial Productivity recommended the following actions:

1. Place less emphasis on short-term financial payoffs and invest more in R&D.
2. Revise corporate strategies to include responses to foreign competition. This, in-turn, calls for greater investment in people and equipment to improve manufacturing capability.
3. Knock down communication barriers within organizations and recognize mutuality of interests with other companies and suppliers (the former relative to international competition, in particular).
4. Recognize that the labor force is a resource to be nurtured, not just a cost to be avoided.
5. Get back to basics in managing production operations. Build in quality at the design stage. Place more emphasis on process innovations rather than focusing sole attention on product innovations.

How are we doing now? Have we taken these suggestions to heart? Apparently so, as evidenced in the box "Red, White, and Boom: U.S. Economy Shines."

Red, White and Boom: U.S. Economy Shines

A 3 percent economic growth rate, a gain of 2 million new jobs in the past year and an inflation rate reminiscent of the 1960s make the United States the envy of the industrialized world. The amount the average U.S. worker can produce, already the highest in the world, is growing faster than in other wealthy countries, including Japan.

The United States has become the world's low-cost provider of many sophisticated products and services, from plastics to software to financial services. And after years of decline, the nation's share of the world export market has been rising.

For the most part, these advantages will continue even after countries such as Japan and Germany snap out of their recessions. It is the United States, not Japan, that is the master of the next generation of commercially important computer and communications technologies as well as leading-edge services from medicine to movie making.

And U.S. managers are not only investing heavily in new equipment, they are also much farther along than those in Europe and Japan in streamlining and re-engineering their companies to make them more competitive.

That's one reason that U.S. industries that recently were losers—such as makers of automobiles, machine tools, steel and computer chips—are back with a vengeance.

The turnaround reflects more than 10 years of sometimes innovative and often wrenching change driven by recession, deregulation, tougher foreign competition, the threat of takeovers, and, not least, new technology.

Foreign leaders and executives who once lectured Americans on their shortcomings now speak enviously of this country's cleverness in churning out everything from jobs to Jeeps.

While such sentiments may seem more common abroad than at home, there are signs that America's self-esteem is recovering. Some polls show that Americans once again see the United States as an economic giant.

Some of the evidence of America's impressive economic performance has been around for years but ignored. Most of it is fairly new.

Start with the most basic yardstick of economic health, the growth of productivity, or output per worker. Productivity determines how fast living standards can rise.

The American worker is already the most productive in the world by far, producing on average $49,600 in goods and services in 1990—$5,000 more than German workers and $10,000 more than their Japanese counterparts.

Moreover, while productivity was growing more quickly abroad than in the United States for most of the 20th century, America has lately been gaining more quickly, as companies here figure out how to provide more and better products and services with new technologies and fewer workers.

Since the start of the economic recovery nearly three years ago, U.S. productivity has been growing at an annual rate of 2.5 percent, more than twice as fast as the average from 1970 to 1990 and markedly better than elsewhere in the world.

Source: Sylvia Nasar, "The American Economy, Back on Top," *The New York Times*, February 27, 1994. Copyright © 1994 by The New York Times Company. Reprinted by permission.

Some Causes of America's Improved Competitiveness

James P. Womack, principal research scientist of the MIT Japan Program, offers some intriguing observations on the specific underlying causes behind the recent improvement in U.S. competitiveness.[9] His thesis is that it is *not* the fact that U.S. firms are better innovators than most foreign competitors. This capability has existed since long before the United States encountered its competitiveness problems. Rather, it is the fact that "we're proving to be very effective copiers. We've spent a decade examining the advan-

---

[9]James P. Womack, "Book Reviews" section, *Sloan Management Review,* Winter 1994, p. 107.

tages of our rivals in product development, production operations, supply chain management and corporate governance (spurred, in many cases, by the demonstration effect of Japanese direct investment) and are putting in place 'functional equivalents' that 'incrementally improve' on their best techniques." Womack cites four examples of where and how this is occurring:

1. New approaches to product development team structure and management that get products to market faster, with better designs and manufacturability. ("Chrysler has been a striking leader in this area with a new product development system initially copied from Honda but then 'improved' into something quite different and now apparently superior. Xerox and Boeing are two more examples of creative adaptation.")

2. Improving performance of manufacturing facilities through dramatic reductions of work-in-process, space, tool costs, and human effort, while improving quality and flexibility. (Womack calls this "focusing on the value stream," which owes much of its philosophy to Japanese JIT concepts.)

3. Adopting new methods of customer–supplier cooperation that borrow from the Japanese **keiretsu** (large holding companies) practices of close linkages, but maintain the independence of the organizations desired by U.S. companies.

4. Better leadership through strong, independent boards of directors that will dismiss managers who are not doing their jobs effectively. (This has achieved results that are comparable to or better than the oversight systems used by the Japanese keiretsu and German banks.)

There are many specific examples of U.S. firms that have risen to the competitive challenge. Monroe Auto Equipment, for example, has succeeded at producing such high-quality shock absorbers that one of its customers, Toyota of Japan, recently gave an appraisal of "defects—zero" in a shipment of 60,000 shocks. Exhibit 2.4 shows how a number of companies are improving the time they take to get their new products to market.

2.6   PRODUCTIVITY MEASUREMENT

Productivity is a common measure of how well a country, industry, or business unit is using its resources (or factors of production). In its broadest sense, productivity is defined as

$$\text{Productivity} = \frac{\text{Outputs}}{\text{Inputs}}$$

To increase productivity, we want to make this ratio of outputs to inputs as large as practical.

Productivity is what we call a *relative measure*. In other words, to be meaningful, it needs to be compared with something else. For example, what can we learn from the fact that we operate a restaurant, and that its productivity last week was 8.4 customers per labor hour? Nothing!

Productivity comparisons can be made in two ways. First, a company can compare itself with similar operations within its industry, or can use industry data when such data are available (e.g., comparing productivity among the different stores in a franchise).

Another approach is to measure productivity over time within the same operation. Here we would compare our productivity in one time period with that of the next.

E X H I B I T 2.4

*Shortening Product
Cycle Times*

Company/Product	Product Cycle Time Reduction
General Motors New Buick model	60 to 40 months
Hewlett-Packard Computer printer	52 to 24 months
IBM Personal computer	48 to 13 months
Honeywell Thermostat	48 to 12 months
Ingersoll Rand Air grinder	42 to 12 months
Warner Electric Clutch brake	36 to 10 months

Source: Data from *Developing Products in Half the Time* by Donald
Relnersen and Preston Smith (New York: Van Nostrand Reinhold,
1990), reported in *Boardroom Reports,* June 15, 1991, p. 7.

E X H I B I T 2.5

*Examples of
Productivity
Measures*

Partial measure
$$\frac{\text{Output}}{\text{Labor}} \text{ or } \frac{\text{Output}}{\text{Capital}} \text{ or } \frac{\text{Output}}{\text{Materials}} \text{ or } \frac{\text{Output}}{\text{Energy}}$$

Multifactor measure
$$\frac{\text{Output}}{\text{Labor} + \text{Capital} + \text{Energy}} \text{ or } \frac{\text{Output}}{\text{Labor} + \text{Capital} + \text{Materials}}$$

Total measure
$$\frac{\text{Output}}{\text{Inputs}} \text{ or } \frac{\text{Goods and services produced}}{\text{All resources used}}$$

Source: David J. Sumanth and Kitty Tang, "A Review of Some Approaches to the Management of Total
Productivity in a Company/Organization," *Institute of Industrial Engineering Conference Proceedings,*
Fall 1984, p. 305. Copyright Institute of Industrial Engineers, 25 Technology Park/Atlanta, Norcross,
Georgia 30092.

As Exhibit 2.5 shows, productivity may be expressed as partial measures, multifactor
measures, or total measures. If we are concerned with the ratio of output to a single input,
we have a *partial productivity measure*. If we want to look at the ratio of output to a group
of inputs (but not all inputs), we have a *multifactor productivity measure*. If we want to express the ratio of all outputs to all inputs, we have a *total factor measure of productivity*
that might be used to describe the productivity of an entire organization or even a nation.

A numerical example of productivity appears in Exhibit 2.6. The data reflect quantitative measures of input and output associated with the production of a certain product.
Notice that for the multifactor and partial measures it is not necessary to use total output
as the numerator. Often it is desirable to create measures that represent productivity as it
relates to some particular output of interest. For example, as in Exhibit 2.6, total units
might be the output of interest to a production control manager whereas total output may
be of key interest to the plant manager. This process of aggregation and disaggregation
of productivity measures provides a means of shifting the level of analysis to suit a variety of productivity measurement and improvement needs.

Exhibit 2.6 shows all units in dollars. Often, however, management can better understand how the company is performing when units other than dollars are used. In these
cases, only partial measures of productivity can be used, as we cannot combine dissimilar units such as labor hours and pounds of material. Some commonly used partial measures of productivity are presented as examples in Exhibit 2.7. Such partial measures of
productivity give managers information in familiar units, allowing them to easily relate
these measures to the actual operations.

E X H I B I T 2.6
Numerical Example of Productivity Measures

Input and Output Production Data ($)		Productivity Measure Examples
Output		Total measure:
1. Finished units	$10,000	$\dfrac{\text{Total output}}{\text{Total input}} = \dfrac{13,500}{15,193} = .89$
2. Work in process	2,500	
3. Dividends	1,000	Multifactor measures:
4. Bonds		$\dfrac{\text{Total output}}{\text{Human + Material}} = \dfrac{13,500}{3,153} = 4.28$
5. Other income		$\dfrac{\text{Finished units}}{\text{Human + Material}} = \dfrac{10,000}{3,153} = 3.17$
Total output	$13,500	
Input		Partial measures:
1. Human	$3,000	$\dfrac{\text{Total output}}{\text{Energy}} = \dfrac{13,500}{540} = 25$
2. Material	153	
3. Capital	10,000	$\dfrac{\text{Finished units}}{\text{Energy}} = \dfrac{10,000}{540} = 18.52$
4. Energy	540	
5. Other expenses	1,500	
Total input	$15,193	

Source: David J. Sumanth and Kitty Tang, "A Review of Some Approaches to the Management of Total Productivity in a Company/Organization," *Institute of Industrial Engineering Conference Proceedings,* Fall 1984, p. 305. Copyright Institute of Industrial Engineers, 25 Technology Park/Atlanta, Norcross, Georgia 30092.

E X H I B I T 2.7
Partial Measures of Productivity

Business	Productivity Measure
Restaurant	Customers (meals) per labor hour
Retail store	Sales per square foot
Chicken farm	Lb. of meat per lb. of feed
Utility plant	Kilowatts per ton of coal
Paper mill	Tons of paper per cord of wood

2.7   CONCLUSION

Operations strategy and competitiveness, particularly as they pertain to manufacturing, are often viewed by non-operations students as not being especially relevant to their specialty areas. We hope that this chapter conveys otherwise, in at least three respects. One is language: The framework for operations strategy shown in Exhibit 2.2 was based upon the one used by AT&T and presents the way that people within management for many high-tech companies view the business. Terms like "order fulfillment" and "support platforms" are now common descriptors in the new language of business. The second respect is in helping you think about how you make decisions within your own field. The concepts of order winners and qualifiers, priorities and capabilities apply to almost any marketing, finance, or personnel decision. And finally, even if you don't wake up in the middle of the night worrying about U.S. manufacturing competitiveness, it doesn't hurt to know what's going on.

2.8   SOLVED PROBLEM

1. A furniture manufacturing company has provided the following data. Compare the labor, raw materials and supplies, and total productivity of 1993 and 1994.

		1993	1994
Output:	Sales value of production	$22,000	$35,000
Input:	Labor	10,000	15,000
	Raw materials and supplies	8,000	12,500
	Capital equipment depreciation	700	1,200
	Other	2,200	4,800

Solution

	1993	1994
Partial productivities		
Labor	2.20	2.33
Raw materials and supplies	2.75	2.80
Total productivity	1.05	1.04

2.9   REVIEW AND DISCUSSION QUESTIONS

1. Can a factory be fast, dependable, and flexible, produce high-quality products, and still provide poor service from a customer's perspective?

2. Why should a service organization worry about being world class if it does not compete outside its own national border?

3. What are the four major categories of manufacturing operations strategy? How has their relationship to each other changed over the years?

4. For each of the different strategies, describe the unique characteristics of the market niche with which it is most compatible.

5. During 1988, for example, the dollar showed relative weakness with respect to foreign currencies such as the yen, mark, and pound. This stimulated exports. Why would long-term reliance on a lower-valued dollar be at best a short-term solution to the competitiveness problem?

6. The MIT Commission on Industrial Productivity identified "preoccupation with short-term financial results" as one of five recurring weaknesses leading to the decline in competitiveness of U.S. industry. If you assume that every U.S. firm's existence is dependent on its financial survival, does the MIT Commission's conclusion predict the demise of U.S. industry?

7. You are president of a computer chip manufacturing firm whose market share is threatened by overseas manufacturers operating at lower cost with higher-quality products. Your manufacturing plant is operating at Stage 1 as defined by the stages in manufacturing in Exhibit 2.1. Would you change the stage in which manufacturing operates? If so, which organizational and strategic changes would be needed to support your decision?

8. In your opinion, do business schools have competitive priorities?

9. Contrast the two four-stage models of manufacturing and services. What parallels and differences do you see relative to the role of operations in the two models?

10. Why does the "proper" operations strategy keep changing for companies that are world-class competitors?

11. What is meant by the expression "Manufacturing is entering the information age"?

12. What do we mean when we say productivity is a "relative" measure?

13. What are the typical performance measures for quality, speed of delivery, and flexibility?

14. What should be the criteria for management to adopt a particular performance measure?

2.10   PROBLEMS

1. Two types of cars (Deluxe and Limited) were produced by a car manufacturer in 1990. Quantities sold, price per unit, and labor hours follow. What is the labor productivity for each car? Explain the problem(s) associated with the labor productivity.

	Quantity	$/Unit
Deluxe Car	4,000 units sold	$8,000/car
Limited Car	6,000 units sold	$9,500/car
Labor, Deluxe	20,000 hours	$12/hour
Labor, Limited	30,000 hours	$14/hour

2. A U.S. manufacturing company operating a subsidiary in an LDC (less developed country) shows the following results:

	U.S.	LDC
Sales (units)	100,000	20,000
Labor (hours)	20,000	15,000
Raw materials (currency)	$ 20,000	FC 20,000
Capital equipment (hours)	60,000	5,000

  a. Calculate partial labor and capital productivity figures for the parent and subsidiary. Do the results seem misleading?
  b. Now compute multifactor labor and capital productivity figures. Are the results better?
  c. Finally, calculate raw material productivity figures (units/$ where $1 = FC 10). Explain why these figures might be greater in the subsidiary.

CASE

2.11 C A S E
Motorola's Plantation Factory

Motorola strives to measure every task performed by every one of its 120,000 employees, and calculates that it saved $1.5 billion by reducing defects and simplifying processes last year. While that figure is hard to verify, here's one that isn't: Since 1986, productivity (sales per employee) has increased 126 percent, even though Motorola has expanded its work force.

What does the company do with all the money it saves? Some goes into R&D, some goes to workers as bonuses keyed to return on net assets, and some goes straight to the bottom line. But mostly, says corporate quality director Richard Buetow, "we've been giving it away at the marketplace." Motorola cut the price of cellular telephones 25 percent last year yet still raised its net profit margins.

At some Motorola factories quality is so high that they've stopped counting defects per million and started working on defects per *billion*. Overall, the company aims to reduce its error rate tenfold every two years and to increase the speed of its processes—cut its cycle time—tenfold every five years. At those levels, says Buetow, "you are hitting the lim-

its of the capabilities of many of your machines." And those of your people as well.

Jerry Mysliwiec, manufacturing director at the Land Mobile Products factory in Plantation, Florida, begins each morning meeting of his factory supervisors with a singular request: "Okay, guys, tell me what records you broke, because if you didn't break records, you didn't improve."

Four years ago the Plantation factory wasn't breaking much of anything except the patience of its managers. It took Motorola as long as 10 days to turn out a finished radio. To decide which models to make, analysts crunched out elaborate forecasts of consumer demand, which were rarely on target. The company began building the radios at a "feeder plant" in Malaysia, where labor costs were low, then shipped them to Plantation for final assembly.

These days Plantation's Jedi line (named after the good guys in *Star Wars*) can make a specific radio—any one of more than 500 variations—for a specific customer in just two hours. They no longer rely on a forecast or a feeder plant. As the radios zip around the U-shaped assembly line, pallets marked with binary codes tell the robots, and the casually clad workers who monitor them, what to do. Plantation's most useful innovation: inventing a computer-controlled soldering process that eliminates the need for costly and time-consuming tool changes. Motorola is now converting the two-way radio plant in Malaysia, along with its other major operation in Ireland, into clones of Plantation's "focused flexible factory."

As part of its quality drive, Motorola has given new meaning to the phrase "team spirit." At the cellular equipment plant in Arlington Heights, Illinois, self-directed teams hire and fire their coworkers, help select their supervisors,

and schedule their own work (in consultation with other teams). Last year, the factory's 1,003 workers also mustered into no fewer than 168 special teams dedicated to improving quality, cutting costs, and reducing cycle time.

Question

1. What operations capabilities is Motorola using to compete?

_____

CASE

2.12 C A S E
Operations Strategy at Compaq Computer

Swaying from the ceiling at its Houston factory is a white banner that reads:

> WE AT COMPAQ COMPUTER ARE ABSOLUTELY COMMITTED TO PROVIDE DEFECT FREE PRODUCTS AND SERVICES TO OUR CUSTOMERS.

The message jibes with what one sees below: a sparkling assembly line, surrounded by potted ficus trees and ferns, washed with light from vast skylights, that looks more like an expensive health club than a factory. Founded in 1982, the company has its ideal inscribed in its name, an amalgam of the words *computer, compact,* and *quality.*

A maker of IBM-compatible PCs as well as ultrafast computers that manage data on office networks, Compaq has grown into an 11,800-employee business that last year [1990] earned $455 million on $3.6 billion in sales. It commands 20 percent of the world PC market, compared with 25 percent each for IBM and Apple Computer, and has almost no foreign rivals, except in the fast-growing field of laptop PCs. Still, competition is ferocious—fighting for sales, Compaq cut prices on its computers this spring as much as 34 percent and warned that second-quarter earnings would drop 80 percent.

Part of Compaq's success derives from its speed at offering the latest processor chips, disk drives, and display screens in its products. Yes, even faster than IBM. A major challenge, says CEO and co-founder Rod Canion, is to keep a breakneck pace of innovation across burgeoning product lines—nine new ones last year alone.

When the company was small, speeding products to market seemed a breeze. Today Compaq tries to maintain its entrepreneurial edge through small product-development teams that include marketers, designers, engineers, and manufacturing experts. Rather than moving a new computer step by step from drawing board to the factory, explains Canion, "The secret is to do all things in parallel."

Compaq's greatest advantage, Canion believes, is that it

buys most components rather than making them itself: "Vertical integration is the old way of doing things. The way to succeed in the 1990s is to be open to technology from anywhere in the world." (Japanese competitors, such as Toshiba, continue to make nearly all their components.)

When Compaq needed a hard disk drive for is first laptop in 1986, it considered building one itself. Instead, it helped finance Conner Peripherals, a Silicon Valley startup with a disk drive already under way. "We worked so closely with Conner that they were literally an extension of our design team," says Canion. "We got all the benefits but weren't tied down. If another company had come along with a better drive, we'd have bought from them as well."

In March [1991], Compaq began a nervy foray beyond the realm of PCs into the $7.5-billion-a-year market for pow-

A product development team at work at Compaq Computer.

erful desktop workstations used primarily by scientists and engineers. Rather than attacking market leaders Sun Microsystems and Hewlett-Packard head-on, Compaq assembled more than a dozen hardware and software companies, including Microsoft and Digital Equipment Corp., in an alliance. The group aims to win by defining a new technical standard for high-speed desktop computing, much like the IBM standard in PCs. Any workstation designed in accordance with the standard would work with any other. That would free customers to buy the latest, fastest machine without fear of being wedded to a single manufacturer.

Industry experts think rivalry among participants may tear the alliance apart. Observes Dick Shaffer, editor of *Computer Letter:* "All the participants are entrepreneurial companies with big egos." The group's prospects may not become clear until late next year, when Compaq and other members are due to roll out the new computers and software. If the products all work together, Compaq's workstation would be a winner. If not, says Stewart Alsop, publisher of *PC Letter,* Compaq may have to lower its sights: "As a $3.6 billion company, Compaq can't keep up a high rate of growth anymore just by building PCs."

Questions

1. Relate the elements of Compaq's strategy to the operations strategy framework shown in Exhibit 2.2. Specifically identify what appear to be the key performance priorities of Compaq's strategy and the required enterprise and support platform capabilities that must be effectively employed for Compaq's strategy to succeed.

2. What are the risks Compaq runs by outsourcing so much of its production?

CASE

2.13 CASE

Memphis Toy Company

The Memphis Toy Company (MTC) views its primary task as making for stock a standardized line of high-quality, unique toys that "last from pablum to puberty." As a rule, MTC introduces one or two new toys a year. In August 1993, the owner and manufacturing manager, Dwight Smith-Daniels, has been informed by his toy inventors that they have designed an M. C. Hammer doll. This doll will stand two feet high and is capable of rapping via an electronic voice synthesizer. One of the company's three manufacturing staff departments, design engineering, states that the product can be made primarily from molded plastic using the firm's new all-purpose molders (now used for making small attachments to the firm's wooden toys). MTC, in its previous initial production of new toys, has relied heavily on its skilled workforce to "debug" the product design as they make the product and to perform quality inspections on the finished product. Production runs have been short runs to fill customer orders.

If the M. C. Hammer doll is to go into production, however, the production run size will have to be large and assembly and testing procedures will have to be more refined. Currently, each toymaker performs almost all processing steps at his or her workbench. The production engineering department believes that the assembly of the new toy is well within the skill levels of the current work force but that the voice synthesizer and battery-operated movement mechanism will have to be subcontracted. MTC has always had good relations with subcontractors, primarily because the firm has placed its orders with sufficient lead time so that its vendors could optimally sequence MTC's orders with those of some larger toy producers in Memphis. Dwight Smith-

Daniels has always favored long-range production planning so that he can keep his 50 toymakers busy all year. (One of the reasons he set up the factory in Memphis was so that he could draw upon the large population of toymakers from the "old country" who lived there.) Smith-Daniels believes the supervisors of the firm's three production departments—castles, puppets, and novelties—are favorable to the new product. The novelty department supervisor, Fred Avide, has stated, "My workers can make any toy—you give us an output incentive, and we'll produce around the clock."

The marketing department has forecast a demand of 50,000 M. C. Hammer dolls for the Christmas rush. The dolls should sell at retail for $29.50. A preliminary cost analysis from the process engineering department is that they will cost no more than $7 each to manufacture. The company is currently operating at 70 percent capacity. Financing is available and there is no problem with cash flow. Dwight Smith-Daniels is wondering if he should go into production of M. C. Hammer dolls.

Questions

1. How consistent is the M. C. Hammer doll order with the current capabilities and focus of MTC?

2. Should MTC (*a*) manufacture the doll itself, (*b*) subcontract the work to a Tijuana, Mexico, manufacturing plant that specializes in high-volume production (at a cost of $8 per doll to MTC), or (*c*) look for another product more in line with its capabilities? The agency that holds the license to M. C. Hammer products wants a decision right away, as does the Mexican supplier.

2.14   SELECTED BIBLIOGRAPHY

Bernstein, A. "Quality Is Becoming Job One in the Office, Too." *Business Week,* April 29, 1991.

———. "The Good Life Isn't Only in America." *Business Week,* November 2, 1992, p. 34.

Blackburn, Joseph D. *Time-Based Competition: The Next Battleground in American Manufacturing.* Homewood, IL: Business One Irwin, 1991.

Bremmer, B., and M. Ivey. "Tough Times, Tough Bosses, Corporate America Calls in New, Cold-Eyed Breed of CEOs." *Business Week,* November 25, 1991, pp. 174–79.

Camp, Robert C. *Benchmarking: The Search for Industry Best Practices That Lead to Superior Performance.* Milwaukee, WI: American Society for Quality Control, Quality Press, 1989.

Cohen, Stephen S., and John Zysman. *Why Manufacturing Matters: The Myth of the Post-Industrial Society.* New York: Basic Books, 1987.

Giffi, Craig A., and Aleda V. Roth. "Winning in Global Markets: Survey of U.S. and Japanese Manufacturing." Paper presented at the 1992 ORSA/TIMS Meeting, San Francisco, November 1–3, 1992.

Giffi, Craig, Aleda V. Roth, and Gregory M. Seal. *Competing in World-Class Manufacturing.* National Center for Manufacturing Sciences. Homewood, IL: Business One Irwin, 1990.

Hart, Christopher W. L., James L. Heskett, and W. Earl Sassar, Jr. *Service Breakthroughs: Changing the Rules of the Game.* New York: Free Press, 1990.

Hayes, Robert H., and Gary P. Pisano. "Beyond World Class: The New Manufacturing Strategy." *Harvard Business Review* 72, no. 1 (January–February 1994), pp. 77–86.

Hayes, Robert H., Steven Wheelwright, and Kim B. Clark. *Dynamic Manufacturing: Creating the Learning Organization.* New York: Free Press, 1988.

Hill, T. J. "Manufacturing Implications in Determining Corporate Policy." *International Journal of Operations & Production Management* 1, no. 1 (1980), pp. 3–11.

Hopp, Wallace, and Mark Spearman. *Factory Physics: A New Approach to Manufacturing Management.* Burr Ridge: Richard D. Irwin, Inc, 1995.

Kim, Jay S., and Jeffrey G. Miller. *Building the Value Factory: A Progress Report for U.S. Manufacturing.* Boston: Boston University Manufacturing Roundtable, 1992.

Main, Jeremy. "How to Steal the Best Ideas Around." *Fortune,* October 19, 1992.

Malhotra, M. K., D. C. Steel, and V. Grover. "Important Strategic and Tactical Manufacturing Issues in the 1990s." *Decision Sciences* 25, no. 2 (March–April 1994), pp. 189–214.

Marucheck, A., R. Pannesi, and C. Anderson. "An Exploratory Study of the Manufacturing Strategy Process in Practice." *Journal of Operations Management* 9, no. 1 (January 1990), pp. 109–18.

Morey, Russell. "Operations Management in Selected Nonmanufacturing Organizations." *Academy of Management Journal* 19, no. 1 (March 1976), pp. 120–24.

Skinner, C. Wickham. *Manufacturing: The Formidable Competitive Weapon.* New York: John Wiley & Sons, 1985.

———. "Manufacturing—The Missing Link in Corporate Strategy." *Harvard Business Review* 47, no. 3 (May–June 1969), pp. 136–45.

———. "The Focused Factory." *Harvard Business Review* 52, no. 3 (May–June 1974), pp. 113–22.

———. "The Productivity Paradox." *Harvard Business Review* 64, no. 4 (July–August 1986), pp. 55–59.

Slack, Nigel. *The Manufacturing Advantage.* London: Mercury Books, 1991.

Solo, S. "Stop Whining and Get Back to Work." *Fortune,* March 12, 1991, pp. 49–50.

Stalk, G., Jr. "Time—The Next Source of Competitive Advantage." *Harvard Business Review,* July–August 1988.

Starr, Martin K. *Global Competitiveness: Getting the U.S. Back on Track.* New York: W. W. Norton, 1988.

———. "Global Production and Operations Strategy." *Columbia Journal of World Business* 19, no. 4 (Winter 1984), pp. 17–32.

Swaim, Jeffery C., and D. Scott Sink. "Current Developments in Firm or Corporate Level Productivity Measurements and Evaluation." *Issues in White Collar Productivity.* Atlanta, GA: Institute of Industrial Engineering, 1984, pp. 8–17.

Templeman, J., G. E. Schares, and D. Greising. "The Exodus of German Industry Is Underway." *Business Week,* May 25, 1992, pp. 42–43.

Thomas, D. R. "Strategy Is Different in a Service Business." *Harvard Business Review,* July–August 1978, pp. 158–65.

Wheelwright, Steven C., and Robert H. Hayes. "Competing through Manufacturing." *Harvard Business Review,* January–February 1985.

II

PRODUCT DESIGN AND PROCESS SELECTION

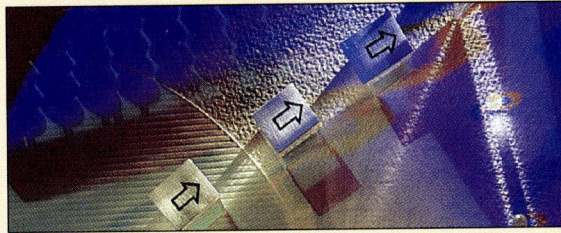

The first decision in creating a production system is selecting or designing the product or service to be produced. The second decision is defining the process technology and supporting organization by which production is to be carried out. The third decision is developing a quality philosophy and integrating it into the operations of the firm. Section II considers these subjects in the two main categories of industry—manufacturing and services.

Chapter

3

Product Design and Process Selection
Manufacturing

CHAPTER OUTLINE

KEY TERMS

Industrial Design

Conversion Processes

Fabrication Processes

Assembly Processes

Testing Processes

Process Flow Structure

Job Shop

Batch

Assembly Line

Continuous Flow

Product-Process Matrix

Virtual Factory

Break-Even Analysis

Process Flow Design

Agile Production

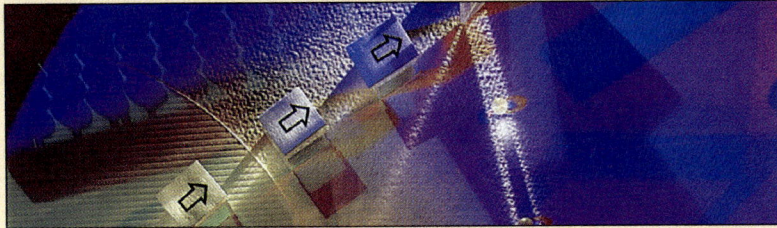

Rubbermaid is known as a new-product machine. Last year it churned out new (not just improved) products at the rate of one a day. No one would admire that, of course, if the products bombed. Few do. Nine out of 10 hit their commercial targets. The company habitually pumps 14 percent of profits into R&D. Admits a competitor in the cookware business, "They're in a class by themselves."

Most ideas for products flow from a single source: teams. Twenty teams, each made up of five to seven people (one each from marketing, manufacturing, R&D, finance, and other departments), focus on specific product lines, such as bathroom accessories. So successful has been the team approach to innovation that the head of Product Development fears to contemplate a world without it. "If we weren't organized that way," he says, a look of concern spreading over his face, "who would be thinking about johnny mops?" Hey, you little trays and johnny mops— rest easy. Rubbermaid has got you covered. Covered, too, are birdhouses (the company makes 25 models, one with a Spanish tile roof) and dustpans. The company's original rubber dustpan is protected, behind glass, at headquarters.

_____

Source: Alan Farnham, *Fortune,* February 7, 1994, p. 52. © 1994 Time Inc. All rights reserved.

E X H I B I T 3.1   *Flow of Activities in Product Design and Process Selection*

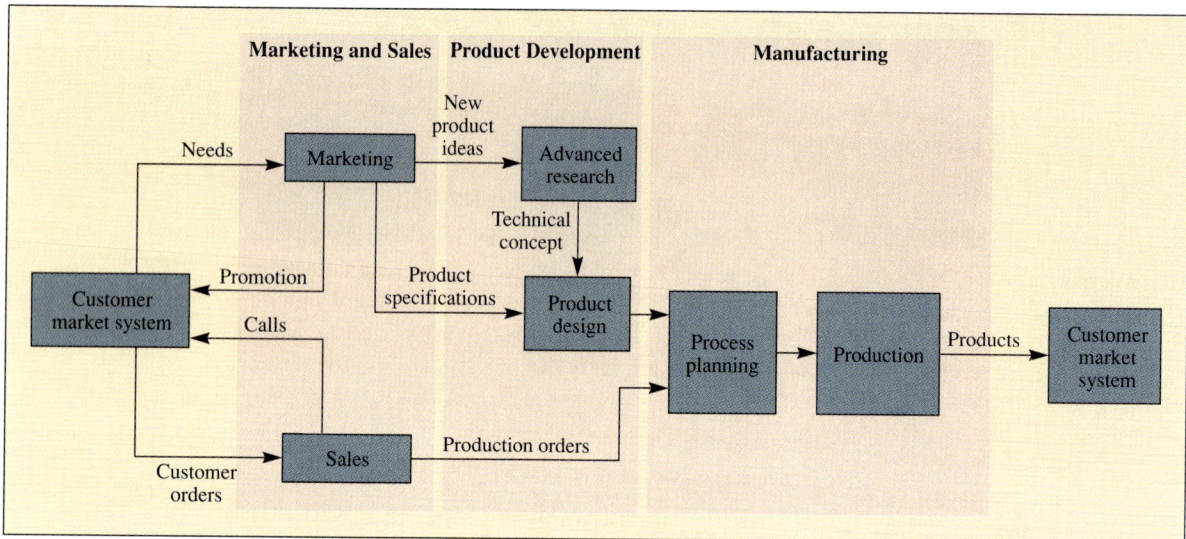

Source: Reprinted with the permission of the Free Press, an imprint of Simon & Schuster from *Fast Cycle Time: How to Align Purpose, Strategy, and Structure for Speed* by Christopher Meyer. Copyright © 1993 by Christopher Meyer.

Designing new products and getting them to market quickly is the challenge facing manufacturers in industries as diverse as computer chips and potato chips. Customers of computer chip manufacturers such as computer companies need ever more powerful semiconductors for their evolving product lines; the grocery company customers of food producers need to provide the new taste sensation to sustain or enlarge their retail market share.

How manufactured products are designed and the process planning required to initiate them into production are the focus of this chapter. As Exhibit 3.1 shows, three major functions are involved in these activities: marketing, product development, and manufacturing. Marketing has the responsibility for suggesting ideas for new products and providing product specifications for existing product lines. Product development has the responsibility for moving the technical concept for the product to its final design. Manufacturing has the responsibility for selecting and/or configuring the processes by which the product is to be manufactured.

Note that with reference to the exhibit, marketing is linked to the product development process, while sales is linked directly to the manufacturing process. This parallels the model in the previous chapter which likewise distinguishes between product development and filling of customer orders.

3.1 DESIGNING FOR THE CUSTOMER

Before we detail the hows and whys of designing and producing products, it is useful to reflect (or, perhaps more accurately, editorialize) on the issue of product design from the user's standpoint. In recent years, companies have been so caught up with technological efforts and advances—especially in the field of electronics—that somewhere along the line consumers were forgotten.

E X H I B I T 3.2
Directions to Set the Channels on a VCR (Can you follow them?)

After pre-tuning, if you wish to change the real channel number to correspond to the actual pre-tuned station, press the CH NO. SET button after calling up the corresponding channel position number on the display and enter the desired channel number using the READ OUT buttons ("10" and "1"). The "1" button changes the figures of the units digit: numerals 0 to 9 are available. The "10" button changes the figure of the tens digit: blank, numerals 1 to 9, U and C are available.

Source: John W. Verity and Jessie Nathan, "I Can't Work This Thing!" *Business Week*, April 29, 1991, p. 60.

Industrial Design

Designing for aesthetics and for the user is generally termed **industrial design.** Industrial design is probably the most abused area by manufacturers. When frustrated with products—setting the VCR, working on the car, or operating a credit card telephone at the airport—most of us have said to ourselves, "The blankety blank person who designed this should be made to work on it!" Often, parts are inaccessible, operation is too complicated, or there is no logic to setting or controlling the unit. Sometimes even worse conditions exist: Metal edges are sharp and consumers cut their hands trying to reach in for adjustments or repairs.

Many products have too many technological features—far more than necessary. The fact is that most purchasers of electronic products cannot fully operate them and only use a small number of the available features. This has occurred because computer chips are inexpensive and adding more controls has negligible cost. Including an alarm clock or a calculator on a microwave oven involves little added cost. But do you need it? What happens when you lose the operator's manual to any of these complex devices?

Written instructions in the operating manuals are often of little help in using the electronic unit. Exhibit 3.2 explains how to set channels for a VCR. Can you figure it out?

Procedures to use technologically advanced devices are often inadequate. For example, using a phone to call firms that force us to do our own routing through their system by way of touch tones often has two common frustrations: (1) If we make a mistake, we cannot backtrack; and (2) we may reach a dead end where none of the choices apply. After several minutes of button pushing on long distance and no option for a live person at the other end, we are disconnected.

One of the best-rated industrial designers is Hartmut Esslinger of frogdesign studios (with a small *f*) in Menlo Park, California. Esslinger's studio has produced designs for General Electric, Eastman Kodak, 3M, Apple Computer, NeXt Computer, and Sony. Exhibit 3.3 shows some designs and Esslinger's comments. He was commissioned to design the new answering machine for AT&T shown in Exhibit 3.4. Simplicity was incorporated in operating the machine. A blue button on top is the "play" button.

3.2   PRODUCT DEVELOPMENT

Generating New Product Ideas

Marketing is typically charged with generating new product ideas through customer surveys, demographic analysis, focus groups, benchmarking competitors, and so on. However, more and more companies are relying on teams from throughout the organization (including marketing) to come up with new concepts. For example, Rubbermaid ("America's most admired company" in 1993 according to *Fortune*), as noted in the opening vignette, uses teams that turn out a new product daily. Hewlett-Packard also uses teams, but in addition encourages its product design engineers to leave whatever they are working on on their desks so that others can come by and tinker with them.

E X H I B I T 3.3   *Examples of Good and Bad Product Designs*

THE WORLD ACCORDING TO ESSLINGER: DESIGN DO'S AND DON'TS

Most consumers are barely aware of the products surrounding them. Tools, toys, and transportation fade into the cluttered background of the material world. But when Hartmut Esslinger looks at products, they often set off passionate reactions. To him, form follows emotion. A sampling of what Esslinger loves—and loathes:

MAZDA MIATA "I love it. It's a wonderful translation of soft shapes from the '50s to the proportions of the '90s. In the '50s, it would have been sleeker, but now it's like a chubby child—much more emotional, like the '90s."

IBM PC "Bland. Just a shame. It's not representing what its company should be. IBM's logo is classy, and it demonstrates what its products could be, but the design has no advantage over any clone."

RAY-BAN SUNGLASSES (aviator style) "They have a drama and a competence because they were invented for the pilots. Vuarnets, I think, are just a little too mean. And Cartiers—just stupid. They have no design."

BRAUN RAZOR "I use it because I'm afraid of cutting myself. It's tactile. It has good technology."

ROLEX OYSTER WATCH "It's a macho watch. It says self-confidence, like a Porsche, but if you don't have confidence, it's phony."

MAYTAG WASHERS "The company talks about quality, but the product doesn't say it. You don't want to touch it because it's so edgy and full of chrome panels."

LEVI'S 501 JEANS "The best American product ever. They're global and a symbol of freedom, ironically made for gold diggers."

1954 CADILLAC "A great statement of the fun of driving. Today's Cadillacs have no emotion. A monument to themselves. They're not dynamic, and you cannot imagine young people being joyful in them."

Source: Joan O'C. Hamilton, "Rebel with a Cause," *Business Week,* December 3, 1990, p. 135.

Developing New Products

Most large companies have their product development staffs evaluate competing new product concepts (and major modifications of current products) and develop their detailed designs and specifications. The evaluation process entails making trade-offs among four criteria:

Source: Joan O'C. Hamilton, "Rebel with a Cause," *Business Week*, December 3, 1990, p. 133.

Product performance—how well the product meets customer needs.

Development speed—how long it takes to get the product to market.

Product cost—the total cost to the customer (including manufacturing costs).

Development program expense—the one-time development costs for the development project.[1]

An example trade-off is seen in Exhibit 3.5, which shows the benefits from improving product performance by adding a product feature versus the cost incurred from a delay in development speed.

The output of the design process is the product's production specifications in the form of blueprints or engineering drawings, often created through computer-aided design methods (CAD), as discussed in the supplement. These specifications provide the basis for decisions such as the purchase of materials, selection of equipment, assignment of workers, and (in some cases) capacity expansion. Note that there is a significant difference between product specifications and customer requirements. Product specs are an outgrowth of understanding customer requirements, but are expressed in technical language. Much of product development teams' work involves translating such customer preferences as "good lighting" into technical terms such as "500 watts." Quality function deployment (QFD)—discussed in Chapter 5—is a methodology to facilitate this translation process by ranking good lighting's importance to the customer relative to other product features, as well as selecting alternative technologies to achieve the desired lighting.[2]

---

[1]Preston G. Smith and Donald G. Reinertsen, *Developing Products in Half the Time* (New York: Van Nostrand Reinhold, 1991), p. 22.

[2]For further discussion of QFD for product development, see Christopher Meyer, *Fast Cycle Time* (New York: Free Press, 1993), pp. 200–1.

E X H I B I T 3.5

Trade-off between Product Performance and Development Speed

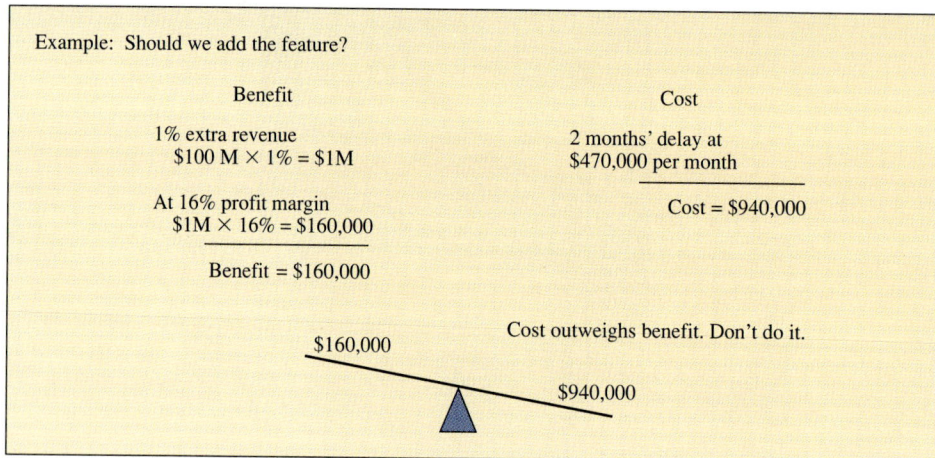

Example: Should we add the feature?

Benefit	Cost

1% extra revenue
$100 M × 1% = $1M

At 16% profit margin
$1M × 16% = $160,000
──────────────
Benefit = $160,000

2 months' delay at
$470,000 per month
──────────────
Cost = $940,000

Cost outweighs benefit. Don't do it.

$160,000

$940,000

Source: Preston G. Smith and Donald G. Reinertsen, *Developing Products in Half the Time* (New York: Van Nostrand Reinhold, 1991), p. 22.

3.3   LINKING DESIGN AND MANUFACTURING

Linking design and manufacturing involves a number of interrelated issues. The more important ones include **design for manufacturability, frequency of design changes, opportunity for product design change,** and **concurrent engineering.**

Design for Manufacturability

In translating the functional product design into a manufacturable product, designers must consider many aspects. They can use many ways and many materials to make a product. Material choices can be ferrous (iron and steel), aluminum, copper, brass, magnesium, zinc, tin, nickel, titanium, or several other metals. The nonmetals include polymers (thermoplastics, thermosetting plastics, and elastomers), wood, leather, rubber, carbon, ceramics, glass, gypsum, and concrete as well as several others. Further, all of these materials can be formed, cut, and shaped in many ways. There are extrusions, stampings, rolling, powder-metal, forgings, castings, and injection molding along with a large variety of machining processes.

In selecting any design for manufacturability, the designers must follow certain rules, depending on the process selected. Many of these rules of design are obvious. For example, Exhibit 3.6 shows two designs to be created through an extrusion process. In an extrusion, the procedure is similar to squeezing toothpaste from a tube. Material squeezed through a die comes out of the other side in the desired shape. To make the squeezing easier, metals are usually heated. A good design avoids sharp points and sharp corners and contains a balance in the pattern. Examples of extrusions are metal screen doors, windows, and picture frames.

In designing for manufacturability, it is also desirable to minimize the number of separate parts. In electronics, manufacturers combine circuits that have been in different components into larger and larger integrated circuits. Not only does this increase speed (because electrons do not have to travel as far), but it also reduces the physical size and increases reliability. Designers increase reliability by eliminating the many connections necessary when circuits were in separate parts. Exhibit 3.7 shows how to reduce a simple bracket from five parts to one by focusing on the purpose of the part, the fabrication, and the assembly procedure used for its manufacture.

E X H I B I T 3.6 *Good and Bad Practice in the Design of Cross Sections to Be Extruded*

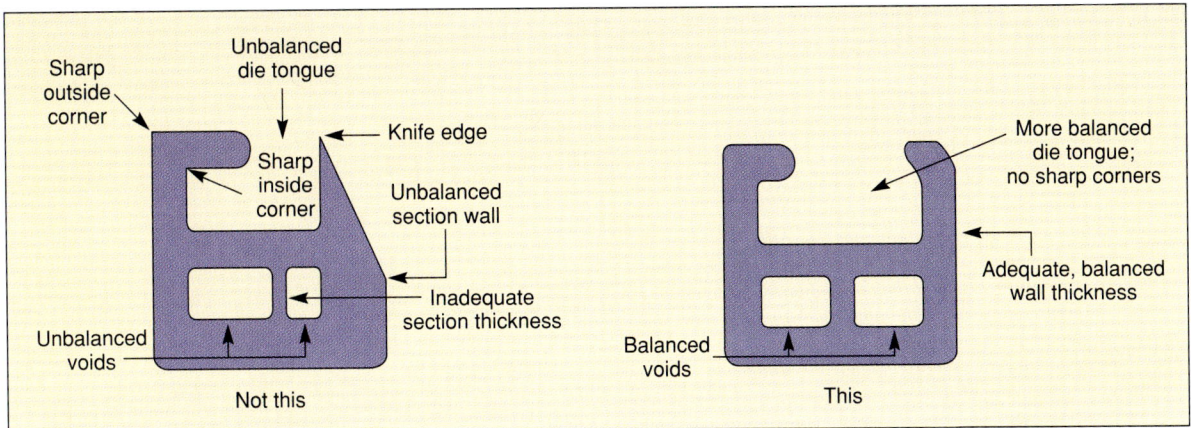

Source: James L. Bralla, ed., *Handbook of Product Design for Manufacturing* (New York: McGraw-Hill, 1986), pp. 3–10.

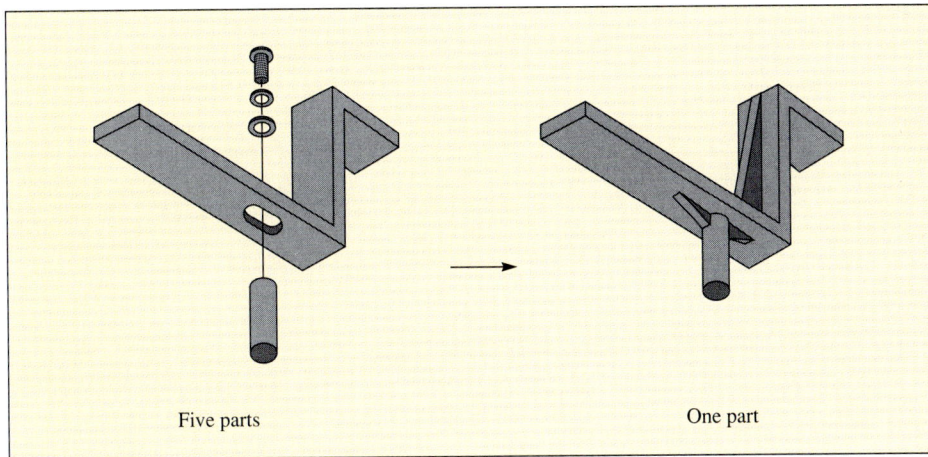

E X H I B I T 3.7

Design Change to Reduce the Number of Parts in a Bracket

Source: Bart Huthwaite, "Managing at the Starting Line: How to Design Competitive Products." Workshop at the University of Southern California–Los Angeles, January 14, 1991, p. 7.

While designing for manufacturability, we must still remember to design for the consumer.

A basic rule in design is

Be obvious. Design a product so that a user can look at it, understand it, and figure out how to use it—quickly, and without an instruction manual.

Frequency of Design Changes

Should products be changed every year, twice a year, every two years? How often a firm changes design depends, in large part, on its marketing strategy. Sony Corporation and its Walkman cassette player provide an example of very frequent design changes. (See Exhibit 3.8.)

Sony introduced its Walkman to the market in 1979. It was an immediate success. Two years later, Sony brought out a new model to keep ahead of its competitors. Since 1979, the rate of new Walkman products introduced by Sony has accelerated. Sony has brought out more than 160 models of the Walkman.

E X H I B I T 3.8

*The Total Number of
Different Walkman-
Type Cassette Players
Produced by Several
Manufacturers*

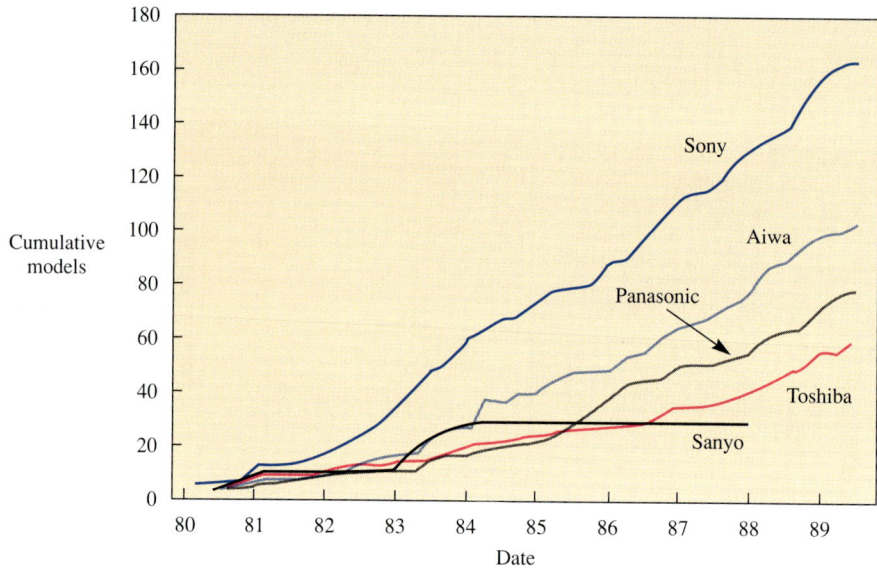

Source: Susan Walsh Sanderson and Vic Uzumeri, "Strategies for New Product Development and Renewal: Design-Based Incrementalism." Center for Science and Technology Policy, School of Management, Rensselaer Polytechnic Institute, Troy, NY 12180, May 1990.

E X H I B I T 3.9

*Cost Committed and
Cost Expended from
Product Concept to
Production*

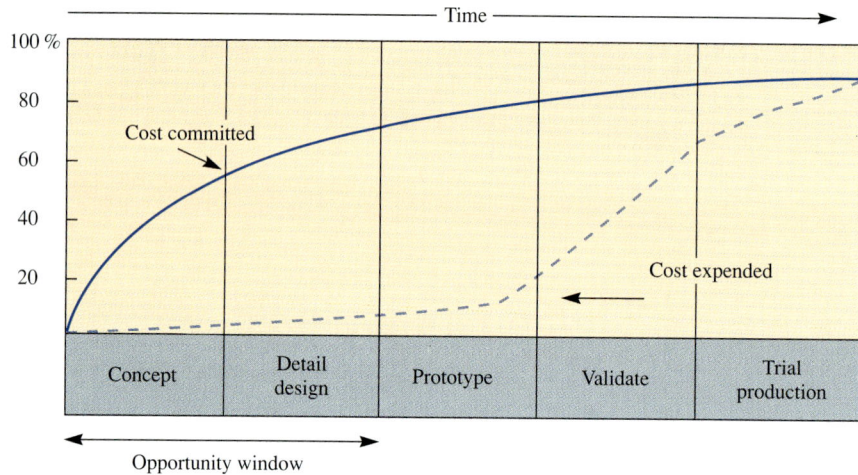

Source: Bart Huthwaite, "Managing at the Starting Line: How to Design Competitive Products." Workshop at the University/Southern California–Los Angeles, January 14, 1991, p. 3.

Sony has relied on "design-based incrementalism." That is, product families are upgraded and enhanced throughout their life cycles. Such changes are small, frequent, and both technological and topological. *Technological innovation* is introducing new technology that enhances the function, adds higher quality, or lowers production cost (for example, developing a new motor). *Topological design* is the rearrangement or remanufacture of well-understood components (for example, making smaller parts, a more compact unit, an easier-functioning unit, or a more appealing unit, or creating product distinction).

Due to its policy of incrementalization, Sony could bring out its "My First Sony" line for children in less than one year because it was built on existing products. One of the

E X H I B I T 3.10
Hewlett-Packard Life Cycle Involvement Activities

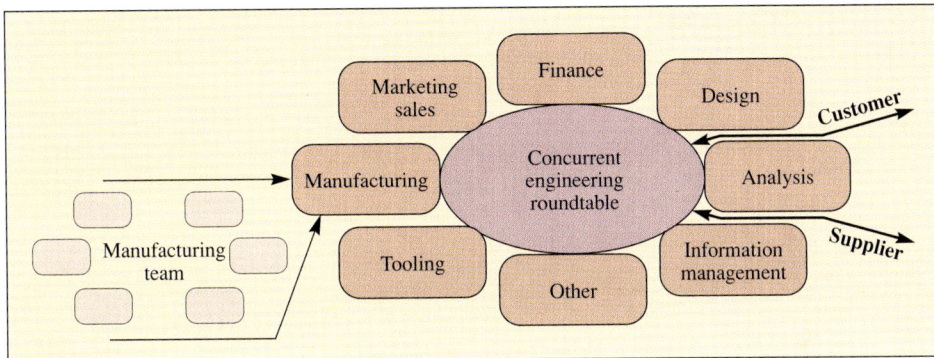

	Development	Transition to Manufacturing	Volume Production	Obsolescence	End Support Life
Product development	We're responsible for design of the product				
Manufacturing engineering	We're responsible for design and support of the processes				
Materials/ materials engineering	We're responsible for sourcing/ management of vendor resources				
Production	We're responsible for building the product				
Marketing	We're responsible for support of the product				

E X H I B I T 3.11
The Concurrent Engineering Roundtable

Source: Dan L. Shunk, *Integrated Process Design and Development* (Homewood, IL: Business One Irwin, 1992), p. 45.

authors was at a Sony dealer recently; and the dealer said there were more than 30 current models of the Walkman! The result is that the average life of a Walkman model is less than 18 months. Sony's other product lines have also been very prolific.

Opportunity for Product Design Change

Exhibit 3.9 shows the design-to-production phases. This cycle extends from concept through full production. Note that Concept and Design commit about 70 percent of the manufacturing cost while expending only about 5 percent of the total cost. Often manufacturers spend far too little time finding all the flaws during the design stage of a new product. Therefore, prudent operation might suggest expending a bit more to ensure a good, sound user-friendly design and expecting to profit through reduced committed cost. Committed cost means the production costs directly resulting from the design. These include materials, processes, and so forth.

Concurrent Engineering

A major trend in manufacturing is early and continuing involvement with new products by production, materials planning, and engineering support groups to ensure that the products are effectively managed throughout their life cycles. At Hewlett-Packard, this responsibility is seen as carrying through product development, transition to manufacturing, volume production, and obsolescence. (See Exhibit 3.10.)

Concurrent engineering can be used interchangeably with the terms *simultaneous engineering* or *concurrent design*. It also refers to the design team often used by firms. Obviously, as these terms imply, continual interaction and parallel actions are necessary throughout the entire product design to the production process. Other areas such as mar-

777 Sets Boeing on New Course

When Boeing Co. unveils the first model of its 777 twin-engine jet this week, it will mark more than a milestone in its most ambitious project since the 747 jumbo jet.

The ceremonial rollout, to be attended by 100,000 Boeing employees, subcontractors, customers and guests, will produce the first tangible evidence of an effort by one of the nation's biggest manufacturers to re-engineer itself for the 21st century.

"There is a different culture at Boeing—a kind of workout ethic that gets you a lot closer to higher productivity," said Nicholas Heymann of County Natwest Securities.

The 777, which will be the world's largest twin-engine jet, is Boeing's first all-new model in more than a decade. It represents other firsts as well.

It is Boeing's first "fly-by-wire" jet, in which moving parts are controlled electronically with no cable connections, and it is the first "paperless" plane, designed entirely on computer.

Boeing officials say the process has resulted in more accurate fittings and fewer adjustments on the floor of its huge assembly plant in Everett, Wash., 30 miles north of Seattle.

If Boeing gets its way with the Federal Aviation Administration—a major "if"—the plane would be the first to go into service with permission to fly immediately on long-haul routes up to three hours from the nearest airport.

And industry analysts and executives say the 777 marks the first time customers and Boeing employees at every level have been so fully involved in the design process.

"In past programs, we didn't really have any contact with Boeing in the design process. This time we sat in from our first day on their basic design teams," said Gordon McKinzie, 777 project manager for Elk Grove Township–based United Airlines.

United has ordered 34 of the jets and is the launch customer for the new plane, which is to make its first flight in June and go into commercial service in May 1995.

Boeing has been forced to change the way it does business in large part to meet growing competition from Europe's Airbus Industrie, which has jets that compete with all Boeing's models except the 747.

"In the past if you wanted a Boeing, you'd have to stand in line," said McKinzie.

But times have changed. While Boeing still dominates the market for new planes, with more than 60 percent of new orders, airlines have cut back drastically and Boeing has had to cut its work force 25 percent since 1989.

Analysts and company officials see the market bottoming out in late 1995, but Boeing still faces a self-imposed challenge of cutting manufacturing expenses by

keting and purchasing need to be involved and interact with all phases of design and development. Their input is critical concerning production planning, productive capacity, and the availability of parts and materials. The sequence from product design to delivery to the marketplace is not a consecutive series of steps. Continual interaction throughout the process ensures that a well-designed product is released to the market at a good price and on time. Exhibit 3.11 shows the concurrent engineering roundtable approach to this interaction. The Breakthrough box "777 Sets Boeing on New Course," discusses this technique at Boeing.

3.4   PROCESS SELECTION

Process Selection Contrasted with Process Planning

Process planning as used in Exhibit 3.1 refers to the tactical planning activities that regularly occur in manufacturing. Process selection, in contrast, refers to the strategic decision of deciding which kind of production processes to have in the plant.

Types of Processes

At the most basic level, the types of processes can be categorized as follows:

> **Conversion processes.** Examples are changing iron ore into steel sheets, or making all the ingredients listed on the box of toothpaste into toothpaste.

reducing the average time it takes to build an aircraft to 6 months from the current 12.

J. A. Donoghue, editor of the trade magazine *Air Transport World,* said airlines, faced with continuing excess capacity in the world market, have become increasingly tightfisted and won't buy new models unless they see operating cost savings.

"If you can't show an advantage over what's currently out there, airlines are getting very reluctant to spend that kind of money," Donoghue said, referring to the 777's price of $116 million to $140 million.

Source: *Chicago Tribune,* April 4, 1994. Reprinted by permission of Reuters.

The 777, the world's largest twin-engine jet, is Boeing's first all-new model in more than a decade. It is set to begin commercial service in 1995.

Fabrication processes. Examples are changing raw materials into some specific form (for example, making sheet metal into a car fender or forming gold into a crown for a tooth).

Assembly processes. Examples are assembling a fender to a car, putting toothpaste tubes into a box, or fastening a dental crown in somebody's mouth.

Testing processes. This is not strictly speaking a fundamental process, but it is so widely mentioned as a standalone major activity that it is included here for completeness.

Process Flow Structures

A **process flow structure** refers to how a factory organizes material flow using one or more of the process technologies just listed.

Hayes and Wheelwright have identified four major process flow structures:

Job shop. Production of small batches of a large number of different products, most of which require a different set or sequence of processing steps. Commercial printing firms, airplane manufacturers, machine tool shops, and plants that make custom-designed printed circuit boards are examples of this type of structure.

Batch. Essentially a somewhat standardized job shop. Such a structure is generally employed when a business has a relatively stable line of products, each of which is produced in periodic batches, either to customer order or for inventory. Most of these items follow the same flow pattern through the plant. Examples include heavy equipment, electronic devices, and specialty chemicals.

Assembly line. Production of discrete parts moving from workstation to workstation at a controlled rate, following the sequence needed to build the product. Examples include manual assembly of toys and appliances, and automatic assembly (called insertion) of components on a printed circuit board. When other processes are employed in a line fashion along with assembly, it is commonly referred to as a *production line*. (See Exhibit 3.12.)

Continuous flow. Conversion or further processing of undifferentiated materials such as petroleum, chemicals, or beer, as the photo above shows. As on assembly lines, production follows a predetermined sequence of steps, but the flow is continuous rather than discrete. Such structures are usually highly automated and in effect constitute one integrated "machine" that must be operated 24 hours a day to avoid expensive shutdowns and start-ups.

The choice of which flow structure to select, with the exception of continuous flow structures, is generally a function of the volume requirements for each product.

Product-Process Matrix

The relationship between process structures and volume requirements is often depicted on a **product-process matrix** (Exhibit 3.13). The way to interpret this matrix is that as volume increases and the product line (the horizontal dimension) narrows, specialized equipment and standardized material flows (the vertical dimension) become economically feasible. Since this evolution in process structure is frequently related to the product's life cycle stage (introduction, growth, and maturity), it is very useful in linking marketing and manufacturing strategies.

E X H I B I T 3.12   *How to Make a Car*

How to make a car
The production process in a modern car plant includes lots of checks on quality and extensive treatment to prevent corrosion.

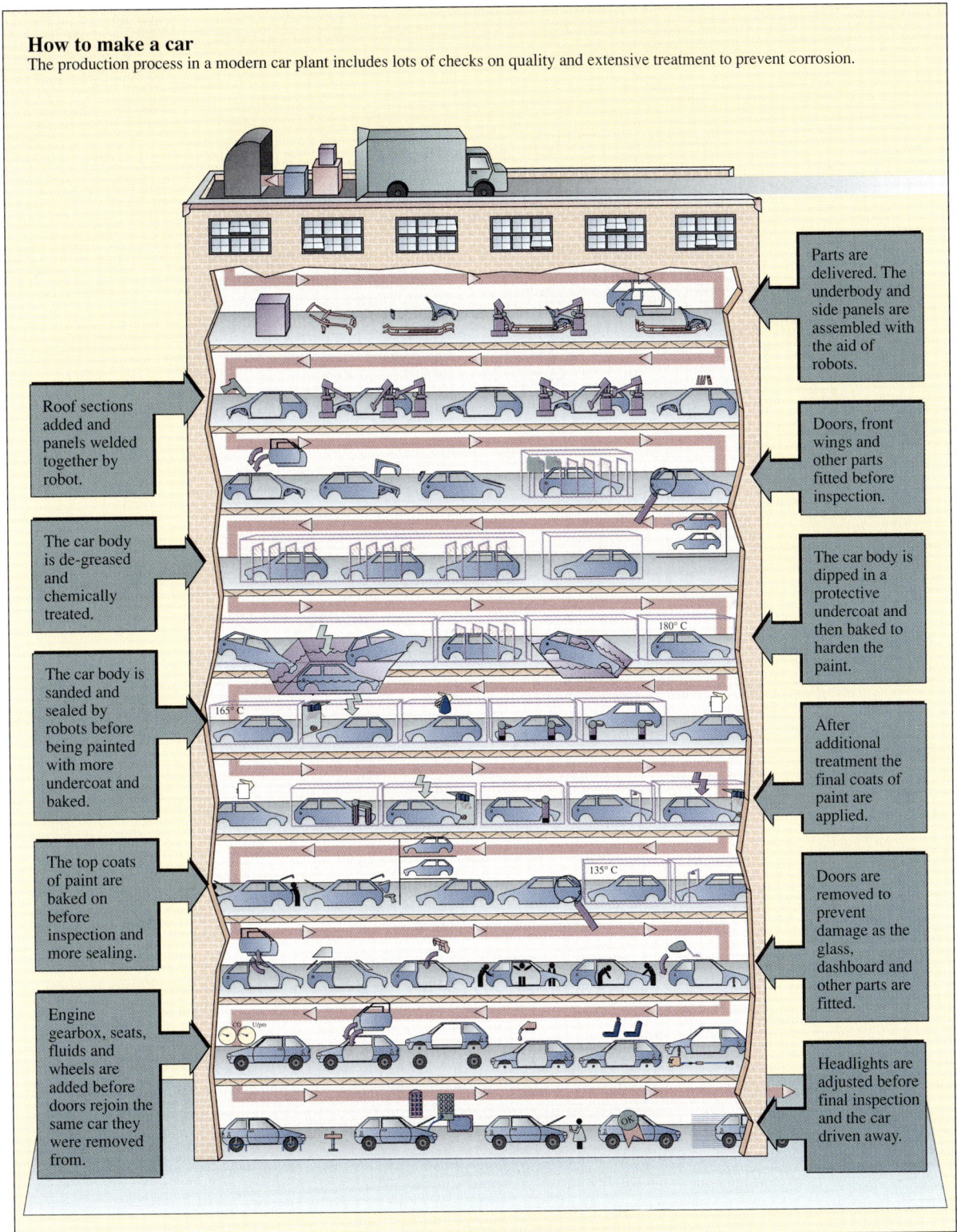

Roof sections added and panels welded together by robot.

The car body is de-greased and chemically treated.

The car body is sanded and sealed by robots before being painted with more undercoat and baked.

The top coats of paint are baked on before inspection and more sealing.

Engine gearbox, seats, fluids and wheels are added before doors rejoin the same car they were removed from.

Parts are delivered. The underbody and side panels are assembled with the aid of robots.

Doors, front wings and other parts fitted before inspection.

The car body is dipped in a protective undercoat and then baked to harden the paint.

After additional treatment the final coats of paint are applied.

Doors are removed to prevent damage as the glass, dashboard and other parts are fitted.

Headlights are adjusted before final inspection and the car driven away.

180° C

165° C

135° C

CO U/pm

OK

Source: General Motor's Opal plant at Eisenach, Germany. *The Economist*, Oct. 17, 1992. © 1992 The Economist Newspaper Group, Inc. Reprinted with permission.

E X H I B I T 3.13   *Matching Major Stages of Product and Process Life Cycles*

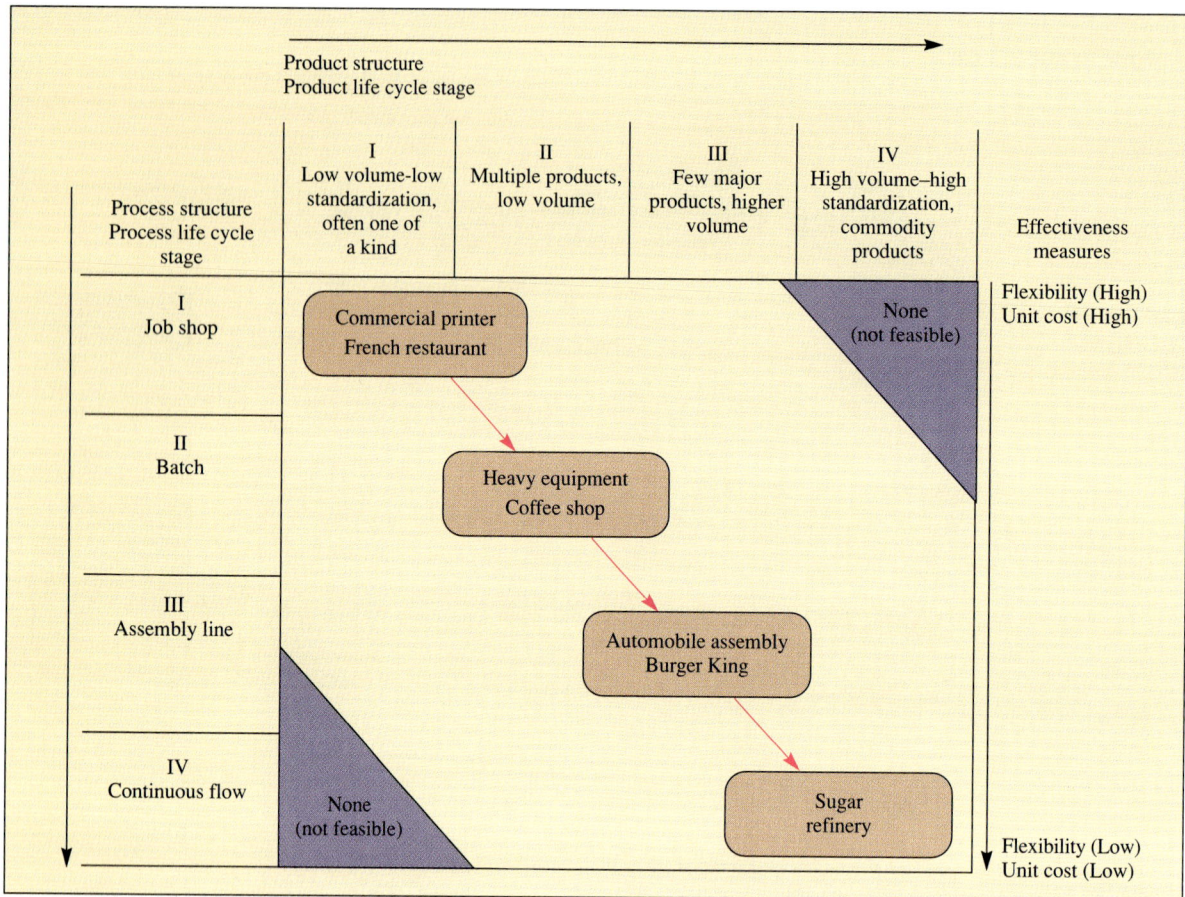

	I Low volume-low standardization, often one of a kind	II Multiple products, low volume	III Few major products, higher volume	IV High volume–high standardization, commodity products	

Product structure
Product life cycle stage

Process structure
Process life cycle stage

| Effectiveness measures |

I Job shop — Commercial printer, French restaurant; None (not feasible) — Flexibility (High), Unit cost (High)

II Batch — Heavy equipment, Coffee shop

III Assembly line — Automobile assembly, Burger King

IV Continuous flow — None (not feasible); Sugar refinery — Flexibility (Low), Unit cost (Low)

Source: Modified from Robert Hayes and Steven Wheelwright, *Restoring Our Competitive Edge: Competing through Manufacturing* (New York: John Wiley & Sons, 1984). p. 209.

The industries listed within the matrix are presented as ideal types that have found their structural niche. (Sample food service systems are included to help readers get a gut feel for the dimensions.) It is certainly possible for an industry member to choose another position on the matrix, however. For example, Volvo makes cars on movable pallets rather than an assembly line. Thus on the matrix it would be at the intersection of process stages II and III. Volvo's production rate is lower than its competitors because it is giving up speed and efficiency of the line. On the other hand, the Volvo system has more flexibility because it uses multiskilled workers who are not paced by a mechanical assembly line.

A major issue in today's manufacturing strategy is to seek benefits of flexibility found in stage I job shop structures along with the cost advantages that go with assembly line or even continuous flow structures of stages III and IV. At the present time, however, this is only feasible when a production system is under complete computer control, using the flexible manufacturing systems (FMS) technology described in the supplement to this chapter.

Decision Variable	Factors to Consider
Initial investment	Price
	Manufacturer
	Availability of used models
	Space requirements
	Need for feeder/support equipment
Output rate	Actual versus rated capacity
Output quality	Consistency in meeting specs
	Scrap rate
Operating requirements	Ease of use
	Safety
	Human factors impact
Labor requirements	Direct to indirect ratio
	Skills and training
Flexibility	General-purpose versus special-purpose equipment
	Special tooling
Setup requirements	Complexity
	Changeover speed
Maintenance	Complexity
	Frequency
	Availability of parts
Obsolescence	State of the art
	Modification for use in other situations
In-process inventory	Timing and need for supporting buffer stocks
Systemwide impacts	Tie-in with existing or planned systems
	Control activities
	Fit with manufacturing strategy

The Virtual Factory

The new term **virtual factory** refers to manufacturing activities carried out—not in one central plant—but rather in multiple locations by suppliers and partner firms as part of a strategic alliance. The role of manufacturing for an auto producer, for example, will shift from solely monitoring activities at one central plant to managing the integration of all steps in the process—no matter where physical production actually takes place. The implications for process planning are profound: The manufacturer must have a deep understanding of the manufacturing capabilities of all parties in the production network, and must excel at the difficult task of coordination.

Specific Equipment Selection

The choice of specific equipment follows the selection of the general type of process structure. Exhibit 3.14 shows some key factors to consider in the selection decision. Firms may have both general-purpose equipment and special-purpose equipment. For example, a machine shop would have lathes and drill presses (general-purpose) and could have transfer machines (special-purpose). An electronics firm may have a single-function test module to perform only one test at a time (general-purpose) and may have a multifunction test unit to perform multiple tests at the same time (special-purpose). As computer-based technology evolves, however, the general-purpose/special-purpose distinction becomes blurred, since a general-purpose machine has the capability to produce just as efficiently as many special-purpose ones.

Choosing among Alternative Processes and Equipment

A standard approach to choosing among alternative processes or equipment is **break-even analysis.** A break-even chart visually presents alternative individual and relative profit and losses due to the number of units produced or sold. The choice obviously depends on anticipated demand. The method is most suitable when processes or equipment entails a

E X H I B I T 3.15

Break-Even Chart of Alternative Processes

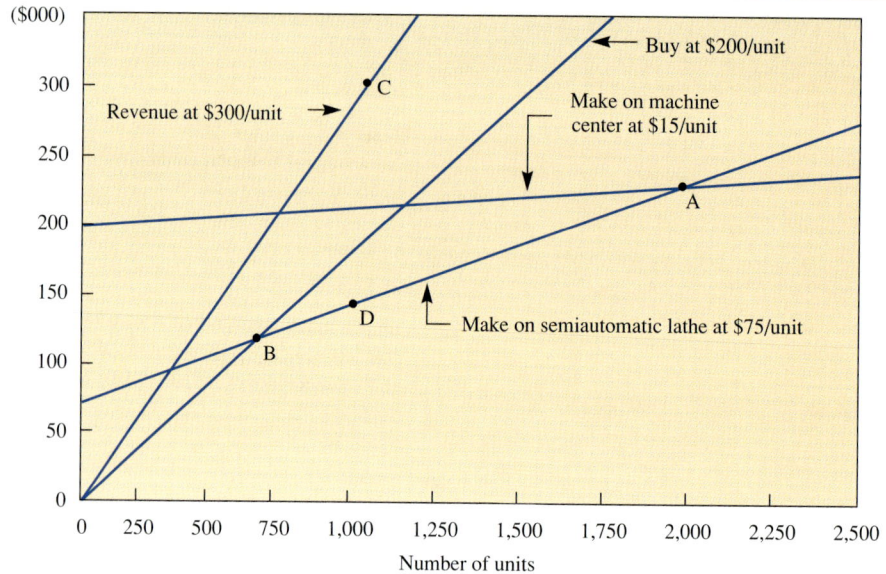

large initial investment and fixed cost, and when variable costs are reasonably proportional to the number of units produced. By way of example, suppose a manufacturer has identified the following options for obtaining a machined part: It can buy the part at $200 per unit (including materials), it can make the part on a numerically controlled semiautomatic lathe at $75 per unit (including materials), or it can make the part on a machining center at $15 per unit (including materials). There is negligible fixed cost if the item is purchased; a semiautomatic lathe costs $80,000, and a machining center costs $200,000.

Whether we approach the solution to this problem as cost minimization or profit maximization really makes no difference as long as the relationships remain linear; that is, variable costs and revenue are the same for each incremental unit. Exhibit 3.15 shows the break-even points for each of the processes. If demand is expected to be more than 2,000 units (point A), the machine center is the best choice since this would result in the lowest total cost. If demand is between 640 (point B) and 2,000 units, the NC lathe is the cheapest. If demand is less than 640 (between 0 and point B), the most economical course is to buy the product.

Consider the effect of revenue, assuming the part sells for $300 each. As Exhibit 3.15 shows, profit (or loss) is the distance between the revenue line and the alternative process cost. At 1,000 units, for example, maximum profit is the difference between the $300,000 revenue (point C) and the semiautomatic lathe cost of $160,000 (point D). For this quantity the semiautomatic lathe is the cheapest alternative available. The optimal choices for both minimizing cost and maximizing profit are the lowest segments of lines: origin to B, to A, and to the right side of the exhibit.

3.5   PROCESS FLOW DESIGN

Process flow design focuses on the specific processes that raw materials, parts, and subassemblies follow as they move through the plant. The most common production management tools used in planning the process flow are assembly drawings, assembly charts, route sheets, and flow process charts. Each of these charts is a useful diagnostic tool and can be used to improve operations during the steady state of the productive system. Indeed, the standard first step in analyzing any production system is to map the flows and

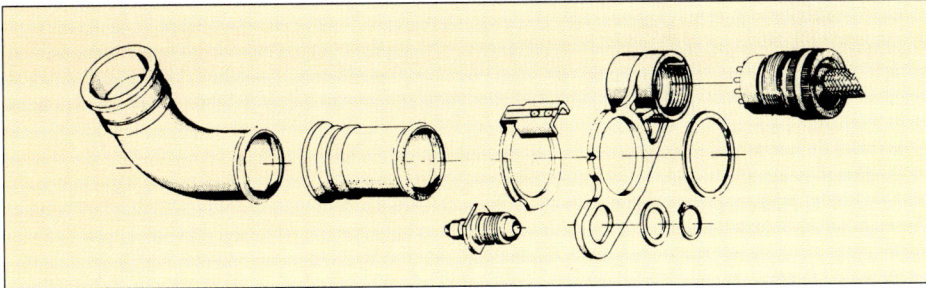

E X H I B I T 3.16
Plug Assembly Drawing

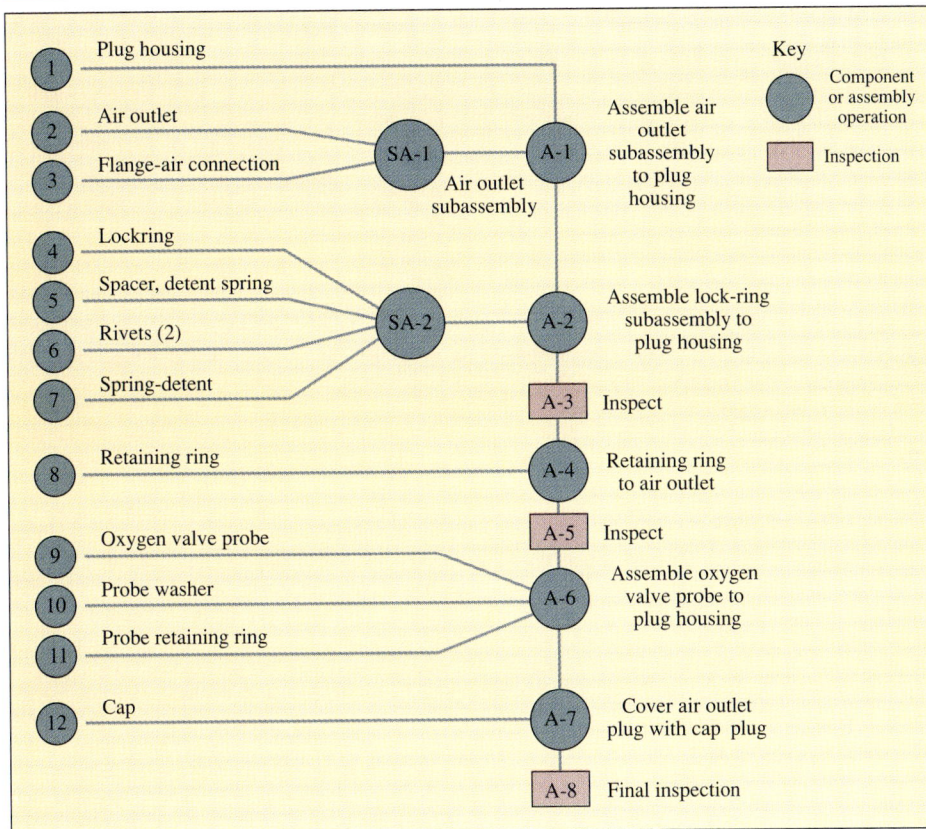

E X H I B I T 3.17
Assembly (or Gozinto) Chart for Plug Assembly

operations using one or more of these techniques. These are the "organization charts" of the manufacturing system.

An *assembly drawing* (Exhibit 3.16) is simply an exploded view of the product showing its component parts. An *assembly chart* (Exhibit 3.17) uses the information presented in the assembly drawing and defines (among other things) how parts go together, their order of assembly, and often the overall material flow pattern.[3] An *operation and route sheet* (Exhibit 3.18), as its name implies, specifies operations and process routing for a particular part. It conveys such information as the type of equipment, tooling, and operations required to complete the part.

---

[3]Also called a *Gozinto chart,* named, so the legend goes, after the famous Italian mathematician Zepartzat Gozinto.

E X H I B I T 3.18

Operation and Route Sheet for Plug Assembly

Material Specs. _____		Part Name	Plug Housing		Part No.	TA 1274
Purchased Stock Size _____		Usage	Plug Assembly		Date Issued	_____
Pcs. Per Pur. Size _____		Assy. No.	TA 1279		Date Sup'd.	_____
Weight _____		Sub. Assy. No.	_____		Issued By	_____

Oper. No.	Operation Description	Dept.	Machine	Set Up Hr.	Rate Pc/Hr.	Tools
20	+.015 Drill 1 hole .32 -.005	Drill	Mach 513 Deka 4	1.5	254	Drill Fixture L-76, Jig #10393
30	+.015 Deburr .312 -.005 Dia. Hole	Drill	Mach 510 Drill	.1	424	Multi-Tooth burring Tool
40	Chamfer .900/.875, Bore .828/.875 dia. (2 Passes), Bore .7600/.7625 (1 Pass)	Lathe	Mach D109 Lathe	1.0	44	Ramet-1, TPG 221, Chamfer Tool
50	Tap Holes as designated - 1/4 Min. Full Thread	Tap	Mach 514 Drill Tap	2.0	180	Fixture #CR-353, Tap. 4 Flute Sp.
60	Bore Hole 1.133 to 1.138 Dia.	Lathe	H & H E107	3.0	158	L44 Turrent Fixture, Hartford
						Superspacer, pl. #45, Holder #L46,
						PDTW-100, Inser #21, Chk. Fixture
70	Deburr .005 to .010, Both Sides, Hand Feed To Hard Stop	Lathe	E162 Lathe	.5	176	Collect #CR179, 1327 RPM
80	Broach Keyway To Remove Thread Burrs	Drill	Mach. 507 Drill	.4	91	B87 Fixture, L59 Broach, Tap. .875120 G-H6
90	Hone Thread I.D. 822/.828	Grind	Grinder		120	
95	Hone .7600/.7625	Grind	Grinder		120	

A flow process chart such as Exhibit 3.19 typically uses standard American Society of Mechanical Engineers (ASME) symbols to denote what happens to the product as it progresses through the productive facility. The symbols for the various processes are explained at the side of the chart. As a rule, the fewer the delays and storages in the process, the better the flow.

3.6   PROCESS ANALYSIS

Detailed process planning entails planning the steps of the process itself. In Chapter 1, we introduced the term *process,* which can be described as a set of tasks that transform inputs into useful outputs. A process usually consists of (1) a set of *tasks,* (2) a *flow* of material and information that connect the set of tasks, and (3) *storage* of material and information.

1. *Task:* Each task in a process accomplishes, to a certain degree, the transformation of input into the desired output.
2. *Flow:* The flow in a process consists of flow of material as well as flow of information. The flow of material involves the transfer of a product from one task to its next task. The flow of information helps in determining how much of the transformation has been done in the previous task and what exactly remains to be completed in the present task.
3. *Storage:* When neither a task is being performed nor a part is being transferred, the part has to be stored. Goods in storage, waiting to be processed by the next task, are often called work-in-process inventory.

An Example of Process Analysis

Process analysis involves adjusting the capacities and balance among different parts of the process to maximize output or minimize the costs with available resources. The XYZ Company supplies a component to several large auto manufacturers.[4] This component is assembled in a shop by 15 workers working an eight-hour shift on an assembly line that

---

[4]This section is modified from Paul W. Marshall et al., *Operations Management: Text and Cases* (Homewood, IL: Richard D. Irwin, 1975), pp. 12–16.

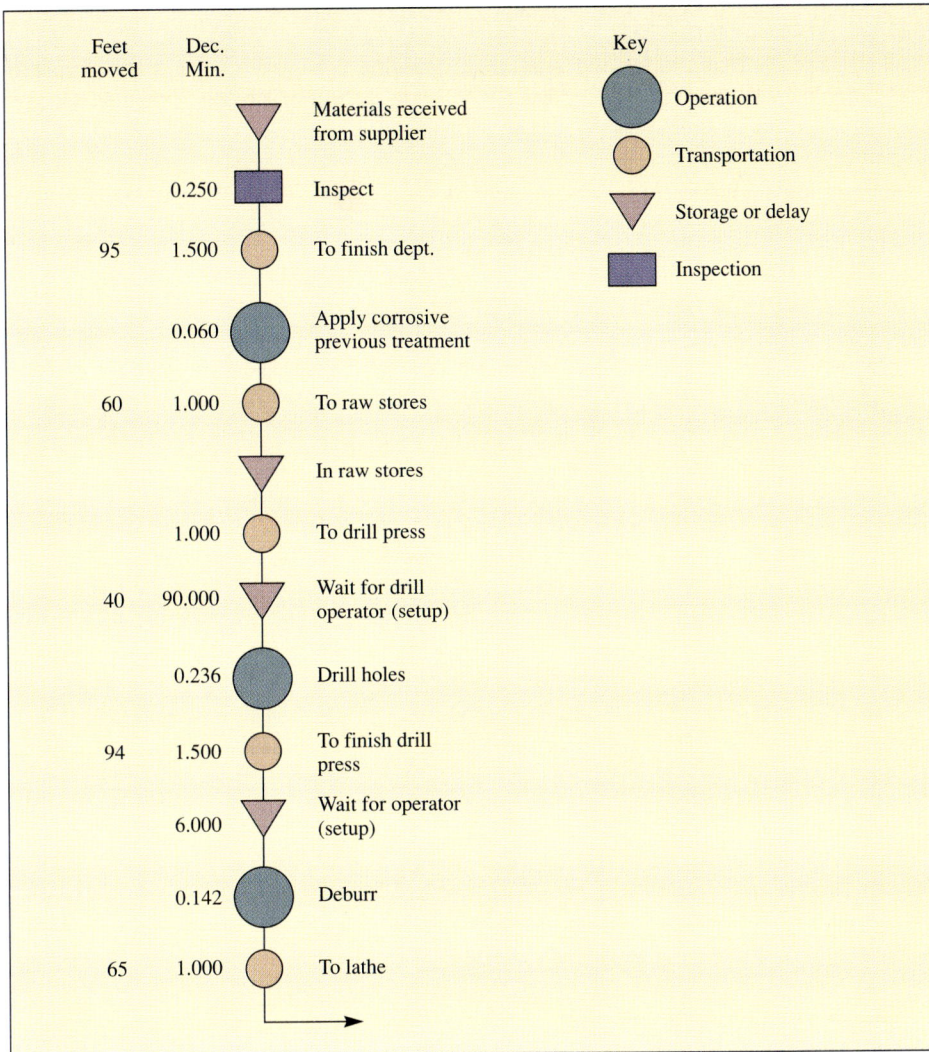

Feet moved	Dec. Min.		
		▽	Materials received from supplier
	0.250	▮	Inspect
95	1.500	○	To finish dept.
	0.060	⬤	Apply corrosive previous treatment
60	1.000	○	To raw stores
		▽	In raw stores
	1.000	○	To drill press
40	90.000	▽	Wait for drill operator (setup)
	0.236	⬤	Drill holes
94	1.500	○	To finish drill press
	6.000	▽	Wait for operator (setup)
	0.142	⬤	Deburr
65	1.000	○	To lathe

Key

⬤ Operation
○ Transportation
▽ Storage or delay
▮ Inspection

Note: These production times were based on a run of 500 items. Source: Arizona Gear & Manufacturing Company.

moves at the rate of 150 components per hour. The workers received their pay in the form of a group incentive amounting to 30 cents per completed good part. This wage is distributed equally among the workers. Management believes that it could hire 15 more workers for a second shift if necessary.

Parts for the final assembly come from two sources. The XYZ molding department makes one very critical part and the rest come from outside suppliers. There are 11 machines capable of molding the one part done in-house, but historically one machine is being overhauled or repaired at any given time. Each machine requires a full-time operator. The machines could each produce 25 parts per hour and the workers are paid on an individual piece rate of 20 cents per good part. The workers will work overtime at a 50 percent increase in rate, or for 30 cents per good part. The workforce for molding is flexible; currently only six workers are on this job. Four more are available from a labor pool within the company. The raw materials for each part molded cost 10 cents per part; a detailed analysis by the accounting department has concluded that 2 cents of electricity is used in making each part. The parts purchased from the outside cost 30 cents for each final component produced.

This entire operation is located in a rented building costing $100 per week. Supervision, maintenance, and clerical employees receive a payroll of $1,000 per week. The accounting department charges depreciation for equipment against this operation at $50 per week.

The accompanying process flow diagram describes the process. The tasks have been shown as rectangles and the storage of goods (inventories) as triangles.

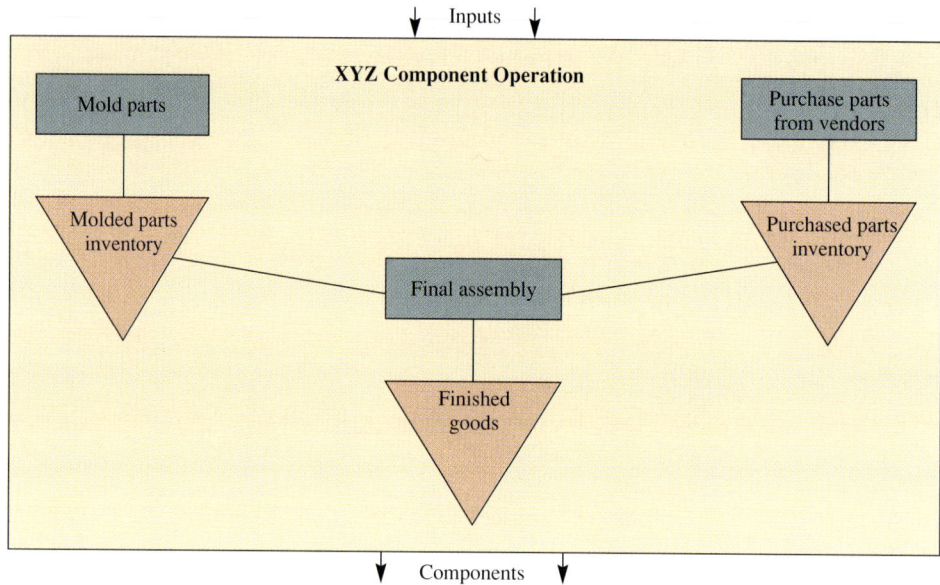

a. Determine the Capacity (number of components produced per week) of the Entire Process. Are the Capacities of All the Processes Balanced?

Capacity of the molding process:

Only six workers are employed for the molding process, each working as a full-time operator for one machine. Thus only 6 of the 11 machines are operational at present.

Molding capacity = 6 machines × 25 parts per hour per machine × 8 hours per day × 5 days per week = 6,000 parts per week

Capacity of the assembly process:

Assembly capacity = 150 components per hour × 8 hours per day × 5 days per week = 6,000 components per week

Since capacity of both the tasks is 6,000 units per week, they are balanced.

b. If the Molding Process Were to Use 10 Machines Instead of 6, and No Change Were to Be Made in the Final Assembly Task, What is the Capacity of the Entire Process?

Molding capacity with 10 machines:

Molding capacity = 10 machines × 25 parts per hour per machine × 8 hours per day × 5 days per week = 10,000 parts per week

Since no change has been made in the final assembly task, the capacity of the assembly process remains 6,000 components per week. Thus, even though the molding capacity is 10,000 per week, the capacity of the entire process is only 6,000 per week because in the long run the overall capacity cannot exceed the slowest task.

c. If XYZ Company Went to a Second Shift of Eight More Hours on Assembly Task, What Would Be the New Capacity?

A second shift on assembly task:

As calculated in the previous section, the molding capacity is 10,000.

Assembly capacity = 150 components per hour × 16 hours per day × 5 days
per week = 12,000 components per week

Here, even though the assembly capacity is 12,000 per week, the capacity of the entire process remains at 10,000 per week because now the slowest task is the molding process, which has a capacity of 10,000 per week. Thus we can note here that capacity of a process is not a constant factor; it depends on the availability of inputs and the sequence of tasks. In fact, it depends on several other factors not covered here.

d. Determine the Cost per Unit Output When the Capacity is (1) 6,000 per Week or (2) 10,000 per Week.

(1) Cost per unit when output per week = 6,000

First, we calculate the cost of producing all the 6,000 parts per week:

Item	Calculation	Cost
Raw material for molding	$0.10 per part × 6,000 =	$ 600
Parts purchased from outside	$0.30 per component × 6,000 =	1,800
Electricity	$0.02 per part × 6,000 =	120
Molding labor	$0.20 per part × 6,000 =	1,200
Assembly labor	$0.30 per part × 6,000 =	1,800
Rent	$100 per week	100
Supervision	$1,000 per week	1,000
Depreciation	$50 per week	50
Total cost		$ 6,670

$$\text{Cost per unit} = \frac{\text{Total cost per week}}{\text{Number of units produced per week}} = \frac{\$6,670}{6,000} = \$1.11$$

(2) Cost per unit when output per week = 10,000

First, we calculate the cost of producing all the 10,000 parts per week:

Item	Calculation	Cost
Raw material for molding	$0.10 per part × 10,000 =	$ 1,000
Parts purchased from outside	$0.30 per component × 10,000 =	3,000
Electricity	$0.02 per part × 10,000 =	200
Molding labor	$0.20 per part × 10,000 =	2,000
Assembly labor	$0.30 per part × 10,000 =	3,000
Rent	$100 per week	100
Supervision	$1,000 per week	1,000
Depreciation	$50 per week	50
Total cost		$ 10,350

The following Breakthrough box provides a walkthrough of Dell Computer's order fulfillment process, which involves order entry, manufacturing, and distribution processes.

Mr. Cozzette Buys a Computer

It's every consumer's dream. You want to make a major purchase, like a car or a computer. You're after high quality at a reasonable price, and you know exactly the features you want. So you call a manufacturer and place an order. Instantly, a modern factory sets to work and custom builds your machine for delivery to your door within a week. (Roll over, Henry Ford!)

You can get it today from Dell Computer, the number 1 direct marketer of PCs. The build-to-order system isn't just a recent addition meant to help the company, based in Austin, Texas, compete in the please-the-consumer Nineties. Dell has specialized in custom PCs since 1984, when founder Michael Dell got his start assembling machines in his college dorm room.

Though Dell lost $36 million last year, partly because of a failed third try at selling notebook computers, its Burger King assembly lines for desktop machines are the envy of the industry. Compaq Computer, Dell's archrival in Houston, is restructuring its entire logistics operation in hopes of achieving similar manufacturing flexibility by 1996.

Dell hasn't forgotten Henry Ford completely. Lately it has expanded into the retail arena, where merchants typically order hundreds of the same model PC. So Dell has jiggered some assembly lines to handle bulk orders. John Varol, director of manufacturing operations, says, "We call it mass customization, and it's a lot easier than sending hundreds of orders down the line." PCs built to order account for over 90 percent of Dell's $2.9 billion in annual sales. *Fortune* followed one machine from the moment a customer ordered it until Dell delivered it 46 hours, 42 minutes later.

Wednesday, 10:49 AM (Central Time)
Dave Cozzette, an accountant at Rothfos Corp., calls in his order for a Dell Dimension PC. At Dell's order center, a sales rep promises the PC will arrive within five business days. (She estimates it will arrive sooner, but sales reps are trained to keep customer expectations low.)

12:50 PM
Dell's financial services unit verifies the charge with Cozzette's credit card company, and the details of his $2,700.22 order print out on the production floor across the street at Dell's factory. An information sheet—called a traveler—lists the 60 items that Cozzette's computer must include, from cables to software. The order is branded with a serial number that will identify the PC for its lifetime.

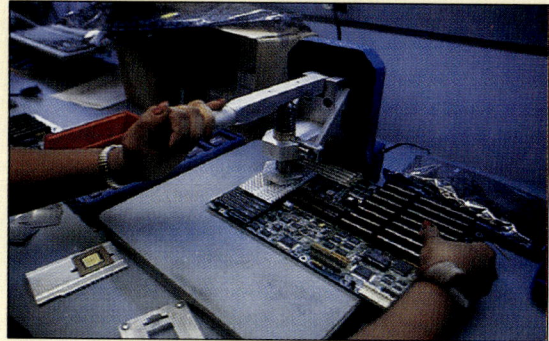

1:00 PM
The assembly process starts with the installation of an Intel 486 DX2 chip—the brains of Cozzette's computer—onto the machine's main circuitboard, known as the motherboard. A worker across the room is readying the floppy drives and hard disk for installation later.

1:55 PM
An employee applies a sticker bearing the nascent PC's serial number to the chassis and then lays in the motherboard, fastening it with screws.

2:01 PM
A fax modem, a device that can send documents created on the PC to fax machines or other computers via telephone lines, is inserted.

2:10 PM
Someone installs the floppy drive that was prepared earlier, along with a tape backup unit. It will let Cozzette make up-to-date duplicates of his hard disk files in the event his machine has a breakdown.

2:20 PM

The power supply, a transformer that converts electrical current for use in the PC, goes into the unit, and the PCs faceplate is attached with the Dell logo subtly displayed.

2:26 PM

A worker scans the computer's bar code to update Dell's inventory. The components that have been installed in Cozzette's PC are now listed as removed from the company's storage facility in another area of the plant.

2:27 PM

The PC gets its first quality inspection. An employee checks the traveler to make sure co-workers have installed every component the computer should have. Then a test diskette is created that will keep track of which software Cozzette has ordered and which components need to be tested.

2:28 PM

The PC powers up for the first time during a "quick test" that checks memory, video circuits, and floppy and hard disk functions. If the test diskette finds a bad sector on the hard disk, a crewmember will install a new hard disk. The test diskette sets the computer's clock to Central Time.

2:45 PM–7:45 PM

Cozzette's computer sits on a rack for an extended test called "burn in." For five hours the diskette runs the PC's components through grueling tests that simulate heavy use. An indicator light hooked to the back of the PC changes color to help workers monitor the testing. Only 2 percent of the PCs fail. Finally, the test diskette uses the network to download the programs Cozzette has ordered, such as Microsoft Windows, and installs them on the hard disk.

8:20 PM

An employee shoots a 25,000-volt charge into the PC's power supply. If the PC handles the jolt without going haywire, it earns a Federal Communications Commission Class B certification that it is safe to use in homes and offices.

8:32 PM

During the PC's final test, the system is hooked up to a monitor and keyboard and operated without its test diskette, just as Cozzette will use it.

8:37 PM

Cozzette's computer is put in a box with its keyboard, manuals, and warranty papers.

9:25 PM

An Airborne Express worker loads the PC onto a truck. If Cozzette had called Dell a few hours earlier, his PC would have made it onto the truck before the 7 PM deadline for next-day delivery. Instead, he'll get it on Friday.

Friday, 10:31 AM (Eastern Time)

Airborne drops off the package at Cozzette's office. He plugs in his PC, and Dell's greeting software offers its congratulations. It's up to Cozzette to reset the computer's clock to Eastern Time.

Source: Stephanie Losee, *Fortune*, April 18, 1994. © 1994 Time Inc. All rights reserved.

$$\text{Cost per unit} = \frac{\text{Total cost per week}}{\text{Number of units produced per week}} = \frac{\$10,350}{10,000} = \$1.04$$

The Breakthrough box provides a walkthrough of Dell computers' order fulfillment process for its build-to-order PC. Note that order fulfillment involves order entry, manufacturing, and distribution processes. Such process analysis calculations are required for many production decisions discussed throughout this book.

3.7   CONCLUSION

Designing a customer-pleasing product is an art. Building the product is a science. Moving the product from design to the customer is management. World-class manufacturers excel at **agile production**—managing for flexibility speed. A key to this is teamwork, not only on the part of marketing, product development, manufacturing, and distribution, but on the part of the supplier and customer as well.

Effective process planning requires clear understanding of what the factory can and cannot do relative to process structures. Many plants use a combination of the structures identified in this chapter—job shops for some parts, batch or assembly operations for others. Frequently a choice exists as to when demand seems likely to favor a switch from one to the other. Making such decisions also requires understanding the nuances of each production process to determine if the process really fits new product specifications. On a day-to-day basis, it requires the ability to systematically analyze capacity capabilities of each processing step, as was done in this chapter.

Finally, there is the issue of technology. While the details of manufacturing processes constitute the world of the engineer, awareness of modern technologies—particularly computer-integrated manufacturing—is now seen as an essential part of a business education. CIM along with other information technologies is discussed in this chapter's supplement.

3.8   SOLVED PROBLEM

1. A company is considering adding a new feature that will increase unit sales by 6 percent and product cost by 10 percent. Profit is expected to increase by 16 percent of the increased sales. Initially the product cost incurred by the company was 63 percent of the sales price. Should the new feature be added?

Solution

Let the sales be $100 M.

Sales increase by 6% = $100 M $\times$ 6% = $6 M.

   Benefits: Profits increase by 16% of the increased sales = $6 M $\times$ 16% = $0.96 M.
   Cost: Increase product cost by 10% = ($100 M $\times$ 63%) $\times$ 10% = $6.3 M.

Since costs exceed benefits, the new feature should not be added.

3.9   REVIEW AND DISCUSSION QUESTIONS

1. Discuss the product design philosophy behind industrial design and design for manufacturability. Which one do you think is more important in a customer-focused product development?

2. Discuss design-based incrementalism, which is frequent product redesign throughout the product's life. What are the pros and cons of this idea?

3. What is the primary production document derived from the product design process? What other types of document does one need to make a product?

4. What factors must be traded off by product development before introducing a new product?

5. What does the product-process matrix tell us? Where would you place a Chinese restaurant on the matrix?

6. It has been noted that during World War II Germany made a critical mistake by having its formidable Tiger tanks produced by locomotive manufacturers, while the less formidable U.S. Sherman tank was produced by American car manufacturers. Use the product-process matrix to explain that mistake and its likely result.

7. What impact does the concept and design stage have on the product's overall cost?

8. Discuss concurrent engineering and how it can benefit a production system.

9. How does the production volume affect break-even analysis?

10. What is meant by a process? Describe its important features.

3.10   PROBLEMS

1. Pick a product and make a list of issues that need to be considered in its design and manufacture. The product can be something like a stereo, telephone, desk, or kitchen appliance. Consider the functional and aesthetic aspects of design as well as the important concerns for manufacturing.

2. Mary Entrepreneur is considering introducing a new novelty item for sale to summer visitors in the Catskill Mountains in upstate New York: a wraparound belt with pockets in which vacationers could carry their suntan lotion, playing cards, and snacks. The belt, which she will market as the "Borscht Belt," was greeted with great enthusiasm by members of a local health club.

   The prototype model consists of six identical naugahyde pockets sewn onto a terrycloth belt, and a metal buckle available in the shape of different astrological signs. Once production begins, Mary will obtain naugahyde and terrycloth in bulk rolls, and buckles will be supplied by a local machine shop. Mary has two heavy-duty sewing machines and a stud-riveting machine (left over from her Bruce Springsteen Levi pants production) to attach the belt buckles. Before entering production, she would like to know

   a. What an assembly chart for the belts would look like.
   b. What a flow process chart for the entire operation, from raw materials receipt to final inspection, would look like.

3. The purpose of this system design exercise is to gain experience in setting up a manufacturing process. (We suggest that this be done as a team project.)
   Assignment:
   a. Get one Ping-Pong paddle.
   b. Specify the type of equipment and raw materials you would need to manufacture that paddle, from the receipt of seasoned wood to packaging for shipment.
   c. Assume that one unit of each type of equipment is available to you and is already placed in a rented hangar at your local airport. Further assume that you have a stock of seasoned wood and other materials needed to produce and box 100 paddles. Making reasonable assumptions about times and distances where necessary,
      (1) Develop an assembly drawing for the paddle.
      (2) Prepare an assembly chart for the paddle.
      (3) Develop a flow process chart for the paddle.
      (4) Develop a route sheet for the paddle.

4. The Goodparts Company produces a component that is subsequently used in the aerospace industry. The component consists of three parts (A, B, and C) that are purchased from outside and cost 40, 35, and 15 cents per piece, respectively. Parts A and B are assembled

first on assembly line 1, which produces 140 components per hour. Part C undergoes a drilling operation before being finally assembled with the output from assembly line 1. There are in total six drilling machines, but at present only three of them are operational. Each drilling machine drills part C at a rate of 50 parts per hour. In the final assembly, the output from assembly line 1 is assembled with the drilled part C. The final assembly line produces at a rate of 160 components per hour. At present, components are produced on a basis of eight hours a day and five days a week. Management believes that if need arises, it can go for a second shift of eight hours for the assembly lines.

The cost of assembly labor is 30 cents per part for each of the assembly lines; the cost of drilling labor is 15 cents per part. For drilling, the cost of electricity is 1 cent per part. The total overhead cost has been calculated as $1,200 per week. The depreciation cost for equipment has been calculated as $30 per week.

a. Draw a process flow diagram (see the XYZ example in Section 3.6) and determine the process capacity (number of components produced per week) of the entire process.

b. Suppose a second shift of eight hours is run for the assembly line 1 and the same is done for the final assembly line. In addition, four of the six drilling machines are made operational. The drilling machines, however, operate for just eight hours a day. What is the new process capacity (number of components produced per week)? Which of the three operations limits the capacity?

c. Management decides to run a second shift of eight hours for assembly line 1 plus a second shift of only four hours for the final assembly line. Five of the six drilling machines operate for eight hours a day. What is the new capacity? Which of the three operations limits the capacity?

d. Determine the cost per unit output for questions *b* and *c*.

e. The product is sold at $4.00 per unit. Assuming that the cost of a drilling machine (fixed cost) is $30,000 and the company produces 8,000 units per week, perform a break-even analysis. Assume that four drilling machines are used for production. If the company had an option to buy the same part at $3.00 per unit, what would be the break-even analysis?

CASE

3.11 C A S E
The Best Engineered Part Is No Part

Putting together NCR Corp.'s new 2760 electronic cash register is a snap. In fact, William R. Sprague can do it in less than two minutes—blindfolded. To get that kind of easy assembly, Sprague, a senior manufacturing engineer at NCR, insisted that the point-of-sale terminal be designed so that its parts fit together with no screws or bolts.

The entire terminal consists of just 15 vendor-produced components. That's 85 percent fewer parts, from 65 percent fewer suppliers, than in the company's previous low-end model, the 2160. And the terminal takes only 25 percent as much time to assemble. Installation and maintenance are also a breeze, says Sprague. "The simplicity flows through to all of the downstream activities, including field service."

The new NCR product is one of the best examples to date of the payoffs possible from a new engineering approach called "design for manufacturability," mercifully shortened to DFM. Other DFM enthusiasts include Ford, General Motors, IBM, Motorola, Perkin-Elmer, and Whirlpool. Since 1981, General Electric Co. has used DFM in more than 100 development programs, from major appliances to gearboxes for jet engines. GE figures that the concept has netted $200 million in benefits, either from cost savings or from increased market shares.

Nuts to Screws

One U.S. champion of DFM is Geoffrey Boothroyd, a professor of industrial and manufacturing engineering at the University of Rhode Island and the co-founder of Boothroyd Dewhurst Inc. This tiny Wakefield (R.I.) company has developed several computer programs that analyze designs for ease of manufacturing.

The biggest gains, notes Boothroyd, come from eliminating screws and other fasteners. On a supplier's invoice, screws and bolts may run mere pennies apiece, and collectively they account for only about 5 percent of a typical product's bill of materials. But tack on all of the associated costs, such as the time needed to align components while screws are inserted and tightened, and the price of using those mundane parts can pile up to 75 percent of total assembly costs. "Fasteners should be the first thing to design out of a product," he says.

Had screws been included in the design of NCR's 2760, calculates Sprague, the total cost over the lifetime of the model would have been $12,500—per screw. "The huge impact of little things like screws, primarily on overhead costs, just gets lost," he says. That's understandable, he admits, because for new-product development projects "the overriding factor is hitting the market window. It's better to be on time and over budget than on budget but late."

But NCR got its simplified terminal to market in record time without overlooking the little details. The product was formally introduced last January, just 24 months after development began. Design was a paperless, interdepartmental effort from the very start. The product remained a computer model until all members of the team—from design engineering, manufacturing, purchasing, customer service, and key suppliers—were satisfied.

That way, the printed-circuit boards, the molds for its plastic housing, and other elements could all be developed simultaneously. This eliminated the usual lag after designers throw a new product "over the wall" to manufacturing, which then must figure out how to make it. "Breaking down the walls between design and manufacturing to facilitate simultaneous engineering," Sprague declares, "was the real breakthrough."

The design process began with a mechanical computer-aided engineering program that allowed the team to fashion three-dimensional models of each part on a computer screen. The software also analyzed the overall product and its various elements for performance and durability. Then the simulated components were assembled on a computer workstation's screen to assure that they would fit together properly. As the design evolved, it was checked periodically with Boothroyd Dewhurst's DFM software. This prompted several changes that trimmed the parts count from an initial 28 to the final 15.

No Mock-Up

After everyone on the team gave their thumbs-up, the data for the parts were electronically transferred directly into computer-aided manufacturing systems at the various suppliers. The NCR designers were so confident everything would work as intended that they didn't bother making a mock-up.

DFM can be a powerful weapon against foreign competition. Several years ago, IBM used Boothroyd Dewhurst's software to analyze dot-matrix printers it was sourcing from Japan—and found it could do substantially better. Its Proprinter has 65 percent fewer parts and slashed assembly time by 90 percent. "Almost anything made in Japan," insists Professor Boothroyd, "can be improved upon with DFM—often impressively."

Question

What development problems has the NCR approach overcome?

—————

Source: Otis Port, "The Best-Engineered Part Is No Part at All," *Business Week,* May 8, 1989, p. 150.

C A S E

3.12 C A S E

Product Development in Japan

Like the wizard of Oz, Japan's giant industrial combines are not what they appear to be. They do not develop all of their own product line, nor do they manufacture it. In reality, these huge businesses are more like "trading companies." That is, rather than design and manufacture their own goods, they actually coordinate a complex design and manufacturing process that involves thousands of smaller companies. The goods you buy with a famous maker's name inscribed on the case are seldom the product of that company's factory— and often not even the product of its own research. Someone else designed it, someone else put it together, someone stuck it in a box with the famous maker's name on it and then shipped it to its distributors.

Does this operation sound unnecessarily complex? Obviously, these huge corporations have their own factories and workers. So why don't they employ their own resources to produce the goods they sell?

They do, of course—but only partially. For instance, it would make very little sense for an electronics giant like Matsushita to farm out the design, manufacture, and assembly of a refrigerator or microwave oven. These products are ideally suited to mass production in the kind of large, highly automated factories that the giant companies can afford. Their factories produce hundreds of thousands of these units every year.

But what about products that companies must continually redesign to compete for public acceptance—like headphone stereos, small compact disc players, or personal computers? Redesigning means retooling a production line. It means sourcing new parts and lots of other things. For a typical product, a company might expect to sell 30,000 units in a few months, retool, sell another 50,000 units, redesign some basic components, retool again, see what the competition brings out, retool again, and on and on, throughout the life cycle of the entire product line. Although some of the giant makers are now employing the newest flexible manufacturing systems (FMS) to allow them more freedom in production, this retooling process is something many big companies want to eliminate.

Thus they farm out much of this business to subcontractors—smaller companies they can depend on. These companies in turn, faced with redesigning and producing a product three or four times a year, will subcontract the design or manufacture of a dozen key components to still smaller companies.

How extensive is this subcontracting pyramid? Would you guess a few dozen companies? A few hundred? Think again. One electronics company I know has well over 6,000 subcontractors in its industrial group, most of them tiny shops that exist just to fill a few little orders for the companies above them.

Welcome to the real world of Japanese manufacturing.

Question

What are the strengths and weakness of the Japanese approach to product development?

Source: Kuniyasu Sakai, "The Feudal World of Japanese Manufacturing," *Harvard Business Review,* November-December 1990, pp. 38–39.

3.13   SELECTED BIBLIOGRAPHY

Adler, Paul S., Henry E. Riggs, and Steven C. Wheelwright. "Product Development Know-How: Trading Tactics for Strategy." *Sloan Management Review,* Fall 1989, pp. 7–17.

Boggs, Robert N. "Rogues' Gallery of 'Aggravating Products'." *Design News,* October 22, 1990, pp. 130–33.

Bolwijn, P. T., and T. Kumpe. "Manufacturing in the 1990's—Productivity, Flexibility, and Innovation." *Long Range Planning* 23, no. 4 (1990), pp. 44–57.

Dixon, John R., and Michael R. Duffy. "The Neglect of Engineering Design." *California Management Review,* Winter 1990, pp. 9–23.

Drucker, Peter F. "The Emerging Theory of Manufacturing." *Harvard Business Review,* May–June 1990, pp. 94–102.

Edmondson, Harold E., and Steven C. Wheelwright. "Outstanding Manufacturing in the Coming Decade." *California Management Review,* Summer 1989, pp. 70–90.

Gardner, Dana. "Tech Toys for Grownups." *Design News,* December 3, 1990, pp. 63–66.

Hamilton, Joan O'C. "Rebel with a Cause." *Business Week,* December 3, 1990, pp. 130–33.

Hammer, Michael. "Reengineering Work: Don't Automate, Obliterate." *Harvard Business Review,* July–August 1990, pp. 104–12.

Hayes, Robert H., and Steven C. Wheelwright. *Restoring Our Competitive Age.* New York: John Wiley & Sons, 1984.

Hill, Terry. *Manufacturing Strategy.* 2d ed. Boston: Richard D. Irwin, 1994.

Huthwaite, Bart. *Design for Competitiveness: A Concurrent Engineering Handbook.* Institute for Competitive Design, 530 N. Pine, Rochester, MI.

Jonas, Norman. "Can America Compete?" *Business Week,* April 20, 1987, pp. 45–69.

Machlis, Sharon. "Three Shortcuts to Better Design." *Design News,* November 19, 1990, pp. 89–91.

Main, Jeremy. "Manufacturing the Right Way." *Fortune,* May 21, 1990, pp. 54–64.

Meyer, Christopher. *Fast Cycle Time.* New York: Free Press, 1993.

Nussbaum, Bruce, and Robert Neff. "I Can't Work This Thing!" *Business Week,* April 29, 1991, pp. 58–66.

Pare, Terence P. "Why Some Do It the Wrong Way." *Fortune,* May 21, 1990, pp. 75–76.

Roehm, Harper A., Donald Klein, and Joseph F. Castellano. "Springing to World-Class Manufacturing." *Management Accounting,* March 1991, pp. 40–44.

Sakai, Kuniyasu. "The Feudal World of Japanese Manufacturing." *Harvard Business Review,* November–December 1990, pp. 38–49.

Sanderson, Susan Walsh, and Vic Uzumeri. "Strategies for New Product Development and Renewal: Design-Based Incrementalism." Center for Science and Technology Policy, School of Management, Rensselaer Polytechnic Institute, May 1990.

Shunk, Dan L. *Integrated Process Design and Development.* Homewood, IL: Business One Irwin, 1992.

Spenser, William J. "Research to Product: A Major U.S. Change." *California Management Review,* Winter 1990, pp. 45–53.

Wheelwright, Steven C., and W. Earl Sasser, Jr. "The New Product Development Map." *Harvard Business Review,* May–June 1989, pp. 112–27.

Ziemke, M. Carl, and Mary S. Spann. "Warning: Don't Be Half-Hearted in Your Efforts to Employ Concurrent Engineering." *Industrial Engineering,* February 1991, pp. 45–49.

Supplement

3

Technology Management

SUPPLEMENT OUTLINE

KEY TERMS

Product Technologies
Process Technologies
Numerically Controlled (NC) Machine
Machining Centers
Industrial Robots
Computer-Aided Design and Manufacturing (CAD/CAM)
Group Technology (GT)
Cellular Manufacturing
Automated Materials Handling (AMH) Systems
Flexible Manufacturing Systems (FMS)
Automated Manufacturing Planning and Control Systems (MP&CS)
Computer-Integrated Manufacturing (CIM)
Service Technologies
Office Automation
Image Processing Systems
Electronic Data Interchange (EDI)
Decision Support and Expert Systems
Client/Server Networks

At first glance, the fry station at the McDonald's restaurant in Mishakawa, Indiana, looks like any other fry station—same size, same silver color. Closer scrutiny, however, reveals that it is no run-of-the-mill spud fryer. Most notably, it has no human attendant. Instead, it weighs, cooks, times, shakes, and dumps fries by itself, without help from crew members.

The fry station, part of a McDonald's program known as ARCH (Automated Restaurant Crew Helper), is one of the country's highest-profile examples of food-service automation. It is also part of a growing trend that is slowly moving the industrial robot into the service sector. "When you look at an automotive assembly line, you realize that it's not much of a stretch to apply automation to fast food or any number of other applications," notes Gay Engelberger, chairman of the International Service Robot Association in Ann Arbor, Michigan.

McDonald's fry-maker is only one prong of a corporate program that has begun to automate the firm's food preparation. The company also has introduced ARCH drink, an automated drink machine that eliminates the need for crew members to grab cups, shovel ice, and operate drink valves. ARCH robots are now employed at 5.5 percent of the company's 9,000 domestic stores. The company's grand plan is to remove as much labor as possible from the kitchen area and move it to the service counter. Robots significantly reduce the time it takes to fill an order, thereby reducing the time a customer waits after placing an order.

The fry-maker automatically drops fries into baskets, lowering the baskets into the cooking oil, shaking them intermittently to remove clumps, and then dumping finished fries for bagging.

Because they were custom-designed to blend with existing cooking equipment, both robots look remarkably unrobotic. They are neither as big nor as complex as the robots often seen on factory floors. Designed for use by people who have never before seen a real robot, let alone worked with one, they have been endowed with special safety features—among them, a shutdown mechanism that is activated when the robot arm encounters human resistance.

The ARCH drink-maker enables crew members to merely push a button and pick up finished drinks seconds later. It is particularly effective in the busiest McDonald's, which often have a crew member handling only drink production.

McDonald's ARCH program is not limited to robots or just automating food production. An automated ARCH production system helps a store manager in sales forecasting and production planning. The system, for example, tells the manager how many hamburgers, cheeseburgers, or fries he or she can expect to sell over the next 10 minutes. It indicates how many packages of tartar or Big Mac sauce the manager should have on hand for the day depending on recent sales patterns. Based on the demand patterns in a day, the system could also help the manager decide how many employees are needed at different time slots and thus assist in staff planning.

Source: Condensed from an article by Chuck Murray, "Robots Roll from Plant to Kitchen, " in the *Chicago Tribune*, October 17, 1993.

Technology is a resource of profound importance not only to operations, but to corporate profitability and growth as well. It also affects the competitive capabilities of national economies. Technology is critical in the global success of U.S. firms such as Wal-Mart, Motorola, McDonald's, and Hewlett-Packard. In firms that have made technology a competitive weapon, technology management could be perceived as the effective integration of the company's technology strategy and business strategy. Also, technology improves the coordination of the research, development, and operations functions with the marketing, finance, accounting, and human resource functions.

Technology management comprises the management of a broad spectrum of areas, including basic research, applied research, product design and development, manufacturing or service operations, and product testing. While technology management is a very broad subject, we largely restrict our discussion here to the use and impact of technologies in improving manufacturing or service operations. In particular, we focus on motives for acquiring new technologies to improve the production process, the major types of technologies, and evaluation of technology investments.

Pictures throughout the book illustrate the profound impact of modern technologies on manufacturing and service industries. Observe in particular the differences between older, labor-intensive plants and newer, automated ones.

S3.1 DRIVE FOR ACQUIRING NEW TECHNOLOGIES

Why do firms acquire new technologies? The reasons can be related directly to the four competitive strategies emphasized in previous chapters: cost, speed of delivery, quality, and flexibility (or customizability).

Cost In this case, the objective is to reduce the cost of the product or service, which in turn enables the firm to make greater profits or lower the price of the product to increase sales volume. Technology can cut costs in many ways: reducing material, labor, or distribution costs. Material costs can be reduced by replacing higher-cost materials used to make a product with lower-cost ones or by reducing the material required to make a product. In general, technology decreases labor costs by reducing the labor time required to make a product. For instance, Johnson and Johnson has developed a new molding technology to make disposable contact lenses that uses almost no labor, giving the firm a sizable cost advantage over its competitors.

Speed of Delivery   In many cases, the key competitive priority may be the speed of delivery, as measured by the lead time required to deliver a product. Technologies may reduce this lead time. For example, automated guidance vehicles (AGVs) are used to rapidly transport materials within Xerox plants, and to move produce items quickly in Ralph's Market's huge Los Angeles warehouse. Technologies such as electronic data interchange (EDI) and now familiar fax machines have dramatically reduced the time required to transmit information from one location to another, thus lowering lead time for both service and manufacturing operations.

Quality   Many technologies improve the quality of the product or service, thereby raising sales volume and lowering costs. For instance, successive innovations in computer tomography (CT) scanners used to obtain CAT scans have improved the quality of the images, which in turn allows radiologists and physicians to make better diagnoses. Firms such as Motorola have benefited immensely from the application of automated testing devices to process control.

Flexibility or Customizability   The global marketplace of the 1990s is characterized by short product life cycles, increased product variety, and extensive customization. To retain and increase market share in such a competitive environment, firms have to be more flexible in their operations and satisfy different market segments. As noted in Chapter 1, the term *mass customization* is now used to describe the strategy of a firm to deliver customized products to consumers at the price of mass-produced items.

The SABRE reservation system developed by American Airlines gives travel agents enormous flexibility in making and changing airline, hotel, and rental car reservations, permitting quick responses to changes in a customer's travel plans.

At Xerox these automated guided vehicles are routed by wires in the floor and move around the warehouse delivering materials and picking and placing inventory.

S3.2   TECHNOLOGY CLASSIFICATIONS

Technologies can be broadly classified into two categories: product and process technologies. **Product technologies** refer to technological efforts to develop new products or services—for example, a VCR or cash management account. These arise typically from product or service design and development activities, which are discussed elsewhere in this book. In this supplement, we focus on process technologies and their impact on operations in manufacturing and service firms. **Process technologies** refer to the collection of equipment and processes (or procedures) used to make the firm's products or services. The distinction between product and process technologies can be ambiguous. Many advances primarily affecting production processes (process changes) consist of quality improvements in some equipment. Technological changes in a process may also be embedded in products that can serve in both production and final consumption (such as personal computers or communication systems and devices).

Another possible classification of technology is in terms of hard and soft technologies, more commonly called hardware and software. **Hardware** refers to the equipment, machine, or tool, while **software** refers to the set of rules, procedures, or guidelines necessary to use the hardware. For instance, automatic check-processing equipment acquired by a bank represents the hardware, including some imbedded software that runs the equipment. However, an operator may follow other procedures to operate the equipment, which represents the software. Hardware and software generally go together in achieving the benefits of technology. Therefore, new technologies may be embodied in the form of advances in either hardware or software or both. In some instances, software exists by itself and technology is represented by changes in the software. For example, a mail-order firm may be using some ad hoc procedures in planning its customer service representative requirements and schedules. In this case, new technology may be represented by sophisticated forecasting and staff scheduling techniques which replace the ad hoc procedures.

S3.3   TECHNOLOGIES IN MANUFACTURING

While technological changes have occurred in almost every industry, many may be unique to each industry. For instance, prestressed concrete blocks are a technological advance unique to the construction industry. But some technological advances in recent decades have had a significant, widespread impact on manufacturing firms in many industries. These advances have generally resulted in greater automation, in which machinery replaces many of the processes performed by humans. Examples of these major types of manufacturing technologies are numerically controlled machine tools, machining centers, industrial robots, computer-aided design and manufacturing systems, automated materials handling systems, flexible manufacturing systems, automated manufacturing planning and control systems, and computer-integrated manufacturing. We describe these technologies next, paying particular attention to computer-aided design and computer-integrated manufacturing.

Numerically controlled (NC) machines are comprised of (1) a typical machine tool used to turn, drill, or grind different types of parts and (2) a computer that controls the sequence of processes performed by the machine. NC machines were first adopted by U.S. aerospace firms in the 1960s and have since proliferated to many other industries. In more recent models, feedback control loops determine the position of the machine tooling during the work, constantly compare the actual location with the programmed location, and correct as needed. This is often called adaptive control.

Numerically Controlled Machines, Machining Centers, and Industrial Robots

Machining centers represent an increased level of automation and complexity relative to NC machines. Machining centers not only provide automatic control of a machine; they may also carry many tools that can be automatically changed depending on the tool required for each operation. For example, a single machine may be equipped with a shuttle system of two worktables that can be rolled into and out of the machine. While work is being done at one table, the next part is mounted on the second table. When machining on the first table is complete, it is moved out of the way and the sec-

The roof of a Lincoln Mark VIII is welded in place by a robotic device. Robots can be operated by humans or run by computers and are particularly beneficial for tasks that are dangerous, dirty, or dull to humans.

E X H I B I T S3.1

Typical Robot Axes of Motion

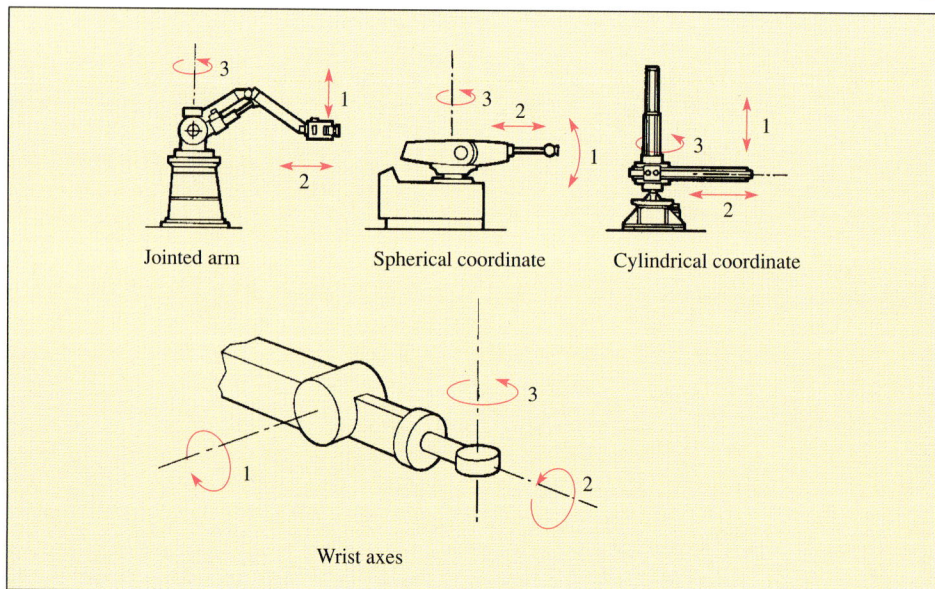

Jointed arm   Spherical coordinate   Cylindrical coordinate

Wrist axes

Source: L. V. Ottinger, "Robotics for the IE: Terminology, Types of Robots," *Industrial Engineering,* November 1981, p. 30. Reprinted with permission.

ond part is moved into position and the required tool is accessed and aligned to perform the next operation.

Industrial robots are substitutes for many repetitive manual activities. A robot is a reprogrammable, multifunctional machine that may be equipped with an end effector (such as a gripper or a tool such as a wrench or welder or sprayer) used to perform repetitive tasks such as picking and placing devices, spot welding, and painting.

Exhibit S3.1 examines the human motions a robot can reproduce. Advanced capabilities have been designed into robots to allow vision, tactile sensing, and hand-to-hand coordination. In addition, some models can be "taught" a sequence of motions in a three-dimensional pattern. As a worker moves the end of the robot arm through the required motions, the robot records this pattern in its memory and repeats them on command.

As productivity increases with robots, workers can be eliminated. (See "Formula for Evaluating a Robot Investment" for a sample financial analysis.) Current estimates set worker displacement at anywhere from 1.7 to 6.0 employees per robot; the potential is especially high in the metalworking industry. It seems just a matter of time before sophisticated robots with vision systems will be viable for assembly and sensitive-touch jobs in other industries. Some experts estimate these robots of the future could replace as many as 3.8 million workers. There are, however, some things a robot will probably never be able to do, as Exhibit S3.2 shows.

Formula for Evaluating a Robot Investment

Many companies use the following modification of the basic payback formula in deciding if a robot should be purchased:

$$P = \frac{I}{L - E + q(L + Z)}$$

Where

P = Payback period in years

I = Total capital investment required in robot and accessories

L = Annual labor costs replaced by the robot (wage and benefit costs per worker times the number of shifts per day)

E = Annual maintenance cost for the robot

q = Fractional speedup (or slowdown) factor

Z = Annual depreciation

Example:

I = $50,000

L = $60,000 (two workers × $20,000 each working one of two shifts; overhead is $10,000 each)

E = $9,600 ($2/hour × 4,800 hours/year)

q = 1.5 (robot works 150 percent as fast as a worker)

Z = $10,000

then

$$P = \frac{\$50,000}{\$60,000 - \$9,600 + 1.5\,(\$60,000 + \$10,000)} = \frac{1}{3}\ \text{year}$$

Things Present (or Past) Robots Can Do	Things Next-Generation Robots Will Be Able to Do	Things a Very Sophisticated Future Robot May Be Able to Do	Things No Robot Will Ever Be Able to Do (Probably)
Play the piano	Vacuum a rug (avoiding obstructions)	Set a table	Cut a diamond
Load/unload CNC machine tools	Load/unload a glass blowing or cutting machine	Clear a table	Polish an opal
Load/unload die casting machines, hammer forging machines, molding machines, etc.	Assemble large and/or complex parts, TVs, refrigerators, air conditioners, microwave ovens, toasters, automobiles	Juggle balls	Peel a grape
		Load a dishwasher	Repair a broken chair or dish
		Unload a dishwasher	
		Weld a cracked casting/forging	Play tennis or Ping-Pong at championship level
Spray paint on an assembly line		Make a bed	
Cut cloth with a laser		Locate and repair leaks inside a tank or pipe	Catch a football or Frisbee at championship level
Make molds	Operate woodworking machines		
Deburr sand castings		Pick a lock	Ride a bicycle in traffic*
Manipulate tools such as welding guns, drills, etc.	Walk on two legs	Knit a sweater	Drive a car in traffic*
	Shear sheep	Make needlepoint design	Tree surgery
	Wash windows	Make lace	Repair a damaged picture
Assemble simple mechanical and electrical parts: small electric motors, pumps, transformers, radios, tape recorders	Scrape barnacles from a ship's hull	Grease a continuous mining machine or similar piece of equipment	Cut hair stylishly
	Sandblast a wall		Apply makeup artistically
		Tune up a car	Set a multiple fracture
		Make a forging die from metal powder	Deliver a baby
		Load, operate, and unload a sewing machine	Cut and trim meat
			Kiss sensuously

Computer-Aided Design

Computer-aided design (CAD) is a contemporary approach to product and process design that utilizes the power of the computer. CAD covers several automated technologies, such as *computer graphics* to examine the visual characteristics of a product and *computer-aided engineering* (CAE) to evaluate its engineering characteristics. CAD also includes technologies associated with manufacturing process design, referred to as *computer-aided process planning (CAPP):* to design numerically controlled part programs that serve as instructions to computer-controlled machine tools, and to design the use of and sequence of machine centers required for the operations on a part, called the process plan. Sophisticated CAD systems may also be able to do on-screen tests, replacing the early phases of prototype testing and modification.

CAD has been used to design everything from computer chips to potato chips. Frito-Lay, for example, used CAD to determine the proper angle and number of ruffles on its O'Grady's double-density, ruffled potato chip to prevent sogginess, burns, and overbrittleness. Another good example of a CAD-designed product is Motorola's new wrist watch pager (Exhibit S3.3). Frequently cited benefits include higher design productivity, shorter design cycle time, higher design quality, and lower manufacturing

Primary
battery

Secondary
battery

Receiver
kit

Antenna

PCB
Insulator

Contact
frame

Decoder
kit

Liquid crystal
display

Bezel
assembly

Display
crystal kit

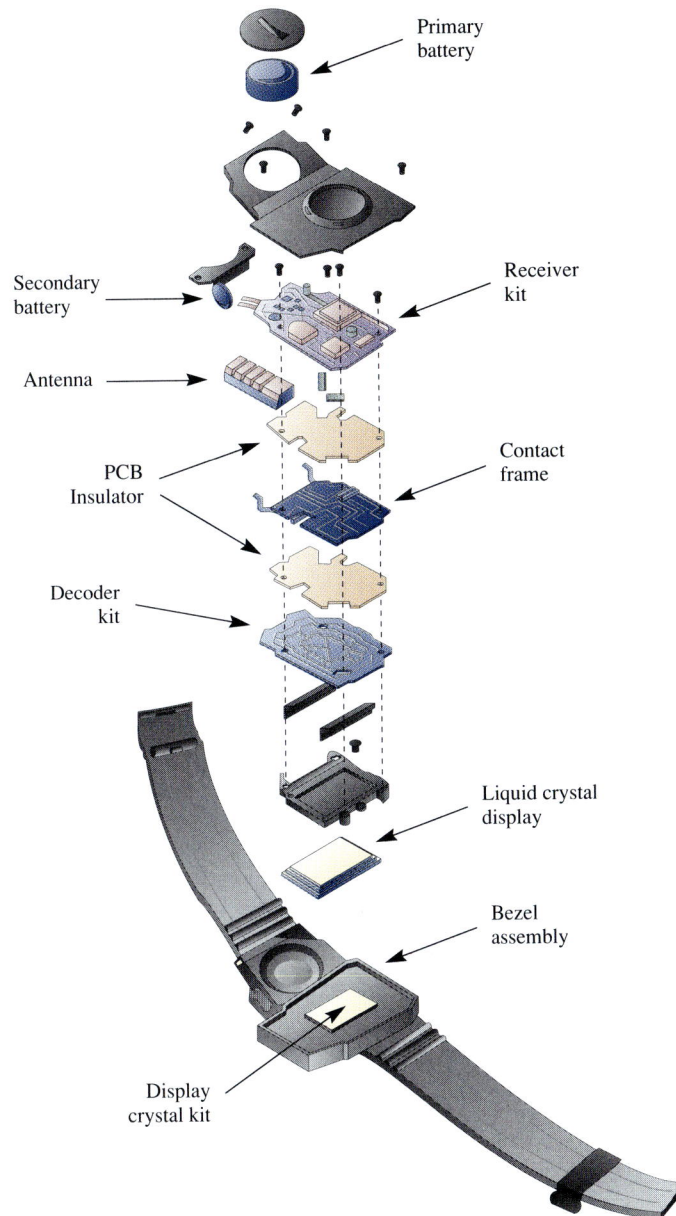

Source: Dana Gardner, "Tech Toys for Grownups." *Design News,* December 3, 1990, p. 64.

costs in the long run due to the ability to uncover potential manufacturing problems at
the design stage itself.

Closely associated with CAD in process design is **group technology (GT),** a production methodology that classifies, codes, and groups parts and processes based on one or
more of such factors as part geometry, materials, and production operations and equipment required. It is widely used in identifying cells of groups of machinery that are closely
associated with each family of parts, also referred to as **cellular manufacturing.** (See
Chapter 10.)

E X H I B I T S3.4

Different Flexible Manufacturing Systems

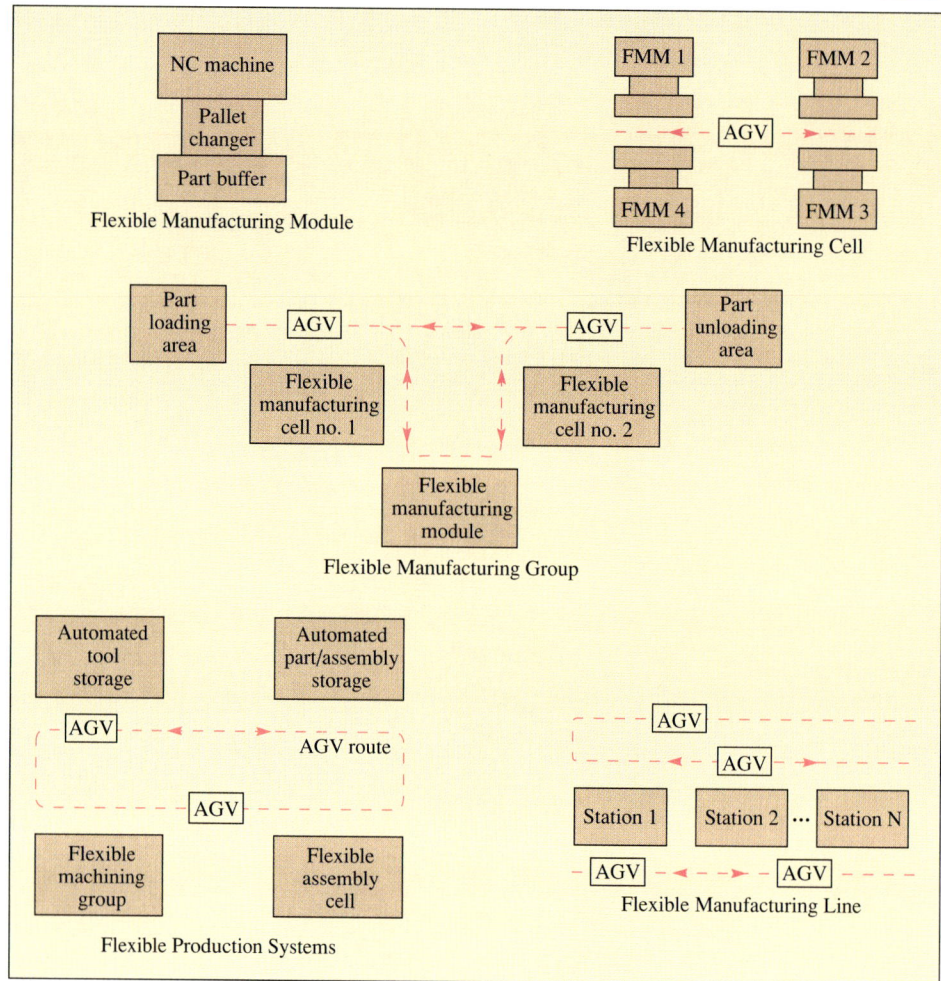

Flexible Manufacturing Module

Flexible Manufacturing Cell

Flexible Manufacturing Group

Flexible Production Systems

Flexible Manufacturing Line

Other Technologies

Automated materials handling (AMH) systems improve the efficiency of transportation, storage, and retrieval of materials. Examples are computerized conveyors, automated storage and retrieval systems (AS/RS) in which computers direct automatic loaders to pick and place items, and automated guided vehicle (AGV) systems, which use embedded floor wires to direct driverless vehicles to various locations in the plant, delivering materials, such as that used at Xerox in the photo on page 82. Benefits of AMH systems include quicker material movement, lower inventories and storage space, reduced product damage, and higher labor productivity.

A **flexible manufacturing system (FMS)** refers to a number of systems that differ in the degree of mechanization, automated transfer, and computer control. Andrew Kusiak has nicely defined and shown five such systems with increasing number of machines and automation: flexible manufacturing module, cell, group, production system, and line (Exhibit S3.4).[1] While a flexible manufacturing module comprises an NC machine supported by a parts inventory, a tool changer, and a pallet changer, a flexible manufactur-

---

[1]Andrew Kusiak, "Flexible Manufacturing Systems: A Structural Approach," *International Journal of Production Research* 23, no. 6 (1985), pp. 1057–73.

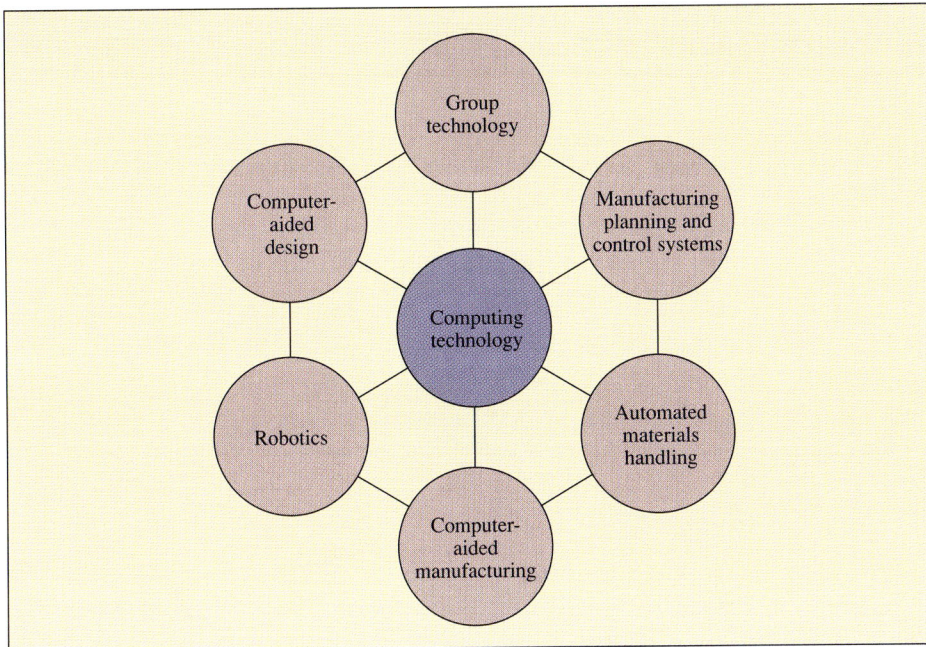

ing line consists of a series of sophisticated machines connected by AGVs, robots, and so on.

In general, the number of different part types produced increases as we go from a flexible manufacturing line toward a module, while the annual production per part decreases. While the conventional belief is that flexible manufacturing systems are best used in low volume and with a high number of different parts, Cummins Engine Company claims a high degree of success and cost savings using FMS in high volumes.[2]

Automated manufacturing planning and control systems (MP&CS) are simply computer-based information systems that help plan, schedule, and monitor manufacturing operations. They obtain information from the shop floor continuously about work status, material arrivals, and so on, and release production and purchase orders. More sophisticated manufacturing planning and control systems also include order-entry processing, shop-floor control, purchasing, and cost accounting. (See Chapters 15 and 16.)

Computer-integrated manufacturing (CIM) is an automation version of the generic manufacturing process, wherein the three major manufacturing functions—product and process design, planning and control, and the manufacturing process itself—are replaced by the automated technologies described so far. (See Exhibit S3.5.) Further, the traditional integration mechanisms of oral and written communication are replaced by computer technology. Such highly automated and integrated manufacturing also goes under other names: *total factory automation* and the *factory of the future.*

All the CIM technologies in Exhibit S3.5 are tied together in a communications link made possible by advanced computing technology. The real power is achieved by linking the data bases of the different components. For instance, data integration allows CAD

Computer-Integrated Manufacturing

---

[2]Ravi Venkatesan, "Cummins Engine Flexes Its Factory," *Harvard Business Review,* March–April 1990, pp. 120–27.

E X H I B I T S3.6
Synergistic Effects of a CIM System

| CIM benefits | = | Benefits of each separate technology | × | Benefits of data integration |

systems to be linked to CAM numerical-control parts programs, and the manufacturing planning and control system can be linked to the AMH systems to facilitate parts pick-list generation. Thus, in a fully integrated system, the areas of design, testing, fabrication, assembly, inspection, and material handling are not only automated, but also integrated with each other and with the manufacturing planning and scheduling function.

Benefits of CIM   Earlier we discussed the benefits of the automated technologies that comprise CIM. These include higher design and manufacturing productivity and quality, lower inventory costs, and savings in space, materials, and so on. The real advantages of CIM are not in the sum of the benefits of each separate technology, although that sum is significant. The real advantage of CIM lies in the integration of these component technologies. The long-term benefits of a data-integrated system like CIM are the individual benefits amplified geometrically by the benefits of integrating each component into a common system, as Exhibit S3.6 shows.

Integration leads to better management of the flow of manufacturing data, better interdepartmental communications, and better resource utilization, all of which can greatly improve product quality, production efficiency, and lead times. Consider these examples of benefits achieved by partial implementation of CIM in five companies:[3]

Achievement	Range of Improvement
Reduction in engineering design cost	15–30%
Reduction in overall lead time	30–60%
Increased product quality as measured by yield of acceptable product	2–5 times previous level
Increased capability of engineers as measured by extent and depth of analysis in same or less time than previously	3–35 times
Increased productivity (complete assemblies)	40–70%
Increased productivity (operating time) of capital equipment	2–3 times
Reduction of work-in-process	30–60%
Reduction of personnel costs	5–20%

As you might surmise, all the component technologies of CIM are further along in their product life cycles than is CIM as a whole. (See Exhibit S3.7.) Since data integration is the essence of CIM, a key to its widespread application will be the refinement and standardization of the programming languages that provide the linkages. Four key management factors will ultimately determine the speed of implementation and, with it, a company's success:

1. *The articulation of a CIM strategy that recognizes CIM's impact on overall corporate competitiveness, not just its short-run financial implications.* This means that the company must clearly identify how it competes (its relative emphasis on price, quality, flexibility, dependability) and how CIM will specifically contribute to its competitiveness.

2. *The need for companywide planning involving all business functions.* The best way to plan for CIM is usually through a multidisciplinary task force with direct involvement of top management.

---

[3]Thomas G. Gunn, *Manufacturing for Competitive Advantage* (Cambridge, MA: Ballinger, 1987), p. 171.

Current Maturity

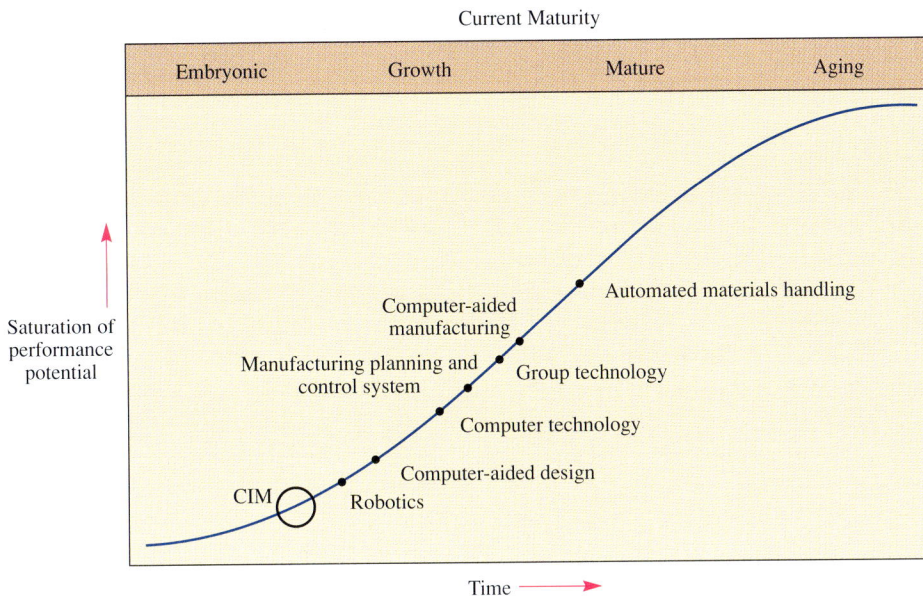

3. The recognition that the administrative structure and the jobs of the workforce may well have to be changed to take full advantage of CIM's capability. CIM is both a new philosophy and a new technology that breaks down departmental barriers and requires new job skills. It is well known that an essential requirement for effective CIM use is close interaction between engineering and manufacturing, resulting in team structures. Similar kinds of groupings or new forms of organizational linkages among marketing, engineering, and manufacturing are also required.

The jobs of the workforce obviously become more computer-based, requiring information processing skills rather than direct production skills. This clearly affects workers in the trades, such as machinists. Finally, there is evidence that CIM leads to job enlargement, and hence new and fewer job titles. According to John Ettlie, "In some [modernized] plants, over 100 job categories have been collapsed into five or even three broad job titles."[4]

4. The recognition that various activities will have to be modified to support CIM technologies. A new GT cell, for example, will require changes in work standards, maintenance procedures, tooling (jigs, dies, and fixtures), and so on.

Examples of CIM   Competition has led many companies to install CIM systems into their manufacturing facilities. It has long been felt that CIM is a trend for the factory of the future, but to use the cliché, the future is now. Each year, *Electronics Business* and *Electronic Packaging & Production* grant their Electronic Factory Automation Award to the U.S.–owned plant they believe is the best example of automation in the electronics industry.[5] One award winner is the Texas Instruments plant in Johnson City, Tennessee. This installation is discussed next, along with the automated Fanuc Company factory, which is well known for its high degree of automation.

---

[4]John Ettlie, speech before the Center for Operations Management Education and Research, University of Southern California, June 27, 1987.

[5]Tony Greene, "CIM Savvy, Tennessee Style," *Electronic Business,* March 6, 1989, pp. 31–36.

Texas Instruments' Johnson City circuit board facility   In responding to customers' demand for higher-quality printed circuit boards and management's demand for higher return on investment, Texas Instruments (TI) created and installed a surface mount technology (SMT) line. The SMT line produces more than 30 types of boards ranging from simple automotive window controllers to high-resolution graphic boards for computer workstations.

The project started with the installation of a flexible electronic manufacturing assembly cell (FEMAC) to produce printed circuit board assemblies. This was to be done with state-of-the-art equipment combined with automated materials handling, and machine programming—all controlled with computers. The facility has worked out so well that other TI plants will install similar lines. TI was also able to enter the contract business.

On this surface mount technology (SMT) line, throughput increased by 21 percent while increased quality improved the yield rate by 20 percent. Electrical rejects decreased from 1,700 ppm to 200 ppm. Cycle time from raw materials to shipping has been cut from five days to three days. Cycle time reduction was due in part to lowering setup time required to change to different boards to under one hour.

The line consists of two assembly lines and one soldering line in parallel, connected by an overhead conveyer running perpendicular to the ends of the three lines. The first step is to apply solder paste to the bare copper pads where the electrical components mounted on the surface must make contact. The components are then dipped in solder paste and then automatically picked up and correctly placed by a machine. The remaining components are also assembled automatically on the board. The board is then soldered, cleaned, and subjected to electrical tests.

The entire process is controlled by computers with minimal human interaction. The system is tied into Texas Instrument's main computer system so that (1) new designs from computer-aided design can be quickly transmitted and (2) to allow for design changes and quick introduction of new products.

TI managers have the attitude that factory automation is a continuous process, not one that ends when some level of automation is installed. The project leader has the belief that CIM is a moving target and, although TI thought it had a 100 percent installation three years ago, right now thinks it is 60 percent CIM. This gives managers the feeling that the opportunity exists to add more improvements and automation to the line.

Fujitsu Fanuc's robot factory   Fujitsu Fanuc has put into operation an entire factory for producing robots, small machining centers, and wire-cut electrodischarge machines. The machining section of the factory operates almost wholly unattended on the night shift.

There are 29 machining cells (22 machining centers served by automatic pallet changes and seven robot-served cells), each consisting of one or more NC machine tools and a robot or pallet changer to keep the machine or machines loaded with parts during the night. Workpieces on pallets are transported to and from the cells and to and from computer-controlled automatic stacker cranes by computer-controlled, wire-guided carts.

During the day there are 19 workers on the machining floor. On the night shift no one is on the machining floor, and there is only one worker in the control room. ("I had some difficulty scheduling a time to visit the plant . . . because the company's managers were concerned about protocol: There would be no one senior enough to receive a visitor on the site during 10 of its 15 operating shifts.")[6] In a 24-hour period, machine

---

[6]Gerald K. O'Neill, "Robots Who Reproduce," *Across the Board,* June 1984, p. 37.

availability is running close to 100 percent, and machine use is averaging 65 to 70 percent. As a result, this 2,050-square-meter factory is producing 100 robots, 75 machining centers, and 75 electrodischarge machines each month.

S3.4   TECHNOLOGIES IN SERVICES

A key element in improving the cost, quality, and speed of service operations is the ability to effectively manage the flow and processing of information.[7] While the 19th century gave birth to the Industrial Revolution, the 20th century has spawned the Information Revolution. The Information Revolution refers to the development of technologies that permit quicker and cheaper transmission, processing, storage, and retrieval of information. Rapid advances in electronics have resulted in a number of new information technologies adopted extensively by the service sector in the past few decades, as we discuss next.

Office automation is achieved by integrating many new office technologies with improved office processes to improve the efficiency and effectiveness of office workers. Office automation is frequently associated with technologies such as personal computers, word processing, spreadsheets, electronic mail, teleconferencing, voice mail, and fax. John Naisbitt wrote in his best-seller *Megatrends,* "We are drowning in information but starved for knowledge and intelligence." Office automation tools help to create knowledge out of the data and transfer that knowledge efficiently.

Office Automation

Word processing and spreadsheets are two of many office systems that help transform ideas and data into intelligence in a form that everyone can easily share. Word processing systems boost productivity by reducing the time it takes to draft, revise, proof, copy, print, and file text material. Spreadsheets reduce the time required to organize, analyze, and interpret large amounts of data. Electronic mail and fax machines help in quickly and efficiently moving and distributing information to others and storing it for later access by a user. Voice mail is similar to electronic mail in its purpose, except that it is meant for communicating, storing, and retrieving verbal rather than nonverbal information. While the tools just described allow information to be communicated easily, teleconferencing technology allows *interactive* communication of information and images on a real-time basis. It is therefore an alternative to in-person meetings, thus reducing travel expenses while allowing fast responses to problems at geographically dispersed sites.

Image processing systems use modern digital and optical technology to scan, capture, store, and reproduce images of any complexity. Banks use image processing equipment extensively in their credit card and check processing operations. In its credit card operations, American Express uses an image processing camera to convert the charge slips (pieces of paper) into digital images. An optical character reader then scans the digital image for the account and invoice number (with 99 percent accuracy). Charge amounts are entered by computer operators using the digital image rather than the paper slip. In addition to improving billing accuracy, the system permits customer service operators to find image records of customer transactions within seconds rather than days (as finding microfilm records sometimes requires).

Image Processing Systems

Barcoding and scanning technologies have helped supermarkets and discount stores reduce inventories and track sales patterns. Wal-Mart has used these technologies, to-

---

[7]Many examples cited in this section are from Blair J. Berkley and A. Gupta, "Improving Service Quality with Information Technology," Working Paper 9-93-9 (Madison: University of Wisconsin, 1993).

gether with electronic data interchange, to increase sales per square foot and improve coordination with suppliers.

Electronic Data Interchange

Electronic data interchange (EDI) is the process by which the output of one firm's information system (for example, in purchasing) is transmitted electronically for direct input to another firm's information system (in sales) without the delay associated with regular mail or the need for data entry in either firm. The Limited clothing store chain has linked all its stores with its textile mills in Hong Kong via an EDI system. The system gathers and processes sales information from the stores and sends it to the factories to initiate production of items that are selling well. Wells Fargo Bank allows its commercial customers to manage their own cash accounts by tapping directly into Wells Fargo's computer account via EDI. Use of EDI is extensive in both service and manufacturing sectors. Overall, it provides an efficient means of transmitting information quickly between suppliers of a product or service and their customers.

Decision Support Systems and Expert Systems

Many technologies we have discussed so far improve the efficiency of information transfer, storage, retrieval, and processing. **Decision support systems** and **expert systems** go one step further by supporting and even supplanting decision making. They are useful in developing decision alternatives, gathering and analyzing the information required for evaluating the decision alternatives, and identifying either the best decision or a set of good decision alternatives. These systems are also useful in assessing the cost or other impacts of a decision alternative proposed by a manager. For instance, Chemical Bank has developed a personal computer–based retail banking expert system, Genesys, that serves each employee group having direct contact with customers. One element of Genesys is the capability to make personal loan decisions through automated credit evaluation, where the expert system analyzes information on the client in many different databases and makes decisions using standard rules set by experienced credit agents.

Networked Computer Systems

It is rare to find an organization now that has a solitary mainframe computer performing all the computing functions. From the smallest microcomputer to the largest mainframe, computers are being interconnected or networked with each other and with printers, copiers, facsimile machines, etc. by telecommunication links. This distribution of computing power throughout the organization is also referred to as distributed processing. This is often achieved by using a client/server approach, with networks of end-user microcomputers (clients) tied together with minicomputers or mainframes or even powerful microcomputers that act as servers or superservers.

John Yormark, Professor of Information Systems at the University of Southern California, describes its benefits nicely: "Client/server systems provide a division of labor between computers—mainframes and powerful minis do what they do best, crunch massive amounts of data, and client PCs do what they do best, analyze and present data in the way the user wants it."

Networked computer systems allow end-users to communicate electronically and share the use of hardware, software, data, and other resources. For instance, end-users in an office local area network (LAN) of microcomputers can share the use of software packages and large data bases that reside on the server and may be connected to a high-quality, expensive laser color printer. The declining cost and the increasing capabilities of microcomputers and telecommunication links in the past two decades have enabled the widespread adoption of such client/server networks in recent years and is likely to be the dominant trend in the future.

S3.5   EVALUATION OF TECHNOLOGY INVESTMENTS

Modern technologies such as a flexible manufacturing system or computerized order processing system represent large capital investments. Hence, a firm has to carefully assess its financial and strategic benefits from a technology before acquiring it. Evaluating such investments is especially hard since the purpose of acquiring new technologies is not just to reduce labor costs, but also to increase product quality and variety, to shorten production lead times, and to increase the flexibility of an operation. Since some of these benefits are intangible relative to labor cost reduction, justification becomes difficult. Further, rapid technological change renders a new equipment obsolete in just a few years, making the cost-benefit evaluation more complex.

But never assume that new automation technologies are always cost-effective. Even when there is no uncertainty about the benefits of automation, it may not be worthwhile to adopt it. For instance, many analysts predicted that integrated CAD/CAM systems would be the answer to all manufacturing problems. But a number of companies investing in such systems lost money in the process. The idea was to take a lot of skilled labor out of the process of tooling up for new or redesigned products and to speed up the process.[8] However, it can take less time to mill complex, low-volume parts than to program the milling machine, and programmer time is more expensive than the milling operator time. Also, it may not always be easy to transfer all the expert knowledge and experience that a milling operator has gained over the years into a computer program. Only recently has CAD/CAM integration software become available that can be cost-effective even in high-variety, low-volume manufacturing environments.

Next, we describe some typical benefits from adopting new technologies, both tangible and intangible, that can be used to develop financial and strategic justifications for their purchase. The tangible benefits can be used in traditional modes of financial analysis like discounted cash flow to justify the investments. A manager can then use the results of the traditional financial analysis, together with the intangible benefits, to make sound investment decisions.

---

[8] From the article "Automating the Automators," *Forbes*, February 14, 1994.

Cost Reductions

Labor Costs   Traditionally, automation helps reduce labor costs by decreasing labor requirements. For instance, an industrial robot may replace a person performing spot welding or painting operations, saving labor costs. Modern steel mills require almost no direct labor at all. In some instances, one person may be required to operate older equipment or a new machine, but the new equipment may have a greater output rate per unit time, thus requiring less labor time per unit of output. A fast copier requires one person to operate it, as does a slow one, but makes more copies per minute. In this case, labor time and labor cost per copy are lower. Do not assume that new technologies always reduce labor costs. They may actually increase labor costs but still have other benefits. While a sophisticated machine may require a more skilled person with higher wages to operate it, it may improve product quality or permit greater product variety.

Material Costs   A new technology may allow the use of alternative materials that are cheaper or can generate greater output. For instance, a major recent technological advance in the telecommunications industry is the replacement of copper cables with fiber-optic cables, which can carry many orders of magnitude as much information. This has drastically lowered unit information transmission costs. In the textile and paper industries, new optimization techniques embedded in computer software have reduced material waste (and costs) when cutting out patterns from large rolls of cloth or paper.

Inventory Costs   In many manufacturing companies, some of the greatest benefits of new technologies may come through reduced inventory holding costs. Automated order processing systems, better scheduling systems, and flexible manufacturing equipment with low setup times can reduce inventories dramatically. But in some cases, firms purchase high-speed machines with (also) high setup times, which actually increase inventory carrying costs. The high setup times force the firm to have long product runs, resulting in high inventories. The reduction in inventories also reduces space requirements.

Transportation or Distribution Costs   Historically, the arrival of the railroad and then the automobile decreased transportation costs substantially, cutting transportation times in the process. Subsequent technological improvements in air, surface, and ocean-going transportation modes too have reduced costs, while major technological changes in recent decades have been in information technologies, tremendously reducing costs and improving the speed of information transfer. This has had a particularly significant impact in service operations, where transfer of information dominates the transfer of goods. Even in the manufacturing sector, these technologies have allowed firms to better integrate with their suppliers and customers and reduce their purchase, distribution, and other transaction costs.

Quality Costs   The adoption of automated process equipment leads to more uniform production and, often, to an order-of-magnitude decline in defects. Many firms have seen 5- to 10-fold reductions in waste, scrap, and rework when manual operations were replaced with automated equipment. Also, as defect rates decrease and process control improves, fewer inspection stations and inspectors are required. These benefits are easy to quantify. These capabilities lead, in turn, to significant reductions in warranty expenditures. The warranty benefits may be more difficult to estimate accurately, but should not be ignored.

Other Costs   Over the years, maintenance costs, energy costs, and so on have also decreased as a result of new technologies. Newer machines, especially in electronics, require little maintenance and repair. Development of new materials and technologies in the construction industry have lowered energy costs in offices.

Other benefits obtained by adopting new technologies are described next. Some benefits may be intangible and harder to estimate than the cost reductions mentioned earlier.

Other Benefits

Increased Product Variety   In the 1920s, consumers flocked to Henry Ford's cars even though they were all black. But this would be unlikely in today's intensely competitive environment. New technologies allow firms to give the customer significant product variety. For instance, flexible manufacturing systems offer the potential for low-cost production of high-variety, low-volume goods, which is generally called economies of scope. Firms introduce new products frequently. For instance, Sony has introduced over 300 versions of its basic Walkman since its inception.

Improved Product Features and Quality   New technologies may allow a firm to significantly improve its product features, the quality of the product or service offerings, and its consistency in quality over time. For instance, new chip-making technologies and machines have allowed firms like Intel to produce more sophisticated and capable microprocessors used in computers. Auto manufacturers have used new painting technologies and robots to improve finishes on their cars.

Shorter Cycle Times   Another benefit frequently cited by firms adopting new technologies like flexible or computer-integrated manufacturing systems is the decrease in manufacturing cycle times or delivery lead times. Generally, reductions in inventories are also accompanied by shorter cycle times. While some benefits of reduced cycle times have been incorporated via inventory savings, the marketing advantages of reduced cycle times have to be recognized. Shorter cycle times have twin benefits: They allow the firm to quote shorter delivery times (which can be an important competitive advantage) and also permit the firm to respond quickly to changes in market demand.

Increased product variety, improved product features and quality, or shorter cycle times normally allow a firm to increase its sales volume or charge a premium price. But these benefits are hard to accurately estimate or predict since they depend so much on competitors' actions, which are not easy to forecast. Despite the difficulty in quantifying such benefits, they should not be ignored as they are strategic in nature and critical to the long-term success of a company. Kaplan says, "Rather than attempt to put a dollar tag on benefits that by their nature are difficult to quantify, managers should reverse the process and estimate first how large these benefits must be in order to justify the proposed investment."[9]

While there may be many benefits in acquiring new technologies, several types of risk accompany the acquisition of new technologies. These risks have to be evaluated and traded off against the benefits before acquiring new technologies. Next, we classify and describe some of these risks.

Risks in Adopting New Technologies

Technological Risks   An early adopter of a new technology has the benefit of being ahead of the competition, but also runs the risk of acquiring an untested technology

---

[9]Robert Kaplan, "Must CIM Be Justified by Faith Alone?" *Harvard Business Review,* March-April 1986, pp. 87–97.

Motorola Pagers: To Each His Own

In the early 1980s, the electronic pager industry in America was stormed by Japanese competitors selling high-quality pagers for $100, half the price charged by the half-dozen American manufacturers. By 1985, most domestic producers were out of the business. Motorola realized that, even if it streamlined its traditional production system, it could not hope for more than a 20 percent increase in productivity. A drastic transformation of the production process was necessary, but it had to be done quickly. Motorola therefore decided to develop a fully automated production process using the best off-the-shelf technology in the world to be sure it worked. The idea was not only to reduce production costs drastically and achieve very high quality, but also to gain the flexibility to make each pager differently and faster than its competitors.

Motorola used many concepts and technologies discussed here to achieve its ambitious goal of *mass customization*. It developed a completely automated, computer-integrated manufacturing process and assembly line to produce its Bravo line of pagers. The pager was designed to have only 134 parts assembled robotically. The electronic devices in the pager provided the customization necessary to allow 29 million possible variations.

The goal was not to transform just the manufacturing line, but rather to transform the entire order-to-delivery process. Instead of taking a month or so to process orders, Motorola now transmits orders for customized pagers by computer to its plant at Boynton Beach, Florida, where pagers can be manufactured, tested, and ready for delivery in less than two hours. A salesperson obtains pager specifications from the customer and transmits them to the plant. Computers in the plant use the order information to determine the exact production schedule plus the machines and robots that will produce the pager. The plant is a showcase facility with automated, minimal setup time and flexible, build-to-order manufacturing operations. The technology is so flexible that

This computer in the Boynton Beach factory is used to communicate with the main computer system and give direction to the robots seen in the photo. The traffic light-like poles are computer linked and indicate conditions on the line.

whose problems could disrupt the firm's operations. There is also the risk of technological obsolescence, especially with electronics-based technologies, where technological progress is rapid. This is particularly true when the fixed cost of acquiring new technologies or the cost of technology upgrades is high. Also, alternative technolgoies may become more cost-effective in the future, negating the benefits of a technology.

Operational Risks   There could also be risks in applying a technology to a firm's operations. Installation of a new technology generally results in significant disruptions, at least in the short run, to a firm's operations in the form of plantwide reorganization, retraining, and so on. Further risks are due to the delays and errors introduced in the production process and the uncertain and sudden calls on various resources.

Break*through*

Motorola has been able to dismantle and use some of the equipment in other pager lines. Here is an example of a firm that has used technology with ingenuity to dramatically improve all four strategic dimensions: cost, quality, speed of delivery, and flexibility.

Effective Use of Information Technology at 7-Eleven (Japan)

7-Eleven—Japan's largest food retailer—is distinct from the U.S. convenience store chain of the same name. There are about 3,900 7-Eleven convenience stores in Japan, most owned by franchise holders. 7-Eleven is a very profitable operation, with its return on equity being the highest among Japanese retailers.

On average, a 7-Eleven has only about 1,000 square feet of shelf space to stock over 3,500 items. Given the limited space and the large variety of products, the mix of products on the shelves is varied according to the time of day. The store owner needs to know what products to sell and when to maximize sales. Electronic point-of-sale terminals at each 7-Eleven are connected by a sophisticated computer network. The POS terminals, which look like simple cash registers, are owned by 7-Eleven to control technical standards across the network. When an item is purchased, the terminal stores information about the sale, such as brand name, manufacturer, and price of the item plus the age and sex of the buyer. The store owner can later obtain information from the machine (in the form of charts) about sales of an item during different hours of the day, days of the week, and so on. Sales patterns can be analyzed and used to change the mix of products stored on the shelves at different times.

Store owners can send orders directly from the terminal to suppliers. This saves on paperwork and time—the only paper they see is the delivery note. They can also check whether a particular supplier has a certain item in stock before placing an order. Inventory is constantly checked by the computer, and orders placed are based on current inventory status. With one or more deliveries per day, the time between order placement and delivery can be as little as eight hours. This enables store owners to carry little inventory and replenish it frequently. This reduces inventory carrying costs and also allows them to carry a greater variety of items on the shelves, maximizing sales effectiveness.

7-Eleven, the parent company, can obtain aggregate statistics about sales patterns from many stores and sell manufacturers purchase information relating to their own products. 7-Eleven also gathers data about regional or national sales patterns and changes in consumer tastes or spending patterns and provides it to store owners, thereby binding them into the organization. 7-Eleven sells about 8,000 different products in a given year. Its sophisticated information system allows it to weed out products selling poorly and replace them with new ones. Thus, the system has proved beneficial in carrying out tactical operations such as order transmission and also for more strategic purposes such as determining who is shopping for which product and when, and how consumer tastes and spending patterns are changing.

Source: Motorola adapted from "The Economist," December 5, 1992, p. 71.
7-Eleven adapted from the Survey on Telecommunications in *The Economist,*" March 10, 1990.

Organizational Risks   Firms may lack the organizational culture and top management commitment required to absorb the short-term disruptions and uncertainties associated with adopting a new technology. In such organizations, there is a risk that the firm's employees or managers may quickly abandon the technology when there are short-term failures or avoid major changes by simply automating the firm's old, inefficient processes and therefore not obtain the benefits of the new technology.

Environmental or Market Risks   In many cases, a firm may invest in a particular technology only to discover a few years later that changes in some environmental or market factors make the investment worthless. For instance, auto firms have been reluctant to invest in technology for making electric cars as they are uncertain about future emission standards of state and federal governments, the potential for decreasing emissions from gasoline-based cars, and the potential for significant improvements in battery technology.

Typical examples of market risks are fluctuations in currency exchange rates and interest rates.

S3.6   CONCLUSION

Technology has played the dominant role in the productivity growth of most nations and has provided the competitive edge to firms that have adopted it early and implemented it successfully. While each of the manufacturing and information technologies described here is a powerful tool by itself and can be adopted separately, their benefits grow exponentially when they are integrated with each other. This is particularly the case with CIM technologies.

With more modern technologies, the benefits are not entirely tangible and many benefits may be realized only on a long-term basis. Thus, typical cost accounting methods and standard financial analysis may not adequately capture all the potential benefits of technologies such as CIM. Hence, we must take into account the strategic benefits in evaluating such investments. Further, since capital costs for many modern technologies are substantial, the various risks associated with such investments have to be carefully assessed.

Implementing flexible manufacturing systems or complex decision support systems requires a significant commitment for most firms. Such investments may even be beyond the reach of small to medium-sized firms. However, as technologies continue to improve and are adopted more widely, their costs may decline and place them within the reach of smaller firms. Given the complex, integrative nature of these technologies, the total commitment of top management and all employees is critical for the successful implementation of these technologies.

S3.7   REVIEW AND DISCUSSION QUESTIONS

1. Give three examples each of companies that have acquired new technologies to achieve the following:
   a. Reduced cost.
   b. Reduced lead time.
   c. Improved quality.
   d. Increased customizability.
2. Give two examples each of recent process and product technology innovations.
3. It is generally believed that the impact of new technologies on service operations is difficult to measure. Why may this be true?
4. What could be the benefits of introducing a computerized registration system at a university? Are these benefits quantifiable?
5. In the McDonald's case at the beginning of this supplement, what are the tangible and intangible benefits?
6. What is the difference between an NC machine and a machining center?
7. How would The Limited apparel chain benefit by using EDI in its operations?
8. The major auto companies are planning to invest millions of dollars on developing new product and process technologies required to make electric cars. Describe briefly why they are investing in these technologies. Discuss the potential benefits and risks involved in these investments.

S3.8 SELECTED BIBLIOGRAPHY

Alden, P. S. "Managing Flexibility." *California Management Review,* Fall 1988.

Alter, Steven. *Information Systems: A Management Perspective.* Reading, MA: Addison-Wesley, 1992.

Avishai, Bernard. "A CEO's Common Sense of CIM: An Interview with J. Tracy O'Rourke." *Harvard Business Review,* January-February 1989, pp. 110–17.

Busby, J. S. *The Value of Advanced Manufacturing Technology.* Oxford, England: Butterworth-Heinemann, 1992.

Flaig, L. Scott. *Integrative Manufacturing: Transforming the Organization through People, Process, and Technology.* Homewood, IL: Business One Irwin, 1993.

Gaynor, Gerard H. *Achieving the Competitive Edge through Integrated Technology Management.* New York: McGraw-Hill, 1991.

Harrington, Joseph J. *Understanding the Manufacturing Process.* New York: Marcel Dekker, 1984.

Noori, Hamid, and Russell W. Radford. *Readings and Cases in the Management of New Technology: An Operations Perspective.* Englewood Cliffs, NJ: Prentice Hall, 1990.

Reynolds, George W. *Information Systems for Managers.* New York: West, 1988.

Tidd, Joseph. *Flexible Manufacturing Technologies and International Competitiveness.* London: Pinter, 1991.

C h a p t e r

4

Product Design and Process Selection—Services

CHAPTER OUTLINE

KEY TERMS

Service Package

Facilities-Based Services

Field-Based Services

Customer

High and Low Degrees of Customer Contact

Service Focus

Service-System Design Matrix

Service Blueprint

Service Poka-Yoke

Service Guarantee

Value

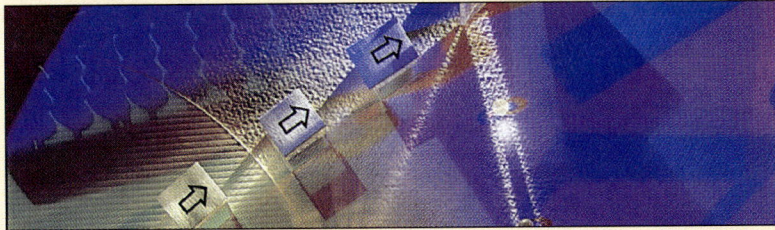

If you've ever languished on hold, enduring Muzak, wondering why you do business with some company that has transferred you six times and still hasn't answered your question, here's a newsflash: Customer phone service stinks.

Management expert Tom Peters, co-author of *In Search of Excellence*, called 13 firms to pose a basic question or file a complaint. His research turned up everything from great service (Nordstrom) to being cut off (General Motors).

"Many of the problems we called [about] weren't all that big," he says. "But we were abused by [some] companies."

Peters' staff targeted organizations from Procter & Gamble to the White House. The results appear in the June issue of his newsletter, *On Achieving Excellence*. Some examples:

Nordstrom. The caller called the switchboard and asked to speak to the CEO about a problem in the shoe department. One transfer later, CEO Bruce Nordstrom was on the line. He listened patiently and promised to call his store and fix the matter.

IBM. Request: an annual report and information regarding IBM's annual meeting. Call was transferred to stockholder relations. "An enthusiastic operator gave way to a disinterested automaton," says Peters' report. Date of request for annual report: March 28. Date it arrived: May 5—two weeks after the annual meeting. IBM's explanation: Unless the caller requests first-class mail, annual reports go bulk mail.

Yoplait. The caller wanted to know the yogurt-maker's position on bovine growth hormone, an additive that boosts milk production in cows. The operator refused to transfer the call. At **Ben & Jerry's,** the same question brought a swift transfer to the public relations department and an eight-minute discussion on why B&J shuns the hormone.

General Motors. Why is it taking automakers so long to develop electric cars, the caller asked. Request to speak to CEO Jack Smith was denied. Transferred to library, then to non-working number and cut off. A GM spokesman says the caller should have been sent to the electric car department, where an official would have answered the question.

Peters admits his survey isn't scientific. In fairness, he called his own circulation department. Service was mediocre.

"Could have been worse, but their performance didn't make my day," Peters says.

Some companies—even big ones like Nordstrom—are thrilling their customers with prompt service, while others are blowing it, Peters says.

"The people answering the phones are major competitive assets—or liabilities."

Source: Ellen Neuborne "Customer Service Flops on the Phone," *Chicago Sun-Times,* May 10, 1994, p. 4. Copyright 1994, Gannet Co., Inc. Reprinted with permission.

It's not just phone service where customers experience problems at the "moment of truth"[1]—the encounter with a service organization; it is at the bank, the restaurant, and the airline as well. While the front-line service workers are often the focal point of criticism (or praise), they are only one part of the often complicated process of service delivery.

In this chapter, after some preliminary comments about services, we address the issue of service delivery system design, starting with the notion of customer contact as a way of classifying service operations. Next, we discuss service organization design, service strategy, and service focus, and describe how marketing and operations interrelate to achieve (or fail to achieve) competitive advantage. We also look at a service-system design matrix that can define the broad features of a service process, and at service blueprints as a way of designing the precise steps of a process. In the latter part of the chapter, we present three service designs used in service industries and discuss how service guarantees can be used as "design drivers." The chapter ends with a case study of a service organization familiar to many readers of this book—Kinko's Copier Stores.

4.1   THE NATURE OF SERVICES

Our study of the nature of services leads to seven generalizations:

1. Everyone is an expert on services. We all think we know what we want from a service organization and, by the very process of living, we have a good deal of experience with the service creation process.

2. Services are idiosyncratic—what works well in providing one kind of service may prove disastrous in another. For example, consuming a restaurant meal in less than half an hour may be exactly what you want at Jack-in-the-Box but be totally unacceptable at an expensive French restaurant.

3. Quality of work is not quality of service. An auto dealership may do good work on your car, but it may take a week to get the job done.

[1]The term *moment of truth* was coined by Jan Carlzon, former president of Scandinavian Airlines System. See in Karl Albrecht and Ron Zemke, *Service America! Doing Business in the New Economy* (Homewood, IL: Dow Jones–Irwin, 1985), p. 19.

4. Most services contain a mix of tangible and intangible attributes that constitute a **service package.** This package requires different approaches to design and management than the production of goods.

5. High-contact services (described later) are *experienced,* whereas goods are *consumed.*

6. Effective management of services requires an understanding of marketing and personnel, as well as operations.

7. Services often take the form of cycles of encounters involving face-to-face, phone, electromechanical, and/or mail interactions. (The term *encounter,* by the way, is defined as "meeting in conflict or battle" and hence is often apt as we make our way through the service economy.)

Service operations management issues exist in two broad organizational contexts:

1. *Service business,* the management of organizations whose primary business requires interaction with the customer to produce the service. These include such familiar services as banks, airlines, hospitals, law firms, retail stores, and restaurants. Within this category, we can make a further major distinction: **facilities-based services,** where the customer must go to the service facility, and **field-based services,** where production and consumption of the service take place in the customer's environment (e.g., cleaning and home repair services).

Technology has allowed for the transfer of many facility-based services to field-based services. Dental vans bring the dentist to your home. Some auto repair services have repair-mobiles. Telemarketing brings the shopping center to your TV screen.

2. *Internal services,* the management of services required to support the activities of the larger organization. These services include such functions as data processing, accounting, engineering, and maintenance. Their customers are the various departments within the organization that require such services. Incidentally, it is not uncommon for an internal service to start marketing its services outside the parent organization and become a service business itself.

Our emphasis in this chapter is on service businesses, but most of the ideas apply equally well to internal services.

Service Businesses and Internal Services

A glance at the management book section in your local book store gives ample evidence of the concern for service among practitioners. The way we now view service parallels the way we view quality: The **customer** is (or should be) the focal point of all decisions and actions of the service organization. This philosophy is captured nicely in the service triangle in Exhibit 4.1. Here, the customer is the center of things—the service strategy, the systems, and the people who serve him or her. From this view, the organization exists to serve the customer, and the systems and the people exist to facilitate the process of service. Some suggest that the service organization also exists to serve the workforce because they generally determine how the service is perceived by the customers. Relative to the latter point, the customer gets the kind of service that management deserves; in other words, how management treats the worker is how the worker will treat the public. If the workforce is well trained and well motivated by management, they will do good jobs for their customers.

The role of operations in the triangle is a major one. Operations is responsible for service systems (procedures, equipment, and facilities) and is responsible for managing the work of the service workforce who typically comprise the majority of employees in large service organizations. But before we discuss this role in depth,

A Contemporary View of Service Management

EXHIBIT 4.1
The Service Triangle

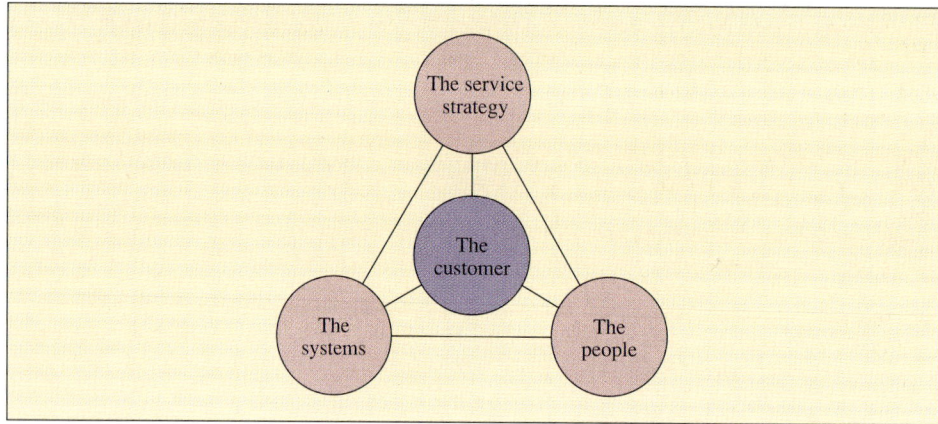

Source: Karl Albrecht and Ron Zemke, *Service America! Doing Business in the New Economy* (Homewood, IL: Dow Jones–Irwin, 1985), p. 41.

it is useful to classify services to show how the customer affects the operations function.

4.2   AN OPERATIONAL CLASSIFICATION OF SERVICES

Service organizations are generally classified according to the service they provide (financial services, health services, transportation services, and so on). These groupings, though useful in presenting aggregate economic data, are not particularly appropriate for OM purposes because they tell us little about the process. In manufacturing, by contrast, there are fairly evocative terms to classify production activities (such as *intermittent* and *continuous production*); when applied to a manufacturing setting, they readily convey the essence of the process. While it is possible to describe services in these same terms, we need one additional item of information to reflect the fact that the customer is involved in the production system. That item, which we believe operationally distinguishes one service system from another in its production function, is the extent of customer contact in the creation of the service.

Customer contact refers to the physical presence of the customer in the system, and *creation of the service* refers to the work process involved in providing the service itself. *Extent of contact* here may be roughly defined as the percentage of time the customer must be in the system relative to the total time it takes to perform the customer service. Generally speaking, the greater the percentage of contact time between the service system and the customer, the greater the degree of interaction between the two during the production process.

From this conceptualization, it follows that service systems with a **high degree of customer contact** are more difficult to control and more difficult to rationalize than those with a **low degree of customer contact.** In high-contact systems, the customer can affect the time of demand, the exact nature of the service, and the quality, or perceived quality, of service since the customer is involved in the process.

Exhibit 4.2 describes the implications of this distinction. Here we see that each design decision is impacted by whether the customer is present during service delivery. We also see that when work is done behind the scenes (in this case in a bank's processing center), it is performed on customer surrogates—reports, databases, and invoices. We can

E X H I B I T 4.2

*Major Differences
between High- and
Low-Contact Systems
in a Bank*

Design Decision	High-Contact System (A branch office)	Low-Contact System (A check processing center)
Facility location	Operations must be near the customer.	Operations may be placed near supply, transport, or labor.
Facility layout	Facility should accommodate the customer's physical and psychological needs and expectations.	Facility should focus on production efficiency.
Product design	Environment as well as the physical product define the nature of the service.	Customer is not in the service environment so the product can be defined by fewer attributes.
Process design	Stages of production process have a direct, immediate effect on the customer.	Customer is not involved in majority of processing steps.
Scheduling	Customer is in the production schedule and must be accommodated.	Customer is concerned mainly with completion dates.
Production planning	Orders cannot be stored, so smoothing production flow will result in loss of business.	Both backlogging and production smoothing are possible.
Worker skills	Direct workforce constitutes a major part of the service product and so must be able to interact well with the public.	Direct workforce need only have technical skills.
Quality control	Quality standards are often in the eye of the beholder and, thus, are variable.	Quality standards are generally measurable and, thus, fixed.
Time standards	Service time depends on customer needs so time standards are inherently loose.	Work is performed on customer surrogates (e.g., forms) so time standards can be tight.
Wage payment	Variable output requires time-based wage systems.	"Fixable" output permits output-based wage systems.
Capacity planning	To avoid lost sales, capacity must be set to match peak demand.	Storable output permits capacity at some average demand level.

thus design it according to the same principles we would use in designing a factory—to maximize the amount of items processed during the production day.

There can be tremendous diversity of customer influence and, hence, system variability within high-contact service systems. For example, a bank branch offers both simple services such as cash withdrawals that take just a minute or so, and complicated services such as loan application preparation that can take in excess of an hour. Moreover, these activities many range from being self-service through an ATM, to coproduction where bank personnel and the customer work as a team to develop the loan application. Subsequent sections of this chapter say more on ways to configure service activities.

4.3 DESIGNING SERVICE ORGANIZATIONS

In designing service organizations we must remember one distinctive characteristic of services—we cannot inventory services. Unlike manufacturing, where we can build up inventory during slack periods for peak demand and thus maintain a relatively stable level of employment and production planning, in services we must (with a few exceptions) meet demand as it arises. Consequently, in services *capacity* becomes a dominant issue. Think about the many service situations you find yourself in—for example, eating in a restaurant or going to a Saturday night movie. Generally speaking, if the restaurant or the theater is full, you will decide to go someplace else. So, an important design parameter in services is "What capacity should we aim for?" Too much capacity generates excessive costs. Insufficient capacity leads to lost customers. In these situations, of course, we seek the assistance of marketing. This is one reason why we have discount airfares, hotel specials on weekends, and so on. This is also a good illustration of why separating the operations management functions from marketing in services is difficult.

Designing a service organization involves four elements of what James Heskett calls the "Strategic Service Vision."[2] The first element is identification of the target market (Who is our customer?); the second is the service concept (How do we differentiate our service in the market?); the third is the service strategy (What is our service package and the operating focus of our service?); and fourth is the service delivery system (What are the actual processes, staff, and facilities by which the service is created?).

Choosing a target market and developing the service package are top management decisions setting the stage for the direct operating decisions of service strategy and delivery system design.

Several major factors distinguish service design and development from typical manufactured product development. First, the process and the product must be developed simultaneously; indeed, in services the process is the product. (We say this with the general recognition that many manufacturers are using such concepts as concurrent engineering and DFM (design for manufacture) as approaches to more closely link product design and process design.)

Second, although equipment and software that support a service can be protected by patents and copyrights, a service operation itself lacks the legal protection commonly available to goods production. Third, the service package, rather than a definable good, constitutes the major output of the development process. Fourth, many parts of the service package are often defined by the training individuals receive before they become part of the service organization. In particular, in professional service organizations (PSOs) such as law firms and hospitals, prior certification is necessary for hiring. Fifth, many service organizations can change their service offerings virtually overnight. Routine service organizations (RSOs) such as barbershops, retail stores, and restaurants have this flexibility.

Service Strategy: Focus and Advantage

Service strategy begins by selecting the operating focus—those performance priorities—by which the service firm will compete. These include

1. Treatment of the customer in terms of friendliness and helpfulness.
2. Speed and convenience of service delivery.
3. Price of the service.
4. Variety of services (essentially a one-stop shopping philosophy).
5. Quality of the tangible goods that are central to or accompany the service. Examples include a "world-class" corned beef sandwich, eyeglasses made while you wait, or an understandable insurance policy.
6. Unique skills that constitute the service offering, such as hair styling, brain surgery, or piano lessons.

---

[2]James Heskett, "Lessons from the Service Sector," *Harvard Business Review,* March–April 1987, pp. 118–26.

Exhibit 4.3 presents what we view as the operating **service focus** choices of a number of well-known companies. If our interpretation is correct, it shows that most companies choose to compete on a relatively few dimensions—that trade-offs have been made. The clear trend now is to focus on value to the customer. Taco Bell, for example, defines value as having two components, quality and price. Their market research showed that to customers, "value" equaled low price and "FACT": fast food *fast;* fast food orders *accurate;* fast food served in restaurants that are *clean;* and fast food at the appropriate *temperature.*

Integrating Marketing and Operations to Achieve Competitive Advantage   Achieving competitive advantage in services requires integration of service marketing with service delivery to meet or exceed customer expectations. This holds true no matter which competitive dimensions are emphasized. Companies that do extremely well (or extremely poorly) in this process create legends and nightmares (Exhibit 4.4).

Exhibit 4.5 gives an overview of the elements leading to service advantage and service oblivion. As it shows, marketing typically has responsibility for communicating the service promise to the customer and thereby creating customer expectations about service outcomes. Operations is responsible for the actions executing the promise and man-

	Treatment	Speed/ Convenience	Price	Variety	Unique Skills/ Tangibles
Nordstrom Department Stores	X				
Federal Express Corporation	X	X			
Merrill Lynch & Company (Cash Management Account)		X		X[a]	
Crown Books			X		
Wal-Mart Stores	X		X[b]	X	
Price Club			X[c]		
Disneyland	X				X
American Express Company	X	X			
McDonald's Corporation		X	X		
Domino's Pizza		X[d]	X		
Marriott Corporation	X				
Club Med Resorts	X[e]		X		
American Airlines		X[f]		X	
Singapore Airlines	X				
Southwest Airlines			X[g]		
Riverside Methodist Hospitals (Columbus, Ohio)	X[h]				
H & R Block		X	X		
American Automobile Association		X[i]			

E X H I B I T 4.3
Operations Focus of Selected Service Firms

[a]A cash management account includes checkbook, credit card, money market fund, and other services in one account.
[b]Wal-Mart controls cost of inventory by driving tough bargains with suppliers.
[c]Price Club converts shoppers into warehouse order pickers in exchange for low-priced volume purchases.
[d]First to use the automated pizza maker where an attendant puts a raw pie in one side and pulls out a cooked pie on the other.
[e]All-inclusive, low-cost resorts where staff known as *Gentils Organisateurs* (GOs) coproduce a fun vacation with the guests, *Gentils Membres* (GMs).
[f]Sabre reservation system makes it easy for travel agents to book seats and for the company to instantaneously change prices to counter competitors' rates.
[g]No-frills service (i.e., no computerized reservation system, no assigned seating, and no meals) allows lowest prices in the industry.
[h]Riverside Hospital treats patients and their families like customers—give adult heart patients teddy bears to hold and colorful smocks with hearts imprinted on them. Holding a teddy bear feels good and helps the healing process.
[i]AAA phone/computer network uses the number of the phone a customer is calling from anywhere in the United States to pinpoint the nearest AAA garage.

Marriot rewards and promotes employees who provide superior customer service and gives employees decision-making authority. The company mails out one million questionnaires a year to keep informed about customer satisfaction and service gaps.

"OUR NEW DESK CLERK LENT HIS CUFF LINKS TO A GUEST FOR A CRUCIAL MEETING. INSTANTLY WE KNEW WE HIRED THE RIGHT GUY."

Bill Marriott

That's a true story. There are many others. They are just one of the many reasons frequent business travelers prefer Marriott. Call your travel agent or 1-800-228-9290.

Marriott
HOTELS · RESORTS · SUITES

WE MAKE IT HAPPEN FOR YOU.

aging the customer experience. The feedback loop indicates that if outcomes are not satisfactory or do not create service advantage, management may alter either the service marketing strategy or the delivery system. The need to monitor and control the execution phase and have a recovery plan to diffuse negative reactions before the customer leaves the system is also indicated.

Monitoring and controlling involve the standard managerial actions of reassigning workers to deal with short-run demand variations (e.g., Lucky Supermarkets opening up another checkout stand when there are more than three people in line); checking with customers and employees as to how things are going; and, for many services, simply being available to customers. (Customers like the idea that they can talk to the manager. . . and few people want to talk to the assistant manager.)

Recovery planning involves training frontline workers to respond to such situations as overbooking, lost luggage, or a bad meal.

A company that can't achieve competitive advantage in its service delivery must at least achieve parity with its competitors. In this regard, Kevin Coyne has made the following observations about investing in improved service:

Investments to reach minimum standards cannot be "traded off" against other investments; they are a cost of doing business and should be considered required investments. However, achieving effective parity often requires less investment than managers might expect, for three reasons: First, most service encounters and attributes do not matter to customers except in extreme situations. Second, most customers are indifferent to a fairly wide variation in the level of service provided for most encounters, once the lower threshold of service is reached. Finally, customers have imprecise impressions as to the actual level of service being

E X H I B I T 4.4

Levels of Satisfaction Achieved Due to Service Performance

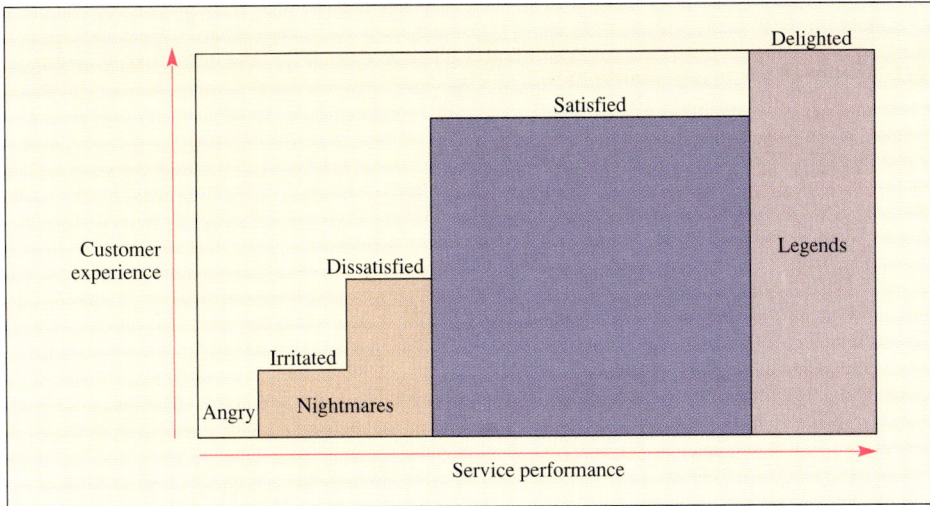

Source: The MAC Group: Building Value through Creating a Service Advantage, 1 Montgomery St., Telesis Tower, Suite 1700, San Francisco, CA 94104, June 1990.

E X H I B I T 4.5

Service Measurement/ Monitoring and Recovery Process

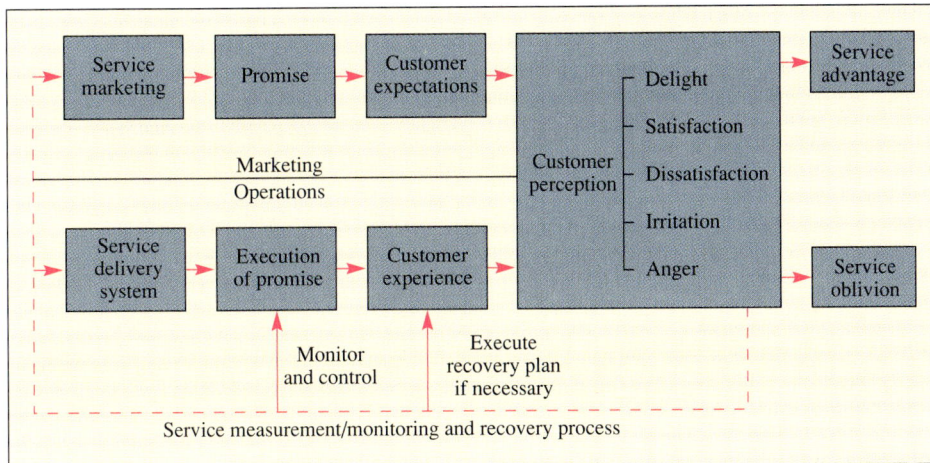

Source: The MAC Group: Building Value through Creating a Service Advantage, 1 Montgomery St., Telesis Tower, Suite 1700, San Francisco, CA 94104, June 1990.

provided, and it is often difficult for customers to compare one provider's service offerings to those of competitors. Thus, two providers may offer significantly different levels of service in a particular encounter, yet be at effective parity.[3]

One approach to measuring the economic value of customer satisfaction is to survey your customers. Ask them to rate each of a list of service and quality dimension items on two scales: importance and satisfaction. The point is to focus your attention on factors that are most important to your customers. Especially, focus on factors where their satisfaction rating is below their importance rating.

---

[3]Kevin Coyne, "Beyond Service Fads—Meaningful Strategies for the Real World," *Sloan Management Review*, Summer 1989, p. 74.

4.4   STRUCTURING THE SERVICE ENCOUNTER: SERVICE-SYSTEM DESIGN MATRIX

Service encounters can be configured in a number of different ways. The **service-system design matrix** in Exhibit 4.6 identifies six common alternatives.

The top of the matrix shows the degree of customer/server contact: the *buffered core,* which is physically separated from the customer; the *permeable system,* which is penetrable by the customer via phone or face-to-face contact; and the *reactive system,* which is both penetrable and reactive to the customer's requirements. The left side of the matrix shows what we believe to be a logical marketing proposition, namely, that the greater the amount of contact, the greater the sales opportunity; the right side shows the impact on production efficiency as the customer exerts more influence on the operation.

The entries within the matrix list the ways in which service can be delivered. At one extreme, service contact is by mail; customers have little interaction with the system. At the other extreme, customers "have it their way," through face-to-face contact. The remaining four entries in the exhibit contain varying degrees of interaction.

As one would guess, production efficiency decreases as the customer has more contact (and therefore more influence) on the system. To offset this, the face-to-face contact provides high sales opportunity to sell additional products. Conversely, low contact, such as mail, allows the system to work more efficiently because the customer is unable to significantly affect (or disrupt) the system. However, there is relatively little sales opportunity for additional product sales.

There can be some shifting in the positioning of each entry. Consider the Exhibit 4.6 entry "face-to-face tight specs." This refers to those situations where there is little variation in the service process—neither customer nor server has much discretion in creating the service. Fast-food restaurants and Disneyland come to mind. Face-to-face loose specs refers to situations where the service process is generally understood but there are options in how it will be performed or the physical goods that are part of it. A full-service restaurant or a car sales agency are examples. Face-to-face total customization refers to service encounters whose specifications must be developed through some interaction between the customer and server. Legal and medical services are of this type, and the degree to which the resources of the system are mustered for the service determines whether the system is reactive or merely permeable. Examples would be the mobilization of an advertising firm's resources in preparation for an office visit by a major client, or an operating team scrambling to prepare for emergency surgery.

Exhibit 4.7 extends the design matrix. It shows the changes in workers, operations, and types of technical innovations as the degree of customer/service system contact changes. For worker requirements, the relationships between mail contact and clerical skills, on-site technology and helping skills, and phone contact and verbal skills are self-evident. Face-to-face tight specs require procedural skills in particular, because the worker must follow the routine in conducting a generally standardized, high-volume process. Face-to-face loose specs frequently call for trade skills (shoemaker, draftsperson, maitred', dental hygienist) to finalize the design for the service. Face-to-face total customization tends to call for diagnostic skills of the professional to ascertain the needs or desires of the client.

Strategic Uses of the Matrix

The matrix in Exhibit 4.6 along with Exhibit 4.7 has both operational and strategic uses. Their operational uses are reflected in their identification of worker requirements, focus of operations, and innovations previously discussed. The strategic uses include

1. Enabling systematic integration of operations and marketing strategy. Trade-offs become more clear-cut, and, more important, at least some of the major design variables are crystalized for analysis purposes. For example, the matrix indicates that it would make little sense relative to sales for a service firm to invest in high-skilled workers if it plans to operate using tight specs.

2. Clarifying exactly which combination of service delivery the firm is in fact providing. As the company incorporates the delivery options listed on the diagonal, it is becoming diversified in its production process.

3. Permitting comparison with how other firms deliver specific services. This helps to pinpoint a firm's competitive advantage.

4. Indicating evolutionary or life cycle changes that might be in order as the firm grows. Unlike the product-process matrix for manufacturing, however, where natural growth moves in one direction (from the job shop to assembly line as a volume increases), evolution of service delivery can move in either direction along the diagonal as a function of a sales-efficiency trade-off.

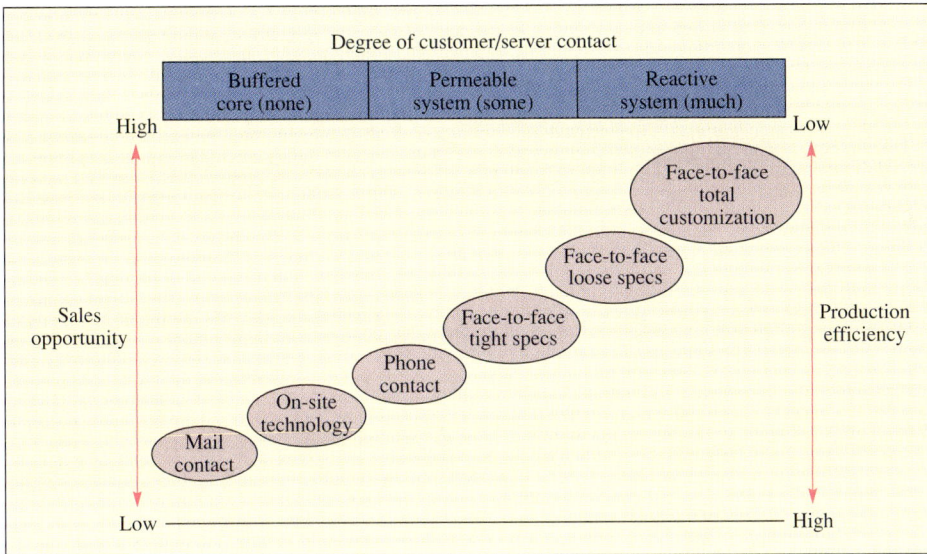

E X H I B I T 4.6

Service-System Design Matrix

E X H I B I T 4.7   *Characteristics of Workers, Operations, and Innovations Relative to the Degree of Customer/Service Contact*

	Degree of customer/server contact					
	Low ←					→ High
Worker requirements	Clerical skills	Helping skills	Verbal skills	Procedural skills	Trade skills	Diagnostic skills
Focus of operations	Paper handling	Demand management	Scripting calls	Flow control	Capacity management	Client mix
Technological innovations	Office automation	Routing methods	Computer databases	Electronic aids	Self-serve	Client/worker teams

4.5   SERVICE BLUEPRINTING

Just as is the case with manufacturing process design, the standard tool for service process design is the flowchart. In 1984, Lynn Shostack added the concept of the *line of visibility* and emphasized the identification of potential fail points in her version of the flowchart called a **service blueprint.**[4] She has also made a compelling case for having blueprints on every aspect of a service, and having the "keeper of the blueprint" as a specific job function in any large service organization. Current practice in some companies is to have blueprints available on computers for senior managers so when problems arise, they can home in on any portion of a service process and thereby make more informed decisions about how to resolve them. The steps involved in developing a blueprint for a simple shoeshine process, including a profitability analysis, are as follows:

1. Identify processes. The first step in creating such a blueprint is mapping the processes that constitute the service. Exhibit 4.8 maps a shoeshine parlor. As the service is simple and clear-cut, the map is straightforward. It might be useful to specify how the proprietor will perform the step called *buff.*

2. Isolate fail points. Having diagrammed the processes involved, the designer can now see where the system might go awry. The shoeshiner may pick up and apply the wrong color wax. So the designer must build in a subprocess to correct this possible error. The identification of fail points and the design of fail-safe processes are critical. The consequences of service failures can be greatly reduced by analyzing fail points at the design stage.

3. Establish a time frame. Since all services depend on time, which is usually the major cost determinant, the designer should establish a standard execution time.

E X H I B I T 4.8

Blueprint for a Corner Shoeshine

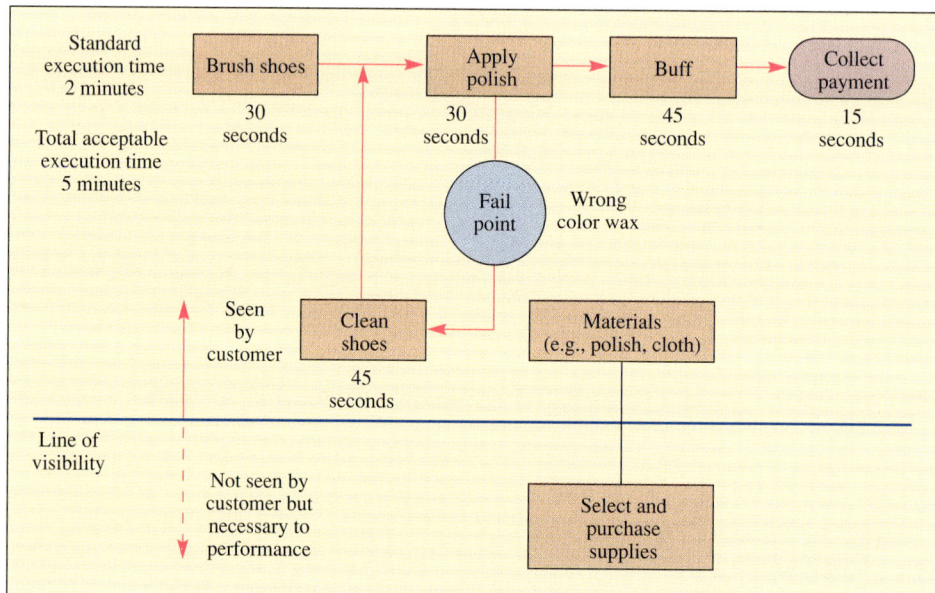

Source: G. Lynn Shostack, "Designing Services that Deliver," *Harvard Business Review* 62, no. 1 (January–February 1984), p. 134.

---

[4]G. Lynn Shostack, "Designing Services that Deliver," *Harvard Business Review* 62, no. 1 (January–February 1984), p. 135.

	Execution Time		
	2 Minutes	**3 Minutes**	**4 Minutes**
Price	$.50	$.50	$.50
Costs			
Time @ $.10 per minute	.20	.30	.40
Wax	.03	.03	.03
Other operating expenses	.09	.09	.09
Total costs	$.32	$.42	$.52
Pretax profit	$.18	$.08	($.02)

Source: G. Lynn Shostack, "Designing Services that Deliver," *Harvard Business Review* 62, no. 1 (January–February 1984), p. 135.

4. Analyze profitability. The customer can spend the three minutes between standard and acceptable execution time at the corner parlor waiting in line or during service, if an error occurs or if the shoeshiner does certain things too slowly. Whatever its source, a delay can affect profits dramatically. Exhibit 4.9 quantifies the cost of delay; after four minutes the proprietor loses money. A service designer must establish a time-of-service-execution standard to assure a profitable business.

In the shoeshine example, the standard execution time is two minutes. Research showed that customers would tolerate up to five minutes of performance before lowering their assessment of quality. Acceptable execution time for a shoeshine is then five minutes.

4.6   SERVICE FAIL-SAFING USING POKA-YOKES

Basic blueprinting describes the features of the service design but does not provide any direct guidance for how to make the process conform to that design. A developing approach to this problem is the application of **poka-yokes**—procedures that block the inevitable mistake from becoming a service defect.[5] Poka-yokes (roughly translated from the Japanese as "avoid mistakes") are common in factories (see Chapter 5 "Total Quality Management," for examples) and consist of such things as fixtures to ensure that parts can only be attached in the right way, electronic switches that automatically shut off equipment if a mistake is made, kitting of parts prior to assembly to make sure the right quantities are used, and checklists to ensure that the right sequence of steps is followed. The Toyota plant in Japan, for example, has an average of 12 poka-yoke devices per machine.[6]

There are many applications of poka-yokes to services as well. These can be classified into warning methods and physical or visual contact methods, and by what we call the **Three T's**—the Task to be done (Was the car fixed right?), the Treatment accorded to the customer (Was the service manager courteous?), and the Tangible or environmental features of the service facility (Was the waiting area clean and comfortable?). Finally (unlike in manufacturing), service poka-yokes often must be applied to fail-safing the actions of the customer as well as the producer (i.e., the service worker).

[5]Richard B. Chase and Douglas M. Stewart, "Make Your Service Fail-Safe," *Sloan Management Review,* Spring 1994, pp. 35–44.

[6]See Alan Robinson and Dean Schroeder, "The Limited Role of Statistical Quality Control in Zero Defect Environment," *Production and Inventory Management Journal,* Third Quarter 1990, pp. 60–65.

Poka-yoke examples include indented trays used by surgeons to ensure that no instruments are left in the patient; chains to configure waiting lines; take-a-number systems; turnstiles; beepers on ATMs to warn people to take their card out of the machine; beepers at restaurants to make sure customers do not miss their table call; mirrors on phones to ensure a "smiling voice"; reminder calls for appointments; locks on airline lavatory doors that activate lights inside; small gifts in comment card envelopes to encourage customers to provide feedback about a service; and pictures of what "a clean room" looks like for kindergarten children. On a lighter note, look at *The Far Side* cartoon on the next page as a customer resolution poka-yoke (not recommended).

Exhibit 4.10 illustrates how a typical automobile service operation might be fail-safed using poka-yokes. As a final comment, while these procedures cannot guarantee the level of error protection found in the factory, they still can reduce such errors in many service situations.

4.7   THREE CONTRASTING SERVICE DESIGNS

The three general approaches to delivering on-site services are the production line approach made famous by McDonald's Corporation, the self-service approach made famous by ATMs and gas stations, and the personal attention approach made famous by Nordstrom department stores and the Ritz-Carlton Hotel Company.

The Production Line Approach

The production line approach pioneered by McDonald's refers to more than just the steps required to assemble a Big Mac. Rather, as Theodore Levitt notes, it is treating the delivery of fast food as a manufacturing process rather than a service process.[7] The value of this philosophy is that it overcomes many problems inherent in the concept of service itself. That is, service implies subordination or subjugation of the server to the served; manufacturing, on the other hand, avoids this connotation because it focuses on things rather than people. Thus in manufacturing and at McDonald's, "the orientation is

---

[7]Theodore Levitt, "Production-Line Approach to Service," *Harvard Business Review* 50, no. 5 (September–October 1972), pp. 41–52.

THE FAR SIDE   By GARY LARSON

THE FAR SIDE © 1992 FarWorks, Inc. Dist. by Universal Press Syndicate.
Reprinted with permission. All rights reserved.

toward the efficient production of results not on the attendance on others." Levitt notes that besides McDonald's marketing and financial skills, the company carefully controls "the execution of each outlet's central function—the rapid delivery of a uniform, high-quality mix of prepared foods in an environment of obvious cleanliness, order, and cheerful courtesy. The systematic substitution of equipment for people, combined with the carefully planned use and positioning of technology, enables McDonald's to attract and hold patronage in proportions no predecessor or imitator has managed to duplicate."

Levitt cites several aspects of McDonald's operations to illustrate the concepts. Note the extensive use of what we term poka-yokes.

- The McDonald's french fryer allows cooking of the optimum number of french fries at one time.

- A wide-mouthed scoop is used to pick up the precise amount of french fries for each order size. (The employee never touches the product.)

- Storage space is expressly designed for a predetermined mix of prepackaged and premeasured products.

- Cleanliness is pursued by providing ample trash cans in and outside each facility. (Larger outlets have motorized sweepers for the parking area.)

- Hamburgers are wrapped in color-coded paper.

- Through painstaking attention to total design and facilities planning, everything is built integrally into the (McDonald's) machine itself—into the technology of the

E X H I B I T 4.10   *Fail-Safing a Typical Automotive Service Operation*

Failure: Customer forgets the need for service.
Poka-Yoke: Send automatic reminders with a 5 percent discount.

Failure: Customer can not find service area, or does not follow proper flow.
Poka-Yoke: Clear and informative signage directing customers.

Failure: Customer has difficulty communicating problem.
Poka-Yoke: Joint inspection — service advisor repeats his/her understanding of the problem for confirmation or elaboration by the customer.

Failure: Customer does not understand the necessary service.
Poka-Yoke: Pre-printed material for most services, detailing work, reasons, and possibly a graphic representation.

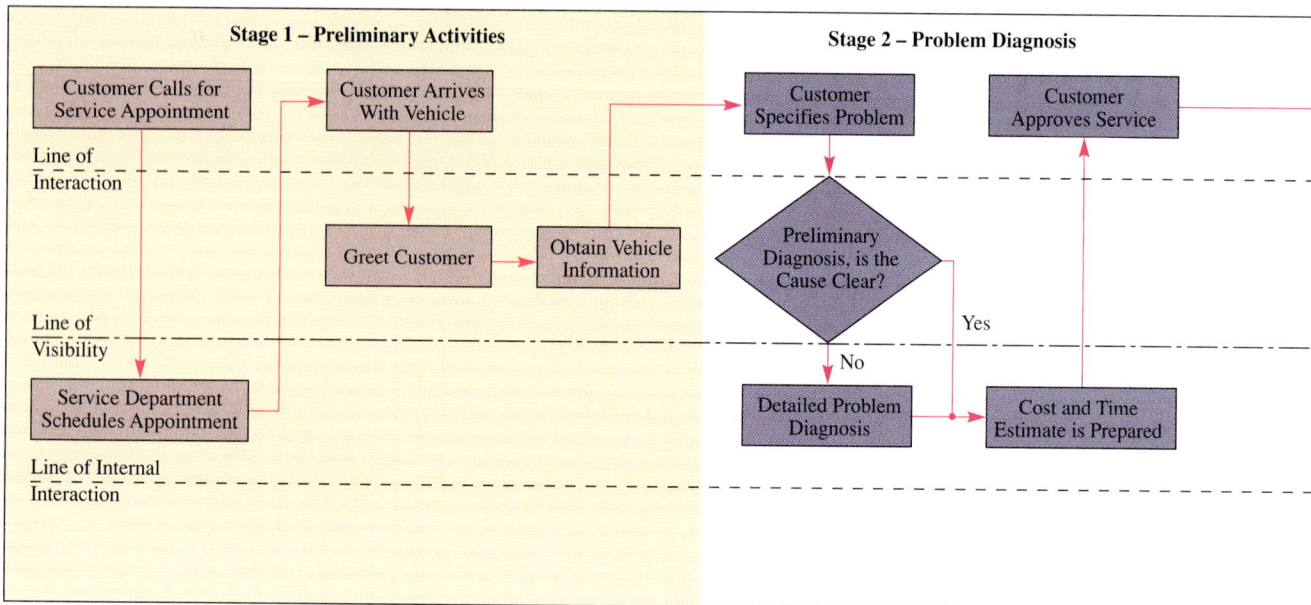

Stage 1 – Preliminary Activities   **Stage 2 – Problem Diagnosis**

Customer Calls for Service Appointment → Customer Arrives With Vehicle → Customer Specifies Problem → Customer Approves Service

Line of Interaction

Greet Customer → Obtain Vehicle Information → Preliminary Diagnosis, is the Cause Clear?

Line of Visibility

Service Department Schedules Appointment

Yes / No

Detailed Problem Diagnosis → Cost and Time Estimate is Prepared

Line of Internal Interaction

Failure: Customer arrival unnoticed.
Poka-Yoke: Use a bell chain to signal arrivals.

Failure: Customers not served in order of arrival.
Poka-Yoke: Place numbered markers on cars as they arrive.
Failure: Vehicle information incorrect and process is time consuming.
Poka-Yoke: Maintain customer database and print forms with historical information.

Failure: Incorrect diagnosis of the problem.
Poka-Yoke: High-tech checklists such as expert systems and diagnostic equipment.

Failure: Incorrect estimate.
Poka-Yoke: Checklists itemizing costs by common repair types.

Source: R. B. Chase and D. M. Stewart, "Make Your Service Fail-Safe," *Sloan Management Review,* Spring 1994, pp. 42–43.

system. The only choice available to the attendant is to operate it exactly as the designers intended.

The Self-Service Approach

In contrast to the production line approach, C. H. Lovelock and R. F. Young propose that the service process can be enhanced by having the customer take a greater role in the production of the service.[8] Automatic teller machines, self-service gas stations, salad bars, and in-room coffee-making equipment in motels are approaches that shift the service burden to the consumer. Many customers like self-service because it puts them in control. For others, this philosophy requires some selling on the part of the service organization to convince customers that it helps them. To this end, Lovelock and Young propose a

[8]C. H. Lovelock and R. F. Young, "Look to Customers to Increase Productivity," *Harvard Business Review* 57, no. 2, pp. 168–78.

Failure: Customer not located.
Poka-Yoke: Issue beepers to
customers who wish to leave facility.

Failure: Bill is illegible.
Poka-Yoke: Top copy to
customer, or plain paper bill.

Failure: Feedback not obtained.
Poka-Yoke: Customer
satisfaction postcard given to
customer with keys to vehicle.

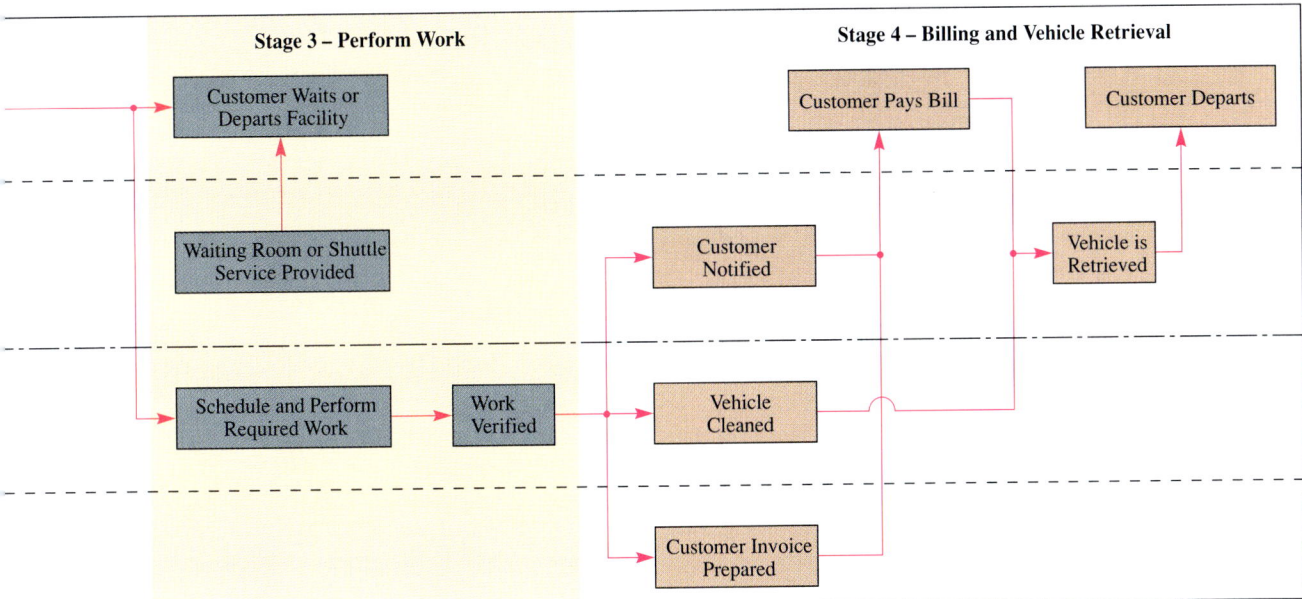

Failure: Service shuttle is inconvenient.
Poka-Yoke: Seating in available shuttles is
allocated when scheduling appointments. Lack
of free spaces indicates that customers needing
shuttle service should be scheduled
for another time.
Failure: Parts are not in stock.
Poka-Yoke: Limit switches activate signal
lamps when part level falls below order point.

Failure: Vehicle not cleaned correctly.
Poka-Yoke: Person retrieving vehicle
inspects, orders a touch-up if necessary,
and removes floor mat in presence of
customer.

Failure: Vehicle takes too long to arrive.
Poka-Yoke: When cashier enters
customer's name in order to print the bill,
information is electronically sent to
runners who retrieve vehicle while the
customer is paying.

number of steps, including developing customer trust, promoting the benefits of cost, speed, and convenience, and following up to make sure that the procedures are being effectively used. In essence, this turns customers into "partial employees" who must be trained in what to do and, as noted earlier, be "fail-safed" in case of mistake.

It is often most profitable to provide both full service and self-service at the same facility. As Globerson and Maggard report, "Analysis of gasoline sales after decontrol of the U.S. gasoline market in 1981 shows that cutting prices for self-service gasoline while increasing prices for full service increased dealer profits, in spite of the fact that self-service gas sales increased by from about 22 percent in 1978 to 41 percent in 1984."[9]

---

[9]S. Globerson and M. J. Maggard, "A Conceptual Model of Self-Service," *International Journal of Production and Operations Management* 11, no. 4 (1991) pp. 33–43.

In this photo, cataract surgery in the Soviet Union is performed in an assembly line fashion.

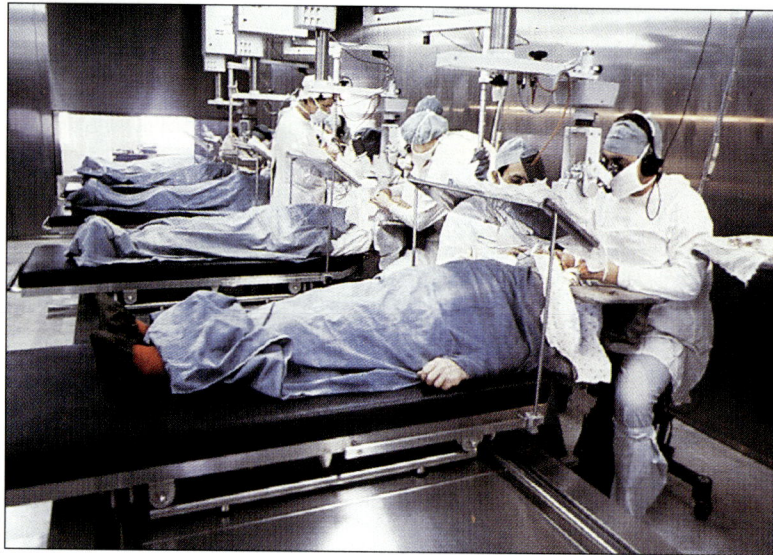

The Personal Attention Approach

An interesting contrast in the way personal attention is provided can be seen in Nordstrom Department Stores and the Ritz-Carlton Hotel Company.

At Nordstrom, a rather loose, unstructured process relies on developing a relationship between the individual salesperson and the customer. At the Ritz-Carlton, the process is virtually scripted, and the information system rather than the employee keeps track of the guest's (customer's) personal preferences. Tom Peters describes Nordstrom's approach here:

> After several visits to a store's men's clothing department, a customer's suit still did not fit. He wrote the company president, who sent a tailor to the customer's office with a new suit for fitting. When the alterations were completed, the suit was delivered to the customer—free of charge.
>
> This incident involved the $1.3 billion, Seattle-based Nordstrom, a specialty clothing retailer. Its sales per square foot are about five times that of a typical department store. Who received the customer's letter and urged the extreme (by others' standards) response? Co-chairman John Nordstrom.
>
> The frontline providers of this good service are well paid. Nordstrom's salespersons earn a couple of bucks an hour more than competitors, plus a 6.75 percent commission. Its top salesperson moves over $1 million a year in merchandise. Nordstrom lives for its customers and salespeople. Its only official organization chart puts the customer at the top, followed by sales and sales support people. Next come department managers, then store managers, and the board of directors at the very bottom.
>
> Salespersons religiously carry a "personal book," where they record voluminous information about each of their customers; senior, successful salespeople often have three or four bulging books, which they carry everywhere, according to Betsy Sanders, the vice president who orchestrated the firm's wildly successful penetration of the tough southern California market. "My objective is to get one new personal customer a day," says a budding Nordstrom star. The system helps him do just that. He has a virtually unlimited budget to send cards, flowers, and thank-you notes to customers. He also is encouraged to shepherd his customer to any department in the store to assist in a successful shopping trip.
>
> He also is abetted by what may be the most liberal returns policy in this or any other business: Return *anything,* no questions asked. Sanders says that "trusting customers," or "our bosses" as she repeatedly calls them, is vital to the Nordstrom philosophy. President Jim Nordstrom told the *Los Angeles Times,* "I don't care if they roll a Goodyear tire into the

E X H I B I T 4.11

*The Ritz-Carlton
Hotel Company
(Three Steps of
Service)*

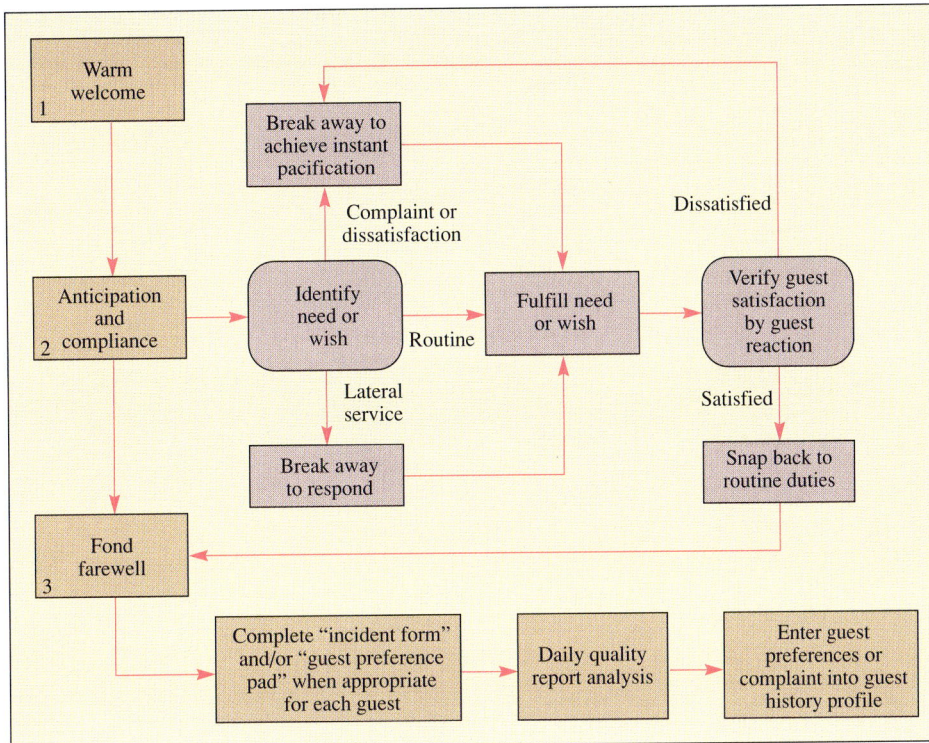

Source: *Ritz-Carlton Malcolm Baldrige National Quality Award Application Summary,* 1993, p. 11.

store. If they say they paid $200, give them $200 (in cash) for it." Sanders acknowledges that a few customers rip the store off—"rent hose from us," to use a common insider's line. But this is more than offset by goodwill from the 99 percent-plus who benefit from the "No Problem at Nordstrom" logo that the company lives up to with unmatched zeal.

No bureaucracy gets in the way of serving the customer. Policy? Sanders explains to a dumbfounded group of Silicon Valley executives, "I know this drives the lawyers nuts, but our whole 'policy manual' is just one sentence, 'Use your own best judgment at all times.' " One store manager offers a translation, "Don't chew gum. Don't steal from us."[10]

The Ritz-Carlton approach is described in the following excerpts from the company's Baldrige Award Application Summary and discussions with Scott Long of Ritz-Carlton's Huntington Hotel in Pasadena, California. Exhibit 4.11 shows the formalized service procedure (the Three Steps of Service). Exhibit 4.12 displays the information system used to capture data about guests ("The Ritz-Carlton Repeat Guest History Program"). Note that the three steps of service are integrated into the guest history information system.

> Systems for the collection and utilization of customer reaction and satisfaction are widely deployed and extensively used throughout the organization. Our efforts are centered on various customer segments and product lines.
>
> Our approach is the use of systems which allow every employee to collect and utilize quality-related data on a daily basis. These systems provide critical, responsive data which includes:
> (1) on-line guest preference information;
> (2) quantity of error free products and services;
> (3) opportunities for quality improvement.

Tom Peters, *Quality!* (Palo Alto, CA: TPC Communications, 1986), pp. 10–12.

E X H I B I T 4.12   *The Ritz-Carlton Repeat Guest History Program (An Aid to Highly Personalized Service Delivery)*

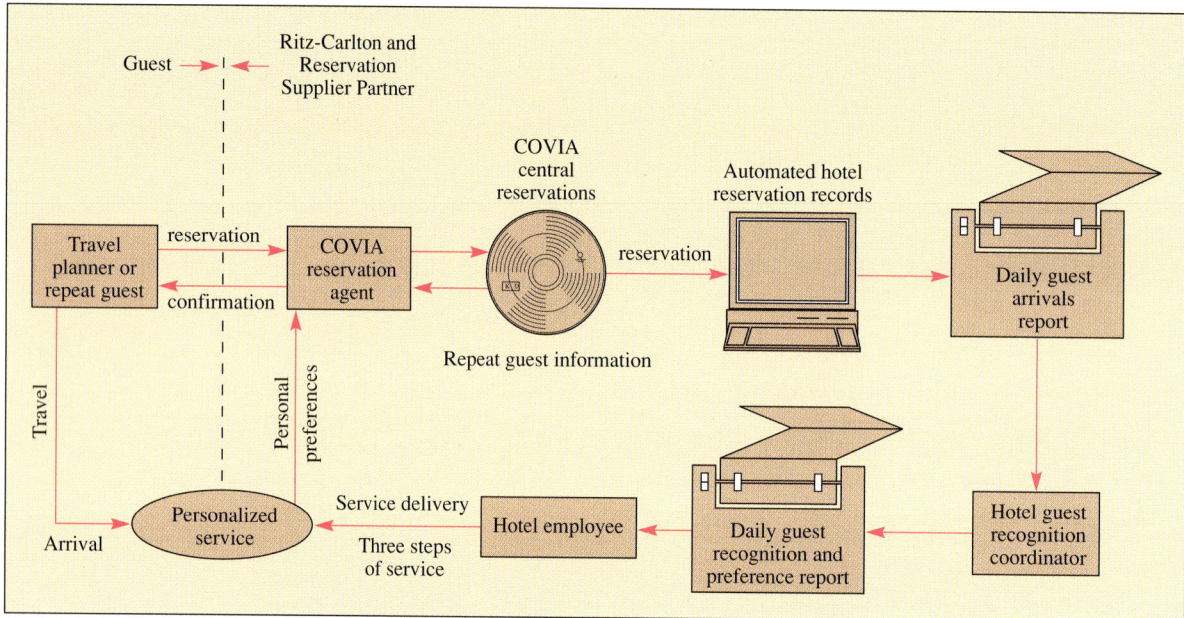

Source: *Ritz-Carlton Malcolm Baldrige National Quality Award Application Summary,* 1993, p. 6.

Our automated property management systems enable the on-line access and utilization of guest preference information at the individual customer level. All employees collect and input this data, and use the data as part of their service delivery with individual guests.

Our quality production reporting system is a method of aggregating hotel level data from nearly two dozen sources into a summary format. It serves as an early warning system and facilitates analysis. The processes employees use to identify quality opportunities for improvement are standardized in a textbook, and available throughout our organization.[11]

No matter what approach is taken to design a service, the need for the service characteristics shown in "Seven Characteristics of a Well-Designed Service System" should be evident.

4.8   SERVICE GUARANTEES AS DESIGN DRIVERS

The phrase "Positively, absolutely, overnight" is an example of a service guarantee most of us know by heart. Hiding behind such marketing promises of service satisfaction are a set of actions that must be taken by the operations organization to fulfill these promises.

Thousands of companies have launched **service guarantees** as a marketing tool designed to provide peace of mind for customers unsure about trying their service. From an operations perspective, a service guarantee can be used not only as an improvement tool but also at the design stage to focus the firm's delivery system squarely on the things it must do so well to satisfy the customer. Consider First Interstate Bank of California's

---

[11]*Ritz-Carlton Malcolm Baldrige National Quality Award Application Summary,* 1993, p. 6.

1. *Each element of the service system is consistent with the operating focus of the firm.* For example, when the focus is on speed of delivery, each step in the process should help to foster speed.

2. *It is user-friendly.* This means that the customer can interact with it easily—that is, it has good signage, understandable forms, logical steps in the process, and service workers available to answer questions.

3. *It is robust.* That is, it can cope effectively with variations in demand and resource availability. For example, if the computer goes down, effective backup systems are in place to permit service to continue.

4. *It is structured so that consistent performance by its people and systems is easily maintained.* This means the tasks required of the workers are doable, and the supporting technologies are truly supportive and reliable.

5. *It provides effective links between the back office and the front office so that nothing falls between the cracks.* In football parlance, there should be "no fumbled handoffs."

6. *It manages the evidence of service quality in such a way that customers see the value of the service provided.* Many services do a great job behind the scenes but fail to make this visible to the customer. This is particularly true where a service improvement is made. Unless customers are made aware of the improvement through explicit communication about it, the improved performance is unlikely to gain maximum impact.

7. *It is cost-effective.* There is minimum waste of time and resources in delivering the service. Even if the service outcome is satisfactory, customers are often put off by a service company that appears inefficient.

service guarantee in Exhibit 4.13. It requires operations to have its back office working well, preventive maintenance for its ATMs, its branch office personnel on their toes, and its loan department working quickly.

Even professional service firms such as Rath and Strong have service guarantees. (Theirs allows the client to choose from a menu of payouts if they do not, for example, cut lead time by *x* percent. Menu options include refunds and no charge for overtime work to get the job done.)

The elements of a good service guarantee are that it is:[12]

Unconditional (no small print).

Meaningful to the customer (the payoff fully covers the customer's dissatisfaction).

Easy to understand and communicate (for employees as well as customers).

Painless to invoke (given proactively).

4.9   REVIEW AND DISCUSSION QUESTIONS

1. Who is the "customer" in a jail? A cemetery? A summer camp for children?

2. How have price and variety competition changed McDonald's basic formula for success?

3. Could a service firm use a production line approach or self-serve design and still keep a high customer focus (personal attention)? Explain and support your answer with examples.

---

[12]Christopher W. L. Hart, "The Power of Unconditional Service Guarantee," *Harvard Business Review.* 56, no. 4 (July–August 1988), p. 55.

GOOF-PROOF BANKING ...OR WE PAY.

Great service should be a lot more than just being greeted with a warm hello and a pleasant smile.

Great service requires professionals who are also dedicated to going out of their way to satisfy your banking needs.

At First Interstate Bank of California, we are committed to going the extra mile for you. Day in and day out.

Perhaps that's why, according to a statewide survey of major banks and savings and loans, First Interstate ranked #1 in overall service. And we intend to remain #1. Because you deserve nothing less.

So, to insure that we continue to provide you with the best banking service in California, we are introducing a comprehensive Service Guarantee. Here's what it means for you:

WE GOOF...WE PAY. If you find any error on your account statement—we'll pay you $5.

WE WAIT...WE PAY. If you have to wait more than 5 minutes in the main teller line—we'll pay you $5.

WE BREAK...WE PAY. If our Day & Night Teller® ATM isn't working when it should be—we'll pay you $5.

WE DAWDLE...WE PAY. If you have a question or problem and one of our Customer Assistance Representatives doesn't respond to you within 24 hours—we'll pay you $5.

WE DELAY...WE PAY. If you apply for a loan and don't get an answer within 24 hours—we'll pay you $5.

Now that's service. The best in California. Our customers know it. Let us prove it to you, too.

Come to First Interstate Bank of California. We go the extra mile for you. Contact any branch for details regarding program qualifications and limitations.

First Interstate Bank

We go the extra mile for you.

4. Why should a manager of a bank home office be evaluated differently than a manager of a bank branch.

5. Identify the high-contact and low-contact operations of the following services:
   a. A dental office.
   b. An airline.
   c. An accounting office.
   d. An automobile agency.

6. Some suggest that customer expectation is the key to service success. Give an example from your own experience to support or refute this assertion.

7. Where would you place a drive-in church, a campus food vending machine, and a bar's automatic mixed drink machine on the service-system design matrix?

8. Can a manufacturer have a service guarantee in addition to a product guarantee?

9. What elements would you like to see guaranteed in addition to those given in First Interstate's guarantee?

10. What are the risks associated with the following guarantee offered by one of the authors of this book for his advanced MBA Service Operations class?

    My service guarantee: If you are not satisfied with the quality of the class, I will refund the cost of books and cases and $250 of your course fees.

11. Suppose you were the manager of a restaurant and you were told honestly that a couple eating dinner had just seen a mouse. What would you say to them—how would you recover from this service crisis?

4.10   PROBLEMS

1. Place the following functions of a department store on the service-system design matrix: mail order (i.e., catalog), phone order, hardware, stationery, apparel, cosmetics, customer service (i.e., complaints).

2. Do the same as in the previous problem for a hospital with the following activities and relationships: physician/patient, nurse/patient, billing, medical records, lab tests, admissions, diagnostic tests (e.g., X-rays).

3. The service designer for the shoeshine shop of Exhibits 4.8 and 4.9 has decided to study the following changes:
   - Add a premium two-coat service, which will repeat Steps 2 and 3 (Apply polish and Buff). The price of the premium service will be set at $.70.
   - Provide each customer (both regular and premium) with a receipt and a sample of shoe polish imprinted with the shop's name. This will add $.01 to operating expenses and 0.5 minutes to the execution time but will provide the customer with some tangible evidence of the service.

   These two changes are to be made simultaneously. Do the following:
   a. Draw the blueprint for the premium service.
   b. Provide a profitability analysis for the premium service.
   c. Provide an updated profitability analysis for the regular service.

4. Perform a quick service audit the next time you go shopping at a department store. Evaluate the three T's of service: the Task, the Treatment and the Tangible features of the service on a 1 (poor), 3 (average), and 5 (excellent). Remember that the tangible features include the environment, layout, and appearance of the store, not the goods you purchased.

5. SYSTEM DESCRIPTION EXERCISE
   The beginning step in studying a productive system is to develop a description of that system. Once a system is described, we can better determine why the system works well or poorly and recommend production-related improvements. Since we are all familiar with fast-food restaurants, try your hand at describing the production system employed at, say, a McDonald's. In doing so, answer the following questions:
   a. What are the important aspects of the service package?
   b. Which skills and attitudes are needed by the service personnel?
   c. How can customer demand be altered?
   d. Provide a rough-cut blueprint of the delivery system. (It is not necessary to provide execution times. Just diagram the basic flow through the system.) Critique the blueprint. Are there any unnecessary steps or can fail points be eliminated?
   e. Can the customer/provider interface be changed to include more technology? More self-serve?
   f. Which measures are being used to evaluate and measure the service? Which could be used?
   g. How does it measure up on the seven characteristics of a well-designed service?

CASE

4.11 CASE
Kinko's Copier Stores

"We're not your average printer," says Annie Odell, Kinko's regional manager for Louisiana. She's right. She may have the only printshops in town where customers come as much for the company as for the copies. It's a free-wheeling, hi-tech operation that marches to the beat of a different drum machine. It looks chaotic; it is chaotic. Yet it produces profit as well as fun.

Odell's copy shop empire has grown from one to seven in six years, including five in the greater New Orleans area.

Kinko's keeps its sales figures a secret, but Odell estimates her New Orleans stores make about 40 million copies a year. At the firm's advertised 4½ cents-per-copy price, that would mean around $1.8 million a year in sales, or an average of over $300,000 per shop. The New Orleans operations rank among Kinko's top 25 percent nationally, reports Becky Barieau of Kinko's of Georgia.

Sales in New Orleans have climbed even while the marketplace has been sinking. At the Carrollton store, revenues increased 10 percent over last year, an excellent showing considering the 4½ cents-per-copy rate has not budged since 1980.

"Depression seems to generate more need for copies," says Wallis Windsor, manager of the Carrollton store, "There are bankruptcies, legal documents and resumes—hundreds of people who want 50 copies of their resumes on specialty paper."

Printers Sneer

Kinko's is unique. For one thing, it doesn't do a lick of offset printing. It makes copies, copies, and almost nothing but copies. On the side it binds, folds, staples, collates, makes pads, and takes passport photos.

Kinko's is also unique among quick printing chains in that it doesn't franchise. All 300 or so Kinko's stores are divided among a few closely held corporations, and founder Paul Orfalea holds a piece of virtually all of them. Odell explains that the company avoids franchising to ensure tight control over quality at its outlets.

Others attribute the structure to a desire to avoid the legal restrictions and paperwork demanded by setting up franchises in different states. How it's been kept together is a management feat in itself.

Even the name sticks out. The Yellow Pages list dozens of quick printers with some reference to speed in their names, often intentionally misspelled. "Kinko's" denotes a place that's . . . well, a little kinky. For the record, Orfalea, who plugged in his first photocopier when he was in college, was nicknamed by classmates as "Kinko" for his curly head of hair.

Broadway and Benihana

Kinko's management style draws on both the restaurant business and the stage. Fast copies are like fast food, say the managers. It's not just that every Big Mac is a copy of every other one. Images of eating come up again and again as they try to explain what keeps their customers coming back.

"Making copies is addictive," says Windsor, and points to her clientele of "regulars," who "have made this their office. They will spend four or five hours here although they don't spend more than $5 or $6. People have suggested we open a bar in here."

"Instant gratification is what Kinko's is offering," says another manager.

The last time managers from around the country huddled in Santa Barbara for the company "picnic," they studied looseleaf binders crammed full of floor plans for McDonald's and Benihana of Tokyo—a variation on the acclaimed art of Japanese management.

"You'd find it hard to believe," says Odell, "but Benihana is a lot like Kinko's. They're masters of efficiency. We'll try to set up the floor to get one person operating two copiers, just like Benihana puts one cook between two tables. Our paper is centrally located, just as they have all the chopping prepared ahead of time. Then there's the floater, who floats around and pops in wherever he's needed."

Both Kinko's and Benihana's use theater to attract clients, charging their employees with putting on a good show as well as putting out good service. At the Japanese restaurant, the show is the cook, who sizzles a sukiyaki right in front of your table. At Kinko's, it's the clatter of copy machines and the Charlie Chaplinlike spectacle of operators running back and forth between them.

"They do it right in front of you and you get instant quality control," says Odell, "There's no way you're going to drop that document with the customer watching you."

She deliberately displays all her machines and personnel in one big room. "We work out with the public. That's why it's fun," says Odell, "The other guys are behind closed doors."

Windsor enjoys working in a fishbowl. "My personality changes," she says. "I'll be a little more dramatic and louder than I would be in a closed group. I walk quickly. I'll wad up and throw papers a lot."

She believes customers unconsciously get into the act. "Some of the mildest-mannered people get aggressive in here. I've seen a little old lady elbow her way in ahead of people, where if she were in a bank she'd stand in line neatly."

Kinko's does no broadcast and little print advertising, counting on price and word-of-mouth to draw customers, and ambience doesn't hurt. Each Kinko's has its "regulars," who get friendly with particular operators and who favor particular machines. The area in front of the counter is strewn with typewriters, lettering machines and light tables, all the better to hook people into making themselves comfortable and coming back.

A recent addition to that melange is the customer comment form. The customer mails the postage-paid form straight to headquarters in Santa Barbara, where senior management review it and send a thank-you note to the author before routing it back to the shop manager for action. Odell has several inches of forms on file, along with notes on the follow-up calls she made to the customers.

"We don't choose our market so much as our market chooses us," she says. Each shop keeps a different mix of machines, depending on the needs of its patrons. An operator learns quickly that the Xerox 1000 series picks up blue but not yellow, while the 9000 series picks up yellow and black but not blue. Thus, the store adjoining the Tulane campus does not have a 9000 because students tend to bring in notes and books highlighted with yellow markers.

Another adaptation to the market is "Professor Publishing," a service which lets professors excerpt chapters from several books and print them up together as a single textbook. During the first two weeks of every semester, the Broadway office works virtually around-the-clock on this specialty.

Odell maintains that her managers clear all material with publishers before printing a professor's anthology. Indeed, Kinko's says it is one of the most scrupulous of the copy chains about observing copyright laws.

Printing in a Fishbowl

If working at the Kinko's shops in New Orleans is like working in a fishbowl, it's a two-way fishbowl where the fish are always peering back at their audience. The crazy-quilt mix of customers provides endless entertainment and a fund of oddball stories to exchange over beers. A sampling:

- One woman insisted that the manager throw away the ribbon on the self-service typewriter she'd just used, fearing that someone might try to use it to recreate her document. Another customer wanted several confidential pages typed, and asked, "Can you get me a typist who won't read them?"

- Some artists enjoy using the photocopiers for the oddest things. One woman brings in stuffed dead birds for reproduction. Another brought in a box of pecans purported to be from the backyard of a house where Tennessee Williams once lived.

- A tipsy woman, about 25 years of age, meandered in from a Mardi Gras parade, curled up next to a window, and fell asleep. There she remained for four hours, while the copiers and binding machines pounded and rattled. Manager Raynell Murphy called the home office. "What should I do?" she asked.

"Get a picture," came the word from California, "We can use it as a promotion, you know, to show what a relaxed atmosphere we have at Kinko's."

Finally, a hulking woman who had just bought some copies walked over to the sleeper, kicked her a couple of times, and asked, "Are you ready yet?" The sleeper arose and groggily headed out the door.

Questions

1. Can general operational standards be developed and implemented in all or a majority of Kinko's shops?

2. Discuss the idea of grouping copiers in machine centers so that certain copiers are available for specific tasks.

3. How do the different services offered (private copying versus copying services provided) present separate types of problems for management?

4. Kinko's Professor Publishing apparently did not pan out. What might have been the cause?

Source: Mark Ballard, "Working in a Fishbowl," *Quick Printing*, May 1987, pp. 30–32. Reprinted by permission.

4.12 SELECTED BIBLIOGRAPHY

Bitran, Gabriel R., and Johannes Hoech. "The Humanization of Service: Respect at the Moment of Truth." *Sloan Management Review*, Winter 1990, pp. 89–96.

Chase, R. B. "The Customer Contact Approach to Services: Theoretical Bases and Practical Extensions." *Operations Research* 21, no. 4 (1981), pp. 698–705.

Chase, R. B. and D. M. Stewart, "Make Your Service Fail-Safe," *Sloan Management Review*, Spring 1994, pp. 35–44.

———. *Mistake-Proofing: How to Design Errors Out,* Productivity Press, Cambridge, MA, 1994.

Cohen, Morris A., and Hau L. Lee. "Out of Touch with Customer Needs?" *Sloan Management Review*, Winter 1990, pp. 55–66.

Collier, D. A. *Service Management: The Automation of Services.* Reston, VA: Reston Publishing, 1986.

———. *The Service/Quality Solution.* Burr Ridge, IL: Irwin Professional Publishing, 1993.

Farsad, Behshid, and Ahmad K. Elshennawy. "Defining Service Quality Is Difficult for Service and Manufacturing Firms." *Industrial Engineering*, March 1989, pp. 17–20.

Firnstahl, Timothy W. "My Employees Are My Service Guarantee." *Harvard Business Review,* July–August 1989, pp. 28–33.

Fitzsimmons, J. A., and R. S. Sullivan. *Service Operations Management.* New York: McGraw-Hill, 1983.

Flint, Jerry, and William Heuslein. "An Urge to Service." *Forbes,* September 18, 1989, pp. 172–74.

Hackett, Gregory P. "Investment in Technology: The Service Sector Sinkhole?" *Sloan Management Review,* Winter 1990, pp. 97–103.

Hart, Christopher W. L. "The Power of Unconditional Service Guarantees." *Harvard Business Review,* July–August 1988, pp. 54–62.

Heskett, J. L. *Managing in the Service Economy.* Cambridge, MA: Harvard University Press, 1986.

Peavey, Dennis E. "It's Time for a Change." *Management Accounting,* February 1990, pp. 31–35.

Pyzdek, Thomas. "Toward Service Systems Engeneering." *Quality Management Journal,* April 1986, pp. 26–42.

Shapiro, Benson P., V. Kasturi Rangan, Rowland T. Moriarty, and Elliot B. Ross. "Manage Customers for Profits, Not Just Sales." *Harvard Business Review,* September–October 1987, pp. 101–8.

Sonnenberg, Frank K. "Service Quality: Forethought, Not Afterthought." *Journal of Business Strategy,* September–October 1989, pp. 54–57.

S u p p l e m e n t

4

Waiting Line Management

SUPPLEMENT OUTLINE

KEY TERMS

Queue

Arrival Rate

Exponential Distribution

Poisson Distribution

Single Channel, Single Phase

Multichannel, Multiphase

Service Rate

Finite queue

Louis Kane hates snakes.

The restaurant executive means the single lines that feed customers one at a time to a group of cashiers. He thinks snakes are much too "institutional." Besides, he says, he would rather try to guess which line will move the fastest. But surveys show that customers prefer snakes to multiple lines because they hate "getting stuck behind some guy ordering nine cappuccinos, each with something different on top," says Mr. Kane, cochairman of the Boston-based Au Bon Pain soup-and-sandwich chain.

The customers have won. Over the past couple of years, Au Bon Pain has instituted snakes at every restaurant that has enough room. But the debate lives on. "We talk about this a great deal," Mr. Kane says.

The issue is queues. Experts suggest that no aspect of customer service is more important than the wait in line to be served. The act of waiting—either in person or on the phone—"has a disproportionately high impact" on customers, says David Maister, a Boston consultant who has studied the psychology of waiting. "The wait can destroy an otherwise perfect service experience."

A customer waiting in line is potentially a lost customer. According to one study, up to 27 percent of customers who can not get through on the telephone will either buy elsewhere or skip the transaction altogether, says Rudy Oetting, a senior partner at Oetting & Co., a New York company that consults on telephone use. Adds Russell James, an official at Avis Rent a Car Inc., "You can't be out-lined by a competitor or you will lose business."

Source: Amanda Bennett, "Their Business Is on the Line," *The Wall Street Journal,* December 7, 1990, p. B1.

Understanding waiting lines or **queues** and learning how to manage them is one of the most important areas in operations management. It is basic to creating schedules, job design, inventory levels, and so on. In our service economy we wait in line every day, from driving to work to checking out at the supermarket. We also encounter waiting lines at factories—jobs wait in lines to be worked on at different machines, and machines themselves wait their turn to be overhauled. In short, waiting lines are pervasive.

In this supplement we discuss the basic elements of waiting line problems and provide standard steady-state formulas for solving them. These formulas, arrived at through queuing theory, enable planners to analyze service requirements and establish service facilities appropriate to stated conditions. Queuing theory is broad enough to cover such dissimilar delays as those encountered by customers in a shopping mall or aircraft in a holding pattern awaiting landing slots.

S4.1   ECONOMICS OF THE WAITING LINE PROBLEM

The central problem in virtually every waiting line situation is a trade-off decision. The manager must weigh the added cost of providing more rapid service (more traffic lanes, additional landing strips, more checkout stands) against the inherent cost of waiting.

Frequently the cost trade-off decision is straightforward. For example, if we find that the total time our employees spend in line waiting to use a copying machine would otherwise be spent in productive activities, we could compare the cost of installing one additional machine to the value of employee time saved. The decision could then be reduced to dollar terms and the choice easily made.

On the other hand, suppose that our waiting line problem centers on demand for beds in a hospital. We can compute the cost of additional beds by summing the costs for building construction, additional equipment required, and increased maintenance. But what is on the other side of the scale? Here we are confronted with the problem of trying to place a dollar figure on a patient's need for a hospital bed that is unavailable. While we can estimate lost hospital income, what about the human cost arising from this lack of adequate hospital care?

Cost Effectiveness Balance

Exhibit S4.1 shows the essential trade-off relationship under typical (steady-state) customer traffic conditions. Initially, with minimal service capacity, the waiting line cost is at a maximum. As service capacity is increased, there is a reduction in the number of customers in the line and in their waiting times, which decreases waiting line cost. The

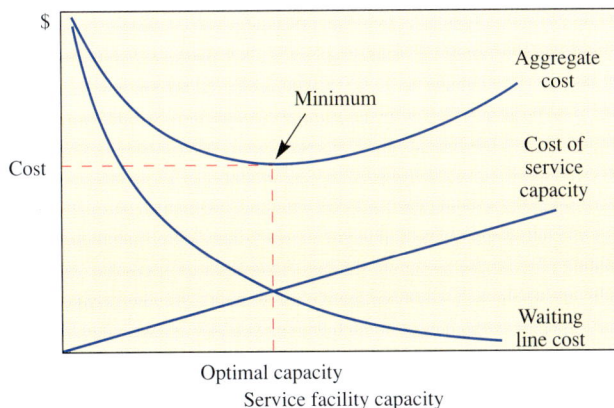

E X H I B I T S4.1

Service Capacity versus Waiting Line Trade-off

E X H I B I T S4.2   *Arrival and Service Profiles*

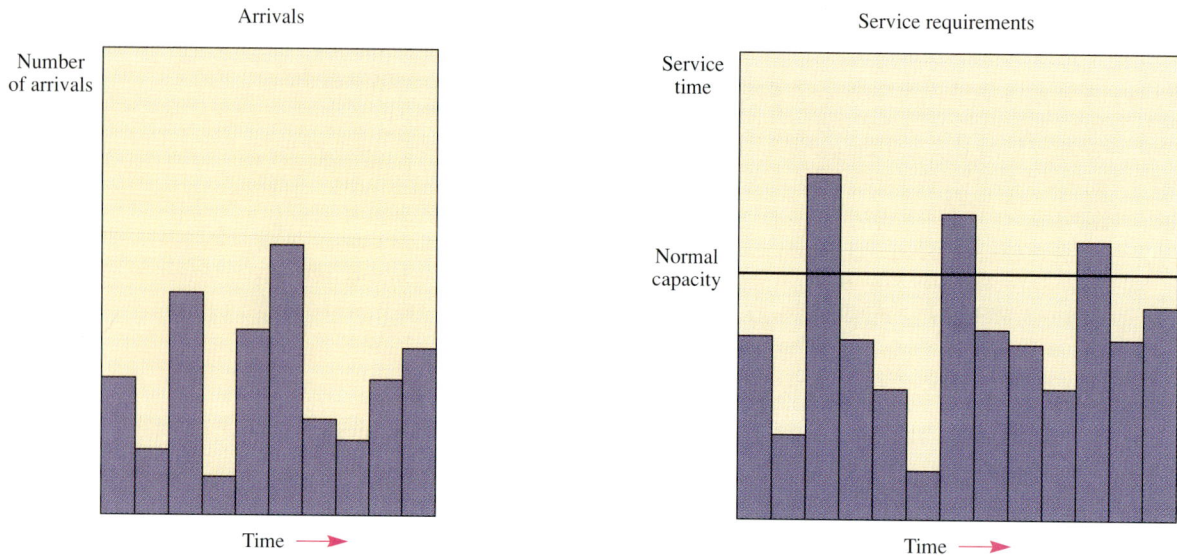

variation in this function is often represented by the negative exponential curve. The cost of installing service capacity is shown simplistically as a linear rather than step function. The aggregate or total cost is shown as a U-shaped curve, a common approximation in such equilibrium problems. The idealized optimal cost is found at the crossover point between the service capacity and waiting line curves.

The Practical View of Waiting Lines

S

Before we precede with a technical presentation of waiting line theory, we need to look at the intuitive side of the issue and what it means. Exhibit S4.2 shows arrivals at a service facility (e.g., a bank) and service requirements at that facility (e.g., tellers, loan officer). One important thing is the number of arrivals over the course of the hours that the service system is open. From the service delivery viewpoint, customers demand varying amounts of service, often exceeding normal capacity. We can have some control over arrivals in a variety of ways. For example, we can have a short line (such as a drive-in at a fast food restaurant with only several spaces), we can establish specific hours for specific customers, or we can run specials. For the server, we can affect service time by using faster or slower servers, faster or slower machines, different tooling, different material, different layout, faster setup time, and so on.

The essential point is waiting lines are *not* a fixed condition of a productive system but are to a very large extent within the control of the system management and design. Professor Richard Larson (the famous "wait-watcher") and his colleagues offer 10 useful suggestions for managing queues based on their research in the banking industry. (See "Ten Suggestions for Managing Queues.")

S4.2   THE QUEUING PHENOMENON

The **queuing phenomenon** consists essentially of three major components: (a) the source population and the way customers arrive at the system, (b) the servicing system, and (c) the condition of the customer exiting the system (back to source population or not?), as Exhibit S4.3 shows. The following sections discuss each of these areas.

We have formulated ten suggestions for managers. Some are direct applications of our research results, while others are based on qualitative observations and previous work in the field of queue psychology.

1. *Do not overlook the effects of perceptions management.* Consumer concern about waiting is growing. There is no limit to the frustration that waiting can cause. Cities are becoming more crowded, the work week is expanding, the economy is worsening, and people need more free time to deal with their frustrations. Now, more then ever, excellent service is the key to success. Using perceptions management to improve customer satisfaction is only a tool, but it's a good tool.

2. *Determine the acceptable waiting time for your customers.* One minute of waiting in a bank will probably go unnoticed, whereas a minute on hold on the telephone can be infuriating. Determining an acceptable waiting period will help managers set operational objectives and, if those are met, will improve customer satisfaction.

3. *Install distractions that entertain and physically involve the customer.* Keep the content light hearted. Piped-in music or live piano players may create a more pleasant atmosphere, but they do not effectively rope the customer into the activity. If the content of the distraction is light, fresh, and engaging, customers remain interested and entertained for many visits. Customers at the bank preferred horoscopes and tabloid headlines to more informative headline news.

    The message screen used in our study managed perceptions effectively. It was inexpensive, easy to operate, and did not disrupt normal operations. In addition, since most customers had to stand still to read the screen, they became physically involved with the distraction and did not mind waiting as much. Screen placement forced customers to turn slightly in order to read it; thus they stood shoulder to shoulder rather than front to back.

4. *Get customers out of line.* Whenever customers can be served without having to stand in line, both company and customer can benefit. For example, queues can be avoided by advance reservations, by mail or telephone service, or by better automation.

    In banking, there are many ways to conduct transactions without using a teller—for example, direct deposit, ATMs, automatic loan payments, and check-cashing machines. The challenge is to increase customer awareness and use of these tools.

5. *Only make people conscious of time if they grossly overestimate waiting times.* There is a trade-off between the accuracy of waiting time perceptions and the awareness of time. In the bank, perceptions were fairly close to reality, perhaps because customers had previous experience with the branch, or because the lines were short. For whatever reason, informing customers of their expected waiting time backfired. The clock made people more aware of the waiting time. It also appeared to increase balking rates.

    However, there may be numerous instances in which information on expected waiting times is helpful. Airline passengers, for example, have no way of knowing when a plane sitting on the runway will take off unless they're told.

6. *Modify customer arrival behavior.* Customers are often aware of peak times before they arrive at a service location, but they show up then anyway. If some customers could be convinced to arrive at other times, everyone would be better off. To achieve this, signs that list off-peak hours could be posted in stores and banks. Servers could also mention off-peak hours to customers who have waited an inordinate amount of time. In addition, incentives could be used to encourage off-peak arrivals.

7. *Keep resources not serving customers out of sight.* Several customers commented that they do not mind waiting so long as the tellers seem to be working as hard as they can. Customers tend to become annoyed if they see several unstaffed teller windows or if tellers

continued

are present but not serving customers. To address this perception, managers can adopt several policies:

- Keep idle employees out of view.
- Conduct activities that do not involve customer interactions out of the customer's sight.
- Staff stations closest to the exit point of the queue first. The practice creates a better first impression for the customer.
- Keep unused physical capacity out of view (e.g., portable cash registers for the Christmas season).

8. *Segment customers by personality types.* The three types of customers we observed—watchers, impatients, and neutrals—want different types of service from the bank. Watchers find the bustle of the bank entertaining and prefer a friendly teller with a smile to a shorter line. The impatient group is more apt to emphasize the length of the queue in their definition of overall satisfaction.

   The needs of the "impatients" can be met through innovative products, services, and educational programs that either avoid or reduce the waiting experience. The airline and hotel industries, for example, have developed club memberships that provide express check-in and check-out policies. Some retailers satisfy convenience-seeking consumers by creating express check-out cashier lines. The emergence of convenience-oriented businesses proves that people are willing to pay more for services that save them time.

9. *Adopt a long-term perspective.* In our research, respondents rated their overall satisfaction significantly lower on a historical basis than on the survey date itself. And, although daily satisfaction improved as the study progressed, historical satisfaction did not. It evidently takes a tremendous number of "good days" before customers' historical opinions change. Managers must take a long-term approach when attempting to improve perceptions.

10. *Never underestimate the power of a friendly server.* Although waiting is an issue worth addressing, managers should not lose perspective. Servers should continually be trained and rewarded for good service, since their efforts can overcome many negative effects of waiting.

Source: K. Katz, B. M. Larson, and R. C. Larson, "Prescription for the Waiting-in-Line Blues," *Sloan Management Review,* Winter 1991, pp. 51–52.

Customer Arrivals

Arrivals at a service system may be drawn from a *finite* or an *infinite* population. The distinction is important because the analyses are based on different premises and require different equations for their solution.

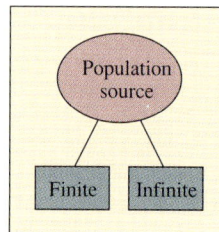

Finite Population   A *finite population* refers to the limited-size customer pool that will use the service and, at times, form a line. The reason this finite classification is important is because when a customer leaves its position as a member of the population of users (by a machine breaking down and requiring service, for example), the size of the

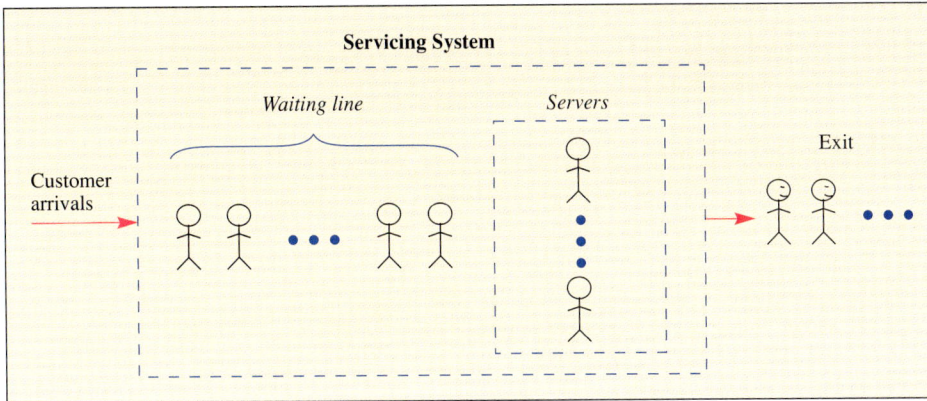

user group is therefore reduced by one, which reduces the probability of the next occurrence. Conversely, when a customer is serviced and returns to the user group, the population increases and the probability of a user requiring service also increases. This finite
class of problems requires a separate set of formulas from that of the infinite population
case.

As an example, consider a group of six machines maintained by one repairperson.
When one machine breaks down, the source population is reduced to five, and the chances
of one of the five breaking down and needing repair is certainly different than the chances
of one out of six, as in the original size. If two machines are down with only four operating, the probability of another breakdown is again changed. Conversely, when a machine is repaired and returned to service, the machine population increases, thus raising
the probability of the next breakdown. A finite population model with one server that
can be used in such cases is presented in Exhibit S4.3.

Infinite Population   An infinite population is one large enough in relation to the service system so that the changes in the population size caused by subtractions or additions to the population (a customer needing service or a serviced customer returning to
the population) does not significantly affect the system probabilities. If, in the preceding
finite explanation, there were 100 machines instead of six, then if one or two machines
broke down, the probabilities for the next breakdowns would not be very different and
the assumption could be made without a great deal of error that the population (for all
practical purposes) was infinite. Nor would the formulas for "infinite" queuing problems
cause much error if applied to a physician with 1,000 patients or a department store with
10,000 customers.

Distribution of Arrivals   When describing a waiting system, we need to define the manner in which customers or the waiting units are arranged for service.

Waiting line formulas generally require an **arrival rate,** or the number of units per
period (such as 10 units per hour). The time between arrivals is the interarrival time
(such as an average of one every six minutes). A *constant* arrival distribution is periodic,
with exactly the same time period between successive arrivals. In productive systems,
about the only arrivals that truly approach a constant interarrival period are those that
are subject to machine control. Much more common are *variable* (random) arrival distributions.

In observing arrivals at a service facility, we can look at them from two viewpoints:
We can analyze the time between successive arrivals to see if the times follow some

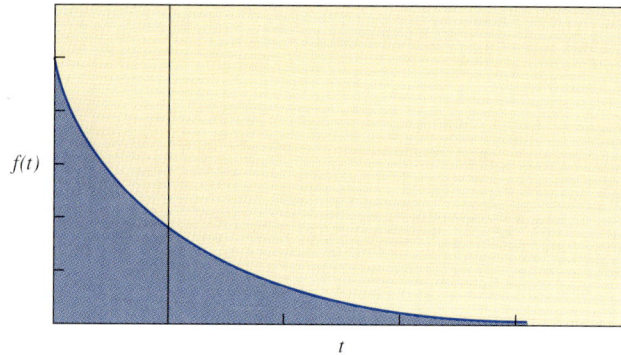

statistical distribution. Usually, we assume that the time between arrivals is exponentially distributed. We can set some time length *(T)* and try to determine how many arrivals might enter the system within *T*. We will typically assume that the number of arrivals per time unit is Poisson distributed.

Exponential distribution   In the first case, when arrivals at a service facility occur in a purely random fashion, a plot of the interarrival times yields an **exponential distribution** such as that shown in Exhibit S4.4. The probability function is

$$f(t) = \lambda e^{-\lambda t} \qquad (S4.1)$$

where λ is the mean number of arrivals per time period.

The cumulative area beneath the curve in Exhibit S4.4 is the summation of Equation S4.1 over its positive range, which is $e^{-\lambda t}$. This integral allows us to compute the probabilities of arrivals within a specified time. For example, for the case of single arrivals to a waiting line ($\lambda = 1$), the following table can be derived either by solving $e^{-\lambda t}$ or by using Appendix F. Column 2 shows the probability that it will be more than *t* minutes until the next arrival. Column 3 shows the probability of the next arrival within *t* minutes (computed as 1 minus column 2).

(1) *t* (minutes)	(2) **Probability That the Next Arrival Will Occur in *t* Minutes or More (from Appendix F or Solving e^{-t})**	(3) **Probability That the Next Arrival Will Occur in *t* Minutes or Less [1 − Column (2)]**
0	1.00	0
0.5	0.61	0.39
1.0	0.37	0.63
1.5	0.22	0.78
2.0	0.14	0.86

Poisson distribution   In the second case, where one is interested in the number of arrivals during some time period *T*, the distribution appears as in Exhibit S4.5 and is obtained by finding the probability of *n* arrivals during *T*. If the arrival process is random, the distribution is the **Poisson,** and the formula is

$$P_T(n) = \frac{(\lambda T)^n e^{-\lambda T}}{n!} \qquad (S4.2)$$

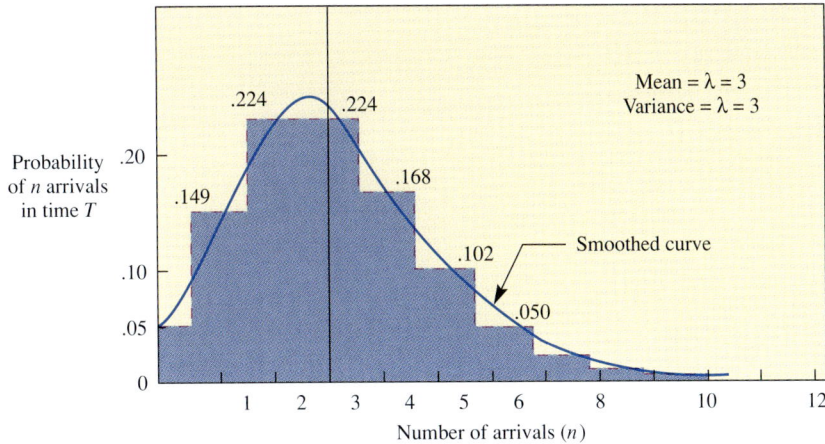

Equation S4.2 shows the probability of exactly n arrivals in time T.[1] For example, if the mean arrival rate of units into a system is three per minute ($\lambda = 3$) and we want to find the probability that exactly five units will arrive within a one-minute period ($n = 5$, $T = 1$), we have

$$P_1(5) = \frac{(3 \times 1)^5 e^{-3 \times 1}}{5!} = \frac{3^5 e^{-3}}{120} = 2.025 e^{-3} = 0.101$$

That is, there is a 10.1 percent chance that there will be five arrivals in any one-minute interval.

Although often shown as a smoothed curve, as in Exhibit S4.5, the Poisson is a discrete distribution. (The curve becomes smoother as n becomes larger.) The distribution is discrete because n refers, in our example, to the number of arrivals in a system, and this must be an integer. (For example, there cannot be 1.5 arrivals.)

Also note that the exponential and Poisson distributions can be derived from one another. The mean and variance of the Poisson are equal and denoted by λ. The mean of the exponential is $1/\lambda$ and its variance is $1/\lambda^2$. (Remember that the time between arrivals is exponentially distributed and the number of arrivals per unit of time is Poisson distributed.)

Other Arrival Characteristics   Other arrival characteristics include arrival patterns, size of arrival units, and degree of patience. (See Exhibit S4.6.)

Arrival patterns   The arrivals at a system are far more *controllable* than is generally recognized. Barbers may decrease their Saturday arrival rate (and supposedly shift it to other days of the week) by charging an extra $1 for adult haircuts or charging adult prices for children's haircuts. Department stores run sales during the off-season or hold one-day-only sales in part for purposes of control. Airlines offer excursion and off-season rates for similar reasons. The simplest of all arrival-control devices is the posting of business hours.

Some service demands are clearly *uncontrollable,* such as emergency medical demands on a city's hospital facilities. But even in these situations, arrivals at emergency rooms in specific hospitals are controllable to some extent by, say, keeping ambulance drivers in the service region informed of the status of their respective host hospitals.

---

[1] $n!$ is defined as $n(n - 1)(n - 2) \ldots (2)(1)$.

E X H I B I T S4.6
*Customer Arrivals
in Queues*

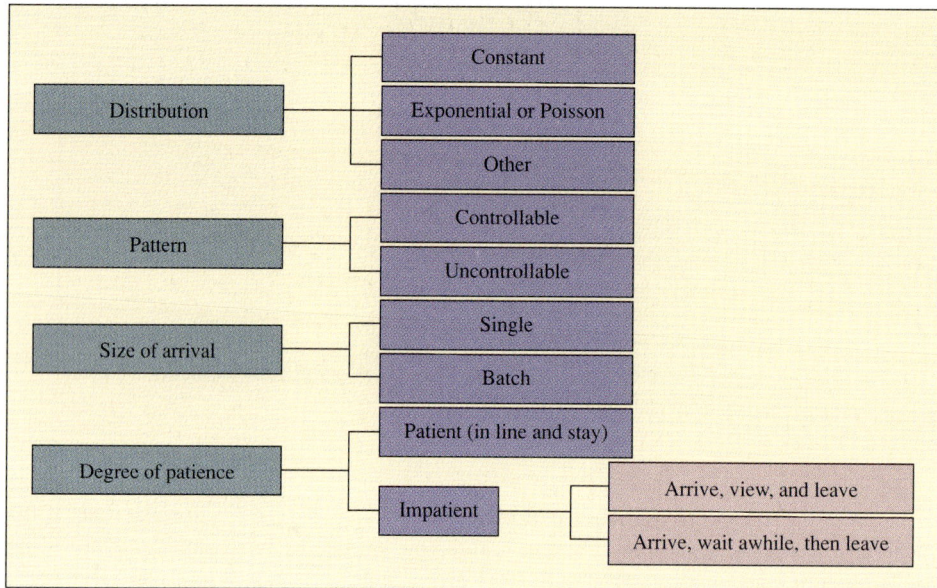

Size of arrival units   A *single arrival* may be thought of as one unit. (A unit is the smallest number handled.) A single arrival on the floor of the New York Stock Exchange (NYSE) is 100 shares of stock; a single arrival at an egg-processing plant might be a dozen eggs or a flat of 2½ dozen; or a single person at a restaurant.

A *batch arrival* is some multiple of the unit, as a block of 1,000 shares on the NYSE, a case of eggs at the processing plant, or a party of five at a restaurant.

Degree of patience   A *patient* arrival is one who waits as long as necessary until the service facility is ready to serve him or her. (Even if arrivals grumble and behave impatiently, the fact that they wait is sufficient to label them as patient arrivals for purposes of waiting line theory.)

There are two classes of *impatient* arrivals. Members of the first class arrive, survey both the service facility and the length of the line, and then decide to leave. Those in the second class arrive, view the situation, join the waiting line, and then, after some period of time, depart. The behavior of the first type is termed *balking,* while the second is termed *reneging.*

**The Queuing
System**

The queuing system consists primarily of the waiting line(s) and the available number of servers. Here we discuss issues pertaining to waiting line characteristics and management, line structure, and service rate.

The Waiting Line   Factors to consider here include the line length, number of lines, and queue discipline.

Length   In a practical sense, an infinite line is very long in terms of the capacity of the service system. Examples of *infinite potential length* are a line of vehicles backed up for miles at a bridge crossing and customers who must form a line around the block as they wait to purchase tickets at a theater.

Gas stations, loading docks, and parking lots have *limited line capacity* caused by legal restrictions or physical space characteristics. This complicates the waiting line prob-

lem not only in service system utilization and waiting line computations but also in the shape of the actual arrival distribution. The arrival denied entry into the line because of lack of space may rejoin the population for a later try or may seek service elsewhere. Either action makes an obvious difference in the finite population case.

Number of lines   A *single line* or single file is, of course, one line only. The term *multiple lines* refers either to the single lines that form in front of two or more servers or to single lines that converge at some central redistribution point. The disadvantage of multiple lines in a busy facility is that arrivals often shift lines if several previous services have been of short duration or if those customers currently in other lines appear to require a short service time.

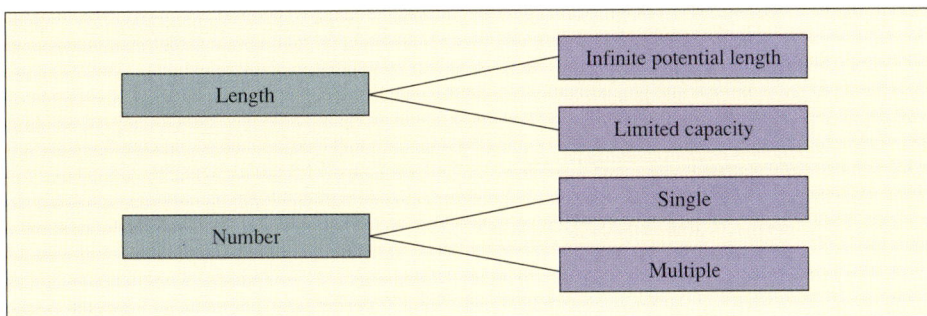

Queue discipline   A queue discipline is a priority rule or set of rules for determining the order of service to customers in a waiting line. The rules selected can have a dramatic effect on the system's overall performance. The number of customers in line, the average waiting time, the range of variability in waiting time, and the efficiency of the service facility are just a few of the factors affected by the choice of priority rules.

Probably the most common priority rule is *first come, first served* (FCFS). This rule states that customers in line are served on the basis of their chronological arrival; no other characteristics have any bearing on the selection process. This is popularly accepted as the fairest rule although in practice, it discriminates against the arrival requiring a short service time.

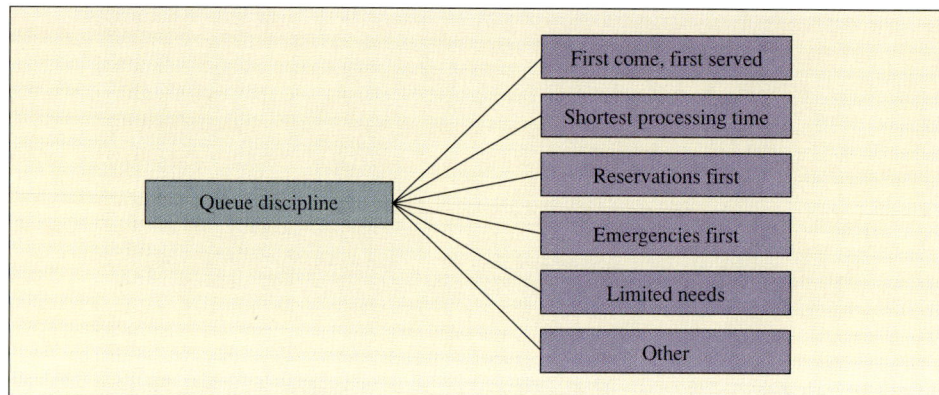

Reservations first, emergencies first, highest-profit customer first, largest orders first, best customers first, longest waiting time in line, and *soonest promised date* are other examples of priority rules. There are two major practical problems in using any rule: One is ensuring that customers know and follow the rule. The other is ensuring that a system exists to enable the employees to manage the line (e.g., take-a-number systems).

Service Time Distribution   Another important feature of the waiting structure is the time the customer or unit spends with the server once the service has started. Waiting line formulas generally specify **service rate** as the capacity of the server in number of units per time period (such as 12 completions per hour) and *not* as service time, which might average five minutes each. A *constant* service time rule states that each service takes exactly the same time. As in constant arrivals, this characteristic is generally limited to machine-controlled operations.

When service times are random, a good approximation of them can be given by the exponential distribution described under the heading "Distribution of Arrivals." When using the exponential distribution as an approximation of the service times, we will refer to μ as the average number of units or customers that can be served per time period.

Line Structures   As the figure on page 141 shows, the flow of items to be serviced may go through a single line, multiple lines, or some mixtures of the two. The choice of format depends partly on the volume of customers served and partly on the restrictions imposed by sequential requirements governing the order in which service must be performed.

Single channel, single phase   This is the simplest type of waiting line structure, and straightforward formulas are available to solve the problem for standard distribution patterns of arrival and service. When the distributions are nonstandard, the problem is easily solved by computer simulation. A typical example of a single-channel, single-phase situation is the one-person barbershop.

Single channel, multiphase   A car wash is an illustration since a series of services (vacuuming, wetting, washing, rinsing, drying, window cleaning, and parking) is performed in a fairly uniform sequence. A critical factor in the single-channel case with service in series is the amount of buildup of items allowed in front of each service, which in turn constitutes separate waiting lines.

Multichannel, single phase   Tellers' windows in a bank and checkout counters in high-volume department stores exemplify this type of structure. The difficulty with this format is that the uneven service time given each customer results in unequal speed or flow among the lines. This results in some customers being served before others who arrived earlier as well as in some degree of line shifting. Varying this structure to ensure the servicing of arrivals in chronological order would require forming a single line, from which, as a server becomes available, the next customer in the queue is assigned.

The major problem of this structure is that it requires rigid control of the line to maintain order and to direct customers to available servers. In some instances, assigning numbers to customers in order of their arrival helps alleviate this problem.

Multichannel, multiphase   This case is similar to the preceding one except that two or more services are performed in sequence. The admission of patients in a hospital follows this pattern because a specific sequence of steps is usually followed: initial contact at the admissions desk, filling out forms, making identification tags, obtaining a room assignment, escorting the patient to the room, and so forth. Since several servers are usually available for this procedure, more than one patient at a time may be processed.

Line Structures

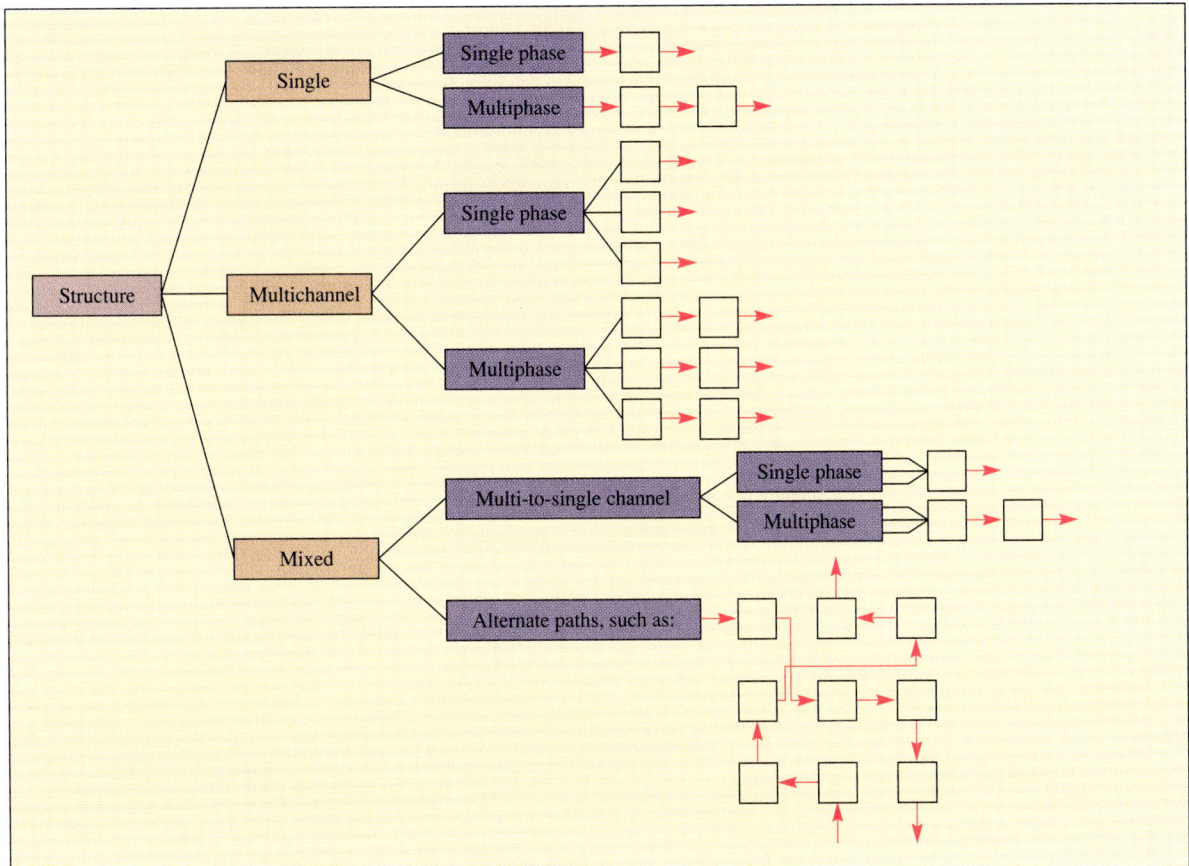

Mixed   Under this general heading, we may consider two subcategories: *(a) multiple-to-single channel structures* and *(b) alternate path structures.* Under *(a),* we find either lines that merge into one for single-phase service, as at a bridge crossing where two lanes merge into one, or lines that merge into one for multiphase service, such as subassembly lines feeding into a main line. Under *(b),* we encounter two structures that differ in directional flow requirements. The first is similar to the multichannel–multiphase case, except that (1) there may be switching from one channel to the next after the first service has been rendered and (2) the number of channels and phases may vary—again—after performance of the first service.

Exit

Once a customer is served, two exit fates are possible. (1) The customer may return to the source population and immediately become a competing candidate for service again. (2) There may be a low probability of reservice. The first case can be illustrated by a machine that has been routinely repaired and returned to duty but may break down again; the second can be illustrated by a machine that has been overhauled or modified and has a low probability of reservice over the near future. In a lighter vein, we might refer to the first as the "recurring-common-cold case" and to the second as the "appendectomy-only-once case."

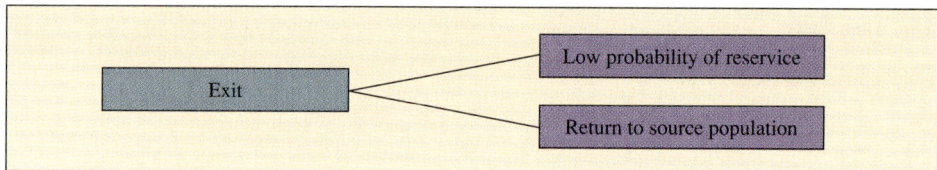

It should be apparent that when the population source is finite, any change in the service performed on customers who return to the population modifies the arrival rate at the service facility. This, of course, alters the characteristics of the waiting line under study and necessitates reanalysis of the problem.

S4.3   WAITING LINE MODELS

In this section we present four sample waiting line problems followed by their solutions. Each has a slightly different structure (see Exhibit S4.7) and solution equation (see Exhibit S4.9). There are more types of models than these four, but the formulas and solutions become quite complicated and those problems are generally solved using computer simulation. Also, in using these formulas, keep in mind that they are steady-state formulas derived on the assumption that the process under study is ongoing. Thus, they may provide inaccurate results when applied to initial operations (such as the start of a new business day by a service firm) until the system settles down to the steady state.

Here is a quick preview of our four problems to illustrate each of the four waiting line models in Exhibits S4.7 and S4.9. Exhibit S4.8 defines the notations used in Exhibit S4.9.)

Problem 1: Customers in line. A bank wants to know how many customers are waiting for a drive-in teller, how long they have to wait, the utilization of the teller, and what the service rate would have to be so that 95 percent of the time there will not be more than three cars in the system at any one time.

Problem 2: Equipment selection. A franchise for Robot Car Wash must decide which equipment to purchase out of a choice of three. Larger units cost more, but wash cars faster. To make the decision, costs are related to revenue.

Problem 3: Determining the number of servers. An auto agency parts department must decide how many clerks to employ at the counter. More clerks cost more money, but there is a savings because mechanics wait less time.

Problem 4: Finite population source. Whereas the previous models assume a large population, finite queuing employs a separate set of equations for those cases where the calling customer population is small. In this last problem, there are just four weaving machines that mechanics must service to keep them operating. Based on the costs associated with machines being idle and the costs of mechanics to service them, the problem is to decide how many mechanics to use.

E X H I B I T   S4.7   *Properties of Some Specific Waiting Line Models*

Model	Layout	Service Phase	Source Population	Arrival Pattern	Queue Discipline	Service Pattern	Permissible Queue Length	Typical Example
1	Single channel	Single	Infinite	Poisson	FCFS	Exponential	Unlimited	Drive-in teller at bank, one-lane toll bridge
2	Single channel	Single	Infinite	Poisson	FCFS	Constant	Unlimited	Automatic car wash, roller coaster rides in amusement park
3	Multichannel	Single	Infinite	Poisson	FCFS	Exponential	Unlimited	Parts counter in auto agency, check out lines in a supermarket
4	Single channel	Single	Finite	Poisson	FCFS	Exponential	Unlimited	Machine breakdown and repair in a factory

E X H I B I T   S4.8   *Notations for Equations (Exhibit S4.9)*

Infinite Queuing Notation: Models 1–3	Finite Queuing Notation: Model 4

Infinite Queuing Notation: Models 1–3

λ = Arrival rate
μ = Service rate
$\dfrac{1}{\mu}$ = Average service time
$\dfrac{1}{\lambda}$ = Average time between arrivals
ρ = Potential utilization of the service facility (defined as λ/μ)
$\bar{n}_l$ = Average number waiting in line
$\bar{n}_s$ = Average number in system (including any being served)
$\bar{t}_l$ = Average time waiting in line
$\bar{t}_s$ = Average total time in system (including time to be served)
n = Number of units in the system
M = Number of identical service channels
P_n = Probability of exactly n units in system
P_w = Probability of waiting in line

Finite Queuing Notation: Model 4

D = Probability that an arrival must wait in line
F = Efficiency factor, a measure of the effect of having to wait in line
H = Average number of units being serviced
J = Population source less those in queuing system $(N - n)$
L = Average number of units in line
M = Number of service channels
n = Average number of units in queuing system (including the one being served)
N = Number of units in population source
P_n = Probability of exactly n units in queuing system
T = Average time to perform the service
U = Average time between customer service requirements
W = Average waiting time in line
X = Service factor, or proportion of service time required

Model 1

$$\bar{n}_l = \frac{\lambda^2}{\mu(\mu - \lambda)} \qquad \bar{t}_l = \frac{\lambda}{\mu(\mu - \lambda)} \qquad P_n = \left(1 - \frac{\lambda}{\mu}\right)\left(\frac{\lambda}{\mu}\right)^n$$

$$\bar{n}_s = \frac{\lambda}{\mu - \lambda} \qquad \bar{t}_s = \frac{1}{\mu - \lambda} \qquad \rho = \frac{\lambda}{\mu}$$

(S4.3)

Model 2

$$\bar{n}_l = \frac{\lambda^2}{2\mu(\mu - \lambda)} \qquad \bar{t}_l = \frac{\lambda}{2\mu(\mu - \lambda)}$$

$$\bar{n}_s = \bar{n}_l + \frac{\lambda}{\mu} \qquad \bar{t}_s = \bar{t}_l + \frac{1}{\mu}$$

(S4.4)

(Exhibit S4.10 provides the value of $\bar{n}_l$ given $\rho = \lambda/\mu$ and the number of servers M.)

Model 3

$$\begin{cases} \bar{n}_s = \bar{n}_l + \lambda/\mu \\ \bar{t}_l = \bar{n}_l/\lambda \\ \bar{t}_s = \bar{n}_l/\lambda + 1/\mu \\ P_w = \bar{n}_l(M - \rho)/\rho \end{cases}$$

(S4.5)

Model 4 is a finite queuing situation that is most easily solved by using finite tables. These tables, in turn, require the manipulation of specific terms.

Model 4

$$X = \frac{T}{T + U} \qquad\qquad H = FNX \qquad\qquad L = N(1 - F) \qquad\qquad n = L + H$$

$$P_n = \frac{N!}{(N - n)!} X^n P_0 \qquad\qquad\qquad\qquad J = NF(1 - X)$$

$$W = \frac{L(T + U)}{N - L} = \frac{LT}{H} \qquad\qquad\qquad F = \frac{T + U}{T + U + W}$$

(S4.6)

E X A M P L E S4.1 / *Customers in Line*   Western National Bank is considering opening a drive-in window for customer service. Management estimates that customers will arrive at the rate of 15 per hour. The teller who will staff the window can service customers at the rate of one every three minutes.

Part 1   Assuming Poisson arrivals and exponential service, find

1. Utilization of the teller.
2. Average number in the waiting line.
3. Average number in the system.
4. Average waiting time in line.
5. Average waiting time in the system, including service.

S O L U T I O N — *PART 1*

1. The average utilization of the teller is

$$\rho = \frac{\lambda}{\mu} = \frac{15}{20} = 75 \text{ percent}$$

2. The average number in the waiting line is

$$\bar{n}_l = \frac{\lambda^2}{\mu(\mu - \lambda)} = \frac{(15)^2}{20(20 - 15)} = 2.25 \text{ customers}$$

3. The average number in the system is

$$\bar{n}_s = \frac{\lambda}{\mu - \lambda} = \frac{15}{20 - 15} = 3 \text{ customers}$$

4. Average waiting time in line is

$$\bar{t}_l = \frac{\lambda}{\mu(\mu - \lambda)} = \frac{15}{20(20 - 15)} = 0.15 \text{ hour, or 9 minutes}$$

5. Average waiting time in the system is

$$\bar{t}_s = \frac{1}{\mu - \lambda} = \frac{1}{20 - 15} = 0.2 \text{ hour, or 12 minutes}$$

Part 2 Because of limited space availability and a desire to provide an acceptable level of service, the bank manager would like to ensure, with 95 percent confidence, that not more than three cars will be in the system at any one time. What is the present level of service for the three-car limit? What level of teller use must be attained and what must be the service rate of the teller to ensure the 95 percent level of service?

S O L U T I O N — *PART 2* The present level of service for three cars or less is the probability that there are 0, 1, 2, or 3 cars in the system. From Model 1, Exhibit S4.9,

$$P_n = \left(1 - \frac{\lambda}{\mu}\right)\left(\frac{\lambda}{\mu}\right)^n$$

at $n = 0$, $P_0 = (1 - 15/20)$ $\quad (15/20)^0 = 0.250$
at $n = 1$, $P_1 = (1/4)$ $\quad\quad\quad (15/20)^1 = 0.188$
at $n = 2$, $P_2 = (1/4)$ $\quad\quad\quad (15/20)^2 = 0.141$
at $n = 3$, $P_3 = (1/4)$ $\quad\quad\quad (15/20)^3 = \underline{0.106}$
$\quad\quad\quad\quad\quad\quad\quad\quad\quad\quad\quad\quad\quad\quad\quad 0.685 \text{ or } 68.5 \text{ percent}$

The probability of having more than three cars in the system is 1.0 minus the probability of three cars or fewer ($1.0 - 0.685 = 31.5$ percent).

For a 95 percent service level to three cars or fewer, this states that $P_0 + P_1 + P_2 + P_3 = 95$ percent.

$$0.95 = \left(1 - \frac{\lambda}{\mu}\right)\left(\frac{\lambda}{\mu}\right)^0 + \left(1 - \frac{\lambda}{\mu}\right)\left(\frac{\lambda}{\mu}\right)^1 + \left(1 - \frac{\lambda}{\mu}\right)\left(\frac{\lambda}{\mu}\right)^2 + \left(1 - \frac{\lambda}{\mu}\right)\left(\frac{\lambda}{\mu}\right)^3$$

$$0.95 = \left(1 - \frac{\lambda}{\mu}\right)\left[1 + \frac{\lambda}{\mu} + \left(\frac{\lambda}{\mu}\right)^2 + \left(\frac{\lambda}{\mu}\right)^3\right]$$

We can solve this by trial and error for values of λ/μ. If $\lambda/\mu = 0.50$,

$0.95 \overset{?}{=} 0.5(1 + 0.5 + 0.25 + 0.125)$
$0.95 \neq 0.9375$

With $\lambda/\mu = 0.45$,

$0.95 \overset{?}{=} (1 - 0.45)(1 + 0.45 + 0.203 + 0.091)$
$0.95 \neq 0.96$

With $\lambda/\mu = 0.47$,

$0.95 \overset{?}{=} (1 - 0.47)(1 + 0.47 + 0.221 + 0.104) = 0.9512$
$0.95 \approx 0.95135$

Therefore, with the utilization $\rho = \lambda/\mu$ of 47 percent, the probability of three cars or fewer in the system is 95 percent.

To find the rate of service required to attain this 95 percent service level, we simply solve the equation $\lambda/\mu = 0.47$, where λ = number of arrivals per hour. This gives $\mu = 32$ per hour.

That is, the teller must serve approximately 32 people per hour (a 60 percent increase over the original 20-per-hour capability) for 95 percent confidence that not more than three cars will be in the system. Perhaps service may be speeded up by modifying the method of service, adding another teller, or limiting the types of transactions available at the drive-in window. Note that with the condition of 95 percent confidence that three or fewer cars will be in the system, the teller will be idle 53 percent of the time. ■

E X A M P L E S4.2 / *Equipment Selection*   The Robot Company franchises combination gas and car wash stations throughout the United States. Robot gives a free car wash for a gasoline fill-up or, for a wash alone, charges $0.50. Past experience shows that the number of customers that have car washes following fill-ups is about the same as for a wash alone. The average profit on a gasoline fill-up is about $0.70, and the cost of the car wash to Robot is $0.10. Robot stays open 14 hours per day.

Robot has three power units and drive assemblies, and a franchisee must select the unit preferred. Unit I can wash cars at the rate of one every five minutes and is leased for $12 per day. Unit II, a larger unit, can wash cars at the rate of one every four minutes but costs $16 per day. Unit III, the largest, costs $22 per day and can wash a car in three minutes.

The franchisee estimates that customers will not wait in line more than five minutes for a car wash. A longer time will cause Robot to lose the gasoline sales as well as the car wash sale.

If the estimate of customer arrivals resulting in washes is 10 per hour, which wash unit should be selected?

S O L U T I O N   Using unit I, calculate the average waiting time of customers in the wash line (μ for unit I = 12 per hour). From the Model 2 equations (Exhibit S4.9),

$$\bar{t}_l = \frac{\lambda}{2\mu(\mu - \lambda)} = \frac{10}{2(12)(12 - 10)} = 0.208 \text{ hour, or } 12\tfrac{1}{2} \text{ minutes}$$

For unit II at 15 per hour,

$$\bar{t}_l = \frac{10}{2(15)(15 - 10)} = 0.067 \text{ hour, or 4 minutes}$$

If waiting time is the only criterion, unit II should be purchased. But before we make the final decision, we must look at the profit differential between both units.

With unit I, some customers would balk and renege because of the 12½-minute wait. And although this greatly complicates the mathematical analysis, we can gain some estimate of lost sales with unit I by inserting $i = 5$ minutes or $\tfrac{1}{12}$ hour (the average length of time customers will wait) and solving for λ. This would be the effective arrival rate of customers:

$$\bar{t}_l = \frac{\lambda}{2\mu(\mu - \lambda)}$$

$$\lambda = \frac{2\bar{t}_l\lambda^2}{1 + 2\bar{t}_l\mu}$$

$$\lambda = \frac{2(\tfrac{1}{12})(12)^2}{1 + 2(\tfrac{1}{12})(12)} = 8 \text{ per hour}$$

Therefore, since the original estimate of λ was 10 per hour, an estimated 2 customers per hour will be lost. Lost profit of 2 customers per hour $\times$ 14 hours $\times$ ½ ($0.70 fill-up profit + $0.40 wash profit) = $15.40 per day.

Because the additional cost of unit II over unit I is only $4 per day, the loss of $15.40 profit obviously warrants installing unit II.

The original five-minute maximum wait constraint is satisfied by unit II. Therefore unit III is not considered unless the arrival rate is expected to increase. ■

E X A M P L E S4.3 / *Determining the Number of Servers*   In the service department of the Glenn-Mark Auto Agency, mechanics requiring parts for auto repair or service present their request forms at the parts department counter. The parts clerk fills a request while the mechanic waits. Mechanics arrive in a random (Poisson) fashion at the rate of 40 per hour, and a clerk can fill requests at the rate of 20 per hour (exponential). If the cost for a parts clerk is $6 per hour and the cost for a mechanic is $12 per hour, determine the optimum number of clerks to staff the counter. (Because of the high arrival rate, an infinite source may be assumed.)

S O L U T I O N   First, assume that three clerks will be used because having only one or two clerks would create infinitely long lines (since $\lambda = 40$ and $\mu = 20$). The equations for Model 3 from Exhibit S4.9 will be used here. But first we need to obtain the average number in line using the table of Exhibit S4.10. Using the table and values $\lambda/\mu = 2$ and $M = 3$, we obtain $\bar{n}_l = 0.8888$ mechanic.

At this point, we see that we have an average of 0.8888 mechanic waiting all day. For an eight-hour day at $12 per hour, there is a loss of mechanic's time worth 0.8888 mechanic $\times$ $12 per hour $\times$ 8 hours = $85.32.

Our next step is to reobtain the waiting time if we add another parts clerk. We then compare the added cost of the additional employee with the time saved by the mechanics. Again, using the table of Exhibit S4.10 but with $M = 4$, we obtain

$\bar{n}_l = 0.1730$ mechanic in line

$0.1730 \times \$12 \times 8$ hours = $16.61 cost of a mechanic waiting in line

Value of mechanics' time saved is $85.32 - $16.61 = $68.71

Cost of additional parts clerk is 8 hour $\times$ $6/hour   =   48.00

Cost reduction by adding fourth clerk   = $20.71

This problem could be expanded to consider the addition of runners to deliver parts to mechanics; the problem then would be to determine the optimal number of runners. This, however, would have to include the added cost of lost time caused by errors in parts receipts. For example, a mechanic would recognize a wrong part at the counter and obtain immediate correction, whereas the parts runner might not. ■

E X H I B I T S4.10 *Expected Number of People Waiting in Line (n_l) for Various Values of M and ρ*

ρ	\multicolumn{15}{c}{Number of Service Channels, M}
	1	2	3	4	5	6	7	8	9	10	11	12	13	14	15
0.10	0.0111														
0.15	0.0264	0.0006													
0.20	0.0500	0.0020													
0.25	0.0833	0.0039													
0.30	0.1285	0.0069													
0.35	0.1884	0.0110													
0.40	0.2666	0.0166													
0.45	0.3681	0.0239	0.0019												
0.50	0.5000	0.0333	0.0030												
0.55	0.6722	0.0449	0.0043												
0.60	0.9090	0.0593	0.0061												
0.65	1.2071	0.0767	0.0084												
0.70	1.6333	0.0976	0.0112												
0.75	2.2500	0.1227	0.0147												
0.80	3.2000	0.1523	0.0189	0.0031											
0.85	4.8165	0.1873	0.0239	0.0041											
0.90	8.1000	0.2285	0.0300	0.0053											
0.95	18.0500	0.2767	0.0371	0.0053											
1.0		0.3333	0.0454	0.0067											
1.2		0.6748	0.0904	0.0158											
1.4		1.3449	0.1778	0.0324	0.0059										
1.6		2.8441	0.3128	0.0604	0.0121										
1.8		7.6731	0.5320	0.1051	0.0227	0.0047									
2.0			0.8888	0.1730	0.0390	0.0090									
2.2			1.4907	0.2770	0.0759	0.0158									
2.4			2.1261	0.4205	0.1047	0.0266	0.0065								
2.6			4.9322	0.6581	0.1609	0.0425	0.0110								
2.8			12.2724	1.0000	0.2411	0.0659	0.0180								
3.0				1.5282	0.3541	0.0991	0.0282	0.0077							
3.2				2.3855	0.5128	0.1452	0.0427	0.0122							
3.4				3.9060	0.7365	0.2085	0.0631	0.0189							
3.6				7.0893	1.0550	0.2947	0.0912	0.0283	0.0084						
3.8				16.9366	1.5181	0.4114	0.1292	0.0412	0.0127						

4.0	2.2164	0.5694	0.1801	0.0590	0.0189			
4.2	3.3269	0.7837	0.2475	0.0827	0.0273	0.0087		
4.4	5.2675	1.0777	0.3364	0.1142	0.0389	0.0128		
4.6	9.2885	1.4857	0.4532	0.1555	0.0541	0.0184		
4.8	21.6384	2.0708	0.6071	0.2092	0.0742	0.0260		
5.0	2.9375	0.8102	0.2785	0.1006	0.0361	0.0125		
5.2	4.3004	1.0804	0.3680	0.1345	0.0492	0.0175		
5.4	6.6609	1.4441	0.5871	0.1779	0.0663	0.0243	0.0085	
5.6	11.5178	1.9436	0.6313	0.2330	0.0683	0.0330	0.0119	
5.8	26.3726	2.6481	0.8225	0.3032	0.1164	0.0443	0.0164	
6.0	3.6878	1.0707	0.3918	0.1518	0.0590	0.0224		
6.2	5.2979	1.3967	0.5037	0.1964	0.0775	0.0300	0.0113	
6.4	8.0768	1.8040	0.6454	0.2524	0.1008	0.0398	0.0153	
6.6	13.7992	2.4198	0.8247	0.3222	0.1302	0.0523	0.0205	
6.8	31.1270	3.2441	1.0533	0.4090	0.1666	0.0679	0.0271	0.0105
7.0	4.4471	1.3471	0.5172	0.2119	0.0876	0.0357	0.0141	
7.2	6.3133	1.7288	0.6521	0.2677	0.1119	0.0463	0.0187	
7.4	9.5102	2.2324	0.8202	0.3364	0.1420	0.0595	0.0245	0.0097
7.6	16.0379	2.9113	1.0310	0.4211	0.1789	0.0761	0.0318	0.0129
7.8	35.8956	3.8558	1.2972	0.5250	0.2243	0.0966	0.0410	0.0168
8.0	5.2264	1.6364	0.6530	0.2796	0.1214	0.0522		
8.2	7.3441	2.0736	0.8109	0.3469	0.1520	0.0663		
8.4	10.9592	2.6470	1.0060	0.4288	0.1891	0.0834		
8.6	18.3223	3.4160	1.2484	0.5236	0.2341	0.1043		
8.8	40.6824	4.4805	1.5524	0.6501	0.2885	0.1208		
9.0	6.0183	1.9366	0.7980	0.3543	0.1603	0.0723		
9.2	8.3869	2.4293	0.9788	0.4333	0.1974	0.0899		
9.4	12.4183	3.0732	1.2010	0.5267	0.2419	0.1111		
9.6	20.6160	3.9318	1.4752	0.5437	0.2952	0.1367		
9.8	45.4769	5.1156	1.8165	0.7827	0.3699	0.1673		
10	6.8210	2.2465	0.9506	0.4352	0.2040			

E X A M P L E S4.4 / *Finite Population Source* Studies of a bank of four weaving machines at the Loose Knit textile mill have shown that, on average, each machine needs adjusting every hour and that the current serviceperson averages 7½ minutes per adjustment. Assuming Poisson arrivals, exponential service, and a machine idle time cost of $40 per hour, determine if a second serviceperson (who also averages 7½ minutes per adjustment) should be hired at a rate of $7 per hour.

S O L U T I O N This is a finite queuing problem that can be solved by using finite queuing tables. (See Exhibit S4.11.) The approach in this problem is to compare the costs of machine downtime (either waiting in line or being serviced) and the cost of one repairperson, to the cost of machine downtime and two repairpeople. We do this by finding the average number of machines that are in the service system and multiply this number by the downtime cost per hour. To this we add the repairpeople's cost.

Before we proceed, we first define some terms:

N = Number of machines in the population

M = Number of repairpeople

T = Time required to service a machine

U = Average time a machine runs before requiring service

X = Service factor, or proportion of service time required for each machine (X = $T/(T + U)$)

L = Average number of machines waiting in line to be serviced ·

H = Average number of machines being serviced

The values to be determined from the finite tables are

D = Probability that a machine needing service will have to wait

F = Efficiency factor, which is a measure of the effect of having to wait in line to be serviced

The tables are arranged according to three variables: N, population size; X, service factor; and M, the number of service channels (repairpeople in this problem). To look up a value, first find the table for the correct N size, then search the first column for the appropriate X, and finally find the line for M. Then read off D and F. (In addition to these values, other characteristics about a finite queuing system can be found by using the finite formulas.)

To solve the problem, consider Case I with one repairperson and Case II with two repairpeople.

Case I: One repairperson. From the problem statement,

$N = 4$

$M = 1$

$T = 7½$ minutes

$U = 60$ minutes

$$X = \frac{T}{T + U} = \frac{7.5}{7.5 + 60} = 0.111$$

From Exhibit S4.11, which displays the table for $N = 4$, F is interpolated as being approximately 0.957 at $X = 0.111$ and $M = 1$.

The number of machines waiting in line to be serviced is L, where

$$L = N(1 - F) = 4(1 - 0.957) = 0.172 \text{ machines}$$

EXHIBIT S4.11
Finite Queuing Tables

Population 4

X	M	D	F
.015	1	.045	.999
.022	1	.066	.998
.030	1	.090	.997
.034	1	.102	.996
.038	1	.114	.995
.042	1	.126	.994
.046	1	.137	.993
.048	1	.143	.992
.052	1	.155	.991
.054	1	.161	.990
.058	1	.173	.989
.060	1	.179	.988
.062	1	.184	.987
.064	1	.190	.986
.066	1	.196	.985
.070	2	.014	.999
	1	.208	.984
.075	2	.016	.999
	1	.222	.981
.080	2	.018	.999
	1	.237	.978
.085	2	.021	.999
	1	.251	.975
.090	2	.023	.999
	1	.265	.972
.095	2	.026	.999
	1	.280	.969
.100	2	.028	.999
	1	.294	.965
.105	2	.031	.998
	1	.308	.962
.110	2	.034	.998
	1	.321	.958
.115	2	.037	.998
	1	.335	.954
.120	2	.041	.997
	1	.349	.950
.125	2	.044	.997
	1	.362	.945
.130	2	.047	.997
	1	.376	.941
.135	2	.051	.996
	1	.389	.936
.140	2	.055	.996
	1	.402	.931
.145	2	.058	.995
	1	.415	.926
.150	2	.062	.995
	1	.428	.921
.155	2	.066	.994
	1	.441	.916
.160	2	.071	.994
	1	.454	.910
.165	2	.075	.993
	1	.466	.904
.170	2	.079	.993
	1	.479	.899
.180	2	.088	.991
	1	.503	.887
.190	2	.098	.990
	1	.526	.874
.200	3	.008	.999
	2	.108	.988
.200	1	.549	.862
.210	3	.009	.999
	2	.118	.986
	1	.572	.849
.220	3	.011	.999
	2	.129	.984
	1	.593	.835
.230	3	.012	.999
	2	.140	.982
	1	.614	.822
.240	3	.014	.999
	2	.151	.980
	1	.634	.808
.250	3	.016	.999
	2	.163	.977
	1	.654	.794
.260	3	.018	.998
	2	.175	.975
	1	.673	.780
.270	3	.020	.998
	2	.187	.972
	1	.691	.766
.280	3	.022	.998
	2	.200	.968
	1	.708	.752
.290	3	.024	.998
	2	.213	.965
	1	.725	.738
.300	3	.027	.997
	2	.226	.962
	1	.741	.724
.310	3	.030	.997
	2	.240	.958
	1	.756	.710
.320	3	.033	.997
	2	.254	.954
	1	.771	.696
.330	3	.036	.996
	2	.268	.950
	1	.785	.683
.340	3	.039	.996
	2	.282	.945
	1	.798	.670
.360	3	.047	.994
	2	.312	.936
	1	.823	.644
.380	3	.055	.993
	2	.342	.926
	1	.846	.619
.400	3	.064	.992
	2	.372	.915
	1	.866	.595
.420	3	.074	.990
	2	.403	.903
	1	.884	.572
.440	3	.085	.986
	2	.435	.891
	1	.900	.551
.460	3	.097	.985
	2	.466	.878
	1	.914	.530
.480	3	.111	.983
	2	.498	.864
.480	1	.926	.511
.500	3	.125	.980
	2	.529	.850
	1	.937	.492
.520	3	.141	.976
	2	.561	.835
	1	.947	.475
.540	3	.157	.972
	2	.592	.820
	1	.956	.459
.560	3	.176	.968
	2	.623	.805
	1	.963	.443
.580	3	.195	.964
	2	.653	.789
	1	.969	.429
.600	3	.216	.959
	2	.682	.774
	1	.975	.415
.650	3	.275	.944
	2	.752	.734
	1	.985	.384
.700	3	.343	.926
	2	.816	.695
	1	.991	.357
.750	3	.422	.905
	2	.871	.657
	1	.996	.333
.800	3	.512	.880
	2	.917	.621
	1	.998	.312
.850	3	.614	.852
	2	.954	.587
	1	.999	.294
.900	3	.729	.821
	2	.979	.555
.950	3	.857	.786
	2	.995	.526

Number of Repair people	Number of Machines Down $(H + L)$	Cost per Hour for Machines Down $[(H + L) \times \$40/\text{hour}]$	Cost of Repairpeople ($7/hour Each)	Total Cost per Hour
1	0.597	$23.88	$ 7.00	$30.88
2	0.451	18.04	14.00	32.04

The number of machines being serviced is H, where

$$H = FNX = 0.957(4)(0.111) = 0.425 \text{ machines}$$

Exhibit S4.12 shows the cost resulting from unproductive machine time and the cost of the repairperson.

Case II: Two repairpeople. From Exhibit S4.11, at $X = 0.111$ and $M = 2$, $F = 0.998$. The number of machines waiting in line, L, is

$$L = N(1 - F) = 4(1 - 0.998) = 0.008 \text{ machines}$$

The number of machines being serviced, H, is

$$H = FNX = 0.998(4)(0.111) = 0.443 \text{ machines}$$

The costs for the machines being idle and for the two repairpeople are shown in Exhibit S4.12. The final column of that exhibit shows that retaining just one repairperson is the best choice. ∎

S4.4   COMPUTER SIMULATION OF WAITING LINES

Some waiting line problems that seem very simple on first impression turn out to be extremely difficult or impossible to solve. Throughout this supplement we have been treating waiting line situations that are independent; that is, either the entire system consists of a single phase, or else each service that is performed in a series is independent. (This could happen if the output of one service location is allowed to build up in front of the next one so that this, in essence, becomes a calling population for the next service.) When a series of services is performed in sequence where the output rate of one becomes the input rate of the next, we can no longer use the simple formulas. This is also true for any problem where conditions do not meet the conditions of the equations, as specified in Exhibit S4.8. The technique best suited to solving this type of problem is computer simulation. We treat the topic of modeling and simulation in the Supplement to Chapter 16, and we also include a waiting line problem that can only be solved on a computer.

S4.5   CONCLUSION

Waiting line problems both challenge and frustrate those who try to solve them. The basic objective is to balance the cost of waiting with the cost of adding more resources. For a service system this means that the utilization of a server may be quite low to provide a short waiting time to the customer. One main concern in dealing with waiting line problems is what procedure or priority rule to use in selecting the next product or customer to be served.

Many queuing problems appear simple until an attempt is made to solve them. This supplement has dealt with the simpler problems. When the situation becomes more complex, when there are multiple phases or where services are performed only in a particular sequence, computer simulation is necessary to obtain the optimal solution.

S4.6 FORMULA REVIEW

Exponential distribution

$$f(t) = \lambda e^{-\lambda t} \tag{S4.1}$$

Poisson distribution

$$P_T(n) = \frac{(\lambda T)^n e^{-\lambda T}}{n!} \tag{S4.2}$$

Model 1 (See Exhibit S4.7.)

$$\bar{n}_l = \frac{\lambda^2}{\mu(\mu - \lambda)} \quad \bar{t}_l = \frac{\lambda}{\mu(\mu - \lambda)} \qquad P_n = \left(1 - \frac{\lambda}{\mu}\right)\left(\frac{\lambda}{\mu}\right)^n \tag{S4.3}$$

$$\bar{n}_s = \frac{\lambda}{\mu - \lambda} \qquad \bar{t}_s = \frac{1}{\mu - \lambda} \qquad \rho = \frac{\lambda}{\mu}$$

Model 2

$$\bar{n}_l = \frac{\lambda^2}{2\mu(\mu - \lambda)} \qquad \bar{t}_l = \frac{\lambda}{2\mu(\mu - \lambda)} \tag{S4.4}$$

$$\bar{n}_s = \bar{n}_l + \frac{\lambda}{\mu} \qquad \bar{t}_s = \bar{t}_l + \frac{1}{\mu}$$

Model 3

$$\bar{n}_s = \bar{n}_l + \lambda/\mu \tag{S4.5}$$
$$\bar{t}_l = \bar{n}_l/\lambda$$
$$\bar{t}_s = \bar{n}_l/\lambda + 1/\mu$$
$$P_w = \bar{n}_l(M - \rho)/\rho$$

Model 4

$$X = \frac{T}{T + U} \qquad H = FNX \qquad L = N(1 - F) \qquad n = L + H \tag{S4.6}$$

$$P_n = \frac{N!}{(N - n)!} X^n P_0 \qquad\qquad J = NF(1 - X)$$

$$W = \frac{L(T + U)}{N - L} = \frac{LT}{H} \qquad F = \frac{T + U}{T + U + W}$$

S4.7 SOLVED PROBLEMS

1. Quick Lube Inc. operates a fast lube and oil change garage. On a typical day, customers arrive at the rate of three per hour, and lube jobs are performed at an average rate of one every 15 minutes. The mechanics operate as a team on one car at a time.

   Assuming Poisson arrivals and exponential service, find

   a. Utilization of the lube team.

   b. The average number of cars in line.

   c. The average time a car waits before it is lubed.

   d. The total time it takes to go through the system (i.e., waiting in line plus lube time.)

Solution

$$\lambda = 3, \ \mu = 4$$

a. Utilization $\rho = \dfrac{\lambda}{\mu} = \dfrac{3}{4} = 75\%$.

b. $\bar{n}_l = \dfrac{\lambda^2}{\mu(\mu - \lambda)} = \dfrac{3^2}{4(4 - 3)} = \dfrac{9}{4} = 2.25$ cars in line.

c. $\bar{t}_l = \dfrac{\lambda}{\mu(\mu - \lambda)} = \dfrac{3}{4(4 - 3)} = \dfrac{3}{4} = 45$ minutes in line.

d. $\bar{t}_s = \dfrac{1}{\mu - \lambda} = \dfrac{1}{1} = 1$ hour (waiting + lube).

2. American Vending Inc. (AVI) supplies vended food to a large university. Because students kick the machines at every opportunity out of anger and frustration, management has a constant repair problem. The machines break down on an average of three per hour, and the breakdowns are distributed in a Poisson manner. Downtime costs the company \$25/hour per machine, and each maintenance worker gets \$4 per hour. One worker can service machines at an average rate of five per hour, distributed exponentially; two workers working together can service seven per hour, distributed exponentially; and a team of three workers can do eight per hour, distributed exponentially.

   What is the optimum maintenance crew size for servicing the machines?

Solution

Case I: One worker.

$\lambda = 3$/hour Poisson, $\mu = 5$/hour exponential

There is an average number of machines in the system of:

$$\bar{n}_s = \frac{\lambda}{\mu - \lambda} = \frac{3}{5 - 3} = \frac{3}{2} = 1\frac{1}{2} \text{ machines}$$

Downtime cost is \$25 × 1.5 = \$37.50 per hour; repair cost is \$4.00 per hour; and total cost per hour for 1 worker is \$37.50 + \$4.00 = \$41.50.

Downtime (1.5 × \$25) = \$37.50
Labor (1 worker × \$4) =   4.00
                         $\overline{\$41.50}$

Case II: Two workers:

$\lambda = 3, \ \mu = 7$

$$\bar{n}_s = \frac{\lambda}{\mu - \lambda} = \frac{3}{7 - 3} = .75 \text{ machines}$$

Downtime (.75 × \$25)   = \$18.75
Labor (2 workers × \$4.00) =   8.00
                            $\overline{\$26.75}$

Case III: Three workers.

$\lambda = 3, \ \mu = 8$

$$\bar{n}_s = \frac{\lambda}{\mu - \lambda} = \frac{3}{8 - 5} = \frac{3}{5} = .60 \text{ machines}$$

Downtime (.60 × \$25) = \$15.00
Labor (3 workers × \$4) = 12.00
                         $\overline{\$27.00}$

Comparing the costs for one, two, or three workers, we see that Case II with two workers is the optimal decision.

S4.8   REVIEW AND DISCUSSION QUESTIONS

1. How many waiting lines did you encounter during your last airline flight?
2. Distinguish between a *channel* and a *phase*.
3. What is the major cost trade-off that must be made in managing waiting line situations?
4. Which assumptions are necessary to employ the formulas given for Model 1?
5. In what way might the first-come, first-served rule be unfair to the customer waiting for service in a bank or hospital?
6. Define, in a practical sense, what is meant by an *exponential service time*.
7. Would you expect the exponential distribution to be a good approximation of service times for
    a. Buying an airline ticket at the airport?
    b. Riding a merry-go-round at a carnival?
    c. Checking out of a hotel?
    d. Completing a midterm exam in your OM class?
8. Would you expect the Poisson distribution to be a good approximation of
    a. Runners crossing the finish line in the Boston Marathon?
    b. Arrival times of the students in your OM class?
    c. Arrival times of the bus to your stop at school?

S4.9   PROBLEMS

1. Burrito King (a new fast food franchise opening up nationwide) has successfully automated burrito production for its drive-up fast food establishments. The Burro-Master 9000 requires a constant 45 seconds to produce a batch of burritos. It has been estimated that customers will arrive at the drive-up window according to a Poisson distribution at an average of one every 50 seconds. To help determine the amount of space needed for the line at the drive-up window, Burrito King would like to know the expected average time in the system, the average line length (in cars), and the average number of cars in the system (both in line and at the window).

2. The Bijou Theater in Hermosa Beach, California, shows vintage movies. Customers arrive at the theater line at the rate of 100 per hour. The ticket seller averages 30 seconds per customer, which includes placing parking validation stamps on customers' parking lot receipts and punching holes in their frequent watcher cards. (Because of these added services, many customers don't get in until after the feature has started.)
    a. What is the average customer waiting time in the system?
    b. What would be the effect on system waiting time of having a second ticket taker doing nothing but validations and card punching, thereby cutting the average service time to 20 seconds?
    c. Would system waiting time be less than you found in *b* if a second window was opened with each server doing all three tasks?

3. To support National Heart Week, the Heart Association plans to install a free blood pressure testing booth in El Con Mall for the week. Previous experience indicates that, on the average, 10 persons per hour request a test. Assume arrivals are Poisson from an infinite population. Blood pressure measurements can be made at a constant time of five minutes each. Assume the queue length can be infinite with FCFS discipline.
    a. What average number in line can be expected?
    b. What average number of persons can be expected to be in the system?
    c. What is the average amount of time that a person can expect to spend in line?
    d. On the average, how much time will it take to measure a person's blood pressure, including waiting time?
    e. On weekends, the arrival rate can be expected to increase to nearly 12 per hour. What effect will this have on the number in the waiting line?

4. A cafeteria serving line has a coffee urn from which customers serve themselves. Arrivals at the urn follow a Poisson distribution at the rate of three per minute. In serving themselves, customers take about 15 seconds, exponentially distributed.

   a. How many customers would you expect to see on the average at the coffee urn?
   b. How long would you expect it to take to get a cup of coffee?
   c. What percentage of time is the urn being used?
   d. What is the probability that three or more people are in the cafeteria?
      If the cafeteria installs an automatic vendor that dispenses a cup of coffee at a constant time of 15 seconds, how does this change your answers to *a* and *b?*

5. An engineering firm retains a technical specialist to assist four design engineers working on a project. The help that the specialist gives engineers ranges widely in time consumption. The specialist has some answers available in memory, others require computation, and still others require significant search time. On the average, each request for assistance takes the specialist one hour.

   The engineers require help from the specialist on the average of once each day. Since each assistance takes about an hour, each engineer can work for seven hours, on the average, without assistance. One further point: Engineers needing help do not interrupt if the specialist is already involved with another problem.

   Treat this as a finite queuing problem and answer the following questions:

   a. How many engineers, on the average, are waiting for the technical specialist for help?
   b. What is the average time that an engineer has to wait for the specialist?
   c. What is the probability that an engineer will have to wait in line for the specialist?

6. L. Winston Martin (an allergist in Tucson) has an excellent system for handling his regular patients who come in just for allergy injections. Patients arrive for an injection and fill out a name slip, which is then placed in an open slot that passes into another room staffed by one or two nurses. The specific injections for a patient are prepared and the patient is called through a speaker system into the room to receive the injection. At certain times during the day, patient load drops and only one nurse is needed to administer the injections.

   Let's focus on the simpler case of the two—namely, when there is one nurse. Also assume that patients arrive in a Poisson fashion and the service rate of the nurse is exponentially distributed. During this slower period, patients arrive with an interarrival time of approximately three minutes. It takes the nurse an average of two minutes to prepare the patients' serum and administer the injection.

   a. What is the average number you would expect to see in Dr. Martin's facilities?
   b. How long would it take for a patient to arrive, get an injection, and leave?
   c. What is the probability that there will be three or more patients on the premises?
   d. What is the utilization of the nurse?
   e. Assume three nurses are available. Each takes an average of two minutes to prepare the patients' serum and administer the injection. What is the average total time of a patient in the system?

7. The NOL Income Tax Service is analyzing its customer service operations during the month prior to the April filing deadline. On the basis of past data it has been estimated that customers arrive according to a Poisson process with an average interarrival time of 12 minutes. The time to complete a return for a customer is exponentially distributed with a mean of 10 minutes. Based on this information, answer the following questions:

   a. If you went to NOL, how much time would you allow for getting your return done?
   b. On average, how much room should be allowed for the waiting area?
   c. If the NOL service were operating 12 hours per day, how many hours on average, per day, would the office be busy?
   d. What is the probability that the system is idle?
   e. If the arrival rate remained unchanged but the average time in system must be 45 minutes or less, what would need to be changed?

8. A graphics reproduction firm has four units of equipment that are automatic, but occasionally become inoperative because of the need for supplies, maintenance, or repair. Each unit requires service roughly twice each hour or, more precisely, each unit of equipment runs an average of 30 minutes before needing service. Service times vary widely, ranging from a simple service (such as hitting a restart switch or repositioning paper) to more involved equipment disassembly. The average service time, however, is five minutes.

   Equipment downtime results in a loss of $20 per hour. The one equipment attendant is paid $6 per hour.

   Using finite queuing analysis, answer the following questions:

   a. What is the average number of units in line?
   b. What is the average number of units still in operation?
   c. What is the average number of units being serviced?
   d. The firm is considering adding another attendant at the same $6 rate. Should the firm do it?

9. Trucks carrying produce for sale in Arizona arrive at the Nogales, Sonora, inspection station at the rate of one every four minutes. Inspectors can inspect about 18 trucks per hour. For simplicity, assume that this is a simple queuing situation so the models assuming Poisson arrivals and exponential service times can apply.

   a. How many trucks would you expect to see in the system?
   b. How long would it take for a truck that just arrived to get through the system?
   c. What is the utilization of the person staffing the check-in point?
   d. What is the probability that there are more than three trucks in the system?

10. Benny the Barber owns a one-chair shop. At barber college, they told Benny that his customers would exhibit a Poisson arrival distribution and that he would provide an exponential service distribution. His market survey data indicate that customers arrive at a rate of two per hour. It will take Benny an average of 20 minutes to give a haircut. Based on these figures, find the following:

   a. The average number of customers waiting.
   b. The average time a customer waits.
   c. The average time a customer is in the shop.
   d. The average utilization of Benny's time.

11. Customers enter the camera department of a department store at the average rate of six per hour. The department is staffed by one employee, who takes an average of six minutes to serve each arrival. Assume this is a simple Poisson arrival exponentially distributed service time situation.

   a. As a casual observer, how many people would you expect to see in the camera department (excluding the clerk)? How long would a customer expect to spend in the camera department (total time)?
   b. What is the utilization of the clerk?
   c. What is the probability that there are *more than* two people in the camera department (excluding the clerk)?
   d. Another clerk has been hired for the camera department who also takes an average of six minutes to serve each arrival. How long would a customer expect to spend in the department now?

12. Arrivals at a free beer dispensing station at an after-finals party come at the rate of one thirsty student or faculty member every 15 seconds. The bartender can pour one beer every 10 seconds.

   a. How many thirsty beer drinkers would you expect to see in the line?
   b. What is the probability that there will be two or more people in line?
   c. How long would you expect to wait to get a beer?

13. Kenny Livingston, bartender at the Tucson Racquet Club, can serve drinks at the rate of one every 50 seconds. During a hot evening recently, the bar was particularly busy and every 55 seconds someone was at the bar asking for a drink.

a. Assuming that everyone in the bar drank at the same rate and that Kenny served people on a first-come, first-served basis, how long would you expect to have to wait for a drink?

b. How many people would you expect to be waiting for drinks?

c. What is the probability that three or more people are waiting for drinks?

d. What is the utilization of the bartender; how busy is he?

e. If the bartender is replaced with an automatic drink dispensing machine, how would this change your answer in part *a?*

14. An office employs several clerks who originate documents and one operator who enters the document information in a word processor. The group originates documents at a rate of 25 per hour. The operator can enter the information with average exponentially distributed time of two minutes. Assume the population is infinite, arrivals are Poisson, and queue length is infinite with FCFS discipline.

a. Calculate the percent of utilization of the operator.

b. Calculate the average number of documents in the system.

c. Calculate the average time in the system.

d. Calculate the probability of four or more documents being in the system.

e. If another clerk were added, the document origination rate would increase to 30 per hour. What would this do to the word processor workload? Show why.

15. A study-aid desk manned by a graduate student has been established to answer students' questions and help in working problems in your OM course. The desk is staffed eight hours per day. The dean wants to know how the facility is working. Statistics show that students arrive at a rate of four per hour, and the distribution is approximately Poisson. Assistance time averages 10 minutes, distributed exponentially. Assume population and line length can be infinite and queue discipline is FCFS.

a. Calculate the percent of utilization of the graduate student.

b. Calculate the average number of students in the system.

c. Calculate the average time in the system.

d. Calculate the probability of four or more students being in line or being served.

e. Before a test, the arrival of students increases to six per hour on the average. What does this do to the average length of the line?

16. At the California border inspection station, vehicles arrive at the rate of 10 per minute in a Poisson distribution. For simplicity in this problem, assume that there is only one lane and one inspector, who can inspect vehicles at the rate of 12 per minute in an exponentially distributed fashion.

a. What is the average length of the waiting line?

b. What is the average time that a vehicle must wait to get through the system?

c. What is the utilization of the inspector?

d. What is the probability that when you arrive there will be three or more vehicles ahead of you?

17. Consider a service system staffed by a person who takes 10 minutes to satisfy a customer's needs. Customers arrive at this system at the rate of five per hour.

a. How many customers would you expect to find in *line* waiting?

b. What total time would you expect a customer to spend in the *system?*

c. What is the probability that there are three or more customers in the system?

18. During the campus Spring Fling, the bumper car amusement attraction has a problem of cars becoming disabled and in need of repair. Repair personnel can be hired at the rate of $5 per hour, but they only work as one team. Thus if one person is hired he or she works alone; two or three people only work together on the same repair.

One repairperson can repair cars in an average time of 30 minutes. Two repairpeople take 20 minutes, and three take 15 minutes each. While these cars are down, lost income is $20 per hour. Cars tend to break down at the rate of two per hour.

How many repairpeople should be hired?

19. The Holland Tunnel under the Hudson River in New York collects tolls for its use. For a portion of a particular day, only one toll booth was open. Cars were arriving at this gate at the rate of 750 per hour. The toll collector took an average of four seconds to collect the fee.

    a. What was the utilization of the toll booth operator?

    b. How much time would you expect to take to arrive, pay your toll, and move on?

    c. How many cars would you expect to see in the system?

    d. What is the probability that there will be more than four cars in the system?

20. A typist in an office can, on the average, type a letter in eight minutes. This typist works for a large number of people, and they tend to send letters to be typed on the average of one every 10 minutes.

    a. What is the utilization of the typist?

    b. If your letter was just sent to the typist's desk, how long would you expect it to take from that point to the completed typed letter?

    c. How many letters would you expect to see in line?

    d. What is the probability that there will be more than three letters in the system?

21. Because it is getting close to flu season, the university is considering setting up a station to dispense flu shots free to all students, staff, and faculty. There is a question of staffing for a variety of possible demands. One option is to hire just one nurse. Assume that the nurse can give 120 shots per hour, exponentially distributed. People arrive about every 36 seconds, on the average.

    a. What is the utilization of the nurse?

    b. How many people would you expect to find in the system (excluding the nurse)?

    c. How long would it take if you just joined the line to get completely through the system (with shot)?

    d. What is the probability that there will be more than three people in the system (excluding the nurse)?

S4.10 SELECTED BIBLIOGRAPHY

Cooper, Robert B. *Introduction to Queuing Theory.* 2d ed. New York: Elsevier–North Holland, 1980.

Davis, Mark M., and M. J. Maggard. "An Analysis of Customer Satisfaction with Waiting Times in a Two-Stage Service Process." *Journal of Operations Management* 9, no. 3 (August 1990), pp. 324–34.

Fitzsimmons, James A. and M. J. Fitzsimmons. *Service Management for Competitive Advantage.* New York: McGraw-Hill, 1994, pp. 264–90.

Hillier, Frederick S. et al. *Queuing Tables and Graphs.* New York: Elsevier–North Holland, 1981.

Katz, K. L., B. M. Larson, and R. C. Larson. "Prescription for the Waiting-in-Line Blues: Entertain, Enlighten, and Engage." *Sloan Management Review* 32, no. 2 (Winter 1991), pp. 44–53.

Larson, Richard C. "Perspectives on Queues: Social Justice and the Psychology of Queuing." *Operations Research* 35, no. 6 (November-December 1987), pp. 895–905.

Newell, Gordon F. *Applications of Queuing Theory.* New York: Chapman and Hall, 1982.

Rising, E. J., R. Baron, and B. Averill. "A Systems Analysis of a University Health-Service Outpatient Clinic." *Operations Research,* September 1973, pp. 1030–47.

Total Quality Management

CHAPTER OUTLINE

KEY TERMS

Total Quality Management (TQM)

Malcolm Baldrige National Quality Award

Deming Prize

Design Quality

Conformance Quality

Quality at the Source

Zero Defects

Dimensions of Quality

Quality Function Deployment (QFD)

House of Quality

Cost of Quality (COQ)

Continuous Improvement (CI) (Kaisen)

PDCA Cycle

Benchmarking

Fail-Safe Design (Poka-Yoke)

ISO 9000

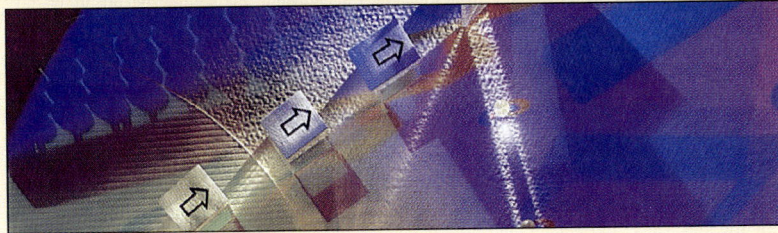

Are you a total quality person? Wouldn't it be great if there were a total quality award for which American citizens could apply—in a contest where all Americans strive for continuous improvement? Suppose there were one. If you are curious as to where you stand, take this test to see whether you meet the criteria for this individual total quality award.

Key	Rarely				Sometimes				Always	
	1	2	3	4	5	6	7	8	9	10

Personal leadership   *Point value*

1. I treat other people fairly and with respect. ☐
2. I actively listen to other people and don't interrupt to give my point of view. ☐
3. I take responsibility for my actions and don't rely on others to plan my future. ☐
4. I volunteer my services to help others in need. ☐
5. I maintain a healthy, positive outlook on life. ☐
6. I understand my values and apply them in my daily living. ☐
7. My long- and short-term goals are tied to my values to ensure that what I am doing in my life is important to me. ☐
8. My daily activities are in harmony with my values. ☐
9. I enjoy the people and things in my environment. ☐
10. I practice good customer service with all the people with whom I come into contact. ☐

Planning

11. I take time to plan my daily activities around what is important to me. ☐
12. I try to align my goals with my values to ensure that my daily activities are in harmony with my goals. ☐

161

13. During my daily planning time I prioritize both important and routine activities that I need to accomplish. ☐

14. Each day I plan to accomplish only those activities for which I have allocated enough time. ☐

15. I strive for continuous learning and have plans to further my education in areas that interest me. ☐

16. I strive to work to the standards set by the most accomplished people in areas that interest me. ☐

17. I try to exceed the expectations of all customers with whom I come into contact in my activities. ☐

18. When I plan my activities, I have knowledge of my environment and take any changing elements into consideration. ☐

19. I have a good sense of how my personal values, strengths, and weaknesses align with what I am doing. ☐

20. I have thought-out, realistic goals with achievable targets for my major activities. ☐

Improvement

21. I can document three major processes that I use in accomplishing my personal goals. ☐

22. I strive to improve my skills, knowledge, and sense of purpose in my life's work. ☐

23. I strive to measure whether I am meeting my goals. ☐

24. I strive to eliminate activities that have no value in my life and focus only on activities that enrich my life. ☐

25. I admit my mistakes, acknowledge the reasons, and then move on with the goal of not making the same mistakes again. ☐

26. I celebrate my successes and improvements. ☐

27. I measure my successes by achieving my goals on time. ☐

28. I strive to improve in areas that are important to me and learn to accept my weaknesses in areas that do not interest me. ☐

29. I am a role model for continuous improvement in everything I do. ☐

30. I am open to changes in my life that will enable me to learn new things. ☐

Scoring

Add up the numbers you have entered and write down the total. Your Score:_____.

Maximum points: 300

How to interpret your score

60–89 points: Grade F. You might want to adopt some of these individual total quality strategies to get your life back on track.

90–128 points: Grade D. You might want to analyze your daily living patterns and goals in life. You do not demonstrate an individual total quality philosophy.

129–158 points: Grade C: You demonstrate some patterns of a total quality person but need to be more consistent on a daily basis.

159–229 points: Grade B. You have a good individual foundation in total quality principles and could serve as a role model for others.

230–300 points: Grade A. You are a great total quality role model, with a solid set of principles in leadership, planning, and continuous improvement.

Source: Craig Nathanson, "Are You a Total Quality Person," *Quality Progress,* September 1993. © 1993 American Society for Quality Control. Reprinted with permission.

The above questionnaire, though directed toward the individual, highlights the three primary dimensions of total quality management—leadership, planning, and improvement. It also conveys the challenging quality values that underlie the contemporary quality movement. After the first few questions it becomes obvious that to score well, you need to have the qualities of an Eagle Scout—brave, thrifty, loyal, reverent, and so on. These are hard enough for scouts, and are often incredibly difficult for the typical organization although, since the quality revolution began in Japan, thousands of organizations have earned their quality merit badges, and a substantial number have achieved what could be viewed as "Eagle Scout rank."

In this chapter, we present a total quality management (TQM) analog of the *Scouts Handbook,* the Malcolm Baldrige National Quality Award criteria. These criteria specify the areas that need to be addressed in any TQM program. We also consider basic quality concepts such as quality specifications and cost of quality, continuous improvement approaches, and the International Society for Standardization (ISO 9000) series for total quality management and continuous improvement approaches. Statistical quality control methods are covered in the chapter supplement.

5.1   OVERVIEW OF TOTAL QUALITY MANAGEMENT

Exhibit 5.1 presents a framework summarizing the important elements of TQM discussed in the chapter and supplement.

We define TQM as "managing the entire organization so that it excels on all dimensions of products and services that are important to the customer." This definition is more applicable than another commonly used one—"conformance to specifications." Though valid for goods production, the second definition is problematic for many services. Precise specifications for service quality are hard to define and measure. It is possible, however, to find out what's important to the customer, and then create the kind of organizational culture that motivates and enables the worker to do what is necessary to deliver a quality service.

The philosophical elements of TQM are from the "Core Values and Concepts" starting at the third heading of the Baldrige Award criteria presented in Exhibit 5.4. The generic tools consist of various statistical process control (SPC) methods which are used for problem solving and continous improvement by quality teams; and quality function deployment typically used by managers. Tools of the QC department consist of statistical quality control (SQC) methods which are used by the quality professionals working in this department.

On August 20, 1987, President Ronald Reagan affixed his signature to Public Law 100-107. This groundbreaking legislation, known commonly as the Malcolm Baldrige National Quality Improvement Act, established the nation's annual award to recognize total quality management in American industry. The **Malcolm Baldrige National Qual-**

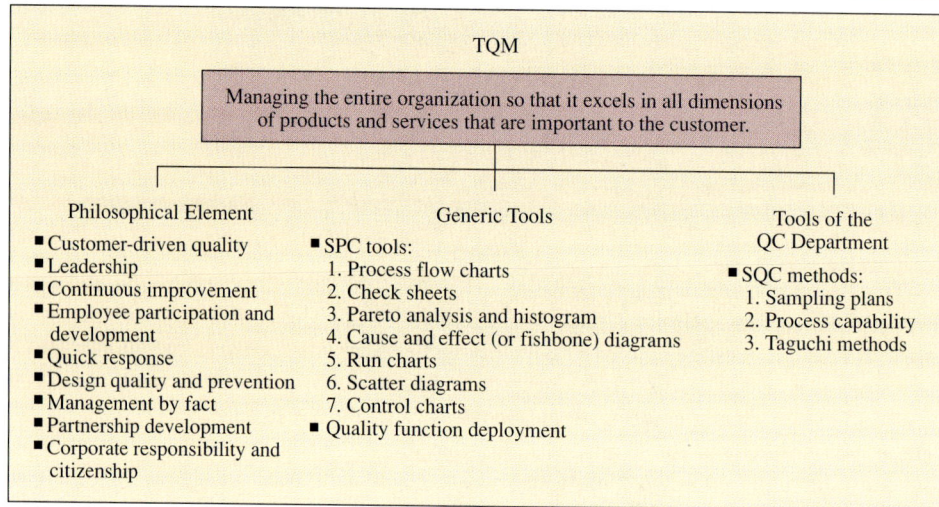

TQM

Managing the entire organization so that it excels in all dimensions
of products and services that are important to the customer.

Philosophical Element	Generic Tools	Tools of the QC Department
▪ Customer-driven quality	▪ SPC tools:	▪ SQC methods:
▪ Leadership	1. Process flow charts	1. Sampling plans
▪ Continuous improvement	2. Check sheets	2. Process capability
▪ Employee participation and	3. Pareto analysis and histogram	3. Taguchi methods
development	4. Cause and effect (or fishbone) diagrams	
▪ Quick response	5. Run charts	
▪ Design quality and prevention	6. Scatter diagrams	
▪ Management by fact	7. Control charts	
▪ Partnership development	▪ Quality function deployment	
▪ Corporate responsibility and		
citizenship		

ity Award represents the United States government's endorsement of quality as an essential part of successful business strategy.

As an instrument of government, the Baldrige Award seeks to improve quality and productivity by

1. Helping to stimulate American companies to improve quality and productivity for the pride of recognition while obtaining a competitive edge through decreased costs and increased profits.

2. Establishing guidelines and criteria that can be used by business, industrial, governmental, and other organizations in evaluating their quality improvement efforts.

3. Recognizing the achievements of those companies that improve the quality of their goods and services and thereby provide an example to others.

4. Providing specific guidance for other American organizations that wish to learn how to manage for high quality by making available detailed information on how winning organizations were able to change their cultures and achieve quality eminence.

The cover of the Malcolm Baldrige National Quality Award 1994 award criteria quotes President Clinton:

> To meet the challenges of the global economy . . . our most successful companies have been eliminating unnecessary layers of management, empowering front-line workers, becoming more responsive to their customers, and seeking constantly to improve the products they make, the services they provide, and the people they employ.

Without question, the Baldrige Award and its comprehensive criteria for evaluating total quality in an organization have had considerable impact. Some observers have begun referring to the award as the Nobel Prize for business.

Applications for the award are reviewed without funding from the U.S. government. Review expenses are paid primarily through application fees and partial support for the reviews is provided by the Baldrige Foundation. Extensive volunteer efforts by members of the Board of Examiners keep application review fees to a minimum. The Baldrige

Award is managed by the U.S. Dept. of Commerce and administered by the American Society for Quality Control (ASQC).

Japan too has an award for outstanding business accomplishment. For over 40 years Japan has recognized its corporate quality leaders by bestowing on them the prestigious **Deming Prize** (see Exhibit 5.2), named after American statistician Dr. W. Edwards Deming, whose quality concepts provided the road map for Japanese success in quality after World War II. The Deming Prize has become so esteemed in Japan that each year, much like America's Academy Awards, millions of Japanese watch the Deming Prize ceremony aired live on television.

There are three categories for the Baldrige Award:

Eligibility for the Baldrige Award

1. Manufacturing companies or subsidiaries that (1) produce and sell manufactured products or manufacturing processes or (2) produce agricultural, mining, or construction products.
2. Service companies or subsidiaries that sell service. Whether a company is classified as manufacturing or service is determined by the larger percentage of sales.
3. Small businesses, which are defined as those that have fewer than 500 employees and that operate independently of any other firm that may have equity ownership.

Up to two awards can be given in each of the three categories. Winners are expected to make themselves available to other firms and openly discuss what they did to achieve quality success. Exhibit 5.3 lists winners through 1993.

Exhibit 5.4A shows the first part of the 1994 award criteria. Note how the Baldrige Award mirrors the broad spectrum of issues necessary for a total quality management system. Scoring for the award falls into the seven categories shown in Exhibit 5.4B. Note that the greatest scoring weight is on customers and operational results.

Description of the 1994 Baldrige Award Criteria[1]

---

[1]Extracted from the Malcolm Baldrige National Quality Award 1994 award criteria.

EXHIBIT 5.2

*Comparison of the
Deming Prize and
Baldrige Award*

Japan's highly coveted Deming Price recognizes successful efforts in instituting companywide quality control (CWQC) principles. The Deming Prize is awarded to all companies that meet a standard based on the evaluation process. For those that do not qualify, the examination process is automatically extended (up to two times over three years). Although both the Deming Prize and the Baldrige Award are designed to recognize outstanding business accomplishments, some notable differences follow:

Topic	Baldrige Award	Deming Prize
Primary focus	Customer satisfaction and quality	Statistical quality control
Grading criteria	Leadership Information and analysis Strategic quality planning Human resource utilization Quality assurance Quality results Customer satisfaction	Policy and objectives Organization and operation Education and extension Data gathering/reporting Analysis Standardization Control Quality assurance Effects Future plans
Winners	Maximum of two per category	All firms meeting standard
Scope	U.S. firms only	Firms from any country
Grading time	Six months	One year
First award	1987	1951
Sponsor	National Institute of Standards and Technology	Union of Japanese Scientists and Engineers

Source: David Bush and Kevin Dooley, "The Deming Prize and Baldrige Award: How They Compare," *Quality Progress,* January 1989, pp. 28–30.

EXHIBIT 5.3

*Baldrige Award
Winners by Category*

Manufacturing	Service	Small Business
Motorola Inc. (1988)	Federal Express (1990)	Globe Metallurgical Inc. (1988)
Westinghouse Commercial Nuclear Fuel Division (1989)	AT&T Universal Card Services (1992)	Wallace Co. (1990)
Milliken & Co. (1989)	Ritz-Carlton Hotel Co. Atlanta (1992)	Marlow Industries (1991)
Xerox Business Products (1989)		Granite Rock Co. (1992)
Cadillac (1990)		Ames Rubber Co. (1993)
IBM Rochester (1990)		
Solectron (1991)		
Zytec Corp. (1991)		
AT&T Network Systems Group Transmission Systems Business Unit (1992)		
Texas Instruments Defense Systems and Electronics Group (1992)		
Eastman Chemical Co. (1993)		

Benchmarking and Baldrige   Measuring an organization's performance against its own historical performance is central to the Baldrige criteria. Tracking performance encourages continuous improvement. Part of the reasoning for emphasizing quality results is the experience that "if it doesn't get measured, it doesn't improve."

To truly create improvement, a firm must continually compare its performance on critical criteria against the best in the business. This is **benchmarking.** Baldrige is a starting point to understand each part of the organization and forces self-evaluation. A company can then adjust its goals and set strategies based on these benchmarks.

Award Criteria Purposes

The Malcolm Baldrige National Quality Award Criteria are the basis for making Awards and for giving feedback to applicants. In addition, the Criteria have three important roles in strengthening U.S. competitiveness:

- to help raise quality performance practices and expectations;

- to facilitate communication and sharing among and within organizations of all types based upon a common understanding of key quality and operational performance requirements; and

- to serve as a working tool for planning, training, assessment, and other uses.

Award Criteria Goals

The Criteria are designed to help companies enhance their competitiveness through focus on dual, results-oriented goals:

- delivery of ever-improving value to customers, resulting in improved marketplace performance; and

- improvement of overall company operational performance.

Core Values and Concepts

The Award Criteria are built upon a set of core values and concepts. These values and concepts are the foundation for integrating the overall customer and company operational performance requirements.

These core values and concepts are:

Customer-Driven Quality

Quality is judged by customers. All product and service characteristics that contribute value to the customer and lead to customer satisfaction and preference must be the focus of a company's management system. Value, satisfaction, and preference may be influenced by many factors throughout the customer's overall purchase, ownership, and service experiences. These factors include the company's relationship with customers that helps build trust, confidence, and loyalty. This concept of quality includes not only the product and service characteristics that meet basic customer requirements, but it also includes those characteristics that enhance them and differentiate them from competing offerings. Such enhancement and differentiation may be based upon new offerings, combinations of product and service offerings, rapid response, or special relationships.

Customer-driven quality is thus a strategic concept. It is directed toward customer retention and market share gain. It demands constant sensitivity to emerging customer and market requirements, and measurement of the factors that drive customer satisfaction and retention. It also demands awareness of developments in technology and of competitors' offerings, and rapid and flexible response to customer and market requirements.

Success requires more than defect and error reduction, merely meeting specifications, and reducing complaints. Nevertheless, defect and error reduction and elimination of causes of dissatisfaction contribute significantly to the customers' view of quality and are thus also important parts of customer-driven quality. In addition, the company's success in recovering from defects and errors ("making things right for the customer") is crucial to building customer relationships and to customer retention.

A company's customer-driven focus needs to address all stakeholders—customers, employees, suppliers, stockholders, the public, and the community.

Leadership

A company's senior leaders must create a customer orientation, clear and visible quality values, and high expectations. Reinforcement of the values and expectations requires substantial personal commitment and involvement. The leaders' basic values and commitment need to include areas of public responsibility and corporate citizenship. The leaders must take part in the creation of strategies, systems, and methods for achieving excellence. The systems and methods need to guide all activities and decisions of the company. The senior leaders must commit to the growth and development of the entire work force and should encourage participation and creativity by all employees. Through their regular personal involvement in visible activities, such as planning, communications, review of company performance, and recognizing employees for quality achievement, the senior leaders serve as role models, reinforcing the values and encouraging leadership in all levels of management.

Continuous Improvement

Achieving the highest levels of quality and competitiveness requires a well-defined and well-executed approach to continuous improvement. The term *continuous improvement* refers to both incremental and "breakthrough" improvement. The approach to improvement needs to be "embedded" in the way the company functions. Embedded means that: (1) improvement is part of the daily work of all work units; (2) improvement processes seek to eliminate problems at their source; and (3) improvement is driven by opportunities to do better, as well as by problems that must be corrected. Opportunities for improvement have four major sources: employee ideas; R&D; customer input; and benchmarking or other comparative information on processes and performance.

Improvements may be of several types: (1) enhancing value to customers through new and improved products and services; (2) reducing errors, defects, and waste; (3) improving responsiveness and cycle time performance; (4) improving productivity and effectiveness in the use of all resources; and (5) improving the company's performance and leadership position in fulfilling its public responsibilities and serving as a role model in corporate citizenship. Thus improvement is driven not only by the objective to provide better product and service quality, but also by the need to be responsive and efficient—both conferring additional marketplace advantages. To meet all of these objectives, the process of continuous improvement must contain regular cycles of planning, execution, and evaluation. This requires a basis—preferably a quantitative basis—for assessing progress, and for deriving information for future cycles of improvement. Such information should provide direct links between desired performance and internal operations.

Employee Participation and Development

A company's success in improving performance depends increasingly on the skills and motivation of its work force. Employee success depends increasingly on having meaningful opportunities to learn and to practice new skills. Companies need to invest in the development of the work force through education, training, and creating opportunities for continuing growth. Such opportunities might include classroom and on-the-job training, job rotation, and pay for demonstrated skills. Structured on-the-job training offers a cost effective way to train and to better link training to work processes. Increasingly, training, development, and work organizations need to be tailored to a more diverse work force and to more flexible, high-performance work environments.

Major challenges in the area of work force development include: (1) integration of human resource management—selection, performance, recognition, training, and career advancement; and (2) aligning human resource management with business plans and strategic change processes. Addressing these challenges requires acquisition and use of employee-related data on skills, satisfaction, motivation, safety, and well-being. Such data need to be tied to indicators of company or unit performance, such as customer satisfaction, customer retention, and productivity. Through this approach, human resource management may be better integrated and aligned with business directions, using continuous improvement processes to refine integration and alignment.

Fast Response

Success in competitive markets increasingly demands ever-shorter cycles for new or improved product and service introduction. Also, faster and more flexible response to customers is now a more critical requirement. Major improvement in response time often requires simplification of work organizations and work processes. To accomplish such improvement, the time performance of work processes should be measured. There are other important benefits derived from this focus: response time improvements often drive simultaneous improvements in organization, quality, and productivity. Hence it is beneficial to consider response time, quality, and productivity objectives together.

Design Quality and Prevention

Business management should place strong emphasis on design quality—problem and waste prevention achieved through building quality into products and services and into production processes. In general, costs of preventing problems at the design stage are much lower than costs of correcting problems which occur "downstream." Design quality includes the creation of fault-tolerant (robust) or error resistant processes and products.

A major issue in the competitive environment is the design-to-introduction ("product generation") cycle time. Meeting the demands of ever-more rapidly changing markets requires that companies carry out stage-to-stage coordination and integration ("concurrent engineering") of functions and activities from basic research to commercialization.

From the point of view of public responsibility, the design stage involves designs regarding resource use and manufacturing processes. Such decisions affect process waste streams and the composition of municipal and industrial wastes. The growing demand by consumers and others for a cleaner environment means that companies will need to develop design strategies that place greater weight on environmental factors.

Consistent with the theme of design quality and prevention, continuous improvement and corrective action need to emphasize interventions "upstream"—at early stages in processes. This approach yields the maximum overall benefits of improvements and corrections. Such upstream intervention also needs to take into account the company's suppliers.

Long-Range Outlook

Achieving quality and market leadership requires a company to have a strong future orientation and a willingness to make long-term commitments to all stakeholders—customers, employees, suppliers, stockholders, the public, and the community. Planning needs to determine or anticipate many types of changes including those that may affect customers' expectations of products and services, technological developments, changing customer segments, evolving regulatory requirements and community/societal expectations, or thrusts by competitors. Plans, strategies, and resource allocations need to reflect these commitments and changes. A major part of the long-term commitment is development of employees and suppliers, fulfilling public responsibilities, and serving as a corporate citizenship role model.

Management by Fact

A modern business management system needs to be built upon a framework of measurement, data and analysis. Measurements must derive from the company's strategy and encompass all key processes and the outputs of those processes. Facts and data needed for quality improvement and quality assessment are of many types, including: customer, product and service performance, operations, market, competitive comparisons, supplier, employee-related, and cost and financial. Analysis refers to the process of extracting larger meaning from data to support evaluation and decision making at various levels within the company. Such analysis may entail using data to reveal information—such as trends, projections, and cause and effect—that might not be evident without analysis. Facts, data, and analysis support a variety of company purposes, such as planning, reviewing company performance, improving operations, and comparing company quality performance with competitors' or with "best practices" benchmarks.

A major consideration relating to use of data and analysis to improve performance involves the creation and use of performance measures or indicators. Performance measures or indicators are measurable characteristics of products, services, processes, and operations the company uses to track and improve performance. The measures or indicators should be selected to best represent the factors that lead to improved customer satisfaction and operational performance. A system of measures or indicators tied to customer and/or company performance requirements represents a clear and objective basis for aligning all activities with the company's strategy and goals. Through the analysis of data from the tracking processes, the measures or indicators themselves may be evaluated and changed. For example, measures or indicators selected to track product and service quality may be judged by how well improvement relative to the quality measures or indicators correlates with improvement in customer satisfaction.

Partnership Development

Companies should seek to build internal and external partnerships to better accomplish their overall goals.

Internal partnerships might include those that promote labor–management cooperation, such as agreements with unions. Agreements might entail employee development, cross-training, or new work organizations, such as high-performance work teams. Internal partnerships might also involve creating network relationships among company units to improve flexibility and responsiveness.

Examples of external partnerships include those with customers, suppliers, and education organizations. An increasingly important kind of external partnership is the strategic partnership or alliance. Such partnerships might offer a company entry into new markets or a basis for new products or services. A partnership might also permit the blending of a company's core competencies or leadership capabilities with complementary strengths and capabilities of partners, thereby enhancing overall capability, including speed and flexibility.

Partnerships should seek to develop longer-term objectives, thereby creating a basis for mutual investments. Partners should address the key requirements for success of the partnership, means of regular communication, approaches to evaluating progress, and means for adapting to changing conditions.

Corporate Responsibility and Citizenship

A company's management objectives should stress corporate responsibility and citizenship. Corporate responsibility refers to basic expectations of the company—business ethics and protection of public health, public safety, and the environment. Healthy, safety and environmental considerations need to take into account the company's operations as well as the life cycles of products and services. Companies need to address factors such as resource conservation and waste reduction at their source. Planning related to public health, safety, and environment should anticipate adverse impacts that may arise in facilities management, production, distribution, transportation, use and disposal of products. Plans should seek to prevent problems, to provide a forthright company response if problems occur, and to make available information needed to maintain public awareness, safety, trust, and confidence. Inclusion of public responsibility areas within a quality system means meeting all local, state, and federal laws and regulatory requirements. It also means treating these and related requirements as areas for continuous improvement "beyond mere compliance."

Corporate citizenship refers to leadership and support—within reasonable limits of a company's resources—of publicly important purposes, including the above-mentioned areas of corporate responsibility. Such purposes might include education, environmental excellence, resource conservation, community services, improving industry and business practices, and sharing of nonproprietary quality-related information. Leadership as a corporate citizen entails influencing other organizations, private and public, to partner for these purposes.

Source: Extracted from the Malcolm Baldrige National Quality Award 1994 Award Criteria.

1.0 Leadership   *Point Values*

The *Leadership* category examines senior executives' *personal* leadership and involvement in creating and sustaining a customer focus and clear and visible quality values. Also examined is how the quality values are integrated into the company's management system, including how the company addresses its public responsibilities and corporate citizenship.

1.1	Senior executive leadership	45
1.2	Management for quality	25
1.3	Public responsibility and corporate citizenship	25

2.0 Information and Analysis

The *Information and Analysis* category examines the scope, management, and use of data and information to maintain a customer focus, to drive quality excellence, and to improve operational competitive performance.

2.1	Scope and management of quality and performance data and information	15
2.2	Competitive comparisons and benchmarking	20
2.3	Analysis and uses of company-level data	40
		60

3.0 Strategic Quality Planning

The *Strategic Quality Planning* category examines the company's planning process and how all key quality and operational performance requirements are integrated into overall business planning. Also examined are the company's short- and longer-term plans and how plan requirements are deployed to all work units.

3.1	Strategic quality and company performance planning process	35
3.2	Quality and performance plans	25

4.0 Human Resource Development and Management

The *Human Resource Development and Management* category examines the key elements of how the work force is enabled to develop its full potential to pursue the company's quality and operational performance objectives. Also examined are the company's efforts to build and maintain an environment for quality excellence conducive to full participation and personal and organizational growth.

4.1	Human resource planning and management	20
4.2	Employee involvement	40
4.3	Employee education and training	40
4.4	Employee performance and recognition	25
4.5	Employee well-being and satisfaction	25

5.0 Management of Process Quality

The *Management of Process Quality* category examines the key elements of process management, including design, management of day-to-day production and delivery, improvement of quality and operational performance, and quality assessment. The category also examines how all work units, including research and development units and suppliers, contribute to overall quality and operational performance requirements.

5.1	Design and introduction of quality products and services	40
5.2	Process management: product and service production and delivery processes	35
5.3	Process management: business and support service processes	30
5.4	Supplier quality	20
5.5	Quality assessment	15

6.0 Quality and Operational Results

The *Quality and Operational Results* category examines the company's achievement levels and improvement trends in quality, company operational performance, and supplier quality. Also examined are current quality and operational performance levels relative to those of competitors.

6.1	Product and service quality results	70
6.2	Company operational results	50
6.3	Business and support service results	25
6.4	Supplier quality results	35

7.0 Customer Focus and Satisfaction

The *Customer Focus and Satisfaction* category examines the company's relationships with customers, and its knowledge of customer requirements and of the key quality factors that drive marketplace competitiveness. Also examined are the company's methods to determine customer satisfaction, current trends and levels of customer satisfaction and retention, and these results relative to competitors.

7.1	Customer expectations: current and future	35
7.2	Customer relationship management	65
7.3	Commitment to customers	15
7.4	Customer satisfaction determination	30
7.5	Customer satisfaction results	85
7.6	Customer satisfaction comparison	70
	Total points	

To Win the Baldrige or Not to Win?

Since its beginning in 1987, over 900,000 applications have been requested for the Baldrige Award. Yet as of mid-1994, only 546 applications have been actually submitted. (The application is 50 to 75 pages long.) This is not to imply that the award's intended motivation toward high quality is failing. In fact, the award is quite successful in that it has provided guidelines against which any firm can measure itself. All award applicants receive the examiners' written evaluation of their strengths and weaknesses. Only about 10 percent of the applicants become finalists and receive site visits from an examination team.

The Board of Examiners evaluates the applications and makes recommendations to the National Institute of Standards and Technology. As of 1994, there are 270 examiners who are quality experts, primarily from the private sector. Exhibit 5.5 shows the number of applications and number of awards from 1988 to 1994.

Not all firms want or should try to win the award. It takes considerable resources to prepare the firm to meet the criteria and to follow through the application and site visits. If a firm does win, the recognition can be quite valuable in sales promotions, attracting outstanding employees, and so on, though this does not guarantee increased profits. In fact, Wallace Co., winner of the award in 1990, found itself in serious financial trouble.

A company should only apply if it (1) has top management's serious commitment to spend the time and resources and (2) wants to be publicly recognized as a customer-focused, quality-conscious company. For anything less than that, it would be best to obtain the Baldrige criteria and use it internally for benchmarking and as guidelines for self-improvement.

Many companies use Baldrige criteria as guidelines either to help them design their quality programs or to see how well they are doing. Bob Lea (a vice president at Paul Revere Insurance Company) says that the company focuses on the Baldrige criteria. Jane Gallagher, Paul Revere's quality manager, says, "If you want greater market share, more new business, and more repeat business, then you do what it takes to focus on the Baldrige criteria."

Bruce Woolpert, president and CEO of Granite Rock Company (a 1992 winner), sees the benefits of using the guidelines. He states,

> The Baldrige application process itself is an investment in future success that every American company should be making. We have applied four consecutive years. Every feedback report that we received contained many suggestions. In fact, one year's report identified 116 areas for improvement. After careful review and discussion, we began working on over 100 of

E X H I B I T 5.5
Baldrige Award Applications Site Visits and Awards, 1988–94

	1988	1989	1990	1991	1992	1993	1994	Total
Manufacturing	45	23	45	38	31	32		
Service	9	6	18	21	15	13		
Small business	12	11	34	47	44	31		
Total	66	40	97	106	90	76	71	546
Site Visits and Award Recipients								
Site visits:	13	10	12	21	17	13	*	86
Award Winners								
Manufacturing	2	2	2	2	2	1	*	11
Service	0	0	1	0	2	0	*	3
Small business	1	0	1	1	1	1	*	5
Total	3	2	4	3	5	1	2	19

*Results for 1994 not in yet.

these ideas immediately. Our hard work and improvements were then reflected in the application the following year.[2]

Hank Hayes, president of Texas Instruments Defense Systems and Electronics Group, states, "The greatest benefit we derived from participating in the Baldrige process was to have access to their objective, outside feedback and specific areas the examiners identified for improvement."[3]

In a survey of 285 firms from a cross section of large and small manufacturing and service firms, companies consistently agreed that the award currently provides the best framework for a total quality management system.[4] They felt that the award "factors quality awareness, promotes the understanding of the requirements for quality excellence, promotes sharing of information on successful quality strategies, and recognizes U.S. companies that excel in quality achievement and quality management."[5]

Baldrige Award Winners' Successes   The following claims by companies that have won the Baldrige Award are contained in the application package. These statements may be biased, but we have no doubt that most winners showed significant benefits.

- At Globe Metallurgical, exports have grown from 2 percent to 20 percent of sales from 1988 to 1992, while overall sales grew by 24 percent.
- In 1990, Xerox Business Products and Systems introduced an industry-leading three-year Total Satisfaction Guarantee, giving the customer the right to return the product.
- Cadillac has received over 15 major awards since winning the Malcolm Baldrige National Quality Award in 1990.
- IBM Rochester had a 25 percent growth in market share from 1988 to 1992, with 1992 new customer installations at twice the rate of 1988.
- The Ritz-Carlton Hotel Company has been honored by the travel industry with 121 quality awards since 1991.
- Granite Rock's customer accounts increased 38 percent from 1989 through mid-1993, while overall construction spending in its market area declined over 40 percent.
- Texas Instruments Defense Systems & Electronics Group had a 21 percent reduction in production cycle time in 1992, with a 56 percent reduction in stock-to-production time.
- At Federal Express, staff Quality Action Teams (QATs) have generated significant savings: $27 million in the Personnel Division since 1986; $1.5 million in recovered revenue by a computer automation QAT; and $462,000 in saved overtime payments in six months by a payroll QAT.
- The Westinghouse Commercial Nuclear Fuel Division's product reliability has continuously improved over the past 10 years, resulting in the industry's best fuel performance and a doubling of orders, compared to eight years ago.
- Motorola's employee productivity has improved 100 percent over the past six years (an annual compounded rate of 12.2 percent) through robust design, continuous

[2]Malcolm Baldrige National Quality Award, *Feedback*, 1994.
[3]Ibid.
[4]Uly S. Knotts, Jr., Leo G. Parrish Jr., and Cheri R. Evans, "What Does the U.S. Business Community Really Think about the Baldrige Award?" *Quality Progress*, May 1993, pp. 49–53.
[5]Ibid., p. 52.

Westinghouse Electric's Commercial Nuclear Fuel Division's 100% on-time delivery record for fuel-rod assemblies can be credited to the division's total quality approach.

Milliken & Company employees work in self-directed teams and are responsible for everything from training to halting production if a quality or safety problem is detected.

improvement in defect reduction, and employee education and empowerment. It claims to save $125 million per year through quality improvements.

- Zytec's internal manufacturing process yields improved fivefold from 1988 to 1992, with customer out-of-box quality up from 99 percent to 99.8 percent. From 1989 to 1992, on-time delivery improved from 75 percent to 98 percent.

- Wallace Company increased sales per associate from $180,000 in 1986 to $294,000 in 1991.

- The AT&T Universal Card program opened its 1 millionth account 78 days after program launch and a month later was one of the top 10 credit card programs in the nation.

- Milliken & Company's associate involvement through its "Opportunity for Improvement" (OFI) process generated 59 ideas per associate in 1992 in areas such as quality improvements, cost reductions, safety, and innovation.

- AT&T Transmission Systems Business Unit reduced time to market by 50 percent in three years.

- Solectron, by focusing on customer satisfaction, has seen average yearly revenue growth of 46.8 percent, and by focusing on process quality has seen average yearly net income growth of 57.3 percent over the past five years.

For the 10 award winners that analyze productivity enhancement as annual increase in revenue per employee, a median average annual compounded growth rate of 9.4 percent and a mean of 9.25 percent have been achieved. According to an October 18, 1993, *Business Week* study, the three publicly traded, whole company Baldrige winners outperformed the Standard & Poor's 500 from the time of their winning through September 30, 1993, by 8.6 to 1.

What Are the Characteristics of a Baldrige Award Winner?[6]   So far no one single approach to achieve high quality appears common. Nor does there seem to be one recipe for firms to follow to ensure success. Some firms send employees to school, some hire

---

[6]This section is based on Richard M. Hodges, *Blueprint for Continuous Improvement: Lessons from the Baldrige Winners* (New York: American Management Association, 1993).

consultants, and some do it themselves internally. However, there were four common elements for all Baldrige winners:

1. The companies formulated a vision of what they thought quality was and how they would achieve it.
2. Senior management was actively involved.
3. Companies carefully planned and organized their quality effort to be sure it would be effectively initiated.
4. They vigorously controlled the overall process.

For each of the winners, the quality drive became more than a program. It penetrated every aspect of corporate life: performance appraisals and incentive pay supported quality objectives, hiring practices, team training, job posting systems, and so on. The quality of human resources was as important as productivity measures such as cycle time reduction and vendor quality assurance.

Baldrige winners carry their commitment to customer satisfaction to extremes. Motorola managers wear pagers so that customers can reach them at any time and any place. Globe responds to all customer questions within 24 hours. Westinghouse's CNFD spends $18 million per year on training specifically devoted to quality improvement processes, principles, technology, and objectives.

One of the intentions of the Baldrige designers was to develop an award that captured the ideas of the leading quality philosophers (or gurus)—Philip Crosby, W. Edwards Deming, and Joseph M. Juran—while at the same time being "nondenominational" with respect to advocating one particular quality view. While there are various nuance differences in many areas among the three philosophies compared in Exhibit 5.6, it is fair to say that this goal was achieved. The reason lies in the nonprescriptive nature of the Baldrige criteria, the fact that the gurus all advocate generally the same thing, and, in our opinion, that they all emphasize top management leadership in the quality effort. The proof is in the pudding as well—different Baldrige winners have been adherents to Deming, Crosby, or Juran approaches.[7]

The Baldrige Award and the Quality Gurus

5.2   Quality Specifications and Quality Costs

Fundamental to any quality program is the determination of quality specifications and the costs of achieving (or *not* achieving) those specifications.

The quality specifications of a product or service derive from decisions and actions made relative to the quality of its design and the quality of its conformance to that design. **Design quality** refers to the inherent value of the product in the marketplace and is thus a strategic decision for the firm. The common dimensions of design quality are listed in Exhibit 5.7.

Conformance quality refers to the degree to which the product or service design specifications are met. Execution of the activities involved in achieving conformance are of a tactical day-to-day nature. It should be evident that a product or service can have high design quality but low conformance quality, and vice versa.

Developing Quality Specifications

$\cdot S \cdot$

---

[7]W. Edwards Deming was active as a consultant, author, and speaker until his death on December 23, 1993, at age 93.

E X H I B I T 5.6   *The Quality Gurus Compared*

	Crosby	Deming	Juran
Definition of quality	Conformance to requirements	A predictable degree of uniformity and dependability at low cost and suited to the market	Fitness for use (satisfies customer's needs)
Degree of senior management responsibility	Responsible for quality	Responsible for 94% of quality problems	Less than 20% of quality problems are due to workers
Performance standard/ motivation	Zero defects	Quality has many "scales": use statistics to measure performance in all areas; critical of zero defects	Avoid campaigns to do perfect work
General approach	Prevention, not inspection	Reduce variability by continuous improvement; cease mass inspection	General management approach to quality, especially human elements
Structure	14 steps to quality improvement	14 points for management	10 steps to quality improvement
Statistical process control (SPC)	Rejects statistically acceptable levels of quality [wants 100% perfect quality]	Statistical methods of quality control must be used	Recommends SPC but warns that it can lead to tool-driven approach
Improvement basis	A process, not a program; improvement goals	Continuous to reduce variation; eliminate goals without methods	Project-by-project team approach; set goals
Teamwork	Quality improvement teams; quality councils	Employee participation in decision making; break down barriers between departments	Team and quality circle approach
Costs of quality	Cost of nonconformance; quality is free	No optimum; continuous improvement	Quality is not free; there is not an optimum
Purchasing and goods received	State requirements; supplier is extension of business; most faults due to purchasers themselves	Inspection too late; sampling allows defects to enter system; statistical evidence and control charts required	Problems are complex; carry out formal surveys
Vendor rating	Yes and buyers; quality audits useless	No, critical of most systems	Yes, but help supplier improve
Single sourcing of supply		Yes	No, can neglect to sharpen competitive edge

Source: Modified from John S. Oakland, *Total Quality Management* (London: Heinemann Professional Publishing Ltd., 1989), pp. 291–92.

Quality at the source is frequently discussed in the context of conformance quality. This means that the person who is doing the production takes responsibility for making sure that his/her output meets specification. If this can be accomplished, then in theory, the ultimate goal of **zero defects** throughout the process is achievable. (Zero defects had been frequently used as the rallying cry for a companywide quality effort. The term has fallen into disrepute because it was often just a slogan, unsupported by quality training and real quality commitment by management.)

Achieving the quality specifications is typically the responsibility of manufacturing management, where a product is involved, and the branch operations management in a service industry, where a service is involved. Exhibit 5.8 shows two examples of the **dimensions of quality.** One is a stereo amplifier that meets the signal-to-noise ratio standard; the second is a checking account transaction in a bank.

Both quality of design and quality of conformance should provide products that meet the customer's objectives for those products. This is often termed the product's *fitness for use,* and it entails identifying the dimensions of the product (or service) that the cus-

Dimension	Meaning
Performance	Primary product or service characteristics
Features	Added touches, bells and whistles, secondary characteristics
Reliability	Consistency of performance over time
Durability	Useful life
Serviceability	Resolution of problems and complaints
Response	Characteristics of the human-to-human interface (timeliness, courtesy, professionalism, etc.)
Aesthetics	Sensory characteristics (sound, feel, look, etc.)
Reputation	Past performance and other intangibles

Source: Modified from Paul E. Pisek, "Defining Quality at the Marketing/Development Interface," *Quality Progress*, June 1987, pp. 28–36.

Dimension	Measures	
	Product Example: Stereo Amplifier	**Service Example: Checking Account at a Bank**
Performance	Signal-to-noise ratio, power	Time to process customer requests
Features	Remote control	Automatic bill paying
Reliability	Mean time to failure	Variability of time to process requests
Durability	Useful life (with repair)	Keeping pace with industry trends
Serviceability	Ease of repair	Resolution of errors
Response	Courtesy of dealer	Courtesy of teller
Aesthetics	Oak-finished cabinet	Appearance of bank lobby

Source: Modified from Paul E. Pisek, "Defining Quality at the Marketing/Development Interface," *Quality Progress*, June 1987, pp. 28–36.

tomer wants (i.e., the voice of the customer) and developing a quality control program to ensure these dimensions are met.

Quality Function Deployment

One approach to getting the voice of the customer into the design specifications of a product is **quality function deployment (QFD).**[8] This approach, which uses interfunctional teams from marketing, design engineering, and manufacturing, has been credited by Toyota Motor Corporation for reducing costs on its cars by more than 60 percent by significantly shortening design times.

The QFD process begins with studying and listening to customers to determine the characteristics of a superior product. Through market research, the consumers' product needs and preferences are defined and broken down into categories called *customer attributes*. One example is an auto manufacturer that would like to improve the design of a car door. Through customer surveys and interviews, it determines that two important customer attributes desired in a car door are that it "stays open on a hill" and is "easy to close from the outside." After the customer attributes are defined, they are weighted based on their relative importance to the customer. Next, the consumer is asked to compare and rate the company's products with the products of competitors. This process helps the

---

[8]The term *quality* is actually a mistranslation of the Japanese word for *qualities*. Because QFD is widely used in the context of quality management, however, we elected to put it in this chapter rather than in Chapter 3 on product design.

company determine the product characteristics that are important to the consumer and to evaluate its product in relation to others. The end result is a better understanding and focus on product characteristics that require improvement.

Customer attribute information forms the basis for a matrix called the **house of quality.** (See Exhibit 5.9.) By building a house of quality matrix, the cross-functional QFD team can use customer feedback to make engineering, marketing, and design decisions. The matrix helps the team to translate customer attribute information into concrete operating or engineering goals. The important product characteristics and goals for improvement are jointly agreed on and detailed in the house. This process encourages the different departments to work closely together and results in a better understanding of one another's goals and issues. However, the most important benefit of

E X H I B I T 5.9

Completed House of Quality Matrix for a Car Door

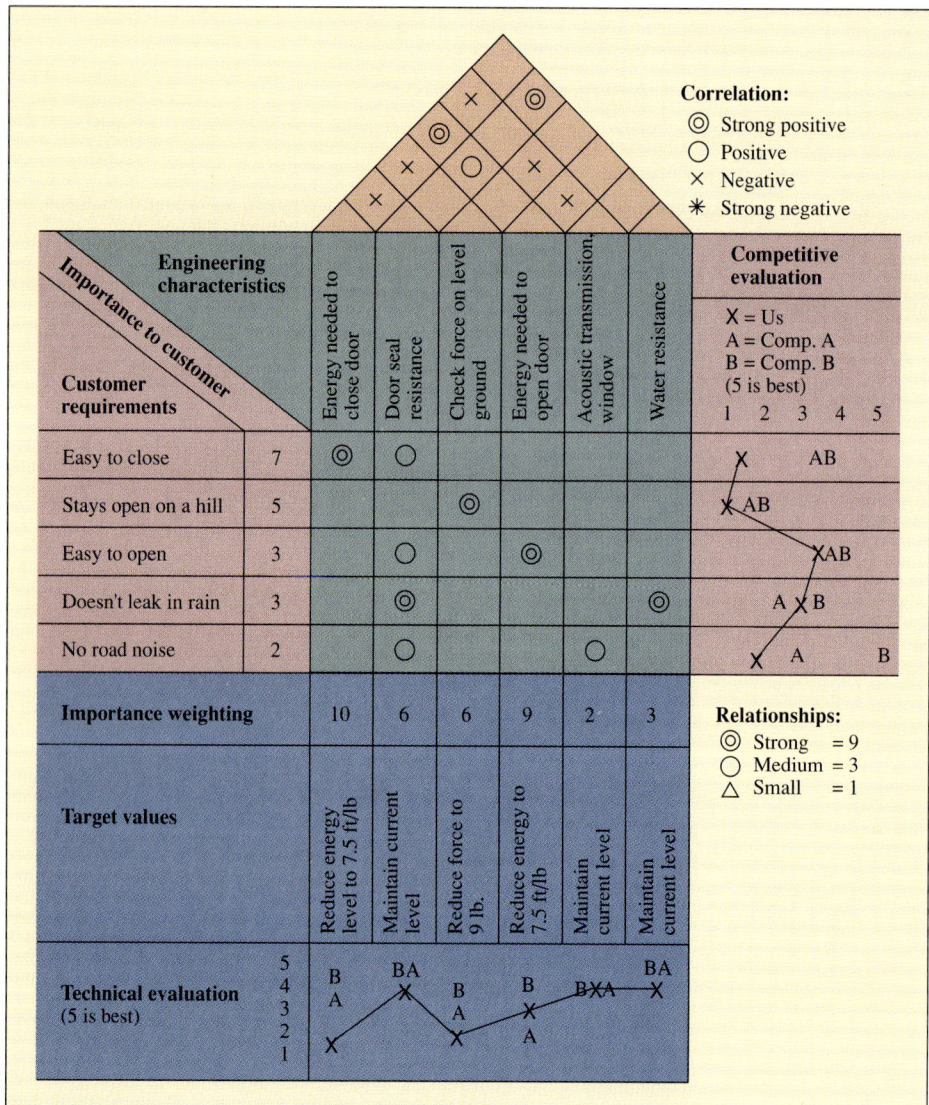

Source: Based on John R. Hauser and Don Clausing, "The House of Quality," *Harvard Business Review,* May–June 1988, pp. 62–73.

the house of quality is that it helps the team to focus on building a product that satisfies customers.

Florida Power & Light (FPL), the nation's third largest utility with 3.4 million customers, used QFD to translate customer requirements into operational issues.[9] FPL wanted to find out what customers expect when they conduct business (such as calling to connect electric service, to discuss rates, to clarify billings, etc.). FPL used focus groups involving customers and what they wanted. It also conducted surveys to quantify the importance of each of these wants. It then formed cross-functional teams to translate these wants and relative values into operational changes.

FPL found that customers want to be treated as valued customers and in a timely manner (as we would have assumed). It also found that customers expect to wait only 94 seconds for service. However, if they know the length of the wait, they are willing to wait an additional 105 seconds, for a total of 199 seconds. FPL's final decision was to create three categories of calls since wait times were noted to be slightly different. FPL then designed a system called Smartqueue, which provided callers with an estimate of wait time and told them how many callers were ahead of them.

Although the house of quality appears complicated, it is not difficult to understand once the house is analyzed in sections. The customer attributes are found on the left side of the house with their relative importances to the customer specified. The customer perceptions of how the product compares to the competition on each characteristic is located on the far right side of the house. The second story of the house lists the engineering or operating characteristics of the product that are likely to affect the customer attributes. The interfunctional team completes the matrix in the middle of the house by indicating how much each engineering or operating characteristic affects each customer attribute. The strength and direction of the relationship is indicated by coded symbols. The roof of the house is also completed by the QFD team, and it indicates the correlations the various engineering or operating characteristics have with one another.

The importance weighting section specifies the significance of the engineering or operating characteristics listed in the matrix. The weight is based on the symbols in the middle of the matrix showing the relationship between the characteristic and the customer attributes. "Target values" for the engineering or operating characteristics are then defined by the QFD team. These are specific goals (often numeric) that the team believes enable it to fulfill the desired customer attributes. Finally, the team compares the technical characteristics of its product to those of the competition.

Value Analysis/Value Engineering   Since it is so important that quality be designed into products we should briefly describe value analysis and value engineering. The purpose of **value analysis/value engineering (VA/VE)** is to simplify products and processes. Its objective is to achieve equivalent or better performance at a lower cost while maintaining all functional requirements defined by the customer. VA/VE does this by identifying and eliminating unnecessary costs. Technically, VA deals with products already in production and is used to analyze product specifications and requirements as shown in production documents and purchase requests. Typically, purchasing departments use VA as a cost reduction technique. Performed before the production stage, value engineering is considered a cost avoidance method. In practice, however, there is a looping back and

---

[9]Bob Graessel and Pete Zeidler, "Using Quality Function Deployment to Improve Customer Service," *Quality Progress,* November 1993, pp. 59–63.

forth between the two for a given product. This occurs due to the fact that new materials, processes, and so forth require the application of VA techniques to products that have previously undergone VE. The VA/VE analysis approach involves brainstorming such questions as

Does the item have any design features that are not necessary?

Can two or more parts be combined into one?

How can we cut down the weight?

Are there nonstandard parts that can be eliminated?

Answers to these questions are converted into ideas to be developed and then proposals for management implementation.

Cost of Quality

While few can quarrel with the notion of prevention, management often needs hard numbers to determine how much prevention activities will cost. This issue was recognized by Joseph Juran, who wrote about it in 1951 in his *Quality Control Handbook*. Today, **cost of quality (COQ)** analyses are common in industry and constitute one of the primary functions of QC departments.

There are a number of definitions and interpretations of the term *cost of quality*. From the purist's point of view, it means all the costs attributable to the production of quality that is not 100 percent perfect. A less stringent definition considers only those costs that are the difference between what can be expected from excellent performance and the current costs that exist.

How significant is the cost of quality? It has been estimated at between 15 and 20 percent of every sales dollar—the cost of reworking, scrapping, repeated service, inspections, tests, warranties, and other quality-related items. Philip Crosby states that the correct cost for a well-run quality management program should be under 2.5 percent.[10] In China, the cost of poor quality can be extremely high, as the following boxed insert relates.

Three basic assumptions justify an analysis of the costs of quality:

1. That failures are caused.
2. That prevention is cheaper.
3. That performance can be measured.

The *costs of quality* are generally classified into four types:

1. Appraisal costs: the costs of the inspection, testing, and other tasks to ensure that the product or process is acceptable.
2. Prevention costs: the sum of all the costs to prevent defects, such as the costs to identify the *cause* of the defect, to implement corrective action to eliminate the cause, to train personnel, to redesign the product or system, and for new equipment or modifications.
3. Internal Failure Costs: The costs for defects incurred within the system: scrap, rework, repair.
4. External Failure Costs: The costs for defects that pass through the system: customer warranty replacements, loss of customer or goodwill, handling complaints, and product repair.

---

[10]Philip B. Crosby, *Quality Is Free* (New York: New American Library, 1979), p. 15.

MANAGERS EXECUTED FOR SHODDY QUALITY

(Beijing)—Eighteen factory managers were executed for poor product quality at Chien Bien Refrigerator Factory on the outskirts of the Chinese capital. The managers—12 men and 6 women—were taken to a rice paddy outside the factory and unceremoniously shot to death as 500 plant workers looked on.

Minister of Economic Reform spokesman, Xi Ten Haun, said the action was required for committing unpardonable crimes against the people of China. He blamed the managers for ignoring quality and forcing shoddy work, saying the factory's output of refrigerators had a reputation for failure. For years, factory workers complained that many component parts did not meet specification and the end product did not function as required. Complaining workers quoted the plant manager as saying, "Ship it." Refrigerators are among the most sought-after consumer items in China. Customers, who waited up to five years for their appliances, were outraged.

"It is understandable our citizens would express shock and outrage when managers are careless in their attitudes toward the welfare of others," Haun says. "Our soldiers are justified in wishing to bring proper justice to these errant managers."

The executed included the plant manager, the quality control manager, the engineering managers and their top staff.

Source: Excerpted from *The Wall Street Journal,* October 17, 1989.

'Exhibit 5.10 illustrates the type of report that might be submitted to show the various costs by categories.

Prevention is the most important influence. The rule of thumb says that for every dollar you spend in prevention, you can save $10 in failure and appraisal costs.

Often, increases in productivity occur as a by-product of efforts to reduce the cost of quality. A bank, for example, set out to improve quality and reduce the cost of quality and found that it had also boosted productivity. The bank developed this productivity measure for the loan processing area: the number of tickets processed divided by the resources required (labor cost, computer time, ticket forms). Before the quality improvement program, the productivity index was 0.2660 [2,080/($11.23 × 640 hours + $0.05 × 2,600 forms + $500 for systems costs)]. After the quality improvement project was completed, labor time fell to 546 hours and the number of forms to 2,100 for a change in the index to 0.3088, or an increase in productivity of 16 percent.

$$\textcircled{S}$$

Generic Tools and Tools of the QC Department

The generic tools of TQM are those developed for statistical process control (SPC), which we include later in this chapter under "Tools and Procedures of CI" and in the supplement to this chapter.

The typical manufacturing QC department has a variety of functions to perform. These include testing designs for their reliability in the lab and the field; gathering performance data on products in the field and resolving quality problems in the field; planning and budgeting the QC program in the plant; and, finally, designing and overseeing quality control systems and inspection procedures, and actually carrying out inspection activities requiring special technical knowledge to accomplish. The tools of the QC department fall under the heading of statistical quality control (SQC) and consist of two main sections: acceptance sampling and process control. These topics are covered in the supplement to this chapter.

E X H I B I T 5.10

Quality Cost Report

	Current Month's Cost	Percent of Total
Prevention costs		
Quality training	$ 2,000	1.3%
Reliability engineering	10,000	6.5
Pilot studies	5,000	3.3
Systems development	8,000	5.2
Total prevention	25,000	16.3
Appraisal costs		
Materials inspection	6,000	3.9
Supplies inspection	3,000	2.0
Reliability testing	5,000	3.3
Laboratory	25,000	16.3
Total appraisal	39,000	25.5
Internal failure costs		
Scrap	15,000	9.8
Repair	18,000	11.8
Rework	12,000	7.8
Downtime	6,000	3.9
Total internal failure	51,000	33.3
External failure costs		
Warranty costs	14,000	9.2
Out-of-warranty repairs and replacement	6,000	3.9
Customer complaints	3,000	2.0
Product liability	10,000	6.5
Transportation losses	5,000	3.3
Total external failure	38,000	24.9
Total quality costs	$153,000	100.0

Source: Harold P. Roth and Wayne J. Morse "Let's Help Measure and Report Quality Costs," *Management Accounting,* August 1983, p. 53.

5.3   CONTINUOUS IMPROVEMENT (CI)

Continuous improvement (CI) is a management philosophy that approaches the challenge of product and process improvement as a never-ending process of achieving small wins. It is an integral part of a Total Quality Management System. Specifically, **continuous improvement** seeks *continual improvement of machinery, materials, labor utilization, and production methods through application of suggestions and ideas of team members.* Though pioneered by U.S. firms, this philosophy has become the cornerstone of the Japanese approach to operations and is often contrasted with the traditional Western approach of relying on major technological or theoretical innovations to achieve "big win" improvements. In a survey of 872 North American manufacturing executives, the majority of world-class manufacturers favored continuous improvement over 11 other management enhancement programs. Clearly, continuous improvement is a subject that warrants a careful look.

In this section we discuss the key managerial elements of continuous improvement and apply some of the basic tools associated with the CI process. We also discuss its impact on quality improvement.

Although management in both Japan and the West historically have implemented CI in manufacturing plants, interest is growing about using it in services as part of the TQM movement. Consider the following *Fortune* excerpt about Federal Express:

At lunch with one team [of back-office employees], this reporter sat impressed as entry-level workers, most with only high school educations, ate their chicken and dropped sophisticated management terms like **kaisen,** the Japanese art of continuous improvement, and *pareto,* a form of problem solving that requires workers to take a logical step-by-step approach. The team described how one day during a weekly meeting, a clerk from quality control pointed out a billing problem. The bigger a package, he explained, the more Fedex charges to deliver it. But the company's wildly busy delivery people sometimes forgot to check whether customers had properly marked the weight of packages on the air bill. That meant that Fedex, whose policy in such cases is to charge customers the lowest rate, was losing money. The team switched on its turbochargers. An employee in billing services found out which field offices in Fedex's labyrinthine 30,000-person courier network were forgetting to check the packages, and then explained the problem to the delivery people. Another worker in billing set up a system to examine the invoices and made sure the solution was working. Last year alone the team's ideas saved the company $2.1 million.[11]

Based on a review of CI programs by Arlyn Melcher et al., two essential features distinguish continuous improvement systems from the traditional systems, which have been termed standard maintaining systems (SMS).[12]

> **Distinguishing Features of CI**

1. *Management's view of performance standards of the organization.* Under continuous improvement, management views the performance level of the firm as something to be "continuously challenged and incrementally upgraded." Exhibit 5.11 shows areas for continuous improvement.

2. *The way management views the contribution and role of its workforce.* The real potency of CI comes from the people management side of the approach. CEOs and operations executives of successful firms believe employee involvement and team efforts are the key to improvement. Such is not always the case with executives who adhere to the standard maintaining approach. Although they certainly say that people are important, they are more likely to be interested in the new generation of automated equipment they contemplate installing. This is not meant to suggest that CI executives do not employ some advanced technology in their plants; indeed, they often do. Rather, it is to point out that the philosophy of continuous improvement makes them think first of how such technology can be used to leverage the work and growth of the workforce. (One specific workforce management difference between the SMS approach and the CIS approach is that the latter is characterized by multifunctional work teams, participative management, a group orientation, and decentralized decision making.)

The approaches companies take to CI as a process range from very structured programs utilizing Statistical Process Control (SPC) tools to simple suggestion systems relying on brainstorming and "back-of-an-envelope" analyses. Exhibit 5.12 shows some common SPC tools used for problem solving and continuous improvement.

> **Tools and Procedures of CI**

Another tool is the **PDCA** (*p*lan-*d*o-*c*heck-*a*ct) **cycle,** often called the Deming Wheel (see Exhibit 5.13), which conveys the sequential and continual nature of the CI process. The *plan* phase of the cycle is where an improvement area (sometimes called a *theme*)

---

[11]Brian Dumaine, "Who Needs a Boss?" *Fortune,* May 7, 1990, p. 54.

[12]Arlyn Melcher, William Acar, Paul Dumont, and Moutaz Khouja, "Standard-Maintaining and Continuous-Improvement Systems: Experiences and Comparisons," *Interfaces* 20, no. 3 (May–June 1990), pp. 24–40.

E X H I B I T 5.11
Continuous Improvement Systems

Areas for Improvement	Method of Improvement
Method for discovering problems	Planned intervention in addition to natural stressors: • Labor reduction • Work-in-progress reduction
Scope of analysis	Holistic: • Problem classifications move from the subsystem toward the whole system
Time frame of solutions	Long term: • Address the root causes of problems
Types of solutions	System improvement: • Change layout • Change product design • Modify machines • Train and educate employees
Generality of solutions	Solutions evaluated for deployment in other areas
Direction of information flow	Upward and horizontal: • Suggestions flow upward for evaluation • Solutions are communicated horizontally for deployment
Frequency of information flow	High, regular: • The suggestion system and its evaluations
Role of operational-level management	Arm's-length supervision: • Acts as a consultant to workers individually • Directs instructions generally to groups of workers engaged in problem solving
Role of middle management	Supports and trains: • Trains workers to solve problems • Evaluates and helps implement suggestions
Role of top management	Futuristic: • Has long-term vision • Watches the environment • Provides the leadership for interactive planning
Environmental scanning and benchmarking	Extensive: • Either through a normal function or by means of shared responsibility

Source: Arlyn Melcher, William Acar, Paul Dumont, and Moutaz Khouja, "Standard-Maintaining and Continuous-Improvement Systems—Experiences and Comparisons," *Interfaces* 20, no. 3 (May–June 1990), p. 27.

and a specific problem with it are identified. It is also where the analysis is done, Exhibit 5.14 is a CI example using the 5W2H method. (5W2H stands for *w*hat, *w*hy, *w*here, *w*hen, *w*ho, *h*ow, and *h*ow much.)

The *do* phase of the PDCA cycle deals with implementing the change. Experts usually recommend that the plan be done on a small scale first, and that any changes in the plan be documented. (Check sheets are useful here too.) The *check* phase deals with evaluating data collected during the implementation. The objective is to see if there is a good fit between the original goal and the actual results. During the *act* phase, the improvement is codified as the new standard procedure and replicated in similar processes throughout the organization.

The group-level CI process is frequently represented as if we were developing a storyboard for a movie. Exhibit 5.15, for example, summarizes the steps just discussed as the "QI (quality improvement) Story."

E X H I B I T 5.12   *SPC Tools Commonly Used for Problem Solving and Continuous Improvement*

These tools do not substitute for judgment and process knowledge. They help deal with complexity and turn raw data into information that can be used to take action.

Process Flow Chart

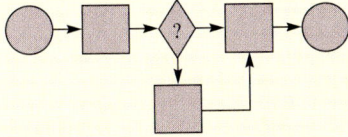

A picture which describes the main steps, branches and eventual outputs of a process.

Pareto Analysis

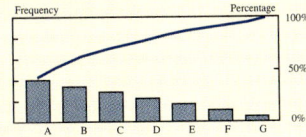

A coordinated approach for identifying, ranking, and working to permanently eliminate defects. Focuses on important error sources. 80/20 rule: 80 percent of the problems are due to 20 percent of the causes.

Run Chart

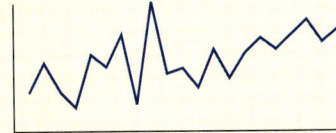

A time sequence chart showing plotted values of a characteristic.

Data Collection

Always have an agreed upon and clear reason for any data you collect. Prepare in advance your strategy for both collecting and analyzing the data. Questions that might be asked of data collection: Why? What? Where? How much? When? How? Who? How long?

Histogram

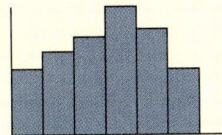

A distribution showing the frequency of occurrences between the high and low range of data.

Scatter Diagram

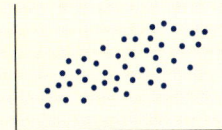

Also known as a correlation chart. A graph of the value of one characteristic versus another characteristic.

Checksheet

An organized method for recording data.

Causes and Effect Diagram

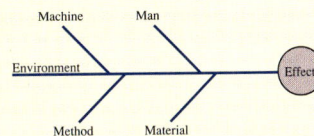

A tool that uses a graphical description of the process elements to analyze potential sources of process variation.

Control Charts

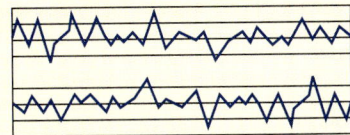

A time sequence chart showing plotted values of a statistic, including a central line and one or more statistically derived control limits.

Source: Coopers and Lybrand, *Quality Practices* brochure, 1989.

The CI approaches described so far are more or less inward looking: They seek to make improvements by analyzing in detail the current practices of the company itself. Benchmarking, however, goes outside the organization to examine what industry competitors and excellent performers outside the industry are doing. Its basic objective is simple: Find the best practices that lead to superior performance and see how you can use them. The practice of benchmarking is a hallmark of Malcolm Baldrige National Quality Award winners and is widely used throughout industry in general. Benchmarking typically involves the following steps:

1. *Identify those processes needing improvement.* This is equivalent to selecting a theme in CI.

2. *Identify a firm that is the world leader in performing the process.* For many processes, this may be a company that is not in the same industry. Examples

Benchmarking for CI

E X H I B I T 5.13

PDCA Cycle (Deming Wheel)

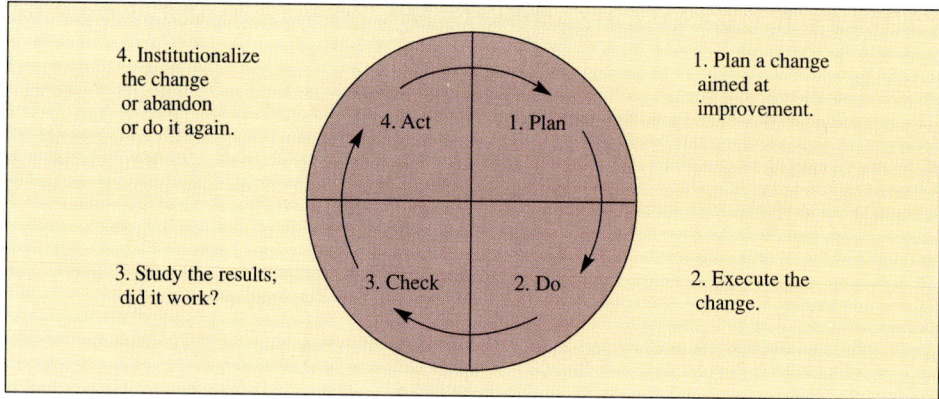

4. Institutionalize the change or abandon or do it again.

4. Act

1. Plan

1. Plan a change aimed at improvement.

3. Study the results; did it work?

3. Check

2. Do

2. Execute the change.

Source: Ernest C. Huge, "Quality of Conformance to Design," in Ernst & Young Quality Consulting Group, *Total Quality: An Executive's Guide for the 1990s* (Homewood, IL: Business One Irwin, 1990), p. 144.

E X H I B I T 5.14

The 5W2H Method

Type	5W2H	Description	Countermeasure
Subject matter	What?	What is being done? Can this task be eliminated?	Eliminate unnecessary tasks.
Purpose	Why?	Why is this task necessary? Clarify the purpose.	
Location	Where?	Where is it being done? Does it have to be done there?	Change the sequence or combination.
Sequence	When?	When is the best time to do it? Does it have to be done then?	
People	Who?	Who is doing it? Should someone else do it? Why am I doing it?	
Method	How?	How is it being done? Is this the best method? Is there some other way?	Simplify the task.
Cost	How much?	How much does it cost now? What will the cost be after improvement?	Select an improvement method.

A number of simple guidelines have been developed to help people or groups generate new ideas. In general, these guidelines urge you to question everything, from every conceivable angle. The figure outlines the 5W2H method. The five "W's" are what, why, where, when, and who; the two "H's" are how and how much.

Source: Alan Robinson, *Continuous Improvement in Operations: A Systematic Approach to Waste Reduction* (Cambridge, MA: Productivity Press, 1991), p. 245.

include Xerox using L. L. Bean as the benchmark in evaluating its order entry system, or ICL (a major British computer maker) benchmarking Marks and Spenser (a large U.K. clothing retailer) to improve its distribution system. A McKinsey study cited a firm that measured pit stops on a motor racing circuit as a benchmark for worker changes on its assembly line.[13]

2. *Contact the managers of that company and make a personal visit to interview managers and workers.* Many companies select a team of workers from that process to be on a benchmarking team as part of a CI program.

---

[13]Steven Walleck, David O'Halloran, and Charles Leader, "Benchmarking World-Class Performance," *McKinsey Quarterly,* 1991, no. 1, p. 7.

E X H I B I T 5.15   *The QI Story*

	QI Story Step	Function	Tools
	1. Select theme.	• Decide theme for improvement. • Make clear why the theme is selected.	"Next processes are our customers." • Standardization • Education • Immediate remedy versus recurrence prevention
	2. Grasp the current situation.	• Collect data. • Find the key characteristics of the theme. • Narrow down the problem area. • Establish priorities: serious problems first.	• Check sheet • Histogram • Pareto
Plan	3. Conduct analysis.	• List all the possible causes of the most serious problem. • Study the relations between possible causes and between causes and problem. • Select some causes and establish hypotheses about possible relations. • Collect data and study cause-and-effect relation.	• Fishbone • Check sheet • Scatter diagram • Stratification
	4. Devise countermeasures.	• Devise countermeasures to eliminate the cause(s) of a problem.	• Intrinsic technology • Experience
Do		• Implement countermeasures. (Experiment.)	
Check	5. Confirm the effect of countermeasures.	• Collect data on the effects of the countermeasures. • Do before–after comparison.	• All seven tools
Act	6. Standardize the countermeasures.	• Amend the existing standards according to the countermeasures whose effects are confirmed.	
	7. Identify the remaining problems and evaluate the whole procedure.		

Source: Paul Lillrank and Noriak Kano, *Continuous Improvement: Quality Control Circles in Japanese Industry* (Ann Arbor: University of Michigan, Center for Japanese Studies, 1989), p. 27.

4. *Analyze data.* This entails looking at gaps between what your company is doing and what the benchmark company is doing. There are two aspects of the study: One is comparing the actual processes; the other is comparing the performance of those processes according to some set of measures. The processes are often described using flow charts or simply written descriptions. (In some cases, companies permit videotaping although there is a tendency now for benchmarked companies to keep things under wraps in fear of giving away process secrets.)

Typical performance measures for process comparisons are breakouts of cost, quality, and service, such as cost per order, percent defectives, and service response time.

The Breakthrough box shows IBM's experience in applying Deming's principles and elements of the Baldrige criteria.

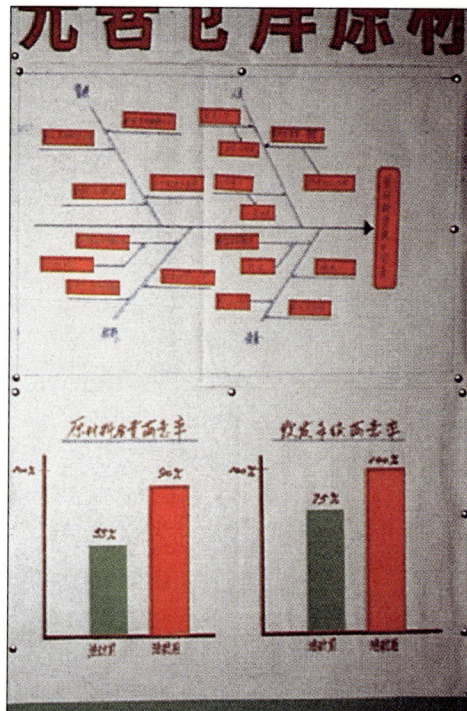

5.4   THE SHINGO SYSTEM: FAIL-SAFE DESIGN

Developing in parallel and in many ways in conflict with the statistically based approach to quality control is the Shingo system. As we discussed in Chapter 4 relating to service applications, this system—or, to be more precise, philosophy of production management—is named after the codeveloper of the Toyota just-in-time system, Shigeo Shingo. Although famous in Japan where he was known as Mr. Improvement, Shingo's work is just now being recognized in the West. Two aspects of the Shingo system in particular have received great attention. One is how to accomplish drastic cuts in equipment setup times by single minute exchange of die (SMED) procedures. The other, and the focus of this section, is the use of source inspection and the poka-yoke system to achieve zero defects.

Shingo has argued that SQC methods do not prevent defects. Although they provide information to tell us probabilistically when a defect will occur, they are after the fact. The way to prevent defects from coming out at the end of a process is to introduce controls within the process. Central to Shingo's approach is the difference between errors and defects. Defects arise because people make errors. Even though errors are inevitable, defects can be prevented if feedback leading to corrective action takes place immediately after the errors are made. Such feedback and action require inspection which should be done on 100 percent of the items produced. This inspection can be one of three types: successive check, self check, and source inspection. *Successive check* inspection is performed by the next person in the process or by an objective evaluator such as a group leader. Information on defects is immediate feedback for the worker who produced the product, who then makes the repair. *Self-check* is done by the individual worker and is appropriate by itself on all but items that require sensory judgment (e.g., existence or severity of scratches, or correct matching of shades of paint). These require successive checks. *Source inspection* is also performed by the individual worker, except instead of

Break*through*

Implementing Quality in a Sales Organization

The Vision of IBM Wisconsin

Constantly Improve Customer Satisfaction
- Improve relationships
- Improve face-to-face contact with customers
- Improve customer business results
- Improve customer feedback

Highest Employee Morale
- Improve skills
- Increase teamwork
- Improve tools
- Provide recognition and rewards
- Increase opportunities for professional growth
- Improve relations with business partners

Constantly Improve Our Quality
- Attain continuous improvement using Baldrige Award methodology
- Have the highest integrity

Increase Our Financial Contribution to IBM
- Increase market share
- Increase our profitability

Increase IBM's Contribution to the Wisconsin Community
- Improve our visibility in the community
- Increase IBM's participation in the community

IBM in Wisconsin

Responsible for marketing IBM customers in Wisconsin and the Upper Peninsula of Michigan, IBM in Wisconsin has about 700 employees in sales, service, administration, and technical support. As part of the overall process of changing the environment, 37 employees developed a vision of the organization's role in the 1990s (as Chart 1 shows). The vision, which is still in place today, calls for IBM in Wisconsin not only to sell computers to data centers but also to help customers gain competitive advantages in the worldwide market.

This vision did not result from a downturn in sales at IBM in Wisconsin or in the information processing industry. In fact, IBM in Wisconsin had experienced several years of significant sales growth. IBM in Wisconsin made the commitment to quality because it was uncertain that it could continue its success into the 1990s and because its customers were asking for more services and skills.

To start the transformation process, the local general manager and a sales branch manager learned about Deming's methodology, the Baldrige Award, and other quality principles. They discovered how IBM and other firms were implementing quality and analyzed how IBM in Wisconsin could incorporate quality principles into its organization.

Based on what the managers learned, IBM in Wisconsin took four initial steps:

1. The six sales branch offices in Wisconsin were given one quota to fill—that of the trading-area manager—to encourage the offices to work as a team. Individual quotas were eliminated.

2. The number of managers was reduced to facilitate a flatter organization and employee empowerment.

3. An education program was started—one that continues to this day. This was the most important step. Managers read Mary Walton's *The Deming Management Method.* Employees were exposed to TQM tools in a class called "Transformation Leadership," which described the need for change and characteristics of that change, such as empowerment and fact-based management decision making. This class is part of IBM's internal training for its Market-Driven Quality program.

4. A new compensation system for sales and technical personnel was developed by sales personnel. It rewarded not only revenue contribution but also customer satisfaction improvement, process improvement, leadership, and skills development. This was a radical change for a sales organization that historically emphasized only revenue volumes and customer satisfaction. But the customer surveys indicated that customers wanted representatives with better skills and an easier company with which to do business.

Teams Make Improvements

Teams were formed to improve customer responsiveness. For example, administrative teams worked on improving trading-area–wide functions such as billing, accounts payable, and telephone usage.

Teams implemented and fine-tuned the new compensation plan. They also developed an employee suggestion system, an employee recognition strategy that is peer-based rather than management-driven, and an employee opinion survey.

Teams were formed to work on tactical marketing issues. For example, they started a management consulting practice and staffed it with highly skilled personnel. They developed new performance plans that specifically

Implementing Quality in a Sales Organization (cont'd)

called for increased education in those skills deemed important by customers.

The technical consulting services organization (which is staffed with technical specialists previously located in the sales branches) designs customized systems and manages projects. The technical specialists were put into this new organization so that their expertise would be available across the state upon request. This move increased IBM's ability to apply the right skill to the right opportunity, regardless of the customer's location in Wisconsin.

Education and Training Continues

While the team efforts were underway, additional education programs were implemented. All employees, from the general manager on down, were required to receive quality instruction. In 1990, employees received, on average, about three days of quality instruction; by the end of 1991 and in 1992, the average rose to more than four days. A variety of classes were offered:

- A two-day "The Journey Continues" class, which covers the concepts of vision, teamwork, empowerment, and recognition and teaches the skills needed to implement each
- Two one-day classes on process management, which are conducted for teams as they are formed
- Three one-day classes on teamwork, empowerment, and the Baldrige Award assessment, which are conducted for natural work groups, such as teams of salesmen and technical personnel assigned to specific customers.

Self-Assessments

In the spring of 1991, IBM in Wisconsin was ready for a thorough self-assessment of its progress. An employee opinion survey conducted in May 1991 indicated that

- Eighty-eight percent of the IBM in Wisconsin employees bought into the quality efforts (up 100 percent in seven months).

- Sixty-seven percent approved of the compensation plan.
- Ninety-one percent endorsed management's leadership.

Using a modified, more detailed version of the Baldrige Award assessment, all organizations within IBM in Wisconsin assessed their operations, and a trading-area–wide assessment report was written. Many of the assessments were performed by quality councils or by teams formed for the exercise.

During 1992, several additional assessment projects were started. Quality indicators were developed to measure the organization's progress in meeting its strategic business initiatives. A benchmarking project was conducted to learn more about customers' requirements. Additional market segmentation work was performed, which provided more precise responses to market opportunities and market demands. Finally, another Baldrige Award assessment was conducted. Chart 2 summarizes IBM in Wisconsin's quality transformation.

Four Lessons

IBM in Wisconsin learned four lessons that are relevant to all sales organizations, regardless of their size or industry:

1. The senior sales executives must support the market-driven quality movement, be prepared to fight off critics, persuade people to join the movement, teach managers, shift resources, and empower and trust employees.

2. Employees closest to the customer know what changes have to be made to serve customers better. Managers must trust that their employees will be impartial and mature in their actions.

3. An enormous investment in education is required to persuade employees of the need for quality improvement and a Baldrige Award assessment. Additional training is needed on how to use quality tools, manage processes, work in teams, and empower em-

checking for defects, the worker checks for the errors that will cause defects. This prevents the defects from ever occurring and hence requiring rework. All three types of inspection rely on controls consisting of fail-safe procedures or devices (called *poka-yoke*). Poka-yoke includes such things as checklists or special tooling that (1) prevents the worker from making an error that leads to a defect before starting a process or (2) gives rapid feedback of abnormalities in the process to the worker in time to correct it.

Implementing Quality in a Sales Organization (cont'd)

ployees. Ongoing education and training are needed, particularly in such areas as interpersonal relations, business acumen, and technical development.

4. Measurement and compensation systems must be changed to reward employees for improving customer satisfaction, simplifying or reengineering business processes, reducing cycle time, and responding quickly to market conditions. Empowerment and teamwork should also be recognized and rewarded by peers.

A Worthwhile Effort

With competition increasing, sales organizations can't afford not to implement quality improvement efforts. IBM in Wisconsin has learned that the business volumes don't have to decline as the quality transformation oc-

curs. The quality transformation does, however, require a great deal of time and effort, and it initially increases education and staffing expenses.

The transformation takes hard work, and not everyone will want to invest the emotion, time, and effort needed. Employees buy in faster than managers; managers embrace the movement unevenly. The latter is a problem since managers control resources and are nervous that the quality transformation might threaten their careers. In the end, however, the majority welcome the ownership they gain for their processes and effectiveness.

Source: James Cortada, "Implementing Quality in a Sales Organization." *Quality Progress*, September 1993, pp. 67–70. © 1993 American Society for Quality Control. Reprinted with Permission.

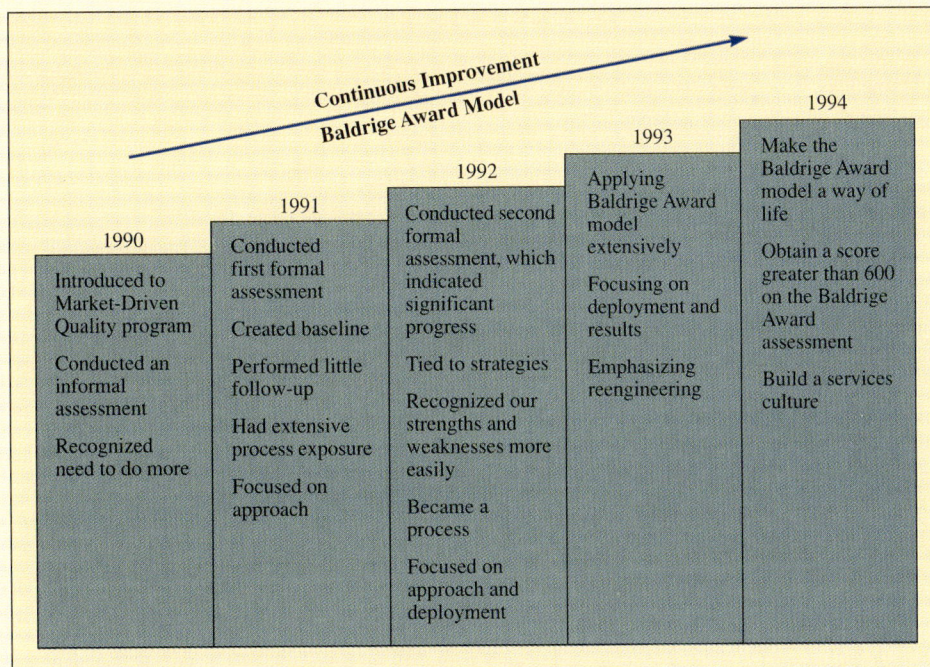

Continuous Improvement — Baldrige Award Model

1990
Introduced to Market-Driven Quality program

Conducted an informal assessment

Recognized need to do more

1991
Conducted first formal assessment

Created baseline

Performed little follow-up

Had extensive process exposure

Focused on approach

1992
Conducted second formal assessment, which indicated significant progress

Tied to strategies

Recognized our strengths and weaknesses more easily

Became a process

Focused on approach and deployment

1993
Applying Baldrige Award model extensively

Focusing on deployment and results

Emphasizing reengineering

1994
Make the Baldrige Award model a way of life

Obtain a score greater than 600 on the Baldrige Award assessment

Build a services culture

There is a wide variety of poka-yoke, ranging from kitting parts from a bin (to ensure that the right number is used in assembly) to sophisticated detection and electronic signaling devices. See an example taken from the writings of Shingo in Exhibit 5.16.

There is a good deal more to say about the work of Shingo. Blasting industry's preoccupation with control charts, Shingo states they are nothing but a mirror reflecting current conditions. When a chemical plant QC manager proudly stated that it had 200 charts

EXHIBIT 5.16

Poka-Yoke Example (Placing labels on parts coming down a conveyor)

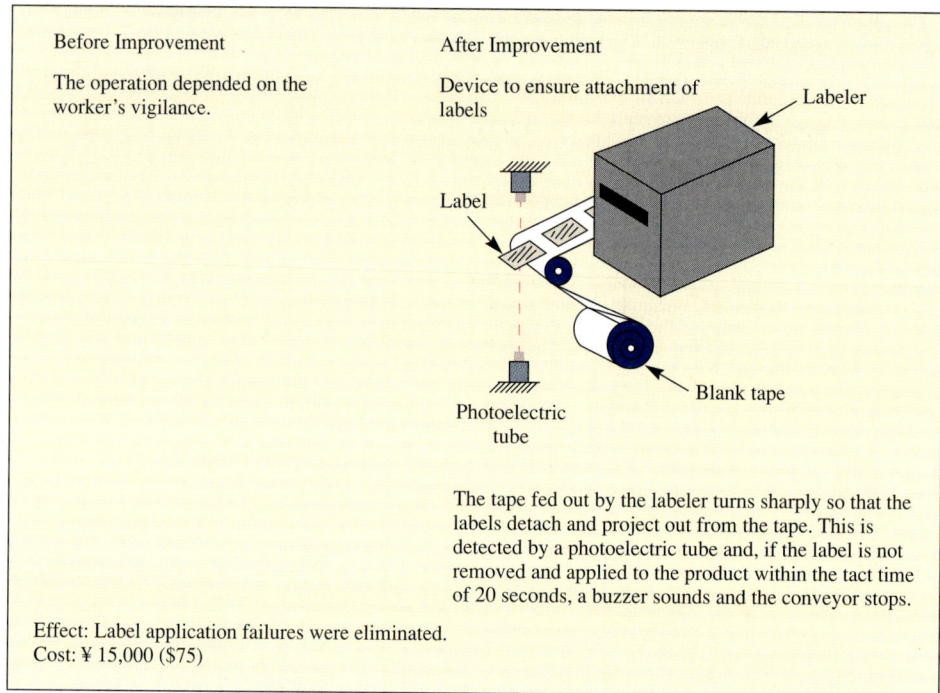

Before Improvement

The operation depended on the worker's vigilance.

After Improvement

Device to ensure attachment of labels

Labeler

Label

Photoelectric tube

Blank tape

The tape fed out by the labeler turns sharply so that the labels detach and project out from the tape. This is detected by a photoelectric tube and, if the label is not removed and applied to the product within the tact time of 20 seconds, a buzzer sounds and the conveyor stops.

Effect: Label application failures were eliminated.
Cost: ¥ 15,000 ($75)

Source: Alan Robinson, *Modern Approaches to Manufacturing Improvement: The Shingo System* (Cambridge, MA: Productivity Press, 1990), p. 272.

in a plant of 150 people, Shingo asked him if "they had a control chart for control charts?"[14] In addition to his insights into the quality area, his work on SMED is must reading for manufacturing executives.

5.5   ISO 9000

ISO 9000 is a series of standards agreed upon by the International Organization for Standardization (ISO) and adopted in 1987. More than 100 countries now recognize the 9000 series for quality standards and certification for international trade. Although ISO 9000 evolved in Europe, International Organization for Standardization members include over 100 firms throughout the world. In the European Common Market (ECM) alone, almost 50,000 companies have been certified as complying with these standards. The United States has been slower to respond, but several hundred U.S. companies have adopted ISO 9000. (Most of these companies have multiple plants and locations.) Certainly, all companies that intend to engage in international trade will have to adopt these standards eventually.

Historians claim that ISO 9000 originated from the quality standards of the U.S. Dept. of Defense (MIL-Q9858) in the late 1950s. The British Standards Institution adopted these standards and expanded them to include the entire business process in 1979 and called

[14]Alan Robinson, *Modern Approaches to Manufacturing Improvement: The Shingo System* (Cambridge, MA: Productivity Press, 1990), p. 234.

Quality System

9001: Model for Quality Assurance in Design, Production Installation, and Servicing. (To be used when conformance to specified requirements is to be assured by the supplier during several stages which *may* include design/development, production, installation, and servicing)

9002: Model for Quality Assurance in Production and Installation. (To be used when conformance to specified requirements is to be assured by the supplier during production and installation)

9003: Model for Quality Assurance in Final Inspection Test. (To be used when conformance to specified requirements is to be assured by the supplier solely at final inspection and test)

Guidelines for Use

9000: Quality Management and Quality Assurance Standards—Guidelines for Selection and Use.

9004: Quality Management and Quality System Elements—Guidelines.

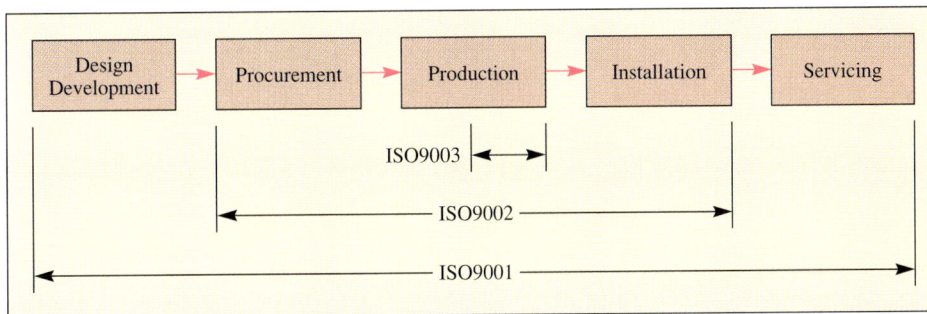

them the British Standard 5750. The International Organization for Standardization adopted the British Standard 5750 in 1987 and called it the ISO 9000 series.

The ISO 9000 Series

ISO 9000 consists of five primary parts numbered as 9000 through 9004 (Exhibit 5.17). If we were to display them on a continuum of an operating firm, the series would range from design and development through procurement, production, installation, and servicing (Exhibit 5.18). While ISO 9000 and 9004 only establish guidelines for operation, ISO 9001, 9002, and 9003 are well-defined standards.

Quite a bit of work and expense may be needed to be accredited at the highest level, which is 9001. Furthermore, some firms may not need ISO 9001 accreditation. For example, note that in Exhibit 5.18, ISO 9003 covers quality in production's final inspection and testing. A firm can be accredited at this level of final production only. This would essentially guarantee the firm's quality of final output and be attractive to customers. A broader accreditation would be 9002, which extends from purchasing and production through installation.

There are 20 elements in the ISO 9000 standards that relate to how the system operates and how well it is performing. These are contained in section 4 of the ISO 9000 Guidelines (Exhibit 5.19). Each of these elements applies in varying degrees to the three standards 9001, 9002, and 9003. (ISO 9001 contains all of them.)

ISO 9000 is somewhat intentionally vague. A *firm* interprets the requirements as they relate to *its* business. From a practical and useful standpoint for businesses, ISO 9000 is valuable to firms because it provides a framework so they can assess where they are and where they would like to be. In its simplest terms, it is sometimes stated that ISO 9000 directs you to "document what you do and then do as you documented." While to some extent this is true, ISO 9000 is much more than that since it promotes awareness and

E X H I B I T 5.19   *The 20 Elements to Be Addressed in an ISO 9000 Quality System*

1. Management Responsibility
a. The quality policy shall be defined, documented, understood, implemented, and maintained.
b. Responsibilities and authorities for all personnel specifying, achieving, and monitoring quality shall be defined. In-house verification resources shall be defined, trained, and funded. A designated management person sees that the Q91 program is implemented and maintained.

2. Quality System
a. Procedures shall be prepared.
b. Procedures shall be implemented.

3. Contract Review
a. Incoming contracts (and purchase orders) shall be reviewed to see whether the requirements are adequately defined, agree with the bid, and can be implemented.

4. Design Control
a. The design project shall be planned.
b. Design input parameters shall be defined.
c. Design output, including crucial product characteristics, shall be documented.
d. Design output shall be verified to meet input requirements.
e. Design changes shall be controlled.

5. Document Control
a. Generation of documents shall be controlled.
b. Distribution of documents shall be controlled.
c. Changes to documents shall be controlled.

6. Purchasing
a. Potential subcontractors and subsuppliers shall be evaluated for their ability to provide stated requirements.
b. Requirements shall be clearly defined in contracting data.
c. Effectiveness of the subcontractor's quality assurance system shall be assessed.

7. Customer-Supplied Material
a. Any customer-supplied material shall be protected against loss or damage.

8. Product Identification and Traceability
a. The product shall be identified and traceable by item, batch, or lot during all stages of production, delivery, and installation.

9. Process Control
a. Production (and installation) processes shall be defined and planned.
b. Production shall be carried out under controlled conditions: documented instructions, in-process controls, approval of processes and equipment, and criteria for workmanship.
c. Special processes that cannot be verified after the fact shall be monitored and controlled throughout the processes.

10. Inspection and Testing
a. Incoming materials shall be inspected or verified before use.
b. In-process inspection and testing shall be performed.
c. Final inspection and testing shall be performed prior to release of finished product.
d. Records of inspection and test shall be kept.

11. Inspection, Measuring, and Test Equipment
a. Equipment used to demonstrate conformance shall be controlled, calibrated, and maintained:
- Identify measurements to be made.
- Identify affected instruments.
- Calibrate instruments (procedures and status indicators).
- Periodically check calibration.
- Assess measurement validity if found out of calibration.
- Control environmental conditions in metrology lab.
b. Measurement uncertainty and equipment capability shall be known.
c. Where test hardware or software is used, it shall be checked before use and rechecked during use.

12. Inspection and Test Status
a. Status of inspections and tests shall be maintained for items as they progress through various processing steps.
b. Records shall show who released conforming product.

13. Control of Nonconforming Product
a. Nonconforming product shall be controlled to prevent inadvertent use or installation.
b. Review and disposition of nonconforming product shall be accomplished in a formal manner.

14. Corrective Action
a. Problem causes shall be identified.
b. Specific problems and their causes shall be corrected.
c. Effectiveness of corrective actions shall be assessed.

15. Handling, Storage, Packaging, and Delivery
a. Procedures for handling, storage, packaging, and delivery shall be developed and maintained.
b. Handling controls shall prevent damage and deterioration.
c. Secure storage shall be provided. Product in stock shall be checked for deterioration.
d. Packing, preservation, and marking processes shall be controlled.
e. Quality of the product after final inspection shall be maintained. This might include delivery controls.

16. Quality Records
a. Quality records shall be identified, collected, indexed, filed, stored, maintained, and dispositioned.

17. Internal Quality Audits
a. Audits shall be planned and performed.
b. Results of audits shall be communicated to management.
c. Any deficiencies found shall be corrected.

18. Training
a. Training needs shall be identified.
b. Training shall be provided.
c. Selected tasks might require qualified individuals.
d. Records of training shall be maintained.

19. Servicing
a. Servicing activities shall be performed to written procedures.
b. Servicing activities shall meet requirements.

20. Statistical Techniques
a. Statistical techniques shall be identified.
b. Statistical techniques shall be used to verify acceptability of process capability and product characteristics.

Source: Dennis R. Arter, "Demystifying the ISO 9000/290 Series Standards," *Quality Progress*, November 1992, p. 66. © 1992 American Society for Quality Control. Reprinted with permission.

continuous improvement. The International Organization for Standardization intended the 9000 series to be more than a standard, reflecting a well-organized operation with trained, motivated people. It is proposed as the new challenge, with firms that move quickly enjoying the benefits of being a leader, while those that delay lose business. In reviewing the parts of ISO 9000 that we show in the exhibits, note that they are common sense principles that have existed for many years.

Why is it important to become ISO 9000–certified? For one reason, it is essential from a purely competitive standpoint. Consider the situation where you need to purchase parts for your firm, and several suppliers offer similar parts at similar prices. Assume that one of these firms has been ISO 9000–certified and the others have not. From whom would you purchase? There is no doubt that the ISO 9000–certified company would have the inside track in your decision making. Why? Because ISO 9000 specifies the way the supplier firm operates as well as its quality standards, delivery times, service levels, and so on.

ISO 9000 has proved invaluable in Europe. Of 19 countries in the European Common Market, 12 are members of the European Community (EC) and 7 are in the bordering countries. This amounts to almost 400 million people!

Two major requirements for the success of the European Common Market are a common currency and a common set of standards for measurement. Prior to the ISO 9000, many standards had been prevalent, discouraging manufacturers from trading outside their own familiar markets.

There are three forms of certification:

1. First party: A firm audits itself against ISO 9000 standards.
2. Second party: A customer audits its supplier.
3. Third party: A "qualified" national or international standards or certifying agency serves as auditor.

The best certification of a firm is through a third party. Once passed by the third-party audit, a firm is certified and may be registered and recorded as having achieved ISO 9000 status and it becomes part of a registry of certified companies. This third-party certification also has legal advantages in the European Community. For example, a manufacturer is liable for injury to a user of the product. The firm, however, can free itself from any liability by showing that it has used the appropriate standards in its production process and carefully selected its suppliers as part of its purchasing requirement. For this reason, there is strong motivation to choose ISO 9000–certified suppliers.

If a manufacturer wants to purchase from a noncertified supplier, the manufacturer should visit the supplier and examine its processes, past performances, workers' credentials, and so on to verify that the supplier can meet the required quality levels and performance schedule. Of course, it is easier, cheaper, quicker, and legally safer to select an already certified supplier.

Certification can take as little as three to six months (if a firm is currently using military standards) or as long as two years (if top management is not fully committed). Certification involves getting the proper documents, initiating the required procedures and practices, and conducting internal audits. This can be followed by a second- or third-party audit as desired.

Currently in the United States, more than 1,000 firm sites have been certified. (Some firms have more than one site.)

ISO 9000 Certification

ISO 9000: An Everyday Example

One example that demonstrates how ISO 9000 applies to an everyday situation is having the brakes of your car worked on at the local garage.[15] You remember a local garage's ad for a special on brake repairs; in addition, you recall a neighbor speaking highly of the place.

As you approach the front counter of the shop, your journey through ISO 9000 begins. The clerk listens to your experience with the brakes as well as about your car. He informs you that your car will require metallic brake pads that will cost extra. You agree to go ahead with the job and the clerk promises your car will be ready in one hour.

As you wait, you mull over your main concerns: Will the car stop properly? Will the repair cost more than was stated? Will they complete the work in an hour? This is what ISO 9000 is all about—confidence that the task will be done *as promised.* The ISO 9000 standard encompasses many details that would easily be taken for granted. As illustrated in the rest of this example, the standard requires that attention be paid to every aspect of the brake job.

You realize that when you picked up the advertisement there was a management structure that made sure the business ran well and that quality methods and practices are used, which gave the garage a good reputation. You want to be confident that the mechanic knows where to get the work order papers for your car, and actually gets *your* car. Hopefully the mechanic has been trained to drive your car onto the ramp properly, disassemble the brakes, and inspect them to ensure nothing else is wrong. Also, you hope the mechanic goes to the proper documents and determines which brake shoes are right for your car and retrieves the parts from a bin with the shoes correctly identified. You would expect that if a mechanic tried to use some parts that ended up not fitting, he would have removed them from stock rather than putting them back in and passing the problem on to you. You hope that this person can assemble the brakes to the proper torque requirements and finally test them by driving your car around the block. You expect to be provided with a check sheet of the items tested and that your car was parked in a safe place. This example covers many of the 20 ISO 9000 elements.

1. *Management responsibility*—Someone is in control ensuring that the organization is selling products and services in the fashion it claims to.

2. *Quality system*—The owners of the operation have a quality system in place to ensure their business operates as indicated. When you approached the counter, the clerk created a contract with you. This person was knowledgeable about the product and communicated with the shop to know approximately how long it would be. The clerk had the training and documents to know that your car required metallic pads, where you should leave your car, and what to do when you returned to pick it up. This person was also willing and able to address your further questions and concerns.

3. *Contract review*—Ensures that the work performed by the mechanic was what you had agreed to with the clerk.

4. *Design control*—Ensures that the brakes placed on your car were properly designed, tested, and documented so as to perform the job as specified.

5. *Document control*—Ensures that the documents and reference books were available to the mechanic for the proper selection of materials and the appropriate testing.

---

[15]This section is from John T. Rabbitt and Peter A. Bergh, *The ISO 9000 Book* (White Plains, NY: Quality Resources, 1993), pp. 17–20.

6. *Purchasing*—Ensures that the mechanic had the correct parts available.

7. *Customer-supplied material*—(In this case, no material was supplied by the customer.)

8. *Product identification and traceability*—Ensures that the brake linings retrieved from the stock bin were marked properly.

9. *Process control*—There were established procedures for the mechanic to do the job, fill out the paperwork, find information on the materials, and access usable assembly instructions.

10. *Inspection and testing*—The mechanic did some form of inspection and test to ensure that your new brakes were acting properly.

11. *Inspection, measuring, and test equipment*—Ensures that the testing and measurement setting devices are calibrated to the correct torques and the right tools are being used to do it.

12. *Inspection and test status*—Ensure that the check-off sheet is a working document and that tests were performed.

13. *Control of nonconforming product*—Ensures that the mechanic knows what to do if a possible problem is detected with the material and how it should be treated and identified to prevent it from ending up on the other side of your car.

14. *Corrective action*—Ensures that the mechanic and his management have a procedure for fixing known problems.

15. *Handling, storage, packaging, and delivery*—The mechanic must know how to handle the brake pads before installation and ensure that they have been stored in a protected area. In addition, the mechanic must know where to put your car, keys, and paperwork when completed.

16. *Quality records*—The mechanic fills out a standard checklist, makes additional notes on the procedure being performed, and perhaps even has a place to record related issues for you to consider and for the shop to note.

17. *Internal quality audits*—The supervisor should be regularly observing the areas to ensure that the mechanic has all the correct materials and documents and is performing tasks correctly.

18. *Training*—This ensures that the mechanic had the proper training before working on your car and that the supervisor went over the task and verified that the mechanic was successful in all aspects of the job.

19. *Servicing*—Ensures that the mechanic knows what to do if something doesn't work correctly with the new brakes.

20. *Statistical techniques*—This ensures that metrics are kept regarding the quality of the service provided at the garage and are reviewed to ensure that the processes remain in control and that problem areas are quickly identified.

You notice an hour has passed. You go to the front desk. The clerk says, "Your car is coming out right now and we noticed that your driver's side windshield wiper was worn, so we replaced it free of charge, as our management believes your safety is paramount. Here are your keys and an itemized check sheet of all the tasks completed. This will also act as your warranty. Please note our toll-free number should you have any problems or wish to make an appointment for any of your other vehicles. Thank you for your patronage and please drive carefully."

This is a simple tale about brakes being fixed and a very happy customer in the end. It illustrated an ISO 9000–compliant organization taking care of the customer in a way that met the customer's expectations.

ISO 9000 versus the Baldrige Criteria

Rabbitt and Bergh nicely answer three questions relating ISO 9000 and the Baldrige award as follows:[16]

1. Should we go for the Baldrige Award or ISO 9000 certification first?   Go for ISO 9000 compliance first. Achieving certification will help you prepare for the Baldrige. The 1992 applications for the Baldrige Award were down, and it was the feeling of the Baldrige committee that this was in response to companies going for ISO 9000 certification first.

2. What's the difference between ISO 9000 and the Baldrige Award?   ISO focuses very closely on your internal processes, especially manufacturing, sales, administration, and technical support and services. The Baldrige places more emphasis on customer satisfaction and business results.

3. Do you have to be certified to ISO 9000 before going for the Baldrige?   The Baldrige assumes you have your processes under control and therefore awards relatively few points in this area. The Baldrige addresses the issues of customer satisfaction, business results, and the competitive aspects of gaining increased sales and profitability. ISO 9000 virtually ignores competitive positioning.

ISO is at the beginning of the quality evolution. ISO 9000 provides stability in the system and the minimum requirements for market survival. Once this is in place, it is easier to build to higher levels as Exhibit 5.20 shows.

5.6   CONCLUSION

This chapter contains a great deal of material that likely will form the basis by which all companies will operate in the future. The idea of a total quality environment including vendors and customers as well as all personnel and operations in the firm itself will probably not be a competitive weapon—it will be a requirement! A TQM environment with defect-free production will be an entry credential even to begin to play the competitive game.

What works best for each company depends on its current level of quality development. As the boxed insert on "Quality Improvement Practices" on page 198 shows, the most effective total quality management methods change as companies develop increasing quality expertise.

ISO 9000 has provided standards for certification and entry into foreign markets. It develops language and confidence for dealing with suppliers and customers and will be used in the United States as well.

The Baldrige Award has greatly helped industry to become aware of problems we have had with quality. It has spilled over to the general public in their sensitivity and

---

[16]Ibid., p. 22.

E X H I B I T 5.20   *ISO 9000—the Basic End of the Quality Evolution*

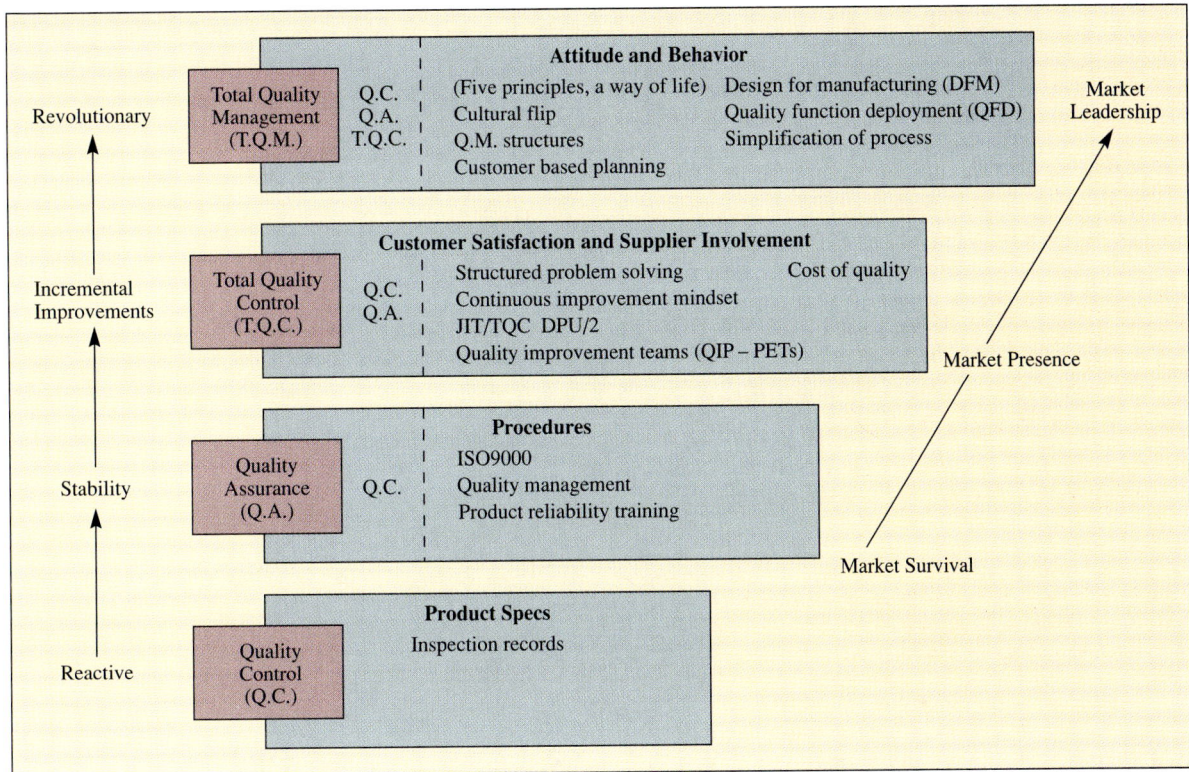

| | | | **Attitude and Behavior** | | **Market** |
| Revolutionary | Total Quality Management (T.Q.M.) | Q.C. Q.A. T.Q.C. | (Five principles, a way of life) Cultural flip Q.M. structures Customer based planning | Design for manufacturing (DFM) Quality function deployment (QFD) Simplification of process | Leadership |

Total Quality Management (T.Q.M.) — Q.C. Q.A. T.Q.C.

Attitude and Behavior
(Five principles, a way of life)   Design for manufacturing (DFM)
Cultural flip   Quality function deployment (QFD)
Q.M. structures   Simplification of process
Customer based planning

Incremental Improvements — Total Quality Control (T.Q.C.) — Q.C. Q.A.

Customer Satisfaction and Supplier Involvement
Structured problem solving   Cost of quality
Continuous improvement mindset
JIT/TQC DPU/2
Quality improvement teams (QIP – PETs)

Market Presence

Stability — Quality Assurance (Q.A.) — Q.C.

Procedures
ISO9000
Quality management
Product reliability training

Market Survival

Reactive — Quality Control (Q.C.)

Product Specs
Inspection records

Source: John. T. Rabbitt and Peter A. Bergh, *The ISO 9000 Book* (White Plains, NY: Quality Resources, 1993), p. 23

concern for quality. But note that only about one out of every 2,000 application packages sent out is finally submitted for the Baldrige Award. There were fewer than 500 completed applications whereas more than 900,000 were mailed out. That is not as bad as it looks, however. Baldrige criteria seem to be the best guidelines so far to develop a total quality management system. Firms are using the application forms for this purpose.

What is next after TQM? We can only speculate, but one thing is certain: It will be based on the presumption that a total quality system is a given.

5.7   REVIEW AND DISCUSSION QUESTIONS

1. What are the commonalities among companies winning the Baldrige Award?
2. How could you apply the Baldrige Award criteria to your university?
3. "Baldrige criteria are more appropriate for evaluating manufacturing firms than service firms." Comment.
4. How is the Baldrige award process beneficial to companies that do not win?
5. What are the limitations of QFD for designing a service encounter?

*Quality
Improvement
Practices and
Current
Company
Performance*

The appropriateness of various quality tools and approaches for a given company depends on its current level of performance. This was the conclusion in a study by *Ernst & Young*.

The Ernst & Young study offers quality-improvement models for companies at three performance levels: lower, medium and higher, ranked by a composite of profitability, productivity, and quality measures. The companies studied divide roughly evenly into three groups.

In general, the study contends, quality efforts work best when companies start with a few, highly focused practices and add more sophisticated ones later. The report's dos and don'ts include:

—Lower Performers: Emphasize teams across and within departments, and increase training of all sorts. Don't use benchmarking or encourage wide participation in quality-related meetings.

—Medium Performers: Simplify such corporate processes as design, and focus training on problem solving. Don't select suppliers based on their reputation; choose them through competitive bidding and by certifying their quality efforts.

—Higher Performers: Use benchmarking to identify new products and services. Encourage companywide quality meetings. Don't increase departmental teams, lest they inhibit cooperation across functions.

Among its other findings, the study reports that disbursing decision-making power—"empowering" individual employees, another fast-growing practice—works best in higher-performing organizations. Lower-performing companies typically "don't have the training or strategy in place to make empowerment work," says Terrence Ozan, head of performance consulting at Ernst & Young. He cites one exception: lower performers can benefit from giving customer representatives more authority to resolve consumer complaints faster.

The study doesn't challenge all conventional wisdom. It identifies a handful of practices that consistently benefit every organization. These so-called "universal truths" include explaining the corporate strategic plan to employees, customers, and suppliers; improving and simplifying production and development processes; and scrutinizing and shortening "cycle time" (how long it takes to get something done—from the design to delivery of a product).

Source: *The Wall Street Journal*, Thursday, October 1, 1992, p. B1.

6. "If line employees are required to assume the quality control function, their productivity will decrease." Discuss this.

7. "You don't inspect quality into a product; you have to build it in." Discuss the implications of this statement.

8. "Before you build quality in, you must think it in." How do the implications of this statement differ from those of Question 7?

9. Business writer Tom Peters has suggested that in making process changes, we should "Try it, test it, and get on with it." How does this philosophy square with the continuous improvement philosophy?

10. How valuable to customers is the improvement developed in this chapter's bank case study about shortening customers' waiting time on the phone?

11. Are there any poka-yokes that could be applied to the bank study referred to in Question 10?

12. Conduct a quick value analysis on a recent purchase you have made. Are you a "happy camper" or do you have buyer's regret?

13. You are the VE person for the company that made the product you analyzed in Question 12. What design changes would you make?

14. Shingo told a story of a poka-yoke he developed to make sure that operators avoided the mistake of putting less than the required four springs in a push button device. The existing method involved assemblers taking individual springs from a box containing several hundred, and then placing two of them behind an ON button and two more behind an OFF button. What was the poka-yoke Shingo created?

15. The typical computerized word processing package is loaded with poka-yokes. List three. Are there any others you wish the packages had?

5.8 PROBLEMS

1. Professor Chase is frustrated by his inability to make a good cup of coffee in the morning. Show how you would use a fishbone diagram to analyze the process he uses to make a cup of his evil brew.

2. Use the benchmarking process and as many CI tools as you can to improve your performance in your weakest course in school.

3. The following is a partial house of quality for a golf club. Provide an importance weighting from your perspective (or that of a golfing friend) in the unshaded areas. If you can, compare it to a club where you or your friend plays using the QFD approach.

WHATs versus HOWs
Strong Relationship: ●
Medium Relationship: ○
Weak Relationship: △

HOWs (columns): Physical Aspects, Course location, Ground maintainance, Landscaping, Pin placement, Course tuning, Tee placement, Service Facilities, Customer-trained attendants, Top quality food, Highly rated chefs, Attractive restaurant, Tournament Activities, Calloway handicapping, Exciting door prizes, Perception Issues, Invitation only, Types of guests, Income level, Celebrity

WHATs (rows):
- Physical Aspects
  - Manicured grounds
  - Easy access
  - Challenging
- Service Facilities
  - Restaurant facilities
  - Good food
  - Good service
  - Good layout
  - Plush locker room
  - Helpful service attendants
- Tournament Facilities
  - Good tournament prize
  - Types of players
  - Fair handicapping system
- Perception Issues
  - Prestigious

5.9 C A S E

Hank Kolb, Director Quality Assurance

Hank Kolb was whistling as he walked toward his office, still feeling a bit like a stranger since he had been hired four weeks before as director, quality assurance. All that week he had been away from the plant at an interesting seminar, entitled "Quality in the 90s," given for quality managers of manufacturing plants by the corporate training department. He was now looking forward to digging into the quality problems at this industrial products plant employing 1,200 people.

Kolb poked his head into Mark Hamler's office, his immediate subordinate as the quality control manager, and asked him how things had gone during the past week. Hamler's muted smile and an "Oh, fine," stopped Kolb in his tracks. He didn't know Hamler very well and was unsure about pursuing this reply any further. Kolb was still uncertain of how to start building a relationship with him since Hamler had been passed over for the promotion to Kolb's job—Hamler's evaluation form had stated "superb technical knowledge; managerial skills lacking." Kolb decided to inquire a little further and asked Hamler what had happened; he replied: "Oh, just another typical quality snafu. We had a little problem on the Greasex line last week [a specialized degreasing solvent packed in a spray can for the high technology sector]. A little high pressure was found in some cans on the second shift, but a supervisor vented them so that we could ship them out. We met our delivery schedule!" Since Kolb was still relatively unfamiliar with the plant and its products, he asked Hamler to elaborate; painfully, Hamler continued:

We've been having some trouble with the new filling equipment and some of the cans were pressurized beyond our AQL [acceptable quality level] on a psi rating scale. The production rate is still 50 percent of standard, about 14 cases per shift, and we caught it halfway into the shift. Mac Evans [the inspector for that line] picked it up, tagged the cases "hold," and went on about his duties. When he returned at the end of the shift to write up the rejects, Wayne Simmons, first-line supervisor, was by a pallet of finished goods finishing sealing up a carton of the rejected Greasex; the reject "hold" tags had been removed. He told Mac that he had heard about the high pressure from another inspector at coffee break, had come back, taken off the tags, individually turned the cans upside down and vented every one of them in the eight rejected cartons. He told Mac that production planning was really pushing for the stuff and they couldn't delay by having it sent through the rework area. He told Mac that he would get on the operator to run the equipment right next time. Mac didn't write it up but came in about three days

ago to tell me about it. Oh, it happens every once in a while and I told him to make sure to check with maintenance to make sure the filling machine was adjusted; and I saw Wayne in the hall and told him that he ought to send the stuff through rework next time.

Kolb was a bit dumbfounded at this and didn't say much—he didn't know if this was a big deal or not. When he got to his office he thought again what Morganthal, general manager, had said when he had hired him. He warned Kolb about the "lack of quality attitude" in the plant, and said that Kolb "should try and do something about this." Morganthal further emphasized the quality problems in the plant: "We have to improve our quality, it's costing us a lot of money, I'm sure of it, but I can't prove it! Hank, you have my full support in this matter; you're in charge of these quality problems. This downward quality-productivity-turnover spiral has to end!"

The incident had happened a week before; the goods were probably out in the customer's hands by now, and everyone had forgotten about it (or wanted to). There seemed to be more pressing problems than this for Kolb to spend his time on, but this continued to nag him. He felt that the quality department was being treated as a joke, and he also felt that this was a personal slap from manufacturing. He didn't want to start a war with the production people, but what could he do? Kolb was troubled enough to cancel his appointments and spend the morning talking to a few people. After a long and very tactful morning, he learned the following information:

1. *From personnel.* The operator for the filling equipment had just been transferred from shipping two weeks ago. He had no formal training in this job but was being trained by Wayne, on the job, to run the equipment. When Mac had tested the high-pressure cans the operator was nowhere to be found and had only learned of the rejected material from Wayne after the shift was over.

2. *From plant maintenance.* This particular piece of automated filling equipment had been purchased two years ago for use on another product. It had been switched to the Greasex line six months ago and maintenance had had 12 work orders during the last month for repairs or adjustments on it. The equipment had been adapted by plant maintenance for handling the lower viscosity of Greasex, which it had not

originally been designed for. This included designing a special filling head. There was no scheduled preventive maintenance for this equipment and the parts for the sensitive filling head, replaced three times in the last six months, had to be made at a nearby machine shop. Nonstandard downtime was running at 15 percent of actual running time.

3. *From purchasing.* The plastic nozzle heads for the Greasex can, designed by a vendor for this new product on a rush order, were often found with slight burrs on the inside rim, and this caused some trouble in fitting the top to the can. An increase in application pressure at the filling head by maintenance adjustment had solved the burr application problem or had at least forced the nozzle heads on despite burrs. Purchasing agents said that they were going to talk to the sales representative of the nozzle head supplier about this the next time he came in.

4. *From product design and packaging.* The can, designed especially for Greasex, had been contoured to allow better gripping by the user. This change, instigated by marketing research, set Greasex apart from the appearance of its competitors and was seen as significant by the designers. There had been no test of the effects of the contoured can on filling speed or filling hydrodynamics from a high-pressured filling head. Kolb had a hunch that the new design was acting as a venturi (carrier creating suction) when being filled, but the packaging designer thought that was unlikely.

5. *From manufacturing manager.* He had heard about the problem; in fact, Simmons had made a joke about it, bragging about how he beat his production quota to the other foremen and shift supervisors. The manufacturing manager thought Simmons was one of the "best foremen we have . . . he always gets his production out." His promotion papers were actually on the manufacturing manager's desk when Kolb dropped by. Simmons was being strongly considered for promotion to shift supervisor. The manufacturing manager, under pressure from Morganthal for cost improvements and reduced delivery times, sympathized with Kolb but said that the rework area would have vented with their pressure gauges what Wayne had done by hand. "But, I'll speak with Wayne about the incident," he said.

6. *From marketing.* The introduction of Greasex had been rushed to market to beat competitors and a major promotional-advertising campaign was underway to increase consumer awareness. A deluge of orders was swamping the order-taking department and putting

Greasex high on the back-order list. Production had to turn the stuff out; even being a little off spec was tolerable because "it would be better to have it on the shelf than not there at all. Who cares if the label is a little crooked or the stuff comes out with a little too much pressure? We need market share now in that high-tech segment."

What bothered Kolb most was the safety issue of the high pressure in the cans. He had no way of knowing how much of a hazard the high pressure was or if Simmons had vented them enough to effectively reduce the hazard. The data from the can manufacturer, which Hamler had showed him, indicated that the high pressure found by the inspector was not in the danger area. But, again, the inspector had only used a sample testing procedure to reject the eight cases. Even if he could morally accept that there was no product safety hazard, could Kolb make sure that this would never happen again?

Skipping lunch, Kolb sat in his office and thought about the morning's events. The past week's seminar had talked about the role of quality, productivity and quality, creating a new attitude, and the quality challenge, but where had they told him what to do when this happened? He had left a very good job to come here because he thought the company was serious about the importance of quality, and he wanted a challenge. Kolb had demanded and received a salary equal to the manufacturing, marketing, and R&D directors, and he was one of the direct reports to the general manager. Yet he still didn't know exactly what he should or shouldn't do, or even what he could or couldn't do under these circumstances.

Questions

1. What are the causes of the quality problems on the Greasex line? Display your answer on a fishbone diagram.

2. What general steps should Hank follow in setting up a CI program for the company? What problems will he have to overcome to make it work?

Source: Copyright 1981 by the President and Fellows of Harvard College, Harvard Business School. Case 681.083. This case was prepared by Frank S. Leonard as the basis for class discussion rather than to illustrate either effective or ineffective handling of an administrative situation. Reprinted by permission of the Harvard Business School.

5.10 C A S E
Shortening Customers' Telephone Waiting Time

This case illustrates how a bank applied some of the basic seven SPC tools shown in Exhibit 5.12 and storyboard concepts to improve customer service. It is the story of a QC program implemented in the main office of a large bank. An average of 500 customers call this office every day. Surveys indicated that callers tended to become irritated if the phone rang more than five times before it was answered, and often would not call the company again. In contrast, a prompt answer after just two rings reassured

the customers and made them feel more comfortable doing business by phone.

Selection of a Theme
Telephone reception was chosen as a QC theme for the following reasons: (1) Telephone reception is the first impression a customer receives from the company, (2) this theme coincided with the company's telephone reception slogan, "Don't make customers wait, and avoid needless

E X H I B I T C5.1
Why Customers Had to Wait

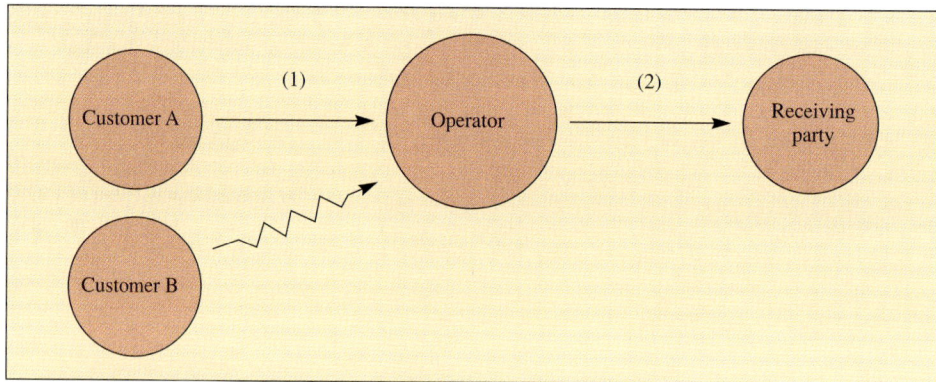

E X H I B I T C5.2   *Cause-and-Effect Diagram*

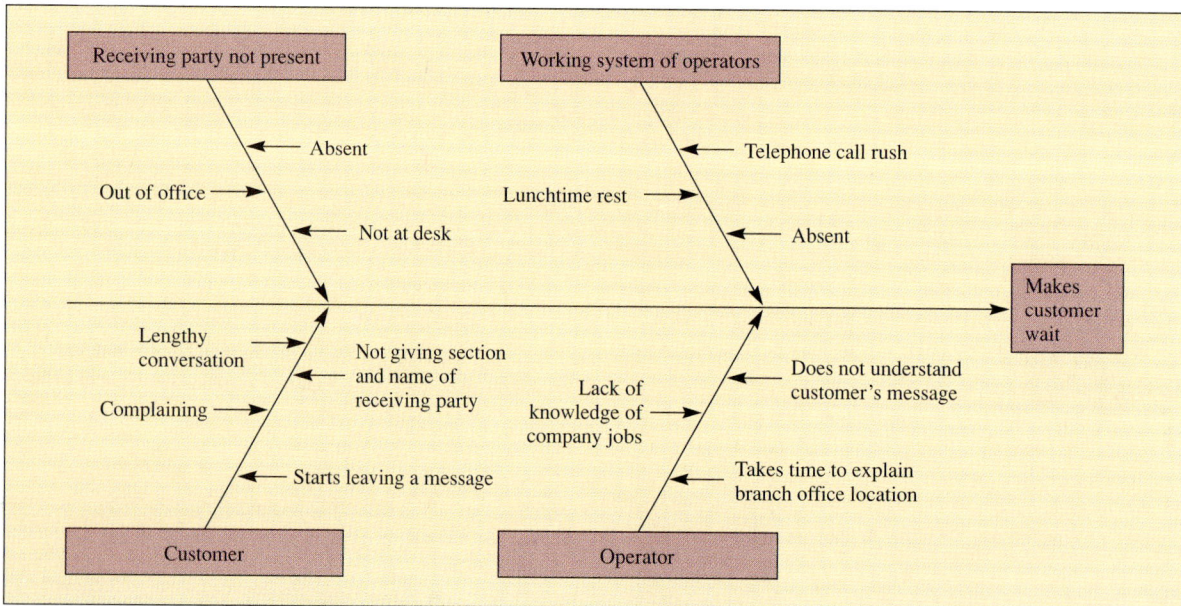

switching from extension to extension," and (3) it also coincided with a companywide campaign being promoted at that time which advocated being friendly to everyone one met.

First, the staff discussed why the present method of answering calls made callers wait. Case Exhibit C5.1 illustrates a frequent situation, where a call from customer B comes in while the operator is talking with customer A. Let's see why the customer has to wait.

At (1), the operator receives a call from the customer but, due to lack of experience, does not know where to connect the call. At (2), the receiving party cannot answer the phone quickly, perhaps because he or she is unavailable, and no one else can take the call. The result is that the operator must transfer the call to another extension while apologizing for the delay.

Cause-and-Effect Diagram and Situation Analysis

To fully understand the situation, the circle members decided to conduct a survey regarding callers who waited for more than five rings. Circle members itemized factors

at a brainstorming discussion and arranged them in a cause-and-effect diagram. (See Exhibit C5.2.) Operators then kept check sheets on several points to tally the results spanning 12 days from June 4 to 16. (See Exhibit C5.3A.)

Results of the Check Sheet Situation Analysis

The data recorded on the check sheets unexpectedly revealed that "one operator (partner out of the office)" topped the list by a big margin, occurring a total of 172 times. In this case, the operator on duty had to deal with large numbers of calls when the phones were busy. Customers who had to wait a long time averaged 29.2 daily, which accounted for 6 percent of the calls received every day. (See Exhibits C5.3B and C5.3C.)

Setting the Target

After an intense but productive discussion, the staff decided to set a QC program goal of reducing the number of waiting callers to zero. That is to say that all incoming

E X H I B I T C5.3   *Causes of Callers' Waits*

A. Checksheet—designed to identify the problems

Reason / Date	No one present in the section receiving the call	Receiving party not present	Only one operator (partner out of the office)	Total
June 4	\\\\	ⅢⅢ \	ⅢⅢ ⅢⅢ \	24
June 5	ⅢⅢ	ⅢⅢ \\\	ⅢⅢ ⅢⅢ \\\\	32
June 6	ⅢⅢ \	\\\\	ⅢⅢ ⅢⅢ \\	28
June 15	ⅢⅢ	ⅢⅢ	ⅢⅢ \\\	25

B. Reasons why callers had to wait

		Daily average	Total number
A	One operator (partner out of the office)	14.3	172
B	Receiving party not present	6.1	73
C	No one present in the section receiving the call	5.1	61
D	Section and name of receiving party not given	1.6	19
E	Inquiry about branch office locations	1.3	16
F	Other reasons	0.8	10
	Total	29.2	351

Period: 12 days from June 4 to 16, 1980

C. Reasons why callers had to wait (Pareto diagram)

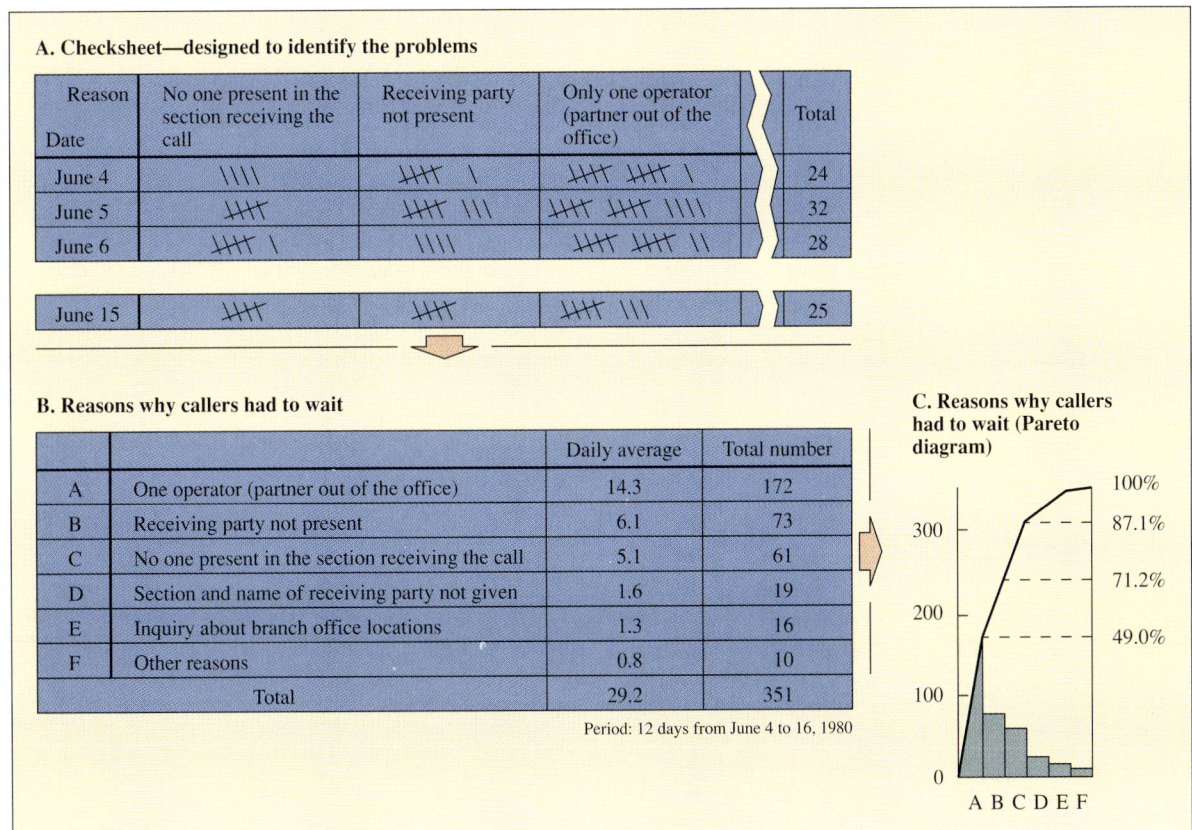

E X H I B I T C5.4

Effects of QC

A. Effects of QC (Comparison of before and after QC)

Reasons why callers had to wait		Total Number Before	Total Number After	Daily Average Before	Daily Average After
A	One operator (partner out of the office)	172	15	14.5	1.2
B	Receiving party not present	73	17	6.1	1.4
C	No one present in the section receiving the call	61	20	5.1	1.7
D	Section and name of receiving party not given	19	4	1.6	0.3
E	Inquiry about branch office locations	16	3	1.3	0.2
F	Others	10	0	0.8	0
	Total	351	59	29.2	4.8

Period: 12 days from Aug. 17 to 30.

Problems are classified according to cause and presented in order of the amount of time consumed. They are illustrated in a bar graph. 100% indicates the total number of time-consuming calls.

B. Effects of QC (Pareto diagram)

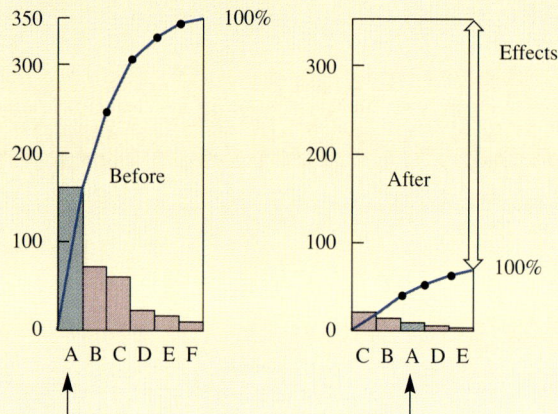

calls would be handled promptly, without inconveniencing the customer.

Measures and Execution

(a) Taking Lunches on Three Different Shifts, Leaving at Least Two Operators on the Job at All Times: Up until this resolution was made, a two-shift lunch system had been employed, leaving only one operator on the job while the other was taking a lunch break. However, since the survey revealed that this was a major cause of customers waiting on the line, the company brought in a helper operator from the clerical section.

(b) Asking All Employees to Leave Messages When Leaving Their Desks: The objective of this rule was to simplify the operator's chores when the receiving party was not at his desk. The new program was explained at the employees' regular morning meetings, and companywide support was requested. To help implement this practice, posters were placed around the office to publicize the new measures.

(c) Compiling a Directory Listing the Personnel and Their Respective Jobs: The notebook was specially designed to aid the operators, who could not be expected to know the details of every employee's job or where to connect her incoming calls.

Confirming the Results

Although the waiting calls could not be reduced to zero, all items presented showed a marked improvement as shown in Exhibits C5.4A and C5.4B. The major cause of delays, "one operator (partner out of the office)," plummeted from 172 incidents during the control period to 15 in the follow-up survey.

Source: From "The Quest for Higher Quality—the Deming Prize and Quality Control," Ricoh Company, Ltd., in Masaaki Imai, *Kaizen: The Key to Japan's Competitive Success* (New York: Random House, 1986), pp. 54–58.

CASE

5.11 C A S E
The First National Bank of Chicago's Quality Program

The skeptics are now believers, and the experts are downright impressed. The First National Bank of Chicago has earned its praise the hard way: by proving that measuring quality in the service industry not only is possible but truly is a formula for success. Since 1981, First Chicago has tracked and charted its performance on a weekly basis in 500 key customer-sensitive areas. Management at the bank felt that a quality-focused strategy is the most effective way to answer the competition, and was delighted to discover that an emphasis on quality helps monitor costs. At First Chicago, the installation and execution of its quality process has resulted in savings of $9 to $12 million annually. In addition to performance measurement, the bank's four-part quality process includes employee involvement, specialized customer service, and reward and recognition.

"We set out to increase the market share of our subsidiary—The First National Bank of Chicago—by positioning ourselves as the quality provider of corporate operating services," says First Chicago President Richard L. Thomas. "These are noncredit services such as corporate checking, funds transfer, shareholder services, and so on. These kinds of services were traditionally thought of as 'giveaways,' designed to help build a relationship for deposits and lending. We believed they could become profit centers on their own, and that the best way to achieve that goal was to emphasize quality and view it as a strategic marketing weapon."

First Chicago Corporation is the largest bank holding company in the Midwest with assets of $48.5 billion. The First National Bank of Chicago (First Chicago), First Chicago Corporation's principal banking subsidiary, is centered on its major businesses—the Global Corporate Bank and the Superregional Bank. The Global Corporate Bank encompasses all financial and operating services oriented to large domestic and international corporate clients. Within the Global Corporate Bank, the Service Products Group provides operating services focused on cash management, securities processing, and trade finance.

First Chicago is the eleventh largest bank in the United States and was founded in 1863. It is the oldest and largest national bank operating under its original name and charter. There are 18,000 employees working worldwide for First Chicago Corporation and 13,000 shareholders.

Since 1971, the required return on equity of the banking industry has been in a free fall decline. So for banks to remain in business, they must alter their business mix, pricing, and/or cost to recover from the free fall.

First Chicago has opted to set itself apart by concentrating on product offerings that meet client needs while generating a high return on equity. Included in its plan of attack is a focus on the high quality of services. For example, service and quality are key controllable buying determinants in operating services, as determined by a major independent research firm. Therefore, First Chicago is determined to be the highest quality provider in the operating services business.

"Satisfying customer needs and expectations is the number one reason for being in any business," says Aleta Holub, Vice President, Manager, Quality Assurance at First Chicago. "Customer responsiveness and loyalty to products and services will ultimately determine a company's success or failure. Customers' standards are constantly rising. A company's failure to respond to raised expectations is like denying the force of the tide. It can leave you high and dry on the beach, while customers sail off to competitors' ports."

"Our formal measurement program really began to take shape back in 1981," Thomas recalls. "We had a particular product quality problem—a system enhancement that was first delayed and then didn't operate as well as it should. We had to make sure the errors we had made in developing the new system didn't recur.

"So we got all the key players into a room and we realized that we needed some form of measurement to judge how we were doing. There was a lot of disparity around the table about just what we should measure, however, and we finally concluded that there was only one valid opinion: the opinion of our clients."

The bank surveyed many of its corporate clients on a product-by-product basis, emphasizing two key questions about each of its nine operating services: (1) What do you consider quality features of each particular service? And (2) what do you consider good quality in the delivery of those services?

"We wanted to make sure we were doing the right things correctly," says Holub. "We didn't want to be doing the wrong things right. By listening to our clients, we learned that what they most wanted and expected from us was timeliness, accuracy, and responsive service."

The first step the bank took in launching its quality process was to create a roadmap for the journey, better described as the company's mission statement: "Our mission is to be the premier bank in the Midwest with a reputation for excellence in serving clients nationwide and throughout the world. . .Our clients are First Chicago's highest priority. . . We are committed to providing our clients with high quality and innovative services."

Next, the bank altered its organizational framework. Separate strategic business units were created—each based on an individual product family. For instance, the Money Transfer unit's product family includes all domestic and international payment services. Operating under the philosophy that bringing the producer and consumer of a product closer together encourages better quality, the strategic business unit manager suddenly became an entrepreneur. The manager was vested with the power to control not only expenses, but also pricing, product features, promotion and quality.

This customer-focused framework was enhanced by the bank in January 1989 in order to further support the Global Corporate Bank, one of First Chicago Corporation's major businesses. In 1989, the Global Corporate Bank comprised $34 billion, or 69 percent of the corporation's total assets. The Service Products Group further articulated its role with a mission statement: "To enhance Global Corporate Bank relationships through service excellence, responsiveness, tailored solutions, high quality, and efficient operations."

A logo in the shape of a star was designed to show employees the key elements of the strategy needed to strengthen the Global Corporate Bank's relationships. All of the star's points represent an action included in the new mission statement—responsiveness, service excellence, tailored solutions, efficiency, and quality. Although responsiveness rests at the top of the star, every point is considered equal. Within the center of the star is the word "teamwork," for teamwork is thought of as central to the execution of the strategy. Without it, First Chicago cannot be a "relationship bank."

"Effective teamwork within the Service Products Group and with the Global Corporate Bank is critical to our success in serving our clients," says Holub.

Each Product Area has its own customer service representatives to handle inquiries and problems, and they act as conduits, communicating client concerns to the product area. Through this specialized customer service approach, the client talks to a knowledgeable service representative who is a product specialist. Because the customer service function and production area are in the same location, the representatives are more efficient and responsive. With the client dealing specifically with a product specialist, a closer relationship is possible, which encourages the client to offer feedback on enhancements and new products.

"We realize the client is the ultimate product specialist," says Holub. "They are the ones using the product on a daily basis. We wanted to make sure that our clients were dealing with a very knowledgeable person who 'spoke their language.'"

The operating services area of First Chicago devised a quality process that's today described as one of America's finest. This area's efforts were revolutionary in the financial industry and have been duplicated by other financial institutions.

In 1981, the bank went to work developing an extensive performance measurement system using nearly 500 charts to track weekly every product's performance in relation to the corresponding client concerns. For example, the accurate processing of money transfers and the turn-around time for letters of credit are measured. By focusing on the attributes of each major product and service, First Chicago learns how to fix a quality problem or sustain a quality advantage. Using the client's perspective and industry standards, managers from each area establish Minimum Acceptable Performance (M.A.P.) standards for each indicator, as well as a goal for exceptional performance. At a weekly performance review, data on how each product area is doing relative to these challenging goals are presented to senior management.

"To encourage performance improvement, the M.A.P. and goal lines are continually adjusted upward similar to the high-jump bar always being raised a little higher for the high jumper," says Holub. Managers' commitment to the program is reinforced because their incentive compensation is linked to reaching M.A.P. and goal levels.

"All of this measuring and charting is not simply to encourage in-house competition," Thomas says. "Nor do we do this solely to provide management information. The chief reason we measure, chart, and analyze is to bring about improvement. The objective is to fix a problem, not to place blame."

A very effective twist on the bank's performance measurement program is the invitation extended to both clients and suppliers to attend the weekly performance measurement meetings. First Chicago receives valuable feedback from clients by having them participate in these sessions. And since suppliers began attending, their service levels have improved.

"A two-fold benefit is gleaned by inviting both clients and suppliers to attend these meetings," says Holub. "First, the bank has an additional forum in which to learn about clients' expectations and concerns involving our products and service. We regularly use that knowledge to refine and improve both. More importantly, we are sending a loud and sincere message that the client is our central interest.

"The second benefit is that service levels from our vendors have also improved. Vendors are invited to see how well they are doing in relation to the bank's performance objectives."

Holub elaborates, "At the weekly performance meetings, competing vendors sit next to each other. For example, the IBM representative may sit beside his or her competitor from Tandem. Each has a chance to see the other's graphically shown performance and then prepare ways to top the other. The result is that the bank receives its 'fair share plus' of the vendors' attention and service. And, of course, our vendors' quality is critical to First Chicago's quality."

Employee involvement is another vital element of the bank's quality process, with more than 30 active quality improvement teams in place. These small groups of employees are brought together to identify problems or opportunities and to recommend actions to improve performance.

For example, when Illinois Bell announced a new area code for suburbs surrounding Chicago, an improvement team assumed a proactive role in guaranteeing a smooth transition for those clients affected. The team formed two months before the new area code went into effect, communicating the conversion to clients and employees alike. The area code change was completely painless for First Chicago clients (and employees) thanks to the work done ahead of time by the team.

The suggestion program within the Service Products Group has generated many excellent ideas for the bank. Handled through the Human Resources Department, suggestion boxes are located throughout the bank and are checked once a week by staff members. Suggestions are numbered and logged, and assigned to a manager and in the Service Products Group or Human Resources to research and respond. The updated log and new suggestions are discussed at the Group head's staff meeting every week. An employee who includes his or her name on the suggestion receives a written response, with a copy sent to the department head of his or her area. The Employee Relations Council also periodically reviews the updated log and those suggestions that are still pending a written response.

One suggestion concerned a work process issue. First shift employees on mail desks in Remittance Banking were working unnecessary overtime, so a proposal was made that changed procedures, improving productivity and lowering costs.

"With the suggestion program, we've learned that follow-up and communication are the most important aspects," Holub stresses. "If you do those two things well, employees will feel they have a voice and can make a change for the better."

The theme of the Service Product Group's Annual Awards Banquet is reward and recognition draped in elegance. The event is as close to the banking world's Oscars as you can get. And that's First Chicago's intention. Impressive is quite an understatement for this evening of celebration.

Positive strokes such as "most improved," "best sustained superior performance," and "most effective in improving quality in a changing environment" are announced emphatically. Yes, First Chicago realizes the importance of recognizing the accomplishments of employee teams within the product areas. These "teams," however, vary in structure. Some employees form a team from their normal work group and address problems affecting their department's productivity.

Then there are teams comprised of employees based on cross functional issues needing attention. These team members might not normally work together. A team can also be a form of recognition for accurate performance by a number of employees. For instance, if an employee consistently does not make errors over a specified time period, he or she is honored by "making" a team. This type of team is an honor group, so to speak, not a problem-solving group.

A dozen employee teams—one for each month—receive this recognition monthly and attend the banquet each year.

"Our objective is to improve the quality of First Chicago's services, recognize groups of employees who have contributed to that improvement, and further develop teamwork," Holub explains.

Each month's winning team receives a plaque and a paid group outing of its choice. The outing is usually dinner, the theater, or a sports event. The group decides on what type of event within the following expense guideline: a maximum of $100 per person with a ceiling of $1,000 per group. Each team member also receives a certificate, and everyone's name is entered in a grand prize drawing held during the annual banquet. The grand prize is round-trip airfare for two to anywhere in the U.S., plus $650 spending money.

"We've created an achievement-oriented culture in which we have asked our employees to work to their potential, rewarding and recognizing them when they do," says Holub.

Last year's November winning team was the Cash Disbursement Team. This group sustained "superior performance in processing currency and coin." The team accepts currency and coin requests from corporate clients and internal bank units. These orders are prepared, verified, packaged, and shipped to their proper destination. In addition, the team maintains an inventory of proper monetary denominations by receiving coin and currency from the Federal Reserve Bank and the bank's Deposit Processing Unit. The team members' accomplishments: since January, 1987, they made only six errors in the 305 million bills, $3.5 billion processed, without a single late delivery.

As mentioned in the opening, First Chicago has fans in respected places, including Tom Peters, who in his syndicated column "On Excellence" cited the bank as having the "quality program of the year." And in 1988, the company became the first financial institution to win the International Customer Service Association's Award of Excellence.

But Holub is quick to put the back-patting into perspective by offering First Chicago's 10 lessons learned during the near decade of quality work. These lessons include:

1. **If you can't measure it, you can't manage it.** Your managers might tell you they can't measure a process. But they've been able to manage it all these years, haven't they?

2. **People respect what you inspect.** And remember to inspect the process. American managers tend to look at problems as though they must be the result of people problems. Japanese managers, on the other hand, look at the process. "It traditionally has been 'whose problem is it?' versus 'what is the problem?'" adds Holub.

3. **Watch out for averages.** Be careful when looking at averages: very hot and very cold can average out to lukewarm. You may be missing important information from "average" performance.

4. **What gets measured gets done.** What you pay for gets done even better, says Holub. The measures included in the bank's annual chartbook give tangible proof of the quality that sets it apart from others.

5. **Make the steak good and don't forget the sizzle.** As an example of this point, Holub refers to a conference of the National Corporate Cash Managers Association. These cash managers—for the most part, treasurers of corporations—are the banks' largest audience. At the close of this conference, the cash managers were asked to rank the best bank exhibit booths. "One bank got the best score for a booth," she recalls. "Only it didn't have a booth at the conference. Obviously, the perception of how that bank does things is well established."

6. **The client is your product specialist.** "We used to have a generalized customer service area. Now we have specialized service representatives—Dedicated Service Reps (DSRs)," says Holub. "This should have been the arrangement from the start." Clients more readily suggest product enhancements to a DSR, who is well informed about their business. And the relationship is just as beneficial for the DSR, because the client directly evaluates his or her job performance by completing an evaluation form. The majority of a DSR's performance appraisal is based on the client's responses to the questionnaire.

7. **Don't underestimate the power of ownership.** "When was the last time you washed a rental car?"

Holub asks. Make your employees accountable for their performance.

8. **Wave the right flag.** "I'm not sure we did this at first," Holub confesses. The quality flag shouldn't be cost reduction/expense savings. It's easier to get employees involved when you wave the flag of Quality of Work Life or say the quality process will "take them out of an error-prone environment," says Holub. Be certain that management understands that quality improvement calls for the empowerment of people at all levels. If First Chicago were given the opportunity to start over again, Holub feels that the bank would make the connection between teamwork and improvement more explicit from the very beginning. Several years ago, changing the culture became more of a priority. One key to this culture change is the chance for an employee's peers from across the bank to evaluate his or her performance.

9. **Know the client's heartbeat so you know when your quality process needs a bypass.** Already well into its quality process, First Chicago began to actively involve clients in resolving problems. "However, we should've involved them (clients) from the outset," Holub says. Benchmarking itself against other service providers also started much later than it should have. After learning the benchmarking process from Xerox, First Chicago benchmarked itself not just against banks but against other companies well known for service quality, including Spiegel and United Airlines. For example, the retail side of the bank adopted one of United's practices: sending a supervisor out to "work the line" in order to speed up processing of customer tickets. Now supervisors work the line in the bank's lobby by preapproving transactions.

10. **Let the quality ship sail.** Trying to get everyone on the quality ship before sailing off to quality land was a mistake, says Holub. If a fresh start were possible, "I'd ask, 'Who wants to get on board?' and then spend our energy on the folks who were listening." And, adds Holub, "the quest for quality is not always going to be easy, so when there is no wind, start rowing."

Performance has been affected in measurable terms, thanks to the bank's quality emphasis. The quality initiatives demonstrate in quantifiable ways the strength and scope of a carefully planned and energetically institutionalized quality measurement program. As proof of improvement, back in 1982 one of the bank's operations experienced an average of one error in every 3,000 transactions. Today, the figure is one in 10,000.

"The success of the quality process within the operating services area alone is telling proof that providing excellent products and services and containing costs can be mutually compatible efforts," says Thomas. "In fact, we've learned firsthand that an emphasis on quality is one of the most effective ways to control costs."

For example, Thomas says, it generally costs First Chicago just under $10 to perform a money transfer. But that's a transfer done right the first time. If the money goes to the wrong place or doesn't make it on schedule, the cost of fixing an error can quickly rocket to $500 or more, depending on the amount of money involved, the complexity of the case, and so on. It's no big surprise, then, that First Chicago's quality effort has saved millions of dollars.

Another reason cost savings are critical is because more and more corporate treasurers are looking at the total cost of using one bank's operating services over another. The bank with the lowest per item price might actually be more expensive to use if its error rate is high. When a bank reduces its error rate, the overall cost a customer pays is reduced. And high quality, customer satisfaction, and competitive prices also mean repeat business, referrals, and new business, which makes the quality effort even more attractive.

First Chicago also realized the importance of communicating the quality commitment to its clients. So, annually, the bank compiles a comprehensive booklet of key performance measurement charts for clients to see what the bank monitors and how it performs in those areas.

"We recognize that when we make errors, both we and our clients have to spend time and money tracking and solving problems," Holub says. "By creating a quality process based on client-sensitive issues, and backing it up with real, quantifiable measurements, we have made a genuine commitment to provide service excellence.

"Although we are proud of the recognition our quality process has received, we realize the ultimate judge of our service is the client. Because of this, we are committed to exceeding every client's expectations."

Question

Evaluate the approach, deployment, and results of First Chicago's quality program. Based on your analysis, do they have Baldrige potential?

Source: Case Study 77, written by Stephen R. Stewart at the Houston-based American Productivity & Quality Center, August 1990.

5.12   SELECTED BIBLIOGRAPHY

Creech, Bill. *The Five Pillars of TQM: How to Make Total Quality Management Work for You.* New York: Truman Talley Books/Dutton, 1994.

Crosby, Philip B. *Quality Is Free.* New York: McGraw-Hill, 1979.

———. *Quality without Tears.* New York: McGraw-Hill, 1984.

———. *Running Things.* New York: McGraw-Hill, 1986.

Deming, Walter E. *Quality, Productivity, and Competitive Position.* Cambridge, MA: MIT Center for Advanced Engineering Study, 1982.

———. *Out of the Crisis.* Cambridge, MA: MIT Center for Advanced Engineering Study, 1986.

Durand, Ian G., Donald W. Marquardt, Robert W. Peach, and James C. Pyle. "Updating the ISO 9000 Quality Standards: Responding to Marketplace Needs." *Quality Progress,* July 1993, pp 23–28.

Ernst & Young Quality Improvement Consulting Group. *Total Quality: An Executive's Guide for the 1990s.* Homewood, IL: Business One Irwin, 1990.

Feigenbaum, A. V. *Total Quality Control.* 3d ed. New York: McGraw-Hill, 1983.

Gitlow, Howard S., and Shelly J. Gitlow. *The Deming Guide to Quality and Competitive Position.* Englewood Cliffs, NJ: Prentice Hall, 1987.

Giffi, Craig, Aleda V. Roth, and Gregory M. Seal. *Competing in World-Class Manufacturing: America's 21st-Century Challenge.* Homewood, IL: Richard D. Irwin, 1990.

Hodges, Richard M. *Blueprints for Continuous Improvement: Lessons from the Baldrige Winners.* New York: American Management Association, 1993.

Hoffherr, Glen D., and Gerald Nadler. *Breakthrough Thinking in Total Quality Management.* Englewood Cliffs, NJ: Prentice Hall, 1993.

Ishikawa, Kaoru (translated by David J. Lu). *What Is Total Quality Control?—the Japanese Way.* Englewood Cliffs, NJ: Prentice Hall, 1985.

Johnson, Richard S. *TQM: Leadership for the Quality Transformation,* vols. 1–4. Milwaukee: ASQC Quality Press, 1993.

Juran, Joseph M. *Quality Control Handbook.* 3d ed. New York: McGraw-Hill, 1979.

Juran, Joseph M., and F. M. Gryna. *Quality Planning and Analysis.* 2nd ed. New York: McGraw-Hill, 1980.

Lamprecht, James L. *Implementing the ISO 9000 Series.* New York: Marcel Dekker, 1993.

Lawler, Edward E., and Susan Albers Mohrman. *Employee Involvement and Total Quality Management: Practices and Results in Fortune 1000 Companies.* San Francisco: Jossey-Bass, 1992.

Mahoney, Francis X., and Carl G. Thor. *The TQM Trilogy: Using ISO 9000, the Deming Prize, and the Baldrige Award to Establish a System for Total Quality Management.* New York: American Management Association, 1994.

The Malcolm Baldrige National Quality Award. Managed by: U.S. Dept. of Commerce, Technology Administration, National Institute of Standards and Technology, Route 270 and Quince Orchard Road, Administration Building, Room A537, Gaithersburg, MD 20899-0001. Administered by: American Society for Quality Control, P.O. Box 3005, Milwaukee, WI 53201-3005.

Rabbitt, John T., and Peter A. Bergh. *The ISO 9000 Book.* White Plains, NY: Quality Resources, 1993.

Robinson, Alan. *Moderate Approaches to Manufacturing Improvement: The Shingo System.* Cambridge, MA: Productivity Press, 1990.

Rothery, Brian. *ISO 9000.* 2d ed. Brookfield, VT: Gower, 1993.

Shingo, Shiego. *Zero Quality Control: Source Inspection and the Poka-Yoke System.* Stamford, CT: Productivity Press, 1986.

Taguchi, G. *On-Line Quality Control during Production.* Tokyo: Japanese Standards Association, 1987.

Weimershirch, Arnold, and Stephen George. *Total Quality Management: Strategies and Techniques Proven at Today's Most Successful Companies.* New York: John Wiley & Sons, 1994.

1994 Malcolm Baldrige National Quality Award: Criteria and Application Instructions.

Supplement

5

Statistical Quality Control Methods

SUPPLEMENT OUTLINE

KEY TERMS

Statistical Quality Control (SQC)

Acceptance Sampling

Statistical Process Control (SPC)

Acceptable Quality Level (AQL)

Operating Characteristic (OC) Curves

Six-Sigma Quality

Design Limits

Capability Index (C_{pk})

Taguchi Methods

The subject of **statistical quality control (SQC)** can be divided into *acceptance sampling* and *process control.* **Acceptance sampling** involves testing a random sample of existing goods and deciding whether to accept an entire lot based on the quality of the random sample. **Statistical process control (SPC)** involves testing a random sample of output from a process to determine whether the process is producing items within a pre-selected range. When the tested output exceeds that range, it is a signal to adjust the production process to force the output back into the acceptable range. This is accomplished by adjusting the process itself. Acceptance sampling is frequently used in a purchasing or receiving situation, while process control is used in a production situation of any type.

Quality control for both acceptance sampling and process control measures either attributes or variables. Goods or services may be observed to be either good or bad, or functioning or malfunctioning. For example, a lawnmower either runs or it doesn't; it attains a certain level of torque and horsepower or it doesn't. This type of measurement is known as sampling by attributes. Alternatively, a lawnmower's torque and horsepower can be measured as an amount of deviation from a set standard. This type of measurement is known as sampling by variables. The following sections describe some standard approaches to developing acceptance sampling plans and process control procedures.

S5.1   ACCEPTANCE SAMPLING

Design of a Single Sampling Plan for Attributes

Acceptance sampling is performed on goods that already exist to determine what percentage of products conform to specifications. These products may be items received from another company and evaluated by the receiving department or they may be components that have passed through a processing step and are evaluated by company personnel either in production or later in the warehousing function. Whether inspection should be done at all is addressed in the following example.

Acceptance sampling is executed through a sampling plan. In this section, we illustrate the planning procedures for a single sampling plan—that is, a plan in which the quality is determined from the evaluation of one sample. (Other plans may be developed

An employee inspects the manufacture of Reece's peanut butter cups. This is the last stage of full quality control where defective cups are removed.

using two or more samples. See J. M. Juran and F. M. Gryna's *Quality Planning and Analysis* for a discussion of these plans.)

E X A M P L E S5.1 / *Costs to Justify Inspection*   Total (100 percent) inspection is justified when the cost of a loss incurred by not inspecting is greater than the cost of inspection. For example, suppose a faulty item results in a $10 loss. If the average percentage of defective items in a lot is 3 percent, the expected cost of faulty items is $0.03 \times \$10$, or $0.30 each. Therefore, if the cost of inspecting each item is less than $0.30, the economic decision is to perform 100 percent inspection. Not all defective items will be removed, however, since inspectors will pass some bad items and reject some good ones.

The purposes of a sampling plan are to test the lot to either (1) find its quality or (2) ensure that the quality is what it is supposed to be. Thus, if a quality control supervisor already knows the quality (such as the 0.03 given in the example), he or she does not sample for defects. Either all of them must be inspected to remove the defects or none of them should be inspected, and the rejects pass into the process. The choice simply depends on the cost to inspect and the cost incurred by passing a reject. ∎

A single sampling plan is defined by n and c, where n is the number of units in the sample and c is the acceptance number. The size of n may vary from one up to all the items in the lot (usually denoted as N) from which it is drawn. The acceptance number c denotes the maximum number of defective items that can be found in the sample before the lot is rejected. Values for n and c are determined by the interaction of four factors (AQL, α, LTPD, and B) that quantify the objectives of the product's producer and its consumer. The objective of the producer is to ensure that the sampling plan has a low probability of rejecting good lots. Lots are defined as good if they contain no more than a specified level of defectives, termed the **acceptable quality level (AQL)**.[1] The objective of the consumer is to ensure that the sampling plan has a low probability of accepting bad lots. Lots are defined as bad if the percentage of defectives is greater than a specified amount, termed *lot tolerance percent defective* (LTPD). The probability associated with rejecting a good lot is denoted by the Greek letter alpha (α) and is termed the *producer's risk*. The probability associated with accepting a bad lot is denoted by the letter beta (β) and is termed the *consumer's risk*. The selection of particular values for AQL, α, LTPD, and β is an economic decision based on a cost trade-off or, more typically, on company policy or contractual requirements.

There is a humorous story supposedly about Hewlett-Packard during its first dealings with Japanese vendors, who place great emphasis on high-quality production. HP had insisted on 2 percent AQL in a purchase of 100 cables. During the purchase agreement some heated discussion took place wherein the Japanese vendor did not want this AQL specification; HP insisted that they would not budge from the 2 percent AQL. The Japanese vendor finally agreed. Later, when the box arrived, there were two packages inside. One contained 100 good cables. The other package had 2 cables with a note stating: "We have sent you 100 good cables. Since you insisted on 2 percent AQL, we have enclosed 2 defective cables in this package, though we do not understand why you want them."

---

[1] There is some controversy surrounding AQLs. This is based on the argument that specifying some acceptable percent of defectives is inconsistent with the philosophical goal of zero defects. In practice, even in the best QC companies, there is an acceptable quality level. The difference is that it may be stated in parts per million rather than in parts per hundred. This is the case in Motorola's six-sigma quality standard which holds that no more than 3.4 defects per million parts are acceptable.

E X H I B I T S5.1

Excerpt from a Sampling Plan Table for α = 0.05, β = 0.10

c	LTPD ÷ AQL	n · AQL	c	LTPD ÷ AQL	n · AQL
0	44.890	0.052	5	3.549	2.613
1	10.946	0.355	6	3.206	3.286
2	6.509	0.818	7	2.957	3.981
3	4.890	1.366	8	2.768	4.695
4	4.057	1.970	9	2.618	5.426

The following example, using an excerpt from a standard acceptance sampling table, illustrates how the four parameters—AQL, α, LTPD, and β—are used in developing a sampling plan.

E X A M P L E S5.2 / *Values of n and c*   Hi-Tech Industries manufactures Z-Band radar scanners used to detect speed traps. The printed circuit boards in the scanners are purchased from an outside vendor. The vendor produces the boards to an AQL of 2 percent defectives and is willing to run a 5 percent risk (α) of having lots of this level or fewer defectives rejected. Hi-Tech considers lots of 8 percent or more defectives (LTPD) unacceptable and wants to ensure that it will accept such poor-quality lots no more than 10 percent of the time (β). A large shipment has just been delivered. What values of n and c should be selected to determine the quality of this lot?

S O L U T I O N   The parameters of the problem are AQL = 0.02, α = 0.05, LTPD = 0.08, and β = 0.10. We can use Exhibit S5.1 to find c and n.

First divide LTPD by AQL (0.08 ÷ 0.02 = 4). Then find the ratio in column 2 that is equal to or just greater than that amount (i.e., 4). This value is 4.057, which is associated with $c = 4$.

Finally, find the value in column 3 that is in the same row as $c = 4$, and divide that quantity by AQL to obtain n (1.970 ÷ 0.02 = 98.5).

The appropriate sampling plan is $c = 4$, $n = 99$. ∎

Operating Characteristic Curves

While a sampling plan such as the one just described meets our requirements for the extreme values of good and bad quality, we cannot readily determine how well the plan discriminates between good and bad lots at intermediate values. For this reason, sampling plans are generally displayed graphically through the use of **operating characteristic (OC) curves.** These curves, which are unique for each combination of n and c, simply illustrate the probability of accepting lots with varying percent defectives. The procedure we have followed in developing the plan, in fact, specifies two points on an OC curve—one point defined by AQL and $1 - α$, and the other point defined by LTPD and β. Curves for common values of n and c can be computed or obtained from available tables.[2]

Shaping the OC Curve

A sampling plan discriminating perfectly between good and bad lots has an infinite slope (vertical) at the selected value of AQL. In Exhibit S5.2, percent defectives to the left of 2 percent would always be accepted and to the right, always rejected. However, such a curve is possible only with complete inspection of all units and thus is not a possibility with a true sampling plan.

---

[2]See, for example, H. F. Dodge and H. G. Romig, *Sampling Inspection Tables—Single and Double Sampling* (New York: John Wiley & Sons, 1959), and *Military Standard Sampling Procedures and Tables for Inspection by Attributes* (MIL-STD-105D) (Washington, DC: U.S. Government Printing Office, 1983).

E X H I B I T S5.2 *Operating Characteristic Curve for AQL = 0.02, α = 0.05, LTPD = 0.08, β = 0.10*

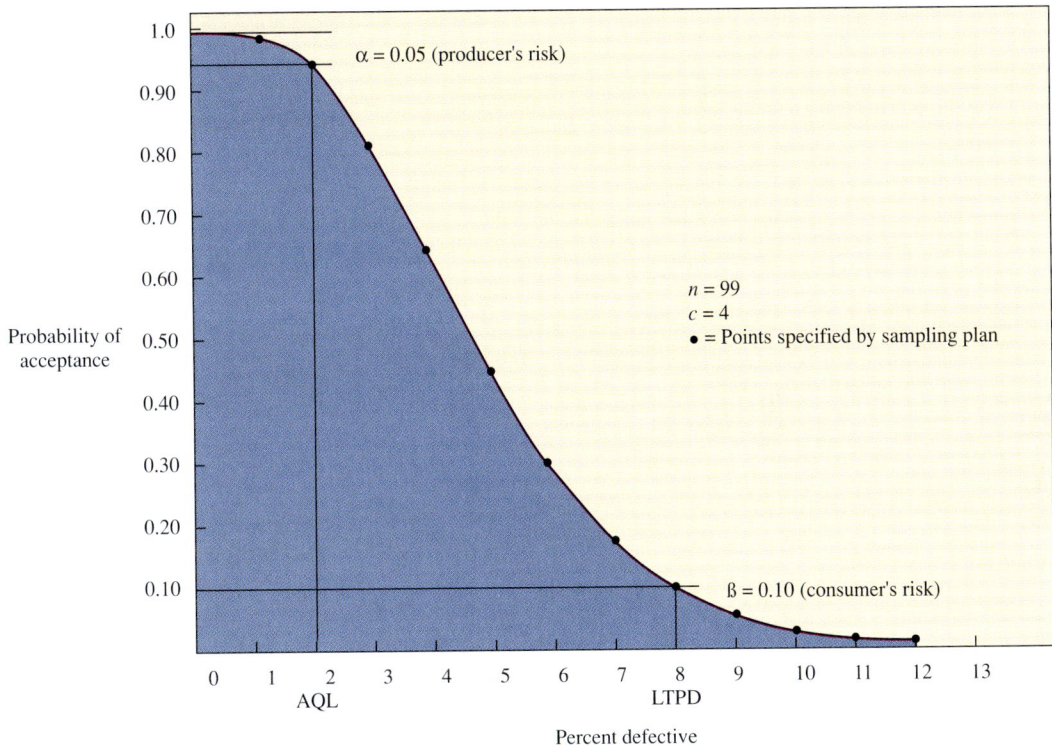

An OC curve should be steep in the region of most interest (between the AQL and the LTPD), which is accomplished by varying n and c. If c remains constant, increasing the sample size n causes the OC curve to be more vertical. While holding n constant, decreasing c (the maximum number of defective units) also makes the slope more vertical, moving closer to the origin.

The Effects of Lot Size

The size of the lot that the sample is taken from has relatively little effect on the quality of protection. Consider, for example, that samples—all of the same size of 20 units—are taken from different lots ranging from a lot size of 200 units to a lot size of infinity. If each lot is known to have 5 percent defectives, the probability of accepting the lot based on the sample of 20 units ranges from about 0.34 to about 0.36. This means that so long as the lot size is several times the sample size, it makes little difference how large the lot is. It seems a bit difficult to accept, but statistically (on the average in the long run) whether we have a carload or box full, we'll get about the same answer. It just seems that a carload should have a larger sample size.

S5.2 PROCESS CONTROL PROCEDURES

Process control is concerned with monitoring quality *while the product or service is being produced*. Typical objectives of process control plans are to provide timely information on whether currently produced items are meeting design specifications and to detect shifts in the process that signal that future products may not meet specifications. The actual control phase of process control occurs when corrective action is taken, such as a worn part replaced, a machine overhauled, or a new supplier found. Process control concepts, especially statistically based control charts, are being used in services as well as in manufacturing.

Process Control Using Attribute Measurements Using *p* Charts

Measurement by attributes means taking samples and using a single decision—the item is good, or it is bad. Because it is a yes–no decision, we can use simple statistics to create a *p* chart with an upper control limit (UCL) and a lower control limit (LCL). We can draw these control limits on a graph and then plot the fraction defective of each individual sample tested. The process is assumed to be working correctly when the samples, which are taken periodically during the day, continue to stay between the control limits.

$$\bar{p} = \frac{\text{Total number of defects from all samples}}{\text{Number of samples} \times \text{Sample size}} \quad \text{(S5.1)}$$

$$s_p = \sqrt{\frac{\bar{p}(1 - \bar{p})}{n}} \quad \text{(S5.2)}$$

$$\text{UCL} = \bar{p} + zs_p \quad \text{(S5.3)}$$

$$\text{LCL} = \bar{p} - zs_p \quad \text{(S5.4)}$$

where $\bar{p}$ is the fraction defective, s is the standard deviation, and z is the number of standard deviations for a specific confidence. Typically, $z = 3$ (99.7 percent confidence) or $z = 2.58$ (99 percent confidence) are used.

Exhibit S5.3 shows information that can be gained from control charts. We do not give an example of attribute process control here so that in the next section we can demonstrate $\bar{X}$ and R charts, which tend to have wider application in process control.

Process Control with Variable Measurements Using $\bar{X}$ and *R* Charts

$\bar{X}$ and R (range) charts are widely used in statistical process control.

In attributes sampling, we determine whether something is good or bad, fit or didn't fit—it is a go/no-go situation. In variables sampling, we measure the weight, volume, number of inches, or other variable measurements, and we develop control charts to determine the acceptability or rejection of the process based on those measurements.

There are four main issues to address in creating a control chart: the size of the samples, number of samples, frequency of samples, and control limits.

Size of Samples   For industrial applications in process control, it is preferable to keep the sample size small. There are two main reasons. First, the sample needs to be taken within a reasonable length of time; otherwise the process might change while the samples are taken. Second, the larger the sample, the more it costs to take.

Sample sizes of four or five units seem to be the preferred numbers. The *means* of samples of this size have an approximately normal distribution, no matter what the distribution of the parent population looks like. Sample sizes greater than five give narrower control limits and thus more sensitivity. For detecting finer variations of a process, it may be necessary, in fact, to use larger sample sizes. However, when sample sizes exceed 15 or so, it would be better to use $\bar{x}$ charts with standard deviation rather than $\bar{x}$ charts with the range R.

Number of Samples   Once the chart has been set up, each sample taken can be compared to the chart and a decision can be made about whether the process is acceptable. To set up the charts, however, prudence (and statistics) suggests that 25 or so samples be taken.

E X H I B I T S5.3   *Control Chart Evidence for Investigation*

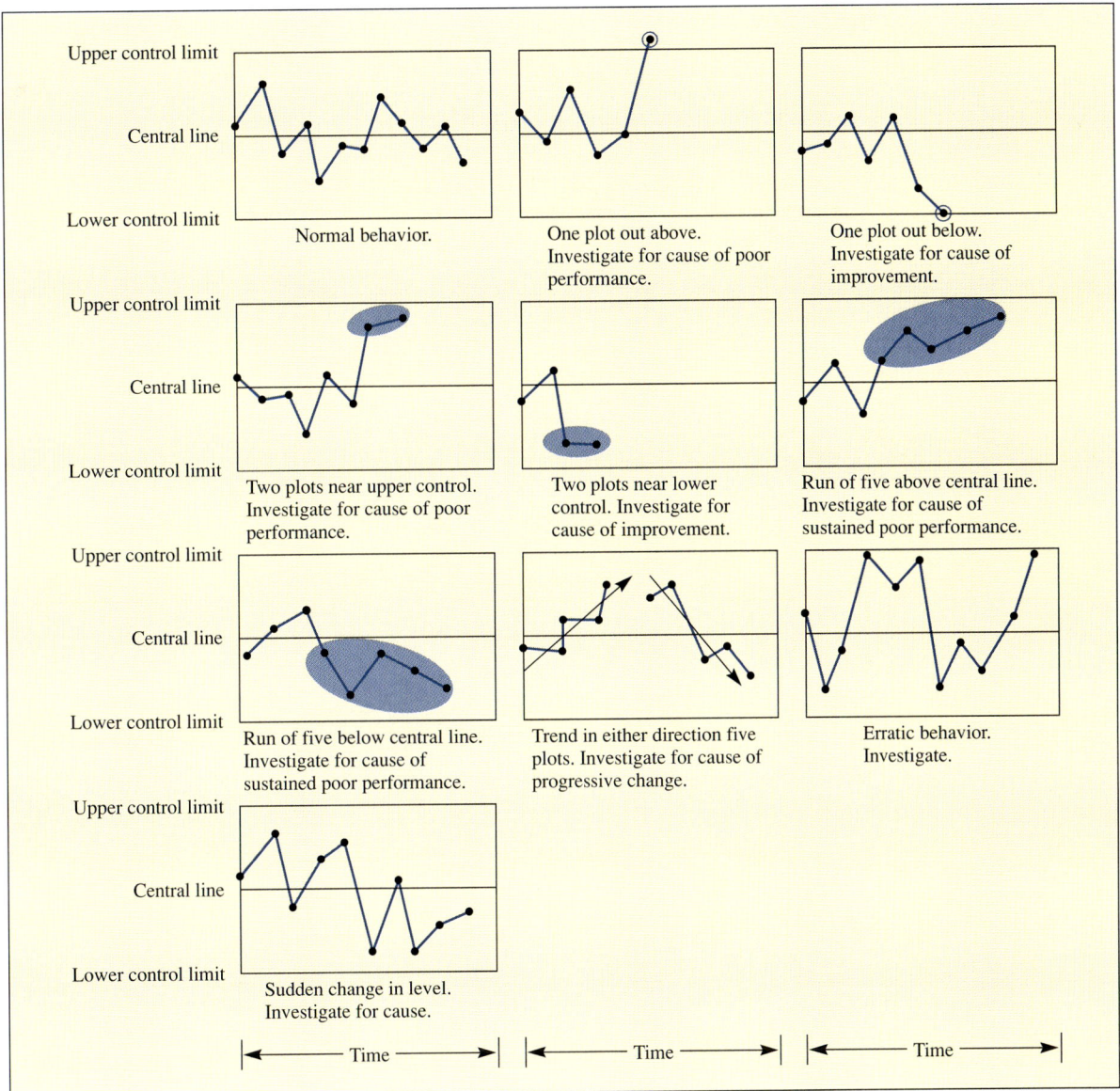

Source: Bertnard L. Hansen, *Quality Control: Theory and Applications,* © 1963, p 65. Reprintedd by permission of Prentice Hall, Inc. Englewood Cliffs, NJ.

Frequency of Samples   How often to take a sample is a trade-off between the cost of sampling (along with the cost of the unit if it is destroyed as part of the test) and the benefit of adjusting the system. Usually, it is best to start off with frequent sampling of a process and taper off as confidence in the process builds. For example, one might start with a sample of five units every half-hour and end up feeling that one sample per day is adequate.

Control Limits   Standard practice in statistical process control for variables is to set control limits three standard deviations above the mean and three standard deviations below. This means that 99.7 percent of the sample means are expected to fall within these control limits (that is, within a 99.7 percent confidence interval). Thus if one sample mean falls outside this obviously wide band, we have strong evidence that the process is out of control.

How to Construct $\overline{X}$ and R Charts

An $\overline{X}$ chart is simply a plot of the means of the samples that were taken from a process. An $\overline{\overline{X}}$ is the average of the means.

An R chart is a plot of the range within each sample. The range is the difference between the highest and the lowest numbers in that sample. R values provide an easily calculated measure of variation used like a standard deviation. An $\overline{R}$ chart is the average of the range of each sample. More specifically defined, these are

$$\overline{X} = \frac{\sum\limits_{i=1}^{n} X_i}{n} \tag{S5.5}$$

where

$\overline{X}$ = Mean of the sample
i = Item number
n = Total number of items in the sample

$$\overline{\overline{X}} = \frac{\sum\limits_{j=1}^{m} X_j}{m} \tag{S5.6}$$

where

$\overline{\overline{X}}$ = The average of the means of the samples
j = Sample number
m = Total number of samples
R_j = Difference between the highest and lowest measurement in the sample
$\overline{R}$ = Average of the measurement differences R for all samples, or

$$\overline{R} = \frac{\sum\limits_{j=1}^{m} R_j}{m} \tag{S5.7}$$

E. L. Grant and R. Leavenworth computed a table that allows us to easily compute the upper and lower control limits for both the $\overline{X}$ chart and the R chart.[3] These are defined as

$$\text{Upper control limit for } \overline{X} = \overline{\overline{X}} + A_2\overline{R} \tag{S5.8}$$
$$\text{Lower control limit for } \overline{X} = \overline{\overline{X}} - A_2\overline{R} \tag{S5.9}$$
$$\text{Upper control limit for } R = D_4\overline{R} \tag{S5.10}$$
$$\text{Lower control limit for } R = D_3\overline{R} \tag{S5.11}$$

---

[3]E. L. Grant and R. Leavenworth, *Statistical Quality Control* (New York: McGraw-Hill, 1964), p. 562. Reprinted by permission.

Number of Observations in Subgroup n	Factor for $\overline{X}$ Chart A_2	Factors for R Chart	
		Lower Control Limit D_3	Upper Control Limit D_4
2	1.88	0	3.27
3	1.02	0	2.57
4	0.73	0	2.28
5	0.58	0	2.11
6	0.48	0	2.00
7	0.42	0.08	1.92
8	0.37	0.14	1.86
9	0.34	0.18	1.82
10	0.31	0.22	1.78
11	0.29	0.26	1.74
12	0.27	0.28	1.72
13	0.25	0.31	1.69
14	0.24	0.33	1.67
15	0.22	0.35	1.65
16	0.21	0.36	1.64
17	0.20	0.38	1.62
18	0.19	0.39	1.61
19	0.19	0.40	1.60
20	0.18	0.41	1.59

Upper control limit for $\overline{X} = UCL_{\overline{X}} = \overline{\overline{X}} + A_2\overline{R}$
Lower control limit for $\overline{X} = LCL_{\overline{X}} = \overline{\overline{X}} - A_2\overline{R}$
Upper control limit for $R = UCL_R = D_4\overline{R}$
Lower control limit for $R = LCL_R = D_3\overline{R}$

E X H I B I T S5.4

Factors for Determining from $\overline{R}$ the Three-Sigma Control Limits for $\overline{X}$ and R Charts

Note: All factors are based on the normal distribution.

Source: E. L. Grant, *Statistical Quality Control*, 6th ed. (New York: McGraw-Hill, 1988). Reprinted by permission of McGraw-Hill, Inc.

E X A M P L E S5.3 / $\overline{X}$ and R Charts   We would like to create $\overline{X}$ and R charts for a process. Exhibit S5.5 shows measurements for all 25 samples. The last two columns show the average of the sample $\overline{X}$ and the range R.

Values for A_2, D_3, and D_4 were obtained from Exhibit S5.4.

Upper control limit for $\overline{X} = \overline{\overline{X}} + A_2\overline{R} = 10.21 + .58(.60) = 10.56$
Lower control limit for $\overline{X} = \overline{\overline{X}} - A_2\overline{R} = 10.21 - .58(.60) = 9.86$
Upper control limit for $R = D_4\overline{R} = 2.11(.60) = 1.27$
Lower control limit for $R = D_3\overline{R} = 0(.60) = 0$

Exhibit S5.6 shows the $\overline{X}$ chart and R chart with a plot of all the sample means and ranges of the samples. All the points are well within the control limits, although sample 23 is close to the $\overline{X}$ lower control limit.

Motorola made process capability and product design famous by adopting its now well-known **six-sigma** limits. Six-sigma limits have 999996.6 good parts per million (3.4 defects per million). As we will show later, though, six sigma can provide quality output all the way up to two defective units per billion. See how dramatically six sigma con-

Process Capability

E X H I B I T S5.5

Measurements in Samples of Five from a Process

Sample Number	Each Unit in Sample					Average $\overline{X}$	Range R
1	10.60	10.40	10.30	9.90	10.20	10.28	.70
2	9.98	10.25	10.05	10.23	10.33	10.17	.35
3	9.85	9.90	10.20	10.25	10.15	10.07	.40
4	10.20	10.10	10.30	9.90	9.95	10.09	.40
5	10.30	10.20	10.24	10.50	10.30	10.31	.30
6	10.10	10.30	10.20	10.30	9.90	10.16	.40
7	9.98	9.90	10.20	10.40	10.10	10.12	.50
8	10.10	10.30	10.40	10.24	10.30	10.27	.30
9	10.30	10.20	10.60	10.50	10.10	10.34	.50
10	10.30	10.40	10.50	10.10	10.20	10.30	.40
11	9.90	9.50	10.20	10.30	10.35	10.05	.85
12	10.10	10.36	10.50	9.80	9.95	10.14	.70
13	10.20	10.50	10.70	10.10	9.90	10.28	.80
14	10.20	10.60	10.50	10.30	10.40	10.40	.40
15	10.54	10.30	10.40	10.55	10.00	10.36	.55
16	10.20	10.60	10.15	10.00	10.50	10.29	.60
17	10.20	10.40	10.60	10.80	10.10	10.42	.70
18	9.90	9.50	9.90	10.50	10.00	9.96	1.00
19	10.60	10.30	10.50	9.90	9.80	10.22	.80
20	10.60	10.40	10.30	10.40	10.20	10.38	.40
21	9.90	9.60	10.50	10.10	10.60	10.14	1.00
22	9.95	10.20	10.50	10.30	10.20	10.23	.55
23	10.20	9.50	9.60	9.80	10.30	9.88	.80
24	10.30	10.60	10.30	9.90	9.80	10.18	.80
25	9.90	10.30	10.60	9.90	10.10	10.16	.70

$\overline{\overline{X}} = 10.21$

$\overline{R} = .60$

E X H I B I T S5.6   *$\overline{X}$ Chart and R Chart*

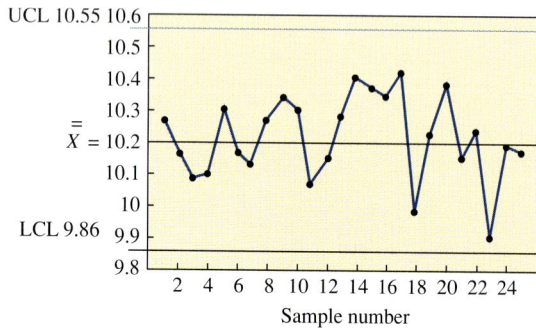

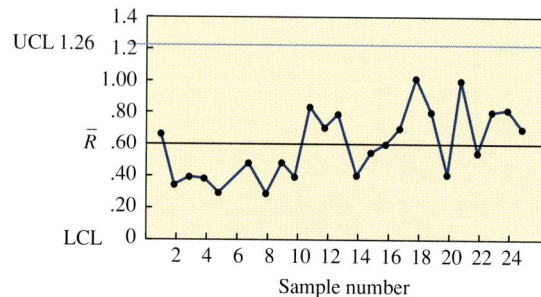

trasts with three sigma, which provides 997 good parts per thousand (or three defects per thousand).

So far in this supplement, we have discussed upper and lower control limits. These control limits deal with the variation in the product. If the product is purchased or

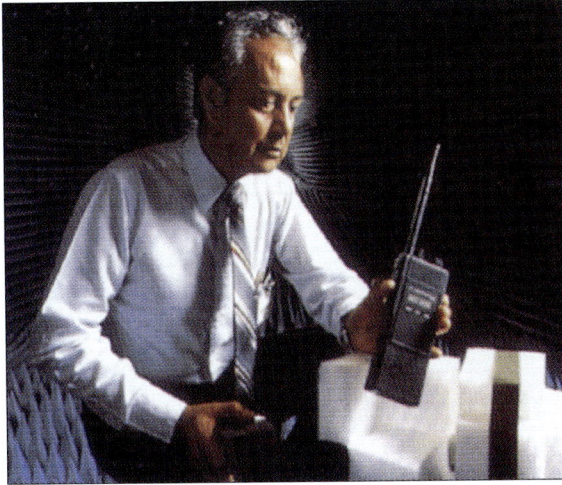

comes in lots, it is acceptance sampling. If the product is being produced, measurement of the product is used to estimate the range of output of the process. Thus we can measure the *process limits* or the expected range of output from a person or machine. Typically, these limits are set as plus or minus three standard deviations, so anything that lies within this range is considered acceptable quality. To understand the six-sigma limits, we need the rest of the story. This product or part will be used somewhere else. The acceptable measurements for where the part or product will be used are the *design limits*. The design limits are also called the **upper and lower specification limits** or **the upper and lower tolerance limits.** Therefore, there are two measurements that play against each other: the where used or design limit, and the production or process limit. Both of these measurements may be controlled—the design limit by making changes in design, and the process limit by making changes in the process.

As a simple example, assume that we are designing a bearing for a rotating shaft—say an axle for the wheel of a car. There are many variables involved for both the bearing and the axle: the metal used and the hardness put in through heat treatment, the width of the bearing, the size of the rollers, the size of the axle, the length of the axle, how it is supported, and so on.

Suppose that initially a design is selected and the diameter of the bearing is set at 1.250 inches $\pm$ 0.005 inches, which means that acceptable parts vary from 1.245 to 1.255 inches. Now, we go on to the process where the bearing will be made. Let's say that by running some tests we determine the machine output to have a variation of sigma equal to 0.001 inch. Bearings will have a variation of $\pm$ 0.003 inch for the three-sigma control limits. If the mean is 1.250 inches, then the output will range from 1.247 to 1.253 inches. Comparing that to our design limits shows that this does not meet Motorola's six-sigma criterion. With a process variation of sigma equal to 0.001, the upper and lower design limits will have to be $\pm$ 0.006, or 1.244 to 1.256, not the 1.245 to 1.255 as originally specified. So either the process has to be changed to reduce the variation, or the axle assembly and supports must be redesigned to accept a slightly larger variation. Whichever is easiest (and equally reliable) should be done.

We can show the six-sigma limits using an exhibit. Assume that the design limits and the process limits are acceptable as just discussed. Let's assume that the measurement of

E X H I B I T S5.7

Process Capability

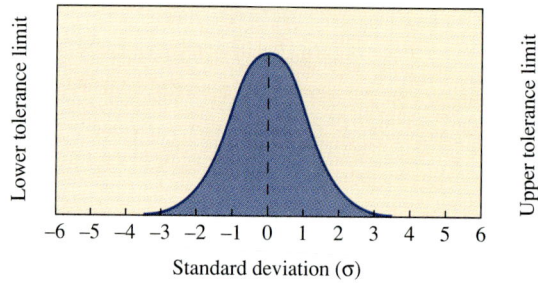

E X H I B I T S5.8

*Process Capability
with a Shift in the
Process Mean*

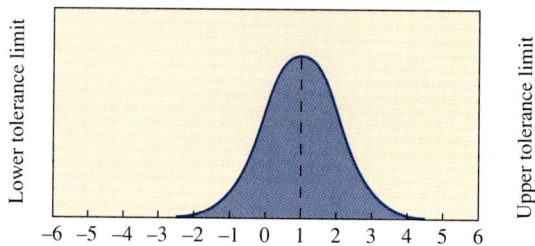

output follows a bell-shaped normal distribution as in Exhibit S5.7. This is the process variation or variation due to the person or machine. We can then set the horizontal sigma scale so that ± 3 sigma includes 99.7 percent of the bell-shaped curve.

The upper and lower specification limits (or tolerance limits) are set by the design as previously discussed. Using Motorola's six-sigma limits, this would be ± 6 sigma, as we have drawn in the exhibit. The question now is, with the mean of our process output in the center, how many defects can we expect (those that fall above or below six sigma). Actually the expected number of defects is two parts per *billion*. We shall explain.

Suppose the central value of the process output shifts away from the mean, where it is now in Exhibit S5.7, by one standard deviation as shown in Exhibit S5.8 This brings the output closer to the upper specification limit so we would expect a slightly greater chance of items falling outside the upper limit. Surprisingly, though, there are still fewer than four parts per million outside the six-sigma limit. In fact, when Motorola calculated its six-sigma limits, at which 3.4 parts per million would lie outside, it did this allowing the process mean to shift as much as 1.5 sigma from the middle (target) value. That is even 0.5 sigma farther to the right than we showed in Exhibit S5.8. Thus the mean value of the process mean lying between ±1.5 sigma guarantees quality greater than 3.4 parts per million.

Look at Exhibit S5.9, a semilogarithmic plot of defect rates versus the sigma level. There are two plots shown. In one the process mean is exactly centered on the design specification mean. This is where there will be the least number of defects. Reading from the graph, where the design specification is six sigma there will be .002 defects per million, which is two parts per billion. The other plot shows where the process mean has shifted 1.5 sigma. At the six-sigma design limits there are 3.4 defects per million. Note that if the design limits were ±3 sigma (on the horizontal) and the process shifts 1.5 sigma (the upper line), there will be 67,000 defects per million.

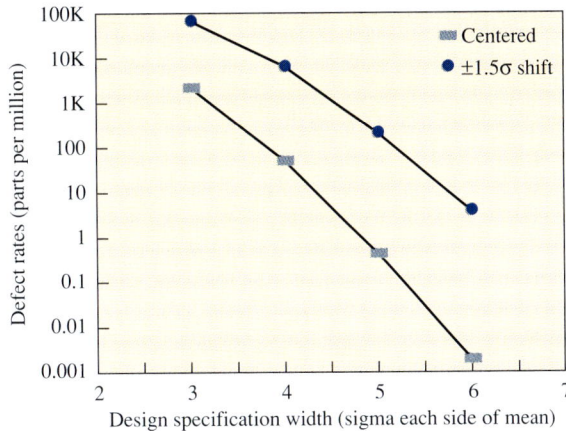

E X H I B I T S5.9

Defect Rates versus the Design Specification Width at a Process Variation of Three Sigma

Source: Fred R. McFadden, "Six-Sigma Quality Programs," *Quality Progress*, June 1993, p. 39. © 1993 American Society for Quality Control. Reprinted with permission.

The **capability index** shows how well the parts being produced fit into the range specified by the design limits. If the design limits are larger than the three sigma allowed in the process, then the mean of the process can be allowed to drift off-center before readjusting, and a high percentage of good parts will still be produced.

Capability Index (C_{pk})

Referring to Exhibits S5.7 and S5.8, the capability index (C_{pk}) is the position of the mean and tails of the process relative to design specifications. The more off-center, the greater the chance to produce defective parts.

Since the process mean can shift in either direction, the direction of shift and its distance from the design specification set the limit on the process capability. The direction of shift is toward the smaller number.

Formally stated, the capability index (C_{pk}) is calculated as the smaller number as follows:

$$C_{pk} = \min \left[\frac{\overline{X} - LTL}{3\sigma} \text{ or } \frac{UTL - \overline{X}}{3\sigma} \right] \qquad (S5.12)$$

For simplicity, let's assume our process mean is one inch and $\sigma = .001$. Further, the process mean is exactly in the center as in Exhibit S5.7. Then for $\overline{x} = 1.000$

$$C_{pk} = \min \left[\frac{1.000 - .994}{3(.001)} \text{ or } \frac{1.006 - 1.000}{3(.001)} \right] =$$

$$= \min \left[\frac{.006}{.003} = 2 \text{ or } \frac{.006}{.003} = 2 \right]$$

Since the mean is in the center, the two calculations are the same and equal to 2. If the mean shifted to $+ 1.5\sigma$ or 1.0015, then for $\overline{x} = 1.0015$

$$C_{pk} = \min \left[\frac{1.0015 - .994}{3(.001)} \text{ or } \frac{1.006 - 1.0015}{3(.001)} \right] =$$

$$= \min [2.5 \text{ or } 1.5]$$

$C_{pk} = 1.5$, which is the smaller number.

This tells us that the process mean has shifted to the right similar to Exhibit S5.8, but parts are still well within design limits.

Assuming that the process is producing within ± 3 sigma and the process is centered exactly between the design limits, as in Exhibit S5.7, Birch calculated the fraction of defective units that would fall outside various design limits as follows:[4]

Design Limit	Defective Parts	Fraction Defective
$\pm 1\sigma$	317 per thousand	.3173
$\pm 2\sigma$	45 per thousand	.0455
$\pm 3\sigma$	2 per thousand	.0027
$\pm 4\sigma$	63 per million	.000063
$\pm 5\sigma$	574 per billion	.000000574
$\pm 6\sigma$	2 per billion	.000000002
$\pm 7\sigma$	.3 per billion	.0000000000003
$\pm 8\sigma$	.001 per billion	.000000000000001

Motorola's design limit of six sigma with a shift of the process off the mean by 1.5 σ ($C_{pk} = 1.5$) gives 3.4 defects per million. If the mean is exactly in the center ($C_{pk} = 2$) then 2 defects per *billion* are expected as the table above shows.

S5.3   TAGUCHI METHODS

We have discussed quality control from the point of view of process adjustments. In what many have termed a revolution in quality thinking, Genichi Taguchi of Japan has suggested the following: Instead of constantly fiddling with production equipment to ensure consistent quality, design the product to be robust enough to achieve high quality despite fluctuations on the production line. This simple idea has been employed by such companies as Ford Motor Company, ITT, and IBM; they have saved millions of dollars in manufacturing costs as a result.

Taguchi methods are basically statistical techniques for conducting experiments to determine the best combinations of product and process variables to make a product. *Best* means lowest cost with highest uniformity. This can be a complicated, time-consuming process. For example, in designing the process for a new product, one might find that a single processing step with only eight process variables (machine speed, cutting angle, and so on) could be combined in up to 5,000 different ways. Thus, finding the combination that makes the product with the highest uniformity at the lowest cost cannot be done by trial and error. Taguchi has found a way around this problem focusing on only a few combinations that represent the spectrum of product/process outcomes.

Taguchi is also known for the development of the concept of a quality loss function (QLF) to tie cost of quality directly to variation in a process. The following discussion from an article by Joseph Turner develops this concept in detail.[5]

IS AN OUT-OF-SPEC PRODUCT REALLY OUT OF SPEC?

VARIATION AROUND US

It is generally accepted that, as variation is reduced, quality is improved. Sometimes that knowledge is intuitive. If a train is always on time, schedules can be planned more precisely. If clothing sizes are consistent, time can be saved by ordering from a catalog. But

---

[4]David Birch, "The True Value of 6 Sigma," *Quality Progress,* April 1993, p. 6.
[5]Adapted from Joseph Turner, "Is an Out-of-Spec Product Really Out of Spec?" *Quality Progress,* December 1990, pp. 57–59.

rarely are such things thought about in terms of the value of low variability. With engineers, the knowledge is better defined. Pistons must fit cylinders, doors must fit openings, electrical components must be compatible, and boxes of cereal must have the right amount of raisins—otherwise quality will be unacceptable and customers will be dissatisfied.

However, engineers also know that it is impossible to have zero variability. For this reason, designers establish specifications that define not only the target value of something, but also acceptable limits about the target. For example, if the aim value of a dimension is 10 inches, the design specifications might then be 10.00 inches $\pm$ 0.02 inch. This would tell the manufacturing department that, while it should aim for exactly 10 inches, anything between 9.98 and 10.02 inches is OK.

A traditional way of interpreting such a specification is that any part that falls within the allowed range is equally good, while any part falling outside the range is totally bad. This is illustrated in Exhibit S5.10. (Note that the cost is zero over the entire specification range, and then there is a quantum leap in cost once the limit is violated.)

Taguchi has pointed out that such a view is nonsense for two reasons:

1. From the customer's view, there is often practically no difference between a product just inside specifications and a product just outside. Conversely, there is a far greater difference in the quality of a product that is the target and the quality of one that is near a limit.

2. As customers get more demanding, there is pressure to reduce variability. However, Exhibit S5.10 does not reflect this logic.

Taguchi suggests that a more correct picture of the loss is shown in Exhibit S5.11. Notice that in this graph the cost is represented by a smooth curve. There are dozens of illustrations of this notion: the meshing of gears in a transmission, the speed of photographic film, the temperature in a workplace or department store. In nearly anything that can be measured, the customer sees not a sharp line, but a gradation of acceptability. Customers see the loss function as Exhibit S5.11 rather than Exhibit S5.10.

What are the elements of loss to society? While different authorities suggest different things, it seems reasonable to think of both internal and external costs. Internally, the more variable the manufacturing process, the more scrap generated and the more a company will have to spend on testing and inspecting for conformance. Externally, customers will find that the product does not last as long or work as well if it is not close to aim. Perhaps, when used in adverse situations, the product will not perform at all, even though it meets specifications that were developed based on normal usage.

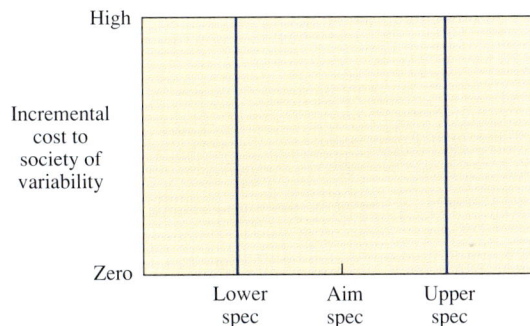

E X H I B I T S5.10
A Traditional View of the Cost of Variability

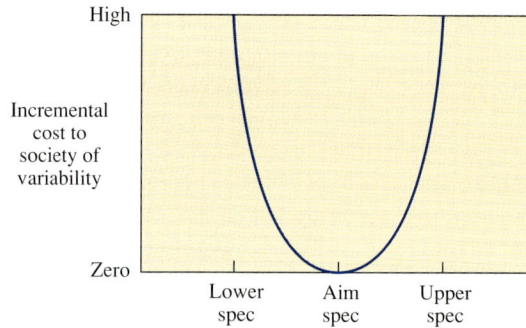

While the actual shape of the loss curve might vary considerably, a simple parabolic curve, as shown in Exhibit S5.11, has a lot of intuitive appeal, especially when specification limits are symmetrical about the target value. With a parabola, the loss is relatively small when we are close to aim and grows at an increasing rate the farther we move from the target.

Of course, if products are consistently scrapped when they are outside specifications, the loss curve flattens out in most cases at a value equivalent to scrap cost in the ranges outside specifications. This is because such products, theoretically at least, will never be sold so there is no external cost to society. However, in many practical situations, either the process is capable of producing a very high percentage of product within specifications and/or 100 percent checking is not done and/or out-of-spec products can be reworked to bring them within specs. In any of these situations, the parabolic loss function is usually a reasonable assumption.

In such cases, the following formula applies:

$$(1)\ L = K(x - a)^2$$

where

L = Loss to society associated with a unit of product produced at a value x

a = Aim or target; assume that at a, $L = 0$

K = A constant

Then, adding the following variables, and solving for K,

c = The loss associated with a unit of product produced at a specification limit, assuming that the loss for a unit at target is zero

d = Distance from the target to the spec limit

$$(2)\ K = c/d^2$$

With n units of product, the average loss per unit becomes

$$(3)\ \overline{L} = K[\Sigma(x - a)^2/n]$$

While this formula assesses average loss, it is somewhat cumbersome because data are not usually collected in a way that makes the computation of $\Sigma(x - a)$ convenient. However, data are often available on the historical mean and standard deviation for the item of interest. When these are known, the average loss is closely approximated by

$$(4)\ \overline{L} = K[s^2 + (\overline{x} - a)^2]$$

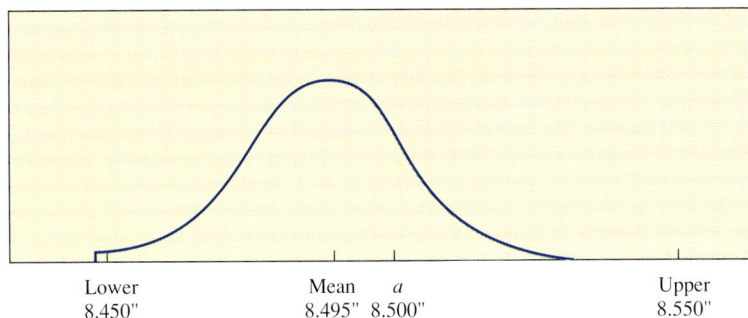

Lower
8.450"

Mean   *a*
8.495" 8.500"

Upper
8.550"

where

$\bar{x}$ = Process average

s = Process standard deviation

The only difficulty in applying the preceding formula to a practical situation is coming up with a valid estimate of c, the incremental loss to society associated with a unit of product produced at the limit, compared to the loss associated with a unit produced at target. While this is, at best, a guesstimate, it is possible for knowledgeable people to suggest a value that represents educated thinking. One group of engineers suggested the value should be one-tenth of the selling price of a particular item. This means that if a unit were right at the limit, there is a reasonable chance that, because of test variability, the unit might fail final inspection. Furthermore, there is a reasonable chance the customer would encounter greater problems with a unit at the limit than with a unit made at target, and this would result in loss to the customer and possible warranty returns. While this estimate was admittedly a bit arbitrary, it seemed a reasonable starting point as a minimum estimate and resulted in a surprisingly high estimated loss value.

The approach is illustrated in the following example: The specification for a key dimension on an automotive part is 8.5 inches ± 0.05 inch. Historical data indicate that over the past several months, the mean value has been 8.492 inches and the standard deviation, 0.016 inch. The part sells for $20, and engineers have estimated the loss to society as $2 for a part that is exactly at the upper or lower limit. Production is 250,000 parts per year. The situation is pictured in Exhibit S5.12.

Applying equation (4), the average loss per part is

$$\bar{L} = [2/(0.05)^2] [(.016)^2 + (.008)^2] = 25.6 \text{ cents}$$

Applying this to the volume of 250,000 units produces a total annual loss of $64,000. If engineers want to reduce this loss, they can pursue three avenues:

1. Shift the mean value so it is on aim (i.e., 8.5 inches).
2. Reduce the variability. (For example, make $s = 0.01$ inch.)
3. Accomplish both 1 and 2.

Applying equation (4) to the three situations produces the following results:

1. By moving the mean value to aim, $\bar{L} = 20.5$ cents; total annual loss = $51,250.
2. By reducing the variability to $s = 0.01$ inch, $\bar{L} = 13.1$ cents; total annual loss = $32,750.
3. By accomplishing both 1 and 2, $\bar{L} = 8$ cents; total annual loss = $20,000.

Note that if higher or lower estimates were used for c, the resulting numbers would be affected proportionately. Thus, it is possible to easily perform a sensitivity analysis assuming a range of values for c. For example, if c were estimated at \$4 rather than \$2, all of the results would be exactly double those shown.

S5.4   CONCLUSION

Statistical quality control is a vital topic. We put it in this supplement rather than Chapter 5 not with the intention of giving it a second class status. Rather, quality has become so important that statistical quality procedures are *expected* to be part of successful firms. Sampling plans and statistical process control are taken as given with the emphasis shifting to broader aspects (such as having suppliers' quality allow eliminating dockside acceptance sampling, and employee empowerment transforming much of the process control). We're finding that world-class manufacturing companies are expecting people to understand the basic concepts of the materials presented in this supplement.

S5.5   FORMULA REVIEW

Process control charts using attribute measurements

$$\bar{p} = \frac{\text{Total number of defects from all samples}}{\text{Number of samples} \times \text{Sample size}} \tag{S5.1}$$

$$s_p = \sqrt{\frac{\bar{p}(1 - \bar{p})}{n}} \tag{S5.2}$$

$$\text{UCL} = \bar{p} + zs_p \tag{S5.3}$$

$$\text{LCL} = \bar{p} - zs_p \tag{S5.4}$$

Process control $\bar{X}$ and R charts

$$\bar{X} = \frac{\sum_{i=1}^{n} X_i}{n} \tag{S5.5}$$

$$\bar{\bar{X}} = \frac{\sum_{j=1}^{m} \bar{X}_j}{m} \tag{S5.6}$$

$$\bar{R} = \frac{\sum_{j=1}^{m} R_j}{m} \tag{S5.7}$$

$$\text{Upper control limit for } \bar{X} = \bar{\bar{X}} + A_2\bar{R} \tag{S5.8}$$

$$\text{Lower control limit for } \bar{X} = \bar{\bar{X}} - A_2\bar{R} \tag{S5.9}$$

$$\text{Upper control limit for } R = D_4\bar{R} \tag{S5.10}$$

$$\text{Lower control limit for } R = D_3\bar{R} \tag{S5.11}$$

Capability index

$$C_{pk} = \min\left[\frac{\bar{X} - \text{LTL}}{3\sigma}, \frac{\text{UTL} - \bar{X}}{3\sigma}\right] \tag{S5.12}$$

S5.6   SOLVED PROBLEMS

1. Completed forms from a particular department of an insurance company were sampled on a daily basis as a check against the quality of performance of that department. To establish a tentative norm for the department, one sample of 100 units was collected each day for 15 days, with these results:

Sample	Sample Size	Number of Forms with Errors	Sample	Sample Size	Number of Forms with Errors
1	100	4	9	100	4
2	100	3	10	100	2
3	100	5	11	100	7
4	100	0	12	100	2
5	100	2	13	100	1
6	100	8	14	100	3
7	100	1	15	100	1
8	100	3			

   a. Develop a *p*-chart using a 95 percent confidence interval (1.96 S_p).

   b. Plot the 15 samples collected.

   c. What comments can you make about the process?

   Solution

   a. $\bar{p} = \dfrac{46}{15(100)} = .0307$

   $$s_p = \sqrt{\frac{\bar{p}(1 - \bar{p})}{n}} = \sqrt{\frac{.0307(1 - .0307)}{100}} = \sqrt{.0003} = .017$$

   $$\text{UCL} = \bar{p} + 1.96s_p = .031 + 1.96(.017) = .064$$

   $$\text{LCL} = \bar{p} - 1.96s_p = .031 - 1.96(.017) = -.003 \text{ or zero}$$

   b. The defectives are plotted here.

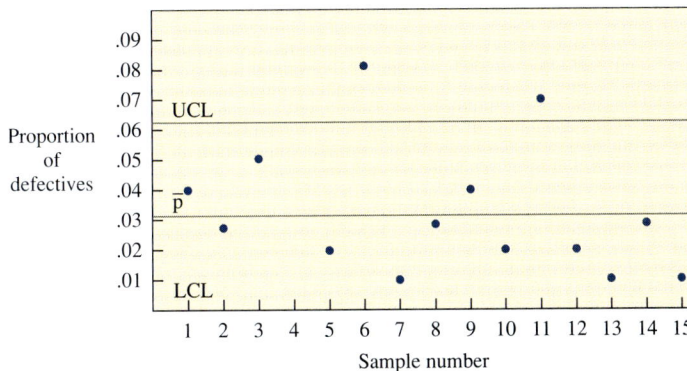

   c. Of the 15 samples, 2 were out of the control limits. Since the control limits were established as 95 percent, or 1 out of 20, we would say that the process is out of control. It needs to be examined to find the cause of such widespread variation.

2. Management is trying to decide whether Part A, which is produced with a consistent 3 percent defective rate, should be inspected. If it is not inspected, the 3 percent defectives will go through a product assembly phase and have to be replaced later. If all Part A's are inspected, one-third of the defectives will be found, thus raising the quality to 2 percent defectives.

   a. Should the inspection be done if the cost of inspecting is $0.01 per unit and the cost of replacing a defective in the final assembly is $4.00?

   b. Suppose the cost of inspecting is $0.05 per unit rather than $0.01. Would this change your answer in *a?*

   Solution

   Should Part A be inspected?
   .03 defective with no inspection.
   .02 defective with inspection.

   a. This problem can be solved simply by looking at the opportunity for 1 percent improvement.

   Benefit = .01($4.00) = $0.04
   Cost of inspection = $0.01

   Therefore, inspect and save $0.03 per unit.

   b. A cost of $0.05 per unit to inspect would be $0.01 greater than the savings so inspection should not be performed.

S5.7   REVIEW AND DISCUSSION QUESTIONS

1. Discuss the trade-off between achieving a zero AQL (acceptable quantity level) and a positive AQL (e.g., an AQL of 2 percent).
2. The capability index allows for some drifting of the process mean. Discuss what this means in terms of product quality output.
3. Discuss the purposes and differences between p-charts and $\overline{X}$ and R charts.
4. In an agreement between a supplier and a customer, the supplier must ensure that all parts are within tolerance before shipment to the customer. What is the effect on the cost of quality to the customer?
5. In the situation described in Question 4, what would be the effect on the cost of quality to the supplier?
6. Discuss the logic of Taguchi methods.

S5.8   PROBLEMS

1. A company currently using an inspection process in its material receiving department is trying to install an overall cost reduction program. One possible reduction is the elimination of one of the inspection positions. This position tests material that has a defective content on the average of 0.04. By inspecting all items, the inspector is able to remove all defects. The inspector can inspect 50 units per hour. Hourly rate including fringe benefits for this position is $9. If the inspection position is eliminated, defects will go into product assembly and will have to be replaced later at a cost of $10 each when they are detected in final product testing.

   a. Should this inspection position be eliminated?
   b. What is the cost to inspect each unit?
   c. Is there benefit (or loss) from the current inspection process? How much?

2. A metal fabricator produces connecting rods with an outer diameter that has a $1 \pm .01$ inch specification. A machine operator takes several sample measurements over time and determines the sample mean outer diameter to be 1.002 inches with a standard deviation of .003 inch.

   a. Calculate the process capability ratio for this example.

   b. What does this figure tell you about the process?

3. Ten samples of 15 parts each were taken from an ongoing process to establish a *p*-chart for control. The samples and the number of defectives in each are shown here.

Sample	*n*	Number of Defects in Sample	Sample	*n*	Number of Defects in Sample
1	15	3	6	15	2
2	15	1	7	15	0
3	15	0	8	15	3
4	15	0	9	15	1
5	15	0	10	15	0

   a. Develop a *p*-chart for 95 percent confidence (1.96 standard deviations).

   b. Based on the plotted data points, what comments can you make?

4. Output from a process contains 0.02 defective units. Defective units that go undetected into final assemblies cost $25 each to replace. An inspection process, which would detect and remove all defectives, can be established to test these units. However, the inspector, who can test 20 units per hour, is paid a rate of $8 per hour, including fringe benefits. Should an inspection station be established to test all units?

   a. What is the cost to inspect each unit?

   b. What is the benefit (or loss) from the inspection process?

5. There is a 3 percent error rate at a specific point in a production process. If an inspector is placed at this point, all the errors can be detected and eliminated. However, the inspector is paid $8 per hour and can inspect units in the process at the rate of 30 per hour.

   If no inspector is used and defects are allowed to pass this point, there is a cost of $10 per unit to correct the defect later on.

   Should an inspector be hired?

6. Resistors for electronic circuits are being manufactured on a high-speed automated machine. The machine is being set up to produce a large run of resistors of 1,000 ohms each.

   To set up the machine and to create a control chart to be used throughout the run, 15 samples were taken with four resistors in each sample. The complete list of samples and their measured values are as follows:

Sample Number	Readings (in ohms)			
1	1010	991	985	986
2	995	996	1009	994
3	990	1003	1015	1008
4	1015	1020	1009	998
5	1013	1019	1005	993
6	994	1001	994	1005
7	989	992	982	1020
8	1001	986	996	996
9	1006	989	1005	1007
10	992	1007	1006	979
11	996	1006	997	989
12	1019	996	991	1011
13	981	991	989	1003
14	999	993	988	984
15	1013	1002	1005	992

Develop an $\bar{X}$ chart and an R chart and plot the values. From the charts, what comments can you make about the process? (Use three-sigma control limits as in Exhibit S5.4.)

7. In the past, Alpha Corporation has not performed incoming quality control inspections but has taken the word of its vendors. However, Alpha has been having some unsatisfactory experience recently with the quality of purchased items and wants to set up sampling plans for the receiving department to use.

   For a particular component, X, Alpha has a lot tolerance percent defective of 10 percent. Zenon Corporation, from whom Alpha purchases this component, has an acceptable quality level in its production facility of 3 percent for component X. Alpha has a consumer's risk of 10 percent and Zenon has a producer's risk of 5 percent.

   a. When a shipment of Product X is received from Zenon Corporation, what is the sample size that the receiving department should test?
   b. What is the allowable number of defects in order to accept the shipment?

8. You are the newly appointed assistant administrator at a local hospital, and your first project is to investigate the quality of the patient meals put out by the food-service department. You conducted a 10-day survey by submitting a simple questionnaire to the 400 patients with each meal, asking that they simply check off that the meal was either satisfactory or unsatisfactory. For simplicity in this problem, assume that the response was 1,000 returned questionnaires from the 1,200 meals each day. The results are

	Number of Unsatisfactory Meals	Sample Size
December 1	74	1,000
December 2	42	1,000
December 3	64	1,000
December 4	80	1,000
December 5	40	1,000
December 6	50	1,000
December 7	65	1,000
December 8	70	1,000
December 9	40	1,000
December 10	75	1,000
	600	10,000

   a. Construct a *p*-chart based on the questionnaire results, using a confidence interval of 95.5 percent, which is two standard deviations.
   b. What comments can you make about the results of the survey?

9. Large-scale integrated (LSI) circuit chips are made in one department of an electronics firm. These chips are incorporated into analog devices that are then encased in epoxy. The yield is not particularly good for LSI manufacture, so the AQL specified by that department is 0.15 while the LTPD acceptable by the assembly department is 0.40.

   a. Develop a sampling plan.
   b. Explain what the sampling plan means; that is, how would you tell someone to do the test?

10. The state and local police departments are trying to analyze areas' crime rates so they can shift their patrols from decreasing-rate areas to areas where rates are increasing. The city and county have been geographically segmented into areas containing 5,000 residences. The police recognize that all crimes and offenses are not reported; people either do not want to become involved, consider the offenses too small to report, are too embarrassed to make a police report, or do not take the time, among other reasons. Every month, because of this, the police are contacting by phone a random sample of 1,000 of the 5,000 residences for

data on crime. (Respondents are guaranteed anonymity.) The data collected for the past 12 months for one area are

Month	Crime Incidence	Sample Size	Crime Rate
January	7	1,000	0.007
February	9	1,000	0.009
March	7	1,000	0.007
April	7	1,000	0.007
May	7	1,000	0.007
June	9	1,000	0.009
July	7	1,000	0.007
August	10	1,000	0.010
September	8	1,000	0.008
October	11	1,000	0.011
November	10	1,000	0.010
December	8	1,000	0.008

Construct a *p*-chart for 95 percent confidence (1.96) and plot each of the months. If the next three months show crime incidences in this area as

    January = 10 (out of 1,000 sampled)
    February = 12 (out of 1,000 sampled)
       March = 11 (out of 1,000 sampled)

what comments can you make regarding the crime rate?

11. Some citizens complained to city council members that there should be equal protection under the law against the occurrence of crimes. The citizens argued that this equal protection should be interpreted as indicating that high-crime areas should have more police protection than low-crime areas. Therefore, police patrols and other methods for preventing crime (such as street lighting or cleaning up abandoned areas and buildings) should be used proportionately to crime occurrence.

In a fashion similar to Problem 10, the city has been broken down into 20 geographic areas, each containing 5,000 residences. The 1,000 sampled from each area showed the following incidence of crime during the past month:

Area	Number of Crimes	Sample Size	Crime Rate
1	14	1,000	0.014
2	3	1,000	0.003
3	19	1,000	0.019
4	18	1,000	0.018
5	14	1,000	0.014
6	28	1,000	0.028
7	10	1,000	0.010
8	18	1,000	0.018
9	12	1,000	0.012
10	3	1,000	0.003
11	20	1,000	0.020
12	15	1,000	0.015
13	12	1,000	0.012
14	14	1,000	0.014
15	10	1,000	0.010
16	30	1,000	0.030
17	4	1,000	0.004
18	20	1,000	0.020
19	6	1,000	0.006
20	30	1,000	0.030
	$\overline{300}$		

Suggest a reallocation of crime protection effort, if indicated, based on a *p*-chart analysis. To be reasonably certain in your recommendation, select a 95 percent confidence level (i.e., $Z = 1.96$).

12. Amalgo Tech engineers are trying to improve the design of a gear that has an outer diameter of 13 inches with a tolerance of $\pm.003$ inch. Available inspection data from the past year indicate that the mean value of the diameter has been 13.001 with standard deviation of .0025 inch. The gear sells for $125. The estimated loss to society is $20 for any gear that has a diameter at the upper or lower tolerance limit. Annual sales of the gear amount to 40,000 units.

    a. Calculate the average loss per unit of production.
    b. What is the expected loss per year?
    c. What happens to the average loss per unit and the expected loss per year if the mean is shifted to the target value of 13 inches?

13. The operations manager of a small metal fabricating company is concerned about the variability of a milling process. Although the average width of a metal connector is identical to the target of .25 inch, the standard deviation of the process is .01 inch. The tolerance limits for the part are $\pm.008$ inch. The expected loss to society for any metal connector that is produced with widths at the limits of tolerance is $1.75 per unit. The specialized connectors sell for $18.00 each.

    a. Calculate the average loss per unit of production.
    b. If the average width shifts from the target value of .25 inch but stays within tolerance, what will happen to value of the average loss per unit of production?
    c. What is the value of the average loss per unit if the standard deviation can be reduced from .01 to .0075?

S5.9   SELECTED BIBLIOGRAPHY

Aslup, Fred, and Ricky M. Watson. *Practical Statistical Process Control: A Tool for Quality Manufacturing.* New York: Van Nostrand Reinhold, 1993.

Hradesky, John L. *Productivity and Quality Improvement: A Practical Guide to Implementing Statistical Process Control.* New York: McGraw-Hill, 1988.

Juran, J. M., and F. M. Gryna. *Quality Planning and Analysis.* 2nd ed. New York: McGraw-Hill, 1980.

Taguchi, G. *On-Line Quality Control during Production.* Tokyo: Japanese Standards Association, 1987.

Thompson, James R., and Jacek Koronacki. *Statistical Process Control for Quality Improvement.* New York: Chapman & Hall, 1993.

Wetherill, G. Barrie, and Don W. Brown. *Statistical Process Control: Theory and Practice.* New York: Chapman & Hall, 1991.

III

DESIGN OF FACILITIES AND JOBS

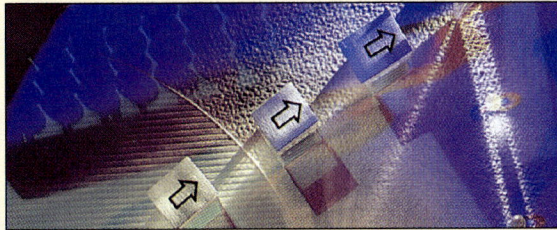

Once a firm decides what it is to make and how to make it, the focus shifts to putting a production system in place. This section addresses this issue, beginning with an integrated approach to production management—just-in-time systems. We then examine such basic questions as: What is the forecasted product demand, where is the plant to be located, how much capacity should it have, how should it be laid out, and how should its jobs be designed? In addition to covering some quantitative techniques for solving specific OM problems, this section introduces four powerful analytical tools—decision trees, linear programming, simulation modeling, and time series techniques—that find application in virtually all areas of business administration.

Chapter

6

Just-in-Time Production Systems

CHAPTER OUTLINE

KEY TERMS

Focused Factory Network
Group Technology
Quality at the Source
Automated Inspection
Uniform Plant Loading
Cycle Times
Kanban Pull System
Bottom Round Management
Quality Circles
Preventive Maintenance
Total Quality Control (TQC)
Level Schedule
Freeze Window
Backflush

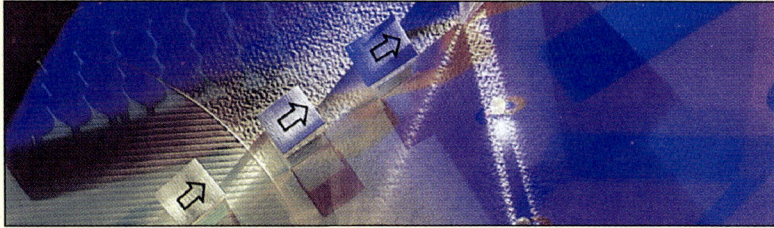

The 100 Yen Sushi House is no ordinary sushi restaurant. It is the ultimate showcase of Japanese productivity. As we entered the shop, there was a chorus of *"irat-sai,"* a welcome from everyone working in the shop—cooks, waitresses, the owner, and the owner's children. The house features an ellipsoid-shaped serving area in the middle of the room, where three or four cooks were busily preparing sushi. Perhaps 30 stools surrounded the serving area. We took seats at the counters and were promptly served with a cup of "misoshiru," which is a bean paste soup, a pair of chopsticks, a cup of green tea, a tiny plate to make our own sauce, and a small china piece to hold the chopsticks. So far, the service was average for any sushi house. Then, I noticed something special. There was a conveyor belt going around the ellipsoid service area, like a toy train track. On it I saw a train of plates of sushi. You can find any kind of sushi that you can think of—from the cheapest seaweed or octopus kind to the expensive raw salmon or shrimp dishes. The price is uniform, however, 100 yen per plate. On closer examination, while my eyes were racing to keep up with the speed of the traveling plates, I found that a cheap seaweed plate had four pieces, while the more expensive raw salmon dish had only two pieces.

I saw a man with eight plates all stacked up neatly. As he got up to leave, the cashier looked over and said, "800 yen, please." The cashier had no cash register, since she can simply count the number of plates and then multiply by 100 yen. As the customer was leaving, once again we heard a chorus of *"Arigato Gosaimas"* (thank you), from all the workers.

The owner's daily operation is based on a careful analysis of information. The owner has a complete summary of demand information about different types of sushi plates, and thus he knows exactly how many of each type of sushi plates he should prepare and when. Furthermore, the whole operation is based on the repetitive manufacturing principle with appropriate just-in-time and quality control systems. For example, the store has a very limited refrigerator capacity (we could see several whole fish or octopus in the glassed chambers right in front of our counter). Thus, the store uses the just-in-time inventory control system. Instead of increasing the refrigeration capacity by purchasing new refrigeration systems, the company has an agreement with the fish vendor to deliver fresh fish several times a day so that materials arrive just in time to be used for sushi making. Therefore, the inventory cost is minimum.

In the just-in-time operation system, the safety stock principle is turned upside down. In other words, the safety stock is deliberately removed gradually, to uncover problems and their possible solutions. The available floor space is for workers and their necessary equipment but not for holding inventory. In the 100 Yen Sushi House, workers and their equipment are positioned so close that sushi making is passed on hand to hand rather than as independent operations. The absence of walls of inventory allows the owner and workers to be involved in the total operation, from greeting the customer to serving what is ordered. Their tasks are tightly interrelated and everyone rushes to a problem spot to prevent the cascading effect of the problem throughout the work process.

The 100 Yen Sushi House is a labor-intensive operation, which is based mostly on simplicity and common sense rather than high technology, contrary to American perceptions. I was very impressed. As I finished my fifth plate, I saw the same octopus sushi plate going around for about the thirtieth time. Perhaps I had discovered the pitfall of the system. So I asked the owner how he takes care of the sanitary problems when a sushi plate goes around all day long, until an unfortunate customer eats it and perhaps gets food poisoning. He bowed with an apologetic smile and said, "Well, sir, we never let our sushi plates go unsold longer than about 30 minutes." Then he scratched his head and said, "Whenever one of our employees takes a break, he or she can take off unsold plates of sushi and either eat them or throw them away. We are very serious about our sushi quality." As we laughed, he laughed, along with a 90-degree bow.

Source: Sang M. Lee, "Japanese Management and the 100 Yen Sushi House," *Operations Management Review* 1, no. 2 (Winter 1983), pp. 45–48.

The 100 Yen Sushi House is a microcosm of the features that characterize the most significant production management approach of the post–World War II era, just-in-time (JIT) production. Developed by the Japanese, this approach integrates the five P's of OM to streamline production of high-quality goods and services. Like TQM, virtually every modern manufacturing organization has used at least some JIT elements in its design.

This chapter relates the logic of JIT. It also details approaches to JIT implementation and JIT's application in service organizations. An accompanying updated version of a classic article by Kenneth A. Wantuck describes the elements of JIT as employed by the Japanese to improve productivity.

6.1   JIT LOGIC

JIT (just-in-time) is an integrated set of activities designed to achieve high-volume production using minimal inventories of raw materials, work in process, and finished goods. Parts arrive at the next workstation "just in time" and are completed and move through the operation quickly. Just-in-time is also based on the logic that nothing will be produced until it is needed. Exhibit 6.1 illustrates the process. Need is created by the product being pulled toward the user. When an item is sold, in theory, the market pulls a replacement from the last position in the system—final assembly in this case. This triggers an order to the factory production line where a worker then pulls another unit from an upstream station in the flow to replace the unit taken. This upstream station then pulls

A vacancy on a subassembly shelf at Saturn Corporation's plant at Spring Hill, Tennessee, generates a purchase order to the vendor to resupply.

E X H I B I T 6.1   *Pull System*

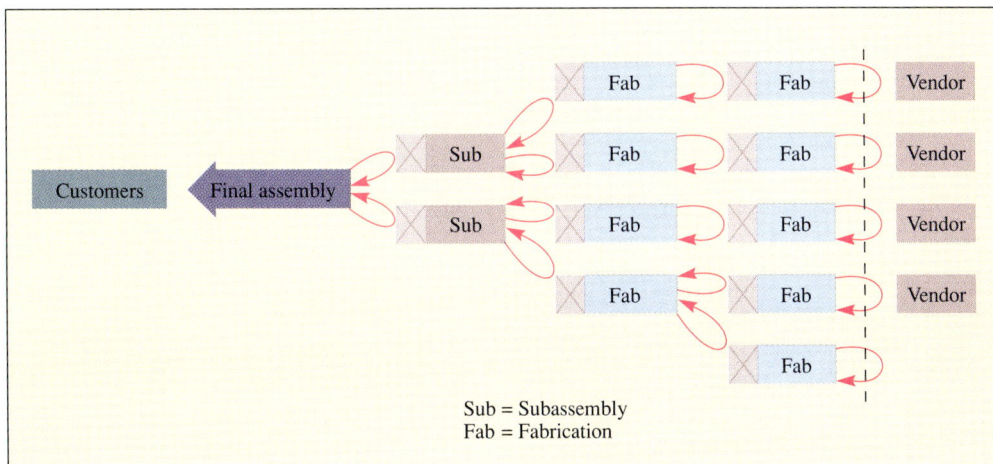

Sub = Subassembly
Fab = Fabrication

Historical Note   JIT gained worldwide prominence in the 1970s, but some of its philosophy can be traced to the early 1900s in the United States. Henry Ford used JIT concepts as he streamlined his moving assembly lines to make automobiles. For example, to eliminate waste he used the bottom of the packing crates for car seats as the floor board of the car. Although elements of JIT were being used by Japanese industry as early as the 1930s, it was not fully refined until the 1970s when Tai-ichi Ohno of Toyota Motors used JIT to take Toyota's cars to the forefront of delivery time and quality. Around the same time, quality experts Deming and Juran lectured on the need for American producers to adopt many JIT principles.

from the next station further upstream and so on back to the release of raw materials. To enable this pull process to work smoothly, JIT demands high levels of quality at each stage of the process, strong vendor relations, and a fairly predictable demand for the end product.

JIT can be viewed colloquially as "big JIT" and "little JIT." Big JIT (often termed lean production[1]) is the philosophy of operations management that seeks to eliminate waste in all aspects of a firm's production activities: human relations, vendor relations, technology, and the management of materials and inventories. Little JIT focuses more narrowly on scheduling goods inventories and providing service resources where and when needed. For example, companies such as Manpower Temporary Services and Pizza Hut essentially use pull signals to fill openings for replacement workers or Big Foot pizzas, respectively. However, they do not necessarily integrate operations around other aspects of the JIT philosophy.

6.2   THE JAPANESE APPROACH TO PRODUCTIVITY[2]

The Japanese have had a national goal of full employment through industrialization since World War II. The strategy for obtaining market dominance has been targeted to specific product areas. When choosing industries to target for improvement, the Japanese Ministry of International Trade and Industry (MITI) selected only industries with a competitive advantage.

To improve their country's competitive posture, they imported technology. Instead of inventing new technology, they avoided major R&D expenditures and corresponding risks by buying licensing agreements frequently from U.S. companies. To make these new products they concentrated their efforts on the factory floor to achieve high productivity and lower unit costs. They directed their best engineering talent to the shop floor, not to product design activities. They also worked to improve product quality and reliability above what competitors could supply. Central to this effort were two philosophies: elimination of waste and respect for people.

Elimination of Waste   The Japanese are true believers in eliminating waste and they practice a great respect for people. Waste in Japan, as defined by Toyota's Fujio Cho, is "anything other than the minimum amount of equipment, materials, parts, and workers (working time) which are absolutely essential to production." [An expanded JIT definition advanced by Fujio Cho

[1]James P. Womack, D. T. Jones, and D. Roos, *The Machine That Changed the World* (New York: R. A. Rawston Associates, 1990).

[2]Kenneth A. Wantuck, "The Japanese Approach to Productivity" (Southfield, MI: Bendix Corporation, 1983. Sections 6.2–6.4 are an edited and updated version of this paper).

identifies seven prominent types of waste to be eliminated: (1) waste from overproduction, (2) waste of waiting time, (3) transportation waste, (4) inventory waste, (5) processing waste, (6) waste of motion, and (7) waste from product defects.[3]]

This definition of JIT leaves no room for surplus or safety stock. No safety stocks are allowed because if you cannot use it now, you do not need to make it now. That would be waste. Hidden inventory in stores, transit systems, carousels, and conveyors are key targets for inventory reduction.

The seven elements that address elimination of waste are

1. Focused factory networks.
2. Group technology.
3. Quality at the source.
4. JIT production.
5. Uniform plant loading.
6. Kanban production control system.
7. Minimized setup times.

Focused Factory Networks   The Japanese build small specialized plants rather than large vertically integrated manufacturing facilities. They find large operations and their bureaucracies difficult to manage and not in line with their management styles. Plants designed for one purpose can be constructed and operated more economically. The bulk of Japanese plants, some 60,000, have between 30 and 1,000 workers.

Group Technology   **Group technology,** while invented in the United States, was most successfully employed in Japan. Instead of transferring jobs from one department to another to specialized workers, the Japanese consider all operations required to make a part and group those machines together. Exhibit 6.2 illustrates the difference between the clus-

E X H I B I T 6.2   *Group Technology versus Departmental Specialty*

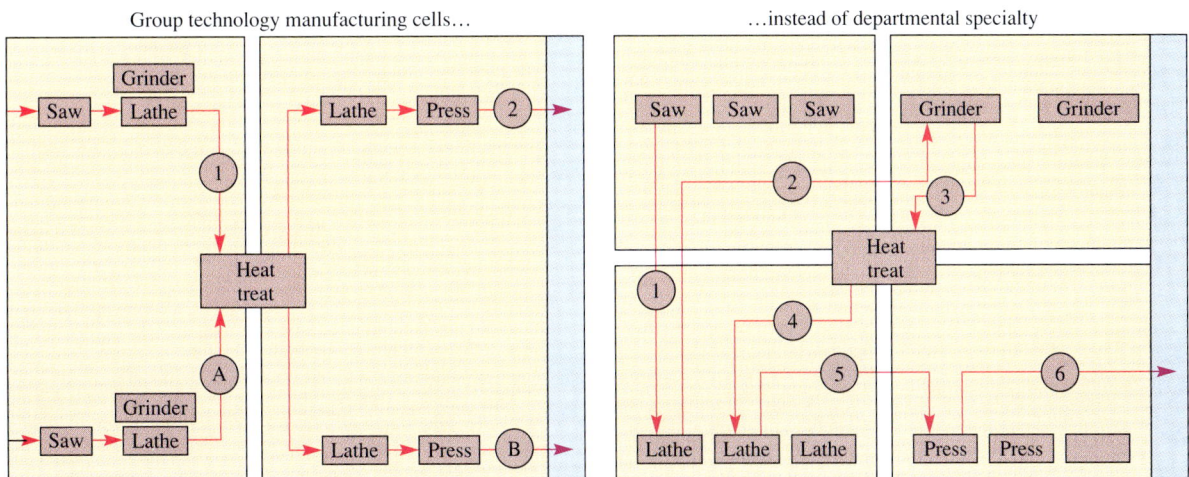

[3]Kiyoshi Suzaki, *The New Manufacturing Challenge: Techniques for Continuous Improvement* (New York: Free Press, 1987), pp. 7–25.

ters of various machines grouped into work centers for parts versus departmental layouts. The group technology cells eliminate movement and queue (waiting) time between operations, reduce inventory, and reduce the number of employees required. Workers, however, must be flexible to run several machines and processes. Due to their advanced skill level, these workers have increased job security.

Quality at the Source   **Quality at the source** means do it right the first time and, when something goes wrong, stop the process or assembly line immediately. Factory workers become their own inspectors, personally responsible for the quality of their outputs. Workers concentrate on one part of the job at a time so quality problems are uncovered. If the pace is too fast, if the worker finds a quality problem, or if a safety issue is discovered, the worker is obligated to push a button to stop the line and turn on a visual signal. People from other areas respond to the alarm and the problem. Workers are empowered to do their own maintenance and housekeeping until the problem is fixed.

This quality at the source includes **autonomation** or **automated inspection.** Japanese prefer to have quality inspections performed by automation or robotics because it is faster, easier, repeatable, and suitable for jobs too redundant for a worker to perform.

JIT Production   JIT means producing what is needed when needed and no more. Anything over the minimum amount necessary is viewed as waste, since effort and material expended for something not needed now cannot be utilized now. This is in contrast to relying on extra material just in case something goes wrong. Exhibit 6.3 shows JIT requirements and assumptions.

JIT has been applied to repetitive manufacturing but does not require large volumes and is not limited to processes that produce the same parts over and over. JIT can be applied to any repetitive segments of a business regardless of where they appear. Under JIT the ideal lot size is one. A worker completes the task and passes it on to the next worker for processing. While workstations may be geographically dispersed, the Japanese minimize transit time and keep transfer quantities small—typically one-tenth of a day's production is a lot size. Vendors even ship several times a day to their customers to keep lot sizes small and inventory low. When all queues are driven to zero, inventory investment is minimized, lead times are shortened, firms can react faster to demand changes, and quality problems are uncovered.

E X H I B I T 6.3
Just-in-Time

WHAT IT IS	WHAT IT DOES
▪ Management philosophy ▪ "Pull" system through the plant	▪ Attacks waste (time, inventory, scrap) ▪ Exposes problems and bottlenecks ▪ Achieves streamlined production

WHAT IT REQUIRES	WHAT IT ASSUMES
▪ Employee participation ▪ Industrial engineering/basics ▪ Continuing improvement ▪ Total quality control ▪ Small lot sizes	▪ Stable environment

Source: Adapted from Chris Gopal (of Price Waterhouse), "Notes on JIT."

Exhibit 6.4 illustrates this idea. If the water in a pond represents inventory, the rocks represent problems that could occur in a firm. A high level of water hides the problems (rocks). Management assumes everything is fine, but as the water level drops in an economic downturn, problems are presented. If you force the water level down on purpose (particularly in good economic times), you can expose and correct problems before they cause worse problems. JIT manufacturing exposes problems otherwise hidden by excess inventories and staff.

Uniform Plant Loading   Smoothing the production flow to dampen the reaction waves that normally occur in response to schedule variations is called **uniform plant loading.** When a change is made in a final assembly, the changes are magnified throughout the line and the supply chain. The only way to eliminate the problem is to make adjustments as small as possible by setting a firm monthly production plan for which the output rate is frozen. (This is how a company addresses the need for a stable demand environment noted in Exhibit 6.3.)

The Japanese found they could do this by building the same mix of products every day in small quantities. Thus they always have a total mix available to respond to variations in demand. A Toyota example is shown in Exhibit 6.5. Monthly car style quantities are reduced to daily quantities (assuming a 20-day month) in order to compute **cycle times** (the time between two identical units completed on a line). The cycle time figure is used to adjust resources to produce the precise quantity needed. Speed of equipment or of the production line is not important. Producing only the needed quantity each day

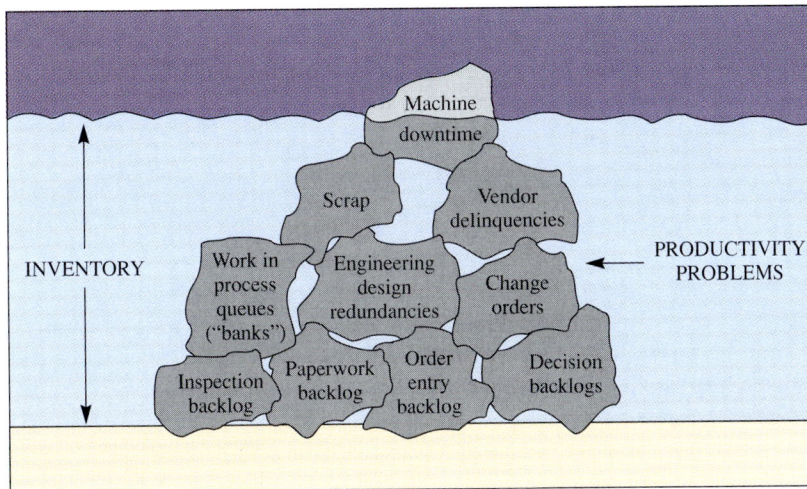

E X H I B I T 6.4
Inventory Hides Problems

Model	Monthly Quantity	Daily Quantity	Cycle Time (minutes)
Sedan	5,000	250	2
Hardtop	2,500	125	4
Wagon	2,500	125	4

Sequence: Sedan, hardtop, sedan, wagon, sedan, hardtop, sedan, wagon, etc.

E X H I B I T 6.5
Toyota Example of Mixed-Model Production Cycle in a Japanese Assembly Plant

At Bernard Welding Equipment, when part bins are emptied, a kanban card is detached from the container and is transferred to the appropriate work cell, and placed on a post to indicate the bin needs to be refilled. The card contains the part number, routing quantity, and bin number.

An empty Kanban square on the factory floor at McDonnell Douglas visually signals the need to be filled by a disk drive unit.

E X H I B I T 6.6

Flow of Two Kanbans

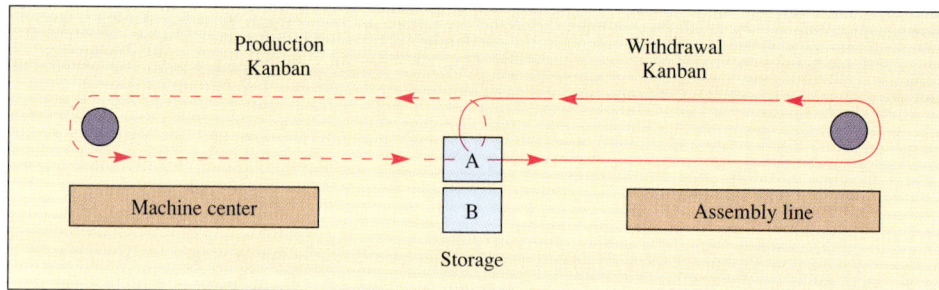

is important. JIT strives to produce on schedule, on cost, and on quality. [Additional discussion of mixed-model assembly is provided in Chapter 10.]

Kanban Production Control Systems   A kanban control system uses a signaling device to regulate JIT flows. In Japanese **Kanban** means "sign" or "instruction card." In a paperless control system, containers can be used instead of cards. The cards or containers make up the **kanban pull system.** The authority to produce or supply additional parts comes from downstream operations. Workers produce to schedule but execute based on kanbans, which are completely manual. Exhibit 6.6 shows kanbans used in two station work centers making parts A and B. These two parts are stored in containers next to the work center. When the line uses part A from a full container, a worker takes the withdrawal kanban from the container and travels to the machining center storage area. There the worker finds a container of part A, removes the production kanban, and replaces it with the withdrawal kanban. This card authorizes movement of the container. The freed production kanban is placed in a rack by the machining center and authorizes another lot of material. Parts are produced in the order of the cards on the rack. The cards become the dispatch list. The same approach is used to authorize vendor shipments. The system requires everyone to do exactly what is authorized and to follow the procedures.

Other signals, rather than cards, are also used to initiate production and can include voice directions, flashing colored lights over a work center, electronic messages sent

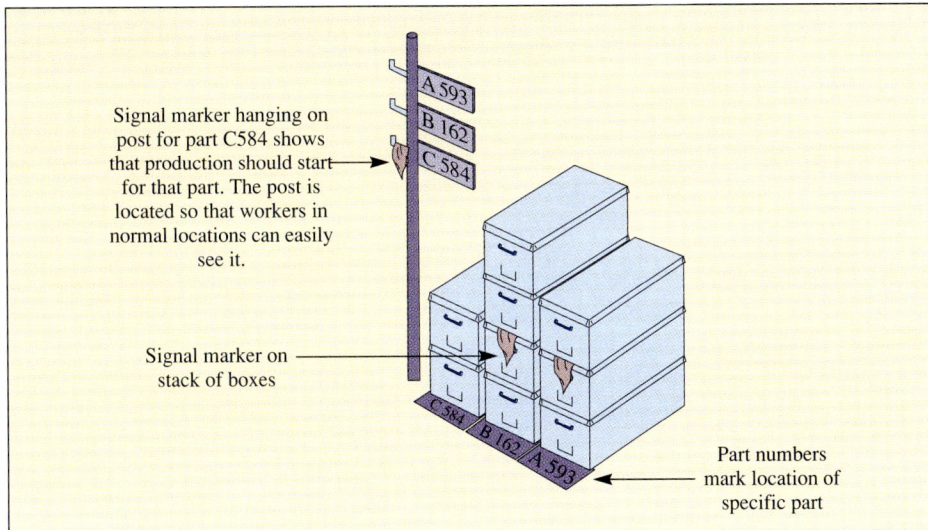

EXHIBIT 6.7

Diagram of Outbound Stockpoint with Warning Signal Marker

Signal marker hanging on post for part C584 shows that production should start for that part. The post is located so that workers in normal locations can easily see it.

Signal marker on stack of boxes

Part numbers mark location of specific part

Source: Robert Hall, *Zero Inventories* (Homewood, IL: Dow Jones-Irwin, 1983), p. 51.

via a computer terminal, or a signal marker hanging on a post by the workstation. Exhibit 6.7 shows a signal marker design. In a system where operations are within sight of each other, no cards are needed at all—only a strict restriction on the inventory between operations. This can be done by marking a space or square between operations called a **kanban square.** If squares are empty, workers fill them up and leave no extras.

A kanban system can set reorder quantities equal to the number of parts held by the inventory bin or equal to the amount withdrawn from the bin. Both approaches can replenish inventory as soon as it is depleted. The standardized containers define the lot size for the reorder point. Both approaches also assume continuous review of inventories, predetermined reorder points, and fixed replenishment quantities.

Minimized Setup Times   Because small lot sizes are the norm, machine setups must be quickly accomplished to produce the mixed models on the line. In a widely cited example from the late 1970s, Toyota teams of press operators producing car hoods and fenders were able to change an 800-ton press in 10 minutes, compared with the average of six hours for U.S. workers and four hours for German workers. [Now, however, such speed is common in most U.S. auto plants. At the John Deere plant, punch press setup time was cut from one hour to one minute back in 1985.] To achieve such setup time reduction, setups are divided into internal and external activities. Internal setups must be done while a machine is stopped. External setups can be done while the machine is running. Other time-saving devices such as duplicate tool holders are also used to reduce setups. It is not unusual for a Japanese setup team to spend a full Saturday practicing changeovers.

Respect for People

Respect for people is a key to the Japanese improvements. They have traditionally stressed lifetime employment for permanent positions within major firms. Companies try to maintain level payrolls even when business conditions deteriorate. Permanent workers (about one-third of the total workforce) have job security and tend to be more flexible, remain with a company, and do all they can to help a firm achieve its goals. [The recent recession in Japan has caused many Japanese companies to move away from this ideal. See the "Toyota Work Contracts" case at the end of this chapter.]

Company unions in Japan exist to foster a cooperative relationship with management. All employees receive two bonuses a year in good times. Employees know if the company performs well, they will get a bonus. This encourages workers to improve productivity. Management views workers as assets, not as human machines. Automation and robotics are used extensively to perform dull or routine jobs so employees are free to focus on important improvement tasks.

Subcontractor networks are very important in Japan. The specialized nature of Japanese factories features little vertical integration. More than 90 percent of all Japanese companies are part of the supplier network of small firms. Some suppliers are specialists in a narrow field serving multiple customers. The other more prominent type are sole-source suppliers that make a small variety of parts for a single customer. Firms have long-term partnerships with their suppliers and customers. Suppliers consider themselves part of a customer's family. [Again, the recession is causing a strain among family members since many small subcontractors are in deep financial trouble.]

They use a **bottom-round management** style made up of consensus management by committees or teams. This decision process is slow but attempts to reach a consensus (not a compromise) by involving all parties, seeking information, and making a decision at the lowest level possible. Unlike in the United States, Japanese top management makes very few operating decisions, but concentrates on strategic planning. This system is effective in the smaller, focused factories of Japan.

Quality circles of volunteer employees meet weekly to discuss their jobs and problems. These **small group improvement activities (SGIA)** attempt to devise solutions to problems and share the solutions with management. They are led by a supervisor or production worker and typically include employees from a given production area. Others are multidiscipline teams and led by a trained group leader or facilitator. Westinghouse Electric Corporation, for example, has 275 quality circles and 25 facilitators. These circles are part of the consensus, bottom-round management approach.

6.3   NORTH AMERICAN MODIFICATIONS OF JIT

Some of these approaches are difficult to implement in North America. Lifetime employment, company unions, and subcontractor networks are not prevalent in the United States and Canada. Also, U.S. and Canadian companies traditionally use a top-down planning and management structure, which is counter to bottom-round management.

What we can (and have) adopted in the United States and Canada is the Japanese general philosophy and approach to JIT. We have discovered that while the process may take many years to implement, reducing setup times, eliminating inventory, identifying problems, and utilizing the expertise of workers are important, practical guidelines for all organizations. Indeed, in a survey on the implementations of 1,035 U.S. manufacturers, 86.4 percent of the respondents agreed that JIT provided an overall net benefit for their organization. Less than 5 percent reported no overall benefit from their JIT implementation. Throughput time (the time it takes to make one product in a plant from start to finish) decreased an average of 59.4 percent. The study found that organizations with 500 or more employees typically implement JIT management practices more often than organizations with fewer than 500 employees. JIT was also practiced for a longer period of time for the larger organizations. Regardless of size or type of process employed, JIT manufacturing was seen as beneficial for U.S. manufacturers.[4]

In Europe as well, many organizations have seen JIT benefits. In a study of 80 European plants, improvements included a 50 percent average reduction in inventory, a 50 to 70 percent reduction in throughput time, a reduction in setup time by as much as 50 percent (without major plant and equipment investments), 20 to 50 percent productivity increases, and a payback for the JIT investment in less than nine months.[5]

6.4   JIT IMPLEMENTATION REQUIREMENTS

This section is structured around the model shown in Exhibit 6.8. It expands on the ideas from the Wantuck paper (Section 6.2) and discusses ways to accomplish JIT production. These suggestions are geared to **repetitive production systems**—those that make the same products again and again. Also, bear in mind that these elements are linked: Any changes in part of the production system impact other features of the system.

JIT Layouts and Design Flows

JIT requires the plant layout to be designed to ensure a balanced work flow with a minimum of work-in-process inventory. Each workstation is part of a production line, whether or not a physical line actually exists. Capacity balancing is done using the same logic for an assembly line and operations are linked through a pull system. In addition, the system designer must have a vision of how all aspects of the internal and external logistics system tie to the layout.

Preventive maintenance is emphasized to ensure that flows are not interrupted by downtime or malfunctioning equipment. Operators perform much of the maintenance because they are most familiar with their machines and because machines are easier to repair as JIT operations favor several simple machines rather than one large complex one.

The reductions in setup and changeover times previously discussed are necessary to achieve a smooth flow. Exhibit 6.9 shows the relationship between lot size and setup costs. Under a traditional approach, setup cost is treated as a constant, and the optimal order quantity is shown as six. Under the kanban approach of JIT, setup cost is treated as a variable and the optimal order quantity is reduced. In the exhibit, the order quantity has been reduced from six to two under JIT by employing setup-time–saving procedures. This organization will ultimately strive for a lot size of one.

JIT Applications for Line Flows

Exhibit 6.10 illustrates a pull system in a simple line flow. In a pure JIT environment, no employee does any work until the product has been pulled from the end of the line by the market. The product could be a final product or a component used in later production. When a product is pulled, a replenishment unit is pulled from upstream operations. In the exhibit, an item of finished goods is pulled from F, the finished goods inventory. The inventory clerk then goes to processing station E and takes replacement product to fill the void. This pattern continues down the line to worker A, who pulls

[4]Richard E. White, "An Empirical Assessment of JIT in U.S. Manufacturers," *Production and Inventory Management Journal* 34, no. 2 (second quarter 1993), pp. 38–42.

[5]Amrik Sohal and Keith Howard, "Trends in Material Management," *International Journal of Production Distribution and Materials Management* 17, no. 5 (1987), pp. 3–41.

E X H I B I T 6.8   *How to Accomplish Just-in-Time Production*

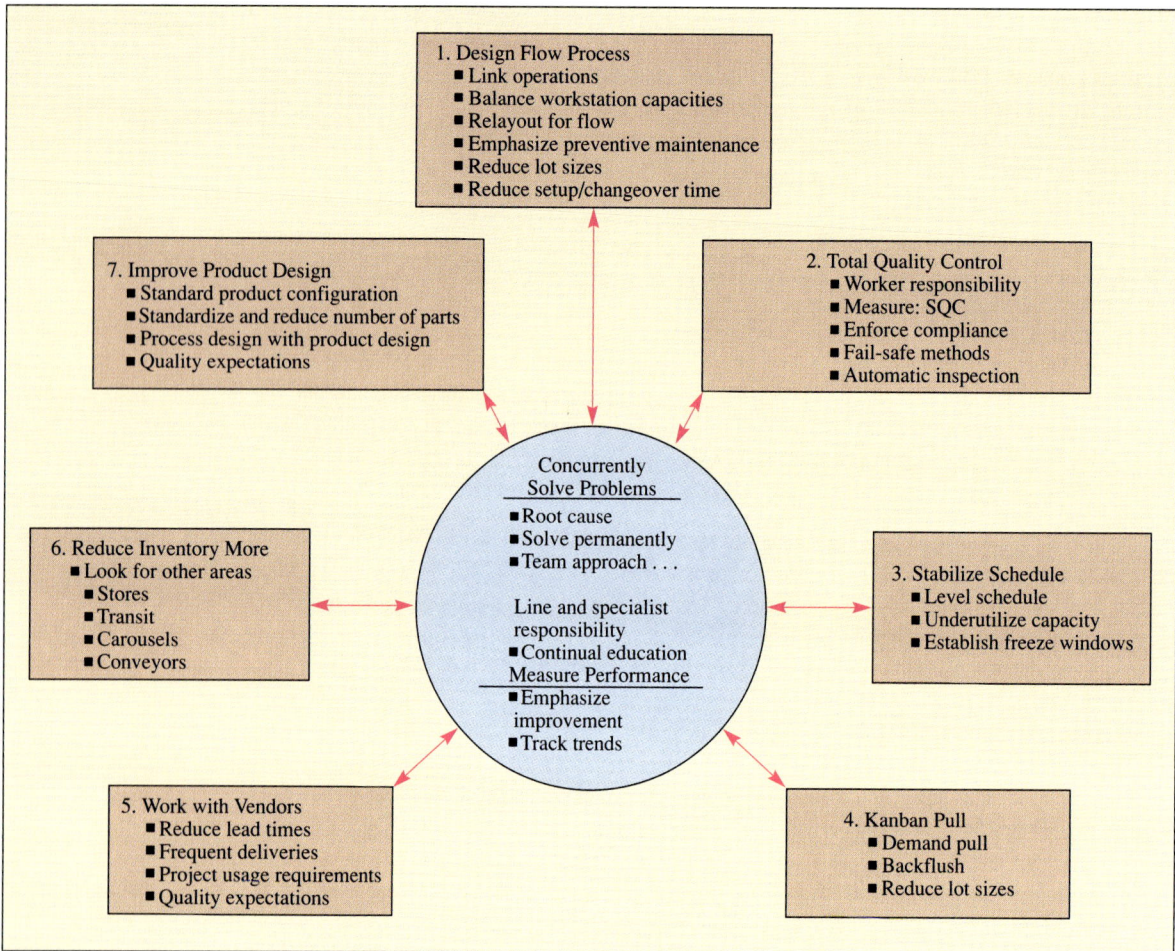

1. Design Flow Process
- Link operations
- Balance workstation capacities
- Relayout for flow
- Emphasize preventive maintenance
- Reduce lot sizes
- Reduce setup/changeover time

7. Improve Product Design
- Standard product configuration
- Standardize and reduce number of parts
- Process design with product design
- Quality expectations

2. Total Quality Control
- Worker responsibility
- Measure: SQC
- Enforce compliance
- Fail-safe methods
- Automatic inspection

Concurrently Solve Problems
- Root cause
- Solve permanently
- Team approach . . .

Line and specialist responsibility
- Continual education

Measure Performance
- Emphasize improvement
- Track trends

6. Reduce Inventory More
- Look for other areas
  - Stores
  - Transit
  - Carousels
  - Conveyors

3. Stabilize Schedule
- Level schedule
- Underutilize capacity
- Establish freeze windows

5. Work with Vendors
- Reduce lead times
- Frequent deliveries
- Project usage requirements
- Quality expectations

4. Kanban Pull
- Demand pull
- Backflush
- Reduce lot sizes

This diagram is modeled after the one used by Hewlett-Packard's Boise plant to accomplish its JIT program.

material from the raw material inventory. The rules of the flow layout require employees to keep completed units at their workstation and if someone takes the completed work away, the employee must move upstream in the flow to get additional work to complete.

JIT Applications for Job Shops

JIT is traditionally applied to line flows, but job shop environments also offer JIT benefits. The focus of JIT is product flow. Though job shops are characterized by low volume and high variety, JIT can be used if demand can be stabilized to permit repetitive manufacture. Stabilizing demand is usually easier to accomplish when the demand is from a downstream production stage rather than an end customer. (The logic is that internal customers can smooth their input requirements far easier than a distributor or individual purchaser.)

Factory machining centers, paint shops, and shirt making are examples of job-shop–type operations that process parts and components before they reach final produc-

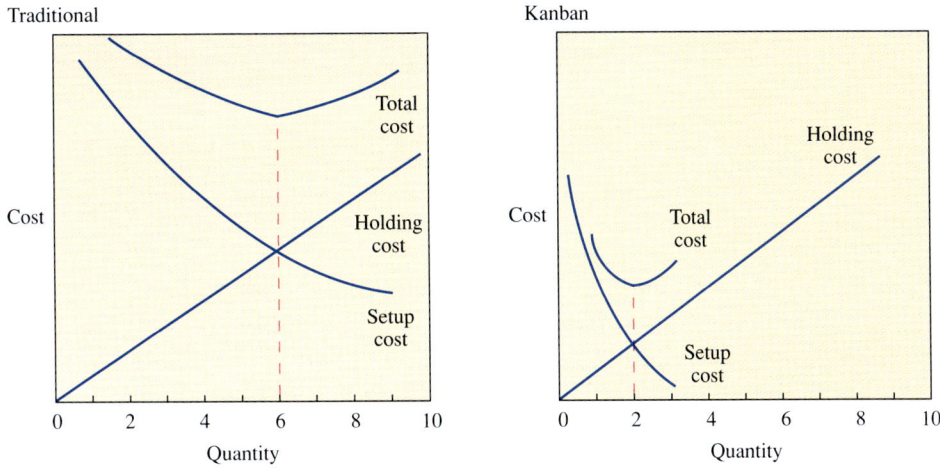

E X H I B I T 6.9
Relationship Between Lot Size and Setup Cost

Definitions: *Holding cost* includes the costs of storing inventory and the cost of money tied up in inventory. *Setup cost* includes the wage costs attributable to workers making the setup, and various administrative and supplies costs. (These are defined in total in Chapter on Independent Demand Inventory.)

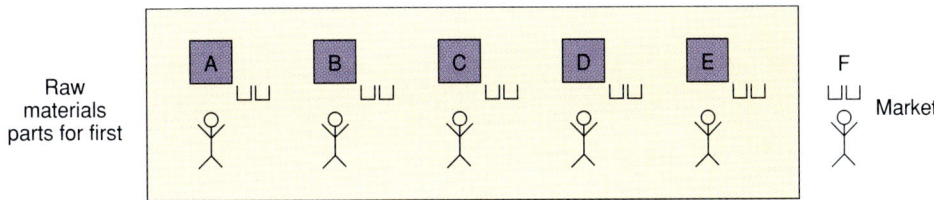

E X H I B I T 6.10
JIT in a Line Flow Layout

tion stages. By way of example, consider the production system in Exhibit 6.11. If a work center produces nine different parts used by several product varieties which are produced just in time, the work center keeps containers of completed output of all nine parts at the center to be picked up by users. Operators could make periodic rounds throughout the facility (hourly or more frequently) to pick up empty containers and drop them off at the corresponding upstream work center and pick up full containers. In Exhibit 6.11 automatic guided vehicles pick up and deliver part numbers M5 and M8 to line two and line three for processing. These handling procedures can be manual or automated, but either way, these periodic pickups and drop-offs allow the system to operate in a just-in-time mode.

JIT and TQC have merged in theory and practice. **Total quality control (TQC)** is the practice of building quality into the process and not identifying quality by inspection. It also refers to the theory of employees assuming responsibility for the quality of their own work. When employees are responsible for quality, JIT works at its best since only good-quality products are pulled through the system. When all products are good, no "just-in-case" extra inventory is needed. Thus organizations can achieve high quality and high productivity as shown in Exhibit 6.12. By using statistical quality control methods and training workers to maintain quality, inspections can be reduced to the first and last units produced. If they are perfect, we can assume the other units between these points are perfect as well.

TQC (Total Quality Control)

E X H I B I T 6.11

JIT in a Job Shop Layout Showing the Materials Handling Vehicle Route Connecting Machine Centers and Line Operations

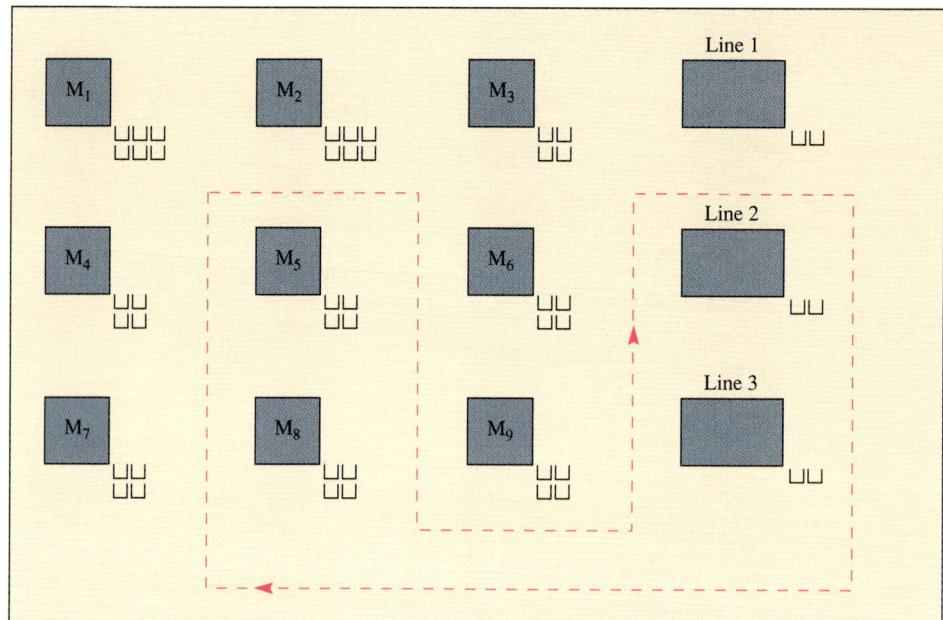

E X H I B I T 6.12

Relationship between JIT and Quality

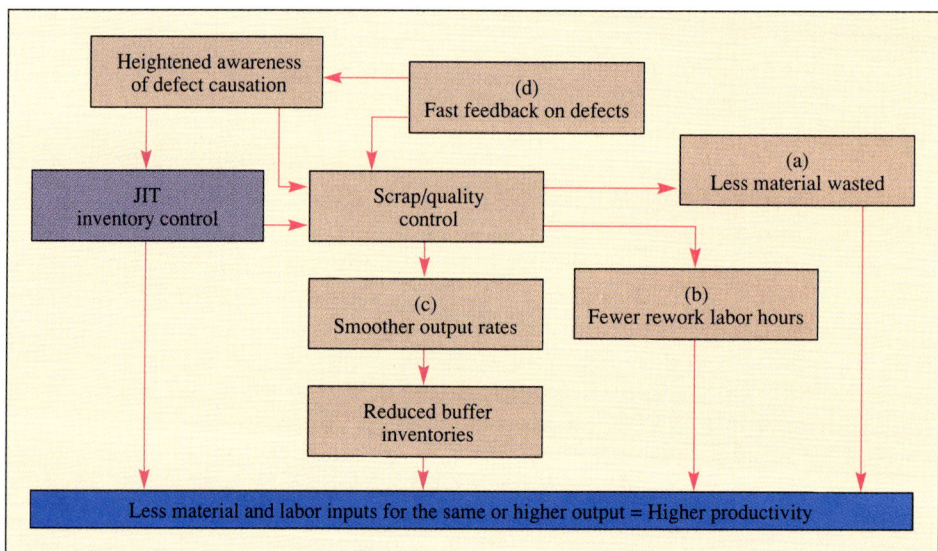

Source: Richard J. Schonberger, "Some Observations on the Advantages and Implementation Issues of Just-in-Time Production Systems," *Journal of Operations Management* 3, no. 1 (November 1982), p. 5.

A component of quality is improved product design. Standard product configurations, fewer parts, and standardized parts are important elements in JIT. These design modifications reduce variability in the end item or in the materials that go into the product. Besides improving the producibility of a product, product design activities can facilitate the processing of engineering changes. Often these engineering changes are introduced in batches in a JIT system rather than one change at a time.

As noted earlier, JIT firms require a stable schedule over a lengthy time horizon. This is accomplished by level scheduling, freeze windows, and underutilization of capacity. A **level schedule**

is one that requires material to be pulled into final assembly in a pattern uniform enough to allow the various elements of production to respond to pull signals. It does not necessarily mean that the usage of every part on an assembly line is identified hour by hour for days on end; it does mean that a given production system equipped with flexible setups and a fixed amount of material in the pipelines can respond.[6]

The term **freeze window** refers to that period of time during which the schedule is fixed and no further changes are possible. An added benefit of the stable schedule is seen in how parts and components are accounted for in a pull system. Here, the concept of **backflush** measurement is used to periodically explode an end item's bill of materials (the parts that go into each product) to calculate how many of each part went into the final product(s). This eliminates much of the shop-floor data collection activity, which is required if each part must be tracked and accounted for during production.

Underutilization of capacity is a controversial feature of JIT. Excess or underutilized capacity is realized as excess inventory buffers are removed from a system. The safety stocks and early deliveries were used as a hedge against production problems like poor quality, machine failures, and unanticipated bottlenecks in traditional manufacturing. Under JIT, excess labor and machines provide the hedge. The excess capacity in labor and equipment that results is much cheaper than carrying excess inventory. During idle periods personnel can be put to work on other activities such as special projects, work group activities, and workstation housekeeping.

Just as customers and employees are key components of the JIT system, vendors are also important to the process. If a firm shares its projected usage requirements with its vendors, they have a long-run picture of the demands that will be placed on their production and distribution systems. Some vendors are linked on-line with a customer to share production scheduling and input needs data. This permits them to develop level production systems. Confidence in the supplier or vendor's delivery commitment allows reductions of buffer inventories. Maintaining stock at a JIT level requires frequent deliveries during the day. Some suppliers even deliver to a location on the production line and not at a receiving dock. When vendors adopt quality practices, incoming receiving inspections of their products can even be bypassed. (See box titled "Saturn.")

To assess JIT progress, performance measures emphasize the number of processes and practices changed to improve materials flow and reduce labor content. If the process physically improves over time, lower costs follow. Other JIT benefits include lower carrying costs, scrap and quality improvements, worker involvement, higher motivation and morale, and productivity increases. According to Hall,[7] in a Japanese JIT system, a department head is likely to be evaluated on six measures:

1. Improvement trends, including the number of improvement projects undertaken, trends in costs, and productivity. Productivity is measured as department output divided by total number of direct and indirect employees.

2. Quality trends, reduction in defect rates, improvement in process capability, and improvement in quality procedures.

A Stable Schedule

Work with Vendors

---

[6]Robert H. Hall, *Zero Inventories* (Homewood, IL: Dow Jones-Irwin, 1983), p. 64.
[7]Ibid., pp. 254–55.

JIT and Cost Accounting   Cost accounting systems have focused on direct labor since the Industrial Revolution. However, under JIT (and computer-integrated manufacturing) overhead costs are dominant, often 20 times as high as direct labor. Moreover, with workers maintaining their own equipment, and other measures, the distinction between direct and indirect labor has become blurred for cost-allocation purposes. Hewlett-Packard has recognized this and has eliminated the cost category of direct labor, now simply using "labor" instead.

It presently appears that the primary difference between traditional and JIT cost accounting is the application of overhead on the basis of product time in the system (cycle time) rather than direct labor or machine hours.

Source: Mohan V. Tatikonda, "Just-in-Time and Modern Manufacturing Environments: Implications for Cost Accounting," *Production and Inventory Management Journal* 28, no. 1 (1988), pp. 1–5.

3. Running to a level schedule and providing parts when others need them.
4. Trends in department inventory levels (e.g., speed or flow).
5. Staying within budgets for expenses.
6. Developing workforce skills, versatility, participation in changes, and morale.

While these quantitative and qualitative improvement measures are realistic and fit the system, many previous cost accounting measures no longer represent the JIT environment. These systems, since the U.S. Industrial Revolution, have focused on direct labor. Under JIT, overhead costs are as much as 20 times as high as direct labor costs. Also, as workers take on maintenance duties, direct and indirect labor distinctions are blurred and cost allocation measures must be changed. (See box insert on "JIT and Cost Accounting.")

6.5   JIT IN SERVICES

Many JIT techniques have been successfully applied by service firms. Just as in manufacturing, the suitability of each technique and the corresponding work steps depends on the characteristics of the firm's markets, production and equipment technology, skill sets, and corporate culture. Service firms are not different in this respect. Here are 10 of the more successful applications:[8]

Organize Problem-Solving Groups   Honeywell is extending its quality circles from manufacturing into its service operations. Other corporations as diverse as First Bank/ Dallas, Standard Meat Company, and Miller Brewing Company are using similar approaches to improve service. British Airways used quality circles as a fundamental part of its strategy to implement new service practices. (See "JIT in an Express Package Service" on the next page for another example of team efforts in JIT.)

Upgrade Housekeeping   Good housekeeping means more than winning the clean broom award. It means that only the necessary items are kept in a work area, that there is a place for everything, and that everything is clean and in a constant state of readiness. The employees clean their own areas.

---

[8]Randall J. Benson, "JIT: Not Just For the Factory!" *APICS 29th Annual International Conference Proceedings* (1986), pp. 370-374.

Saturn

Like clockwork. According to Saturn's VP of purchasing, Alec Bedricky, Saturn "runs the tightest JIT system in the auto business." Certainly, no one at GM will argue the point. Indeed, one will find little buffer anywhere in the Saturn plant. For instance, the number of powertrains on the floor between the engine plant and vehicle assembly at any time will be less than 140, or barely enough to cover two hours of production, which is in sharp contrast to the two-week float that one likely will find at other GM plants. Elsewhere, it's the same story. Less than 95 body frames will be found in transit at any time between body fabrication and the start of trim operations.

"You can't build out-of-sequence here." says Bedricky. "If there is a hiccup in the powertrain plant, it will be felt immediately on the assembly line."

All material arrives at the Saturn plant directly from the supplier's dock without passing through a consolidation point, which is a typical practice at the Japanese transplants. Production parts are delivered daily, some more frequently (e.g., large items like radiators and front-end modules). Seats arrive in sequence from the seating supplier every 30 minutes. The scheduling of dock times and truck routes is all plotted by Saturn's logistics partner, namely Ryder, from its office inside the assembly plant.

Suppliers are paid as the parts are consumed in production ("pay on production" or "POP"). While the supplier community at large generally has resisted such an idea, Saturn's suppliers have bought into the concept, says Curt Gibbs, director of material flow and logistics, because "the pipeline at Saturn is so short."

Source: Ernest Raia, "Saturn: Rising Star," *Purchasing*, September 9, 1993, pp. 44–47. Copyright by Cahners Publishing Company.

Ryder Systems worked with Saturn to design a state of the art JIT delivery system. Ryder picks up components for Saturn from over 200 suppliers and delivers directly to the assembly line as needed. Then Ryder transports finished cars to dealers across the country.

Service organizations such as McDonald's, Disneyland, and Speedi-Lube have recognized the critical nature of housekeeping. Their dedication to housekeeping has meant that service processes work better, the attitude of the continuous improvement is easier to develop, and customers perceive that they are receiving better service.

Upgrade Quality   The only cost-effective way to improve quality is to develop reliable process capabilities. Process quality is quality at the source—it guarantees first-time production of consistent and uniform products and services.

JIT in an Express Package Service

Company A, an overnight package delivery service, retains an inventory of supplies (shipping airbills, sorting bags, service guides, overnight envelopes, boxes, tubes, and employee uniforms). White utilizing a traditional inventory system, Company A saw their inventory investment swell from $16 million to $34 million.

Since Company A is a service industry, there is no real "conversion process." But being a service industry does not disqualify a firm from benefiting from a JIT program. After becoming aware of the potential benefits of JIT, Company A's CEO began a push to see it implemented at his firm.

After researching the issue further, Company A's management issued this statement

*The strategic objective of the JIT program at Company A is not to decrease inventory; it is to increase profit by providing a 99.9% service level to our customers in ful-*filling their revenue document need. Inventory will fall, but as an effect of JIT, not as an achieved objective. Another important strategic objective is to further enhance Company A's competitive position against other express package delivery companies.

This statement emphasizes the customer focus that underlies JIT implementation within a service industry. A JIT team (composed of members from all affected departments) met weekly to work out communication and coordination problems encountered by the JIT effort. All involved personnel were educated on all aspects of JIT and were made aware of the company's corresponding goals. All vendors were brought in for a formal presentation on delivery and quality expectations. Vendors were even encouraged to attend the weekly meetings of the JIT team to offer input and support. In order to facilitate a better vendor relationship, the length of vendor contracts was extended to a more long-term period than in the past. Through the education and coordination efforts of the JIT team, the JIT philosophy was implemented at Company A based on prerequisites of communication, quality and commitment.

By dividing the weekly number of items filled by the number of items requested, Company A was able to compute a service level ratio for gauging their service performance. Prior to JIT implementation, their service level ran a respectable 79%. After JIT, the service level increased to 99%, with the expectation of an eventual 99.9%.

In addition to an increased service level, Company A's JIT program yielded enhanced forecasts, reduced traffic time, a more proactive expediter function, enhanced buyer awareness, improved quality, a stronger focus on customer service, improved communication, price reductions, improved processing of paperwork, and a sense of team spirit.

Source: R. Anthony Inman and Satish Mehra, "JIT Applications for Service Environments," *Production and Inventory Management Journal,* third quarter, 1991, pp. 16–20.

McDonald's is famous for building quality into its service delivery process. It literally "industrialized" the service delivery system so that part-time, casual workers could provide the same eating experience anywhere in the world. Quality doesn't mean producing the best; it means consistently producing products and services that give the customers their money's worth.

Clarify Process Flows   Clarification of the flows, based on the JIT themes, can dramatically improve the process performance. Here are examples.

First, Federal Express Corporation changed air flight patterns from origin-to-destination to origin-to-hub where the freight is transferred to an outbound plane heading for the destination. This revolutionized the air transport industry. Second, the order entry department of a manufacturing firm converted from functional subdepartments to customer-centered work groups and reduced the order processing lead time from eight to two days. Third, a county government used the JIT approach to cut the time to record a deed transfer by 50 percent. Finally, Supermaids sends in a team of house cleaners, each with a specific responsibility, to clean each house quickly with parallel processes. Changes in process flows can literally revolutionize service industries.

Revise Equipment and Process Technologies   Revising technologies involves evaluation of the equipment and processes for their ability to meet the process requirements, to process consistently within tolerance, and to fit the scale and capacity of the work group.

Speedi-Lube converted the standard service station concept to a specialized lubrication and inspection center by changing the service bays from drive-in to drive-through and by eliminating the hoists and instead building pits under the cars where employees have full access to the lubrication areas on the vehicle.

A hospital reduced operating room setup time so that it had the flexibility to perform a wider range of operations without reducing the operation room availability.

Level the Facility Load   Service firms synchronize production with demand. They have developed unique approaches to leveling demand so they can avoid making customers wait for service. CompuServe sells time for less during the evening. McDonald's offers a special breakfast menu in the morning. Retail stores use take-a-number systems. The post office charges more for next-day delivery. These are all examples of the service approach for creating uniform facility loads.

Eliminate Unnecessary Activities   A step that does not add value is a candidate for elimination. A step that does add value may be a candidate for reengineering to improve the process consistency or to reduce the time to perform the tasks.

A hospital discovered that during an operation significant time was spent waiting for an instrument that was not available when the operation began. It developed a checklist of instruments required for each category of operation. Speedi-Lube eliminated steps, but it also added steps that did not improve the lubrication process but did make customers feel more assured about the work being performed.

Reorganize Physical Configuration   Work area configurations frequently require reorganization during a JIT implementation. Often manufacturers accomplish this by setting up manufacturing cells to produce items in small lots, synchronous to demand. These cells amount to "microfactories" inside the plant.

Most service firms are far behind manufacturers in this area. However, a few interesting examples do come out of the service sector. Some hospitals—instead of routing patients all over the building for tests, exams, X-rays, and injections—are reorganizing their services into work groups based on the type of problem. Teams that treat only trauma are common, but other work groups have been formed to treat less immediate conditions like hernias. These amount to microclinics within the hospital facility.

Introduce Demand-Pull Scheduling   Due to the nature of service production and consumption, demand-pull (customer-driven) scheduling is necessary for operating a service business. Moreover, many service firms are separating their operations into "back room" and "customer contact" facilities. This approach creates new problems in coordinating schedules between the facilities. The original Wendy's restaurants were set up so cooks could see cars enter the parking lot. They put a preestablished number of hamburger patties onto the grill for each car. This pull system was designed to have a fresh patty on the grill before the customer even placed an order.

Develop Supplier Networks   Supplier networks in the JIT context refer to the cooperative association of suppliers and customers working over the long term for mutual benefit. (See Breakthrough, "A New Type of Partnership," on next page.) Service firms have not emphasized supplier networks for materials because the service costs are often predomi-

Breakthrough

A New Type of Partnership

A partnership between customers and suppliers has evolved at companies such as Honeywell, Bose, and AT&T. This partnership was conceived by Lance Dixon, director of purchasing at Bose Corporation. His system, entitled JIT II, brings the vendor into the plant to participate in the customer's purchasing office on a full-time daily basis. Whereas the typical JIT process eliminated inventory and brought the customer and supplier closer, this system adds such benefits as eliminating the buyer and sales representative from the customer–supplier relationship. This vendor replaces the buyer and salesperson. He or she is directed to use the customer's purchase orders and to practice concurrent design and engineering. By being in-plant, this empowered employee, or facilitator, can raise the level of communication between the supplier and the customer company employees. Following JIT principles, the practices are customer-focused, cost-effective, quality-driven, and team-based.

Having vendor representatives work with Bose engineers on designs has led to substantial improvements in design quality and productivity for the component-quality high fidelity loudspeakers Bose manufactures. The major advantage is that the customer representative at the Bose location is empowered to use its system. Bose also applied these concepts to its transportation system and plans material in transit just like its inventory in the warehouse. AT&T and Honeywell have adopted JIT II and have been able to save money and improve productivity by combining the voice of the customer with that of the employee.

Source: Martin M. Stein, "The Ultimate Customer–Supplier Relationship at Bose, Honeywell, and AT&T," *National Productivity Review* 12, no. 4 (Autumn 1993), pp. 543–48; and Sherwin Greenblatt, "Continuous Improvement in Supply Chain Management," *Chief Executive* 86 (June 1993), pp. 40–43.

nantly labor. Notable exceptions must include service organizations like McDonald's, one of the biggest food products purchasers in the world. A small manufacturer recognized that it needed cooperative relationships for temporary employees as well as for parts. It is considering a campaign to establish JIT-type relationships with a temporary employment service and a trade school to develop a reliable source of trained assemblers.

6.6   CONCLUSION

JIT represents a powerful tool for reducing inventory and improving production and service operations. Its principles can result in many improvements, but users are cautioned that JIT applications are not universal. Like TQM, JIT implementation faces many problems led by a resistance to change shown by many employees. Education of top management is important. Visible initial pilot programs (rather than a plantwide implementation of JIT all at once) are a good beginning. Management should use care in choosing an implementation team who will be responsible for making the major changes on the plant floor. The team can include 5 to 15 individuals from quality control, engineering, manufacturing, traffic, purchasing, marketing, and other areas. Ongoing team education is important to help employees discard practices that block JIT progress. Again, like TQM, JIT is series of small improvements that take time. It requires the patience of all involved parties.

JIT is an encompassing philosophy considering product design, process design, equipment, selection, material management, quality assurance, job design, and productivity improvements. The goal of synchronized, streamlined one-piece-at-a-time production is a world-class standard seldom achieved in practice. Because zero lead time and zero idle time are hard to accomplish, some JIT projects are put quickly in place and later forgotten. Management support, commitment, and training to continue JIT progress are needed.

6.7   REVIEW AND DISCUSSION QUESTIONS

1. What JIT principles are being used by the 100 Yen Sushi House? Use the categories in Exhibit 6.8 to develop your answer. What else could the restaurant do in a JIT service?

2. Is it possible to achieve zero inventories? Why?

3. Stopping waste is a vital part of JIT. Identify some sources of waste and discuss how they may be eliminated.

4. Discuss JIT in a job-shop layout and in a line layout.

5. Why must JIT have a stable schedule?

6. Will JIT work in service environments? Why?

7. Discuss ways to use JIT to improve one of the following: a pizza restaurant, a hospital, or an auto dealership.

8. Which objections might a marketing manager have against uniform plant loading?

9. What are the implications for cost accounting of JIT production?

10. What are the roles of suppliers and customers in a JIT system?

11. Explain how cards are used in a kanban system.

12. In which ways, if any, are the following systems analogous to kanban: returning empty bottles to the supermarket and picking up filled ones; running a hot dog stand at lunchtime; withdrawing money from a checking account; raking leaves into bags?

13. How is a U.S. JIT system different from a Japanese one?

14. Why is JIT hard to implement in practice?

15. Explain the relationship between quality and productivity under the JIT philosophy.

C A S E

6.8 C A S E
Quick Response Apparel

Imagine walking into a store and ordering clothing manufactured to your size and specifications. This phenomenon—called "apparel on demand"—is an extension of JIT linking retailers and manufacturers for a just-in-time responsiveness. With this quick response, retailers can send their point-of-sale information directly to the factory floor to minimize downtime. Clothing is delivered to the purchaser through normal retail channels. Custom Clothing Technology Corporation (CCTC) is making reasonably priced custom jeans for women. This apparel-on-demand concept could result in 30 percent production savings. It also reduces the need for inventory and markdowns. CCTC was launched by Sung Park, who feels women will pay the $48 price for a pair of jeans guaranteed to fit.

Women are electronically measured and select their jeans' style in stores contracting with CCTC's JIT service. The jeans are cut in Vermont, sewed in Texas, and shipped to the customer in less than two weeks. The current market for women's jeans is $2 billion so Park feels this is a great market to test JIT jeans.

Questions

1. If you were a traditional retailer selling jeans, how worried would you be about this new trend?

2. Do you think customers will be willing to wait two weeks for product delivery?

3. How can CCTC compete on customer service if delivery takes two weeks?

4. Discuss what other strategic variables CCTC is competing on.

5. How can JIT concepts be used to improve customer service and flexibility in other industries? Choose one of the following industries and brainstorm creating JIT solutions: health care, grocery stores, physical fitness, or home repair and maintenance.

6. Another example of quick response clothing is Second Skin Swimwear in North Palm Beach, Florida. The firm custom manufactures 10,000 bathing suits annually using a body scanning system to eliminate embarrassment in bathing suit shopping. Delivery is in two to three weeks. Given these examples, what other clothing styles or types could benefit from just-in-time customization?

7. What other improvements can retailers experience with these new systems? Discuss end-of-season inventory, size of department store or retail floor space, and inventory record keeping and cycle counting.

8. How must other organizational functions change their strategies to support this manufacturing shift to JIT apparel?

Source: Martha E. Manglesdorf, "Quick-Response Apparel," *Inc.,* November 1993, p. 35.

CASE

6.9 C A S E
EDI and JIT

In the transportation industry communication can best be identified by the ever increasing use of EDI or electronic data interchange. Procter & Gamble handles around 90,000 freight bills a month. This requires a staggering amount of paper plus time and personnel to handle the paper. But with the ever improving EDI systems, a freight company could become an EDI partner with suppliers and factories, leading to many improvements.

A transportation company could use EDI to lock itself in with factories and at the same time improve its ability to meet its just-in-time needs. It takes time to communicate via paper, but EDI allows immediate communication between the three partners.

The link between the physical locations would be the EDI system. With JIT, errors must be reduced and speed must increase for quick response. Procter & Gamble and Schneider Transport work together and, through EDI, Schneider always knows exactly where its individual trucks are. This enables Schneider to meet an important need of just in time. Because of the multiple deliveries, a factory needs to know that material will be delivered within its window time. By knowing the exact location of its trucks at all times, Schneider can meet these needs. Tracing is done by placing in each tractor a computer that is in contact by satellite with the company.

This system also enables carriers to handle another problem with industry carriers—backhauls. Transporting of just-in-time loads many times entails carrying less than full truckloads. Backhauls thus play an important part in transportation as it is very expensive to operate with loads going in only one direction.

With EDI and a quick response time, transportation firms contract with other companies in the same area so backhauls can be scheduled for their trailers. Certain cases may require multiple and sequenced deliveries. Several companies have used the close proximity of the suppliers to accomplish mul-tiple deliveries by the use of so-called milk runs. An example is the auto industry in Detroit.

The use of sequenced deliveries by trucking companies has allowed Chrysler Corporation to reduce more than $1 billion of inventory. Chrysler's use of single sourcing for its car lines allows its transportation company to improve on delivery times. The factory attempts to give as much advance notice as possible to suppliers. Sequenced deliveries by transportation companies allow Chrysler to time its deliveries so red car seats are being delivered at the exact time red cars are being produced.

Roadway Express of Akron, Ohio, adjusts its operation to meet the needs of its JIT suppliers and factories by scheduling dedicated tractor-trailers to make pickups at specific times to several suppliers and then deliver to the factory. This avoids the use of terminals to separate and mix loads. Control and tracking are accomplished by a system it calls Quicktrak.

For companies to meet the needs of JIT customers, several variables must be in place: communication, tracking, and EDI. Also, the companies should be timely, reliable, and flexible, and must provide cost-effective service.

Questions

1. Why is EDI important in a JIT environment?

2. Why is it important to know the exact location of products and deliveries at all times?

3. Why did Chrysler adopt sequenced deliveries?

Source: Walter Weart, "Procter & Gamble's War on Paper," *Distribution,* 1988, pp. 88–89; Francis J. Quinn, "Why You Should Know About EDI," *Traffic Management,* July 1991, pp. 45–48, 89; "Not Just a Buzzword Anymore," *Traffic Management,* September 1988, pp. 42–45; and Ernest Raia, "JIT in Detroit," *Purchasing,* September 1988, pp. 68–77.

CASE

6.10 C A S E
Toyota Work Contracts

While lifetime employment has been the norm for a portion of the workers in Japan, recessionary economic systems have made this trend difficult if not impossible for some corporations. In an effort to eliminate the costly lifetime-employment contracts while at the same time avoiding layoffs, organizations led by Toyota Motor Corporation have created a new category of temporary professional worker for its labor force in Japan.

These temporary workers will have a limited number of one-year contracts. Employees like automotive designers will not be offered the customary lifelong employment. The company will pay these employees a salary based on individual merit rather than the past pay practice of linking pay to seniority and overall company performance.

According to Toyota, "As the business conditions surrounding Japanese corporations underwent radical change . . . it was inevitable that the rigid organizational structure of the past would impose limits on corporate growth."

Toyota President Tatsuro Toyoda plans to gradually increase the number of white-collar contract workers in Japan. Other Japanese organizations may follow Toyota's trend. The number of white-collar contract employees is increasing and this class of worker is easier to terminate than lifetime workers.

Contract workers in blue- and white-collar segments increased from 14 percent in 1989 to 19 percent in 1993. These temporary workers will be a safety valve during cyclical economic conditions. The practice will reduce the number of white-collar workers blamed for many corporate earnings declines. According to a leading Japanese business organization, executives agree Japan "must thoroughly revise the lifetime employment system."

Questions

1. Why do you think the Japanese are reversing their employment trend?
2. What are the advantages and disadvantages of this new employment practice?
3. Are the Japanese attempting to adopt an American-style employment and evaluation policy?
4. Would the former lifetime employment system work for U.S. companies? Why?

Source: Michael Williams, "Toyota Creates Work Contracts Challenging Lifetime-Job System," *The Wall Street Journal*, January 24, 1994, p. A8.

CASE

6.11 C A S E
Quality Parts Company

Quality Parts Company is a supplier of gizmos for a computer manufacturer located a few miles away. The company produces two different models of gizmos in production runs ranging from 100 to 300 units.

The production flow of models X and Y is shown in Exhibit C6.1. Model Z requires milling as its first step, but otherwise follows the same flow pattern as X and Y. Skids can hold up to 20 gizmos at a time. Approximate times per unit by operation number and equipment setup times are shown in Exhibit C6.2.

Demand for gizmos from the computer company ranges between 125 and 175 per month, equally divided among X, Y, and Z. Subassembly builds up inventory early in the month to make certain that a buffer stock is always available. Raw materials and purchased parts for subassemblies each constitute 40 percent of the manufacturing cost of a gizmo. Both categories of parts are multiple-sourced from about 80 vendors and are delivered at random times. (Gizmos have 40 different part numbers.)

Scrap rates are about 10 percent at each operation, inventory turns twice yearly, employees are paid on a day rate, employee turnover is 25 percent per year, and net profit from operations is steady at 5 percent per year. Maintenance is performed as needed.

The manager of Quality Parts Company has been contemplating installing an automated ordering system to help control inventories and to "keep the skids filled." (He feels that two days of work in front of a workstation motivates the worker to produce at top speed.) He is also planning to add three inspectors to clean up the quality problem. Further, he is thinking about setting up a rework line to speed repairs. While he is pleased with the high utilization of most of his equipment and labor, he is concerned about the idle time of his milling machine. Finally, he has asked his industrial engineering department to look into high-rise shelving to store parts coming off machine 4.

E X H I B I T C6.1

Gizmo Production Flow

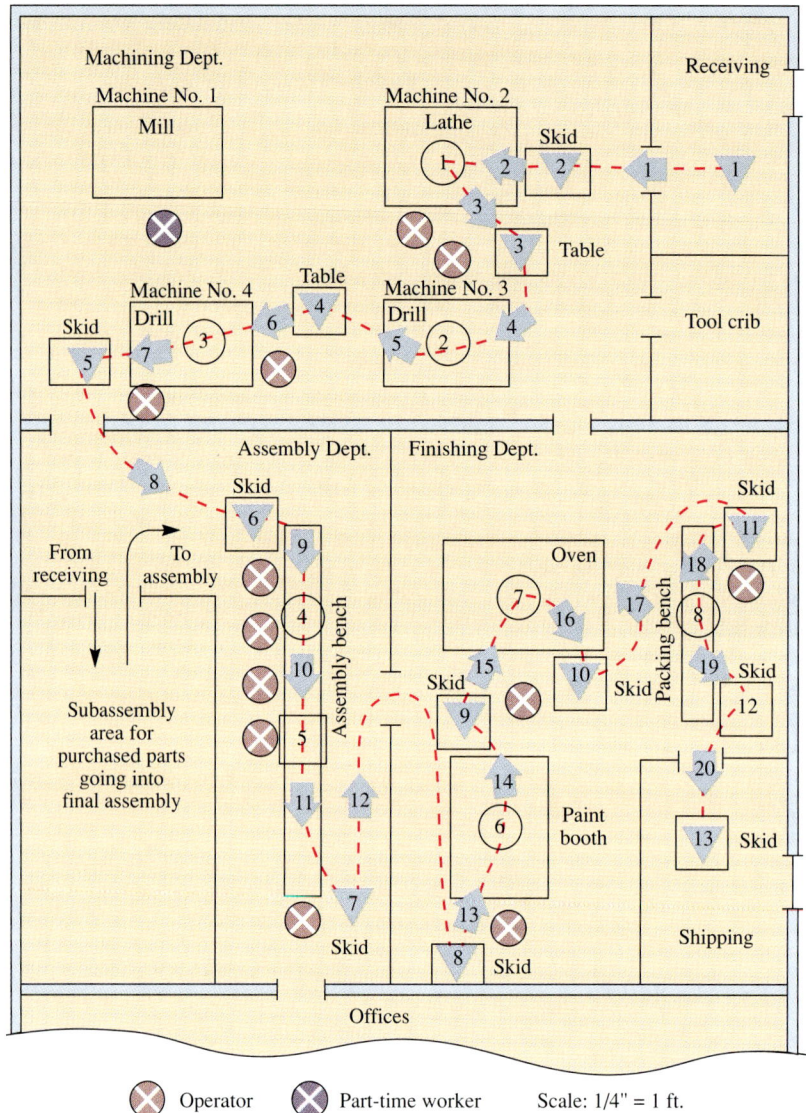

E X H I B I T C6.2

Operations and Setup Time

Operation Number and Name	Operation Time (minutes)	Setup Time (minutes)
— Milling for Z	20	60
1 Lathe	50	30
2 Mod. 14 drill	15	5
3 Mod. 14 drill	40	5
4 Assembly step 1	50	
Assembly step 2	45	
Assembly step 3	50	
5 Inspection	30	
6 Paint	30	20
7 Oven	50	
8 Packing	5	

Questions

1. Which of the changes being considered by the manager of Quality Parts Company go counter to the JIT philosophy?

2. Make recommendations for JIT improvements in such areas as scheduling, layout, kanban, task groupings, and inventory. Use quantitative data as much as possible; state necessary assumptions.

3. Sketch the operation of a pull system for quality for Quality Parts Company's current system.

4. Outline a plan for the introduction of JIT at Quality Parts Company.

6.12   SELECTED BIBLIOGRAPHY

Ansari, A., and B. Modarress. *Just in Time Purchasing.* New York: Free Press, 1990, pp. 105–6.

Blackburn, Joseph D. *Time-Based Competition.* Homewood, IL: Business One Irwin, 1991.

Davidson, William H. *The Amazing Race: Winning the Technorivalry with Japan.* New York: John Wiley & Sons, 1984.

Fucini, Joseph J., and Suzy Fucini. *Working for the Japanese.* New York: Free Press, 1990.

Giunipero, Larry C. "Motivating and Monitoring JIT Supplier Performance." *Journal of Purchasing and Material Management,* Winter 1990, pp. 19–24.

Hall, Robert. *Attaining Manufacturing Excellence.* Homewood, IL: Dow Jones-Irwin, 1987.

———. *Zero Inventories.* Homewood, IL: Dow Jones-Irwin, 1983.

Inman, R. Anthony, and Satish Mehra. "JIT Applications for Service Environments." *Production and Inventory Management Journal* (third quarter 1991), pp. 16–20.

———. "The Transferability of Just-in-Time Concepts to American Small Business." *Interfaces* 20, no. 2 (March–April 1990), pp. 30–37.

Klein, Janice. "A Re-Examination of Autonomy in Light of New Manufacturing Practices." *Human Relations* 43 (1990).

Monden, Yasuhiro. *Toyota Production System, Practical Approach to Production Management.* Atlanta, GA: Industrial Engineering and Management Press, 1983.

———. "What Makes the Toyota Production System Really Tick?" *Industrial Engineering* 13, no. 1 (January 1981), pp. 36–46.

Ohno, Taiichi. *Toyota Production System: Beyond Large-Scale Production.* Cambridge, MA: Productivity Press, 1988.

Ohno, Taiichi, and Setsuo Mito. *Just-in-Time for Today and Tomorrow.* Cambridge, MA: Productivity Press, 1988.

Schonberger, Richard J. *Building a Chain of Customers: Linking Business Functions to Create a World-Class Company.* New York: Free Press, 1989.

———. *Japanese Productivity Techniques.* New York: Free Press, 1982.

———. *World-Class Manufacturing: The Lessons of Simplicity Applied.* New York: Free Press, 1986.

Sewell, G. "Management Information Systems for JIT Production." *Omega* 18, no. 5 (1990), pp. 481–503.

Shingo, Shigeo. *A Revolution in Manufacturing: The SMED System.* Tokyo: Japan Management Association, 1983.

———. *A Study of the Toyota Production System from an Industrial Engineering Viewpoint.* Cambridge, MA: Productivity Press, 1989.

Suzaki, Kiyoshi. *The New Manufacturing Challenge: Techniques for Continuous Improvement.* New York: Fress Press, 1987.

Wantuck, Kenneth A. "The Japanese Approach to Productivity." Southfield, MI: Bendix Corporation, 1983.

Weiss, Andrew. "Simple Truths of Japanese Manufacturing." *Harvard Business Review* 62, no. 4 (July–August 1984), pp. 119–25.

White, Richard E. "An Empirical Assessment of JIT in U.S. Manufacturers." *Production and Inventory Management Journal.* 34, no. 2 (second quarter 1993).

Womack, James P., D. T. Jones, and D. Roos. *The Machine That Changed the World.* New York: R. A. Rawston Associates, 1990.

Zipkin, Paul H. "Does Manufacturing Need a JIT Revolution?" *Harvard Business Review,* January–February 1991, pp. 40–50.

Chapter

Forecasting

CHAPTER OUTLINE

KEY TERMS

Dependent Demand

Independent Demand

Time Series Analysis

Grass Roots

Executive Judgment

Delphi Method

Moving Average

Exponential Smoothing

Smoothing Constants Alpha (α) and Delta (δ)

Mean Absolute Deviation (MAD)

Tracking Signal

Linear Regression Forecasting

Trend Effect

Seasonal Factor

Deseasonalization of Demand

Causal Relationship

Focus Forecasting

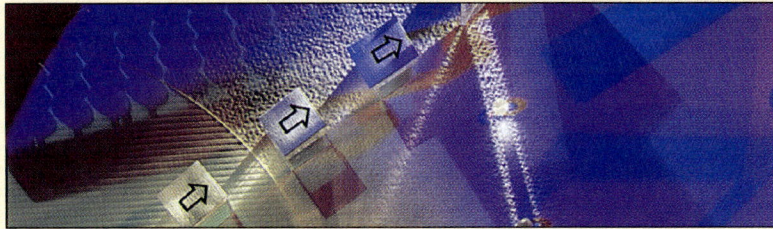

In 22 of the 25 years that a team from the original National Football League has won the Super Bowl, the stock market has risen. Such accuracy in predicting the stock market is far better than we get from forecasting techniques and stock market advisors.

The difficulty of accurately forecasting the future of physics has caused scientists to accompany forecasts with disclaimers.

Accounting firms involved in budgeting and forecasting could be liable for damages if their predictions are far off. Recent court cases in Canada warn that data should be qualified and documented, while budgets and forecasts should be accompanied by a disclaimer.

Many peculiar incidents occur in forecasting—some humorous, some contrary to logic, some very serious, and some based on old wives' tales or folklore. "Red sky at night, a sailor's delight." (A red sky predicted calm seas the following day.) Your nose itching means someone is talking about you. Your palm itching means you will come into some money. There are many of these beliefs and tales.

While folklore is interesting, what is fascinating is how things happen contrary to logic. In February 1994, the statistic came out that the inventory of manufactured finished goods went down. The stock market reacted by going down! Logic states that decreasing inventory means that consumers are buying and manufacturers need to increase production. This should drive the stock market up—not down.

Any way you look at it, forecasting is a bit of everything—some art, some science, some mystery, but, most of all, much luck. As one anonymous source stated, "forecasting is difficult—especially about the future."

Sources: Robert H. Stovall, "Of Redskins and Wampum," *Financial World* 161, no. 4 (February 18, 1992) p. 88; Daniel Kleppner, "A Lesson in Humility," *Physics Today* 44, no. 12 (December 1991), pp. 9–10; and Mindy Paskell-Mede, "Foul Forecasts," *CA Magazine* 126, no. 4 (April 1993), pp. 42–44.

Forecasts are vital to every business organization and for every significant management decision. Forecasting is the basis of corporate long-run planning. In the functional areas of finance and accounting, forecasts provide the basis for budgetary planning and cost control. Marketing relies on sales forecasting to plan new products, compensate sales personnel, and make other key decisions. Production and operations personnel use forecasts to make periodic decisions involving process selection, capacity planning, and facility layout as well as for continual decisions about production planning, scheduling, and inventory.

Bear in mind that a perfect forecast is usually impossible. Too many factors in the business environment cannot be predicted with certainty. Therefore, rather than search for the perfect forecast, it is far more important to establish the practice of continual review of forecasts and to learn to live with inaccurate forecasts. This is not to say that we should not try to improve the forecasting model or methodology, but that we should try to find and use the best forecasting method available, *within reason.*

When forecasting, a good strategy is to use two or three methods and look at them for the commonsense view. Are there expected changes in the general economy that will affect the forecast? Are there changes in industrial and private consumer behaviors? Will there be a shortage of essential complementary items? Continual review and updating in light of new data are basic to successful forecasting. In this chapter we look at *qualitative* and *quantitative* forecasting and concentrate primarily on several quantitative time series techniques. We cover in some depth moving averages, linear regression, trends, seasonal ratios (including deseasonalization), and focused forecasting. We also discuss sources and measurements of errors.

7.1   DEMAND MANAGEMENT

The purpose of demand management is to coordinate and control all of the sources of demand so the productive system can be used efficiently and the product delivered on time.

Where does demand for a firm's product or service come from, and what can a firm do about it? There are two basic sources of demand: dependent demand and independent

The National Science Foundation forecasts electronic traffic measured in billions of bytes. Traffic volume range is depicted from zero bytes (purple) to 100 billion bytes (white). Such forecasts aid companies in planning their product development, as well as inventory and production levels and a variety of strategic and tactical decisions.

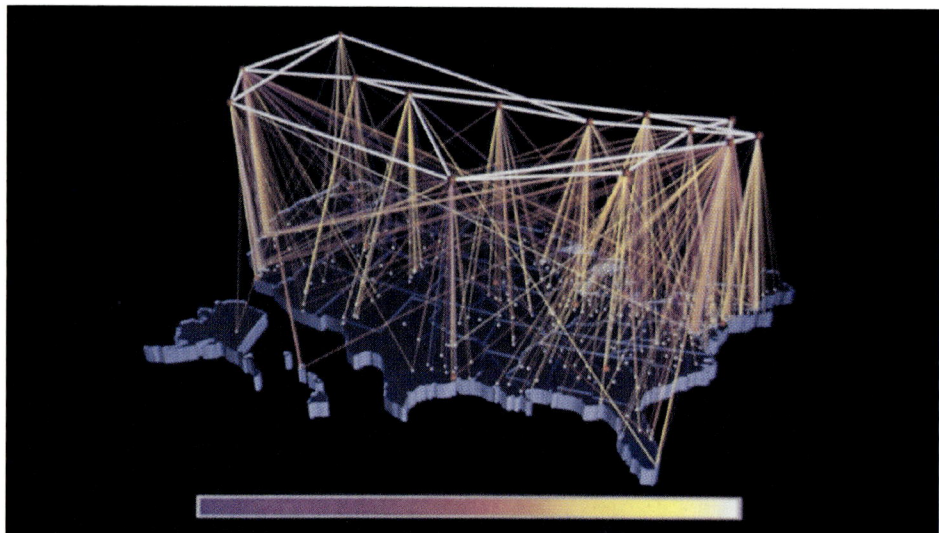

demand. **Dependent demand** is the demand for a product or service caused by the demand for other products or services. For example, if a firm sells 1,000 tricycles, then 1,000 front wheels and 2,000 rear wheels are needed. This type of internal demand does not need a forecast, simply a tabulation. As to how many tricycles the firm might sell, this is called **independent demand** because its demand cannot be derived directly from that of other products.[1] We discuss dependence and independence more fully in Chapters 14 and 15.

There is not much a firm can do about dependent demand. It must be met (although the product or service can be purchased rather than produced internally). But there is a lot a firm can do about independent demand—if it wants to. The firm can

1. *Take an active role to influence demand.* The firm can apply pressure on its sales force, it can offer incentives both to customers and to its own personnel, it can wage campaigns to sell products, and it can cut prices. These actions can increase demand. Conversely, demand can be decreased through price increases or reduced sales efforts.

2. *Take a passive role and simply respond to demand.* There are several reasons a firm may not try to change demand but simply accept what happens. If a firm is running at full capacity, it may not want to do anything about demand. Other reasons are a firm may be powerless to change demand because of the expense to advertise; the market may be fixed in size and static; or demand is beyond its control (e.g., sole supplier). There are other competitive, legal, environmental, ethical, and moral reasons why market demand is passively accepted.

A great deal of coordination is required to manage these dependent and independent, and active and passive demands. These demands originate both internally and externally in the form of new product sales from marketing, repair parts for previously sold products from product service, restocking from the factory warehouses, and supply items for manufacturing. In this chapter, our primary interest is in forecasting for independent items.

7.2   TYPES OF FORECASTING

Forecasting can be classified into four basic types: *qualitative, time series analysis, causal relationships, and simulation.*

Qualitative techniques are subjective or judgmental and are based on estimates and opinions. **Time series analysis,** the primary focus of this chapter, is based on the idea that data relating to past demand can be used to predict future demand. Past data may include several components, such as trend, seasonal, or cyclical influences, and is described in the following section. Causal forecasting, which we discuss using the linear regression technique, assumes that demand is related to some underlying factor or factors in the environment. Simulation models allow the forecaster to run through a range of assumptions about the condition of the forecast. Exhibit 7.1 describes a variety of the four basic types of forecasting models. In this chapter we discuss the first four time series analysis methods in the exhibit and the first of the causal techniques.

---

[1] In addition to dependent and independent demands, other product relationships include complementary products and causal relationships where demand for one causes the demand for another.

E X H I B I T 7.1   *Forecasting Techniques and Common Models*

I. Qualitative	Subjective; judgmental. Based on estimates and opinions.
Grass roots	Derives a forecast by compiling input from those at the end of the hierarchy who deal with what is being forecast. For example, an overall sales forecast may be derived by combining inputs from each salesperson, who is closest to his or her own territory.
Market research	Sets out to collect data in a variety of ways (surveys, interviews, etc.) to test hypotheses about the market. This is typically used to forecast long-range and new-product sales.
Panel consensus	Free open exchange at meetings. The idea is that discussion by the group will produce better forecasts than any one individual. Participants may be executives, salespeople, or customers.
Historical analogy	Ties what is being forecast to a similar item. Important in planning new products where a forecast may be derived by using the history of a similar product.
Delphi method	Group of experts responds to questionnaire. A moderator compiles results and formulates a new questionnaire which is submitted to the group. Thus, there is a learning process for the group as it receives new information and there is no influence of group pressure or dominating individual.
II. Time series analysis	Based on the idea that the history of occurrences over time can be used to predict the future.
Simple moving average	A time period containing a number of data points is averaged by dividing the sum of the point values by the number of points. Each, therefore, has equal influence.
Weighted moving average	Specific points may be weighted more or less than the others, as seen fit by experience.
Exponential smoothing	Recent data points are weighted more with weighting declining exponentially as data become older.
Regression analysis	Fits a straight line to past data generally relating the data value to time. Most common fitting technique is least squares.
Box Jenkins technique	Very complicated but apparently the most accurate statistical technique available. Relates a class of statistical models to data and fits the model to the time series by using Bayesian posterior distributions.
Shiskin time series	(Also called X-11). Developed by Julius Shiskin of the Census Bureau. An effective method to decompose a time series into seasonals, trends, and irregular. It needs at least three years of history. Very good in identifying turning points, for example, in company sales.
Trend projections	Fits a mathematical trend line to the data points and projects it into the future.
III. Causal	Tries to understand the system underlying and surrounding the item being forecast. For example, sales may be affected by advertising, quality, and competitors.
Regression analysis	Similar to least squares method in time series but may contain multiple variables. Basis is that forecast is caused by the occurrence of other events.
Econometric models	Attempts to describe some sector of the economy by a series of interdependent equations.
Input/output models	Focuses on sales of each industry to other firms and governments. Indicates the changes in sales that a producer industry might expect because of purchasing changes by another industry.
Leading indicators	Statistics that move in the same direction as the series being forecast but move before the series, such as an increase in the price of gasoline indicating a future drop in the sale of large cars.
IV. Simulation models	Dynamic models, usually computer-based, that allow the forecaster to make assumptions about the internal variables and external environment in the model. Depending on the variables in the model, the forecaster may ask such questions as: What would happen to my forecast if price increased by 10 percent? What effect would a mild national recession have on my forecast?

7.3   COMPONENTS OF DEMAND

In most cases, demand for products or services can be broken down into six components: average demand for the period, a trend, seasonal element, cyclical elements, random variation, and autocorrelation. Exhibit 7.2 illustrates a demand over a four-year period, showing the average, trend, and seasonal components, and randomness around the smoothed demand curve.

Cyclical factors are more difficult to determine since the time span may be unknown or the cause of the cycle may not be considered. Cyclical influence on demand may come from such occurrences as political elections, war, economic conditions, or sociological pressures.

Random variations are caused by chance events. Statistically, when all the known causes for demand (average, trend, seasonal, cyclical, and autocorrelative) are subtracted from total demand, what remains is the unexplained portion of demand. If we cannot identify the cause of this remainder, it is assumed to be purely random chance.

E X H I B I T 7.2 *Historical Product Demand Consisting of a Growth Trend and Seasonal Demand*

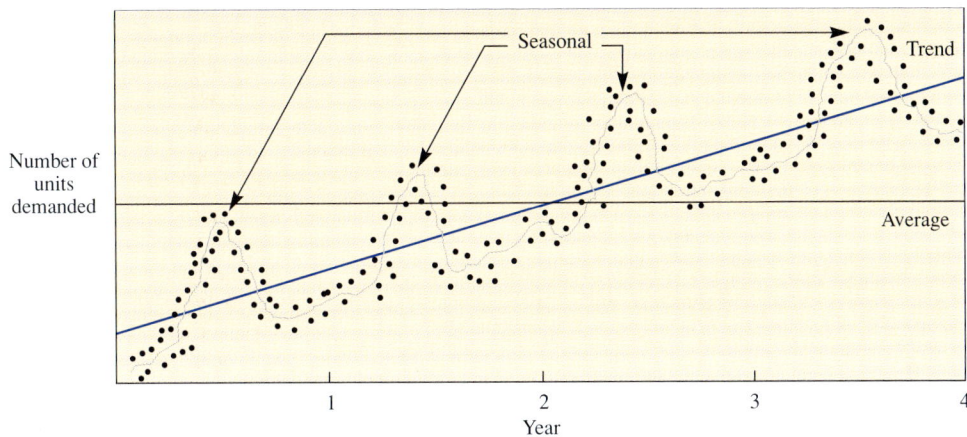

Autocorrelation denotes the persistence of occurrence. More specifically, the value expected at any point is highly correlated with its own past values. In waiting line theory, the length of a waiting line is highly autocorrelated. That is, if a line is relatively long at one time, then shortly after that time we would expect the line still to be long.

When demand is random, it may vary widely from one week to another. Where high autocorrelation exists, demand is not expected to change very much from one week to the next.

Trend lines are the usual starting point in developing a forecast. These trend lines are then adjusted for seasonal effects, cyclical, and any other expected events that may influence the final forecast. Exhibit 7.3 shows four of the most common types of trends. A linear trend is obviously a straight continuous relationship. An S-curve is typical of a product growth and maturity cycle. The most important point in the S-curve is where the trend changes from a slow growth to a fast growth, or from fast to slow. An asymptotic trend starts with the highest demand growth at the beginning, but then tapers off. Such a curve could happen when a firm enters an existing market with the objective of saturating and capturing a large share of the market. An exponential curve is common in products with explosive growth. The exponential trend suggests that sales will continue to increase—an assumption that may not be safe to make.

A widely used forecasting method plots data and then searches for the standard distribution (such as linear, S-curve, asymptotic, or exponential) that fits best. The attractiveness of this method is that the mathematics for the curve are known so solving for values for future time periods is easy.

Sometimes our data do not seem to fit any of the standard curves. This may be due to several causes essentially beating the data from several directions at the same time. For these cases, a simplistic but often effective forecast can be obtained by simply plotting data.

7.4 QUALITATIVE TECHNIQUES IN FORECASTING

As stated in Exhibit 7.1, **grass roots** forecasting builds the forecast by adding successively from the bottom. The assumption here is that the person closest to the customer or end use of the product knows its future needs best. Though this is not always true, in many instances it is a valid assumption and is the basis for this method.

Grass Roots

E X H I B I T 7.3
Common Types of Trends

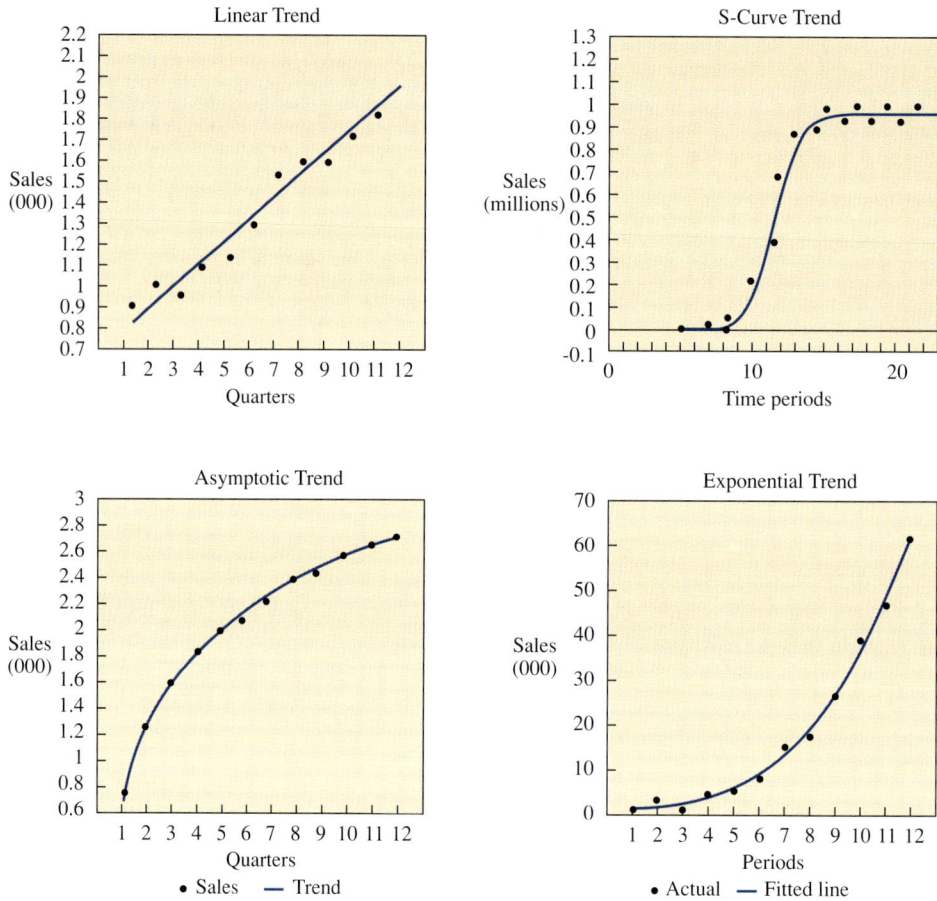

Linear Trend

S-Curve Trend

Asymptotic Trend

Exponential Trend

• Sales — Trend

• Actual — Fitted line

Forecasts at this bottom level are summed and given to the next higher level. This is usually a district warehouse which then adds in safety stocks and any effects of ordering quantity sizes. This amount is then fed to the next level, which may be a regional warehouse. The procedure repeats until it becomes an input at the top level which, in the case of a manufacturing firm, would be the input to the production system.

Market Research

Firms often hire outside companies that specialize in **market research** to conduct this type of forecasting. You yourself may have been involved in market surveys through a marketing class. Certainly you have not escaped phone calls asking you about product preferences, your income, habits, and so on.

Market research is used mostly for product research in the sense of looking for new product ideas, likes and dislikes about existing products, which competitive products within a particular class are preferred, and so on. Again, the data collection methods are primarily surveys and interviews.

Panel Consensus

In a **panel consensus,** the idea that two heads are better than one is extrapolated to the idea that a panel of people from a variety of positions can develop a more reliable forecast than a narrower group. Panel forecasts are developed through open meetings with free exchange of ideas from all levels of management and individuals.

The difficulty with this open style is that lower employee levels are intimidated by higher levels of management. For example, a salesperson in a particular product line may have a good estimate of future product demand but may not speak up to refute a much different estimate given by the vice president of marketing. The Delphi technique (which we discuss shortly) was developed to try to correct this impairment to free exchange.

When decisions in forecasting are at a broader and higher level (as when introducing a new product line or concerning strategic product decisions such as new marketing areas), the term **executive judgment** is generally used. The term is self-explanatory since a higher level of management is involved.

Historical Analogy

In trying to forecast demand for a new product, an ideal situation would be where an existing product or generic product could be used as a model. There are many ways to classify such analogies—for example, complementary products, substitutable or competitive products, and products as a function of income. Again, you have surely gotten a deluge of mail advertising products in a similar category when you purchase via catalog or mail order. If you buy a CD through the mail, you will receive more mail about new CDs and CD players. A causal relationship (listed in Exhibit 7.1, Part III) would be that demand for compact discs is caused by demand for CD players. An analogy would be the demand for VCRs or TVs to be generated by CDs. While the products are in the same general category of electronics, they are different enough so as not to compete or be causal. A simpler example would be toasters and coffee pots. A firm that already produces toasters and wants to produce coffee pots could use the toaster history as a likely growth model.

Delphi Method

As we mentioned under panel consensus, a statement or opinion of a higher-level person will likely be weighted more than that of a lower-level person. The worst case is where lower-level people feel threatened and do not contribute their true beliefs. To prevent this problem, the **Delphi method** conceals the identity of the individuals participating in the study. Everyone has the same weight. Procedurally, a moderator creates a questionnaire and distributes it to participants. Their responses are summed and given back to the entire group along with a new set of questions.

The Delphi method was developed by the Rand Corporation in the 1950s. The step-by-step procedure is

1. Choose the experts to participate. There should be a variety of knowledgeable people in different areas.
2. Through a questionnaire (or E-mail), obtain forecasts (and any premises or qualifications for the forecasts) from all participants.
3. Summarize the results and redistribute them to the participants along with appropriate new questions.
4. Summarize again, refining forecasts and conditions, and again develop new questions.
5. Repeat Step 4 if necessary. Distribute the final results to all participants.

The Delphi technique can usually achieve satisfactory results in three rounds. The time required is a function of the number of participants, how much work is involved for them to develop their forecasts, and their speed in responding.

7.5   TIME SERIES ANALYSIS

Time series forecasting models try to predict the future based on past data. For example, sales figures collected for each of the past six weeks can be used to forecast sales for the seventh week. Quarterly sales figures collected for the past several years can be used to forecast future quarters. Even though both examples contain sales, different forecasting time series models would likely be used for forecasting.

Exhibit 7.4 shows the time series models and some of their characteristics. The simple moving average forecast is not shown in this table, but it would have the same characteristics as simple exponential smoothing. The weighted moving average can be more tricky if the forecaster includes seasonality or other cyclic influences. Its characteristics would lie somewhere between Holt's exponential smoothing and Winter's exponential smoothing. Though we do not cover the Holt and Winter's models in detail, the reader may want to investigate these variations if exponential smoothing seems to apply to the data. Note that the models vary from simple to complex.

While recognizing that terms such as *short, medium,* and *long* are relative to the context in which they are used, in business forecasting *short-term* usually refers to under three months, *medium-term* to three months to two years, and *long-term* to greater than two years. In general, the short-term models compensate for random variation and adjust for short-term changes (such as consumers' responses to a new product). Medium-term forecasts are useful for seasonal effects, and long-term models detect general trends and are especially useful in identifying major turning points.

E X H I B I T 7.4   *A Guide to Selecting an Appropriate Forecasting Method*

Forecasting Method	Amount of Historical Data	Data Pattern	Forecast Horizon	Preparation Time	Personnel Background
Simple exponential smoothing	5 to 10 observations to set both weights	Data should be stationary	Short	Short	Little sophistication
Holt's exponential smoothing	10 to 15 observations to set both weights	Trend but no seasonality	Short to medium	Short	Slight sophistication
Winter's exponential smoothing	At least 4 or 5 observations per season	Trend and seasonality	Short to medium	Short	Moderate sophistication
Regression trend models	10 to 20; for seasonality at least 5 per season	Trend and seasonality	Short to medium	Short	Moderate sophistication
Causal regression models	10 observations per independent variable	Can handle complex patterns	Short, medium, or long	Long development time, short time for implementation	Considerable sophistication
Time-series decomposition	Enough to see 2 peaks and troughs	Handles cyclical and seasonal patterns; may identify turning points	Short to medium	Short to moderate	Little sophistication
Box Jenkins	50 or more observations	Must be stationary or be transformed to stationarity	Short, medium, or long	Long	High sophistication

Source: J. Holton Wilson and Deborah Allison-Koerber, "Combining Subjective and Objective Forecasts Improves Results," *The Journal of Business Forecasting,* Fall 1992, p. 4.

Which forecasting model a firm should choose depends on

1. Time horizon to forecast.
2. Data availability.
3. Accuracy required.
4. Size of forecasting budget.
5. Availability of qualified personnel.

In selecting a forecasting model, there are other issues such as the firm's degree of flexibility. (The greater the ability to react quickly to changes the less accurate the forecast needs to be.) Another item is the consequence of a bad forecast. If a large capital investment decision is to be based on a forecast, it should be a good forecast.

Simple Moving Average

When demand for a product is neither growing nor declining rapidly, and if it does not have seasonal characteristics, a moving average can be useful in removing the random fluctuations for forecasting. Although **moving averages** are frequently centered, it is more convenient to use past data to predict the following period directly. To illustrate, a centered five-month average of January, February, March, April, and May gives an average centered on March. However, all five months of data must already exist. If our objective is to forecast for June, we must project our moving average—by some means—from March to June. If the average is not centered but is at the forward end, we can forecast more easily, though we may lose some accuracy. Thus if we want to forecast June with a five-month moving average, we can take the average of January, February, March, April, and May. When June passes, the forecast for July would be the average of February, March, April, May, and June. This is how Exhibits 7.5 and 7.6 were computed.

Although it is important to select the best period for the moving average, there are several conflicting effects of different period lengths: The longer the moving-average period, the greater the random elements are smoothed (which may be desirable in many cases). But if there is a trend in the data—either increasing or decreasing—the moving

E X H I B I T 7.5
Forecast Demand Based on a Three- and a Nine-Week Simple Moving Average

Week	Demand	3 Week	9 Week	Week	Demand	3 Week	9 Week
1	800			16	1,700	2,200	1,811
2	1,400			17	1,800	2,000	1,800
3	1,000			18	2,200	1,833	1,811
4	1,500	1,067		19	1,900	1,900	1,911
5	1,500	1,300		20	2,400	1,967	1,933
6	1,300	1,333		21	2,400	2,167	2,011
7	1,800	1,433		22	2,600	2,233	2,111
8	1,700	1,533		23	2,000	2,467	2,144
9	1,300	1,600		24	2,500	2,333	2,111
10	1,700	1,600	1,367	25	2,600	2,367	2,167
11	1,700	1,567	1,467	26	2,200	2,367	2,267
12	1,500	1,567	1,500	27	2,200	2,433	2,311
13	2,300	1,633	1,556	28	2,500	2,333	2,311
14	2,300	1,833	1,644	29	2,400	2,300	2,378
15	2,000	2,033	1,733	30	2,100	2,367	2,378

E X H I B I T 7.6
*Moving Average
Forecast of Three-
and Nine-Week
Periods versus Actual
Demand*

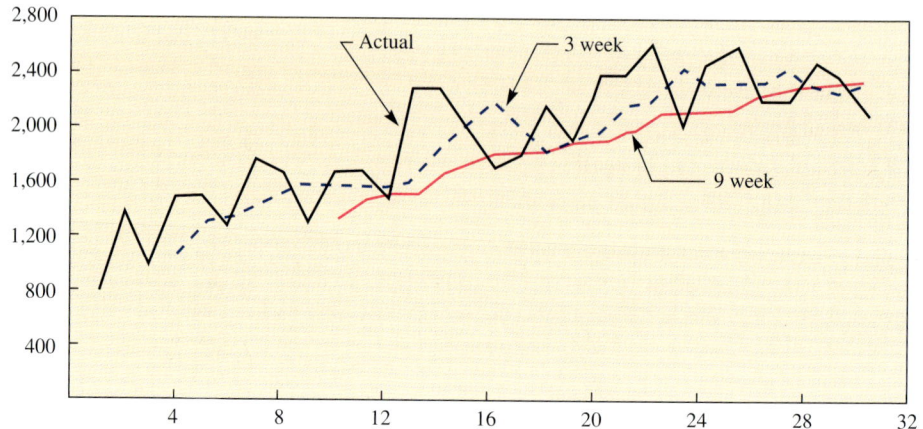

average has the adverse characteristic of lagging the trend. Therefore, while a shorter time span produces more oscillation, there is a closer following of the trend. Conversely, a longer time span gives a smoother response but lags the trend.

The formula for a simple moving average is

$$F_t = \frac{A_{t-1} + A_{t-2} + A_{t-3} + \ldots + A_{t-n}}{n} \tag{7.1}$$

where

F_t = Forecast for the coming period

n = Number of periods to be averaged

A_{t-1} = Actual occurrence in the past period

A_{t-2}, A_{t-3}, and A_{t-n} = Actual occurrences two periods ago, three periods ago, and so on up to n periods ago

Exhibit 7.6, a plot of the data in Exhibit 7.5, shows the effects of various lengths of the period of a moving average. We see that the growth trend levels off at about the 23rd week. The three-week moving average responds better in following this change than the nine-week average, although overall, the nine-week average is smoother.

The main disadvantage in calculating a moving average is that all individual elements must be carried as data since a new forecast period involves adding new data and dropping the earliest data. For a three- or six-period moving average, this is not too severe. But plotting a 60-day moving average for the usage of each of 20,000 items in inventory would involve a significant amount of data.

**Weighted
Moving Average**

Whereas the simple moving average gives equal weight to each component of the moving-average database, a weighted moving average allows any weights to be placed on each element, providing, of course, that the sum of all weights equals 1. For example, a department store may find that in a four-month period the best forecast is derived by using 40 percent of the actual sales for the most recent month, 30 percent of two months ago, 20 percent of three months ago, and 10 percent of four months ago. If actual sales experience was

Month 1	Month 2	Month 3	Month 4	Month 5
100	90	105	95	?

the forecast for month 5 would be

$$F_5 = 0.40(95) + 0.30(105) + 0.20(90) + 0.10(100)$$
$$= 38 + 31.5 + 18 + 10$$
$$= 97.5$$

The formula for weighted moving average is

$$F_t = w_1 A_{t-1} + w_2 A_{t-2} + \ldots + w_n A_{t-n} \qquad (7.2)$$

where

w_1 = Weight to be given to the actual occurrence for the period $t - 1$
w_2 = Weight to be given to the actual occurrence for the period $t - 2$
w_n = Weight to be given to the actual occurrence for the period $t - n$
n = Total number of periods in the forecast

While many periods may be ignored (i.e., their weights are zero) and the weighting scheme may be in any order (e.g., more distant data may have greater weights than more recent data), the sum of all the weights must equal 1.

$$\sum_{i=1}^{n} w_i = 1$$

Suppose sales for month 5 actually turned out to be 110. Then the forecast for month 6 would be

$$F_6 = 0.40(110) + 0.30(95) + 0.20(105) + 0.10(90)$$
$$= 44 + 28.5 + 21 + 9$$
$$= 102.5$$

Choosing Weights   Experience and trial and error are the simplest ways to choose weights. As a general rule, the most recent past is the most important indicator of what to expect in the future and therefore should get higher weighting. The past month's revenue or plant capacity, for example, would be a better estimate for the coming month than the revenue or plant capacity of several months ago.

However, if the data are seasonal, for example, weights should be established accordingly. Bathing suit sales in July of last year should be weighted more heavily than bathing suit sales in December (in the northern hemisphere).

The weighted moving average has a definite advantage over the simple moving average in being able to vary the effects of past data. However, it is more inconvenient and costly to use than the exponential smoothing method, which we will examine next.

Exponential Smoothing

In the previous methods of forecasting (simple and weighted moving average), the major drawback is the need to continually carry a large amount of historical data. (This is also true for regression analysis techniques, which we soon will cover.) As each new piece of data is added in these methods, the oldest observation is dropped, and the new forecast is calculated. In many applications (perhaps in most), the most recent occurrences are more indicative of the future than those in the more distant past. If this premise is valid—that the importance of data diminishes as the past becomes more distant—then **exponential smoothing** may be the most logical and easiest method to use.

The reason this is called exponential smoothing is because each increment in the past is decreased by $(1 - \alpha)$. If α is 0.05, for example, weights for various periods would be as follows:

	Weighting at $\alpha = 0.05$
Most recent weighting $= \alpha(1 - \alpha)^0$	0.0500
Data one time period older $= \alpha(1 - \alpha)^1$	0.0475
Data two time periods older $= \alpha(1 - \alpha)^2$	0.0451
Data three time periods older $= \alpha(1 - \alpha)^3$	0.0429

Therefore, the exponents 0,1,2,3 . . . ., and so on give it its name.

Exponential smoothing is the most used of all forecasting techniques. It is an integral part of virtually all computerized forecasting programs, and is widely used in ordering inventory in retail firms, wholesale companies, and service agencies.

Exponential smoothing techniques have become well accepted for six major reasons:

1. Exponential models are surprisingly accurate.
2. Formulating an exponential model is relatively easy.
3. The user can understand how the model works.
4. Little computation is required to use the model.
5. Computer storage requirements are small because of the limited use of historical data.
6. Tests for accuracy as to how well the model is performing are easy to compute.

In the exponential smoothing method, only three pieces of data are needed to forecast the future: the most recent forecast, the actual demand that occurred for that forecast period, and a **smoothing constant alpha (α).** This smoothing constant determines the level of smoothing and the speed of reaction to differences between forecasts and actual occurrences. The value for the constant is determined both by the nature of the product and by the manager's sense of what constitutes a good response rate. For example, if a firm produced a standard item with relatively stable demand, the reaction rate to differences between actual and forecast demand would tend to be small, perhaps just 5 or 10 percentage points. However, if the firm were experiencing growth, it would be desirable to have a higher reaction rate, perhaps 15 to 30 percentage points, to give greater importance to recent growth experience. The more rapid the growth, the higher the reaction rate should be. Sometimes users of the simple moving average switch to exponential smoothing but like to keep the forecasts about the same as the simple moving average. In this case, α is approximated by $2 \div (n + 1)$ where n is the number of time periods.

The equation for a single exponential smoothing forecast is simply

$$F_t = F_{t-1} + \alpha(A_{t-1} - F_{t-1}) \tag{7.3}$$

where

F_t = The exponentially smoothed forecast for period t

F_{t-1} = The exponentially smoothed forecast made for the prior period

A_{t-1} = The actual demand in the prior period

α = The desired response rate, or smoothing constant

This equation states that the new forecast is equal to the old forecast plus a portion of the error (the difference between the previous forecast and what actually occurred).[2]

To demonstrate the method, assume that the long-run demand for the product under study is relatively stable and a smoothing constant (α) of 0.05 is considered appropriate. If the exponential method were used as a continuing policy, a forecast would have been made for last month.[3] Assume that last month's forecast (F_{t-1}) was 1,050 units. If 1,000 actually were demanded, rather than 1,050, the forecast for this month would be

$$F_t = F_{t-1} + \alpha(A_{t-1} - F_{t-1})$$
$$= 1,050 + 0.05(1,000 - 1,050)$$
$$= 1,050 + 0.05(-50)$$
$$= 1,047.5 \text{ units}$$

Because the smoothing coefficient is small, the reaction of the new forecast to an error of 50 units is to decrease the next month's forecast by only 2½ units.

Single exponential smoothing has the shortcoming of lagging changes in demand. Exhibit 7.7 presents actual data plotted as a smooth curve to show the lagging effects of the exponential forecasts. The forecast lags during an increase or decrease, but overshoots when a change in the direction occurs. Note that the higher the value of alpha, the more closely the forecast follows the actual. To more closely track actual demand, a trend factor may be added. Adjusting the value of alpha also helps. This is termed *adaptive fore-*

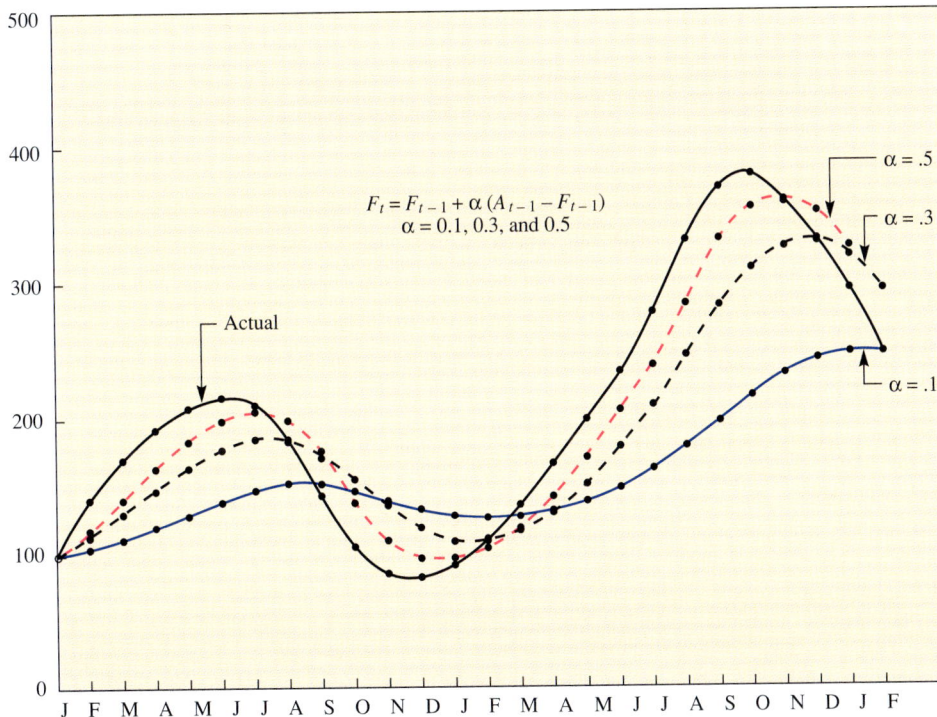

E X H I B I T 7.7
Exponential Forecasts versus Actual Demands for Units of a Product over Time Showing the Forecast Lag

$F_t = F_{t-1} + \alpha(A_{t-1} - F_{t-1})$
$\alpha = 0.1, 0.3, \text{ and } 0.5$

---

[2]Some writers prefer to call F_t a smoothed average.
[3]When exponential smoothing is first introduced, the initial forecast or starting point may be obtained by using a simple estimate or an average of preceding periods such as the average of the first two or three periods.

casting. Both trend effects and adaptive forecasting are briefly explained in following sections.

Trend Effects in Exponential Smoothing   Remember that an upward or downward trend in data collected over a sequence of time periods causes the exponential forecast to always lag behind (be above or below) the actual occurrence. Exponentially smoothed forecasts can be corrected somewhat by adding in a trend adjustment. To correct the trend, we need two smoothing constants. Besides the smoothing constant α, the trend equation also uses a **smoothing constant delta (δ).** The delta reduces the impact of the error that occurs between the actual and the forecast. If both alpha and delta are not included, the trend would overreact to errors.

To get the trend equation going, the first time it is used the trend value must be entered manually. This initial trend value can be an educated guess or a computation based on observed past data.

The equation to compute the forecast including trend (FIT) is

$$FIT_t = F_t + T_t \tag{7.4}$$
$$F_t = FIT_{t-1} + \alpha(A_{t-1} - FIT_{t-1}) \tag{7.5}$$
$$T_t = T_{t-1} + \alpha\delta(A_{t-1} - FIT_{t-1}) \tag{7.6}$$

where

F_t = The exponentially smoothed forecast for period t
T_t = The exponentially smoothed trend for period t.
FIT_t = The forecast including trend for period t.
FIT_{t-1} = The forecast including trend made for the prior period.
A_{t-1} = The actual demand for the prior period.
α = Smoothing constant.
δ = Smoothing constant.

E X A M P L E   7.1 / *Forecast Including Trend*   Assume an initial starting F_t of 100 units, a trend of 10 units, an alpha of .20, and a delta of .30. If actual demand turned out to be 115 rather than the forecast 100, calculate the forecast for the next period.

S O L U T I O N   Adding the starting forecast and the trend, we have

$FIT_{t-1} = F_{t-1} + T_{t-1} = 100 + 10 = 110$

The actual A_{t-1} is given as 115. Therefore,

$F_t = FIT_{t-1} + \alpha(A_{t-1} - FIT_{t-1})$
    $= 110 + .2(115 - 110) = 111.0$
$T_t = T_{t-1} + \alpha\delta(A_{t-1} - FIT_{t-1})$
    $= 10 + (.2)(.3)(115 - 110) = 10.3$
$FIT_t = F_t + T_t = 111.0 + 10.3 = 121.3$

If, instead of 121.3, the actual turned out to be 120, the sequence would be repeated and the forecast for the next period would be

$F_{t+1} = 121.3 + .2(120 - 121.3) = 121.04$
$T_{t+1} = 10.3 + (.2)(.3)(120 - 121.3) = 10.22$
$FIT_{t+1} = 121.04 + 10.22 = 131.26$ ∎

Choosing the Appropriate Value for Alpha   Exponential smoothing requires that the smoothing constant alpha (α) be given a value between 0 and 1. If the real demand is stable (such as demand for electricity or food), we would like a small alpha to lessen the effects of short-term or random changes. If the real demand is rapidly increasing or decreasing (such as in fashion items or new small appliances), we would like a large alpha to try to keep up with the change. It would be ideal if we could predict which alpha we should use. Unfortunately, two things are going against us. First, it would take some passage of time to determine the alpha that would best fit our actual data. This would be tedious to follow and revise. Second, because demands do change, the alpha we pick this week may need to be revised in the near future. Therefore, we need some automatic method to track and change our alpha values.

Adaptive forecasting   There are two approaches to controlling the value of alpha. One uses various values of alpha. The other uses a tracking signal.

1. *Two or more predetermined values of alpha.* The amount of error between the forecast and the actual demand is measured. Depending on the degree of error, different values of alpha are used. If the error is large, alpha is 0.8; if the error is small, alpha is 0.2.

2. *Computed values for alpha.* A tracking signal computes whether the forecast is keeping pace with genuine upward or downward changes in demand (as opposed to random changes). In this application, the tracking signal is defined as the exponentially smoothed actual error divided by the exponentially smoothed absolute error. Alpha is set equal to this tracking signal so it changes from period to period within the possible range of 0 to 1.

Forecast Errors

In using the word *error,* we are referring to the difference between the forecast value and what actually occurred. In statistics, these errors are called residuals. So long as the forecast value is within the confidence limits, as we discuss later in "Measurement of Error," this is not really an error. But common usage refers to the difference as an error.

Demand for a product is generated through the interaction of a number of factors too complex to describe accurately in a model. Therefore, all forecasts certainly contain some error. In discussing forecast errors, it is convenient to distinguish between *sources of error* and the *measurement of error.*

Sources of Error

Errors can come from a variety of sources. One common source that many forecasters are unaware of is projecting past trends into the future. For example, when we talk about statistical errors in regression analysis, we are referring to the deviations of observations from our regression line. It is common to attach a confidence band (i.e., statistical control limits) to the regression line to reduce the unexplained error. But when we then use this regression line as a forecasting device by projecting it into the future, the error may not be correctly defined by the projected confidence band. This is because the confidence interval is based on past data; it may or may not hold for projected data points and therefore cannot be used with the same confidence. In fact, experience has shown that the actual errors tend to be greater than those predicted from forecast models.

Errors can be classified as bias or random. *Bias errors* occur when a consistent mistake is made. Sources of bias include failing to include the right variables; using the wrong relationships among variables; employing the wrong trend line; mistakenly shifting the seasonal demand from where it normally occurs; and the existence of some undetected secular trend. *Random errors* can be defined as those that cannot be explained by the forecast model being used.

Measurement of Error

Several of the common terms used to describe the degree of error are *standard error, mean squared error* (or *variance*), and *mean absolute deviation*. In addition, tracking signals may be used to indicate any positive or negative bias in the forecast.

Standard error is discussed in the section on linear regression in this chapter. Since the standard error is the square root of a function, it is often more convenient to use the function itself. This is called the mean square error or variance.

The **mean absolute deviation (MAD)** was in vogue in the past but subsequently was ignored in favor of standard deviation and standard error measures. In recent years, MAD has made a comeback because of its simplicity and usefulness in obtaining tracking signals. MAD is the average error in the forecasts, using absolute values. It is valuable because MAD, like the standard deviation, measures the dispersion of some observed value from some expected value.

MAD is computed using the differences between the actual demand and the forecast demand without regard to sign. It equals the sum of the absolute deviations divided by the number of data points, or, stated in equation form,

$$\text{MAD} = \frac{\sum\limits_{t=1}^{n} |A_t - F_t|}{n} \tag{7.7}$$

where

t = Period number

A = Actual demand for the period

F = Forecast demand for the period

n = Total number of periods

$|\ \ |$ = A symbol used to indicate the absolute value disregarding positive and negative signs

When the errors that occur in the forecast are normally distributed (the usual case), the mean absolute deviation relates to the standard deviation as

$$1 \text{ standard deviation} = \sqrt{\frac{\pi}{2}} \times \text{MAD, or approximately 1.25 MAD.}$$

Conversely,

1 MAD = 0.8 standard deviation

The standard deviation is the larger measure. If the MAD of a set of points was found to be 60 units, then the standard deviation would be 75 units. In the usual statistical manner, if control limits were set at plus or minus 3 standard deviations (or ± 3.75 MADs), then 99.7 percent of the points would fall within these limits.

A **tracking signal** is a measurement that indicates whether the forecast average is keeping pace with any genuine upward or downward changes in demand. As used in forecasting, the tracking signal is the *number* of mean absolute deviations that the forecast value is above or below the actual occurrence. Exhibit 7.8 shows a normal distribution with a mean of zero and a MAD equal to 1. Thus, if computing the tracking signal and finding it equal to minus 2, we can notice that the forecast model is providing forecasts that are quite a bit above the mean of the actual occurrences.

A tracking signal (TS) can be calculated using the arithmetic sum of forecast deviations divided by the mean absolute deviation:

$$TS = \frac{\text{RSFE}}{\text{MAD}} \qquad\qquad (7.8)$$

where

RSFE is the running sum of forecast errors, considering the nature of the error. (For example, negative errors cancel positive errors and vice versa)

MAD is the average of all of the forecast errors (disregarding whether the deviations are positive or negative). It is the average of the absolute deviations

Exhibit 7.9 illustrates the procedure for computing MAD and the tracking signal for a six-month period where the forecast had been set at a constant 1,000 and the actual demands that occurred are as shown. In this example, the forecast, on the average, was off by 66.7 units and the tracking signal was equal to 3.3 mean absolute deviations.

We can get a better feel for what the MAD and tracking signal mean by plotting the points on a graph. Though this is not completely legitimate from a sample size standpoint, we plotted each month in Exhibit 7.10 to show the drift of the tracking signal.

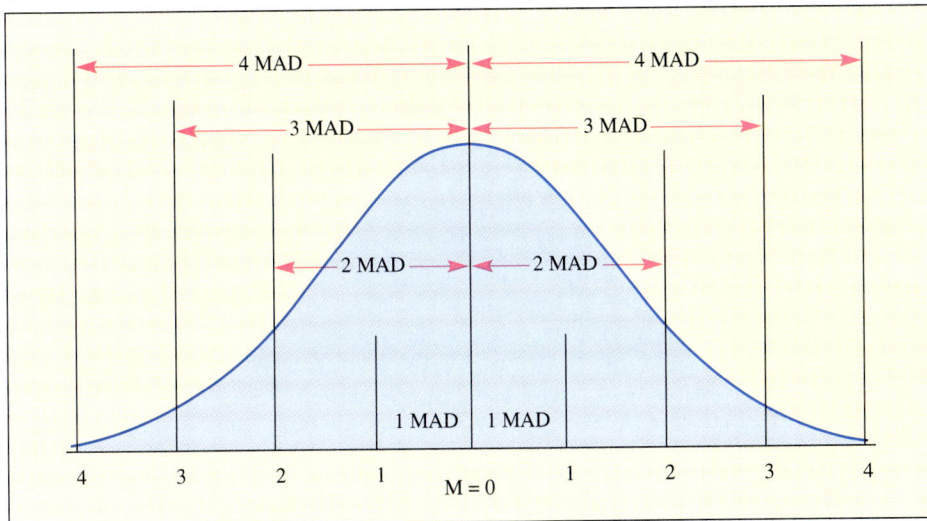

E X H I B I T 7.8
A Normal Distribution with Mean = 0 and MAD = 1

E X H I B I T 7.9 *Computing the Mean Absolute Deviation (MAD), the Running Sum of Forecast Errors (RSFE), and the Tracking Signal (TS) from Forecast and Actual Data*

Month	Demand Forecast	Actual	Deviation	RSFE	Abs. Dev.	Sum of Abs. Dev.	MAD*	$TS = \frac{\text{RSFE†}}{\text{MAD}}$
1	1,000	950	−50	−50	50	50	50	−1
2	1,000	1,070	+70	+20	70	120	60	.33
3	1,000	1,100	+100	+120	100	220	73.3	1.64
4	1,000	960	−40	+80	40	260	65	1.2
5	1,000	1,090	+90	+170	90	350	70	2.4
6	1,000	1,050	+50	+220	50	400	66.7	3.3

*For Month 6, MAD = 400 ÷ 6 = 66.7.

†For Month 6, TS = $\frac{\text{RSFE}}{\text{MAD}} = \frac{220}{66.7} = 3.3$ MADs.

E X H I B I T 7.10

A Plot of the Tracking Signals Calculated in Exhibit 7.9

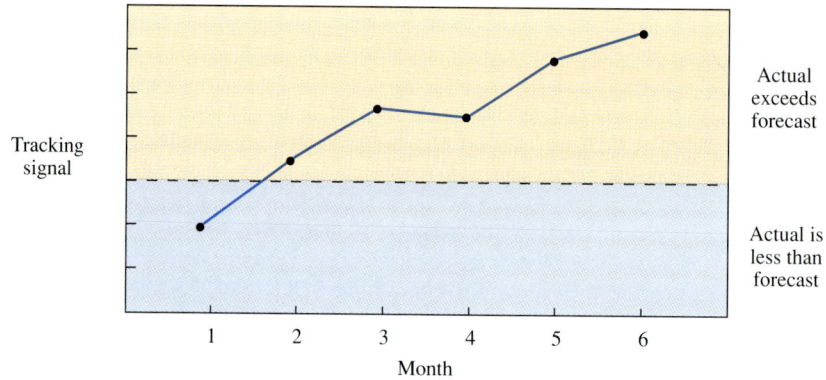

Note that it drifted from minus 1 MAD to plus 3.3 MADs. This happened because actual demand was greater than the forecast in four of the six periods. If the actual demand does not fall below the forecast to offset the continual positive RSFE, the tracking signal would continue to rise and we would conclude that assuming a demand of 1,000 is a bad forecast.

Acceptable limits for the tracking signal depend on the size of the demand being forecast (high-volume or high-revenue items should be monitored frequently) and the amount of personnel time available (narrower acceptable limits cause more forecasts to be out of limits and therefore require more time to investigate). Exhibit 7.11 shows the area within the control limits for a range of zero to four MADs.

In a perfect forecasting model, the sum of the actual forecast errors would be zero; the errors that result in overestimates should be offset by errors that are underestimates. The tracking signal would then also be zero, indicating an unbiased model, neither leading nor lagging the actual demands.

Often, MAD is used to forecast errors. It might then be desirable to make the MAD more sensitive to recent data. A useful technique to do this is to compute an exponentially smoothed MAD as a forecast for the next period's error range. The procedure is similar to single exponential smoothing covered earlier in this chapter. The value of the MAD forecast is to provide a range of error. In the case of inventory control, this is useful in setting safety stock levels.

$$\text{MAD}_t = \alpha | A_{t-1} - F_{t-1} | + (1 - \alpha)\text{MAD}_{t-1}$$

where

MAD_t = Forecast MAD for the *t*th period

α = Smoothing constant (normally in the range of 0.05 to 0.20)

A_{t-1} = Actual demand in the period $t - 1$

F_{t-1} = Forecast demand for period $t - 1$

Linear Regression Analysis

Regression can be defined as a functional relationship between two or more correlated variables. It is used to predict one variable given the other. The relationship is usually developed from observed data. The data should be plotted first to see if they appear linear or at least parts of the data are linear. Linear regression refers to the special class of regression where the relationship between variables forms a straight line.

	Control Limits	
Number of MADs	**Related Number of Standard Deviations**	**Percentage of Points Lying within Control Limits**
±1	0.798	57.048
±2	1.596	88.946
±3	2.394	98.334
±4	3.192	99.856

E X H I B I T 7.11

The Percentages of Points Included within the Control Limits for a Range of 0 to 4 MADs

The linear regression line is of the form $Y = a + bX$, where Y is the value of the dependent variable that we are solving for, a is the Y intercept, b is the slope, and X is the independent variable. (In time series analysis, X is units of time.)

Linear regression is useful for long-term forecasting of major occurrences and aggregate planning. For example, linear regression would be very useful to forecast demands for product families. Even though demand for individual products within a family may vary widely during a time period, demand for the total product family is surprisingly smooth.

The major restriction in using **linear regression forecasting** is, as the name implies, that past data and future projections are assumed to fall about a straight line. While this does limit its application, sometimes, if we use a shorter period of time, linear regression analysis can still be used. For example, there may be short segments of the longer period which are approximately linear.

Linear regression is used for both time series forecasting and for causal relationship forecasting. When the dependent variable (usually the vertical axis on a graph) changes as a result of time (plotted as the horizontal axis), it is time series analysis. If one variable changes because of the change in another variable, this is a causal relationship (such as the number of deaths from lung cancer increasing with the number of people who smoke).

We use the following example several times in this chapter to compare forecasting models and types of analysis. We use it for hand fitting a line, for the least squares analysis, and for a decomposition example.

E X A M P L E 7.2 / *Hand Fitting a Trend Line* A firm's sales for a product line during the 12 quarters of the past three years were as follows:

Quarter	Sales	Quarter	Sales
1	600	7	2,600
2	1,550	8	2,900
3	1,500	9	3,800
4	1,500	10	4,500
5	2,400	11	4,000
6	3,100	12	4,900

The firm wants to forecast each quarter of the fourth year, that is, quarters 13, 14, 15, and 16. In hand fitting a curve, we plot the data and use simple eyeballing or OHA (ocular heuristic approximation).

S O L U T I O N The procedure is quite simple: Lay a straightedge (clear plastic rulers are nice) across the data points until the line seems to fit well, and draw the line. This is the regression line. The next step is to determine the intercept a and slope b.

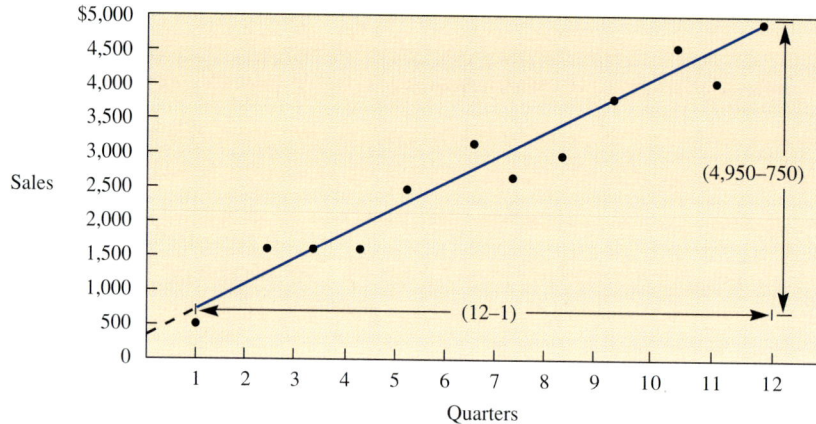

Exhibit 7.12 shows a plot of the data and the straight line we drew through the points. The intercept a, where the line cuts the vertical axis, appears to be about 400. The slope b is the "rise" divided by the "run" (the change in the height of some portion of the line divided by the number of units in the horizontal axis). Any two points can be used, but two points some distance apart give the best accuracy because of the errors in reading values from the graph. We use values for the 1st and 12th quarters.

In Exhibit 7.12, by reading from the points on the line the Y values for quarter 1 and quarter 12 are about 750 and 4,950. Therefore,

$$b = (4,950 - 750) / (12 - 1) = 382$$

The hand fitted regression equation is therefore

$$Y = 400 + 382x$$

The forecasts for quarters 13 through 16 are

Quarter	Forecast
13	$400 + 382(13) = 5,366$
14	$400 + 382(14) = 5,748$
15	$400 + 382(15) = 6,130$
16	$400 + 382(16) = 6,512$

These forecasts are based on the line only and do not identify or adjust for elements such as seasonal or cyclical elements. ∎

Least Squares Method   The least squares equation for linear regression is the same as we used in our hand fitted example:

$$Y = a + bx \qquad (7.9)$$

where

Y = Dependent variable computed by the equation

y = The actual dependent variable data point

a = Y intercept

b = Slope of the line

x = Time period

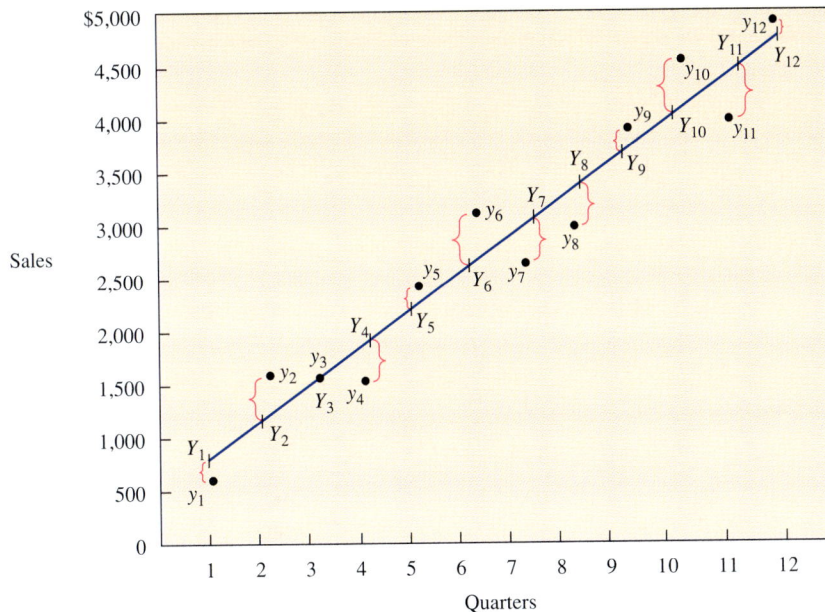

The least squares method tries to fit the line to the data *that minimize the sum of the squares of the vertical distance* between each data point and its corresponding point on the line. Exhibit 7.12 showed the 12 data points. If a straight line is drawn through the general area of the points, the difference between the point and the line is $y - Y$. Exhibit 7.13 shows these differences. The sum of the squares of the differences between the plotted data points and the line points is

$$(y_1 - Y_1)^2 + (y_2 - Y_2)^2 + \ldots + (y_{12} - Y_{12})^2$$

The best line to use is the one that minimizes this total.

As before, the straight line equation is

$$Y = a + bx$$

Previously we determined a and b from the graph. In the least squares method, the equations for a and b are

$$a = \bar{y} - b\bar{x} \tag{7.10}$$

$$b = \frac{\Sigma xy - n\bar{x} \cdot \bar{y}}{\Sigma x^2 - n\bar{x}^2} \tag{7.11}$$

where

$a = Y$ intercept

$b =$ Slope of the line

$\bar{y} =$ Average of all ys

$\bar{x} =$ Average of all xs

$x = x$ value at each data point

$y = Y$ value at each data point

$n =$ Number of data points

$Y =$ Value of the dependent variable computed with the regression equation

E X H I B I T 7.14

Least Squares
Regression Analysis

(1) x	(2) y	(3) xy	(4) x^2	(5) y^2	(6) Y
1	600	600	1	360,000	801.3
2	1,550	3,100	4	2,402,500	1,160.9
3	1,500	4,500	9	2,250,000	1,520.5
4	1,500	6,000	16	2,250,000	1,880.1
5	2,400	12,000	25	5,760,000	2,239.7
6	3,100	18,600	36	9,610,000	2,599.4
7	2,600	18,200	49	6,760,000	2,959.0
8	2,900	23,200	64	8,410,000	3,318.6
9	3,800	34,200	81	14,440,000	3,678.2
10	4,500	45,000	100	20,250,000	4,037.8
11	4,000	44,000	121	16,000,000	4,397.4
12	4,900	58,800	144	24,010,000	4,757.1
78	33,350	268,200	650	112,502,500	

$\bar{x} = 6.5$ $b = 359.6153$

$\bar{y} = 2,779.17$ $a = 441.6666$

Therefore $Y = 441.66 + 359.6x$

$S_{yx} = 363.9$

Exhibit 7.14 shows these computations carried out for the 12 data points in Exhibit 7.12. Note that the final equation for Y shows an intercept of 441.6 and a slope of 359.6. The slope shows that for every unit change in X, that Y changes by 359.6.

Strictly based on the equation, forecasts for periods 13 through 16 would be

$Y_{13} = 441.6 + 359.6 (13) = 5,116.4$

$Y_{14} = 441.6 + 359.6 (14) = 5,476.0$

$Y_{15} = 441.6 + 359.6 (15) = 5,835.6$

$Y_{16} = 441.6 + 359.6 (16) = 6,195.2$

The standard error of estimate, or how well the line fits the data, is[4]

$$S_{yx} = \sqrt{\frac{\sum_{i=1}^{n} (y_i - Y_i)^2}{n - 2}} \tag{7.12}$$

The standard error of estimate is computed from the second and last columns of Exhibit 7.14:

$$S_{yx} = \sqrt{\frac{(600 - 801.3)^2 + (1,550 - 1,160.9)^2 + (1,500 - 1,520.5)^2 + \ldots + (4,900 - 4,757.1)^2}{10}}$$

$$= 363.9$$

We discuss the possible existence of seasonal components in the next section on decomposition of a time series.

---

[4]An equation for the standard error that is often easier to compute is $S_{yx} = \sqrt{\dfrac{\Sigma y^2 - a\Sigma y - b\Sigma xy}{n - 2}}$

E X H I B I T 7.15   *Additive and Multiplicative Seasonal Variation Superimposed on Changing Trend*

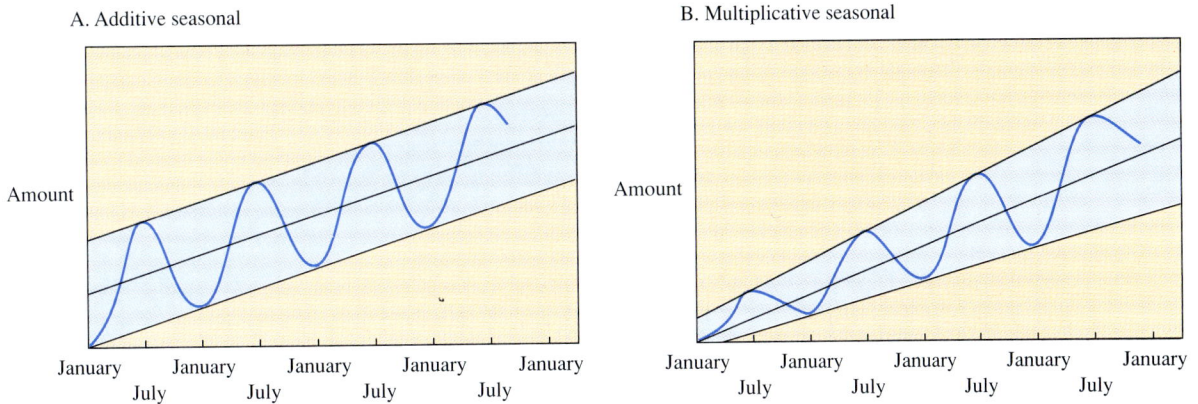

A. Additive seasonal

Amount

January   January   January   January   January
   July   July   July   July

B. Multiplicative seasonal

Amount

January   January   January   January   January
   July   July   July   July

A *time series* can be defined as chronologically ordered data that may contain one or more components of demand: trend, seasonal, cyclical, autocorrelation, and random. *Decomposition* of a time series means identifying and separating the time series data into these components. In practice, it is relatively easy to identify the trend (even without mathematical analysis, it is usually easy to plot and see the direction of movement) and the seasonal component (by comparing the same period year to year). It is considerably more difficult to identify the cycles (these may be many months or years long), autocorrelation, and random components. (The forecaster usually calls random anything left over that cannot be identified as another component.)

When demand contains both seasonal and **trend effects** at the same time, the question is how they relate to each other. In this description, we examine two types of seasonal variation: *additive* and *multiplicative*.

Additive Seasonal Variation   Additive seasonal variation simply assumes that the seasonal amount is a constant no matter what the trend or average amount is.

Forecast including trend and seasonal = Trend + Seasonal

Exhibit 7.15A shows an example of increasing trend with constant seasonal amounts.

Multiplicative Seasonal Variation   In multiplicative seasonal variation, the trend is multiplied by the seasonal factors.

Forecast including trend and seasonal = Trend × Seasonal factor

Exhibit 7.15B shows the seasonal variation increasing as the trend increases since its size depends on the trend.

The multiplicative seasonal variation is the usual experience. Essentially, this says that the larger the basic amount projected, the larger the variation around this that we can expect.

Seasonal Factor (or Index)   A **seasonal factor** is the amount of correction needed in a time series to adjust for the season of the year.

We usually associate *seasonal* with a period of the year characterized by some particular activity. We use the word *cyclical* to indicate other than annual recurrent periods of repetitive activity.

Decomposition of a Time Series

The following examples show where seasonal indexes are determined and used to forecast (1) a simple calculation based on past seasonal data and (2) the trend and seasonal index from a hand fitted regression line. We follow this with a more formal procedure for the decomposition of data and forecasting using least squares regression.

E X A M P L E 7.3 / *Simple Proportion*   Assume that a firm in past years sold an average of 1,000 units of a particular product line each year. On the average, 200 units were sold in the spring, 350 in the summer, 300 in the fall, and 150 in the winter. The seasonal factor (or index) is the ratio of the amount sold during each season divided by the average for all seasons.

S O L U T I O N   In this example, the yearly amount divided equally over all seasons is $1,000 \div 4 = 250$. The seasonal factors therefore are

	Past Sales	Average Sales for Each Season (1,000/4)	Seasonal Factor
Spring	200	250	200/250 = 0.8
Summer	350	250	350/250 = 1.4
Fall	300	250	300/250 = 1.2
Winter	150	250	150/250 = 0.6
Total	1,000		

Using these factors, if we expected demand for next year to be 1,100 units, we would forecast the demand to occur as

	Expected Demand for Next Year	Average Sales for Each Season (1,100/4)		Seasonal Factor		Next Year's Seasonal Forecast
Spring		275	×	0.8	=	220
Summer		275	×	1.4	=	385
Fall		275	×	1.2	=	330
Winter		275	×	0.6	=	165
Total	1,100					

The seasonal factor may be periodically updated as new data are available. The following example shows the seasonal factor and multiplicative seasonal variation.

E X A M P L E 7.4 / *Computing Trend and Seasonal Factor from a Hand Fit Straight Line*   Here we must compute the trend as well as the seasonal factors.

S O L U T I O N   We solve this problem by simply hand fitting a straight line through the data points and measuring the trend and intercept from the graph. Assume the history of data is

Quarter	Amount	Quarter	Amount
I—1993	300	I—1994	520
II—1993	200	II—1994	420
III—1993	220	III—1994	400
IV—1993	530	IV—1994	700

First, we plot as in Exhibit 7.16 and then fit a straight line through the data simply by eyeballing. (Naturally this line and the resulting equation are subject to variation.) The equation for the line is

$$\text{Trend}_t = 170 + 55t$$

Our equation was derived from the intercept 170 plus a rise of $(610 - 170) \div 8$ periods. Next we can derive a seasonal index by comparing the actual data with the trend line as in Exhibit 7.17. The seasonal factor was developed by averaging the same quarters in each year.

We can compute the 1994 forecast including trend and seasonal factors (FITS) as follows:

$$\text{FITS}_t = \text{Trend} \times \text{Seasonal}$$

I—1994 $\text{FITS}_9 = [170 + 55(9)]1.25 = 831$

II—1994 $\text{FITS}_{10} = [170 + 55(10)]0.78 = 562$

III—1994 $\text{FITS}_{11} = [170 + 55(11)]0.69 = 535$

IV—1994 $\text{FITS}_{12} = [170 + 55(12)]1.25 = 1,038$ ∎

Decomposition Using Least Squares Regression Decomposition of a time series means to find the series' basic components of trend, seasonal, and cyclical. Indexes are calculated for seasons and cycles. The forecasting procedure then reverses the process by

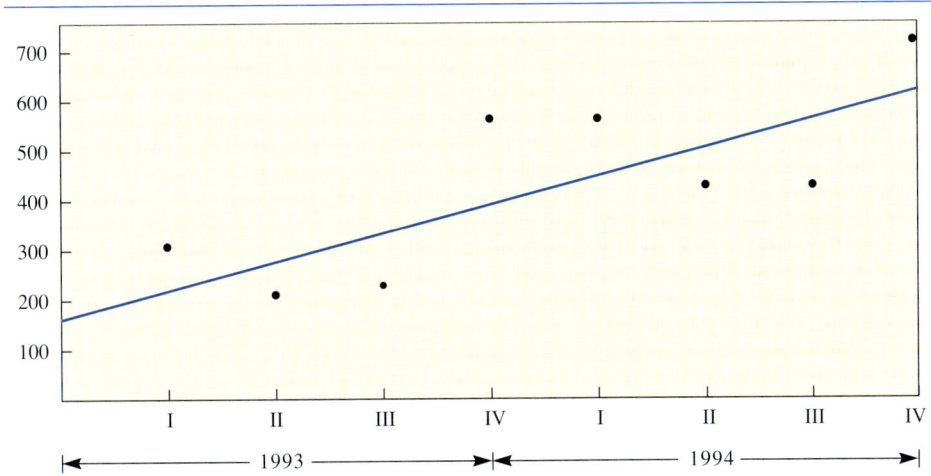

E X H I B I T 7.16

A Plot of Quarterly Demand History

E X H I B I T 7.17

Computing a Seasonal Factor from the Actual Data and Trend Line

Quarter	Actual Amount	From Trend Equation $T_t = 170 + 55t$	Ratio of Actual ÷ Trend	Seasonal Factor (average of same quarters in both years)
1993				
I	300	225	1.33	I—1.25
II	200	280	.71	II—0.78
III	220	335	.66	III—0.69
IV	530	390	1.36	IV—1.25
1994				
I	520	445	1.17	
II	420	500	.84	
III	400	555	.72	
IV	700	610	1.15	

projecting the trend and adjusting it by the seasonal and cyclical indices, which were determined in the decomposition process. More formally the process is

1. Decompose the time series into its components.
   - *a.* Find seasonal component.
   - *b.* Deseasonalize the demand.
   - *c.* Find trend component.
2. Forecast future values of each component.
   - *a.* Project trend component into the future.
   - *b.* Multiply trend component by seasonal component.

Note that the random component is not included in this list. We implicitly remove the random component from the time series when we average as in Step 1. It is pointless to attempt a projection of the random component in Step 2 unless we have information about some unusual event, such as a major labor dispute, that could adversely affect product demand (and this would not really be random).

Exhibit 7.18 shows the decomposition of a time series using least squares regression and the same basic data we used in our earlier examples. Each data point corresponds to using a single three-month quarter of the three-year (12-quarter) period. Our objective is to forecast demand for the four quarters of the fourth year.

E X H I B I T 7.18 *Deseasonalized Demand*

(1) Period (x)	(2) Quarter	(3) Actual Demand (y)	(4) Average of the Same Quarters of Each Year	(5) Seasonal Factor	(6) Deseasonalized Demand (y_d) Col (3) ÷ Col (5)	(7) x^2 (Col. 1)^2	(8) $x \times y_d$ Col (1) × Col (6)
1	I	600	(600 + 2,400 + 3,800)/3 = 2,266.7	0.82	735.7	1	735.7
2	II	1,550	(1,550 + 3,100 + 4,500)/3 = 3,050	1.10	1,412.4	4	2,824.7
3	III	1,500	(1,500 + 2,600 + 4,000)/3 = 2,700	0.97	1,544.0	9	4,631.9
4	IV	1,500	(1,500 + 2,900 + 4,900)/3 = 3,100	1.12	1,344.8	16	5,379.0
5	I	2,400		0.82	2,942.6	25	14,713.2
6	II	3,100		1.10	2,824.7	36	16,948.4
7	III	2,600		0.97	2,676.2	49	18,733.6
8	IV	2,900		1.12	2,599.9	64	20,798.9
9	I	3,800		0.82	4,659.2	81	41,932.7
10	II	4,500		1.10	4,100.4	100	41,004.1
11	III	4,000		0.97	4,117.3	121	45,290.1
12	IV	4,900		1.12	4,392.9	144	52,714.5
78		33,350		12	33,350.1*	650	265,706.9

$$\bar{x} = \frac{78}{12} = 6.5 \qquad b = \frac{\Sigma xy_d - n\bar{x}\bar{y}_d}{\Sigma x^2 - n\bar{x}^2} = \frac{265,706.9 - 12(6.5)2,779.2}{650 - 12(6.5)^2} = 342.2$$

$\bar{y}_d = 33,350/12 = 2,779.2 \qquad a = \bar{y}_d - b\bar{x} = 2,779.2 - 342.2(6.5) = 554.9$

Therefore $Y = a + bx = 554.9 + 342.2x$

*Column 3 and Column 6 totals should be equal at 33,350. Differences are due to rounding. Column 5 was rounded to two decimal places.

Step 1. Determine the seasonal factor (or index). Exhibit 7.18 summarizes all of the calculations needed. Column 4 develops an average for the same quarters in the three-year period. For example, the first quarters of the three years are added together and divided by three. A seasonal factor is then derived by dividing that average by the general average for all 12 quarters $\left(\dfrac{33{,}350}{12} \text{ or } 2{,}779\right)$. These are entered in column 5. Note that the seasonal factors are identical for similar quarters in each year.

Step 2. Deseasonalize the original data. To remove the seasonal effect on the data, we divide the original data by the seasonal factor. This step is called the **deseasonalization of demand** and is shown in column 6 of Exhibit 7.18.

Step 3. Develop a least squares regression line for the deseasonalized data. The purpose here is to develop an equation for the trend line Y, which we then modify with the seasonal factor. The procedure is the same as we used before:

$$Y = a + bx$$

where

y = actual data point

y_d = Deseasonalized demand

x = Quarter

Y = Demand computed using the regression equation $Y = a + bx$

a = Y intercept

b = Slope of the line

The least squares calculations using columns 1, 7, and 8 of Exhibit 7.18 are shown in the lower section of the exhibit. The final deseasonalized equation for our data is $Y = 554.9 + 342.2x$. This straight line is shown in Exhibit 7.19.

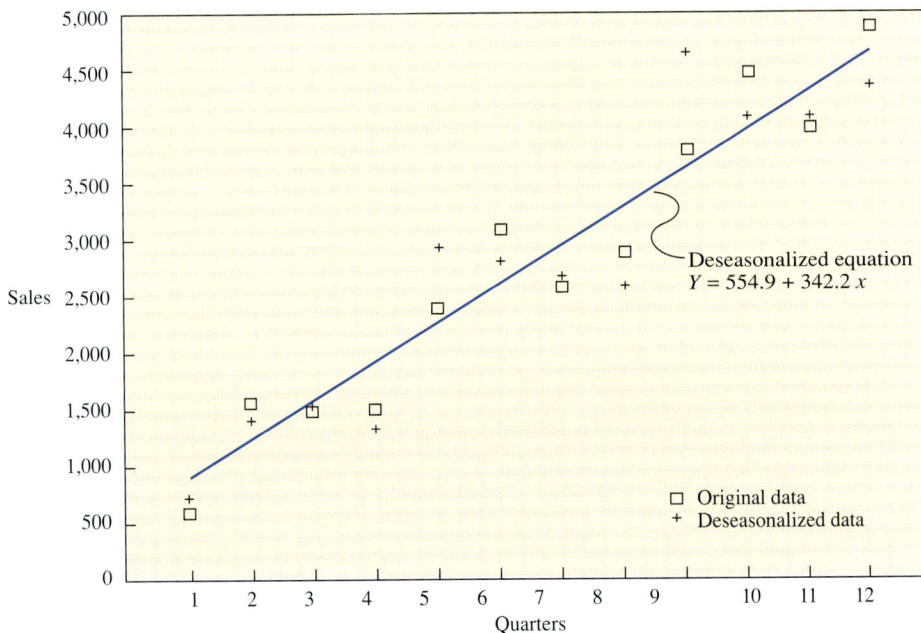

E X H I B I T 7.19
Straight Line Graph of Deseasonalized Equation

Step 4. Project the regression line through the period to be forecast. Our purpose is to forecast periods 13 through 16. We start by solving the equation for Y at each of these periods (shown in step 5, column 3).

Step 5. Create the final forecast by adjusting the regression line by the seasonal factor. Recall that the Y equation has been deseasonalized. We now reverse the procedure by multiplying the quarterly data we derived by the seasonal factor for that quarter:

Period	Quarter	Y from Regression Line	Seasonal Factor	Forecast ($Y \times$ Seasonal Factor)
13	1	5,003.5	0.82	4,080.8
14	2	5,345.7	1.10	5,866.6
15	3	5,687.9	0.97	5,525.9
16	4	6,030.1	1.12	6,726.2

Our forecast is now complete. The procedure is generally the same as what we did in the hand fit previous example. In the present example, however, we followed a more formal procedure and computed the least squares regression line as well.

Error Range   When a straight line is fitted through data points and then used for forecasting, errors can come from two sources. First, there are the usual errors similar to the standard deviation of any set of data. Second, there are errors that arise because the line is wrong. Exhibit 7.20 shows this error range. Instead of developing the statistics here, we will briefly show why the range broadens. First, visualize that one line is drawn that has some error in that it slants too steeply upward. Standard errors are then calculated for this line. Now visualize another line that slants too steeply downward. It also has a standard error. The total error range, for this analysis, consists of errors resulting from both lines as well as all other possible lines. We included this exhibit to show how the error range widens as we go further into the future.

E X H I B I T 7.20
Prediction Intervals for Linear Trend

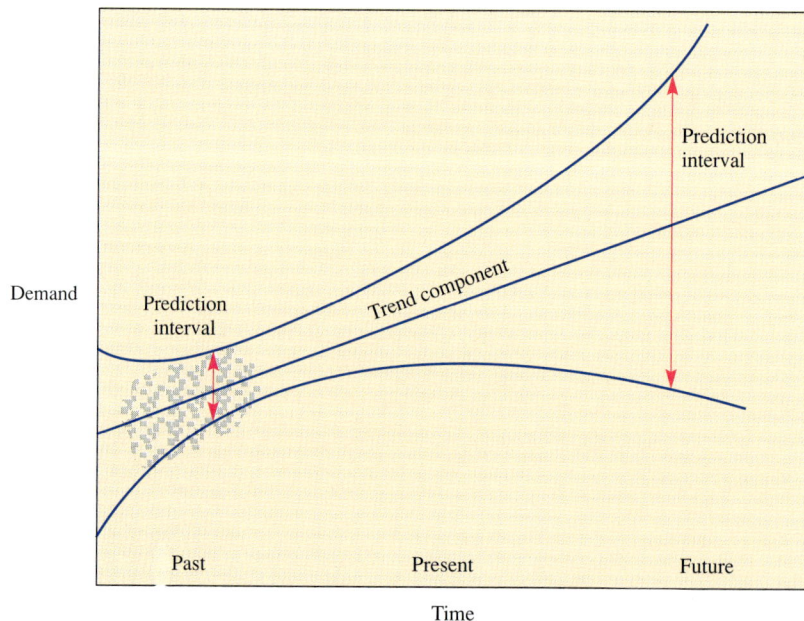

7.6   CAUSAL RELATIONSHIP FORECASTING

To be of value for the purpose of forecasting, any independent variable must be a leading indicator. For example, we can expect that an extended period of rainy days will increase sales of umbrellas and raincoats. The rain causes the sale of rain gear. This is a **causal relationship** where one occurrence causes another. If the causing element is far enough in advance, it can be used as a basis for forecasting.

The first step in causal relationship forecasting is to find those occurrences that are really the causes. Often leading indicators are not causal relationships, but in some indirect way they may suggest that some other things might happen. Other noncausal relationships just seem to exist as a coincidence. One study some years ago showed that the amount of alcohol sold in Sweden was directly proportional to teachers' salaries. Presumably this was a spurious (false) relationship. Following shows one example of a forecast using a causal relationship.

E X A M P L E 7.5 / *Forecast Using a Causal Relationship*   The Carpet City Store in Carpenteria has kept records of its sales (in square yards) each year, along with the number of permits for new houses in its area.

Year	Number of Housing Start Permits	Sales (in sq. yds.)
1986	18	13,000
1987	15	12,000
1988	12	11,000
1989	10	10,000
1990	20	14,000
1991	28	16,000
1992	35	19,000
1993	30	17,000
1994	20	13,000

Carpet City's operations manager believes forecasting sales is possible if housing starts are known for that year. First, the data are plotted in Exhibit 7.21, with

x = Number of housing start permits

y = Sales of carpeting

Since the points appear to be in a straight line, the manager decides to use the linear relationship $Y = a + bx$. We solve this problem by hand fitting a line. We could also solve for this equation using least squares regression as we did earlier.

S O L U T I O N   Projecting the hand fit line causes it to intercept the Y axis at about 7,000 yards. This could be interpreted as the demand when no new houses are built; that is, probably as replacement for old carpeting. To estimate the slope, two points are selected, such as

Year	x	y
1989	10	10,000
1993	30	17,000

E X H I B I T 7.21

Causal Relationship: Sales to Housing Starts

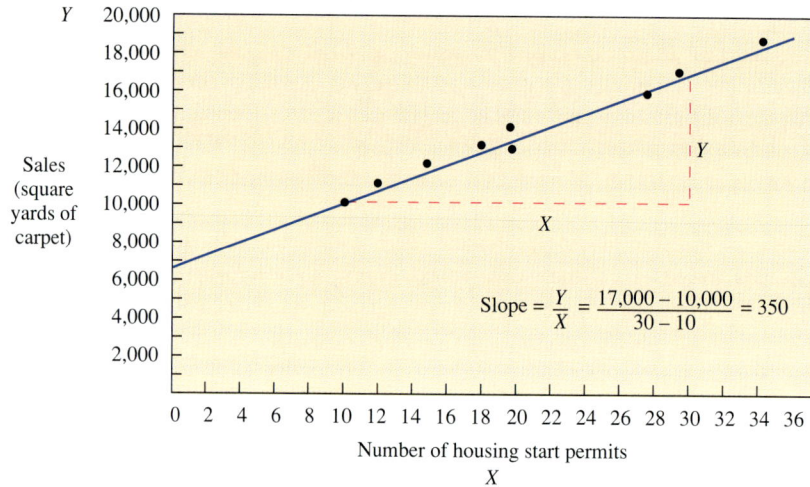

From algebra the slope is calculated as

$$b = \frac{y(93) - y(89)}{x(93) - x(89)} = \frac{17,000 - 10,000}{30 - 10} = \frac{7,000}{20} = 350$$

The manager interprets the slope as the average number of square yards of carpet sold for each new house built in the area. The forecasting equation is therefore

$$Y = 7,000 + 350x$$

Now suppose that there are 25 permits for houses to be built in 1995. The 1995 sales forecast would therefore be

$$7,000 + 350(25) = 15,750 \text{ square yards}$$

In this problem, the lag between filing the permit with the appropriate agency and the new homeowner coming to Carpet City to buy carpet makes a causal relationship feasible for forecasting. ■

Multiple Regression Analysis

Another forecasting method is multiple regression analysis, in which a number of variables are considered, together with the effects of each on the item of interest. For example, in the home furnishings field, the effects of the number of marriages, housing starts, disposable income, and the trend can be expressed in a multiple regression equation, as

$$S = B + B_m(M) + B_h(H) + B_i(I) + B_t(T)$$

where

S = Gross sales for year

B = Base sales, a starting point from which other factors have influence

M = Marriages during the year

H = Housing starts during the year

I = Annual disposable personal income

T = Time trend (first year = 1, second = 2, third = 3, and so forth)

B_m, B_h, B_i, and B_t represent the influence on expected sales of the numbers of marriages and housing starts, income, and trend.

Forecasting by multiple regression is appropriate when a number of factors influence a variable of interest—in this case, sales. Its difficulty lies with the data gathering—particularly with the mathematical computation. Fortunately, standard computer programs for multiple regression analysis are available, relieving the need for tedious manual calculation.

7.7 CHOOSING A FORECASTING METHOD

The first question is, Do you need a forecasting system? The system can range from simple inexpensive tools (such as moving averages or exponential smoothing) to expensive programs requiring extensive commitments of resources and personnel.

A business uses forecasting in planning its inventory and production levels as well as for new product development, staffing, and budgets. At the product level, it is inexpensive to develop forecasts using simple moving average, weighted moving average, or exponential smoothing. These methods would apply to the large bulk of standard inventory items carried by a firm. The choice of which of these three methods to use is based on market conditions. Moving averages weights each period the same, exponential smoothing weights the recent past more, and weighted moving average allows the weights to be determined by the forecaster. Which is better? One test would be to use each method on sample data and measure the errors using the MAD and RSFE as previously discussed.

In any case, all forecasts should be passed on to the appropriate area to have someone familiar with the product adjust or modify the forecast. In using regression analysis, it is critical to assure that the data fit the model. If they do not, extrapolations will create serious errors.

A survey of users and uses of forecasting methods was performed by Herbig, Milewicz, and Golden.[5] There were 150 responses from manufacturing and service companies ranging in size from $10 million to over $500 million. Questionnaires were addressed to the "Forecasting/Marketing Managers," so the findings stated in Exhibit 7.22 have their biased views.

As expected, because of the marketing emphasis, we find executive opinion, sales force, and customer survey near the top of the list. Also, valuable forecast indicators are trends and market share.

In comparing manufacturing and service firms, manufacturing firms tend to be more thorough and provide more iterations in circulating and adjusting the forecast. The most important forecasts are by product lines and product life cycles. Manufacturers tend to use more quantitative techniques and are more satisfied with the forecasting process. They also tend to rate forecasting as well as the level of accuracy more important than service firms rate them.

Service firms tend to involve more people in forecasting and have a higher percentage of executive involvement. Service firms also tend to (1) view the weighted moving average as an important technique and (2) use subjective forecasting much more than manufacturers. Because of the different techniques each uses, service firms also reported

---

[5]Paul Herbig, John Milewicz, and James E. Golden, "Forecasting: Who, What, When and How," *The Journal of Business Forecasting,* Summer 1993, pp. 16–21.

E X H I B I T 7.22

*A Survey of
Forecasting
Techniques*

	Mentioned (%)[a]	Average Importance[b]	Rate of Usage[c]
Executive opinion	86%	6	2.9
Sales force	68	5	2.2
Customer survey	72	4.7	2.2
Trends	91	5.6	2.9
Market share	70	4.6	2.5
Regression	52	4.2	1.7
Econometric	52	4.2	1.4
Naive	41	2.0	1.1
Indust. survey	45	3.2	1.4
Own computer model	68	5.2	2.2
Lead/lag	38	3	0.8
Simple correlation	42	3.6	1.2
Multiple correlation	34	1.8	0.6
Probabilistic	40	3.7	0.6
Time series	45	4.3	1.5
3 chart	28	1.4	1.45
Weighted moving	46	3.8	1.4
Exponential smoothing	36	2.8	0.9
Simple linear regression	38	4.0	1.3
Mult. linear regression	35	3.6	1.0
Mult. nonlinear regression	32	2.5	0.6
Product life cycle	47	3.0	1.3

[a]Percentage of respondents mentioned as using technique.
[b]Average importance rating based on 1 = Low, 4 = Average, 7 = Highest.
[c]Usage score based on 3 = Regularly used, 2 = Frequently used, 1 = Previously used, and 0 = Never used.
Source: Paul Herbig, John Milewicz, and James E. Golden, "Forecasting: Who, What, When and How," *The Journal of Business Forecasting,* Summer 1993, p. 20.

that their forecasting process is more cumbersome than manufacturers'. Additionally, service firms are less satisfied with the forecast.

7.8   FOCUS FORECASTING

Focus forecasting is the creation of Bernie Smith, who claims that this method of forecasting is a revolutionary concept.[6] He uses it primarily in finished-goods inventory management, and he has laid such significant claims to its success that we feel obligated to cover it here. Smith substantiates strong arguments that statistical approaches used in forecasting do not give the best results. He states that simple techniques that work well on past data also prove the best in forecasting the future.

**Methodology
of Focus
Forecasting**

Focus forecasting simply tries several rules that seem logical and easy to understand to project past data into the future. Each of these rules is used in a computer simulation program to actually project demand and then measure how well that rule performed when compared to what actually happened. Therefore, the two components of the focus forecasting system are (1) several simple forecasting rules and (2) computer simulation of these rules on past data.

These are simple, commonsense rules made up and then tested to see whether they should be kept. Examples of simple forecasting rules could include

[6]Bernard T. Smith, *Focus Forecasting: Computer Techniques for Inventory Control* (Boston: CBI Publishing, 1984).

1. Whatever we sold in the past three months is what we will probably sell in the next three months.

2. What we sold in the same three-month period last year, we will probably sell in that three-month period this year. (This would account for seasonal effects.)

3. We will probably sell 10 percent more in the next three months than we sold in the past three months.

4. We will probably sell 50 percent more over the next three months than we did for the same three months of last year.

5. Whatever percentage change we had for the past three months this year compared to the same three months last year will probably be the same percentage change that we will have for the next three months of this year.

These forecasting rules are not hard and fast. If a new rule seems to work well, it is added. If one has not been working well, it is deleted.

The second part of the process is computer simulation. To use the system, a data history should be available—for example, 18 to 24 months of data. The simulation process then uses each of the forecasting rules to predict some recent past data. The rule that did best in predicting the past is the rule used to predict the future. Example 7.5 is an exercise used by Smith.[7]

E X A M P L E   7.6 / *Demand in Units for a Broiler Pan*   The following table shows unit demand for a broiler pan over an 18-month period. (Try to guess what demand might be for July, August, and September, and compare your guess to the actual data presented later.)

	Last Year	**This Year**
January	6	72
February	212	90
March	378	108
April	129	134
May	163	92
June	96	137
July	167	
August	159	
September	201	
October	153	
November	76	
December	30	

S O L U T I O N   For brevity, we will use only two rules to demonstrate the method: 1 and 5. In practice, they would all be used.

Using focus forecasting, we first try forecasting rule 1—whatever we sold in the past three months is what we will probably sell in the next three months. (We are using the terms *demand* and *sales* interchangeably, assuming that demands culminate in actual sales.) We first test this rule on the past three months:

$$\text{Forecast (April, May, June)} = \text{Demand (January + February + March)}$$
$$= 72 + 90 + 108 = 270$$

---

[7] We use this exercise because it is real data from the records of American Hardware Supply Company where Smith was inventory manager. This forecasting exercise has been played by many people: buyers for American Hardware, inventory consultants, and numerous participants at national meetings of the American Production and Inventory Control Society. Further, data for the remainder of the year exist that allow for checking the results.

Since what actually occurred was 363 (134 + 92 + 137), the forecast was 270/363 = 74 percent. In other words, it was 26 percent low.

Let's try another, say rule 5—whatever percentage change we had over last year in the past three months will probably be our percentage change over last year in the next three months.

Forecast (April + May + June)

$$= \frac{\text{Demand (January + February + March) this year}}{\text{Demand (January + February + March) last year}} \times \text{Demand (April + May + June) last year}$$

$$= \frac{72 + 90 + 108}{6 + 212 + 378} \times (129 + 163 + 96)$$

$$= \frac{270}{596}(388) = 175.77$$

What actually occurred during April, May, and June this year was 363 so the forecast was 175/363, or only 48 percent of the actual demand.

Since rule 1 was better in predicting the past three months, we use that rule in predicting July, August, and September of this year. Rule 1 says that whatever we sold in the past three months is what we will probably sell in the next three months.

Forecast (July + August + September) = Demand (April + May + June)
$$= 134 + 92 + 137 = 363$$

The actual demand for the period was 357, as seen in the table, which shows the completed demand history for this year and serves as a basis for comparison.

	Last Year	This Year
January	6	72
February	212	90
March	378	108
April	129	134
May	163	92
June	96	137
July	167	120
August	159	151
September	201	86
October	153	113
November	76	97
December	30	40

Forecasts made using focus forecasting logic are then reviewed and modified (if necessary) by buyers or inventory control personnel who have responsibility over these items. When they see the forecasts made by the computer, they know which method was used and can either accept it or change the forecast if they do not agree. Smith says that about 8 percent of the forecasts are changed by the buyers because they know something that the computer does not (such as the cause of a previous large demand, or that the next forecast is too high because a competitor is introducing a competing product).

Smith states that in all the forecast simulations he has run using variations of exponential smoothing (including adaptive smoothing), focus forecasting gave significantly better results.

Here are suggestions for developing a focus forecasting system:

1. Don't try to add a seasonality index. Let the forecasting system find out seasonality by itself, especially with new items, since seasonality may not apply until the pipeline is filled and the system is stable. The forecasting rules can handle it.

2. When a forecast is unusually high or low (such as two or three times the previous period, or the previous year if there is seasonality), print out an indicator such as the letter *R* telling the person affected by this demand to review it. Do not just disregard unusual demands since they may, in fact, be valid changes in the demand pattern.

3. Let the people who will be using the forecasts (such as buyers or inventory planners) participate in creating the rules. Smith plays his "can you outguess focus forecasting" game with all the company's buyers. Using two years of data and 2,000 items, focus forecasting makes forecasts for the past six months. Buyers are asked to forecast the past six months using any rule they prefer. If they are consistently better than the existing forecasting rules, their rules are added to the list.

4. Keep the rules simple. That way, they will be easily understood and trusted by users of the forecast.

In summary, it appears that focus forecasting has significant merit when demand is generated outside the system, such as in forecasting end-item demand, spare parts, and materials and suppliers used in a variety of products.

Computer time apparently is not very large since Smith forecasts 100,000 items every month using his focus forecasting rules.

7.9 COMPUTER PROGRAMS

Many commercial forecasting programs are available. Some exist as library routines within a mainframe computer system, some may be purchased separately from a vendor, and some are part of larger programs. Many programs are available for microcomputers. Most computer manufacturers either produce their own, team up with a software company, or entice software companies to write programs for their computers.

All but the most sophisticated forecasting formulas are quite easy to understand. Anyone who can use a spreadsheet such as Lotus® 1-2-3®, SuperCalc®, Quattro®, or Excel® can create a forecasting program on a PC. Depending on one's knowledge of the spreadsheet, a simple program can be written in anywhere from a few minutes to a couple of hours. How this forecast is to be used by the firm could be the bigger challenge. If demand for many items is to be forecast, this becomes a data-handling problem, not a problem in the forecasting logic.

Two authors, Aghazadeh and Romal, provide a list of 66 packages for forecasting and statistical analysis for personal computer (PC) use.[8] Some are simple to use and others are advanced with a large capacity for graphics and graphical interface. The accompanying "The Evolution of a Forecasting Department" (written by the director of sales forecasting at Warner-Lambert Company) discusses the development, methods, and benefits of his firm's forecasting system.

---

[8]Seyed-Mahmoud Aghazadeh and Jane B. Romal, "A Directory of 66 Packages for Forecasting and Statistical Analysis," *The Journal of Business Forecasting,* Summer 1992, pp. 14–18.

Break*through*

The Evolution of a Forecasting Department

At Warner-Lambert Company, the Consumer Health Product Group (CHPG) generated $732 million in 1992 sales. The products are divided into three main categories: oral care, upper respiratory, and women and skin care. The product line includes the mouth rinses, Listerine and Cool Mint Listerine, plus Benadryl cold and allergy products, Lubriderm skin lotion, and e.p.t home pregnancy test. Each of the businesses is highly promoted and subject to considerable seasonal swings, constituting a formidable challenge to the forecasting professional.

The CHPG Sales Forecasting Department was established in the late 1980s to improve forecast accuracy and customer service levels. However, the role of the forecaster, with no formal process or forecasting tools, was limited to attending forecast review meetings and performing ad-hoc analysis.

Though a step in the right direction, these efforts fell short of fulfilling the department's objectives and management's expectations. A project was initiated to identify and implement a forecasting system, tailored to our line of products and logistics needs. Key here was a robust tool set (i.e., seasonality decomposition, promotional analysis, and "what-if" capability) as well as the ability to integrate with the order processing and logistic systems.

After one year of developmental efforts, the main components of the system were "completed" and we began training the marketing staff. As we proceeded with the training and roll-out plan, it became increasingly evident that the system was overwhelming to the users. This was due to

1. The statistical and forecasting knowledge required to generate and interpret the models. The system provides eight "modified" trend analysis models, with a user override interface. Although designed to minimize the need for heavy statistics, the user must possess a good understanding of moving averages, trends, seasonal decomposition, random noise, and so on.

However, marketing professionals are generalists and often lack statistical training.

2. Time investment by the marketing assistants. Although the system was designed to maximize productivity, it constituted a substantial investment of their time to properly generate the models. This was next to impossible, given their hectic schedules.

In the mean time, the forecast accuracy worsened and customer service was suffering. In addition, management's frustrations with the total forecasting process and the system's inability to deliver grew exponentially. We, therefore, focused our total efforts on the implementation process, redesigning and adding new features on the way.

How We Did It

We enlisted the assistance of Sales, Marketing, Manufacturing, MIS, forecasting consultants, and academia to develop a vision statement and strategic plan.

Our vision states that "We will be the best Sales Forecasting Department in the industry." To support it, the strategic plan calls for establishing a forecasting "center of excellence" consisting of professionals who (1) possess superior analytical and statistical skills, (2) have a solid understanding of our businesses and marketplace, and (3) possess solid communication and interpersonal skills. The plan further recommends the implementation of a forecast analyst program. In this scenario, each business category would have one forecast analyst totally dedicated to developing the sales forecast, conducting macro-economic analysis, developing customer specific models, and performing competitive benchmarks. The strategic plan and supporting ROI analysis were approved by management late in 1992.

In early 1993 we began to implement the plan with the Oral Care Category, since it is the most representative of our "flagship" brands. First, we embarked on identifying a qualified candidate for the analyst position. This was a challenging task since we were pursuing an analytical individual with strong interpersonal skills, a com-

---

7.10   **CONCLUSION**

As shown in our "Breakthrough," developing a forecasting system is not easy. However, it must be done since forecasting is fundamental to any planning effort. In the short run, a forecast is needed to predict the requirements for materials, products, services, or other resources to respond to changes in demand. Forecasts permit adjusting schedules and

bination not easily found. Once on board, the analyst began a rigorous training program and, in May 1993, assumed full responsibility for the Oral Care forecasting process.

Two of the principle success factors underlining the new process are a solid understanding of the business and marketplace, and a strong relationship with the sales, marketing, finance and manufacturing organizations. At the same time, we must maintain a high degree of objectivity—a most difficult undertaking. The analysts work with the sales planning and marketing colleagues in every step of the forecasting process, incorporating their input in the models and conducting "what-if" scenarios.

Our Forecasting Process

Our forecasting cycle is monthly, culminating with a consensus forecast review meeting on the third workday of the month. After the review meeting, all changes are incorporated in the models and the final forecast is transmitted to manufacturing on the fifth workday. The models are continuously improved on throughout the month and, importantly, weekly customer service meetings are conducted to discuss the monthly forecast progress as well as any manufacturing or distribution issues.

The forecast is developed at the pack level (i.e., Listerine 32 oz) and is exploded to all component SKUs (open stock, floor displays, etc.). Currently in Oral Care alone there are close to 50 models, supporting 30 packs. For most packs, there are two models. One forecasts market consumption and the second trade demand. On an average, each model is comprised of 10 economic and event-specific variables.

How We Benefited from the System

Since the new process was implemented in May, we have realized benefits in two forms. First, forecast accuracy has improved substantially. Second, we have freed marketing resources from the arduous process of generating the forecast and can now focus on other value-added ac-

tivities for business growth. And as we master the analytical process, we will reap a by-product benefit in the form of "learning" that will help grow the business.

The forecast analyst program has been extended and is currently being implemented for the Upper Respiratory Category; we estimate assuming the forecasting responsibilities by early fourth quarter 1993. In addition, the role of the department is expanding.

We are currently spearheading several projects to improve Field Sales input, as well as the timing and execution of the forecast. We have also established forecasting relationships with key customers to work with them in developing their forecast. Additionally, we plan to redesign the forecasting data base to improve the regional and customer-specific analysis/forecasting tool set.

The forecasting process at Warner-Lambert's Consumer Products Division has experienced substantial successful evolution. It all started with a rudimentary process, evolving to the current "center of excellence" status, fully supported by a clear vision and strategic direction. Clearly, there are several morals to this evolution. First, the focus should be on the total forecasting process. It is paramount that the forecasting professionals have a solid knowledge of the business and marketplace, and that they translate this knowledge to the model development realm. It is equally critical that the forecasters are capable of making a smooth transition from the analytical to the business realm. You will certainly not build credibility if you talk "R-square" language to Sales and Marketing. Importantly, management's expectations should be managed carefully. It is necessary that all assumptions and payback analysis are documented and updated, as dictated by your "learning" and changing business conditions and priorities. Also, the forecasting professional must play the role of "salespeople," continuously marketing the "learning" and positive results to the organization.

Source: Luis Reyes, "The Evolution of a Forecasting Department," *The Journal of Business Forecasting,* Fall 1993, pp. 22–24.

varying labor and materials. In the long run, forecasting is required as a basis for strategic changes, such as developing new markets, developing new products or services, and expanding or creating new facilities.

For long-term forecasts that lead to heavy financial commitments, great care should be taken to derive the forecast. Several approaches should be used. Causal methods such as regression analysis or multiple regression analysis are beneficial. These provide a basis for discussion. Economic factors, product trends, growth factors, and competition, as well as a myriad of other possible variables, need to be considered and the forecast adjusted to reflect the influence of each.

Short- and intermediate-term forecasting (such as required for inventory control as well as staffing and material scheduling) may be satisfied with simpler models, such as exponential smoothing with perhaps an adaptive feature or a seasonal index. In these applications, thousands of items are usually being forecast. The forecasting routine should therefore be simple and run quickly on a computer. The routines should also detect and respond rapidly to definite short-term changes in demand while at the same time ignoring the occasional spurious demands. Exponential smoothing, when monitored by management to control the value of alpha, is an effective technique.

Focus forecasting appears to offer a reasonable approach to short-term forecasting, say, monthly or quarterly but certainly less than a year. If there is one thing focus forecasting offers, it is close monitoring and rapid response.

In summary, forecasting is tough. A perfect forecast is like a hole in one in golf: great to get but we should be satisfied just to get close to the cup—or, to push the analogy, just to land on the green. The ideal philosophy is to create the best forecast that you reasonably can and then hedge by maintaining flexibility in the system to account for the inevitable forecast error.

7.11 FORMULA REVIEW

Simple moving average

$$F_t = \frac{A_{t-1} + A_{t-2} + A_{t-3} + \ldots + A_{t-n}}{n} \tag{7.1}$$

Weighted moving average

$$F_t = w_1 A_{t-1} + w_2 A_{t-2} + \ldots + w_n A_{t-n} \tag{7.2}$$

Single exponential smoothing

$$F_t = F_{t-1} + \alpha(A_{t-1} - F_{t-1}) \tag{7.3}$$

Exponential smoothing with trend

$$\text{FIT}_t = F_t + T_t \tag{7.4}$$
$$F_t = \text{FIT}_{t-1} + \alpha(A_{t-1} - \text{FIT}_{t-1}) \tag{7.5}$$
$$T_t = T_{t-1} + \alpha\delta(A_{t-1} - \text{FIT}_{t-1}) \tag{7.6}$$

Mean absolute deviation

$$\text{MAD} = \frac{\sum_{t=1}^{n} |A_t - F_t|}{n} \tag{7.7}$$

Tracking signal

$$\text{TS} = \frac{\text{RSFE}}{\text{MAD}} \tag{7.8}$$

Least squares regression

$$Y = a + bx \tag{7.9}$$

$$a = \bar{y} - b\bar{x} \tag{7.10}$$

$$b = \frac{\Sigma xy - n\bar{x} \cdot \bar{y}}{\Sigma x^2 - n\bar{x}^2} \tag{7.11}$$

Standard error of estimate

$$S_{xy} = \sqrt{\frac{\sum_{i=1}^{n} (y_i - Y_i)^2}{n - 2}} \tag{7.12}$$

7.12 SOLVED PROBLEMS

1. Sunrise Baking Company markets doughnuts through a chain of food stores. It has been experiencing over- and underproduction because of forecasting errors. The following data are its demand in dozens of doughnuts for the past four weeks. Donuts are made for the following day, such as Sunday's donut production is for Monday's sales, Monday's production for Tuesday's sales, etc. The bakery is closed Saturday, so Friday's production must satisfy demand for both Saturday and Sunday.

	4 Weeks Ago	3 Weeks Ago	2 Weeks Ago	Last Week
Monday	2,200	2,400	2,300	2,400
Tuesday	2,000	2,100	2,200	2,200
Wednesday	2,300	2,400	2,300	2,500
Thursday	1,800	1,900	1,800	2,000
Friday	1,900	1,800	2,100	2,000
Saturday Sunday	2,800	2,700	3,000	2,900

Make a forecast for this week on the following basis:

 a. Daily, using a simple four-week moving average.
 b. Daily, using a weighted average of 0.40, 0.30, 0.20, and 0.10 for the past four weeks.
 c. Sunrise is also planning its purchases of ingredients for bread production. If bread demand had been forecast for last week at 22,000 loaves and only 21,000 loaves were actually demanded, what would Sunrise's forecast be for this week using exponential smoothing with $\alpha = 0.10$?
 d. Supposing, with the forecast made in (c), this week's demand actually turns out to be 22,500. What would the new forecast be for the next week?

Solution

 a. Simple moving average, four-week.

Monday $\dfrac{2,400 + 2,300 + 2,400 + 2,200}{4} = \dfrac{9,300}{4} = 2,325$ doz.

Tuesday $= \dfrac{8,500}{4} = 2,125$ doz.

Wednesday $= \dfrac{9,500}{4} = 2,375$ doz.

Thursday $= \dfrac{7,500}{4} = 1,875$ doz.

Friday $= \dfrac{7,800}{4} = 1,950$ doz.

Saturday and Sunday $= \dfrac{11,400}{4} = 2,850$ doz.

b. Weighted average with weights of .40, .30, .20, and .10.

	(.10)		(.20)		(.30)		(.40)		
Monday	220	+	480	+	690	+	960	=	2,350
Tuesday	200	+	420	+	660	+	880	=	2,160
Wednesday	230	+	480	+	690	+	1,000	=	2,400
Thursday	180	+	380	+	540	+	800	=	1,900
Friday	190	+	360	+	630	+	800	=	1,980
Saturday and Sunday	280	+	540	+	900	+	1,160	=	2,880
	1,300	+	2,660	+	4,110	+	5,600	=	13,670

c. Exponentially smoothed forecast for bread demand

$$F_t = F_{t-1} + \alpha(A_{t-1} - F_{t-1})$$
$$= 22,000 + 0.10(21,000 - 22,000)$$
$$= 22,000 - 100 = 21,900 \text{ loaves}$$

d. Exponentially smoothed forecast

$$F_{t+1} = 21,900 + .10(22,500 - 21,900)$$
$$= 21,900 + .10(600) = 21,960 \text{ loaves}$$

2. Here are the actual demands for a product for the past six quarters. Using forecasting rules 1 to 5, find the best rule to use in predicting the third quarter of this year.

	Quarter			
	I	**II**	**III**	**IV**
Last year	1,200	700	900	1,100
This year	1,400	1,000		

Solution

Rule 1: Next three months' demand = Last three months' demand.
   Testing this on the last three months, $F_{II} = A_I$; therefore $F_{II} = 1,400$.
   Actual demand was 1,000, so $\dfrac{1,000}{1,400} = 71.4\%$.

Rule 2: This quarter's demand equals demand in the same quarter last year.
The forecast for the second quarter this year will therefore be 700, the amount for that quarter last year.
   Actual demand was 1,000, and $\dfrac{1,000}{700} = 142.9\%$.

Rule 3: 10 percent more than last quarter.
   $F_{II} = 1,400 \times 1.10 = 1,540$.
   Actual was 1,000, and $\dfrac{1,000}{1,540} = 64.9\%$.

Rule 4: 50 percent more than same quarter last year.
   $F_{II} = 700 \times 1.50 = 1,050$.
   Actual was 1,000, and $\dfrac{1,000}{1,050} = 95.2\%$.

Rule 5: Same rate of increase or decrease as last three months.
   $\dfrac{1,400}{1,200} = 1.167$.
   $F_{II} = 700 \times 1.167 = 816.7$
   Actual was 1,000 so $\dfrac{1,000}{816.7} = 122.4\%$.

Rule 4 was the closest in predicting the recent quarter—95.2 percent or just 4.8 percent under. Using this rule (50 percent more than the same quarter last year), we would forecast the third quarter this year as 50 percent more than the third quarter last year, or
   This year $F_{III} = 1.50\, A_{III}$ (last year)
   $F_{III} = 1.50\,(900) = 1,350 \text{ units}$

3. A specific forecasting model was used to forecast demand for a product. The forecasts and the corresponding demand that subsequently occurred are shown below. Use the MAD and tracking signal technique to evaluate the accuracy of the forecasting model.

	Actual	Forecast
October	700	660
November	760	840
December	780	750
January	790	835
February	850	910
March	950	890

Solution

Evaluate the forecasting model using MAD and tracking signal.

	Actual Demand	Forecast Demand	Actual Deviation	Cumulative Deviation (RSFE)	Absolute Deviation
October	700	660	40	40	40
November	760	840	−80	−40	80
December	780	750	30	−10	30
January	790	835	−45	−55	45
February	850	910	−60	−115	60
March	950	890	60	−55	60
				Total dev. =	315

$$MAD = \frac{315}{6} = 52.5$$

$$Tracking\ signal = \frac{-55}{52.5} = -1.05$$

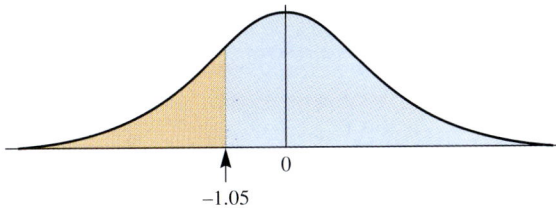

Forecast model is well within the distribution.

4. Here are quarterly data for the past two years. From these data prepare a forecast for the upcoming year using decomposition.

Period	Actual
1	300
2	540
3	885
4	580
5	416
6	760
7	1191
8	760

Solution

(1) x Period	(2) Y Actual	(3) Period Average	(4) Seasonal Factor	(5) Deseasoned Demand
1	300	358	0.527	568.99
2	540	650	0.957	564.09
3	885	1,038	1.529	578.92
4	580	670	0.987	587.79
5	416		0.527	789.01
6	760		0.957	793.91
7	1,191		1.529	779.08
8	760		0.987	770.21
Total	5,432	2,716	8.0	
Average	679	679	1	

Column 3 is seasonal average. For example, the first-quarter average is

$$\frac{300 + 416}{2} = 358$$

Column 4 is the quarter average (column 3) divided by the overall average (679). Column 5 is the actual data divided by the seasonal index.
To determine x^2 and xy we can construct a table as follows:

	x Period	Deseasoned Demand (y_d)	x^2	xy
	1	568.99	1	569.0
	2	564.09	4	1128.2
	3	578.92	9	1736.7
	4	587.79	16	2351.2
	5	789.01	25	3945.0
	6	793.91	36	4763.4
	7	779.08	49	5453.6
	8	770.21	64	6161.7
Sums	36	5,432	204	26,108.8
Average	4.5	679		

Now we calculate regression results for deseasonalized data.

$$b = \frac{(26108) - (8)(4.5)(679)}{(204) - (8)(4.5)^2} = 39.64$$
$$a = \overline{Y} - b\overline{x}$$
$$a = 679 - 39.64(4.5) = 500.6$$

Therefore, the deseasonalized regression results are

$$Y = 500.6 + 39.64x$$

Period	Trend Forecast	Seasonal Factor	Final Forecast
9	857.4	0.527	452.0
10	897.0	0.957	858.7
11	936.7	1.529	1431.9
12	976.3	0.987	963.4

7.13 REVIEW AND DISCUSSION QUESTIONS

1. What is the difference between dependent and independent demand?
2. Examine Exhibit 7.4 and suggest which model you might use for (1) bathing suit demand, (2) demand for new houses, (3) electrical power usage, (4) new plant expansion plans.
3. What is the logic in the least squares method of linear regression analysis?
4. Explain the procedure to create a forecast using the decomposition method of least squares regression.
5. Give some very simple rules you might use to manage demand for a firm's product. (An example is "limited to stock on hand.")
6. What strategies are used by supermarkets, airlines, hospitals, banks, and cereal manufacturers to influence demand?
7. All forecasting methods using exponential smoothing, adaptive smoothing, and exponential smoothing including trend require starting values to get the equations going. How would you select the starting value for, say, F_{t-1}?
8. From the choice of simple moving average, weighted moving average, exponential smoothing, and linear regression analysis, which forecasting technique would you consider the most accurate? Why?
9. Give some examples that you can think of that have a multiplicative seasonal trend relationship.
10. What is the main disadvantage of daily forecasting using regression analysis?
11. What are the main problems with using adaptive exponential smoothing in forecasting?
12. How is a seasonal index computed from a regression line analysis?
13. Discuss the basic differences between the mean absolute deviation and standard deviation.
14. What implications do forecast errors have for the search for ultrasophisticated statistical forecasting models?
15. What are the strongest selling points of focused forecasting?
16. Causal relationships are potentially useful for which component of a time series?

7.14 PROBLEMS

1. Demand for stereo headphones and CD players for joggers has caused Nina Industries to grow almost 50 percent over the past year. The number of joggers continues to expand, so Nina expects demand for headsets to also expand, since, as yet, no safety laws have been passed to prevent joggers from wearing them.

Demand for the stereo units for last year were as follows:

Month	Demand (units)	Month	Demand (units)
January	4,200	July	5,300
February	4,300	August	4,900
March	4,000	September	5,400
April	4,400	October	5,700
May	5,000	November	6,300
June	4,700	December	6,000

a. Using least squares regression analysis, what would you estimate demand to be for each month next year? Follow the general format in Exhibit 7.14.

b. To be reasonably confident of meeting demand, Nina decides to use three standard errors of estimate for safety. How many additional units should be held to meet this level of confidence?

2. Historical demand for a product is:

	Demand
January	12
February	11
March	15
April	12
May	16
June	15

a. Using a weighted moving average with weights of 0.60, 0.30, and 0.10, find the July forecast.

b. Using a simple three-month moving average, find the July forecast.

c. Using single exponential smoothing with $\alpha = 0.2$ and a June forecast $= 13$, find the July forecast. Make whatever assumptions you wish.

d. Using simple linear regression analysis, calculate the regression equation for the preceding demand data.

e. Using the regression equation in (d), calculate the forecast for July.

3. The following tabulations are actual sales of units for six months and a starting forecast in January.

a. Calculate forecasts for the remaining five months using simple exponential smoothing with $\alpha = 0.2$.

b. Calculate MAD for the forecasts.

	Actual	Forecast
January	100	80
February	94	
March	106	
April	80	
May	68	
June	94	

4. Zeus Computer Chips, Inc., used to have major contracts to produce the 286 and 386-type chips. The market has been declining during the past three years because of the 486 and pentium-type chips, which it cannot produce, so Zeus has the unpleasant task of forecasting next year. The task is unpleasant because the firm has not been able to find replacement chips for its product lines. Here is demand over the past 12 quarters:

1992		1993		1994	
I	4,800	I	3,500	I	3,200
II	3,500	II	2,700	II	2,100
III	4,300	III	3,500	III	2,700
IV	3,000	IV	2,400	IV	1,700

Use the decomposition technique to forecast the four quarters of 1995.

5. Sales data for two years are as follows. Data are aggregated with two months of sales in each "period."

	Sales
January–February	109
March–April	104
May–June	150
July–August	170
September–October	120
November–December	100
January–February	115
March–April	112
May–June	159
July–August	182
September–October	126
November–December	106

a. Plot the data.

b. Fit a simple linear regression model to the sales data.

c. In addition to the regression model, determine multiplicative seasonal index factors. A full cycle is assumed to be a full year.

d. Using the results from parts *(b)* and *(c)* prepare a forecast for the next year.

6. The tracking signals computed using past demand history for three different products are as follows. Each product used the same forecasting technique.

	TS 1	**TS 2**	**TS 3**
1	−2.70	1.54	0.10
2	−2.32	−0.64	0.43
3	−1.70	2.05	1.08
4	−1.1	2.58	1.74
5	−0.87	−0.95	1.94
6	−0.05	−1.23	2.24
7	0.10	0.75	2.96
8	0.40	−1.59	3.02
9	1.50	0.47	3.54
10	2.20	2.74	3.75

Discuss the tracking signals for each product and what the implications are.

7. Prepare a forecast for each quarter of the next year from the following past two years' quarterly sales information. Assume that there are both trend and seasonal factors and that the season cycle is one year. Use time series decomposition.

Quarter	**Sales**
1	160
2	195
3	150
4	140
5	215
6	240
7	205
8	190

8. Tucson Machinery, Inc., manufactures numerically controlled machines, which sell for an average price of $0.5 million each. Sales for these NCMs for the past two years were as follows:

Quarter	Quantity (units)
1993	
I	12
II	18
III	26
IV	16
1994	
I	16
II	24
III	28
IV	18

a. Hand fit a line (or do a regression if your calculator has that feature).
b. Find the trend and seasonal factors.
c. Forecast sales for 1995.

9. Not all the items in your office supply store are evenly distributed as far as demand is concerned, so you decide to forecast demand to help plan your stock. Past data for legal-sized yellow tablets for the month of August are

Week 1	300
Week 2	400
Week 3	600
Week 4	700

a. Using a three-week moving average, what would you forecast the next week to be?
b. Using exponential smoothing with $\alpha = 0.20$, if the exponential forecast for week 3 was estimated as the average of the first two weeks $[(300 + 400)/2 = 350]$, what would you forecast week 5 to be?

10. Given the following history, use focus forecasting to forecast the third quarter of this year. Use three focus forecasting strategies.

	Jan	Feb	Mar	Apr	May	Jun	Jul	Aug	Sep	Oct	Nov	Dec
Last year	100	125	135	175	185	200	150	140	130	200	225	250
This year	125	135	135	190	200	190						

11. Here are the actual tabulated demands for an item for a nine-month period (January through September). Your supervisor wants to test two forecasting methods to see which method was better over this period.

	Actual
January	110
February	130
March	150
April	170
May	160
June	180
July	140
August	130
September	140

a. Forecast April through September using a three-month moving average.
b. Use simple exponential smoothing to estimate April through September.

c. Use MAD to decide which method produced the better forecast over the six-month period.

12. A particular forecasting model was used to forecast a six-month period. Here are the forecasts and actual demands that resulted.

	Forecast	Actual
April	250	200
May	325	250
June	400	325
July	350	300
August	375	325
September	450	400

Find the tracking signal and state whether you think the model being used is giving acceptable answers.

13. Harlen Industries has a simple forecasting model: Take the actual demand for the same month last year and divide that by the number of fractional weeks in that month. This gives the average weekly demand for that month. This weekly average is used as the weekly forecast for the same month this year. This technique was used to forecast the eight weeks for this year which are shown below along with the actual demand that occurred.

The following eight weeks shows the forecast (based on last year) and the demand that actually occurred.

Week	Forecast Demand	Actual Demand
1	140	137
2	140	133
3	140	150
4	140	160
5	140	180
6	150	170
7	150	185
8	150	205

a. Compute the MAD of forecast errors.
b. Using the RSFE, compute the tracking signal.
c. Based on your answers to (a) and (b), comment on Harlen's method of forecasting.

14. Historical demand for a product is January, 80; February, 100; March, 60; April, 80; and May, 90.
a. Using a simple four-month moving average, what is the forecast for June? If June experienced a demand of 100, what would your forecast be for July?
b. Using single exponential smoothing with $\alpha = 0.20$, if the forecast for January had been 70, compute what the exponentially smoothed forecast would have been for the remaining months through June.
c. Using least squares regression analysis, compute a forecast for June, July, and August.
d. Using a weighted moving average with weights of 0.30, 0.25, 0.20, 0.15, and 0.10, what is June's forecast?

15. In this problem, you are to test the validity of your forecasting model. Here are the forecasts for a model you have been using and the actual demands that occurred.

Week	Forecast	Actual
1	800	900
2	850	1,000
3	950	1,050
4	950	900
5	1,000	900
6	975	1,100

Use the method stated in the text to compute the MAD and tracking signal. Then decide whether the forecasting model you have been using is giving reasonable results.

16. Assume that your stock of sales merchandise is maintained based on the forecast demand. If the distributor's sales personnel call on the first day of each month, compute your forecast sales by each of the three methods requested here.

	Actual
June	140
July	180
August	170

  a. Using a simple three-month moving average, what is the forecast for September?
  b. Using a weighted moving average, what is the forecast for September with weights of .20, .30, and .50 for June, July, and August, respectively?
  c. Using single exponential smoothing and assuming that the forecast for June had been 130, forecast sales for September with a smoothing constant alpha of .30.

17. Historical demand for a product is:

	Demand
April	60
May	55
June	75
July	60
August	80
September	75

  a. Using a simple four-month moving average, calculate a forecast for October.
  b. Using single exponential smoothing with $\alpha = 0.2$ and a September forecast $= 65$, calculate a forecast for October.
  c. Using simple linear regression, calculate the trend line for the historical data. Say the X axis is April $= 1$, May $= 2$, and so on, while the Y axis is demand.

$$n = 6 \qquad\qquad \Sigma x^2 = 91$$
$$\Sigma x = 21 \qquad\qquad \Sigma y^2 = 27,875$$
$$\Sigma y = 405 \qquad\qquad \Sigma xy = 1,485$$

  d. Calculate a forecast for October.

18. Sales by quarter for last year and the first three quarters of this year were as follows:

	\multicolumn{4}{c}{Quarter}

	I	II	III	IV
Last year	23,000	27,000	18,000	9,000
This year	19,000	24,000	15,000	

Using the focus forecasting procedure described in the text, forecast expected sales for the fourth quarter of this year.

19. The following table shows predicted product demand using your particular forecasting method along with the actual demand that occurred.

Forecast	Actual
1,500	1,550
1,400	1,500
1,700	1,600
1,750	1,650
1,800	1,700

   a. Compute the tracking signal using the mean absolute deviation and running sum of forecast errors.

   b. Discuss whether your forecasting method is giving good predictions.

20. Sales during the past six months have been

January	115
February	123
March	132
April	134
May	140
June	147

   a. Using a simple three-month moving average, make forecasts for April through July. What is the main weakness of using a simple moving average with data patterned like this?

   b. Using single exponential smoothing with $\alpha = 0.70$, if the forecast for January had been 110, compute the exponentially smoothed forecasts for each month through July. Is this method more accurate for this data? Why or why not?

   c. Using least squares regression analysis, compute the forecasts for the rest of the year. Does your regression line seem to fit the January through June data well? If so, briefly describe a pattern of data with which linear regression would not work well.

   d. Calculate the mean absolute deviation for January through June using the trend equation from *(c)*.

21. Use regression analysis on deseasonalized demand to forecast demand in summer 1995, given the following historical demand data:

Year	Season	Actual Demand
1993	Spring	205
	Summer	140
	Fall	375
	Winter	575
1994	Spring	475
	Summer	275
	Fall	685
	Winter	965

22. Here are the data for the past 21 months for actual sales of a particular product.

	1993	1994
January	300	275
February	400	375
March	425	350
April	450	425
May	400	400
June	460	350
July	400	350
August	300	275
September	375	350
October	500	
November	550	
December	500	

Develop a forecast for the fourth quarter using three different focus forecasting rules. (Note that to correctly use this procedure, the rules are first tested on the third quarter; the best performing one is used to forecast the fourth quarter.) Do the problem using quarters, as opposed to forecasting separate months.

23. Actual demand for a product for the past three months was

Three months ago	400 units
Two months ago	350 units
Last month	325 units

a. Using a simple three-month moving average, make a forecast for this month.
b. If 300 units actually occurred this month, what would your forecast be for next month?
c. Using simple exponential smoothing, what would your forecast be for this month if the exponentially smoothed forecast for three months ago was 450 units and the smoothing constant was 0.20?

24. After using your forecasting model for six months, you decide to test it using MAD and a tracking signal. Here are the forecasted and actual demands for the six-month period:

Period	Forecast	Actual
May	450	500
June	500	550
July	550	400
August	600	500
September	650	675
October	700	600

a. Find the tracking signal.
b. Decide whether your forecasting routine is acceptable.

25. Goodyear Tire and Rubber Company is the world's largest rubber manufacturer, with automotive products accounting for 82 percent of sales. Cooper Tire and Rubber Company is the ninth largest tire manufacturer in the world, with tires accounting for about 80 percent of sales.

Here are earnings per share for each company by quarter from the first quarter of 1988 through the second quarter of 1991. Forecast earnings per share for the rest of 1991 and 1992. Use exponential smoothing to forecast the third period of 1991, and the time series decomposition method to forecast the last two quarters of 1991 and all four quarters of 1992. (It is much easier to solve this problem on a computer spreadsheet so you can see what is happening.)

Earnings per Share

	Quarter	Goodyear Tire	Cooper Tire
1988	I	$ 1.67	$0.17
	II	2.35	0.24
	III	1.11	0.26
	IV	1.15	0.34
1989	I	1.56	0.25
	II	2.04	0.37
	III	1.14	0.36
	IV	0.38	0.44
1990	I	0.29	0.33
	II	d0.18 (loss)	0.40
	III	d0.97 (loss)	0.41
	IV	0.20	0.47
1991	I	d1.54 (loss)	0.30
	II	0.38	0.47

a. For the exponential smoothing method, choose the first quarter of 1988 as the beginning forecast. Make two forecasts: one with $\alpha = 0.10$ and one with $\alpha = 0.30$.

b. Using the MAD method of testing the forecasting model's performance, plus actual data from 1988 through the second quarter of 1991, how well did the model perform?

c. Using the decomposition of a time series method of forecasting, forecast earnings per share for the last two quarters of 1991 and all four quarters of 1992. Is there a seasonal factor in the earnings?

d. Using your forecasts, comment on each company: Cooper Tire and Goodyear Tire.

26. Consolidated Edison Company of New York, Inc., sells electricity, gas, and steam to New York City and Westchester County. Here are sales revenues for 1981 through 1991. (The last four months of 1991 are estimated.) Forecast revenues for 1992 through 1995. Use your own judgment, intuition, or common sense concerning which model or method to use, as well as the period of data to include.

Revenue (millions)

1981	$4,865.9
1982	5,067.4
1983	5,515.6
1984	5,728.8
1985	5,497.9
1986	5,197.7
1987	5,094.4
1988	5,108.8
1989	5,550.6
1990	5,738.9
1991	5,860.0

7.15   SELECTED BIBLIOGRAPHY

Bowerman, Bruce L., and Richard T. O'Connell. *Forecasting and Time Series: An Applied Approach,* 3d ed. Belmont, CA: Duxbury Press, 1993.

Hudson, William J. *Executive Economics: Forecasting and Planning for the Real World of Business.* New York: John Wiley & Sons, 1993.

Jain, Chaman. "Developing Forecasts for Better Planning." *Long Range Planning* 26, no. 5 (October 1993), pp. 121–29.

The Journal of Business Forecasting. See various issues for interesting topics.

Niemira, Michael P. *Forecasting Financial and Economic Cycles.* New York: John Wiley & Sons, 1994.

Zarnowitz, Victor. *Business Cycles: Theory, History, Indicators, and Forecasting.* National Bureau of Economic Research Monograph. Chicago: University of Chicago Press, 1992.

Chapter

8

Strategic Capacity Planning

CHAPTER OUTLINE

KEY TERMS

Capacity

Strategic Capacity Planning

Capacity Utilization Rate

Experience Curves

Capacity Focus

Capacity Flexibility

Economies of Scope

Capacity Cushion

Decision Tree

Multisite Service Growth

"Bermuda triangle" of operational complexity

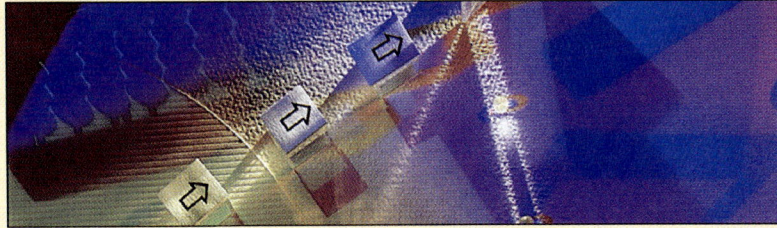

Disney's "kick-the-door-down" attitude in the planning, building, and financing of Euro Disney accounts for many of the huge problems facing the resort as of early 1994, including losses of $1 million per day. As of December 31, 1993, Euro Disney (opened in April 1992 just outside Paris, France) had a cumulative loss of 6.04 billion francs ($1.03 billion). This has triggered a costly rescue attempt by Disney and its bankers. Euro Disney is, in the words of one senior French banker familiar with the company, "a good theme park married to a bankrupt real-estate company—and the two can't be divorced." Operational errors related to capacity just made things worse.

1. Euro Disney, with one theme park, is a two-day experience at the most. This is much less than the typical stay of more than four days at Florida's Disney with three theme parks. The excessive checking in and out that resulted required additional installation of computer stations in the park's hotels.

2. Euro Disney has 5,200 hotel rooms—more than the entire French city of Cannes. Disney priced the rooms more to meet revenue targets than to meet demand. The hotels have been just over half-full on average. Disney has now changed its approach and announced separate peak, shoulder, and low season rates.

3. Disney thought that Monday would be a light day for visitors and Friday a heavy one so it allocated staff accordingly; the reality was the reverse. The problem is compounded by the fact that the number of visitors in the high season can be 10 times the number in the low season. Inflexible labor schedules in France also aggravate the problem.

4. Disney built an 18-hole golf course and then added 9 holes to adjoin 600 planned new homes. The homes have not been built, and the golf courses, which cost $15 to $20 million, are under-used.

5. Disney built expensive trams along a lake to take guests from the hotels to the park. But people prefer to walk.

6. "We were told that Europeans don't take breakfast, so we downsized the restaurants," recalls one executive. But crowds showed up for a full breakfast. Disney was trying to serve 2,500 breakfasts in 350-seat restaurants at some hotels. Lines were horrendous. Disney reacted quickly with prepackaged breakfast delivery services.

7. The parking space was too small for buses. Restrooms were built for 50 drivers, though there were 200 drivers on peak days.

From impatient drivers to grumbling bankers, Disney stepped on European toe after European toe.

Source: Peter Gumbel and Richard Turner, "Mouse Trap," *The Wall Street Journal,* March 10, 1994, p. A1.

How much should a plant be able to produce? How many customers should a service facility be able to serve? What kinds of problems arise as the production system expands? Whether we are talking about Euro Disney near Paris, France, or Clint's Machine Shop in Paris, Texas, such capacity questions are of major concern to their managers. In this chapter, we look at capacity from a strategic perspective—that is, how manufacturing and service firms plan capacity over the long run. We begin by discussing the nature of capacity from an OM perspective.

8.1   NATURE OF CAPACITY RELATIVE TO OM

A dictionary definition of **capacity** is "the ability to hold, receive, store, or accommodate." In a general business sense, it is most frequently viewed as the amount of output that a system is capable of achieving at a particular time. An operations management view tends to modify these definitions to account for the factors that determine output achieved. That is, when looking at capacity, operations managers need to look at both resource inputs *and* product outputs. The reason is that, for planning purposes, real (or effective) capacity is dependent on what is to be produced. For example, a firm that makes multiple products inevitably can produce more of one kind than of another with a given level of resource inputs. Thus, while factory management may state that their facility has 10,000 labor hours available per year, they are also thinking that these labor hours can be used to make either 50,000 X's or 20,000 Y's (or, more likely, some mix of X's and Y's). This reflects their knowledge of what their current technology and labor force inputs can produce and the product mix that is to be demanded from these resources. An operations management view also emphasizes the time dimension of capacity. This is evidenced in the common distinction drawn between long-range, intermediate-range, and short-range capacity planning. (See "Time Horizons for Capacity Planning.") Finally, capacity planning itself has different meanings to individuals at different levels within the operations management hierarchy. The vice president of manufacturing is concerned with aggregate capacity of all factories within the firm, the plant manager is concerned with the capacity of the individual plant, and the first-level supervisor is concerned with capacity of the equipment and manpower mix at the department level. Thus, while there is

Time Horizons for Capacity Planning

Capacity planning is generally viewed in three time durations:

Long range—greater than one year. Where productive resources take a long time to acquire or dispose of, such as buildings, equipment, or facilities. Long-range capacity planning requires top management participation and approval.

Intermediate range—monthly or quarterly plans for the next 6 to 18 months. Here, capacity may be varied by such alternatives as hiring, layoffs, new tools, minor equipment purchases, and subcontracting.

Short range—less than one month. This is tied into the daily or weekly scheduling process and involves making adjustments to eliminate the variance between planned output and actual output. This includes alternatives such as overtime, personnel transfers, and alternate production routings.

no one with the job title of "capacity manager," there are several managerial positions charged with the effective use of capacity.

In summary, capacity is a relative term that, in an operations management context, may be defined as *the amount of resource inputs available relative to output requirements at a particular time*. Note that this definition makes no distinction between efficient and inefficient use of capacity. In this respect, it is consistent with how the government, through the Bureau of Economic Analysis, defines "maximum practical capacity" used in its surveys: "That output attained within the normal operating schedule of shifts per day and days per week including the use of high cost inefficient facilities"[1]

Strategic Capacity Planning (Long-Range)

The objective of **strategic capacity planning** is to specify the overall capacity level of resources—facilities, equipment, and labor force size— that best supports the company's long-range competitive strategy for production. The capacity level selected has a critical impact on the firm's response rate, its cost structure, its inventory policies, and its management and staff support requirements. If capacity is inadequate, a company may lose customers through slow service or by allowing competitors to enter the market. If capacity is excessive, a company may have to reduce its prices to stimulate demand or else underutilize its workforce, carry excess inventory, or seek additional, less profitable products to stay in business. (The box insert on page 320 gives examples of how earlier capacity decisions can come back to haunt a company or industry.)

8.2   IMPORTANT CAPACITY PLANNING CONCEPTS

Best Operating Level

The term *capacity* implies an attainable rate of output but says nothing about how long that rate can be sustained. Thus, if we say that a given plant has a capacity of x units, we do not know if this is a one-day peak or a six-month average. To avoid this problem, the concept of *best operating level* is used. This is the level of capacity for which the process was designed and thus is the volume of output at which average unit cost is at a minimum. When the output of the facility falls below this level (underutilization), average unit cost will increase as overhead must be allocated to fewer units. Above this level

---

[1]In gathering capacity statistics, the Bureau of Economic Analysis asks two questions of surveyed firms: (1) At what percentage of manufacturing capacity did your company operate in (month and year)? (2) At what percentage of (month and year) manufacturing capacity would your company have preferred to operate in order to achieve maximum profits or other objectives? See "Survey of Current Business," *U.S. Department of Commerce Journal.*

E X H I B I T 8.1
Best Operating Level

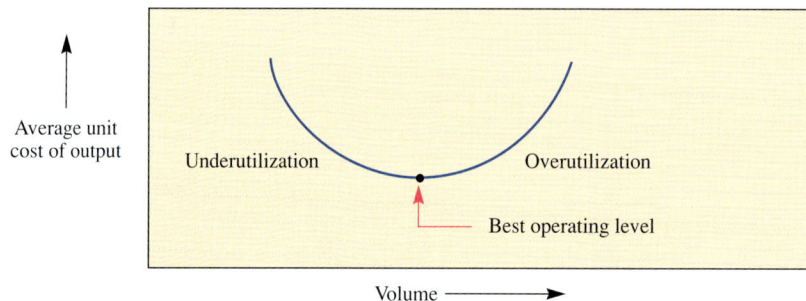

The **capacity utilization rate** reveals how close a firm is to its design capacity (i.e., best operating point):

$$\text{Capacity Utilization Rate} = \frac{\text{Capacity used}}{\text{Design capacity}}$$

The capacity utilization rate is expressed as a percentage and requires that the numerator and denominator be measured in similar units and time periods (machine hours/day, barrels of oil/day, patients/day, dollar of output/day).

(overutilization), average unit cost also increases—here due to overtime, increased equipment wear, and heightened defect rates. These relationships are shown in Exhibit 8.1.

**Economies
of Scale**

The basic notion of economies of scale is well known: As a plant gets larger and volume increases, the average cost per unit of output drops. This is partially due to operating and capital costs' decline since a piece of equipment with twice the capacity of another piece does not cost twice as much to purchase or operate. Plants also gain efficiencies when they become large enough to fully utilize dedicated resources for tasks such as material handling. The remaining cost reductions come from the ability to distribute nonmanufacturing costs such as marketing and R&D over a greater number of products.

This reduction in average unit cost continues until the plant gets so big that coordination of material flow and staffing becomes so expensive that new sources of capacity must be found. This concept can be related to best operating levels by comparing the average unit cost of different sized plants. Exhibit 8.2 shows the best operating levels for 100-, 200-, 300-, and 400-unit (per year) plants. The average unit cost is shown as dropping from best operating level to best operating level as we move from 100 to 300 units. Diseconomies of scale would be evidenced if we had, say, a 400-unit plant where cost was higher than for the 300-unit plant. However, moving to the right along any of the

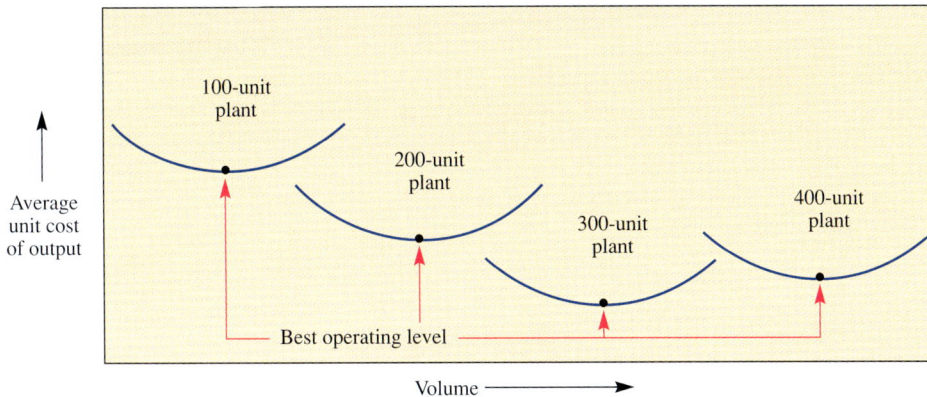

E X H I B I T 8.2
Economies of Scale

E X H I B I T 8.3   *The Experience Curve*

a. Costs per unit produced fall by a specific percentage each time cumulative production doubles. This relationship can be expressed through a linear scale:

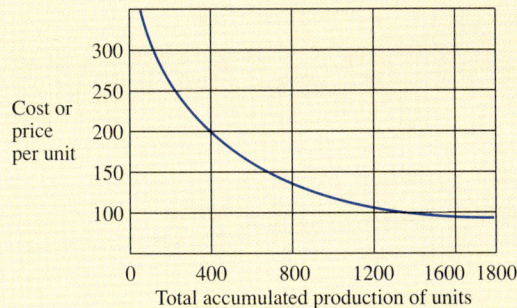

b. It can also be expressed through logarithms:

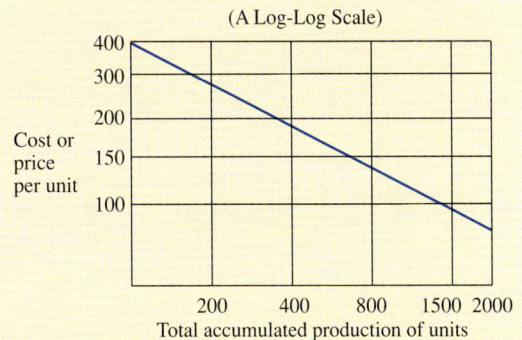

(A Log-Log Scale)

The experience-curve percentage varies across industries.

To apply this concept to the restaurant industry, consider a hypothetical fast food chain that has produced five million hamburgers. Given a current variable cost of $0.55 per burger, what will the cost per burger be when cumulative production reaches ten million burgers? If the firm has a 90-percent experience curve, costs will fall to 90 percent of $0.55, or $0.495, when accumulated production reaches ten million.

Note that sales volume becomes an important issue in achieving cost savings. If firm A serves twice as many hamburgers daily as firm B, it will accumulate "experience" twice as fast.

Source: C. Hart, G. Spizizen, and D. Wyckoff, "Scale Economies and the Experience Curve: Is Bigger Better for Restaurant Companies?" *The Cornell HRA Quarterly,* May 1984, p. 96.

three average cost curves would not be evidence of diseconomy of scale because the plant size has not increased. Rather, it would indicate that management has tried to get more from the plant than it can most efficiently provide.

The Experience Curve

This is another well-known concept. As plants produce more products, they gain experience in the best production methods, which reduce their costs of production in a predictable manner. Every time a plant's cumulative production doubles, its production costs decline by a specific percentage depending on the nature of the business. Exhibit 8.3 demonstrates the effect of a 90 percent experience curve on the production costs of hamburgers. (Additional discussion of experience or learning curves is provided in Chapter 11.)

Where Economies of Scale Meet the Experience Curve

The astute reader will realize that larger plants can have a two-way cost advantage over their competitors. Not only does a larger plant gain from economies of scale, but it will also produce more, giving it experience curve advantages as well. Companies often use this dual advantage as a competitive strategy by first building a large plant with substantial economies of scale, and then using its lower costs to price aggressively and increase sales volume. The increased volume moves them down the experience curve more quickly than their competitors, allowing the company to lower prices further, gaining still more volume. There are, however, two criteria that must be met for this strategy to be successful: The product must fit customers' needs and the demand must be sufficiently large to support the volume. Consider the case of Chrysler. By the 1970s, economies of scale and experience had given Chrysler the lowest production costs of all of the U.S. auto manufacturers. Unfortunately, its cars no longer fit customers' needs so Chrysler could not sell enough of them to operate its large plants at their design levels, driving their costs up to the highest level among the other U.S. producers in the United States. It appears that Korean auto manufacturers are now aggressively trying to cash in on this cycle, as "Risky Expansion in Korea" relates. Their success or failure remains to be seen.

Capacity Focus

As noted in Chapter 2, the concept of the focused factory holds that a production facility works best when it focuses on a fairly limited set of production objectives.[2] This means, for example, that a firm should not expect to excel in every aspect of manufacturing performance: cost, quality, flexibility, new-product introductions, reliability, short lead times, and low investment. Rather, it should select a limited set of tasks that contribute the most to corporate objectives. However, given the breakthroughs in manufacturing technology, there is an evolution in factory objectives toward trying to do everything well. How do we deal with these apparent contradictions? One way is to say that if the firm does not have the technology to master multiple objectives, then a narrow focus is the logical choice. Another way is to recognize the practical reality that not all firms are in industries that require them to use their full range of capabilities to compete.

The **capacity focus** concept can also be operationalized through the mechanism of plants within plants—*PWPs* in Skinner's terms. A focused plant may have several PWPs, each of which may have separate suborganizations, equipment and process policies, workforce management policies, production control methods, and so forth for different prod-

---

[2]Wickham Skinner, "The Focused Factory," *Harvard Business Review,* May–June 1974, pp. 113–21.

The Xerox focus factory concept creates a flexible and efficient work environment where teams of employees are responsible for the end-to-end manufacturing of specific products. The factory was designed with input from the industrial staff, working in tandem with engineers and management.

ucts—even if they are made under the same roof. This, in effect, permits finding the best operating level for each department of the organization and thereby carries the focus concept down to the operating level.

Capacity flexibility means having the ability to rapidly increase or decrease production levels, or to shift production capacity quickly from one product or service to another. Such flexibility is achieved through flexible plants, processes, and workers as well as through strategies that use the capacity of other organizations.

Capacity Flexibility

Flexible Plants   Perhaps the ultimate in plant flexibility is the *zero-changeover-time* plant. Using movable equipment, knockdown walls, and easily accessible and reroutable utilities, such a plant can adapt to change in real time. An analogy to a familiar service business captures the flavor quite well—a plant with equipment "that is easy to install and easy to tear down and move—like the Ringling Bros.–Barnum and Bailey Circus in the old tent-circus days."[3]

Flexible Processes   Flexible processes are epitomized by flexible manufacturing systems on the one hand and simple, easily setup equipment on the other. (See box "Capacity Flexibility at Aladan Corp.") Both of these technological approaches permit rapid low-cost switching from one product line to another, enabling what is sometimes referred to as **economies of scope.** (By definition, economies of scope exist when multiple products can be produced at a lower cost in combination than they can separately.)

---

[3]See R. J. Schonberger, "The Rationalization of Production," *Proceedings of the 50th Anniversary of the Academy of Management* (Chicago: Academy of Management, 1986), pp. 64–70.

*Capacity
Flexibility at
Aladan Corp.*

Julian Danielly and Larry Povlacs began the Aladan Corp., based in Dothan, Alabama, in 1986. By late 1987, AIDS awareness had created what appeared to be a shortage of gloves, as hospitals and dentists began hoarding inventory. Aladan now holds 17 percent of the global market, and its revenues for 1993 are closing in on $55 million for latex exam gloves.

From the outset, Danielly recognized the commodity status of gloves and that someday Aladan would be competing with offshore manufacturers because of the labor-intensive nature of glove making. Equipment designed and built in-house played a big role in factory efficiency. By redesigning machines to hold twice as many glove molds, Povlacs doubled machine capacity at negligible cost, giving Aladan a substantial edge over all its competitors. Each machine holds 8,000 hand forms, which complete a revolution in 17 minutes, resulting in 200 million gloves per machine per year. Being the first to reach the market with additional supplies during a shortage certainly has its advantages! Shrewd payment terms and long-term contracts helped fund the building of additional machinery that would fulfill customers' demands. At the same time, $11 million in industrial-development bonds were issued by Eufaula, Alabama, to build a second factory there.

By February 1989, two months after the Eufaula facility had doubled the company's factory capacity, the glove market was glutted and the distribution pipeline was choked with imported products. Aladan was operating at 25 percent capacity. The Eufaula project was pursued even though it was fairly certain that a glut was in the offing. Danielly was willing to let factory capacity go idle in order to bank on the long-term relationship with customers willing to buy a quality product.

Povlacs stared at the idle machinery and knew condoms were the answer. Although Danielly was reluctant to pursue the condom business, Povlacs established the first contracts in 1990 to address the idle capacity problem. Condom sales revved up Aladan's idle machines and have grown to represent almost 20 percent of the company's revenues today. Aladan reached 100 percent capacity utilization in November 1991 and closed that year with $50 million in revenue—after having reached just $27 million in the previous year. Today six machines run gloves, and two run condoms. Recently, the company has cut back on glove sales to meet the growing demand for condoms. As long as the machines are humming, Larry Povlacs is happy. But Danielly is shopping for items that are more high tech and less price-sensitive to keep out of the commodity trap and to grow out of being a two-product company. This is essential to remain a preferred supplier and to maintain the 10 to 20 percent profit margins that Aladan enjoys today—impressive numbers for a manufacturer.

Source: Terry Lammers, "What's Luck Got to Do with It?" *Inc.* 15, no. 13 (December 1993), pp. 90–98.

Flexible Workers   Flexible workers have multiple skills and the ability to switch easily from one kind of task to another. They require broader training than specialized workers and need managers and staff support to facilitate quick changes in their work assignments.

8.3   CAPACITY PLANNING

**Considerations in
Adding Capacity**

Many issues must be considered when adding capacity. Three important ones are maintaining system balance, frequency of capacity additions, and the use of external capacity.

Maintaining System Balance   In a perfectly balanced plant, the output of stage 1 provides the exact input requirement for stage 2. Stage 2's output provides the exact input requirement for stage 3, and so on. In practice, however, achieving such a "perfect" design is usually both impossible and undesirable. One reason is that the best operating levels for each stage generally differ. For instance, department 1 may operate most efficiently over a range of 90 to 110 units per month while department 2, the next stage in the process, is most efficient at 75 to 85 units per month, and Department 3, the third stage, works best over a range of 150 to 200 units per month. Another reason is that variability in product demand and the processes themselves generally lead to imbalance except in automated production lines which, in essence, are just one big machine. There are various ways of dealing with imbalance. One is to add capacity to those stages that are the bottlenecks. This can be done by temporary measures such as scheduling overtime, leasing equipment, or going outside the system and purchasing additional capacity through subcontracting. A second way is through the use of buffer inventories in front of the bottleneck stage to ensure that it always has something to work on. (This is a central feature of the synchronous manufacturing approach detailed in Chapter 19.) A third approach involves duplicating the facilities of one department on which another is dependent.

Frequency of Capacity Additions   There are two types of costs to consider when adding capacity: the cost of upgrading too frequently and that of upgrading too infrequently. Upgrading capacity too frequently is expensive. First there are direct costs, such as removing and replacing old equipment, and training employees on the new equipment.

In addition, the new equipment must be purchased, often for considerably more than the selling price of the old. Finally, there is the opportunity cost of idling the plant or service site during the changeover period.

Conversely, upgrading capacity too infrequently is also expensive. Infrequent expansion means that capacity is purchased in larger chunks. Any excess capacity that is purchased must be carried as overhead until it is utilized. (Exhibit 8.4 illustrates frequent versus infrequent capacity expansion.)

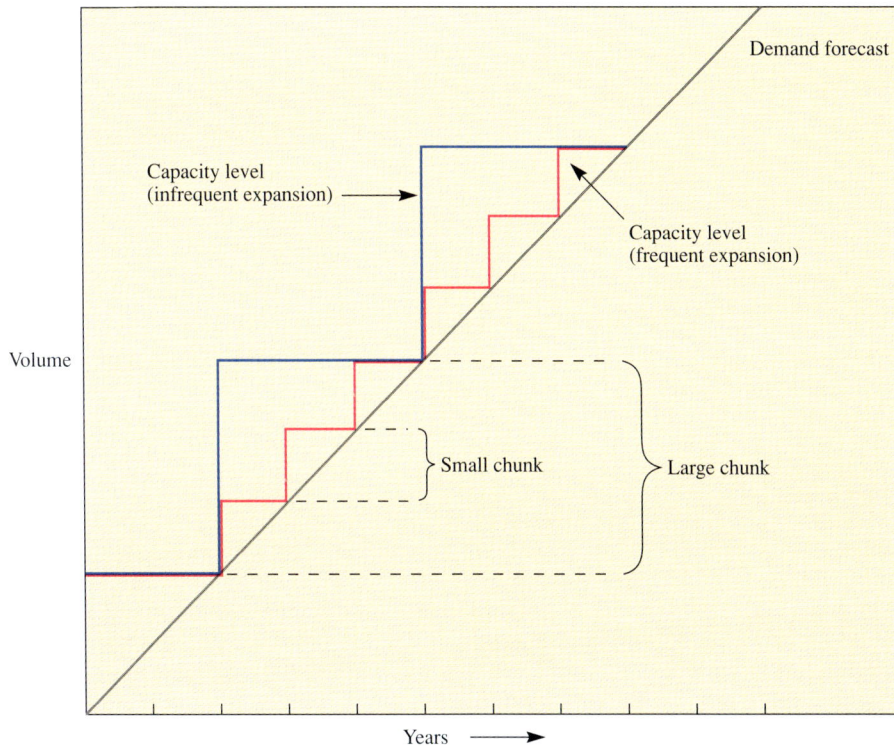

E X H I B I T 8.4

Frequent versus Infrequent Capacity Expansion

Time-Share Manufacturing

With the support of the U.S. Dept. of Commerce (DOC) and other U.S. government agencies and universities, microfactories are now being built for use by consortiums of small and medium-sized U.S. businesses. The essential aspect of such a flexible computer-integrated factory is that its manufacturing facilities are shared. A company can buy time in a facility equipped to make thousands of products for different companies in different industries through the frequent reprogramming of software. The facility can make 1, 10 or 1,000 of a kind at essentially the cost and economies of scale of a dedicated plant, but it also has the reproducibility and

quality control that is needed for a world-class operation. In addition, the high entry costs for new product manufacturing can be greatly reduced because a dedicated plant operating at partial capacity is no longer necessary. A flexible factory can also support new business development and test marketing. Time-shared manufacturing provides an alternative approach to capacity addition.

Source: Excepted from Shirley B. Dreifus (ed.), *Business International's Global Management Desk Reference* (New York: McGraw-Hill, 1992), pp. 242–43.

External Sources of Capacity   In some cases, it may be less expensive to not add capacity at all, but rather to use some existing external source of capacity. Two common strategies used by organizations are subcontracting and sharing capacity. An example of subcontracting is Japanese banks in California subcontracting check-clearing operations to the First Interstate Bank of California's check clearinghouse. An example of sharing capacity is two domestic airlines flying different routes with different seasonal demands exchanging aircraft (suitably repainted) when one's routes are heavily used and the other's are not. A new approach to sharing capacity involves consortiums' time-sharing flexible factories. (See the *Breakthrough* above "Time-Share Manufacturing.")

Determining Capacity Requirements

In determining capacity requirements, we must address the demands for individual product lines, individual plant capabilities, and allocation of production throughout the plant network. Typically this is done according to the following steps:

1. Use forecasting techniques (see Chapter 7) to forecast sales for individual products within each product line.
2. Calculate equipment and labor requirements to meet product line forecasts.
3. Project labor and equipment availabilities over the planning horizon.

Often the firm then decides on some **capacity cushion** that will be maintained between the projected requirements and the actual capacity. A capacity cushion is an amount in excess of expected demand. For example, if the expected annual demand on a facility is $10 million in products per year and the design capacity is $12 million per year, it has a 20 percent capacity cushion. A 20 percent capacity cushion equates to an 83 percent utilization rate (100%/120%).

When a firm's design capacity is less than the capacity required to meet its demand, it is said to have a negative capacity cushion. If, for example, a firm has a demand of $12 million in products per year but can only produce $10 million per year, it has a negative capacity cushion of 20 percent.

We now apply these three steps to an example.

E X A M P L E   8.1 / ***Determining Capacity Requirements***   The Stewart Company produces two flavors of salad dressings: Paul's and Newman's. Each is available in bottles and single-serving plastic bags. Management would like to determine equipment and labor requirements for the next five years.

S O L U T I O N   *Step 1. Use forecasting techniques to forecast sales for individual products within each product line.* The marketing department, which is now running a promotional campaign for Newman's dressing, provided the following forecasted demand values (in thousands) for the next five years. The campaign is expected to continue for the next two years.

	Year				
	1	**2**	**3**	**4**	**5**
Paul's					
Bottles (000s)	60	100	150	200	250
Plastic bags (000s)	100	200	300	400	500
Newman's					
Bottles (000s)	75	85	95	97	98
Plastic bags (000s)	200	400	600	650	680

Step 2. Calculate equipment and labor requirements to meet product line forecasts. Currently, three machines that can package up to 150,000 bottles each per year are available. Each machine requires two operators and can produce bottles of both Newman's and Paul's dressings. Six bottle machine operators are available. Also, five machines that can package up to 250,000 plastic bags each per year are available. Three operators are required for each machine, which can produce plastic bags of both Newman's and Paul's dressings. Currently, 20 plastic bag machine operators are available.

Total product line forecasts can be calculated from the preceding table by adding the yearly demand for bottles and plastic bags as follows:

	Year				
	1	**2**	**3**	**4**	**5**
Bottles	135	185	245	297	348
Plastic bags	300	600	900	1,050	1,180

We can now calculate equipment and labor requirements for the current year (year 1). Since the total available capacity for packaging bottles is 450,000/year (3 machines × 150,000 each), we will be using 135/450 = 0.3 of the available capacity for the current year or 0.3 × 3 = 0.9 machines. Similarly we will need 300/1250 = 0.24 of the available capacity for plastic bags for the current year or 0.24 × 5 = 1.2 machines. The number of crew required to support our forecasted demand for the first year will consist of the crew required for the bottle and the plastic bag machines:

The labor requirement for year 1's bottle operation is

0.9 bottle machines × 2 operators = 1.8 operators
1.2 bag machines × 3 operators = 3.6 operators

Step 3. Project labor and equipment availabilities over the planning horizon. We repeat the preceding calculations for the remaining years:

	Year				
	1	**2**	**3**	**4**	**5**
Plastic Bag Operation					
Percent capacity utilized	24	48	72	84	94
Machine requirement	1.2	2.4	3.6	4.2	4.7
Labor requirement	3.6	7.2	10.8	12.6	14.1
Bottle Operation					
Percent capacity utilized	30	41	54	66	77
Machine requirement	.9	1.23	1.62	1.98	2.31
Labor requirement	1.8	2.46	3.24	3.96	4.62

A positive capacity cushion exists for all five years since the available capacity for both operations is always in excess of the expected demand. The Stewart Company can now begin to develop the intermediate range or aggregate plan for the two production lines. (See Chapter 13 for a discussion of aggregate planning.) ■

Using Decision Trees to Evaluate Capacity Alternatives

A convenient way to lay out the steps of a capacity problem is through the use of *decision trees*. The tree format helps not only in understanding the problem but also in finding a solution. A **decision tree** is a schematic model of the sequence of steps in a problem and the conditions and consequences of each step.

Decision trees are composed of decision nodes with branches to and from them. By convention, squares represent decision points and circles represent chance events. Branches from decision points show the choices available to the decision maker; branches from chance events show the probabilities for their occurrence.

In solving decision tree problems, we work from the end of the tree backward to the start of the tree. As we work back, we calculate the expected values at each step.

Once the calculations are made, we prune the tree by eliminating from each decision point all branches except for the one with the highest payoff. This process continues to the first decision problem, and the decision problem is thereby solved.

We now demonstrate an application to capacity planning for Hackers Computer Store.

E X A M P L E   8.2 / *Decision Trees*   The owner of Hackers Computer Store is considering what to do with his business over the next five years. Sales growth over the past couple of years has been good, but sales could grow substantially if a major electronics firm is built in his area as proposed. Hackers' owner sees three options. The first is to enlarge his current store, the second is to locate at a new site, and the third is to simply wait and do nothing. The decision to expand or move would take little time and, therefore, the store would not lose revenue. If nothing were done the first year and strong growth occurred, then the decision to expand would be reconsidered. Waiting longer than one year would allow competition to move in and make expansion no longer feasible.

The assumptions and conditions are

1. Strong growth as a result of the increased population of computer fanatics from the electronics firm has a 55 percent probability.
2. Strong growth with a new site would give annual returns of $195,000 per year. Weak growth with a new site would mean annual returns of $115,000.

3. Strong growth with an expansion would give annual returns of $190,000 per year. Weak growth with an expansion would mean annual returns of $100,000.

4. At the existing store with no changes, there would be returns of $170,000 per year if there is strong growth and $105,000 per year if growth is weak.

5. Expansion at the current site would cost $87,000.

6. The move to the new site would cost $210,000.

7. If growth is strong and the existing site is enlarged during the second year, the cost would still be $87,000.

8. Operating costs for all options are equal.

S O L U T I O N   We construct a decision tree to advise Hackers' owner on the best action. Exhibit 8.5 shows the decision tree for this problem. There are two decision points (square nodes) and three chance occurrences (round nodes). The values of the nodes and decision points are as follows:

Node A. Move to new location.

Return with strong growth	$195,000/yr. × 5 yrs. = $975,000
Return with weak growth	$115,000/yr. × 5 yrs. = $575,000
Expected return at A =	($975,000 × .55) + ($575,000 × .45) =
	$795,000
Less new site costs =	−210,000
New site net return	$585,000

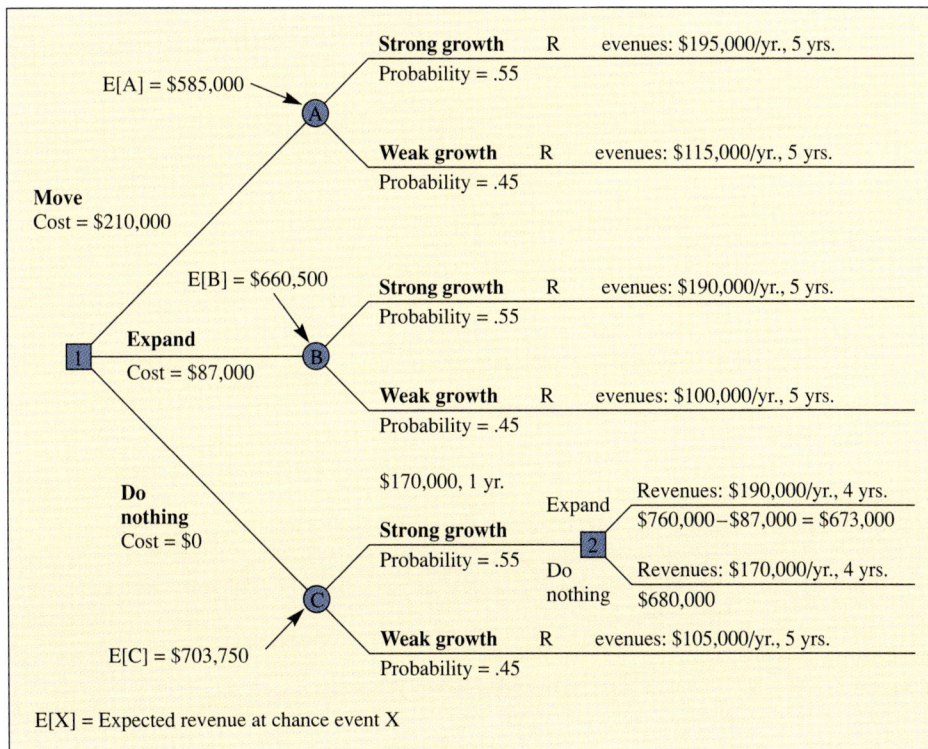

E X H I B I T 8.5

Decision Tree for Hackers Computer Store

E[X] = Expected revenue at chance event X

Node B. Enlarge the existing store.

Return with strong growth	$190,000/yr. × 5 yrs. = $950,000
Return with weak growth	$100,000/yr. × 5 yrs. = $500,000
Expected return at B =	($950,000 × .55) + ($500,000 × .45) =
	$747,500
Less costs of expansion =	−87,000
Expansion net return	$660,500

Decision point 2. After one year, reconsider:
Enlarging existing store:

Return with strong growth	$190,000/yr. × 4 yrs. = $760,000
Less expansion costs	−87,000
Net return	$673,000

Keeping existing store the same:

Return with strong growth	$170,000/yr. × 4 yrs. = $680,000

Decision point 2 shows the choice of $673,000 if the existing store is enlarged versus $680,000 if the existing store is kept the same. Therefore, we would prune the expansion branch because it is less.

Node C. Do nothing.

Strong growth in first year = $170,000/yr. × 1 yr. =		$170,000
Value of best decision of not to expand	=	680,000
		$850,000
Weak growth in first year	=	$105,000
Keep store the same next four years (4 × $105,000) =		420,000
		$525,000

Expected return at Node C = (.55 × $850,000) + (.45 × $525,000)
= $703,750

The best choice is to do nothing with a value of $703,750 compared to $585,000 for the new site and $660,500 for the expansion. ■

8.4   PLANNING SERVICE CAPACITY

Capacity Planning in Service versus Manufacturing

Although capacity planning in services is subject to many of the same issues as manufacturing capacity planning, and facility sizing can be done in much the same way, there are several important differences. Service capacity is more time- and location-dependent, it is subject to more volatile demand fluctuations, and utilization directly impacts service quality.

Time   Unlike goods, services cannot be stored for later use. The capacity must be available to produce a service at the time when it is needed. For example, a customer cannot be given a seat that went unoccupied on a previous airline flight if the current flight is full. Nor could the customer purchase a seat on a particular day's flight and take it home to be used at some later date.

Location   The service capacity must be located near the customer. In manufacturing, production takes place, and then the goods are distributed to the customer. With services, however, the opposite is true. The capacity to deliver the service must first be distributed to the customer (either physically or through some communications media such as the telephone); then the service can be produced. A hotel room or rental car that is available in another city is not much use to the customer—it must be where she is when she needs it.

Volatility of Demand   The volatility of demand on a service delivery system is much higher than that on a manufacturing production system for three reasons. First, as just mentioned, services cannot be stored. This means that inventory cannot be used to smooth the demand as in manufacturing. The second reason is that the customers interact directly with the production system—and each of these customers often has different needs, will have different levels of experience with the process, and may require different numbers of transactions. This contributes to greater variability in the processing time required for each customer and hence greater variability in the minimum capacity needed. The third reason for the greater volatility in service demand is that it is directly affected by consumer behavior. Influences on customer behavior ranging from the weather to a major event can directly affect demand for different services. Go to any restaurant near your campus during spring break and it will probably be almost empty. Or try to book a room at a local hotel during Homecoming weekend. This behavioral effect can be seen over even shorter time frames such as the lunch-hour rush at a bank's drive-through window or the sudden surge in pizza orders at Domino's during halftime on Superbowl Sunday. Because of this volatility, planning capacity in services is often done in increments as small as 10 to 30 minutes, as opposed to the one-week increments more common in manufacturing.

Planning capacity levels for services must consider the day-to-day relationship between service utilization and service quality. Exhibit 8.6 shows a service situation cast in waiting line terms (arrival rates and service rates).[4] As noted by Haywood-Farmer and Nollet, the best operating point is near 70 percent of the maximum capacity. This is "enough

Capacity Utilization and Service Quality

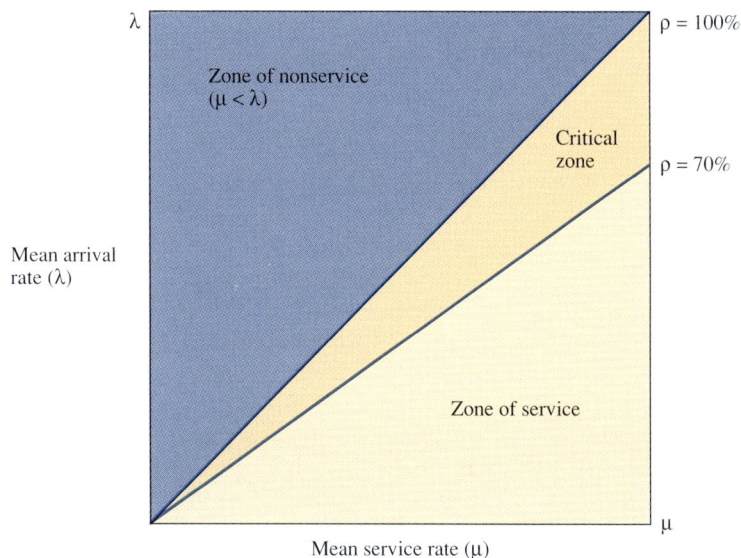

E X H I B I T 8.6
Relationship between the Rate of Service Utilization (ρ) and Service Quality

Source: John Haywood-Farmer and Jean Nollet, *Service Plus: Effective Services Management* (Boucherville, Quebec, Canada: G. Morin Publisher Ltd., 1991), p. 59.

---

[4]Waiting lines are discussed in the supplement to Chapter 4.

to keep servers busy but allows enough time to serve customers individually and keep enough capacity in reserve so as not to create too many managerial headaches."[5] In the critical zone, customers are processed through the system, but service quality declines. Above the critical zone, the line builds up and it is likely that many customers may never be served.

Haywood-Farmer and Nollet also note that the optimal utilization rate is very context-specific. Low rates are appropriate when both the degree of uncertainty and the stakes are high. For example, hospital emergency rooms and fire departments should aim for low utilization because of the high level of uncertainty and the life-or-death nature of their activities. Relatively predictable services such as commuter trains or service facilities without customer contact, such as postal sorting operations, can plan to operate much nearer 100 percent utilization. Interestingly, there is a third group for which high utilization is desirable. All sports teams like sellouts, not only because of the virtually 100 percent contribution margin of each customer, but because a full house creates an atmosphere that pleases customers, motivates the home team to perform better, and boosts future ticket sales. Stage performances and bars share this phenomenon. On the other hand, many airline passengers feel that a flight is too crowded when the seat next to theirs is occupied. Airlines capitalize on this response to sell more business-class seats.[6]

8.5   ADDING CAPACITY THROUGH MULTISITE SERVICE GROWTH

Many services, particularly franchises, start with one unit and grow by adding similar units at different locations. Research by Sasser, Olsen, and Wycoff indicated that this growth followed four life cycle stages: entrepreneurial, multisite rationalization, (rapid) growth, and maturity.[7]

Entrepreneurial Stage

Services are conceived in the entrepreneurial stage. Services generally offer a single service at a single location. Many services such as small groceries, specialty stores, and restaurants never grow out of this stage. Capacity expansion consists of the addition of equipment and personnel at the current site to meet a growing demand for the service. Planning issues revolve around (1) equipment cost and (2) how the addition of equipment and personnel into a normally already cramped facility will affect service delivery.

Two strategies are commonly used by a single-site firm to cope with the highly volatile demand typical of services. The first is cultivating the ability to shift resources from other tasks to where they are needed. Services will commonly cross-train personnel to fill in at other positions when they are needed, such as training a bank clerk to fill in as a teller during the lunch-hour rush or teaching a salesperson to run a register whenever a line forms.

The second strategy is the use of customer coproduction. Coproduction takes place when the customer does some or all of the work required in a service transaction, as with self-serve drink fountains or self-bussing tables in restaurants. Coproduction tends to smooth the demands on the system because whenever demand increases, these additional customers also provide labor to help meet this demand.

---

[5]John Haywood-Farmer and Jean Nollet, *Services Plus: Effective Service Management* (Boucherville, Quebec, Canada: G. Morin Publisher Ltd., 1991), p. 58.

[6]Ibid.

[7]W. E. Sasser, R. P. Olsen, and D. D. Wycoff, *Management of Service Operations: Text, Cases, and Readings*, 1978, pp. 534–66. Reprinted by permission of Prentice Hall, Englewood Cliffs, New Jersey.

At the multisite rationalization stage, the service firm has exhausted the local market for its existing service and must make a decision about continued growth. The firm can duplicate its existing service in additional locations (which is often called cookie cutter growth), it can add new services at its current location, or it can attempt to do both.

Multisite Rationalization Stage

If a firm decides to grow by adding services to the existing site, it manages capacity expansion in much the same manner as firms at the entrepreneurial stage. Service firms that choose multiple sites have an additional option for managing the demand volatility—by shifting resources between sites to cover the peak demands. Car and truck rental firms will shift vehicles from slow locations to where the demand is currently highest. In fact, through the use of select discount fares on one-way rentals, these firms actually have the customers transport the vehicles to where they are most needed. Companies with multiple telephone call handling centers will often reroute the overload during peak hours to call centers in other time zones that peak earlier or later in the day. One engineering firm is able to handle rush jobs by electronically moving the work among sites around the globe. By passing work on at the end of one site's day to a new site where the day is just beginning, the company is able to work 24 hours a day on an important project, even though none of its offices actually keep those hours.

As shown in Exhibit 8.7, some firms (such as resorts, universities, and hospitals) manage to grow quite large without ever becoming multisite operations by adding more and more services at their existing site. Other firms (such as chain restaurants and hotels) replicate a more focused concept in a large number of different sites. Despite the success of a limited number of firms, those that try to expand in both directions most often fail. In some cases, this is because the complexity of managing a large variety of services at multiple sites becomes overwhelming. In other cases, some or all components of a complex package of services that evolve to serve customers in one location may simply not be appropriate for customers in another. The opening vignette shows how one of the most successful multiservice firms learned this the hard way when it added a site in Europe.

Different types of economies apply depending on how the service firm expands. As the capacity of a service at a given site increases, there will be economies of scale, just as in a manufacturing plant. Adding sites to a service firm, however, produces more limited economies of scale. Fixed costs are still distributed over a greater volume, but we do not expect to see the capital and operating cost reductions. This is because adding a site does not actually increase the "plant" size, it merely adds another small "plant." Diseconomies of scale are also evident as service firms acquire too many sites and the complexity becomes increasingly unmanageable. Exhibit 8.8 shows an empirical study of how the perceived quality of food services deteriorates as the number of sites

	Single-service	Multiservice
Multisite	Chain restaurants Hotels Car and truck rentals Airlines Specialty stores	Department stores Banks HMOs
Single-site	Dry cleaners Restaurants Mom and pop stores	Hospitals Resorts Universities

E X H I B I T 8.7
Service Growth Matrix

E X H I B I T 8.8

Food Service Quality Relative to Number of Units

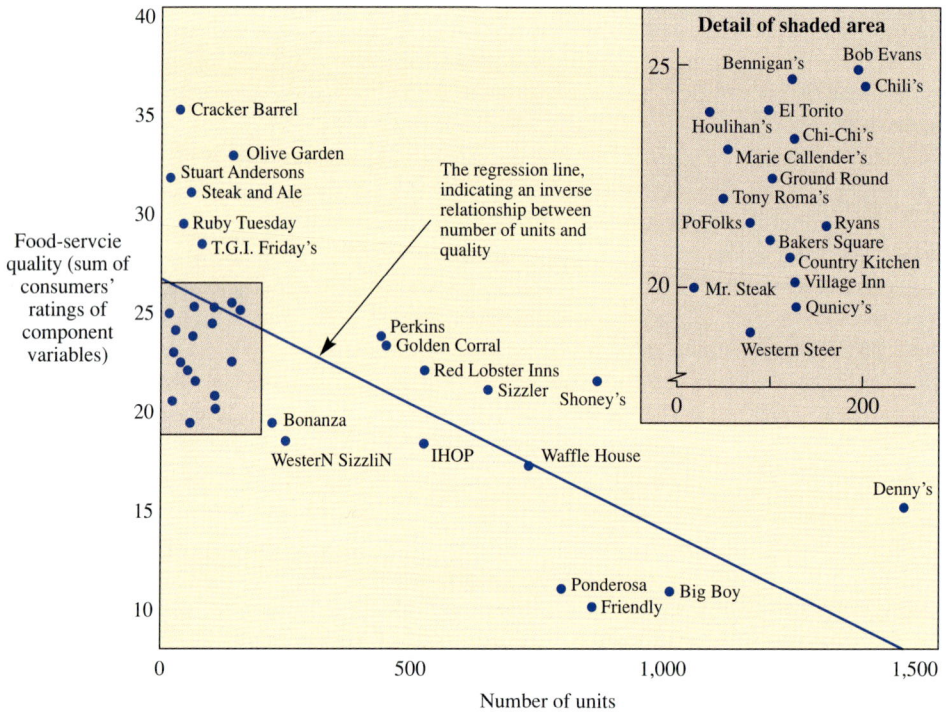

Source: Michael S. Morgan, "Benefit Dimensions of Midscale Restaurant Chains," *The Cornell Hotel and Restaurant Quarterly,* April 1993, pp. 40–45.

grows very large. Multiservice firms often experience the other type of economy, economies of scope. In other words, offering related services at a single site can be less expensive than offering the services independently at separate sites. This is possible because some common resources such as databases or specific employee skills that have been developed and maintained to support a particular service can support additional related services at little or no additional cost. To take full advantage of economies of scope, therefore, it is important to focus on adding new services that can efficiently use existing resources.

Growth Stage

When the service firm enters its rapid growth stage, its sales volume typically increases exponentially. Unfortunately, so does the operational complexity of running the firm. This is what Sasser, Olsen, and Wycoff refer to as the **"Bermuda triangle" of operational complexity,** where the difficulty in running the business outstrips the manager's ability to handle it. (See Exhibit 8.9.) Other new capacity planning challenges at this stage include (1) the need to incorporate fresh ideas into the existing facilities and (2) the need to upgrade older facilities that are nearing the end of their useful life or that require remodeling or expansion.

Maturity Stage

By the mature stage, a service firm has tapped most of its potential market and may have lost much of its original uniqueness. At this stage, operational efficiencies become particularly important as the competition becomes largely price based. Because of the age of the facilities, capacity issues generally focus on remodeling and replacement.

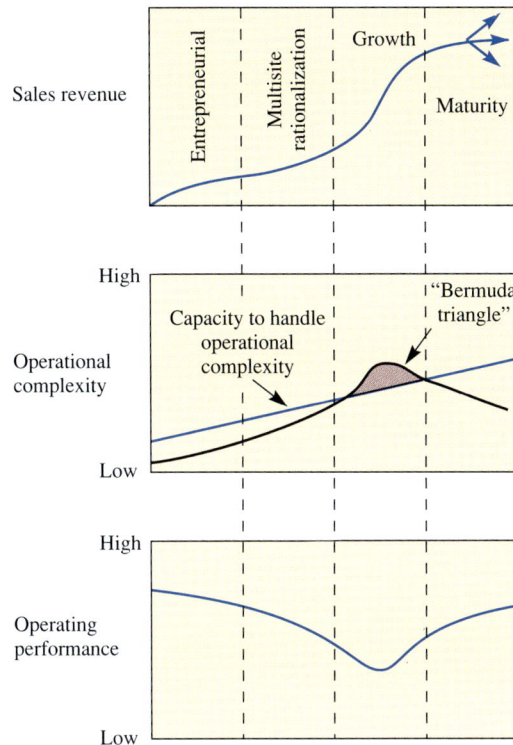

E X H I B I T 8.9
*Operational
Complexity*

Source: Sasser, Olsen, and Wycoff, *Op. Cit,* p. 561.

Sometimes, however, it is necessary to modify the service concept because it has become stale over time. If the concept is revitalized, capacity planning must address the complicated issue of duplicating any required changes across the entire existing system.

8.6   CONCLUSION

Strategic capacity planning involves an investment decision that must match resource capabilities to a long-term demand forecast. As discussed in this chapter, factors to be taken into account in selecting capacity additions for both manufacturing and services include

- The likely effects of economies of scale.
- The effects of experience curves.
- The impact of changing facility focus and balance among production stages.
- The degree of flexibility of facilities and the workforce.

For services in particular, key considerations include (1) the effect of capacity changes on the quality of the service offering and (2) the implications of increasing the number of services in parallel with increasing the number of service outlets. In the next chapter, we discuss the related issue of where to locate the firm's facilities.

8.7   SOLVED PROBLEM

Calcom (a new hand-held calculator manufacturing company based in Los Angeles) has demand from both domestic and foreign markets. Currently Calcom has produced 100,000 calculators, and the unit production cost is $3.50. The company believes that an 85 percent experience curve is about right for its production capacity.

a. What is Calcom's unit production cost if the cumulative production volume reaches 800,000?

b. At approximately what cumulative production volume can Calcom reduce production cost to below $2.55?

Solution

a. An 85 percent learning curve means that Calcom's production cost will fall 15 percent when the cumulative production doubles. We can tabulate the calculation as follows:

Cumulative Production Volume	Unit Production Cost
100,000	$3.5
200,000	$3.5 × 0.85 = $2.98
400,000	$2.98 × 0.85 = $2.53
800,000	$2.53 × 0.85 = $2.15

Therefore, when Calcom's cumulative production volume reaches 800,000, the unit cost will be $2.15.

b. As the preceding table shows, unit cost falls to $2.53 when cumulative production volume is 400,000. Hence unit production cost drops below $2.55 when cumulative volume approaches 400,000.

8.8   REVIEW AND DISCUSSION QUESTIONS

1. What were the capacity problems encountered at the opening of Euro Disney? What lessons are there for other service companies in planning capacity?

2. List some practical limits to economies of scale; that is, when should a plant stop growing?

3. What are some capacity balance problems faced by the following organizations or facilities?
   a. An airline terminal.
   b. A university computing center.
   c. A clothing manufacturer.

4. What is the cause of the "Bermuda triangle" phenomenon in multisite services? Does it exist in growing manufacturing firms?

5. What are some major capacity considerations in a hospital? How do they differ from those of a factory?

6. Management may choose to build up capacity in anticipation of demand or in response to developing demand. Cite the advantages and disadvantages of both approaches.

7. What is capacity balance? Why is it hard to achieve? What methods are used to deal with capacity imbalances?

8. What are some reasons for a plant to maintain a capacity cushion? How about a negative capacity cushion?

9. At first glance, the concepts of the focused factory and capacity flexibility may seem to contradict each other. Do they really?

8.9   PROBLEMS

1. AlwaysRain Irrigation, Inc., would like to determine capacity requirements for the next four years. Currently two production lines are in place for bronze and plastic sprinklers. Three types of sprinklers are available in both bronze and plastic: 90-degree nozzle sprinklers, 180-degree nozzle sprinklers, and 360-degree nozzle sprinklers. Management has forecasted demand for the next four years as follows:

	Yearly Demand			
	1 (in 000s)	**2 (in 000s)**	**3 (in 000s)**	**4 (in 000s)**
Plastic 90	32	44	55	56
Plastic 180	15	16	17	18
Plastic 360	50	55	64	67
Bronze 90	7	8	9	10
Bronze 180	3	4	5	6
Bronze 360	11	12	15	18

Both production lines can produce all the different types of nozzles. Each bronze machine requires two operators to run and can produce up to 12,000 sprinklers. The plastic injection molding machine requires four operators to run and can produce up to 200,000 sprinklers. Three bronze machines and only one injection molding machine are available. What are the capacity requirements for the next four years?

2. Suppose that AlwaysRain Irrigation's marketing department will undertake an intense ad campaign for the bronze sprinklers, which are more expensive but also more durable than the plastic ones. Forecasted demand for the next four years is

	Yearly Demand			
	1 (in 000s)	**2 (in 000s)**	**3 (in 000s)**	**4 (in 000s)**
Plastic 90	32	44	55	56
Plastic 180	15	16	17	18
Plastic 360	50	55	64	67
Bronze 90	11	15	18	23
Bronze 180	6	5	6	9
Bronze 360	15	16	17	20

What are the capacity implications of the marketing campaign?

3. In anticipation of the ad campaign, AlwaysRain bought an additional bronze machine. Will this be enough to ensure that enough capacity is available?

4. Suppose that operators have enough training to operate both the bronze machines and the injection molding machine for the plastic sprinklers. Currently AlwaysRain has 10 such employees. In anticipation of the ad campaign described in Problem 2, management approved the purchase of two additional bronze machines. What are the labor requirement implications?

5. A builder has located a piece of property that he would like to buy and eventually build on. The land is currently zoned for four homes per acre, but he is planning to request new zoning. What he builds depends on approval of zoning requests and your analysis of this

problem to advise him. With his input and your help, the decision process has been reduced to the following costs, alternatives, and probabilities:

Cost of land: $2 million.

Probability of rezoning: .60.

If the land is rezoned, there will be additional costs for new roads, lighting, and so on, of $1 million.

If the land is rezoned, the contractor must decide whether to build a shopping center or 1,500 apartments that the tentative plan shows would be possible. If he builds a shopping center, there is a 70 percent chance that he can sell the shopping center to a large department chain for $4 million over his construction cost, which excludes the land; and there is a 30 percent chance that he can sell it to an insurance company for $5 million over his construction cost (also excluding the land). If, instead of the shopping center, he decides to build the 1,500 apartments, he places probabilities on the profits as follows: There is a 60 percent chance that he can sell the apartments to a real estate investment corporation for $3,000 each over his construction cost; there is a 40 percent chance that he can get only $2,000 each over his construction cost. (Both exclude his land cost.)

If the land is not rezoned, he will comply with the existing zoning restrictions and simply build 600 homes on which he expects to make $4,000 over his construction cost on each one (excluding his cost of land).

Draw a decision tree of the problem and determine the best solution and the expected net profit.

C A S E

8.10 C A S E
Shouldice Hospital—A Cut Above

Shouldice Hospital in Canada is widely known for one thing—hernia repair! In fact, that is the only operation it performs, and it performs a great many of them. Over the past two decades this small 90-bed hospital has averaged 7,500 operations annually. Patients' ties to Shouldice do not end when they leave the hospital. Every year the gala Hernia Reunion dinner (with complimentary hernia inspection) draws in excess of 1,000 former patients, some of who have been attending the event for over 30 years.

A number of notable features in Shouldice's service delivery system contribute to its success. (1) Shouldice only accepts patients with the uncomplicated external hernias, and it uses a superior technique developed for this type of hernia by Dr. Shouldice during World War II. (2) Patients are subject to early ambulation which promotes healing. (Patients literally walk off the operating table and engage in light exercise throughout their stay, which lasts only three days.) (3) Its country club atmosphere, gregarious nursing staff, and built-in socializing make a surprisingly pleasant experience out of an inherently unpleasant medical problem. Regular times are set aside for tea, cookies, and socializing. All patients are paired up with a roommate with similar background and interests.

The Production System

The medical facilities at Shouldice consist of five operating rooms, a patient recovery room, a laboratory, and six

Shouldice Hospital is set in a 17,000-square-foot manor house on a 130-acre estate 15 miles north of Toronto. Patients are encouraged to stroll the grounds, play billiards, and practice on the putting green—all of which foster patient bonding as well as healing.

examination rooms. In addition to the 90 regular hospital beds, Shouldice has 14 hostel rooms that are used during busy periods for patients waiting overnight before their surgery.

Shouldice performs, on average, 150 operations per week, with patients generally staying at the hospital for three days. Although operations are performed only five days a week, the remainder of the hospital is in operation continuously to attend to recovering patients.

An operation at Shouldice Hospital is performed by one of the 12 full-time surgeons assisted by one of seven part-time assistant surgeons. Surgeons generally take about one hour to prepare for and perform each hernia operation, and they operate on four patients per day. During the afternoon, between 1 and 3 PM, up to six of those surgeons who do not have afternoon operations scheduled spend their time examining incoming patients. The surgeons' day ends at 4 PM, although they can expect to be on call every 14th night and every 10th weekend.

The Shouldice Experience

All patients undergo a screening exam prior to setting a date for their operation. Patients in the Toronto area are encouraged to walk in to have the diagnosis done. Out-of-town patients are mailed a medical information questionnaire, which is used for the diagnosis. A small percentage of the patients who are overweight or otherwise represent an undue medical risk are refused treatment. The remaining patients receive a confirmation card with the scheduled date for their operation. A patient's folder is transferred to the reception desk once he has confirmed his arrival date.

Patients arrive at the clinic between 1 and 3 PM the day before their surgery. After a short wait, they receive a brief pre-operative examination. They are then sent to see an admissions clerk to complete any necessary paperwork. Patients are next directed to one of the two nurses' stations for blood and urine tests and then are shown to their rooms. They spend the remaining time before orientation getting settled and acquainting themselves with their roommates.

Orientation begins at 5 PM, followed by dinner in the common dining room. Later in the evening, at 9 PM, patients gather in the lounge area for tea and cookies. Here new patients can talk with patients who have already had their surgery. Bedtime is between 9:30 and 10 PM.

On the day of the operation, patients with early operations are awakened at 5:30 AM for pre-operative sedation. The first operations begin at 7:30 AM. Shortly before an operation starts, the patient is administered a local anesthetic, leaving him alert and fully aware of the proceedings. At the conclusion of the operation, the patient is invited to walk from the operating table to a nearby wheelchair, waiting to return him to his room. After a brief period of rest, he is

encouraged to get up and start exercising. By 9 PM that day, he is in the lounge having cookies and tea, and talking with new, incoming patients.

The skin clips holding the incision together are loosened and some are removed the next day. The remainder are removed the following morning just before the patient is discharged.

Future Plans

The management of Shouldice is thinking of expanding the hospital's capacity to serve considerable unsatisfied demand. To this effect, the vice president is seriously considering two options. The first involves adding one more day of operations (Saturday) to the existing five-day schedule, which would increase capacity by 20 percent. The second option is to add another floor of rooms to the hospital, increasing the number of beds by 50 percent. This would require more aggressive scheduling of the operating rooms.

The administrator of the hospital, however, is concerned about maintaining control over the quality of the service delivered. He thinks the facility is already getting very good utilization. The doctors and the staff are happy with their jobs and the patients are satisfied with the service. According to him, further expansion of capacity might make it hard to maintain the same kind of working relationships and attitudes.

Questions

Exhibit C8.1 is a room occupancy table for the existing system. Each row in the table follows the patients that checked in on a given day. The columns indicate the number of patients in the hospital on a given day. For example, the first row of the table shows that 30 people checked in on Monday and were in the hospital for Monday, Tuesday, and Wednesday. By summing the columns of the table for Wednesday, we see that there are 90 patients staying in the hospital that day.

1. How well is the hospital currently utilizing its beds?

2. Develop a similar table to show the effects of adding operations on Saturday. (Assume that 30 operations would still be performed each day.) How would this affect the utilization of the bed capacity? Is this capacity sufficient for the additional patients?

3. Now look at the effect of increasing the number of beds by 50 percent. How many operations could the hospital perform per day before running out of bed capacity? (Assume five operations per week, the same number performed on each day.) How well would the new resources be utilized relative to the current operation? Could the hospital really perform this many operations? Why? (Hint: Look at the capacity of the 12 surgeons and the five operating rooms.)

Source: This case is based on S. Oliver, "A Canadian Hospital Does Brisk Business in Rupture Repairs," *The Wall Street Journal,* February 7, 1978; James L. Heskitt, W. Earl Sasser, and Christopher W. L. Hart, *Service Breakthroughs* (New York: The Free Press, 1990; "Shouldice Hospital Limited," Harvard Business School Case 5-686-120 (Boston: Harvard Business School, 1986); and personal interviews.

E X H I B I T C8.1   *Operations with 90 beds (30 patients per day)*

		Beds Required							
		Monday	**Tuesday**	**Wednesday**	**Thursday**	**Friday**	**Saturday**	**Sunday**	
	Monday	30	30	30					
	Tuesday		30	30	30				
	Wednesday			30	30	30			
Check-in on	Thursday				30	30	30		
	Friday								
	Saturday								
	Sunday	30	30					30	
	Total	60	90	90	90	60	30	30	450

8.11   SELECTED BIBLIOGRAPHY

Bakke, Nils Arne, and Ronald Hellberg. "The Challenges of Capacity Planning." *International Journal of Production Economics* 31–30 (1993), pp. 243–64.

Hammesfahr, R. D. Jack, James A. Pope, and Alireza Ardalan. "Strategic Planning for Production Capacity." *International Journal of Operations and Production Management* 13, no. 5 (1993), pp. 41–53.

Haywood-Farmer, John, and Jean Nollet. *Services Plus: Effective Services Management.* Boucherville, Quebec, Canada: G. Morin Publisher Ltd., 1991.

Johnston, Robert, Stuart Chambers, Christine Harland, Alan Harrison, and Nigel Slack. *Cases in Operations Management.* London, England: Pitman, 1993.

Martin, Hugh F. "Mass Customization at Personal Lines Insurance Center". Planning Review 21, no. 4 (July–August 1993), pp. 27, 56.

Meyer, Christopher. *Fast Cycle Time: How to Align Purpose, Strategy and Structure for Speed.* New York: Free Press, 1993.

National Center for Manufacturing Sciences. *Competing in World-Class Manufacturing: Amber's 21st Century Challenge.* Homewood, IL: Irwin, 1990.

Pine II, B. Joseph. *Mass Customization: The New Frontier in Business Competition.* Boston: Harvard Business School Press, 1993.

Linear Programming

SUPPLEMENT OUTLINE

KEY TERMS

Objective Function

Constraint Equation

Slack Variable

Pivot Method

Maximization

Minimization

Sensitivity Analysis

Shadow Price

Degeneracy

Union Rescue Mission

Charitable institutions that feed the homeless face the difficult problems of meeting the minimal daily requirements for nutrition and providing for preferences in human taste, while operating on very limited funds. The Union Rescue Mission of Knoxville, Tennessee, uses linear programming tools to determine the minimal cost of providing dietary and intangible needs. Such analysis also supports purchasing decisions by attaching a relative dollar figure on how increased variety and taste in food materials will be valued.[1]

Judging Performance Appraisal Consistency

Three researchers used linear programming to determine consistency of performance appraisals of major league baseball players. The model calculated weights for objective performance measures that best fit the subjective ranking assigned to each player. Comparison of the LP results with the appraisal ranking made comparisons within the league possible. Such an application of LP would be equally applicable to evaluating the consistency of business managers' performance appraisals of employees.[2]

Valuing Forest Resources

When the New Zealand government was privatizing the state-run forest plantations they needed to value the expected cash flows from the forests to determine a fair selling price. Using linear programming, a forest estate modeling system was developed that calculated renewable harvesting and log allocation of the 14 districts over a 40 to 70 year time horizon. The expected cash flows from these operations were used to help set reserve prices, and indicative valuations. The potential buyers also used the system to help develop their bidding strategies.[3]

---

[1]Mary C. Holcomb and Elden L. DePorter, "A Linear Programming Application Helps Feed the Homeless," *Computers & Industrial Engineering* 19, no. 1-4 (1990), pp. 548–52.

[2]Christopher Zappe, William Webster, and Ira Horowitz, "Using Linear Programming to Determine Post-Facto Consistency in Performance Evaluations of Major League Baseball Players," *Interfaces,* November/December 1993, pp. 107–113.

[3]Bruce R. Manley and John A. Threadgill, "LP Used for Valuation and Planning of New Zealand Plantation Forests," *Interfaces,* November/December, 1991, pp. 66–79.

Simplex Method

Aggregate production planning: Finding the minimum-cost production schedule, including production rate change costs, given constraints on size of workforce and inventory levels.

Service productivity analysis: Comparing how efficiently different service outlets are using their resources compared to the best performing unit. (This approach is called data envelopment analysis).

Product planning: Finding the optimal product mix where several products have different costs and resource requirements (e.g., finding the optimal blend of constituents for gasolines, paints, human diets, animal feeds).

Product routing: Finding the optimal routing for a product that must be processed sequentially through several machine centers, with each machine in a center having its own cost and output characteristics.

Process control: Minimizing the amount of scrap material generated by cutting steel, leather, or fabric from a roll or sheet of stock material.

Inventory control: Finding the optimal combination of products to stock in a warehouse or store.

Transportation Method

Aggregate production planning: Finding the minimum-cost production schedule (excluding production rate change costs).

Distribution scheduling: Finding the optimal shipping schedule for distributing products between factories and warehouses or warehouses and retailers.

Plant location studies: Finding the optimal location of a new plant by evaluating shipping costs between alternative locations and supply and demand sources.

Materials handling: Finding the minimum-cost routings of material handling devices (e.g., forklift trucks) between departments in a plant and of hauling materials from a supply yard to work sites by trucks, with each truck having different capacity and performance capabilities.

*Grouped by the two primary methods covered in the supplement. (The graphical method is not included in this lising since it is limited to problems with two variables.)

Tool time! In this supplement we present the basics of one of the most powerful tools of management science, linear programming.

Linear programming (or simply **LP**) refers to several related mathematical techniques that are used to allocate limited resources among competing demands in an optimal way. LP is the most popular of the approaches falling under the general heading of mathematical optimization techniques, and, as can be seen in "Typical Operations Management Applications of Linear Programming" above, has been applied to a myriad of operations management problems. Our focus here is on the simplex method (which can solve any type of linear programming problem) and the graphical and transportation methods (which are useful in dealing with certain special cases). In addition to illustrating how linear programming methods lead to an optimum solution for a given problem, we will discuss shadow prices and other valuable "free information" provided by the simplex method.

There are five essential conditions in a problem situation for linear programming to pertain. First, there must be *limited resources* (e.g., a limited number of workers, equipment, finances, and material); otherwise there would be no problem. Second, there must be an *explicit objective* (such as maximize profit or minimize cost). Third, there must be *linearity* (two is twice as good as one; if it takes three hours to make a part, then two parts would take six hours, three parts would take nine hours). Fourth, there must be *homogeneity* (the products produced on a machine are identical, or all the hours available from a worker are equally productive). Fifth is *divisibility:* Normal linear programming assumes that products and resources can be subdivided into fractions. If this subdivision is not possible (such as flying half an airplane or hiring one-fourth of a person), a modification of linear programming, called *integer programming,* can be used.

When a single objective is to be maximized (e.g., profit) or minimized (e.g., costs), we can use *linear programming.* When multiple objectives exist, *goal programming* is used. If a problem is best solved in stages or time frames, this is *dynamic programming.* Other restrictions on the nature of the problem may require that it be solved by other variations of the technique, such as *nonlinear programming* or *quadratic programming.*

S8.1   THE LINEAR PROGRAMMING MODEL

Stated formally, the linear programming problem entails an optimizing process in which nonnegative values for a set of decision variables $X_1, X_2. . . X_n$ are selected so as to maximize (or minimize) an objective function in the form

$$\text{Maximize (minimize) } Z = C_1X_1 + C_2X_2 + . . . + C_nX_n$$

subject to resource constraints in the form

$$A_{11} X_1 + A_{12}X_2 + . . . + A_{1n}X_n \leq B_1$$
$$A_{21}X_1 + A_{22}X_2 + . . . + A_{2n}X_n \leq B_2$$
$$.$$
$$.$$
$$.$$
$$A_{m1}X_1 + A_{m2}X_2 + . . . + A_{mn}X_n \leq B_m$$

where C_n, A_{mn}, and B_m are given constants.

Depending on the problem, the constraints may also be stated with equal-to signs ($=$) or greater-than-or-equal-to signs ($\geq$).

S8.2   GRAPHICAL LINEAR PROGRAMMING

Though limited in application to problems involving two decision variables (or three variables for three-dimensional graphing), **graphical linear programming** provides a quick insight into the nature of linear programming and illustrates what takes place in the general simplex method described later.

We describe the steps involved in the graphical method in the context of a sample problem, that of the Puck and Pawn Company, which manufactures hockey sticks and chess sets. Each hockey stick yields an incremental profit of $2 and each chess set, $4. A hockey stick requires four hours of processing at machine center A and two hours at machine center B. A chess set requires six hours at machine center A, six hours at machine center B, and one hour at machine center C. Machine center A has a maximum of 120 hours of available capacity per day, machine center B has 72 hours, and machine center C has 10 hours.

If the company wishes to maximize profit, how many hockey sticks and chess sets should be produced per day?

1. Formulate the Problem in Mathematical Terms   If H is the number of hockey sticks and C is the number of chess sets, to maximize profit the **objective function** may be stated as

Maximize $Z = \$2H + \$4C$

The maximization will be subject to the following constraints:

$4H + 6C \leq 120$ (machine center A constraint)
$2H + 6C \leq 72$ (machine center B constraint)
$\quad 1C \leq 10$ (machine center C constraint)
$\quad H, C \geq 0$

This formulation satisfies the five requirements for standard LP stated in the second paragraph of this supplement:

1. There are limited resources (a finite number of hours available at each machine center).
2. There is an explicit objective function (we know what each variable is worth and what the goal is in solving the problem).
3. The equations are linear (no exponents or cross products).
4. The resources are homogeneous (everything is in one unit of measure, machine hours).
5. The decision varibles are divisible and non-negative (we can make a fractional part of a hockey stick or chess set; however, if this were deemed undesirable, we would have to use integer programming).

2. Plot Constraint Equations   The **constraint equations** are easily plotted by letting one variable equal zero and solving for the axis intercept of the other. (The inequality portions of the restrictions are disregarded for this step.) For the machine center A constraint equation when $H = 0$, $C = 20$, and when $C = 0$, $H = 30$. For the machine center B constraint equation, when $H = 0$, $C = 12$, and when $C = 0$, $H = 36$. For the machine center C constraint equation, $C = 10$ for all values of H. These lines are graphed in Exhibit S8.1.

3. Determine the Area of Feasibility   The direction of inequality signs in each constraint determines the area where a feasible solution is found. In this case, all inequalities are of the less-than-or-equal-to variety, which means that it would be impossible to produce any combination of products that would lie to the right of any constraint line on the graph. The region of feasible solutions is unshaded on the graph and forms a convex polygon. A convex polygon exists when a line drawn between any two points in the polygon stays within the boundaries of that polygon. If this condition of convexity does not exist, the problem is either incorrectly set up or not amenable to linear programming.

4. Plot the Objective Function   The objective function may be plotted by assuming some arbitrary total profit figure and then solving for the axis coordinates, as was done for the constraint equations. Other terms for the objective function, when used in this context, are the *iso-profit* or *equal contribution line,* because it shows all possible production combinations for any given profit figure. For example, from the dotted line closest to the origin on the graph, we can determine all possible combinations of hockey sticks and chess sets that yield $32 by picking a point on the line and reading the num-

E X H I B I T S8.1

Graph of Hockey Stick and Chess Set Problem

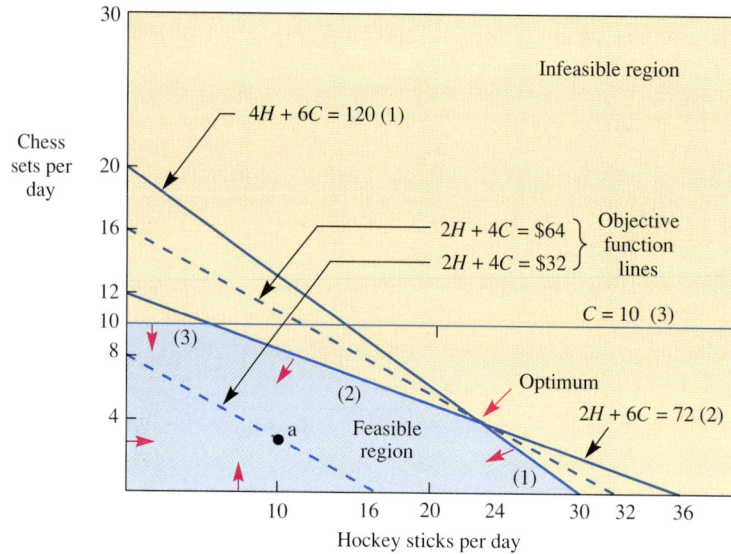

H	C	Explanation
0	120/6 = 20	Intersection of Constraint (1) and *C* axis
120/4 = 30	0	Intersection of Constraint (1) and *H* axis
0	72/6 = 12	Intersection of Constraint (2) and *C* axis
72/2 = 36	0	Intersection of Constraint (2) and *H* axis
0	10	Intersection of Constraint (3) and *C* axis
0	32/4 = 8	Intersection of $32 iso-profit line (objective function) and *C* axis
32/2 = 16	0	Intersection of $32 iso-profit line and *H* axis
0	64/4 = 16	Intersection of $64 iso-profit line and *C* axis
64/2 = 32	0	Intersection of $64 iso-profit line and *H* axis

ber of each product that can be made at that point. The combination yielding $32 at point *a* would be 10 hockey sticks and three chess sets. This can be verified by substituting $H = 10$ and $C = 3$ in the objective function:

$$\$2(10) + \$4(3) = \$20 + \$12 = \$32$$

5. Find the Optimum Point It can be shown mathematically that the optimal combination of decision variables is always found at an extreme point (corner point) of the convex polygon. In Exhibit S8.1 there are four corner points (excluding the origin), and we can determine which one is the optimum by either of two approaches. The first approach is to find the values of the various corner solutions algebraically. This entails simultaneously solving the equations of various pairs of intersecting lines and substituting the quantities of the resultant variables in the objective function. For example, the calculations for the intersection of $2H + 6C = 72$ and $C = 10$ are as follows:

Substituting $C = 10$ in $2H + 6C = 72$ gives $2H + 6(10) = 72$, $2H = 12$, or $H = 6$. Substituting $H = 6$ and $C = 10$ in the objective function, we get

$$\text{Profit} = \$2H + \$4C = \$2(6) + \$4(10)$$
$$= \$12 + \$40 = \$52$$

A variation of this approach is to read the *H* and *C* quantities directly from the graph and substitute these quantities into the objective function, as shown in the previous calculation. The drawback in this approach is that in problems with a large number of constraint equations, there will be many possible points to evaluate, and the procedure of testing each one mathematically is inefficient.

The second and generally preferred approach entails using the objective function or iso-profit line directly to find the optimum point. The procedure involves simply drawing a straight line *parallel* to any arbitrarily selected initial iso-profit line so that the iso-profit line is farthest from the origin of the graph. (In cost-minimization problems, the objective would be to draw the line through the point closest to the origin.) In Exhibit S8.1, the dashed line labeled $2H + $4C = $64 intersects the most extreme point. Note that the initial arbitrarily selected iso-profit line is necessary to display the slope of the objective function for the particular problem.[4] This is important since a different objective function (try profit $= 3H + 3C$) might indicate that some other point is farthest from the origin. Given that $2H + $4C = $64 is optimal, the amount of each variable to produce can be read from the graph: 24 hockey sticks and four chess sets. No other combination of the products yields a greater profit.

S8.3   THE SIMPLEX METHOD

The **simplex method** is an algebraic procedure that, through a series of repetitive operations, progressively approaches an optimal solution.[5] Theoretically, the simplex method can solve a problem consisting of any number of variables and constraints, although for problems containing more than, say, four variables or four constraint equations, the actual calculations are best left to the computer. Still, to know how to construct equations that would be put into a program, and to be able to use the output from the computer program, it is well worth the effort to go through the simplex method manually.

There are a number of technical steps in the simplex method, and each one is described in detail and summarized at the end of the section. We use the hockey stick and chess set problem to demonstrate the procedure involved.

The Six-Step Solution Procedure

Step 1: Formulate the Problem   Recall that to maximize profit we had

Maximize $Z = \$2H + \$4C$

subject to
(1) $4H + 6C \leq 120$ (machine center A constraint)
(2) $2H + 6C \leq 72$ (machine center B constraint)
(3) $1C \leq 10$ (machine center C constraint)
          $H, C \geq 0$ (nonnegativity requirement)

Step 2: Set Up Initial Tableau with Slack Variables in Solution   To use the simplex method requires two major adjustments to the problem as stated: (1) the introduction of slack variables and (2) the establishment of a solution table or tableau.

---

[4]The slope of the objective function is -2. If $P =$ profit, $P = \$2H + \$4C$; $\$2H = P - \$4C$; $H = p/2 - 2C$. Thus the slope is -2.
[5]Simplex does not mean "simple"; it is a term used in *n*-space geometry.

Introduce slack variables Each constraint equation is expanded to include a slack variable. A **slack variable,** which may be thought of as an idle resource in a practical sense, computationally represents the amount required to make one side of a constraint equation equal to the other—in other words, to convert the inequalities to equalities. For our problem, we need three slack variables: S_1 for the first constraint equation, S_2 for the second, and S_3 for the third.

The constraint equations are

$$4H + 6C + 1S_1 = 120$$
$$2H + 6C + 1S_2 = 72$$
$$1C + 1S_3 = 10$$

So that all variables are represented in each equation, each slack variable not originally associated with a constraint equation is given a zero coefficient and added to that equation. Adjusting the system of equations in this way gives

$$4H + 6C + 1S_1 + 0S_2 + 0S_3 = 120$$
$$2H + 6C + 0S_1 + 1S_2 + 0S_3 = 72$$
$$0H + 1C + 0S_1 + 0S_2 + 1S_3 = 10$$

Note that the variable H, with a zero coefficient, is entered in the third equation to ensure that it also will be represented in all equations. Likewise, the objective function reflects the addition of slack variables, but since they yield no profit, their coefficient is $0:

$$Z = \$2H + \$4C + \$0S_1 + \$0S_2 + \$0S_3$$

Construct initial tableau A tableau (see Exhibit S8.2) is a convenient way of setting up the problem for simplex computation. A tableau tells us

1. The variables in the solution at that point.
2. The profit associated with the solution.
3. The variable (if any) that adds most to profit if brought into the solution.
4. The amount of reduction in the variables in the solution that results from introducing one unit of each variable. This amount is termed the *substitution rate*.
5. The worth of an additional unit (e.g., hour) of resource capacity. This is called a *shadow price*.

The first four features are discussed in reference to the first tableau; the last one is considered later.

E X H I B I T S8.2
Initial Tableau of the Hockey Stick and Chess Set Problem

C_j	C_j Row	$2	$4	$0	$0	$0		Machine
Column	Solution Mix	H	C	S_1	S_2	S_3	Quantity	Center
$0	S_1	4	6	1	0	0	120	A
$0	S_2	2	6	0	1	0	72	B
$0	S_3	0	1	0	0	1	10←	C
	Z_j	$0	$0	$0	$0	$0	$0	
	$C_j - Z_j$	$2	$4	$0	$0	$0		
			↑					

The top row of Exhibit S8.2 contains the C_j's (the contribution to total profit associated with the production of one unit of each alternative product). This row is a direct restatement of the coefficients of the variables in the objective function, and therefore remains the same for all subsequent tableaus. The first column, headed by C_j, merely lists, for convenience, the profit per unit of the variables included in the solution at any stage of the problem.

The variables chosen for the first tableau are listed under Solution Mix. As you can see, only slack variables are considered in the initial solution, and their profit coefficients are zero, which is indicated by the C_j column.

The constraint variables are listed to the right of Solution Mix, and under each one is the particular variable's coefficient in each constraint equation. That is, 4, 6, 1, 0, and 0 are the coefficients of the machine center A constraint; 2, 6, 0, 1, and 0 for machine center B; and 0, 1, 0, 0, and 1 for machine center C.

Substitution rates can be ascertained from the numbers as well. For example, consider 4, 2, and 0, listed under H in the third column. For every unit of product H introduced into the solution, four units of S_1, two units of S_2, and zero units of S_3 must be withdrawn from the quantities available. The entries in the Quantity column refer to how many units of each resource are available in each machine center. In the initial tableau, this is a restatement of the right side of each constraint equation. With the exception of the value in the quantity column, the Z_j values in the second row from the bottom refer to the amount of *gross* profit that is given up by introducing one unit of that variable into the solution. The subscript j refers to the specific variable being considered. The Z_j value under the quantity column is the total profit for the solution. In the initial solution of a simplex problem, all values of Z_j are zero because no real product is being produced (all machines are idle), and hence there is no gross profit to be lost if they are replaced.

The bottom row of the tableau contains the *net* profit per unit, obtained by introducing one unit of a given variable into the solution. This row is designated the $C_j - Z_j$ row. The procedure for calculating Z_j and each $C_j - Z_j$ appears in Exhibit S8.3.

The initial solution to the problem is read directly from Exhibit S8.2: The company produces 120 units of S_1, 72 units of S_2, and 10 units of S_3. Total profit from this solution is $0. Thus, no capacity has yet been allocated and no real product produced.

Step 3: Determine Which Variable to Bring into Solution   An improved solution is possible if there is a positive value in the $C_j - Z_j$ row. Recall that this row provides the net profit obtained by adding one unit of its associated column variable in the solution. In this example, there are two positive values to choose from: $2, associated with H, and $4, associated with C. Since our objective is to maximize profit, the logical choice is to

---

EXHIBIT S8.3

Calculations of Z_j and $C_j - Z_j$

C_j H	C_j C	C_j S_1	C_j S_2	C_j S_3	C_j Quantity
$0 × 4 = 0	$0 × 6 = 0	$0 × 1 = 0	$0 × 0 = 0	$0 × 0 = 0	$0 × 120 = 0
+	+	+	+	+	+
$0 × 2 = 0	$0 × 6 = 0	$0 × 0 = 0	$0 × 1 = 0	$0 × 0 = 0	$0 × 72 = 0
+	+	+	+	+	+
$0 × 0 = 0	$0 × 1 = 0	$0 × 0 = 0	$0 × 0 = 0	$0 × 1 = 0	$0 × 10 = 0
Z_H = $0	Z_C = $0	Z_{S_1} = $0	Z_{S_2} = $0	Z_{S_3} = $0	Z_Q = $0

$C_j - Z_j$ calculations:

$C_H - Z_H = \$2 - 0 = \$2$ $C_{S_1} - Z_{S_1} = \$0 - 0 = \$0$

$C_C - Z_C = \$4 - 0 = \$4$ $C_{S_2} - Z_{S_2} = \$0 - 0 = \$0$

$C_{S_3} - Z_{S_3} = \$0 - 0 = \$0$

pick the variable with the largest payoff to enter the solution, so variable C will be introduced. The column associated with this variable is designated by the small arrow beneath column C in Exhibit S8.2. (Only one variable at a time can be added in developing each improved solution.)

Step 4: Determine Which Variable to Replace

Given that it is desirable to introduce C into the solution, the next question is to determine which variable it will replace. To make this determination, we divide each amount in the Quantity column by the amount in the comparable row of the C column and choose the variable associated with the smallest positive quotient as the one to be replaced:

For the S_1 row: $120/6 = 20$
For the S_2 row: $72/6 = 12$
For the S_3 row: $10/1 = 10$

Since the smallest quotient is 10, S_3 will be replaced, and its row is identified by the small arrow to the right of the tableau in Exhibit S8.2. This is the maximum amount of C that can be brought into the solution. That is, production of more than 10 units of C would exceed the available capacity of machine C. This can be verified mathematically by considering the constraint $C \le 10$ and visually by examining the graphical representation of the problem in Exhibit S8.1. The graph also shows that the 20 and 12 are the C intercepts of the other two constraints, and if $C \le 10$ were removed, the amount of C introduced could be increased by two units.

Step 5: Calculate New Row Values for Entering Variable

The introduction of C into the solution requires that the entire S_3 row be replaced. The values for C, the replacing row, are obtained by dividing each value presently in the S_3 row by the value in column C in the same row. This value is termed the *intersectional element* since it occurs at the intersection of a row and column. This intersectional relationship is abstracted from the rest of the tableau and the necessary divisions are shown in Exhibit S8.4.

E X H I B I T S8.4
Calculation of New Row Values for Entering Variable

	C	
	6	
	6	
S_3	0 ① 0 0 1 10	$0/1 = 0,\ 1/1 = 1,\ 0/1 = 0,\ 0/1 = 0,\ 1/1 = 1,\ 10/1 = 10$
	\$4	

E X H I B I T S8.5   *Pivot Method*

Old S_1 Row	−	Inter- sectional Element of Old S_1 Row	×	Corre- sponding Element of New C Row	=	Updated S_1 Row	Old S_2 Row	−	Inter- sectional Element of Old S_2 Row	×	Corre- sponding Element of New C Row	=	Updated S_2 Row
4	−	(6	×	0)	=	4	2	−	(6	×	0)	=	2
6	−	(6	×	1)	=	0	6	−	(6	×	1)	=	0
1	−	(6	×	0)	=	1	0	−	(6	×	0)	=	0
0	−	(6	×	0)	=	0	1	−	(6	×	0)	=	1
0	−	(6	×	1)	=	−6	0	−	(6	×	1)	=	−6
120	−	(6	×	10)	=	60	72	−	(6	×	10)	=	12

Step 6: Revise Remaining Rows   The new third-row values (now associated with C) are 0, 1, 0, 0, 1, and 10, which in this case are identical to those of the old third row.

Introducing a new variable into the problem affects the values of the remaining variables, and a second set of calculations must be performed to update the tableau. Specifically, we want to determine the effect of introducing C on the S_1 and S_2 rows. These calculations can be carried out by using what is termed the **pivot method** or by algebraic substitution. The pivot method is a more mechanical procedure and is generally used in practice, while algebraic substitution is more useful in explaining the logic of the updating process. The procedure using the pivot method to arrive at new values for S_1 and S_2 is shown in Exhibit S8.5. (In essence, the method subtracts six times row 3 from both the S_1 and S_2 rows.)

Updating by algebraic substitution entails substituting the entire equation for the entering row into each of the remaining rows and solving for the revised values for each row's variable. The procedure, summarized in Exhibit S8.6, illustrates the fact that linear programming via the simplex method is essentially the solving of a number of simultaneous equations.

Isolating the variable coefficients yields the same values for the new S_1 row as did the pivot method: 4, 0, 1, 0, -6, 60.

The results of the computations carried out in Steps 3 through 6, along with the calculations of Z_j and $C_j - Z_j$ are shown in the revised tableau, Exhibit S8.7. In mathematical programming terminology, we have completed one *iteration* of the problem.

In evaluating this solution, we note two things: The profit is $40, but, more important, further improvement is possible since there is a positive value in the $C_j - Z_j$ row.

To find new values for S_1,
1. Reconstruct old S_1 row as a constraint with slack variables added (from first tableau).
   $$4H + 6C + 1S_1 + 0S_2 + 0S_3 = 120$$

2. Write entering row as a constraint with slack variables added. (These are the values computed in Exhibit S8.4.)
   $$0H + C + 0S_1 + 0S_2 + 1S_3 = 10$$

3. Rearrange entering row in terms of C, the entering variable.
   $$10 - S_3$$

4. Substitute $10 - S_3$ for C in the first equation (the old S_1 row) and solve for each variable coefficient.
   $$4H + 6(10 - S_3) + 1S_1 = 120$$
   $$4H + 60 - 6S_3 + 1S_1 = 120$$
   $$4H + 1S_1 - 6S_3 = 120 - 60$$
   $$4H + 1S_1 - 6S_3 = 60$$
   or
   $$4H + 0C + 1S_1 + 0S_2 - 6S_3 = 60$$

E X H I B I T   S8.6

Algebraic Substitution

C_j		$2	$4	$0	$0	$0	
	Solution Mix	H	C	S_1	S_2	S_3	Quantity
$0	S_1	4	0	1	0	-6	60
$0	S_2	2	0	0	1	-6	12←
$4	C	0	1	0	0	1	10
	Z_j	$0	$4	$0	$0	$ 4	$40
	$C_j - Z_j$	$2 ↑	$0	$0	$0	$-4	

E X H I B I T   S8.7

Second Tableau of the Hockey Stick and Chess Problem

E X H I B I T S8.8   *Updating S_1 and C Rows*

Old S_1 Row	−	Intersectional Element of Old S_1 Row	×	Corresponding Element of New H Row	=	New S_1 Row	Old C Row	−	Intersectional Element of Old C Row	×	Corresponding Element of New H Row	=	New C Row
4	−	(4	×	1)	=	0	0	−	(0	×	1)	=	0
0	−	(4	×	0)	=	0	1	−	(0	×	0)	=	1
1	−	(4	×	0)	=	1	0	−	(0	×	0)	=	0
0	−	(4	×	½)	=	−2	0	−	(0	×	½)	=	0
−6	−	(4	×	−3)	=	6	1	−	(0	×	−3)	=	1
60	−	(4	×	6)	=	36	10	−	(0	×	6)	=	10

E X H I B I T S8.9

Third Tableau of the Hockey Stick and Chess Set Problem

C_j		$2	$4	$0	$0	$0	
	Solution Mix	H	C	S_1	S_2	S_3	Quantity
$0	S_1	0	0	1	−2	6	36←
$2	H	1	0	0	½	−3	6
$4	C	0	1	0	0	1	10
	Z_j	$2	$4	$0	$ 1	$−2	$52
	$C_j − Z_j$	$0	$0	$0	$−1	$ 2	
						↑	

36/6 = 6   6/−3 = −2 (negative)*   10/1 = 10

*Since there are three constraint equations, there must be three variables with non-negative values in the solution. Therefore a negative amount cannot be considered for introduction into the solution.

Second iteration   The entering variable is H because it has the largest $C_j − Z_j$ amount (2). The replaced variable is S_2 since it has the smallest quotient when the Quantity column values are divided by their comparable amounts in the H column:

$$S_1 = 60/4 = 15, S_2 = 12/2 = 6, C_3 = 10/0 = \infty$$

Values of entering *(H)* row are

2/2 = 1, 0/2 = 0, 0/2 = 0, 1/2 = 1/2, −6/2 = −3, 12/2 = 6
Updated S_1 row from Exhibit S8.8: 0, 0, 1, −2, 6, 36.
Updated C row from Exhibit S8.8: 0, 1, 0, 0, 1, 10.

Using the result from Exhibit S8.8, we obtain the third tableau, Exhibit S8.9.
Examining the third tableau, we see that further improvement is possible by introducing the maximum amount of S_3 that is technically feasible. From the computation at the bottom of Exhibit S8.9, the maximum amount of S_3 that can be brought into the solution is six units because of the limited supply of S_1. Replacing S_1 by S_3 and performing the updating operations yields the tableau in Exhibit S8.10. Since the $C_j − Z_j$ row contains only negative numbers, no further improvement is possible, and an optimal solution ($H = 24$, $C = 4$) has been achieved in three iterations. See boxed insert on the next page for a summary of steps.

Minimization Problems   The Puck and Pawn example dealt with maximization. An identical procedure is followed for solving minimization problems. Since the objective is to minimize rather than maximize, a negative $C_j − Z_j$ value indicates potential improve-

1. Formulate problem in terms of an objective function and a set of constraints.
2. Set up initial tableau with slack variables in the solution mix and calculate the Z_j and $C_j - Z_j$ rows.
3. Determine which variable to bring into solution (largest $C_j - Z_j$ value).
4. Determine which variable to replace (smallest positive ratio of quantity column to its comparable value in the column selected in Step 3).
5. Calculate new row values for entering variable and insert into new tableau (row to be replaced plus intersectional element).
6. Update remaining rows and enter into new tableau; compute new Z_j and $C_j - Z_j$ rows (old row minus intersectional element of old row times corresponding element in new row). If no positive $C_j - Z_j$ value is found, solution is optimal. If there is a positive value of $C_j - Z_j$, repeat Steps 3 to 6.

Summary of Steps in the Simplex Method: Maximization Problems

C_j		$2	$4	$0	$0	$0	
	Solution Mix	H	C	S_1	S_2	S_3	Quantity
$0	S_3	0	0	1/6	−1/3	1	6
$2	H	1	0	1/2	−1/2	0	24
$4	C	0	1	−1/6	1/3	0	4
	Z_j	$2	$4	$ 1/3	$ 1/3	$0	$64
	$C_j - Z_j$	$0	$0	$−1/3	$−1/3	$0	

EXHIBIT S8.10

Fourth Tableau of the Hockey Stick and Chess Set Problem (Optimal Solution)

ment; therefore the variable associated with the largest negative $C_j - Z_j$ value would be brought into solution first. Additional variables must be brought in to set up such problems, however, since minimization problems include greater-than-or-equal-to constraints, which must be treated differently from less-than-or-equal-to constraints, which typify maximization problems. (See section dealing with greater-than-or-equal-to and equal-to constraints in the simplex method.)

As mentioned earlier, the optimal solution to linear programming problems is obtained by finding the extreme corner point. The simplex procedure starts with an initial solution, searches for the most profitable direction to follow, and hops from point to point of intersecting lines (or planes in multidimensional space). The evaluation of a corner point takes one iteration, and when the furthermost point is reached (in the case of profit-maximization problems as shown by the next point's decreasing profit), the solution is complete.

Search Path Followed by the Simplex Method

Consider the graph of the example problem shown in Exhibit S8.11, where the simplex method began at point *a* (profit = $0). In the first iteration, 10 units of *C* were introduced at point *b* (profit = $40). In the second iteration, six units of *H* were introduced at point *c* (profit = $52). The third iteration left the problem at point *d* (profit = $64), which is optimal. Note that the solution procedure did not calculate profit for all corners of this problem. It did, however, *look ahead*—by virtue of the $C_j - Z_j$ calculations—to see if further improvement was possible by moving to another point (point *e*), but no improvement was indicated by such a change. These two characteristics—evaluating corner points and looking ahead for improvements—are the essential features of the simplex method.

Another feature that is also characteristic of the basic simplex method is that it does not necessarily converge on the optimum point by the shortest route around the feasible area. Reference to the graph shows that if the solution procedure had proceeded along the path $a \rightarrow e \rightarrow d$, an optimum would have been reached in two iterations rather than three.

The reason why this route was not followed was that the profit per chess set was higher than profit per hockey stick so the simplex method indicated that C, rather than H, be introduced in the first iteration. This, in turn, set the pattern for subsequent iterations to points c and d. Note that since the solution space forms a convex polygon (as previously defined), profit cannot increase, decrease, and then again increase.

Shadow Prices, Ranging, and Sensitivity

By examining the final (optimal) simplex tableau, we can learn a great deal. Besides showing the solution, the final tableau provides valuable information about the resources used, the range where the optimal decision remains unchanged, and the range where the coefficients in the objective function do not change the optimal solution. Specifically, it enables us to answer such questions as: Would you like to buy any more of a resource? If so, what price should you pay? How many units should you buy at that price? Similar questions can be answered about selling resources; even though a resource may be currently used in making products, at some price it is worthwhile to forgo production and sell it. These considerations are of interest because they lead to decisions that can increase profit or reduce cost. These profit increases or cost decreases are *in addition* to the optimal solution calculated in the final tableau objective function.

Other questions are of the sort: If we change the profit per unit (by changing the coefficient in the objective function), will this change the optimal solution? This is **sensitivity analysis,** and refers to how much the solution changes for a small change in the objective function or, conversely, for a small change in the solution, the change that occurs in the objective function.

Referring to Exhibit S8.10, the $C_j - Z_j$ values associated with the slack variables are termed **shadow prices,** *marginal values, incremental values,* or *break-even prices.* Note that the shadow prices for S_1 and S_2 were $ \frac{1}{3}$ (or 33 cents) each, and the shadow price for S_3 was $0. Above each price, management would be willing to sell resources, and below each price, it would be willing to buy. Let's take another look at this problem and all the information available in a computer printout.

Computer Program Output

Exhibit S8.12 shows the output from a computer program for the same hockey stick and chess set problem. This output differs somewhat from the hand-solved simplex solution in that the rows and columns are rotated as well as some other minor differences in the way it is displayed. The top line shows the objective function value of

---

E X H I B I T S8.11

Graph of Hockey Stick and Chess Set Problem Showing Successive Corner Evaluations

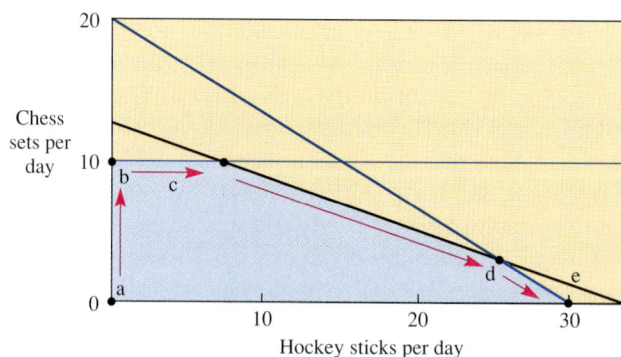

OBJECTIVE FUNCTION VALUE = 64

ROW	EQUATION	SLACK	RIGHT HAND SIDE	SHADOW PRICE
1	MACHINE A	0	120	.33
2	MACHINE B	0	72	.33
3	MACHINE C	6	10	0

COL	VARIABLE	VALUE	RELATIVE PROFIT
1	HOCKEY	24	0
2	CHESS	4	0

RIGHT HAND SENSITIVITY

ROW	EQUATION	RANGE	LEAVE	RATE
1	MACHINE A	144	CHESS	.33
1	MACHINE A	84	MACHINE C	−.33
2	MACHINE B	90	MACHINE C	.33
2	MACHINE B	60	CHESS	−.33
3	MACHINE C	INF		
3	MACHINE C	4	MACHINE C	0

OBJECTIVE SENSITIVITY

COL	VARIABLE	RANGE	ENTER	RATE
1	HOCKEY	2.67	MACHINE B	24
1	HOCKEY	1.33	MACHINE A	−24
2	CHESS	6.0	MACHINE A	4
2	CHESS	3.0	MACHINE B	− 4

$64. Row 1 has machine A with no slack and therefore all 120 units being used up. The shadow price is $.33 per unit. Row 2 shows no slack also with all 72 units used up and a shadow price of $.33. Row 3 shows machine 3 has 6 of the 10 units slack (and therefore only 4 units being used). Since there are excess units, it has zero shadow price.

In the next section of Exhibit S8.12, column 1 shows that there are 24 hockey sticks in solution. (The zero relative profit indicates that it is in solution; if it were not in solution the relative profit would show as $2—the value shown in the objective function.) Column 2 shows that there are four chess sets in solution.

The Right-Hand Sensitivity section shows that as resources are added or subtracted, there is a point where the problem changes. For example, row 1 shows that additional machine A time can be purchased at a rate less than $.33 per hour up to a total of 144 hours. As we add more machine A time, however, we make more hockey sticks and fewer chess sets (shown as Chess leaving the solution). To see this pictorially, look at Exhibit S8.1, which shows that as the $4H + 6C = 120$ equation shifts to the right, the optimum point goes up with more hockey sticks and fewer chess sets. If we decide to sell machine A time at a price greater than $.33, we can sell up to the point where we have 84 left. In this case we would make fewer hockey sticks and more chess sets. If all 36 resource units of A were sold, all resource units of C would be used and machine center C slack would become zero.

The purpose of buying or selling resources is to try to obtain profit (in this case) greater than the $64 currently given by the objective function. To be optimal, the changes are constrained to lie on the boundary of the bounded area of feasibility. In this example, the optimal solution lies on a segment of the line $4H + 6C = K$, where K is the number of resource units for machine center A within the range 84 to 144. (The value of doing the analysis the way we have in this section is that we can obtain optimal solutions for changes in the equations without re-solving the simplex algorithm.)

E X H I B I T S8.13   *Final Tableau for Hockey Stick and Chess Set Buy and Sell Questions*

A. For the S_1 decisions to buy if the price is less than $ $\frac{1}{3}$.

S_1	Quantity	Limit
$\frac{1}{6}$	6	No limit
$\frac{1}{2}$	24	No limit
$-\frac{1}{6}$	4	24 (4 divided by $\frac{1}{6}$)

B. For the S_1 decisions to sell if the price is more than $ $\frac{1}{3}$.

S_1	Quantity	Limit
$\frac{1}{6}$	6	36 (6 divided by $\frac{1}{6}$)
$\frac{1}{2}$	24	48 (24 divided by $\frac{1}{2}$)
$-\frac{1}{6}$	4	No limit

H	C	S_1	S_2	S_3	Quantity
0	0	$\frac{1}{6}$	$-\frac{1}{3}$	1	6
1	0	$\frac{1}{2}$	$-\frac{1}{2}$	0	24
0	1	$-\frac{1}{6}$	$\frac{1}{3}$	0	4
		$-\frac{1}{3}$	$-\frac{1}{3}$		

Using the same logic, machine B hours can be sold or purchased so long as the total remains within the range of 60 to 90. If we buy units of B, we make fewer hockey sticks but more chess sets. In the limit, slack for machine center C becomes zero. If we sell units of B, we would make more hockey sticks and fewer chess sets. The limit would be where we would use 60 units of resource B and would make 30 hockey sticks and zero chess sets.

Recall that machine C had excess capacity. We can therefore add an infinite supply if it is offered at a price below zero (someone pays us to take it), but we can only sell up to four units at a price greater than zero.

The objective sensitivity shows the effect of changing the profit of each hockey stick and chess set as stated in the objective equation. If hockey sticks are increased in price, the slope becomes less steep (in Exhibit S8.1). Above $2.67, the optimal solution shifts, producing 30 hockey sticks and no chess sets and machine B is used less. When the profit drops below $1.33 each, the solution shifts to 10 chess sets and six hockey sticks and machine A has idle time. The same logic exists for the chess set profit. So long as the profit of the chess set stays within the range of $3 to $6, the optimum point does not change. The Rate column in this section simply refers to the change in the value of the objective function per unit. Since there are 24 hockey sticks in solution, for example, an increase in the profit of $1 increases the value of the profit equation (objective function) by $24.

Let's look at the final simplex tableau in Exhibit S8.13. S_1 has a shadow price of $ $\frac{1}{3}$ per unit. If the price is less than $ $\frac{1}{3}$, we would be willing to buy 24 units. (See Exhibit S8.13A.) The S_1 column shows that for every S_1 produced, $\frac{1}{6}$ of a chess set must be given up. Therefore, since four exist, giving up $\frac{1}{6}$ at a time means we can add 24 units.

If we sell S_1 (at a price greater than $ $\frac{1}{3}$) we would have to give up $\frac{1}{6}$ of an S_2 and $\frac{1}{2}$ of an H for each S_1 sold. Therefore, our limit would be the smaller of 36 or 48, which would limit our selling to just 36 units.

The same analysis of S_2 (not shown in the exhibit) would show that $18S_2$ could be purchased or $12S_2$ sold. This corresponds to the Right-Hand Sensitivity section of Exhibit S8.12 where there would be a total of 90 machine B hours as the upper range (the original 72 plus the 18 purchased), and 60 as the lower range (the original 72 less 12 sold).

Dealing with Greater-than-or-Equal-to and Equal-to Constraints in the Simplex Method   Greater-than-or-equal-to constraints ($\geq$) and equal-to constraints ($=$) must be handled somewhat differently from the less-than-or-equal-to constraints ($\leq$) in setting up and solving simplex problems.

Recall that with $\leq$ constraints, we added a slack variable to convert the inequality to an equality. For example, in converting the inequality $4H + 6C \leq 120$ to an equality, we added S_1, giving us $4H + 6C + S_1 = 120$. Now suppose that the sign was changed to a greater-than-or-equal-to sign, yielding $4H + 6C \geq 120$. Initially, we would surmise that subtracting a slack variable would convert this to an equality and it would be written as $4H + 6C - 1S_1 = 120$.

Unfortunately, this adjustment would lead to difficulties in the simplex method, because the initial simplex solution starts with fictitious variables and hence a negative value $(-1S_1)$ would be in the solution—a condition not permitted in linear programming. To overcome this problem, the simplex procedure requires that a different type of variable—an artificial variable—be added to each equal-to-or-greater-than equation. An artificial variable may be thought of as representing a fictitious product having a very high cost, which, though permitted in the initial solution to a simplex problem, would never appear in the final solution. Defining A as the artificial variable, the constraint given above would now appear as

$$4H + 6C - 1S_1 + 1A_1 = 120$$

Assuming that we were minimizing cost rather than maximizing profit, the objective function would appear as

$$\$2H + \$4C + \$0S_1 + \$MA_1$$

where $\$M$ is assumed to be a very large cost—for example, a million or a billion dollars.[6] (Note that S_1 is added to the objective function even though it is negative in the constraint equation.)

An artificial variable must also be included in constraints with equality signs. For example, if $4H + 6C = 120$, this must be changed to $4H + 6C + 1A_1 = 120$ to satisfy the simplex requirement that each constraint equation have a non-negative variable in the initial solution. It would be reflected in the objective function, again as $\$MA_1$, but would have no slack variable accompanying it in the constraint equation.

Procedurally, where such constraints exist, the simplex method starts with artificial variables in the initial solution but otherwise treats them the same as it would real or slack variables.

As mentioned previously, spreadsheets can be used to solve linear programming problems. Most spreadsheets have built-in optimization routines that are very easy to use and understand. For example, Microsoft Excel for Windows 5.0 has an optimization tool called Solver that we will demonstrate by using it to solve the hockey stick and chess problem completed earlier.

First, we define the problem by identifying a target cell (or objective function), the changing cells (or decision variables), and the constraints that we want in the analysis. Exhibit S8.14 presents the input data sheet for the problem. Our objective function (total profit) cell contains a formula that multiplies the quantities of hockey sticks and chess sets produced by their corresponding profit. Similarly, the constraint cells contain formulas for the machine constraints. Since we must provide an initial set of quantities produced, we will randomly select to produce two of each. This will provide a starting point for Solver.

Linear Programming on a Spreadsheet— Microsoft Excel 5.0

---

[6]When a $\geq$ or $=$ constraint is encountered in a maximization problem, an artificial variable is assumed to have a large negative profit coefficient in the objective function to ensure that it would not appear in the final solution.

EXHIBIT S8.14

Microsoft Excel 5.0—Input Data and Initial Setup

Total Profit	12
Hockey sticks produced	2
Chess sets produced	2
Constraint 1 (machine A)	20
Constraint 2 (machine B)	16
Constraint 3 (machine C)	2
Data	
Hockey sticks unit profit ($)	2
Chess sets unit profit ($)	4
Machine A availability	120
Machine B availability	72
Machine C availability	10

EXHIBIT S8.15

Excel Answer and Sensitivity Report

Target Cell (Max)

Cell	Name	Original Value	Final Value		
B3	Total profit	12	64.00000		

Adjustable Cells

Cell	Name	Original Value	Final Value		
B4	Hockey sticks produced	2	24.00000		
B5	Chess sets produced	2	4.00000		

Constraints

Cell	Name	Cell Value	Formula	Status	Slack
B7	Constraint 1 (machine A)	120	B7 < = 120	Binding	0
B8	Constraint 2 (machine B)	72.0000	B8 < = 72	Binding	0
B9	Constraint 3 (machine C)	4.0000	B9 < = 10	Not binding	6.00000

Changing Cells

Cell	Name	Final Value	Reduced Gradient
B4	Hockey sticks produced	24.00000	0
B5	Chess sets produced	4.00000	0

Constraints

Cell	Name	Final Value	Lagrange Multiplier
B7	Constraint 1 (machine A)	120.00000	0.33333
B8	Constraint 2 (machine B)	72.00000	0.33333
B9	Constraint 3 (machine C)	4.00000	0.00000

Next we can invoke Solver from the tools menu. A dialogue box will request the changing cells (decision variables) and the constraints. After we input these cells in the dialogue box, we can choose the solve button that will create at least two reports: an answer report and a sensitivity report, Exhibit S8.15. The answer report shows the final answers for the total profit ($64) and the amounts produced (24 hockey sticks and 4 chess sets). Also shown are the binding constraints and the associated slack for each constraint. The sensitivity report presents the Lagrange Multipliers (shadow prices) for the constraints

				Shipping Costs per Case (in Dollars)				
Factory	Supply	Warehouse	Demand	From	To E	To F	To G	To H
A	15	E	10	A	$25	$35	$36	$60
B	6	F	12	B	55	30	45	38
C	14	G	15	C	40	50	26	65
D	11	H	9	D	60	40	66	27

and the reduced gradient (relative profit) for the coefficients. What-if questions can also be answered by using another tool, the Scenario Manager, also built in Excel.

S8.4   TRANSPORTATION METHOD

The **transportation method** is a simplified special case of the simplex method. It gets its name from its application to problems involving transporting products from several sources to several destinations.[7] The two common objectives of such problems are either (1) minimize the cost of shipping n units to m destinations or (2) maximize the profit of shipping n units to m destinations. There are three general steps in solving transportation problems. We will now discuss each one in the context of a simple example.

Suppose the Puck and Pawn Company has four factories supplying four warehouses and its management wants to determine the minimum-cost shipping schedule for its monthly output of chess sets. Factory supply, warehouse demands, and shipping costs per case of chess sets are shown in Exhibit S8.16.

The transportation matrix for this example appears in Exhibit S8.17, where supply availability at each factory is shown in the far right column and the warehouse demands are shown in the bottom row. The unit shipping costs are shown in the small boxes within the cells. It is important at this step to make sure that the total supply availabilities and total demand requirements are equal. In this case they are both the same, 46 units, but often there is an excess supply or demand. In such situations, for the transportation method to work, a dummy warehouse or factory must be added. Procedurally, this involves inserting an extra row (for an additional factory) or an extra column (for an additional

Step 1: Set Up Transportation Matrix

---

[7]For other applications, see Exhibit S8.24.

EXHIBIT S8.18
Northwest-Corner Assignment

From \ To	E	F	G	H	Factory supply
A	25 — 10	35 — 5	36	60	15
B	55	30 — 6	45	38	6
C	40	50 — 1	26 — 13	65	14
D	60	40	66 — 2	27 — 9	11
Destination requirements	10	12	15	9	46 / 46

Total cost = 10($25) + 5($35) + 6($30) + 1($50) + 13($26) + 2($66) + 9($27) = $1,368

warehouse). The amount of supply or demand required by the dummy equals the difference between the row and column totals.

For example, the following problem might be restated to indicate a total demand of 36 cases, and therefore, a new column would be inserted with a demand of 10 cases to bring the total up to 46 cases. The cost figures in each cell of the dummy row would be set at zero so any units sent there would not incur a transportation cost. Theoretically, this adjustment is equivalent to the simplex procedure of inserting a slack variable in a constraint inequality to convert it to an equation, and, as in the simplex, the cost of the dummy would be zero in the objective function.

Step 2: Make Initial Allocations

Initial allocation entails assigning numbers to cells to satisfy supply and demand constraints. Next we will discuss several methods for doing this: the northwest-corner method, least-cost method, and Vogel's approximation method.

Northwest-Corner Method of Allocation   The northwest-corner method, as the name implies, begins allocation by starting at the northwest corner of the matrix and assigning as much as possible to each cell in the first row.[8] The procedure is then repeated for the second row, third row, and so on, until all row and column requirements are met. Exhibit S8.18 shows a northwest-corner assignment. (Cell *A-E* was assigned first, *A-F* second, *B-F* third, and so forth.)

Inspection of Exhibit S8.18 indicates some high-cost cells were assigned and some low-cost cells bypassed by using the northwest-corner method. Indeed, this is to be expected since this method ignores costs in favor of following an easily programmable allocation algorithm.

Least-Cost Method of Allocation   This method allocates as much as possible to the least-cost cell. Ties may be broken arbitrarily. Rows and columns that have been completely allocated are not considered, and the process of allocation is continued. The procedure is completed when all row and column requirements are addressed. Exhibit S8.19 shows a least-cost assignment. (Cell A-E was assigned first, C-G second, D-H third, B-F fourth, and so on.)

---

[8] Assign as many units as possible to each cell to meet the requirements of having no more than $m + n - 1$ filled cells, where m = number of rows and n = number of columns.

From \ To	E	F	G	H	Factory supply
A	25 10	35 5	36	60	15
B	55	30 6	45	38	6
C	40	50	26 14	65	14
D	60	40 1	66 1	27 9	11
Destination requirements	10	12	15	9	46 46

Total cost = 10($25) + 14($26) + 9($27) + 6($30) + 5($35) + 1($40) + 1($66) = $1,318

Vogel's Approximation Method of Allocation This method also takes costs into account in allocation. Five steps are involved in applying this heuristic:

Step 1: Determine the difference between the lowest two cells in all rows and columns, including dummies.

Step 2: Identify the row or column with the largest difference. Ties may be broken arbitrarily.

Step 3: Allocate as much as possible to the lowest-cost cell in the row or column with the highest difference.

Step 4: Stop the process if all row and column requirements are met. If not, go to the next step.

Step 5: Recalculate the differences between the two lowest cells remaining in all rows and columns. Any row and column with zero supply or demand should not be used in calculating further differences. Then go to Step 2.

The Vogel's approximation method (VAM) usually produces an optimal or near-optimal starting solution. One study found that VAM yields an optimum solution in 80 percent of the sample problems tested. (Our students have observed that the remaining 20 percent of sample problems are found on examinations.) Exhibit S8.20 shows the VAM assignments for the chess set problem. (Cell A-E was assigned first, C-G second, D-H third, D-F fourth, and so on.) Note that this starting solution is the same as the optimal solution obtained after making all possible improvements to the starting solution obtained using the northwest-corner method. (See Exhibit S8.23.)

To develop an optimal solution in a transportation problem involves evaluating each unused cell to determine whether a shift into it is advantageous from a total-cost standpoint. If it is, the shift is made, and the process is repeated. When all cells have been evaluated and appropriate shifts made, the problem is solved.

Step 3: Develop Optimal Solution

Stepping Stone Method of Evaluation One approach to making this evaluation is the stepping stone method. The term *stepping stone* appeared in early descriptions of the method, in which unused cells were referred to as "water" and used cells as "stones"— from the analogy of walking on a path of stones half-submerged in water. We now apply

E X H I B I T S8.20   *Vogel's Approximation Method*

From \ To	E	F	G	H	Factory supply
A	25 10	35 4	36 1	60	15
B	55	30 6	45	38	6
C	40	50	26 14	65	14
D	60	40 2	66	27 9	11
Destination requirements	10	12	15	9	46 / 46

Difference Iterations	1	2	3	4	5	6	7
	10	1	1	1	1	(25)	–
	8	8	8	8	8	8	8
	14	(14)	–	–	–	–	–
	13	13	(13)	(20)	–	–	–

Difference Iterations				
1	(15)	5	10	11
2	–	5	10	11
3	–	5	9	11
4	–	5	9	–
5	–	5	(9)	–
6	–	5	–	–
7	–	20	–	–

Total cost = 10($25) + 14($26) + 9($27) + 2($40) + 1($36) + 4($35) + 6($30) = $1,293

the method to the northwest-corner solution to the sample problem, as shown in Exhibit S8.19.

Step 1: Pick any empty cell and identify the closed path leading to that cell. A closed path consists of horizontal and vertical lines leading from an empty cell back to itself.[9] In the closed path there can only be one empty cell that we are examining. The 90-degree turns must therefore occur at those places that meet this requirement. Two closed paths are identified in Exhibit S8.21. Closed path *a* is required to evaluate empty cell *B-E;* closed path *b* is required to evaluate empty cell *A-H.*

Step 2: Move one unit into the empty cell from a filled cell at a corner of the closed path and modify the remaining filled cells at the other corners of the closed path to reflect this move.[10] Modifying entails adding to and subtracting from filled cells in such a way that supply and demand constraints are not violated. This requires that one unit always be subtracted in a given row or column for each unit added to that row or column. Thus, the following additions and subtractions would be required for path *a:*

Add one unit to *B-E* (the empty cell).

Subtract one unit from *B-F.*

Add one unit to *A-F.*

Subtract one unit from *A-E.*

---

[9]If assignments have been made correctly, the matrix has only one closed path for each empty cell.
[10]More than one unit could be used to test the desirability of a shift. However, since the problem is linear, if it is desirable to shift one unit, it is desirable to shift more than one, and vice versa.

From \ To	E	F	G	H	Factory supply
A	25 10 *a*	35 5	*b* 36	60	15
B	55	30 6	45	38	6
C	40	50 1	26 13	65	14
D	60	40	66 2	27 9	11
Destination requirements	10	12	15	9	46 46

E X H I B I T S8.21
Stepping Stone Method—Identification of Closed Paths

For the longer path *b*,

> Add one unit to *A-H* (the empty cell).
> Subtract one unit from *D-H*.
> Add one unit to *D-G*.
> Subtract one unit from *C-G*.
> Add one unit to *C-F*.
> Subtract one unit from *A-F*.

Step 3: Determine desirability of the move. This is easily done by (1) summing the cost values for the cell to which a unit has been added, (2) summing the cost values of the cells from which a unit has been subtracted, and (3) taking the difference between the two sums to determine if there is a cost reduction. If the cost is reduced by making the move, as many units as possible should be shifted out of the evaluated filled cells into the empty cell. If the cost is increased, no move should be made and the empty cell should be crossed out or otherwise marked to show that it has been evaluated. (A large plus sign is typically used to denote a cell that has been evaluated and found undesirable in cost-minimizing problems. A large minus sign is used for this purpose in profit-maximizing problems.) For cell *B-E*, the pluses and minuses are

+		−	
$55	(*B-E*)	$30	(*B-F*)
35	(*A-F*)	25	(*A-E*)
$90		$55	

For cell *A-H* they are

+		−	
$60	(*A-H*)	$27	(*D-H*)
66	(*D-G*)	26	(*C-G*)
50	(*C-F*)	35	(*A-F*)
$176		$88	

Thus in both cases it is apparent that no move into either empty cell should be made.

E X H I B I T S8.22

Revised
Transportation
Matrix

From \ To	E	F	G	H	Factory supply
A	25 / 10	35 / 5	36	60 / +	15
B	55 / +	30 / 6	45	38	6
C	40	50 / +	26 / 14	65	14
D	60	40 / 1	66 / 1	27 / 9	11
Destination requirements	10	12	15	9	46 / 46

Total cost = 10($25) + 5($35) + 6($30) + 14($26) + 1($40) + 1($66) + 9($27) = $1,318

Step 4: Repeat Steps 1 through 3 until all empty cells have been evaluated. To illustrate the mechanics of carrying out a move, consider cell *D-F* and the closed path leading to it, which is a short one: *C-F, C-G,* and *D-G.* The pluses and minuses are

+	−
$40 (*D-F*)	$50 (*C-F*)
26 (*C-G*)	66 (*D-G*)
$66	$116

Since there is a savings of $50 per unit from shipping via *D-F,* as many units as possible should be moved into this cell. In this case, however, the maximum amount that can be shifted is one unit—because the maximum amount added to any cell may not exceed the quantity found in the lowest-amount cell from which a subtraction is to be made. To do otherwise would violate the supply and demand constraints of the problem. Here we see that the limiting cell is *C-F* since it contains only one unit.

The revised matrix, showing the effects of this move and the previous evaluations, is presented in Exhibit S8.22. Applying the stepping stone method to the remaining unfilled cells and making shifts where indicated yields an optimal solution.

In particular, the empty cell *A-G* in Exhibit S8.22 has closed path *D-G, D-F,* and *A-F.* The pluses and minuses are

+	−
36 (*A-G*)	35 (*A-F*)
40 (*D-F*)	66 (*D-G*)
76	101

Since savings = 101 − 76 = $25, we shift one unit to *A-G.* Exhibit S8.23 shows the optimal matrix, with minimum transportation cost of $1,293.

To verify that we have the optimum, we should evaluate each empty cell to see if it is desirable to bring in that cell. If we did this, we would have a plus sign in each of these cells.

Degeneracy   **Degeneracy** exists in a transportation problem when the number of filled cells is less than the number of rows plus the number of columns minus one (i.e., $m + n − 1$). Degeneracy may be observed during the initial allocation when the first entry in a

EXHIBIT S8.23

Optimal Solution to Transportation Problem

From \ To	E	F	G	H	Factory supply
A	25 / **10**	35 / **5 − 1 = 4**	36 / **0 + 1 = 1**	60	15
B	55	30 / **6**	45	38	6
C	40	50	26 / **14**	65	14
D	60	40 / **1 + 1 = 2**	66 / **1 − 1 = 0**	27 / **9**	11
Destination requirements	10	12	15	9	46 / 46

Total cost = 10($25) + 4($35) + 1($36) + 6($30) + 14($26) + 2($40) + 9($27) = $1,293

EXHIBIT S8.24

Degenerate Transportation Problem with Theta Added

From \ To	W	X	Y	Factory supply
T	8 / **3**	6 / **8**	4 / **θ**	11
U	9	8	0 / **9**	9
V	5 / **3**	3	10	3
Destination requirements	6	8	9	23 / 23

m + n − 1 = 5 filled cells

Actual allocation = 4 filled cells

row or column satisfies *both* the row and column requirements. Degeneracy requires some adjustment in the matrix to evaluate the solution achieved. The form of this adjustment involves inserting some value in an empty cell so a closed path can be developed to evaluate other empty cells. This value may be thought of as an infinitely small amount, having no direct bearing on the cost of the solution.

Procedurally, the value (often denoted by the Greek letter theta, θ) is used in exactly the same manner as a real number except that it may initially be placed in any empty cell, even though row and column requirements have been met by real numbers. A degenerate transportation problem showing an optimal minimum cost allocation is presented in Exhibit S8.24, where we can see that if θ were not assigned to the matrix, it would be impossible to evaluate several cells (including the one where it is added). Once a θ has been inserted into the solution, it remains there until it is removed by subtraction or until a final solution is reached.

While the choice of where to put a θ is arbitrary, it saves time if it is placed where it may be used to evaluate as many cells as possible without being shifted. In this regard, verify for yourself that θ is optimally allocated in Exhibit S8.24.

Alternate Optimal Solutions   When the evaluation of an empty cell yields the same cost as the existing allocation, an alternate optimal solution exists.[11] In such cases, management has additional flexibility and can invoke nontransportation cost factors in decid-

---

[11] Assuming that all other cells are optimally assigned.

ing on a final shipping schedule. (A large zero is commonly placed in an empty cell that has been identified as an alternate optimal route.)

S8.5 CONCLUSION

This supplement has dealt mainly with the mechanics of solution procedures for linear programming problems. It would be a rare instance when a linear programming problem would actually be solved by hand. There are too many computers around and too many LP software programs to justify spending time for manual solution.[12] We firmly believe, though, that to truly understand the computer output, it is useful to take the time to solve some simple problems, as we have done here.

S8.6 SOLVED PROBLEMS

1. Two products, X and Y, both require processing time on machines I and II. Machine I has 200 hours available, and machine II has 400 hours available. Product X requires one hour on machine I and four hours on machine II. Product Y requires one hour on machine I and one hour on machine II. Each unit of product X yields $10 profit and each unit of Y yields $5 profit. These statements reduce to the following set of equations:

$X + Y \leq 200$ (Machine I)

$4X + Y \leq 400$ (Machine II)

Maximize $10X + $5Y$

Solve the problem graphically showing the optimal utilization of machine time.

Solution

The optimal point, as shown on the graph, is $X = 67$ and $Y = 133$. Profit at this point would be $10(67) + $5(133) = $1,335.

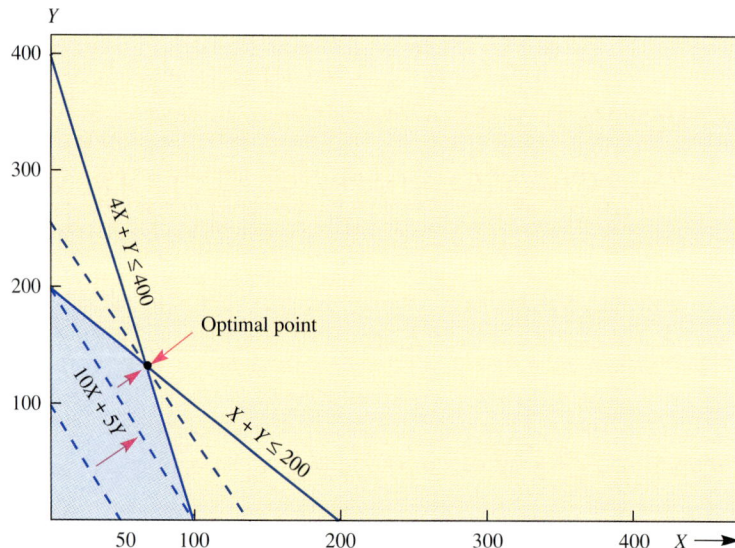

[12]There are also programs that assist in the construction of the LP model itself. Probably the best known is GAMS—General Algebraic Modeling System (GAMS–General, San Francisco, CA). This provides a high-level language for easy respresentation of complex problems.

To plot first isoprofit line, assume:

$$10X + 5Y = 500$$
$$@X = 0, Y = 100$$
$$@Y = 0, X = 50$$

Continue to move this isoprofit line outward until it reaches the furthest point in the feasible region (at approximately $X = 67$, $Y = 133$).

2. Solve Problem 1 using the simplex method.

Solution

The simplex solution to Problem 1 is

		$10 X	$5 Y	0 S_1	0 S_2	
	S_1	1	1	1	0	200
	S_2	4	1	0	1	400
		$10	$5	0	0	
First iteration	S_1	0	3/4	1	$-1/4$	100
	X	1	1/4	0	1/4	100
		0	2.50	0	-2.50	
Second iteration	Y	0	1	4/3	$-1/3$	133
	X	1	0	$-1/3$	1/3	67
				$-3.33	$-1.66	

With $X = 67$ and $Y = 133$, the value of the objective function would be $Z = \$10(67) + \$5(133) = \$1,335$.

S8.7 REVIEW AND DISCUSSION QUESTIONS

1. What structural requirements of a problem are needed to solve it by linear programming?
2. What type of information is provided in a solved simplex tableau?
3. What type of information is provided by shadow prices?
4. What are slack variables? Why are they necessary in the simplex method? When are they used in the transportation method?
5. It has been stated in this chapter that an optimal solution for a simplex problem always lies at a corner point. Under what conditions might an equally desirable solution be found anywhere along a constraint line?
6. What is a convex polygon? How is it identified?
7. How do you know if a transportation problem is degenerate? What must be done if a degenerate problem is to be tested for optimality?

S8.8 PROBLEMS

1. Solve the following problem using the graphical method of linear programming.

$$4A + 6B \geq 120$$
$$2A + 6B \geq 72$$
$$B \geq 10$$

Minimize $2A + 4B$

2. Bindley Corporation has a one-year contract to supply motors for all washing machines produced by Rinso Ltd. Rinso manufactures the washers at four locations around the

country: New York, Fort Worth, San Diego, and Minneapolis. Plans call for the following numbers of washing machines to be produced at each location:

New York	50,000
Fort Worth	70,000
San Diego	60,000
Minneapolis	80,000

Bindley has three plants that can produce the motors. The plants and production capacities are

Boulder	100,000
Macon	100,000
Gary	150,000

Due to varying production and transportation costs, the profit Bindley earns on each 1,000 units depends on where they were produced and where they were shipped. The following table gives the accounting department estimates of the dollar profit per unit. (Shipment will be made in lots of 1,000.)

	Shipped to			
Produced at	**New York**	**Fort Worth**	**San Diego**	**Minneapolis**
Boulder	7	11	8	13
Macon	20	17	12	10
Gary	8	18	13	16

Given profit *maximization* as a criterion, Bindley would like to determine how many motors should be produced at each plant and how many motors should be shipped from each plant to each destination.

   a. Develop a transportation tableau for this problem.

   b. Find the optimal solution.

3. Solve the problem using the graphical method of linear programming.

$$16X + 10Y \leq 160$$
$$12X + 14Y \leq 168$$
$$Y \geq 2$$

Maximize $2X + 10Y$

4. A manufacturing firm has discontinued production of a certain unprofitable product line. Considerable excess production capacity was created as a result. Management is considering devoting this excess capacity to one or more of three products: X_1, X_2, and X_3.

   Machine hours required per unit are

	Product		
Machine Type	X_1	X_2	X_3
Milling machine	8	2	3
Lathe	4	3	0
Grinder	2	0	1

The available time in machine hours per week are

	Machine Hours per Week
Milling machines	800
Lathes	480
Grinders	320

The salespeople estimate that they can sell all the units of X_1 and X_2 that can be made.

But the sales potential of X_3 is 80 units per week maximum.

Unit profits for the three products are

Unit Profits

X_1	$20
X_2	6
X_3	8

a. Set up the equations that can be solved to maximize the profit per week.

b. Solve these equations using the simplex method.

c. What is the optimal solution? How many of each product should be made and what should the resultant profit be?

d. What is the situation with respect to the machine groups? Would they work at capacity, or would there be unused available time? Will X_3 be at maximum sales capacity?

e. Suppose that an additional 200 hours per week can be obtained from the milling machines by working overtime. The incremental cost would be $1.50 per hour. Would you recommend doing this? Explain how you arrived at your answer.

5. Rent'R Cars is a multi-site car rental company in the city. It is trying out a new "return the car to the location most convenient for you" policy to improve customer service. But this means that the company has to constantly move cars around the city to maintain required levels of vehicle availability. The supply and demand for economy cars, and the total cost of moving these vehicles between sites, are shown below.

From \ To	D	E	F	G	Supply
A	$9	$8	$6	$5	50
B	9	8	8	0	40
C	5	3	3	10	75
Demand	50	60	25	30	165 / 165

a. Find the solution that minimizes moving costs.

b. What would you have to do to the costs to assure that A always sends a car to D as part of the optimal solution?

6. A diet is being prepared for the University of Arizona dorms. The objective is to feed the students at the least possible cost, but the diet must have between 1,800 and 3,600 calories. No more than 1,400 calories can be starch, and no fewer than 400 can be protein. The varied diet is to be made of two foods: A and B. Food A costs $0.75 per pound and contains 600 calories, 400 of which are protein and 200 starch. No more than two pounds of food A can be used per resident. Food B costs $0.15 per pound and contains 900 calories, of which 700 are starch, 100 are protein, and 100 are fat.

a. Write out the equations representing this information.

b. Solve the problem graphically for the amounts of each food that should be used.

7. Do Problem 6 with the added constraint that not more than 150 calories shall be fat, and that the price of food has escalated to $1.75 per pound for food A and $2.50 per pound for food B.

8. Logan Manufacturing wants to mix two fuels (A and B) for its trucks to minimize cost. It needs no fewer than 3,000 gallons to run its trucks during the next month. It has a

maximum fuel storage capacity of 4,000 gallons. There are 2,000 gallons of fuel A and 4,000 gallons of fuel B available. The mixed fuel must have an octane rating of no less than 80.

When mixing fuels, the amount of fuel obtained is just equal to the sum of the amounts put in. The octane rating is the weighted average of the individual octanes, weighted in proportion to the respective volumes.

The following is known: Fuel A has an octane of 90 and costs $1.20 per gallon. Fuel B has an octane of 75 and costs $0.90 per gallon.

a. Write out the equations expressing this information.

b. Solve the problem graphically, giving the amount of each fuel to be used. State any assumptions necessary to solve the problem.

9. Here is a solved simplex tableau.

X	Y	Z	S_1	S_2	S_3	
0	5	0	-2	1	1	40
0	-3	1	3	-2	0	90
1	4	0	-4	3	0	60
0	-7	0	-2	-3	0	

a. What are the values of X, Y, Z, S_1, S_2, and S_3?

b.

	Would you buy?	At what price?	How many?
S_1			
S_2			
S_3			

	Would you sell?	At what price?	How many?
S_1			
S_2			
S_3			

10. You are trying to create a budget to optimize the use of a portion of your disposable income. You have a maximum of $700 per month to be allocated to food, shelter, and entertainment. The amount spent on food and shelter combined must not exceed $500. The amount spent on shelter alone must not exceed $100. Entertainment cannot exceed $300 per month. Each dollar spent on food has a satisfaction value of 2, each dollar spent on shelter has a satisfaction value of 3, and each dollar spent on entertainment has a satisfaction value of 5.

Assuming a linear relationship, use the simplex method of linear programming to determine the optimal allocation of your funds.

S8.9   SELECTED BIBLIOGRAPHY

Eppen, G. D., and F. J. Gould. *Introductory Management Science.* 4th ed. Englewood Cliffs, NJ: Prentice Hall, 1993.

Greeberg, H. J. "How to Analyze the Results of Linear Programs—Part 2: Price Interpretation." *Interfaces* 23, no. 5, September–October 1993, pp. 97–114.

Llewellyn, John, and Ramesh Sharda. "Linear Programming Software for Personal Computers: 1990 Survey." *OR/MS Today,* October 1990, pp. 35–47.

Sharda, R. "Mathematical Programming on Microcomputers:

Directions in Performance and User Interfaces." In *Mathematical Models for Decision Support*, ed. G. Mitra. New York: Springer-Verlag, 1988, pp. 279–93.

———. "Linear Programming Software for the Microcomputer: Recent Advances." In *Decision-Aiding Software and Decision Analysis,* ed. S. Nagel. Cambridge, England: Cambridge University Press, 1990.

Taha, Hamdy A. *Operations Research.* New York: Macmillan, 1992.

Chapter

9

Facility Location

CHAPTER OUTLINE

KEY TERMS

Virtual Office

Free Trade Zone

Trading Blocks

Factor-Rating Systems

Center of Gravity Method

Analytic Delphi Model

Regression Model

Ardalan Heuristic

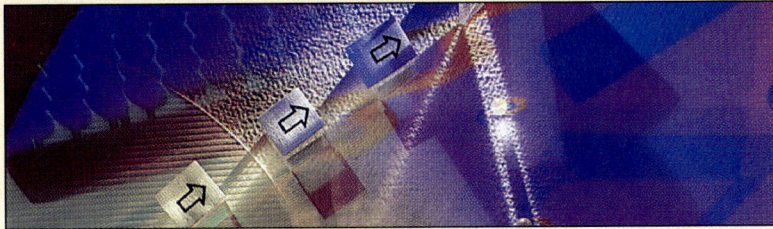

When asked, "Where is your office?" you may reply, "Everywhere and nowhere!"

Welcome to the world of the **"virtual office"** that facilitates whatever work needs to be done whenever and wherever one chooses. AT&T's intended acquisition of McCaw Cellular signals the advent of the individual-based communications services market of the 1990s. In addition, the trend toward a highly mobile, flexible, information-supported, and networked workforce is growing exponentially in today's knowledge-based economy. As a result, an estimated 25 million Americans generated their primary income from their homes in 1992. Of that total, nearly seven million telecommute. That number's expected growth will be partly due to the U.S. Clean Air Act of 1992 that requires reduced commuting mileage in many targeted areas.

Big firms like Ernst & Young and Arthur Andersen are adopting the virtual office, but many small companies too are embracing nonterritorial concepts. All are increasing productivity while slashing occupancy costs. AT&T launched its virtual office program in 1991, placing thousands of marketing representatives on the street, armed with Safari workstations and cellular phones. When sales representatives need an office at the office, they call ahead and reserve one for the day. AT&T reports a potential reduction in facilities costs of hundreds of millions per year. Sales productivity has gone up 15 to 20 percent. Dun and Bradstreet has launched a pilot project called Telecommunicating and Sharing at its software unit. Computer consultants are invited to work from home and use nonterritorial offices when they are in town at the office for team meetings or client sessions. The firm estimates a $30 million occupancy-cost saving per year.

Looking into the future, we predict that the location of offices will undergo fundamental change. Fully integrated office/residential communes will emerge, turning many people's commute into an elevator ride or a walk across the hall. The virtual office will unalterably change how, where, and when we work.

Source: Adapted from Michael Bell, "The Virtual Office: Hit or Myth?" *Site Selection,* December 1993, pp. 296–302.

Where should a plant or service facility be located? This is a top question on the strategic agendas of contemporary manufacturing and service firms, particularly in this age of global markets and global production. Dramatic changes in communication technology (as described in the vignette) have made the world truly a "global village," allowing companies greater flexibility in their location choices. In practice, however, the question of location is very much linked to two competitive imperatives:

1. The need to produce close to the customer due to time-based competition, trade agreements, and shipping costs.
2. The need to locate near the appropriate labor pool to take advantage of low wage costs and/or high technical skills.

This chapter discusses these and other issues in facility location decisions. Examples cover different industries with a global perspective. The chapter presents typical techniques involved in facility location analysis. Two cases on global location decisions are presented at the end of the chapter.

9.1   ISSUES IN FACILITY LOCATION

The problem of facility location is common to new and existing businesses. This planning is critical to a company's eventual success. For instance, 3M has moved a significant part of its corporate activity, including R&D, to the more temperate climate of Austin, Texas. Toys "R" Us has opened a new location in Japan as a part of its global strategy. Disney chose Paris, France, for its EuroDisney theme park, though this site has not met with the same success as the U.S. and Japanese locations. Manufacturing and service companies' location decisions are guided by a variety of criteria defined by competitive imperatives. Criteria that influence manufacturing plant and warehouse location planning are discussed next.

Proximity to Customers   A location close to the customer is important because of the ever-increasing need to be customer-responsive. This enables faster delivery of goods to customers. In addition, it ensures that customers' needs are incorporated into the products being developed and built. Population characteristics provide a basis for decision making on these criteria.

Business Climate   A favorable business climate can include the presence of similar-sized businesses, the presence of companies in the same industry, the presence of other foreign companies in the case of international locations. Probusiness government legislation, and local government intervention to facilitate businesses locating in an area via subsidies, tax abatements, and other support are also factors. (See "The Quality Business Base in Europe.")

The Quality Business Base in Europe

Within the past 25 years Ireland has been transformed from a predominantly agricultural country into one of the most vibrant industrial economies in Europe. Today Ireland has a trade surplus in excess of IR£ 1.7 billion (equivalent to more than 7 percent of GNP), an overall balance of payment surplus of 2 percent of GNP, and an above average rate of GNP growth.

The consistency of government policies for industrial development has been a major contributor toward growth. Industrial policy consists of specific incentives and programs, infrastructure support, and wider economic measures. A corporate tax rate of 10 percent (guaranteed to the end of year 2010) is available to manufacturing and internationally traded service companies. The attractive climate for investment created by such measures has attracted a variety of companies from different sectors including information technology, engineering, health care and pharmaceutical products, consumer products, financial services, and telemarketing-based services. (See the following table.)

Some Overseas Companies in Ireland

From the United States	From the Far East	From Europe
Apple	Brother	Braun
Claris	Daiwa Bank	Cadbury-Schweppes
Chase Bank	Fujitsu	Deutsche Bank
Dell	Goldstar	Ericsson
Digital Equipment	Hitachi	Moulinex
Fruit of the Loom	Mitsubishi Trust	Nestlé
IBM	Mitsumi	Phillips
Intel	NEC	Sandoz
Merck	Saehan Media	Siemens
Microsoft	Sumitomo Bank	Unilever
Pratt & Whitney	Yamanouchi	
Thermoking		

A strong, capable, competitive local supplier base in Ireland is also of great importance to the overseas firms. This involves not just the availability and quality of components, but also the physical proximity and ability to establish long-term partnership relationships. For instance, foreign companies operating locally spend about IR£ 1.3 billion annually on raw materials, components, and subassemblies sourced from local suppliers in the areas of electronics, engineering, food, and health care. A well-educated workforce is an additional advantage.

Ireland's membership in the European Economic Community (EEC) certainly has added value to locating in that country!

Source: IDA Ireland advertisement, *Site Selection*, June 1993, p. 643.

Total Costs   The objective is to select a site with the lowest total cost. This includes regional costs, inbound distribution costs, outbound distribution costs, and regional costs. Land, construction, labor, taxes, and energy costs comprise the regional costs. In addition, there are hidden costs that are difficult to measure. These involve (1) excessive moving of preproduction material between locations before final delivery to the customers and (2) loss of customer responsiveness arising from locating away from the main customer base.

Infrastructure   Adequate road, rail, air, and sea transportation is vital. Energy and telecommunications requirements must also be met. In addition, the local government's willingness to invest in upgrading infrastructure to the levels required may be an incentive to select a specific location.

Archer Daniels Midland (ADM) is a major processor of agricultural products. ADM's Eurooport plant in Rotterdam, the Netherlands, is the largest grain processing facility in the world and positions ADM to play a role in meeting Europe's agricultural product needs. It can ship by land, rail, river, and sea.

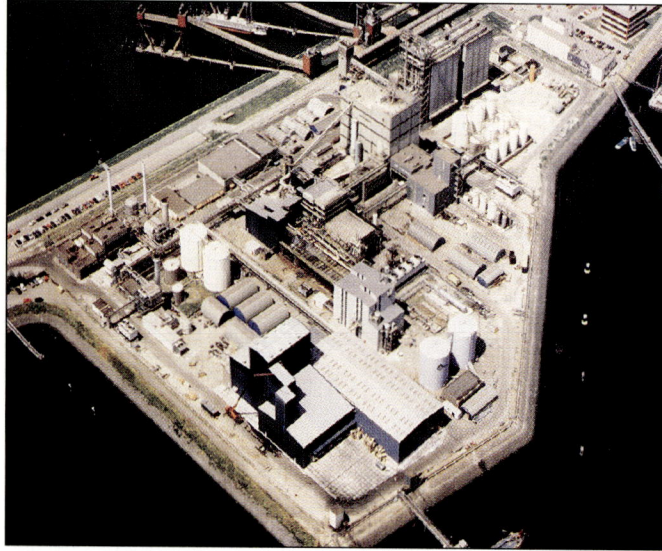

Quality of Labor   The educational and skill levels of the labor pool must match the company's needs. Even more important are the willingness and ability to learn.

Suppliers   A high-quality and competitive supplier base makes a given location suitable. The proximity of important suppliers' plants also supports lean production methods.

Other Facilities   The location of other plants or distribution centers of the same company may influence a new facility's location in the network. Issues of product mix and capacity are strongly interconnected to the location decision in this context.

Free Trade Zones   A foreign trade zone or a **free trade zone** is typically a closed facility (under the supervision of the customs department) into which foreign goods can be brought without being subject to the necessary customs requirements. There are about 170 such free trade zones in the United States today. Such specialized locations also exist in other countries. Manufacturers in free trade zones can use imported components in the final product and delay payment of customs duties until the product is shipped into the host country.

Political Risk   The fast-changing geopolitical scenes in numerous nations present exciting, challenging opportunities. But the extended phase of transformation that many countries are undergoing makes the decision to locate in those areas extremely difficult. Political risks in both the country of location and the host country influence location decisions. See Chapter 17 section on Global Sourcing for more on this.

Government Barriers   Barriers to enter and locate in many countries are being removed today through legislation. Yet many nonlegislative and cultural barriers should be considered in location planning. (See "Toys 'R' Us in Japan")

Toys "R" Us in Japan

On December 20, 1991, Toys "R" Us—the world's largest toy retailer—opened its first retail store in Japan. What may now sound like an American success story in Japan traveled a difficult road for two years. The retailer had established locations in Canada, the United Kingdom, Germany, France, Singapore, Hong Kong, Malaysia, and Taiwan well before it attempted to enter the Japanese market.

In January 1990, Toys "R" Us formally applied to open its first (large) toy store in Niigata, Japan. This caused local toy retailers to proclaim their opposition by invoking provisions contained in the Large-Scale Retail Store Act. Then they organized a lobbying group to mobilize support against the American firm. Toys "R" Us appealed for help directly through the U.S. trade representative and other channels. Sustained American political pressure and widespread publicity finally forced MITI to confront the local lobby and limit to 18 months the application process under the restrictive retail law. It was April 1990, and Toys "R" Us had overcome its first major hurdle.

But there was another hurdle to cross. Toys "R" Us succeeds in large part by selling below suggested retail price. It accomplishes this mainly through exploiting economies it obtains through volume purchases. Anticipating the threat posed by that strategy to their own profit margins, Japanese toy manufacturers banded together and vowed not to sell their wares to Toys "R" Us. But Nintendo depends heavily on Toys "R" Us for the distribution of its products in the United States and other major markets. Nintendo's defection triggered an ultimate end to this boycott.

Private sector countermeasures consciously adopted by numerous major Japanese corporations are replacing the falling barriers to entry of public sector regulation.

Toys "R" Us has successfully entered the Japanese toy market through private-sector help—in this case, with the help of Nintendo.

Source: Mark Mason, "United States Direct Investment in Japan: Trends and Prospects," *California Management Review,* Fall 1992, pp. 98–115.

Trading Blocs   The world of **trading blocs** gained a new member with the ratification of the North American Free Trade Agreement (NAFTA). Such agreements influence location decisions, both within and outside trading bloc countries. Firms typically locate, or relocate, within a bloc to take advantage of new market opportunities or lower total costs afforded by the trading agreement. Other companies (those outside the trading bloc countries) decide on locations within the bloc so as not to be disqualified from competing in the new market. Examples include the location of various Japanese auto manufacturing plants in Europe before 1992 as well as recent moves by many communications and financial services companies into Mexico in a post-NAFTA environment.

Environmental Regulation   The environmental regulations that impact a certain industry in a given location should be included in the location decision. Besides measurable cost implications, this influences the relationship with the local community.

Host Community   The host community's interest in having the plant in its midst is a necessary part of the evaluation process. Local educational facilities and the broader issue of quality of life are important too.

Competitive Advantage   An important decision for multinational companies is the nation in which to locate the home base for each distinct business. Porter suggests that a company can have different home bases for distinct businesses or segments. Competitive advantage is created at a home base where strategy is set, the core product and process technology is created, and a critical mass of production takes place. So a company should move its home base to a country that stimulates innovation and provides the best environment for global competitiveness.[1] This concept can also be applied to domestic companies seeking to gain sustainable competitive advantage. It partly explains the southeastern states' recent emergence as the preferred corporate destination within the United States (i.e., its business climate fosters innovation and low cost production).

9.2   PLANT LOCATION METHODS

"If the boss likes Bakersfield, I like Bakersfield." Exhibit 9.1 summarizes the set of decisions that a company must make in choosing a plant location. While the exhibit implies a step-by-step process, virtually all activities listed take place simultaneously. As suggested by the preceding vote for Bakersfield, political decisions may occasionally override systematic analysis.

Evaluation of alternative regions, subregions, and communities is commonly termed *macro analysis*. Evaluation of specific sites in the selected community is termed *micro analysis*. Techniques used to support macro analyses include factor-rating

---

[1]Michael E. Porter, "The Competitive Advantage of Nations," *Harvard Business Review,* March–April 1990, pp. 73–93.

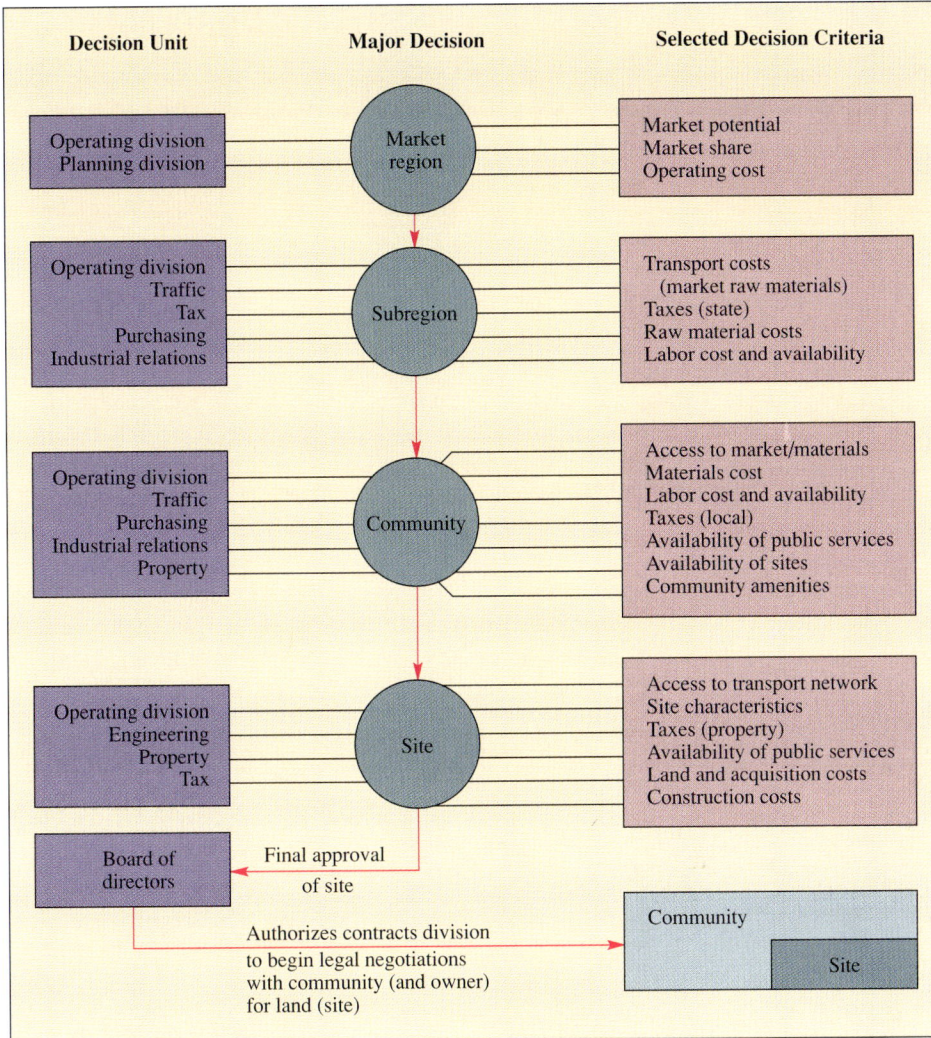

EXHIBIT 9.1
*Plant Search:
Company XYZ*

Source: Thomas M. Carroll and Robert D. Dean, "A Bayesian Approach to Plant-Location Decisions," *Decision Sentences* 11, no. 1 (January 1980), p. 87.

systems, linear programming, and center of gravity. A detailed cost analysis would accompany each of these methods, and they must, of course, be related to business strategy. (See the box inserts on AM/PM stores and Mercedes Benz later in the chapter for examples.

Factor-rating systems are perhaps the most widely used of the general location techniques because they provide a mechanism to combine diverse factors in an easy-to-understand format.

   By way of example, a refinery assigned the following range of point values to major factors affecting a set of possible sites.

**Factor-Rating
Systems**

	Range
Fuels in region	0 to 330
Power availability and reliability	0 to 200
Labor climate	0 to 100
Living conditions	0 to 100
Transportation	0 to 50
Water supply	0 to 10
Climate	0 to 50
Supplies	0 to 60
Tax policies and laws	0 to 20

Each site was then rated against each factor, and a point value was selected from its assigned range. The sums of assigned points for each site were then compared. The site with the most points was selected.

A major problem with simple point-rating schemes is that they do not account for the wide range of costs that may occur within each factor. For example, there may be only a few hundred dollars' difference between the best and worst locations on one factor and several thousands of dollars' difference between the best and the worst on another. The first factor may have the most points available to it but provide little help in making the location decision; the latter may have few points available but potentially show a real difference in the value of locations. To deal with this problem, Phillip Hicks and Areen Kumtha suggest that points possible for each factor be derived using a weighting scale based on standard deviations of costs rather than simply total cost amounts.[2] Interested readers should consult the original article for details of calculation in this useful method.

Linear Programming

The transportation method of linear programming (discussed in the supplement to Chapter 8) can be used to test the cost impact of different candidate locations on the entire production-distribution network. The way it works can be seen by reference to the Puck and Pawn Company example in the supplement. Here, we might add a new row which contains the unit shipping costs from a factory in a new location, *X*, to warehouses *E, F, G,* and *H*, along with the total amount it could supply. We could then solve this particular matrix for minimum total cost. Next we would replace the factory located in *X* in the same row of the matrix with a factory at a different location, say *Y*, and again solve for minimum total cost. Assuming factories in *X* and *Y* would be identical in other important respects, the location resulting in the lowest total cost for the network would be selected. This method is easy to use but it does require that at least subregional locations be identified before a solution can be found.

Center of Gravity Method

The **center of gravity method** is a technique for locating single facilities that considers the existing facilities, the distances between them, and the volumes of goods to be shipped. The technique is often used to locate intermediate or distribution warehouses. In its simplest form, this method assumes that inbound and outbound transportation costs are equal, and it does not include special shipping costs for less than full loads.

The center of gravity method begins by placing the existing locations on a coordinate grid system. The choice of coordinate systems is entirely arbitrary. The purpose is to

---

[2]Phillip E. Hicks and Areen M. Kumtha, "One Way to Tighten Up Plant Location Decisions," *Industrial Engineering* 9 (April 1971), pp. 19–23.

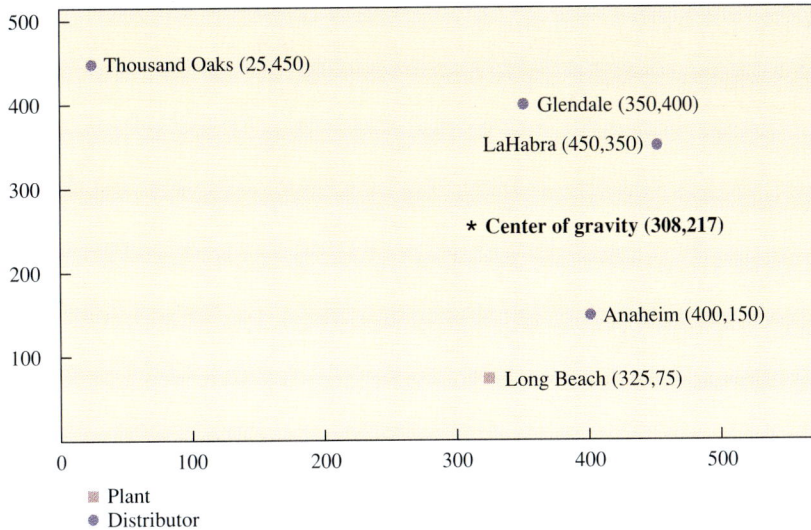

establish relative distances between locations. Using longitude and latitude coordinates might be helpful in international decisions. Exhibit 9.2 shows an example of a grid layout.

The center of gravity is found by calculating the *X* and *Y* coordinates that result in the minimal transportation cost. We use the formulas

$$C_x = \frac{\Sigma d_{ix} V_i}{\Sigma V_i}$$

$$C_y = \frac{\Sigma d_{iy} V_i}{\Sigma V_i}$$

(9.1)

where

C_x = X coordinate of the center of gravity

C_y = Y coordinate of the center of gravity

d_{ix} = X coordinate of the *i*th location

d_{iy} = Y coordinate of the *i*th location

V_i = Volume of goods moved to or from the *i*th location

E X A M P L E 9.1 / *HiOctane Refining Company*   The HiOctane Refining Company needs to locate an intermediate holding facility between its refining plant in Long Beach and its major distributors. Exhibit 9.2 shows the coordinate map. The amount of gasoline shipped to or from the plant and distributors appears in Exhibit 9.3.

In this example, for the Long Beach location (the first location),

$d_{1x} = 325$

$d_{1y} = 75$

$V_1 = 1,500$

E X H I B I T 9.3

*Shipping Volumes,
Center of Gravity
Example*

Locations	Gallons of Gasoline per Month (000,000)
Long Beach	1,500
Anaheim	250
LaHabra	450
Glendale	350
Thousand Oaks	450

S O L U T I O N   Using the information in Exhibits 9.2 and 9.3, we can calculate the coordinates of the center of gravity:

$$C_x = \frac{(325 \times 1,500) + (400 \times 250) + (450 \times 450) + (350 \times 350) + (25 \times 450)}{1,500 + 250 + 450 + 350 + 450}$$

$$= \frac{923,750}{3,000} = 307.9$$

$$C_y = \frac{(75 \times 1,500) + (150 \times 250) + (350 \times 450) + (400 \times 350) + (450 \times 450)}{1,500 + 250 + 450 + 350 + 450}$$

$$= \frac{650,000}{3,000} = 216.7$$

This gives management the X and Y coordinates of approximately 308 and 217, respectively, and provides an initial starting point to search for a new site. By examining the location of the calculated center of gravity on the grid map, we can see that it might be more cost-efficient to ship directly between the Long Beach plant and the Anaheim distributor than to ship via a warehouse near the center of gravity. Before a location decision is made, management would probably recalculate the center of gravity, changing the data to reflect this (i.e., decrease the gallons shipped from Long Beach by the amount Anaheim needs and remove Anaheim from the formula). ■

Analytic Delphi Model

Typical location analyses consider single-facility locations and are based on criteria such as minimizing travel time or distance between demand and supply points, minimization of the cost function, or minimizing the average response time. But multiple facilities and varied objectives have subsequently been added to this problem scenario. Some decision criteria are based on intangible—even emotional—issues. One approach to address the more complex location decision is by using the **Analytic Delphi Model** that incorporates tangible and intangible factors into the decision-making process.[3] This method integrates the Delphi Method (discussed in Chapter 7) and the Analytic Hierarchy Process, a mathematical model for multicriteria decision making. The Analytic Delphi Model has five steps:

1. Form two Delphi panels.
2. Identify threats and opportunities.
3. Determine direction and strategic goals of the organization.
4. Develop alternatives.
5. Prioritize alternatives.

---

[3]Hossein Azani and Reza Khorramshahgol, *Engineering Costs & Production Economics* 20, no. 1 (July 1990), pp. 23–28.

9.3   LOCATING SERVICE FACILITIES

Because of the variety of service firms and the relatively low cost of establishing a service facility compared to one for manufacturing, new service facilities are far more common than new factories and warehouses. Indeed, there are few communities in which
rapid population growth has not been paralleled by concurrent rapid growth in retail outlets, restaurants, municipal services, and entertainment facilities.

Services typically have multiple sites to maintain close contact with customers. The
location decision is closely tied to the market selection decision. If the target market is
college-age groups, locations in retirement communities—despite desirability in terms of
cost, resource availability, and so forth—are not viable alternatives. Market needs also
affect the number of sites to be built, the size, and the characteristics of the sites.
Whereas manufacturing location decisions are often made by minimizing costs, many
service location decision techniques maximize the profit potential of various sites.
Below we present two examples of analytical approaches that can be used to help select
good sites. The first employs regression modeling and the second a simple heuristic
procedure.

E X A M P L E 9.2 / *Screening Location Sites at La Quinta Motor Inns*   Selecting
good sites is crucial to a hotel chain's success. Of the four major marketing considerations (price, product, promotion, and location), location and product have been shown
to be most important for multisite firms. As a result, hotel chain owners who can pick
good sites quickly have a distinct competitive advantage.

Exhibit 9.4 shows the initial list of variables included in a study to help La Quinta
Motor Inns screen potential locations for its new hotels.[4] Data were collected on 57 existing La Quinta Inns. Analysis of the data identified the variables that correlated with
operating profit in 1983 and 1986. (See Exhibit 9.5)

S O L U T I O N   A **regression model** was constructed. Its final form was

$$
\begin{aligned}
\text{Profitability} = 39.05 &- 5.41 \times \text{State population per inn (1,000)} \\
&+ 5.86 \times \text{Price of the inn} \\
&- 3.91 \times \text{Square root of the median income of the} \\
&\qquad \text{area (1,000)} \\
&+ 1.75 \times \text{College students within four miles}
\end{aligned}
$$

The model shows that profitability is affected by market penetration, positively affected by price, negatively affected by higher incomes (the inns do better in
lower–median-income areas), and positively affected by colleges nearby.

La Quinta implemented the model on a Lotus 1-2-3 spreadsheet and routinely uses
the spreadsheet to screen potential real estate acquisitions. The founder and president of
La Quinta has accepted the model's validity and no longer feels obligated to personally
select the sites.

This example shows that a specific model can be obtained from the requirements
of service organizations and used to identify the most important features in site
selection.   ■

---

[4]Sheryl E. Kimes and James A. Fitzsimmons, "Selecting Profitable Hotel Sites at La Quinta Motor Inns,"
Interfaces 20 (March–April 1990), pp. 12–20.

Category	Name	Description
Competitive	INNRATE	Inn price
	PRICE	Room rate for the inn
	RATE	Average competitive room rate
	RMS1	Hotel rooms within 1 mile
	RMSTOTAL	Hotel rooms within 3 miles
	ROOMSINN	Inn rooms
Demand generators	CIVILIAN	Civilian personnel on base
	COLLEGE	College enrollment
	HOSP1	Hospital beds within 1 mile
	HOSPTOTL	Hospital beds within 4 miles
	HVYIND	Heavy industrial employment
	LGTIND	Light industrial acreage
	MALLS	Shopping mall square footage
	MILBLKD	Military base blocked
	MILITARY	Military personnel
	MILTOT	MILITARY + CIVILIAN
	OFC1	Office space within 1 mile
	OFCTOTAL	Office space within 4 miles
	OFCCBD	Office space in Central Business District
	PASSENGR	Airport passengers enplaned
	RETAIL	Scale ranking of retail activity
	TOURISTS	Annual tourists
	TRAFFIC	Traffic count
	VAN	Airport van
Demographic	EMPLYPCT	Unemployment percentage
	INCOME	Average family income
	POPULACE	Residential population
Market awareness	AGE	Years inn has been open
	NEAREST	Distance to nearest inn
	STATE	State population per inn
	URBAN	Urban population per inn
Physical	ACCESS	Accessibility
	ARTERY	Major traffic artery
	DISTCBD	Distance to downtown
	SIGNVIS	Sign visibility

Source: Reprinted by permission of Sheryl E. Kimes and James A. Fitzsimmons, "Selecting Profitable Hotel Sites at La Quinta Motor Inns," *Interfaces* 20 (March–April 1990). Copyright 1990, The Institute of Management Sciences, 290 Westminster Street, Providence, Rhode Island 02903 USA.

A common problem encountered by service-providing organizations is deciding how many service outlets to establish within a geographic area, and where. The problem is complicated by the many possible locations and several options in the absolute number of service centers. Thus, attempting to find a good solution, much less an optimal one, can be extremely time consuming even for a relatively small problem. For example, there would be 243 possible solutions for a problem involving choosing among one, two, or three retail outlets to serve four geographically dispersed customer populations, even where there are only three possible locations for the outlets. To illustrate one approach to searching for feasible solutions to such problems, we apply to a sample problem a heuristic method based on one described by Alireza Ardalan.[5]

_____

[5]Alireza Ardalan, "An Efficient Heuristic for Service Facility Location," *Proceedings, Northeast Decision Sciences Institute Conference,* 1984, pp. 181–82.

E X H I B I T 9.5

A Summary of the Variables That Correlated with Operating Margin in 1983 and 1986

Variable	1983	1986
ACCESS	.20	
AGE	.29	.49
COLLEGE		.25
DISTCBD		−.22
EMPLYPCT	−.22	−.22
INCOME		−.23
MILTOT		.22
NEAREST	−.51	
OFCCBD	.30	
POPULACE	.30	.35
PRICE	.38	.58
RATE		.27
STATE	−.32	−.33
SIGNVIS	.25	
TRAFFIC	.32	
URBAN	−.22	−.26

Source: Reprinted by permission of Sheryl E. Kimes and James A. Fitzsimmons. "Selecting Profitable Hotel Sites at La Quinta Motor Inns," *Interfaces* 20 (March–April 1990). Copyright 1990, The Institute of Management Sciences, 290 Westminster Street, Providence, Rhode Island 02903 USA.

E X H I B I T 9.6

Distances, Population, and Relative Weights

From Community	Miles to Clinic				Population of Community (thousands)	Relative Weighting of Population
	A	B	C	D		
A	0	11	8	12	10	1.1
B	11	0	10	7	8	1.4
C	8	10	0	9	20	0.7
D	9.5	7	9	0	12	1.0

E X H I B I T 9.7

Weighted Population Distances

From Community	To Clinic			
	A	B	C	D
A	0	121	88	132
B	123.2	0	112	78.4
C	112	140	0	126
D	114	84	108	0

E X A M P L E 9.3 / *Locating Two Medical Clinics Using Ardalan Heuristic*   Suppose that a medical consortium wishes to establish two clinics to provide medical care for people living in four communities in Off Tackle County, Ohio. Assume that the sites under study are in each community and that the population of each community is evenly distributed within the community's boundaries. Further, assume that the potential use of the clinics by members of the various communities has been determined and weighting factors reflecting the relative importance of serving members of the population of each community have been developed. (This information appears in Exhibit 9.6.) The objective of the problem is to find the two clinics that can serve all communities at the lowest weighted travel-distance cost.

AM/PM convenience stores are a subsidiary of the ARCO Corporation. These stores are usually connected with service stations. The goals of AM/PM International are to leverage the existing AM/PM program through brand licensing agreements in foreign countries and joint venture participation. Furthermore, ARCO wants to participate aggressively in emerging international markets and leverage its international presence. ARCO also wants to generate additional long-term profits.

To select a new potential country, AM/PM International looks at four main criteria:

1. The population should be over 1 million in a targeted city.
2. Annual per capita income should be over $2,000.
3. The political system should be fairly stable.
4. The host country should have minimal restrictions on hard currency repatriation.

Once AM/PM has selected a potential country for its business, it evaluates the country's

1. Stage of industrial development.
2. People/car ratio. (This is important because the AM/PM stores are located in service stations.)
3. Population density in rural and urban areas.
4. Availability and cost of labor.
5. Infrastructure (supply and distribution, equipment availability, real estate cost, and reliability of utilities).
6. Tax regulations.
7. Legal issues.

AM/PM International uses franchising as a rapid and convenient way to expand in the Pacific Rim, Europe, and North America. The company's prospect list for the next expansion includes Italy, France, Denmark, Mexico, Brazil, Malaysia, and Canada.

AM/PM's international expansion strategy is based on three points:

1. Use the existing service station staff to run the convenience store.
2. For the first year an American-trained manager works closely with the new licensee.
3. Develop new stores in selected countries as quickly as possible.

Source: ARCO presentation to University of Southern California MBA students, June 5, 1991.

S O L U T I O N   *Step 1.* Construct a weighted population-distance table from initial data table, multiplying distance times weighting factor (Exhibit 9.7). For example, Community A to Clinic B is $11 \times 1.1 \times 10 = 121$.

Step 2. Add the amounts in each column. Choose the community with the lowest cost and locate a facility there (Community C in our example). (Recall that costs are expressed in weighted population-distance units.)

| | **To Clinic Located in Community** | | | |
From Community	**A**	**B**	**C**	**D**
A	0	121	88	132
B	123.2	0	112	78.4
C	112	140	0	126
D	114	84	108	0
	349.2	345	308	336.4

Step 3. For each row, compare the cost of each column entry to the community clinics already located. If the cost is less, do not change them. If the cost is greater, reduce the cost to the lowest of the sites already selected.

To Clinic Located in Community

From Community	A	B	C	D
A	0	88	88	88
B	112	0	112	78.4
C	0	0	0	0
D	108	84	108	0
	$\overline{220}$	$\overline{172}$	$\overline{308}$	$\overline{166.4}$

Step 4. If additional locations are desired, choose the community with the lowest cost from those not already selected (Community D in our example).

Step 5. Repeat Step 3, reducing each row entry that exceeds the entry in the column just selected.

To Clinic Located in Community

From Community	A	B	D
A	0	88	88
B	78.4	0	78.4
C	0	0	0
D	0	0	0
	$\overline{78.4}$	$\overline{88}$	$\overline{166.4}$

Continue repeating Steps 4 and 5 until the desired number of locations is selected. If we wished to compute the complete list, it would be:

To Clinic Located in Community

From Community	A	B
A	0	0
B	78.4	0
C	0	0
D	0	0
	$\overline{78.4}$	$\overline{0}$

The problem has now been solved for all four possible locations. Choose C first, then D, then A, then B.

The logic in this procedure is as follows:

1. We select the least total cost column since this column location represents the lowest travel cost of all communities traveling to that location.

2. Once a location is chosen, no rational member of a community would travel to any other community that was more costly. In Step 2, for example, Community A residents would certainly prefer going to a clinic located in Community C (88), which has already been decided on, than to B (121) or D (132). Therefore, the maximum number of weighted population-distance units that residents of A would be willing to pay is 88, and we can use this amount as

Mercedes-Benz Parks in Vance, Alabama

Mercedes has always pursued automotive excellence with little regard to costs. But it now has a 30 percent cost disadvantage against Japanese and U.S. competitors, and has seen its share of the luxury market slip since the late 1980s. As a key element in reinventing itself, Mercedes decided to go ahead with its luxury sports-utility vehicle project. The Multi-Purpose Vehicle (MPV), as the vehicle is known, is aimed mainly at the United States because it is the world's largest market for this type of automobile. Andreas Renschler, the relatively new deputy to Chairman Helmut Werner, was named to head the project and was given a bold brief: Find a site outside Germany for the project. A worldwide selection process began in January 1993.

In April 1993, Mercedes announced that it would locate the MPV plant in the United States. Studies showed that combined costs of labor, shipping, and components would be lowest there. Mercedes considered more than 100 sites in 35 states before narrowing the search in August 1993 to Alabama, North Carolina, and South Carolina. One of the main criteria was transportation costs because Mercedes expects to export about half the vehicles produced. The U.S. site will be the only production facility for the MPV.

In September 1993, the Mercedes-Benz board approved the project team's selection of Vance, Alabama, for the $300 million, 1,500-employee, 65,000-vehicles-per-year manufacturing plant. Vance is located along Interstate 20/59 between Tuscaloosa and Birmingham, Alabama. State officials have even offered to rename a section of I-20/59 the Mercedes-Benz Autobahn.

According to Mercedes, the state's probusiness climate was significant to the site selection process. Other selection criteria included

- Access to interstate highways.
- Access to railroads and ports.
- Adequate available labor.
- A lucrative package of financial incentives and tax breaks.

- Proximity to schools and universities in Tuscaloosa and Birmingham.
- The quality of life.

Alabama's incentive package totaled about $253 million, more than twice what South Carolina gave BMW in 1992. Alabama's package included

- $92.2 million to buy and build the 966-acre site, create a foreign trade zone, and build an employee training center.
- $77.5 million to extend water, gas, and sewer lines to the site and provide other infrastructure.
- $60 million to train Mercedes employees, suppliers, and workers in related industries.
- $15 million from private business.
- $8.7 million in sales/use tax abatements on machinery, equipment, and construction material.

Studies show that this money is well spent. The plant's economic impact is estimated at $365 million for the first year and $7.3 billion over 20 years.

The three finalists in the site selection process were in a dead heat when it came to business climate, education levels, and transportation. Long-term operating costs at all three locations were approximately equal, despite slight differences in incentive packages. Right-to-work laws and low unionization were not factors in the decision-making process. The deciding factor was Alabama's dedication to the project. One final factor did not hurt: The wooded, rolling hills around the site reminded the Germans of the Swabian countryside near Stuttgart, home of their headquarters.

Construction of the facility began in spring 1994, with vehicle production to start in January 1997.

Source: David Woodruff and John Templeman, "Why Mercedes Is Alabama Bound," *Business Week,* October 11, 1993, pp. 138–39; and Tim Venable, "Mercedes-Benz Parks $300 Million Plant in Alabama," *Site Selection,* December 1993, p. 1292.

our top limit. If a clinic is located in A, however, residents of A would patronize their own community clinic (at a cost of 0). Residents in Community B would prefer C (112) to A (123.2) but not to B (0) or D (78.4). Therefore, the cost 123.2 is reduced to 112, but 0 and 78.4 remain unchanged.

3. Once a community location is selected and the matrix costs adjusted, that community can be dropped from the matrix since the column costs are no longer relevant. ■

9.4 CONCLUSION

Facility location decisions are a key element in any firm's overall strategic plan. Dramatic changes in the global geopolitical environment, coupled with rapid advances in technology, have provided decision makers with a variety of options and opportunities for locating their businesses. The criteria for selecting appropriate locations have also evolved beyond the singular focus on minimizing cost or distance. Today, a number of quantitative and qualitative issues impact location decisions. A company's long-term success depends on its managers' ability to make a comprehensive synthesis of the various dimensions of the multifaceted location problem.

9.5 FORMULA REVIEW

Center of gravity

$$C_x = \frac{\Sigma d_{ix} V_i}{\Sigma V_i}$$

$$C_y = \frac{\Sigma d_{iy} V_i}{\Sigma V_i}$$

(9.1)

9.6 SOLVED PROBLEM

1. Cool Air, a manufacturer of automotive air conditioners, currently produces its XB-300 line at three different locations: Plant A, Plant B, and Plant C. Recently management decided to build all compressors, a major product component, in a separate dedicated facility, Plant D.

   Using the center of gravity method and the information displayed in Exhibits 9.8 and 9.9, determine the best location for Plant D. Assume a linear relationship between volumes shipped and shipping costs (no premium charges).

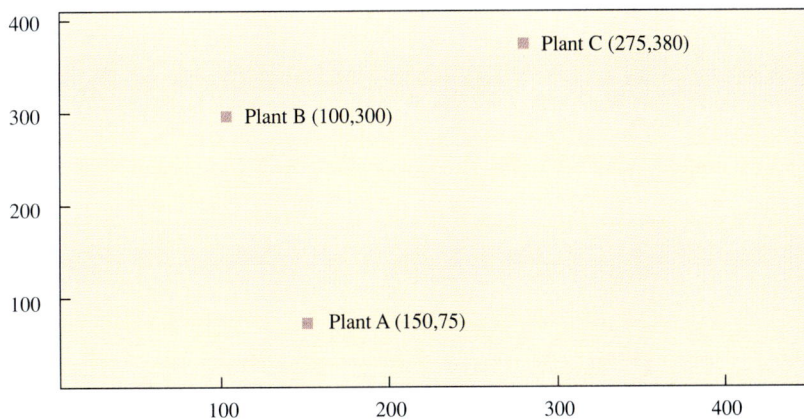

EXHIBIT 9.8

Plant Location Matrix

E X H I B I T 9.9

Quantity of Compressors Required by Each Plant

Plant	Compressors Required per Year
A	6,000
B	8,200
C	7,000

Solution

$d_{1x} = 150$ $d_{1y} = 75$ $V_1 = 6,000$

$d_{2x} = 100$ $d_{2y} = 300$ $V_2 = 8,200$

$d_{3x} = 275$ $d_{3y} = 380$ $V_3 = 7,000$

$$C_x = \frac{\Sigma d_{ix} V_i}{\Sigma V_i} = \frac{(150 \times 6,000) + (100 \times 8,200) + (275 \times 7,000)}{6,000 + 8,200 + 7,000} = 172$$

$$C_y = \frac{\Sigma d_{iy} V_i}{\Sigma V_i} = \frac{(75 \times 6,000) + (300 \times 8,200) + (380 \times 7,000)}{21,200}$$

$$= \frac{5,570,000}{21,200} = 262.7$$

Plant $D[C_x, C_y] = D[172, 263]$

9.7 REVIEW AND DISCUSSION QUESTIONS

1. What motivations typically cause firms to initiate a facilities location or relocation project?

2. List five major reasons why a new electronic components manufacturing firm should move into your city or town.

3. How do facilities location decisions differ for service facilities and manufacturing plants?

4. What are the pros and cons of relocating a small or midsized manufacturing firm (that makes mature products) from the United States to Mexico in the post-NAFTA environment?

5. If you could locate your new software development company anywhere in the world, which place would you choose, and why?

9.8 PROBLEMS

1. Refer to the information given in the Solved Problem. Suppose management decides to shift 2,000 units of production from Plant B to Plant A. Does this change the proposed location of Plant D, the compressor production facility? If so, where should Plant D be located?

2. A drugstore chain plans to open four stores in a medium-sized city. However, funds are limited, so only two can be opened this year.

    a. Given the following matrix showing the weighted population distance costs for each of the four areas and four store sites, select the two to be opened up first.

    b. If additional funds become available, which store should be the third to open?

		Store			
		1	2	3	4
Geographic Area	1	0	20	160	60
	2	80	0	40	80
	3	120	80	0	100
	4	80	100	60	0

3. A firm is considering four possible office locations within a particular city. The firm would like to have an office in each location eventually, but at present its managers would like to open just one. They want to know the sequence in which they should open all four offices. The accompanying matrix shows costs for opening each office in each area. Determine the order in which they should be opened.

Office

Geographic Area		A	B	C	D
	A	0	34	40	30
	B	24	0	36	54
	C	60	20	0	36
	D	50	40	60	0

CASE

9 . 9   C A S E
Is It Russian Roulette?

Dramatic changes in the former Soviet Union have turned business conditions there into a roller-coaster ride. The unstable situation has created a great deal of uncertainty for firms that look to this part of the world as a market for goods and services. Yet the size of the market and the potential for international expansion remain tempting. Russia, with all its uncertainties, remains the most popular destination among the Commonwealth of Independent States (CIS).

Exhibit C9.1 on page 392 shows the risks of doing business in the former USSR based on responses to a 1992 survey of U.S.–based businesses.

"Only put in what you can afford to lose. Decide up front what you want—profits, market share, and the like," advises Erich Zarnfaller, senior international treasury analyst at EG&G, Inc., a Wellesley, Massachusetts–based provider of environmental management services and manufacturer of radiation and security devices. Adds Kathy Creculius, a vice president at BayBank in Boston, "The former USSR presents . . . great risks. However, for those with ethnic and linguistic ties to the CIS countries, with solid business experience and capital to invest—and risk—there are now opportunities." A recent survey of CFOs of leading companies also echoes such sentiments of risk.

Also, most firms view host governments as being neutral toward U.S. firms. Some firms even found them to be a barrier to doing business. The following incidents are reported by Intertech International Corporation, a Boston-based firm whose Austrian subsidiary was involved in a joint venture to install air-conditioning systems in new buildings in the Republic of Georgia. The Soviet embassy in Wash-

ington, DC, said a letter from the Soviet partner was not sufficient to provide work and travel visas. But the Soviet embassy in Vienna, home of Intertech's joint venture partner, did agree to provide visas based on the same letter. Furthermore, in an attempt to send cargo by air freight to the Black Sea via Moscow, Intertech lost six precious weeks waiting for bureaucrats in Moscow to "find" the shipment. In that time, the goods could have been delivered by ocean freight to Odessa or air freight to Vienna and trucked to the site. Such are the remnants of an incredibly complex web of bureaucracy left in the aftermath of decentralized control in the Soviet Union!

Yet the majority of firms surveyed—including manufacturing, service, and sales and distribution companies—plan to either maintain or expand current levels of investment in their existing activities.

Questions

1. Discuss advantages and disadvantages of facility location in the old Soviet Union with reference to the typical location selection criteria.

2. Discuss the issues involved in locating a specific company in Russia.

Source: Daniel J. McCarthy, Sheila M. Puffer, and Peter J. Simmonds, "Riding the Russian Roller Coaster: U.S. Firms' Recent Experience and Future Plans in the Former USSR," *California Management Review,* Fall 1993, pp. 99–115. © 1993 Regents of the University of California. Reprinted from the *California Management Review,* Vol. 36, No. 1. By permission of The Regents.

EXHIBIT   C9.1

Risk Faced by
Western Businesses

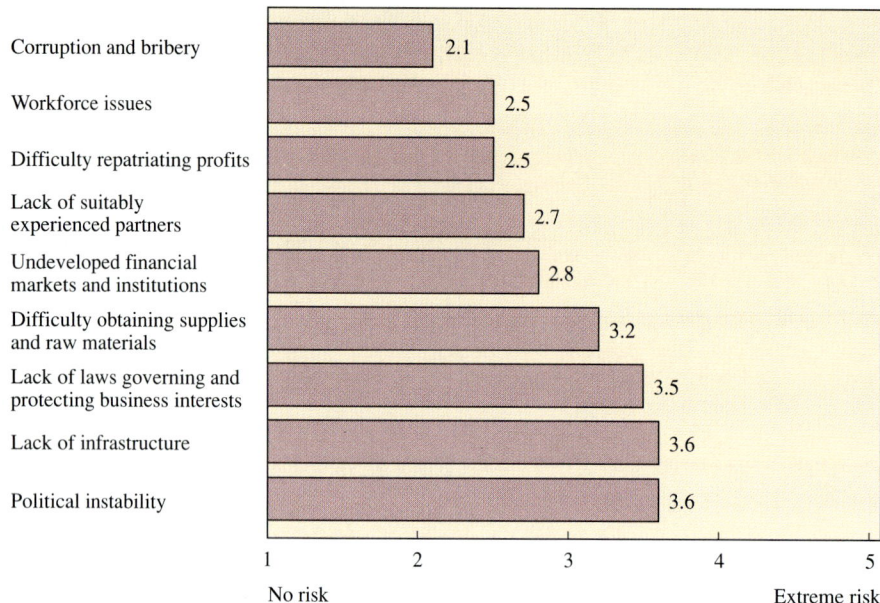

Corruption and bribery — 2.1
Workforce issues — 2.5
Difficulty repatriating profits — 2.5
Lack of suitably experienced partners — 2.7
Undeveloped financial markets and institutions — 2.8
Difficulty obtaining supplies and raw materials — 3.2
Lack of laws governing and protecting business interests — 3.5
Lack of infrastructure — 3.6
Political instability — 3.6

1   2   3   4   5
No risk   Extreme risk

CASE

9.10 C A S E
The Plant Location Puzzle*

Ann Reardon made her way across the crowded trade-show floor, deep in thought and oblivious to the noisy activity all around her. As CEO of the Eldora Company (EDC) for the previous 13 years, she had led her organization through a period of extraordinary success. While larger bicycle makers had moved their manufacturing operations overseas to take advantage of lower labor costs, Eldora had stuck with a domestic manufacturing strategy, keeping its plant on the same campus as its corporate offices in Boulder, Colorado. Ann felt that her strategy of keeping all the parts of the company in the same location, while unconventional, had contributed greatly to cooperation among various departments and, ultimately, to the company's growth: EDC had become the largest and most profitable bicycle company in the United States. Yet her manufacturing vice president, Sean Andrews, was now urging her to build a plant in China.

"Look at the number of companies here," he had said that morning, as they helped several other EDC staffers stack brochures on the exhibit table and position the company's latest models around the perimeter of their area. Manufacturing heads rarely attended trade shows; in fact, this was Sean's first, but he had wanted to attend, and Ann had supported his interest. "There are too many players in this mar-

ket," he had said. "I've been saying this for two months now, and you know the forecasters' numbers back me up. But if they weren't enough to convince you, just look around. The industry is reaching the saturation point here in the States. We have to break into Asia."

"Leave it alone, Sean," Ann had replied. "I know this is something you're pushing; you've said so in the past. But let's set up a time to talk about it in detail later. This isn't the time or the place."

Now, three hours later, with the show in full swing, Ann understood why Sean had been compelled to speak up again. Having all their competitors in the same room at the same time was a powerful visual reminder of how the industry had changed. She thought about what Sean had said about the U.S. market. In 1992, EDC's sales and earnings had hit record levels. The company now produced almost 30% of the bicycles sold in the United States. But U.S. mass-market bicycle sales were growing by only 2% per year, while the Asian market for those same bikes was nearly doubling on an annual basis. And Eldora could not competitively serve those markets from its U.S. manufacturing facility. Two of the largest bike manufacturers in the world, located in rapidly growing Asian markets, enjoyed a significant labor and distribution cost advantage.

---

*This is a broad top-management–oriented strategy case designed to elicit debate.

She stopped at a mountain bike display set up by a fast-growing, young bike company. Mountain bikes with front suspension were the latest trend—the added support and cushion allowed riders to better absorb the shocks inherent in off-road riding without slowing down or losing balance. Most of these bikes were still prohibitively expensive. But Eldora, too, had an entry in this product category, retailing for about $190, and Ann was proud of it. For years, the company had concentrated its efforts on inexpensive bicycles, which retailed through mass merchandisers for between $100 and $200. Eldora's prices were slightly higher than other low-end competitors, but large retailers were willing to pay the premium because EDC had consistently been able to offer many state-of-the-art styles and features with quick, timely deliveries that competitors building overseas couldn't match.

One of the reasons the company had been so successful was that Boulder, Colorado, was a bicyclists' mecca. Eldora employees at all levels shared a genuine love of bicycling and eagerly pursued knowledge of the industry's latest trends and styles. Someone was always suggesting a better way to position the hand brakes, or a new toe grip that allowed for better traction and easier dismounts. And Eldora never had a shortage of people willing to test out the latest prototypes.

Another reason was that all marketing staff, engineers, designers, and manufacturing personnel worked on one campus, within a 10-minute walk of one another. Ann had bet big on that strategy, and it had paid off. Communication was easy, and changes in styles, production plans, and the like could be made quickly and efficiently. Mountain bikes, for example, had gone from 0 percent to more than 50 percent of the market volume since 1988, and Eldora had met the increased demand with ease. And when orders for cross-bikes—a mountain/road bike hybrid that had enjoyed a spurt of popularity—began to fall off, Eldora had been able to adjust its production run with minimal disruption.

EDC had also benefited from its foray into the high-end market (bicycles retailing for between $400 and $700) 12 years earlier. One of Ann's first moves as CEO had been to enter into a joint venture with Rinaldi, a high-end Italian bicycle manufacturer that at the time was specializing in racing models. As part of the agreement, EDC had begun importing Rinaldi bikes under the brand name Summit and selling them through specialty bike dealers. Similarly, Rinaldi had begun marketing EDC bikes in Europe. That arrangement had had lasting rewards: although racing bikes were no longer very popular, EDC's offerings had taken off. About 20 percent of EDC's sales were now made outside the United States (primarily in Europe and Canada) through this and other agreements.

The relationships with Rinaldi and the specialty bike shops also helped keep EDC management aware of the latest industry trends over the years. Most recently, those trends had included a move toward more exotic frame materials like aluminum and carbon fiber and more advanced components, including the new front-fork suspension systems. Ann examined another rival's brochure touting a soon-to-be-released high-end model with these advances. EDC engineers were clearly ahead of the curve.

Her satisfaction was quickly tempered with thoughts of foreign sales performance. Between 1987 and 1991, EDC's foreign sales had grown at an annual rate of over 80 percent. But during the previous two years they had been flat.

Sean appeared at Ann's side, jolting her out of her thoughts and into the reality of her surroundings. "Dale just finished up the first round of retailers' meetings," he said. "We'd like to get some lunch back over at the hotel and talk about our options." Dale Stewart was Eldora's marketing vice president. His views of what was best for the company often differed from Sean's, but the two had an amiable working relationship and enjoyed frequent spirited verbal sparring matches.

"You won't let this go, will you," Ann said, throwing up her hands in a gesture of surrender. "Fine, let's talk. But you know I won't make a decision until we've had a more formal round of discussions back in Boulder next month."

Over sandwiches, Sean made his case. "Our primary markets in North America and western Europe represent less than a quarter of the worldwide demand. Of the 200 million bicycles made in the world last year, 40 million were sold in China, 30 million in India, and 9 million in Japan. Historically, bikes sold in Asia's developing markets were low-end products used as primary modes of transportation. But the economic picture is changing fast. There's a growing middle class. Suddenly people have disposable income. Many consumers there are now seeking higher quality and trendier styles. Mountain bikes with suspension are in. And cross-bikes are still holding their own. In fact, the demand in these markets for the product categories we produce has been doubling annually, and the growth rates seem sustainable.

"If we're going to compete in Asia, though, we need a local plant. My staff has evaluated many locations there. We've looked at wage rates, proximity to markets, and materials costs, and we feel that China is our best bet. We'd like to open a plant there as soon as possible, and start building our position."

Dale jumped in. "Two of our largest competitors, one from China, one from Taiwan, have been filling the demand so far," he said. "In 1990, 97 percent of the volume produced by these companies was for export. In 1994, they are projecting that 45 percent of their production will be for local markets. We can't compete with them from here. About 20% of our product cost is labor, and the hourly wages of the manufacturing workforce in these countries are between 5 percent and 15 percent of ours. It also costs us an additional 20 percent in transportation and duties to get our bicycles to these markets."

He glanced at Sean quickly and continued. "But here's where I disagree with Sean. I think we need a short-term solution. These companies have a big lead on us, and the more I think about it, the more I believe we need to put a direct sales operation in Asia first."

"Dale, you're crazy," Sean said, pouring himself some ice water from the pitcher on the table. "What good would an Asian sales operation do without a manufacturing plant? I know we source components in Asia now, but we could save another 10 percent of those parts if we were located there. Then we would really be bringing Eldora to Asia. If we want to compete there, we have to play from our greatest strength—quality. If we did it your way, you wouldn't be selling Eldora bikes. You'd just be selling some product with our label on it. You wouldn't get the quality. You wouldn't build the same kind of reputation we have here. It wouldn't really be Eldora. Over the long term, it couldn't work."

"We're building bicycles, not rocket ships," Dale countered. "There are lots of companies in Asia that could provide us with a product very quickly if we gave them our designs and helped them with their production process. We could outsource production in the short term, until we made more permanent arrangements." He turned to Ann. "We could even outsource the product permanently, despite what Sean says. What do we know about building and running a plant in China? All I know is we're losing potential share even as we sit here. The trading companies aren't giving our products the attention they deserve, and they also aren't giving us the information we need on the features that consumers in these markets want. A sales operation would help us learn the market even as we're entering it. Setting up a plant first would take too long. We need to be over there now, and opening a sales operation is the quickest way."

Ann cut in. "Dale has a good point, Sean," she said. "We've been successful here in large part because our entire operation is in Boulder, on one site. We've had complete control over our own flexible manufacturing operation, and that's been a key factor in our ability to meet rapid change in the local market. How would we address the challenges inherent in manufacturing in a facility halfway around the world? Would you consider moving there? And for how long?

"Also, think about our other options. If the biggest issue keeping up out of these markets right now is cost, then both of you are ignoring a few obvious alternatives. Right now, only our frame-building operation is automated. We could cut labor costs significantly by automating more processes. And why are you so bent on China? Frankly, when I was there last month touring facilities, a lot of what I saw worried me. You know, that day I was supposed to tour a production facility, there was a power failure. Judging by the reactions of the personnel in the plant the next day, these outages are common. The roads to the facility are in very poor condition. And wastewater and cleaning solvents are regularly dumped untreated into the waterways. We could operate differently if we located there, but what impact would that have on costs?

"Taiwan has a better developed infrastructure than China. What about making that our Asian base? And I've heard that Singapore offers attractive tax arrangements to new manufacturing operations. Then there's Mexico. It's closer to home, and aside from distribution costs, the wage rates are similar to Asia's and many of the other risks would be minimized. You both feel strongly about this, I know, but this isn't a decision we can make based on enthusiasm." Ann crumpled up her sandwich wrapper and drank the last of her soda. "Let's get back over to the exhibits. I'm attending the IT seminar at 1:30. We'll schedule a formal meeting on this subject soon. I was going to say next month, but how about bumping it up two weeks?"

Walking back to the convention center with Dale and Sean, Ann realized that she wasn't just frustrated because she didn't know which course EDC should pursue. She was concerned that she really didn't know which aspects of the decision were important and which were irrelevant. Should she establish a division in China? If so, which functions should she start with? Manufacturing? Marketing? And what about engineering? Or should she consider a different location? Would China's low labor costs offset problems caused by a poor infrastructure?

Growth had always been vitally important to Eldora, both in creating value to shareholders and in providing a work environment that could attract and retain the most talented people. Now it appeared that Ann would have to choose between continued growth and a domestic-only manufacturing strategy that had served her well. Ann knew the plant location decision she had made years earlier had been critical to the company's success, and she felt the company's next move would be just as crucial.

Questions

1. What is the competitive environment facing EDC?
2. What are EDC's strengths in manufacturing?
3. Should EDC establish a manufacturing division in Asia?
4. What plan of action would you recommend to Ann Reardon?

9.11 SELECTED BIBLIOGRAPHY

Blackburn, Joseph, D. *Time-Based Competition: The Next Battle Ground in American Manufacturing.* Homewood, IL: Richard D. Irwin, 1991.

Coyle, John J., and Edward J. Bardi. *The Management of Logistics,* 2d ed. St. Paul: West Publishing, 1980, pp. 294–98.

Francis, R. L., and J. A. White. *Facilities Layout and Location: An Analytical Approach.* Englewood Cliffs, NJ: Prentice Hall, 1987.

Heskett, J. L., W. E. Sasser, Jr., and C. W. L. Hart. *Service Breakthroughs: Changing the Rules of the Game.* New York: Free Press, 1990.

Shycon, Harvey N. "Site Location Analysis, Cost and Customer Service Consideration." *Proceedings of the Seventeenth Annual International Conference,* American Production and Inventory Control Society, 1974, pp. 335–47.

Skinner, Wickham. "The Focused Factory." *Harvard Business Review,* May–June 1974, pp. 113–21.

Tompkins, James A., and John A. White. *Facilities Planning.* New York: John Wiley & Sons, 1984.

Chapter

10

Facility Layout

CHAPTER OUTLINE

KEY TERMS

Process Layout

Product Layout

Group Technology (Cellular) Layout

Fixed-Position Layout

CRAFT

Systematic Layout Planning

Cycle Time

Assembly-Line Balancing

Precedence Relationship

Retail Service Layout

Servicescape

Office Layout

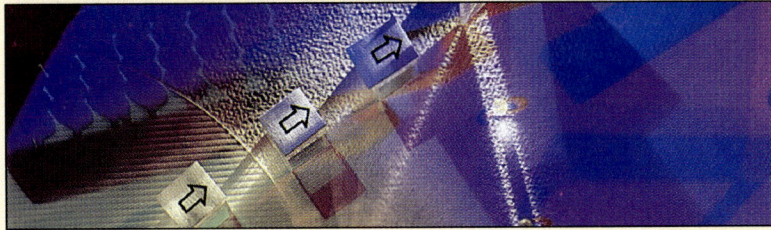

As they developed their first franchised restaurant, the McDonald brothers anticipated that it would be the model for many others like it. The plans called for a new, distinctive building with large golden arches plus a kitchen that was twice as large as the original San Bernardino restaurant's. Because the McDonald's production system had five cooks working in a limited area at a frantic pace, a good kitchen layout was vital to prevent the cooks from running into each other or having to move any further than necessary. To determine the best positions for the equipment in the new kitchen, the brothers invited the night crew from the original restaurant over to their house after work. The brothers drew a full-size outline of the new kitchen on their tennis court in red chalk. The crew then moved around in this imaginary kitchen, making hamburgers, shakes, and fries, while the brothers marked out the best positions for each piece of equipment. By late that night, they had created an efficient layout for the new kitchen for much less than the normal engineering costs. The new layout was to be recorded by a draftsman the following morning. Unfortunately, a rare desert rainstorm came through San Bernardino that night, washing away the chalk, and the work had to be redone.

Source: John F. Love, *McDonald's: Behind the Arches* (New York: Bantam Books, 1986), pp. 21–22.

The McDonald's brothers recognized the fundamental importance of a good layout to their production system's success. A good layout is crucial for virtually any organization that creates a product or delivers a service within a production facility.

As indicated in the McDonald's vignette, the layout decision entails determining the placement of departments, workstations, machines, and stock-holding points within a productive facility. Its general objective is to arrange these elements in a way that ensures a smooth work flow (in a factory) or a particular traffic pattern (in a service organization). The inputs to the layout decision are

1. Specification of objectives of the system in terms of output and flexibility.
2. Estimation of product or service demand on the system.
3. Processing requirements in terms of number of operations and amount of flow between departments and work centers.
4. Space availability within the facility itself.

All these inputs are, in fact, outputs of process selection and capacity planning, discussed in previous chapters. In our treatment of layout in this chapter, we examine how layouts are developed under various formats (or work-flow structures). Our emphasis will be on quantitative techniques used in locating departments within a facility and on workstation arrangements and balance in the important area of assembly lines. We will also discuss layout issues in nonmanufacturing facilities.

10.1   BASIC PRODUCTION LAYOUT FORMATS

The formats by which departments are arranged in a facility are defined by the general pattern of work flow, and are of three basic types (process layout, product layout, and fixed-position layout) and one hybrid type (group technology or cellular layout).

A **process layout** (also called a *job-shop* or *functional layout*) is one where similar equipment or functions are grouped together, such as all lathes in one area and all stamping machines in another. A part being worked on then travels, according to the established sequence of operations, from area to area, where the proper machines are located for each operation. This type of layout is typical of hospitals, for example, where we find areas dedicated to particular types of medical care, such as maternity wards and intensive care units.

A **product layout** (also called a *flow-shop layout*) is one in which equipment or work processes are arranged according to the progressive steps by which the product is made. The path for each part is, in effect, a straight line. Production lines for shoes, chemical plants, and car washes are all product layouts.

A **group technology (cellular) layout** groups dissimilar machines into work centers (or cells) to work on products that have similar shapes and processing requirements. A GT layout is similar to process layout in that cells are designed to perform a specific set of processes, and it is similar to product layout in that the cells are dedicated to a limited range of products. (*Group technology* also refers to the parts classification and coding system used to specify machine types that go into a cell.)

In a **fixed-position layout,** the product (by virtue of its bulk or weight) remains at one location. Manufacturing equipment is moved to the product rather than vice versa. Shipyards, construction sites, and movie lots, are examples of this format.

Many manufacturing facilities present a combination of two layout types. For example, a given floor may be laid out by process, while another floor may be laid out by product. It is also common to find an entire plant arranged according to product layout (fabrication, subassembly, and final assembly), with process layout within fabrication and product layout within the assembly department. Likewise, group technology layout is frequently found within a department that itself is located according to a plantwide product-oriented layout.

10.2 PROCESS LAYOUT

The most common approach in developing a process layout is to arrange departments consisting of like processes in a way that optimizes their relative placement. In many installations, optimal placement often means placing departments with large amounts of interdepartment traffic adjacent to one another.

Consider the following example. Suppose that we want to arrange the eight departments of a toy factory to minimize the interdepartmental material handling cost. Initially, let us make the simplifying assumption that all departments have the same amount of space (say, 40 feet by 40 feet) and that the building is 80 feet wide and 160 feet long (and thus compatible with the department dimensions). The first things we would want to know are the nature of the flow between departments and how the material is transported. If the company has another factory that makes similar products, information about flow patterns might be abstracted from the records. On the other hand, if this is a new product line, such information would have to come from routing sheets or from estimates by knowledgeable personnel such as process or industrial engineers. Of course, these data, regardless of their source, will have to be modified to reflect the nature of future orders over the projected life at the proposed layout.

Let us assume that this information is available. We find that all material is transported in a standard-size crate by forklift truck, one crate to a truck (which constitutes one "load"). Now suppose that transportation costs are $1 to move a load between adjacent departments and $1 extra for each department in between. The expected loads between departments for the first year of operation are tabulated in Exhibit 10.1; available plant space is depicted in Exhibit 10.2.

Given this information, our first step is to illustrate the interdepartmental flow by a model, such as Exhibit 10.3. This provides the basic layout pattern, which we will try to improve.

Flow between departments (number of moves)									Department	Activity
	1	2	3	4	5	6	7	8		
1		175	50	0	30	200	20	25	1	Shipping and receiving
2			0	100	75	90	80	90	2	Plastic molding and stamping
3				17	88	125	99	180	3	Metal forming
4					20	5	0	25	4	Sewing department
5						0	180	187	5	Small toy assembly
6							374	103	6	Large toy assembly
7								7	7	Painting
8									8	Mechanism assembly

E X H I B I T 10.1

Interdepartmental Flow

E X H I B I T 10.2

Building Dimensions and Departments

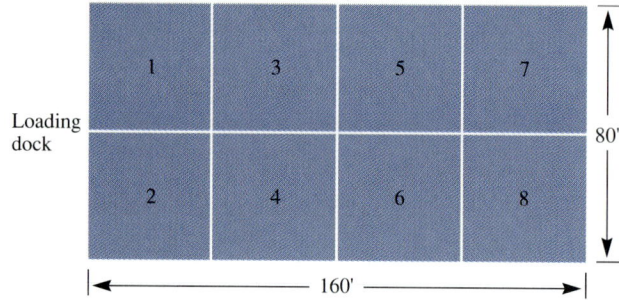

E X H I B I T 10.3

Interdepartmental Flow Graph with Number of Annual Movements

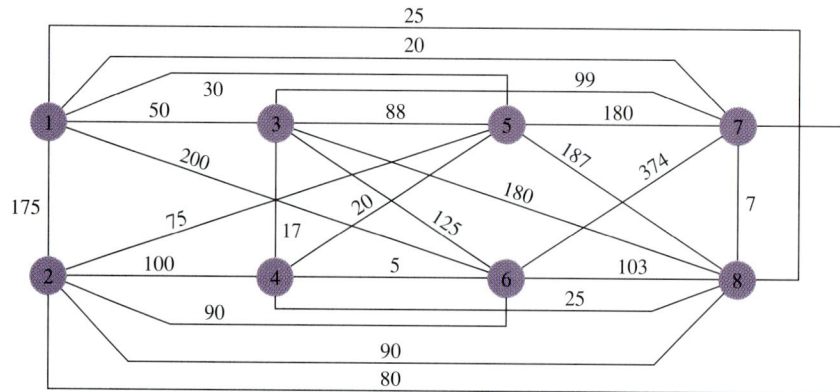

E X H I B I T 10.4

Cost Matrix—First Solution

$	1	2	3	4	5	6	7	8
1		175	50	0	60	400	60	75
2			0	100	150	180	240	270
3				17	88	125	198	360
4					20	5	0	50
5						0	180	187
6							374	103
7								7
8								

Total cost: $3,474

The second step is to determine the cost of this layout by multiplying the material handling cost by the number of loads moved between each department. Exhibit 10.4 presents this information, which is derived as follows: The annual material handling cost between Departments 1 and 2 is $175 ($1 × 175 moves), $60 between Departments 1 and 5 ($2 × 30 moves), $60 between Departments 1 and 7 ($3 × 20 moves), $240 between diagonal Departments 2 and 7 ($3 × 80), and so forth. (The "distances" are taken from Exhibit 10.2 or 10.3, not Exhibit 10.1.)

The third step is a search for departmental changes that will reduce costs. On the basis of the graph and the cost matrix, it seems desirable to place Departments 1 and 6 closer together to reduce their high move-distance costs. However, this requires shifting

E X H I B I T 10.5

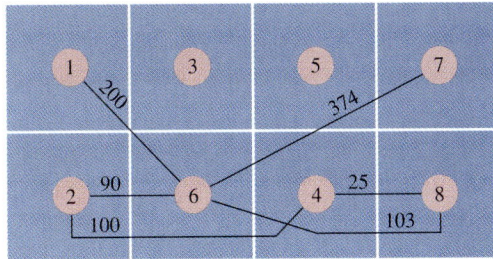

Revised Interdepartmental Flow Chart (Only interdepartmental flow with effect on cost is depicted.)

E X H I B I T 10.6

Cost Matrix—Second Solution

several other departments, thereby affecting their move-distance costs and the total cost of the second solution. Exhibit 10.5 shows the revised layout resulting from relocating Department 6 and an adjacent department. (Department 4 is arbitrarily selected for this purpose.) The revised cost matrix for the exchange, showing the cost changes, is given in Exhibit 10.6. Note the total cost is $262 *greater* than in the initial solution. Clearly, doubling the distance between Departments 6 and 7 accounted for the major part of the cost increase. This points out the fact that, even in a small problem, it is rarely easy to decide the correct "obvious move" on the basis of casual inspection.

Thus far, we have shown only one exchange among a large number of potential exchanges; in fact, for an eight-department problem there are 8! (or 40,320) possible arrangements. Therefore, the procedure we have employed would have only a remote possibility of achieving an optimal combination in a "reasonable" number of tries. Nor does our problem stop here.

Suppose that we *do* arrive at a good cut-and-try solution solely on the basis of material handling cost, such as that shown in Exhibit 10.7 (whose total cost is $3,244). We would note, first of all, that our shipping and receiving department is near the center of the factory—an arrangement that probably would not be acceptable. The sewing department is next to the painting department, introducing the hazard that lint, thread, and cloth particles might drift onto painted items. Further, small-toy assembly and large-toy assembly are located at opposite ends of the plant, which would increase travel time for assemblers (who very likely would be needed in both departments at various times of the day) and for supervisors (who might otherwise supervise both departments simultaneously).

E X H I B I T 10.7

A Feasible Layout

Small toy assembly 5	Mechanism assembly 8	Shipping and receiving 1	Large toy assembly 6
Metal forming 3	Plastic molding and stamping 2	Sewing 4	Painting 7

Computerized Layout Techniques— CRAFT

A number of computerized layout programs have been developed since the 1970s to help devise good process layouts. Of these, the most widely applied is the Computerized Relative Allocation of Facilities Technique (**CRAFT**).[1]

The CRAFT method follows the same basic idea we developed in the layout of the toy factory, but with some significant operational differences. Like the toy factory example, it requires a load matrix and a distance matrix as initial inputs, but in addition requires a cost-per-unit distance traveled, say $.10 per foot moved. (Remember, we made the simplifying assumption that cost doubled when material had to jump one department, tripled when it had to jump two departments, and so forth.) With these inputs and an initial layout in the program, CRAFT then tries to improve the relative placement of the departments as measured by total material handling cost for the layout. (Material handling cost between departments = Number of loads × Rectilinear distance between department centroids × Cost-per-unit distance.) It makes improvements by exchanging pairs of departments in an iterative manner until no further cost reductions are possible. That is, the program calculates the effect on total cost of exchanging departments; if this yields a reduction, the exchange is made, which constitutes an iteration. As we saw in the manual method, the departments are part of a material flow network, so even a simple pairwise exchange generally will affect flow patterns among many other departments.

Applying CRAFT to the Toy Factory

A CRAFT layout solution to the toy factory problem is shown in Exhibit 10.8. It provides a higher-cost layout than the manual one ($3,497 versus $3,244). Note, however, that these costs are not precisely comparable because CRAFT uses rectilinear distances as opposed to Euclidean (straight-line) distances, and links centroids of departments instead of "entrances." Because we were not given cost-per-unit distances in this example, CRAFT simply broke the stated $1-per-unit cost of movement between departments into 50-cent segments. Exhibit 10.8 shows two example calculations of the CRAFT movement costs. (Having square departments in the toy factory makes this calculation method a reasonable one for example purposes.) Also note that we fixed the location of the shipping and receiving department in the CRAFT solution so that it would be adjacent to the loading dock.

Distinguishing features of CRAFT and issues relating to it are

1. It is a heuristic program; it uses a simple rule of thumb in making evaluations: "Compare two departments at a time and exchange them if it reduces the total cost of the layout." This type of rule is obviously necessary to analyze even a modest-size layout.

---

[1] For a discussion of CRAFT and other methods, see R. L. Francis and J. A. White, *Facility Layout and Location: An Analytical Approach* (Englewood Cliffs, NJ: Prentice-Hall, 1974).

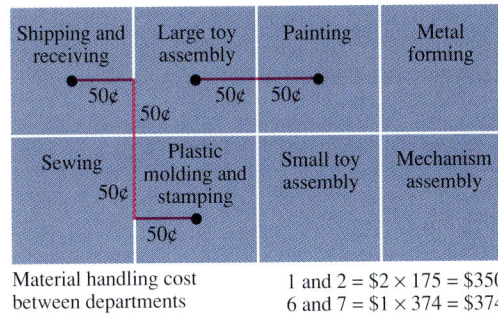

Shipping and receiving	Large toy assembly	Painting	Metal forming
Sewing	Plastic molding and stamping	Small toy assembly	Mechanism assembly

50¢   50¢ 50¢

50¢

50¢

50¢

Material handling cost between departments

1 and 2 = $2 × 175 = $350
6 and 7 = $1 × 374 = $374

2. It does not guarantee an optimal solution.

3. CRAFT is "biased" by its starting conditions: Where you start (i.e., the initial layout) will determine the final layout.

4. Starting with a reasonably good solution is more likely to yield a lower-cost final solution, but it does not always. This means that a good strategy for using CRAFT is to generate a variety of different starting layouts to expose the program to different pairwise exchanges.

5. It can handle up to 40 departments and rarely exceeds 10 iterations in arriving at a solution.

6. CRAFT departments consist of combinations of square modules (typically representing floor areas 10 feet by 10 feet). This permits multiple departmental configurations, but often results in strange departmental shapes that have to be modified manually to obtain a realistic layout.

7. A modified version called SPACECRAFT has been developed to handle multistory layout problems.[2]

8. CRAFT assumes the existence of variable path material handling equipment such as forklift trucks. Therefore, when computerized fixed-path equipment is employed, CRAFT's applicability is greatly reduced.

Systematic Layout Planning

In certain types of layout problems, numerical flow of items between departments either is impractical to obtain or does not reveal the qualitative factors that may be crucial to the placement decision. In these situations, the venerable technique known as **systematic layout planning** (SLP) can be used.[3] It involves developing a relationship chart showing the degree of importance of having each department located adjacent to every other department. From this chart is developed an activity relationship diagram similar to the flow graph used for illustrating material handling between departments. The activity relationship diagram is then adjusted by trial and error until a satisficing adjacency pattern is obtained. This pattern, in turn, is modified department by department to meet building space limitations. Exhibit 10.9 illustrates the technique with a simple five-department problem involving laying out a floor of a department store.

The SLP approach has been quantified for ease of evaluating alternative layouts. This entails assigning numerical weights to the closeness preferences and then trying different

---

[2]Roger Johnson, "Spacecraft for Multi-Floor Layout Planning," *Management Science* 28, no. 4 (April 1982), pp. 407–17.
[3]See Richard Muther and John D. Wheeler, "Simplified Systematic Layout Planning," *Factory* 120, nos. 8, 9, 10 (August, September, October 1962), pp. 68–77, 111–19, 101–13.

EXHIBIT 10.9

Systematic Layout Planning for a Floor of a Department Store

A. Relationship chart (based upon Tables B and C)

From	To				Area (sq. ft.)
	2	3	4	5	
1. Credit department	I 6	U —	A 4	U —	100
2. Toy department		U —	I 1	A 1,6	400
3. Wine department			U —	X 1	300
4. Camera department				X 1	100
5. Candy department					100

Letter — Closeness rating
Number — Reason for rating

B.

Code	Reason*
1	Type of customer
2	Ease of supervision
3	Common personnel
4	Contact necessary
5	Share same space
6	Psychology

*Others may be used.

C.

Value	Closeness	Line code*	Numerical weights
A	Absolutely necessary	≡≡≡	16
E	Especially important	≡≡	8
I	Important	═	4
O	Ordinary closeness OK	—	2
U	Unimportant		0
X	Undesirable	∧∧∧	80

*Used for example purposes only.

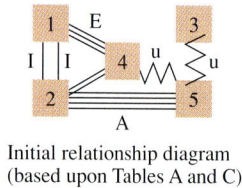

Initial relationship diagram (based upon Tables A and C)

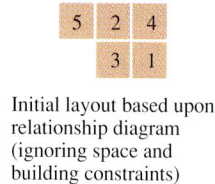

Initial layout based upon relationship diagram (ignoring space and building constraints)

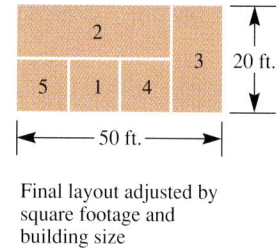

Final layout adjusted by square footage and building size

layout arrangements. The layout with the highest total closeness score is selected. For example, Lofti and Pegels' educational software program[4] assigns weights of 16 for "A," 8 for "E," 4 for "I," 2 for "O," 0 for "U," and −80 for "X." The choice of this weight structure is rather ad hoc but the logic is that the most undesirable preference weighting (−80 for "X") is five times worse than the most desirable weighting of 16 for "A." Applying this weighting scheme using the software gives a score of 40 to the final layout in Exhibit 10.9. (The score is the summation of the preference scores for each pair—in this case, 10 pairs. Exchanges may be made randomly, by user choice, or by pairs in this software program.)

Integrating Factory Layout Software with Layout Planning   The Breakthrough on "Improving a Manufacturing Process" illustrates how layout planning is currently conducted using one of the many new software packages. This represents an interesting con-

[4]Vahid Lofti and C. Carl Pegels, *Decision Support Systems for Operations Management,* 2d ed. (Homewood, IL: Richard D. Irwin, 1991), Chapter 8.

trast to the 1980s attempts to model the preferences of layout planners through massive artificial intelligence systems.[5]

10.3   PRODUCT LAYOUT

The basic difference between product layout and process layout is the pattern of work-flow. As we have seen in process layout, the pattern can be highly variable, since material for any given job may have to be routed to the same processing department several times during its production cycle. In product layout, equipment or departments are dedicated to a particular product line, duplicate equipment is employed to avoid backtracking, and a straight-line flow of material movement is achievable. Adopting a product makes sense when the batch size of a given product or part is large relative to the number of different products or parts produced.

Assembly Lines

Assembly lines are a special case of product layout. In a general sense, the term *assembly line* refers to progressive assembly linked by some material handling device. The usual assumption is that some form of pacing is present and the allowable processing time is equivalent for all workstations. Within this broad definition, there are important differences among line types. A few of these are material handling devices (belt or roller conveyor, overhead crane); line configuration (U-shape, straight, branching); pacing (mechanical, human); product mix (one product or multiple products); workstation characteristics (workers may sit, stand, walk with the line, or ride the line); and length of the line (few or many workers).

The range of products partially or completely assembled on lines includes toys, appliances, autos, planes, guns, garden equipment, clothing, and a wide variety of electronic components. In fact, it is probably safe to say that virtually any product that has multiple parts and is produced in large volume uses assembly lines to some degree. Clearly, lines are an important technology; to really understand their managerial requirements, we should have some familiarity with how a line is balanced.

Assembly-Line Balancing

Though primarily a scheduling issue, assembly-line balancing often has implications for layout. This would occur when for balance purposes, workstation size or the number used would have to be physically modified.

The most common assembly line is a moving conveyor that passes a series of workstations in a uniform time interval called the **cycle time** (which is also the time between successive units coming off the end of the line). At each workstation, work is performed on a product either by adding parts or by completing assembly operations. The work performed at each station is made up of many bits of work, termed *tasks, elements,* and *work units.* Such tasks are described by motion-time analysis. Generally, they are groupings that cannot be subdivided on the assembly line without paying a penalty in extra motions.

The total work to be performed at a workstation is equal to the sum of the tasks assigned to that workstation. The **assembly-line balancing** problem is one of assigning all tasks to a series of workstations so that each workstation has no more than can be done in the cycle time, and so that the unassigned (i.e., idle) time across all workstations is minimized. The problem is complicated by the relationships among tasks imposed by product design and process technologies. This is called the **precedence relationship,** which specifies the order in which tasks must be performed in the assembly process.

---

[5]See, for example, the discussion of Facilities Design Expert System (FADES) in Edward L. Fisher, "An AI Based Methodology for Factory Design," *AI Magazine,* Fall 1986, pp. 72–85.

Improving a Manufacturing Process Using Planning Software

A challenge many facilities planners face today is finding a way to quickly and effectively evaluate proposed layout changes and material handling systems, so that the material handling costs and distances are minimized. This challenge was addressed during a three-day on-site software training session conducted at an appliance manufacturer. The facilities planners were learning the basics on using the FactoryFLOW software package, a computer-based facilities planning tool developed by Cimtechnologies Corp. The training group evaluated a current layout proposal of a console assembly area to see if any improvements could be made.

The FactoryFLOW software quantitatively evaluates facility layouts and material handling systems by showing the material flow paths and costs, both in output text reports and in a graphic overlay of an AutoCAD layout drawing. FactoryFLOW evaluates the material flow and material handling costs and distances using the following input information: an AutoCAD layout drawing, part routing data (i.e. part names, from/to locations, and move quantities), and material handling system characteristics (i.e. fixed and variable costs, load/unload times, and speeds).

The facilities planners had a drawing of the area and the industrial engineers supplied the part routing and material equipment information; therefore data entry and analysis of the current layout took about one half of a day. Output diagrams and reports showed material handling distances of over 407 million feet per year and material handling costs of just over $900,000 per year.

The second half of the day was used to come up with alternative layouts by analyzing the output text reports and the material flow lines. One alternative was to rotate a line of 16 plastic presses 90-degrees, so they fed right into the subassembly area, and to rotate the main console assembly lines 90-degrees, so they were closer to the same area. Since the primary material handling system was an overhead conveyor, minimizing the length of conveyor was a major concern. FactoryFLOW was used to evaluate the alternative layout and the output reports showed the material handling costs had been reduced by over $100,000 to $792,265 per year. Also, by decreasing the material travel distance, the length of overhead conveyor needed had been reduced from 3,600 feet to just over 700 feet.

The FactoryFLOW software made it possible to complete this project in such a short amount of time and the facilities planners at this company now have a tool for further evaluation of facility layouts and material handling systems.

Source: "Factory Planning Software Cimtechnologies Corp. (Ames, IA)," *Industrial Engineering,* December 1993, p. SS3.

FactoryFLOW integrates material handling data and a layout drawing to compute material handling distances, costs, and equipment utlization.

Steps in Assembly-Line Balancing The steps in balancing an assembly line are straight-forward:

1. Specify the sequential relationships among tasks using a precedence diagram. The diagram consists of circles and arrows. Circles represent individual tasks; arrows indicate the order of task performance.

2. Determine the required cycle time *(C)*, using the formula

$$C = \frac{\text{Production time per day}}{\text{Required output per day (in units)}}$$

3. Determine the theoretical minimum number of workstations *(N_t)* required to satisfy the cycle time constraint using the formula

$$N_t = \frac{\text{Sum of task times } (T)}{\text{Cycle time } (C)}$$

4. Select a primary rule by which tasks are to be assigned to workstations, and a secondary rule to break ties.

5. Assign tasks, one at a time, to the first workstation until the sum of the task times is equal to the cycle time, or no other tasks are feasible because of time or sequence restrictions. Repeat the process for Workstation 2, Workstation 3, and so on, until all tasks are assigned.

6. Evaluate the efficiency of the balance derived using the formula

$$\text{Efficiency} = \frac{\text{Sum of task times } (T)}{\text{Actual number of workstations } (N_a) \times \text{Cycle time } (C)}$$

7. If efficiency is unsatisfactory, rebalance using a different decision rule.

E X A M P L E 10.1 / *Assembly-Line Balancing* The Model J Wagon is to be assembled on a conveyor belt. Five hundred wagons are required per day. Production time per day is 420 minutes, and the assembly steps and times for the wagon are given in Exhibit 10.10. Assignment: Find the balance that minimizes the number of workstations, subject to cycle time and precedence constraints.

Task	Performance Time (in seconds)	Description	Tasks that Must Precede
A	45	Position rear axle support and hand fasten four screws to nuts.	—
B	11	Insert rear axle.	A
C	9	Tighten rear axle support screws to nuts.	B
D	50	Position front axle assembly and hand fasten with four screws to nuts.	—
E	15	Tighten front axle assembly screws.	D
F	12	Position rear wheel #1 and fasten hubcab.	C
G	12	Position rear wheel #2 and fasten hubcab.	C
H	12	Position front wheel #1 and fasten hubcap.	E
I	12	Position front wheel #2 and fasten hubcap.	E
J	8	Position wagon handle shaft on front axle assembly and hand fasten bolt and nut.	F, G, H, I
K	9	Tighten bolt and nut.	
	195		

E X H I B I T 10.11
Precedence Graph for
Model J Wagon

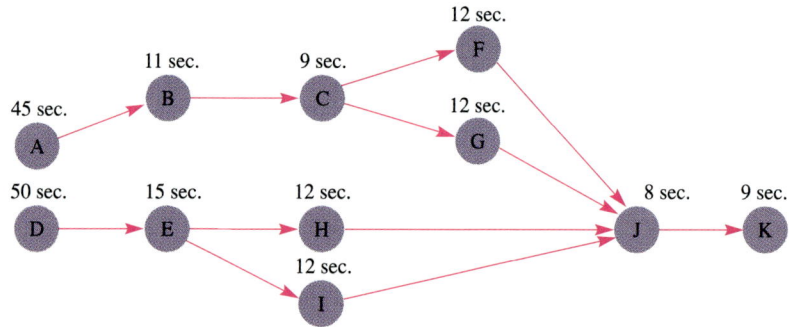

S O L U T I O N

1. Draw a precedence diagram. Exhibit 10.11 illustrates the sequential relationships identified in Exhibit 10.10. (The length of the arrows has no meaning.)

2. Cycle time determination. Here we have to convert to seconds since our task times are in seconds.

$$C = \frac{\text{Production time per day}}{\text{Output per day}} = \frac{60 \text{ sec.} \times 420 \text{ min.}}{500 \text{ wagons}} = \frac{25{,}200}{500} = 50.4$$

3. Theoretical minimum number of workstations required (the actual number may be greater):

$$N_t = \frac{T}{C} = \frac{195 \text{ seconds}}{50.4 \text{ seconds}} = 3.87$$

4. Select assignment rules. Research has demonstrated that some rules are better than others for certain problem structures. In general, the strategy is to use a rule assigning tasks that either have many followers or are of long duration since they effectively limit the balance achievable. In this case, we use as our primary rule:

   a. Assign tasks in order of the largest number of following tasks. Our secondary rule, to be invoked where ties exist from our primary rule, is

   b. Assign tasks in order of longest operating time.

$$\text{Efficiency} = \frac{T}{NC} = \frac{195}{(5)\,(50.4)} = 77, \text{ or } 77\%$$

Task	Number of Following Tasks
A	6
B or D	5
C or E	4
F, G, H, or I	2
J	1
K	0

	Task	Task Time (in seconds)	Remaining Unassigned Time (in seconds)	Feasible Remaining Tasks	Task with Most Followers	Task with Longest Operation Time
Station 1	A	45	5.4 idle	None		
Station 2	D	50	0.4 idle	None		
Station 3	B	11	39.4	C, E	C, E	E
	E	15	24.4	C, H, I	C	
	C	9	15.4	F, G, H, I	F, G, H, I	F, G, H, I
	F*	12	3.4 idle	None		
Station 4	G	12	38.4	H, I	H, I	H, I
	H*	12	26.4	I		
	I	12	14.4	J		
	J	8	6.4 idle	None		
Station 5	K	9	41.4 idle	None		

* Denotes task arbitrarily selected where there is a tie between longest operation times.

E X H I B I T 10.12

A. Balance Made According to Largest Number of Following Tasks Rule

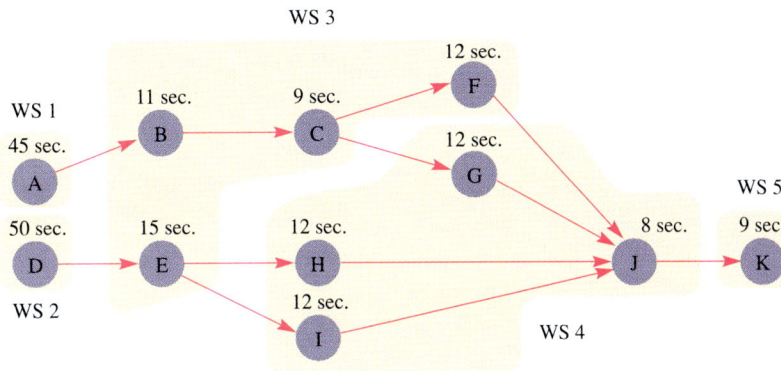

B. Precedence Graph for Model J Wagon

$$\text{Efficiency} = \frac{T}{NC} = \frac{195}{(5)(50.4)} = .77, \text{ or } 77\%$$

C. Efficiency Calculation

5. Make task assignments to form Workstation 1, Workstation 2, and so forth until all tasks are assigned. The actual assignment is given in Exhibit 10.12A and is shown graphically in Exhibit 10.12B.

6. Do the efficiency calculation. This is shown in Exhibit 10.12C.

7. Evaluate solution. An efficiency of 77 percent indicates an imbalance or idle time of 23 percent (1.0 − .77) across the entire line. From Exhibit 10.12A we can see that there are 57 total seconds of idle time, and the "choice" job is at Workstation 5.

Is a better balance possible? In this case, yes. Try balancing the line with rule *b* and breaking ties with rule *a*. (This will give you a feasible four-station balance.) ∎

Splitting Tasks

Often the longest required task time forms the shortest cycle time for the production line. This task time is the lower time bound unless it is possible to split the task into two or more workstations.

Consider the following illustration: Suppose that an assembly line contains the following task times in seconds: 40, 30, 15, 25, 20, 18, 15. The line runs for 7½ hours per day and demand for output is 750 per day.

The cycle time required to produce 750 per day is 36 seconds ([7½ hours × 60 minutes × 60 seconds]/750). How do we deal with the task that is 40 seconds long?

There are several ways that we may be able to accommodate the 40-second task in a 36-second cycle. Possibilities are

1. *Split the task.* Can we split the task so that complete units are processed in two workstations?

2. *Share the task.* Can the task somehow be shared so an adjacent workstation does part of the work? This differs from the split task in the first option because the adjacent station acts to assist, not to do some units containing the entire task.

3. *Use a more skilled worker.* Since this task exceeds the cycle time by just 11 percent, a faster worker may be able to meet the 36-second time.

4. *Work overtime.* Producing at a rate of one every 40 seconds would produce 675 per day, 75 short of the needed 750. The amount of overtime required to do the additional 75 is 50 minutes (75 × 40 seconds/60 seconds).

5. *Redesign.* It may be possible to redesign the product to reduce the task time slightly.

Other possibilities to reduce the task time include equipment upgrading, a roaming helper to support the line, a change of materials, and multiskilled workers to operate the line as a team rather than as independent workers.

Flexible Line Layouts

As we saw in the preceding example, assembly line balances frequently result in unequal workstation times. Flexible line layouts such as shown in Exhibit 10.13 are a common way of dealing with this problem. In our toy company example, the U-shaped line with work sharing at the bottom of the figure could help resolve the imbalance.

Computerized Line Balancing

Companies engaged in assembly methods commonly employ a computer for line balancing. Most develop their own computer programs, but commercial package programs are also widely applied. One of these is General Electric Company's *Assembly-Line Configuration (ASYBL$),* which uses the "ranked positional weight" rule in selecting tasks

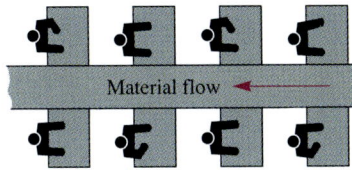

Bad: Operators caged. No chance
to trade elements of work
between them.
(subassembly line layout
common in American plants)

Better: Operators can trade elements of
work. Can add and subtract
operators. Trained ones can
nearly self-balance at different
output rates.

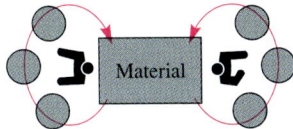

Bad: Operators birdcaged. No chance
to increase output with a
third operator

Better: Operators can help
each other. Might
increase output with
a third operator.

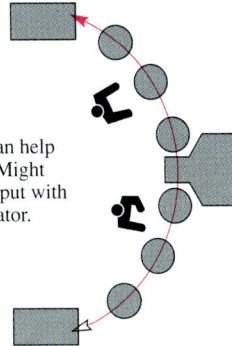

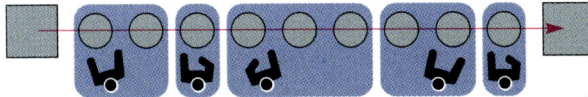

Bad: Straight line difficult to balance.

Better: One of several advantages
of U-Line is better operator
access. Here, five operators
were reduced to four.

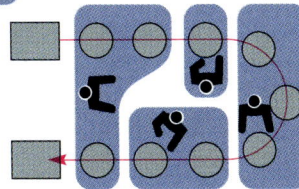

Source: Robert W. Hall, *Attaining Manufacturing Excellence* (Homewood, IL: Dow Jones-Irwin, 1987),
p. 125.

for workstations. Specifically, this rule states that tasks are assigned according to their positional weights, which is the time for a given task plus the task times of all those that follow it. Thus, the task with the highest positional weight would be assigned to the first workstation (subject to time, precedence, and zoning constraints). As is typical with such software, the user has several options for how the problem is to be solved. Exhibit 10.14 illustrates a portion of program output when a target level of efficiency is used as a basis for deriving and comparing different balances for a 35-task assembly line. (The program can handle up to 450 tasks.) Note the trade-offs that take place as the number of workstations changes. In this case, the larger number of workstations allows for a better balance and, therefore, a higher efficiency.

Mixed-Model Line Balancing

This approach is used by JIT manufacturers such as Toyota. Its objective is to meet the demand for a variety of products and to avoid building high inventories of one product model. It involves scheduling several different models to be produced over a given day or week on the same line.in a cyclical fashion.

E X H I B I T 10.14
Sample Computer
Output

```
ENTER OPTION NUMBER?3

ENTER TARGET EFFICIENCY?.85


TOTAL EFFICIENCY   = 82%
STANDARD DEVIATION =   0.0153
TARGET CYCLE TIME  =   0.347
MINIM. CYCLE TIME  =   0.343
NO. OF STATIONS =  19

TOTAL EFFICIENCY   = 80%
STANDARD DEVIATION =   0.0175
TARGET CYCLE TIME  =   0.368
MINIM. CYCLE TIME  =   0.368
NO. OF STATIONS =  18

TOTAL EFFICIENCY   = 75%
STANDARD DEVIATION =   0.0214
TARGET CYCLE TIME  =   0.417
MINIM. CYCLE TIME  =   0.415
NO. OF STATIONS =  17
```

Source: General Electric Company, *Assembly-Line Configuration, ASYBL$ User's Guide,* Revised (1985), p. 17.

E X A M P L E 10.2 / *Mixed-Model Line Balancing*   To illustrate how this is done, suppose our toy company has a fabrication line to bore holes in its Model J wagon frame and its Model K wagon frame. The time required to bore the holes is different for each wagon type.

Assume that the final assembly line downstream requires equal numbers of Model J and Model K wagon frames. Assume also that we want to develop a cycle time for the fabrication line that is balanced for the production of equal numbers of J and K frames. Of course, we could produce Model J frames for several days and then produce Model K frames until an equal number of frames has been produced. However, this would build up unnecessary work in process inventory.

If we want to reduce the amount of in-process inventory, we could develop a cycle mix that greatly reduces inventory buildup while keeping within the restrictions of equal numbers of J and K wagon frames.

Process times: 6 minutes per J and 4 minutes per K.

The day consists of 480 minutes (8 hours × 60 minutes).

S O L U T I O N

$$6J + 4K = 480$$

Since equal numbers of J and K are to be produced (or J = K), produce 48J and 48K per day, or 6J and 6K per hour.

The following shows one balance of J and K frames.

Balanced Mixed-Model Sequence

Model sequence	J J	K K K	J J	J J	K K K	
Operation time	6 6	4 4 4	6 6	6 6	4 4 4	Repeats 8 times per day
Minicycle time	1 2	1 2	1 2	1 2	1 2	
Total cycle time			60			

This line is balanced at six frames of each type per hour with a minicycle time of 12 minutes.

Another balance is J K K J K J, with times of 6, 4, 4, 6, 4, 6. This balance produces three J and three K every 30 minutes with a minicycle time of 10 minutes (JK, KJ, KJ). ■

The simplicity of mixed-model balancing (under conditions of a level of production schedule) is seen in Yasuhiro Mondon's description of Toyota Motor Corporation's operations:

> Final assembly lines of Toyota are mixed product lines. The production per day is averaged by taking the number of vehicles in the monthly production schedule classified by specifications, and dividing by the number of working days.
>
> In regard to the production sequence during each day, the cycle time of each different specification vehicle is calculated. To have all specification vehicles appear at their own cycle time, different specification vehicles are ordered to follow each other.[6]

It is true that the widespread use of assembly-line methods in manufacturing has dramatically increased output rates. Historically, the focus has almost always been on full utilization of human labor; that is, to design assembly lines minimizing human idle time. Equipment and facility utilization stood in the background as much less important. Past research has tried to find optimal solutions as if the problem stood in a never-changing world.

Current Thoughts on Assembly Lines

Newer views of assembly lines take a broader perspective. The intentions are to incorporate greater flexibility in products produced on the line, more variability in workstations (such as size and number of workers), improved reliability (through routine preventive maintenance), and high-quality output (through improved tooling and training). Exhibit 10.15 compares some old and new ideas about production lines.

10.4 GROUP TECHNOLOGY (CELLULAR) LAYOUT

Group technology (or cellular) layout allocates dissimilar machines into cells to work on products that have similar shapes and processing requirements. Group technology (GT) layouts are now widely used in metal fabricating, computer chip manufacture, and assembly work. The overall objective is to gain the benefits of product layout in job-shop kind of production. These benefits include

---

[6]Yasuhiro Mondon, *Toyota Production System: Practical Approach to Production Management* (Atlanta, GA: Industrial Engineering and Management Press, Institute of Industrial Engineers, 1983), p. 208.

Traditional	Contemporary
1. Top priority: line balance	Top priority: flexibility
2. Strategy: stability—long production runs so that the need to rebalance seldom occurs	Strategy: flexibility—except to rebalance often to match output to changing demand
3. Assume fixed labor assignments	Flexible labor: move to the problems or to where the current workload is
4. Use inventory buffers to cushion effects of equipment failure	Employ maximal preventive maintenance to keep equipment from breaking down
5. Need sophisticated analysis (e.g., using computers) to evaluate and cull the many options	Need human ingenuity to provide flexibility and ways around bottlenecks
6. Planned by staff	Supervisor may lead design effort and will adjust plan as needed
7. Plan to run at fixed rate; send quality problems off line	Slow for quality problems; speed up when quality is right
8. Linear or L-shaped lines	U-shaped or parallel lines
9. Conveyorized material movement is desirable	Put stations close together and avoid conveyors
10. Buy "supermachines" and keep them busy	Make (or buy) small machines; add more copies as needed
11. Applied in labor-intensive final assembly	Applied even to capital-intensive subassembly and fabrication work
12. Run mixed models where labor content is similar from model to model	Strive for mixed-model production, even in subassembly and fabrication

Source: Richard J. Schonberger, *Japanese Manufacturing Techniques: Nine Hidden Lessons in Simplicity* (New York: Free Press, 1982), p. 133.

1. Better human relations. Cells consist of a few workers who form a small work team; a team turns out complete units of work.

2. Improved operator expertise. Workers see only a limited number of different parts in a finite production cycle so repetition means quick learning.

3. Less in-process inventory and material handling. A cell combines several production stages so fewer parts travel through the shop.

4. Faster production setup. Fewer jobs mean reduced tooling and hence faster tooling changes.

Developing a GT Layout

Shifting from process layout to a GT cellular layout entails three steps:

1. Grouping parts into families that follow a common sequence of steps. This step requires developing and maintaining a computerized parts classification and coding system. This is often a major expense with such systems, although many companies have developed short-cut procedures for identifying parts families.

2. Identifying dominant flow patterns of parts families as a basis for location or relocation of processes.

3. Physically grouping machines and processes into cells. Often there will be parts that cannot be associated with a family and specialized machinery that cannot be placed in any one cell because of its general use. These unattached parts and machinery are placed in a "remainder cell."

Exhibit 10.16 illustrates the cell development process followed by Rockwell's Telecommunication Division, maker of wave-guide parts. Part A shows the

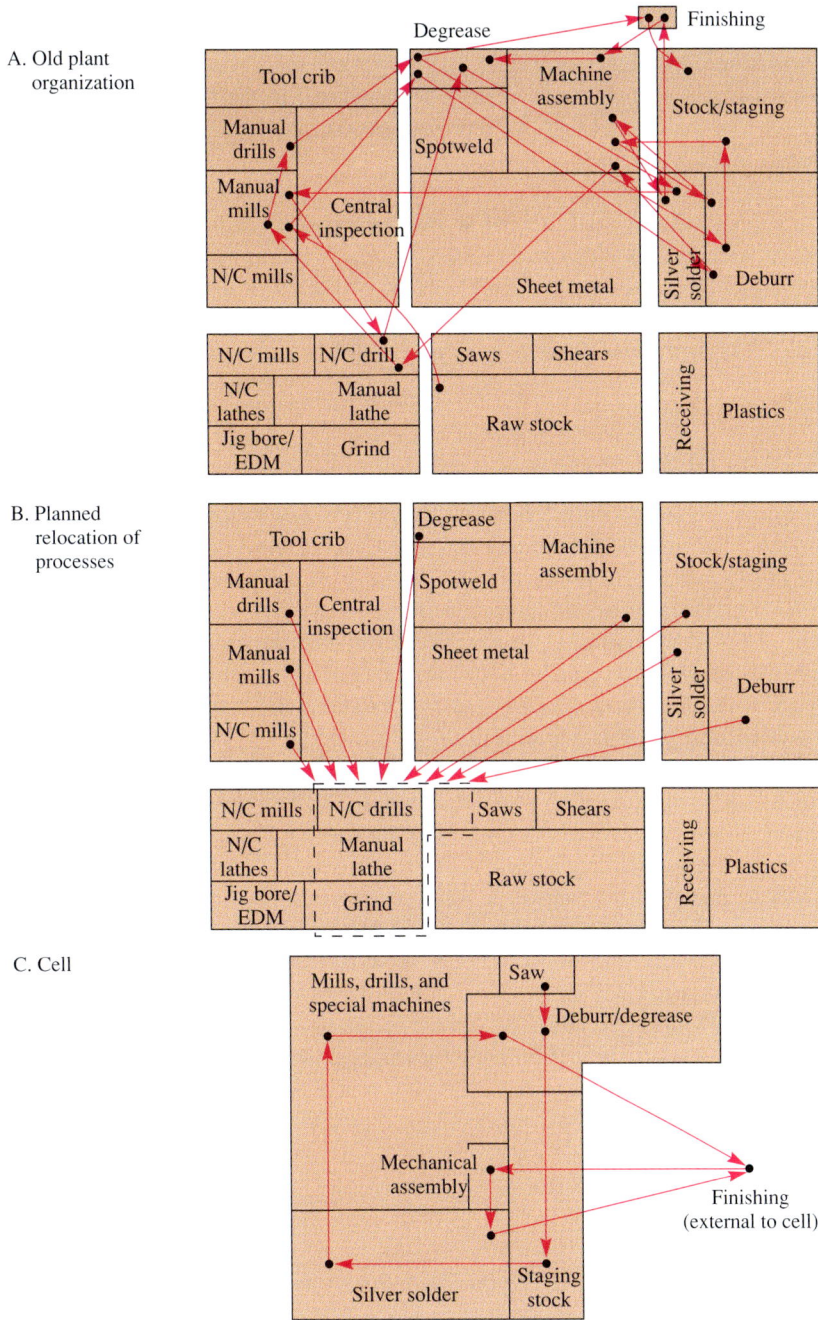

E X H I B I T 10.16

Developing a Cell to Produce Wave-Guide Parts

A. Old plant organization

B. Planned relocation of processes

C. Cell

Source: Reprinted with permission of The Free Press, an imprint of Simon and Schuster, from *World Class Manufacturing* by Richard J. Schonberger. Copyright © 1986 by Schonberger & Associates.

original process-oriented layout; part B the planned relocation of process based on parts-family production requirements; and part C an enlarged layout of the cell designed to perform all but the finishing operation. According to Schonberger, cellular organization was practical here because (1) distinct parts families existed; (2) there were several of each type of machine so taking a machine out of a cluster did not rob the cluster of all its capacity, leaving no way to produce other products; (3) the work centers were easily movable stand-alone machine tools—heavy, but anchored to the floor rather simply. He adds that these three features represent general guidelines for deciding where cells make sense.[7]

"Conceptual" GT Layout

When equipment is not easily movable, many companies dedicate a given machine out of a set of identical machines in a process layout. A conceptual GT cell for, say, a two-month production run for the job might consist of Drill 1 in the drills area, Mill 3 in the mill area, and Assembly Area 1 in the machine assembly area. To approximate a GT flow, all work on the particular part family would be done only on these specific machines.

10.5   FIXED-POSITION LAYOUT

Fixed-position layout is characterized by a relatively low number of production units in comparison with process and product layout formats. In developing a fixed-position layout, we may visualize the product as the hub of a wheel with materials and equipment arranged concentrically around the production point in their order of use and movement difficulty. Thus in shipbuilding, for example, rivets that are used throughout construction would be placed close to or in the hull; heavy engine parts, which must travel to the hull only once, would be placed at a more distant location; and cranes would be set up close to the hull because of their constant use.

In fixed-position layout, a high degree of task ordering is common, and to the extent that this precedence determines production stages, a fixed-position layout might be developed by arranging materials according to their technological priority. This procedure would be expected in making a layout for a large machine tool, such as a stamping machine, where manufacture follows a rigid sequence; assembly is performed from the ground up, with parts being added to the base in almost a building-block fashion.

As far as quantitative layout techniques are concerned, there is little in the literature devoted to fixed-position formats, even though they have been utilized for thousands of years. In certain situations, however, it may be possible to specify objective criteria and develop a fixed-position layout through quantitative means. For instance, if the material handling cost is significant and the construction site permits more or less straight-line material movement, the CRAFT process layout technique might be advantageously employed.

10.6   RETAIL SERVICE LAYOUT

The objective of a **retail service layout** (as is found in stores, banks, and restaurants) is to maximize net profit per square foot of store space. A company that has been very successful in leveraging every inch of its layout space to achieve this objective is Taco Bell Restaurants. Exhibit 10.17 illustrates Taco Bell store layouts used in 1986 and from 1991 to the present. The nature of layout changes reflects actions required to support the company's value strategy of speed and low prices. Key operational modifications include elimination of many on-site food preparation steps, which simultaneously increased the

---

[7]Richard C. Schonberger, *World Class Manufacturing* (New York: Free Press, 1986), p. 112.

E X H I B I T 10.17   *Taco Bell Restaurant Floor Plans*

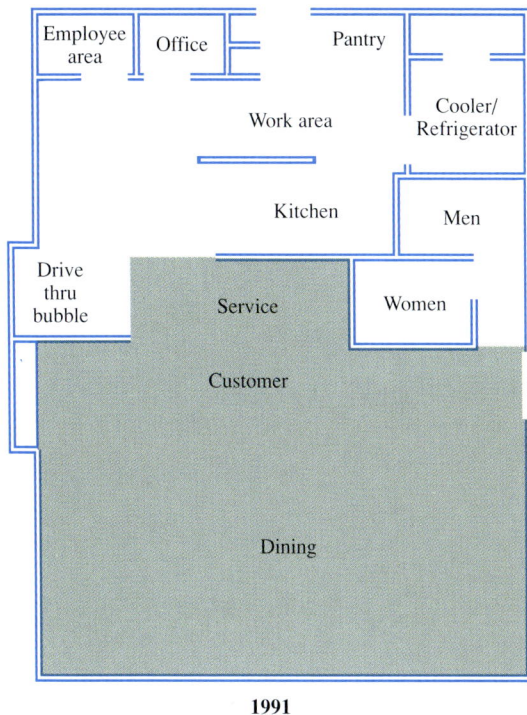

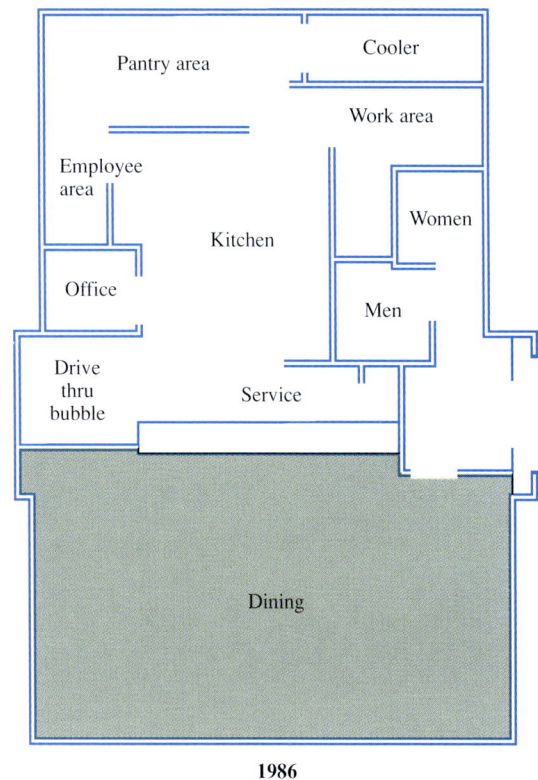

1991

1986

Source: Courtesy of Taco Bell Corp., Los Angeles, CA.

speed of service while reducing the amount of working space needed. For example, chopping and bagging of lettuce and precooking and seasoning of meats, beans, and hard tortilla products are now done at central kitchens or by suppliers. The restaurant kitchens are now heating and assembly units only. In addition to such outsourcing, changes were made in queue structures, such as moving from a single line running parallel to the counter, to a double line running perpendicular to it. This improved product flow facilitated serving drive-through windows, increased capacity, and allowed customers to see assembly workers' faces (as opposed to just their backsides, as was the case before).

As previously noted, the broad objective of layout in retail services is generally to maximize net profit per square foot of floor space. Operationally, this goal is often translated into such criteria as "minimize handling cost" or "maximize product exposure." Although as Sommers and Kernan observed almost 30 years ago, employing these and similar criteria in service layout planning "results in stores that look like warehouses and requires shoppers to approach the task like order pickers or display case stockers."[8] There are other more humanistic aspects of the service that must also be considered in the layout.

Servicescapes

---

[8]Montrose S. Sommers and Jerome B. Kernan, "A Behavioral Approach to Planning, Layout and Display," *Journal of Retailing,* Winter 1965–66, pp. 21–27.

Mary Jo Bitner coined the term **servicescape** to refer to the physical surroundings in which the service takes place, and how these surroundings affect customers and employees. An understanding of the servicescape is necessary to create a good layout for the service firm (or the service-related portions of the manufacturing firm). The servicescape has three elements that must be considered: the ambient conditions; the spatial layout and functionality; and the signs, symbols, and artifacts.[9]

Ambient Conditions

Ambient conditions refer to background characteristics such as the noise level, music, lighting, temperature, and scent that can affect employee performance and morale as well as customers' perceptions of the service, how long they stay, and how much money they spend. Although many of these characteristics are influenced primarily by the design of the building (e.g., the placement of light fixtures, acoustic tiles, and exhaust fans), the layout within a building can also have an effect. Areas near food preparation will smell like food, lighting in a hallway outside a theater must be dim, tables near a stage will be noisy, and locations near an entrance will be drafty.

Spatial Layout and Functionality

Two aspects of the *spatial layout and functionality* are especially important: planning the circulation path of the customers, and grouping the merchandise. The goal of circulation planning is to provide a path for the customers that exposes them to as much of the merchandise as possible while placing any needed services along this path in the sequence they will be needed. For example, the above photo shows a bank reception area placed where the customer will encounter it immediately upon entering the bank. Aisle characteristics are of particular importance. Aside from determining the number of aisles to be provided, decisions must be made as to the width of

---

[9]Mary Jo Bitner, "Servicescapes: The Impact of Physical Surroundings on Customers and Employees," *Journal of Marketing* 56 (April 1992), pp. 57–71.

Why are these people smiling? Removable, magnetic, life-size cut-outs featuring "balloon" comments are mounted on the wall next to the teller machines. All figures have "fact tags" with printed product features popping out of hidden pockets, back-packs, and purses. These figures add an element of entertainment to the task of shopping product features.-

the aisles since this is a direct function of expected or desired traffic. Aisle width can also affect the direction of flow through the service. Stu Leonard's Dairy Store in Norwalk, Connecticut, is designed so that it is virtually impossible to turn around a shopping cart once you have entered the shopping flow path. Focal points that catch the customers' attention in the layout can also be used to draw the customers in the desired direction. The famous blue light at Kmart is an example. Another is shown in the photo above.

To enhance shoppers' view of merchandise as they proceed down a main aisle, secondary and tertiary aisles may be set at an angle. Consider the two layouts in Exhibit 10.18. The rectangular layout would probably require less expensive fixtures and contain more display space. If storage considerations are important to the store management, this would be the more desirable layout. On the other hand, the angular layout provides the shopper with a much clearer view of the merchandise and, other things being equal, presents a more desirable selling environment.

It is common practice now to base merchandise groupings on the shopper's view of related items, as opposed to the physical characteristics of the products or shelf-space and servicing requirements. This grouping-by-association philosophy is seen in boutiques in department stores and gourmet sections in supermarkets.

Special mention is in order for a few guidelines derived from marketing research and relating to circulation planning and merchandise grouping.

1. People in supermarkets tend to follow a perimeter pattern in their shopping behavior. Placing high-profit items along the walls of a store will enhance their probability of purchase.
2. Sale merchandise placed at the end of an aisle in supermarkets almost always sells better than the same sale items placed in the interior portion of an aisle.
3. Credit and other nonselling departments that require customers to wait for the completion of their services should be placed either on upper floors or in "dead" areas.

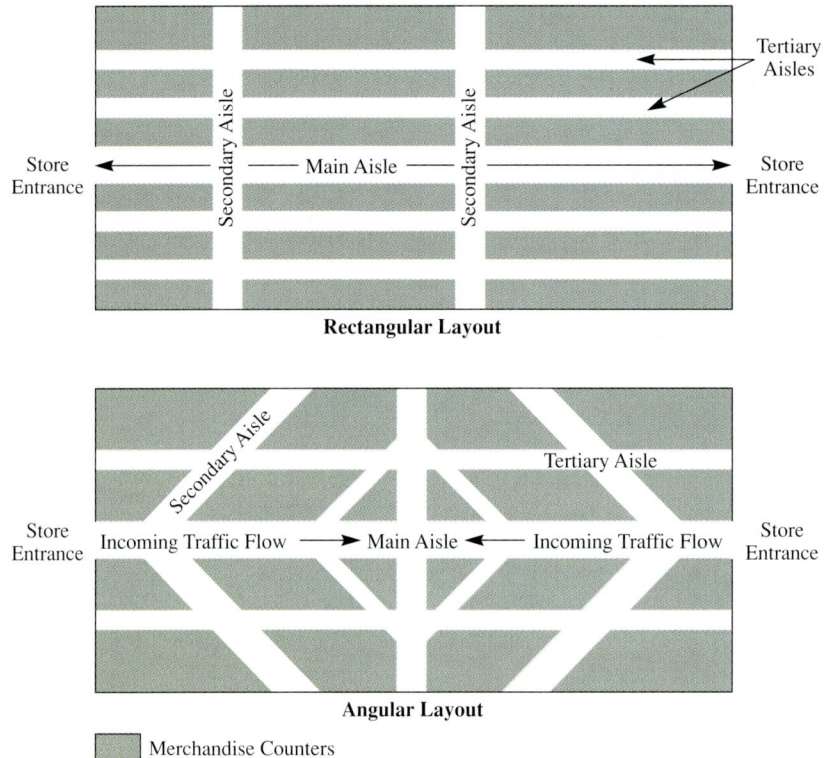

Rectangular Layout

Angular Layout

☐ Merchandise Counters

4. In department stores, locations nearest the store entrances and adjacent to front-window displays are most valuable in terms of sales potential.

Signs, Symbols, and Artifacts

Signs, symbols, and artifacts refer to the parts of the service that have social significance. As with the ambiance, these are often a characteristic of the design of the building, although the orientation, location, and size of many objects and areas can carry special meaning. As examples,

- In the old days, bank loan officers were easily identified because their desks were located on a raised section of the bank floor called the platform.
- A person seated at the desk closest to the entrance is usually in charge of greeting customers and directing them to their destination.
- In a department store, the tiled areas indicate the aisles for travel, while carpeted areas indicate departments for browsing.
- Some car salespeople have blackboards installed in their offices because a person writing on a blackboard symbolizes someone who should be listened to and trusted (e.g., a teacher).

As you might have gathered from these examples, the influence of behavioral factors makes the development of hard and fast rules for servicescape layout rather difficult. Suffice it to say that making the layout choice is not simply a matter of choosing between display space and ease of operation.

10.7   OFFICE LAYOUT

Computerization has had a tremendous effect on **office layout** requirements. In the past, layouts were designed in part around the flow of paperwork. There was also, of course, the need to keep work centers that required face-to-face interaction between their staffs close together. Now, however, local area networks and computer workstations have made layout by paper flow unnecessary in many offices, and much face-to-face–type interaction is done by electronic mail and imaging technology.

Another recent trend in office layout is toward more open offices, with personal work spaces separated only by low divider walls. Popular belief has it that companies have removed fixed walls to foster greater communication and teamwork. Shoshana Zuboff, however, disagrees. Her belief is that the pervasive divider walls are, in reality, techniques used by management to enforce isolation on previously open clerical office areas, management's motive being to gain efficiencies by removing the social component of the clerical task, transforming the job into one of pure physical labor.[10]

Signs, symbols, and artifacts, as discussed in the section on service layout, are possibly even more important in office layout than in retailing. For instance, size and orientation of desks can indicate the importance or professionalism of the people behind them. (See, for example, the box "Office Layout in Japan" on the next page about the layout of a Japanese office.)

Central administration offices are often designed and laid out so as to convey the desired image of the company. For example, Scandinavian Airlines System's (SAS) administrative office complex outside of Stockholm is a two-story collection of glass-walled pods that provide the feeling of open communication and flat hierarchy (few levels of organization) that characterize the company's management philosophy.

Service-Master (the highly profitable janitorial management company) positions its "Know-How Room" at the center of its headquarters. This room contains all of the physical products, operations manuals, and pictorial displays of career paths and other symbols for the key knowledge essential to the business. "From this room, the rest of the company can be seen as a big apparatus to bring the knowledge of the marketplace [to its employees and potential customers]."[11]

10.8   CONCLUSION

Facility layout is where the rubber meets the road in the design and operation of a production system. A good factory (or office) layout can provide real competitive advantage by facilitating material and information flow processes. It can also enhance employees' work life. A good service layout can be an effective "stage" for playing out the service encounter. In conclusion, here are some marks of a good layout in these environments:

Marks of a good layout for manufacturing and back-office operations

1. Straight-line flow pattern (or adaptation).
2. Backtracking kept to a minimum.
3. Production time predictable.
4. Little interstage storage of materials.
5. Open plant floors so everyone can see what is happening.

---

[10]Shoshana Zuboff, *In the Age of the Smart Machine: The Future of Work and Power* (New York: Basic Books, 1984), pp. 138–39.

[11]Richard Norman, *Service Management,* 2d ed. (New York: John Wiley & Sons, 1991), p. 28.

***Office Layout
in Japan***

The positioning of the desks in Japanese offices symbolizes the importance of those who sit behind them. The rank-and-file workers sit, facing each other, in a column of adjacent desks (as shown in the accompanying figure). The employee who sits closest to the door is lowest in the hierarchy and must get up to open the door and greet all visitors. At the top of this column of desks sits the head of the office, with the second and third in command at the desks to either side. Seats by the window, so coveted by western managers, are reserved for those who have been passed over for promotion and are now no longer on the career track. They will spend the remainder of their days at the company doing work of little consequence and looking out the window.

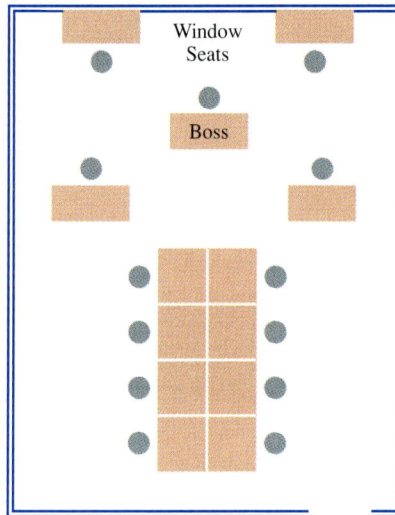

6. Bottleneck operations under control.
7. Workstations close together.
8. Orderly handling and storage of materials.
9. No unnecessary rehandling of materials.
10. Easily adjustable to changing conditions.

Marks of a good layout for face-to-face services

1. Easily understood service flow pattern.
2. Adequate waiting facilities.
3. Easy communication with customers.
4. Easily maintained customer surveillance.
5. Clear exit and entry points with adequate checkout capabilities.
6. Departments and processes arranged so that customers see only what you want them to see.
7. Balance between waiting areas and service areas.
8. Minimum walking and material movement.
9. Lack of clutter.
10. High sales volume per square foot of facility.

10.9   **SOLVED PROBLEMS**

1. A university advising office has four rooms, each dedicated to specific problems: petitions (Room A), schedule advising (Room B), grade complaints (Room C), and student counseling (Room D). The office is 80 feet long and 20 feet wide. Each room is 20 feet by 20 feet. The present location of rooms is A, B, C, D; that is, a straight line. The load summary shows the number of contacts that each advisor in a room has with other advisors in the other rooms. Assume that all advisors are equal in this value.

Load summary: $AB = 10$, $AC = 20$, $AD = 30$,
  $BC = 15$, $BD = 10$, $CD = 20$.

a. Evaluate this layout according to the material handling cost method.

b. Improve the layout by exchanging functions within rooms. Show your amount of improvement using the same method as in *(a)*.

Solution

a.

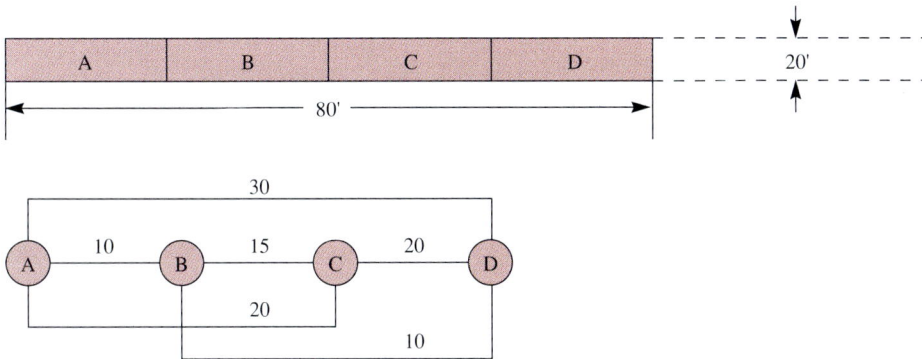

Using the material handling cost method shown in the toy company example we obtain the following costs, assuming that every nonadjacency doubles the initial cost/unit distance:

AB = 10 × 1 = 10
AC = 20 × 2 = 40
AD = 30 × 3 = 90
BC = 15 × 1 = 15
BD = 10 × 2 = 20
CD = 20 × 1 = 20
Current cost = 195

b. A better layout would be BCDA.

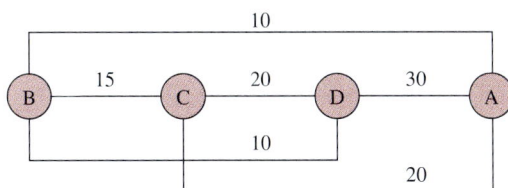

AB = 10 × 3 = 30
AX = 20 × 2 = 40
AΔ = 30 × 1 = 30
BX = 15 × 1 = 15
BΔ = 10 × 2 = 20
XΔ = 20 × 1 = 20
Improved cost = 155

2. The following tasks must be performed on an assembly line in the sequence and times specified.

Task	Task Time (seconds)	Tasks That Must Precede
A	50	—
B	40	—
C	20	A
D	45	C
E	20	C
F	25	D
G	10	E
H	35	B, F, G

a. Draw the schematic diagram.

b. What is the theoretical minimum number of stations required to meet a forecasted demand of 400 units per eight-hour day?

c. Use the longest operating time rule and balance the line in the minimum number of stations to produce 400 units per day.

Solution

a.

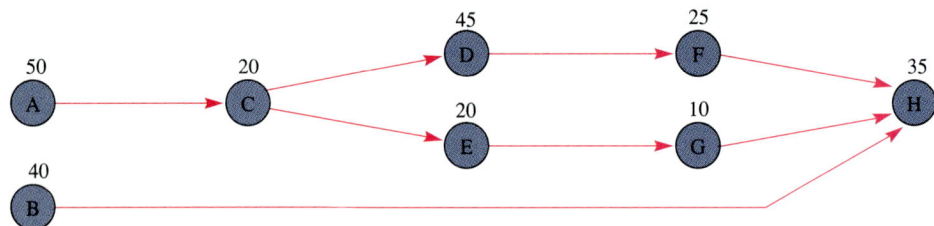

b. Theoretical minimum number of stations to meet D = 400 is

$$N_t = \frac{T}{C} = \frac{245 \text{ seconds}}{\left(\dfrac{60 \text{ seconds} \times 480 \text{ minutes}}{400 \text{ units}}\right)} = \frac{245}{72} = 3.4 \text{ stations}$$

c.

	Task	Task Time (seconds)	Remaining Unassigned Time	Feasible Remaining Task
Station 1	A	50	22	C
	C	20	2	None
Station 2	D	45	27	E, F
	F	25	2	None
Station 3	B	40	32	E
	E	20	12	G
	G	10	2	None
Station 4	H	35	37	None

10.10 REVIEW AND DISCUSSION QUESTIONS

1. What kind of layout is used in a physical fitness center?

2. What is the key difference between SLP and CRAFT?

3. What is the objective of assembly-line balancing? How would you deal with the situation where one worker, although trying hard, is 20 percent slower than the other 10 people on a line?

4. How do you determine the idle-time percentage from a given assembly-line balance?

5. What information of particular importance do route sheets and process charts (discussed in Chapter 3) provide to the layout planner?

6. What is the essential requirement for mixed-model lines to be practical?

7. Why might it be difficult to develop a GT layout?

8. In what respects is facility layout a marketing problem in services? Give an example of a service system layout designed to maximize the amount of time the customer is in the system.

9. Consider a department store. Which departments probably should not be located near each other? Would any departments benefit from close proximity?

10. How would a flowchart help in planning the servicescape layout? What sorts of features would act as focal points or otherwise draw customers along certain paths through the service? In a supermarket, what departments should be located first along the customers' path? Which should be located last?

10.11 PROBLEMS

1. The Cyprus Citrus Cooperative ships a high volume of individual orders for oranges to northern Europe. The paperwork for the shipping notices is done in the accompanying layout. Revise the layout to improve the flow and conserve space if possible.

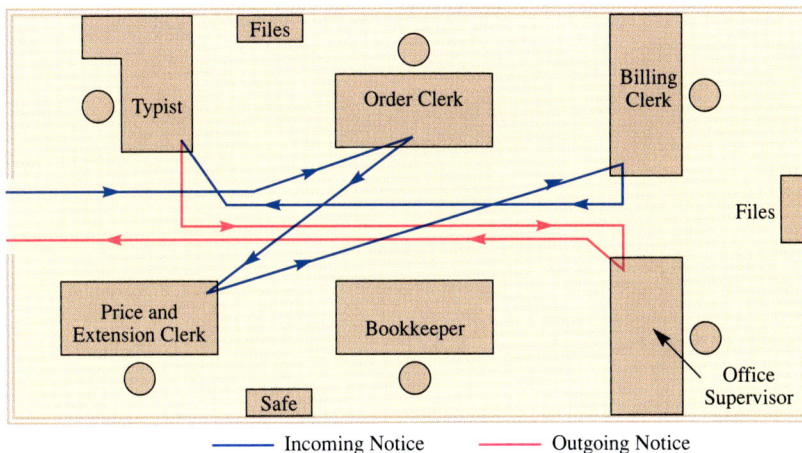

— Incoming Notice   — Outgoing Notice

2. An assembly line makes two models of trucks: a Buster and a Duster. Busters take 12 minutes each and Dusters take 8 minutes each. The daily output requirement is 24 of each per day. Develop a perfectly balanced mixed-model sequence to satisfy demand.

3. The following tasks and the order in which they must be performed according to their assembly requirements are shown in the following table. These are to be combined into workstations to create an assembly line. The assembly line operates 7½ hours per day. The output requirement is 1,000 units per day.

Task	Preceding Tasks	Time (seconds)
A	—	15
B	A	24
C	A	6
D	B	12
E	B	18
F	C	7
G	C	11
H	D	9
I	E	14
J	F, G	7
K	H, I	15
L	J, K	10

a. What is the cycle time?

b. Balance the line using longest operating time based on the 1,000 unit forecast, stating which tasks would be done in each workstation.

c. For *b* above, what is the efficiency of your line balance?

d. After production was started, Marketing realized that they understated demand and must increase output to 1,100 units. What action would you take? Be specific in quantitative terms, if appropriate.

4. An assembly line is operated seven hours per day and produces 420 units per day. Following are the tasks performed with their performance time and preceding tasks.

Task	Time (seconds)	Preceding Tasks
A	15	None
B	15	None
C	45	A, B
D	45	C

Compute the cycle time and the theoretical minimum number of workstations, and prepare an initial line configuration. Determine the efficiency of your layout.

5. An initial solution has been given to the following process layout problem. Given the flows described and a cost of $2.00 per unit per foot, compute the total cost for the layout. Each location is 100 feet long and 50 feet wide as shown on the following figure. Use the centers of departments for distances.

		Department			
		A	B	C	D
Department	A	0	10	25	55
	B		0	10	5
	C			0	15
	D				0

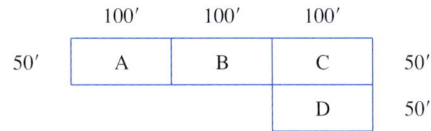

6. An assembly line will operate eight hours per day and produce 480 units per day. The accompanying table shows task times and precedence relationships. Prepare an initial line configuration and determine the efficiency of your layout.

Task	Time (seconds)	Preceding Tasks
A	20	None
B	40	A
C	35	B
D	35	B
E	35	C, D

7. An assembly line is to be designed to operate 7½ hours per day and supply a steady demand of 300 units per day. Here are the tasks and their performance times.

Task	Preceding Tasks	Performance Time (seconds)	Task	Preceding Tasks	Performance Time (seconds)
a	—	70	g	d	60
b	—	40	h	e	50
c	—	45	i	f	15
d	a	10	j	g	25
e	b	30	k	h, i	20
f	c	20	l	j, k	25

    a. Draw the precedence diagram.

    b. What is the cycle time?

    c. What is the theoretical minimum number of workstations?

    d. Assign tasks to workstations stating your logical rules.

    e. What is the efficiency of your line balance?

    f. Suppose demand increases by 10 percent. How would you react to this?

8. S. L. P. Craft would like your help in developing a layout for a new outpatient clinic to be built in California. Based on analysis of another recently built clinic, he obtains the data on page 428. This includes the number of trips made by patients between departments on a typical day (shown above the diagonal line) and the numbered weights (defined in Exhibit 10.9, page 404) between departments as specified by the new clinic's physicians (below the diagonal). The new building will be 60 feet by 20 feet.

    a. Develop an interdepartmental flow graph that minimizes patient travel.

    b. Develop a "good" relationship diagram using systematic layout planning.

    c. Choose either of the layouts obtained in *a* or *b* and sketch the departments to scale within the building.

    d. Will this layout be satisfactory to the nursing staff? Explain.

Departments	2	3	4	5	6	Area requirement (sq. ft.)
1 Reception	A / 2	O / 5	E / 200	U / 0	O / 10	100
2 X-ray		E / 10	I / 300	U / 0	O / 8	100
3 Surgery			I / 100	U / 0	A / 4	200
4 Examining rooms (5)				U / 0	I / 15	500
5 Lab					O / 3	100
6 Nurses' station						100

9. The following tasks are to be performed on an assembly line:

Task	Seconds	Tasks that Must Precede
A	20	—
B	7	A
C	20	B
D	22	B
E	15	C
F	10	D
G	16	E, F
H	8	G

The workday is seven hours long.
Demand for completed product is 750 per day.

a. Find the cycle time.
b. What is the theoretical number of workstations?
c. Draw the precedence diagram.
d. Balance the line using sequential restrictions and the longest operating time rule.
e. What is the efficiency of the line balanced as in *d?*
f. Suppose that demand rose from 750 to 800 units per day. What would you do? Show any amounts or calculations.
g. Suppose that demand rose from 750 to 1,000 units per day. What would you do? Show any amounts or calculations.

10. The Dorton University president has asked the OM department to assign eight biology professors (A, B, C, D, E, F, G, and H) to eight offices (numbered 1 to 8 in the diagram) in the new Biology Building.

The following distances and two-way flows are given:

Distances between Offices (feet)

	1	2	3	4	5	6	7	8
1	—	10	20	30	15	18	25	34
2		—	10	20	18	15	18	25
3			—	10	25	18	15	18
4				—	34	25	18	15
5					—	10	20	30
6						—	10	20
7							—	10
8								—

Two-Way Flows (units per period)

	A	B	C	D	E	F	G	H
A	—	2	0	0	5	0	0	0
B		—	0	0	0	3	0	2
C			—	0	0	0	0	3
D				—	4	0	0	0
E					—	1	0	0
F						—	1	0
G							—	4
H								—

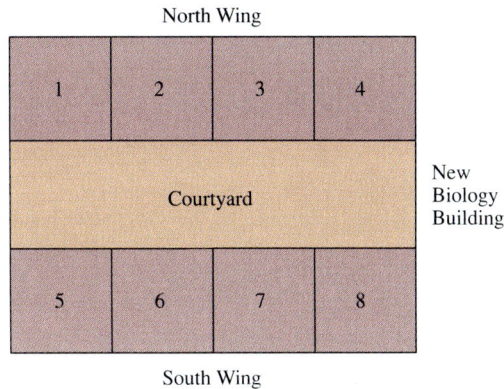

North Wing / Courtyard / New Biology Building / South Wing

a. If there are no restrictions (constraints) on the assignment of professors to offices, how many alternative assignments are there to evaluate?

b. The biology department has sent the following information and requests to the OM department:

Offices 1, 4, 5, and 8 are the only offices with windows.
A must be assigned Office 1.
D and E, the biology department co-chairpeople, must have windows.
H must be directly across the courtyard from D.
A, G, and H must be in the same wing.
F must *not* be next to D or G or directly across from G.

Find the optimal assignment of professors to offices that meets all the requests of the biology department and minimizes total material handling cost. You may use the path flow list as a computational aid.

Path	Flow	Path	Flow	Path	Flow	Path	Flow	Path	Flow
A–B	2	B–C	0	C–D	0	D–E	4	E–F	1
A–C	0	B–D	0	C–E	0	D–F	0	E–G	0
A–D	0	B–E	0	C–F	0	D–G	0	E–H	0
A–E	5	B–F	3	C–G	0	D–H	0	F–G	1
A–F	0	B–G	0	C–H	3			F–H	0
A–G	0	B–H	2					G–H	4
A–H	0								

CASE

1 0 . 1 2   C A S E
Soteriou's Souvlaki

Mr. Soteriou looks up from cleaning the floor—the lights are on. This means that the power has finally been hooked up, and soon his restaurant will reopen here in its new location.

Soteriou's Souvlaki is typical of many of the small dining establishments scattered around the perimeter of the university. Specializing in Greek cuisine—souvlaki (lamb kabobs), gyros, tiropita (cheese-filled pastries), and baklava (a honey and pistachio nut dessert)—the restaurant has been very popular with the student body.

The operations are similar to those of most fast-food restaurants. Customers enter and queue near the register to place their orders and pay. Food is prepared and given to the customer over the main counter. Drinks are self-serve, and the tables are bussed by the customers upon leaving. The kitchen is normally run by Mr. Soteriou with help from an assistant working the cash register.

Until recently Soteriou's had been located in a local food court, but earthquake damage, space constraints, and deteriorating sanitary conditions prompted him to move the restaurant to these new quarters. The new facility is a small, free-standing building, formerly a hamburger joint. Although the previous owners have removed all equipment and tables, the large fixed service counter remains, physically marking out the kitchen and dining areas. (See the accompanying figure.)

Aware of students' growing health consciousness (and possibly a little heady with the extra floor space in the new building), Mr. Soteriou has decided to add a self-service salad bar to the new restaurant. The salad bar will be much like those in other restaurants, but with a more Mediterranean flair.

The new kitchen does not appear to be much larger than the old one, though it is narrower. To prepare his Greek specialties in this new kitchen, Mr. Soteriou will need a grill/oven, a storage refrigerator, a preparation table (with hot and cold bins for the condiments, side dishes, and pita bread), a vertical spit broiler for the gyros meat, and a display case to hold the tiropitas, baklava, and cups for the self-serve drink machines.

The new dining area will include smoking and nonsmoking seating, the salad bar, self-serve drink machines, and an area for the register queues. Of course, the location of the cash register will be important to both the kitchen and dining area layouts.

Leaning against the mop handle, Mr. Soteriou looks around the clean, empty floor. Eager to open the new location, he has already ordered all the necessary equipment, but where will he put it? Unfortunately, the equipment will be arriving tomorrow morning. Once it is placed by the delivery crew, it will be hard for Mr. Soteriou and his assistant to rearrange it by themselves.

QUESTION

The matrices in Exhibits C10.1 and C10.2 show the importance of proximity for the kitchen equipment and dining area features. Use systematic layout planning (with numerical reference weightings) to develop a floor layout for the kitchen and the dining area for Soteriou's Souvlaki.

Source: This case was prepared by University of Southern California doctoral student Douglas Stewart. It is not intended to show proper or improper handling of food.

Soteriou's Souvlaki

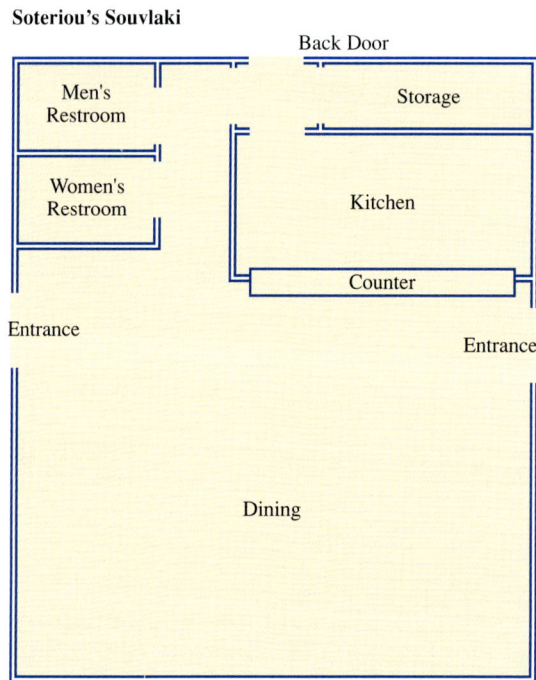

	Grill	Prep. Table	Refrig.	Vertical Broiler	Display Case
Cash register	X	A	X	U	A
Grill	—	A	A	U	E
Prep. table	—	—	I	A	U
Refrigerator	—	—	—	U	X
Vertical broiler	—	—	—	—	U
Display case	—	—	—	—	—

E X H I B I T C10.1
The Kitchen

	No Smk.	Smoking	Drinks	Salad Bar	Waiting Area
Cash register	U	U	I	I	A
No smk.	—	X	E	E	U
Smoking	—	—	I	I	U
Drinks	—	—	—	U	U
Salad bar	—	—	—	—	X
Waiting area	—	—	—	—	—

E X H I B I T C10.2
The Dining Area

C A S E

1 0 . 1 3   C A S E
State Automobile License Renewals

Henry Coupe, manager of a metropolitan branch office of the state department of motor vehicles, attempted to perform an analysis of the driver's license renewal operations. Several steps were to be performed in the process. After examining the license renewal process, he identified the steps and associated times required to perform each step as shown in Exhibit C10.3.

Coupe found that each step was assigned to a different person. Each application was a separate process in the sequence shown in the exhibit. Coupe determined that his office should be prepared to accommodate the maximum demand of processing 120 renewal applicants per hour.

He observed that the work was unevenly divided among the clerks, and that the clerk who was responsible for checking violations tended to shortcut her task to keep up with the other clerks. Long lines built up during the maximum demand periods.

Coupe also found that jobs 1, 2, 3, and 4 were handled by general clerks who were each paid $6.00 per hour. Job 5 was by a photographer paid $8 per hour. Job 6, the issuing of temporary licenses, was required by state policy to be handled by a uniformed motor vehicle officer. Officers were paid $9 per hour, but they could be assigned to any job except photography.

A review of the jobs indicated that job 1, reviewing the application for correctness, had to be performed before any other step could be taken. Similarly, job 6, issuing the temporary license, could not be performed until all the other steps were completed. The branch offices were charged $10 per hour for each camera to perform photography.

Henry Coupe was under severe pressure to increase productivity and reduce costs, but he was also told by the regional director of the Department of Motor Vehicles that he had better accommodate the demand for renewals. Otherwise, "heads would roll."

QUESTIONS

1. What is the maximum number of applications per hour that can be handled by the present configuration of the process?
2. How many applications can be processed per hour if a second clerk is added to check for violations?
3. Assuming the addition of one more clerk, what is the maximum number of applications the process can handle?
4. How would you suggest modifying the process to accommodate 120 applications per hour?

Source: P. R. Olsen, W. E. Sasser, and D. D. Wyckoff, *Management of Service Operations: Text, Cases, and Readings,* pp. 95–96. © 1978. Reprinted by permission of Prentice Hall, Englewood Cliffs, New Jersey.

E X H I B I T C10.3

State Automobile
License Renewals
Process Times

Job	Average Time to Perform (seconds)
1. Review renewal application for correctness	15
2. Process and record payment	30
3. Check file for violations and restrictions	60
4. Conduct eye test	40
5. Photograph applicant	20
6. Issue temporary license	30

10.14   SELECTED BIBLIOGRAPHY

Bachman, Timothy A. "Information and Advice: Innovations and Product Delivery for Financial Service." *Design Management Journal* 3, no. 1 (Winter 1992), pp. 103–10.

Bitner, Mary Jo. "Servicescapes: The Impact of Physical Surroundings on Customers and Employees." *Journal of Marketing* 56 (April 1992), pp. 57–71.

Bonett, Douglas G., and Robert E. D. Woolsey. "Load-Distance Analysis with Variable Loads." *Production and Inventory Management Journal,* 1st quarter 1993, pp. 32–34.

Choobineh, F. "A Framework for the Design of Cellular Manufacturing Systems." *International Journal of Production Research* 26, no. 7 (1988), pp. 1161–72.

Francis, R. L., and J. A. White. *Facility Layout and Location: An Analytical Approach.* Englewood Cliffs, NJ: Prentice Hall, 1987.

Gosh, Soumen, and Roger Gagnon. "A Comprehensive Literature Review and Analysis of the Design, Balancing and Scheduling of Assembly Systems." *International Journal of Production Research* 27, no. 4 (1989), pp. 637–70.

Green, Timothy J., and Randall P. Sadowski. "A Review of Cellular Manufacturing Assumptions, Advantages and Design Techniques." *Journal of Operations Management* 4, no. 2 (February 1984), pp. 85–97.

Gunther, R. E., G. D. Johnson, and R. S. Peterson. "Currently Practiced Formulations for the Assembly Line Balance Problem." *Journal of Operations Management* 3, no. 4 (August 1983), pp. 209–21.

Hyer, Nancy Lea. "The Potential of Group Technology for U.S. Manufacturing." *Journal of Operations Management* 4, no. 3 (May 1984), pp. 183–202.

Johnson, Roger. "Optimally Balancing Large Assembly Lines with FABLE." *Management Science* 34, no. 2 (February 1988), pp. 240–53.

Love, John F. *McDonald's: Behind the Arches.* New York: Bantam, 1986.

Mondon, Yasuhiro. *Toyota Production System: Practical Approach to Production Management.* Atlanta: Industrial Engineering and Management Press, 1983.

Norman, Richard. *Service Management.* 2d ed. New York: John Wiley & Sons, 1991.

Schonberger, Richard J. *Japanese Manufacturing Techniques.* New York: Free Press, 1982.

Zuboff, Shoshana. *In the Age of the Smart Machine: The Future of Work and Power.* New York: Basic Books, 1984, pp. 138–39.

Chapter

11

Job Design, Work Measurement, and Learning Curves

CHAPTER OUTLINE

KEY TERMS

Job Design

Specialization of Labor

Sociotechnical Systems

Job Enrichment

Work Physiology

Work Measurement

Time Study

Normal Time

Standard Time

Work Sampling

Financial Incentive Plans

Profit Sharing

Gain Sharing

Learning Curve

Individual Learning

Organizational Learning

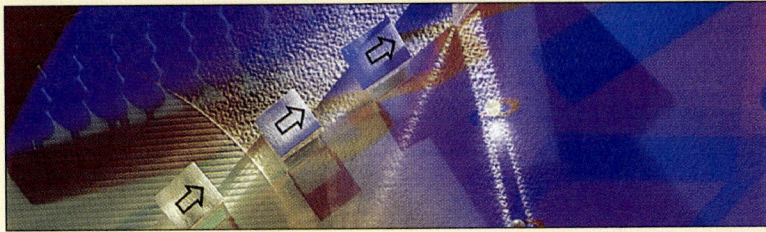

JOB DESIGN THEN . . .

Frederick W. Taylor recounts his "motivation" of his trusty worker, Schmidt (in *Principles of Scientific Management*, 1910):

"Schmidt, are you a high-priced man?"

"Vell, I don't know vat you mean."

"Oh yes you do. What I want to know is whether you are a high-priced man or not. . . . What I want to find out is whether you want to earn $1.85 a day or whether you are satisfied with $1.15, just the same as all those cheap fellows are getting?"

"Vell, yes I vas a high-priced man."

"Now come over here. You see that pile of pig iron?"

"Yes."

"You see that car?"

"Yes."

"Well, if you are a high-priced man, you will load that pig iron on that car tomorrow for $1.85."

"You see that man over there? . . . Well, if you are a high-priced man, you will do exactly as this man tells you tomorrow, from morning till night. When he tells you to pick up a pig and walk, you pick it up and you walk, and when he tells you to sit down and rest, you sit down. You do that straight through the day. And what's more, no back talk."

AND NOW . . .

Researcher Paul S. Adler describes job design at New United Motor Manufacturing Inc.'s (NUMMI) Freemont, California, plant. NUMMI is a joint venture between General Motors and Toyota.

Team members hold the stopwatch and design their own jobs. Team members begin by timing one another, seeking the most efficient way to do each task at a sustainable pace. They pick the best performance, break it down into its component parts, and then look for ways of improving each element. The team then takes the resulting methods, compares them with those used by teams working on the other shift at the same workstation, and writes detailed specifications that become the standard work definition for everyone on both teams.

Source: Discussions with Paul S. Adler; Paul S. Adler, "Time and Motion Regained," *Harvard Business Review* 71, no. 1 (January–February 1993), pp. 97–110; and "Return of the Stopwatch," *The Economist,* January 23, 1993, p. 69.

The operations manager's job, by definition, deals with managing the personnel that create the firm's products and services. To say that this is a challenging job in today's complex environment is an understatement. The diversity of the workforce's cultural and educational background, coupled with frequent organization restructuring, calls for a much higher level of people management skills than have been required in even the recent past.

The objective in managing the personnel is to obtain the highest productivity possible without sacrificing quality, service, or responsiveness. The operations manager uses job design techniques to structure the work so that it will be conducive to both the physical and behavioral needs of the human worker. Work measurement methods are used to determine the most efficient means of performing a given task, as well as to set reasonable standards for performing it. People are motivated by many things, only one of which is financial reward. Operations managers can structure such rewards, not only to motivate consistently high performance, but also to reinforce the most important aspects of the job. A working knowledge of learning curves is also needed to allow the operations manager to anticipate the gains in efficiency that naturally arise as workers gain experience.

11.1   JOB DESIGN DECISIONS

Job design may be defined as the function of specifying the work activities of an individual or group in an organizational setting. Its objective is to develop job structures that meet the requirements of the organization and its technology, and that satisfy the jobholder's personal and individual requirements. Exhibit 11.1 summarizes the decisions involved. These decisions are being affected by the following trends:

1. *Quality control as part of the worker's job.* Now often referred to as "quality at the source" (see Chapters 5 and 6), quality control is linked with the concept of *empowerment.* Empowerment, in turn, refers to workers being given authority to stop a production line if there is a quality problem, or to give a customer an on-the-spot refund if service was not satisfactory.

2. *Cross-training workers to perform multiskilled jobs.* As companies engage in downsizing, the remaining workforce is expected to do more and different tasks.

3. *Employee involvement and team approaches to designing and organizing work.* This is a central feature in total quality management (TQM) and continuous improvement efforts. In fact, it is safe to say that virtually all TQM programs are team-based.

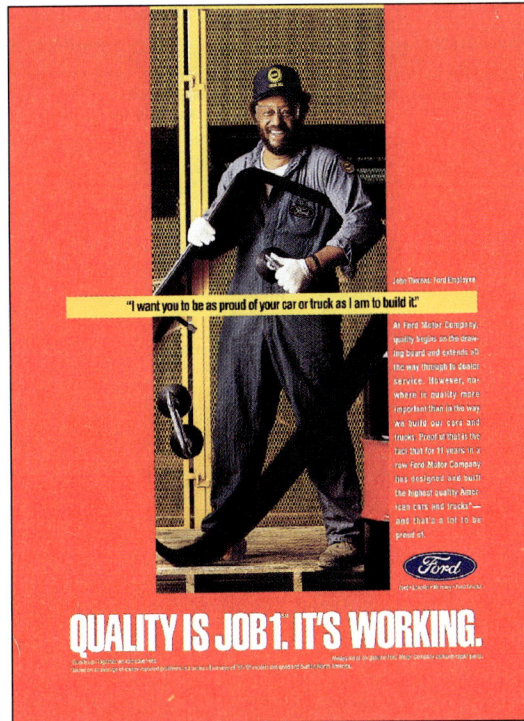

Ford and other U.S. auto manufacturers emphasize the importance of quality at the source and employee involvement. These have been factors in the resurgence of the American automobile industry.

E X H I B I T 11.1   *Job Design Decisions*

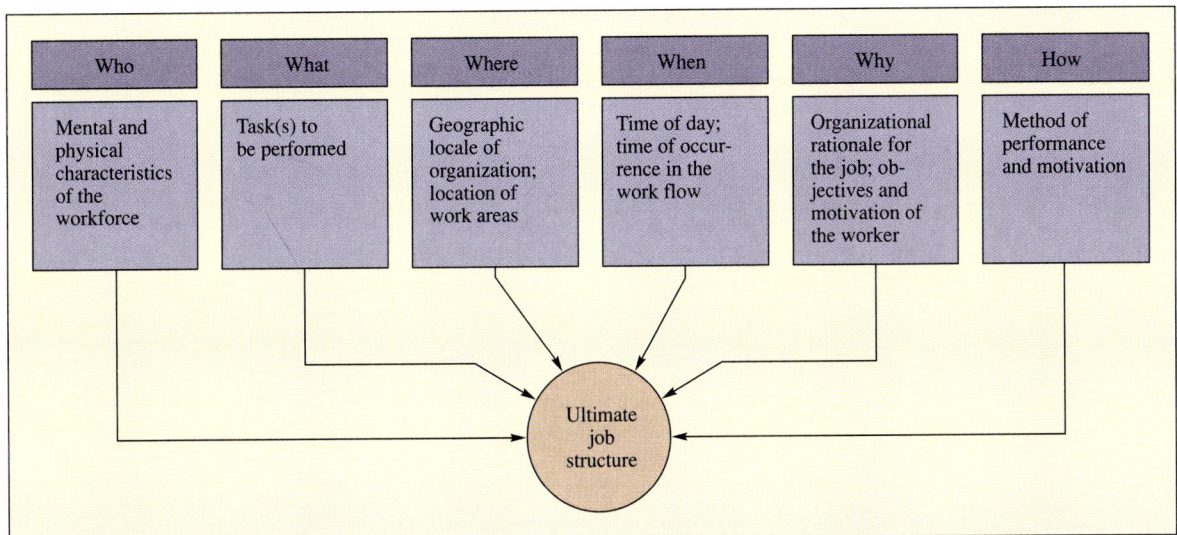

4. *"Informating" ordinary workers through telecommunication networks and computers, thereby expanding the nature of their work and their ability to do it.* In this context, informating is more than just automating work—it is revising work's fundamental structure. Northeast Utilities' computer system, for example, can pinpoint a problem in a service area before the customer service

representative answers the phone. The rep uses the computer to troubleshoot serious problems, to weigh probabilities that other customers in the area have been affected, and to dispatch repair crews before other calls are even received.

5. *Extensive use of temporary workers.* Manpower, a company specializing in providing temporary employees, is vying with McDonald's as the largest private employer in the United States with over 500,000 workers on its payroll.

6. *Automation of heavy manual work.* Examples abound in both services (one-person trash pickup trucks) and manufacturing (robot spray painting on auto lines). These changes are driven by safety regulations as well as economics and personnel reasons.

7. *Most important of all, organizational commitment to providing meaningful and rewarding jobs for all employers.* Hewlett-Packard's mission statement lists three "People related objectives: (1) Belief in our people; (2) Emphasis on working together and sharing rewards (teamwork and partnership); and (3) A superior working environment which other companies seek but few achieve."

11.2   BEHAVIORAL CONSIDERATIONS IN JOB DESIGN

Degree of Labor Specialization

Specialization of labor is the two-edged sword of job design. On one hand, specialization has made possible high-speed, low-cost production, and, from a materialistic standpoint, has greatly enhanced our standard of living. On the other hand, extreme specialization (as we see in mass-production industries) often has serious adverse effects on workers, which in turn are passed on to the production systems. In essence, the problem is to determine how much specialization is enough. At what point do the disadvantages outweigh the advantages? (See Exhibit 11.2.)

Recent research suggests that the disadvantages dominate the advantages much more commonly than was thought in the past. However, simply stating that, for purely humanitarian reasons, specialization should be avoided is risky. The reason, of course, is

E X H I B I T 11.2

Advantages and Disadvantages of Specialization of Labor

Advantages of Specialization	
To Management	**To Labor**
1. Rapid training of the workforce 2. Ease in recruiting new workers 3. High output due to simple and repetitive work 4. Low wages due to ease of substitutability of labor 5. Close control over work flow and workloads	1. Little or no education required to obtain work 2. Ease in learning job

Disadvantages of Specialization	
To Management	**To Labor**
1. Difficulty in controlling quality since no one person has responsibility for entire product 2. Worker dissatisfaction leading to hidden costs arising from turnover, absenteeism, tardiness, grievances, and intentional disruption of production process 3. Reduced likelihood of improving the process because of workers' limited perspective	1. Boredom stemming from repetitive nature of work 2. Little gratification from work itself because of small contribution to each item 3. Little or no control over the workpace, leading to frustration and fatigue (in assembly-line situations) 4. Little opportunity to progress to a better job since significant learning is rarely possible on fractionated work

that people differ in what they want from their work and what they are willing to put into it. Some workers prefer not to make decisions about their work, some like to day-dream on the job, and others are simply not capable of performing more complex work. Still, there is much worker frustration with many jobs' structures, leading organizations to try different approaches to job design. Two popular contemporary approaches are job enrichment and sociotechnical systems.

Job Enrichment

Job enlargement generally entails adjusting a specialized job to make it more interesting to the jobholder. A job is said to be enlarged *horizontally* if the worker performs a greater number or variety of tasks, and it is said to be enlarged *vertically* if the worker is involved in planning, organizing, and inspecting his own work. Horizontal job enlargement is intended to counteract oversimplification and to permit the worker to perform a "whole unit of work." Vertical enlargement (traditionally termed job enrichment) attempts to broaden workers' influence in the transformation process by giving them certain managerial powers over their own activities. Today, common practice is to apply both horizontal and vertical enlargement to a given job and refer to the total approach as **job enrichment.**

The organizational benefits of job enrichment occur both in quality and productivity. Quality in particular improves dramatically because when individuals are responsible for their work output, they take ownership of it and simply do a better job. Also, because they have a broader understanding of the work process, they are more likely to catch errors and make corrections than if the job is narrowly focused. Productivity improvements also occur from job enrichment, but they are not as predictable or as large as the improvements in quality. The reason is that enriched work invariably contains a mix of tasks that (for manual labor) causes interruptions in rhythm and different motions when switching from one task to the next. Such is the not the case for specialized jobs.[1]

Sociotechnical Systems

Consistent with the job enrichment philosophy but focusing more on the interaction between technology and the work group is the **sociotechnical systems** approach. It attempts to develop jobs that adjust the needs of the production process technology to the needs of the worker and work group. The term was developed from studies of weaving mills in India and coal mines in England in the early 1950s. These studies revealed that work groups could effectively handle many production problems better than management if they were permitted to make their own decisions on scheduling, work allocation among members, bonus sharing, and so forth. This was particularly true when there were variations in the production process requiring quick reactions by the group or when one shift's work overlapped with other shifts' work.

Since these pioneering studies, the sociotechnical approach has been applied in many countries—often under the heading of "autonomous work groups," "Japanese-style work groups," or employee involvement (EI) teams. Most major American manufacturing companies have work teams as the basic building block in so-called high employee involvement plants. They are now becoming common in service organizations as well. The benefits of teams are similar to those of individual job enrichment: they provide higher quality and greater productivity (they often set higher production goals than general management), do their own support work and equipment maintenance, and have increased chances to make meaningful improvements.[2]

---

[1]Edward E. Lawler III, *The Ultimate Advantage: Creating the High Involvement Organizations* (San Francisco: Jossey-Bass Publishers, 1992), pp. 85–86.

[2]Ibid., pp. 98–99.

One major conclusion from these applications is that the individual or work group requires a logically integrated pattern of work activities that incorporates the following job design principles:

Task Variety   An attempt must be made to provide an optimal variety of tasks within each job. Too much variety can be inefficient for training and frustrating for the employee. Too little can lead to boredom and fatigue. The optimal level is one that allows the employee to take a rest from a high level of attention or effort while working on another task or, conversely, to stretch after periods of routine activity.

Skill Variety   Research suggests that employees derive satisfaction from using a number of skill levels.

Feedback   There should be some means for informing employees quickly when they have achieved their targets. Fast feedback aids the learning process. Ideally, employees should have some responsibility for setting their own standards of quantity and quality.

Task Identity   Sets of tasks should be separated from other sets of tasks by some clear boundary. Whenever possible, a group or individual employee should have responsibility for a set of tasks that is clearly defined, visible, and meaningful. In this way, work is seen as important by the group or individual undertaking it, and others understand and respect its significance.

Task Autonomy   Employees should be able to exercise some control over their work. Areas of discretion and decision making should be available to them.[3]

11.3   PHYSICAL CONSIDERATIONS IN JOB DESIGN

Beyond the behavioral components of job design, another aspect warrants consideration: the physical side. Indeed, while motivation and work group structure strongly influence job performance, they may be of secondary importance if the job is too demanding from a physical (or "human factors") standpoint. One approach to incorporating the physical costs of moderate to heavy work in job design is **work physiology.** Pioneered by Eastman Kodak in the 1960s, work physiology sets work-rest cycles according to the energy expended in various parts of the job. For example, if a job entails caloric expenditure above five calories per minute (the rough baseline for sustainable work), the required rest period must equal or exceed the time spent working. Obviously, the harder the work, the more frequent and longer the rest periods. (Exhibit 11.3 shows caloric requirements for various activities.)

11.4   WORK METHODS

In contemporary industry, responsibility for developing work methods in large firms is typically assigned either to a staff department designated *methods analysis* or to an industrial engineering department. In small firms, this activity is often performed by consulting firms that specialize in work methods design.

---

[3]This summary is taken from Enid Mumford and Mary Weir, *Computer Systems in Work Design—the ETHICS Method* (New York: Halstead, 1979), p. 42.

Type of Activity	Typical Energy Cost in Calories per Minute*	Required Minutes of Rest for Each Minute of Work
Sitting at rest	1.7	—
Writing	2.0	—
Typing on a computer	2.0	—
Medium assembly work	2.9	—
Shoe repair	3.0	—
Machining	3.3	—
Ironing	4.4	—
Heavy assembly work	5.1	—
Chopping wood	7.5	1
Digging	8.9	2
Tending furnace	12.0	3
Walking upstairs	12.0	3

*Five calories per minute is generally considered the maximum sustainable level throughout the workday.

Activity	Objective of Study	Study Techniques
Overall productive system	Eliminate or combine steps; shorten transport distance; identify delays	Flow diagram, service blueprint, process chart
Worker at fixed workplace	Simplify method; minimize motions	Operations charts, simo charts; apply principles of motion economy
Worker's interaction with equipment	Minimize idle time; find number or combination of machines to balance cost of worker and machine idle time	Activity chart, worker-machine charts
Worker's interaction with other workers	Maximize productivity; minimize interference	Activity charts, gang process charts

The principal approach to the study of work methods is the construction of charts, such as operations charts, worker-machine charts, simo (simultaneous motion) charts, and activity charts, in conjunction with time study or standard time data. The choice of which charting method to use depends on the task's activity level; that is, whether the focus is on (1) the overall productive system, (2) the worker at a fixed workplace, (3) a worker interacting with equipment, or (4) a worker interacting with other workers (see Exhibit 11.4). (Several of these charting techniques were introduced in Chapter 3, where they were used to aid in manufacturing process design. Chapter 4 introduced the service blueprint that accounts for customer interactions.)

The objective in studying the overall productive system is to identify delays, transport distances, processes, and processing time requirements to simplify the entire operation. The underlying philosophy is to eliminate any step in the process that does not add value to the product. The approach is to flow chart the process and then ask the following questions:

What is done? Must it be done? What would happen if it were not done?

Where is the task done? Must it be done at that location or could it be done somewhere else?

When is the task done? Is it critical that it be done then or is there flexibility in time and sequence? Could it be done in combination with some other step in the process?

How is the task done? Why is it done this way? Is there another way?

Who does the task? Can someone else do it? Should the worker be of a higher or lower skill level?

Overall Productive System

These thought-provoking questions usually help to eliminate much unnecessary work and simplify the remaining work, by combining a number of processing steps and changing the order of performance.

The process chart is valuable in studying an overall system, though care must be taken to follow the same item throughout the process. The subject may be a product being manufactured, a service being created, or a person performing a sequence of activities. Exhibit 11.5 shows a process chart (and flow diagram) for a clerical operation. Exhibit 11.6 shows common notation in process charting.

Worker at a Fixed Workplace

Many jobs require the worker to remain at a specified workstation. When the nature of the work is primarily manual (such as sorting, inspecting, making entries, or assembly operations), the focus of work design is on simplifying the work method and making the required operator motions as few and as easy as possible.

There are two basic ways to determine the best method when a method analyst studies a single worker performing an essentially manual task. The first is to search among the workers and find the one who performs the job best. That person's method is then accepted as the standard, and others are trained to perform it in the same way. This was basically F. W. Taylor's approach, though after determining the best method, he searched for "first-class men" to perform according to the method. (A first-class man possessed the natural ability to do much more productive work in a particular task than the average. Men who were not first class were transferred to other jobs.) The second way is to observe the performance of a number of workers, analyze in detail each step of their work, and pick out the superior features of each worker's performance. This results in a composite method that combines the best elements of the group studied. Frank Gilbreth, the father of motion study, used this procedure to determine the "one best way" to perform a work task.

Taylor observed actual performance to find the best method; Frank Gilbreth and his wife Lillian relied on movie film. Through micromotion analysis—observing the filmed work performance frame by frame—the Gilbreths studied work very closely and defined its basic elements, which were termed *therbligs* ("Gilbreth" spelled backward, with the *t* and *h* transposed). Their study led to the rules or principles of motion economy, such as "The hands should begin and complete the motions at the same time," and "Work should be arranged to permit natural rhythm."

Once the motions for performing the task have been identified, an *operations chart* may be made, listing the operations and their sequence of performance. For greater detail, a *simo* (simultaneous motion) *chart* may be constructed, listing not only the operations but also the times for both left and right hands. This chart may be assembled from the data collected with a stopwatch, from analysis of a film of the operation, or from predetermined motion-time data (discussed later in the chapter). Many aspects of poor design are immediately obvious: a hand being used as a holding device (rather than a jig or fixture), an idle hand, or an exceptionally long time for positioning.

Worker Interacting with Equipment

When a person and equipment operate together to perform the productive process, interest focuses on the efficient use of the person's time and equipment time. When the operator's working time is less than the equipment run time, a worker-machine chart is a useful device in analysis. If the operator can operate several pieces of equipment, the problem is to find the most economical combination of operator and equipment, when the combined cost of the idle time of a particular combination of equipment and the idle time for the worker is at a minimum.

Worker-machine charts are always drawn to scale, the scale being time as measured by length. Exhibit 11.7 shows a worker-machine chart in a service setting. The question here is, Whose use is most important?

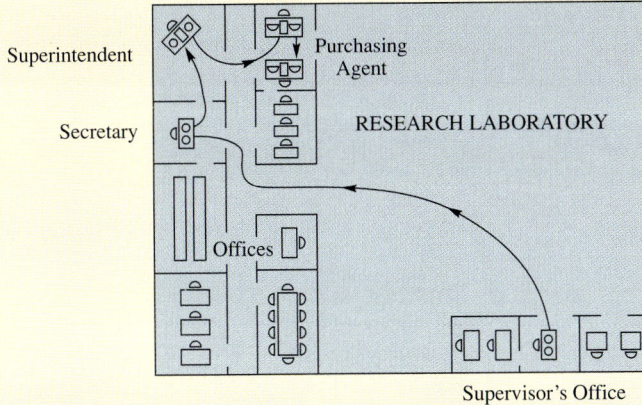

E X H I B I T 11.5

Flow Diagram and Process Chart of an Office Procedure— Present Method

PROCESS CHART

Present Method ☒
Proposed Method ☐

SUBJECT CHARTED Requisition for small tools

Chart begins at supervisor's desk and ends at

typist's desk in purchasing department

DEPARTMENT Research laboratory

DATE _____

CHART BY J.C.H.

CHART NO. R136

SHEET NO. 1 OF 1

DIST. IN FEET	TIME IN MINS.	CHART SYMBOLS	PROCESS DESCRIPTION
		● ⇨ □ D ▽	Requisitions written by supervisor (one copy)
		○ ⇨ □ D ▽	On supervisor's desk (awaiting messenger)
65		○ ⇨ □ D ▽	By messenger to superintendent's secretary
		○ ⇨ □ D ▽	On secretary's desk (awaiting typing)
		● ⇨ □ D ▽	Requisition typed (original requisition copied)
15		○ ⇨ □ D ▽	By secretary to superintendent
		○ ⇨ □ D ▽	On superintendent's desk (awaiting messenger)
		○ ⇨ □ D ▽	Examined and approved
		○ ⇨ □ D ▽	On superintendent's desk (awaiting messenger)
20		○ ⇨ □ D ▽	To purchasing department
		○ ⇨ □ D ▽	On purchasing agent's desk (awaiting approval)
		○ ⇨ □ D ▽	Examined and approved
		○ ⇨ □ D ▽	On purchasing agent's desk (awaiting messenger)
5		○ ⇨ □ D ▽	To typist's desk
		○ ⇨ □ D ▽	On typist's desk (awaiting typing of purchase order)
		● ⇨ □ D ▽	Purchase order typed
		○ ⇨ □ D ▽	On typist's desk (awaiting transfer to main office)
		○ ⇨ □ D ▽	
105		3 4 2 8	Total

Source: Ralph M. Barnes, *Motion and Time Study* (New York: John Wiley & Sons, 1980), pp. 76-79.

Note: Requisition is written by a supervisor, typed by a secretary, approved by a superintendent, and approved by a purchasing agent. Then a purchase order is prepared by a stenographer.

E X H I B I T 11.6
Common Notation in Process Charting

● Operation. Something is actually being done. This may be work on a product, some support activity or anything that is directly productive in nature.

➡ Transportation. The subject of the study (product, service, or person) moves from one location to another.

■ Inspection. The subject is observed for quality and correctness.

◗ Delay. The subject of the study must wait before starting the next step in the process.

▼ Storage. The subject is stored, such as finished products in inventory or completed papers in a file. Frequently, a distinction is made between temporary storage and permanent storage by inserting a T or P in the triangle.

E X H I B I T 11.7   *Worker-Machine Chart for a Gourmet Coffee Store*

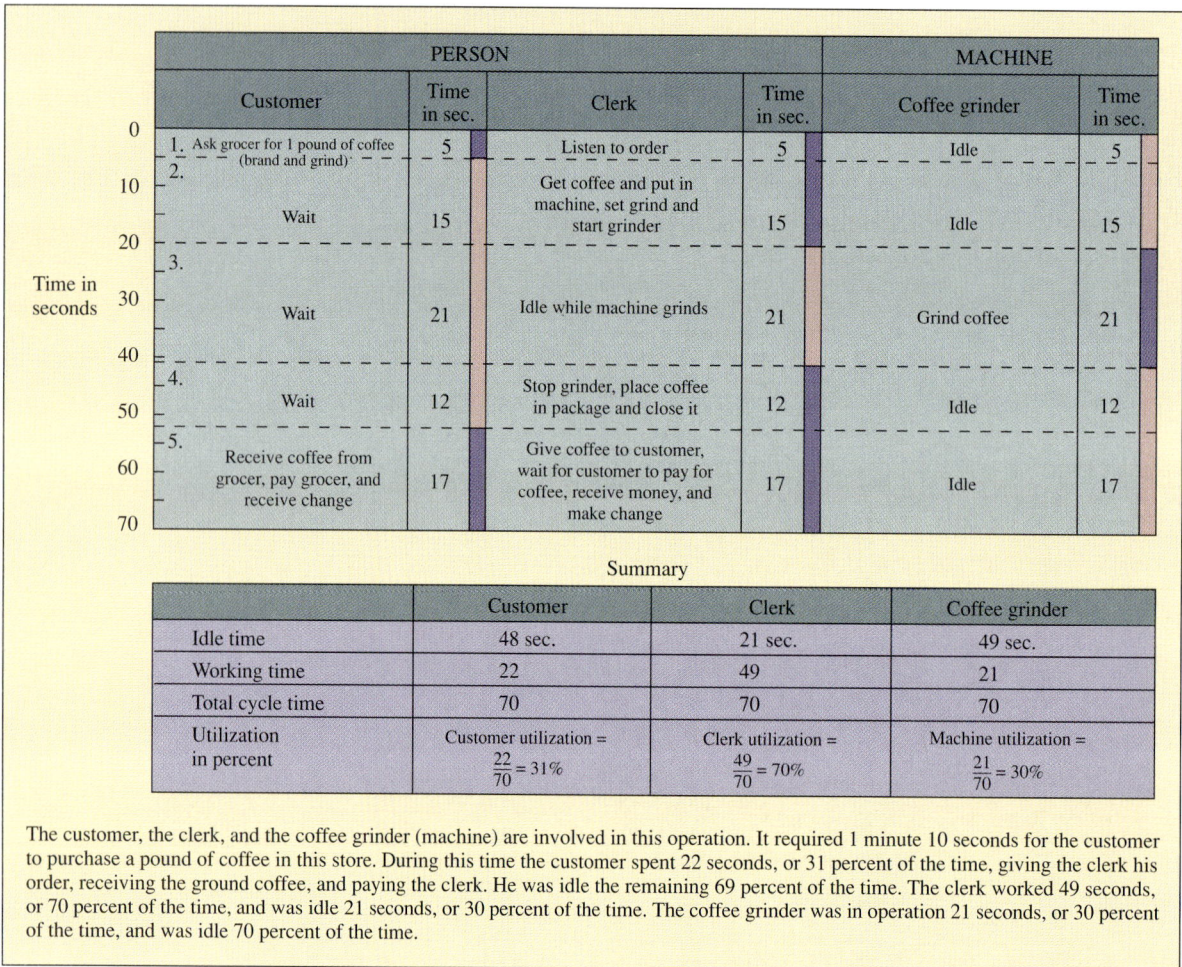

		PERSON				MACHINE	
Time in seconds	Customer	Time in sec.	Clerk	Time in sec.	Coffee grinder	Time in sec.
0	1. Ask grocer for 1 pound of coffee (brand and grind)	5	Listen to order	5	Idle	5
10	2. Wait	15	Get coffee and put in machine, set grind and start grinder	15	Idle	15
20 30 40	3. Wait	21	Idle while machine grinds	21	Grind coffee	21
50	4. Wait	12	Stop grinder, place coffee in package and close it	12	Idle	12
60 70	5. Receive coffee from grocer, pay grocer, and receive change	17	Give coffee to customer, wait for customer to pay for coffee, receive money, and make change	17	Idle	17

Summary

	Customer	Clerk	Coffee grinder
Idle time	48 sec.	21 sec.	49 sec.
Working time	22	49	21
Total cycle time	70	70	70
Utilization in percent	Customer utilization = $\frac{22}{70}=31\%$	Clerk utilization = $\frac{49}{70}=70\%$	Machine utilization = $\frac{21}{70}=30\%$

The customer, the clerk, and the coffee grinder (machine) are involved in this operation. It required 1 minute 10 seconds for the customer to purchase a pound of coffee in this store. During this time the customer spent 22 seconds, or 31 percent of the time, giving the clerk his order, receiving the ground coffee, and paying the clerk. He was idle the remaining 69 percent of the time. The clerk worked 49 seconds, or 70 percent of the time, and was idle 21 seconds, or 30 percent of the time. The coffee grinder was in operation 21 seconds, or 30 percent of the time, and was idle 70 percent of the time.

Workers Interacting with Other Workers

A great amount of our productive output in manufacturing and service industries is performed by teams. The degree of interaction may be as simple as one operator handing a part to another, or as complex as a cardiovascular surgical team of doctors, nurses, anesthesiologist, operator of an artificial heart machine, X-ray technician, standby blood donors, and pathologist (and perhaps a minister to pray a little).

E X H I B I T 11.8 *Activity Chart of Emergency Tracheotomy*

	Nurse	First doctor	Orderly	Second doctor	Nurse supervisor	Scrub nurse	
0							0
1	Detects problem Notifies doctor						1
2							2
3	Gets mobile cart	Makes diagnosis					3
4							4
5							5
6	Notifies nurse supervisor	Assists patient to breathe			Opens OR Calls scrub nurse		6
7	Notifies second doctor			Assures availability of laryngoscope and endotracheal tube			7
8	Notifies orderly	Moves to OR					8
9	Moves patient to OR	Scrubs	Moves patient to OR			Moves to OR Sets up equipment	9
10		Dons gown and gloves					10
11				Operates laryngoscope and inserts endotracheal tube			11
12				Calls for IPPB machine			12
13		Performs tracheotomy					13
14							14
15							15
16							16

Source: Data taken from Harold E. Smalley and John Freeman, *Hospital Industrial Engineering* (New York: Reinhold, 1966), p. 409.

An activity or a gang process chart is useful in plotting each individual's activities on a time scale similar to that of the worker-machine chart. A gang process chart is usually employed to trace the interaction of a number of workers with machines of a specified operating cycle, to find the best combination of workers and machines. An activity chart is less restrictive and may be used to follow the interaction of any group of operators, with or without equipment being involved. Such charts are often used to study and define each operation in an ongoing repetitive process, and they are extremely valuable in developing a standardized procedure for a specific task. Exhibit 11.8, for example, shows an activity chart for a hospital's emergency routine in performing a tracheotomy (opening a patient's throat surgically to allow her to breathe), where detailed activity analysis is critical and any delay could be fatal.

11.5 WORK MEASUREMENT AND STANDARDS

The fundamental purpose of **work measurement** is to set time standards for a job. Such standards are necessary for four reasons:

1. *To schedule work and allocate capacity.* All scheduling approaches require some estimate of how much time it takes to do the work being scheduled.

2. *To provide an objective basis for motivating the workforce and measuring their performance.* Measured standards are particularly critical where output-based incentive plans are employed.

3. *To bid for new contracts and to evaluate performance on existing ones.* Questions such as "Can we do it?" and "How are we doing?" presume the existence of standards.

4. *To provide benchmarks for improvement.* In addition to internal evaluation, benchmarking teams regularly compare work standards in their company with those of similar jobs in other organizations.

Work measurement and its resulting work standards have been controversial since Taylor's time. Much of this criticism has come from unions, which argue that management often sets standards that cannot be achieved on a regular basis. (To counter this, in some contracts the industrial engineer who sets the standard must demonstrate that she can do the job over a representative period of time at the rate she sets.) There is also the argument that workers who find a better way of doing the job get penalized by having a revised rate set. (This is commonly called rate cutting.)

With the widespread adoption of W. Edwards Deming's ideas, the subject has received renewed criticism. Deming argued that work standards and quotas inhibit process improvement and tend to focus the worker's efforts on speed rather than quality.

Despite these criticisms, work measurement and standards have proven to be effective. Much depends on sociotechnical aspects of the work. Where the job requires work groups to function as teams and create improvements, the NUMMI approach of worker-set standards discussed in the opening vignette makes sense. On the other hand, where the job really boils down to doing the work quickly, with little need for creativity (such as delivering packages for UPS as the box insert on page 447 relates), tightly engineered standards set by pros are appropriate.

Work Measurement Techniques

There are four basic techniques for measuring work: time study (stopwatch and filmed micromotion analysis), elemental standard time data, predetermined motion time data, and work sampling. The choice of techniques depends on the level of detail desired and the nature of the work itself. Highly detailed, repetitive work usually calls for time study and predetermined motion-time data analysis. When work is done in conjunction with fixed processing time equipment, elemental data are often used to reduce the need for direct observation. When work is infrequent or entails a long cycle time, work sampling is the tool of choice.

Time Study   A **time study** is generally made with a stopwatch, either on the spot or by analyzing a videotape of the job. The job or task to be studied is separated into measurable parts or elements, and each element is timed individually.

Some general rules for breaking down the elements are

1. Define each work element to be short in duration but long enough so it can be timed with a stopwatch and the time can be written down.

2. If the operator works with equipment that runs separately (meaning the operator performs a task and the equipment runs independently), separate the actions of the operator and of the equipment into different elements.

3. Define any delays by the operator or equipment into separate elements.

After a number of repetitions, the collected times are averaged. (The standard deviation may be computed to give a measure of variance in the performance times.) The averaged times for each element are added, yielding the performance time for the operator. However, to make this operator's time usable for all workers, a measure of speed or *performance rating* must be included to "normalize" the job. The application of a rating factor gives what is called *normal time*. For example, if an operator performs a task in

Grabbing a package under his arm, Joseph Polise, a driver for United Parcel Service (UPS), bounds from his brown delivery truck and toward an office building here. A few paces behind him, Marjorie Cusack, a UPS industrial engineer, clutches a digital timer.

Her eyes fixed on Mr. Polise, she counts his steps and times his contact with customers. Scribbling on a clipboard, Ms. Cusack records every second taken up by stoplights, traffic, detours, doorbells, walkways, stairways, and coffee breaks. "If he goes to the bathroom, we time him," she says.

Seventy-five thousand UPS drivers travel 1.8 billion miles per year and deliver more than 11 million packages a day. On average, UPS drivers move in and out of the truck 200 times a day. An unnecessary step or indirect travel path reduces the effectiveness of the driver and impacts service to the customer. One minute saved each day saves the company $5 million annually. For this reason, UPS spends millions each year to train its drivers in proper, efficient, and safe work methods.

Approximately 3,200 industrial engineers at UPS ensure efficient and reliable customer service by conducting time studies on drivers' routes to provide job method instruction. They have measured even the finest details of the drivers' job including determining on which finger drivers should consistently carry their key rings to avoid losing them.

In addition to developing specific job methods, UPS provides drivers with custom-built package cars with features including:

- Domed seats which allow the driver to slide on and off easily at each delivery stop.
- A drop floor well located behind the rear wheel housing making the rear of the vehicle only a short step from the ground for easy entry.
- Bulkhead doors that allow easy access to the package compartment and save the driver steps in selecting parcels for delivery.

Source: Abstracted from Daniel Machalaba, "Up to Speed: United Parcel Service Gets Deliveries Done by Driving Its Workers," *The Wall Street Journal*, April 22, 1986, p. 1, Information provided by UPS, 1994.

Work Measurement at United Parcel Service

---

two minutes and the time study analyst estimates him to be performing about 20 percent faster than normal, the normal time would be computed as 2 minutes + 0.20(2 minutes), or 2.4 minutes. In equation form,

Normal time = Observed performance time per unit $\times$ Performance rating

In this example, denoting normal time by *NT*,

$$NT = 2(1.2) = 2.4 \text{ minutes}$$

When an operator is observed for a period of time, the number of units produced during this time, along with the performance rating, gives

$$NT = \frac{\text{Time worked}}{\text{Number of units produced}} \times \text{Performance rating}$$

Standard time is derived by adding to normal time allowances for personal needs (e.g., washroom and coffee breaks), unavoidable work delays (e.g., equipment breakdown, lack of materials), and worker fatigue (physical or mental). Two such equations are

$$\text{Standard time} = \text{Normal time} + (\text{Allowances} \times \text{Normal time})$$

or

$$ST = NT(1 + \text{Allowances}) \qquad (11.1)$$

E X H I B I T 11.9

*Time-Study
Observation Sheet*

Time Study Observation Sheet															
Identification of operation		*Assemble 24" x 36" chart blanks*										Date *10/9*			
Began timing: *9:26* Ended timing: *9:32*		Operator *109*				Approval *BqR*						Observer *f.D.f.*			
Element description and breakpoint			Cycles										Summary		
			1 0.00	2	3	4	5	6	7	8	9	10	ΣT	T̄	PR	NT

	Element description and breakpoint		1 0.00	2	3	4	5	6	7	8	9	10	ΣT	T̄	PR	NT
1	*Fold over end (grasp stapler)*	T	.07	.07	.05	.07	.09	.06	.05	.08	.08	.06	.68	.07	.90	.06
		R	.07	.61	.14	.67	.24	.78	.33	.88	.47	.09				
2	*Staple five times (drop stapler)*	T	.16	.14	.14	.15	.16	.16	.14	.17	.14	.15	1.51	.15	1.05	.16
		R	.23	.75	.28	.82	.40	.94	.47	.05	.61	.24				
3	*Bend and insert wire (drop pliers)*	T	.22	.25	.22	.25	.23	.23	.21	.26	.25	.24	2.36	.24	1.00	.24
		R	.45	.00	.50	.07	.63	.17	.68	.31	.86	.48				
4	*Dispose of finished chart (touch next sheet)*	T	.09	.09	.10	.08	.09	.11	.12	.08	.17	.08	1.01	.10	.90	.09
		R	.54	.09	.60	.15	.72	.28	.80	.39	.03	.56				
5		T													*0.55 normal minute for cycle*	
		R														
6		T														
10		T														
		R														

Normal cycle time ___0.55___ + Allowance *(0.55 ∞ 0.143) or 0.08* = Std. time ___0.63 min./pc.___

and

$$ST = \frac{NT}{1 - \text{Allowances}}$$ (11.2)

Equation (11.1) is most often used in practice. If one presumes that allowances should be applied to the total work period, then equation (11.2) is the correct one. To illustrate, suppose that the normal time to perform a task is 1 minute and that allowances for personal needs, delays, and fatigue total 15 percent; then by equation (11.1)

$ST = 1(1 + 0.15) = 1.15$ minutes

In an eight-hour day, a worker would produce $8 \times 60/1.15$, or 417 units. This implies 417 minutes working and $480 - 417$ (or 63) minutes for allowances.

With equation (11.2),

$$ST = \frac{1}{1 - 0.15} = 1.18 \text{ minutes}$$

In the same eight-hour day, $8 \times 60/1.18$ (or 408) units are produced with 408 working minutes and 72 minutes for allowances. Depending on which equation is used, there is a difference of 9 minutes in the daily allowance time.

Exhibit 11.9 shows a time study of 10 cycles of a four-element job. For each element, there is a space for the watch reading in 100ths of a minute *(R)* and each element subtracted time *(T)*. The value for *T* is obtained after the time study observations are completed, since in this case the watch is read continuously.[4] *PR* denotes the performance rating and *T* the average time for each element. The standard time, calculated according to equation (11.1), is given at the bottom of the time study sheet shown above.

How many observations are enough? Time study is really a sampling process, that is, we take relatively few observations as being representative of many subsequent cycles to be performed by the worker. Based on a great deal of analysis and experience, Benjamin

---

[4]Not surprisingly, this is called the *continuous method* of timing. When the watch is reset after each element is recorded, it is called the *snapback method*.

When Time per Cycle Is More than	Minimum Number of Cycles of Study (Activity)		
	Over 10,000 per Year	**1,000–10,000**	**Under 1,000**
8 hours	2	1	1
3	3	2	1
2	4	2	1
1	5	3	2
48 minutes	6	3	2
30	8	4	3
20	10	5	4
12	12	6	5
8	15	8	6
5	20	10	8
3	25	12	10
2	30	15	12
1	40	20	15
.7	50	25	20
.5	60	30	25
.3	80	40	30
.2	100	50	40
.1	120	60	50
Under .1	140	80	60

E X H I B I T 11.10

Guide to Number of Cycles to Be Observed in a Time Study

Source: Benjamin W. Niebel, *Motion and Time Study,* 9th ed. (Homewood, Ill.: Richard D. Irwin, 1993), p. 390.

Niebel's table shown in Exhibit 11.10 indicates that enough is a function of cycle length and number of repetitions of the job over a one-year planning period.

Elemental Standard-Time Data   **Elemental standard-time data** are obtained from previous time studies and codified in tables in a handbook or computer data bank. Such data are used to develop time standards for new jobs or to make time adjustments to reflect changes in existing jobs. They are more correctly viewed as *normal-time data,* because tabled values have been modified by an average performance rating, and allowances must be added to obtain a standard time.

Calculating a time standard for a new job using elemental standard-time data tables entails four steps:

1. Break down the new job into its basic elements (such as shown in Exhibit 11.9's time-study sheet).
2. Match these elements to the time for similar elements in the table.
3. Adjust element times for special characteristics of the new job. (In metal cutting, for instance, this is often done by a formula that modifies the time required as a function of type of metal, size of the cutting tool, depth of the cut, and so forth.)
4. Add element times together and add delay and fatigue allowances as specified by company policy for the given class of work.

The obvious benefit of elemental standard data is cost savings. It eliminates the need for a new time study for each new job. This saves staff time and avoids disruption of the workforce. The main practical requirement of the approach is that elemental data must be kept up to date and easily accessible.

Predetermined Motion-Time Data Systems   **Predetermined motion-time data systems (PMTS)** also use existing tabled data to artificially create a time standard. These systems differ from elemental standard data systems in several respects. First, they provide times for basic motions rather than job-specific work elements. Second, they are generic to a wide range of manual work; elemental standard data are company- or industry-specific. Finally, since they typically require the use of many basic motions to describe even a short-duration job, they require far more analyst time to develop a standard. For this reason, the systems discussed next are being simplified as much as possible to facilitate their use, and new, faster versions with computer support are being marketed.

The three predetermined motion-time data systems that are most often used are **methods time measurement (MTM), most work measurement systems (MOST),** and **work factor.** Each was developed in the laboratory, and all are proprietary. MTM even has its own journal, user certification program, and an association of MTM organizations (the International MTM Directorate).

The sample MTM table in Exhibit 11.11 describes the movement designated as Reach, stipulating the different times allowed for varying conditions. (Other standard movement categories in the basic version of the system, MTM-1, are Grasp, Move, Position, and Release.) Note that times are measured in *time measurement units* (TMUs) of .0006 minute. To derive an MTM standard time for a job, you would list all the movements that go into it, find the appropriate TMU value for each, sum the times, and add allowances.

PMTS have been used successfully for more than 40 years. Among their advantages are

1. They enable development of standards before the job is started.
2. They have been tested extensively in the laboratory and field.
3. They include performance rating in the times given in the tables, so users need not calculate them.
4. They can be used to audit time studies for accuracy.
5. They are accepted as part of many union contracts.

Work Sampling   As the name suggests, **work sampling** involves observing a portion or sample of the work activity. Then, based on the findings in this sample, statements can be made about the activity. For example, if we were to observe a fire department

---

E X H I B I T   11.11   *MTM Predetermined Motion-Time Data for the Hand and Arm Movement "Reach" (1 TMU = .0006 minute)*

REACH—R

Distance moved (inches)	Time TMU				Hand in motion		CASE AND DESCRIPTION	
	A	B	C or D	E	A	B		
3/4 or less	2.0	2.0	2.0	2.0	1.6	1.6	A	Reach to object in fixed location, or to object in other hand or on which other hand rests.
1	2.5	2.5	3.6	2.4	2.3	2.3		
2	4.0	4.0	5.9	3.8	3.5	2.7		
3	5.3	5.3	7.3	5.3	4.5	3.6		
4	6.1	6.4	8.4	6.8	4.9	4.3	B	Reach to single object in location which may vary slightly from cycle to cycle.
5	6.5	7.8	9.4	7.4	5.3	5.0		
6	7.0	8.6	10.1	8.0	5.7	5.7		
7	7.4	9.3	10.8	8.7	6.1	6.5		
8	7.9	10.1	11.5	9.3	6.5	7.2	C	Reach to object jumbled with other objects in a group so that search and select occur.
9	8.3	10.8	12.2	9.9	6.9	7.9		
10	8.7	11.5	12.9	10.5	7.3	8.6		
12	9.6	12.9	14.2	11.8	8.1	10.1		
14	10.5	14.4	15.6	13.0	8.9	11.5		
16	11.4	15.8	17.0	14.2	9.7	12.9	D	Reach to a very small object or where accurate grasp is required.
18	12.3	17.2	18.4	15.5	10.5	14.4		
20	13.1	18.6	19.8	16.7	11.3	15.8		
22	14.0	20.1	21.2	18.0	12.1	17.3		
24	14.9	21.5	22.5	19.2	12.9	18.8	E	Reach to indefinite location to get hand in position for body balance or next motion or out of way.
26	15.8	22.9	23.9	20.4	13.7	20.2		
28	16.7	24.4	25.3	21.7	14.5	21.7		
30	17.5	25.8	26.7	22.9	15.3	23.2		

Source: Copyright by the MTM Association for Standards and Research. Reprinted with permission from the MTM Association, 9–10 Saddle River Road, Fair Lawn, New Jersey 07410.

rescue squad 100 random times during the day and found it was involved in a rescue mission for 30 of the 100 times (en route, on site, or returning from a call), we would estimate that the rescue squad spends 30 percent of its time directly on rescue mission calls. (The time it takes to make an observation depends on what is being observed. Many times only a glance is needed to determine the activity, and the majority of studies require only several seconds' observation.)

Observing an activity even 100 times may not, however, provide the accuracy desired in the estimate. To refine this estimate, three main issues must be decided. (These points are discussed later in this section, along with an example.)

1. What level of statistical confidence is desired in the results?
2. How many observations are necessary?
3. Precisely when should the observations be made?

The three primary applications for work sampling are

1. *Ratio delay* to determine the activity-time percentage for personnel or equipment. For example, management may be interested in the amount of time a machine is running or idle.
2. *Performance measurement* to develop a performance index for workers. When the amount of work time is related to the quantity of output, a measure of performance is developed. This is useful for periodic performance evaluation.
3. *Time standards* to obtain the standard time for a task. When work sampling is used for this purpose, however, the observer must be experienced since he must attach a performance rating to the observations.

The number of observations required in a work sampling study can be fairly large, ranging from several hundred to several thousand, depending on the activity and desired degree of accuracy. Although the number can be computed from formulas, the easiest way is to refer to a table such as Exhibit 11.12, which gives the number of observations needed for a 95 percent confidence level in terms of absolute error. Absolute error is the actual range of the observations. For example, if a clerk is idle 10 percent of the time and the designer of the study is satisfied with a 2.5 percent range (meaning that the true percentage lies between 7.5 and 12.5 percent), the number of observations required for the work sampling is 576. A 2 percent error (or an interval of 8 to 12 percent) would require 900 observations.

Five steps are involved in making a work sampling study.

1. Identify the specific activity or activities that are the main purpose for the study. For example, determine the percentage of time that equipment is working, idle, or under repair.
2. Estimate the proportion of time of the activity of interest to the total time (e.g., that the equipment is working 80 percent of the time). These estimates can be made from the analyst's knowledge, past data, reliable guesses from others, or a pilot work sampling study.
3. State the desired accuracy in the study results.
4. Determine the specific times when each observation is to be made.
5. At two or three intervals during the study period, recompute the required sample size by using the data collected thus far. Adjust the number of observations if appropriate.

E X H I B I T 11.12   *Determining Number of Observations Required for a Given Absolute Error at Various Values of p, with 95 Percent Confidence Level*

Percentage of Total Time Occupied by Activity or Delay, p	Absolute Error					
	±1.0%	±1.5%	±2.0%	±2.5%	±3.0%	±3.5%
1 or 99	396	176	99	63	44	32
2 or 98	784	348	196	125	87	64
3 or 97	1,164	517	291	186	129	95
4 or 96	1,536	683	384	246	171	125
5 or 95	1,900	844	475	304	211	155
6 or 94	2,256	1,003	564	361	251	184
7 or 93	2,604	1,157	651	417	289	213
8 or 92	2,944	1,308	736	471	327	240
9 or 91	3,276	1,456	819	524	364	267
10 or 90	3,600	1,600	900	576	400	294
11 or 89	3,916	1,740	979	627	435	320
12 or 88	4,224	1,877	1,056	676	469	344
13 or 87	4,524	2,011	1,131	724	503	369
14 or 86	4,816	2,140	1,204	771	535	393
15 or 85	5,100	2,267	1,275	816	567	416
16 or 84	5,376	2,389	1,344	860	597	439
17 or 83	5,644	2,508	1,411	903	627	461
18 or 82	5,904	2,624	1,476	945	656	482
19 or 81	6,156	2,736	1,539	985	684	502
20 or 80	6,400	2,844	1,600	1,024	711	522
21 or 79	6,636	2,949	1,659	1,062	737	542
22 or 78	6,864	3,050	1,716	1,098	763	560
23 or 77	7,084	3,148	1,771	1,133	787	578
24 or 76	7,296	3,243	1,824	1,167	811	596
25 or 75	7,500	3,333	1,875	1,200	833	612
26 or 74	7,696	3,420	1,924	1,231	855	628
27 or 73	7,884	3,504	1,971	1,261	876	644
28 or 72	8,064	3,584	2,016	1,290	896	658
29 or 71	8,236	3,660	2,059	1,318	915	672
30 or 70	8,400	3,733	2,100	1,344	933	686
31 or 69	8,556	3,803	2,139	1,369	951	698
32 or 68	8,704	3,868	2,176	1,393	967	710
33 or 67	8,844	3,931	2,211	1,415	983	722
34 or 66	8,976	3,989	2,244	1,436	997	733
35 or 65	9,100	4,044	2,275	1,456	1,011	743
36 or 64	9,216	4,096	2,304	1,475	1,024	753
37 or 63	9,324	4,144	2,331	1,492	1,036	761
38 or 62	9,424	4,188	2,356	1,508	1,047	769
39 or 61	9,516	4,229	2,379	1,523	1,057	777
40 or 60	9,600	4,266	2,400	1,536	1,067	784
41 or 59	9,676	4,300	2,419	1,548	1,075	790
42 or 58	9,744	4,330	2,436	1,559	1,083	795
43 or 57	9,804	4,357	2,451	1,569	1,089	800
44 or 56	9,856	4,380	2,464	1,577	1,095	804
45 or 55	9,900	4,400	2,475	1,584	1,099	808
46 or 54	9,936	4,416	2,484	1,590	1,104	811
47 or 53	9,964	4,428	2,491	1,594	1,107	813
48 or 52	9,984	4,437	2,496	1,597	1,109	815
49 or 51	9,996	4,442	2,499	1,599	1,110	816
50	10,000	4,444	2,500	1,600	1,111	816

Note: Number of observations is obtained from the formula $E = Z \sqrt{\dfrac{p(1-p)}{N}}$ and the required sample (N) is $N = \dfrac{Z^2 p(1-p)}{E^2}$

where E = Absolute error

p = Percentage occurrence of activity or delay being measured

N = Number of random observations (sample size)

Z = Number of standard deviations to give desired confidence level (e.g., for 90 percent confidence, Z = 1.65; for 95 percent, Z = 1.96; for 99 percent, Z = 2.23). In this table Z = 2

The number of observations to be taken in a work sampling study is usually divided equally over the study period. Thus, if 500 observations are to be made over a 10-day period, observations are usually scheduled at 500/10 or 50 per day. Each day's observations are then assigned a specific time by using a random number table.

Work Sampling Applied to Nursing   There has been a long-standing argument that a large amount of nurses' hospital time is spent on nonnursing activities. This, the argument goes, creates an apparent shortage of well-trained nursing personnel, wastes talent, hinders efficiency, and increases hospital costs, because nurses' wages are the highest single cost in the operation of a hospital. Further, pressure is growing for hospitals and hospital administrators to contain costs. With that in mind, let us use work sampling to test the hypothesis that a large portion of nurses' time is spent on nonnursing duties.

Assume at the outset that we have made a list of all the activities that are part of nursing and will make our observations in only two categories; nursing and nonnursing activities.[5] (An expanded study could list all nursing activities to determine the portion of time spent in each.) Therefore, when we observe a nurse during the study and find her performing one of the duties on the nursing list, we simply place a tally mark in the nursing column. If we observe her doing anything besides nursing, we place a tally mark in the nonnursing column.

We can now proceed to plan the study. Assume that we (or the nursing supervisor) estimate that nurses spend 60 percent of their time in nursing activities. Assume that we would like to be 95 percent confident that findings of our study are within the absolute error range of ±3 percent; that is, that if our study shows nurses spend 60 percent of their time on nursing duties, we are 95 percent confident that the true percentage lies between 57 and 63 percent. From Exhibit 11.12, we find that 1,067 observations are required for 60 percent activity time and ±3 percent error. If our study is to take place over 10 days, we start with 107 observations per day.

To determine when each day's observations are to be made, we assign specific numbers to each minute and a random number table to set up a schedule. If the study extends over an eight-hour shift, we can assign numbers to correspond to each consecutive minute.[6] Exhibit 11.13A shows the assignment of numbers to corresponding minutes. For simplicity, because each number corresponds to one minute, a three-number scheme is used, with the second and third numbers corresponding to the minute of the hour. A number of other schemes would also be appropriate.[7]

If we refer to a random number table and list three-digit numbers, we can assign each number to a time. The random numbers in Exhibit 11.13B demonstrate the procedure for seven observations.

This procedure is followed to generate 107 observation times, and the times are rearranged chronologically for ease in planning. Rearranging the times determined in Exhibit 11.13B gives the total observations per day shown in Exhibit 11.13C (for our sample of seven).

To be perfectly random in this study, we should also "randomize" the nurse we observe each time. (The use of various nurses minimizes the effect of bias.) In the study, our first observation is made at 7:13 AM for Nurse X. We walk into his area and, on

---

[5]Actually, there is much debate on what constitutes nursing activity. For instance, is talking to a patient a nursing duty?

[6]For this study, it is likely that the night shift (11:00 PM to 7:00 AM) would be run separately since the nature of nighttime nursing duties is considerably different from that of daytime duties.

[7]If a number of studies are planned, a computer program may be used to generate a randomized schedule for the observation times.

A.

Time	Assigned Numbers	B. Random Number	Corresponding Time from the List in 11.13A
7:00–7:59 AM	100–159	669	Nonexistent
8:00–8:59 AM	200–259	831	2:31 PM
9:00–9:59 AM	300–359	555	11:55 AM
10:00–10:59 AM	400–459	470	Nonexistent
11:00–11:59 AM	500–559	113	7:13 AM
12:00–12:59 PM	600–659	080	Nonexistent
1:00–1:59 PM	700–759	520	11:20 AM
2:00–2:59 PM	800–859	204	8:04 AM
		732	1:32 PM
		420	10:20 AM

C.

Observation	Schedule Time	Nursing Activity (✔)	Nonnursing Activity (✔)
1	7:13 AM		
2	8:04 AM		
3	10:20 AM		
4	11:20 AM		
5	11:55 AM		
6	1:32 PM		
7	2:31 PM		

seeing him, check either a nursing or a nonnursing activity. Each observation need be only long enough to determine the class of activity—in most cases only a glance is needed. At 8:04 AM we observe Nurse Y. We continue in this way to the end of the day and the 107 observations. At the end of the second day (and 214 observations), we decide to check for the adequacy of our sample size.

Let us say we made 150 observations of nurses working and 64 of them not working, which gives 70.1 percent working. From Exhibit 11.12, this corresponds to 933 observations. Since we have already taken 214 observations, we need take only 719 over the next eight days, or 90 per day.

When the study is half over, another check should be made. For instance, if Days 3, 4, and 5 showed 55, 59, and 64 working observations, the cumulative data would give 328 working observations of a total 484, or a 67.8 percent working activity. For a ± 3% error, Exhibit 11.12 shows the sample size to be about 967, leaving 483 to be made—at 97 per day—for the following five days. Another computation should be made before the last day to see if another adjustment is required. If after the tenth day several more observations are indicated, these can be made on Day 11.

If at the end of the study we find that 66 percent of nurses' time is involved with what has been defined as nursing activity, there should be an analysis to identify the remaining 34 percent. Approximately 12 to 15 percent is justifiable for coffee breaks and personal needs, which leaves 20 to 22 percent of the time that must be justified and compared to what the industry considers ideal levels of nursing activity. To identify the nonnursing activities, a more detailed breakdown could have been originally built into the sampling plan. Otherwise, a follow-up study may be in order.

Setting time standards using work sampling   As mentioned earlier, work sampling can be used to set time standards. To do this, the analyst must record the subject's performance rate (or index) along with working observations. Exhibit 11.14 gives the additional data required and the formula for calculating standard time.

Information	Source of Data	Data for One Day
Total time expended by operator (working time and idle time)	Time cards	480 min.
Number of parts produced	Inspection Department	420 pieces
Working time in percent	Work sampling	85%
Idle time in percent	Work sampling	15%
Average performance index	Work sampling	110%
Total allowances	Company time-study manual	15%

$$\text{Standard time per piece} = \frac{\left(\begin{array}{c}\text{Total time}\\ \text{in minutes}\end{array}\right) \times \left(\begin{array}{c}\text{Working time}\\ \text{proportion}\end{array}\right) \times (\text{Performance index})}{\text{Total number of pieces produced}} \times \frac{1}{1 - \text{Allowances}}$$

$$= \left(\frac{480 \times 0.85 \times 1.10}{420}\right) \times \left(\frac{1}{1 - 0.15}\right) = 1.26 \text{ minutes}$$

Source: R. M. Barnes, *Working Sampling*, 2d ed. (New York: John Wiley & Sons, 1966), p. 81.

Work sampling compared to time study Work sampling offers several advantages:

1. Several work sampling studies may be conducted simultaneously by one observer.
2. The observer need not be a trained analyst unless the purpose of the study is to determine a time standard.
3. No timing devices are required.
4. Work of a long cycle time may be studied with fewer observer hours.
5. The duration of the study is longer, which minimizes effects of short-period variations.
6. The study may be temporarily delayed at any time with little effect.
7. Since work sampling needs only instantaneous observations (made over a longer period), the operator has less chance to influence the findings by changing her work method.

When the cycle time is short, time study (or PMTS) is more appropriate than work sampling. One drawback of work sampling is that it does not provide as complete a breakdown of elements as time study. Another difficulty with work sampling is that observers, rather than following a random sequence of observations, tend to develop a repetitive route of travel. This may allow the time of the observations to be predictable and thus invalidate the findings. A third factor—a potential drawback—is that the basic assumption in work sampling is that all observations pertain to the same static system. If the system is in the process of change, work sampling may give misleading results.

11.6 FINANCIAL INCENTIVE PLANS

The third piece of the job design equation is the paycheck. In this section we briefly review common methods for setting financial incentives.

Basic Compensation Systems

The main forms of basic compensation are hourly pay, straight salary, piece rate, and commissions. The first two are based on time spent on the job, with individual performance rewarded by an increase in the base rate. Piece-rate plans reward on the basis of direct daily output. (A worker is paid $5 a unit so if he produces 10 units per day, he earns $50). Sometimes a guaranteed base is included in a piece-rate plan; a worker would receive this base amount regardless of output, plus her piece-rate bonus. (For example, the worker's hourly base pay is $8, so this coupled with $50 piece-rate earnings gives her $114 for an eight-hour day.) Commissions may be thought of as sales-based piece rates and are calculated in the same general way.

The two broad categories of **financial incentive plans** are individual or small-group incentive plans and organizationwide plans.

Individual and Small-Group Incentive Plans

Individual and work group plans traditionally have rewarded performance by using output (often defined by piece rates) and quality measures. Quality is accounted for by a quality adjustment factor, say percentage of rework.[8] (For example: Incentive pay = Total output × [1 − Percent deduction for rework].) In recent years skill development has also been rewarded. Sometimes called *pay for knowledge,* this means a worker is compensated for learning new tasks. This is particularly important in job shops using group technology as well as in banking, where supervisors' jobs require knowledge of new types of financial instruments and selling approaches.

AT&T, for example, instituted incentive programs for its managers—an Individual Incentive Award (IIA) and a Management Team Incentive Award (MTIA). The IIA provides lump-sum bonuses to outstanding performers. These outstanding performers were determined by individual performance ratings accompanied by extensive documentation. The lump-sum bonus could range between 15 and 30 percent of base pay.

MTIAs are granted to members of specific divisions or units. Appropriate division or unit goals are established at the beginning of the year. The goals include department service objectives and interdepartmental goals. A typical MTIA could call for a standard amount equivalent to 1.5 percent of wages plus overtime for the next three years based on performance in the current year.

Organizationwide Plans

Profit sharing and gain sharing are the major types of organizationwide plans. **Profit sharing** is simply distributing a percentage of corporate profits across the workforce. In the United States, at least one-third of all organizations have profit sharing. In Japan, most major companies give profit-based bonuses twice a year to all employees. Such bonuses may range from 50 percent of salaries in good years, to nothing in bad years.

Gain sharing also involves giving organizationwide bonuses, but differs from profit sharing in two important respects. First, it typically measures controllable costs or units of output, not profits, in calculating a bonus. Second, gain sharing is always combined with a participative approach to management. The original and best-known gainsharing plan is the Scanlon Plan.

Scanlon Plan   In the late 1930s, the Lapointe Machine and Tool Company was on the verge of bankruptcy, but through the efforts of union president Joseph Scanlon and company management, a plan was devised to save the company by reducing labor costs. In essence, this plan started with the normal labor cost within the firm. Workers as a group were rewarded for any reductions in labor cost below this base cost. The plan's success depended on committees of workers throughout the firm whose purpose was to search out areas for cost saving and to devise ways of improvement. There were many improvements, and the plan did, in fact, save the company.

---

[8]For a complete discussion of incentive plans including quality measures, see S. Globerson and R. Parsons, "Multi-Factor Incentive Systems: Current Practices," *Operations Management Review* 3, no. 2 (Winter 1985).

The basic elements of the Scanlon Plan are

1. *The ratio.* The ratio is the standard that serves as a measure for judging business performance. It can be expressed as

$$\text{Ratio} = \frac{\text{Total labor cost}}{\text{Sales value of production}}$$

2. *The bonus.* The amount of bonus depends on the reduction in costs below the preset ratio.

3. *The production committee.* The production committee is formed to encourage employee suggestions to increase productivity, improve quality, reduce waste, and so forth. The purpose of a production committee is similar to that of a QC circle.

4. *The screening committee.* The screening committee consists of top management and worker representatives who review monthly bonuses, discuss production problems, and consider improvement suggestions.

Gain-sharing plans are now used by more than a thousand firms in the United States and Europe, and are growing in popularity. One survey in the United States indicated that about 13 percent of all firms have them, and that more than 70 percent were started after 1982.[9] Though originally established in small companies such as Lapointe, Lincoln Electric Company, and Herman Miller, gain sharing has been installed by large firms such as TRW, General Electric, Motorola, and Firestone. These companies apply gain sharing to organizational units. Motorola, for example, has virtually all its plant employees covered by gain sharing. These plans are increasing because "they are more than just pay incentive plans; they are a participative approach to management and are often used as a way to install participative management."[10]

A comparison of the typical applications of the plans is discussed, along with merit pay, in Exhibit 11.15.

Next we will discuss learning curves, which are widely used in work measurement.

11.7   LEARNING CURVES

A **learning curve** is a line displaying the relationship between unit production time and the number of consecutive units produced.

Application of Learning Curves

Learning (or experience) curve theory has a wide range of application in the business world. In manufacturing, it can be used to estimate the time for product design and production, as well as costs. Learning curves are important and sometimes overlooked as one of the trade-offs in Just-in-Time systems, where sequencing and short runs achieve lower inventories by forfeiting some advantages of experience benefits from long product runs. Learning curves are also an integral part in planning corporate strategy, such as decisions concerning pricing, capital investment, and operating costs based on experience curves.

Learning curves can be applied to individuals or organizations. **Individual learning** is improvement that results when people repeat a process and gain skill or efficiency from their own experience. That is, "practice makes perfect." **Organizational learning** results from practice as well but also comes from changes in administration, equipment, and product design. In organizational settings, we expect to see both kinds of learning occurring simultaneously and often describe the combined effect with a single learning curve.

---

[9]C. O'Dell, *People, Performance, and Pay* (Houston: American Productivity Center, 1987).

[10]E. E. Lawler III, "Paying for Organizational Performance," Report G 87-1 (92) (Los Angeles: Center for Effective Organizations, University of Southern California, 1987).

E X H I B I T 11.15

Comparison of Common Reward/Incentive Plans

Type of Plan	Application	Advantages	Disadvantages
Merit Pay	Individual	• Allows management to target specific behavior and to easily evolve criteria over time.	• Criteria tend toward arbitrary and unbiased when incorrectly administered. • Often not clearly tied to business goals.
Profit Sharing	Group	• Ties business performance to employee reward.	• Often individual or group behavior is not correlated to business performance.
Gains-Sharing	Group	• Specific group performance directly tied to employee reward.	• Often focuses excessively on cost control. • More applicable for tactical improvements than strategic changes.
Lump-Sum Bonuses and Individual Bonuses	Either	• Allows management to vary criteria and magnitude of reward; able to target specific actions and behavior.	• Often used for and seen as deferred compensation. • Not always a tie to business goals or performance.
Pay-for-Knowledge	Individual	• Allows management to target specific types of skills and personal growth.	• May not impact business performance unless management targets correct skills and applies new skills effectively.
Piece Rate	Either	• Allows management to target specific output goals	• May lead to undesirable competition among workers • Standards must be kept up to date.

Source: Modified from Ted Olson, C. Giffi, A. Roth, and G. Seal, *Competing in World-Class Manufacturing: America's 21st Century Challenge* (Homewood, Ill.: Richard D. Irwin, 1990).

Learning curve theory is based on three assumptions:

1. The amount of time required to complete a given task or unit of a product will be less each time the task is undertaken.
2. The unit time will decrease at a decreasing rate.
3. The reduction in time will follow a predictable pattern.

Each of these assumptions was found to hold true in the airplane industry, where learning curves were first applied. In this application, it was observed that, as output doubled, there was a 20 percent reduction in direct production worker-hours per unit between doubled units. Thus, if it took 100,000 hours for Plane 1, it would take 80,000 hours for Plane 2, 64,000 hours for Plane 4, and so forth. Since the 20 percent reduction meant that, say, Unit 4 took only 80 percent of the production time required for Unit 2, the line connecting the coordinates of output and time was referred to as an "80 percent learning curve." (By convention, the percentage learning rate is used to denote any given exponential learning curve.)

E X H I B I T 11.16   *Learning Curves Plotted as Times and Numbers of Units*

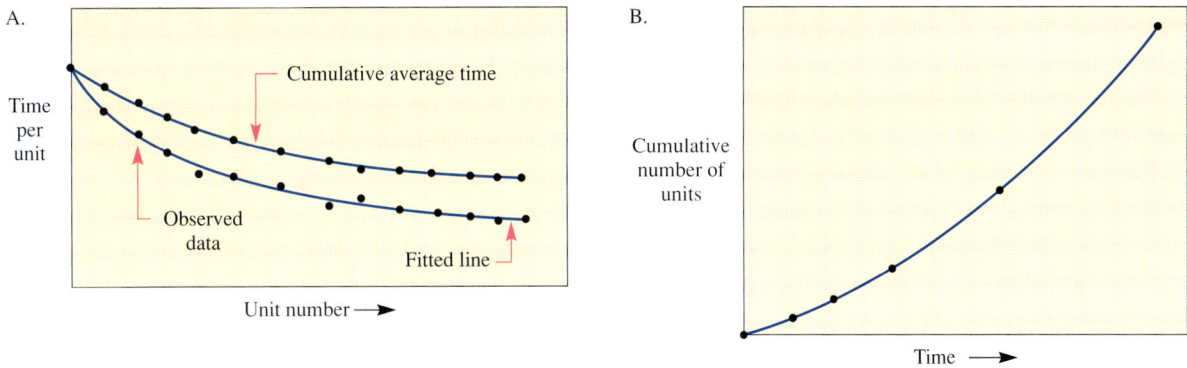

A. Learning Curve plotted with Time per unit on vertical axis and Unit number on horizontal axis, showing Cumulative average time, Observed data, and Fitted line.

B. Learning Curve plotted with Cumulative number of units on vertical axis and Time on horizontal axis.

A learning curve may be developed from an arithmetic tabulation, by logarithms, or by some other curve-fitting method, depending on the amount and form of the available data.

There are two ways to think about the improved performance that comes with learning curves; that is time per unit (as in Exhibit 11.16A) or as units of output per time period (as in 11.16B). *Time per unit* shows the decrease in time required for each successive unit. *Cumulative average time* shows the cumulative average performance times as the total number of units increases. Time per unit and cumulative average times are also called *progress curves* or *product learning,* and are useful for complex products or products with a longer cycle time. *Units of output per time period* is also called *industry learning* and is generally applied to high-volume production (short cycle time).

Note in Exhibit 11.16A that the cumulative average curve does not decrease as fast as the time per unit because the time is being averaged. For example, if the time for Units 1, 2, 3, and 4 were 100, 80, 70, and 64, they would be plotted that way on the time per unit graph, but would be plotted as 100, 90, 83.3, and 78.5 on the cumulative average time graph.

Plotting Learning Curves

There are many ways to analyze past data to fit a useful trend line. We will use the simple exponential curve first as an arithmetic procedure and then by a logarithmic analysis. In an arithmetical tabulation approach, a column for units is created by doubling, row by row, as: 1, 2, 4, 8, 16. . . . The time for the first unit is multiplied by the learning percent to obtain the time for the second unit. The second unit is multiplied by the learning percent for the fourth unit, and so on. Thus, if we are developing an 80 percent learning curve, we would arrive at the figures listed in column 2 of Exhibit 11.17. Since it is often desirable for planning purposes to know the cumulative direct labor hours, column 4, which lists this information, is also provided. The calculation of these figures is straightforward; for example, for Unit 4, cumulative average direct labor hours would be found by dividing cumulative direct labor hours by 4, yielding the figure given in column 4.

Exhibit 11.18 shows three curves with different learning rates: 90 percent, 80 percent, and 70 percent. Note that if the cost of the 1st unit was $100, the 30th unit would cost $59.63 at the 90 percent rate and $17.37 at the 70 percent rate. Differences in learning rates can have dramatic effects.

In practice, learning curves are plotted on log-log paper, with the results that the unit curves become linear throughout their entire range and the cumulative curve becomes linear after the first few units. The property of linearity is desirable because it facilitates

E X H I B I T 11.17

Unit, Cumulative, and
Cumulative Average
Direct Labor
Worker-Hours
Required for an 80
Percent Learning
Curve

(1) Unit Number	(2) Unit Direct Labor Hours	(3) Cumulative Direct Labor Hours	(4) Cumulative Average Direct Labor Hours
1	100,000	100,000	100,000
2	80,000	180,000	90,000
4	64,000	314,210	78,553
8	51,200	534,591	66,824
16	40,960	892,014	55,751
32	32,768	1,467,862	45,871
64	26,214	2,392,453	37,382
128	20,972	3,874,395	30,269
256	16,777	6,247,318	24,404

E X H I B I T 11.18   *Arithmetic Plot of 70, 80, and 90 Percent Learning Curves*

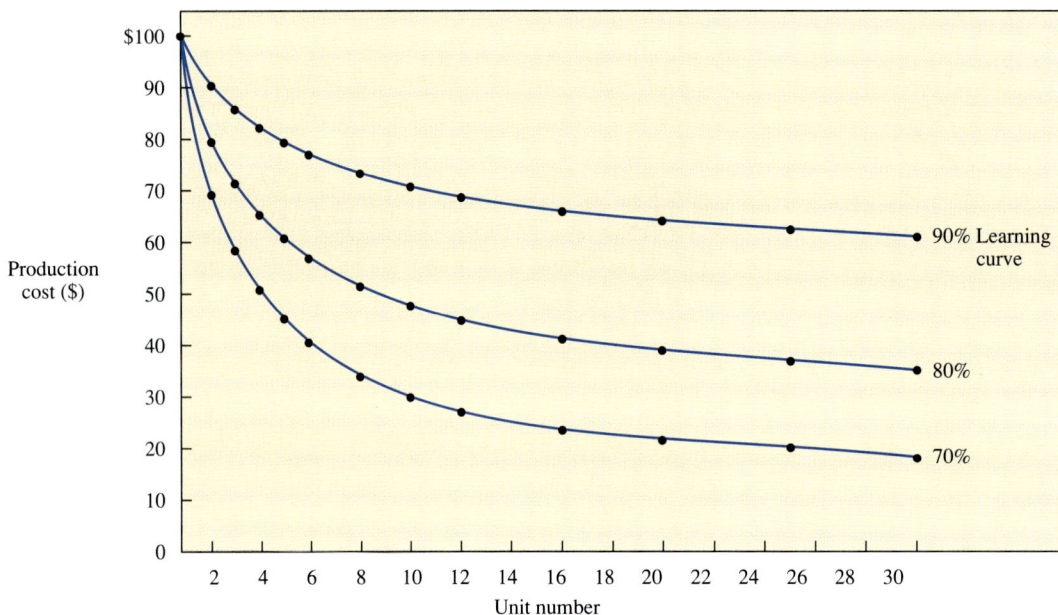

extrapolation and permits a more accurate reading of the cumulative curve. Exhibit 11.19 shows the 80 percent unit cost curve and average cost curve on logarithmic paper. Note that the cumulative average cost is essentially linear after the eighth unit.

While the arithmetic tabulation approach is useful, direct logarithmic analysis of learning curve problems is generally more efficient since it does not require a complete enumeration of successive time-output combinations. Moreover, where such data are not available, an analytical model that uses logarithms may be the most convenient way of obtaining output estimates.

Logarithmic Analysis   The normal form of the learning curve equation is[11]:

$$Y_x = Kx^n \qquad (11.3)$$

---

[11]This equation says that the number of direct labor hours required for any given unit is reduced exponentially as more units are produced.

E X H I B I T 11.19   *Logarithmic Plot of an 80 Percent Learning Curve*

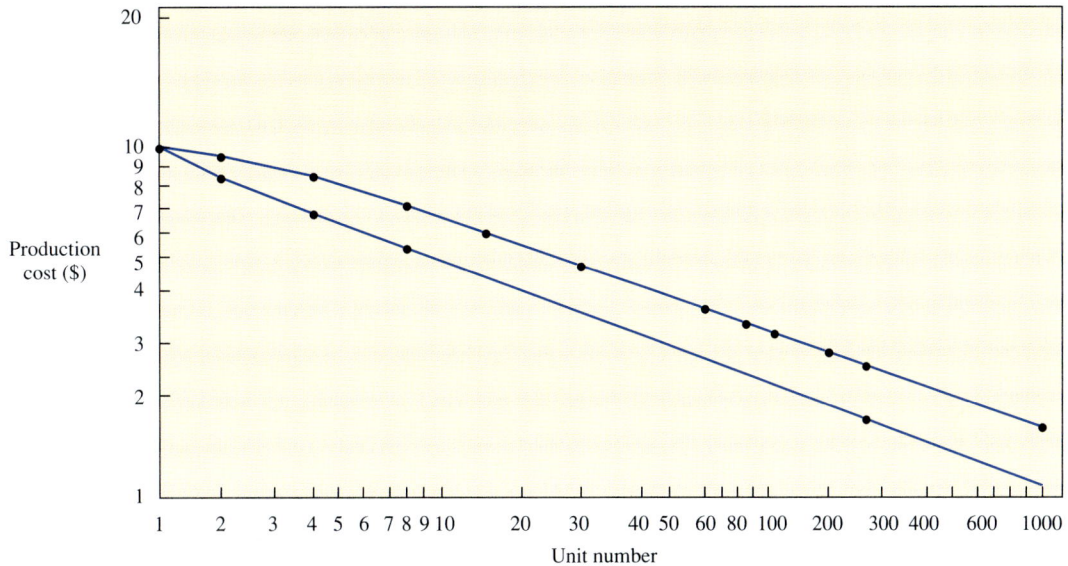

where

   x = Unit number

   Y_x = Number of direct labor hours required to produce the xth unit

   K = Number of direct labor hours required to produce the first unit

   n = Log b/log 2 where b = Learning percentage

Thus to find the labor-hour requirement for the eighth unit in our example (Exhibit 11.17), we would substitute as follows:

   $Y_8 = (100,000) (8)^n$

This may be solved by using logarithms:

$$Y_8 = 100,000 (8)^{\log 0.8/\log 2}$$

$$= 100,000(8)^{-0.322} = \frac{100,000}{(8)^{0.322}}$$

$$= \frac{100,000}{1.9535} = 51,192$$

Therefore, it would take 51,192 hours to make the eighth unit.

Learning Curve Tables   When the learning percentage is known, Exhibits 11.20 and 11.21 can be easily used to calculate estimated labor hours for a specific unit or for cumulative groups of units. We need only multiply the initial unit labor hour figure by the appropriate tabled value.

To illustrate, suppose we want to double check the figures in Exhibit 11.17 for unit and cumulative labor hours for Unit 16. From Exhibit 11.20, the improvement factor for Unit 16 at 80 percent is .4096. This multiplied by 100,000 (the hours for Unit 1) gives 40,960, the same as in Exhibit 11.17. From Exhibit 11.21, the improvement factor for

E X H I B I T 11.20

Improvement Curves: Table of Unit Values

				Improvement Ratios				
Unit	60%	65%	70%	75%	80%	85%	90%	95%
1	1.0000	1.0000	1.0000	1.0000	1.0000	1.0000	1.0000	1.0000
2	.6000	.6500	.7000	.7500	.8000	.8500	.9000	.9500
3	.4450	.5052	.5682	.6338	.7021	.7729	.8462	.9219
4	.3600	.4225	.4900	.5625	.6400	.7225	.8100	.9025
5	.3054	.3678	.4368	.5127	.5956	.6857	.7830	.8877
6	.2670	.3284	.3977	.4754	.5617	.6570	.7616	.8758
7	.2383	.2984	.3674	.4459	.5345	.6337	.7439	.8659
8	.2160	.2746	.3430	.4219	.5120	.6141	.7290	.8574
9	.1980	.2552	.3228	.4017	.4930	.5974	.7161	.8499
10	.1832	.2391	.3058	.3846	.4765	.5828	.7047	.8433
12	.1602	.2135	.2784	.3565	.4493	.5584	.6854	.8320
14	.1430	.1940	.2572	.3344	.4276	.5386	.6696	.8226
16	.1290	.1785	.2401	.3164	.4096	.5220	.6561	.8145
18	.1188	.1659	.2260	.3013	.3944	.5078	.6445	.8074
20	.1099	.1554	.2141	.2884	.3812	.4954	.6342	.8012
22	.1025	.1465	.2038	.2772	.3697	.4844	.6251	.7955
24	.0961	.1387	.1949	.2674	.3595	.4747	.6169	.7904
25	.0933	.1353	.1908	.2629	.3548	.4701	.6131	.7880
30	.0815	.1208	.1737	.2437	.3346	.4505	.5963	.7775
35	.0728	.1097	.1605	.2286	.3184	.4345	.5825	.7687
40	.0660	.1010	.1498	.2163	.3050	.4211	.5708	.7611
45	.0605	.0939	.1410	.2060	.2936	.4096	.5607	.7545
50	.0560	.0879	.1336	.1972	.2838	.3996	.5518	.7486
60	.0489	.0785	.1216	.1828	.2676	.3829	.5367	.7386
70	.0437	.0713	.1123	.1715	.2547	.3693	.5243	.7302
80	.0396	.0657	.1049	.1622	.2440	.3579	.5137	.7231
90	.0363	.0610	.0987	.1545	.2349	.3482	.5046	.7168
100	.0336	.0572	.0935	.1479	.2271	.3397	.4966	.7112
120	.0294	.0510	.0851	.1371	.2141	.3255	.4830	.7017
140	.0262	.0464	.0786	.1287	.2038	.3139	.4718	.6937
160	.0237	.0427	.0734	.1217	.1952	.3042	.4623	.6869
180	.0218	.0397	.0691	.1159	.1879	.2959	.4541	.6809
200	.0201	.0371	.0655	.1109	.1816	.2887	.4469	.6757
250	.0171	.0323	.0584	.1011	.1691	.2740	.4320	.6646
300	.0149	.0289	.0531	.0937	.1594	.2625	.4202	.6557
350	.0133	.0262	.0491	.0879	.1517	.2532	.4105	.6482
400	.0121	.0241	.0458	.0832	.1453	.2454	.4022	.6419
450	.0111	.0224	.0431	.0792	.1399	.2387	.3951	.6363
500	.0103	.0210	.0408	.0758	.1352	.2329	.3888	.6314
600	.0090	.0188	.0372	.0703	.1275	.2232	.3782	.6229
700	.0080	.0171	.0344	.0659	.1214	.2152	.3694	.6158
800	.0073	.0157	.0321	.0624	.1163	.2086	.3620	.6098
900	.0067	.0146	.0302	.0594	.1119	.2029	.3556	.6045
1,000	.0062	.0137	.0286	.0569	.1082	.1980	.3499	.5998
1,200	.0054	.0122	.0260	.0527	.1020	.1897	.3404	.5918
1,400	.0048	.0111	.0240	.0495	.0971	.1830	.3325	.5850
1,600	.0044	.0102	.0225	.0468	.0930	.1773	.3258	.5793
1,800	.0040	.0095	.0211	.0446	.0895	.1725	.3200	.5743
2,000	.0037	.0089	.0200	.0427	.0866	.1683	.3149	.5698
2,500	.0031	.0077	.0178	.0389	.0806	.1597	.3044	.5605
3,000	.0027	.0069	.0162	.0360	.0760	.1530	.2961	.5530

Source: R. C. Meier, *Cases in Production and Operations Management* (New York: McGraw-Hill), pp. 310–14.

cumulative hours for the first 16 units is 8.920. When multiplied by 100,000, this gives 892,000, which is reasonably close to the exact value of 892,014 shown in Exhibit 11.17.

Following is a more involved example of the application of a learning curve to a production problem.

				Improvement Ratios				
Unit	60%	65%	70%	75%	80%	85%	90%	95%
1	1.000	1.000	1.000	1.000	1.000	1.000	1.000	1.000
2	1.600	1.650	1.700	1.750	1.800	1.850	1.900	1.950
3	2.045	2.155	2.268	2.384	2.502	2.623	2.746	2.872
4	2.405	2.578	2.758	2.946	3.142	3.345	3.556	3.774
5	2.710	2.946	3.195	3.459	3.738	4.031	4.339	4.662
6	2.977	3.274	3.593	3.934	4.299	4.688	5.101	5.538
7	3.216	3.572	3.960	4.380	4.834	5.322	5.845	6.404
8	3.432	3.847	4.303	4.802	5.346	5.936	6.574	7.261
9	3.630	4.102	4.626	5.204	5.839	6.533	7.290	8.111
10	3.813	4.341	4.931	5.589	6.315	7.116	7.994	8.955
12	4.144	4.780	5.501	6.315	7.227	8.244	9.374	10.62
14	4.438	5.177	6.026	6.994	8.092	9.331	10.72	12.27
16	4.704	5.541	6.514	7.635	8.920	10.38	12.04	13.91
18	4.946	5.879	6.972	8.245	9.716	11.41	13.33	15.52
20	5.171	6.195	7.407	8.828	10.48	12.40	14.61	17.13
22	5.379	6.492	7.819	9.388	11.23	13.38	15.86	18.72
24	5.574	6.773	8.213	9.928	11.95	14.33	17.10	20.31
25	5.668	6.909	8.404	10.19	12.31	14.80	17.71	21.10
30	6.097	7.540	9.305	11.45	14.02	17.09	20.73	25.00
35	6.478	8.109	10.13	12.72	15.64	19.29	23.67	28.86
40	6.821	8.631	10.90	13.72	17.19	21.43	26.54	32.68
45	7.134	9.114	11.62	14.77	18.68	23.50	29.37	36.47
50	7.422	9.565	12.31	15.78	20.12	25.51	32.14	40.22
60	7.941	10.39	13.57	17.67	22.87	29.41	37.57	47.65
70	8.401	11.13	14.74	19.43	25.47	33.17	42.87	54.99
80	8.814	11.82	15.82	21.09	27.96	36.80	48.05	62.25
90	9.191	12.45	16.83	22.67	30.35	40.32	53.14	69.45
100	9.539	13.03	17.79	24.18	32.65	43.75	58.14	76.59
120	10.16	14.11	19.57	27.02	37.05	50.39	67.93	90.71
140	10.72	15.08	21.20	29.67	41.22	56.78	77.46	104.7
160	11.21	15.97	22.72	32.17	45.20	62.95	86.80	118.5
180	11.67	16.79	24.14	34.54	49.03	68.95	95.96	132.1
200	12.09	17.55	25.48	36.80	52.72	74.79	105.0	145.7
250	13.01	19.28	28.56	42.08	61.47	88.83	126.9	179.2
300	13.81	20.81	31.34	46.94	69.66	102.2	148.2	212.2
350	14.51	22.18	33.89	51.48	77.43	115.1	169.0	244.8
400	15.14	23.44	36.26	55.75	84.85	127.6	189.3	277.0
450	15.72	24.60	38.48	59.80	91.97	139.7	209.2	309.0
500	16.26	25.68	40.58	63.68	98.85	151.5	228.8	340.6
600	17.21	27.67	44.47	70.97	112.0	174.2	267.1	403.3
700	18.06	29.45	48.04	77.77	124.4	196.1	304.5	465.3
800	18.82	31.09	51.36	84.18	136.3	217.3	341.0	526.5
900	19.51	32.60	54.46	90.26	147.7	237.9	376.9	587.2
1,000	20.15	34.01	57.40	96.07	158.7	257.9	412.2	647.4
1,200	21.30	36.59	62.85	107.0	179.7	296.6	481.2	766.6
1,400	22.32	38.92	67.85	117.2	199.6	333.9	548.4	884.2
1,600	23.23	41.04	72.49	126.8	218.6	369.9	614.2	1001.
1,800	24.06	43.00	76.85	135.9	236.8	404.9	678.8	1116.
2,000	24.83	44.84	80.96	144.7	254.4	438.9	742.3	1230.
2,500	26.53	48.97	90.39	165.0	296.1	520.8	897.0	1513.
3,000	27.99	52.62	98.90	183.7	335.2	598.9	1047.	1791.

E X H I B I T 11.21

Improvement Curves: Table of Cumulative Values

E X A M P L E 11.1 / *Sample Learning Curve Problem*   Captain Nemo, owner of the Suboptimum Underwater Boat Company (SUB), is puzzled. He has a contract for 11 boats and has completed 4 of them. He has observed that his production manager, young Mr. Overick, has been reassigning more and more people to torpedo assembly after the construction of the first four boats. The first boat, for example, required 225 workers, each working a 40-hour week, while 45 fewer workers were required for the second boat.

Overick has told them that "this is just the beginning" and that he will complete the last boat in the current contract with only 100 workers!

Overick is banking on the learning curve, but has he gone overboard?

S O L U T I O N   Since the second boat required 180 workers and using a simple exponential curve, then the learning percentage is 80 percent (180 ÷ 225). To find out how many workers are required for the 11th boat, we look up unit 11 for an 80 percent improvement ratio in Exhibit 11.21 and multiply this value by the number required for the first sub. By interpolating between Unit 10 and Unit 12 we find the improvement ratio equal to 0.4629. This yields 104.15 workers (.4629 interpolated from table × 225). Thus, Overick's estimate missed the boat by 4 people.

SUB has produced the first unit of a new line of minisubs at a cost of $500,000—$200,000 for materials and $300,000 for labor. It has agreed to accept a 10 percent profit, based on cost, and it is willing to contract on the basis of a 70 percent learning curve. What will be the contract price for three minisubs?

Cost of first sub		$ 500,000
Cost of second sub		
Materials	$200,000	
Labor: $300,000 × .70	210,000	410,000
Cost of third sub		
Materials	200,000	
Labor: $300,000 × .5682	170,460	370,460
Total cost		1,280,460
Markup: $1,280,460 × .10		128,046
Selling price		$1,408,506

If the operation is interrupted, then some relearning must occur. How far to go back up the learning curve can be estimated in some cases.   ■

Estimating the Learning Percentage   If production has been underway for some time, the learning percentage is easily obtained from production records. Generally speaking, the longer the production history, the more accurate the estimate. Since a variety of other problems can occur during the early stages of production, most companies do not begin to collect data for learning curve analysis until some units have been completed.

Statistical analysis should also be used. For example, in an exponential learning curve to find out how well the curve fits past data, it can be converted to a straight-line logarithmic (data plotted on log-log graph paper).

If production has not started, estimating the learning percentage becomes enlightened guesswork. In these cases the analyst has these options:

1. Assume that the learning percentage will be the same as it has been for previous applications within the same industry.

2. Assume that it will be the same as it has been for the same or similar products.

3. Analyze the similarities and differences between the proposed startup and previous startups and develop a revised learning percentage that appears best to fit the situation.

There are two reasons for disparities between a firm's learning rate and that of its industry. First, there are the inevitable differences in operating characteristics between any two firms, stemming from the equipment, methods, product design, plant organization, and so forth. Second, procedural differences are manifested in the development of the learning percentage itself, such as whether the industry rate is based on a single product or on a product line, and the manner in which the data were aggregated.

How Long Does Learning Go On?   Does output stabilize, or is there continual improvement? Some areas can be shown to improve continually even over decades—radios, computers, and other electronic devices; and, if we allow for the effects of infla-

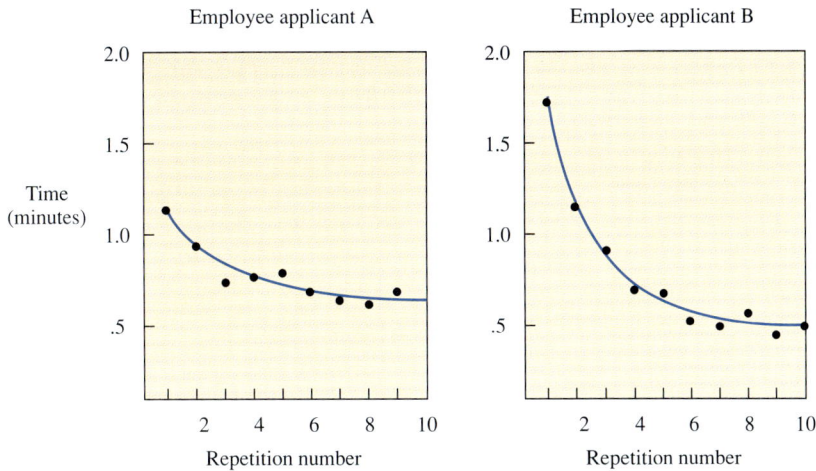

E X H I B I T 11.22
Test Results of Two Job Applicants

Employee applicant A

Employee applicant B

tion, also automobiles, washing machines, refrigerators, and most other manufactured goods. If the learning curve has been valid for several hundreds or thousands of units, it will probably be valid for several hundreds or thousands more. On the other hand, highly automated systems may have a near zero learning curve since, after installation, they quickly reach a constant volume.

In this section we offer guidelines for two categories of "learners": individuals and organizations.

General Guidelines for Learning

Individual Learning   A number of factors affect an individual's performance and rate of learning. Remember that there are two elements involved: the rate of learning and the initial starting level. To explain this more clearly, compare the two learning curves in Exhibit 11.22. Suppose these were the times for two individuals who performed a simple mechanical test administered by the personnel department as part of their application for employment in the assembly area of manufacturing.

Which applicant would you hire? Applicant A had a much lower starting point but a slower learning rate. Applicant B, although starting at a much higher rate, is clearly the better choice. This points out that performance times are important—not just the learning rate by itself.

Some general guidelines to improve individual performance based on learning curves:

1. *Proper selection of workers.* A test should be administered to help choose the workers. These tests should be representative of the planned work: A dexterity test for assembly work, a mental ability test for mental work, tests for interaction with customers for front office work, and so on.

2. *Proper training.* The more effective the training, the faster the learning rate.

3. *Motivation.* Productivity gains based on learning curves are not achieved unless there is a reward. Rewards can be money (individual or group incentive plans) or nonmonetary (such as employee of the month, etc.).

4. *Work specialization.* As a general rule, the simpler the task, the faster the learning. Be careful that boredom doesn't interfere; if it does, redesign the task.

5. *Do one or very few jobs at a time.* Learning is faster on each job if completed one at a time, rather than working on all jobs simultaneously.

6. *Use tools or equipment that assists or supports performance.*

7. *Provide quick and easy access for help.* The benefits from training are realized and continue when assistance is available.

8. *Allow workers to help redesign their tasks.* Taking more performance factors into the scope of the learning curve can, in effect, shift the curve downward.

Organizational Learning   Organizations learn as well. For example, in a manufacturing unit the learning curve would include technology, equipment, engineering, and training.

Learning rates differ among firms and across industries. These differences are due to the peculiarities and opportunities in various industries, as well as individual firms' performances. Exhibit 11.23 depicts the learning rates in 108 firms in various industries. While the majority of firms had learning rates of 70 to 80 percent, several were lower and higher. One firm had a very rapid learning rate of 55 to 56 percent. At the other extreme, one firm had a learning rate of 107 to 108 percent. (We wonder if this firm is still in business.) Any learning rate greater than 100 percent means dislearning; or, the more times a task is done, the longer it takes or the more it costs.

An example of learning curve theory is in contract negotiations. For example, there can be a wide difference between delivery of a product in one lot or in spaced lots involving subsequent contracts, because of learning rates. The spacing of contracts for identical items can lead to problems between buyer and seller. While the buyer may expect that subsequent contracts are simply continuations of previous contracts, the seller may have significant relearning efforts. The longer the spacing between contracts, the greater the opportunity for forgetting and for other changes such as shifting of personnel to other areas, equipment changes, and so forth. For example, new studies are coming out showing organizational learning rates in quality defects and productivity gains. These types of studies should have widespread benefits.

E X H I B I T 11.23

Learning Curve Rates Observed in 22 Field Studies in Different Industries (n = 108)

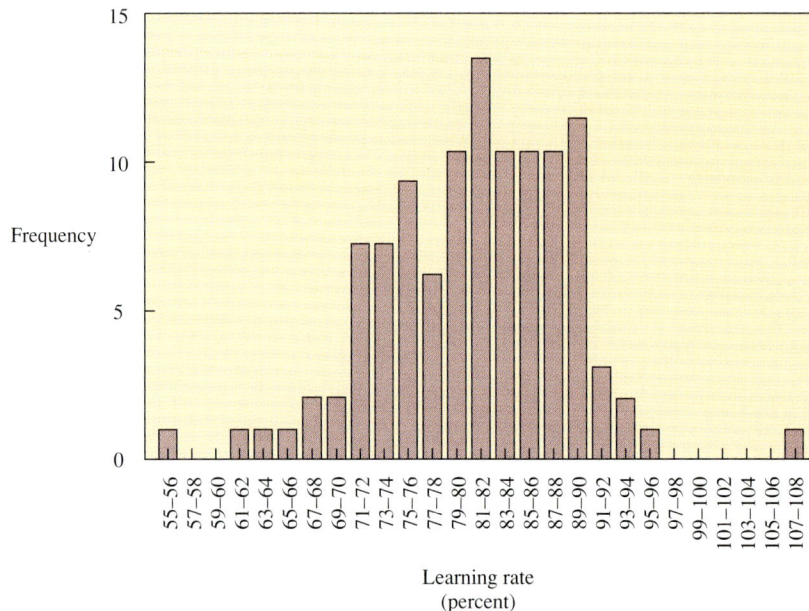

Source: J. M. Dutton and A. Thomas, "Treating Progress Functions as a Managerial Opportunity," *Academy of Management Review* 9 (1984), p. 235.

Why do organizations differ in their performance, even when they produce the same product or service? There are a number of reasons, some of these are:

1. *Position on the learning curve.* All other things being equal, the firm that has the higher cumulative output should have the lower cost.

2. *Rate of output.* Studies have shown that recent experience has much more effect in reducing cost than more distant experience.

3. *Employee participation in productivity and cost reduction.* Programs such as employee stock purchases, profit sharing, and group incentive plans can significantly improve the rate of learning.

4. *Existence of standards.* Without a comparison base, performance cannot be measured.

5. *Presence of similar experiences.* If two organizations produce the same product, the one with a related product has a higher learning rate.

6. *Ability to learn from other firms.* Much can be learned from industry or other data about competitor's performances. However, once underway, a firm's learning is dominated by its own experiences.

7. *Simplification of work tasks.* The simpler the task, the easier it is to learn.

8. *Avoiding discontinuity.* Interruptions require relearning even if it only involves a simple restart of an operation.

9. *Avoid employee turnover.* New employees require training and thereby affect the learning rate.

10. *Standard design of work tasks for an entire industry.* There are numerous rewards when firms in an industry develop standard designs and procedures. A simple example is when a company can hire a worker with prior experience from another firm and benefit from that employee's experience.

11. *Attending meetings, conferences, and professional associations results in a transfer of knowledge across organizations.*

12. *Hire experienced personnel (especially from the competition).* The value of outside experience is very important during the early stages of a learning curve.

13. *Effects of calendar time.* It is interesting that calendar time is not as good a predictor of performance as cumulative output.

14. *Separate the work when operating two or more shifts.* Rather than having two or three shifts with duplicate learning rates for the same jobs, assign different jobs to each of them. Each shift achieves higher productivity by producing more units and moving further down the learning curve.

15. *Economies of scale.* The benefits of increasing output through economies of scale in equipment, personnel, and operations are added to the productivity gains from learning.

Learning curves provide an excellent means to examine performance. The best comparison for one's performance would be the learning rates for competitors in the industry. Even when a standard or expected level is unknown, much can still be learned by simply using and plotting data in a learning curve fashion. As an illustration of this ability to learn about one's performance, we present the experience of a heart transplant facility in a hospital.[12]

Learning Curves Applied to Heart Transplant Mortality

⟨*S*⟩

---

[12] David B. Smith, and Jan L. Larsson, "The Impact of Learning on Cost: The Case of Heart Transplantation," *Hospital and Health Sciences Administration* 34, no. 1 (Spring 1989), pp. 85–97.

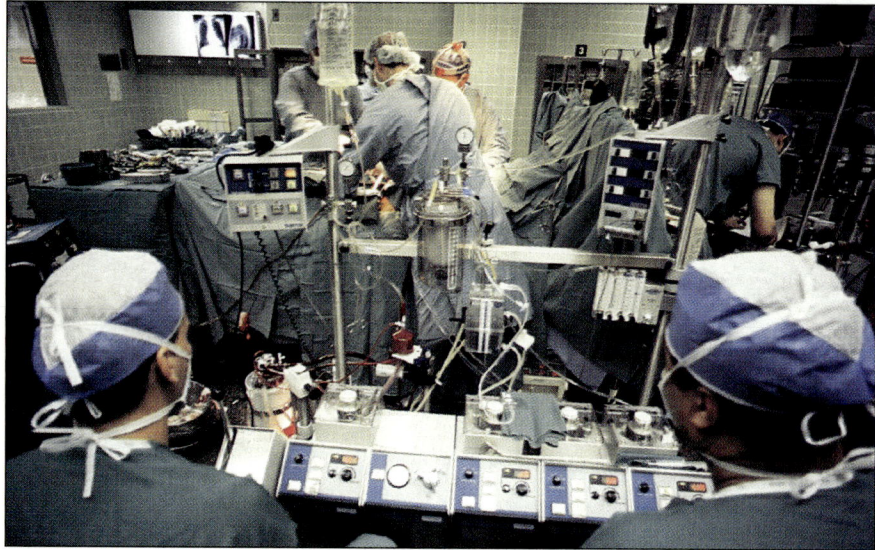

Learning curve theory can affect such complex processes as heart transplants. This highly trained surgical team gets better results each time the procedure is repeated.

E X H I B I T 11.24

Consumption Coefficients for Heart Transplant Learning Model

	B_0 (asymptote)	B_1 (range)	B_2 (rate)	Percent Decrease
Death rate	.2329	.8815	.2362	21.04%
Length of stay	28.26	23.76	.0943	9.00
Units of service	1,282.84	592.311	.0763	7.35
Adjusted charges	$96,465.90	$53,015.80	.0667	6.45

The learning curve model in the heart transplant analysis was of the form

$$Y_i = B_0 + B_1^{-xB_2}$$

Y_i is the cumulative average resource consumption (the total number of deaths, costs, etc. divided by the number of transplants), B_0 is the asymptote (the minimum), B_1 is the maximum possible reduction (the difference between the first unit and minimum B_0), x is the total number of units produced, and B_2 is the rate of change for each successive unit as it moves toward the lower bound.

Exhibit 11.24 shows the coefficients which were obtained for the model. Exhibit 11.25 shows the cumulative death rate. This seems to follow an industrial learning curve with a rate just over 80 percent. Seven of the first 23 transplant patients died within a year after transplant surgery. Only 4 of the next 39 patients died within a year. For the cumulative average length of stay, shown in Exhibit 11.26, the death reduction rate is approximately 9 percent.

The least sloping curve (the lowest learning rate) is the cost of heart transplants. Exhibit 11.27 shows that the initial costs were in the vicinity of $150,000. After 51 surviving patients (62 procedures, 11 died), the average cost was still close to $100,000. (A learning rate of 80 percent would result in an average cost of $40,000; a 90 percent rate would result in a cost of $80,000.)

Why are learning rates high in death rate reduction and low in average length of stay and the lowest rate in cost reduction? David Smith and Jan Larsson question whether the low learning rates may be related to conservatism in dealing with human lives. Or could it be due to the power and insulation of the heart transplant team from pressure to

E X H I B I T 11.25   *Death Rates, Less than One Year Survival*

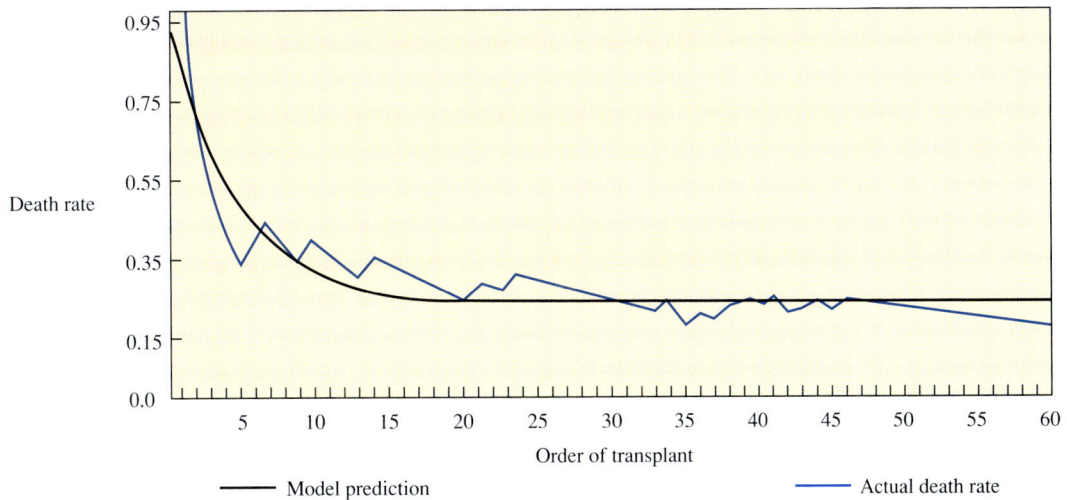

Source: David B. Smith and Jan L. Larsson, "The Impact of Learning on Cost: The Case of Heart Transplantation," *Hospital and Health Services Administration* 34, no. 1 (Spring 1989), p. 92.

E X H I B I T 11.26   *Average Length of Stay (ALOS) for Heart Transplant Survivors*

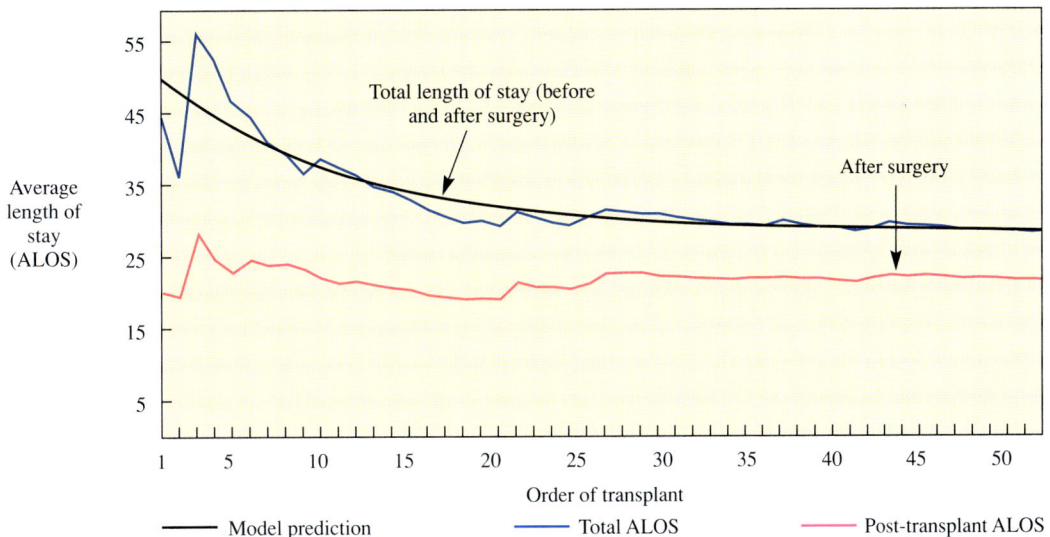

For transplant admission only, actual costs are approximately 50 percent of charges.
Source: David B. Smith and Jan L. Larsson, "The Impact of Learning on Cost: The Case of Heart Transplantation," *Hospital and Health Services Administration* 34, no. 1 (Spring 1989), p. 93.

reduce cost? The importance and purpose of this study on learning curves was to make institutions and administrators aware of learning. Institutions need to behave in a learning curve logic—that is, in pricing as well as a motivation for continuous improvement.

We hope that you learn from this discussion that it is generally not wise to be among the first in any new procedures such as a heart transplant (if you are the patient). Before

E X H I B I T 11.27 *Cost for Heart Transplant Survivors*

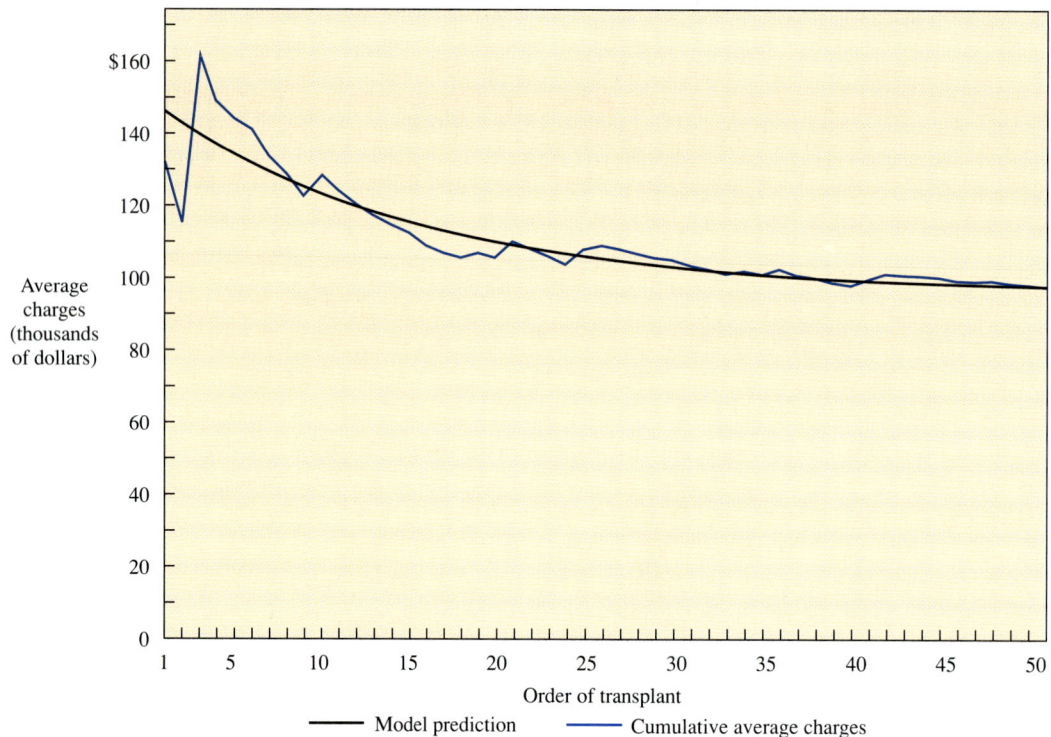

For transplant admission only, actual costs are approximately 50 percent of charges.
Source: David B. Smith and Jan L. Larsson, "The Impact of Learning on Cost: The Case of Heart Implantation," *Hospital and Health Services Administration* 34, no. 1 (Spring 1989), p. 95.

getting involved your first questions should be "How many have you done before and what were the results?"

11.8 CONCLUSION

At the outset of the chapter we identified current trends in job design. What will the future hold? One thing is clear: Globalization and the successful application of sophisticated process technologies will make the human element even more important to operations competitiveness than before. Giffi, Roth, and Seal speculate that "the twenty-first century will be marked by the human resource renaissance." In their view, this renaissance will be characterized by companies actively cultivating their human resources through careful selection and training of the best and brightest employees, implementing innovative team-based employee involvement programs, developing genuinely participative management approaches, and continually retraining their employees.[13] (See "Breakthrough at AT&T Credit Corp." for an example.)

What is the future of the industrial engineering approaches also addressed in this chapter? In our opinion, they will always have application to analyzing work methods and,

---

[13]C. Giffi, A. Roth, and G. M. Seal, *Competing in World-Class Manufacturing: America's 21st Century Challenge* (Homewood, Ill. Richard D. Irwin, 1990), p. 299.

Breakthrough at AT&T Credit Corp.

Millions of clerical employees toil in the back offices of financial companies, processing applications, claims, and customer accounts on what amounts to electronic assembly lines. The jobs are dull and repetitive, and efficiency gains are minuscule—when they come at all.

That was the case with AT&T Credit Corp. (ATTCC) when it opened shop in 1985 as a newly created subsidiary of American Telephone & Telegraph Co. Based in Morristown, New Jersey, ATTCC provides financing for customers who lease equipment from AT&T and other companies. A bank initially retained by ATTCC to process lease applications would not keep up with the volume of new business.

ATTCC President Thomas C. Wajnert saw that the fault lay in the bank's method of dividing labor into narrow tasks and organizing work by function. One department handled applications and checked the customer's credit standing, a second drew up contracts, and a third collected payments. So no one person or group had responsibility for providing full service to a customer. "The employees had no sense of how their jobs contributed to the final solution for the customer," Wajnert says.

Wajnert decided to hire his own employees and give them "ownership and accountability." His first concern was to increase efficiency, not to provide more rewarding jobs. But in the end, he did both.

In 1986, ATTCC set up 11 teams of 10 to 15 newly hired workers in a high-volume division serving small businesses. The three major lease-processing functions were combined in each team. No longer were calls from customers shunted from department to department. The company also divided its national staff of field agents into seven regions and assigned two or three teams to handle business from each region. That way, the same teams always worked with the same sales staff, establishing a personal relationship with them and their customers. Above all, team members took responsibility for solving customers' problems. ATTCC's new slogan was "Whoever gets the call owns the problem."

The teams largely manage themselves. Members make most decisions on how to deal with customers, schedule their own time off, reassign work when people are absent, and interview prospective new employees. The only supervisors are seven regional managers who advise the team members, rather than give orders. The result: The teams process up to 800 lease applications a day versus 400 under the old system. Instead of taking several days to give a final yes or no, the teams do it in 24 to 48 hours. As a result, ATTCC is growing at a 40 to 50 percent compound annual rate, Wajnert says.

The teams also have economic incentives for providing good service. A bonus plan tied to each team's costs and profits can produce extra cash. The employees, most of whom are young college graduates, can add $1,500 a year to average salaries of $28,000. Pay rises as employees learn new skills. "It's a phenomenal learning opportunity," says 24-year-old team member Michael LoCastro.

Source: John Hoerr, "The Payoff from Teamwork," *Business Week,* July 10, 1989, p. 59.

selectively, to setting work standards. The UPS (page 447) and the NUMMI (page 435) examples show how these classic tools are used quite differently, but effectively, by two very successful organizations.

11.9   FORMULA REVIEW

Standard time

$$ST = NT(1 + \text{Allowances}) \tag{11.1}$$

$$ST = \frac{NT}{1 - \text{Allowances}} \tag{11.2}$$

Logarithmic curve

$$Y_x = Kx^n \tag{11.3}$$

11.10   SOLVED PROBLEMS

1. Brandon is very organized and wants to plan his day perfectly. To do this, he has his friend Kelly time his daily activities. Here are the results of her timing Brandon on polishing two pairs of black shoes using the snapback method of timing. What is the standard time for polishing two pair? (Assume a 5 percent allowance factor for Brandon to put something mellow on the CD player. Account for noncyclically recurring elements by dividing their observed times by the total number of cycles observed.)

		Observed Times						
Element	**1**	**2**	**3**	**4**	**ΣT**	**T**	**Performance Rating**	**NT**
Get shoeshine kit	0.50						125%	
Polish shoes	0.94	0.85	0.80	0.81			110	
Put away kit				0.75			80	

Solution

	ST	**$\overline{T}$**	**Performance Rating**	**NT**
Get shoeshine kit	.50	.50/2 = .25	125%	.31
Polish shoes (2 pair)	3.40	3.40/2 = 1.70	110	1.87
Put away kit	.75	.75/2 = .375	80	.30
Normal time for one pair of shoes				2.48

Standard time for the pair = 2.48 × 1.05 = 2.60 minutes.

2. A total of 15 observations have been taken on a head baker for a school district. The numerical breakdown of her activities is

Make Ready	**Do**	**Clean Up**	**Idle**
2	6	3	4

Based on this information, how many work sampling observations are required to determine how much of the baker's time is spent in "doing"? Assume a 5 percent desired absolute accuracy and 95 percent confidence level.

Solution

To calculate the number of observations, use the formula at the bottom of Exhibit 11.12, since the 95 percent confidence is required (i.e., $Z \cong 2$).

p = "Doing" = 6/15 = 40%
E = 5% (given)

$$N = \frac{4p(1 - p)}{E^2} = \frac{4(.4)(1 - .4)}{(.05)(.05)} = \frac{.96}{.0025} = 384$$

3. After completing a total of 10 minisubs, SUB (see the example in the chapter) receives an order for two subs from a Loch Ness Monster search team. Given the fact that a 70 percent learning curve prevailed for the previous order, what price should SUB quote the search team, assuming that SUB wishes to make the same percentage profit as before?

Solution

The solution is found by applying learning curve (LC) values to labor costs for the 11th and 12th subs and adding these amounts to the material requirements. A 10 percent markup is then added to the sum. LC of the 11th is estimated as the average of the 10th and 12th.

Cost of the 11th sub:
Materials	$ 200,000
Labor: 300,000 (.3058 + .2784) ÷ 2	87,630
	$ 287,630

Cost of the 12th sub:
Materials:	$ 200,000
Labor: .2784 × 300,000	83,520
	$ 283,520

Selling price: 1.10 × (287,630 + 283,520) $ 628,265

4. A job applicant is being tested for an assembly line position. Management feels that steady-state times have been approximately reached after 1,000 performances. Regular assembly line workers are expected to perform the task within four minutes.

   a. If the job applicant performed the first test operation in 10 minutes and the second one in 9 minutes, should this applicant be hired?

   b. What is the expected time that the job applicant would finish the 10th unit?

Solution

a. Learning rate $= \dfrac{9 \text{ minutes}}{10 \text{ minutes}} = 90\%$

   From Exhibit 11.20, the time for the 1,000th unit is .3499 × 10 minutes = 3.499 minutes.

   Yes, hire the person.

b. From Exhibit 11.20, unit 10 at 90% is .7047. Therefore, time for 10th unit = .7047 × 10 = 7.047 minutes.

11.11   REVIEW AND DISCUSSION QUESTIONS

1. Why might practicing managers and industrial engineers be skeptical about job enrichment and sociotechnical approaches to job design?

2. Chase and Aquilano commonly complain to their families that book writing is hard work and that they should be excused from helping out with the housework so that they can rest. Which exhibit in this chapter should they never let their families see?

3. Is there an inconsistency when a company requires precise time standards and encourages job enlargement?

4. Match the following techniques to their most appropriate application:

MTM	Washing clothes at laundromat
SIMO chart	Tracing your steps in getting a parking permit
Worker-machine chart	Faculty office hours kept
Process chart	Development of a new word processor keyboard
Work sampling	Planning the assembly process for a new electronic device

5. You have timed your friend, Lefty, assembling widgets. His time averaged 12 minutes for the two cycles you timed. He was working very hard, and you believe that none of the nine other operators doing the same job can beat his time. Are you ready to put this time forth as the standard for making an order of 5,000 widgets? If not, what else should you do?

6. Comment on the following:

   a. "Work measurement is old hat. We have automated our office, and now we run every bill through our computer (after our 25 clerks have typed the data into our computer database)."

   b. "It's best that our workers don't know that they are being time studied. That way, they can't complain about us getting in the way when we set time standards."

    c. "Once we get everybody on an incentive plan, then we will start our work measurement program."

    d. "Rhythm is fine for dancing, but it has no place on the shop floor."

7. Organizationwide financial incentive plans cover all the workers. Some units or individuals may have contributed more to corporate profits than others. Does this detract from the effectiveness of the incentive plan system? How would your incentive scheme for a small software development firm compare to an established auto manufacturing firm?

8. If you kept any of your old exam grades from last semester, get them out and write down the grades. Use Exhibits 11.20 and 11.21 or use log-log graph paper to find whether the exponential curve fits showing that you experienced learning over the semester (insofar as your exam performance is concerned). If not, can you give some reasons why not?

9. How might the following business specialists use learning curves: accountants, marketers, financial analysts, personnel managers, and computer programmers?

10. As a manager, which learning percentage would you prefer (other things being equal), 110 percent or 60 percent? Explain.

11. Discuss the influence of the learning curve forgetting factor on a company's contract bidding.

12. What difference does it make if a customer wants a 10,000 unit order produced and delivered all at one time or in 2,500 unit batches?

11.12   PROBLEMS

1. Use the following form to evaluate a job you have held relative to the five principles of job design given in the chapter. Develop a numerical score by summing the numbers in parentheses.

	Poor (0)	Adequate (1)	Good (2)	Outstanding (3)
Task variety				
Skill variety				
Feedback				
Task identity				
Task autonomy				

    a. Compute the score for your job. Does the score match your subjective feelings about the job as a whole? Explain.

    b. Compare your score with the scores generated by your classmates. Is there one kind of job that everybody likes and one kind that everybody dislikes?

2. Examine the process chart in Exhibit 11.5. Can you recommend some improvements to cut down on delays and transportation? (Hint: The research laboratory can suggest changes in the requisition form.)

3. A time study was made of an existing job to develop new time standards. A worker was observed for 45 minutes. During that period, 30 units were produced. The analyst rated the worker as performing at a 90 percent performance rate. Allowances in the firm for rest and personal time are 12 percent.

    a. What is the normal time for the task?

    b. What is the standard time for the task?

    c. If the worker produced 300 units in an eight-hour day, what would the day's pay be if the basic rate was $6 per hour and the premium payment system paid on a 100 percent basis?

4. The Bullington Company wants a time standard established on the painting operation of souvenir horseshoes for the local Pioneer Village. Work sampling is to be used. It is estimated that working time averages 95 percent of total time (working time plus idle time). A co-op student is available to do the work sampling between 8:00 AM and 12:00 noon.

Sixty working days are to be used for the study. Use Exhibit 11.12 and an absolute error of 2.5 percent. Use the table of random numbers (Appendix B) to calculate the sampling schedule for the first day (i.e., show the times of day that an observation of working/idle should be made). Hint: Start random number selection with the first tour.

5. The final result of the study in Problem 4 estimated working time at 91.0 percent. In a 480-minute shift the best operator painted 1,000 horseshoes. The student's performance index was estimated to be 115 percent. Total allowances per company standard are 10 percent. Calculate the standard time per piece.

6. Suppose you want to set a time standard for the baker making her specialty, square donuts. A work sampling study of her on "donut day" yielded the following results:

Time spent (working and idle)	320 minutes
Number of donuts produced	5,000
Working time	280 minutes
Performance rating	125%
Allowances	10%

What is the standard time per donut?

7. In an attempt to increase productivity and reduce costs, Rho Sigma Corporation is planning to install an incentive pay plan in its manufacturing plant. In developing standards for one operation, time-study analysts observed a worker for a 30-minute period. During that time the worker completed 42 parts. The analysts rated the worker as producing at 130 percent. The base wage rate of the worker is $5 per hour. The firm has established 15 percent as a fatigue and personal time allowance.

   a. What is the normal time for the task?
   b. What is the standard time for the task?
   c. If the worker produced 500 units during an eight-hour day, what wages would the worker have earned?

8. Since new regulations will greatly change the products and services offered by savings and loan associations, time studies must be performed on tellers and other personnel to determine the number and types of personnel needed and incentive wage payment plans that might be installed.

   As an example of the studies that the various tasks will undergo, consider the following problem and come up with appropriate answers.

   A hypothetical case was set up in which the teller (to be retitled later as an *account adviser*) was required to examine a customer's portfolio and determine whether it was more beneficial for the customer to consolidate various CDs into a single issue currently offered, or to leave the portfolio unaltered. A time study made of the teller yielded the following findings:

Time of study	90 minutes
Number of portfolios examined	10 portfolios
Performance rating	130 percent
Rest for personal time	15 percent
Teller's proposed new pay rate	$ 12 per hour

   a. What is the normal time for the teller to do a portfolio analysis for the CDs?
   b. What is the standard time for the analysis?
   c. If the S&L decides to pay the new tellers on a 100 percent premium payment plan, how much would a teller earn for a day in which he analyzed 50 customer portfolios?

9. A time standard was set as .20 hour per unit after observing 50 cycles. If the task has a 90 percent learning curve, what would be the average time per unit after 100, 200, and 400 cycles?

10. You have just received 10 units of a special subassembly from an electronics manufacturer at a price of $250 per unit. A new order has also just come in for your company's product that uses these subassemblies, and you wish to purchase 40 more to be shipped in lots of 10

units each. (The subassemblies are bulky, and you need only 10 a month to fill your new order.)

a. Assuming a 70 percent learning curve by your supplier on a similar product last year, how much should you pay for each lot? Assume that the learning rate of 70 percent applies to each lot of 10 units, not per unit.

b. Suppose you are the supplier and can produce 20 units now but cannot start production on the second 20 units for two months. What price would you try to negotiate?

11. Johnson Industries received a contract to develop and produce four high-intensity long-distance receiver/transmitters for cellular telephones. The first took 2,000 labor hours and $39,000 worth of purchased and manufactured parts, the second took 1,500 labor hours and $37,000 in parts, the third took 1,450 labor hours and $31,000 in parts, and the fourth took 1,270 labor hours and $31,000 in parts.

Johnson was asked to bid on a follow-on contract for another dozen receiver/transmitter units. Ignoring any forgetting factor effects, what should Johnson estimate their time and parts costs to be for the dozen units? Estimate the learning curve using log-log paper. (Hint: There are two learning curves—one for labor and one for parts.)

12. Lambda Computer Products competed for and won a contract to produce two prototype units of a new type of computer, based on optics using lasers rather than electronic binary bits.

The first unit produced by Lambda took 5,000 hours to produce and required $250,000 worth of material, equipment usage, and supplies. The second unit took 3,500 hours and used $200,000 worth of materials, equipment usage, and supplies. Labor is $30 per hour.

a. You were asked by your customer to present a bid for 10 additional units as soon as the second unit was completed. Production would start immediately. What would your bid be?

b. Suppose there was a significant delay between both contracts. During this time, personnel and equipment were reassigned to other projects. Explain how this would affect your subsequent bid.

13. You've just completed a pilot run of 10 units of a major product and found the processing time for each unit was as follows:

Unit Number	Time (hours)
1	970
2	640
3	420
4	380
5	320
6	250
7	220
8	240
9	190
10	190

a. According to the pilot run, what would you estimate the learning rate to be?

b. Based on *a,* how much time would it take for the next 190 units, assuming no loss of learning?

c. How much time would it take to make the 1,000th unit?

14. Lazer Technologies, Inc. (LTI), has produced a total of 20 high-power laser systems that could be used to destroy any approaching enemy missiles or aircraft. The 20 units have been produced, funded in part as private research within the research and development arm of LTI, but the bulk of the funding came from a contract with the U.S. Department of Defense (DOD).

Testing of the laser units has shown that they are effective defense weapons, and, through redesign to add portability and easier field maintenance, the units could be truck-mounted.

DOD has asked LTI to submit a bid for 100 units.

The 20 units that LTI built so far cost the following amounts and are listed in the order in which they were produced:

Unit Number	Cost ($ millions)	Unit Number	Cost ($ millions)	Unit Number	Cost ($ millions)	Unit Number	Cost ($ millions)
1	$ 12	6	$ 6	11	$ 3.9	16	$ 2.6
2	10	7	5	12	3.5	17	2.3
3	6	8	3.6	13	3.0	18	3.0
4	6.5	9	3.6	14	2.8	19	2.9
5	5.8	10	4.1	15	2.7	20	2.6

a. Based on past experience, what is the learning rate? (Hint: You may use log-log paper to plot the values and make estimates.)

b. What bid should LTI submit for the total order of 100 units, assuming that learning continues?

c. What is the cost expected to be for the last unit, under the learning rate you estimated?

15. Jack Simpson, contract negotiator for Nebula Airframe Company, is currently involved in bidding on a follow-up government contract. In gathering cost data from the first three units, which Nebula produced under a research and development contract, he found that the first unit took 2,000 labor hours, the second took 1,800 labor hours, and the third took 1,692 hours.

In a contract for three more units, how many labor hours should Simpson plan for?

16. Honda Motor Company has discovered a problem in the exhaust system of one of its automobile lines and has voluntarily agreed to make the necessary modifications to conform with government safety requirements. Standard procedure is for the firm to pay a flat fee to dealers for each modification completed.

Honda is trying to establish a fair amount of compensation to pay dealers and has decided to choose a number of randomly selected mechanics and observe their performance and learning rate. Analysis demonstrated that the average learning rate was 90 percent, and Honda then decided to pay a $60 fee for each repair (3 hours × $20 per flat-rate hour).

Southwest Honda, Inc., has complained to Honda Motor Company about the fee. Six mechanics, working independently, have completed two modifications each. All took 9 hours on the average to do the first unit and 6.3 hours to do the second. Southwest refuses to do any more unless Honda allows at least 4½ hours.

What is your opinion of Honda's allowed rate and the mechanics' performance?

17. United Research Associates (URA) had received a contract to produce two units of a new cruise missile guidance control. The first unit took 4,000 hours to complete and cost $30,000 in materials and equipment usage. The second took 3,200 hours and cost $21,000 in materials and equipment usage. Labor cost is charged at $18 per hour.

The prime contractor has now approached URA and asked to submit a bid for the cost of producing *another* 20 guidance controls.

a. What will the last unit cost to build?

b. What will be the average time for the 20 missile guidance controls?

c. What will the average cost be per guidance control for the 20 in the contract?

18. United Assembly Products (UAP) has a personnel screening process for job applicants to test their ability to perform at the department's long-term average rate. UAP has asked you to modify the test by incorporating learning theory. From the company's data, you discovered that if people can perform a given task in 30 minutes or less on the 20th unit, they achieve the group long-run average. Obviously, all job applicants cannot be subjected to 20 performances of such a task, so you are to determine whether they will likely achieve the desired rate based only on two performances.

a. Suppose a person took 100 minutes on the first unit and 80 minutes on the second. Should this person be hired?

b. What procedure might you establish for hiring (i.e., how to evaluate the job applicant for his or her two performances)?

19. A potentially large customer offered to subcontract assembly work which is profitable only if you can perform the operations at an average time of less than 20 hours each. The contract is for 1,000 units.

    You run a test and do the first one in 50 hours and the second one in 40 hours.

    a. How long would you expect it to take to do the third one?

    b. Would you take the contract? Explain.

20. Western Turbine, Inc., has just completed the production of the 10th unit of a new high-efficiency turbine/generator. Its analysis showed that a learning rate of 85 percent existed over the production of the 10 units. If the 10th unit contained labor costs of $2.5 million, what price should Western Turbine charge for labor on the 11th and 12th units to make a profit of 10 percent of the selling price?

CASE

11.13 C A S E
Teamwork at Volvo

Volvo is trying to determine if the assembly line has become outdated as mass markets disappear. In 1974 the Swedish automaker dismantled the assembly line at its plant in Kalmar, Sweden. The line was replaced with a system in which cars are built by small, decentralized work teams that produce sections of cars. Volvo officials believe strongly that teams, and a return to craftsmanship, will improve quality and increase employees' pride in their work. In fact, Volvo believes so strongly in teamwork that this system is also being put into place at the company's new plant in Uddevalla, Sweden.

The Uddevalla plant was completed in 1990 to build the 740 and 940 models. By the end of 1991 the plant was producing about 22,000 cars annually; at full capacity it will employ 1,000 workers and produce 40,000 cars annually. At the Uddevalla facility, self-managed teams of 8 to 10 members assemble complete cars from start to finish. Cars being assembled are not moved on a conveyor line from worker to worker but rather are assembled in a stationary position. A special device tilts the car as needed so that workers can perform their tasks. Each team has a high degree of autonomy and responsibility; they set their own break times and vacation schedules and reassign work when a team member is absent. Teams also participate in policy-making decisions and are responsible for a variety of tasks, including quality control, production planning, developing work procedures, servicing equipment, and ordering supplies.

Workers at the Uddevalla plant are paid for performance. In addition to wages, bonuses are paid for maintaining quality and productivity and for meeting weekly delivery targets. There are no supervisors and plant foremen; each of six "production workshops" houses 80 to 100 employees who are divided into assembly teams. Each assembly team has a coordinator (chosen on a rotating basis), who has direct contact with the managers. To make sure the system works, employees are provided with abundant information. Volvo also goes to great lengths to ensure that workers have an in-depth understanding of company history, tradition, and its strategy. The free flow of information is encouraged and workers have input on everything from assembly processes to new-product innovations.

The new system at Uddevalla isn't totally successful. Although morale is up and absenteeism is down, productivity is not as high as at Volvo's plant in Ghent, Belgium, where building a car on the assembly line takes about half the time. Lennert Ericson, president of the metal workers' union at the Uddevalla plant, thinks the approach there will work: "I am convinced that our ways [teams] will be successful and competitive. Our next goal is to be better than Kalmar, and when we get to that, our goal will be to get to Ghent."

Volvo has invested heavily in training workers at the Uddevalla plant. First, employees attend a 16-week initiation course as part of a 16-month training program in which workers learn about auto assembly. Workers are encouraged to share experiences with one another and exchange ideas.

Both union and management feel confident that the new system will improve the organization. But it will take time. The system puts numerous demands on everyone, and there has been some resistance. And like other automakers, Volvo hasn't escaped the current worldwide slump in car sales. But several experts pick Volvo as the company to invest in once the economy rebounds. Stock in the firm climbed from 35 in early 1991 to 60 about a year later, while shares of GM, Ford, and Chrysler were still down from their 1991 highs.

Investment firm Bear Stearns thinks the Swedish automaker's profits will boom. In the meantime, striving to become the world's first truly global auto producer, Volvo has developed alliances with French automaker Renault and Japan's Mitsubishi.

Questions

1. What is the difference between teams at the Kalmar plant and self-managed teams at Uddevalla?

2. How important is empowerment in Volvo's Uddevalla facility?

3. Why do you think there is resistance to the team approach at Uddevalla? How can Volvo overcome this resistance?

4. Do you believe that the Uddevalla plant will eventually be able to produce cars at the same speed as the Ghent assembly line? Why or why not?

Source: J. M. Ivancevich, P. Lorenzi, and S. Skinner, *Management Quality and Competitiveness* (Homewood Ill.: Richard D. Irwin, 1994), pp. 279–80.

11.14   SELECTED BIBLIOGRAPHY

Argote, Linda, and Dennis Epple. "Learning Curves in Manufacturing." *Science* 247 (February 1990), pp. 920–24.

Bailey, Charles D. "Forgetting and the Learning Curve: A Laboratory Study." *Management Science* 35, no. 3 (March 1989), pp. 340–52.

Barnes, Ralph M. *Motion and Time Study: Design and Measurement of Work.* 8th ed. New York: John Wiley & Sons, 1980.

Carlisle, Brian. "Job Design Implications for Operations Managers." *International Journal of Operations and Production Management* 3, no. 3 (1983), pp. 40–48.

Globerson, Shlomo. "The Influence of Job-Related Variables on the Predictability Power of Three Learning Curve Models." *AIIE Transactions* 12, no. 1 (March 1980), pp. 64–69.

Irving, Robert. "A Convenient Method for Computing the Learning Curve." *Industrial Engineering* 14, no. 5 (May 1982), pp. 52–54.

Konz, Stephan. *Work Design: Industrial Ergonomics.* 2d ed. New York: John Wiley & Sons, 1983.

Kopsco, David P., and William C. Nemitz. "Learning Curves and Lot Sizing for Independent and Dependent Demand." *Journal of Operations Management* 4, no. 1 (November 1983), pp. 73–83.

Kostiuk, Peter F., and Dean A. Follmann. "Learning Curves, Personal Characteristics, and Job Performance," *Journal of Labor Economics* 7, no. 2 (April 1989), pp. 129–46.

Logan, Gordon D. "Shapes of Reaction-Time Distribution and Shapes of Learning Curves." *Journal of Experimental Psychology: Learning, Memory, and Cognition* 18, no. 5 (Sept. 1992), pp. 883–915.

Niebel, Benjamin W. *Motion and Time Study.* 9th ed. Homewood, IL: Richard D. Irwin, 1993.

Ramsey, Jr., George F. "Using Self-Administered Work Sampling in a State Agency." *Industrial Engineering,* February 1993, pp. 44–45.

Rutter, Rick. "Work Sampling: As a Win/Win Management Tool." *Industrial Engineering,* February 1994, pp. 30–31.

Sasser, W. Earl, and William E. Fulmer. "Creating Personalized Service Delivery Systems." In *Service Management Effectiveness,* ed. D. Bowen, R. Chase, and T. Cummings. San Francisco: Jossey-Bass, 1990, pp. 213–33.

Smith, David B., and Jan L. Larsson. "The Impact of Learning on Cost: The Case of Heart Transplantation." *Hospital and Health Services Administration* 34, no. 1 (Spring 1989), pp. 85–97.

Smunt, Timothy L. "A Comparison of Learning Curve Analysis and Moving Average Ratio Analysis for Detailed Operational Planning." *Decision Sciences* 17, no. 4 (Fall 1986), pp. 475–95.

Towill, D. R. "The Use of Learning Curve Models for Prediction of Batch Production Performance." *International Journal of Operations and Production Management* 5, no. 2 (1985), pp. 13–24.

Yelle, Louie E. "The Learning Curves: Historical Review and Comprehensive Survey." *Decision Sciences* 10, no. 2 (April 1979), pp. 302–28.

Zandin, Kjell. *Most Work Measurement Systems.* New York: Marcel Dekker, 1990.

Zuboff, Shoshana. *In the Age of the Smart Machine: The Future of Work and Power.* New York: Basic Books, 1984.

IV

STARTUP OF THE SYSTEM

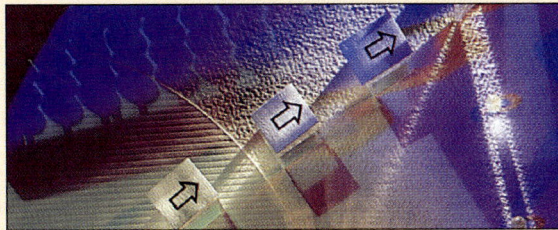

12 Project Planning and Control

Once designed, it is no easy task to bring a production system up to full operation: Numerous problems are experienced in this phase of the system life cycle. One discovers that tasks and activities were not well defined, some aspects of the system were overlooked, and unexpected incidents occur.

Perhaps the most appropriate way to guide this transitional period between the design of the system and its steady-state operation is through the techniques of project management. Within this section, we discuss project management and how it differs from traditional management—in purpose, structure, and operation. We also discuss the scheduling techniques of PERT and CPM, which provide a logical analysis of activity performance times and help in estimating the time for project completion.

Chapter

12

Project Planning and Control

CHAPTER OUTLINE

KEY TERMS

Project

Project Management

Program

Milestone

Work Breakdown Structure

Gantt Chart

Pure Project

Functional Project

Matrix

PERT

CPM

Early Start/Late Start Schedules

Time–Cost Model

"I'll have an order of tacos and one rebuilt store, please."

Taco Bell of Compton, California, a quick-service Mexican restaurant, was destroyed by fire during the Los Angeles riots. In a dramatic effort to restore services and jobs to the community, Taco Bell and the City of Compton decided to launch a 48-hour rebuilding plan.

Taco Bell hired Fluor Daniel Inc., an international engineering, construction, maintenance, and technical services company, less than three weeks before the building was to begin. Ahmad Kanawi, Fluor Daniel's project manager, had his work cut out for him. The typical building schedule for a Taco Bell restaurant was 60 days, not two. Considering that Taco Bell wanted everything done on site with nothing prefabricated, having the restaurant open and ready for business at the 48-hour mark would be a race against the clock. As the project required planning increments smaller than the one day that most software allows, Primavera's Finest Hour was used.

"The night before we started," says Kanawi, "I just lay awake going over the plan in my mind, moving certain activities around in my head, thinking about how they would affect the rest of the project. With other planning software and traditional bar charts, it was almost a game. I would go over all the what-if questions in my head and try to come up with the same outcomes along with the computer. But I couldn't think that fast for this project. Luckily, the scheduling software could."

Because of the tight time frame, the plan could not be changed once the project was underway, so Kanawi and the rest of the team had to firmly set the schedule before the zero hour. The software's detailed scheduling capacity alerted the team to the high-risk components of the project while providing information on alternative procedures and fallback positions. Because certain activities would need to be pooled together to complete the construction in the allotted 45 hours, the software gave the workers their options, allowing them to decide together what to cut, what to keep, and what to change—all before actually starting the project. The software's easy-to-understand graphics allowed everyone to get involved with such decisions.

Fluor Daniel organized a dry run of everything three days before construction started to ensure that all team members knew the plan. "There was no time in this project for errors," says Kanawi. "Everyone was so pumped up about the project that no one would risk making a mistake for fear of jeopardizing the schedule."

The first few hours of the project were critical. If anything went wrong, it would cast a negative light on the entire rebuilding. As this time passed with no delays, everyone realized that the project had a good chance of proceeding according to schedule. Progress meetings were held every three hours to distribute the earned value report, just one of the software's several productivity reports, comparing plans versus actuals in terms of both budget and work accomplished. Finally, at hour 46 the health inspector gave his okay. Then at hour 47 the certificate of occupancy was signed. Finally, just as planned, at hour 48 the first new tacos were served.

Adds Kanawi, "Not even this software could have done a job like this alone. Team effort was the key. We knew we weren't just building a restaurant, but helping rebuild a destroyed community."

Source: "Riot-Ravaged Taco Bell Rebuilt in 48 Hours using Project Planning Software." Reprinted from *Industrial Engineering* 24, no. 9 (September 1992), p. 18. © 1992 Institute of Industrial Engineers, 25 Technology Park/Atlanta, Norcross, Georgia 30092.

The approach followed in rebuilding the Taco Bell restaurant—developing a highly motivated project team and supporting it with advanced project management software—is now standard in many organizations. On an everyday basis, planning and execution of projects using project management tools are common responsibilities of managers in both the public and private sectors. From an organizational perspective, companies ranging from Andersen Consulting to Xerox organize major parts of their businesses by project or programs.

In this chapter, we first focus on how projects are structured and then provide a detailed discussion of the tools commonly used to help managers run such projects.

12.1   DEFINITION OF PROJECT MANAGEMENT

A **project** may be defined as a series of related jobs usually directed toward some major output and requiring a significant period of time to perform. **Project management** can be defined as planning, directing, and controlling resources (people, equipment, material) to meet the technical, cost, and time constraints of the project.

While projects are often thought to be one-time occurrences, the fact is that many projects can be repeated or transferred to other settings or products. The result will be another project output. A contractor building houses or a firm producing low-volume products such as supercomputers, locomotives, or linear accelerators can effectively consider these as projects.

A project starts out as a *statement of work* (SOW). The SOW may be a written description of the objectives to be achieved, with a brief statement of the work to be done and a proposed schedule specifying the start and completion dates. It could also contain performance measures in terms of budget and completion steps (milestones) and the written reports to be supplied.

If the proposed work is a large endeavor, it is often referred to as a **program,** although the terms *project* and *program* are often used interchangeably. A program is the highest order of complexity, may take some years to complete, and may be made up of interrelated projects completed by many organizations. As examples, development of a missile system would be best termed a program, and the introduction of a new statewide medical health care system is a program.

As implied earlier, a project is similar to a program, but is less complex and of shorter duration. A program may be to build a missile system; a project may be to develop the guidance control portion. In a health care system, one project is to develop a bid proposal system for health care providers.

A *task* is a further subdivision of a project. It is usually not longer than several months in duration and is performed by one group or organization.

A *subtask* may be used if needed to further subdivide the project into more meaningful pieces.

A *work package* is a group of activities combined to be assignable to a single organizational unit. It still falls into the format of all project management—that the package provides a description of what is to be done, when it is to be started and completed, the budget, measures of performance, and specific events to be reached at points in time (called **milestones**). Typical milestones might be the completion of the design, the production of a prototype, the completed testing of the prototype, and the approval of a pilot run.

Work Breakdown Structure

The **work breakdown structure** (WBDS) is the heart of project management. This subdivision of the objective into smaller and smaller pieces clearly defines the system and contributes to its understanding and success. Conventional use shows the work breakdown structure decreasing in size from top to bottom and shows this level by indentation to the right:

Level	
1	Program
2	Project
3	Task
4	Subtask
5	Work Package

Exhibit 12.1 shows the work breakdown structure for a project. Note the ease in identifying activities through the level numbers. For example, telescope design (the third item down) is identified as 1.1.1 (the first item in level 1, the first item in level 2, and the first item in level 3). Data recording (the 13th item down) is 1.2.4.

The keys to a good work breakdown structure are

- Allow the elements to be worked on independently.
- Make them manageable in size.
- Give authority to carry out the program.
- Monitor and measure the program.
- Provide the required resources.

E X H I B I T 12.1

Work Breakdown Structure, Large Optical Scanner Design

1	2	3	4	5	
x					Optical simulator design
	x				Optical design
		x			Telescope design/fab
		x			Telescope/simulator optical interface
		x			Simulator zoom system design
		x			Ancillary simulator optical component specification
	x				System performance analysis
		x			Overall system firmware and software control
			x		Logic flow diagram generation and analysis
			x		Basic control algorithm design
		x			Far beam analyzer
		x			System inter- and intra-alignment method design
		x			Data recording and reduction requirements
	x				System integration
	x				Cost analysis
		x			Cost/system schedule analysis
		x			Cost/system performance analysis
	x				Management
		x			System design/engineering management
		x			Program management
	x				Long lead item procurement
		x			Large optics
		x			Target components
		x			Detectors

(Level is shown across columns 1–5)

12.2 PROJECT CONTROL

Reporting Mechanisms

The U.S. Dept. of Defense (one of the earliest large users of project management) has published a variety of helpful standard forms. Many are used directly or have been modified by firms engaged in project management. Since those early days, however, graphics programs have been written for most computers, so management, the customer, and the project manager have a wide choice of how data are presented. Exhibit 12.2 shows a sample of available presentations.

Exhibit 12.2A is a sample **Gantt chart** showing both the amount of time involved and the sequence in which activities can be performed. For example, "long lead procurement" and "manufacturing schedules" are independent activities and can occur simultaneously. All other activities must be done in the sequence from top to bottom. Exhibit 12.2B graphically shows the amounts of money spent on labor, material, and overhead over time. Its value is its clarity in identifying sources and amounts of cost.

Exhibit 12.2C shows the percentage of the project's labor hours that come from the various areas of manufacturing, finance, and so on. These labor hours are related to the proportion of the project's total labor cost. For example, manufacturing is responsible for 50 percent of the project's labor hours, but this 50 percent is allocated just 40 percent of the total labor dollars charged.

The top half of Exhibit 12.2D shows the degree of completion of these projects. The dotted vertical line signifies today. Project 1, therefore, is already late since it still has work to be done. Project 2 is not being worked on temporarily so there is a space before the projected work. Project 3 continues to be worked on without interruption. The bottom of Exhibit 12.2D compares actual total costs and projected costs. As we see, two cost overruns occurred.

Exhibit 12.2E is a milestone chart. The three milestones mark specific points in the project where checks can be made to see if the project is on time and where it should be. The best place to locate milestones is at the completion of a major activity. In this ex-

E X H I B I T 12.2   *A Sample of Graphic Project Reports*

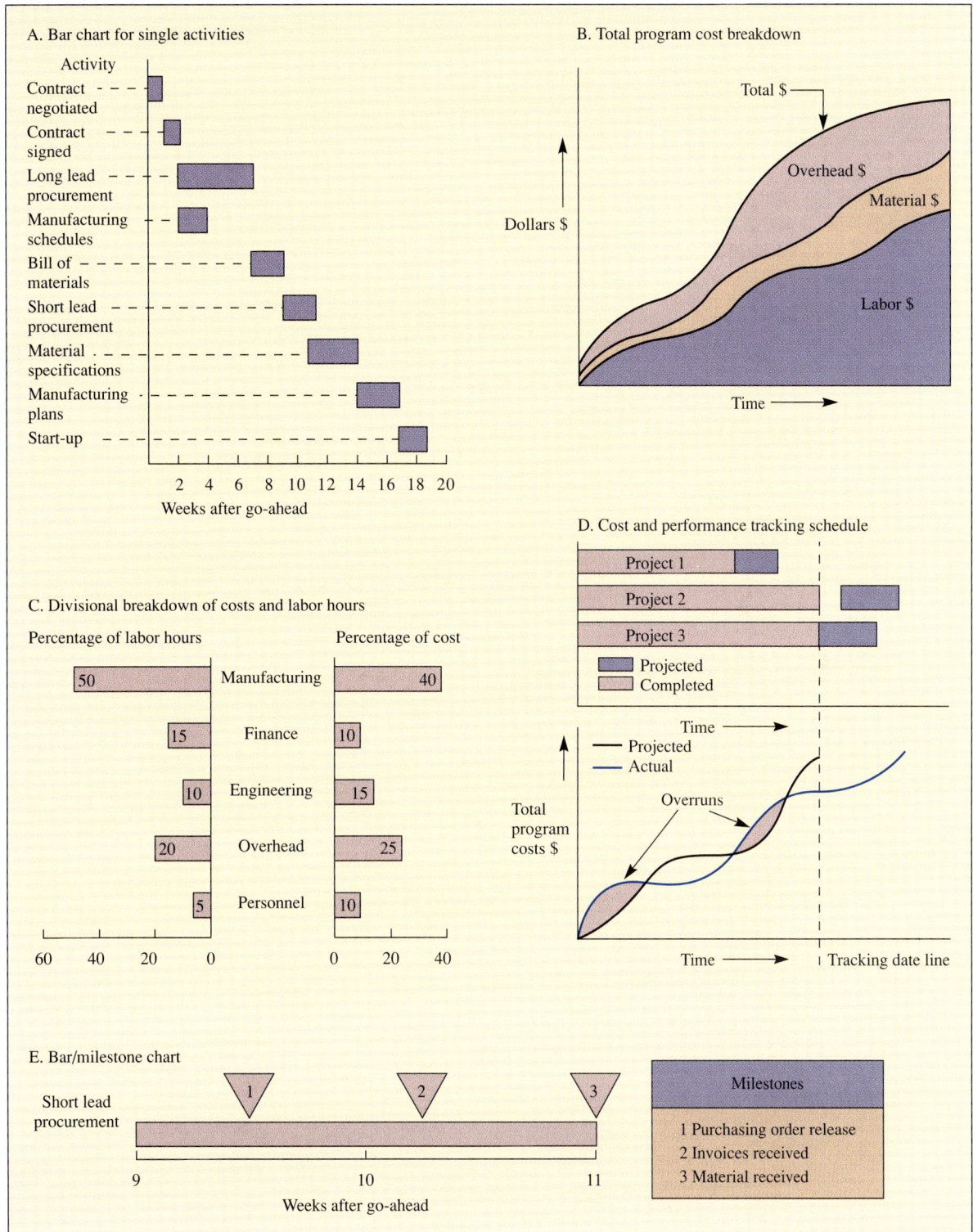

A. Bar chart for single activities

Activity:
- Contract negotiated
- Contract signed
- Long lead procurement
- Manufacturing schedules
- Bill of materials
- Short lead procurement
- Material specifications
- Manufacturing plans
- Start-up

Weeks after go-ahead: 2 4 6 8 10 12 14 16 18 20

B. Total program cost breakdown

Total $
Overhead $
Material $
Labor $
Dollars $
Time

C. Divisional breakdown of costs and labor hours

Percentage of labor hours / Percentage of cost

	Percentage of labor hours		Percentage of cost
Manufacturing	50		40
Finance	15		10
Engineering	10		15
Overhead	20		25
Personnel	5		10

60 40 20 0   0 20 40

D. Cost and performance tracking schedule

- Project 1
- Project 2
- Project 3

Projected
Completed

Time

Total program costs $
Projected
Actual
Overruns

Time   Tracking date line

E. Bar/milestone chart

Short lead procurement

1   2   3

9   10   11

Weeks after go-ahead

Milestones
1 Purchasing order release
2 Invoices received
3 Material received

hibit, the major activities completed were "purchase order release," "invoices received," and "material received."

Other standard reports can be used for a more detailed presentation comparing cost to progress (such as cost schedule status report—CSSR) or reports providing the basis for partial payment (such as "earned value" report).

12.3   ORGANIZATIONAL STRUCTURES

Senior management, before the project starts, must decide which of three organizational structures will be used to tie the project to the parent firm: pure project, functional project, or matrix project. If the matrix form is chosen, where different projects (rows of the matrix) borrow resources from functional areas (columns), another choice is made among the weak, balanced, or strong form of a matrix, depending on whether project managers have little, equal, or more authority than the functional managers with whom they negotiate for resources. Here are the strengths and weaknesses of the three main forms.

Pure Project

Tom Peters predicts that "most of the world's work will be 'brainwork,' done in semipermanent networks of small project oriented teams, each one an autonomous, entrepreneurial center of opportunity; where the necessity for speed and flexibility dooms to the dodo's fate the hierarchical management structures we and our ancestors grew up with."[1] Thus, out of the three basic project organizational structures, Peters favors the **pure project** (nicknamed skunk works) where a self-contained team works full time on the project.

Advantages

- The project manager has full authority over the project.
- Team members report to one boss. They do not have to worry about dividing loyalty with a functional area manager.
- Lines of communication are shortened. Decisions are made quickly.
- Team pride, motivation, and commitment are high.

Disadvantages

- Duplication of resources. Equipment and people are not shared across projects.
- Organizational goals and policies are ignored, since team members are often both physically and psychologically removed from headquarters.
- The organization falls behind in its knowledge of new technology due to weakened functional divisions.
- Since team members have no functional area "home," they worry about life-after-project, and project termination is delayed.

Functional Project

At the other end of the project organization spectrum is housing the project within a functional division.

Advantages

- A team member can work on several projects.
- Technical expertise is maintained within the functional area even if individuals leave the project or organization.

[1]Tom Peters, *Liberation Management* (New York: Alfred A. Knopf, 1992), p. 5 and cover flyleaf.

- The functional area is a home after the project is completed. Functional specialists can advance vertically.
- A critical mass of specialized functional area experts creates synergystic solutions to a project's technical problems.

Disadvantages

- Aspects of the project that are not directly related to the functional area get short-changed.
- Motivation of team members is often weak.
- Needs of the client are secondary and are responded to slowly.

The classic specialized organizational form—the **matrix**—attempts to blend properties of functional and pure project structures. Each project utilizes people from different functional areas. The project manager (PM) decides what and when tasks will be performed, but the functional managers control which people and technologies are used.

Matrix Project

Advantages

- Communication between functional divisions is enhanced.
- A project manager is held responsible for successful completion of the project.
- Duplication of resources is minimized.
- Team members have a functional "home" after project completion so they are less worried about "life-after-project," than if they were a pure project organization.
- Policies of the parent organization are followed. This increases support for the project.

Disadvantages

- There are two bosses. Often the functional manager will be listened to before the project manager. After all, who can promote you or give you a raise?
- It is doomed to failure unless the PM has strong negotiating skills.
- Suboptimization is a danger, as PMs hoard resources for their own project, thus harming other projects.

Note that regardless of which of the three major organizational forms is used, the project manager is the primary contact point with the customer. Communication and flexibility are greatly enhanced, as one person is responsible for successful completion of the project.

12.4 CRITICAL PATH SCHEDULING

Critical path scheduling refers to a set of graphic techniques used in planning and controlling projects. In any given project, the three factors of concern are time, cost, and resource availability. Critical path techniques have been developed to deal with each of these, individually and in combination. The rest of this chapter focuses on time-based models, time–cost models, and limited-resource models.

PERT *(program evaluation and review technique)* and **CPM** *(critical path method)*, the two best-known techniques, were both developed in the late 1950s. PERT was developed under the sponsorship of the U.S. Navy Special Projects Office in 1958 as a management tool for scheduling and controlling the Polaris missile project. CPM was developed in 1957 by J. E. Kelly of Remington-Rand and M. R. Walker of Du Pont to aid in scheduling maintenance shutdowns of chemical processing plants.

Critical path scheduling techniques display a project in graphic form and relate its component tasks in a way that focuses attention on those crucial to the project's completion. For critical path scheduling techniques to be most applicable, a project must have the following characteristics:

1. It must have well-defined jobs or tasks whose completion marks the end of the project.
2. The jobs or tasks are independent; they may be started, stopped, and conducted separately within a given sequence.
3. The jobs or tasks are ordered; they must follow each other in a given sequence.

Construction, airplane manufacture, and shipbuilding industries commonly meet these criteria, and critical path techniques find wide application within them. We previously noted also that applications of project management and critical path techniques are becoming much more common within firms in rapidly changing industries.

12.5 TIME-ORIENTED TECHNIQUES

The basic forms of PERT and CPM focus on finding the longest time-consuming path through a network of tasks as a basis for planning and controlling a project. Both PERT and CPM use nodes and arrows for display. Originally, the basic differences between PERT and CPM were that PERT used the arrow to represent an activity and CPM used the node. The other original difference was that PERT used three estimates—optimistic, pessimistic, and best—of an activity's required time, whereas CPM used just the best estimate. This distinction reflects PERT's origin in scheduling advanced projects that are characterized by uncertainty and CPM's origin in the scheduling of the fairly routine activity of plant maintenance. As years passed, these two features no longer distinguished PERT from CPM. This is because CPM users started to use three time estimates and PERT users often placed activities on the nodes.

We believe the activity on the node is much easier to follow logically than the activity on the arrow. However, the three time estimates are often valuable to measure the probability of completion times. Therefore, in this book we use the activity on the node and either a single estimate for activity time or three time estimates depending on our objective. We use the terms *CPM* and *PERT* interchangeably and mean the same thing, although we tend to use *CPM* more frequently.

In a sense, both techniques owe their development to their widely used predecessor, the Gantt chart. While the Gantt chart is able to relate activities to time in a usable fashion for very small projects, the interrelationship of activities, when displayed in this form, becomes extremely difficult to visualize and to work with for projects with more than 25 or 30 activities. Also, the Gantt chart provides no direct procedure for determining the critical path, which, despite its theoretical shortcomings, is of great practical value.

Here is an example of a project that we will develop in a normal project scheduling manner. The times for each activity have been given as a single best estimate (rather than three estimates, which we discuss in a later example).

CPM with a Single Time Estimate

E X A M P L E 12.1 / *Single Time Estimate*   Many firms that have tried to enter the laptop and briefcase computer market have failed. Suppose your firm believes that there is a big demand in this market because existing products have not been designed correctly. They are either too heavy, too large, or too small to have standard-size keyboards. Your intended computer will be small enough to carry inside a jacket pocket if need be. The ideal size will be no larger than 4 inches $\times$ $9\frac{1}{2}$ inches $\times$ 1 inch with a standard typewriter keyboard. It should weigh no more than 15 ounces, have a 4-to-8–line $\times$ 80-character LCD display, have a micro disk drive, and a micro printer. It should be aimed toward word processing use but have plug-in ROMs for an assortment of languages and programs. This should appeal to traveling businesspeople, but it could have a much wider market. If it can be priced to sell retail in the $175–$200 range, it should appeal to anyone who uses a typewriter. A big market is also expected to be students. College students could use this to create reports; college, high school, and elementary schoolchildren could take notes during class and during library research.

The project, then, is to design, develop, and produce a prototype of this small computer. In the rapidly changing computer industry, it is crucial to hit the market with a product of this sort in less than a year. Therefore, the project team has been allowed approximately eight months (35 weeks) to produce the prototype.

S O L U T I O N   The first charge of the project team is to develop a project network chart and estimate the likelihood of completing the prototype computer within the 35 weeks. Let's follow the steps in the development of the network.

1. Activity identification. The project team decides that the following activities are the major components of the project: design of the computer, prototype construction, prototype testing, methods specification (summarized in a report), evaluation studies of automatic assembly equipment, an assembly equipment study report, and a final report summarizing all aspects of the design, equipment, and methods.

2. Activity sequencing and network construction. On the basis of discussion with his staff, the project manager develops the precedence table and sequence network shown in Exhibit 12.3. Activities are indicated as nodes while arrows show the sequence in which the activities must be completed.

When constructing a network, take care to ensure that the activities are in the proper order and that the logic of their relationships is maintained. For example, it would be illogical to have a situation where Event A precedes Event B, B precedes C, and C precedes A.

CPM ACTIVITY DESIGNATIONS AND TIME ESTIMATES

Activity	Designation	Immediate predecessors	Time in weeks
Design	A	–	21
Build prototype	B	A	5
Evaluate equipment	C	A	7
Test prototype	D	B	2
Write equipment report	E	C, D	5
Write methods report	F	C, D	8
Write final report	G	E, F	2

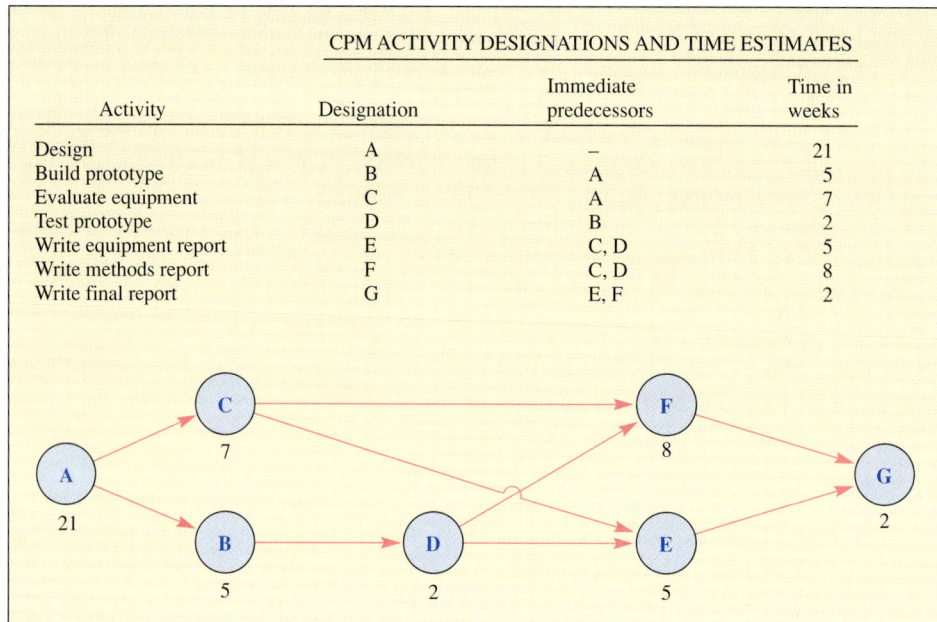

3. *Determine the critical path.* The critical path is the longest sequence of connected activities through the network and is defined as the path with zero slack time. (The numbers are consecutive.) *Slack time,* in turn, is calculated for each activity; it is the difference between the latest and the earliest expected completion time for an event. Slack may be thought of as the amount of time the start of a given activity may be delayed without delaying the completion of the project. To arrive at slack time, we must calculate four time values for each activity:

- *Early start time* (ES), the earliest possible time that the activity can begin.
- *Early finish time* (EF), the early start time plus the time needed to complete the activity.
- *Late finish time* (LF), the latest time an activity can end without delaying the project.
- *Late start time* (LS), the late finish time minus the time needed to complete the activity.

The procedure for arriving at these values and for determining slack and the critical path can best be explained by reference to the simple network shown in Exhibit 12.4. The letters denote the activities; the numbers denote the activity times.

a. Find ES time. Take 0 as the start of the project and set this equal to ES for activity A. To find ES for B, we add the duration of A (which is 2) to 0 and obtain 2. Likewise, ES for C would be $0 + 2 = 2$. To find ES for D, we take the larger ES and duration time for the preceding activities. Since $B = 2 + 5 = 7$ and $C = 2 + 4 = 6$, ES for D = 7. These values are entered on the diagram (Exhibit 12.4, Step a). The largest value is selected since activity D cannot begin until the longest time-consuming activity preceding it is completed.

b. Find EF times. The EF for A is its ES time, 0, plus its duration of 2. B's EF is its ES of 2 plus its duration of 5, or 7. C's is $2 + 4$, or 6, and D's is $7 + 3$, or 10 (Exhibit

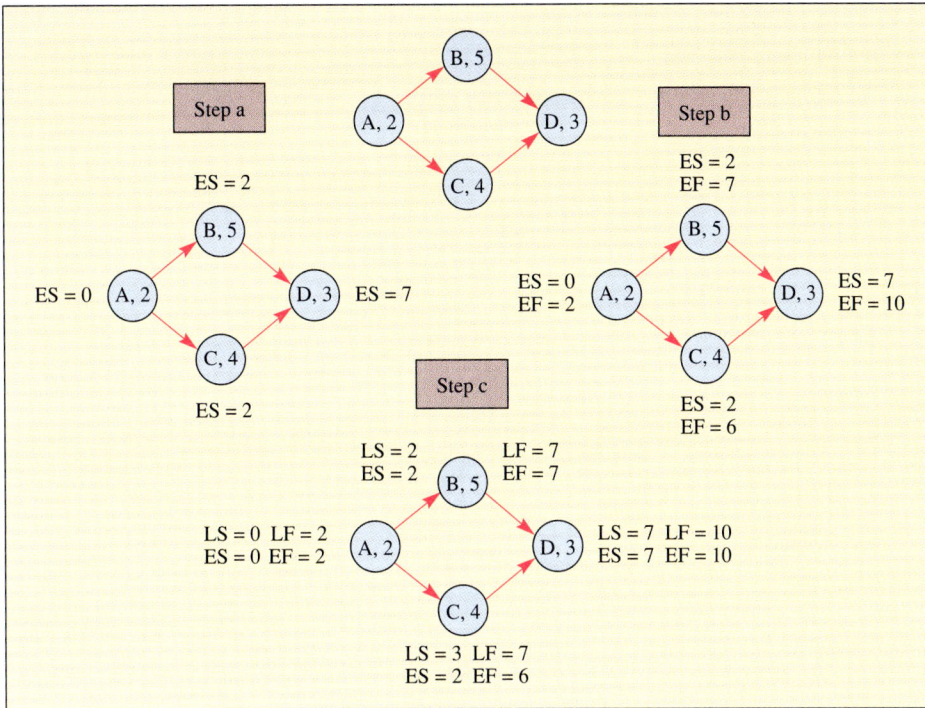

E X H I B I T 12.4

Steps to Develop and Solve a CPM Network

12.4, Step b). In practice, one computes ES and EF together while proceeding through the network. Since ES plus activity time equals EF, the EF becomes the ES of the following event, and so forth.

c. Find late start and late finish times. While the procedure for making these calculations can be presented in mathematical form, the concept is much easier to explain and understand if it is presented in an intuitive way. The basic approach is to start at the end of the project with some desired or assumed completion time. Working back toward the beginning, one activity at a time, we determine how long the starting of this activity may be delayed without affecting the start of the one that follows it.

In reference to the sample network in Exhibit 12.4, Step c, let us assume that the late finish time for the project is equal to the early finish time for activity D, that is, 10. If this is the case, the latest possible starting time for D is 10 − 3, or 7. The latest time C can finish without delaying the LS of D is 7, which means that C's LS is 7 − 4, or 3. The latest time B can finish without delaying the LS of D is also 7, which means that B's LS is 7 − 5, or 2. Since A precedes two activities, the choice of LS and LF values depends on which of those activities must be started first. Clearly, B determines the LF for A since its LS is 2, whereas C can be delayed one day without extending the project. Finally, since A must be finished by day 2, it cannot start any later than day 0, so its LS is 0.

d. Determine slack time for each activity. Slack for each activity is defined as either LS − ES or LF − EF. In this example, only activity C has slack (one day) so the critical path is A, B, D. ■

Early Start and Late Start Schedules An **early start schedule** is one that lists all of the activities by their early start times. For activities not on the critical path, there is slack time between the activity completion and the start of the next activity that suc-

E X H I B I T 12.5   *CPM Network for Computer Design Project*

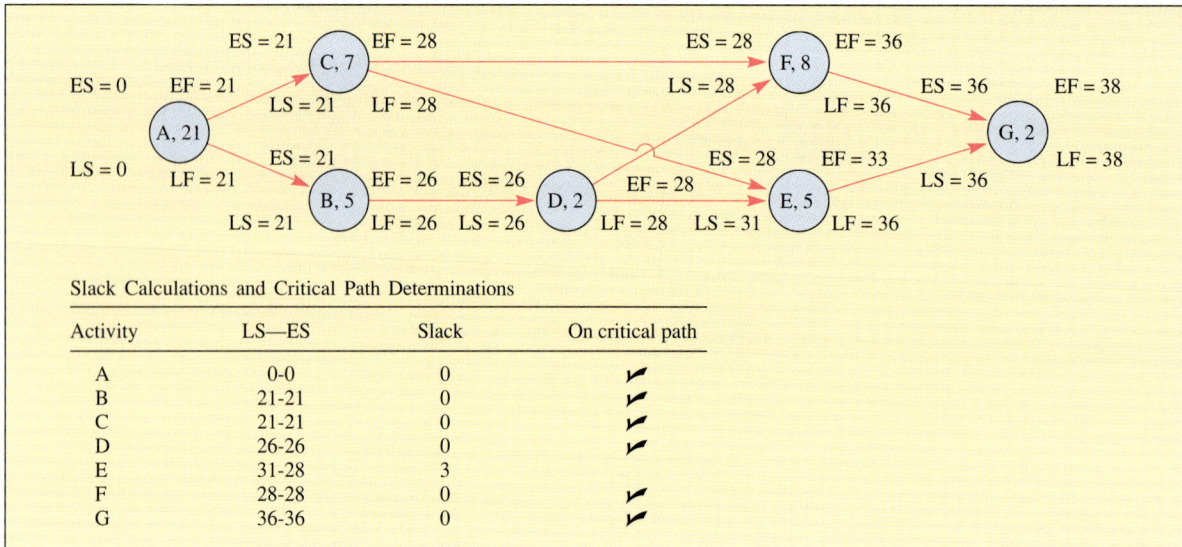

Slack Calculations and Critical Path Determinations

Activity	LS—ES	Slack	On critical path
A	0-0	0	✔
B	21-21	0	✔
C	21-21	0	✔
D	26-26	0	✔
E	31-28	3	
F	28-28	0	✔
G	36-36	0	✔

ceeds it. The early start schedule completes the project and all of its activities as soon as possible.

A **late start schedule** lists the activities to start as late as possible without delaying the completion date of the project. One motivation for using a late start schedule is that savings are realized by postponing purchases of materials, the use of labor, and other costs until necessary.

Applying CPM to the Computer Design Project   Following through the steps just described, we find the critical path and early and late start times as shown in Exhibit 12.5.

CPM with Three Activity Time Estimates

If a single estimate of the time required to complete an activity is not reliable, the best procedure is to use three time estimates. These three times not only allow us to estimate the activity time but also let us obtain a probability estimate for completion time for the entire network. Briefly, the procedure is as follows: The estimated activity time is a weighted average, with more weight given to the best estimate and less to the maximum and minimum times. The ratio generally used is 4, 1, 1 as shown later. The estimated completion time of the network is computed using basic statistics, which states that the standard deviation of a sequence of events is the square root of the sum of the variances of each event. This is the logic of Z shown in step 7 below. Then, simply by locating Z (the number of standard deviations) in a probability table (as in Appendix E) we obtain the probability of completion.

E X A M P L E 12.2 / *Three Time Estimates*   We use the same information as in Example 12.1 with the exception that activities have three time estimates.

S O L U T I O N

1. Identify each activity to be done in the project.
2. Determine the sequence of activities and construct a network reflecting the precedence relationships.
3. The three estimates for an activity time are

a = Optimistic time: the minimum reasonable period of time in which the activity can be completed. (There is only a small probability, typically assumed to be 1 percent, that the activity can be completed in less time.)

m = Most likely time: the best guess of the time required. Since *m* would be the time thought most likely to appear, it is also the mode of the beta distribution discussed in step 4.

b = Pessimistic time: the maximum reasonable period of time the activity would take to be completed. (There is only a small probability, typically assumed to be 1 percent, that it would take longer).

    Typically, this information is gathered from those people who are to perform the activity.

4. *Calculate the expected time (ET) for each activity.* The formula for this calculation is

$$ET = \frac{a + 4m + b}{6} \tag{12.1}$$

This is based on the beta statistical distribution and weights the most likely time *(m)* four times more than either the optimistic time *(a)* or the pessimistic time *(b).* The beta distribution is extremely flexible; it can take on the variety of forms that typically arise, it has finite end points (which limit the possible activity times to the area between *a* and *b*) and, in the simplified version, permits straightforward computation of the activity mean and standard deviation.

5. *Determine the critical path.* Using the estimated times, a critical path is calculated in the same way as the single time case.

6. *Calculate the variances (σ^2) of the activity times.* Specifically, this is the variance, σ^2, associated with each ET, and is computed as follows:

$$\sigma^2 = \left(\frac{b - a}{6}\right)^2 \tag{12.2}$$

As you can see, the variance is the square of one-sixth the difference between the two extreme time estimates. Of course, the greater this difference, the larger the variance.

7. *Determine the probability of completing the project on a given date.* A valuable feature of using three time estimates is that it enables the analyst to assess the effect of uncertainty on project completion time. The mechanics of deriving this probability are as follows:

   a. Sum the variance values associated with each activity on the critical path.

   b. Substitute this figure, along with the project due date and the project expected completion time, into the Z transformation formula. This formula is

$$Z = \frac{D - T_E}{\sqrt{\Sigma \sigma_{cp}^2}} \tag{12.3}$$

where

       $D =$ Desired completion date for project

      $T_E =$ Earliest expected completion time for the project

   $\Sigma\sigma_{cp}^2 =$ Sum of the variances along the critical path

Activity	Activity Designation	Time Estimates			Expected Times (ET) $\dfrac{a + 4m + b}{6}$	Activity Variances (σ^2) $\left(\dfrac{b - a}{6}\right)^2$
		a	*m*	*b*		
Design	A	10	22	28	21	9
Build prototype	B	4	4	10	5	1
Evaluate equipment	C	4	6	14	7	2⅞
Test prototype	D	1	2	3	2	⅑
Write report	E	1	5	9	5	1⅞
Write methods report	F	7	8	9	8	⅑
Write final report	G	2	2	2	2	0

c. *Calculate the value of Z,* which is the number of standard deviations the project due date is from the expected completion time.
d. Using the value for *Z,* find the probability of meeting the project due date (using a table of normal probabilities such as Appendix E). The *earliest expected completion time* is the starting time plus the sum of the activity times on the critical path.

Following the steps just outlined, we developed Exhibit 12.6 showing expected times and variances. The project network was created the same as we did previously. The only difference is that the activity times are weighted averages. We determine the critical path as before, using these values as if they were single numbers. The difference between the single time estimate and range of three times is in computing probabilities of completion. Exhibit 12.7 shows the network and critical path.

Since there are two critical paths in the network, we must decide which variances to use in arriving at the probability of meeting the project due date. A conservative approach dictates using the path with the largest total variance since this would focus management's attention on the activities most likely to exhibit broad variations. On this basis, the variances associated with activities A, C, E, and G would be used to find the probability of completion. Thus $\Sigma\sigma_{cp}^2 = 9 + 2\frac{7}{9} + \frac{1}{9} + 0 = 11.89$. Suppose management asks for the probability of completing the *project* in 35 weeks. D, then, is 35. The earliest expected completion time was found to be 38. Substituting into the Z equation and solving, we obtain

$$Z = \frac{D - T_E}{\sqrt{\Sigma\sigma_{cp}^2}} = \frac{35 - 38}{\sqrt{11.89}} = -0.87$$

Looking at Appendix E we see that a *Z* value of -0.87 yields a probability of 0.19, which means that the project manager has only about a 19 percent chance of completing the project in 35 weeks. Note that this probability is really the probability of completing the critical path ACEG. Since there is another critical path and other paths that might become critical, the probability of completing the project in 35 weeks is actually less than .19. ■

**Maintaining
Ongoing Project
Schedules**

It is important to keep a project schedule accurate and current. The schedule tracks progress and identifies problems as they occur while corrective time may still be available. It also monitors the progress of cost and is often the basis for partial payments. Yet, schedules are often sloppily kept or even totally abandoned.

Excuses for failing to maintain project schedules include

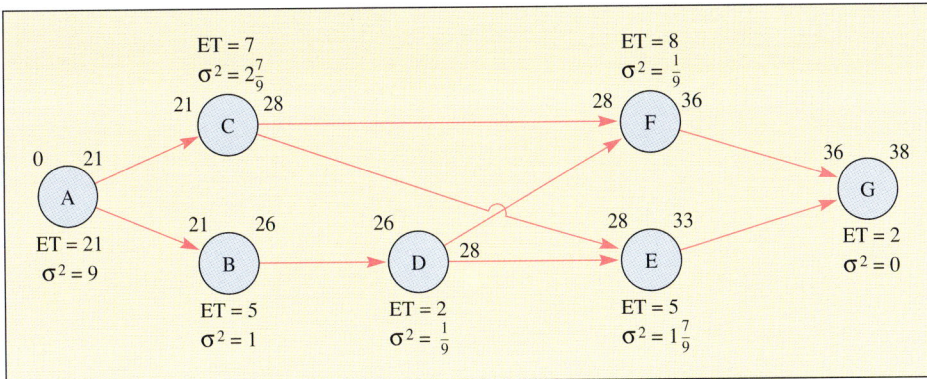

"The project schedule was required by the contractor for us to get the contract, but we don't really need it to operate."

"I don't have the time to send in a report every week and neither do my personnel."

"The time and cost estimates we gave you were only wild guesses anyway, and what do you get when you revise and report on guesses?"

Perhaps the major reason is that managers are not committed enough to the technique to insist that schedules be kept up, with the resulting poor schedules giving project scheduling a bad name. Experience in project scheduling techniques is important so this job should not be carelessly relegated to the closest warm body. The project manager must support the schedule and see to it that it is maintained.

12.6   TIME–COST MODELS

In practice, project managers are as much concerned with the cost to complete a project as with the time to complete the project. For this reason, **time–cost models** have been devised. These models—extensions of PERT and CPM—attempt to develop a minimum-cost schedule for an entire project and to control expenditures during the project.

**Minimum-Cost
Scheduling
(Time–Cost
Trade-off)**

The basic assumption in minimum-cost scheduling is that there is a relationship between activity completion time and the cost of a project. On one hand, it costs money to expedite an activity; on the other, it costs money to sustain (or lengthen) the project. The costs associated with expediting activities are termed *activity direct costs* and add to the project direct cost. Some may be worker-related, such as overtime work, hiring more workers, and transferring workers from other jobs, while others are resource-related, such as buying or leasing additional or more efficient equipment and drawing on additional support facilities.

The costs associated with sustaining the project are termed *project indirect costs:* overhead, facilities, and resource opportunity costs, and, under certain contractual situations, penalty costs or lost incentive payments. Since *activity direct costs* and *project indirect costs* are opposing costs dependent on time, the scheduling problem is essentially one of finding the project duration that minimizes their sum or, in other words, finding the optimum point in a time–cost trade-off.

E X H I B I T 12.8

Example of Time–Cost Trade-off Procedure

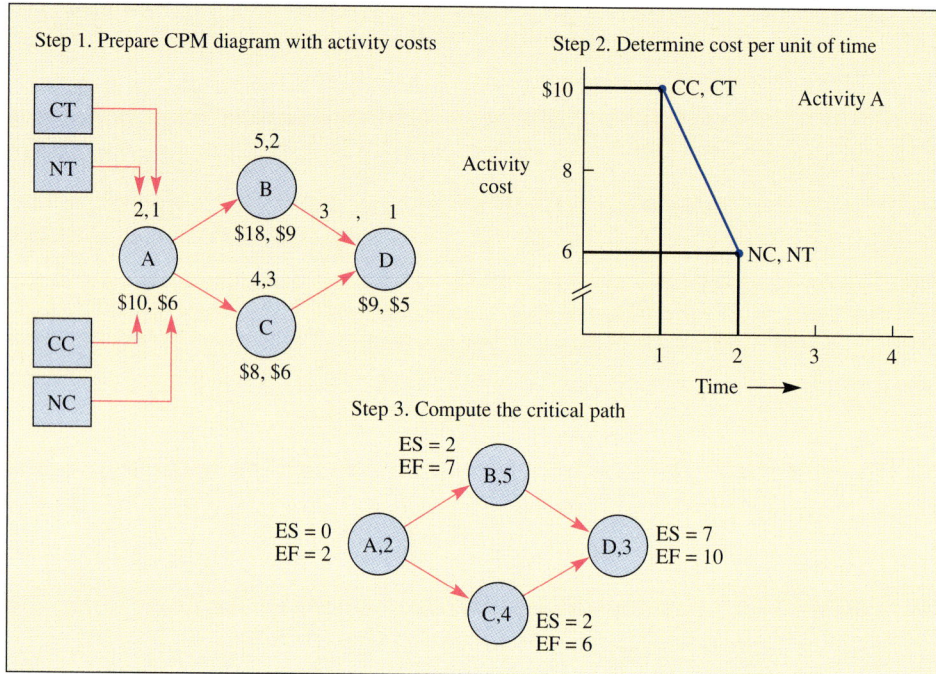

Step 1. Prepare CPM diagram with activity costs

Step 2. Determine cost per unit of time

Step 3. Compute the critical path

The procedure for finding this point consists of the following five steps; it is explained by using the simple four-activity network that we expanded from Exhibit 12.4 and it is shown in Exhibit 12.8. Assume that the indirect costs remain constant for eight days and then increase at the rate of $5 per day.

1. *Prepare a CPM-type network diagram.* For each activity this diagram should list
   a. Normal cost (NC): the lowest expected activity cost. (These are the lesser of the cost figures shown under each node in Exhibit 12.8.)
   b. Normal time (NT): the time associated with each normal cost.
   c. Crash time (CT): the shortest possible activity time.
   d. Crash cost (CC): the cost associated with each crash time.

2. *Determine the cost per unit of time (assume days) to expedite each activity.* The relationship between activity time and cost may be shown graphically by plotting CC and CT coordinates and connecting them to the NC and NT coordinates by a concave, convex, or straight line—or some other form, depending on the actual cost structure of activity performance, as in Exhibit 12.8. For activity A, we assume a linear relationship between time and cost. This assumption is common in practice and helps us derive the cost per day to expedite since this value may be found directly by taking the slope of the line using the formula Slope = (CC − NC) ÷ (NT − CT). (When the assumption of linearity cannot be made, the cost of expediting must be determined graphically for each day the activity may be shortened.)

The calculations needed to obtain the cost of expediting the remaining activities are shown in Exhibit 12.9.

3. *Compute the critical path.* For the simple network we have been using, this schedule would take 10 days. The critical path is A, B, D.

Activity	CC − NC	NT − CT	$\dfrac{CC - NC}{NT - CT}$	Cost per Day to Expedite	Number of Days Activity May Be Shortened
A	$10 − $6	2 − 1	$\dfrac{\$10 - \$6}{2 - 1}$	$4	1
B	$18 − $9	5 − 2	$\dfrac{\$18 - \$9}{5 - 2}$	$3	3
C	$ 8 − $6	4 − 3	$\dfrac{\$8 - \$6}{4 - 3}$	$2	1
D	$ 9 − $5	3 − 1	$\dfrac{\$9 - \$5}{3 - 1}$	$2	2

Current Critical Path	Remaining Number of Days Activity May Be Shortened	Cost per Day to Expedite Each Activity	Least Cost Activity to Expedite	Total Cost of All Activities in Network	Project Completion Time
ABD	All activity times and costs are normal.			$26	10
ABD	A–1, B–3, D–2	A–4, B–3, D–2	D	28	9
ABD	A–1, B–3, D–1	A–4, B–3, D–2	D	30	8
ABD	A–1, B–3	A–4, B–3	B	33	7
ABCD	A–1, B–2, C–1	A–4, B–3, C–2	A*	37	6
ABCD	B–2, C–1	B–3, C–2	B&C†	42	5
ABCD	B–1	B–3	B	45	5

*To reduce the critical path by one day, reduce either A alone, or B and C together at the same time (since either B or C by itself just modifies the critical path without shortening it).
†B&C must be crashed together to reduce the path by one day.

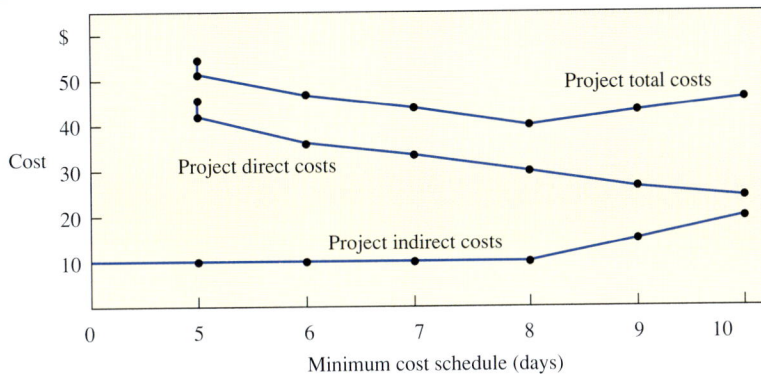

4. *Shorten the critical path at the least cost.* The easiest way to proceed is to start with the normal schedule, find the critical path, and reduce the path time by one day using the lowest-cost activity. Then recompute and find the new critical path and reduce it by one day also. Repeat this procedure until the time of completion is satisfactory, or until there can be no further reduction in the project completion time. Exhibit 12.10 shows the reduction of the network one day at a time.

5. *Plot project direct, indirect, and total-cost curves and find minimum-cost schedule.* Exhibit 12.11 shows the indirect cost plotted as a constant $10 per day for eight days and increasing $5 per day thereafter. The direct costs are plotted from Exhibit 12.10 and the total project cost is shown as the total of the two costs.

Summing the values for direct and indirect costs for each day yields the project total cost curve. As you can see, this curve is at its minimum with an eight-day schedule, which costs $40 ($30 direct + $10 indirect).

12.7   MANAGING RESOURCES

In addition to scheduling each task, we must assign resources. Modern software quickly highlights overallocations—situations in which allocations exceed resources.

To resolve overallocations manually, you can either add resources or reschedule. Moving a task within its slack can free up resources.

Mid- to high-level project management information systems software (PMIS) can resolve overallocations through a "leveling" feature. Several rules of thumb can be used. You can specify that low-priority tasks should be delayed until higher-priority ones are complete, or that the project end before or after the original deadline.

12.8   TRACKING PROGRESS

The real action starts after the project gets underway. Actual progress will differ from your original, or baseline, planned progress. Software can hold several different baseline plans, so you can compare monthly snapshots.

A *tracking Gantt chart* superimposes the current schedule onto a baseline plan so deviations are easily noticed. If you prefer, a spreadsheet view of the same information could be output. Deviations between planned start/finish and newly scheduled start/finish also appear, and a "slipping filter" can be applied to highlight or output only those tasks that are scheduled to finish at a later date than the planned baseline.

Management by exception can also be applied to find deviations between budgeted costs and actual costs.

12.9   PICKING ON PERT AND CPM

Several assumptions need to be made to use project networks and CPM or PERT analysis. This section summarizes some significant assumptions and their criticisms. One particularly difficult point for operating personnel is understanding the statistics when three time estimates are used. The beta distribution of activity times, the three time estimates, the activity variances, and the use of normal distribution to arrive at project completion probabilities are all potential sources of misunderstandings, and with misunderstanding comes distrust and obstruction. Thus, management must be sure that the people charged with monitoring and controlling activity performance understand the statistics.

1. *Assumption:* Project activities can be identified as entities. (There is a clear beginning and ending point for each activity.)
   Criticism: Projects, especially complex ones, change in content over time so a network made at the beginning may be highly inaccurate later on. Also, the very fact that activities are specified and a network is formalized tends to limit the flexibility that is required to handle changing situations as the project progresses.

2. *Assumption:* Project activity sequence relationships can be specified and networked.
   Criticism: Sequence relationships cannot always be specified beforehand. In some projects, in fact, ordering certain activities is conditional on previous activities. (PERT and CPM, in their basic form, have no provision for treating

Break*through*

Project Management Information Systems in Everyday Use

The 1990s have seen an explosion of interest in the techniques and concepts of project management—with a parallel increase in project management software offerings. A few years ago, there were but a handful of microcomputer-based project management software packages. By 1994, however, there were over 100 such project management information systems—and the use of these tools is proliferating exponentially. Within our own MBA-level project management classes, about half of the students now enter having had some exposure to such software; all leave knowing at least one package and having been exposed to several others (Microsoft Project for Windows, Primavera Project Planner, Time Line, Project Scheduler, Milestone, Schedule Publisher, Texim Project). As recently as the early 1990s, perhaps one student per class would have prior experience with a PMIS, and our only in-class software was incapable of managing costs, leveling resources, or even displaying a PERT or Gantt chart. Here are examples of three PMISs leading this operations breakthrough.

Microsoft Project comes with an excellent on-line tutorial, which is one reason for its overwhelming popularity with project managers tracking midsized projects. This package aids in scheduling, allocating, and leveling resources as well as in controlling costs and producing presentation-quality graphics and reports. Exhibit 12.12 shows a Microsoft Project 4.0 sample plotter output.

If the focus is primarily in scheduling, Kidasa's Milestones, Etc. produces Gantt charts that can even show dependencies among activities. As the project unfolds and schedules need updating, a Gantt chart's activity start or end dates can easily be modified.

Finally, for managing very large projects or programs having several projects, Primavera Project Planner is often the choice. A companion product to Finest Hour (see the Taco Bell case at the beginning of this chapter), Project Planner was selected to track the multihundred-million–dollar rebuilding of the World Trade Center after the terrorist bombing of February 26, 1993. Primavera's Monte Carlo risk analysis program was also used to determine how much time and money were risked under different assumptions.

Ever more user-friendly software will continue to push this operations breakthrough. After all, as Tom Peters' book, *Liberation Management,* points out, complexity and urgency issues dictate that work be handled more and more in a project format. To manage projects, a PMIS is no longer a luxury, but a necessity.

---

this problem, although some other techniques have been proposed that allow the project manager several contingency paths, given different outcomes from each activity.)

3. *Assumption:* Project control should focus on the critical path.
   Criticism: It is not necessarily true that the longest time-consuming path (or the path with zero slack) obtained from summing activity expected time values ultimately determines project completion time. What often happens as the project progresses is that some activity not on the critical path becomes delayed to such a degree that it extends the entire project. For this reason it has been suggested that a "critical activity" concept replace the critical path concept as focus of managerial control. Under this approach, attention would center on those activities that have a high potential variation and lie on a "near-critical path." A near-critical path is one that does not share any activities with the critical path and, though it has slack, could become critical if one or a few activities along it become delayed. Obviously, the more parallelism in a network, the more likely that one or more near-critical paths exist. Conversely, the more a network approximates a single series of activities, the less likely it is to have near-critical paths.

4. *Assumption:* The activity times in PERT follow the beta distribution, with the variance of the project assumed to equal the sum of the variances along the critical path.

E X H I B I T 12.12

Microsoft Project 4.0 Sample Plotter Output

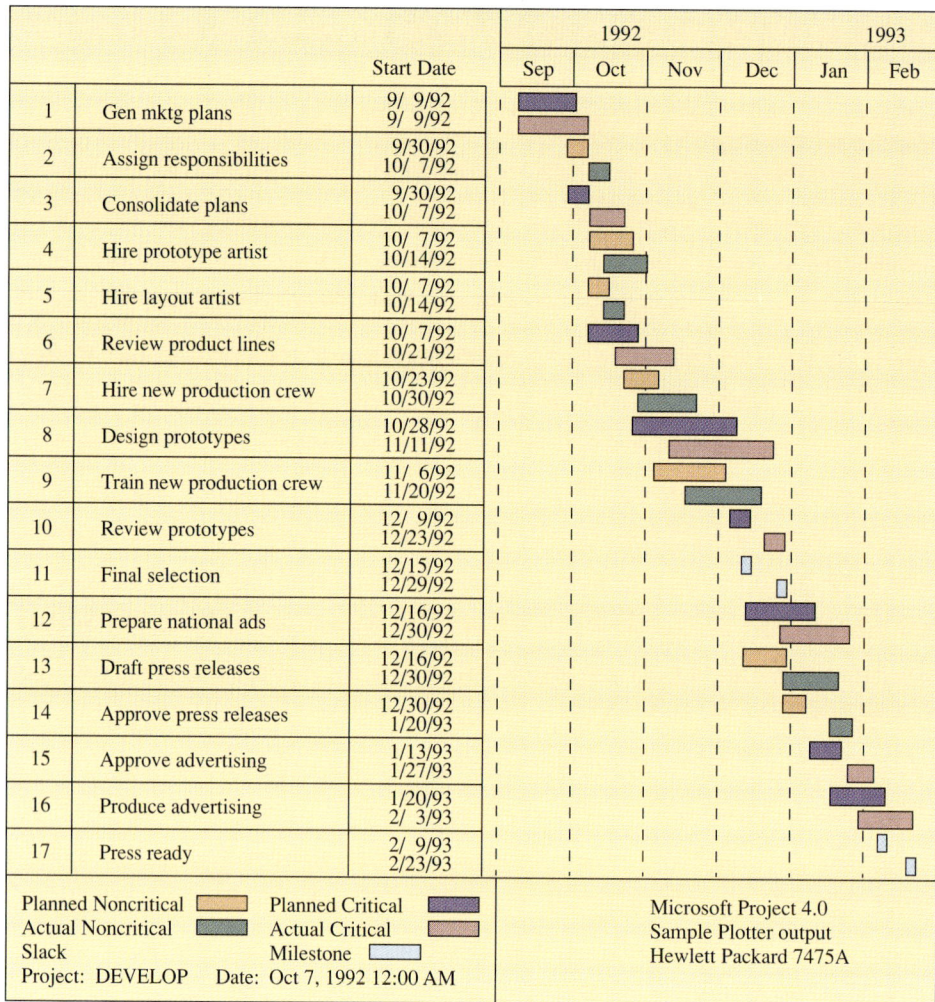

			1992				1993	
		Start Date	Sep	Oct	Nov	Dec	Jan	Feb
1	Gen mktg plans	9/ 9/92 9/ 9/92						
2	Assign responsibilities	9/30/92 10/ 7/92						
3	Consolidate plans	9/30/92 10/ 7/92						
4	Hire prototype artist	10/ 7/92 10/14/92						
5	Hire layout artist	10/ 7/92 10/14/92						
6	Review product lines	10/ 7/92 10/21/92						
7	Hire new production crew	10/23/92 10/30/92						
8	Design prototypes	10/28/92 11/11/92						
9	Train new production crew	11/ 6/92 11/20/92						
10	Review prototypes	12/ 9/92 12/23/92						
11	Final selection	12/15/92 12/29/92						
12	Prepare national ads	12/16/92 12/30/92						
13	Draft press releases	12/16/92 12/30/92						
14	Approve press releases	12/30/92 1/20/93						
15	Approve advertising	1/13/93 1/27/93						
16	Produce advertising	1/20/93 2/ 3/93						
17	Press ready	2/ 9/93 2/23/93						

Planned Noncritical [ ] Planned Critical [ ]
Actual Noncritical [ ] Actual Critical [ ]
Slack Milestone [ ]
Project: DEVELOP   Date: Oct 7, 1992 12:00 AM

Microsoft Project 4.0
Sample Plotter output
Hewlett Packard 7475A

Criticism: Although originally the beta distribution was selected for a variety of good reasons, each component of the statistical treatment has been brought into question. First, the formulas are in reality a modification of the beta distribution mean and variance, which, when compared to the basic formulas, could be expected to lead to absolute errors on the order of 10 percent for ET and 5 percent for the individual variances. Second, given that the activity-time distributions have the properties of unimodality, continuity, and finite positive end points, other distributions with the same properties would yield different means and variances. Third, obtaining three "valid" time estimates to put into the formulas presents operational problems—it is often difficult to arrive at one activity time estimate, let alone three, and the subjective definitions of *a* and *b* do not help the matter. (How optimistic and pessimistic should one be?)

Finally, the cost of applying critical path methods to a project is sometimes used as a basis for criticism. However, the cost of applying PERT or CPM rarely exceeds 2 percent of total project cost. When used with added features of a work breakdown structure and various reports, it is more expensive but rarely exceeds 5 percent of total project costs. Thus, this added cost is generally outweighed by the savings from improved scheduling and reduced project time.

12.10 CONCLUSION

The 1990s have seen an explosion of interest in the techniques and concepts of project management—with a parallel increase in project management software offerings. Although much of this chapter has dealt with networking techniques we would like to emphasize the importance of teamwork. Effective project management involves much more than simply setting up a CPM or PERT schedule. It also requires clearly identified project responsibilities, a simple and timely progress reporting system, and good people-management practices.

Projects fail for a number of reasons. The most important reason is insufficient effort in the planning phase. In addition, the implementation of a project will fail unless the team has the commitment of top management and has a talented project manager.

12.11 FORMULA REVIEW

Expected time

$$ET = \frac{a + 4m + b}{6} \tag{12.1}$$

Variance (σ^2) of the activity times

$$\sigma^2 = \left(\frac{b - a}{6}\right)^2 \tag{12.2}$$

Z transformation formula

$$Z = \frac{D - T_E}{\sqrt{\Sigma \sigma_{cp}^2}} \tag{12.3}$$

12.12 SOLVED PROBLEMS

1. A project has been defined to contain the following list of activities, along with their required times for completion:

Activity	Time (days)	Immediate Predecessors
A	1	—
B	4	A
C	3	A
D	7	A
E	6	B
F	2	C, D
G	7	E, F
H	9	D
I	4	G, H

 a. Draw the critical path diagram.
 b. Show the early start and early finish times.
 c. Show the critical path.
 d. What would happen if activity F was revised to take four days instead of two?

Solution

The answers to *a, b,* and *c* are shown in the following diagram.

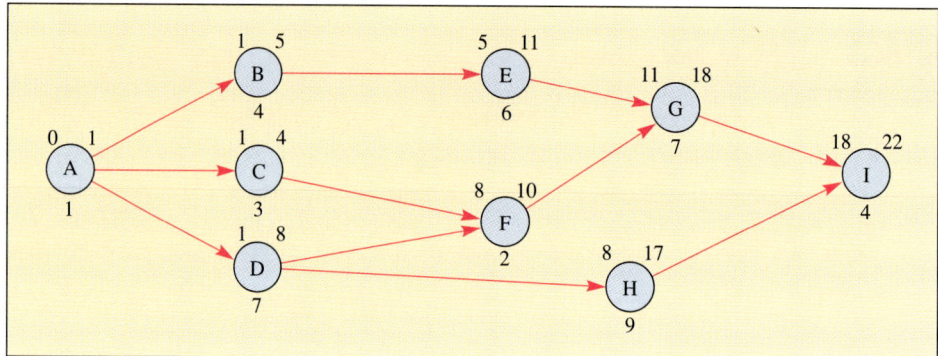

d. New critical path: A, D, F, G, I. Time of completion is 23 days.

2. Here are the precedence requirements, normal and crash activity times, and normal and crash costs for a construction project.

Activity	Preceding Activities	Required Time (weeks)		Cost	
		Normal	Crash	Normal	Crash
A	—	4	2	$10,000	$11,000
B	A	3	2	6,000	9,000
C	A	2	1	4,000	6,000
D	B	5	3	14,000	18,000
E	B, C	1	1	9,000	9,000
F	C	3	2	7,000	8,000
G	E, F	4	2	13,000	25,000
H	D, E	4	1	11,000	18,000
I	H, G	6	5	20,000	29,000

a. What is the critical path and the estimated completion time?

b. To shorten the project by three weeks, which tasks would be shortened and what would the final total project cost be?

Solution

Construction project network is shown below.

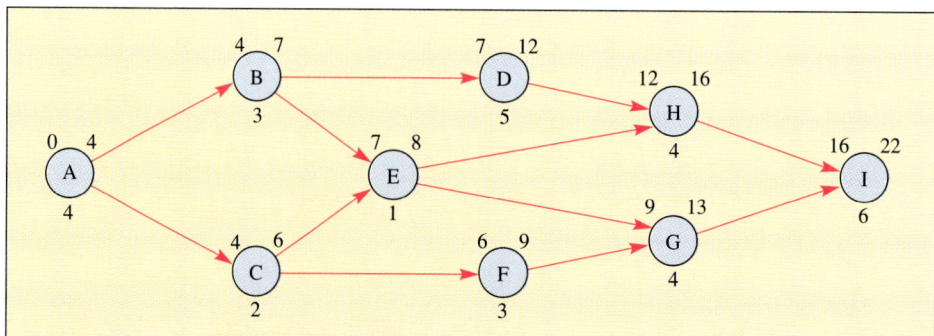

a. Critical path A, B, D, H, I.

Normal completion time is 22 weeks.

b.

Activity	Crash Cost	Normal Cost	Normal Time	Crash Time	Cost per Week	Weeks
A	$11,000	$10,000	4	2	$ 500	2
B	9,000	6,000	3	2	3,000	1
C	6,000	4,000	2	1	2,000	1
D	18,000	14,000	5	3	2,000	2
E	9,000	9,000	1	1		0
F	8,000	7,000	3	2	1,000	1
G	25,000	13,000	4	2	6,000	2
H	18,000	11,000	4	1	2,333	3
I	29,000	20,000	6	5	9,000	1

1. 1st week: CP = A B D H I. Cheapest is A at $500. Critical path stays the same.

2. 2d week: A is still the cheapest at $500. Critical path stays the same.

3. 3d week: Since A is no longer available, the choices are B (at $3,000), D (at $2,000), H (at $2,333), or I (at $9,000).

Therefore, choose D at $2,000.

Total project cost shortened three weeks is

A	$ 11,000
B	6,000
C	4,000
D	16,000
E	9,000
F	7,000
G	13,000
H	11,000
I	20,000
	$ 97,000

12.13 REVIEW AND DISCUSSION QUESTIONS

1. Define project management.

2. Describe or define work breakdown structure, program, project, task, subtask, and work package.

3. What are some reasons project scheduling is not done well?

4. Discuss the graphic presentations in Exhibit 12.2. Are there any other graphic outputs you would like to see if you were project manager?

5. Which characteristics must a project have for critical path scheduling to be applicable? What types of projects have been subjected to critical path analysis?

6. What are the underlying assumptions of minimum-cost scheduling? Are they equally realistic?

7. "Project control should always focus on the critical path." Comment.

8. Why would subcontractors for a government project want their activities on the critical path? Under what conditions would they try to avoid being on the critical path?

12.14 PROBLEMS

1. The following activities are part of a project to be scheduled using CPM:

Activity	Intermediate Predecessor	Time (weeks)
A	—	6
B	A	3
C	A	7
D	C	2
E	B, D	4
F	D	3
G	E, F	7

   a. Draw the network.
   b. What is the critical path?
   c. How many weeks will it take to complete the project?
   d. How much slack does activity B have?

2. American Steam Turbine and Generator Company manufactures electric power generating systems for the major electric power companies. Turbine/generator sets are made to specific order and generally require a three-to-five–year lead time. Costs range from $8 to $15 million per set.

   Management has been planning its production using traditional planning techniques such as planning charts, Gantt charts, and other shop-floor control methods. However, management would now like to introduce CPM project planning and control methods where each turbine/generator set is considered a separate project.

   Here is a segment of the total activities involved in the turbine/generator production:

Activity	Time (weeks)	Immediate Predecessors
a	8	—
b	16	a
c	12	a
d	7	a
e	22	b, c
f	40	c, d
g	15	e, f
h	14	—
i	9	h
j	13	i
k	7	i
l	36	j
m	40	k
n	9	l, m
o	10	g, n

   a. Draw the network.
   b. Find the critical path.
   c. If the project is to be cut by two weeks, show which activities would be on the list to be investigated for cutting performance time.
   d. If the project is to be cut by 10 weeks, show which activities would be on the list to be investigated for cutting performance time.

3. The R&D Department is planning to bid on a large project for the development of a new communication system for commercial planes. The accompanying table shows the activities, times, and sequences required.

Activity	Immediate Predecessor	Time (weeks)
A	—	3
B	A	2
C	A	4
D	A	4
E	B	6
F	C, D	6
G	D, F	2
H	D	3
I	E, G, H	3

  a. Draw the network diagram.
  b. What is the critical path?
  c. Suppose you want to shorten the completion time as much as possible, and have the option of shortening any or all of B, C, D, and G each two weeks. Which would you shorten?
  d. What is the new critical path and earliest completion time?

4. A construction project is broken down into the following 10 activities:

Activity	Preceding Activity	Time (weeks)
1	—	4
2	1	2
3	1	4
4	1	3
5	2, 3	5
6	3	6
7	4	2
8	5	3
9	6, 7	5
10	8, 9	7

  a. Draw the network diagram.
  b. Find the critical path.
  c. If activities 1 and 10 cannot be shortened, but activities 2 through 9 can be shortened to a minimum of one week each at a cost of $10,000 per week, which activities would you shorten to cut the project by four weeks?

5. A manufacturing concern has received a special order for a number of units of a special product that consists of two component parts: X and Y. The product is a nonstandard item that the firm has never produced before, and scheduling personnel have decided that the application of CPM is warranted. A team of manufacturing engineers has prepared the following table:

Activity	Description	Immediate Predecessors	Expected Time (days)
A	Plan production	—	5
B	Procure materials for Part X	A	14
C	Manufacture Part X	B	9
D	Procure materials for Part Y	A	15
E	Manufacture Part Y	D	10
F	Assemble Parts X and Y	C, E	4
G	Inspect assemblies	F	2
H	Completed	G	0

  a. Construct a graphic representation of the CPM network.
  b. Identify the critical path.
  c. What is the length of time to complete the project?
  d. Which activities have slack, and how much?

6. Here is a CPM network with activity times in weeks:

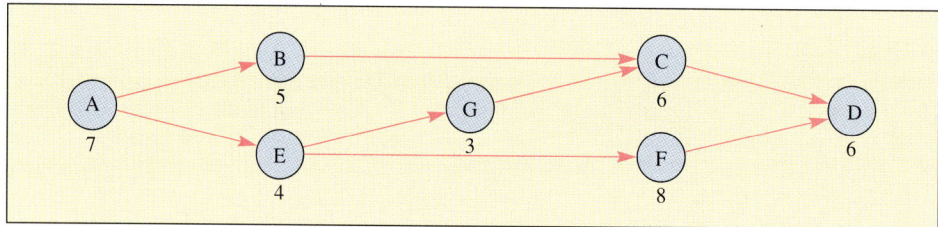

   a. Determine the critical path.
   b. How many weeks will the project take to complete?
   c. Suppose F could be shortened by two weeks and B by one week. How would this affect the completion date?

7. The following table represents a plan for a project:

Job No.	Predecessor Job(s)	*a*	*m*	*b*
1	—	2	3	4
2	1	1	2	3
3	1	4	5	12
4	1	3	4	11
5	2	1	3	5
6	3	1	2	3
7	4	1	8	9
8	5, 6	2	4	6
9	8	2	4	12
10	7	3	4	5
11	9, 10	5	7	8

   a. Construct the appropriate network diagram.
   b. Indicate the critical path.
   c. What is the expected completion time for the project?
   d. You can accomplish any one of the following at an additional cost of $1,500:
      (1) Reduce job 5 by two days.
      (2) Reduce job 3 by two days.
      (3) Reduce job 7 by two days.
      If you will save $1,000 for each day that the earliest completion time is reduced, which action, if any, would you choose?
   e. What is the probability that the project will take more than 30 days to complete?

8. Here is a network with the activity times shown under the nodes in days:

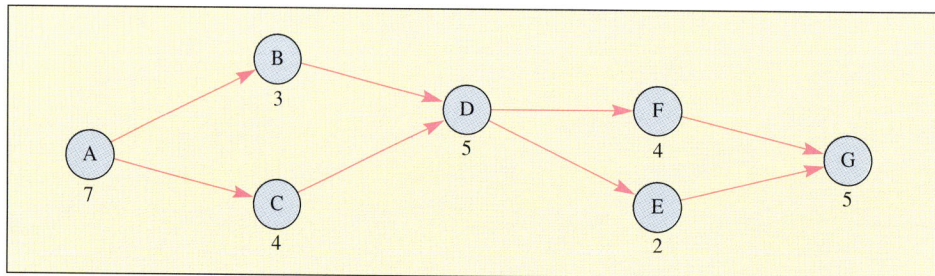

   a. Find the critical path.
   b. The following table shows the normal times and the crash times, along with the associated costs for each activity.

Activity	Normal Time	Crash Time	Normal Cost	Crash Cost
A	7	6	$7,000	$ 8,000
B	3	2	5,000	7,000
C	4	3	9,000	10,200
D	5	4	3,000	4,500
E	2	1	2,000	3,000
F	4	2	4,000	7,000
G	5	4	5,000	8,000

If the project is to be shortened by four days, show which activities in order of reduction would be shortened and the resulting cost.

9. The home office billing department of a chain of department stores prepares monthly inventory reports for use by the stores' purchasing agents. Given the following information, use the critical path method to determine

   a. How long the total process will take.

   b. Which jobs can be delayed without delaying the early start of any subsequent activity.

	Job and Description	Immediate Predecessors	Time (hours)
a	Start	—	0
b	Get computer printouts of customer purchases	a	10
c	Get stock records for the month	a	20
d	Reconcile purchase printouts and stock records	b, c	30
e	Total stock records by department	b, c	20
f	Determine reorder quantities for coming period	e	40
g	Prepare stock reports for purchasing agents	d, f	20
h	Finish	g	0

10. For the network shown:

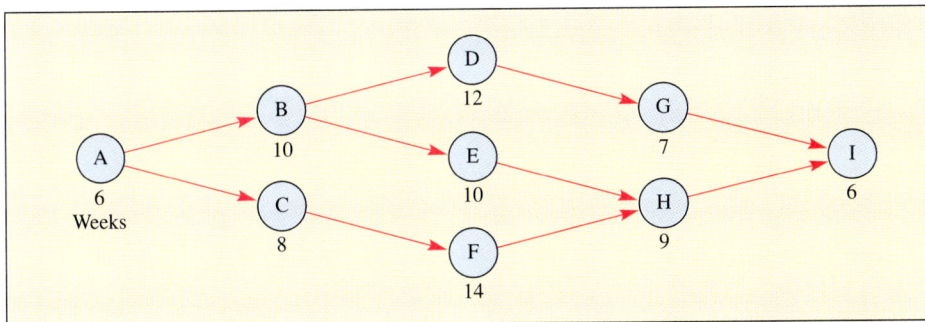

a. Determine the critical path and the early completion time for the project.

Activity*	Normal Time (weeks)	Normal Cost	Crash Time (weeks)	Crash Cost
A	6	$ 6,000	4	$12,000
B	10	10,000	9	11,000
C	8	8,000	7	10,000
D	12	12,000	10	14,000
E	10	10,000	7	12,000
F	14	14,000	12	19,000
G	7	7,000	5	10,000
H	9	9,000	6	15,000
I	6	6,000	5	8,000

*An activity cannot be shortened to less than its crash time.

b. Using the data shown, reduce the project completion time by four weeks. Assume a linear cost per day shortened and show, step by step, how you arrived at your schedule. Also indicate the critical path.

11. The following CPM network has estimates of the *normal time* listed for the activities:

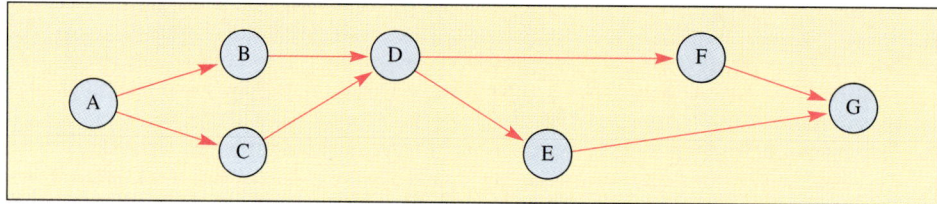

Activity	Time (weeks)
A	7
B	2
C	4
D	5
E	2
F	4
G	5

a. Identify the critical path.
b. What is the length of time to complete the project?
c. Which activities have slack, and how much?
d. Here is a table of normal and crash times and costs. Which activities would you shorten to cut two weeks from the schedule in a rational fashion? What would be the incremental cost? Is the critical path changed?

Activity	Normal Time	Crash Time	Normal Cost	Crash Cost	Possible Number of Weeks Decrease	Cost/Week to Expedite
A	7	6	$7,000	$ 8,000		
B	2	1	5,000	7,000		
C	4	3	9,000	10,200		
D	5	4	3,000	4,500		
E	2	1	2,000	3,000		
F	4	2	4,000	7,000		
G	5	4	5,000	8,000		

12.15   SELECTED BIBLIOGRAPHY

Cleland, David I., and William R. King. *Project Management Handbook.* New York: Van Nostrand Reinhold, 1983.

Goodman, Louis J., and Ralph N. Love. *Project Planning and Management: An Integrated Approach.* New York: Pergamon Press, 1980.

Hughes, Michael William. "Why Projects Fail: The Effects of Ignoring the Obvious." *Industrial Engineering* 18, no. 4 (April 1986), pp. 14–18.

Kerzner, Harold. *Project Management for Executives.* New York: Van Nostrand Reinhold, 1984.

O'Neal, Kim. "Project Management Computer Software Buyer's Guide." *Industrial Engineering* 19, no. 1 (January 1987).

Peterson, P., "Project Management Software Survey." *PMNETwork* 8, no. 5 (May 1994), pp. 33–41.

Rogers, Tom. "Project Management: Emerging as a Requisite for Success." *Industrial Engineering,* June 1993, pp. 42–43.

Smith-Daniels, Dwight E., and Nicholas J. Aquilano. "Constrained Resource Project Scheduling." *Journal of Operations Management* 4, no. 4 (1984), pp. 369–87.

Smith-Daniels, Dwight E., and Vikki L. Smith-Daniels. "Optimal Project Scheduling with Materials Ordering." *IIE Transactions* 19, no. 2 (June 1987), pp. 122–29.

V

THE SYSTEM IN STEADY STATE

The steady-state period is the longest phase of the typical system's life cycle, and managing it constitutes the heart of the operations manager's job. The focus of this period is on production planning and control activities: aggregate planning, inventory control, and scheduling.

For most manufacturers, the steady-state period consists of recurring manufacturing cycles: materials acquisition, fabrication, assembly, testing, and distribution of the end product to field.

For most service firms, the steady-state period consists of daily cycles in which system capacity is made available to the public.

Chapter

13

Aggregate Planning

CHAPTER OUTLINE

KEY TERMS

Long-, Intermediate-, and Short-Range Planning

Master Production Schedule (MPS)

Rough-Cut Capacity Planning

Capacity Requirements Planning

Order Scheduling

Production Rate

Workforce Level

Inventory on Hand

Demand Management

Production Planning Strategies

Pure Strategy

Mixed Strategy

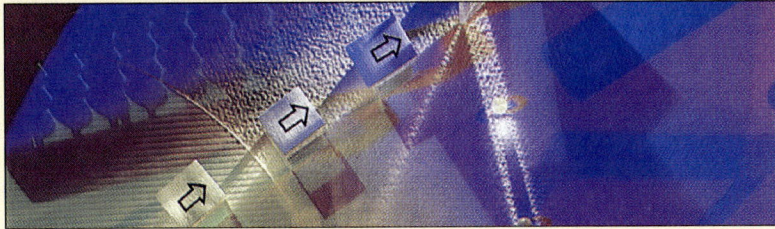

Managing Overtime at Hertz Rental Equipment

Overtime is a critical factor not only in our business but in every service business. All service businesses run overtime, and overtime is expensive because it usually involves a time-and-a-half pay rate. A service business is not like a factory, where under ordinary circumstances you can pretty much plan your scheduling and minimize overtime. In the service industry, scheduling tends to be erratic and operating on overtime is the normal condition. We build this expectation into our planning, and we staff our branches on the assumption that overtime will run at a rate of 10 percent of payroll. The basic reason for this is that customer needs arise and you have to satisfy them or make a customer unhappy and lose the business.

A number of problems (some understandable and others remediable) can cause excessive overtime:

- *A sudden surge in business or unusual repair requirements (unexpected breakage, for example) may have occurred.* If either of these is the case, we accept the situation for what it is.

- *Staffing was inadequate.* The branch may not have enough drivers or mechanics to handle the normal workload, let alone a surge in activity. If we determine that the overtime is due to inadequate staffing, the regional office can authorize the branch manager to increase the size of the workforce.

- *There is a pattern of abuse.* The fact of life is that people get used to overtime as it gets built into their standard of living. A truck driver who has been running 5 to 10 hours overtime on a regular basis won't let that go easily when you try to take it away; the driver will find ways to court that overtime.

We have a lot of younger managers because of our policy of training our own managerial cadre, and many of them find that the hardest thing they have to learn is managing overtime. They are dealing with people who are senior to them, and they are confronted with basic standard-of-living issues, often involving heavy family or similar responsibilities.

Source: Daniel I. Kaplan and Carl Rieser, *Service Success!* (New York: John Wiley & Sons, 1994), pp. 124–126. Reprinted by permission of John Wiley & Sons, Inc.

The problems of managing overtime discussed in the preceding vignette by the president of Hertz Equipment Rental, Daniel I. Kaplan, reflect one of the major areas addressed in aggregate planning. **Aggregate planning** involves translating annual and quarterly business plans into broad labor and output categories for the intermediate term (6 to 18 months). Its objective is to minimize the cost of resources required to meet demand over that period.

13.1   OVERVIEW OF OPERATIONS PLANNING ACTIVITIES

Exhibit 13.1 positions aggregate planning relative to other major operations planning activities presented in the text. The time dimension is shown as long, intermediate, and short range. **Long-range planning** is generally done annually, focusing on a horizon greater than one year. **Intermediate-range planning** usually covers a period from 6 to 18 months, with time increments that are monthly or sometimes quarterly. **Short-range planning** covers a period from one day or less to six months, with the time increment usually weekly.

E X H I B I T 13.1

Overview of Major Operations Planning Activities

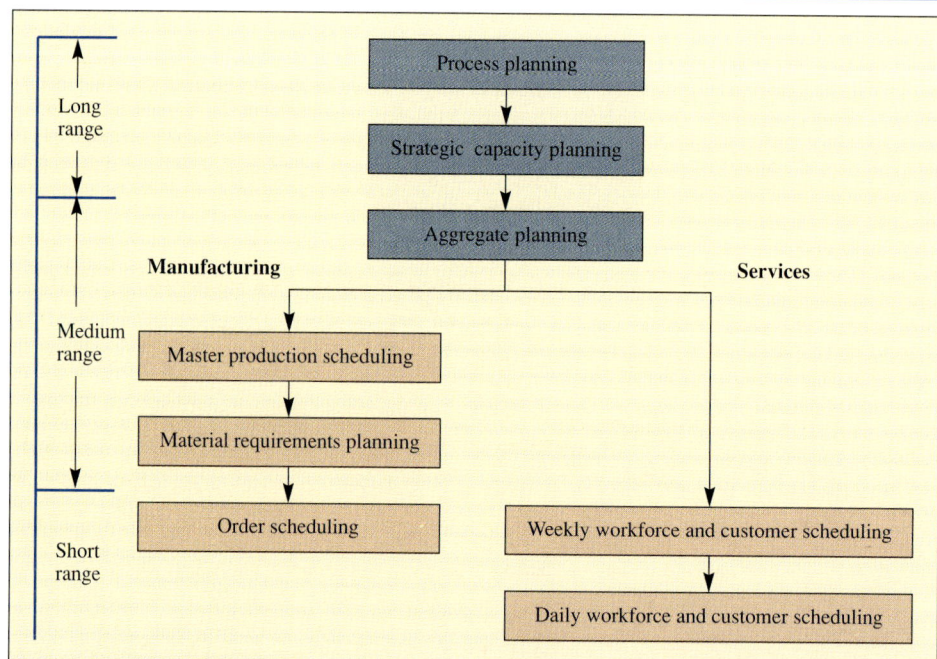

Process planning deals with determining the specific technologies and procedures required to produce a product or service. (See Chapters 3 and 4.) **Strategic capacity planning** deals with determining the long-term capabilities (e.g., size and scope) of the production system. (See Chapter 8.) The aggregate planning process is essentially the same for services and manufacturing, the major exception being manufacturing's use of inventory buildups and cutbacks to smooth production (as we discuss shortly). After the aggregate planning stage, manufacturing and service planning activities are generally quite different.

In manufacturing, the planning process can be summarized as follows: The production control group inputs existing or forecast orders into a **master production schedule (MPS).** The MPS generates the amounts and dates of specific items required for each order. **Rough-cut capacity planning** is then used to verify that production and warehouse facilities, equipment, and labor are available and that key vendors have allocated sufficient capacity to provide materials when needed. As Chapter 15 details, **material requirements planning (MRP)** takes the end product requirements from the MPS and breaks them down into their component parts and subassemblies to create a materials plan. This plan specifies when production and purchase orders must be placed for each part and subassembly to complete the products on schedule. Most MRP systems also allocate production capacity to each order. (This is called **capacity requirements planning.**) The final planning activity is daily or weekly **order scheduling** of jobs to specific machines, production lines, or work centers. (See Chapter 16 for details.)

In services, once the aggregate staffing level is determined, the focus is on workforce and customer scheduling during the week or even hour by hour during the day. Workforce schedules are a function of the hours the service is available to a customer, the particular skills needed at particular times over the relevant time period, and so on. Many service jobs have unique time and legal restrictions affecting scheduling that typical manufacturing work lacks. Airline flight crews are a good example of such constraints that make their scheduling far more complicated than scheduling manufacturing personnel. (Again, see Chapter 16.) Customer (or demand) scheduling deals with setting appointments and reservations for customers to use the service, and assigning priorities when they arrive at the service facility. These obviously range from formal reservation systems to simple sign-up sheets.

We now turn our attention back to manufacturing.

13.2   HIERARCHICAL PRODUCTION PLANNING

We have looked at manufacturing planning activities within a framework of long range, medium range, and short range. If we were to overlay the organization chart of a firm onto Exhibit 13.1, we would note that higher levels within the organization deal with long-range planning and lower levels deal with short-range planning. In a more formal way, Harlan Meal uses the term *hierarchical production planning (HPP)* to tailor the planning structure to the organization.[1] As Exhibit 13.2 shows, higher levels of management would use aggregate data for top-level decisions, while shop-floor decisions would be made using detailed data. In the extreme case HPP logically states that top management should not become involved in determining the production lot size at a machine

---

[1]Harlan C. Meal, "Putting Production Decisions Where They Belong," *Harvard Business Review* 62, no. 2 (March–April 1984), pp. 102–11.

E X H I B I T 13.2

Hierarchical
Planning Process

Decision level	Decision process	Forecasts needed
Corporate	Allocates production among plants	Annual demand by item and by region
Plant manager	Determines seasonal plan by product type	Monthly demand for 15 months by product type
Shop superintendent	Determines monthly item production schedules	Monthly demand for 5 months by item

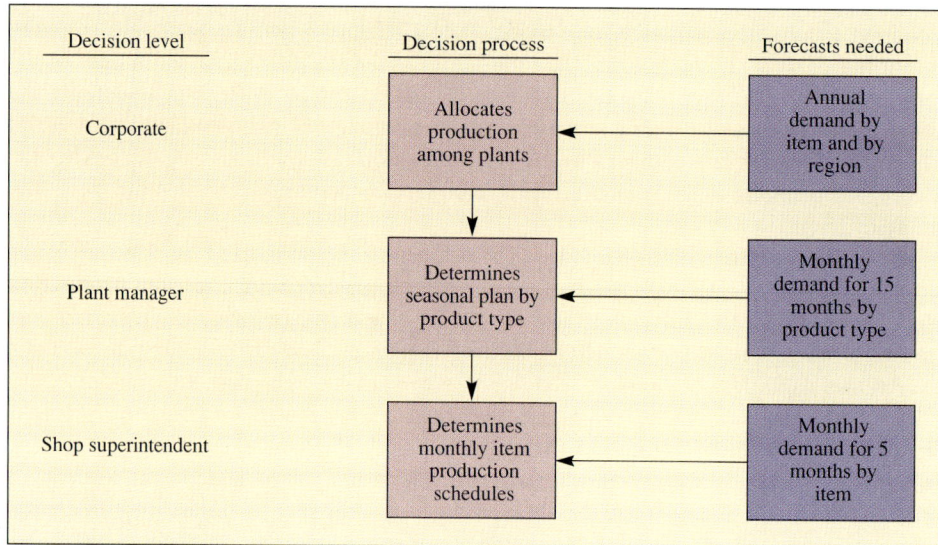

Source: Harlan C. Meal, "Putting Production Decisions Where They Belong," *Harvard Business Review* 62, no. 2 (March–April 1984), p. 104.

center. By the same token, the production line supervisor should not become involved in planning new product lines.

Meal cites as an example a tire manufacturer with several plants. With a *conventional* approach, each plant would tend to build a stock of tires it was confident of selling. An unsatisfactory consequence was that slow-moving items were produced in small quantities during peak season when capacity was scarce.

By centralizing the decision, top managers expected that they could somehow decide which plants would produce which tires in what quantities. This became impossible; not only was the number of detailed variables much too large to review but also it took the decision-making power away from plant management where it rightly belonged.

The hierarchical procedure divided the decision making, with top management allocating tire production among the plants on an annual basis. Plant management in each of the plants would decide on seasonal effects, buildup of inventory, hiring, and so on. Shop management would perform the detailed scheduling of individual items. Shop supervisors, knowing the proportion of time they needed to spend on each product group, could then fill up available capacity.

An advantage of hierarchical planning is that each successive level has a smaller database and a simpler structure.

13.3   AGGREGATE PRODUCTION PLANNING

Again, aggregate production planning is concerned with setting production rates by product group or other broad categories for the intermediate term (6 to 18 months). Note again from Exhibit 13.1 that the aggregate plan precedes the master schedule. *The main purpose of the aggregate plan is to specify the optimal combination of production rate,*

Kawasaki Motors U.S.A. produces utility vehicles, motorcycles, all-terrain vehicles, and Jet Ski watercraft at its plant in Lincoln, Nebraska.

While the corporate plan would specify how many units in each product line, the aggregate plan would determine how to meet this requirement with available resources.

the workforce level, and inventory on hand. **Production rate** refers to the number of units completed per unit of time (such as per hour or per day). **Workforce level** is the number of workers needed for production. **Inventory on hand** is the balance of unused inventory carried over from the previous period.

Here is a formal statement of the aggregate planning problem: Given the demand forecast F_t for each period t in the planning horizon that extends over T periods, determine the production level P_t, inventory level I_t, and workforce level W_t for periods $t = 1, 2, \ldots, T$ that minimize the relevant costs over the planning horizon.[2]

The form of the aggregate plan varies from company to company. In some firms, it is a formalized report containing planning objectives and the planning premises on which it is based. In other companies, particularly smaller ones, "it may take shape in verbal directives or writings on the back of matchbook covers."[3]

The process by which the plan itself is derived also varies. One common approach is to derive it from the corporate annual plan, as shown in Exhibit 13.1. A typical corporate plan contains a section on manufacturing that specifies how many units in each major product line need to be produced over the next 12 months to meet the sales forecast. The planner takes this information and attempts to determine how best to meet these requirements with available resources. Alternatively, some organizations combine output requirements into equivalent units and use this as the basis for aggregate planning. For example, a division of General Motors may be asked to produce a certain number of cars of all types at a particular facility. The production planner would then take the average labor

---

[2]J. M. Mellichamp and R. M. Love, "Production Switching Heuristics for the Aggregate Planning Problem," *Management Science* 24, no. 12 (1978), p. 1242.

[3]M. Nelson, "I Read the Book: The Master Scheduler Did It" (21st Annual American Production and Inventory Control Society Conference proceedings, 1978), p. 666.

hours required for all models as a basis for the overall aggregate plan. Refinements to this plan, specifically model types to be produced, would be reflected in shorter-term production plans.

Another approach is to develop the aggregate plan by simulating various master production schedules and calculating corresponding capacity requirements to see if adequate labor and equipment exist at each work center. If capacity is inadequate, additional requirements for overtime, subcontracting, extra workers, and so forth are specified for each product line and combined into a rough-cut plan. This plan is then modified by cut-and-try or mathematical methods to derive a final and (one hopes) lower-cost plan.

Production Planning Environment

Exhibit 13.3 illustrates the internal and external factors that constitute the production planning environment. In general, the external environment is outside the production planner's direct control, but in some firms, demand for the product can be managed as noted in Chapter 7. In general, there are two primary means for accomplishing **demand management:** (1) *pricing and promotion* and (2) *complementary products.*

Through close cooperation between marketing and operations, promotional activities and price cutting can be used to build demand during slow periods. Conversely, when demand is strong, promotional activities can be curtailed and prices raised to maximize the revenues from those products or services that the firm has the capacity to provide.

Complementary products may work for firms facing cyclical demand fluctuations. For instance, lawnmower manufacturers will have strong demand for spring and summer, but weak demand during fall and winter. Demands on the production system can be smoothed out by producing a complementary product with high demand during fall and winter, and low demand during spring and summer (for instance, snowmobiles, snowblowers, or leafblowers). With services, cycles are more often measured in hours than months. Restaurants with strong demand during lunch and dinner will often add a breakfast menu to increase demand during the morning hours.

But even so, there are limits to how much demand can be controlled. Ultimately, the production planner must live with the sales projections and orders promised by the marketing function, leaving the internal factors as variables that can be manipulated in deriving a production plan. A new approach to facilitate managing these internal factors is termed *accurate response*. This entails refined measurement of historical demand patterns blended with expert judgment to determine when to begin production of particular items. The key element of the approach is clearly identifying those products for which demand is relatively predictable from those for which demand is relatively unpredictable.[4]

The internal factors themselves differ in their controllability. Current physical capacity (plant and equipment) is usually nearly fixed in the short run; union agreements often constrain what can be done in changing the workforce; physical capacity cannot always be increased; and top management may set limits on the amount of money that can be tied up in inventories. Still, there is always some flexibility in managing these factors, and production planners can implement one or a combination of the **production planning strategies** discussed here.

---

[4]Marshall L. Fisher, Janice H. Hammond, Walter R. Obermeyer, and Anath Raman, "Making Supply Meet Demand in an Uncertain World," *Harvard Business Review* 72, no. 3 (May–June 1994), p. 84.

E X H I B I T 13.3   *Required Inputs to the Production Planning System*

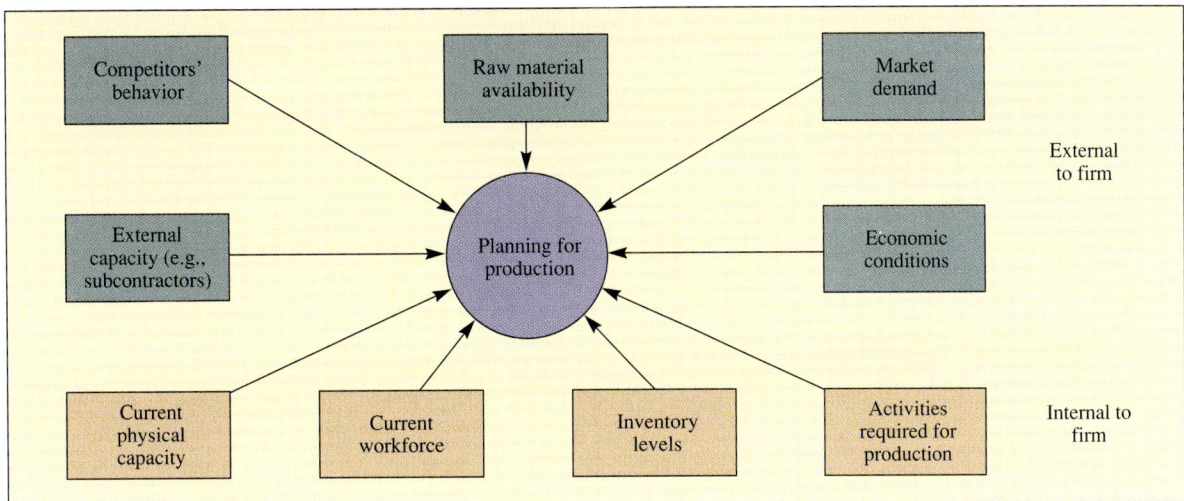

Production Planning Strategies   There are essentially three production planning strategies. These strategies involve trade-offs among the workforce size, work hours, inventory, and backlogs.

1. *Chase strategy.*[5] Match the production rate to the order rate by hiring and laying off employees as the order rate varies. The success of this strategy depends on having a pool of easily trained applicants to draw on as order volumes increase. There are obvious motivational impacts. When order backlogs are low, employees may feel compelled to slow down out of fear of being laid off as soon as existing orders are completed.

2. *Stable workforce—variable work hours.* Vary the output by varying the number of hours worked through flexible work schedules or overtime. By varying the number of work hours, you can match production quantities to orders. This strategy provides workforce continuity and avoids many of the emotional and tangible costs of hiring and firing associated with the chase strategy.

3. *Level strategy.* Maintain a stable workforce working at a constant output rate. Shortages and surpluses are absorbed by fluctuating inventory levels, order backlogs, and lost sales. Employees benefit from stable work hours at the costs of potentially decreased customer service levels and increased inventory costs. Another concern is the possibility of inventoried products becoming obsolete.

When just one of these variables is used to absorb demand fluctuations, it is termed a **pure strategy;** one or more used in combination is a **mixed strategy.** As you might suspect, mixed strategies are more widely applied in industry.

---

[5]No relation to one of the authors of this text.

Subcontracting   In addition to these strategies, managers may also choose to subcontract some portion of production. This strategy is similar to the chase strategy, but hiring and laying off are translated into subcontracting and not subcontracting. Some level of subcontracting can be desirable to accommodate demand fluctuations. However, unless the relationship with the supplier is particularly strong, a manufacturer can lose some control over schedule and quality. For this reason, extensive subcontracting may be viewed as a high-risk strategy.

Relevant Costs

There are four costs relevant to aggregate production planning. These relate to the production cost itself as well as the cost to hold inventory and to have unfilled orders. More specifically, these are

1. *Basic production costs.* These are the fixed and variable costs incurred in producing a given product type in a given time period. Included are direct and indirect labor costs and regular as well as overtime compensation.
2. *Costs associated with changes in the production rate.* Typical costs in this category are those involved in hiring, training, and laying off personnel. Hiring temporary help is a way of avoiding these costs. See the Breakthrough box, "Now You Have Them, Now You Don't."
3. *Inventory holding costs.* A major component is the cost of capital tied up in inventory. Other components are storing, insurance, taxes, spoilage, and obsolescence.
4. *Backlogging costs.* Usually these are very hard to measure and include costs of expediting, loss of customer goodwill, and loss of sales revenues resulting from backlogging.

Budgets   To receive funding, operations managers are generally required to submit annual, and sometimes quarterly, budget requests. Aggregate planning activities are key to the success of the budgeting process. Recall that the goal of aggregate planning is to minimize the total production-related costs over the planning horizon by determining the optimal combination of workforce levels and inventory levels. Thus aggregate planning provides justification for the requested budget amount. Accurate medium-range planning increases the likelihood of (1) receiving the requested budget and (2) operating within the limits of the budget.

In the next section, we provide examples of medium-range planning in both manufacturing and service settings. These examples illustrate the trade-offs associated with different production planning strategies.[6]

13.4   AGGREGATE PLANNING TECHNIQUES

Companies still use simple cut-and-try charting and graphic methods in developing their aggregate plans. A cut-and-try approach involves costing out various production planning alternatives and selecting the one with the lowest cost. In addition, there are more sophisticated approaches, including linear programming, the Linear Decision Rule, and various heuristic methods. Of these, only linear programming has seen broad application; we discuss it later.

---

[6]For an interesting application of aggregate planning in nonprofit humanitarian organizations, see Chwen Sheu and John G. Wacker, "A Planning and Control Framework for Non-profit Humanitarian Organizations," *International Journal of Operations and Production Management* 14, no. 4 (1994), pp. 64–77.

A firm with pronounced seasonal variation normally plans production for a full year to capture the extremes in demand during the busiest and slowest months. But we can illustrate the general principles involved with a shorter horizon. Suppose we wish to set up a production plan for the C&A Company for the next six months. We are given the following information:

Month	Demand Forecast	Number of Working Days
January	1,800	22
February	1,500	19
March	1,100	21
April	900	21
May	1,100	22
June	1,600	20
	8,000 units	125 days

Costs

Materials	$100/unit
Inventory holding cost	$1.50/unit/month
Marginal cost of stockout	$5/unit/month
Marginal cost of subcontracting	$20/unit ($120 subcontracting cost less $100 material savings)
Hiring and training cost	$200/worker
Layoff cost	$250/worker
Labor hours required	5/unit
Straight-line cost (first eight hours each day)	$4/hour
Overtime cost (time and a half)	$6/hour

Inventory

Beginning inventory	400 units

In solving this problem, we can exclude the material costs. We could have included this $100 cost in all our calculations, but if we assume that a $100 cost is common to each demanded unit, then we need only to concern ourselves with the marginal costs. Since the subcontracting cost is $120, our true cost for subcontracting is just $20 because we save the materials.

	(1)	(2)	(3) =	(4) =	(5) =
			.25 × (2)	(2) + (3) − (1)	(1) + (4) − (2)
Month	Beginning Inventory	Demand Forecast	Safety Stock	Production Requirement	Ending Inventory
January	400	1,800	450	1,850	450
February	450	1,500	375	1,425	375
March	375	1,100	275	1,000	275
April	275	900	225	850	225
May	225	1,100	275	1,150	275
June	275	1,600	400	1,725	400
				8,000	

E X H I B I T 13.4

Aggregate Production Planning Requirements

Now You Hire Them, Now You Don't

Across the country, companies of all kinds have been trying to accommodate the demands of a world economy that is highly volatile and yet insistent on strict standards of quality.

In this environment, the full-time payrolls of large corporations have shrunk, and temporary employment has mushroomed. From 1991 to 1993, the number of people working as temporary employees in the United States on any given day grew by 350,000—from approximately 1.15 million to almost 1.5 million, according to the National Association of Temporary Services (NATS), a trade association based in Alexandria, VA.

Even though temporary employment still accounts for only a small percentage of the nation's workforce, its rapid growth has provoked doomsaying from commentators who see in it the severing of a precious bond between employer and employee. Others, like author Tom Peters, scoff at this notion, pointing out that at the beginning of this century, half of all Americans were self-employed. What is happening, they say, is simply the return to an earlier pattern.

The rise in temporary employment can thus be interpreted as a harbinger of an economy with a more entrepreneurial character, in which millions of workers carry their highly portable skills with them from job to job.

Typically, a temporary-help contract provides that a temp will work for an employer for a set period—long enough for the temporary-help company to recover any investment in training. If the employer wants to hire the temp permanently before that period is up, it pays "liquidated damages" to the temporary-help company. Until the past few years, temporary-help companies tried much harder not to lose their workers, NATS' Bruce Steinberg, media relations manager says, but "you can't swim against the tide." The temporary-help companies "are going to accommodate the customer," he says, and increasingly that means that "the selling of temporary help has evolved into human-resource consulting."

Such customer-specific services are the sort of thing that niche companies have always been good at providing, and temporary employment is no exception. In the temporary-employment field, the most striking recent success stories are those of niche companies.

For example, On Assignment, a temporary-help firm in Canoga Park, Calif., grew from $7.4 million in revenues in 1988 to $3?.7 million in 1992; it now fields more than 1,200 scientific professionals, whose average assignment to customers' laboratories is for $3\frac{1}{2}$ months. On Assignment's typical employee is someone with a bachelor's degree in the sciences and less than five years' experience.

On Assignment thrives on the fact that some jobs are temporary by nature. "We work with a food company that does cheese analysis," says H. Tom Buelter, On Assignment's chairman and CEO. "Our people change every four months—not because the job changes, but because after four months, if that person never sees another piece of cheese in front of him, it'll be too soon."

Today, Buelter says, American companies are staffing "for the valleys, and they use a contingent work force to staff for the peaks." With temps available, a company can consider taking on a project that may last only a few months—too short a time to justify going through the expensive and time-consuming process of hiring permanent employees.

As Steinberg says, "The economies of using temporaries come because you're not recruiting; you're not handling the massive interviewing process and filtering out all the people who shouldn't be there in the first place."

Annually, Buelter says, 20 percent of On Assignment's temps move on to permanent jobs. That figure is significantly lower than the average of about one-third for all temporary employees, even though more than 90 percent of On Assignment's temps serve out the full term of their assignments.

That suggests, for one thing, that a sizable number of On Assignment's professionals are in no hurry to move to a permanent job, but it also suggests that their tempo-

Note that many costs are expressed in a different form than typically found in the accounting records of a firm. Therefore, do not expect to obtain all these costs directly from such records, but obtain them indirectly from management personnel, who can help interpret the data.

Inventory at the beginning of the first period is 400 units. Because the demand forecast is imperfect, the C&A Company has determined that a *safety stock* (buffer inventory) should be established to reduce the likelihood of stockouts. For this example, as-

rary employers are building the use of temps into the structure of their companies. "In a company that understands the benefits of using temporary help," Steinberg says, "the amount of temp-to-perm activity is far less than the amount of temporary activity."

As the demand for temporary workers—and highly skilled workers in particular—grows, remaining a temporary worker is becoming a more attractive option for the workers themselves. By making health insurance available (at the employee's expense), for example, companies such as On Assignment are not only attracting high-quality temporaries but are also making it easier for them to continue working *as temps.*

Even the idea that temporary workers are paid only when they work is eroding. "Because there is such a shortage of nurses," Steinberg says, a temporary-help company might pay a nurse for an idle week between assignments.

Buelter foresees a two-tiered system, one tier made up of relatively small, high-margin companies like On Assignment, offering specialized services, and the other consisting of the much larger companies that provide clerical and light-industrial temps.

It seems equally conceivable, though, that temporary employment of all kinds will take on a more professional cast, with temporary workers motivated not so much by loyalty to a particular employer as by loyalty to themselves—and by the close connection between their work and the pay they receive for it. Workers of that kind can fit very easily into a quality-oriented company.

In a large organization, after all, "loyalty" can be a sort of camouflage for the lazy and the incompetent. "Our people do real work," Tom Buelter says, "and that's what's needed in America today—not middle management, not supervisors. Before you hire a temp, you know exactly what they need to do."

Planning for Temporary Help

Think about the kind of temporary-help company you need. Is a specialized niche company most likely to have someone available for the work you have in mind? Or does the work require skills that are in plentiful supply?

If the latter is the case, you may want to look to a large, established company. In any event, you should ask several companies to outline what they can do for you.

Ask each temporary-help company the right questions, such as these: Do you have insurance? Do you check on the progress of your temporaries? How do you recruit your temps? How much training do you give them? What benefits do you offer your temps? What kinds of guarantees does the company offer in case a temporary employee it provides doesn't work out? And don't foreget to ask for references.

When you've settled on a temporary-help company, use it as a consultant. Let it know from the beginning if you're interested in having someone try out for a permanent job. That way, they will only send you people who are interested in such a position.

When you are trying out a temporary worker for permanent employment, evaulate not just the person but also the position itself.

You may hire a full-time temp, for example, and learn that there is only enough work for a part-timer; or vice versa. Or you may learn that the job's responsibilities should be different from what you had planned.

Source: Michael Barrier, "Now You Hire Them, Now You Don't," *Nation's Business,* January 1994, pp. 30–32. Reprinted by permission Nation's Business. Copyright 1994, U.S. Chamber of Commerce.

---

sume the safety stock should be one-quarter of the demand forecast. (Chapter 14 covers this topic in more depth.)

Before investigating alternative production plans, it is often useful to convert demand forecasts into *production requirements,* which take into account the safety stock estimates. In Exhibit 13.4, note that these requirements implicitly assume that the safety stock is never actually used, so that the ending inventory each month equals the safety stock for that month. For example, the January safety stock of 450 (25 percent of January demand

E X H I B I T 13.5 Costs of Four Production Plans

Production Plan 1: Exact Production; Vary Workforce

Month	(1) = (4) in Exhibit 13.4 Production Requirement	(2) = (1) × 5 Hr./Unit Production Hours Required	(3) Working Days per Month	(4) = (3) × 8 Hr./Day Hours per Month per Worker	(5) = (2) ÷ (4) Workers Required	(6) New Workers Hired	(7) = (6) × $200 Hiring Cost	(8) Workers Laid Off	(9) = (8) × $250 Layoff Cost	(10) = (2) × $4 Straight-Time Cost
Jan.	1,850	9,250	22	176	53	0*	—	—	—	$ 37,000
Feb.	1,425	7,125	19	152	47	0	0	6	$1,500	28,500
Mar.	1,000	5,000	21	168	30	0	0	17	4,250	20,000
Apr.	850	4,250	21	168	25	0	0	5	1,250	17,000
May	1,150	5,750	22	176	33	8	$1,600	0	0	23,000
June	1,725	8,625	20	160	54	21	4,200	0	0	34,500
							$5,800		$7,000	$160,000

*Assuming opening workforce equal to first month's requirement of 53 workers.

Production Plan 2: Constant Workforce; Vary Inventory and Stockout

Month	(1) Beginning Inventory	(2) Working Days per Month	(3) = (2) × 8 Hr./Day × 40 Workers* Production Hours Available	(4) = (3) ÷ 5 Hr./Unit Actual Production	(5) = (2) in Exhibit 13.4 Demand Forecast	(6) = (1) + (4) − (5) Ending Inventory	(7) Units Short	(8) = (7) × $5 Shortage Cost	(9) = (3) in Exhibit 13.4 Safety Stock	(10) = (6) − (9) Units Excess	(11) = (10) × $1.50 Inventory Cost	(12) = (3) × $4 Straight-Time Cost
Jan.	400	22	7,040	1,408	1,800	8	0	0	450	0	0	$ 28,160
Feb.	8	19	6,080	1,216	1,500	−276	276	$1,380	375	0	0	$ 24,320
Mar.	−276	21	6,720	1,344	1,100	−32	32	160	275	0	0	$ 26,880
Apr.	−32	21	6,720	1,344	900	412	0	0	225	187	$281	$ 26,880
May	412	22	7,040	1,408	1,100	720	0	0	275	445	667	$ 28,160
June	720	20	6,400	1,280	1,600	400	0	0	400	0	0	$ 25,600
		125						$1,540			$948	$160,000

*(Sum of Col. (4) in Exhibit 13.4 × 5/hr./unit) ÷ (Sum of Col. (2) × 8 hr./day) = (8,000 × 5) ÷ (125 × 8) = 40

Production Plan 3: Constant Low Workforce; Subcontract

	(1) =	(2)	(3) =	(4) =	(5) =	(6) =	(7) =
Month	(4) in Exhibit 13.4 Production Requirement	Working Days per Month	(2) × 8 Hr./Day × 25 Workers* Production Hours Available	(3) ÷ 5 Hr./Unit Actual Production	(1) − (4) Units Subcontracted	(5) × $20 Subcontracting Cost	(3) × $4 Straight-Time Cost
Jan.	1,850	22	4,400	880	970	$19,400	$ 17,600
Feb.	1,425	19	3,800	760	665	13,300	15,200
Mar.	1,000	21	4,200	840	160	3,200	16,800
Apr.	850	21	4,200	840	10	200	16,800
May	1,150	22	4,400	880	270	5,400	17,600
June	1,725	20	4,000	800	925	18,500	16,000
						$60,000	$100,000

*Minimum production requirement. For example, (Col. (1) for April × 6 months × 5 hr./unit) ÷ (Sum of Col. 2 × 8 hr./day) = (850 × 6 × 5) ÷ (125 × 8) = 25 workers.

Production Plan 4: Constant Workforce; Overtime

	(1)	(2)	(3) =	(4) =	(5) =	(6) =	(7)	(8) =	(9) =	(10) =	(11) =	(12) =
Month	Beginning Inventory	Working Days per Month	(2) × 8 Hr./Day × 38 Workers Production Hours Available	(3) ÷ 5 Hr./Unit Regular Shift Production	(2) in Exhibit 13.4 Demand Forecast	(1) + (4) − (5) Units Available before Overtime	From (6) Units Overtime	(7) × 5 Hr./Unit × $6/Hr. Overtime Cost	(3) in Exhibit 13.4 Safety Stock	(6) − (9) Units Excessive	(10) × $1.50 Inventory Cost	(3) × $4 Straight-Time Cost
Jan.	400	22	6,688	1,338	1,800	−62	62	$ 1,860	450	0	0	$ 26,752
Feb.	0	19	5,776	1,155	1,500	−345	340	10,350	375	0	0	23,104
Mar.	0	21	6,384	1,277	1,100	177	0	0	275	0	0	25,536
Apr.	177	21	6,384	1,277	900	554	0	0	225	329	$ 493	25,536
May	554	22	6,688	1,338	1,100	792	0	0	275	517	776	26,752
June	792	20	6,080	1,216	1,600	408	0	0	400	8	12	24,320
								$12,210			$1,281	$152,000

E X H I B I T 13.6

*Comparison of Four
Plans*

Cost	Plan 1: Exact Production; Vary Workforce	Plan 2: Constant Workforce; Vary Inventory and Stockout	Plan 3: Constant Low Workforce; Subcontract	Plan 4: Constant Workforce; Overtime
Hiring	$ 5,800	$ 0	$ 0	0
Layoff	7,000	0	0	0
Excess inventory	0	948	0	$ 1,281
Shortage	0	1,540	0	0
Subcontract	0	0	60,000	0
Overtime	0	0	0	12,210
Straight time	160,000	160,000	100,000	152,000
	$172,800	$162,488	$160,000	$165,491

of 1,800) becomes the inventory at the end of January. The production requirement for January is demand plus safety stock minus beginning inventory (1,800 + 450 − 400 = 1,850).

Now we must formulate alternative production plans for the C&A Company. We investigate four different plans with the objective of finding the one with the lowest total cost.

Plan 1. Produce to exact monthly production requirements using a regular eight-hour day by varying workforce size.

Plan 2. Produce to meet expected average demand over the next six months by maintaining a constant workforce. This constant number of workers is calculated by *averaging* the demand forecast over the horizon. Take the total production requirements for all six months and determine how many workers would be needed if each month's requirements were the same [(8,000 units × 5 hours per unit) ÷ (125 days × 8 hours per day) = 40 workers]. Inventory is allowed to accumulate, with shortages filled from next month's production by back ordering.

Plan 3. Produce to meet the minimum expected demand (April) using a constant workforce on regular time. Subcontract to meet additional output requirements. The number of workers is calculated by locating the minimum monthly production requirement and determining how many workers would be needed for that month [(850 units × 6 months × 5 hours per unit) ÷ (125 days × 8 hours per day) = 25 workers] and subcontracting any monthly difference between requirements and production.

Plan 4. Produce to meet expected demand for all but the first two months using a constant workforce on regular time. Use overtime to meet additional output requirements. The number of workers is more difficult to compute for this plan, but the goal is to finish June with an ending inventory as close as possible to the June safety stock. By trial and error it can be shown that a constant workforce of 38 workers is the closest approximation.

The next step is to calculate the cost of each plan. This requires the series of simple calculations shown in Exhibit 13.5. Note that the headings in each column are different for each plan because each is a different problem requiring its own data and calculations.

The final step is to tabulate and graph each plan and make a comparison of their costs. From Exhibit 13.6 we can see that making use of subcontracting resulted in the lowest cost (Plan 3). Exhibit 13.7 shows the effects of the four plans. This is a cumulative graph illustrating the expected results on the total production requirement.

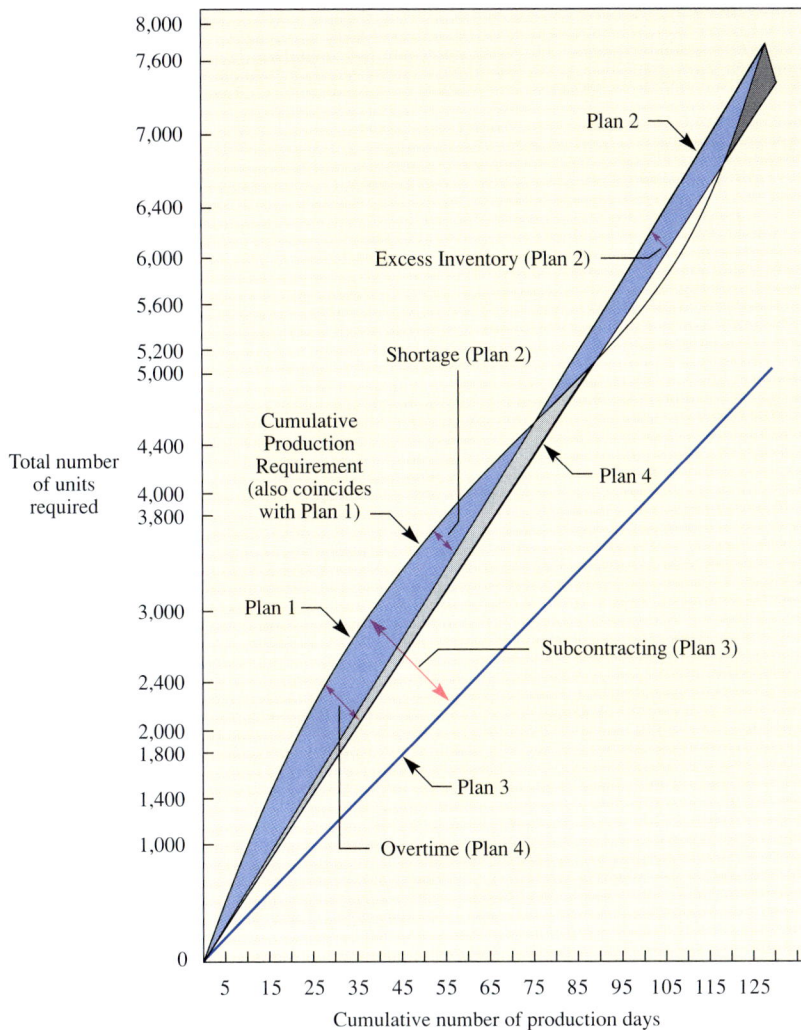

Note that we have made one other assumption in this example: The plan can start with any number of workers with no hiring or layoff cost. This usually is the case since an aggregate plan draws on existing personnel, and we can start the plan that way. However, in an actual application, the availability of existing personnel transferable from other areas of the firm changes the assumptions in this example.

Each of these four plans focused on one particular cost, and the first three were simple pure strategies. Obviously, there are many other feasible plans, some of which would use a combination of workforce changes, overtime, and subcontracting. The problems at the end of this chapter include examples of such mixed strategies. In practice, the final plan chosen would come from searching a variety of alternatives and future projections beyond the six-month planning horizon we have used.

Keep in mind that the cut-and-try approach does not guarantee finding the minimum-cost solution. However, spreadsheet programs, such as Lotus or Excel, can perform cut-and-try cost estimates in seconds and have elevated this kind of what-if analysis to a fine art. More sophisticated programs can generate much better solutions without the user having to intercede, as in the cut-and-try method.

Aggregate Planning Applied to Services: Tucson Parks and Recreation Department

Charting and graphic techniques are also very useful for aggregate planning in service applications. The following example shows how a city's parks and recreation department could use the alternatives of full-time employees, part-time employees, and subcontracting to meet its commitment to provide a service to the city.

Tucson Parks and Recreation Department has an operation and maintenance budget of $9,760,000. The department is responsible for developing and maintaining open space, all public recreational programs, adult sports leagues, golf courses, tennis courts, pools, and so forth. There are 336 full-time-equivalent employees (FTEs). Of these, 216 are full-time permanent personnel who provide the administration and year-round maintenance to all areas. The remaining 120 year-long FTE positions are part-time; about three-quarters of them are used during the summer and the remaining quarter in the fall, winter, and spring seasons. The three-fourths (or 90 FTE positions) show up as approximately 800 part-time summer jobs: lifeguards, baseball umpires, and instructions in summer programs for children. Eight hundred part-time jobs came from 90 FTEs because many last only for a month or two while the FTEs are a year long.

Currently, the only parks and recreation work subcontracted amounts to less than $100,000. This is for the golf and tennis pros and for grounds maintenance at the libraries and veterans cemetery.

Because of the nature of city employment, the probable bad public image, and civil service rules, the option to hire and fire full-time help daily or weekly to meet seasonal demand is out of the question. However, temporary part-time help is authorized and traditional. Also, it is virtually impossible to have regular (full-time) staff for all the summer jobs. During the summer months, the approximately 800 part-time employees are staffing many programs that occur simultaneously, prohibiting level scheduling over a normal 40-hour week. Also, a wider variety of skills are required than can be expected from full-time employees (e.g., umpires, coaches, lifeguards, and teachers of ceramics, guitar, karate, belly dancing, and yoga).

Three options are open to the department in its aggregate planning.

1. The present method, which is to maintain a medium-level full-time staff and schedule work during off-seasons (such as rebuilding baseball fields during the winter months) and to use part-time help during peak demands.

2. Maintain a lower level of staff over the year and subcontract all additional work presently done by full-time staff (still using part-time help).

3. Maintain an administrative staff only and subcontract all work, including part-time help. (This would entail contracts to landscaping firms and pool-maintenance companies as well as to newly created private firms to employ and supply part-time help.)

The common unit of measure of work across all areas is full-time equivalent jobs or employees. For example, assume in the same week that 30 lifeguards worked 20 hours each, 40 instructors worked 15 hours each, and 35 baseball umpires worked 10 hours each. This is equivalent to $(30 \times 20) + (40 \times 15) + (35 \times 10) = 1,550 \div 40 = 38.75$ FTE positions for that week. Although a considerable amount of workload can be shifted to off-season, most of the work must be done when required.

Full-time employees consist of three groups: (1) the skeleton group of key department personnel coordinating with the city, setting policy, determining budgets, measuring performance, and so forth; (2) the administrative group of supervisory and office personnel who are responsible for or whose jobs are directly linked to the direct-labor workers; and (3) the direct-labor workforce of 116 full-time positions. These workers physically maintain the department's areas of responsibility, such as cleaning up, mowing golf greens and ballfields, trimming trees, and watering grass.

Cost information needed to determine the best alternative strategy is

Full-time direct-labor employees	
Average wage rate	$4.45 per hour
Fringe benefits	17% of wage rate
Administrative costs	20% of wage rate
Part-time employees	
Average wage rate	$4.03 per hour
Fringe benefits	11% of wage rate
Administrative costs	25% of wage rate
Subcontracting all full-time jobs	$1.6 million
Subcontracting all part-time jobs	$1.85 million

June and July are the peak demand seasons in Tucson. Exhibits 13.8 and 13.9 show the high requirements for June and July personnel. The part-time help reaches 575 full-time-equivalent positions (although in actual numbers, this is approximately 800 different employees). After a low fall and winter staffing level, the demand shown as "full-time direct" reaches 130 in March (when grounds are reseeded and fertilized) and then increases to a high of 325 in July. The present method levels this uneven demand over the year to an average of 116 full-time year-round employees by early scheduling of work. As previously mentioned, no attempt is made to hire and lay off full-time workers to meet this uneven demand.

Exhibit 13.10 shows the cost calculations for all three alternatives. Exhibit 13.11 compares the total costs for each alternative. From this analysis, it appears that the department is already using the lowest-cost alternative (Alternative 1).

Level Scheduling

In this chapter we looked at four primary strategies for production planning: vary workforce size to meet demand, work overtime and undertime, vary inventory through excesses and shortages, and subcontract.

The just-in-time approach concentrates on keeping a *level production schedule*. A level schedule holds production constant over a period of time. It is something of a combination of the strategies we have mentioned here: For that period it keeps the workforce

E X H I B I T 13.8 *Actual Demand Requirement for Full-Time Direct Employees and Full-Time-Equivalent (FTE) Part-Time Employees*

	Jan.	Feb.	Mar.	Apr.	May	June	July	Aug.	Sept.	Oct.	Nov.	Dec.	Total
Days	22	20	21	22	21	20	21	21	21	23	18	22	252
Full-time employees	66	28	130	90	195	290	325	92	45	32	29	60	
Full-time days*	1,452	560	2,730	1,980	4,095	5,800	6,825	1,932	945	736	522	1,320	28,897
Full-time-equivalent part-time employees	41	75	72	68	72	302	576	72	0	68	84	27	
FTE days	902	1,500	1,512	1,496	1,512	6,040	12,096	1,512	0	1,564	1,512	594	30,240

Note: Some work weeks are staggered to include weekdays, but this does not affect the number of workdays per employee.
*Full-time days derived by multiplying the number of days in each month by the number of workers.

E X H I B I T 13.9

Monthly Requirement for Full-Time Direct-Labor Employees (Other than Key Personnel) and Full-Time-Equivalent Part-Time Employees

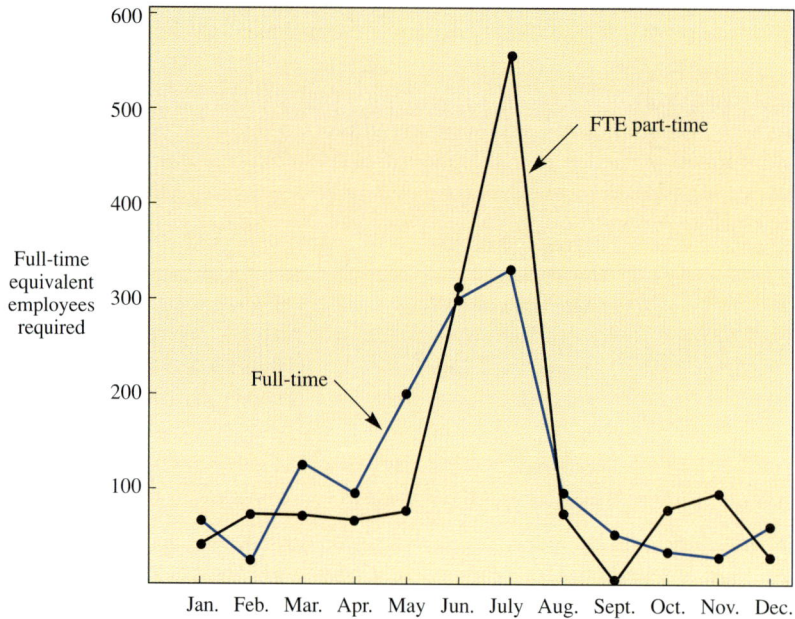

E X H I B I T 13.10   *Three Possible Plans for the Parks and Recreation Department*

Alternative 1: Maintain 116 full-time regular direct workers. Schedule work during off-seasons to level workload throughout the year. Continue to use 120 full-time-equivalent (FTE) part-time employees to meet high demand periods.

Costs	Days per Year (Exhibit 13.8)	Hours (employees × days × 8 hours)	Wages (full-time, $4.45; part-time, $4.03)	Fringe Benefits (full-time, 17%; part-time, 11%)	Administrative Cost (full-time, 20%; part-time, 25%)
116 full-time regular employees	252	233,856	$1,040,659	$176,912	$208,132
120 part-time employees	252	241,920	974,938	107,243	243,735
Total cost = $2,751,619			$2,015,597	$284,155	$451,867

Alternative 2: Maintain 50 full-time regular direct workers and the present 120 FTE part-time employees. Subcontract jobs releasing 66 full-time regular employees. Subcontract cost, $1,100,000.

Cost	Days per year (Exhibit 13.8)	Hours (employees × days × 8 hours)	Wages (full-time, $4.45; part-time, $4.03)	Fringe Benefits (full-time, 17%; part-time, 11%)	Administrative Cost (full-time, 20%; part-time, 25%)	Subcontract Cost
50 full-time employees	252	100,800	$ 448,560	$ 76,255	$ 89,712	$1,100,000
120 FTE part-time employees						
subcontracting cost	252	241,920	974,938	107,243	243,735	
Total cost = $3,040,443			$1,423,498	$183,498	$333,447	$1,100,000

Alternative 3: Subcontract all jobs previously performed by 116 full-time regular employees. Subcontract cost $1,600,000. Subcontract all jobs previously performed by 120 full-time-equivalent part-time employees. Subcontract cost $1,850,000.

Cost	Subcontract Cost
0 full-time employees	
0 part-time employees	
Subcontract full-time jobs	$1,600,000
Subcontract part-time jobs	1,850,000
Total cost	$3,450,000

constant and inventory low, and depends on demand to pull products through. Level production has a number of advantages:

1. The entire system can be planned to minimize inventory and work in process.
2. Product modifications are up-to-date because of the low amount of work in process.
3. There is a smooth flow throughout the production system.
4. Purchased items from vendors can be delivered when needed, and, in fact, often directly to the production line.

Toyota Motor Corporation, for example, creates a yearly production plan that shows the total number of cars to be made and sold. The aggregate production plan creates the system requirements to produce this total number with a level schedule. The secret to success in the Japanese level schedule is *production smoothing*. The aggregate plan is translated into monthly and daily schedules that *sequence* products through the production system. The procedure is essentially this: Two months in advance, the car types and quantities needed are established. This is converted to a detailed plan one month ahead. These quantities are given to subcontractors and vendors so that they can plan on meeting Toyota's needs. The monthly needs of various car types are then translated into daily schedules. For example, if 8,000 units of car type A are needed in one month, along with 6,000 type B, 4,000 type C, and 2,000 type D, and if we assume the line operates 20 days per month, then this would be translated to a daily output of 400, 300, 200, and 100, respectively. Further, this would be sequenced as four units of A, three of B, two of C, and one of D each 9.6 minutes of a two-shift day (960 minutes).

Each worker operates a number of machines, producing a sequence of products. To use this level scheduling technique,

1. Production should be repetitive (assembly-line format).
2. The system must contain excess capacity.
3. Output of the system must be fixed for a period of time (preferably a month).
4. There must be a smooth relationship among purchasing, marketing, and production.
5. The cost of carrying inventory must be high.

E X H I B I T 13.11   *Comparison of Costs for All Three Alternatives*

	Alternative 1: 116 Full-Time Direct Labor Employees, 120 Full-Time Equivalent Part-Time Employees	Alternative 2: 50 Full-Time Direct Labor Employees, 120 Full-Time Equivalent Part-Time Employees, Subcontracting	Alternative 3: Subcontracting Jobs Formerly Performed by 116 Direct Labor Full-Time Employees and 120 FTE Part-Time Employees
Wages	$2,015,597	$1,423,498	—
Fringe benefits	284,155	183,498	—
Administrative costs	451,867	333,447	—
Subcontracting, full-time jobs		1,100,000	$1,600,000
Subcontracting, part-time jobs			1,850,000
Total	$2,751,619	$3,040,443	$3,450,000

E X H I B I T 13.12   *Aggregate Planning by the Transportation Method of Linear Programming*

Production periods (sources)		1	2	3	4	Ending inventory	Unused capacity	Total capacity
			Sales periods					
Beginning inventory		0 — 50	5	10	15	20	0	50
1	Regular time	50 — 700	55	60	65	70	0	700
1	Overtime	75 — 50	80	85	90	95 — 50	0 — 250	350
2	Regular time	X	50 — 700	55	60	65	0	700
2	Overtime	X	75 — 100	80	85	90 — 150	0	250
3	Regular time	X	X	50 — 700	55	60	0	700
3	Overtime	X	X	75 — 100	80	85 — 150	0	250
4	Regular time	X	X	X	50 — 700	55	0	700
4	Overtime	X	X	X	75 — 100	80 — 150	0	250
Total requirements		800	800	800	800	500	250	3,950

6. Equipment costs must be low.

7. The workforce must be multiskilled.

For more about level scheduling, see uniform plant loading in Chapter 6 on just-in-time production systems. Also see the discussion on mixed model line balancing in Chapter 10 on layout.

Mathematical Techniques

Linear Programming   Linear programming (LP) is appropriate to aggregate planning if the cost and variable relationships are linear and demand can be treated as deterministic. For the general case, the simplex method can be used. For the special case where hiring and firing are not considerations, the more easily formulated transportation method can be applied.

The application of an LP transportation matrix to aggregate planning is illustrated by the solved problem in Exhibit 13.12. This formulation is termed a *period model* since it relates production demand to production capacity by periods.[7] In this case, there are four subperiods with demand forecast as 800 units in each. The total capacity available is 3,950 or an excess capacity of 750 (3,950 − 3,200). However, the bottom row of the matrix indicates a desire for 500 units in inventory at the end of the planning period, so unused capacity is reduced to 250. The left side of the matrix indicates the means by which production is made available over the planning period (that is, beginning inven-

---

[7]The analogy used here to the standard transportation problem is that (1) production periods are factories and sales periods are warehouses, (2) wages and holding costs are the transportation costs, and (3) ending inventory and unused capacity are dummy warehouses.

EXHIBIT 13.13

*Additional Factors
That Can Be
Included in the
Transportation
Method for Aggregate
Planning*

1. **Multiproduct production.** When more than one product shares common facilities, additional columns are included corresponding to each product. For each month, the number of columns will equal the number of products, and the cost entry in each cell will equal the cost for the corresponding product.

2. **Backlogging.** The backlog time and the cost of backlogging can be included by treating the shaded assignments in Exhibit 13.12 as feasible. If a product demanded in period 1 is delivered in period 2, this is equivalent to meeting period 1's demand with production in period 2. For, say, a $10 unit cost associated with such a backlog, the cost entry in the cell corresponding to period 2 regular time row and period 1 column will be $60 ($10 plus the $50 cost of regular-time production in period 2).

3. **Lost sales.** When stockouts are allowed and a part of the demand is not met, the firm incurs opportunity cost equal to the lost revenue. This can be included in the matrix by adding a "lost-sales" row for each period. The cost entry in the cell will be equal to lost revenue per unit.

4. **Perishability.** When perishability does not permit the sale of a product after it has been in stock for a certain period, the corresponding cells in the matrix are treated as infeasible. If the product in Exhibit 13.12 cannot be sold after it has been in stock for two periods, the cells occupying the intersection of period 1 rows and columns beyond period 3 will be infeasible.

5. **Subcontracting.** This can be included by adding a "subcontracting" row for each period. Cost values in each cell would be the unit cost to subcontract plus any inventory holding cost (incremented in the same fashion as regular time and overtime costs).

6. **Learning effects.** Learning effects result in increased capacity and lower cost per unit. These changes are incorporated by making corresponding adjustments in capacity (total amount available from source) column and cost entry in the cells.

Source: K. Singhal, "A Generalized Model for Production Scheduling by Transportation Method of LP," *Industrial Management* 19, no. 5 (September–October 1977), pp. 1–6.

tory and regular and overtime work during each period). An X indicates a period where production cannot be backlogged. That is, you cannot produce in, say, Period 3 to meet demand in Period 2. (This is feasible if the situation allows back orders.) Finally, the costs in each cell are incremented by a holding cost of $5 for each period. Thus, if one produces on regular time in Period 1 to satisfy demand for Period 4, there will be a $15 holding cost. Overtime is, of course, more expensive to start with, but holding costs in this example are not affected by whether production is on regular time or overtime. The solution shown is an optimal one. The same allocation and evaluation methods (e.g., the stepping stone method) applied to the transportation problems in the Supplement to Chapter 8 can be applied to the period model.

The transportation matrix is remarkably versatile and can incorporate a variety of aggregate planning factors as described in Exhibit 13.13.

Observations on Linear Programming and Mathematical Techniques   Linear programming is appropriate when the cost and variable relationships are linear or can be cut into approximately linear segments. Regarding application of sophisticated aggregate planning techniques in industry (see Exhibit 13.14), only linear programming has seen wide usage. Commenting on this issue, R. Peterson and E. A. Silver suggest that the answer lies in the decision-making style of management.[8] The basic issue, in their view, is management's attitude toward models in general. Those companies where modeling is a way of life are likely to try the more sophisticated methods; in those where it is not, we would suspect that graphic and charting approaches would be used. Somewhere in the middle ground lie companies that have substantial experience in data processing and use the computer primarily for detailed scheduling. In these firms, we

[8]R. Peterson and E. A. Silver, *Decision Systems for Inventory Management and Production Planning* (New York: John Wiley & Sons, 1979), p. 662.

E X H I B I T   13.14   *Summary Data on Aggregate Planning Methods*

Methods	Assumptions	Technique
1. Graphic and charting	None	Tests alternative plans through trial and error. Nonoptimal, but simple to develop and easy to understand.
2. Simulation of master schedule	Existence of a computer-based production system	Tests aggregate plans developed by other methods.
3. Linear programming—transportation method	Linearity, constant workforce	Useful for the special case where hiring and firing costs are not a consideration. Gives optimal solution.
4. Linear programming—simplex method	Linearity	Can handle any number of variables but often is difficult to formulate. Gives optimal solution.
5. Linear decision rules*	Quadratic cost functions	Uses mathematically derived coefficient to specify production rates and workforce levels in a series of equations.
6. Management coefficients†	That managers are basically good decision makers	Uses statistical analysis of past decisions to make future decisions. Applies, therefore, to just one group of managers; nonoptimal.
7. Search decision rules‡	Any type of cost structure	Uses pattern search procedure to find minimum points on total cost curves. Complicated to develop; nonoptimal.

*Charles C. Holt et al., *Planning Production, Inventories, and Work Force* (Englewood Cliffs, NJ: Prentice Hall, 1960).
†Edward H. Bowman and Robert B. Fetter, *Analysis for Production and Operations Management*, 3rd ed. (Homewood, IL: Richard D. Irwin, 1957).
‡William H. Taubert, "A Search Decision Rule for the Aggregate Scheduling Problem," *Management Science*, February 1978, pp. B343–59.

would expect to see experimentation with alternative cut-and-try plans in developing master schedules.

13.5   CONCLUSION

Remember that aggregate planning translates the corporate strategic and capacity plans into broad categories of workforce size, inventory quantity, and production levels. It does not do detailed planning. It is also useful to point out some practical considerations in aggregate planning.

First, demand variations are a fact of life so the planning system must include sufficient flexibility to cope with such variations. Flexibility can be achieved by developing alternative sources of supply, cross-training workers to handle a wide variety of orders, and engaging in more frequent replanning during high demand periods.

Second, decision rules for production planning should be adhered to once they have been selected. However, they should be carefully analyzed prior to implementation by such checks as simulation of historical data to see what really would have happened if they had been in operation in the past.

13.6   SOLVED PROBLEM

Jason Enterprises (JE) is producing video telephones for the home market. Quality is not quite as good as it could be at this point, but the selling price is low and Jason can study market response while spending more time on R&D.

At this stage, however, JE needs to develop an aggregate production plan for the six months from January through June. As you can guess, you have been commissioned to create the plan. The following information should help you:

	January	**February**	**March**	**April**	**May**	**June**
Demand Data						
Beginning inventory	200					
Forecast demand	500	600	650	800	900	800
Cost Data						
Holding cost		$10/unit/month				
Stockout cost		$20/unit/month				
Subcontracting cost/unit		$100				
Hiring cost/worker		$50				
Layoff cost/worker		$100				
Labor cost/hour—straight time		$12.50				
Labor cost/hour—overtime		$18.75				
Production Data						
Labor hours/unit	4					
Workdays/month	22					
Current workforce	10					

What is the cost of each of the following production strategies?

a. Exact production; vary workforce (assuming a starting workforce of 10).

b. Constant workforce; vary inventory and stockout only (assuming a starting workforce of 10).

c. Constant workforce of 10; vary overtime only.

Solution

    a. Plan 1: Exact production; vary workforce. (Assume 10 in work force to start.)

	(1)	**(2)**	**(3)**	**(4)**	**(5)**	**(6)**
		Production Hours Required	**Hours/Month per Worker**	**Workers Required**	**Workers**	
Month	**Production Required**	**(1) × 4**	**22 × 8**	**(2) ÷ (3)**	**Hired**	**Fired**
January	300	1,200	176	7	0	3
February	600	2,400	176	14	7	0
March	650	2,600	176	15	1	0
April	800	3,200	176	19	4	0
May	900	3,600	176	21	2	0
June	800	3,200	176	19	0	2

	(7)	**(8)**	**(9)**
Month	**Hiring Cost (5) × $50**	**Layoff Cost (6) × $100**	**Straight-Time Cost (2) × $12.50**
January	0	$300	$ 15,000
February	$350	0	30,000
March	50	0	32,500
April	200	0	40,000
May	100	0	45,000
June	0	200	40,000
	$700	$500	$202,500

Total cost for plan:

Hiring cost	$	700
Layoff cost		500
Straight-time cost		202,500
Total		$203,700

b. Plan 2: Constant workforce; vary inventory and stockout only.

	(1)	**(2)**	**(3)**	**(4)**
Month	**Cumulative Production Requirement**	**Production Hours Available 22 × 8 × 10**	**Units Produced (2) ÷ 4**	**Cumulative Production**
January	300	1,760	440	440
February	900	1,760	440	880
March	1,550	1,760	440	1,320
April	2,350	1,760	440	1,760
May	3,250	1,760	440	2,200
June	4,050	1,760	440	2,640

	(5)	**(6)**	**(7)**	**(8)**	**(9)**
Month	**Units Short (1) − (4)**	**Shortage Cost (5) × $20**	**Units Excess (4) − (1)**	**Inventory Cost (7) × $10**	**Straight-Time Cost (2) × $12.50**
January	$ 0	0	140	$1,400	$ 22,000
February	20	400	0	0	22,000
March	230	4,600	0	0	22,000
April	590	11,800	0	0	22,000
May	1,050	21,000	0	0	22,000
June	1,410	28,200	0	0	22,000
		$66,000		$1,400	$132,000

Total cost for plan:

Shortage cost	$ 66,000
Inventory cost	1,400
Straight-time cost	132,000
Total	$199,400

c. Plan 3A: Constant workforce of 10; vary overtime only; inventory carryover permitted.

	(1)	**(2)**	**(3)**	**(4)**
Month	**Production Requirement**	**Standard-Time Production Hours Available 22 × 8 × 10**	**Standard-Time Units Produced (2) ÷ 4**	**Overtime Required in Units (1) − (3)**
January	300	1,760	440	0
February	460*	1,760	440	20
March	650	1,760	440	210
April	800	1,760	440	360
May	900	1,760	440	460
June	800	1,760	440	360
				1,410

Month	(5) Overtime Required Hours (4) × 4	(6) Overtime Cost (5) × $18.75	(7) Straight-Time Cost (2) × $12.50	(8) Excess Inventory Costs (3) − (1) × $10
January	0	0	$ 22,000	$1,400
February	80	$ 1,500	22,000	
March	840	15,750	22,000	
April	1,440	27,000	22,000	
May	1,840	34,500	22,000	
June	1,440	27,000	22,000	
		$105,750	$132,000	$1,400

*600 − 140 units of beginning inventory in February.

Total cost for plan:

Straight-time cost	$132,000
Overtime cost	105,750
Inventory cost	1,400
Total	$239,150

Plan 3B: Constant workforce of 10; vary overtime only; no inventory carryover.

Month	(1) Production Requirement	(2) Standard-Time Hours Available 22 × 8 × 10	(3) Standard-Time Units Produced Min. [(2) ÷ 4; (1)]	(4) Overtime Required in Units (1) − (3)
January	300	1,760	300	0
February	600	1,760	440	160
March	650	1,760	440	210
April	800	1,760	440	360
May	900	1,760	440	460
June	800	1,760	440	360

Month	(5) Overtime Required in Hours (4) × 4 Hours	(6) Overtime Cost (5) × $18.75	(7) Standard-Time Cost (2) × $12.50	(8) Excess Inventory Cost (3) − (1) × $10
January	0	0	$ 22,000	0
February	640	$ 12,000	22,000	
March	840	15,750	22,000	
April	1,440	27,000	22,000	
May	1,840	34,500	22,000	
June	1,440	27,000	22,000	
		$116,250	$132,000	0

Total cost for plan:

Straight-time cost	$132,000
Overtime cost	116,250
	$248,250

Summary.

	Costs					
Plan Description	**Hiring**	**Layoff**	**Straight Time**	**Shortage**	**Excess Inventory**	**Total Cost**
1 Exact production; vary workforce	$700	$ 500	$202,500	—	—	$203,700
2 Constant workforce; vary inventory and shortages		—	132,000	$66,000	$1,400	199,400
3A Constant workforce; vary overtime with carryover of inventory	—	105,750	132,000	—	1,400	239,150
3B Constant workforce; vary overtime (carryover not permitted)	—	116,250	132,000	—	0	248,250

13.7   REVIEW AND DISCUSSION QUESTIONS

1. What is the major difference between aggregate planning in manufacturing and aggregate planning in services?
2. What are the basic controllable variables of a production planning problem? What are the four major costs?
3. Distinguish between pure and mixed strategies in production planning.
4. Define level scheduling. How does it differ from the pure strategies in production planning?
5. Compare the best plans in the C&A Company and the Tucson Parks and Recreation Department. What do they have in common?
6. Under which conditions would you have to use the general simplex method rather than the period model in aggregate planning?
7. How does forecast accuracy relate, in general, to the practical application of the aggregate planning models discussed in the chapter?
8. In which way does the time horizon chosen for an aggregate plan determine whether it is the best plan for the firm?

13.8   PROBLEMS

1. For the Solved Problem, devise the least costly plan you can. You may choose your starting workforce level.
2. Assume that Alan Industries has purchased Jason Enterprises (see the Solved Problem) and has instituted Japanese-style management in which workers are guaranteed a job for life (with no layoffs). Based on the data in Problem 1 (and additional information provided here), develop a production plan using the transportation method of linear programming. To keep things simple, plan for the first three months only and convert costs from hours to units in your model. Additional information: overtime is limited to 11 units per month per worker, and up to 5 units per month may be subcontracted at a cost of $100 per unit.
3. Develop a production plan and calculate the annual cost for a firm whose demand forecast is fall, 10,000; winter, 8,000; spring, 7,000; summer, 12,000. Inventory at the beginning of fall is 500 units. At the beginning of fall you currently have 30 workers, but you plan to hire temporary workers at the beginning of summer and lay them off at the end of the summer. In addition, you have negotiated with the union an option to use the regular workforce on overtime during winter or spring if overtime is necessary to prevent stockouts at the end of those quarters. Overtime is *not* available during the fall. Relevant costs are:

hiring, $100 for each temp; layoff, $200 for each worker laid off; inventory holding, $5 per unit-quarter; back order, $10 per unit; straight time, $5 per hour; overtime, $8 per hour. Assume that the productivity is two worker hours per unit, with eight hours per day and 60 days per season.

4. Plan production for a four-month period: February through May. For February and March, you should produce to exact demand forecast. For April and May, you should use overtime and inventory with a stable workforce; *stable* means that the number of workers needed for March will be held constant through May. However, government constraints put a maximum of 5,000 hours of overtime labor per month in April and May (zero overtime in February and March). If demand exceeds supply, then back orders occur. There are 100 workers on January 1. You are given the following demand forecast: February, 80,000; March, 64,000; April, 100,000; May, 40,000. Productivity is four units per worker hour, eight hours per day, 20 days per month. Assume zero inventory on February 1. Costs are: hiring, $50 per new worker; layoff, $70 per worker laid off; inventory holding, $10 per unit-month; straight-time labor, $10 per hour; overtime, $15 per hour; back order, $20 per unit. Find the total cost of this plan.

5. Plan production for the next year. The demand forecast is spring, 20,000; summer, 10,000; fall, 15,000; winter, 18,000. At the beginning of spring you have 70 workers and 1,000 units in inventory. The union contract specifies that you may lay off workers only once a year, at the beginning of summer. Also, you may hire new workers only at the end of summer to begin regular work in the fall. The number of workers laid off at the beginning of summer and the number hired at the end of summer should result in planned production levels for summer and fall that equal the demand forecasts for summer and fall, respectively. If demand exceeds supply, use overtime in spring only, which means that back orders could occur in winter. You are given these costs: hiring, $100 per new worker; layoff, $200 per worker laid off; holding, $20 per unit-quarter; back-order cost, $8 per unit; straight-time labor, $10 per hour; overtime, $15 per hour. Productivity is two worker hours per unit, eight hours per day, 50 days per quarter. Find the total cost.

6. DAT, Inc. needs to develop an aggregate plan for its product line. Relevant data are

Production time	1 hour per unit
Average labor cost	$10 per hour
Workweek	5 days, 8 hours each day
Days per month	Assume 20 workdays per month
Beginning inventory	500 units
Safety stock	One half month
Shortage cost	$20 per unit per month
Carry cost	$5 per unit per month

The forecast for 1995 is

Jan.	Feb.	Mar.	Apr.	May	June	July	Aug.	Sept.	Oct.	Nov.	Dec.
2,500	3,000	4,000	3,500	3,500	3,000	3,000	4,000	4,000	4,000	3,000	3,000

Management prefers to keep a constant workforce and production level, absorbing variations in demand through inventory excesses and shortages. Demand not met is carried over to the following month.

Develop an aggregate plan that will meet the demand and other conditions of the problem. Do not try to find the optimum; just find a good solution and state the procedure you might use to test for a better solution. Make any necessary assumptions.

7. Old Pueblo Engineering Contractors creates six-month "rolling" schedules, which are recomputed monthly. For competitive reasons (they would need to divulge proprietary

design criteria, methods, etc.), Old Pueblo does not subcontract. Therefore, its only options to meet customer requirements are (1) work on regular time; (2) work on overtime, which is limited to 30 percent of regular time; (3) do customers' work early, which would cost an additional $5 per hour per month; and (4) perform customers' work late, which would cost an additional $10 per hour per month penalty, as provided by their contract.

Old Pueblo has 25 engineers on its staff at an hourly rate of $30. Customers' hourly requirements for the six months from January to June are

January	February	March	April	May	June
5,000	4,000	6,000	6,000	5,000	4,000

Develop an aggregate plan using the transportation method of linear programming. Assume 20 working days in each month.

8. Alan Industries is expanding its product line to include new models: Model A, Model B, and Model C. These are to be produced on the same productive equipment and the objective is to meet the demands for the three products using overtime where necessary. The demand forecast for the next four months, in required hours, is

Product	April	May	June	July
Model A	800	600	800	1,200
Model B	600	700	900	1,100
Model C	700	500	700	850

Because the products deteriorate rapidly, there is a high loss in quality and, consequently, a high carryover cost into subsequent periods. Each hour's production carried into future months costs $3 per productive hour of Model A, $4 for Model B, and $5 for Model C.

Production can take place during either regular working hours or during overtime. Regular time is paid at $4 when working cn Model A, $5 for Model B, and $6 for Model C. Overtime premium is 50 percent.

The available production capacity for regular time and overtime is

	April	May	June	July
Regular time	1,500	1,300	1,800	1,700
Overtime	700	650	900	850

a. Set the problem up in matrix form and show appropriate costs.
b. Show a feasible solution.

9. Shoney Video Concepts produces a line of videodisc players to be linked to personal computers for video games. Videodiscs have much faster access time than tape. With such a computer/video link, the game becomes a very realistic experience. In a simple driving game where the joystick steers the vehicle, for example, rather than seeing computer graphics on the screen, the player is actually viewing a segment of a videodisc shot from a real moving vehicle. Depending on the action of the player (hitting a guard rail, for example), the disc moves virtually instantaneously to that segment and the player becomes part of an actual accident of real vehicles (staged, of course).

Shoney is trying to determine a production plan for the next 12 months. The main criterion for this plan is that the employment level is to be held constant over the period. Shoney is continuing in its R&D efforts to develop new applications and prefers not to cause any adverse feeling with the local workforce. For the same reasons, all employees should put in full workweeks, even if this is not the lowest-cost alternative. The forecast for the next 12 months is

Month	Forecast Demand	Month	Forecast Demand
January	600	July	200
February	800	August	200
March	900	September	300
April	600	October	700
May	400	November	800
June	300	December	900

Manufacturing cost is $200 per set, equally divided between materials and labor. Inventory storage cost is $5 per month. A shortage of sets results in lost sales and is estimated to cost an overall $20 per unit short.

The inventory on hand at the beginning of the planning period is 200 units. Ten labor hours are required per videodisc player. The workday is eight hours.

Develop an aggregate production schedule for the year using a constant workforce. For simplicity, assume 22 working days each month except July, when the plant closes down for three weeks' vacation (leaving seven working days). Make any assumptions you need.

10. Develop a production schedule to produce the exact production requirements by varying the workforce size for the following problem. Use the example in the chapter as a guide (Plan 1).

The monthly forecast for Product X for January, February, and March is 1,000, 1,500, and 1,200, respectively. Safety stock policy recommends that half of the forecast for that month be defined as safety stock. There are 22 working days in January, 19 in February, and 21 in March. Beginning inventory is 500 units.

Manufacturing cost is $200 per unit, storage cost is $3 per unit per month, standard pay rate is $6 per hour, overtime rate is $9 per hour, cost of stockout is $10 per unit per month, marginal cost of subcontracting is $10 per unit, hiring and training cost is $200 per worker, layoff cost is $300 per worker, and production worker hours required per unit are 10. Make whatever assumptions are necessary.

CASE

13.9 CASE
XYZ Brokerage Firm

Consider the national operations group of the XYZ brokerage firm. The group, housed in an office building located in the Wall Street area, handles the transactions generated by registered representatives in more than 100 branch offices throughout the United States. As with all firms in the brokerage industry, XYZ's transactions must be settled within five trading days. This five-day period allows operations managers to smooth out the daily volume fluctuations.

Fundamental shifts in the stock market's volume and mix can occur overnight, so the operations manager must be prepared to handle extremely wide swings in volume. For example, on the strength of an international peace rumor, the number of transactions for XYZ rose from 5,600 one day to 12,200 the next.

Managers of XYZ, not unlike their counterparts in other firms, have trouble predicting volume. In fact, a random number generator can predict volume a week or even a month into the future almost as well as the managers can.

How do the operations managers in XYZ manage capacity when there are such wide swings? The answer differs according to the tasks and constraints facing each manager. Here's what two managers in the same firm might say:

Manager A: The capacity in our operation is currently 12,000 transactions per day. Of course, what we should gear up for is always a problem. For example, our volume this year ranged from 4,000 to 15,000 transactions per day. It's a good thing we have a turnover rate; in periods of low volume, it helps us reduce our personnel without the morale problems caused by layoffs. [The labor turnover rate in this department is over 100 percent per year.]

Manager B: For any valid budgeting procedure, we need to estimate volume within 15 percent. Correlations between actual and expected volume in the brokerage industry have been so poor that I question the value of budgeting at all. I maintain our capacity at a level of 17,000 transactions per day.

Why the big difference in capacity management in the same firm? Manager A is in charge of the cashiering operation—the handling of certificates, checks, and cash. The personnel in cashiering are messengers, clerks, and supervisors. The equipment—file cabinets, vaults, calculators—is uncomplicated.

Manager B, however, is in charge of handling orders, an information processing function. The personnel are keypunch operators, EDP specialists, and systems analysts. The equipment is complex: computers, LANs, file servers, and communication devices that link national operations with the branches. The employees under B's control had performed their tasks manually until decreased volume and a standardization of the information needs made it worthwhile to install computers.

Because the lead times required to increase the capacity of the information processing operation are long, however, and the incremental cost of the capacity to handle the last 5,000 transactions is low (only some extra peripheral equipment is needed), Manager B maintains the capacity to handle 17,000 transactions per day. He holds to this level even though the average number of daily transactions for any month has never been higher than 11,000 and the number of

transactions for any one day has never been higher than 16,000.

Because a great deal of uncertainty about the future status of the stock certificate exists, the situation is completely different in cashiering. Attempts to automate the cashiering function to the degree reached by the order processing group have been thwarted because of the high risk of selecting a system not compatible with the future format of the stock certificate.

In other words, Manager A is tied to the "chase demand" strategy, and his counterpart, Manager B in the adjacent office, is locked into the "level capacity" strategy. However, each desires to incorporate more of the other's strategy into his own. A is developing a computerized system to handle the information processing requirements of cashiering; B is searching for some variable costs in the order processing operation that can be deleted in periods of low volume.

Questions

1. What appear to be the primary differences between the departments?
2. Do these differences eliminate certain strategy choices for either manager?
3. Which factors cause the current strategy to be desirable for each manager?
4. What are the mixed or subcontracting possibilities?
5. What are the problems associated with low standardization?

Source: W. E. Sasser, R. P. Olsen, and D. D. Wyckoff, *Management of Service Operations* © 1978, pp. 303–4. Reprinted by permission of Prentice Hall, Englewood Cliffs, New Jersey.

13.10   SELECTED BIBLIOGRAPHY

Fisher, Marshall L., Janice H. Hammond, Walter Obermeyer, and Anath Raman. "Making Supply Meet Demand in an Uncertain World." *Harvard Business Review* 72, no. 3 (May–June 1994) pp. 83–93.

Fisk, J. C., and J. P. Seagle. "Integration of Aggregate Planning with Resource Requirements Planning." *Production and Inventory Management,* 3d quarter 1978, p. 87.

McLeavy, D., and S. Narasimhan. *Production Planning and Inventory Control.* Boston: Allyn & Bacon, 1985.

Monden, Yasuhiro. *Toyota Production System.* Atlanta, GA: Industrial Engineering and Management Press, 1983.

Plossl, G. W. *Production and Inventory Control: Principles and Techniques.* 2d ed. Englewood Cliffs, NJ: Prentice Hall, 1985.

Silver, E. A., and R. Peterson. *Decision Systems for Inventory Management and Production Planning.* 2d ed. New York: John Wiley & Sons, 1985.

Smith-Daniels, V., S. Schweikhar and D. Smith-Daniels, "Capacity Management in Health Care Services: Review and Future Research Directions." *Decision Sciences.* 19 (1988), pp. 889–919.

Vollmann, T. E., W. L. Berry, and D. C. Whybark. *Manufacturing Planning and Control Systems.* 3rd ed. Homewood, IL: Richard D. Irwin, 1992.

Wight, Oliver W. *Production and Inventory Management in the Computer Age.* Boston: Cahners, 1974.

Chapter

14

Inventory Systems for Independent Demand

CHAPTER OUTLINE

KEY TERMS

Raw Materials

Finished Goods

Work in Process

Independent and Dependent Demand

Fixed-Order Quantity Models (Q Models)

Fixed-Time Period Models (P Models)

Service Level

Safety Stock

Price-Break Order Quantity

ABC Analysis

Optimal Replenishment System

One-Bin System

Two-Bin System

Inventory Accuracy

Cycle Counting

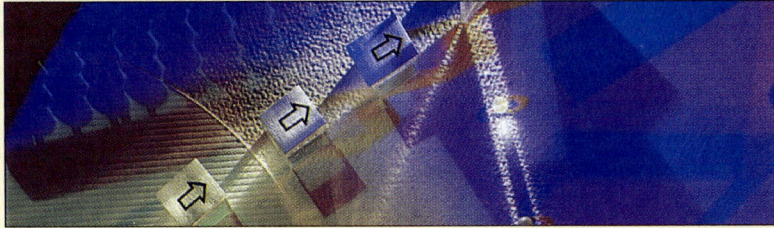

"**I**nventory Chicanery Tempts More Firms, Fools More Auditors," a 1992 *Wall Street Journal* headline announced. The accompanying article continued, "Why do so many accountants fail to warn the public that the companies that they audit are on the verge of collapse? Interestingly, experts are blaming inventory fraud."

The Wall Street Journal article went on to state that the problem worsens when companies struggle during tougher economic times. Shareholders, banks, and other creditors add pressure to show good operating performance and bottom-line profits. Among firms charged with inventory fraud were Laribee Wire Manufacturing, Comptronix, L.A. Gear, Digital Equipment, and Phar-Mor.

While improvements in inventory control and just-in-time production and deliveries are beginning to reduce inventory supplies, inventory is still one of the firm's largest costs in both manufacturing and service sectors. The balance sheet of Boeing Aircraft Company, for example, shows that of $20.45 billion in total assets, inventory constituted $10.485 billion—slightly more than half of all assets. Sales for 1993 totaled $25.438 billion.

Schering-Plough, the pharmaceutical company, also showed heavy investment in inventories. As of December 31, 1993, its inventories came to $404.6 million, with assets of $4.317 billion. Sales for 1993 totaled $4.341 billion.

Boeing's production system is much slower than Schering-Plough's, so there is a proportionally larger investment in inventory compared to sales.

Source: "Inventory Chicanery Tempts More Firms, Fools More Auditors," *The Wall Street Journal,* December 14, 1992, pp. A1, A4; The Boeing Company 1993 Annual Report, p. 39; and Schering-Plough Annual Report 1993.

Question: Why do companies cheat on their inventory?

Answer: Because inventory costs so much and the quickest way to dress up the balance sheet is to fudge on the numbers.

Consider this, the average cost of inventory across all manufacturing in the United States is 30 to 35 percent of its value. For example, if a firm carries an inventory of $20 million, it costs the firm more than $6 million per year. These costs are due to obsolescence, insurance, opportunity costs, and so forth. If the amount of inventory could be reduced to $10 million, for instance, the firm would save over $3 million which goes directly to the bottom line. That is, the savings from reduced inventory shows as increased profit.

In this chapter, we present standard inventory models designed to help management keep the cost down while still meeting production and customer service requirements. Also included are special purpose models, such as price-break, as well as the ABC technique. In addition, we discuss inventory accuracy and show applications of the models in department stores and auto parts supply.

There are conflicting views concerning the teaching of classical inventory models. On one side, articles claim that economic order quantity (EOQ) models are invalid. The other side defends their use. We believe both sides are correct—from within their own arenas. While you must be careful in their application, there certainly are situations in manufacturing where EOQ models can be successfully used. Just-in-time manufacturing (JIT), for example, is based on the classical production–consumption inventory model discussed here. Classical models are quite valid for the many thousands of companies engaged in product and parts distribution.

Concerning JIT and safety stocks, recall that JIT does have safety stock! It shows up as the size of containers and the number of containers between each station in a production sequence. Further, all manufacturers that supply parts cannot have similar JIT schedules. A manufacturer using a JIT system utilizing twice-per-day deliveries by a supplier to the production line might be surprised that the supplier produces those supplies a month's worth at a time using an EOQ formula! How we compute inventory requirements depends on many factors—all methods are valid given the correct set of circumstances. Therefore, we should become familiar with them all.

14.1   DEFINITION OF INVENTORY

Inventory is the stock of any item or resource used in an organization. An *inventory system* is the set of policies and controls that monitors levels of inventory and determines what levels should be maintained, when stock should be replenished, and how large orders should be.

By convention, manufacturing inventory generally refers to materials entities that contribute to or become part of a firm's product output. Manufacturing inventory is typically classified into **raw materials, finished products, component parts, supplies,** and **work in process.** In services, inventory generally refers to the tangible goods to be sold and the supplies necessary to administer the service.

The basic purpose of inventory analysis in manufacturing and stockkeeping services is to specify (1) when items should be ordered and (2) how large the order should be. Many firms are tending to enter into longer-term relationships with vendors to supply their needs for perhaps the entire year. This changes the "when" and "how many to order" to "when" and "how many to deliver."

14.2   PURPOSES OF INVENTORY

All firms (including JIT operations) keep a supply of inventory for the following reasons:

1. To maintain independence of operations. A supply of materials at a work center allows that center flexibility in operations. For example, because there are costs for making each new production setup, this inventory allows management to reduce the number of setups.

Independence of workstations is desirable on assembly lines as well. The time that it takes to do identical operations will naturally vary from one unit to the next. Therefore, it is desirable to have a cushion of several parts within the workstation so that shorter performance times can compensate for longer performance times. This way the average output can be fairly stable.

2. To meet variation in product demand. If the demand for the product is known precisely, it may be possible (though not necessarily economical) to produce the product to exactly meet the demand. Usually, however, demand is not completely known, and a safety or buffer stock must be maintained to absorb variation.

3. To allow flexibility in production scheduling. A stock of inventory relieves the pressure on the production system to get the goods out. This causes longer lead times, which permit production planning for smoother flow and lower-cost operation through larger lot-size production. High setup costs, for example, favor the production of a larger number of units once the setup has been made.

4. To provide a safeguard for variation in raw material delivery time. When material is ordered from a vendor, delays can occur for a variety of reasons: a normal variation in shipping time, a shortage of material at the vendor's plant causing backlogs, an unexpected strike at the vendor's plant or at one of the shipping companies, a lost order, or a shipment of incorrect or defective material.

5. To take advantage of economic purchase-order size. There are costs to place an order: labor, phone calls, typing, postage, and so on. Therefore, the larger the size of

each order, the fewer the number of orders that need be written. Also, shipping costs favor larger orders—the larger the shipment, the lower the per-unit cost.

For each of the preceding reasons (especially for items 3, 4, and 5) be aware that inventory is costly and large amounts are generally undesirable. Long cycle times are caused by large amounts of inventory and are undesirable as well.

14.3   INVENTORY COSTS

In making any decision that affects inventory size, the following costs must be considered.

1. Holding (or carrying) costs. This broad category includes the costs for storage facilities, handling, insurance, pilferage, breakage, obsolescence, depreciation, taxes, and the opportunity cost of capital. Obviously, high holding costs tend to favor low inventory levels and frequent replenishment.

2. Setup (or production change) costs. To make each different product involves obtaining the necessary materials, arranging specific equipment setups, filling out the required papers, appropriately charging time and materials, and moving out the previous stock of material. In addition, other costs may be involved in hiring, training, or laying off workers, and in idle time or overtime.

If there were no costs or loss of time in changing from one product to another, many small lots would be produced. This would reduce inventory levels, with a resulting savings in cost. One challenge today is to try to reduce these setup costs to permit smaller lot sizes. (This is the goal of a JIT system.)

3. Ordering costs. These costs refer to the managerial and clerical costs to prepare the purchase or production order. Ordering costs included all the details, such as counting items and calculating order quantities.

4. Shortage costs. When the stock of an item is depleted, an order for that item must either wait until the stock is replenished or be canceled. There is a trade-off between carrying stock to satisfy demand and the costs resulting from stockout. This balance is sometimes difficult to obtain, since it may not be possible to estimate lost profits, the effects of lost customers, or lateness penalties. Frequently, the assumed shortage cost is little more than a guess, although it is usually possible to specify a range of such costs.

Establishing the correct quantity to order from vendors or the size of lots submitted to the firm's productive facilities involves a search for the minimum total cost resulting from the combined effects of four individual costs: holding costs, setup costs, ordering costs, and shortage costs.

14.4   INDEPENDENT VERSUS DEPENDENT DEMAND

In inventory management it is important to understand the difference between dependent and independent demand. The reason is that entire inventory systems are predicated on whether demand is derived from an end item or is related to the item itself.

Briefly, the distinction between **independent and dependent demand** is this: In independent demand, the demands for various items are unrelated to each other. For example, a workstation may produce many parts that are unrelated but meet some external demand requirement. In dependent demand, the need for any one item is a direct result of the need for some other item, usually a higher-level item of which it is part.

In concept, dependent demand is a relatively straightforward computational problem. Needed quantities of a dependent-demand item are simply computed, based on the number needed in each higher-level item where it is used. For example, if an automobile company plans on producing 500 cars per day, then obviously it will need 2,000 wheels and tires (plus spares). The number of wheels and tires needed is *dependent* on the production levels and not derived separately. The demand for cars, on the other hand, is *independent*—it comes from many sources external to the automobile firm and is not a part of other products and so is unrelated to the demand for other products.

To determine the quantities of independent items that must be produced, firms usually turn to their sales and market research departments. They use a variety of techniques, including customer surveys, forecasting techniques, and economic and sociological trends, as we discussed in Chapter 7 on forecasting. Because independent demand is uncertain, extra units must be carried in inventory. This chapter presents models to determine how many units need to be ordered, and how many extra units should be carried to provide a specified *service level* (percentage of independent demand) that the firm would like to satisfy.

14.5   INVENTORY SYSTEMS

An inventory system provides the organizational structure and the operating policies for maintaining and controlling goods to be stocked. The system is responsible for ordering and receipt of goods: timing the order placement and keeping track of what has been ordered, how much, and from whom. The system must also follow up to answer such questions as: Has the vendor received the order? Has it been shipped? Are the dates correct? Are the procedures established for reordering or returning undesirable merchandise?

There are two general types of inventory systems: **fixed-order quantity models** (also called the *economic order quantity,* EOQ, and **Q model**) and **fixed-time period models** (also referred to variously as the *periodic* system, *periodic review* system, *fixed-order interval* system, and **P model**).

The basic distinction is that fixed-order quantity models are "event triggered" and fixed-time period models are "time triggered." That is, a fixed-order quantity model initiates an order when the event of reaching a specified reorder level occurs. This event

Classifying Models by Fixed-Order Quantity or Fixed-Time Period

Feature	*Q* **Fixed-Order Quantity Model**	*P* **Fixed-Time Period Model**
Order quantity	*Q*—constant (the same amount ordered each time)	*q*—variable (varies each time order is placed)
When to place order	*R*—when quantity on hand drops to the reorder level	*T*—when the review period arrives
Recordkeeping	Each time a withdrawal or addition is made	Counted only at review period
Size of inventory	Less than fixed-time period model	Larger than fixed-order quantity model
Time to maintain	Higher due to perpetual recordkeeping	
Type of items	Higher-priced, critical, or important items	

may take place at any time, depending on the demand for the items considered. In contrast, the fixed-time period model is limited to placing orders at the end of a predetermined time period; only the passage of time triggers the model.

To use the fixed-order quantity model (which places an order when the remaining inventory drops to a predetermined order point, *R*), the inventory remaining must be continually monitored. Thus, the fixed-order quantity model is a *perpetual* system, which requires that every time a withdrawal from inventory or an addition to inventory is made, records must be updated to ensure that the reorder point has or has not been reached. In a fixed-time period model counting takes place only at the review period. (We will discuss some variations of systems that combine features of both.)

Some additional differences that tend to influence the choice of systems are (also see Exhibit 14.1):

- The fixed-time period model has a larger average inventory since it must also protect against stockout during the review period, *T;* the fixed-quantity model has no review period.

- The fixed-order quantity model favors more expensive items since average inventory is lower.

- The fixed-order quantity model is more appropriate for important items such as critical repair parts since there is closer monitoring and therefore quicker response to potential stockout.

- The fixed-order quantity model requires more time to maintain since every addition or withdrawal is logged.

Exhibit 14.2 shows what occurs when each of the two models is put into use and becomes an operating system. As we can see, the fixed-order quantity system focuses on order quantities and reorder points. Procedurally, each time a unit is taken out of stock, the withdrawal is logged and the amount remaining in inventory is immediately compared to the reorder point. If it has dropped to this point, an order for *Q* items is placed. If it has not, the system remains in an idle state until the next withdrawal.

In the fixed-time period system, a decision to place an order is made after the stock has been counted or reviewed. Whether an order is actually placed depends on the inventory status at that time.

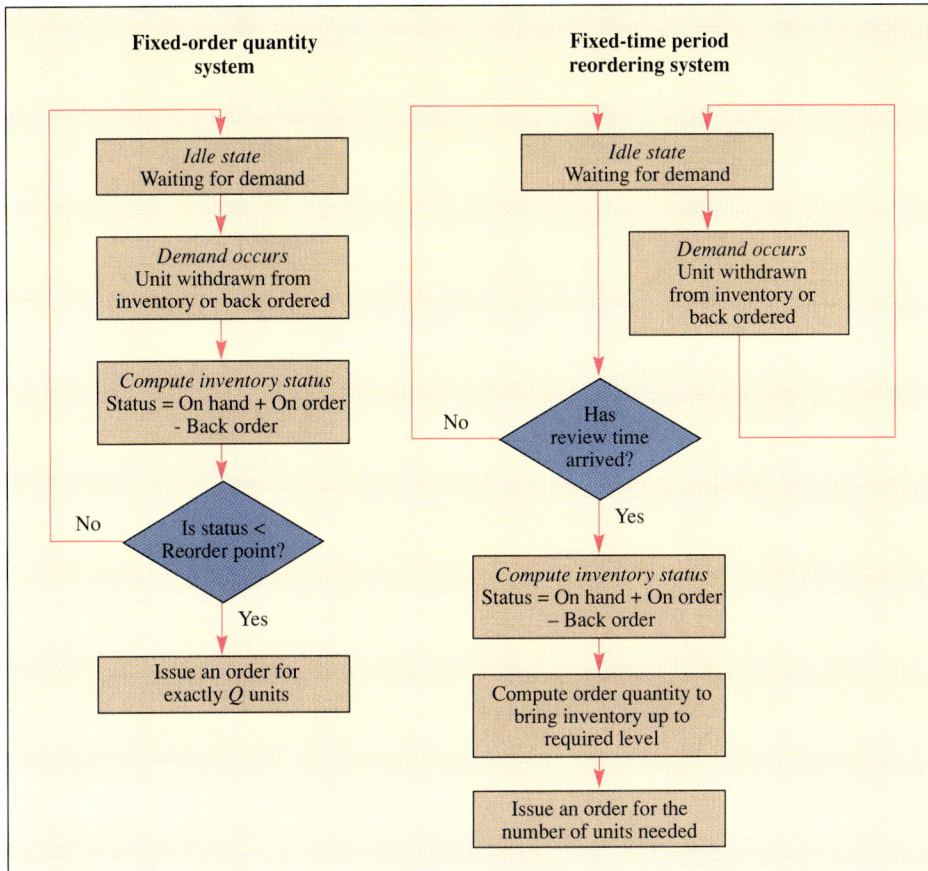

E X H I B I T 14.2

Comparison of Fixed-Order Quantity and Fixed-Time Period Reordering Inventory Systems

14.6   FIXED ORDER QUANTITY MODELS

Fixed-Order Quantity Models   Fixed-order quantity models attempt to determine the specific point, *R*, at which an order will be placed and the size of that order, *Q*. The order point, *R*, is always a specified number of units actually in inventory. The solution to a fixed-order quantity model may stipulate something like this: When the number of units of inventory on hand drops to 36, place an order for 57 more units.

The simplest models in this category occur when all aspects of the situation are known with certainty. If the annual demand for a product is 1,000 units, it is precisely 1,000— not 1,000 plus or minus 10 percent. The same is true for setup costs and holding costs. Although the assumption of complete certainty is rarely valid, it provides a good starting point for our coverage of inventory models.

Exhibit 14.3 and the discussion about deriving the optimal order quantity are based on the following characteristics of the model. These assumptions are unrealistic, but they represent a starting point and allow us to use a simple example.

- Demand for the product is constant and uniform throughout the period.
- Lead time (time from ordering to receipt) is constant.

E X H I B I T 14.3

Basic Fixed-Order
Quantity Model

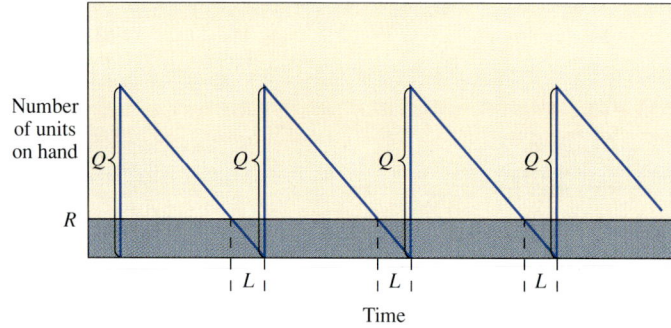

- Price per unit of product is constant.
- Inventory holding cost is based on average inventory.
- Ordering or setup costs are constant.
- All demands for the product will be satisfied. (No back orders are allowed.)

The "sawtooth effect" relating Q and R in Exhibit 14.3 shows that when inventory drops to point R, a reorder is placed. This order is received at the end of time period L, which does not vary in this model.

In constructing any inventory model, the first step is to develop a functional relationship between the variables of interest and the measure of effectiveness. In this case, since we are concerned with cost, the following equation pertains:

$$
\begin{array}{ccccc}
\text{Total} & & \text{Annual} & \text{Annual} & \text{Annual} \\
\text{annual} & = & \text{purchase} + & \text{ordering} + & \text{holding} \\
\text{cost} & & \text{cost} & \text{cost} & \text{cost}
\end{array}
$$

or

$$ TC = DC + \frac{D}{Q}S + \frac{Q}{2}H \qquad (14.1) $$

where

TC = Total annual cost

D = Demand (annual)

C = Cost per unit

Q = Quantity to be ordered (The optimum amount is termed the *economic order quantity*—EOQ—or Q_{opt}.)

S = Setup cost or cost of placing an order

R = Reorder point

L = Lead time

H = Annual holding and storage cost per unit of average inventory (Often, holding cost is taken as a percentage of the cost of the item, such as

H = iC where i is the percent carrying cost.)

On the right side of the equation, DC is the annual purchase cost for the units, $(D/Q)S$ is the annual ordering cost (the actual number of orders placed, D/Q, times the cost of

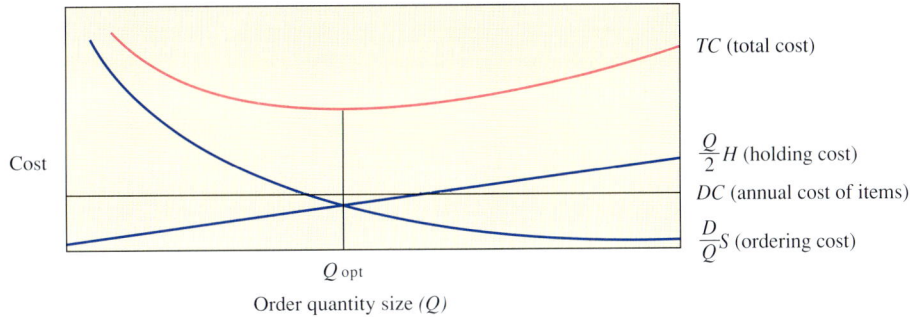

E X H I B I T 14.4
Annual Product Costs, Based on Size of the Order

each order, S), and $(Q/2)H$ is the annual holding cost (the average inventory, $Q/2$, times the cost per unit for holding and storage, H). These cost relationships are graphed in Exhibit 14.4.

The second step in model development is to find that order quantity Q_{opt}, at which total cost is a minimum. In Exhibit 14.4, the total cost is minimum at the point where the slope of the curve is zero. Using calculus, we take the derivative of total cost with respect to Q and set this equal to zero. For the basic model considered here, the calculations are

$$TC = DC + \frac{D}{Q}S + \frac{Q}{2}H$$

$$\frac{dTC}{dQ} = 0 + \left(\frac{-DS}{Q^2}\right) + \frac{H}{2} = 0$$

$$Q_{opt} = \sqrt{\frac{2DS}{H}} \tag{14.2}$$

Since this simple model assumes constant demand and lead time, no safety stock is necessary, and the reorder point, R, is simply

$$R = \bar{d}L \tag{14.3}$$

where

$\bar{d}$ = Average daily demand [constant]

L = Lead time in days [constant]

E X A M P L E 14.1 / *Economic Order Quantity and Reorder Point*   Find the economic order quantity and the reorder point, given

Annual demand (D) = 1,000 units

Average daily demand $(\bar{d})$ = 1,000/365

Ordering cost (S) = $5 per order

Holding cost (H) = $1.25 per unit per year

Lead time (L) = 5 days

Cost per unit (C) = $12.50

What quantity should be ordered?

S O L U T I O N   The optimal order quantity is

$$Q_{\text{opt}} = \sqrt{\frac{2DS}{H}} = \sqrt{\frac{2(1,000)5}{1.25}} = \sqrt{8,000} = 89.4 \text{ units}$$

The reorder point is

$$R = \bar{d}L = \frac{1,000}{365}(5) = 13.7 \text{ units}$$

Rounding to the nearest unit, the inventory policy is as follows: When the number of units in inventory drops to 14, place an order for 89 more.

The total annual cost will be

$$TC = DC + \frac{D}{Q}S + \frac{Q}{2}H$$

$$= 1,000(12.50) + \frac{1,000}{89}(5) + \frac{89}{2}(1.25)$$

$$= \$12,611.81$$

Note that in this example, the purchase cost of the units was not required to determine the order quantity and the reorder point since the cost was constant and unrelated to order size. ■

Fixed-Order Quantity Model with Usage

Example 14.1 assumed that the quantity ordered would be received in one lot, but frequently this is not the case. In many situations, in fact, production of an inventory item and usage of that item take place simultaneously. This is particularly true where one part of a production system acts as a supplier to another part. For example, while aluminum extrusions are being made to fill an order for aluminum windows, the extrusions are cut and assembled before the entire extrusion order is completed. Also, companies are beginning to enter longer-term arrangements with vendors. Under such contracts, a single order may cover product or material needs over a six-month or year period, with the vendor making deliveries weekly or sometimes even more frequently. If we let d denote a constant demand rate for some item going into production and let p be the production rate of that process that uses the item, we may develop the total cost equation[1]

$$TC = DC + \frac{D}{Q}S + \frac{(p-d)QH}{2p}$$

Again differentiating with respect to Q and setting the equation equal to zero, we obtain

$$Q_{\text{opt}} = \sqrt{\frac{2DS}{H} \cdot \frac{p}{(p-d)}} \tag{14.4}$$

This model is shown in Exhibit 14.5. We can see that the number of units on hand is always less than the order quantity, Q.

---

[1]Clearly, the production rate must exceed the rate of usage. Otherwise Q would be infinite, resulting in continual production.

E X H I B I T 14.5
Fixed-Order Quantity Model with Usage during Production Time

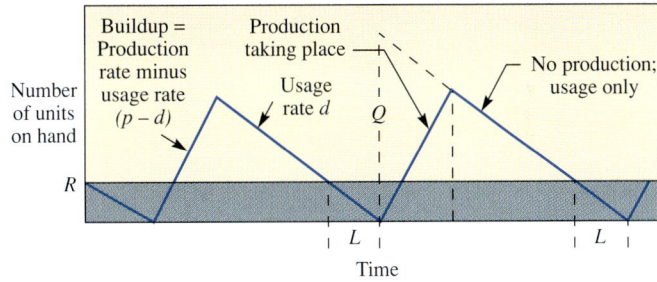

E X A M P L E 14.2 / *Optimal Lot Size* Product X is a standard item in a firm's inventory. Final assembly of the product is performed on an assembly line that is in operation every day. One component of product X (call it component X_1) is produced in another department. This department, when it produces X_1, does so at the rate of 100 units per day. The assembly line uses component X_1 at the rate of 40 units per day.

Given the following data, what is the optimal lot size for production of component X_1?

$$\text{Daily usage rate } (d) = 40 \text{ units}$$
$$\text{Annual demand } (D) = 10,000 \ (40 \text{ units} \times 250 \text{ working days})$$
$$\text{Daily production } (p) = 100 \text{ units}$$
$$\text{Cost for production setup } (S) = \$50$$
$$\text{Annual holding cost } (H) = \$0.50 \text{ per unit}$$
$$\text{Cost of component } X_1 \ (C) = \$7 \text{ each}$$
$$\text{Lead time } (L) = 7 \text{ days}$$

S O L U T I O N The optimal order quantity and the reorder point are calculated as follows:

$$Q_{opt} = \sqrt{\frac{2DS}{H} \cdot \frac{p}{p-d}} = \sqrt{\frac{2(10,000)50}{0.50} \cdot \frac{100}{100-40}} = 1,826 \text{ units}$$
$$R = dL = 40(7) = 280 \text{ units}$$

This states that an order for 1,826 units of component X_1 should be placed when the stock drops to 280 units.

At 100 units per day, this run would take 18.26 days and provide a 45.65-day supply for the assembly line (1,826/40). Theoretically, the department would be occupied with other work for the 27.39 days when component X_1 is not being produced. ■

Establishing Safety Stock Using Service Levels

The previous model assumed that demand was constant and known. In the majority of cases, though, demand is not constant but varies from day to day. Safety stock must therefore be maintained to provide some level of protection against stockouts. The general literature on the subject of safety stocks contains two approaches relating to the demand for the inventory that is to be protected. First is the *probability* that demand will exceed some specified amount. For example, an objective may be something like "Set the safety stock level so that there will only be a 5 percent chance that demand will exceed 300 units."

The second approach deals with the *expected number* of units that will be out of stock. For example, an objective might be to set the inventory level so that we can meet 95 percent of the orders for that unit (or be out of stock 5 percent of the time). Again, the first approach deals with the *probability* of exceeding a value and the second approach is concerned with *how many* units were short.

In this chapter on inventory, we deal primarily with the expected number of units short since it is a far more realistic approach.

Here is an analogy that may help conveying why this is so. Suppose the weather forecaster predicts rain tomorrow. Are you satisfied with this yes/no (rain/no rain) prediction—or would you prefer to know if the prediction is for a light sprinkle or for heavy rains with possible flooding? If it happens to be winter, would you be satisfied with a simple forecast of snow (with an associated probability of being correct)? Would you like to know whether this is a light snow flurry or a heavy snowfall resulting in hazardous driving and, probably, closed airports? That is the same idea for our inventory model. We are interested not only in whether we will be out of stock (possibility of rain or snow), but also in how many units we will be short (how much total rain or snow).

We are now ready to define service level: **Service level** refers to the number of units that can be supplied from stock currently on hand. For example, if annual demand for an item is 1,000 units, a 95 percent service level means that 950 can be supplied immediately from stock and 50 units are short. (This concept assumes that orders are small and randomly distributed—one or several at a time. This model would not apply, for example, where the entire annual demand might be sold to just a few customers.)

Safety stock can be defined as inventory carried to assure that the desired service level is met. Safety stock is also called *buffer stock*.

The discussion in this section on service levels is based on a statistical concept known as Expected z or E(z). E(z) is the expected number of units short during each lead time.

To compute service level, we need to know *how many* units are short. For example, assume that the average weekly demand for an item is 100 units with a standard devia-

E X H I B I T   14.6

Expected Number Out of Stock versus the Standard Deviation (This table is normalized to a standard deviation of 1.)

E(z)	z	E(z)	z	E(z)	z	E(z)	z
4.500	−4.50	2.205	−2.20	0.399	0.00	0.004	2.30
4.400	−4.40	2.106	−2.10	0.351	0.10	0.003	2.40
4.300	−4.30	2.008	−2.00	0.307	0.20	0.002	2.50
4.200	−4.20	1.911	−1.90	0.267	0.30	0.001	2.60
4.100	−4.10	1.814	−1.80	0.230	0.40	0.001	2.70
4.000	−4.00	1.718	−1.70	0.198	0.50	0.001	2.80
3.900	−3.90	1.623	−1.60	0.169	0.60	0.001	2.90
3.800	−3.80	1.529	−1.50	0.143	0.70	0.000	3.00
3.700	−3.70	1.437	−1.40	0.120	0.80	0.000	3.10
3.600	−3.60	1.346	−1.30	0.100	0.90	0.000	3.20
3.500	−3.50	1.256	−1.20	0.083	1.00	0.000	3.30
3.400	−3.40	1.169	−1.10	0.069	1.10	0.000	3.40
3.300	−3.30	1.083	−1.00	0.056	1.20	0.000	3.50
3.200	−3.20	1.000	−0.90	0.046	1.30	0.000	3.60
3.100	−3.10	0.920	−0.80	0.037	1.40	0.000	3.70
3.000	−3.00	0.843	−0.70	0.029	1.50	0.000	3.80
2.901	−2.90	0.769	−0.60	0.023	1.60	0.000	3.90
2.801	−2.80	0.698	−0.50	0.018	1.70	0.000	4.00
2.701	−2.70	0.630	−0.40	0.014	1.80	0.000	4.10
2.601	−2.60	0.567	−0.30	0.011	1.90	0.000	4.20
2.502	−2.50	0.507	−0.20	0.008	2.00	0.000	4.30
2.403	−2.40	0.451	−0.10	0.006	2.10	0.000	4.40
2.303	−2.30	0.399	0.00	0.005	2.20	0.000	4.50

z = Number of standard deviations of safety stock
$E(z)$ = Expected number of units short
Source: Revised from Robert G. Brown, *Decision Rules for Inventory Management* (New York: Holt, Rinehart & Winston, 1967), pp. 95–103.

tion of 10 units. If we stock 110 units, how many will we expect to be short? To do this we need to summarize the probability that 111 are demanded (1 short), the probability that 112 are demanded (2 short), plus the probability that 113 are demanded (3 short), and so on. This summary would give us the number of units we would expect to be short by stocking 110 units.

While the concept is simple, the equations are impractical to solve by hand. Fortunately, Robert Brown has provided tables of expected values (Exhibit 14.6).

Exhibit 14.7 plots the numbers in Exhibit 14.6. This shows the expected number of units short each order cycle (whether it is a periodic model P or an order quantity model Q). Using our previous examples, suppose the average demand for an item was 100 units and the standard deviation of that demand was 10 units. In Exhibit 14.7 we must multiply the vertical axis by 10 since the chart is based on a standard deviation of one unit. Reading from either the numbers in Exhibit 14.6 or the plot of these numbers in Exhibit 14.7, at $z = 1$, if we carry a safety stock of 10 units (one standard deviation), we should expect to be out of stock just .83 units total (.083 times 10 since the exhibits are based on a standard deviation of 1). Since normal demand during the period is 100 and we were only short .83 (less than one unit), our service level is $100 - .83$ or 99.17 percent.

If in the same example we did not carry any safety stock (i.e., order just 100 units), we would be short 3.99 units (.399 times 10). Our service level would be $100 - 3.99$ or 96.01 percent.

The concept becomes tricky when safety stock become negative. This simply states that our service level is too good and we are not running out of stock often enough. Again, from our same example, note that if we have a safety stock of minus one standard deviation, this just says to order 90 units ($100 - 10$ safety stock). At 90 units we would run short 10.83 units and our service level would be 89.17 percent. Carrying this further, if we order 80 units, we will be short 20.08 units; if we order 70 units, we will be short 30 units; and so on. Since these exhibits are based on a standard deviation of one unit, all we need to do is to multiply the figures by the actual data to be used. Another example, if demand was 550 units and the standard deviation was 36 units, then

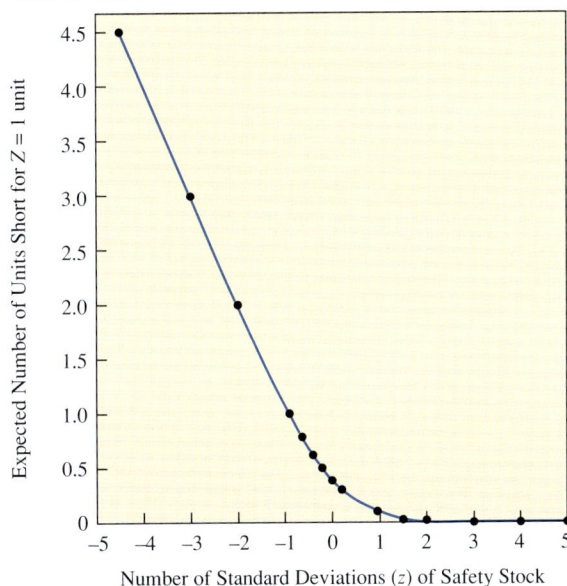

E X H I B I T 14.7

Expected Numbers Out of Stock per Order Cycle

E X H I B I T 14.8

Fixed-Order Quantity Model

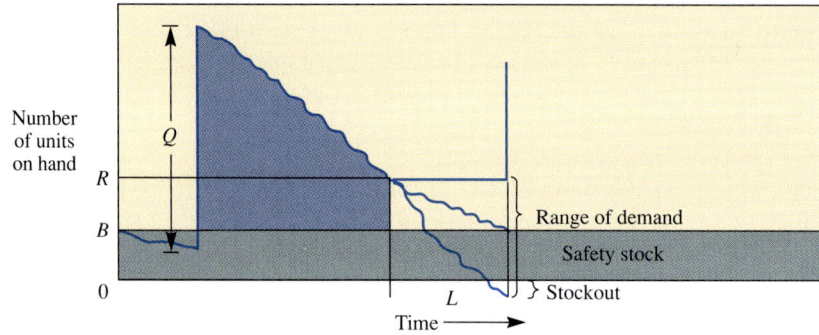

ordering 568 would give a .5 standard deviation of safety stock with an expected number of units short of .198 × 36 = 7.128 units. The service level would therefore be (550 − 7.128)/550 = 98.7 percent.

To summarize the preceding discussion, what we did was simply to convert the existing standard deviation to a base of one unit and to calculate the planned number of units short for a particular service level.

We will carry the explanations further within the context of our two basic model types: the fixed-order quantity and fixed-time period. We will discuss important questions such as how to control our inventory to provide a customer service level of 95 percent?

Fixed-Order Quantity Model with Specified Service Level

A fixed-order quantity system perpetually monitors the inventory level and places a new order when stock reaches some level, R. The danger of stockout in this model occurs only during the lead time, between the time an order is placed and the time it is received. As shown in Exhibit 14.8, an order is placed when the inventory level drops to the reorder point, R. During this lead time *(L)*, a range of demands is possible. This range is determined either from an analysis of past demand data or from an estimate (if past data are not available).

The amount of safety stock depends on the service level desired, as previously discussed. The quantity to be ordered, Q, is calculated in the usual way considering the demand, shortage cost, ordering cost, holding cost, and so forth. A fixed-order quantity model can be used to compute Q such as the simple Q_{opt} model previously discussed. The reorder point is then set to cover the expected demand during the lead time plus a safety stock determined by the desired service level. Thus, *the key difference between a fixed-order quantity model, where demand is known and one where demand is uncertain is in computing the reorder point. The order quantity is the same in both cases.* The uncertainty element is taken into account in the safety stock.

The reorder point is

$$R = \bar{d}L + z\sigma_L \tag{14.5}$$

where

R = Reorder point in units

$\bar{d}$ = Average daily demand

L = Lead time in days (time between placing an order and receiving the items)

z = Number of standard deviations for a specified service level

σ_L = Standard deviation of usage during lead time.

The term $z\sigma_L$ is the amount of safety stock. Note that if safety stock is positive, the effect is to place a reorder sooner. That is, R without safety stock is simply the average demand during the lead time. If lead time usage was expected to be 20, for example, and safety stock was computed to be 5 units, then the order would be placed sooner, when 25 units remained. The greater the safety stock, the sooner the order is placed.

Computing $\bar{d}$, σ_L and z Demand during the lead time to receive a replenishment order is really an estimate or forecast of what is expected. It may be a single number (for example, if the lead time is a month, the demand may be taken as the previous year's demand divided by 12), or it may be a summation of expected demands over the lead time (such as the sum of daily demands over a 30-day lead time). For the daily demand situation, d can be a forecasted demand using any of the models in Chapter 7 on forecasting. For example, if a 30-day period was used to calculate d, then a simple average would be

$$\bar{d} = \frac{\sum\limits_{i=1}^{n} d_i}{n} \tag{14.6}$$

$$= \frac{\sum\limits_{i=1}^{30} d_i}{30}$$

where n is the number of days.

The standard deviation of the average $\bar{d}$ is:

$$\sigma_d = \sqrt{\frac{\sum\limits_{i=1}^{n} (d_i - \bar{d})^2}{n}} \tag{14.7}$$

$$= \sqrt{\frac{\sum\limits_{i=1}^{30} (d_i - \bar{d})^2}{30}}$$

Since σ_d refers to one day, if lead time extends over several days we can use the statistical premise that the standard deviation of a series of independent occurrences is equal to the square root of the sum of the variances. That is, in general,

$$\sigma_s = \sqrt{\sigma_1^2 + \sigma_2^2 + \ldots + \sigma_i^2} \tag{14.8}$$

For example, suppose we computed the standard deviation of demand to be 10 units per day. If our lead time to get an order is five days, the standard deviation for the five-day period, since each day can be considered independent, is

$$\sigma_L = \sqrt{(10)^2 + (10)^2 + (10)^2 + (10)^2 + (10)^2} = 22.36$$

Next we need to compute z. We do this by computing $E(z)$, the number of units short that meets our desired service level, and then looking this up in Exhibit 14.6 for the appropriate z.

Suppose we wanted a service level of P. (For example, P might be 95 percent.) In the course of a year we would be short $(1 - P)\,D$ units, or $0.05D$, where D is the annual demand. If we ordered Q units each time, we would be placing D/Q orders per year. Exhibit 14.6 is based on $\sigma_L = 1$. Therefore, any $E(z)$ that we read from the table needs to be multiplied by σ_L if it is other than 1. The number of units short per order, therefore, is $E(z)\sigma_L$. For the year, the number of units short is $E(z)\sigma_L D/Q$. Stated again, we have,

$$\begin{array}{ccccc}
\text{Percentage} & & \text{Annual} & & \text{Number short} & & \text{Number of} \\
\text{short} & \times & \text{demand} & = & \text{per order} & \times & \text{orders per year} \\
(1 - P) & \times & D & = & E(z)\sigma_L & \times & \dfrac{D}{Q}
\end{array}$$

which simplifies to

$$E(z) = \frac{(1 - P)Q}{\sigma_L} \tag{14.9}$$

where

$P =$ Service level desired (such as satisfying 95 percent of demand from items in stock)

$(1 - P) =$ Unsatisfied demand

$D =$ Annual demand

$\sigma_L =$ Standard deviation of demand during lead time

$Q =$ Economic order quantity calculated in the usual way (such as $Q = \sqrt{2DS/H}$)

$E(z) =$ Expected number of units short each order cycle from a normalized table where $\sigma = 1$

Note that D (annual demand) drops out of Equation 14.9. This is because $E(z)$ is the number short *each order cycle*. (There are D/Q cycles per year.)

We now compare two examples. The difference between them is that in the first, the variation in demand is stated in terms of standard deviation over the entire lead time, while in the second, it is stated in terms of standard deviation per day.

E X A M P L E   14.3 / *Economic Order Quantity*   Consider an economic order quantity case where annual demand $D = 1,000$ units, economic order quantity $Q = 200$ units, the desired service level $P = .95$, the standard deviation of demand during lead time $\sigma_L = 50$ units, and lead time $L = 15$ days. Determine the reorder point.

S O L U T I O N   In our example, $\bar{d} = 4$ (1,000 over a 250-workday year), and lead time is 15 days. We use the equation

$$R = \bar{d}L + z\sigma_L$$
$$= 4(15) + z(50)$$

To find z, we use equation 14.9 above for $E(z)$ and look this value up in the table. Our problem data gave us $Q = 200$, service level $P = .95$, and standard deviation of demand during lead time $= 50$. Therefore,

$$E(z) = \frac{(1 - P)Q}{\sigma_L} = \frac{(1 - .95)200}{50} = .2$$

From Exhibit 14.6, and through interpolation at $E(z) = .2$, we find $z = .49$. Completing the solution for R, we find

$$R = 4(15) + z(50) = 60 + .49(50) = 84.5 \text{ units}$$

This says that when the stock on hand gets down to 85 units, order 200 more.

Just to satisfy any skepticism, we can calculate the number served per year to see if it really is 95 percent. $E(z)$ is the expected number short on each order based on a standard deviation of 1. The number short on each order for our problem is $E(z)\sigma_L = .2(50) = 10$. Since there are five orders per year (1,000/200), this results in 50 units short. This verifies our achievement of a 95 percent service level, since 950 out of 1,000 demand were filled from stock.   ■

E X A M P L E 14.4 / *Order Quantity and Reorder Point*   Daily demand for a certain product is normally distributed with a mean of 60 and standard deviation of 7. The source of supply is reliable and maintains a constant lead time of six days. The cost of placing the order is $10 and annual holding costs are $0.50 per unit. There are no stock-out costs, and unfilled orders are filled as soon as the order arrives. Assume sales occur over the entire year. Find the order quantity and reorder point to satisfy 95 percent of the customers.

S O L U T I O N   In this problem we need to calculate the order quantity Q as well as the reorder point R.

$$\bar{d} = 60 \qquad\qquad S = \$10$$
$$\sigma_d = 7 \qquad\qquad H = \$0.50$$
$$D = 60(365) \qquad L = 6$$

The optimal order quantity is

$$Q_{\text{opt}} = \sqrt{\frac{2DS}{H}} = \sqrt{\frac{2(60)365(10)}{0.50}} = \sqrt{876,000} = 936 \text{ units}$$

To compute the reorder point, we need to calculate the amount of product used during the lead time and add this to the safety stock.

The standard deviation of demand during the lead time of six days is calculated from the variance of the individual days. Since each day's demand is independent[2]

$$\sigma_L = \sqrt{\sum_{i=1}^{L} \sigma_{d_i}{}^2} = \sqrt{6(7)^2} = 17.2$$

Next we need to know how many standard deviations are needed for a specified service level. As previously defined,

$$E(z) = \frac{Q(1 - P)}{\sigma_L}$$

Therefore

$$E(z) = \frac{936(1 - .95)}{17.2} = 2.721$$

----

[2]As previously discussed, the standard deviation of a sum of independent variables equals the square root of the sum \of the variances.

From Exhibit 14.6, interpolating at $E(z) = 2.721$, $z = -2.72$. The reorder point is

$$R = \bar{d}L + z\sigma_L = 60(6) + (-2.72)(17.2) = 313.2 \text{ units}$$

To summarize the policy derived in this example, an order for 936 units is placed whenever the number of units remaining in inventory drops to 313.

Note that in this case the safety stock $(z\sigma_L)$ turns out to be negative. This means that if we had ordered the average demand of 360 units during the lead time (60×6), we would have had a higher service level than we wanted. To get down to 95 percent service, we need to create more shortages by ordering less. While this may seem strange, it is nevertheless true. Our service is too good and we need to run out of stock more often!

We can verify our service level in this example by noting that we would place 23.4 orders per year [$60(365)/936$]. Each period would experience 46.8 units out of stock (2.72×17.2). Thus we would be out of stock 1,095 units per year (46.8×23.4). Service level, therefore, is 0.95 as we intended [$(21,900 - 1,095)/21,900$]. ■

As shown in these two examples, this technique of determining safety stock levels is relatively simple and straightforward. It allows us to control inventory to meet our desired service levels.

14.7   FIXED TIME PERIOD MODELS

Fixed-Time Period Model with Specified Service Level

In a fixed-time period system, inventory is counted only at particular times, such as every week or every month. Counting inventory and placing orders on a periodic basis is desirable in situations such as when vendors make routine visits to customers and take orders for their complete line of products, or when buyers want to combine orders to save transportation costs. Other firms operate on a fixed-time period to facilitate planning their inventory count; for example, Distributor X calls every two weeks and employees know that all Distributor X's product must be counted.

Fixed-time period models generate order quantities that vary from period to period, depending on the usage rates. These generally require a higher level of safety stock than a fixed-order quantity system. The fixed-order quantity system assumes continual counting of inventory on hand, with an order immediately placed when the reorder point is reached. In contrast, the standard fixed-time period models assume that inventory is counted only at the time specified for review. It is possible that some large demand will draw the stock down to zero right after an order is placed. This condition could go unnoticed until the next review period. Then the new order, when placed, still takes time to arrive. Thus, it is possible to be out of stock throughout the entire review period, T, and order lead time, L. Safety stock, therefore, must protect us against stockouts during the review period itself as well as during the lead time from order placement to order receipt.

In a fixed-time period system, reorders are placed at the time of review (T), and the safety stock that must be reordered is

$$\text{Safety stock} = z\sigma_{T+L}$$

Exhibit 14.9 shows a fixed-time period system with a review cycle of T and a constant lead time of L. In this case, demand is randomly distributed about a mean $\bar{d}$. The quantity to order, q, is

$$
\begin{array}{ccccc}
\text{Order} & \text{Average demand} & & & \text{Inventory currently} \\
\text{quantity} = & \text{over the vulner-} & + & \text{Safety} & - & \text{on hand (plus on} & \quad (14.10) \\
& \text{able period} & & \text{stock} & & \text{order, if any)} \\
q \quad = & \bar{d}(T + L) & + & z\sigma_{T+L} & - & I
\end{array}
$$

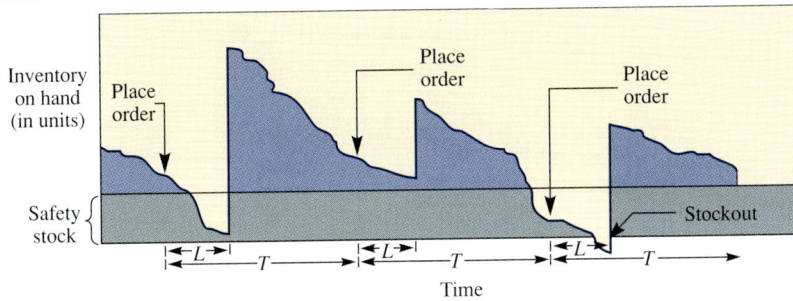

where

q = Quantity to be ordered

T = The number of days between reviews

L = Lead time in days (time between placing an order and receiving it)

$\bar{d}$ = Forecasted average daily demand

z = Number of standard deviations for a specified service level

σ_{T+L} = Standard deviation of demand over the review and lead time

I = Current inventory level (includes items on order)

Note: The demand, lead time, review period, and so forth can be any time units such as days, weeks, or years so long as it is consistent throughout the equation.

In this model, demand $(\bar{d})$ can be forecast and revised each review period if desired, or the yearly average may be used if appropriate.

The value of z can be obtained by solving the following equation for $E(z)$ and reading the corresponding z value from Exhibit 14.6:

$$E(z) = \frac{\bar{d}T(1 - P)}{\sigma_{T+L}} \qquad (14.11)$$

where

$E(z)$ = Expected number units short from a formalized table where $\sigma = 1$

P = Service level desired

$\bar{d}T$ = Demand during the review period where $\bar{d}$ is daily demand and T is the number of days

σ_{T+L} = Standard deviation over the review period and lead time

E X A M P L E 14.5 / *Quantity to Order* Daily demand for a product is 10 units with a standard deviation of three units. The review period is 30 days, and lead time is 14 days. Management has set a policy of satisfying 98 percent of demand from items in stock. At the beginning of this review period, there are 150 units in inventory.

How many units should be ordered?

S O L U T I O N The quantity to order is

$$q = \bar{d}(T + L) + z\sigma_{T+L} - I$$
$$= 10(30 + 14) + z\sigma_{T+L} - 150$$

Before we can complete the solution, we need to find σ_{T+L} and z. To find σ_{T+L}, we use the notion, as before, that the standard deviation of a sequence of independent random variables equals the square root of the sum of the variances. Therefore, the standard deviation during the period $T + L$ is the square root of the sum of the variances for each day:

$$\sigma_{T+L} = \sqrt{\sum_{i=1}^{T+L} \sigma_{d_i}^2} \qquad (14.12)$$

Since each day is independent and σ_d is constant,

$$\sigma_{T+L} = \sqrt{(T + L)\,\sigma_d^2} = \sqrt{(30 + 14)(3^2)} = 19.90$$

Now to find z, we first need to find $E(z)$ and look this value up in the table. In this case, demand during the review period is $\bar{d}T$ so

$$E(z) = \frac{\bar{d}T(1 - P)}{\sigma_{T+L}} = \frac{10(30)(1 - .98)}{19.90} = 0.30151$$

From Exhibit 14.6 at $E(z) = 0.30151$, by interpolation $z = .21$.
   The quantity to order, then, is

$$q = \bar{d}(T + L) + z\sigma_{T+L} - I = 10(30 + 14) + .21(19.90) - 150 = 294 \text{ units}$$

To satisfy 98 percent of the demand for units, order 294 at this review period.   ■

14.8   SPECIAL PURPOSE MODELS

The fixed-order quantity and the fixed-time period models presented thus far differed in their assumptions but had two characteristics in common: (1) The cost of units remained constant for any order size. (2) The reordering process was continuous; that is, the items were ordered and stocked with the expectation that the need would continue.

   This section presents two new models. The first illustrates the effect on order quantity when unit price changes with order size. The second is a single-period model (sometimes called a *static model*) in which ordering and stocking require a cost trade-off each time. This type of model is amenable to solution by marginal analysis.

Price-Break Models   Price-break models deal with the fact that generally the selling price of an item varies with the order size. This is a discrete or step change rather than a per-unit change. For example, wood screws may cost $0.02 each for 1 to 99 screws, $1.60 per 100, and $13.50 per 1,000. To determine the optimal quantity of any item to order, we simply solve for the economic order quantity for each price and at the point of price change. But not all the economic order quantities determined by the formula are feasible. In the wood screw example, the Q_{opt} formula might tell us that the optimal decision at the price of 1.6 cents is to order 75 screws. This would be impossible, however, because 75 screws would cost 2 cents each.

   The total cost for each feasible economic order quantity and **price-break order quantity** is tabulated, and the Q that leads to the minimum cost is the optimal order size. If holding cost is based on a percentage of unit price, it may not be necessary to compute economic order quantities at each price. Procedurally, the largest order quantity (lowest unit price) is solved first; if the resulting Q is valid, that is the answer. If not, the next largest order quantity (second lowest price) is derived. If that is feasible, the cost of this Q is compared to the cost of using the order quantity at the price break above, and the lowest cost determines the optimal Q.

E X H I B I T 14.10   *Curves for Three Separate Order Quantity Models in a Three-Price-Break Situation (Color line depicts feasible range of purchases.)*

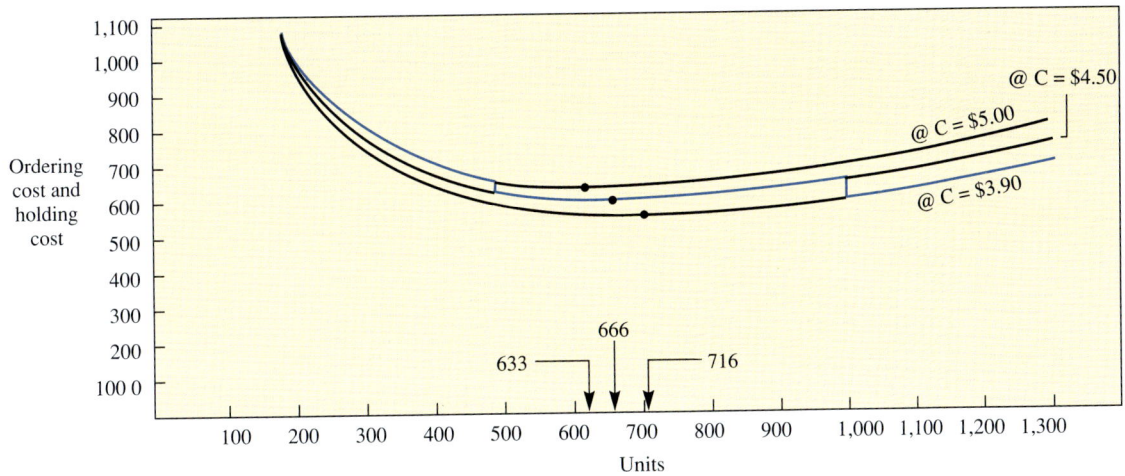

Looking at Exhibit 14.10, we see that order quantities are solved from right to left, or from the lowest unit price to the highest, until a valid Q is obtained. Then the order quantity at each *price break* above this Q is used to find which order quantity has the least cost—the computed Q or the Q at one of the price breaks.

E X A M P L E 14.6 / Price-Break   Consider the following case, where

D = 10,000 units (annual demand)
S = $20 to place each order
i = 20 percent of cost (annual carrying cost, storage, interest, obsolescence, etc.)
C = Cost per unit (according to the order size; orders of 0 to 499 units, $5.00 per unit; 500 to 999, $4.50 per unit; 1,000 and up, $3.90 per unit)

What quantity should be ordered?

S O L U T I O N   The appropriate equations from the basic fixed-quantity case are

$$TC = DC + \frac{D}{Q}S + \frac{Q}{2}iC$$

and

$$Q = \sqrt{\frac{2DS}{iC}} \qquad (14.13)$$

Solving for the economic order size at each price, we obtain

@ C = $5.00, Q = 633
@ C = $4.50, Q = 666
@ C = $3.90, Q = 716

In Exhibit 14.10, which displays the cost relationship and order quantity range, note that most of the order quantity–cost relationships lie outside the feasible range and that

E X H I B I T 14.11   *Relevant Costs in a Three-Price-Break Model*

	$Q = 633$ where $C = \$5$	$Q = 666$ where $C = \$4.50$	$Q = 716$ where $C = \$3.90$	Price Break 1,000
Holding cost $\left(\dfrac{Q}{2}iC\right)$		$\dfrac{666}{2}(0.20)4.50$ $= \$299.70$		$\dfrac{1,000}{2}(0.20)3.90$ $= \$390$
Ordering cost $\left(\dfrac{D}{Q}S\right)$	Not feasible	$\dfrac{10,000(20)}{666}$ $= \$300$	Not feasible	$\dfrac{10,000(20)}{1,000}$ $= \$200$
Holding and ordering cost		$\$599.70$		$\$590$
Item cost (DC)		$10,000(4.50)$		$10,000(3.90)$
Total cost		$\$45,599.70$		$\$39,590$

only a single, continuous range results. This should be readily apparent since, for example, the first order quantity specifies buying 633 units at $5.00 per unit. However, if 633 units are ordered, the price is $4.50, not $5.00. The same holds true for the third order quantity, which specifies an order of 716 units at $3.90 each. This $3.90 price is not available on orders of less than 1,000 units.

Exhibit 14.11 itemizes the total costs at the economic order quantities and at the price breaks. The optimal order quantity is shown to be 1,000 units. ■

One practical consideration in price-break problems is that the price reduction from volume purchases frequently makes it seemingly economical to order amounts larger than the Q_{opt}. Thus, when applying the model we must be particularly careful to obtain a valid estimate of product obsolescence and warehousing costs.

Single-Period Models   Some inventory situations involve placing orders to cover only one demand period or to cover short-lived items at frequent intervals. Sometimes called single-period or "newsboy" problems (for example, how many papers should a newsboy order each day), they are amenable to solution through the classic economic approach of marginal analysis. The optimal stocking decision, using marginal analysis, occurs at the point where the benefits derived from carrying the next unit are less than the costs for that unit. Of course, the selection of the specific benefits and costs depends on the problem. For example, we may be looking at costs of holding versus shortage costs or (as we develop further) marginal profit versus marginal loss.

When stocked items are sold, the optimal decision—using marginal analysis—is to stock that quantity where the profit from the sale or use of the last unit is equal to or greater than the losses if the last unit remains unsold. In symbolic terms, this is the condition where $MP \geq ML$, where

MP = Profit resulting from the nth unit if it is sold

ML = Loss resulting from the nth unit if it is not sold

Marginal analysis is also valid when we are dealing with probabilities of occurrence. In these situations we are looking at expected profits and expected losses. By introducing probabilities, the marginal profit–marginal loss equation becomes

$$P(MP) \geq (1 - P)ML$$

where P is the probability of the unit's being sold and $1 - P$ is the probability of it not being sold, since one or the other must occur. (The unit is sold or is not sold.)[3]

Then, solving for P, we obtain

$$P \geq \frac{ML}{MP + ML} \qquad (14.14)$$

This equation states that we should continue to increase the size of the inventory so long as the probability of selling the last unit added is equal to or greater than the ratio $ML/(MP + ML)$.

Salvage value   Salvage value, or any other benefits derived from unsold goods, can easily be included in the problem. This simply reduces the marginal loss, as the following example shows.

E X A M P L E 14.7 / *Salvage Value*   A product is priced to sell at $100 per unit, and its cost is constant at $70 per unit. Each unsold unit has a salvage value of $30. Demand is expected to range between 35 and 40 units for the period: 35 units definitely can be sold and no units over 40 will be sold. The demand probabilities and the associated cumulative probability distribution (P) for this situation are shown in Exhibit 14.12.

The marginal profit if a unit is sold is the selling price less the cost, or $MP = \$100 - \$70 = \$30$.

The marginal loss incurred if the unit is not sold is the cost of the unit less the salvage value, or $ML = \$70 - \$30 = \$40$.

How many units should be ordered?

S O L U T I O N   The optimal probability of the last unit being sold is

$$P \geq \frac{ML}{MP + ML} = \frac{40}{30 + 40} = 0.57$$

According to the cumulative probability table (the last column in Exhibit 14.12), the probability of selling the unit must be equal to or greater than 0.57 so 37 units should be stocked. The probability of selling the 37th unit is 0.75. The net benefit from stocking the 37th unit is the expected marginal profit minus the expected marginal loss.

Number of Units Demanded	(p) Probability of This Demand	(P) Probability of Selling This Unit Is	
35	0.10	1 to 35	1.00
36	0.15	36	0.90
37	0.25	37	0.75
38	0.25	38	0.50
39	0.15	39	0.25
40	0.10	40	0.10
41	0	41 or more	0

E X H I B I T 14.12
Demand and Cumulative Probabilities

[3]P is actually a cumulative probability since the sale of the nth unit depends not only on exactly n being demanded but also on the demand for any number greater than n.

E X H I B I T 14.13   *Marginal Inventory Analysis for Units Having Salvage Value*

(N) Units of Demand	(p) Probability of Demand	(P) Probability of Selling nth Unit	(MP) Expected Marginal Profit of nth Unit $P(100 - 70)$	(ML) Expected Marginal Loss of nth Unit $(1 - P)(70 - 30)$	(Net) (MP) − (ML)
35	0.10	1.00	$30	$ 0	$ 30.00
36	0.15	0.90	27	4	23.00
37	0.25	0.75	22.50	10	12.50
38	0.25	0.50	15	20	(5.00)
39	0.15	0.25	7.50	30	(22.50)
40	0.10	0.10	3	36	(33.00)
41	0	0			(40.00)

Note: Expected marginal profit is the selling price of $100 less the unit cost of $70 times the probability the unit will be sold. Expected marginal loss is the unit cost of $70 less the salvage value of $30 times the probability the unit will not be sold.

$$\text{Net} = P(MP) - (1 - P)(ML)$$
$$= 0.75(\$100 - \$70) - (1 - 0.75)(\$70 - \$30)$$
$$= \$22.50 - \$10.00 = \$12.50$$

For the sake of illustration, Exhibit 14.13 shows all possible decisions. From the last column, we can confirm that the optimum decision is 37 units. ∎

14.9 MISCELLANEOUS SYSTEMS AND ISSUES

Obtaining actual order, setup, carrying, and shortage costs is difficult—sometimes impossible. Even the assumptions are sometimes unrealistic. For example, Exhibit 14.14 compares ordering costs assumed to the real case where staff additions cause a step function.

All inventory systems are plagued by two major problems: maintaining adequate control over each inventory item and ensuring that accurate records of stock on hand are kept. In this section, we present three simple systems (an optional replenishment system, a one-bin system, and a two-bin system) and **ABC analysis** (an inventory system offering a control technique and inventory cycle counting that can improve record accuracy).

Three Simple Inventory Systems

Optional Replenishment System   An **optional replenishment system** forces reviewing the inventory level at a fixed frequency (such as weekly) and ordering a replenishment supply if the level has dropped below some amount. In Exhibit 14.1, this is a *P* model. For example, the maximum inventory level (which we will call *M*) can be computed based on demand, ordering costs, and shortage costs. Because it takes time and costs money to place an order, a minimum order of size *Q* can be established. Then, whenever this item is reviewed, the number in inventory (we will call it *I*) is subtracted from the replenishment level (*M*). If that number (call it *q*) is equal to or greater than *Q,* order *q.* Otherwise, forget it until the next review period. Stated formally,

$q = M - I$

If $q \geq Q$, order *q.*

Otherwise, do not order any.

Two-Bin System   In a **two-bin system,** items are used from one bin, and the second bin provides the replenishment supply. In Exhibit 14.1, this is a *Q* model. The second bin is the same as an order size *Q* with instant arrival. As soon as the second bin supply

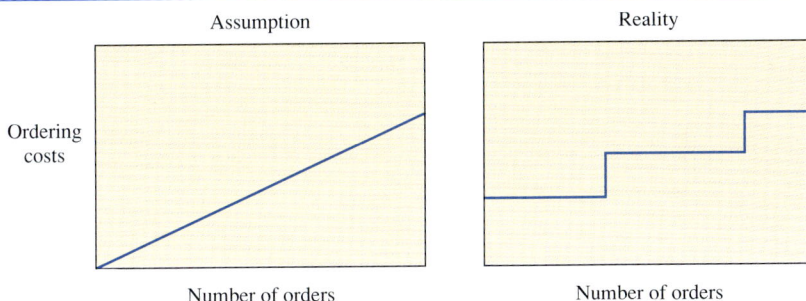

E X H I B I T 14.14
*Cost to Place Orders
versus the Number
of Orders Placed:
Linear Assumption
and Normal Reality*

is brought to the first bin, an order is placed to replenish the second bin. Actually, these bins can be located together. In fact, there could be just one bin with a divider between. The key to a two-bin operation is to separate the inventory so that part of it is held in reserve until the rest is used first.

One-Bin System   A **one-bin** inventory **system** involves periodic replenishment no matter how few are needed. At fixed periods (such as weekly), the inventory is brought up to its predetermined maximum level. The one bin is always replenished and therefore differs from the optional replenishment system which only reorders when the inventory used is greater than some minimum amount. This is a *P* model in Exhibit 14.1.

ABC Inventory Planning

Maintaining inventory through counting, placing orders, receiving stock, and so on takes personnel time and costs money. When there are limits on these resources, the logical move is to try to use the available resources to control inventory in the best way. In other words, focus on the most important items in inventory.

In the 19th century, Vilfredo Pareto, in a study of the distribution of wealth in Milan, found that 20 percent of the people controlled 80 percent of the wealth. This logic of the few having the greatest importance and the many having little importance has been broadened to include many situations and is termed the *Pareto principle*.[4] This is true in our everyday lives (most of our decisions are relatively unimportant, but a few shape our future) and is certainly true in inventory systems (where a few items account for the bulk of our investment).

Any inventory system must specify when an order is to be placed for an item and how many units to order. Most inventory control situations involve so many items that it is not practical to model and give thorough treatment to each item. To get around this problem, the ABC classification scheme divides inventory items into three groupings: high dollar volume (A), moderate dollar volume (B), and low dollar volume (C). Dollar volume is a measure of importance; an item low in cost but high in volume can be more important than a high-cost item with low volume.

ABC Classification   If the annual usage of items in inventory is listed according to dollar volume, generally the list shows that a small number of items account for a large dollar volume and that a large number of items account for a small dollar volume. Exhibit 14.15 illustrates the relationship.

The ABC approach divides this list into three groupings by value: A items constitute roughly the top 15 percent of the items, B items the next 35 percent, and C items the last

---

[4]The Pareto principle is also widely applied in quality problems through the use of Pareto charts. (See Chapter 5.)

E X H I B I T 14.15

Annual Usage of Inventory by Value

Item Number	Annual Dollar Usage	Percentage of Total Value
22	$ 95,000	40.8%
68	75,000	32.1
27	25,000	10.7
03	15,000	6.4
82	13,000	5.6
54	7,500	3.2
36	1,500	0.6
19	800	0.3
23	425	0.2
41	225	0.1
	$ 233,450	100.0%

E X H I B I T 14.16

ABC Grouping of Inventory Items

Classification	Item Number	Annual Dollar Usage	Percentage of Total
A	22, 68	$ 170,000	72.9%
B	27, 03, 82	53,000	22.7
C	54, 36, 19, 23, 41	10,450	4.4
		$ 233,450	100.0%

50 percent. From observation, it appears that the list in Exhibit 14.15 may be meaningfully grouped with A including 20 percent (2 of the 10), B including 30 percent, and C including 50 percent. These points show clear delineations between sections. The result of this segmentation is shown in Exhibit 14.16 and plotted in Exhibit 14.17.

Segmentation may not always occur so neatly. The objective, though, is to try to separate the important from the unimportant. Where the lines actually break depends on the particular inventory under question and on how much personnel time is available. (With more time, a firm could define larger A or B categories.)

The purpose of classifying items into groups is to establish the appropriate degree of control over each item. On a periodic basis, for example, class A items may be more clearly controlled with weekly ordering, B items may be ordered biweekly, and C items may be ordered monthly or bimonthly. Note that the unit cost of items is not related to their classification. An A item may have a high dollar volume through a combination of either low cost and high usage or high cost and low usage. Similarly, C items may have a low dollar volume because of either low demand or low cost. In an automobile service station, gasoline would be an A item with daily or weekly tabulation; tires, batteries, oil, grease, and transmission fluid may be B items and ordered every two to four weeks; and C items would consist of valve stems, windshield wiper blades, radiator caps, hoses, fan belts, oil and gas additives, car wax, and so forth. C items may be ordered every two or three months or even be allowed to run out before reordering since the penalty for stockout is not serious.

Sometimes, an item may be critical to a system if its absence creates a sizable loss. In this case, regardless of the item's classification, sufficiently large stocks should be kept on hand to prevent runout. One way to ensure closer control is to designate this item an A or a B, forcing it into the category even if its dollar volume does not warrant such inclusion.

Inventory Accuracy and Cycle Counting

Inventory records usually differ from the actual physical count; **inventory accuracy** refers to how well the two agree. The question is, How much error is acceptable? If the record shows a balance of 683 of part X and an actual count shows 652, is this within reason? Suppose the actual count shows 750, an excess of 67 over the record; is this any better?

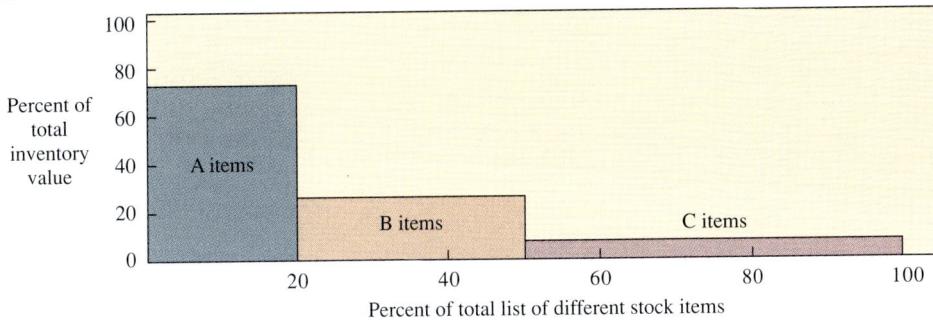

E X H I B I T 14.17
ABC Inventory Classification (Inventory value for each group versus the group's portion of the total list)

Every production system must have agreement, within some specified range, between what the record says is in inventory and what actually is in inventory. There are many reasons why records and inventory may not agree. For example, an open stockroom area allows items to be removed for both legitimate and unauthorized purposes. The legitimate removal may have been done in a hurry and simply not recorded. Sometimes parts are misplaced, turning up months later. Parts are often stored in several locations, but records may be lost or the location recorded incorrectly. Sometimes stock replenishment orders are recorded as received, when in fact they never were. Occasionally, a group of parts is recorded as removed from inventory, but the customer order is canceled and the parts are replaced in inventory without canceling the record. To keep the production system flowing smoothly without parts shortages and efficiently without excess balances, records must be accurate.

How can a firm keep accurate, up-to-date records? The first general rule is to keep the storeroom locked. If only storeroom personnel have access, and one of their measures of performance when it comes time for personnel evaluation and merit increases is record accuracy, there is a strong motivation to comply. Every location of inventory storage, whether in a locked storeroom or on the production floor, should have a recordkeeping mechanism. A second way is to convey the importance of accurate records to all personnel and depend on them to assist in this effort. (What this all boils down to is: Put a fence that goes all the way to the ceiling around the storage area so that workers cannot climb over to get parts; put a lock on the gate and give one person the key. Nobody, but nobody, can pull parts without having the transaction authorized and recorded.)

Another way to ensure accuracy is to count inventory frequently and match this against records. A widely used method is called *cycle counting.*

Cycle counting is a physical inventory-taking technique in which inventory is counted on a frequent basis rather than once or twice a year. The key to effective cycle counting and, therefore, to accurate records lies in deciding which items are to be counted, when, and by whom.

Virtually all inventory systems these days are computerized. The computer can be programmed to produce a cycle count notice in the following cases:

1. When the record shows a low or zero balance on hand. (It is easier to count fewer items.)

2. When the record shows a positive balance but a backorder was written (indicating a discrepancy).

3. After some specified level of activity.

4. To signal a review based on the importance of the item (as in the ABC system) such as in the following table:

Annual Dollar Usage	Review Period
$10,000 or more	30 days or less
$3,000–$10,000	45 days or less
$250–3,000	90 days or less
Less than $250	180 days or less

The easiest time for stock to be counted is when there is no activity in the stockroom or on the production floor. This means on the weekends or during the second or third shift, when the facility is less busy. If this is not possible, more careful logging and separation of items are required to do an inventory count while production is going on and transactions are occurring.

The counting cycle depends on the available personnel. Some firms schedule regular stockroom personnel to do the counting during lull times in the regular working day. Other companies contract out to private firms that come in and count inventory. Still other firms use full-time cycle counters who do nothing but count inventory and resolve differences with the records. While this last method sounds expensive, many firms believe that it is actually less costly than the usual hectic annual inventory count generally performed during the two- or three-week annual vacation shutdown.

The question of how much error is tolerable between physical inventory and records has been much debated. While some firms strive for 100 percent accuracy, others accept 1, 2, or 3 percent error. The accuracy level recommended by the American Production and Inventory Control Society (APICS) is ±0.2 percent for A items, ±1 percent for B items, and ±5 percent for C items. Regardless of the specific accuracy decided on, the important point is that the level be dependable so that safety stocks may be provided as a cushion. Accuracy is important for a smooth production process so that customer orders can be processed as scheduled and not held up because of the unavailability of parts.

Inventory Control in Services

To demonstrate how inventory control is conducted in service organizations, we have selected two areas to describe: a department store and an automobile service agency.

Department Store Inventory Policy   The common term used to identify an inventory item in a department store is the *stockkeeping unit (SKU)*. The SKU identifies each item, its manufacturer, and its cost. The number of SKUs becomes large even for small departments. For example, if towels carried in a domestic items department are obtained from three manufacturers in three quality levels, three sizes (hand towel, face towel, and bath towel), and four colors, there are 108 different items ($3 \times 3 \times 3 \times 4$). Even if towels are sold only in sets of three pieces (hand towel, face towel, and bath towel), the number of SKUs needed to identify the towel sets is $3 \times 3 \times 1 \times 4 = 36$. Depending on the store, a housewares department may carry 3,000 to 4,000 SKUs, and a linen and domestic items department may carry 5,000 to 6,000.

Such large numbers mean that individual economic order quantities cannot be calculated for each item by hand. How, then, does a department keep tabs on its stock and place orders for replenishment? We answer this question in the context of an example dealing with a housewares department and an auto service department.

Housewares department   Generally, housewares are divided into staple and promotional items. Within these major divisions, further classifications are used, such as cookware and tableware. Also, items are frequently classified by price, as $5 items, $4, $3, and so forth.

The housewares department usually purchases from a distributor rather than directly from a manufacturer. The use of a distributor, who handles products from many manufacturers, has the advantage of fewer orders and faster shipping time (shorter lead time). Further, the distributor's sales personnel may visit the housewares department weekly and count all the items they supply to this department. Then, in line with the replenishment level that has been established by the buyer, the distributor's salesperson places orders for the buyer. This saves the department time in counting inventory and placing orders. The typical lead time for receipt of stock from a housewares distributor is two or three days. The safety stock, therefore, is quite low, and the buyer establishes the replenishment level so as to supply only enough items for the two- to three-day lead time, plus expected demand during the period until the distributor's salesperson's next visit.

Note that a formal method of estimating stockout and establishing safety stock levels is usually not followed because the number of items is too great. Instead, the total value of items in the department is monitored. Thus, replenishment levels are set by dollar allocation.

Through planning, each department has an established monthly value for inventory. By tabulating inventory balance, monthly sales, and items on order, an "open-to-buy" figure is determined. ("Open-to-buy" is the unspent portion of the budget.) This dollar amount is the sum available to the buyer for the following month. When an increase in demand is expected (Christmas, Mother's Day, and so forth), the allocation of funds to the department is increased, resulting in a larger open-to-buy position. Then the replenishment levels are raised in line with the class of goods, responding to the demand increase, thereby creating a higher stock of goods on hand.

In practice, the open-to-buy funds are largely spent during the first days of the month. However, the buyer tries to reserve some funds for special purchases or to restock fast-moving items. Promotional items in housewares are controlled individually (or by class) by the buyer.

Maintaining an Auto Replacement Parts Inventory   A firm in the automobile service business purchases most of its parts supplies from a small number of distributors. Franchised new-car dealers purchase the great bulk of their supplies from the auto manufacturer. A dealer's demand for auto parts originates primarily from the general public and other departments of the agency, such as the service department or body shop. The problem, in this case, is to determine the order quantities for the several thousand items carried.

A franchised auto agency of medium size may carry a parts inventory valued in the area of $500,000. Because of the nature of this industry, alternate uses of funds are plentiful so opportunity costs are high. For example, dealers may lease cars, carry their own contracts, stock a larger new-car inventory, or open sidelines such as tire shops, trailer sales, or recreational vehicle sales—all with potentially high returns. This creates pressure to try to carry a low inventory level of parts and supplies while still meeting an acceptable service level.

While some dealers still perform their inventory ordering by hand, most use computers and software packages provided by car manufacturers. For both manual and computerized systems, an ABC classification works well. Expensive and high-turnover supplies are counted and ordered frequently; low-cost items are ordered in large quantities at infrequent intervals. A common drawback of frequent order placement is the extensive amount of time needed to physically put the items on the shelves and log them in. (However, this restocking procedure does not greatly add to an auto agency's cost because parts department personnel generally do this during slow periods.)

A great variety of computerized systems are currently in use. One program gives a choice of using either a simple weighted average or exponential smoothing to forecast the next period's demand. In a monthly reordering system, for example, the items to be ordered are counted and the number on hand is entered into the computer. By subtracting the number on hand from the previous month's inventory and adding the orders received during the month, the usage rate is determined. Some programs use exponential smoothing forecasts while others use a weighted-average method. For the weighted-average method the computer program stores the usage rate for, say, four previous months. Then, with the application of a set of weighting factors, a forecast is made in the same manner as described in Chapter 7. This works as follows: Suppose usage of a part during January, February, March, and April was 17, 19, 11, and 23, respectively, and the set of corresponding weights was 0.10, 0.20, 0.30, and 0.40. Thus, the forecast for May is 0.10(17) + 0.20(19) + 0.30(11) + 0.40(23), or 18 units. If safety stock were included and equal to one-month demand, then 36 units would be ordered (one-month demand plus one-month safety stock) less whatever is on hand at the time of order placement. This simple two-month rule allows for forecasted usage during the lead time plus the review period, with the balance providing the safety stock.

The computer output provides a useful reference file, identifying the item, cost, order size, and number of units on hand. The output itself constitutes the purchase order and is sent to the distributor or factory supply house. The simplicity in this is attractive since, once the forecast weighting is selected, all that needs to be done is to input the number of units of each item on hand. Thus, negligible computation is involved, and very little preparation is needed to send the order out.

14.10 CONCLUSION

This chapter introduced the two main classes of demand: (1) independent demand referring to the external demand for a firm's end product and (2) dependent demand, usually referring—within the firm—to the demand for items created because of the demand for more complex items of which they are a part. Most industries have items in both classes. In manufacturing, for example, independent demand is common for finished products, service and repair parts, and operating supplies; and dependent demand is common for those parts and materials needed to produce the end product. In wholesale and retail sales of consumer goods, most demand is independent—each item is an end item, with the wholesaler or retailer doing no further assembly or fabrication.

Independent demand, the focus of this chapter, is based on statistics. In the fixed-order quantity and fixed-time period models, the influence of service level was shown on safety stock and reorder point determinations. Two special-purpose models—price-break and single-period—were also presented.

To distinguish among item categories for analysis and control, the ABC method was offered. The importance of inventory accuracy was also noted, and cycle counting was described. Finally, brief descriptions of inventory procedures in a department store and an auto parts shop illustrated some of the simpler ways nonmanufacturing firms carry out their inventory control functions.

In this chapter we also pointed out that inventory reduction requires a knowledge of the operating system. It is not simply a case of selecting a model off the shelf and plugging in some numbers. In the first place, a model might not even be appropriate. In the second case, the numbers might be full of errors or even based on erroneous data. It is vital to understand that this is also not a trade-off compromise. Likewise, determining order quantities is often referred to as a trade-off problem; that is, trading off holding costs for setup costs. Note that companies really want to reduce both.

The simple fact is that firms have very large investments in inventory, and the cost to carry this inventory runs from 25 to 35 percent of the inventory's worth annually. Therefore, a major goal of most firms today is to reduce inventory.

A caution is in order, though. The formulas in this chapter try to minimize cost. Bear in mind that a firm's objective should be something like "making money" so be sure that reducing inventory cost does, in fact, support this. Usually, correctly reducing inventory lowers cost, improves quality and performance, and enhances profit.

14.11 FORMULA REVIEW

Q model. Total annual cost for an order quantity Q, a per unit cost C, setup cost S, and per unit holding cost H.

$$TC = DC + \frac{D}{Q}S + \frac{Q}{2}H \qquad (14.1)$$

Q model. Optimum (or economic) order quantity.

$$Q_{opt} = \sqrt{\frac{2DS}{H}} \qquad (14.2)$$

Q model. Reorder point R based on average daily demand $\bar{d}$ and lead time L in days.

$$R = \bar{d}L \qquad (14.3)$$

Q model (production-consumption model). Optimum order size when items are used at rate *d*, as they are produced at rate *p*.

$$Q_{\text{opt}} = \sqrt{\frac{2DS}{H} \cdot \frac{p}{(p-d)}} \tag{14.4}$$

Q model. Reorder point providing a safety stock of $z\sigma_L$.

$$R = \bar{d}L + z\sigma_L \tag{14.5}$$

Average daily demand over a period of *n* days.

$$\bar{d} = \frac{\sum\limits_{i=1}^{n} d_i}{n} \tag{14.6}$$

Standard deviation of demand over a period of *n* days.

$$\sigma_d = \sqrt{\frac{\sum\limits_{i=1}^{n} (d_i - \bar{d})^2}{n}} \tag{14.7}$$

Standard deviation of a series of independent demands.

$$\sigma_s = \sqrt{\sigma_1^2 + \sigma_2^2 + \ldots + \sigma_i^2} \tag{14.8}$$

Q model. Expected number of units short in one order cycle for a service level *P* and optimum order quantity *Q*.

$$E(z) = \frac{(1-P)Q}{\sigma_L} \tag{14.9}$$

P model. Optimum order quantity in a fixed period system with a review period of *T* days and lead time of *L* days.

$$q = \bar{d}(T + L) + z\sigma_{T+L} - I \tag{14.10}$$

P model. Expected number of units short in one period of a fixed period system.

$$E(z) = \frac{\bar{d}T(1-P)}{\sigma_{T+L}} \tag{14.11}$$

P model. Standard deviation of a series of independent demands over the review period *T* and lead time *L*.

$$\sigma_{T+L} = \sqrt{\sum\limits_{i=1}^{T+L} \sigma_{d_i}^2} \tag{14.12}$$

Q model. Optimum order quantity based on an order cost *S*, holding cost as a percent (*i*) of the unit cost (*C*).

$$Q = \sqrt{\frac{2DS}{iC}}$$

(14.13)

Single period model. Probability of selling the last unit as a ratio of marginal loss and marginal profit.

$$P \geq \frac{ML}{MP + ML}$$

(14.15)

14.12   SOLVED PROBLEMS

1. Items purchased from a vendor cost $20 each, and the forecast for next year's demand is 1,000 units. If it costs $5 every time an order is placed for more units and the storage cost is $4 per unit per year, what quantity should be ordered each time?

   a. What is the total ordering cost for a year?

   b. What is the total storage cost for a year?

   Solution

   The quantity to be ordered each time is

   $$Q = \sqrt{\frac{2DS}{H}} = \sqrt{\frac{2(1,000)5}{4}} = 50 \text{ units}$$

   a. The total ordering cost for a year is

   $$\frac{D}{Q}S = \frac{1,000}{50}(\$5) = \$100$$

   b. The storage cost for a year is

   $$\frac{Q}{2}H = \frac{50}{2}(\$4) = \$100$$

2. Daily demand for a product is 120 units, with a standard deviation of 30 units. The review period is 14 days and the lead time is 7 days. At the time of review there are 130 units in stock. If 99 percent of all demand is to be satisfied from items in stock, how many units should be ordered?

   Solution

   $$\sigma_{T+L} = \sqrt{(14 + 7)(30)^2} = \sqrt{18,900} = 137.5$$

   $$E(z) = \frac{120(14)(1 - .99)}{137.5} = 0.122$$

   From Exhibit 14.6, $z = .80$

   $$q = \bar{d}(T + L) + z\sigma_{T+L} - I$$
   $$= 120(14 + 7) + .80(137.5) - 130$$
   $$= 2,500 \text{ units}$$

3. A company currently has 200 units of a product on hand which it orders every two weeks when the salesperson visits the premises. Demand for the product averages 20 units per day with a standard deviation of five units. Lead time for the product to arrive is seven days. Management has a goal of providing a 99 percent service level for this product.

The salesperson is due to come in late this afternoon when there are 180 units left in stock (assuming that 20 are sold today). How many units should be ordered?

Solution

Given $I = 186$, $T = 14$, $L = 7$, $\bar{d} = 20$

$$\sigma_{T+L} = \sqrt{21(5)^2} = 23$$

$$E(z) = \frac{\bar{d}T(1-P)}{\sigma_{T+L}} = \frac{20(14)(1-.99)}{23} = .1217$$

From Table 14.6, $z = .80$

$$q = \bar{d}(T + L) + z\sigma_{T+L} - I$$
$$= 20(14 + 7) + .80(23) - 180$$
$$q = 258.4 \text{ units}$$

14.13 REVIEW AND DISCUSSION QUESTIONS

1. Distinguish between dependent and independent demand in a McDonald's, in an integrated manufacturer of personal copiers, and in a pharmaceutical supply house.
2. Distinguish between in-process inventory, safety stock inventory, and seasonal inventory.
3. Discuss the nature of the costs that affect inventory size.
4. Under which conditions would a plant manager elect to use a fixed-order quantity model as opposed to a fixed-time period model? What are the disadvantages of using a fixed-time period ordering system?
5. Discuss the general procedure for determining the order quantity when price breaks are involved. Would there be any differences in the procedure if holding cost were a fixed percentage of price rather than a constant amount?
6. What two basic questions must be answered by an inventory-control decision rule?
7. Discuss the assumptions that are inherent in production setup cost, ordering cost, and carrying costs. How valid are they?
8. "The nice thing about inventory models is that you can pull one off the shelf and apply it so long as your cost estimates are accurate." Comment.
9. Which type of inventory system would you use in the following situations?
   a. Supplying your kitchen with fresh food.
   b. Obtaining a daily newspaper.
   c. Buying gas for your car.
   To which of these items do you impute the highest stockout cost?
10. Why is it desirable to classify items into groups, as the ABC classification does?
11. What kind of policy or procedure would you recommend to improve the inventory operation in a department store? What advantages and disadvantages does your system have vis-à-vis the department store inventory operation described in this chapter?

14.14 PROBLEMS

1. Annual demand for an item is 2,500 units. The cost to place an order is $5, and holding cost is 20 percent of the cost of the item. Items have the following cost schedule:

1 to 99	$10.00 each
100 to 199	$ 9.80 each
over 200	$ 9.60 each

What is the optimal number to order each time?

2. Electronic Memos, Inc. (EMI), produces pocket-size microcassette recorders for business and professional people to record notes and for transcribing. These recorders are sold through retailers nationally.

   EMI would like to give its retailers guidelines to help them determine what size orders to place, what safety stocks to carry, the reorder points, and so forth. EMI has just hired you to develop a set of charts to distribute to its retailers for use during their reordering periods.

   Because technology in the entire electronics area is changing so rapidly (recorders included), EMI is recommending that its dealers review their inventory on hand and place orders monthly.

   During an interview for a job with EMI, the recruiter has explained this reordering situation to you and has asked you to demonstrate that you are qualified to take on this task as your first assignment with the company. You happen to have your operations management text with you and she is allowing you to use its equations and tables.

   The tables cover a wide variety of possibilities. The problem you are to solve has the following features:

   Demand for the coming 30-day month is 40 units.

   Standard deviation of daily demand is four units.

   The firm is open every day.

   It takes 10 calendar days to receive an order.

   The firm would like to satisfy 95 percent of the customers.

   There are currently 30 units in stock.

   How many units should be ordered?

3. Dunstreet's Department Store would like to develop an inventory ordering policy to satisfy 95 percent of its customers' demands for products directly from inventory stock on hand. To illustrate your recommended procedure, use as an example the ordering policy for white percale sheets.

   Demand for white percale sheets is 5,000 per year. The store is open 365 days per year. Every two weeks (14 days) an inventory count is made and a new order is placed. It takes 10 days for the sheets to be delivered. Standard deviation of demand for the sheets is five per day. There are currently 150 sheets on hand.

   How many sheets should you order?

4. Charlie's Pizza orders all of its pepperoni, olives, anchovies, and mozzarella cheese to be shipped directly from Italy. An American distributor stops by every four weeks to take orders. Since the orders are shipped directly from Italy, it takes three weeks to arrive.

   Charlie's Pizza uses an average of 150 pounds of pepperoni each week, with a standard deviation of 30 pounds. Since Charlie's prides itself on offering only the best-quality ingredients and a high level of service, it wants to ensure that it can satisfy 99 percent of the customers who demand pepperoni on their pizza.

   Assume that the sales representative just walked in the door and there is currently 500 pounds of pepperoni in the walk-in cooler. How many pounds of pepperoni would you order?

5. Given the following information, formulate an inventory management system. The item is demanded 50 weeks a year.

Item cost	$10.00
Order cost	$250.00
Holding cost (%)	33% of item cost
Annual demand	25,750
Average demand	515 per week
Standard deviation of demand	25 per week
Lead time	1 week
Service level	95%

    a. State the order quantity and the reorder point.

    b. Determine the annual holding and order costs.

    c. How many units per order cycle would you expect to be short?

    d. If a price break of $50 per order was offered for purchase quantities of over 2,000, would you take advantage of it? How much would you save on an annual basis?

6. Lieutenant Commander Data is planning to make his monthly (every 30 days) trek to Gamma Hydra City to pick up a supply of isolinear chips. The trip will take Data about two days. Before he leaves, he calls in the order to the GHC Supply Store. He uses chips at an average rate of five per day (seven days per week) with a standard deviation of demand of one per day. He needs a 99 percent service level. If he currently has 35 chips in inventory, how many should he order? What is the most he will ever have to order?

7. Jill's Job Shop buys two parts (Tegdiws and Widgets) for use in its production system from two different suppliers. The parts are needed throughout the entire 52-week year. Tegdiws are used at a relatively constant rate and are ordered whenever the remaining quantity drops to the reorder level. Widgets are ordered from a supplier who stops by every three weeks. Data for both products are as follows:

Item	Tegdiw	Widget
Annual demand	10,000	5,000
Holding cost (% of item cost)	20%	20%
Setup or order cost	$150.00	$25.00
Lead time	4 weeks	1 week
Safety stock	55 units	5 units
Item cost	$10.00	$2.00

    a. What is the inventory control system for Tegdiws; that is, what is the reorder quantity and what is the reorder point?

    b. What is the inventory control system for Widgets?

8. Demand for an item is 1,000 units per year. Each order placed costs $10; the annual cost to carry items in inventory is $2 each.

    a. In what quantities should the item be ordered?

    b. Supposing a $100 discount on each order is given if orders are placed in quantities of 500 or more. Should orders be placed in quantities of 500, or should you stick to the decision you made in *a?*

9. The annual demand for a product is 15,600 units. The weekly demand is 300 units with a standard deviation of 90 units. The cost to place an order is $31.20, and the time from ordering to receipt is four weeks. The annual inventory carrying cost is $0.10 per unit. Find the reorder point necessary to provide a 99 percent service level.

    Suppose the production manager is ordered to reduce the safety stock of this item by 50 percent. If he does so, what will the new service level be?

10. Daily demand for a product is 100 units, with a standard deviation of 25 units. The review period is 10 days and the lead time is 6 days. At the time of review there are 50 units in stock. If 98 percent of all demand is to be satisfied from items in stock, how many units should be ordered?

11. Item X is a standard item stocked in a company's inventory of component parts. Each year, the firm, on a random basis, uses about 2,000 of item X, which costs $25 each. Storage costs, which include insurance and cost of capital, amount to $5 per unit of average inventory. Every time an order is placed for more item X, it costs $10.

    a. Whenever item X is ordered, what should the order size be?

    b. What is the annual cost for ordering item X?

    c. What is the annual cost for storing item X?

12. Annual demand for a product is 13,000 units; weekly demand is 250 units with a standard deviation of 40 units. The cost of placing an order is $100, and the time from ordering to receipt is four weeks. The annual inventory carrying cost is $0.65 per unit. To provide a 99 percent service level, what must the reorder point be?

    Suppose the production manager is told to reduce the safety stock of this item by 10 units. If this is done, what will the new service level be?

13. A particular raw material is available to a company at three different prices, depending on the size of the order:

Less than 100 pounds	$20 per pound
100 pounds to 999 pounds	$19 per pound
More than 1,000 pounds	$18 per pound

    The cost to place an order is $40. Annual demand is 3,000 units. Holding (or carrying) cost is 25 percent of the material price.

    What is the economic order quantity to buy each time?

14. In the past, Taylor Industries has used a fixed-time inventory system that involved taking a complete inventory count of all items each month. However, increasing labor costs are forcing Taylor Industries to examine alternate ways to reduce the amount of labor involved in inventory stockrooms, yet without increasing other costs, such as shortage costs. Here is a random sample of 20 of Taylor's items.

Item Number	Annual Usage	Item Number	Annual Usage
1	$ 1,500	11	$13,000
2	12,000	12	600
3	2,200	13	42,000
4	50,000	14	9,900
5	9,600	15	1,200
6	750	16	10,200
7	2,000	17	4,000
8	11,000	18	61,000
9	800	19	3,500
10	15,000	20	2,900

    a. What would you recommend Taylor do to cut back its labor cost? (Illustrate using an ABC plan.)
    b. Item 15 is critical to continued operations. How would you recommend it be classified?

15. Gentle Ben's Bar and Restaurant uses 5,000 quart bottles of an imported wine each year. The effervescent wine costs $3 per bottle and is served in whole bottles only since it loses its bubbles quickly. Ben figures that it costs $10 each time an order is placed, and holding costs are 20 percent of the purchase price. It takes three weeks for an order to arrive. Weekly demand is 100 bottles (closed two weeks per year) with a standard deviation of 30 bottles.

    Ben would like to use an inventory system that minimizes inventory cost and will satisfy 95 percent of his customers who order this wine.

    a. What is the economic order quantity for Ben to order?
    b. At what inventory level should he place an order?
    c. How many bottles of wine will be short during each order cycle?

16. Retailers Warehouse (RW) is an independent supplier of household items to department stores. RW attempts to stock enough items to satisfy 98 percent of the requests from its customers.

    A stainless steel knife set is one item it stocks. Demand (2,400 sets per year) is relatively stable over the entire year. Whenever new stock is ordered, a buyer must assure that numbers are correct for stock on hand and then phone in a new order. The total cost involved to place an order is about $5. RW figures that to hold inventory in stock and to pay for interest on borrowed capital, insurance, and so on adds up to about $4 holding cost per unit per year.

Analysis of the past data shows that the standard deviation of demand from retailers is about four units per day for a 365-day year. Lead time to get the order once placed is seven days.

a. What is the economic order quantity?

b. What is the reorder point?

17. Daily demand for a product is 60 units with a standard deviation of 10 units. The review period is 10 days, and lead time is 2 days. At the time of review there are 100 units in stock. If 98 percent of all demand is to be satisfied from items in stock, how many units should be ordered?

18. University Drug Pharmaceuticals orders its antibiotics every two weeks (14 days) when a salesperson visits from one of the pharmaceutical companies. Tetracycline is one of its most prescribed antibiotics, with average daily demand of 2,000 capsules. The standard deviation of daily demand was derived from examining prescriptions filled over the past three months and was found to be 800 capsules. It takes five days for the order to arrive. University Drug would like to satisfy 99 percent of the prescriptions. The salesperson just arrived, and there are currently 25,000 capsules in stock.

How many capsules should be ordered?

19. Several machine centers in SJM Manufacturing, Inc., produce a number of parts on each machine that are then used internally elsewhere in the production process. The question is whether parts could be transferred in several smaller batches, as a machine makes the parts, rather than waiting for the entire process batch to be finished. Currently the process batch is transferred only after it is totally completed.

SJM would like to know the potential benefits and resulting costs of using smaller transfer batch sizes.

Note: The basic EOQ equations on pages 552 and 553 are slightly modified to consider that the average holding cost would become $QH/(2n)$ rather than $QH/2$, where Q is the process batch size which will be divided into n separate transfer lots, or Q/n at a time.

The resulting equations are:

$$Q = \sqrt{\frac{2nDS}{H}} \text{ and } TC = DC + \frac{D}{Q} + \frac{Q}{2n}H$$

One item was selected to use for a quick calculation of costs. This item has annual demand of 24,000 units and manufacturing cost of $8 each. Carrying cost is 25 percent of manufacturing cost, and setup cost is estimated to be $40.

a. While ignoring materials handling costs, what would the process batch size be if parts could be transferred in 2 batches, 5 batches, and 10 batches, rather than in one batch containing the entire process batch?

b. What would the total costs be for each batch size?

c. Discuss the results.

20. Magnetron, Inc., manufactures microwave ovens for the commercial market. Currently, Magnetron is producing part 2104 in its fabrication shop for use in the adjacent unit assembly area. Next year's requirement for part 2104 is estimated at 20,000 units. Part 2104 is valued at $50 per unit, and the combined storage and handling cost is $8 per unit per year. The cost of preparing the order and making the production setup is $200. The plant operates 250 days per year. The assembly area operates every working day, completing 80 units, and the fabrication shop produces 160 units per day when it is producing part 2104.

a. Compute the economic order quantity.

b. How many orders will be placed each year?

c. If part 2104 could be purchased from another firm with the same costs as described, what would the order quantity be? (The order is received all at once.)

d. If the average lead time to order from another firm is 10 working days and a safety stock level is set at 500 units, what is the reorder point?

21. Garrett Corporation, a turbine manufacturer, works an 18-hour day, 300 days a year. Titanium blades can be produced on its turbine blade machine number 1, TBM1, at a rate of 500 per hour, and the average usage rate is 5,000 per day. The blades cost $15 apiece, and storage costs $0.10 per day per blade because of insurance, interest on investments, and space allocation. TBM1 costs $250 to set up for each run. Lead time requires production to begin after stock drops to 500 blades. What is the optimal production run for TBM1?

22. Famous Albert prides himself on being the Cookie King of the West. Small, freshly baked cookies are the specialty of his shop. Famous Albert has asked for help to determine the number of cookies he should make each day. From an analysis of past demand he estimates demand for cookies as

Demand	Probability of Demand
1,800 dozen	0.05
2,000	0.10
2,200	0.20
2,400	0.30
2,600	0.20
2,800	0.10
3,000	0.05

Each dozen sells for $.69 and costs $.49, which includes handling and transportation. Cookies that are not sold at the end of the day are reduced to $0.29 and sold the following day as day-old merchandise.

a. Construct a table showing the profits or losses for each possible quantity.
b. What is the optimal number of cookies to make?
c. Solve this problem by using marginal analysis.

23. The text described how one department store conducted its inventory ordering for a housewares department. How would you apply the theory and models in this chapter to enhance the operation of that store's system?

24. Alpha Products, Inc., is having a problem trying to control inventory. There is insufficient time to devote to all its items equally. Here is a sample of some items stocked, along with the annual usage of each item expressed in dollar volume.

Item	Annual Dollar Usage	Item	Annual Dollar Usage
a	$ 7,000	k	$80,000
b	1,000	l	400
c	14,000	m	1,100
d	2,000	n	30,000
e	24,000	o	1,900
f	68,000	p	800
g	17,000	q	90,000
h	900	r	12,000
i	1,700	s	3,000
j	2,300	t	32,000

a. Can you suggest a system for allocating control time?
b. Specify where each item from the list would be placed.

25. After graduation you decide to go into a partnership in an office supply store that has existed for a number of years. Walking through the store and stockrooms, you find a great discrepancy in service levels. Some spaces and bins for items are completely empty; others have supplies that are covered with dust and have obviously been there a long time. You decide to take on the project of establishing consistent levels of inventory to meet customer demands. Most of your supplies are purchased from just a few distributors that call on your store once every two weeks.

You choose, as your first item for study, computer printer paper. You examine the sales records and purchase orders and find that demand for the past 12 months was 5,000 boxes.

Using your calculator you sample some days' demands and estimate that the standard deviation of daily demand is 10 boxes. You also search out these figures:

Cost per box of paper: $11.

Desired service level: 98 percent.

Store is open every day.

Salesperson visits every two weeks.

Delivery time following visit is three days.

Using your procedure, how many boxes of paper would be ordered if, on the day the salesperson calls, there are 60 boxes on hand?

26. A distributor of large appliances needs to determine the order quantities and reorder points for the various products it carries. The following data refer to a specific refrigerator in its product line:

Cost to place an order	$30
Holding cost	20 percent of product cost per year
Cost of refrigerator	$300 each
Annual demand	500 refrigerators
Standard deviation during lead time	10 refrigerators
Lead time	7 days

Consider an even daily demand and a 365-day year.

a. What is the economic order quantity?

b. If the distributor wants to satisfy 97 percent of its demand, what reorder point, *R,* should be used?

27. It is your responsibility, as the new head of the automotive section of Nichols Department Store, to ensure that reorder quantities for the various items have been correctly established. You decide to test one of the items and choose Michelin tires, XW size 185 × 14 BSW. A perpetual inventory system has been used so you examine this as well as other records and come up with the following data:

Cost per tire	$35 each
Holding cost	20 percent of tire cost per year
Demand	1,000 per year
Ordering cost	$20 per order
Standard deviation of daily demand	3 tires
Delivery lead time	4 days

Because customers generally do not wait for tires but go elsewhere, you decide on a service level of 98 percent.

a. Determine the order quantity.

b. Determine the reorder point.

28. UA Hamburger Hamlet (UAHH) places an order for its high-volume items daily (hamburger patties, buns, milk, etc.). UAHH counts its current inventory on hand once per day and phones in its order for delivery 24 hours later. Determine the number of hamburgers UAHH should order for the following conditions:

Average daily demand	600
Standard deviation of demand	100
Desired service level	99%
Hamburger inventory	800

29. CU, Incorporated (CUI), produces copper contacts that it uses in switches and relays. CUI needs to determine the order quantity, *Q,* to meet the annual demand at the lowest cost. The price of copper depends on the quantity ordered. Here are price-break data and other data for the problem:

> Price of copper: $0.82 per pound up to 2,499 pounds
> $0.81 per pound for orders between 2,500 and 4,999 pounds
> $0.80 per pound for orders greater than 5,000 pounds
> Annual demand: 50,000 pounds per year
> Holding cost: 20 percent per unit per year of the price of the copper
> Ordering cost: $30

Which quantity should be ordered?

30. DAT, Inc., produces digital audiotapes to be used in the consumer audio division. DAT lacks sufficient personnel in its inventory supply section to closely control each item stocked, so it has asked you to determine an ABC classification. Here is a sample from the inventory records:

Item	Average Monthly Demand	Price per Unit
1	700	$ 6.00
2	200	4.00
3	2,000	12.00
4	1,100	20.00
5	4,000	21.00
6	100	10.00
7	3,000	2.00
8	2,500	1.00
9	500	10.00
10	1,000	2.00

Develop an ABC classification for these 10 items.

31. A local service station is open 7 days per week, 365 days per year. Sales of 10W40 grade premium oil average 20 cans per day. Inventory holding costs are $0.50 per can per year. Ordering costs are $10 per order. Lead time is two weeks. Back orders are not practical—the motorist drives away.

   a. Based on this data, choose the appropriate inventory model and calculate the economic order quantity and reorder point. Describe in a sentence how the plan would work. Hint: Assume demand is deterministic.

   b. The boss is concerned about this model because demand really varies. The standard deviation of demand was determined from a data sample to be 6.15 cans per day. The manager wants to satisfy 99.5 percent of his customers (practically all) when they ask for oil. Determine a new inventory plan based on this new information and the data in *(a)*. Use Q_{opt} from *(a)*.

14.15   SELECTED BIBLIOGRAPHY

Anderson, Edward J. "Testing Feasibility in a Lot Scheduling Problem." *Operations Research,* November–December 1990, pp. 1079–89.

Brooks, Roger B., and Larry W. Wilson. *Inventory Record Accuracy: Unleashing the Power of Cycle Counting.* Essex Junction, VT: Oliver Wight, 1993.

Davis, Samuel G. "Scheduling Economic Lot Size Production Runs." *Management Science,* August 1990, pp. 985–99.

Fogarty, Donald W., John H. Blackstone, and Thomas R. Hoffmann. *Production and Inventory Management.* 2d ed. Cincinnati, OH: South-Western, 1991.

Freeland, James R., John P. Leschke, and Elliott N. Weiss. "Guidelines for Setup Reduction Programs to Achieve Zero Inventory." *Journal of Operations Management,* January 1990, pp. 75–80.

Graves, Steven C., A. H. G. Rinnoy Kan, and Paul H. Zipkin. *Logistics of Production and Inventory.* New York: North-Holland, 1993.

Harris, Ford Whitman. "How Many Parts to Make at Once." *Operations Research,* November–December 1990, pp. 947–51.

Tersine, Richard J. *Principles of Inventory and Materials Management.* 4th ed. New York: North-Holland, 1994.

Vollmann, T. E., W. L. Berry, and D. C. Whybark. *Manufacturing Planning and Control Systems.* 3d ed. Homewood, IL: Richard D. Irwin, 1992.

Young, Jan B. *Modern Inventory Operations: Methods for Accuracy and Productivity.* New York: Van Nostrand Reinhold, 1991.

Chapter

15

Inventory Systems for Dependent Demand
MRP-Type Systems

CHAPTER OUTLINE

KEY TERMS

Material Requirements Planning (MRP)

Manufacturing Resource Planning (MRP II)

Master Production Schedule (MPS)

Bill of Materials (BOM)

Net Change System

Closed-Loop MRP

Advanced MRP-Type Systems

Enterprise Resource Planning (ERP)

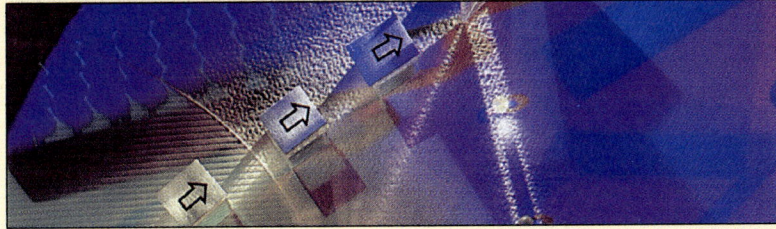

Two companies ready for next-generation MRP systems are FMC Corp. and Dow Corning Corp.

FMC Corp. is a $3.75 billion global producer of food machinery, chemicals, and defense equipment. Already skilled at producing high-quality, low-cost products, the company now wants to take advantage of emerging, worldwide markets while being its customers' best supplier.

To do that, FMC plans to supply the sales force with up-to-date information about the markets, the company's product lines, and product availability across their plants. This will allow the sales force to access current information from 112 plants in 20 countries.

In addition, sales representatives will be given tools to analyze available inventory, capacity, cost, and currency considerations in order to achieve the most favorable economics in delivering products to customers. But first, FMC needs to get the right information from the company's multiple ManMan MRP II systems from The Ask Cos. Currently, FMC is working with Ask to develop the capabilities to support its goals.

Customer service is the primary focus at Dow Corning Corp. The company has launched 30 cross-functional teams across five of its eight divisions. These teams are working to change Dow's operational processes, work flows, and the way people perform to increase customer satisfaction and reduce resource consumption.

Of utmost importance is shortening the time-to-market of new products and placing operational activities, such as order entry, into the hands of customers. Key to these plans is an EDI system for the entire supply chain. Dow also plans to replace its 20-year-old, in-house–developed MRP II system with an advanced system that can balance its production resources across all of its divisions.

_____

Source: Alice Greene, "Two Ready for the Next Generation," *Computerworld,* June 8, 1992, p. 77.

As Virginia Slims ads used to say, "You've come a long way, baby." So has material requirements planning (MRP) come a long way. From humble beginnings computing the schedules and amounts of materials required, MRP is growing to become fully integrated, interactive, real time systems capable of multisite global applications.

In this chapter we go back to the beginning and introduce the basic MRP system and take you through the logic and calculations of time bucket scheduling and materials ordering. We conclude the chapter by discussing the latest MRP-type systems being developed today.

Material requirements planning (MRP) systems have been installed almost universally in manufacturing firms, even those considered small. The reason is that MRP is a logical, easily understandable approach to the problem of determining the number of parts, components, and materials needed to produce each end item. MRP also provides the time schedule specifying when each of these materials, parts, and components should be ordered or produced.

The original MRP planned only materials. However, as computer power grew and applications expanded, so did the breadth of MRP. Soon it considered resources as well as materials and was called **MRP II,** standing for **manufacturing resource planning.** A complete MRP program included 20 or so modules controlling the entire system from order entry through scheduling, inventory control, finance, accounting, accounts payable, and so on. Today MRP impacts the entire system and is including just-in-time, Kanban, and computer-integrated manufacturing (CIM).

All firms maintain a bill of materials file (BOM) which is simply the sequence of everything that goes into the final product. It can be called a *product structure tree,* a *schematic,* or a *flow diagram,* which shows the order of creating the item. Also maintained by all firms is an inventory file. This database contains specifications about each item, where it is purchased or produced, and how long it takes. MRP in its basic form is a computer program determining how much of each item is needed and when it is needed to complete a specified number of units in a specific time period. MRP does this by reaching into the bill of materials file and inventory records file to create a time schedule and the number of units needed at each step in the process.

MRP is based on dependent demand. Dependent demand is that demand caused by the demand for a higher-level item. Tires, wheels, and engines are dependent demand items that depend on the demand for automobiles.

Determining the number of dependent demand items needed is essentially a straightforward multiplication process. If one Part A takes five parts of B to make, then five parts of A require 25 parts of B. The basic difference in independent demand covered in the previous chapter and dependent demand covered in this chapter is as follows: If Part A is sold outside of the firm, the amount of Part A that we sell is uncertain. We need to create a forecast using past data or do something like a market analysis. Part A is an independent item. However, Part B is a dependent part and its use depends on Part A. The number of B needed is simply the number of A times five. As a result of this type of multiplication, the requirements of other dependent demand items tend to become more and more lumpy as we go farther down into the product creation sequence. Lumpiness means that the requirements tend to bunch or lump rather than having an even disbursement. This is also caused by the way manufacturing is done. When manufacturing occurs in lots, items needed to produce the lot are withdrawn from inventory in quantities (perhaps all at once) rather than one at a time.

The main purpose of this chapter is to explain MRP more thoroughly and to demonstrate its use. We show that just-in-time (JIT) systems and MRP are not necessarily com-

Industry Type	Examples	Expected Benefits
Assemble-to-stock	Combines multiple component parts into a finished product, which is then stocked in inventory to satisfy customer demand. Examples: watches, tools, appliances.	High
Fabricate-to-stock	Items are manufactured by machine rather than assembled from parts. These are standard stock items carried in anticipation of customer demand. Examples: piston rings, electrical switches.	Low
Assemble-to-order	A final assembly is made from standard options that the customer chooses. Examples: trucks, generators, motors.	High
Fabricate-to-order	Items manufactured by machine to customer order. These are generally industrial orders. Examples: bearings, gears, fasteners.	Low
Manufacture-to-order	Items fabricated or assembled completely to customer specification. Examples: turbine generators, heavy machine tools.	High
Process	Industries such as foundries, rubber and plastics, specialty paper, chemicals, paint, drug, food processors.	Medium

peting ways for production but can work effectively together. Finally we discuss advanced MRP-type systems including enterprisewide and industrywide modules and data requirements.

15.1   WHERE MRP CAN BE USED

MRP is being used in a variety of industries with a job-shop environment (meaning that a number of products are made in batches using the same productive equipment). The list in Exhibit 15.1 includes process industries, but note that the processes mentioned are confined to job runs that alternate output product and do not include continuous processes such as petroleum or steel.

As you can see in the exhibit, MRP is most valuable to companies involved in assembly operations and least valuable to those in fabrication.

One more point to note: MRP does not work well in companies that produce a low number of units annually. Especially for companies producing complex expensive products requiring advanced research and design, experience has shown that lead times tend to be too long and too uncertain, and the product configuration too complex for MRP to handle. Such companies need the control features that network scheduling techniques offer; they would be better off using project scheduling methods (covered previously in Chapter 12).

Exhibit 15.2 shows the percentage of companies in the United States that have installed MRP II-type systems. Pharmaceuticals lead the list at 80 percent. Aerospace is second with 70 percent. Next come automotive with 60 percent, electronics with 44 percent, and fabricated metals with 25 percent. Since there are about 65,000 total installed MRP II-type systems in the United States (90,000 worldwide) out of 550,000 manufacturing firms, this gives an overall installation rate of just 11 percent. Since the concept of MRP has expanded to include a very wide data management and information flow, there is a high likelihood for further expansion.

E X H I B I T 15.2

Percentage of Companies in 11 Industries with Installed MRP II Systems

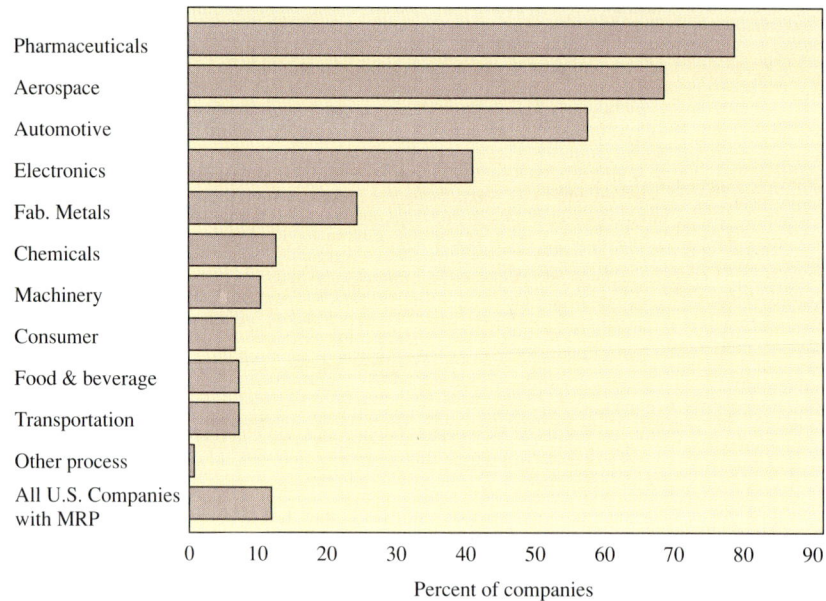

Source: David A. Turbide, *MRP+: The Adaptation, Enhancement, and Application of MRPII* (New York: Industrial Press, 1993), p. 11.

It is interesting to note that the expectation that microcomputers would lead the expansion did not materialize. In 1990, 70 percent of the installations were on minicomputers, and microcomputer installation rates declined.

MRP started in the late 1960s. Many systems have since been developed and sold by many software and consulting firms. While other competing-type integrated information programs have been and will probably continue to be developed, MRP-based systems will likely stay in the lead. This is because the firms currently in MRP systems are continuing to develop and enhance them.[1]

15.2   A SIMPLE MRP EXAMPLE

Before discussing details of an MRP system, we briefly explain how quantities are calculated, lead times are offset, and order releases and receipts are established.

Suppose that we are to produce Product T, which is made of two parts U and three parts V. Part U, in turn, is made of one part W and two parts X. Part V is made of two parts W and two parts Y. Exhibit 15.3 shows the product structure tree of Product T. By simple computation, we calculate that if 100 units of T are required, we need

Part U:	2 × number of Ts =	2 × 100	= 200
Part V:	3 × number of Ts =	3 × 100	= 300
Part W:	1 × number of Us =	1 × 200	= 800
	+2 × number of Vs =	+2 × 300	
Part X:	2 × number of Us =	2 × 200	= 400
Part Y:	2 × number of Vs =	2 × 300	= 600

---

[1]David A. Turbide, *MRP+: The Adaptation, Enhancement, and Application of MRPII* (New York: Industrial Press, 1993), p. 12.

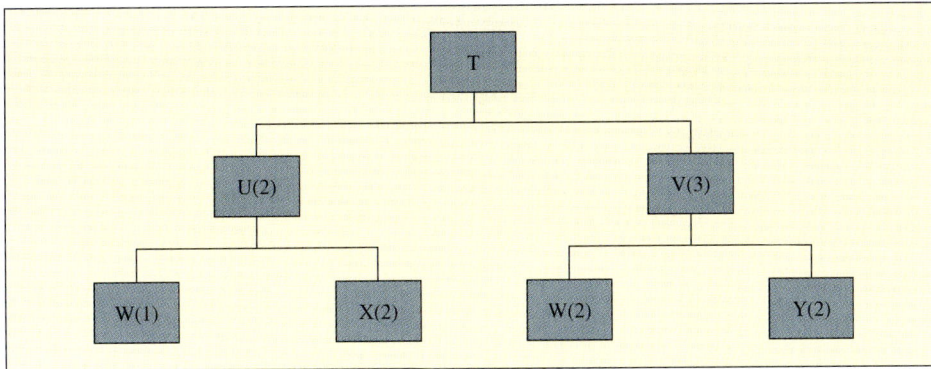

E X H I B I T 15.3

Product Structure Tree for Product T

E X H I B I T 15.4

Material Requirements Plan for Completing 100 Units of Product T in Period 7

Now, consider the time needed to obtain these items, either to produce the part internally or to obtain it from an outside vendor. Assume, now, that T takes one week to make; U, 2 weeks; V, 2 weeks; W, 3 weeks; X, 1 week; and Y, 1 week. If we know when Product T is required, we can create a time schedule chart specifying when all materials must be ordered and received to meet the demand for T. Exhibit 15.4 shows which items are needed and when. We have thus created a material requirements plan based on the demand for Product T and the knowledge of how T is made and the time needed to obtain each part.

From this simple illustration, it is apparent that developing a material requirements plan manually for thousands or even hundreds of items would be impractical—a great deal of computation is needed, and a tremendous amount of data must be available about the inventory status (number of units on hand, on order, and so forth) and about the product structure (how the product is made and how many units of each material are required). Because we are compelled to use a computer, our emphasis from here on in this chapter is to discuss the files needed for a computer program and the general makeup of the system. However, the basic logic of the program is essentially the same as that for our simple example.

Generally, the master schedule deals with end items. If the end item is quite large or quite expensive, however, the master schedule may schedule major subassemblies or components instead.

All production systems have limited capacity and limited resources. This presents a challenging job for the master scheduler. While the aggregate plan provides the general range of operation, the master scheduler must specify exactly what is to be produced. These decisions are made while responding to pressures from various functional areas such as the sales department (meet the customer's promised due date), finance (minimize inventory), management (maximize productivity and customer service, minimize resource needs), and manufacturing (have level schedules and minimize setup time).

To determine an acceptable feasible schedule to be released to the shop, trial master production schedules are run through the MRP program. The resulting planned order releases (the detailed production schedules) are checked to make sure that resources are available and the completion times are reasonable. What appears to be a feasible master schedule may turn out to require excessive resources once the product explosion has taken place and materials, parts, and components from lower levels are determined. If this does happen (the usual case), the master production schedule is then modified with these limitations and the MRP program is run again. To ensure good master scheduling, the master scheduler (the human being) must

Include all demands from product sales, warehouse replenishment, spares, and interplant requirements.

Never lose sight of the aggregate plan.

Be involved with customer order promising.

Be visible to all levels of management.

Objectively trade off manufacturing, marketing, and engineering conflicts.

Identify and communicate all problems.

15.3   MASTER PRODUCTION SCHEDULE

The upper portion of Exhibit 15.5 shows an aggregate plan for the total number of mattresses planned per month, without regard for mattress type. The lower portion shows a master production schedule specifying the exact type of mattress and the quantity planned for production by week. The next level down (not shown) would be the MRP program that develops detailed schedules showing when cotton batting,

E X H I B I T 15.5

The Aggregate Plan and the Master Production Schedule for Mattresses

Aggregate Production Plan for Mattresses

Month	1	2
Mattress production	900	950

Master Production Schedule for Mattress Models

	1	2	3	4	5	6	7	8
Model 327	200			400		200	100	
Model 538		100	100		150		100	
Model 749			100			200		200

springs, and hardwood are needed to make the mattresses. If carried further, this mattress example would look like Exhibit 15.17, which shows parts and subassemblies for electrical meters.

The aggregate production plan, discussed in Chapter 13, specifies product groups. It does not specify exact items. The next level down in the planning process is the master production schedule. The **master production schedule (MPS)** is the time-phased plan specifying how many and when the firm plans to build each end item. For example, the aggregate plan for a furniture company may specify the total volume of mattresses it plans to produce over the next month or next quarter. The MPS goes the next step down and identifies the exact size mattresses and their qualities and styles. All the mattresses sold by the company would be specified by the MPS. The MPS also states period by period (usually weekly) how many and when each of these mattress types is needed.

Still further down the disaggregation process is the MRP program, which calculates and schedules all raw materials, parts, and supplies needed to make the mattress specified by the MPS.

Time Fences

The question of flexibility within a master production schedule depends on several factors: production lead time, commitment of parts and components to a specific end item, relationship between the customer and vendor, amount of excess capacity, and the reluctance or willingness of management to make changes.

The purpose of time fences is to maintain a reasonably controlled flow through the production system. Unless some operating rules are established and adhered to, the system could be chaotic and filled with overdue orders and constant expediting.

Exhibit 15.6 shows an example of a master production schedule time fence. Management defines *time fences* as periods of time having some specified level of opportunity for the customer to make changes. (The customer may be the firm's own marketing department which may be considering product promotions, broadening variety, etc.) Note in the exhibit that for the next eight weeks this particular master schedule is frozen. Each firm has its own time fences and operating rules. Under these rules, *frozen* could be defined as anything from absolutely no changes in one firm to only the most minor of changes in another. *Moderately firm* may allow changes in specific products within a product group so long as parts are available. *Flexible* may allow almost any variations in products, with the provision that capacity remains about the same and that there are no long lead time items involved.

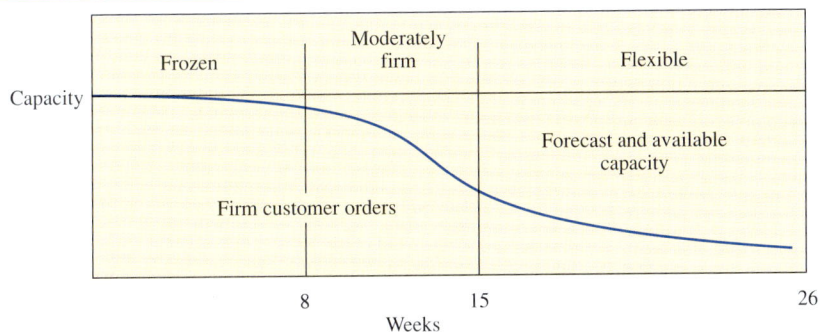

E X H I B I T 15.6
Master Production Schedule Time Fences

15.4   MATERIAL REQUIREMENTS PLANNING (MRP) SYSTEMS

As we stated previously, based on a *master schedule* derived from a *production plan,* a *material requirements planning (MRP) system* creates schedules identifying the specific parts and materials required to produce end items, the exact numbers needed, and the dates when orders for these materials should be released and be received or completed within the production cycle. MRP systems use a computer program to carry out these operations. Most firms have used computerized inventory systems for years, but they were independent of the scheduling system; MRP links them together.

Purposes, Objectives, and Philosophy of MRP

The main purposes of a basic MRP system are to control inventory levels, assign operating priorities for items, and plan capacity to load the production system. These may be briefly expanded as follows:

Inventory

Order the right part.

Order in the right quantity.

Order at the right time.

Priorities

Order with the right due date.

Keep the due date valid.

Capacity

Plan for a complete load.

Plan an accurate load.

Plan for an adequate time to view future load.

The *theme* of MRP is "getting the right materials to the right place at the right time."

The *objectives* of inventory management under an MRP system are the same as under any inventory management system: to improve customer service, minimize inventory investment, and maximize production operating efficiency.

The *philosophy* of material requirements planning is that materials should be expedited (hurried) when their lack would delay the overall production schedule and de-expedited (delayed) when the schedule falls behind and postpones their need. Traditionally, and perhaps still typically, when an order is behind schedule, significant effort is spent trying to get it back on schedule. However, the opposite is not always true; when an order, for whatever reason, has its completion date delayed, the appropriate adjustments are not made in the schedule. This results in a one-sided effort—later orders are hurried, but early orders are not rescheduled for later. Aside from perhaps using scarce capacity, it is preferable not to have raw materials and work in process before the actual need since inventories tie up finances, clutter up stockrooms, prohibit design changes, and prevent the cancellation or delay of orders.

Advantages of an MRP System

In past years, when firms switched from existing manual or computerized systems to an MRP system, they realized many benefits:

Ability to price more competitively.

Reduced sales price.

Reduced inventory.

Better customer service.

The MRP system at Allen-Bradley, a manufacturer of circuit boards, receives an order and schedules appropriate production. Panels are automatically routed to the required process such as this robotic cell that inserts nonstandard components.

Better response to market demands.

Ability to change the master schedule.

Reduced setup and tear-down costs.

Reduced idle time.

In addition, the MRP system:

Gives advance notice so managers can see the planned schedule before actual release orders.

Tells when to de-expedite as well as expedite.

Delays or cancels orders.

Changes order quantities.

Advances or delays order due dates.

Aids capacity planning.

During their conversions to MRP systems, many firms claimed as much as 40 percent reductions in inventory investment.

Disadvantages of an MRP System

MRP is very well developed technically, and implementation of an MRP system should be pretty straightforward. Yet there are many problems with the MRP systems and many "failures" in trying to install them. Why do such problems and outright failures occur with a "proven" system?

The answer partially lies with organizational and behavioral factors. Three major causes have been identified: the lack of top management commitment, the failure to recognize that MRP is only a software tool that needs to be used correctly, and the integration of MRP and JIT.

Part of the blame for the lack of top management's commitment may be MRP's image. It sounds like a manufacturing system rather than a business plan. However, an MRP system is used to plan resources and develop schedules. Also, a well-functioning schedule can use the firm's assets effectively, thus increasing profits. MRP should be accepted

E X H I B I T 15.7

Overall View of the Inputs to a Standard Material Requirements Planning Program and the Reports Generated by the Program

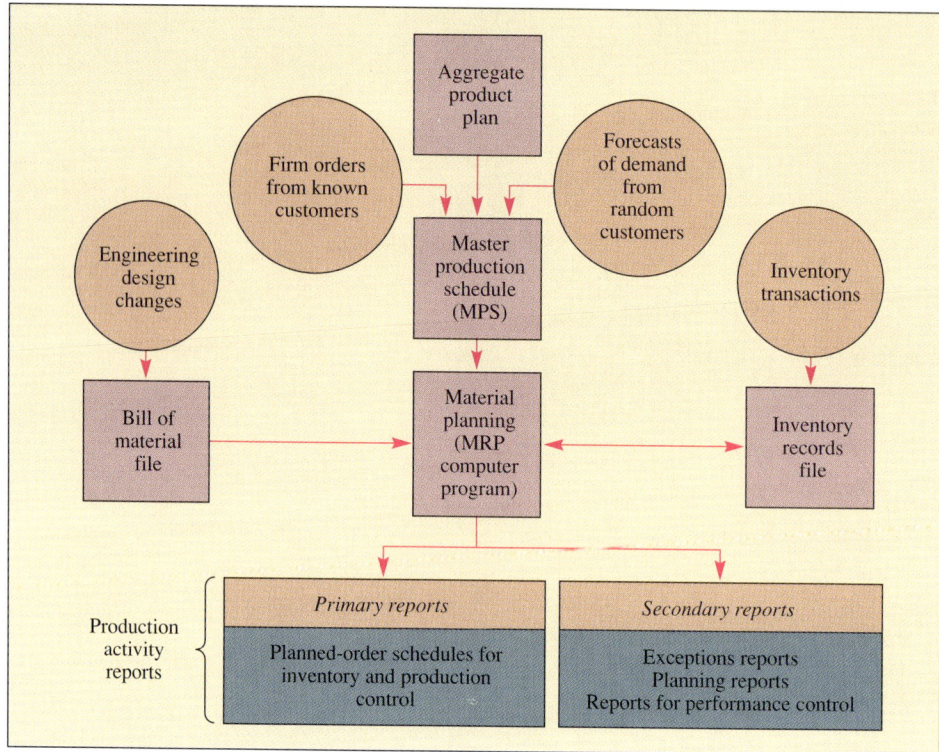

by top management as a planning tool with specific reference to profit results. Intensive executive education is needed, emphasizing the importance of MRP as a closed-loop, integrated, strategic planning tool.

The second cause of the problem concerns the MRP proponents that overdid themselves in selling the concept. MRP was presented and perceived as a complete and stand-alone system to run a firm, rather than as part of the total system. The third issue is how MRP can be made to function with JIT, which we discuss later in this chapter.

MRP also needs a high degree of accuracy for operation, which often requires (1) changing how the firm operates and (2) updating files. For example, many firms have had open access to inventory stores. This causes differences between recorded inventory and actual inventory on hand. Also, many engineering drawings and bills of materials become outdated, and MRP requires accuracy to function correctly.

Perhaps one of the biggest complaints by users is that MRP is too rigid. When MRP develops a schedule, it is quite difficult to veer away from the schedule if need arises.

15.5   MATERIAL REQUIREMENTS PLANNING SYSTEM STRUCTURE

The material requirements planning portion of manufacturing activities most closely interacts with the master schedule, bill of materials file, inventory records file, and the output reports. Exhibit 15.7 shows a different perspective of Exhibit 13.1 in Chapter 13 with several additions. Note that capacity is not considered in this exhibit, nor are there any feedback loops to higher levels. We discuss these elements later in this chapter under MRP II and capacity requirements planning.

E X H I B I T 15.8
*Bill of Materials
(Product Structure
Tree) for Product A*

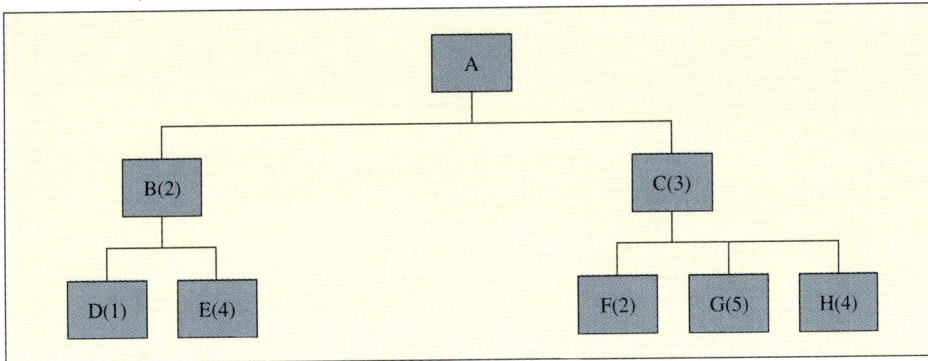

Each facet of Exhibit 15.7 is detailed in the following sections, but essentially the MRP system works as follows: Orders for products are used to create a master production schedule, which states the number of items to be produced during specific time periods. A bill of materials file identifies the specific materials used to make each item and the correct quantities of each. The inventory records file contains data such as the number of units on hand and on order. These three sources—master production schedule, bill of materials file, and inventory records file—become the data sources for the material requirements program, which expands the production schedule into a detailed order scheduling plan for the entire production sequence.

Demand for Products

Product demand for end items stems primarily from two main sources. The first is known customers who have placed specific orders, such as those generated by sales personnel, or from interdepartment transactions. These orders usually carry promised delivery dates. There is no forecasting involved in these orders—simply add them up. The second source is forecast demand. These are the normal independent-demand orders; the forecasting models presented in Chapter 7 can be used to predict the quantities. The demand from the known customers and the forecast demand are combined and become the input for the master production schedule.

Demand for Repair Parts and Supplies   In addition to the demand for end products, customers also order specific parts and components either as spares, or for service and repair. These demands for items less complex than the end product are not usually part of the master production schedule; instead, they are fed directly into the material requirements planning program at the appropriate levels. That is, they are added in as a gross requirement for that part or component.

Bill of Materials File

The **bill of materials (BOM)** file contains the complete product description, listing not only the materials, parts, and components but also the sequence in which the product is created. This BOM file is one of the three main inputs to the MRP program. (The other two are the master schedule and the inventory records file.)

The BOM file is often called the *product structure file* or *product tree* because it shows how a product is put together. It contains the information to identify each item and the quantity used per unit of the item of which it is a part. To illustrate this, consider Product A shown in Exhibit 15.8. Product A is made of two units of Part B and three units of Part C. Part B is made of one unit of Part D and four units

E X H I B I T 15.9

*Parts List in an
Indented Format and
in a Single-Level List*

Indented Parts List			Single-Level Parts List		
A			A		
	B(2)				B(2)
		D(1)			C(3)
		E(4)	B		
	C(3)				D(1)
		F(2)			E(4)
		G(5)	C		
		H(4)			F(2)
					G(5)
					H(4)

of Part E. Part C is made of two units of Part F, five units of Part G, and four units of Part H.

In the past, bill of materials files have often listed parts as an indented file. This clearly identifies each item and the manner in which it is assembled because each indentation signifies the components of the item. A comparison of the indented parts in Exhibit 15.9 with the item structure in Exhibit 15.8 shows the ease of relating the two displays. From a computer standpoint, however, storing items in indented parts lists is very inefficient. To compute the amount of each item needed at the lower levels, each item would need to be expanded ("exploded") and summed. A more efficient procedure is to store parts data in a single-level explosion. That is, each item and component is listed showing only its parent and the number of units needed per unit of its parent. This avoids duplication because it includes each assembly only once. Exhibit 15.9 shows both the indented parts list and the single-level parts list for Product A.

A *modular* bill of materials is the term for a buildable item that can be produced and stocked as a subassembly. It is also a standard item with no options within the module. Many end items that are large and expensive are better scheduled and controlled as modules (or subassemblies). It is particularly advantageous to schedule subassembly modules when the same subassemblies appear in different end items. For example, a manufacturer of cranes can combine booms, transmissions, and engines in a variety of ways to meet a customer's needs. Using a modular bill of materials simplifies the scheduling and control and also makes it easier to forecast the use of different modules. Another benefit in using modular bills is that if the same item is used in a number of products, then the total inventory investment can be minimized.

A *planning* bill of materials includes items with fractional options. (A planning bill can specify, for example, 0.3 of a part. What that means is that 30 percent of the units produced contain that part and 70 percent do not.)

Low-Level Coding   If all identical parts occur at the same level for each end product, the total number of parts and materials needed for a product can be computed easily. Consider Product L shown in Exhibit 15.10a. Notice that Item N, for example, occurs both as an input to L and as an input to M. Item N therefore needs to be lowered to level 2 (Exhibit 15.10b) to bring all Ns to the same level. If all identical items are placed at the same level, it becomes a simple matter for the computer to scan across each level and summarize the number of units of each item required.

E X H I B I T 15.10   *Product L Hierarchy in (a) Expanded to the Lowest Level of Each Item in (b)*

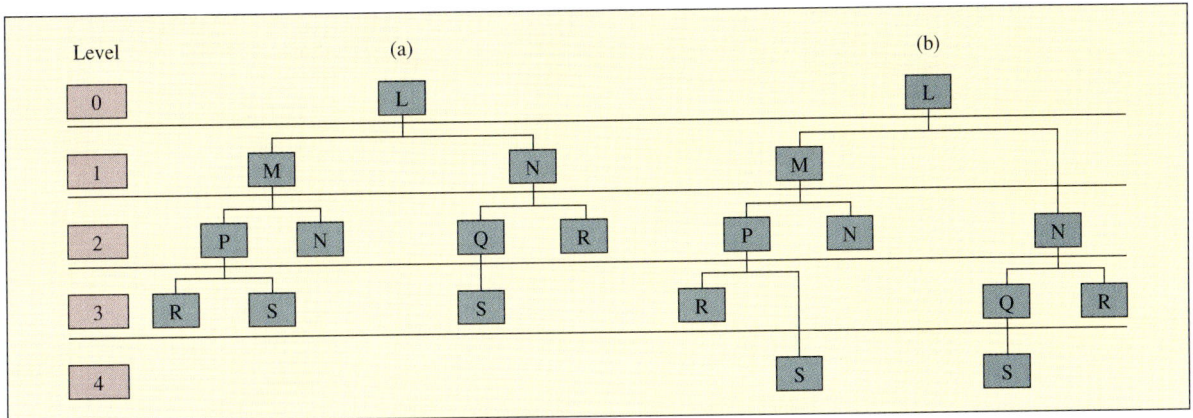

E X H I B I T 15.11

The Inventory Status Record for an Item in Inventory

The **inventory records file** under a computerized system can be quite lengthy. Each item in inventory is carried as a separate file and the range of details carried about an item is almost limitless. Though Exhibit 15.11 is from the earlier versions of the MRP, it shows the variety of information contained in the inventory records files. The MRP program accesses the *status* segment of the file according to specific time periods (called *time buckets* in MRP slang). These files are accessed as needed during the program run.

The MRP program performs its analysis from the top of the product structure downward, exploding requirements level by level. There are times, however, when it is desir-

Inventory Records File

able to identify the parent item that caused the material requirement. The MRP program allows the creation of a *peg record* file either separately or as part of the inventory record file. Pegging requirements allows us to retrace a material requirement upward in the product structure through each level, identifying each parent item that created the demand.

Inventory Transactions File   The inventory status file is kept up to date by posting inventory transactions as they occur. These changes occur because of stock receipts and disbursements, scrap losses, wrong parts, canceled orders, and so forth.

MRP Computer Program

The material requirements planning program operates on the inventory file, the master schedule, and the bill of materials file. It works in this way: A list of end items needed by time periods (as in the discussion of master scheduling in this chapter) is specified by the master schedule. A description of the materials and parts needed to make each item is specified in the bill of materials file. The number of units of each item and material currently on hand and on order are contained in the inventory file. The MRP program "works" on the inventory file (which is segmented into time periods) while continually referring to the bill of materials file to compute the quantities of each item needed. The number of units of each item required is then corrected for on-hand amounts, and the net requirement is "offset" (set back in time) to allow for the lead time needed to obtain the material.

(One obstacle that many potential users of an MRP program have found is that their current bill of materials files and inventory records files are not adequate to provide data in the format required by the program. Thus they must modify these files before installing an MRP system. We discuss other problems as well later in the chapter.)

If the MRP program being used does not consider capacity constraints, the master scheduler must do some capacity balancing by hand. Through an iterative process, the master scheduler feeds a tentative master schedule into the MRP system (along with other items requiring the same resources) and the output is examined for production feasibility. The master schedule is adjusted to try to correct any imbalances, and the program is executed again. This process is repeated until the output is acceptable. Although it would seem to be a simple matter to have the computer simulate some schedules that consider resource limitations, in reality it is a very large and very time-consuming problem.

To further complicate the problem today, there is not simply one master scheduler; there are a number of them. Often firms divide the scheduling work among the schedulers by assigning one master scheduler for each major product line. The result of this is competition: Each master scheduler competes for limited resources for his or her own product line. As a group, however, they are trying to balance resource usage and due dates for the production system as a whole.

Output Reports

Because the MRP program has access to the bill of materials file, the master production schedule, and the inventory records file, outputs can take on an almost unlimited range of format and content. These reports are usually classified as *primary* and *secondary* reports. (With the expansion of MRP into MRP II and later versions, many additional reports are available.)

Primary Reports   Primary reports are the main or normal reports used for inventory and production control. These reports consist of

1. *Planned orders* to be released at a future time.
2. *Order release notices* to execute the planned orders.

3. *Changes in due dates* of open orders due to rescheduling.
4. *Cancellations or suspensions* of open orders due to cancellation or suspension of orders on the master production schedule.
5. *Inventory status data.*

Secondary Reports   Additional reports, which are optional under the MRP system, fall into three main categories:

1. *Planning reports* to be used, for example, in forecasting inventory and specifying requirements over some future time horizon.
2. *Performance reports* for purposes of pointing out inactive items and determining the agreement between actual and programmed item lead times and between actual and programmed quantity usage and costs.
3. *Exceptions reports* that point out serious discrepancies, such as errors, out-of-range situations, late or overdue orders, excessive scrap, or nonexistent parts.

Net Change Systems

Ordinarily an MRP system is initiated from a master schedule every week or two. This results in the complete explosion of items and the generation of the normal and exception reports. Some MRP programs, however, offer the option of generating intermediate schedules, called *net change* schedules. Net change systems are "activity" driven. Only if a transaction is processed against a particular item would that item be reviewed in a **net change system.** However, net change systems can be modified to respond only to unplanned or exception occurrences. Rather than being buried in paperwork output from an MRP system (which can easily happen), management may elect not to have the expected occurrences reported, but only deviations that should be noted. For example, if orders are received on time, a report is not produced. On the other hand, if the quantity delivered differs significantly from the order, this item is included in the net change report. Other reasons to include an item in a net change run might be to note a lost shipment, scrap losses, lead time changes, or a counting error in inventory. Based on these changes, new reports are generated.

On the surface, it appears that a daily net change program run would be highly satisfactory. In practice, however, few companies elect to use the net change option; instead, most rely on their weekly or biweekly complete MRP schedule run. It seems that more frequent net change runs may not be worth the added effort required to perform them, and too-frequent runs cause overreaction or "system nervousness."

15.6   AN EXAMPLE USING MRP

Ampere, Inc., produces a line of electric meters installed in residential buildings by electric utility companies to measure power consumption. Meters used on single-family homes are of two basic types for different voltage and amperage ranges. In addition to complete meters, some parts and subassemblies are sold separately for repair or for changeovers to a different voltage or power load. The problem for the MRP system is to determine a production schedule that would identify each item, the period it is needed, and the appropriate quantities. This schedule is then checked for feasibility, and the schedule is modified if necessary.

EXHIBIT 15.12

Future Requirements for Meters A and B, Subassembly D, and Part E Stemming from Specific Customer Orders and from Random Sources

Month	Meter A Known	Meter A Random	Meter B Known	Meter B Random	Subassembly D Known	Subassembly D Random	Part E Known	Part E Random
3	1,000	250	400	60	200	70	300	80
4	600	250	300	60	180	70	350	80
5	300	250	500	60	250	70	300	80
6	700	250	400	60	200	70	250	80
7	600	250	300	60	150	70	200	80
8	700	250	700	60	160	70	200	80

EXHIBIT 15.13

A Master Schedule to Satisfy Demand Requirements as Specified in Exhibit 15.12

	Week 9	10	11	12	13	14	15	16	17
Meter A	1,250				850				550
Meter B	460				360				560
Subassembly D	270				250				320
Part E	380				430				380

Forecasting Demand

Demand for the meters and components originates from two sources: regular customers that place firm orders, and unidentified customers that make the normal random demands for these items. The random requirements were forecast using one of the usual classical techniques described in Chapter 7 and past demand data. Exhibit 15.12 shows the requirement for Meters A and B, Subassembly D, and Part E for a six-month period (months three through eight).

Developing a Master Production Schedule

For the meter and component requirements specified in Exhibit 15.12, assume that the quantities to satisfy the known demands are to be delivered according to customers' delivery schedules throughout the month, but that the items to satisfy random demands must be available during the first week of the month.

Our schedule assumes that *all* items are to be available the first week of the month. This assumption trial is reasonable since management (in our example) prefers to produce meters in one single lot each month rather than a number of lots throughout the month.

Exhibit 15.13 shows the trial master schedule that we use under these conditions, with demands for months 3 and 4 listed in the first week of each month, or as weeks 9 and 13. For brevity, we work only with these two demand periods. The schedule we develop should be examined for resource availability, capacity availability, and so on, and then revised and run again. We will stop with our example at the end of this one schedule, however.

Bill of Materials (Product Structure) File

The product structure for Meters A and B is shown in Exhibit 15.14 in the typical way using low-level coding, in which each item is placed at the lowest level at which it appears in the structure hierarchy. Meters A and B consist of two subassemblies, C and D, and two parts, E and F. Quantities in parentheses indicate the number of units required per unit of the parent item.

E X H I B I T 15.14 *Product Structure for Meters A and B*

Exhibit shows the subassemblies and parts that make up the meters and shows the numbers of units required per unit of parent in parentheses.

E X H I B I T 15.15

Indented Parts List for Meter A and Meter B, with the Required Number of Items per Unit of Parent Listed in Parentheses

Exhibit 15.15 shows an indented parts list for the structure of Meters A and B. As mentioned earlier in the chapter, the BOM file carries all items without indentation for computational ease, but the indented printout clearly shows the manner of product assembly.

Inventory Records (Item Master) File

The inventory records file would be similar to the one shown in Exhibit 15.11. The differences, as we saw earlier in this chapter, are that the inventory records file also contains much additional data, such as vendor identity, cost, and lead times. For this example, the pertinent data contained in the inventory records file are the on-hand inventory at the start of the program run and the lead times. Taken from the inventory records file, these data are shown in Exhibit 15.16.

Running the MRP Program

The correct conditions are now set to run the MRP computer program—end-item requirements have been established through the master production schedule, while the status of inventory and the order lead times are contained in the inventory item master file, and the bill of materials file contains the product structure data. The MRP program now explodes the item requirements according to the BOM file, level by level, in conjunction with the inventory records file. A release data for the net requirements order is offset to an earlier time period to account for the lead time. Orders for parts and

E X H I B I T 15.16

Number of Units on Hand and Lead Time Data that Would Appear on the Inventory Record File

Item	On-Hand Inventory	Lead Time (weeks)
A	50	2
B	60	2
C	40	1
D	30	1
E	30	1
F	40	1

subassemblies are added through the inventory file, bypassing the master production schedule, which, ordinarily, does not schedule at a low enough level to include spares and repair parts.

Exhibit 15.17 shows the planned order release dates for this particular run. The following analysis explains the program logic. (We confine our analysis to the problem of meeting the gross requirements for 1,250 units of Meter A, 460 units of Meter B, 270 units of Subassembly D, and 380 units of Part E, all in Week 9.)

The 50 units of A on hand result in a net requirement of 1,200 units of A. To receive Meter A in Week 9, the order must be placed in Week 7 to account for the two-week lead time. The same procedure follows for Item B, resulting in a planned 400-unit order released in Period 7.

The rationale for these steps is that for an item to be released for processing, all its components must be available. The planned order release date for the parent item therefore becomes the same gross requirement period for the subitems.

Referring to Exhibit 15.14, level 1, one unit of C is required for each A and each B. Therefore, the gross requirements for C in Week 7 are 1,600 units (1,200 for A and 400 for B). Taking into account the 40 units on hand and the one-week lead time, 1,560 units of C must be ordered in Week 6.

Level 2 of Exhibit 15.14 shows that one unit of D is required for each A and each C. The 1,200 units of D required for A are gross requirements in Week 7, and the 1,560 units of D for item C are the gross requirements for Week 6. Using the on-hand inventory first and the one-week lead time results in the planned order releases for 1,530 units in Week 5 and 1,200 units in Week 6.

Level 3 contains Items E and F. Because E and F are each used in several places, Exhibit 15.18 is presented to identify more clearly the parent item, the number of units required for each parent item, and the week in which it is required. Two units of Item E are used in each Item A. The 1,200-unit planned order release for A in Period 7 becomes the gross requirement for 2,400 units of E in the same period. One unit of E is used in each B, so the planned order release for 400 units of B in Period 7 becomes the gross requirement for 400 units of E in Week 7. Item E is also used in Item D at the rate of one per unit. The 1,530-unit planned order release for D in Period 5 becomes the gross requirement for 1,530 units of E in Period 5 and a 1,500-unit planned order release in Period 4 after accounting for the 30 units on hand and the one-week lead time. The 1,200-unit planned order release for D in Period 6 results in gross requirements for 1,200 units of E in Week 6 and a planned order release for 1,200 units in Week 5.

Item F is used in B, C, and D. The planned order releases for B, C, and D become the gross requirements for F for the same week, except that the planned order release for 400 units of B and 1,560 of C become gross requirements for 800 and 3,120 units of F, since the usage rate is two per unit.

E X H I B I T 15.17   *Material Requirements Planning Schedule for Meters A and B, Subassemblies C and D, and Parts E and F*

Item		Week											
		4	5	6	7	8	9	10	11	12	13
A	Gross requirements						1,250				850
	On hand 50						50				
	Net requirements						1,200				
(LT = 2)	Planned-order receipt						1,200				
	Planned-order release				1,200						
B	Gross requirements						460				360
	On hand 60						60				
	Net requirements						400				
(LT = 2)	Planned-order receipt						400				
	Planned-order release				400						
C	Gross requirements				400						
					1,200						
	On hand 40				40						
	Net requirements				1,560						
(LT = 1)	Planned-order receipt				1,560						
	Planned-order release			1,560							
D	Gross requirements				1,560	1,200	270				250
	On hand 30				30	0	0				
	Net requirements				1,530	1,200	270				
(LT = 1)	Planned-order receipt				1,530	1,200	270				
	Planned-order release		1,530	1,200		270					
E	Gross requirements			1,530	1,200	2,400	270	380			430
						400					
	On hand 30			30	0	0	0	0			
	Net requirements			1,500	1,200	2,800	270	380			
(LT = 1)	Planned-order receipt			1,500	1,200	2,800	270	380			
	Planned-order release	1,500	1,200	2,800	270	380					
F	Gross requirements			1,530	3,120	800	270				
					1,200						
	On hand 40			40	0	0	0				
	Net requirements			1,490	4,320	800	270				
(LT = 1)	Planned-order receipt			1,490	4,320	800	270				
	Planned-order release	1,490	4,320	800	270						

The independent order for 270 units of subassembly D in Week 9 is handled as an input to D's gross requirements for that week. This is then exploded into the derived requirements for 270 units of E and F. The 380-unit requirement for Part E to meet an independent repair part demand is fed directly into the gross requirements for Part E.

The independent demands for Week 13 have not been expanded as yet.

The bottom line of each item in Exhibit 15.17 is taken as a proposed load on the productive system. The final production schedule is developed manually or with the firm's computerized production package. If the schedule is infeasible or the loading unacceptable, the master production schedule is revised and the MRP package is run again with the new master schedule.

E X H I B I T   15.18

The Identification of the Parent of Items C, D, E, and F and Item Gross Requirements Stated by Specific Weeks

Item	Parent	Number of Units per Parent	Resultant Gross Requirement	Gross Requirement Week
C	A	1	1,200	7
C	B	1	400	7
D	A	1	1,200	7
D	C	1	1,560	6
E	A	2	2,400	7
E	B	1	400	7
E	D	1	1,530	5
E	D	1	1,200	6
F	B	2	800	7
F	C	2	3,120	6
F	D	1	1,200	6
F	D	1	1,530	5

15.7   IMPROVEMENTS IN THE BASIC MRP SYSTEM

MRP, as it was originally introduced and as we have discussed it so far in this chapter, considered only materials. Revising the schedule because of capacity considerations was done external to the MRP software program. The schedule was revised because of the capacity constraints and the MRP program was run again. (The Nichols case at the end of this chapter requires that the schedule be revised manually in Question 2 of the case.) The response to all other elements and resource requirements were not part of the system. Later refinements included the capacity of the work centers as part of the software program. Feedback of information was also being introduced. We will give an example of capacity planning at a work center and a closed-loop system. Following that we will discuss MRP II systems and advanced versions of MRP.

Computing Work Center Load

The place to start in computing capacity requirements is right from the routing sheets for the jobs scheduled to be processed. Exhibit 3.18 in Chapter 3 shows the routing sheet for a plug assembly. Note that the routing sheet specifies where a job is to be sent, the particular operations involved, and the standard setup time and run time per piece. These are the types of figures used to compute the total work at each work center.

While the routing sheet is a "job view" that follows a particular job around the productive facility, a work center file is the view seen from a work center. Each work center is generally a functionally defined center so that jobs routed to it require the same type of work and the same equipment. From the work center view, if there is adequate capacity, the issue is just sequencing since all jobs will be done on time. (We discuss priority scheduling rules in Chapter 16.) If there is insufficient capacity, however, the problem must be resolved since some jobs will be late unless the schedule is adjusted.

Exhibit 15.19 shows a work center that has various jobs assigned to it. Note that the capacity per week was computed at the bottom of the exhibit at 161.5 hours. The jobs scheduled for the three weeks result in two weeks planned under work center capacity, and one week over capacity.

Exhibit 15.19 uses the terms **utilization** and **efficiency.** Both of these terms have been defined and used in a variety of ways, some conflicting. In this exhibit, utilization refers to the actual time that the machines are used. Efficiency refers to how well the machine is performing while it is being used. Efficiency is usually defined as a comparison to a defined standard output or an engineering design rate. For instance, a machine used for six hours of an eight-hour shift was utilized % or 75 percent. If the standard output for that machine is defined as 200 parts per hour and an average of 250 parts were made, then efficiency is 125 percent. Note that in these definitions, efficiency can be more than 100 percent, but utilization cannot be.

Exhibit 15.20 shows a loading representation of Work Center A for the three weeks. The scheduled work exceeds capacity for Week 11. There are several options available:

1. Work overtime.
2. Select an alternate work center that could perform the task.
3. Subcontract to an outside shop.
4. Try to schedule part of the work of Day 2 earlier into Day 1, and delay part of the work into Day 3.
5. Renegotiate the due date and reschedule.

An MRP program with a capacity requirements planning module allows rescheduling to try to level capacity. Two techniques used are backward scheduling and forward sched-

E X H I B I T 15.19

Workload for Work Center A

Week	Job No.	Units	Setup Time	Run Time per Unit	Total Job Time	Total for Week
10	145	100	3.5	.23	26.5	
	167	160	2.4	.26	44.0	
	158	70	1.2	.13	10.3	
	193	300	6.0	.17	57.0	137.8
11	132	80	5.0	.36	33.8	
	126	150	3.0	.22	36.0	
	180	180	2.5	.30	56.5	
	178	120	4.0	.50	64.0	190.3
12	147	90	3.0	.18	19.2	
	156	200	3.5	.14	31.5	
	198	250	1.5	.16	41.5	
	172	100	2.0	.12	14.0	
	139	120	2.2	.17	22.6	128.8

Computing Work Center Capacity

The available capacity in standard hours is 161.5 hours per five-day week, calculated as (2 machines) × (2 shifts) (10 hours/shift) (85% machine utilization) (95% efficiency).

E X H I B I T 15.20

Scheduled Workload for Work Center A

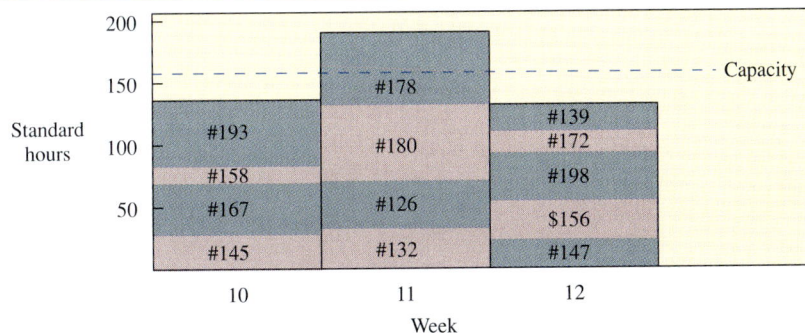

E X H I B I T 15.21   *Closed-Loop MRP System Showing Feedback*

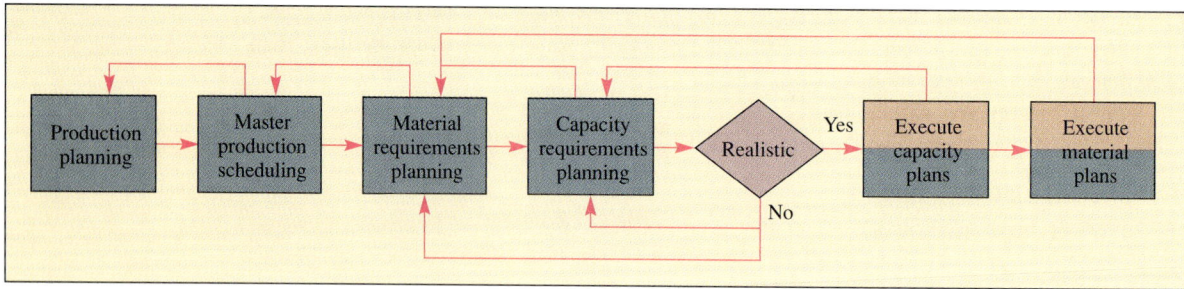

uling—the fourth option on the preceding list. The objective of the master scheduler is to try to spread the load in Exhibit 15.20 more evenly to remain within the available capacity.

Closed-Loop MRP

When the material requirements planning (MRP) system has information feedback from its module outputs, this is termed **closed-loop MRP.** The American Production and Inventory Control Society defines closed-loop MRP as

> A system built around material requirements that includes the additional planning functions of sales and operations (production planning, master production scheduling, and capacity requirements planning). Once this planning phase is complete and the plans have been accepted as realistic and attainable, the execution functions come into play. These include the manufacturing control functions of input-output (capacity) measurement, detailed scheduling and dispatching, as well as anticipated delay reports from both the plant and suppliers, supplier scheduling, etc. The term "closed-loop" implies that not only is each of these elements included in the overall system, but also that feedback is provided by the execution functions so that the planning can be kept valid at all times.[2]

Exhibit 15.21 shows a closed-loop MRP system. The closed loop means that questions and output data are looped back up the system for verification and, if necessary, modification. Recognize that the input to the MRP system is the master production schedule, as was stated earlier in the chapter. The MRP program does an explosion of all the parts, components, and other resources needed to meet this schedule. The capacity requirements planning module then checks the MRP output to see if sufficient capacity exists. If it does not, feedback to the MRP module indicates that the schedule needs to be modified. Continuing through the MRP system, orders are released to the production system by executing the capacity and material plans. From that point on, it is a matter of monitoring, data collection, completing the order, and evaluating results. Any changes in production, capacity, or material are fed back into the system.

15.8   MRP II (MANUFACTURING RESOURCE PLANNING)

An expansion of the material requirements planning system to include other portions of the productive system was natural and to be expected. One of the first to be included was the purchasing function. At the same time, there was a more detailed inclusion of the production system itself—on the shop floor, in dispatching, and in the detailed sched-

---

[2]Dictionary definitions are reprinted with the permission of APICS, Inc., *APICS Dictionary,* 7th ed., 1992.

uling control. MRP had already included work center capacity limitations so it was obvious the name *material requirements planning* no longer was adequate to describe the expanded system. Someone (probably Ollie Wight) introduced the name *manufacturing resource planning (MRP II)* to reflect the idea that more and more of the firm was becoming involved in the program. To quote Wight,

> The fundamental manufacturing equation is:
> What are we going to make?
> What does it take to make it?
> What do we have?
> What do we have to get?[3]

The initial intent for MRP II was to plan and monitor all the resources of a manufacturing firm—manufacturing, marketing, finance, and engineering—through a closed-loop system generating financial figures. The second important intent of the MRP II concept was that it simulate the manufacturing system.

For more than a decade, efforts continued in MRP II systems along the lines of adding some modules and making continuing small improvements. The basic system and its operating logic remained intact. IBM's Manufacturing Accounting and Production Information Control System (MAPICS), for example, contains 19 interrelated modules:

Accounts payable.	Location/lot management.
Accounts receivable.	Master production scheduling
Capacity requirements planning.	planning.
Cross-application support.	Material requirements planning.
Data collection system support.	Order entry and invoicing.
Financial analysis.	Payroll.
Forecasting.	Product data management.
General ledger.	Production control and costing.
Inventory management.	Purchasing.
Inventory management for process.	Sales analysis.

This system is still widely used and, in fact, IBM has a Partners Program where some universities have MAPICS programs set up and courses taught using this software. This gives a hands-on experience. Universities in the Partners Program as of 1993 include Iowa, Iowa State, Mankato State, Minnesota, North Dakota, North Dakota State, Penn State, Purdue, St. Cloud State, South Dakota, Texas A&M, Washington (St. Louis), Winona State, and Wisconsin–Madison.[4]

15.9   EMBEDDING JIT INTO MRP

MRP and JIT each have benefits. The question is: Can they work together successfully, and how would one go about combining them? As stated earlier in the chapter, most major manufacturing firms use MRP. Of the firms using MRP, many in repetitive manufacturing are also implementing JIT techniques. Although JIT is best suited to repetitive manufacturing, MRP is used in everything from custom job shops to assembly-line pro-

---

[3]Oliver Wight, *The Executive's Guide to Successful MRP II* (Williston, VT: Oliver Wight, 1982), pp. 6, 17.

[4]Henry W. Kroebber, Jr., "Teaching MP&C on Campus Using an 'Industrial Grade' System," *Industrial Engineering,* July 1993, p. 61.

duction. Most firms that have successfully implemented MRP systems are not interested in discarding MRP to try JIT. A new challenge arises in integrating the shop-floor improvement approaches of JIT with an MRP-based planning and control system. The MRP/JIT combination creates what might be considered a hybrid manufacturing system. Efforts to integrate MRP and JIT are now popular enough to justify a regular column titled "MRP/JIT Report" in *Modern Materials Handling* magazine.

MRP is a very large computerized production planning system. Trying to add JIT to this system is very difficult. Some firms are trying to create add-on modules but at present there is no standard way.

Part of the difficulty in trying to integrate both systems into a computer program is caused by their different objectives and conflicting purposes, such as:

	MRP	**JIT**
Based on:	MPS, BOM, and inventory records	MPS, Kanban
Objective:	Plan and control	Eliminate waste; continuous improvement
Involvement process:	Passive—no efforts toward change	Active—tries to improve and change system, and to lower inventory
Data requirements:	Detailed and strict data accuracy	Much lower and tend to be visible
Operation:	Computerized	Simple, manual shop-floor controls such as Kanban

Exhibit 15.22 shows a master production schedule with an MRP system on the left. MRP systems can help create the master production schedule. From that point on, it stays as a pure MRP system. Scheduling resources such as inventory are continuously controlled and monitored.

The right side of Exhibit 15.22 shows a master production schedule at the top feeding a JIT system. Computer control has been severed and the JIT portion operates as its own separate pull method drawing from preceding stages. MRP may well be used to help create the master production schedule, but MRP's involvement stops there.

Exhibit 15.23 shows a hybrid MRP/JIT system. The top half shows a conventional MRP system with its standard inputs such as forecasted demand, inventory status, and bills of materials. It produces a plan. The system in the bottom portion of the exhibit, in a JIT manner, controls when vendors should deliver material, when product is to be produced, and when completed product is to be distributed. The middle section—the shop schedule and Kanban system—is the interfaces coupling the MRP and JIT systems along with the capacity control and group technology planning.

Phasing MRP into JIT

Assume an existing production system is currently being planned and scheduled using an MRP system. The firm's management believes JIT should be introduced because various parts of the firm produce the same products repetitively. To convert those repetitive areas into just-in-time manufacturing, S. D. P. Flapper, G. J. Miltenburg, and J. Wijngaard propose this three-step approach:

Step 1. Create a logical flow line through rapid material handling.

Step 2. Use a pull production control system on the logical line.

Step 3. Create a physical line flow.[5]

---

[5]S. D. P. Flapper, G. J. Miltenburg, and J. Wijngaard, "Embedding JIT into MRP," *International Journal of Production Research* 29, no. 2 (1991), pp. 329–41.

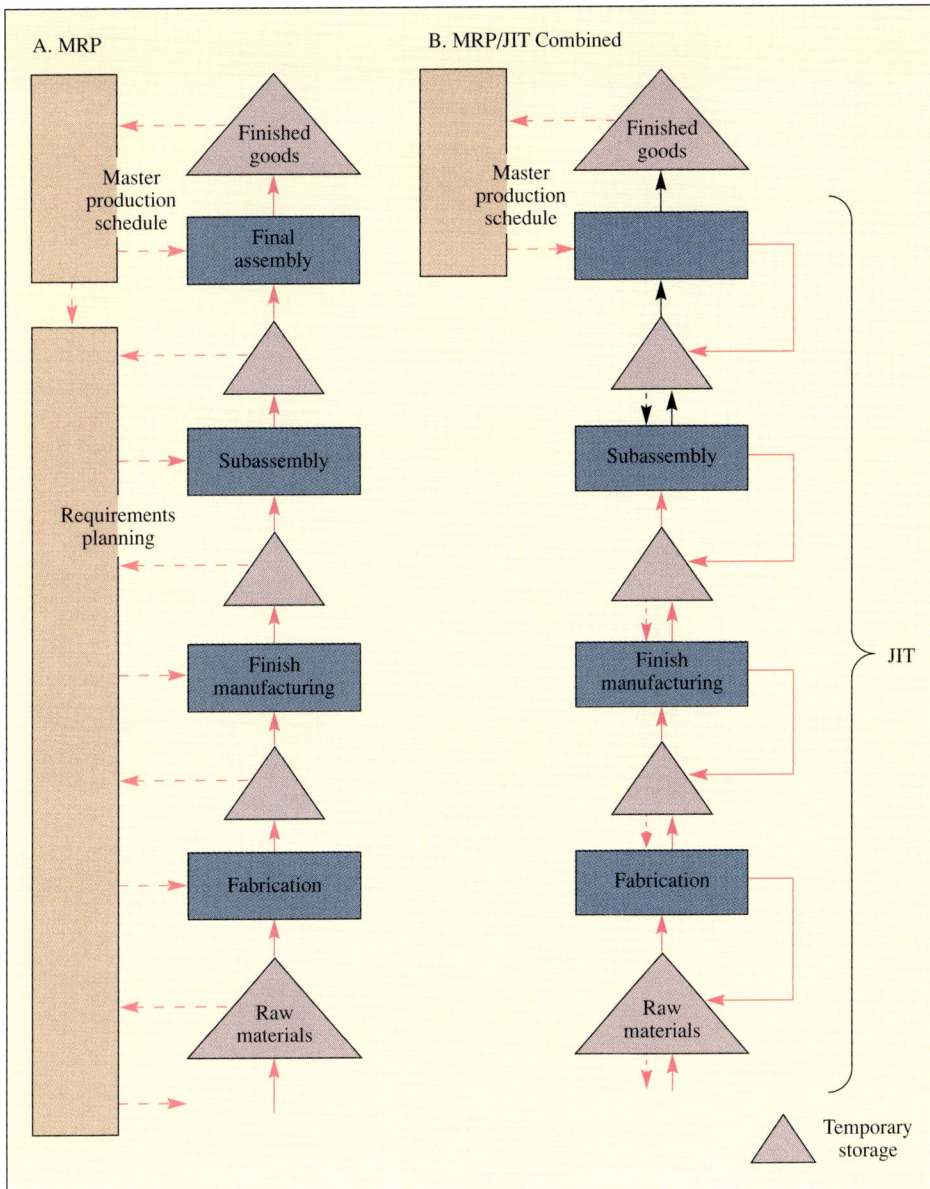

Exhibit 15.24A shows the existing pure MRP system. It operates in its conventional fashion with work located at work centers and the main stockroom. Orders are generated by the main MRP system, and all operations are continuously monitored.

Step 1—Relocate Inventory The first step (Exhibit 15.24B) is to discontinue using the stockroom and locate all inventory on the shop floor. A materials handling system then connects all areas of the shop floor with an automatic guided vehicle (AGV) or material handling personnel driving a vehicle. This material handling procedure replaces the discontinued method of MRP drawing inventory from main stock. The MRP system needs to be informed of the new locations of inventory, but it is still in control. Major changes

EXHIBIT 15.23

An MRP Planning System with JIT Production and Distribution

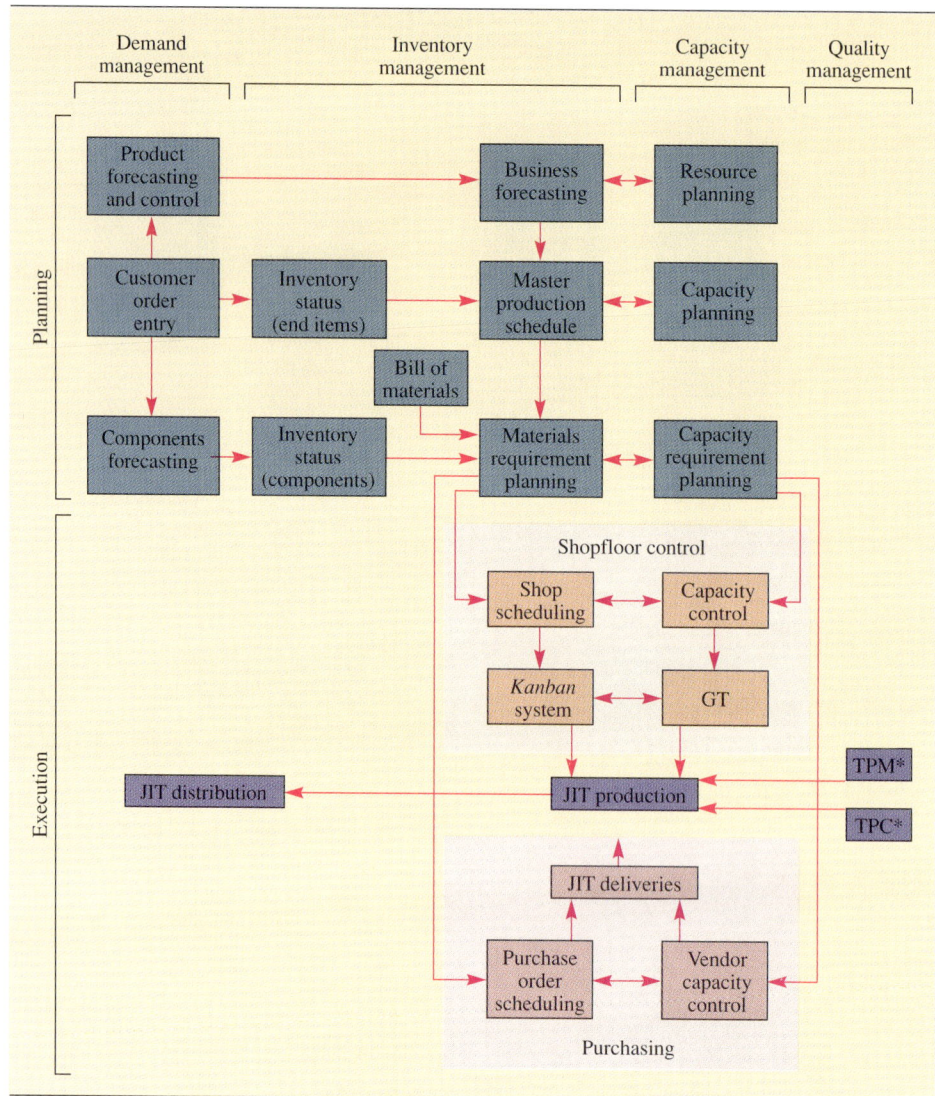

*TPC—Total Process Control. TPM—Total Preventive Maintenance.
Source: Choong Y. Lee, "A Recent Development of the Integrated Manufacturing System: A Hybrid of MRP and JIT,"
International Journal of Operations and Production Management 13, no. 4 (1993), p. 9.

need to be made in the process, such as improvements in quality, tooling, lead times, and setup times. As the system improves, inventory levels are reduced.

Step 2—Introduce a Pull System   A pull system is implemented (Exhibit 15.24C). Kanban cards, container sizes, and so forth are used in the conventional JIT manner. Pulling containers from work areas creates authorization to produce replacements. To be successful in this step, setup time must be greatly reduced and quality must be improved.

The MRP's position in this transition phase is to do the ordering but not the scheduling. MRP releases orders external to the firm for parts and other components that are needed. Since the internal system operates as a JIT system, MRP does not do detailed scheduling. This is taken care of by the JIT system itself.

E X H I B I T 15.24 *Embedding JIT into an MRP System*

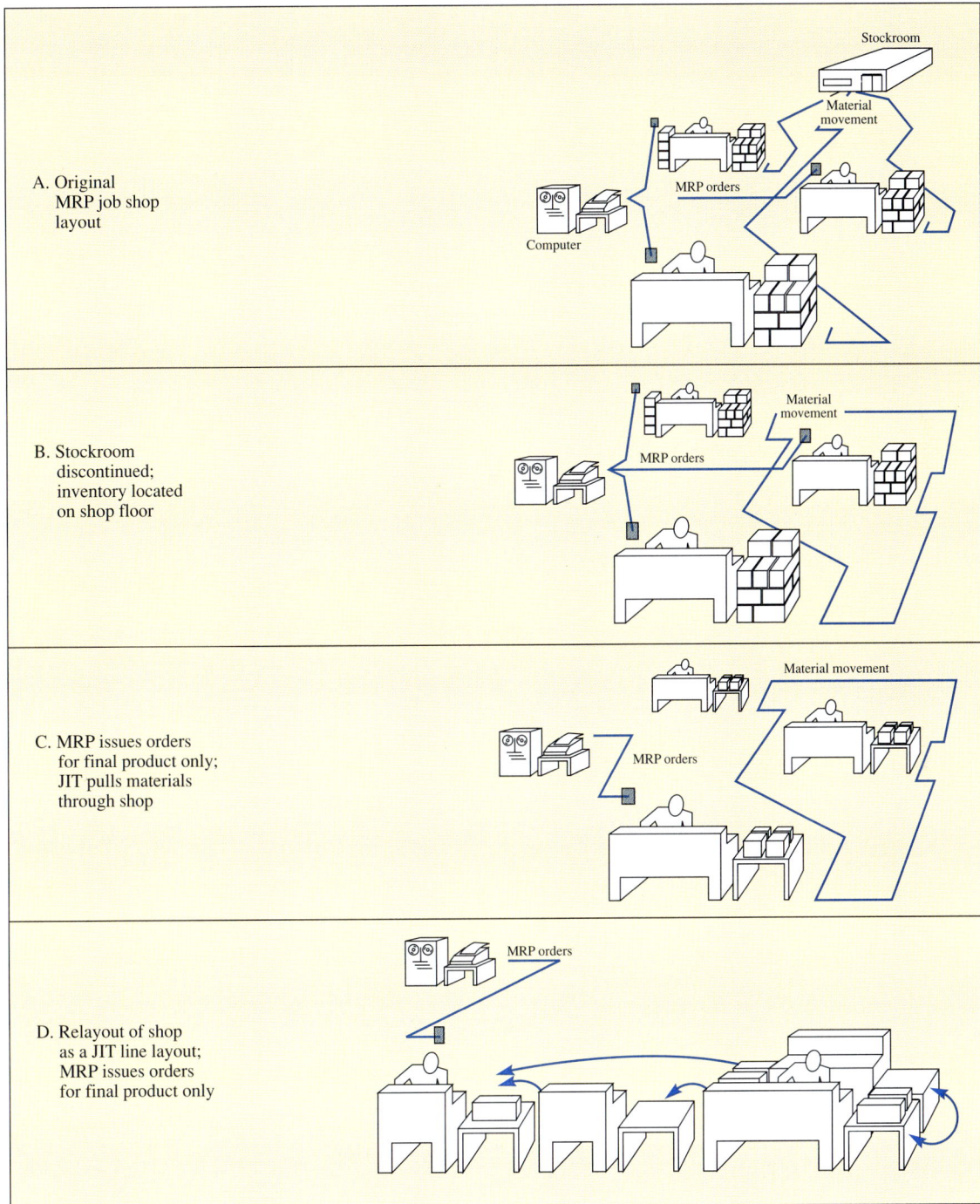

Source: S. D. P. Flapper, G. J. Miltenburg, and J. Wijngaard, "Embedding JIT into MRP," *International Journal of Production Research* 29, no. 2 (1991), p. 331.

Step 3—Create a New Layout   When the pull system is balanced for a product group and demand is sufficient and stable, a new layout may be created. All equipment needed is arranged into a line flow as shown in Exhibit 15.24D. Efforts continue to improve the individual processes and reduce inventory. MRP's position now is (1) involvement to create the master production schedule, (2) ordering external parts and components, (3) updating inventories through backflushing, which is to compute material used based on the number of units completed.

Flapper et al. state that few companies advance beyond Step 1 (relocating stock on the shop floor) because

1. They do not want to lose control of inventories (which happens within a JIT system).
2. They are not prepared to commit resources to training, engineering time, maintenance, and so on to make JIT improvements.
3. Management is satisfied with achievements already made in cost, lead time, quality, and inventory reduction.[6]

15.10   LOT SIZING IN MRP SYSTEMS

The determination of lot sizes in an MRP system is a complicated and difficult problem. Lot sizes are the part quantities issued in the planned order receipt and planned order release sections of an MRP schedule. For parts produced in-house, lot sizes are the production quantities or batch sizes. For purchased parts, these are the quantities ordered from the supplier. Lot sizes generally meet part requirements for one or more periods.

Most lot-sizing techniques deal with how to balance the setup or order costs and holding costs associated with meeting the net requirements generated by the MRP planning process. Many MRP systems have options for computing lot sizes based on some of the more commonly used techniques. It should be obvious, though, that the use of lot-sizing techniques increases the complexity in generating MRP schedules. When fully exploded, the numbers of parts scheduled can be enormous.

Next, we explain four lot-sizing techniques using a common example. The lot-sizing techniques presented are lot-for-lot (L4L), economic order quantity (EOQ), least total cost (LTC), and least unit cost (LUC).

Consider the following MRP lot-sizing problems; the net requirements are shown for eight scheduling weeks:

Cost per item					$10.00		
Order or setup cost					$47.00		
Inventory carrying cost/week					0.5%		
Weekly net requirements:							
1	2	3	4	5	6	7	8
50	60	70	60	95	75	60	55

Lot-for-Lot

Lot-for-lot (L4L) is the most common technique. It

- Sets planned orders to exactly match the net requirements.
- Produces exactly what is needed each week with none carried over into future periods.

---

[6]Ibid., p. 340.

E X H I B I T 15.25 *Lot-for-Lot Run Size for an MRP Schedule*

Week	Net Requirements	Production Quantity	Ending Inventory	Holding Cost	Setup Cost	Total Cost
1	50	50	0	$0.00	$47.00	$ 47.00
2	60	60	0	0.00	47.00	94.00
3	70	70	0	0.00	47.00	141.00
4	60	60	0	0.00	47.00	188.00
5	95	95	0	0.00	47.00	235.00
6	75	75	0	0.00	47.00	282.00
7	60	60	0	0.00	47.00	329.00
8	55	55	0	0.00	47.00	376.00

- Minimizes carrying cost.
- Does not take into account setup costs or capacity limitations.

Exhibit 15.25 shows the lot-for-lot calculations. The net requirements are given in column 2. Since the logic of lot-for-lot says the production quantity (column 3) will exactly match the required quantity (column 2), then there will be no inventory left at the end (column 4). Without any inventory to carry over into the next week, there is zero holding cost (column 5). However, lot-for-lot will require a setup cost each week (column 6). Incidentally, there is a setup cost each week because this is a work center where a variety of items are worked on each week. This is not a case where the work center is committed to one product and sits idle when it is not working on that product (and therefore only one setup would result). Lot-for-lot causes high setup costs.

In Chapter 14 we already discussed the EOQ model that explicitly balances setup and holding costs. In an EOQ model, either fairly constant demand must exist or safety stock must be kept to provide for demand variability. The EOQ model uses an estimate of total annual demand, the setup or order cost, and the annual holding cost. EOQ was not designed for a system with discrete time periods such as MRP. The lot-sizing techniques used for MRP assume that part requirements are satisfied at the start of the period. Holding costs are then charged only to the ending inventory for the period, not to the average inventory used in the EOQ model. EOQ assumes that parts are used on a continuous basis during the period. The lot sizes generated by EOQ do not always cover the entire number of periods. For example, the EOQ might provide the requirements for 4.6 periods.

Economic Order Quantity

Annual demand based on the 8 weeks $= D = \dfrac{525}{8} \times 52 = 3{,}412.5$ units

Annual holding cost $= H = 0.5\% \times \$10 \times 52$ weeks $= \$2.60$ per unit

Setup cost $= S = \$47$ (given)

$\therefore \text{EOQ} = \sqrt{\dfrac{2\,DS}{H}} = \sqrt{\dfrac{2(3{,}412.5)\,(\$47)}{\$2.60}} = 351$ units

Exhibit 15.26 shows the MRP schedule using an EOQ of 351 units. The EOQ lot size in Week 1 is enough to meet requirements for Weeks 1 through 5 and a portion of Week 6. Then, in Week 6 another EOQ lot is planned to meet the requirements for Weeks 6 through 8. Notice that the EOQ plan leaves some inventory at the end of Week 8 to carry forward into Week 9.

E X H I B I T 15.26   *Economic Order Quantity Run Size for an MRP Schedule*

Week	Net Requirements	Production Quantity	Ending Inventory	Holding Cost	Setup Cost	Total Cost
1	50	351	301	$15.05	$47.00	$ 62.05
2	60	0	241	12.05	0.00	74.10
3	70	0	171	8.55	0.00	82.65
4	60	0	111	5.55	0.00	88.20
5	95	0	16	0.80	0.00	89.00
6	75	351	292	14.60	47.00	150.60
7	60	0	232	11.60	0.00	162.20
8	55	0	177	8.85	0.00	171.05

E X H I B I T 15.27   *Least Total Cost Run Size for an MRP Schedule*

Weeks	Net Requirements	Production Quantity	Ending Inventory	Holding Cost	Setup Cost	Total Cost
1	50	335	285	$14.25	$47.00	$ 61.25
2	60	0	225	11.25	0.00	72.50
3	70	0	155	7.75	0.00	80.25
4	60	0	95	4.75	0.00	85.00
5	95	0	0	0.00	0.00	85.00
6	75	190	115	5.75	47.00	137.75
7	60	0	55	2.75	0.00	140.50
8	55	0	0	0.00	0.00	140.50

Weeks	Quantity Ordered	Carrying Cost	Order Cost	Total Cost
1	50	$ 0.00	$47.00	$ 47.00
1–2	110	3.00	47.00	50.00
1–3	180	10.00	47.00	57.00
1–4	240	19.00	47.00	66.00
1–5	335	38.00	47.00	85.00 ← Least total cost
1–6	410	56.75	47.00	103.75
1–7	470	74.75	47.00	121.75
1–8	525	94.00	47.00	141.00
6	75	0.00	47.00	47.00
6–7	135	3.00	47.00	50.00
6–8	190	8.50	47.00	55.50 ← Least total cost

Least Total Cost

The least total cost method (LTC) is a dynamic lot-sizing technique that calculates the order quantity by comparing the carrying cost and the setup (or ordering) costs for various lot sizes and then selects the lot in which these are most nearly equal.

The bottom half of Exhibit 15.27 shows the least total cost lot size results. The procedure to compute least total cost lot sizes is to compare order costs and holding costs for various numbers of weeks. For example, costs are compared for producing in Week 1 to cover the requirements for Week 1; producing in Week 1 for Weeks 1 and 2; producing in Week 1 to cover Weeks 1, 2, and 3, and so on. The correct selection is the lot size where the ordering costs and holding costs are approximately equal. In Exhibit 15.27 the best lot size is 335 since a $38 carrying cost and a $47 ordering cost are closer than $56.25

E X H I B I T 15.28 *Least Unit Cost Run Size for an MRP Schedule*

Week	Net Requirements	Production Quantity	Ending Inventory	Holding Cost	Setup Cost	Total Cost
1	50	410	360	$18.00	$47.00	$ 65.00
2	60	0	300	15.00	0.00	80.00
3	70	0	230	11.50	0.00	91.50
4	60	0	170	8.50	0.00	100.00
5	95	0	75	3.75	0.00	103.75
6	75	0	0	0	0	103.75
7	60	115	55	2.75	47.00	153.50
8	55	0	0	0	0	153.50

Weeks	Quantity Ordered	Carrying Cost	Order Cost	Total Cost	Unit Cost	
1	50	$ 0.00	$47.00	$ 47.00	$0.9400	
1–2	110	3.00	47.00	50.00	0.4545	
1–3	180	10.00	47.00	57.00	0.3167	
1–4	240	19.00	47.00	66.00	0.2750	
1–5	335	38.00	47.00	85.00	0.2537	
1–6	410	56.75	47.00	103.75	0.2530	← Least unit cost
1–7	470	74.75	47.00	121.75	0.2590	
1–8	525	94.00	47.00	141.00	0.2686	
7	60	0.00	47.00	47.00	0.7833	
7–8	115	2.75	47.00	49.75	0.4326	← Least unit cost

and $47 ($9 versus $9.25). This lot size covers requirements for Weeks 1 through 5. Unlike EOQ, the lot size covers only whole numbers of periods.

Based on the Week 1 decision to place an order to cover five weeks, we are now located in Week 6, and our problem is to determine how many weeks into the future we can provide for from here. Exhibit 15.27 shows that holding and ordering costs are closest in the quantity that covers requirements for Weeks 6 through 8. Notice that the holding and ordering costs here are far apart. This is because our example extends only to Week 8. If the planning horizon were longer, the lot size planned for Week 6 would likely cover more weeks into the future beyond Week 8. This brings up one of the limitations of both LTC and LUC (discussed below). Both techniques are influenced by the length of the planning horizon.

Least Unit Cost (LUC)

The least unit cost method is a dynamic lot-sizing technique that adds ordering and inventory carrying cost for each trial lot size and divides by the number of units in each lot size, picking the lot size with the lowest unit cost. The lower half of Exhibit 15.28 calculates the unit cost for ordering lots to meet the needs of Weeks 1 through 8. Note that the minimum occurred when the quantity 410, ordered in Week 1, was sufficient to cover Weeks 1 through 6. The lot size planned for Week 7 covers through the end of the planning horizon.

Which Lot Size to Choose

Using the lot-for-lot method, the total cost for the eight weeks is $376; the EOQ total cost is $171.05; the least total cost method is $140.50; and the least unit cost is $153.50. The lowest cost was obtained using the least total cost method of $140.50. If there were more than eight weeks, the lowest cost could differ.

The advantage of the least unit cost method is that it is a more complete analysis and would take into account ordering or setup costs that might change as the order size increases. If the ordering or setup costs remain constant, the lowest total cost method is more attractive because it is simpler and easier to compute; yet it would be just as accurate under that restriction.

15.11   ADVANCED MRP-TYPE SYSTEMS

For more than two decades, MRP systems were the first choice for firms that focused at the plant production level. MRP took as its input the product demands, inventory levels, and resource availability and produced production schedules as well as inventory ordering quantities. During this time the world was changing, with new global competition, multiplant international sites, wide global product demand, international subcontracting, and varying political environments and currency markets. Existing MRP software programs in their standard form could not handle these widened applications.

In today's environment, MRP users want instant access to information on customers' needs, which plants can meet these needs, and companywide inventory levels and available capacity.

What has been the response to these needs? There are more than 300 vendors for MRP systems. While most of these were involved with MRP systems from years ago and are still selling and maintaining their existing systems, many others are changing their systems to accommodate the new requirements; other firms are at the state of the art in developing new advanced systems based on MRP logic. In an expected response, many existing firms are modifying their current software programs while others are making major changes in the basic logic and databases.

Various names have been given to this new generation of MRP. The Gartner Group called the new MRP **Enterprise Resource Planning (ERP).** To fully operate in an enterprise sense, there needs to be distributed applications for planning, scheduling, costing, and so on to the multiple layers of the organization: work centers, sites, divisions, corporate. Multiple languages and currencies are also being included for global applications.

Advanced MRP systems (also called next-generation MRP II) will include[7]

Client/server architecture.

Relational database with SQL.

Graphic user interface.

Multiple database support.

Front-end systems for decision support.

Automated EDI.

Interoperability with multiple platforms.

Standard application programming interfaces.

Electronic data interchange (EDI) needs to be included for better communication with customers and suppliers.

Distributed MRP Processing versus Centralized Processing

Many companies want to retain their mainframes and centralized processing systems. To do this and be able to give users throughout the firm reliable real-time information, relational databases are being implemented. Oracle Corp., for example, has a widely used relational database system and fourth-generation language that is being incorporated to

---

[7]Alice Greene, "MRPII: Out with the Old," *Computerworld,* June 8, 1992, p. 74.

enhance existing MRP systems. Sequent Computer Systems is using Oracle's manufacturing software on its computer and is expanding into other areas as need arises, such as JIT (just-in-time manufacturing) and TQI (total quality through incremental improvements).

Existing MRP systems are limited in access and quite self-contained.

A *centralized process operation* controls such features as engineering, production scheduling, forecasting, order processing, purchasing, and materials planning for multiple plants at one central location. A *decentralized processing operation* distributes these responsibilities among the plants for autonomous operation. A *distributed processing operation* uses a combination of centralized and decentralized controls to allocate resources where they are logically needed and where they can be executed most efficiently.[8]

In distributed MRP processing, remote stations can access data, manipulate it, do local processing, and feed it back into the system. High-performance workstations such as Hewlett-Packard and Sun Microsystems are based on Unix, allowing fairly open communications and exchange. Mainframes, minicomputers, and microcomputers are a mixture that will become common in a truly distributed environment. Other open communication systems include IBM's OS/2, DEC's VMS, and Hewlett-Packard's MPE/iX.

Focus is on the total organization, but local computation and control are allowed. Local managers get quicker feedback on their performance and can therefore improve themselves by doing their own analysis.

There are two opposing views about centralization versus decentralization. One argument is that shifting to global manufacturing will encourage more decentralized MRP to allow more local control. The counterargument is that global manufacturing will cause centralization since more decision making will take place concerning multiple markets, customers, sources, and so on. Both can be satisfied by perhaps using an OSI (open systems interconnect) providing for a fully distributed system. OSI uses a common data architecture that permits both decentralization and data sharing.[9]

Exhibit 15.29 shows a sample of new and innovative MRP-type software. The list from which this was taken has about 60 entries.

SAP America, Inc.'s R/3

SAP America, Inc., recently came out with its R/3 MRP software package for open systems. It is a client/server application. The software includes a full variety of manufacturing and financial applications such as financial and fixed asset accounting, materials management, sales and distribution, human resources, production planning, quality assurance, and plant maintenance. R/3 runs on UNIX, Dec VMS, HP MPE/IX, and IBM OS/2.

Many companies are justifiably reluctant to install drastically new systems. They know that being first in new software applications has more disadvantages than advantages. Previously unknown system bugs and errors in logic creep in and can create havoc during the installation and startup phases. Rather than adopting the R/3 package, many firms are installing SAP's earlier R/2 instead. SAP's R/2 system is used by more than 2,300 customers as of 1994. Many of these will switch over to R/3 as needs arise. OS/2-based R/3 software improves the graphic user interface.

Use of R/3 is more widespread in Europe, since SAP AG is a German firm. Companies are responding in different ways. Eastman Chemical, a $3.9-billion company, is installing R/2 and just a very small part of R/3 to see how it runs. However, $40-billion Chevron is planning to use R/3 on a corporatewide basis.

---

[8]Richard Costello, "Available: Real-Time EDI, Multiplant Functions, More," *Computerworld*, June 8, 1992, p. 79.

[9]William F. McSpadden, "OSI, Distributed MRPII and You," *Industrial Engineering*, February 1992, pp. 38–39.

E X H I B I T 15.29   *A Sample of the New and Functionally Innovative MRP-Type Software Systems*

Vendor	Product	Type of Manufacturing	Top 5 Customers	Number of Modules/Top Modules	Hardware Required	Client/Server Platform	DBMSS Supported
The Ask Cos. (415) 969-4442	ManMan HP	Batch, discrete, repetitive, make to order	Contact vendor	20/ManMan/MFG, ManMan/Omar, ManMan/AP, ManMan GL	HP 3000 HP (Unix)	No	Turbo Image
Avalon Software, Inc. (602) 790-4214	CIIM	Batch, process, discrete, defense, repetitive, make to order	John Deere, Reed Tool Autolite Division of Allied-Signal, AT&T, Teleco Oilfield	12/Inventory, bill of materials, purchasing, order entry, general ledger	VAX, all Unix machines	Yes	Oracle, Sybase
Cincom Systems, Inc. (513) 662-2300 (800) 543-3010	Control Manufacturing	Batch, process, discrete, repetitive, make to order	Contact vendor	21/MRP, master production scheduling, bill of materials and routings, material control, project manufacturing control	IBM MVS/VSE, VAX, Ultrix, HP (Unix)	Yes	Supra
IBM (404) 835-8355	Mapics/DB	Discrete, repetitive	Bally Engineered Structures, Sybron Chemicals, Lovejoy, Inc., Siemens Burdick, Weiler and Co.	19/Inventory management, product data management, MRP, purchasing, repetitive production management	AS/400	Yes	OS/400 relational database
MCBA (818) 242-9600	Classic	Discrete	Sold to resellers	20/MRP, inventory, shop floor control, general ledger, payroll	IBM PCs and compatibles, all Unix	Yes	Oracle
Micro-MRP, Inc. (415) 345-6000	Micro-Max	Batch, discrete, repetitive, make to order, assemble to order	IBM, Intel, HP, Dresser, United Technologies	55/Sales order entry, inventory, shop floor control, MRP, purchasing (MRP II)	IBM PCs and compatibles	Yes	Btrieve
SAP America, Inc. (215) 595-4500	R/2 System	Batch, process, discrete, repetitive, make to order	Kodak, Du Pont, ICI, Mobil, Bristol-Meyers	10/Financials, assets accounting, sales, material control, MRP	IBM 370	No	VSAM, IMS, DB2
System Software Associates, Inc. (312) 641-2900	Business Planning and Control System	Batch, process, discrete, repetitive, make to order	Contact vendor	32/MRP, order processing, general ledger	AS/400, System/34 to 38	Yes	AS/400

Source: "Product Spotlight," *Computerworld,* June 8, 1992, pp. 82–85. Copyright 1992 by Computerworld, Inc. Framingham, MA 01701.

E X H I B I T 15.29   *A Sample of the New and Functionally Innovative MRP-Type Software Systems–cont'd*

SQL Access	GUIS Supported	Interfaces that Are Automated Interactive	Application Development Tool Used to Build Product	Multilingual Capabilities	Graphics-Based Decision Support Tools	Activity-Based Costing	Integrated Supply Chain Inventory Management	Worldwide Installed Base (Approx.)	Price Per Module
No	NA	CAD, data collection	NA	None	No	No	Yes	1,500	$39,400 starting price
Yes	Windows 3.0, X Window, OSF/Motif (depends on the database)	EDI, data collection	4GL, CASE	Screen, database, documentation	No	Yes	No	130	$56,000–$700,000
No	Windows 3.0, Macintosh	EDI, data collection	4GL, CASE	Screens, database, documentation	Yes	No	NP	400	Contact vendor
Yes	Windows 3.0, OS/2, GDDM	EDI, data collection	IBM CASE tool	Screens, database, documentation	Yes	No	Yes	10,000	Contact vendor
Yes	None	EDI	4GL	None	No	No	Yes	30,000	$2,000–$12,000
Yes	Windows 3.0	EDI, CAD, data collection	Microsoft development tools	Screens	Yes	Yes	Yes	4,000	Contact vendor
Yes	Windows 3.0, OS/2, OSF/Motif	EDI, CAD, data collection	4GL	Screens, database, documentation	Yes	Yes	Yes	1,600	Contact vendor
Yes	OS/2	EDI, data collection	CASE	Screens, database, documentation	Yes	No	Yes	5,500	$2,000–$90,000

E X H I B I T 15.30

A Customer-Oriented Manufacturing Management System (COMMS)

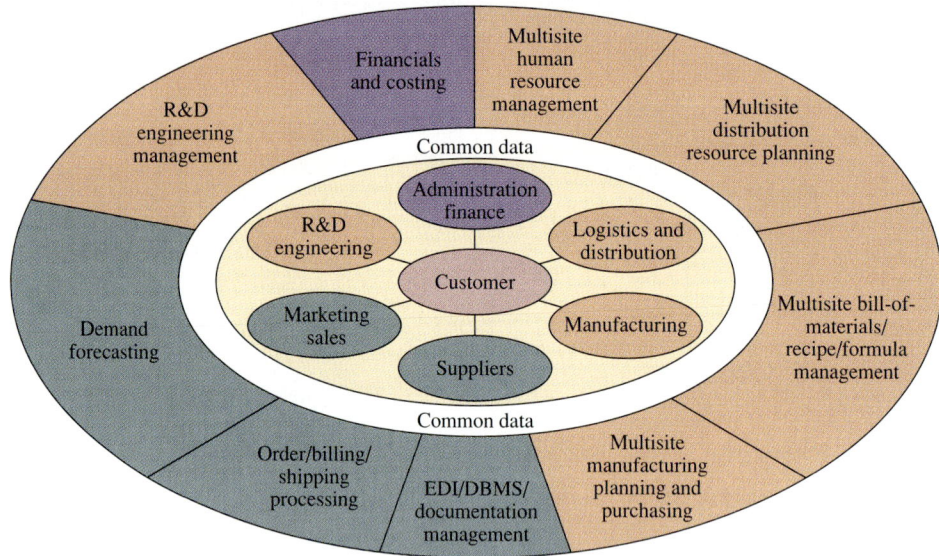

Source: Chris Staiti, "Customers Drive New Manufacturing Software," *Datamation,* November 15, 1993, p. 72. Reprinted with permission. © 1993 by Cahners Publishing Co.

ManMan/X

ManMan/X in a Unix-based software from Ask Computer Systems, Inc. It is based on the Enterprise Resource Planning logic and uses the fourth-generation language (4GL). ManMan/X also supports Digital Equipment Corp.'s OSF/1, Hewlett-Packard's MPR/iX, Oracle Corp.'s database, and Informix Inc.'s database.

ManMan/X provides stronger planning and forecasting features including simulation and net change than most other MRP systems. ManMan/X will exchange information with other systems. It also includes languages and currency features for global operation.

COMMS (Customer-Oriented Manufacturing Management System)

Vendors are taking many different approaches to develop new MRP-type advanced programs. A new model of an advanced integrated MRP-type system is being created by Advanced Manufacturing Research, Inc. (AMR), a Boston-based consulting firm. AMR's model is called **COMMS (Customer-Oriented Manufacturing Management System).** COMMS has added in real-time interaction with the manufacturing plants throughout the supply chain. Currently in development, this model is shown in Exhibit 15.30. It places the customer in the center with the objective of giving customers what they want, when, how, where, and at the price they want. This is a distributed-type system.

The firms that AMR represents believe that we are entering an era of "customerized" manufacturing where the customer can specify anything and the manufacturer must be able to respond to remain competitive. Note that Exhibit 15.30 shows AMR's COMMS model uniting the departments of the chain around the customer. In practice, when a customer's order is taken, the salesperson can give all the necessary information to the customer: any engineering changes, the schedule, price, and so on. This is possible because the salesperson has direct access to all the databases and schedules.

EDI (Electronic Data Interface)

Roughly 80 percent of MRP packages have either an EDI module or an EDI interface that allows manufacturers to import and export documents. The new addition to EDI is that it is beginning to be *real-time* interchange rather than batch processing. It is valuable for multiplant MRP. EDI vendors include American Software, IBM, Andersen Consulting, and Symix Computer Systems.

Furniture Maker Uses MRP II to Cut Lead Time

For a manufacturer like Harpers, Inc., it was the ultimate in good news/bad news: The company's sales kept going up, but its profits kept going down.

That was January 1988. By March, Harpers' plant in Torrance, California, experienced the manufacturing equivalent of a nervous breakdown. It was accustomed to a 12-week raw-material-to-market cycle (also known as lead time) to make its freestanding office furniture.

Meanwhile, its competitors—Herman Miller, Inc., Steelcase, Inc., and Haworth, Inc., all in Michigan and all nationwide suppliers—were taking just six weeks to convert raw plastic and metal into modular "systems furniture," the pastel, rat-maze furniture that was becoming popular.

"We were forced to either become a 'systems furniture' manufacturer or sell the company to other manufacturers," says Joe Wisniewski, executive vice president and general manager at Harpers. "We chose systems."

Executives and managers at Harpers did something many faltering firms only talk about doing: "We actually had a strategic planning meeting and determined a number of critical success factors," Wisniewski says.

The first success factor was the most predictable. Harpers decided to cut manufacturing costs by 15 percent. One way to do that was to reduce lead time to three weeks or less versus the new industry standard of six weeks.

Second, the firm decided to cut product design and development lead time—a critical phase for a company bent on being responsive to its marketplace—to six months instead of the three *years* Harpers had previously enjoyed.

It wasn't going to be easy.

For one thing, Harpers' material requirements processing (formerly known as MRP I, or "little" MRP) system was homemade with no forecasting, "no real integration between order processing and accounting and no inventory location system in the plant," Wisniewski says.

Wisniewski and his managers drew up a detailed plan of objectives to complement Harpers' lofty goals of reducing money and lead times.

First was a marketing objective. The company decided it would carve out a niche for "custom furniture solu-

tions," which would appeal to companies that were, for example, converting their engineering staff from drawing boards to computers. Such projects often demand products that are not of a standard size. Wisniewski decided on a design lead time of two weeks, with custom furniture "shippable in no more than four weeks."

The second objective was to acquire "flexible manufacturing" machinery. The system would be able to increase or decrease the number of features a particular furniture system offered at the customer's whim.

But what would make the whole system work was a manufacturing resource planning (MRP II, or "big" MRP) system that would "integrate our engineering, marketing, manufacturing, and accounting efforts and simultaneously engineer and deliver those custom products," Wisniewski says.

Harpers took a look at its hardware requirements, narrowed the possibilities down to Digital Equipment Corp. and IBM, determined that more solutions were available on the IBM platform, and selected IBM's Application System/400, which was new at the time.

Finding MRP II software became a contest between IBM, Systems Software Associates, Inc. in Chicago, Andersen Consulting in Chicago, and Pansophic Systems, Inc., now a subsidiary of Computer Associates International, Inc., in Lisle, Illinois. Andersen Consulting's Mac-Pac won, partly because it included an expert system, Expert Configurator, that was developed to improve order accuracy and response time.

By October 1990, the system was installed and running.

Harpers has not yet met its goal of a three-week manufacturing lead time, but 20 percent of its furniture is out within two weeks, with the remainder clocking in at four weeks.

Harpers, which was bought by Jasper, Indiana–based Kimball International last January, now makes modular furniture at the rate of $60 million a year. Wisniewski says the company accomplishes that with only 350 factory employees, compared with an output of $50 million in 1988 with 580 employees.

Source: Robert M. Knight, "Furniture Maker Uses MRP II to Cut Lead Time," *Computerworld*, June 8, 1992, p. 80. Copyright 1992 by Computerworld, Inc., Framingham, MA 01701.

About 85 percent of MRP II packages include an interface with at least one CAD (computer-aided design) system. The CAD integration solutions such as those by Cincom and Micro-MRP are two of the most popular.

Transition to Advanced MRP-Type Systems

How do firms change from existing MRP systems to the advanced ones? That depends on the new system they want. Some systems are easier to use than others, such as Cincom's Control Manufacturing, which uses existing data and transaction processing methods. Others (such as Datalogix and Dunn and Bradstreet software) are more difficult in requiring re-implementation. Still other firms are waiting by the sidelines until more clear paths and possible results are visible. Most larger firms eventually will have to expand their MRP system to remain competitive.

15.12   CONCLUSION

Since the 1970s, MRP has grown from its purpose of determining simple time schedules, to its present advanced types that tie together all major functions of an organization. During its growth and its application, MRP's disadvantages as a scheduling mechanism have been well recognized. This is largely because MRP tries to do too much in light of the dynamic, often jumpy system in which it is trying to operate.

MRP is recognized, however, for its excellent databases and linkages within the firm. MRP also does a good job in helping to produce master schedules. Many firms in repetitive manufacturing are installing JIT systems to link with the MRP system. JIT takes the master production schedule as its pulling force but does not use MRP's generated schedule. Results indicate that this is working very well.

Many newer MRP-type software programs have been developed since the early 1990s. Several others are currently in the development stage. These allow more open exchange of data than the earlier systems, embrace a larger part of the firm's operation (such as multiple sites, global customers, languages, and currency rates), and operate in real time.

MRP's service applications have not fared well, even though it seems that they should have. The MRP approach would appear to be valuable in producing services since service scheduling consists of identifying the final service and then tracing back to the resources needed, such as equipment, space, and personnel. Consider, for example, a hospital operating room planning an open-heart surgery. The master schedule can establish a time for the surgery (or surgeries, if several are scheduled). The BOM could specify all required equipment and personnel—MDs, nurses, anesthesiologist, operating room, heart/lung machine, defibrillator, and so forth. The inventory status file would show the availability of the resources and commit them to the project. The MRP program could then produce a schedule showing when various parts of the operation are to be started, expected completion times, required materials, and so forth. Checking this schedule would allow "capacity planning" in answering such questions as "Are all the materials and personnel available?" and "Does the system produce a feasible schedule?"

We still believe that MRP systems will eventually find their way into service applications. But after a number of years of believing this, we still have not seen development and implementation. One reason is that even service managers who are aware of it believe that MRP is just a manufacturing tool. Also, service managers tend to be people-oriented and skeptical of tools from outside their industry.

15.13 SOLVED PROBLEMS

1. Product X is made of two units of Y and three of Z. Y is made of one unit of A and two units of B. Z is made of two units of A and four units of C.

   Lead time for X is one week; Y, two weeks; Z, three weeks; A, two weeks; B, one week; and C, three weeks.

   a. Draw the bill of materials (product structure tree).
   b. If 100 units of X are needed in week 10, develop a planning schedule showing when each item should be ordered and in what quantity.

Solution

a.

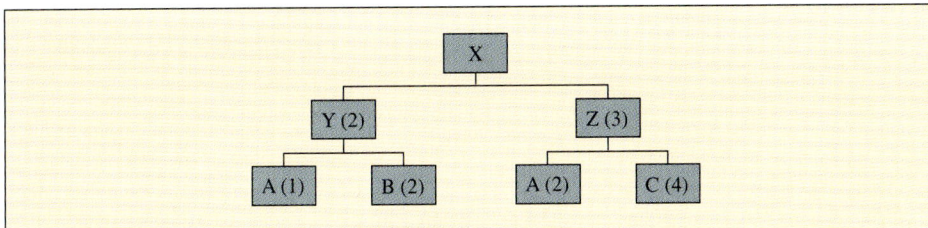

b.

		3	4	5	6	7	8	9	10
X	LT = 1							100	100
Y	LT = 2					200		200	
Z	LT = 3				300			300	
A	LT = 2		600	200	600	200			
B	LT = 1				400	400			
C	LT = 3	1200			1200				

2. Product M is made of two units of N and three of P. N is made of two units of R and four units of S. R is made of one unit of S and three units of T. P is made of two units of T and four units of U.

   a. Show the bill of materials (product structure tree).
   b. If 100 M are required, how many units of each component are needed?
   c. Show both a single-level parts list and an indented parts list.

Solution

a.

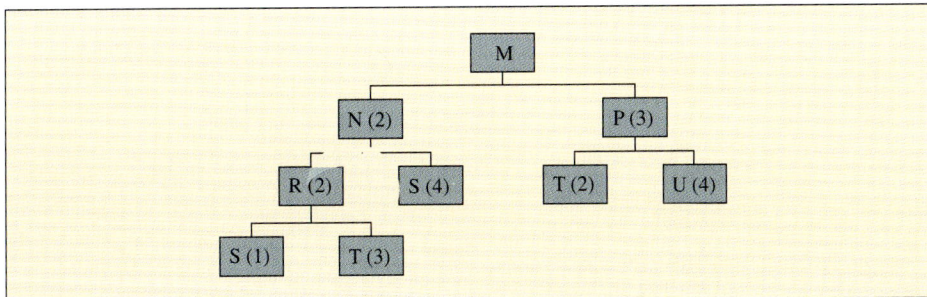

b. M = 100
N = 200
P = 300
R = 400
S = 800 + 400 = 1,200
T = 600 + 1,200 = 1,800
U = 1,200

c.

Single-level Parts List		**Indented Parts List**			
M		M			
	N (2)		N (2)		
	P (3)			R (2)	
N					S (1)
	R (2)				T (3)
	S (4)			S (4)	
R			P (3)		
	S (1)			T (2)	
	T (3)			U (4)	
P					
	T (2)				
	U (4)				

15.14 REVIEW AND DISCUSSION QUESTIONS

1. Since material requirements planning appears so reasonable, discuss why it did not become popular until recently.

2. Discuss the·meaning of MRP terms such as *planned order release* and *scheduled order receipts.*

3. Most practitioners currently update MRP weekly or biweekly. Would it be more valuable if it were updated daily? Discuss.

4. What is the role of safety stock in an MRP system?

5. How does MRP relate to CIM? (See the supplement to Chapter 3.)

6. Contrast the significance of the term *lead time* in the traditional EOQ context and in an MRP system.

7. Discuss the importance of the master production schedule in an MRP system.

8. "MRP just prepares shopping lists. It does not do the shopping or cook the dinner." Comment.

9. What are the sources of demand in an MRP system? Are these dependent or independent, and how are they used as inputs to the system?

10. State the types of data that would be carried in the bill of materials file and the inventory record file.

11. How do the advanced versions of MRP differ from the basic system?

15.15 PROBLEMS

1. In the following MRP planning schedule for Item J, indicate the correct net requirements, planned order receipts, and planned order releases to meet the gross requirements. Lead time is one week.

Week Number

Item J	0	1	2	3	4	5
Gross requirements			75		50	70
On hand 40						
Net requirements						
Planned order receipt						
Planned order releases						

2. Repeat Solved Problem 1 using current on-hand inventories of 20 X, 40 Y, 30 Z, 50 A, 100 B, and 900 C.

3. Assume that Product Z is made of two units of A and four units of B. A is made of three units of C and four of D. D is made of two units of E.

   Lead times for purchase or fabrication of each unit to final assembly are: Z takes two weeks; A, B, C, and D take one week each; and E takes three weeks.

   Fifty units are required in Period 10. (Assume that there is currently no inventory on hand of any of these items.)

   a. Show the bill of materials (product structure tree).

   b. Develop an MRP planning schedule showing gross and net requirements, order release and order receipt dates.

4. *Note:* For Problems 4 through 7, to simplify data handling to include the receipt of orders that have actually been placed in previous periods, the following six-level scheme can be used. (There are a number of different techniques used in practice, but the important issue is to keep track of what is on hand, what is expected to arrive, what is needed, and what size orders should be placed.) One way to calculate the numbers is as follows:

Week

Gross requirements								
Scheduled receipts								
On hand from prior period								
Net requirements								
Planned order receipt								
Planned order release								

   One unit of A is made of three units of B, one unit of C, and two units of D. B is composed of two units of E and one unit of D. C is made of one unit of B and two units of E. E is made of one unit of F.

   Items B, C, E, and F have one-week lead times; A and D have lead times of two weeks.

   Assume that lot-for-lot (L4L) lot sizing is used for items A, B, and F; lots of size 50, 50, and 200 are used for items C, D, and E, respectively. Items C, E, and F have on-hand (beginning) inventories of 10, 50, and 150, respectively; all other items have zero beginning inventory. We are scheduled to receive 10 units of A in Week 5, 50 units of E in Week 4, and also 50 units of F in Week 4. There are no other scheduled receipts. If 30 units of A are required in Week 8, use the low-level-coded bill of materials to find the necessary planned order releases for all components.

5. One unit of A is made of two units of B, three units of C, and two units of D. B is composed of one unit of E and two units of F. C is made of two units of F and one unit of D. E is made of two units of D. Items A, C, D, and F have one-week lead times; B and E have lead times of two weeks. Lot-for-lot (L4L) lot sizing is used for Items A, B, C, and D; lots of size 50 and 180 are used for items E and F, respectively. Item C has an on-hand (beginning) inventory of 15; D has an on-hand inventory of 50; all other items have zero beginning inventory. We are scheduled to receive 20 units of Item E in week 4; there are no other scheduled receipts.

   Construct simple and low-level-coded bills of materials (product structure tree) and indented and summarized parts list.

If 20 units of A are required in Week 8, use the low-level-coded bill of materials to find the necessary planned order releases for all components. (See note in Problem 4.)

6. One unit of A is made of one unit of B and one unit of C. B is made of four units of C and one unit of E and F. C is made of two units of D and one unit of E. E is made of three units of F. Item C has a lead time of one week; Items A, B, E, and F have two-week lead times; and Item D has a lead time of three weeks. Lot-for-lot lot sizing is used for Items A, D, and E; lots of size 50, 100, and 50 are used for Items B, C, and F, respectively. Items A, C, D, and E have on-hand (beginning) inventories of 20, 50, 100, and 10, respectively; all other items have zero beginning inventory. We are scheduled to receive 10 units of A in week 5, 100 units of C in Week 6, and 100 units of D in Week 4; there are no other scheduled receipts. If 50 units of A are required in Week 10, use the low-level-coded bill of materials (product structure tree) to find the necessary planned order releases for all components. (See note in Problem 4.)

7. One unit of A is made of two units of B and one unit of C. B is made of three units of D and one unit of F. C is composed of three units of B, one unit of D, and four units of E. D is made of one unit of E. Item C has a lead time of one week; Items A, B, E, and F have two-week lead times; and Item D has a lead time of three weeks. Lot-for-lot lot sizing is used for Items C, E, and F; lots of size 20, 40, and 160 are used for items A, B, and D, respectively. Items A, B, D, and E have on-hand (beginning) inventories of 5, 10, 100, and 100, respectively; all other items have zero beginning inventories. We are scheduled to receive 10 units of A in Week 3, 20 units of B in Week 7, 40 units of F in week 5, and 60 units of E in Week 2; there are no other scheduled receipts. If 20 units of A are required in Week 10, use the low-level-coded bill of materials (product structure tree) to find the necessary planned order releases for all components. (See note in Problem 4.)

8. The MRP gross requirements for Item A are shown here for the next 10 weeks. Lead time for A is three weeks and setup cost is $10 per setup. There is a carrying cost of $0.01 per unit per week. Beginning inventory is 90 units.

	Week									
	1	**2**	**3**	**4**	**5**	**6**	**7**	**8**	**9**	**10**
Gross requirements	30	50	10	20	70	80	20	60	200	50

Use the least total cost or the least unit cost lot-sizing method to determine when and for what quantity the first order should be released.

9. (This problem is intended as a very simple exercise to go from the aggregate plan to the master schedule to the MRP.) Gigamemory Storage Devices, Inc., produces CD ROMs (read only memory) and WORMs (write once read many) for the computer market. Aggregate demand for the WORMs for the next two quarters are 2,100 units and 2,700 units. Assume that demand is distributed evenly for each month of the quarter.

There are two models of the WORM: an internal model and an external model. The drive assemblies in both are the same but the electronics and housing are different. Demand is higher for the external model and currently is 70 percent of the aggregate demand.

The bill of materials and the lead times follow. One drive assembly and one electronic and housing unit go into each WORM.

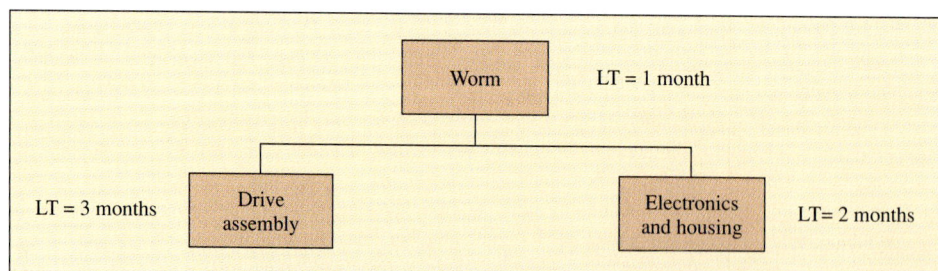

The MRP system is run monthly. Currently, 200 external WORMs and 100 internal WORMs are in stock. Also in stock are 250 drive assemblies, 50 internal electronic and housing units, and 125 external electronic and housing units.

Problem: Show the aggregate plan, the master production schedule, and the full MRP with the gross and net requirements and planned order releases.

10. Product A is an end item and is made from two units of B and four of C. B is made of three units of D and two of E. C is made of two units of F and two of E.

    A has a lead time of one week. B, C, and E have lead times of two weeks, and D and F have lead times of three weeks.

    a. Show the bill of materials (product structure tree).

    b. If 100 units of A are required in week 10, develop the MRP planning schedule, specifying when items are to be ordered and received. There are currently no units of inventory on hand.

11. Product A consists of two units of subassembly B, three units of C, and one unit of D. B is composed of four units of E and three units of F. C is made of two units of H and three units of D. H is made of five units of E and two units of G.

    a. Construct a simple bill of materials (product structure tree).

    b. Construct a product structure tree using low-level coding.

    c. Construct an indented parts list.

    d. To produce 100 units of A, determine the numbers of units of B, C, D, E, F, G, and H required.

12. The MRP gross requirements for Item X are shown here for the next 10 weeks. Lead time for A is two weeks, and setup cost is $9 per setup. There is a carrying cost of $0.02 per unit per week. Beginning inventory is 70 units.

					Week					
	1	**2**	**3**	**4**	**5**	**6**	**7**	**8**	**9**	**10**
Gross requirements	20	10	15	45	10	30	100	20	40	150

Use the least total cost or the least unit cost lot-sizing method to determine when and for what quantity the first order should be released.

13. Audio Products, Inc., produces two AM/FM/CD players for cars. The radio/CD units are identical, but the mounting hardware and finish trim differ. The standard model fits intermediate and full-size cars, and the sports model fits small sports cars.

    Audio Products handles the production in the following way. The chassis (radio/CD unit) is assembled in Mexico and has a manufacturing lead time of two weeks. The mounting hardware is purchased from a sheet steel company and has a three-week lead time. The finish trim is purchased from a Taiwan electronics company with offices in Los Angeles as prepackaged units consisting of knobs and various trim pieces. Trim packages have a two-week lead time. Final assembly time may be disregarded since adding the trim package and mounting are performed by the customer.

    Audio Products supplies wholesalers and retailers, who place specific orders for both models up to eight weeks in advance. These orders, together with enough additional units to satisfy the small number of individual sales, are summarized in the following demand schedule:

				Week				
	1	**2**	**3**	**4**	**5**	**6**	**7**	**8**
Standard model				300				400
Sports model					200			100

There are currently 50 radio/CD units on hand but no trim packages or mounting hardware.

Prepare a material requirements plan to meet the demand schedule exactly. Specify the gross and net requirements, on-hand amounts, and the planned order release and receipt periods for the radio/CD chassis, the standard trim and sports car model trim, and the standard mounting hardware and the sports car mounting hardware.

14. Brown and Brown Electronics manufactures a line of digital audiotape (DAT) players. While there are differences among the various products, there are a number of common parts within each player. The bill of materials, showing the number of each item required, lead times, and the current inventory on hand for the parts and components, follows:

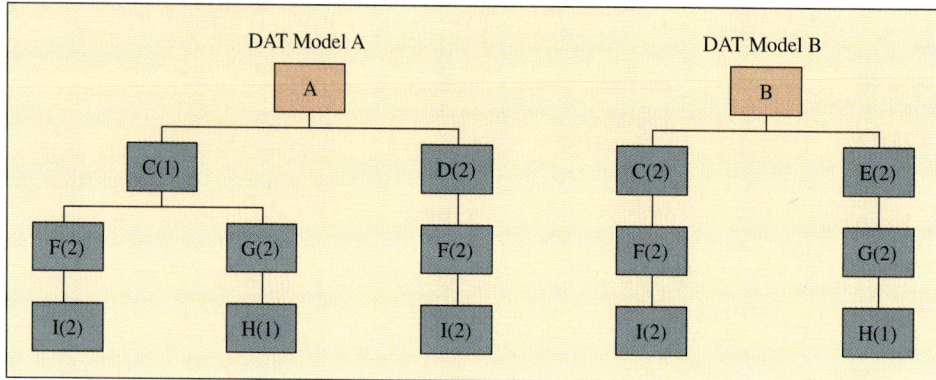

	Number Currently in Stock	Lead Time (weeks)
DAT Model A	30	1
DAT Model B	50	2
Subassembly C	75	1
Subassembly D	80	2
Subassembly E	100	1
Part F	150	1
Part G	40	1
Raw material H	200	2
Raw material I	300	2

Brown and Brown created a forecast that it plans to use as its master production schedule, producing exactly to schedule. Part of the MPS shows a demand for 700 units of Model A and 1,200 units of Model B in Week 10.

Develop an MRP schedule to meet that demand.

CASE

15.16 C A S E
Nichols Company

This particular December day seemed bleak to Joe Williams, president of Nichols Company (NCO). He sat in his office watching the dying embers in his fireplace, hoping to clear his mind. Suddenly there came a tapping by someone gently rapping, rapping at his office door. "Another headache," he muttered, "tapping at my office door. Only that and nothing more."[10]

The intruder was Barney Thompson, director of marketing. "A major account has just canceled a large purchase of A units because we are back ordered on tubing. This can't continue. My sales force is out beating the bushes for customers and our production manager can't provide the product."

For the past several months, operations at NCO have been unsteady. Inventory levels have been high, while at the same time there have been stockouts. This has resulted in late deliveries, complaints, and cancellations. To compound the problem, overtime has been excessive.

History

Nichols Company was started by Joe Williams and Peter Schaap, both with MBAs from the University of Arizona. Much has happened since Williams and Schaap formed the company. Schaap has left the company and is working in real estate development in Queensland, Australia. Under the direction of Williams, NCO has diversified to include a number of other products.

NCO currently has 355 full-time employees directly involved in manufacturing the three primary products: A, B, and C. Final assembly takes place in a converted warehouse adjacent to NCO's main plant.

The Meeting

Williams called a meeting the next day to get input on the problems facing NCO and to lay the groundwork for some solutions. Attending the meeting, besides himself and Barney Thompson, were Phil Bright of production and inventory control, Trevor Hansen of purchasing, and Steve Clark of accounting.

The meeting lasted all morning. Participation was vocal and intense.

Bright said, "The forecasts that marketing sends us are always way off. We are constantly having to expedite one product or another to meet current demand. This runs up our overtime."

Thompson said, "Production tries to run too lean. We need a larger inventory of finished goods. If I had the merchandise, my salespeople could sell 20 percent more product."

Clark said, "No way! Our inventory is already uncomfortably high. We can't afford the holding costs, not to mention how fast technology changes around here causing even more inventory, much of it obsolete."

Bright said, "The only way I can meet our stringent cost requirement is to buy in volume."

At the end of the meeting, Williams had lots of input but no specific plan. What do you think he should do? Use Exhibits C15.1 through C15.4 showing relevant data to answer the specific questions at the end of the case.

QUESTIONS

Use Lotus (or another spreadsheet if you prefer) to solve the Nichols Company case. (Note that if you start from scratch, it will take several hours to answer Question 1, about the same for Question 2, and perhaps double that for Question 3).

Simplifying assumption: To get the program started, some time is needed at the beginning since MRP backloads the system. For simplicity, assume that the forecasts (and therefore demands) are zero for Periods 1 through 3. Also assume that the starting inventory specified in Exhibit C15.3 is available from Week 1. For the master production schedule, use only End Items A, B, and C.

To modify production quantities, adjust only Products A, B, and C. Do not adjust the quantities of D, E, F, G, H, and I.

E X H I B I T C15.1

Bills of Materials for Products A, B, and C

Product A	Product B	Product C
.A	.B	.C
.D(4)	.F(2)	.G(2)
.I(3)	.G(3)	.I(2)
.E(1)	.I(2)	.H(1)
.F(4)		

E X H I B I T C15.2

Work Center Routings for Products and Components

Item	Work Center Number	Standard Time (hours per unit)
Product A	1	0.20
	4	0.10
Product B	2	0.30
	4	0.08
Product C	3	0.10
	4	0.05
Component D	1	0.15
	4	0.10
Component E	2	0.15
	4	0.05
Component F	2	0.15
	3	0.20
Component G	1	0.30
	2	0.10
Component H	1	0.05
	3	0.10

E X H I B I T C15.3
Inventory Levels and Lead Times for Each Item on the Bill of Materials at the Beginning of Week 1

Product/Component	On Hand (units)	Lead Time (weeks)
Product A	100	1
Product B	200	1
Product C	175	1
Component D	200	1
Component E	195	1
Component F	120	1
Component G	200	1
Component H	200	1
I (Raw material)	300	1

E X H I B I T C15.4
Forecasted Demand for Weeks 4 to 27

Week	Product A	Product B	Product C
1			
2			
3			
4	1,500	2,200	1,200
5	1,700	2,100	1,400
6	1,150	1,900	1,000
7	1,100	1,800	1,500
8	1,000	1,800	1,400
9	1,100	1,600	1,100
10	1,400	1,600	1,800
11	1,400	1,700	1,700
12	1,700	1,700	1,300
13	1,700	1,700	1,700
14	1,800	1,700	1,700
15	1,900	1,900	1,500
16	2,200	2,300	2,300
17	2,000	2,300	2,300
18	1,700	2,100	2,000
19	1,600	1,900	1,700
20	1,400	1,800	1,800
21	1,100	1,800	2,200
22	1,000	1,900	1,900
23	1,400	1,700	2,400
24	1,400	1,700	2,400
25	1,500	1,700	2,600
26	1,600	1,800	2,400
27	1,500	1,900	2,500

These should be linked so that changes in A, B, and C automatically adjust them.

1. Disregarding machine-center limitations, develop an MRP schedule and also capacity profiles for the four machine centers.

2. Work center capacities and costs follow. Repeat (1) creating a *feasible* schedule (within the capacities of the machine centers) and compute the relevant costs. Do this by adjusting the MPS only. Try to minimize the total cost of operation for the 27 weeks.

3. Suppose end items had to be ordered in multiples of 100 units, components in multiples of 500 units, and raw materials in multiples of 1,000 units. How would this change your schedule?

	Capacity	Cost
Work Center 1	6,000 hours available	$20 per hour
Work Center 2	4,500 hours available	$25 per hour
Work Center 3	2,400 hours available	$35 per hour
Work Center 4	1,200 hours available	$65 per hour
Inventory carrying cost		
End Items A, B, and C	$2.00 per unit	
Components D, E, F, G, and H	$1.50 per unit	
Raw Material I	$1.00 per unit	
Back order cost		
End Items A, B, and C	$20 per unit	
Components D, E, F, G, and H	$14 per unit	
Raw Material I	$ 8 per unit	

[10] With apologies to E. A. P. (Edgar Allen Poe)

15.17 SELECTED BIBLIOGRAPHY

Flapper, S. D. P., G. J. Miltenburg, and J. Wijngaard. "Embedding JIT into MRP." *International Journal of Production Research* 29, no. 2 (1991), pp. 329–41.

Goodrich, Thomas. "JIT & MRP Can Work Together." *Automation,* April 1989, pp. 46–47.

Journal of American Institute of Decision Science. (Articles appear discussing MRP and MRP II from an analytical basis, examining topics such as lot sizing, safety stocks, and multi-echelon inventory.)

Journal of American Production and Inventory Control Society. (Numerous articles on MRP and MRP II appear. Most cite practitioners' difficulties and experiences.)

Lee, Choong Y. "A Recent Development of the Integrated Manufacturing System: A Hybrid of MRP and JIT." *International Journal of Operations and Production Management* 13, no. 4 (1993), pp. 3–17.

McSpadden, William F. "OSI, Distributed MRP II and You." *Industrial Engineering,* February 1992, pp. 38–39.

Mittenberg, J. "On the Equivalence of JIT and MRP as Technologies for Reducing Wastes in Manufacturing." *Naval Research Logistics* 40, no. 7 (1993), pp. 905–24.

Orlicky, Joseph. *Materials Requirements Planning.* New York: McGraw-Hill, 1975. (This is the classic book on MRP.)

Primrose, P. L. "Selecting and Evaluating Cost-Effective MRP and MRP II." *International Journal of Operations and Production Management* 10, no. 1 (1990), pp. 51–66.

Sillince, J. A. A., and G. M. H. Sykes. "Integrating MRP II and JIT: A Management Rather Than a Technical Challenge." *International Journal of Operations and Production Management* 13, no. 4 (April 1993), pp. 18–30.

Staiti, Chris. "Customers Drive New Manufacturing Software." *Datamation,* November 15, 1993, pp. 71–74.

Turbide, David A. *MRP+: The Adaptation, Enhancement, and Application of MRP.* New York: Industrial Press, 1993.

Wallace, Thomas F. "MRP II & JIT Work Together in Plan and Practice." *Automation,* March 1990, pp. 40–42.

———. *MRP II: Making It Happen.* 2d ed. Essex Junction, VT: Oliver Wight, 1990.

Chapter

16

Operations Scheduling

CHAPTER OUTLINE

KEY TERMS

Machine-Limited and Labor-Limited Systems

Priority Rules

Assignment Method

Interactive Scheduling

Input/Output (I/O) Control

Optimized Production Technology (OPT)

Q Control

First Hour Principle

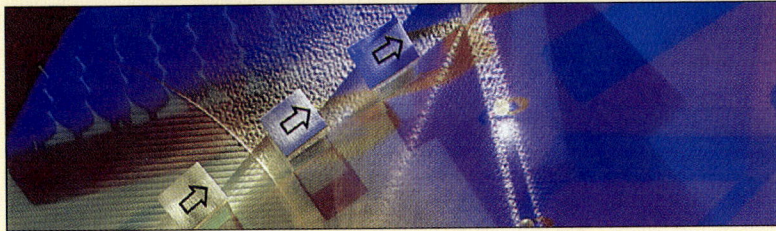

Why should accounting and finance types worry about the nitty gritty problems of scheduling, such as long queue times? Answer: Workflow equals cash flow, and workflow is driven by the schedule!

Consider the following figure. In poorly scheduled job shops, it is not at all uncommon for jobs to wait for 95 percent of their total production cycle (a). This results in a long workflow cycle (b). Add inventory time and receivables collection time to this and you get a long cash flow cycle (c). But if you can do a good job of scheduling, you can eliminate, say, 75 percent of the queue time (d,e) and cut your cash flow cycle by the same amount of time.

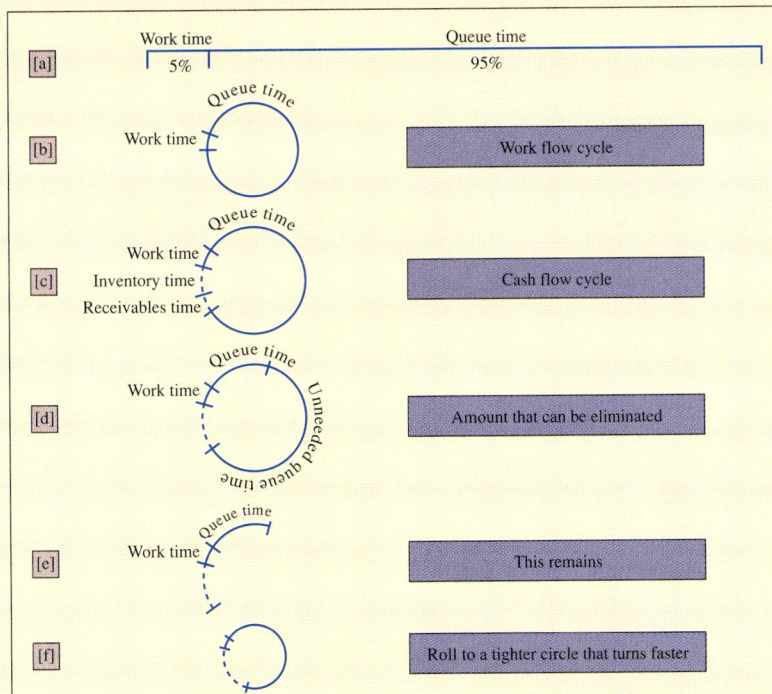

_____

Source: Modified from William E. Sandman with J.P. Hayes, *How to Win Productivity in Manufacturing* (Dresher, Pa: Yellow Book of Pennsylvania), 1980. p. 57.

635

Again, workflow equals cash flow and scheduling lies at the heart of the process. A schedule is a timetable for performing activities, utilizing resources, or allocating facilities. In this chapter, we discuss short-run scheduling and control of orders with emphasis on job-shop manufacturing. We also introduce some basic approaches to short-term scheduling of workers in services.

16.1   THE NATURE AND IMPORTANCE OF JOB SHOPS

A **job shop** may be defined as a form of manufacturing (or service) organization in which productive resources are organized according to function. Jobs pass through the functional departments in lots and each lot may have a different routing.[1] In a sense, each job order constitutes a "miniproject" that must be individually planned, its progress closely monitored, and separate records kept on its cost. Exhibit 16.1 contrasts additional characteristics of job shops with other manufacturing environments we have discussed in previous chapters.

Job shops are well worth studying, not only because they are pervasive, but because so many of the innovative and custom-made products that have been the hallmark of North American manufacturing over the years are produced in them. Moreover, most high tech start-up manufacturers work in a job-shop mode.

In the service sector, medical centers, licensing bureaus, department stores, and all manner of large and small offices process people and paperwork in small lots by their unique needs rather than via standardized routings for all. Whenever you have a significant amount of back-and-forth movement between departments or you choose your own path in a service, you are in a job shop.

Objectives of Job-Shop Scheduling in Manufacturing

The objectives of job-shop scheduling are (1) to meet due dates, (2) to minimize lead time, (3) to minimize setup time or cost, (4) to minimize work-in-process inventory, and (5) to maximize machine utilization. (The last objective is controversial since simply keeping all equipment busy may not be the most effective way to manage flow

---

[1] *APICS Dictionary* (Falls Church, VA: American Production and Inventory Control Society, 1992), p. 22.

Type	Product	Characteristics	Typical Scheduling Tools
1. Pure process	Chemicals, steel, wire and cables, liquids (beer, soda), canned goods	Full automation, low labor content in product costs, high-volume output, facilities dedicated to one product	Linear programming
2. High-volume manufacturing	Automobiles, telephones, fasteners, textiles, motors, household fixtures	Automated equipment, partial automated handling, moving assembly lines, most equipment in line, factories dedicated to various models of product	Just-in-time scheduling (Kanban) Line balancing algorithms
3. Job shops (low-volume)	Capital goods, hand tools, hardware, instruments	Machining centers organized by manufacturing function (not in line), high labor content in product costs, general-purpose machinery with significant changeover time, little automation of material handling, large variety of product	MRP-based scheduling software Simulation Assignment method
4. Projects (very low volume)	Offices, roads, theme parks, homes	Production at the point of use rather than in a factory	PERT/CPM

Source: Modified from Romeyn Everdell, "Lowell to Sunnyvale: Manufacturing in the United States," in *Strategic Manufacturing,* ed. Patrica E. Moody (Homewood, IL: Dow Jones-Irwin, 1990), p. 34.

through the shop. See the discussion of optimized production technology later in the chapter.)

16.2 SCHEDULING AND CONTROL IN THE JOB SHOP

The following functions must be performed in scheduling and controlling a job shop:

1. Allocating orders, equipment, and personnel to work centers or other specified locations. Essentially, this is short-run capacity planning.
2. Determining the sequence of order performance (that is, establishing job priorities).
3. Initiating performance of the scheduled work. This is commonly termed the dispatching of orders.
4. Shop-floor control (or production activity control) involving
   a. Reviewing the status and controlling the progress of orders as they are being worked on.
   b. Expediting late and critical orders.[2]
5. Revising the schedule in light of changes in order status.

A simple shop-scheduling process is shown in Exhibit 16.2. At the start of the day, the scheduler (in this case, a production control person assigned to this department) selects and sequences available jobs to be run at individual workstations. The scheduler's

---

[2]Despite the fact that expediting is frowned on by production control specialists, it is nevertheless a reality of life. In fact, a very typical entry-level job in production control is that of expediter or "stock-chaser." In some companies, a good expediter—one who can negotiate a critical job through the system or can scrounge up materials nobody thought were available—is a prized possession.

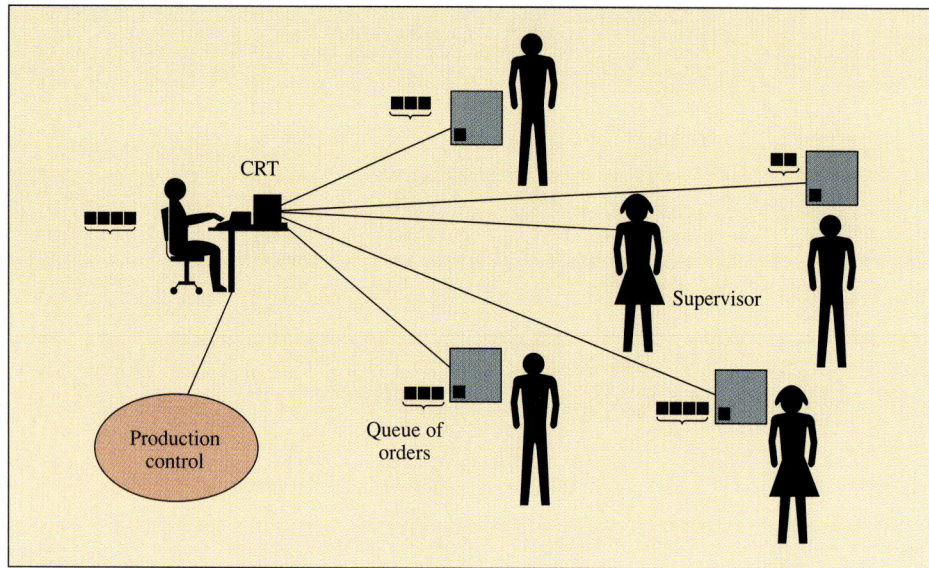

decisions would be based on the operations and routing requirements of each job, the status of existing jobs on the machines, the queue of work before each machine, job priorities, material availability, anticipated job orders to be released later in the day, and worker and machine capabilities. To help organize the schedule, the scheduler would draw on shop-floor information from the previous day and external information provided by central production control, process engineering, and so on. The scheduler would also confer with the supervisor of the department about the feasibility of the schedule, especially workforce considerations and potential bottlenecks.

16.3   ELEMENTS OF THE JOB-SHOP SCHEDULING PROBLEM

The classic approach to job-shop scheduling focuses on the following six elements, with a great deal of research invested in evaluating which priority rules are best at satisfying various performance criteria.

1. Job arrival patterns.
2. Number and variety of machines in the shop.
3. Ratio of workers to machines in the shop.
4. Flow pattern of jobs through the shop.
5. Priority rules for allocating jobs to workers or machines.
6. Schedule evaluation criteria.

Job Arrival Patterns

Jobs can arrive at the scheduler's desk either in a batch or over a time interval according to some statistical distribution. The first arrival pattern is termed *static,* the second *dynamic*. Static arrival does not mean that orders are placed by customers at the same moment; it only means that they are subject to being scheduled at one time. Such a situation occurs when a production control clerk makes out a schedule (say, once a week) and does not dispatch any jobs until all the previous week's incoming orders are on hand. In

E X H I B I T 16.3
Workflow Patterns for a Hypothetical Job Shop

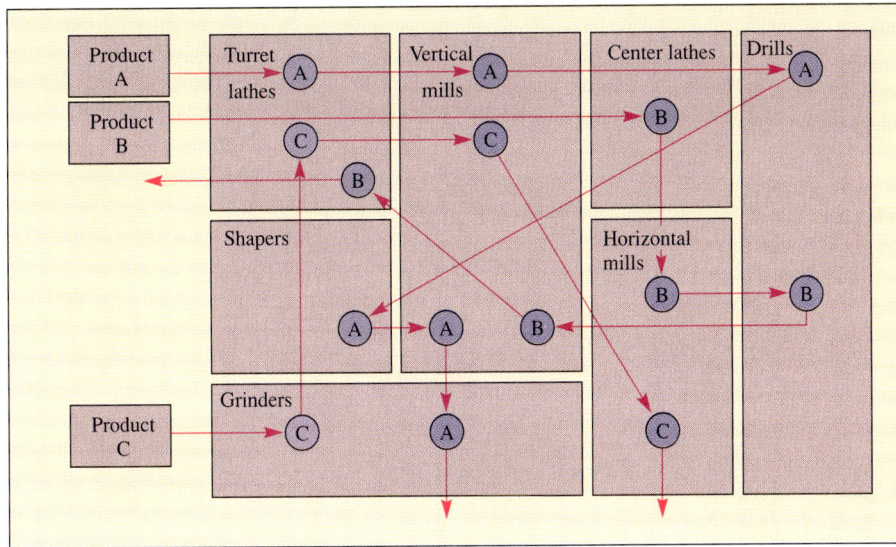

Note: First work center for each product is termed the gateway work center.

a dynamic arrival, jobs are dispatched as they arrive, and the overall schedule is updated to reflect their effect on the production facility.

Number and Variety of Machines

The number of machines in the shop obviously affects the scheduling process. If there is but one machine, or if a group of machines can be treated as one, the scheduling problem is greatly simplified. On the other hand, as the number and variety of machines increase, the more complex the scheduling problem is likely to become.

Ratio of Workers to Machines

If there are more workers than machines or an equal number of workers and machines, the shop is referred to as a **machine-limited system.** If there are more machines than workers, it is referred to as a **labor-limited system.** The machine-limited system has received a far greater amount of study, although recent investigations suggest that labor-limited systems are more pervasive in practice. In studying labor-limited systems, the primary areas of concern are the utilization of the worker on several machines and determination of the best way to allocate workers to machines.

Flow Patterns of Jobs

The pattern of flow through the shop ranges from what is termed a **flow shop,** where all the jobs follow the same path from one machine to the next, to a **randomly routed job shop,** where there is no similar pattern of movement of jobs from one machine to the next. (Exhibit 16.3 approximates the latter situation.) Most shops fall somewhere in between. The extent to which a shop is a flow shop or a randomly routed job shop can be determined by noting the statistical probability of a job's moving from one machine to the next. Frequently such probabilities are expressed in a transitional probability matrix derived from historical data on the percentage of jobs in say, turret lathes (TL), going next to vertical mills (VM), center lathes (CL), and so on. A pure flow shop would show a probability of 1.0 for a job going from TL to VM, 1.0 from VM to CL, 1.0 from CL to drills, and so on. A pure random job shop would show equal probabilities of a job going from TL to any other machine center. Likewise, if a job were in say VM, the pure jobshop case would show it had an equal probability of going back to either TL or CL. (Clearly, the pure random job shop is an unlikely configuration in the real world.)

Job Sequencing

The process of determining which job is started first on some machine or work center is known as **sequencing** or priority sequencing. **Priority rules** are the rules used in obtaining a job sequence. These can be very simple, requiring only that jobs be sequenced according to one piece of data, such as processing time, due date, or order of arrival. Other rules, though equally simple, may require several pieces of information, typically to derive an index number such as in the least slack rule and the critical ratio rule (both defined later). Still others, such as Johnson's rule (discussed later), apply to job scheduling on a sequence of machines and require a computational procedure to specify the order of performance. Ten of the more common priority rules are shown in "Ten Priority Rules for Job Sequencing."

Priority Rule Evaluation Criteria

The following standard measures of schedule performance are used to evaluate priority rules:

1. Meeting due dates of customers or downstream operations.
2. Minimizing flow time (the time a job spends in the shop).
3. Minimizing work in process.
4. Minimizing idle time of machines and workers.

16.4   PRIORITY RULES AND TECHNIQUES

Scheduling *n* Jobs on One Machine

Let's look at some of the 10 priority rules compared in a static scheduling situation involving four jobs on one machine. (In scheduling terminology, this class of problems is referred to as an "*n* job—one-machine problem" or simply "*n*/1"). The theoretical difficulty of scheduling problems increases as more machines are considered rather than as more jobs must be processed; therefore, the only restriction on *n* is that it be a specified, finite number. Consider the following example.

E X A M P L E   16.1 / ***n Jobs on One Machine***   Mike Morales is the supervisor of Legal Copy-Express, which provides copy services for downtown Los Angeles law firms. Five customers submitted their orders at the beginning of the week. Specific scheduling data are as follows:

Job (in order of arrival)	Processing Time (days)	Due Date (days hence)
A	3	5
B	4	6
C	2	7
D	6	9
E	1	2

All orders require the use of the only color copy machine available; Morales must decide on the processing sequence for the five orders. The evaluation criterion is minimum flow time. Suppose that Morales decides to use the FCFS rule in an attempt to make Legal Copy-Express appear fair to its customers.

1. FCFS (first-come, first-served). Orders are run in the order they arrive in the department.

2. SOT (shortest operating time). Run the job with the shortest completion time first, next shortest second, and so on. This is identical to SPT (shortest processing time).

3. Due date—earliest due date first; run the job with the earliest due date first. DDate—when referring to the entire job; OPNDD—when referring to the next operation.

4. Start date—due date minus normal lead time. (Run the job with the earliest start date first.)

5. STR (slack time remaining). This is calculated as the difference between the time remaining before the due date minus the processing time remaining. Orders with the shortest STR are run first.

6. STR/OP (slack time remaining per operation). Orders with shortest STR/OP are run first. STR/OP is calculated as follows:

$$\text{STR/OP} = \frac{\begin{matrix}\text{Time remaining} \\ \text{before due date}\end{matrix} - \begin{matrix}\text{Remaining} \\ \text{processing time}\end{matrix}}{\text{Number of remaining operations}}$$

7. CR (critical ratio). This is calculated as the difference between the due date and the current date divided by the number of work days remaining. Orders with the smallest CR are run first.

8. QR (queue ratio). This is calculated as the slack time remaining in the schedule divided by the planned remaining queue time. Orders with the smallest QR are run first.

9. LCFS (last-come, first-served). This rule occurs frequently by default. As orders arrive they are placed on the top of the stack; the operator usually picks up the order on top to run first.

10. Random order or whim. The supervisors or the operators usually select whichever job they feel like running.

Source: List modified from Donald W. Fogarty, John H. Blackstone, Jr., and Thomas R. Hoffmann, *Production and Inventory Management* (Cincinnati: South-Western Publishing, 1991), pp. 452–53.

S O L U T I O N :   FCFS RULE: The FCFS rule results in the following flow times:

FCFS Schedule

Job	Processing Time (days)	Due Date (days hence)	Flow Time (days)
A	3	5	0 + 3 = 3
B	4	6	3 + 4 = 7
C	2	7	7 + 2 = 9
D	6	9	9 + 6 = 15
E	1	2	15 + 1 = 16

Total flow time = 3 + 7 + 9 + 15 + 16 = 50 days

Mean flow time = $\dfrac{50}{5}$ = 10 days

Comparing the due date of each job with its flow time, we observe that only Job A will be on time. Jobs B, C, D, and E will be late by 1, 2, 6, and 14 days, respectively. On the average, a job will be late by (0 + 1 + 2 + 6 + 14)/5 = 4.6 days. ∎

S O L U T I O N :   SOT RULE: Let's now consider the SOT rule. Here Morales gives a highest priority to the order that has the shortest processing time. The resulting flow times are

SOT Schedule

Job	Processing Time (days)	Due Date (days hence)	Flow Time (days)
E	1	2	0 + 1 = 1
C	2	7	1 + 2 = 3
A	3	5	3 + 3 = 6
B	4	6	6 + 4 = 10
D	6	9	10 + 6 = 16

Total flow time = 1 + 3 + 6 + 10 + 16 = 36 days

Mean flow time = $\dfrac{36}{5}$ = 7.2 days

SOT results in lower average flow time. In addition, Jobs E and C will be ready before the due date, and Job A is late by only one day. On the average a job will be late by (0 + 0 + 1 + 4 + 7)/5 = 2.4 days. ∎

S O L U T I O N :   DDATE RULE: If Morales decides to use the DDate rule, the resulting schedule is

DDate Schedule

Job	Processing Time (days)	Due Date (days hence)	Flow Time (days)
E	1	2	0 + 1 = 1
A	3	5	1 + 3 = 4
B	4	6	4 + 4 = 8
C	2	7	8 + 2 = 10
D	6	9	10 + 6 = 16

Total completion time = 1 + 4 + 8 + 10 + 16 = 39 days

Mean flow time = 7.8 days

In this case Jobs B, C, and D will be late. On the average, a job will be late by (0 + 0 + 2 + 3 + 7)/5 = 2.4 days. ∎

S O L U T I O N S :   LCFS, RANDOM, AND STR RULES: Here are the resulting flow times of the LCFS, random, and STR rules:

Job	Processing Time (days)	Due Date (days hence)	Flow Time (days)
LCFS schedule			
E	1	2	0 + 1 = 1
D	6	9	1 + 6 = 7
C	2	7	7 + 2 = 9
B	4	6	9 + 4 = 13
A	3	5	13 + 3 = 16
Total flow time = 46 days			
Mean flow time = 9.2 days			
Average lateness = 4.0 days			
Random Schedule			
D	6	9	0 + 6 = 6
C	2	7	6 + 2 = 8
A	3	5	8 + 3 = 11
E	1	2	11 + 1 = 12
B	4	6	12 + 4 = 16
Total flow time = 53 days			
Mean flow time = 10.6 days			
Average lateness = 5.4 days			

Job	Processing Time (days)	Due Date (days hence)	Flow Time (days)
STR Schedule			
E	1	2	$0 + 1 = 1$
A	3	5	$1 + 3 = 4$
B	4	6	$4 + 4 = 8$
D	6	9	$8 + 6 = 14$
C	2	7	$14 + 2 = 16$

Total flow time = 43 days
Mean flow time = 8.6 days
Average lateness = 3.2 days

■

Comparison of Priority Rules

Here are some of the results summarized for the rules that Morales examined:

Rule	Total Completion Time (days)	Average Completion Time (days)	Average Lateness (days)
FCFS	50	10	4.6
SOT	36	7.2	2.4
DDate	39	7.8	2.4
LCFS	46	9.2	4.0
Random	53	10.6	5.4
STR	43	8.6	3.2

Obviously, here SOT is better than the rest of the rules, but is this always the case? The answer is yes. Moreover, it can be shown mathematically that the SOT rule yields an optimum solution for the $n/1$ case in such other evaluation criteria as mean waiting time and mean completion time. In fact, so powerful is this simple rule that it has been termed "the most important concept in the entire subject of sequencing."[3]

Scheduling *n* Jobs on Two Machines

The next step up in complexity of job-shop types is the $n/2$ flow-shop case, where two or more jobs must be processed on two machines in a common sequence. As in the $n/1$ case, there is an approach that leads to an optimal solution according to certain criteria. The objective of this approach, termed *Johnson's rule* or *method* (after its developer), is to minimize the flow time, from the beginning of the first job until the finish of the last. Johnson's rule consists of the following steps:

1. List the operation time for each job on both machines.
2. Select the shortest operation time.
3. If the shortest time is for the first machine, do the job first; if it is for the second machine, do the job last.
4. Repeat Steps 2 and 3 for each remaining job until the schedule is complete.

E X A M P L E 16.2 / *n Jobs on Two Machines* We can illustrate this procedure by scheduling four jobs through two machines.

S O L U T I O N *Step 1:* List operation times.

Job	Operation Time on Machine 1	Operation Time on Machine 2
A	3	2
B	6	8
C	5	6
D	7	4

[3]R. W. Conway, William L. Maxwell, and Louis W. Miller, *Theory of Scheduling* (Reading, MA: Addison-Wesley, 1967), p. 26. A classic book on the subject.

E X H I B I T 16.4

Optimal Schedule of Jobs Using Johnson's Rule

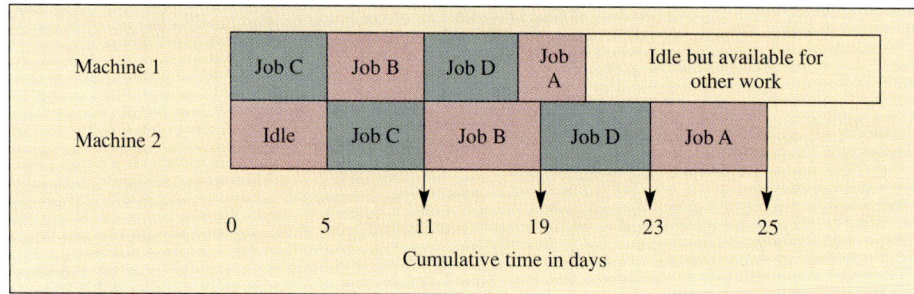

Steps 2 and 3: Select shortest operation time and assign. Job A is shortest on Machine 2 and is assigned first and performed last. (Job A is no longer available to be scheduled.)

Step 4: Repeat Steps 2 and 3 until completion of schedule. Select the shortest operation time among the remaining jobs. Job D is second shortest on Machine 2 so it is performed second to last. (Remember, Job A is last.) Now Jobs A and D are not available anymore for scheduling. Job C is the shortest on Machine 1 among the remaining jobs. Job C is performed first. Now only Job B is left with the shortest operation time on Machine 1. Thus, according to Step 3, it is performed first among the remaining, or second overall. (Job C was already scheduled first.)

In summary, the solution sequence is C → B → D → A, and the flow time is 25 days, which is a minimum. Also minimized are total idle time and mean idle time. The final schedule appears in Exhibit 16.4.

These steps result in scheduling the jobs having the shortest time in the beginning and ending of the schedule. As a result, the concurrent operating time for the two machines is maximized, thus minimizing the total operating time required to complete the jobs. ∎

Johnson's method has been extended to yield an optimal solution for the *n*/3 case. When flow-shop scheduling problems larger than *n*/3 arise (and they generally do), analytical solution procedures leading to optimality are not available. The reason for this is that even though the jobs may arrive in static fashion at the first machine, the scheduling problem becomes dynamic, and series of waiting lines start to form in front of machines downstream.

Scheduling a Set Number of Jobs to the Same Number of Machines

Some job shops have enough of the right kinds of machines to start all jobs at the same time. Here the problem is not which job to do first, but rather which particular assignment of individual jobs to individual machines will result in the best overall schedule. In such cases, we can use the assignment method.

The **assignment method** is a special case of the transportation method of linear programming. It can be applied to situations where there are *n* supply sources and *n* demand uses (e.g., five jobs on five machines) and the objective is to minimize or maximize some measure of effectiveness. This technique is convenient in applications involving allocation of jobs to work centers, people to jobs, and so on. The assignment method is appropriate in solving problems that have the following characteristics:

1. There are *n* "things" to be distributed to *n* "destinations."
2. Each thing must be assigned to one and only one destination.
3. Only one criterion can be used (minimum cost, maximum profit, or minimum completion time, for example).

E X H I B I T 16.5

Assignment Matrix Showing Machine Processing Costs for Each Job

	Machine				
Job	**A**	**B**	**C**	**D**	**E**
I	$5	$6	$4	$8	$3
II	6	4	9	8	5
III	4	3	2	5	4
IV	7	2	4	5	3
V	3	6	4	5	5

E X A M P L E 16.3 / *Assignment Method* Suppose that a scheduler has five jobs that can be performed on any of five machines ($n = 5$). The cost of completing each job–machine combination is shown in Exhibit 16.5. The scheduler would like to devise a minimum-cost assignment.
(There are 5!, or 120, possible assignments.)

S O L U T I O N This problem may be solved by the assignment method, which consists of four steps:

1. Subtract the smallest number in each *row* from itself and all other numbers in that row. (There will then be at least one zero in each row.)
2. Subtract the smallest number in each *column* from all other numbers in that column.
3. Determine if the *minimum* number of lines required to cover each zero is equal to n. If so, an optimum solution has been found since job machine assignments must be made at the zero entries and this test proves that this is possible. If the minimum number of lines required is less than n, go to Step 4.
4. Draw the least possible number of lines through all the zeros. (These may be the same lines used in Step 3.) Subtract the smallest number not covered by lines from itself and all other uncovered numbers, and add it to the number at each intersection of lines. Repeat Step 3.

For the example problem, the steps listed in Exhibit 16.6 would be followed.

Note that even though there are two zeros in three rows and three columns, the solution shown in Exhibit 16.6 is the only one possible for this problem since Job III must be assigned to machine C to meet the "assign to zero" requirement. Other problems may have more than one optimum solution, depending, of course, on the costs involved. The nonmathematical rationale of the assignment method is one of minimizing opportunity costs.[4] ∎

For example, if we decided to assign Job I to machine A instead of to machine E, we would be sacrificing the opportunity to save $2 ($5 − $3). The assignment algorithm in effect performs such comparisons for the entire set of alternative assignments by means

---

[4]The underlying rationale of the procedure of adding and subtracting the smallest cell values is as follows: Additional zeros are entered into the matrix by subtracting an amount equal to one of the cells from all cells. Negative numbers, which are not permissible, occur in the matrix. To get rid of the negative numbers, an amount equal to the maximum negative number must be added to each element of the row or column in which it occurs. This results in adding this amount twice to any cell that lies at the intersection of a row and a column that were both changed. The net result is that the lined rows and columns revert to their original amounts, and the intersections increase by the amount subtracted from the uncovered cells. (The reader may wish to prove this by solving the example without using lines.)

E X H I B I T 16.6 *Procedure to Solve an Assignment Matrix*

Step 1: Row reduction—the smallest number is subtracted from each row.

Machine

Job	A	B	C	D	E
I	2	3	1	5	0
II	2	0	5	4	1
III	2	1	0	3	2
IV	5	0	2	3	1
V	0	3	1	2	2

Step 2: Column reduction—the smallest number is subtracted from each column.

Machine

Job	A	B	C	D	E
I	2	3	1	3	0
II	2	0	5	2	1
III	2	1	0	1	2
IV	5	0	2	1	1
V	0	3	1	0	2

Step 3: Apply line test—the number of lines to cover all zeros is 4; since 5 are required, go to Step 4.

Machine

Job	A	B	C	D	E
I	2	3	1	3	0
II	2	0	5	2	1
III	2	1	0	1	2
IV	5	0	2	1	1
V	0	3	1	0	2

Step 4: Subtract smallest uncovered number and add to intersection of lines—using lines drawn in Step 3, smallest uncovered number is 1.

Machine

Job	A	B	C	D	E
I	1	3	0	2	0
II	1	0	4	1	1
III	2	2	0	1	3
IV	4	0	1	0	1
V	0	4	1	0	3

Optimum solution—by "line test."

Machine

Job	A	B	C	D	E
I	1	3	0	2	0
II	1	0	4	1	1
III	2	2	0	1	3
IV	4	0	1	0	1
V	0	4	1	0	3

Optimum assignments and their costs.

Job I to Machine E	$ 3
Job II to Machine B	4
Job III to Machine C	2
Job IV to Machine D	5
Job V to Machine A	3
Total cost	$17

of row and column reduction, as described in Steps 1 and 2. It makes similar comparisons in Step 4. Obviously, if assignments are made to zero cells, no opportunity cost, with respect to the entire matrix, is incurred.

Scheduling n Jobs on m Machines: Complex Job Shops

Complex job shops are characterized by multiple machine centers processing a variety of different jobs arriving at the machine centers in an intermittent fashion throughout the day. If there are n jobs to be processed on m machines and all jobs are processed on all machines, then there are $(n!)^m$ alternative schedules for this job set. Because of the large number of schedules that exist for even small job shops, computer simulation (see the supplement to this chapter) is the only practical way to determine the relative merits of different priority rules in such situations. As in the case of n jobs on one machine, the 10 priority rules (and more) have been compared relative to their performance on the evaluation criteria previously mentioned. By way of example, John Kanet and Jack Hayya focused on due date–oriented priority rules to see which one was best. Their simulation of a complex job shop led to the finding that total job competition rules of "DDATE, STR, and CR were outperformed by their 'operation'

Interactive Scheduling Using the JOB System

The JOB system developed by Pruett and Schartner uses a simulation model that allows for human interaction in scheduling jobs and balancing workloads across machine centers. It involves three scheduling approaches: successive, interactive, and semi-interactive.

The *successive approach* is characterized by the computer scheduling work orders automatically according to a priority rule (e.g., earliest due date), ignoring load balancing considerations. The *interactive approach* is characterized by a human scheduling one work order at a time. The schedule is developed interactively through JOB by the scheduler who simultaneously considers both work order scheduling needs and machine group load capacities. The *semi-interactive approach* is a combination of the interactive and successive approaches. Work orders are automatically scheduled using the successive approach criteria, but with prespecified machine group load thresholds (usually set at 100 percent). When a machine-group load threshold is exceeded, the algorithm pauses and human intervention (interactive approach) is required to rectify the overload. Once the loading problem for that one work order is corrected, the algorithm (successive approach) is allowed to resume the scheduling process.

The interactive process entails the use of computer generated bar chart schedules shown on the computer screen. The system is menu driven and provides such statistics as average work in process, average cycle time, overloaded and underloaded machine groups, and late and early work orders.

Source: James M. Pruett and Andreas Schartner, "JOB: An Instructive Job Shop Scheduling Environment," *International Journal of Operations & Production Management* 13, no. 11, 1993, pp. 4–34.

counterparts OPNDD, STR/OP, and OPCR" for all seven of the performance criteria used.[5]

Which priority rule should be used? We believe that the needs of most manufacturers are reasonably satisfied by a relatively simple priority scheme that embodies the following principles:

1. It should be dynamic, that is, computed frequently during the course of a job to reflect changing conditions.
2. It should be based in one way or another on slack (the difference between the work remaining to be done on a job and the time remaining to do it in). This embodies the due-date features suggested by Kanet and Hayya.

Newer approaches combine simulation with human schedulers to create schedules on standard PCs. See "Interactive Scheduling Using the JOB System."

16.5 SHOP-FLOOR CONTROL

Scheduling job priorities is just one aspect of **shop-floor control** (now often called *production activity control*). The *APICS Dictionary* defines *shop-floor control system* as

A system for utilizing data from the shop floor as well as data processing files to maintain and communicate status information on shop orders and work centers. The major functions of shop-floor control are:

1. Assigning priority of each shop order.
2. Maintaining work-in-process quantity information.

---

[5]John K. Kanet and Jack C. Hayya, "Priority Dispatching with Operation Due Dates in a Job Shop," *Journal of Operations Management* 2, no. 3 (May 1982), p. 170.

3. Conveying shop-order status information to the office.
4. Providing actual output data for capacity control purposes.
5. Providing quantity by location by shop order for WIP inventory and accounting purposes.
6. Providing measurement of efficiency, utilization, and productivity of manpower and machines.

Gantt Charts

Smaller job shops and individual departments of large ones employ the venerable Gantt chart to help plan and track jobs. As described in Chapter 12 it is a type of bar chart that plots tasks against time. Gantt charts are used for project planning as well as to coordinate a number of scheduled activities. The example in Exhibit 16.7 indicates that Job A is behind schedule by about four hours, Job B is ahead of schedule, and Job C has been completed, after a delayed start for equipment maintenance. Note that whether the job is ahead of schedule or behind schedule is based on where it stands compared to where we are now. In Exhibit 16.7 we are at the end of Wednesday and Job A should have been completed. Job B has already had some of Thursday's work completed.

Tools of Shop-Floor Control

The basic tools of shop-floor control are

1. The *daily dispatch list,* which tells the supervisor what jobs are to be run, their priority, and how long each will take. (See Exhibit 16.8A.)
2. Various *status and exception reports,* including
   a. The anticipated delay report, made out by the shop planner once or twice a week and reviewed by the chief shop planner to see if there are any serious delays that could affect the master schedule. (See Exhibit 16.8B.)
   b. Scrap reports.
   c. Rework reports.
   d. Performance summary reports giving the number and percentage of orders completed on schedule, lateness of unfilled orders, volume of output, and so on.
   e. Shortage list.
3. An *input/output control report,* which is used by the supervisor to monitor the workload–capacity relationship for each workstation. (See Exhibit 16.8C.)

Input/Output Control

Input/output (I/O) control is a major feature of a manufacturing planning and control system. Its major precept is that the planned work input to a work center should never exceed the planned work output. When the input exceeds the output, backlogs build up at the work center, which in turn increases the lead-time estimates for jobs upstream. Moreover, when jobs pile up at the work center, congestion occurs, processing becomes

---

E X H I B I T 16.7   *Gantt Chart*

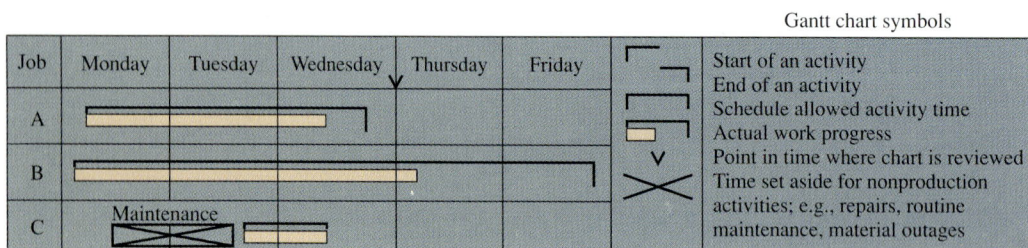

Job	Monday	Tuesday	Wednesday	Thursday	Friday
A					
B					
C	Maintenance				

Gantt chart symbols

Start of an activity
End of an activity
Schedule allowed activity time
Actual work progress
Point in time where chart is reviewed
Time set aside for nonproduction activities; e.g., repairs, routine maintenance, material outages

inefficient, and the flow of work to downstream work centers becomes sporadic. (The water flow analogy to shop capacity control in Exhibit 16.9 illustrates the general phenomenon.) Exhibit 16.8C shows an I/O report for a downstream work center. Looking first at the lower or output half of the report, we see that output is far below plan. It would seem that a serious capacity problem exists for this work center. However, looking at the input part of the plan, it becomes apparent that the serious capacity problem exists at an upstream work center feeding this work center. The control process would entail finding the cause of upstream problems and adjusting capacity and inputs accordingly. The basic solution is simple: Either increase capacity at the bottleneck station, or reduce the input to it. (Input reduction at bottleneck work centers, incidentally, is usually the first step recommended by production control consultants when job shops get into trouble.)

E X H I B I T 16.8

Some Basic Tools of Shop-Floor Control

A. Dispatch list

Work center 1501—Day 205

Start date	Job #	Description	Run time
201	15131	Shaft	11.4
203	15143	Stud	20.6
205	15145	Spindle	4.3
205	15712	Spindle	8.6
207	15340	Metering rod	6.5
208	15312	Shaft	4.6

B. Anticipated delay report

Dept. 24 April 8

Part #	Sched. date	New date	Cause of delay	Action
17125	4/10	4/15	Fixture broke	Toolroom will return on 4/15
13044	4/11	5/1	Out for plating—plater on strike	New lot started
17653	4/11	4/14	New part-holes don't align	Engineering laying out new jig

C. Input/output control report

Work center 0162

Week ending	505	512	519	526
Planned input	210	210	210	210
Actual input	110	150	140	130
Cumulative deviation	−100	−160	−230	−310
Planned output	210	210	210	210
Actual output	140	120	160	120
Cumulative deviation	−70	−160	−210	−300

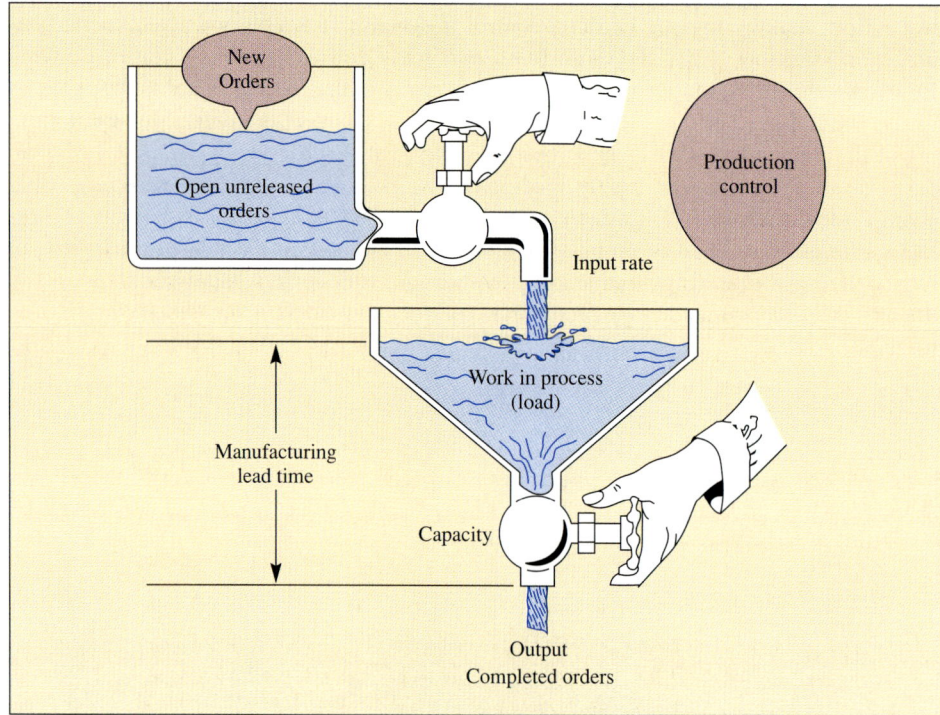

New
Orders

Open unreleased
orders

Production
control

Input rate

Work in process
(load)

Manufacturing
lead time

Capacity

Output
Completed orders

Source: American Production and Inventory Control Society, "Training Aid—Shop Floor Control," undated.

OPT and "Q Control" Approaches

A logical extension of I/O control is **optimized production technology (OPT).** One of OPT's main focuses is that the output capacity of a production system is controlled by the processes that have the least capacity.[6] A machine working continually with work to be processed still waiting would be called a *bottleneck.* Machines that have significant excess capacity are called *nonbottlenecks.* The objective is to control the flow and inventory levels in the system to always make sure the bottleneck does not stop working because its output is directly related to the output of the system. For the nonbottlenecks, the objective is to permit as little inventory as possible with the result that the flow of goods through the system is rapid, while the total inventory in the system is small. Chapter 19, "Synchronous Manufacturing," discusses these concepts in detail.

A similar though less well-known approach to scheduling is **"Q Control"** developed by William Sandman. Sandman strongly advocates (in addition to carefully managing bottlenecks) working with customers to develop a range of acceptable delivery dates. This permits scheduling jobs completely through each work center, eliminating interruptions for higher-priority jobs. He calls this the "string of pearls" concept where each shop order is scheduled with all its processing steps threaded on a string, like a pearl necklace.[7]

---

[6]See the articles by R. E. Fox, "OPT—An Answer for America, Part II," *Inventories and Production Magazine* 2, no. 6 (November–December 1982); and "OPT vs. MRP: Thoughtware vs. Software," *Inventories and Production Magazine* 3, no. 6 (November–December 1983).

[7]*Solving the Job Shop Problem* (Dresher, PA: Sandman Associates, 1979), p. 7. Also, see William E. Sandman, *How to Win Productivity in Manufacturing* (Dresher, PA: Yellow Book of Pennsylvania, 1980).

Shop-floor control systems in most modern plants are now computerized, with job status information entered directly into a CRT terminal as the job enters and leaves a work center. Many plants have gone heavily into bar coding and optical scanners to speed up the reporting process and to cut down on data-entry errors.[8] As you might guess, the key problems in shop-floor control are data inaccuracy and lack of timeliness. When these occur, data fed back to the overall planning system are wrong and incorrect production decisions are made. Typical results are excess inventory or stockout problems or both, missed due dates, and inaccuracies in job costing.

Data Integrity

Of course, maintaining data integrity requires that a sound data-gathering system be in place; but more important, it requires adherence to the system by everybody interacting with it. Most firms recognize this, but maintaining what is variously referred to as *shop discipline, data integrity,* or *data responsibility* is not always easy. And despite periodic drives to publicize the importance of careful shop-floor reporting by creating data-integrity task forces, inaccuracies can still creep into the system in many ways: A line worker drops a part under the workbench and pulls a replacement from stock without recording either transaction. An inventory clerk makes an error in a cycle count. A manufacturing engineer fails to note a change in the routing of a part. A department supervisor decides to work jobs in a different order than specified in the dispatch list.

16.6   EXAMPLE OF A SHOP FLOOR CONTROL SYSTEM: H.P.'S MANUFACTURING MANAGEMENT II[9]

HP's Manufacturing Management II (MMII) program illustrates the features available for shop floor control. MMII is a fully integrated system interacting with the various functions within the firm and with external customers.

Exhibit 16.10 shows the logic of the Shop Floor Scheduling Model that addresses the following areas:

- Routings and workcenters.
- Work-in-process (WIP) control.
- Work order scheduling.
- Shop floor dispatching.
- Work order tracking.
- Input/output analysis.
- Labor collection and reporting.

The capacity requirements planning features of MMII interact with this shop floor model to assure that scheduling is within the capacity limits of the facility.

The routings to work centers have on-line entry through terminals and various screen views available on a CRT. There are a number of different screens that can be reviewed covering various conditions for shop floor control. A screen called PARTROUTINGS, for example, shows all the parts, operation numbers, routings, labor, alternate workstations, parallel sequences, common parts routings, available capacity at each work center, and exception or repair steps in routings.

---

[8]Some companies also use "smartshelves" (inventory bins with weight sensors beneath each shelf). When an item is removed from inventory, a signal is sent to a central computer that notes the time, date, quantity, and location of the transaction.

[9]From H.P. Manufacturing Management II Sales Guide 1993.

E X H I B I T 16.10
Hewlett-Packard's Shop Floor Control System

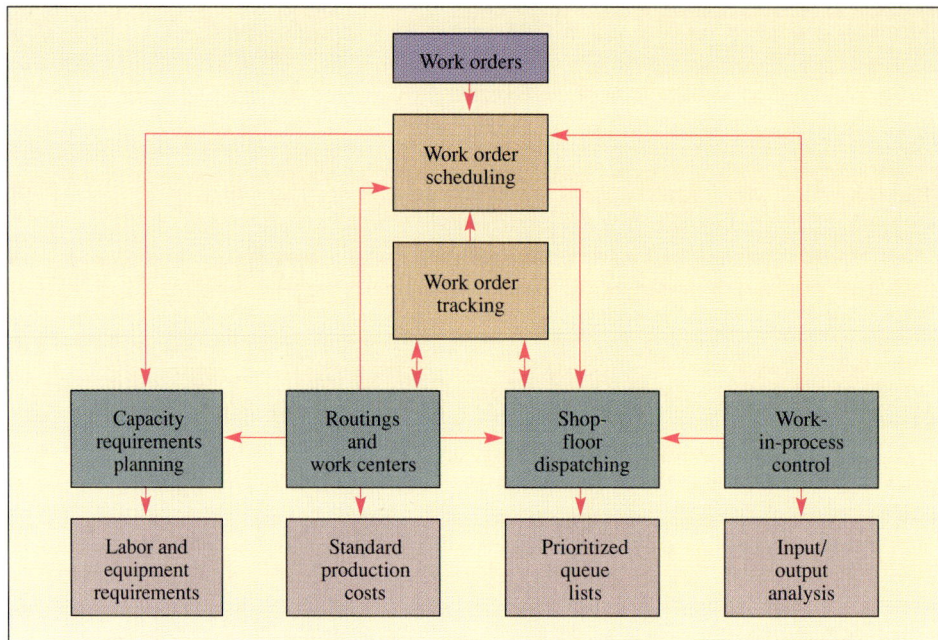

Source: Adapted from H. P. Manufacturing Management II Sales Guide 1993.

For production scheduling, the orders scheduling function calculates start and completion times for each production sequence. For on-line use, screen to review the tentative order routing (REVTENT ROUTING) allows a production scheduler to review a work order's scheduled dates and times.

There are other screens such as shop floor dispatching and STEP COMPLETION which shows a continuous picture of the status and location of each work order. From the screen, any information shown can be updated manually or by using barcoded data entry methods.

Principles of Job Shop Scheduling

Much of our discussion of job shop scheduling systems can be summarized in the following principles:

1. There is a direct equivalence between work flow and cash flow.
2. The effectiveness of any job shop should be measured by speed of flow through the shop.
3. Schedule jobs as a string, with process steps back to back.
4. A job once started should not be interrupted.
5. Speed of flow is most efficiently achieved by focusing on bottleneck work centers and jobs.
6. Reschedule every day.
7. Obtain feedback each day on jobs that are not completed at each work center.
8. Match work center input information to what the worker can actually do.
9. When seeking improvement in output, look for incompatibility between engineering design and process execution.

10. Certainty of standards, routings, and so forth is not possible in a job shop, but always work towards achieving it.

16.7   IMPROVING PERFORMANCE IN JOB SHOPS

Managing a job shop is more than just priorities and systems—it requires an integrative philosophy of production management and communication of that philosophy to the managers and workers. The breakthrough box on the next page, "Improving Job Shop Performance at Schlumberger," provides an example of what this entails, with particular emphasis on the evils of batching.

16.8   PERSONNEL SCHEDULING IN SERVICES

The scheduling problem in most service organizations revolves around setting weekly, daily, and hourly personnel schedules. In this section we present simple analytical approaches for developing such schedules.

A practical problem encountered in many services is setting schedules so that employees can have two consecutive days off. The importance of the problem stems from the fact that the Fair Labor Standards Act requires overtime for any work hours (by hourly workers) in excess of 40 hours per week. Obviously, if two consecutive days off cannot be scheduled each week for each employee, the likelihood of unnecessary overtime is quite high. In addition, most people probably prefer two consecutive days off per week. The following heuristic procedure was modified from that developed by James Browne and Rajen Tibrewala to deal with this problem.[10]

Scheduling Consecutive Days Off

Objective   Find the schedule that minimizes the number of five-day workers with two consecutive days off, subject to the demands of the daily staffing schedule.

Procedure   Starting with the total number of workers required for each day of the week, create a schedule by adding one worker at a time. This is a two-step procedure:

Step 1. Circle the lowest pair of consecutive days off. The lowest pair is the one where the highest number in the pair is equal to or lower than the highest number in any other pair. This ensures that the days with the highest requirements are covered by staff. (Monday and Sunday may be chosen even though they are at opposite ends of the array of days.) In case of ties, choose the days-off pair with the lowest requirement on an adjacent day. This day may be before or after the pair. If a tie still remains, choose the first of the available tied pairs. (Do not bother using further tie-breaking rules, such as second lowest adjacent days.)

Step 2. Subtract 1 from each of the remaining five days (i.e., the days not circled). This indicates that one less worker is required on these days since the first worker has just been assigned to them.

The two steps are repeated for the second worker, the third worker, and so forth, until no more workers are required to satisfy the schedule.

---

[10]James J. Browne and Rajen K. Tibrewala, "Manpower Scheduling," *Industrial Engineering* 7, no. 8 (August 1975), pp. 22–23.

The HDS (Houston Downhole Sensors) Division of Schlumberger builds electromechanical sensors (logging tools) that collect and process geological data for oil and gas exploration. The division operates under all the demands facing the classic job shop. Its Houston factory turns out 200 different products with 30,000 line items in inventory. Engineering changes—sometimes major changes—are an inescapable fact of life. Logging tools must be customized to reflect the kind of drilling they are used for, the underground formations they operate in, and other geological, climatic, and performance factors. Monthly output of each product ranges from 1 to 20 units; prices range from $5,000 to $15,000. Monthly sales volume has ranged from $15 million to less than $1 million, a reflection of the cyclical nature of the oil and gas business.

In the summer of 1985, HDS was struggling. Operations were costly, chaotic, and falling short of acceptable standards. Customers were dissatisfied. About 15 percent of the logging tools failed on final acceptance test. Most products were built to schedules established far in advance, but on-time delivery was no better than 70 percent. The average lead times exceeded 12 months.

Senior management was also dissatisfied. Cost of sales was unacceptably high (as exemplified by the nearly two-to-one ratio of overhead to direct labor), and the plant was bulging with inventories. WIP alone averaged five months of output.

Most job shop managers will instantly recognize these troubled conditions; the situation at HDS has been the rule for job shops, not the exception. In our experience, on-time delivery for master-scheduled items seldom exceeds 75 percent and can be as low as 20 percent. Lead times have grown insidiously over the past decade, and most job shops cannot respond effectively to swings in the business cycle. Backlogs (and lead times) shrink during recessions but soar during periods of robust economic growth—a phenomenon that managers explain away with the slogan, "Backlogs always grow in expansionary periods."

What explains the chronic and intractable problems afflicting job shops? At HDS, most products were batched for final assembly and test in lots that usually represented two to three months' requirements. Therefore, lead times on orders were at least two to three months—and in reality much longer—even though many logging tools could be assembled and tested in two weeks.

So why batch? Because management wanted to be as efficient as possible—with efficiency defined as minimizing direct labor charges. Batching generated short-term savings in virtually every phase of the production process. Batching, in effect, allowed all the factory's workers to be busy all the time.

In the long term, however, batching becomes a big obstacle to the very efficiencies it seeks to achieve. The long lead-time, large-lot, long-queue philosophy invariably results in split lots, broken setups, lost and defective parts, late deliveries, and large WIP. The results are visible in job shops everywhere: the monthly shipments

E X A M P L E 16.5 / *Scheduling Days Off*

	M	Tu	W	Th	F	S	Su
Requirement	4	3	4	2	3	1	2
Worker 1	4	3	4	2	3	1	2
Worker 2	3	2	3	1	2	1	2
Worker 3	2	1	2	0	2	1	1
Worker 4	1	0	1	0	1	1	1
Worker 5	0	0	1	0	0	0	0

S O L U T I O N   This solution consists of five workers covering 19 worker days, although slightly different assignments may be equally satisfactory.

The schedule is Worker 1 assigned S–Su off, Worker 2 F–S off, Worker 3 S–Su off, Worker 4 Tu–W off, and Worker 5 works only on Wednesday since there are no further requirements for the other days.   ■

hockey stick, where a large volume of product leaves the factory at the end of each measurement period, relaxation of quality standards under pressure to make quotas; secret high-rework jobs hidden in WIP; ever-changing production priorities; and daily crises on the shop floor.

We believe the real solution lies in eliminating batching, smoothing, and artificial economies of scale, and organizing a job shop that can quickly and efficiently "change over" from one product to another without incurring large delays and cost penalties.

HDS adopted just such a production philosophy. It emphasizes shorter lead times (down from an average of three months under the batching system to two weeks today), small to nonexistent queues, low inventories, and quick recognition and correction of defects. The factory is now more responsive to external changes in product mix and volumes. It is also more manageable. The number of work orders open at any particular time is small, so their status is easier to monitor. Likewise, the number of open problems is modest, so they can, and are, handled with greater urgency.

Getting control over the shop floor has allowed us to slash overhead. In the summer of 1985, 520 of the division's 830 employees were salaried or indirect personnel. The overhead count now stands at 220 employees. The largest reductions came from three departments—quality control; shipping, receiving, and warehousing; and production control (expediters, dispatchers)—whose roles diminish as quality and on-time performance improves.

The specific directives and actions HDS followed to implement its philosophy included

* *Making quality mandatory.* Quality was defined to include both product defects and late and partial shipments.
* *Making the schedule, every time.* On-schedule was defined as having every job start and complete on schedule. An accompanying policy was to never start jobs early.
* *Capacity should not be sacrificed for cost.* This required that managers plan for realistic manpower requirements rather than for ideal productivity levels.
* *Reduce setup times.* This involved extensive worker cross-training, simplification of manufacturing instructions, and JIT layouts.
* *Focus on making parts rather than running machines.* Machine utilization was taken out of the shop performance measures.
* *Make performance visible.* All workers were made aware of the progress of each job, speed of correction of defects, and current and anticipated parts shortages.
* *Improve feeder shop and vendor responsiveness.* All supplying operations were made aware of the master schedule and aggressively pursued reductions in planned lead times for their operations.

Source: Reprinted by permission of the *Harvard Business Review.* An excerpt "Time to Reform Job Shop Manufacturing," by James E. Ashton and Frank X. Cook, Jr., (March/April 1989). Copyright 1989 by the President and Fellows of Harvard College; All Rights Reserved.

Scheduling Daily Work Times

The example below shows how bank clearinghouses and back-office operations of large bank branches establish daily work times. Basically, management wants to derive a staffing plan that (1) requires the least number of workers to accomplish the daily workload and (2) minimizes the variance between actual output and planned output.

In structuring the problem, bank management defines inputs (checks, statements, investment documents, and so forth), as *products,* which are routed through different processes or *functions* (receiving, sorting, encoding, and so forth).

To solve the problem, a daily demand forecast is made by product for each function. This is converted to labor hours required per function, which in turn is converted to workers required per function. These figures are then tabled, summed, and adjusted by an absence and vacation factor to give planned hours. Then they are divided by the number of hours in the workday to yield the number of workers required. This yields the daily staff hours required. (See Exhibit 16.11.) This becomes the basis for a departmental staffing plan that lists the workers required, workers available, variance, and managerial action in light of variance. (See Exhibit 16.12.)

E X H I B I T 16.11   *Daily Staff Hours Required to Schedule Daily Work Times*

Product	Daily Volume	Receive		Preprocess		Microfilm		Verify		Totals
		P/H	H_{std}	P/H	H_{std}	P/H	H_{std}	P/H	H_{std}	H_{std}
Checks	2,000	1,000	2.0	600	3.3	240	8.3	640	3.1	16.7
Statements	1,000	—	—	600	1.7	250	4.0	150	6.7	12.4
Notes	200	30	6.7	15	13.3		—			20.0
Investments	400	100	4.0	50	8.0	200	2.0	150	2.7	16.7
Collections	500	300	1.7			300	1.7	60	8.4	11.8
			—		—		—		—	—
Total hours required			14.4		26.3		16.0		20.9	77.6
Times 1.25 (absences and vacations)			18.0		32.9		20.0		26.1	
			—		—		—		—	
Divided by 8 hours equals staff required			2.3		4.1		2.5		3.3	12.2

Note: P/H indicates production rate per hour; H_{std} indicates required hours.

E X H I B I T 16.12
Staffing Plan

Function	Staff Required	Staff Available	Variance (±)	Management Actions
Receive	2.3	2.0	−0.3	Use overtime.
Preprocess	4.1	4.0	−0.1	Use overtime.
Microfilm	2.5	3.0	+0.5	Use excess to verify.
Verify	3.3	3.0	−0.3	Get 0.3 from microfilm.

Scheduling Hourly Work Times

Services such as restaurants face changing requirements from hour to hour. More workers are needed for peak hours, and fewer are needed in between. Management must continuously adjust to this changing requirement. This kind of personnel scheduling situation can be approached by applying a simple rule, the **"first-hour" principle.**[11] This procedure can be best explained using the following example. Assume that each worker works continuously for an eight-hour shift. The first-hour rule says that for the first hour, we will assign a number of workers equal to the requirement in that period. For each subsequent period, assign the exact number of additional workers to meet the requirements. When in a period one or more workers come to the end of their shifts, add more workers only if they are needed to meet the requirement. The following table shows the worker requirements for the first 12 hours in a 24-hour restaurant:

	Period											
	10AM	11AM	Noon	1PM	2PM	3PM	4PM	5PM	6PM	7PM	8PM	9PM
Requirement	4	6	8	8	6	4	4	6	8	10	10	6

[11] Ibid. Also, see the Nanda and Browne text on employer scheduling listed in the Bibliography for a discussion of this as well as many other techniques and software.

The schedule shows that four workers are assigned at 10 AM, and two are added at 11 AM, and another two are added at noon to meet the requirement. From noon to 5 PM, we have eight workers on duty. However, the four workers assigned at 10 AM finish their eight-hour shifts by 6 PM, and four more workers are added to start their shifts. The two workers starting at 11 AM leave by 7 PM, and the number of workers available drops to six. Therefore four new workers are assigned at 7 PM. At 9 PM, there are 10 workers on duty, which is more than the requirement, so no worker is added. This procedure continues as new requirements are given.

					Period							
	10AM	**11**AM	**Noon**	**1**PM	**2**PM	**3**PM	**4**PM	**5**PM	**6**PM	**7**PM	**8**PM	**9**PM
Requirement	4	6	8	8	6	4	4	6	8	10	10	6
Assigned	4	2	2	0	0	0	0	0	4	4	2	0
On duty	4	6	8	8	8	8	8	8	8	10	10	10

Another option is splitting shifts. For example, the worker can come in, work for four hours, then come back two hours later for another four hours. The impact of this option in scheduling is essentially similar to that of changing lot size in production. When workers start working, they have to log in, change uniforms, and probably get necessary information from workers in the previous shift. This preparation can be considered as the "setup cost" in a production scenario. Splitting shifts is like having smaller production lot sizes and thus more preparation (more setups). This problem can be solved by linear programming methods described in the Nanda and Browne bibliographic reference.

16.9   CONCLUSION

In manufacturing job shops, scheduling now relies heavily on simulation to estimate the flow of work through the system to determine bottlenecks and adjust job priorities. Various software packages are available to do this. In services, the focus is typically on employee scheduling using mathematical tools that can be used to set work schedules in light of expected customer demand. No matter what the scheduling situation is, it is important to avoid suboptimization—a schedule that works well for one part of the organization, but creates problems for other parts or most importantly, for the customer.

16.10   SOLVED PROBLEM

Joe's Auto Seat Cover and Paint Shop is bidding on a contract to do all the custom work for Smiling Ed's used car dealership. One of the main requirements in obtaining this contract is rapid delivery time, since Ed—for reasons we shall not go into here—wants the cars facelifted and back on his lot in a hurry. Ed has said that if Joe can refit and repaint five cars that Ed has just received (from an unnamed source) in 24 hours or less, the contract will be his. Following is the time (in hours) required in the refitting shop and the paint shop for each of the five cars. Assuming that cars go through the refitting operations before they are repainted, can Joe meet the time requirements and get the contract?

Car	Refitting Time (hours)	Repairing Time (hours)
A	6	3
B	0	4
C	5	2
D	8	6
E	2	1

Solution

This problem can be viewed as a two-machine flow shop and can be easily solved using "Johnson's method."

	Original Data			Johnson Method	
Car	Refitting Time (hours)	Repainting Time (hours)		Order of Selection	Position in Sequence
A	6	3		4th	3d
B	0	4		1st	1st
C	5	2		3d	4th
D	8	6		5th	2d
E	2	1		2d	5th

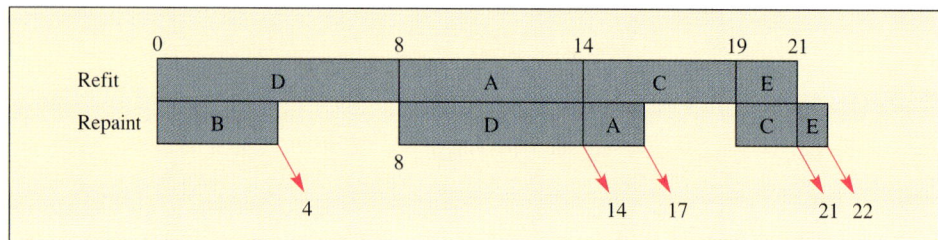

16.11 REVIEW AND DISCUSSION QUESTIONS

1. What are the objectives of job-shop scheduling?
2. Distinguish between a job shop and a flow shop.
3. What practical considerations are deterrents to using the SOT rule?
4. What priority rule do you use in scheduling your study time for midterm examinations? If you have five exams to study for, how many alternative schedules exist?
5. The SOT rule provides an optimal solution in a number of evaluation criteria. Should the manager of a bank use the SOT rule as a priority rule? Why?
6. Data integrity is a big deal in industry. Why?
7. Why does batching cause so much trouble in job shops? (Hint: See breakthrough box on Schlumberger (page 654).)
8. What job characteristics would lead you to schedule jobs according to "longest processing time first"?
9. Why is managing bottlenecks so important in job shop scheduling?
10. Under what conditions is the assignment method appropriate?
11. How might planning for a special customer affect the personnel schedule in a service?

16.12 PROBLEMS

1. Joe has three cars that must be overhauled by his ace mechanic, Jim. Given the following data about the cars, use least slack per remaining operation to determine Jim's scheduling priority for each.

Car	Customer Pick-Up Time (hours hence)	Remaining Overhaul Time (hours)	Remaining Operations
A	10	4	Painting
B	17	5	Wheel alignment, painting
C	15	1	Chrome plating, painting, seat repair

2. A hotel has to schedule its receptionists according to hourly loads. Management has identified the number of receptionists needed to meet the hourly requirement, which changes from day to day. Assume each receptionist works a four-hour shift. Given the following staffing requirement in a certain day, use the first-hour principle to find the personnel schedule.

	Period											
	8AM	**9**AM	**10**AM	**11**AM	**Noon**	**1**PM	**2**PM	**3**PM	**4**PM	**5**PM	**6**PM	**7**PM
Requirement	2	3	5	8	8	6	5	8	8	6	4	3

	Period											
	8AM	**9**AM	**10**AM	**11**AM	**Noon**	**1**PM	**2**PM	**3**PM	**4**PM	**5**PM	**6**PM	**7**PM
Requirement	2	3	5	8	8	6	5	8	8	6	4	3
Assigned												
On duty												

3. There are seven jobs that must be processed in two operations: A and B. All seven jobs must go through A and B in that sequence—A first, then B. Determine the optimal order in which the jobs should be sequenced through the process using these times:

Job	Process A Time	Process B Time
1	9	6
2	8	5
3	7	7
4	6	3
5	1	2
6	2	6
7	4	7

4. This problem requires use of simulation as discussed in the supplement to this chapter. Joe has the opportunity to do a big repair job for a local motorcycle club. (Their cycles were accidentally run over by a garbage truck.) The compensation for the job is good, but it is vital that the total repair time for the five cycles be less than 40 hours. (The leader of the club has stated that he would be very distressed if the cycles were not available for a planned rally.) Joe knows from experience that repairs of this type often entail several trips between processes for a given cycle, so estimates of time are difficult to provide. Still, Joe has the following historical data about the probability that a job will start in each process, processing time in each process, and transitional probabilities between each pair of processes:

Process	Probability of Job Starting in Process	Processing Time Probability (hours)			Probability of Going from Process to Other Processes or Completion (out)				
		1	**2**	**3**	**Frame**	**Engine**	**Work**	**Painting**	**Out**
Frame repair	0.5	0.2	0.4	0.4	—	0.4		0.4	0.2
Engine work	0.3	0.6	0.1	0.3	0.3	—		0.4	0.3
Painting	0.2	0.3	0.3	0.4	0.1	0.1		—	0.8

Given this information, use simulation to determine the repair times for each cycle. Display your results on a Gantt chart showing an FCFS schedule. (Assume that only one cycle can be worked on at a time in each process.) Based on your simulation, what do you recommend Joe do next?

5. The following list of jobs in a critical department includes estimates of their required times:

Job	Required Time (days)	Days to Delivery Promise	Slack
A	8	12	4
B	3	9	6
C	7	8	1
D	1	11	10
E	10	−10	—
F	6	10	4
G	5	−8	—
H	4	6	2

   a. Use the shortest operation time rule to schedule these jobs:

       What is the schedule?

       What is the mean flow time?

   b. The boss does not like the schedule in *(a)*. Jobs E and G must be done first, for obvious reasons. (They are already late.) Reschedule and do the best you can while scheduling Jobs E and G first and second, respectively.

       What is the new schedule?

       What is the new mean flow time?

6. The following matrix shows the costs for assigning individuals A, B, C, and D to do jobs 1, 2, 3, and 4. Solve the problem showing your final assignments in order to minimize cost.

	1	2	3	4
A	7	9	3	5
B	3	11	7	6
C	4	5	6	2
D	5	9	10	12

7. A manufacturing facility has five jobs to be scheduled into production. The following table gives the processing times plus the necessary wait times and other necessary delays for each of the jobs. Assume that today is April 3 and the jobs are due on the dates shown:

Job	Days of Actual Processing Time Required	Days of Necessary Delay Time	Total Time Required	Date Job Due
1	2	12	14	April 30
2	5	8	13	April 21
3	9	15	24	April 28
4	7	9	16	April 29
5	4	22	28	April 27

   Determine *two* schedules, stating the order in which the jobs are to be done. Use the critical ratio priority rule for one. You may use any other rule for the second schedule as long as you state what it is.

8. An accounting firm, Debits 'R Us, would like to keep its auditing staff to a maximum of four people and still satisfy the staffing needs and the policy of two days off per week. Given the following requirements, is this possible? What should the schedule be?

   Requirements (Monday through Sunday): 4, 3, 3, 2, 2, 4, 4.

9. Jobs A, B, C, D, and E must go through Processes I and II in that sequence (i.e., Process I first, then Process II). Use Johnson's rule to determine the optimal sequence to schedule the jobs to minimize the total required time.

Job	Required Processing Time on A	Required Processing Time on B
A	4	5
B	16	14
C	8	7
D	12	11
E	3	9

10. In a job shop operation, six machinists were uniquely qualified to operate certain machines in the shop. However, they were all able to operate any one of the five machines in the shop. The job shop had considerable backlog and all five machines were kept busy at all times. The one machinist not operating a machine was usually occupied doing clerical or routine maintenance work. Given the value schedule below for each machinist on each of the five machines, develop an optimal assignment. (Hint: Add a dummy column with zero cost values, and solve using the assignment method.)

	Machine				
Machinist	1	2	3	4	5
A	65	50	60	55	80
B	30	75	125	50	40
C	75	35	85	95	45
D	60	40	115	130	110
E	90	85	40	80	95
F	145	60	55	45	85

11. Joe has achieved a position of some power in the institution in which he currently resides and works. In fact, things have gone so well that he has decided to divide the day-to-day operations of his business activities among four trusted subordinates: Big Louie, Dirty Dave, Baby Face Nick, and Tricky Dick. The question is how he should do this in order to take advantage of his associates' unique skills and to minimize the costs from running all areas for the next year. The following matrix summarizes the costs that arise under each possible combination of men and areas.

	Area			
	1	2	3	4
Big Louie	$1,400	$1,800	$ 700	$1,000
Dirty Dave	600	2,200	1,500	1,300
Baby Face Nick	800	1,100	1,200	500
Tricky Dick	1,000	1,800	2,100	1,500

12. Joe has now been released from his government job. Based on his excellent performance, he was able to land a job as production scheduler in a brand-new custom refinishing auto service shop located near the border. Techniques have improved in the several years he was out of circulation so processing times are considerably faster. This system is capable of handling 10 cars per day. The sequence now is customizing first, followed by repainting.

Car	Customizing Time (hours)	Painting (hours)
1	3.0	1.2
2	2.0	0.9
3	2.5	1.3
4	0.7	0.5
5	1.6	1.7
6	2.1	0.8
7	3.2	1.4
8	0.6	1.8
9	1.1	1.5
10	1.8	0.7

In what sequence should Joe schedule the cars?

CASE

16.13 C A S E

Keep Patients Waiting? Not in My Office

Good doctor–patient relations begin with both parties being punctual for appointments. This is particularly important in my specialty—pediatrics. Mothers whose children have only minor problems don't like them to sit in the waiting room with really sick ones, and the sick kids become fussy if they have to wait long.

But lateness—no matter who's responsible for it—can cause problems in any practice. Once you've fallen more than slightly behind, it may be impossible to catch up that day. And although it's unfair to keep someone waiting who may have other appointments, the average office patient cools his heels for almost 20 minutes, according to one recent survey. Patients may tolerate this, but they don't like it.

I don't tolerate that in my office, and I don't believe you have to in yours. I see patients *exactly* at the appointed hour more than 99 times out of 100. So there are many GPs (grateful patients) in my busy solo practice. Parents often remark to me, "We really appreciate your being on time. Why can't other doctors do that too?" My answer is "I don't know, but I'm willing to tell them how I do it."

Booking Appointments Realistically

The key to successful scheduling is to allot the proper amount of time for each visit, depending on the services required, and then stick to it. This means that the physician must pace himself carefully, receptionists must be corrected if they stray from the plan, and patients must be taught to respect their appointment times.

By actually timing a number of patient visits, I found that they break down into several categories. We allow half an hour for any new patient, 15 minutes for a well-baby checkup or an important illness, and either 5 or 10 minutes

for a recheck on an illness or injury, an immunization, or a minor problem like warts. You can, of course, work out your own time allocations, geared to the way you practice.

When appointments are made, every patient is given a specific time, such as 10:30 or 2:40. It's an absolute no-no for anyone in my office to say to a patient, "Come in 10 minutes" or "Come in a half-hour." People often interpret such instructions differently, and nobody knows just when they'll arrive.

There are three examining rooms that I use routinely, a fourth that I reserve for teenagers, and a fifth for emergencies. With that many rooms, I don't waste time waiting for patients, and they rarely have to sit in the reception area. In fact, some of the younger children complain that they don't get time to play with the toys and puzzles in the waiting room before being examined, and their mothers have to let them play awhile on the way out.

On a light day I see 20 to 30 patients between 9 AM and 5 PM. But our appointment system is flexible enough to let me see 40 to 50 patients in the same number of hours if I have to. Here's how we tighten the schedule:

My two assistants (three on the busiest days) have standing orders to keep a number of slots open throughout each day for patients with acute illnesses. We try to reserve more such openings in the winter months and on the days following weekends and holidays, when we're busier than usual.

Initial visits, for which we allow 30 minutes, are always scheduled on the hour or the half-hour. If I finish such a visit sooner than planned, we may be able to squeeze in a patient who needs to be seen immediately. And, if necessary, we can book two or three visits in 15 minutes between well checks. With these cushions to fall back on, I'm free to spend an extra 10 minutes or so on a serious case, knowing that the lost time can be made up quickly.

Parents of new patients are asked to arrive in the office a few minutes before they're scheduled in order to get the preliminary paperwork done. At that time the receptionist informs them, "The doctor always keeps an accurate appointment schedule." Some already know this and have chosen me for that very reason. Others, however, don't even know that there *are* doctors who honor appointment times, so we feel that it's best to warn them on the first visit.

Fitting in Emergencies

Emergencies are the excuse doctors most often give for failing to stick to their appointment schedules. Well, when a child comes in with a broken arm or the hospital calls with an emergency Caesarean section, naturally I drop everything else. If the interruption is brief, I may just scramble to catch up. If it's likely to be longer, the next few patients are given the choice of waiting or making new appointments. Occasionally my assistants have to reschedule all appointments for the next hour or two. Most such interruptions, though, take no more than 10 to 20 minutes, and the patients usually choose to wait. I then try to fit them into the spaces we've reserved for acute cases that require last-minute appointments.

The important thing is that emergencies are never allowed to spoil my schedule for the whole day. Once a delay has been adjusted for, I'm on time for all later appointments. The only situation I can imagine that would really wreck my schedule is simultaneous emergencies in the office and at the hospital—but that has never occurred.

When I return to the patient I've left, I say, "Sorry to have kept you waiting, I had an emergency—a bad cut" (or whatever). A typical reply from the parent: "No problem, Doctor. In all the years I've been coming here, you've never made me wait before. And I'd surely want you to leave the room if *my* kid were hurt."

Emergencies aside, I get few walk-ins, because it's generally known in the community that I see patients only by appointment except in urgent circumstances. A non-emergency walk-in is handled as a phone call would be. The receptionist asks whether the visitor wants advice or an appointment. If the latter, he or she is offered the earliest time available for non-acute cases.

Taming the Telephone

Phone calls from patients can sabotage an appointment schedule if you let them. I don't. Unlike some pediatricians, I don't have a regular telephone hour, but my assistants will handle calls from parents at any time during office hours. If the question is a simple one, such as "How much aspirin do you give a one-year-old?" the assistant will answer it. If the question requires an answer from me, the assistant writes it in the patient's chart and brings it to me while I'm seeing

another child. I write the answer in—or she enters it in the chart. Then she relays it to the caller.

What if the caller insists on talking with me directly? The standard reply is "Doctor will talk with you personally if it won't take more than one minute. Otherwise you'll have to make an appointment and come in." I'm rarely called to the phone in such cases, but if the mother is very upset, I prefer to talk with her. I don't always limit her to one minute; I may let the conversation run two or three. But the caller knows I've left a patient to talk with her, so she tends to keep it brief.

Dealing with Latecomers

Some people are habitually late; others have legitimate reasons for occasional tardiness, such as a flat tire or "He threw up on me." Either way, I'm hard-nosed enough not to see them immediately if they arrive at my office more than 10 minutes behind schedule, because to do so would delay patients who arrived on time. Anyone who is less than 10 minutes late is seen right away, but is reminded of what the appointment time was.

When it's exactly 10 minutes past the time reserved for a patient and he hasn't appeared at the office, a receptionist phones his home to arrange a later appointment. If there's no answer and the patient arrives at the office a few minutes later, the receptionist says pleasantly, "Hey, we were looking for you. The doctor's had to go ahead with his other appointments, but we'll squeeze you in as soon as we can." A note is then made in the patient's chart showing the date, how late he was, and whether he was seen that day or given another appointment. This helps us identify the rare chronic offender and take stronger measures if necessary.

Most people appear not to mind waiting if they know they themselves have caused the delay. And I'd rather incur the anger of the rare person who *does* mind than risk the ill will of the many patients who would otherwise have to wait after coming in on schedule. Although I'm prepared to be firm with parents, this is rarely necessary. My office in no way resembles an army camp. On the contrary, most people are happy with the way we run it, and tell us so frequently.

Coping with No-Shows

What about the patient who has an appointment, doesn't turn up at all, and can't be reached by telephone? Those facts, too, are noted in the chart. Usually there's a simple explanation, such as being out of town and forgetting about the appointment. If it happens a second time, we follow the same procedure. A third-time offender, though, receives a letter reminding him that time was set aside for him and he failed to keep three appointments. In future, he's told, he'll be billed for such wasted time.

That's about as tough as we ever get with the few people who foul up our scheduling. I've never dropped a patient for doing so. In fact, I can't recall actually billing a no-show;

the letter threatening to do so seems to cure them. And when they come back—as nearly all of them do—they enjoy the same respect and convenience as my other patients

Questions

1. What features of the appointment scheduling system were crucial in capturing "many grateful patients"?

2. What procedures were followed to keep the appointment system flexible enough to accommodate

the emergency cases, and yet be able to keep up with the appointment with other patients?

3. How were the special cases such as latecomers and no-shows handled?

Source: W. B. Schafer, "Keep Patients Waiting? Not in My Office," *Medical Economics,* May 12, 1986, pp. 137–141. Copyright © 1986 and published by Medical Economics Company, Inc., Oradell, NJ 07649. Reprinted by permission.

CASE

16.14 C A S E

McCall Diesel Motor Works (Need for a Complete System of Production Control)

McCall Diesel Motor Works has been a pioneer in the manufacture of a particular internal combustion engine. The plant is located on tidewater in the state of New Jersey because the company originally built engines for the marine field, chiefly fishing boats and pleasure craft. Subsequently, its activities were extended to the stationary type of engines used primarily for production of power in small communities, in manufacturing plants, or on farms.

During the earlier years of the company's operation, its engines were largely special-order jobs. Even at the present time about 60 percent of the output is made to order. There has been in recent years, however, a trend toward standardization of component parts and reduction in the variety of engines produced. The Engineering Department has followed the principle of simplification and standardization in the case of minor parts, such as studs, bolts, and springs, giving a degree of interchangeability of these components among the various sizes and types of engines. Sizes of marine engines have been standardized to some extent, although customer requirements still necessitate some designs. In the small engines for agricultural use there has been a genuine effort to concentrate sales on a standard line of engines of three sizes: 20, 40, and 60 HP.

The company has always been advanced in its engineering development and design. The production phase, on the other hand, has not been progressive. The heritage of job-shop operation persists, and despite the definite trend toward standardization, manufacture continues largely on a made-to-order basis. The increasing popularity of diesel engines has brought many new producing companies into the field, with a consequent tightening of the competitive situation.

High manufacturing costs and poor service have been reflected in the loss of orders. Customer complaints, together with pressure from the Sales Department, prompted management to call in a consulting engineer to make a survey of the Manufacturing Department and recommend a plan of action.

The report of the engineer showed the following:

1. *Manufacturing methods,* while still largely of the job-shop character, are in the main good, and no wholesale change should be made. As production is still 60 percent special, a complete shift to line manufacture or departmentalization by product is not feasible.

2. *Machinery and equipment* are for the most part general-purpose in line with manufacturing requirements. Some machine tools are approaching obsolescence, and for certain operations high-production, single-purpose machines would be advisable. Extensive replacement of machine tools is not a pressing need, but an increased use of jigs and fixtures should be undertaken immediately. There are many bottlenecks existing in the plant, but contrary to your belief, as well as that of your foreman and other shop executives, there is no serious lack of productive equipment. The trouble lies in the improper utilization of the machine time available.

3. *Production control* is the major element of operating weakness, and improvement is imperative. The lack of proper control over production shows up in many ways:
   a. High in-process inventory, as indicated by piles of partially completed parts over the entire manufacturing floor areas.
   b. Absence of any record concerning the whereabouts of orders in the process from their initiation to delivery at assembly.
   c. Inordinate number of rush orders, particularly in assembly but also in parts manufacture.
   d. Too many parts chasers who force orders through the shops by pressure methods.
   e. Piecemeal manufacture—a lot of 20 parts usually is broken up into four or five lots before it is finished. Not infrequently the last sublot remains on the shop floor for months and, in a number of instances, is lost as far as records are concerned.

Subsequent orders for the same part are issued and new lots pass through to completion while the remains of the old lot lie in partially fabricated condition.

f. Excessive setup costs resulting from the piecemeal methods mentioned in *(e)*, as well as failure to use proper lot sizes, even when lots are not broken up during manufacture.

g. Failure of all necessary component parts to reach assembly at approximately the same time. The floor of the assembly department is cluttered with piles of parts awaiting receipt of one or more components before engines can be assembled.

h. Lack of definite sequence of manufacturing operations for a given part. Responsibility for the exact way by which a part is to be made rests entirely on the various department foremen; these men are able machinists, but, burdened with detail, their memories cannot be relied on to ensure that parts will always be manufactured in the best, or even the same, sequence of operations. Moreover, they have the responsibility for determining the department to which a lot of parts should be sent when it has been completed in their department.

i. In the case of certain small standard parts, shop orders have been issued as many as six or eight times in a single month.
Information is lacking from which to estimate, with any degree of close approximation, the overall manufacturing time for an engine. The result is failure to meet delivery promises or high production cost due to rush or overtime work.

j. Parts in process or in stores, and destined for imminent assembly, are frequently taken by the Service Department to supply an emergency repair order. The question here is not the academic determination of priority between the customer whose boat may be lying idle because of a broken part and the customer who has not yet received an engine; the question is why there should be any habitual difficulty in rendering adequate repair service and at the same time meeting delivery promises.

k. Virtually all basic manufacturing data reside in the heads of the superintendent, department foreman, assistant foremen, and setup men.

l. Delivery dates are set by the Sales Department and generally are dates that customers arbitrarily stipulate.

m. The general superintendent shows little enthusiasm for the idea of a system of production control; in fact, he is opposed to such an installation. He is of the opinion that reasonably satisfactory results are now being obtained by placing responsibility on the foremen and maintaining contact

between them and the parts chasers, who in turn are held responsible for meeting delivery promises. He believes that no system can be substituted for the foremen's knowledge of the ability of the workers. He feels that operation of a production control system requires time studies of all jobs. Time study, he points out, is difficult because of the many operations involved, the high degree of special work, the probable resistance of the workers, and the cost. He further protests that emergencies and rush orders would upset any rigid scheduling of work through the plant. Finally, he is convinced that any system of production control involves an excessive amount of clerical detail to which the foremen, who are practical shop men, object.

The state of affairs the consultant found had, he realized, two main causes:

1. The strong influence of the original job-shop character of manufacture and the very slow evolution to large-scale operation.

2. The fact that the top management of the company was essentially sales minded.

His recommendations, therefore, had to be a simple, straightforward program that would provide adequate control over production and could be instituted gradually and logically.

Questions

1. Outline the essential features of a production control system for this company, giving sufficient detail to make clear how the system will function.

2. Indicate which part of your procedure should be centralized and which part decentralized. What functions should be handled by a central production control office and what functions should be carried out in the various production and assembly departments?

3. What data must be compiled before your system can become fully effective?

4. Enumerate the benefits the company will derive when your production control system is in operation.

5. Set forth in proper order the steps that should be taken and the departments that should be involved in the determination of delivery promises to customers.

6. What arguments would you advance in answer to the general superintendent's objections, as presented in paragraph *n* of the consultant's report?

7. Generally speaking, what is the foremen's place in the scheme of things when a fully developed production control system is in operation and when a production control department has been established?

16.15 SELECTED BIBLIOGRAPHY

Ashton, James E., and Frank X. Cook, Jr. "Time to Reform Job Shop Manufacturing." *Harvard Business Review,* March–April 1989, pp. 106–111.

Baker, K. R. "The Effects of Input Control in a Simple Scheduling Model." *Journal of Operations Management* 4, no. 2 (February 1984), pp. 99–112.

Berry, W. L., R. Penlesky, and T. E. Vollmann. "Critical Ratio Scheduling: Dynamic Due-Date Procedures under Demand Uncertainty." *IIE Transactions* 16, no. 1 (March 1984), pp. 81–89.

Conway, R. W., William L. Maxwell, and Louis W. Miller. *Theory of Scheduling.* Reading, MA: Addison-Wesley, 1967.

Fox, R. E. "OPT—An Answer for America, Part II." *Inventories and Production Magazine* 2, no. 6 (November–December 1982).

———. "OPT vs. MRP: Thoughtware vs. Software." *Inventories and Production Magazine* 3, no. 6 (November–December 1983).

Gershkoff, I. "Optimizing Flight Crew Schedules." *Interfaces* 19, no. 4 (July–August 1989), pp. 29–43.

Goldratt, E. M., and J. Cox. *The Goal: A Process of Ongoing Improvement.* Great Barrington, MA: North River Press, 1992.

Johnson, S. M. "Optimal Two Stage and Three Stage Production Schedules with Setup Times Included." *Naval Logistics Quarterly* 1, no. 1 (March 1954), pp. 61–68.

Moody, P. E. *Strategic Manufacturing: Dynamic New Directions for the 1990s.* Homewood, IL: Richard D. Irwin, 1990.

Nanda, Ravinder, and Jim Browne. *Introduction to Employee Scheduling.* New York: Van Nostrand Reinhold, 1992.

Richter, H. "Thirty Years of Airline Operations Research." *Interfaces* 19, no. 4 (July–August 1989), pp. 3–9.

Sandman, W. E., with J. P. Hayes. *How to Win Productivity in Manufacturing.* Dresher, PA: Yellow Book of Pennsylvania, 1980.

Wild, Ray. *International Handbook of Production and Operations Management.* London, England: Cassell Educational Ltd., 1989.

Supplement

16

Simulation

KEY TERMS

Variables

Parameters

Decision Rules

Probability Distributions

Time Incrementing

Run Length (Run Time)

Computer Models

Simulation Brings Productivity Enhancements to the Social Security Administration

Approximately 25 million people visit Social Security Administration field offices each year. It is not unusual to find a line of people stretching the length of a city block waiting at an office door prior to opening time. Waiting time experienced by these people and others arriving once the office opens is an important measure of quality service delivery to the SSA, and obviously, a matter of concern to those waiting in line.

Thus, a primary application of the simulation modeling initiative has been to analyze field offices and system dynamics to determine staffing and workflow variables effects on service. The required degree of insight into the field office system dynamics encompasses a widely dispersed range of individual characteristics particular to each location. These characteristics coincide with the demographics of respective offices, which are found in urban, suburban and rural communities. For example, an office located in an urban setting serves people who may have entirely different needs from those arriving at a rural or suburban office. Thus, differing skills and specialties of the staff are required for the many types of workloads that result.

The study effort has involved a two-phased concurrent approach. One phase, using the simulation language *SLAMSYSTEM,* developed by Pritsker Corp., Indianapolis, has involved a macroscopic, agency-level analysis of field offices, thereby dealing with categorical groupings of offices according to office size, regionally and nationally.

The other phase, using *ProModel PC,* a simulation software package with animation capability, and *ServiceModel,* an object-oriented, *Windows*-based graphical simulation package from PRO-MODEL Corp., Orem, Utah, has focused on examining the elemental dynamics taking place within individual field offices upon which staffing levels vs. service level criteria are analyzed, and staffing levels subsequently established.

The inherent graphics and animation in these packages has been utilized to model office activity such that the layouts are depicted with patrons shown arriving and being served by SSA personnel while the simulation model statistics, including waiting time and staff utilization calculations, are concurrently handled by the software.

Source: Julian Swedish, "Simulation Brings Productivity Enhancements to the Social Security Administration," *Industrial Engineering,* May 1993, pp. 28, 30.

Functional Area	Percent
Production	59%
Corporate planning	53
Engineering	46
Finance	41
Research and development	37
Marketing	24
Data processing	16
Personnel	10

E X H I B I T S16.1

Use of Simulation by Functional Areas of Business

Simulation has become a standard tool in business. In manufacturing simulation is used to determine production schedules, inventory levels, and maintenance procedures; to do capacity planning, resource requirements planning, and process planning; and more. In service, it is widely used to analyze waiting line and paper processing operations such as discussed in the opening vignette. Often, when a mathematical technique fails, we turn to simulation to save us. A survey of nonacademic members of the Institute of Management Science showed that 89 percent of their firms use simulation.[1] (If the survey was repeated today, the percentage would undoubtedly be higher.) Exhibit S16.1 shows the functional areas where it is applied. Note that production heads the list, with 59 percent. Another interesting finding of the study is that 54 percent of the respondents said that simulation models are created within the functional areas themselves.

S16.1   DEFINITION OF SIMULATION

While the term *simulation* can have various meanings depending on its application, in business it generally refers to using a digital computer to perform experiments on a model of a real system.[2] These experiments may be undertaken before the real system is operational, to aid in its design to see how the system might react to changes in its operating rules, or to evaluate the system's response to changes in its structure. Simulation is particularly appropriate to situations in which the size or complexity of the problem makes the use of optimizing techniques difficult or impossible. Thus, job shops, which are characterized by complex queuing problems, have been studied extensively via simulation, as have certain types of inventory, layout, and maintenance problems (to name but a few). Simulation can also be used in conjunction with traditional statistical and management science techniques.

In addition, simulation is useful in training managers and workers in how the real system operates, in demonstrating the effects of changes in system variables, in real-time control, and in developing new ideas about how to run the business.

S16.2   SIMULATION METHODOLOGY

Exhibit S16.2 is a flowchart of the major phases in a simulation study. In this section, we develop each phase with particular reference to the key factors noted at the right of the chart.

---

[1] David P. Christy and Hugh J. Watson, "The Application of Simulation: A Survey of Industry Practice," *Interfaces* 13, no. 5 (October 1983), pp. 47–52.

[2] Examples of other types of simulation are airplane flight simulators, video games, and virtual reality animation.

E X H I B I T S16.2
*Major Phase in a
Simulation Study*

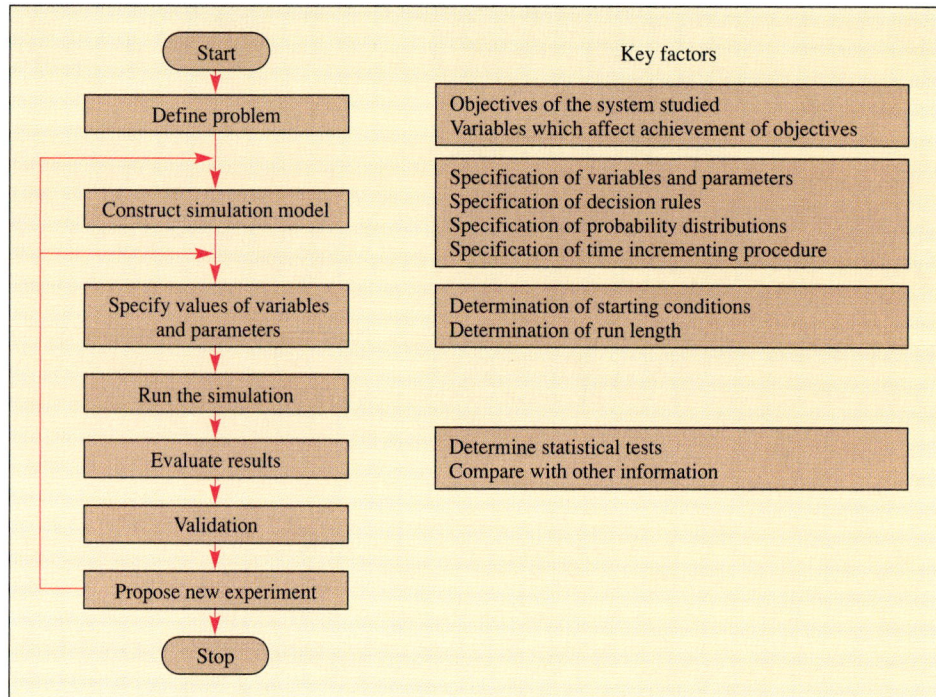

Start

Define problem → Objectives of the system studied / Variables which affect achievement of objectives

Construct simulation model → Specification of variables and parameters / Specification of decision rules / Specification of probability distributions / Specification of time incrementing procedure

Specify values of variables and parameters → Determination of starting conditions / Determination of run length

Run the simulation

Evaluate results → Determine statistical tests / Compare with other information

Validation

Propose new experiment

Stop

Key factors

**Problem
Definition**

Problem definition for purposes of simulation differs little from problem definition for any other tool of analysis. Essentially, it entails specifying the objectives and identifying the relevant controllable and uncontrollable variables of the system to be studied. The objective of a fish market owner is maximizing the profit on sales of fish. The relevant controllable variable (i.e., under the control of the decision maker) is the ordering rule; the relevant uncontrollable variables are the daily demand levels for fish and the amount of fish sold. Other possible objectives could also be specified, such as to maximize profit from the sale of lobsters or to maximize sales revenue.

**Constructing a
Simulation
Model**

A feature that distinguishes simulation from techniques such as linear programming or queuing theory is the fact that a simulation model must be custom built for each problem situation. (A linear programming model, in contrast, can be used in a variety of situations with only a restatement of the values for the objective function and constraint equations.) There are simulation languages that make the model building easier, however. We discuss this subject later in the chapter. The unique nature of each simulation model means that the procedures discussed later for building and executing a model represent a synthesis of various approaches to simulation and are guidelines rather than rigid rules.

Specification of Variables and Parameters   The first step in constructing a simulation model is determining which properties of the real system should be fixed (called **parameters**) and which should be allowed to vary throughout the simulation run (called **variables**). In the fish market example, the variables are the amount of fish ordered, the

E X H I B I T S16.3   *Actual Distribution of Demand and Normal Distribution with the Same Mean*

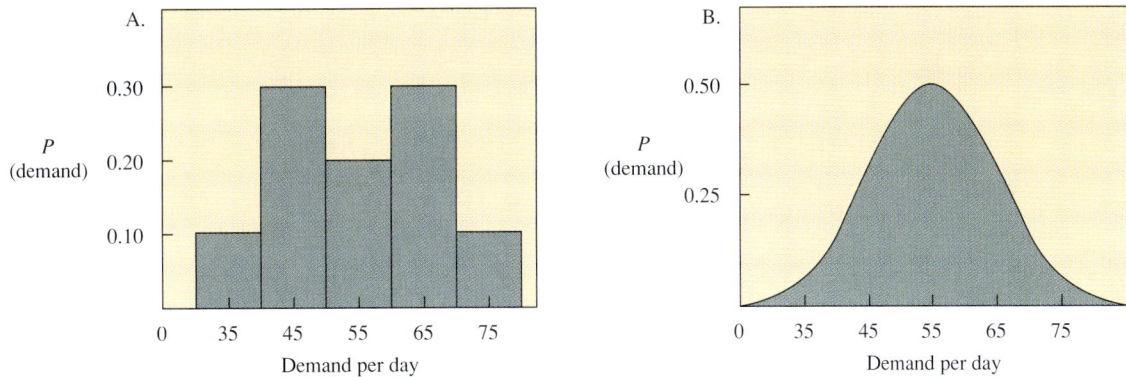

amount demanded, and the amount sold; the parameters are the cost of the fish and the selling price of the fish. In most simulations, the focus is on the status of the variables at different points in time, such as the number of pounds of fish demanded and sold each day.

Specification of Decision Rules   **Decision rules** (or operating rules) are sets of conditions under which the behavior of the simulation model is observed. These rules are either directly or indirectly the focus of most simulation studies. In many simulations, decision rules are priority rules (for example, which customer to serve first, which job to process first). In certain situations these can be quite involved, taking into account a large number of variables in the system. For example, an inventory ordering rule could be stated in such a way that the amount to order would depend on the amount in inventory, the amount previously ordered but not received, the amount back ordered, and the desired safety stock.

Specification of Probability Distributions   Two categories of **distributions** can be used for simulation: empirical frequency distributions and standard mathematical distributions. An empirical distribution is one derived from observing the relative frequencies of some event such as arrivals in a line or demand for a product. In other words, it is a custom-built demand distribution that is relevant only to a particular situation. It might appear like the one shown on the left side of Exhibit S16.3. Such distributions have to be determined by direct observation or detailed analysis of records. (We will show how to use these later in the waiting line simulation example.) But often demand, for example, can reasonably be assumed to closely approximate a standard mathematical distribution such as the normal or Poisson. This greatly simplifies data collection and computerization.

E X A M P L E S16.1 / *Relating Random Numbers to a Standard Distribution*   To illustrate how to relate random numbers to a standard distribution, let us suppose that daily demand for newspapers from a vending machine is normally distributed with a mean of 55 and standard deviation of 10. (This distribution is shown on the right side of Exhibit S16.3.) Under this assumption, the generation of daily demand would employ a table of randomly distributed normal numbers (or deviates) in conjunction with the sta-

E X H I B I T S16.4

Randomly Distributed
Normal Numbers

1.23481	−1.66161	1.49673	−.26990	−.23812	.34506
1.54221	.02629	1.22318	.52304	.18124	.20790
.19126	1.18250	1.00826	.24826	−1.35882	.70691
−.54929	−.87214	−2.75470	−1.19941	−1.45402	.16760
1.14463	−.23153	1.11241	1.08497	−.28185	−.17022
−.63248	−.04776	−.55806	.04496	1.16515	2.24938
−.29988	.31052	−.49094	−.00926	−.28278	−.95339
−.32855	−.93166	−.04187	−.94171	1.64410	−.96893
.35331	.56176	−.98726	.82752	.32468	.36915
.72576					
.04406					

tistical formula $D_n = \bar{x} + Z_n \sigma$ (terms defined later), derived from the Z transform used to enter a standard normal table.[3] The specific steps are

S O L U T I O N

1. Draw a five- or six-digit figure from Exhibit S16.4. The entries in this table are randomly developed deviate values that pertain to a normal distribution having a mean of zero and a standard deviation of 1. The term *deviate* refers to the number of standard deviations some value is from the mean and, in this case, represents the number of standard deviations that any day's demand is from the mean demand. In the preceding formula for D_n, it would be the value for Z on day n. If we are simulating Day 1 and using the first entry in Exhibit S16.4, then $Z_1 = 1.23481$. A negative deviate value means simply that the particular level of demand to be found by using it will be less than the mean, not that demand will be a negative value.

2. Substitute the value of Z_1, along with the predetermined values for x and σ, into the formula

    $$D_n = \bar{x} + Z_n \sigma$$

    where

    > D_n = Demand on day n
    > $\bar{x}$ = Mean demand (55 in this example)
    > σ = Estimated standard deviation (10 in this example)
    > Z_n = Number of standard deviations from the mean on day n

    Thus $D_n = 55 + (1.23481)(10)$.

3. Solve for D_n:

    $$D_n = 55 + 12.3481$$
    $$D_n = 67.3481$$

4. Repeat Steps 1 to 3, using different normal deviates from the table until the desired number of days have been simulated. ■

---

[3]The basic formula is $Z = x − \mu/\sigma$, which, when restated in terms of x, appears as $x = \mu + Z\sigma$. We then substituted D_n for x and $\bar{x}$ for μ to relate the method more directly to the sample problem.

Specification of Time-Incrementing Procedure   In a simulation model, time can be advanced by one of two methods: (1) fixed-time increments or (2) variable-time increments. Under both methods of **time incrementing,** the concept of a simulated clock is important. In the fixed-time increment method, uniform clock-time increments (e.g., minutes, hours, days) are specified and the simulation proceeds by fixed intervals from one time period to the next. At each point in clock time, the system is scanned to determine if any events are to occur. If they are, the events are simulated, and time is advanced; if they are not, time is still advanced by one unit.

In the variable-time increment method, clock time is advanced by the amount required to initiate the next event.

Which method is most appropriate? Experience suggests that the fixed-time increment is desirable when events of interest occur with regularity or when the number of events is large, with several commonly occurring in the same time period. The variable-time increment method is generally desirable, taking less computer run time when there are relatively few events occurring within a considerable amount of time.[4]

Determining Starting Conditions   A variable, by definition, changes in value as the simulation progresses, but must be given an initial starting value. The value of a parameter, remember, stays constant; however, it may be changed as different alternatives are studied in other simulations.

Specifying Values of Variables and Parameters

Determining starting conditions for variables is a major tactical decision in simulation. This is because the model is biased by the set of initial starting values until the model has settled down to a steady state. To cope with this problem, analysts have followed various approaches, such as (1) discarding data generated during the early parts of the run, (2) selecting starting conditions that reduce the duration of the warm-up period, or (3) selecting starting conditions that eliminate bias. To employ any of these alternatives, however, the analyst must have some idea of the range of output data expected. Therefore, in one sense, the analyst biases results. On the other hand, one of the unique features of simulation is that it allows judgment to enter into the design and analysis of the simulation; so if the analyst has some information that bears on the problem, it should be included.

Determining Run Length   The length of the simulation run (**run length** or **run time**) depends on the purpose of the simulation. Perhaps the most common approach is to continue the simulation until it has achieved as equilibrium condition. In the context of the fish market mentioned earlier, this would mean that simulated demands correspond to their historical relative frequencies. Another approach is to run the simulation for a set period, such as a month, a year, or a decade, and see if the conditions at the end of the period appear reasonable. A third approach is to set run length so that a sufficiently large sample is gathered for purposes of statistical hypothesis testing. This alternative is considered further in the next section.

Determining Statistical Tests   The types of conclusions that can be drawn from a simulation depend, of course, on the degree to which the model reflects the real system, but they also depend on the design of the simulation in a statistical sense. Indeed, many analysts view simulation as a form of hypothesis testing, with each simulation run providing

Evaluating Results

---

[4]It ignores time intervals where nothing happens and immediately advances to the next point when some event does take place.

one or more pieces of sample data that are amenable to formal analysis through inferential statistical methods.[5]

Comparison with Other Information   In most situations, the analyst has other information available with which to compare the simulation results: past operating data from the real system, operating data from the performance of similar systems, and the analyst's own intuitive understanding of the real system's operation. Admittedly, however, information obtained from these sources is probably not sufficient to validate the conclusions derived from the simulation. Thus the only true test of a simulation is how well the real system performs after the results of the study have been implemented.

Validation

In this context, *validation* refers to testing the computer program to ensure that the simulation is correct. Specifically, it is a check to see whether the computer code is a valid translation of the flowchart model and whether the simulation adequately represents the real system. Errors may arise in the program from mistakes in the coding or from mistakes in logic. Mistakes in coding are usually easily found since the program is most likely not executed by the computer. Mistakes in logic, however, present more of a challenge. In these cases, the program runs, but it fails to yield correct results.

To deal with this problem, the analyst has three alternatives: (1) have the program print out all calculations and verify these calculations by separate calculation, (2) simulate present conditions and compare the results with the existing system, or (3) pick some point in the simulation run and compare its output to the answer obtained from solving a relevant mathematical model of the situation at that point. Even though the first two approaches have obvious drawbacks, they are more likely to be employed than the third, because if we had a relevant mathematical model in mind, we would probably be able to solve the problem without the aid of simulation.

Proposing a New Experiment

Based on the simulation results, a new simulation experiment may be in order. We might like to change many of the factors: parameters, variables, decision rules, starting conditions, and run length. As for parameters, we might be interested in replicating the simulation with several different costs or prices of a product to see what changes would occur. Trying different decision rules would obviously be in order if the initial rules led to poor results or if these runs yielded new insights into the problem. (The procedure of using the same stream of random numbers is a good general approach in that it sharpens the differences among alternatives and permits shorter runs.) Also, the values from the previous experiment may be useful starting conditions for subsequent simulations.

Finally, whether trying different run lengths constitutes a new experiment rather than a replication of a previous experiment depends on the types of events that occur in the system operation over time. It might happen, for example, that the system has more than one stable level of operation and that reaching the second level is time-dependent. Thus, while the first series of runs of, say, 100 periods shows stable conditions, doubling the length of the series may provide new and distinctly different, but equally stable, conditions. In this case, running the simulation over 200 time periods could be thought of as a new experiment.

---

[5]Statistical procedures commonly used in evaluating simulation results include analysis of variance, regression analysis, and *t* tests.

When using a **computer model** we reduce the system to be studied to a symbolic representation to be run on a computer. Although it is beyond this book's scope to detail the technical aspects of computer modeling, some that bear directly on simulation are

Computerization

1. Computer language selection.
2. Flowcharting.
3. Coding.
4. Data generation.
5. Output reports.
6. Validation.

We will say more about simulation programs and languages at the end of this supplement.

Output Reports   General-purpose languages permit the analyst to specify any type of output report (or data) desired, providing one is willing to pay the price in programming effort. Special-purpose languages have standard routines that can be activated by one or two program statements to print out such data as means, variances, and standard deviations. Regardless of language, however, our experience has been that too much data from a simulation can be as dysfunctional to problem solving as too little data; both situations tend to obscure important, truly meaningful information about the system under study.

S16.3   EXAMPLE: SIMULATING WAITING LINES

Waiting lines that occur in series and parallel (such as in assembly lines and job shops) usually cannot be solved mathematically. However, since waiting lines are often easily simulated on a computer, we have chosen a two-stage assembly line as our second simulation example.

Consider manufacturing a product on an assembly line that has a significant physical size, such as for a refrigerator, stove, car, boat, TV, or furniture. Exhibit S16.5 shows two workstations on such a line.

A Two-Stage Assembly Line

The size of the product is an important consideration in assembly-line analysis and design because the number of products that can exist at each workstation affects worker performance. If the product is large, then the workstations are dependent on each other.

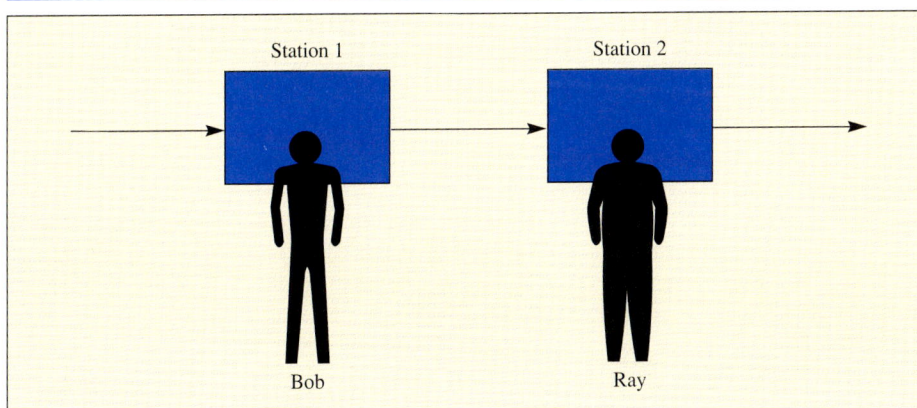

E X H I B I T S16.5
Two Workstations on an Assembly Line

Station 1   Station 2

Bob   Ray

Seconds	Bob		Totals	Ray	Totals
5–14.99	IIII		4	IIII	4
15–24.99	ЖH I		6	ЖH	5
25–34.99	ЖH ЖH		10	ЖH I	6
35–44.99	ЖH ЖH ЖH ЖH		20	ЖH II	7
45–54.99	ЖH ЖH ЖH ЖH ЖH ЖH ЖH ЖH		40	ЖH ЖH	10
55–64.99	ЖH ЖH I		11	ЖH III	8
65–74.99	ЖH		5	ЖH I	6
75–84.99	IIII		4	IIII	4
			100		50

Exhibit S16.5, for example, shows Bob and Ray working on a two-stage line where Bob's output in Station 1 is fed to Ray in Station 2. If the workstations are adjacent so that there is no room for items in between, then Bob, by working slowly, would cause Ray to wait. Conversely, if Bob completes a product quickly (or if Ray takes longer to finish the task) then Bob must wait for Ray.

In this simulation, assume that Bob, the first worker on the line, can pull over a new item to work on whenever needed. We concentrate our analysis on the interaction between Bob and Ray.

Objective of the Study There are a number of questions we would like to have answered about the assembly line from this study. A partial list would be

What is the average performance time of each worker?

What is the output rate of product through this line?

How much time does Bob wait for Ray?

How much time does Ray wait for Bob?

If the space between the two stations were increased so that items could be stored there and give workers some independence, how would this affect output rates, wait times, and so on?

Data Collection To simulate this system, we need the performance times of Bob and Ray. One way to collect this data is to divide the range of performance times into segments, and then observe each worker. A simple check or tally mark in each of these segments results in a useful histogram of data.

Exhibit S16.6 shows the data collection form used to observe the performances of Bob and Ray. To simplify the procedure, performance time was divided into 10-second intervals. Bob was observed for 100 repetitions of the work task, and Ray was observed just 50 times. The number of observations does not have to be the same, but the more there are and the smaller the size of the time segments, the more accurate the study will be. The trade-off is that more observations and smaller segments take more time and more people (as well as more time to program and run a simulation).

Exhibit S16.7 contains the random number intervals assigned that correspond to the same ratio as the actual observed data. For example, Bob had 4 out of 100 times at 10 seconds. Therefore, if we used 100 numbers, we would assign 4 of those numbers as

Seconds	Time Frequencies for Bob (Operation 1)	RN Intervals	Time Frequencies for Ray (Operation 2)	RN Intervals
10	4	00–03	4	00–07
20	6	04–09	5	08–17
30	10	10–19	6	18–29
40	20	20–39	7	30–43
50	40	40–79	10	44–63
60	11	80–90	8	64–79
70	5	91–95	6	80–91
80	4	96–99	4	92–99
	100		50	

E X H I B I T S16.7

Random Number Intervals for Bob and Ray

E X H I B I T S16.8   *Simulation of Bob and Ray—Two-Stage Assembly Line*

Item Number	Bob						Ray				
	Random Number	Start Time	Performance Time	Finish Time	Wait Time	Storage Space	Random Number	Start Time	Performance Time	Finish Time	Wait Time
1	56	00	50	50		0	83	50	70	120	50
2	55	50	50	100	20	0	47	120	50	170	
3	84	120	60	180		0	08	180	20	200	10
4	36	180	40	220		0	05	220	10	230	20
5	26	220	40	260		0	42	260	40	300	30
6	95	260	70	330		0	95	330	80	410	30
7	66	330	50	380	30	0	17	410	20	430	
8	03	410	10	420	10	0	21	430	30	460	
9	57	430	50	480		0	31	480	40	520	20
10	69	480	50	530		0	90	530	70	600	10
			470		60				430		170

corresponding to 10 seconds. We could have assigned any four numbers, for example, 42, 18, 12, and 93. However, these would be a nuisance to search for so we assign consecutive numbers, such as 00, 01, 02, and 03.

There were 50 observations of Ray. There are two ways we could assign random numbers. First, we could use just 50 numbers (say 00–49) and ignore any numbers over that. However, this is wasteful since we would discard 50 percent of all the numbers from the list. Another choice would be to double the frequency number. For example, rather than assign, say, numbers 0–03 to account for the 4 observations out of 50 that took 10 seconds, we could assign numbers 00–07 to represent 8 observations out of 100, which is double the observed number but the same frequency. Actually, for this example and the speed of computers, the savings of time by doubling is insignificant.

Exhibit S16.8 shows a hand simulation of 10 items processed by Bob and Ray. The random numbers used were from Appendix B, starting at the first column of two numbers and working downward.

Assume that we start out at time 00 and run it in continuous seconds (not bothering to convert this to hours and minutes). The first random number is 56 and corresponds to Bob's performance at 50 seconds on the first item. The item is passed to Ray, who starts at 50 seconds. Relating the next random number 83 to Exhibit S16.7, we find that Ray takes 70 seconds to complete the item. In the meantime, Bob starts on the next item at time 50 and takes 50 seconds (random number 55), finishing at time 100. However, Bob cannot start on the third item until Ray gets through with the first item at time 120. Bob, therefore, has a wait time of 20 seconds. (If there was storage space between Bob and Ray, this item could have been moved out of Bob's workstation and Bob could have started the next item at time 100.) The remainder of the exhibit was calculated following the same pattern: obtaining a random number, finding the corresponding processing time, noting the wait time (if any), and computing the finish time. Note that with no storage space between Bob and Ray, there was considerable waiting time for both workers.

We can now answer some questions and make some statements about the system. For example,

> The output time averages 60 seconds per unit (the complete time 600 for Ray divided by 10 units).
>
> Utilization of Bob is $^{470}\!/_{530} = 88.7$ percent.
>
> Utilization of Ray is $^{430}\!/_{550} = 78.2$ percent (disregarding the initial startup wait for the first item of 50 seconds).
>
> The average performance time for Bob is $^{470}\!/_{10} = 47$ seconds.
>
> The average performance time for Ray is $^{430}\!/_{10} = 43$ seconds.

We have demonstrated how this problem would be solved in a simple manual simulation. A sample of 10 is really too small to place much confidence in so this problem should be run on a computer for several thousand iterations. (We extend this same problem further in the next section of this supplement).

It is also vital to study the effect of item storage space between workers. The problem would be run to see what the throughput time and worker utilization times are with no storage space between workers. A second run should increase this storage space to one unit, with the corresponding changes noted. Repeating the runs for two, three, four, and so on offers management a chance to compute the additional cost of space compared with the increased use. Such increased space between workers may require a larger building, more materials and parts in the system, material handling equipment, and transfer machine plus added heat, light, building maintenance, and so on.

This would also be useful data for management to see what changes in the system would occur if one of the worker positions was automated. The assembly line could be simulated using data from the automated process to see if such a change would be cost-justified.

S16.4 SPREADSHEET SIMULATION

As we have stated throughout this book, spreadsheets such as Lotus, Quattro, Excel, and SuperCalc are very useful for a variety of problems. Exhibit S16.9 shows Bob and Ray's two-stage assembly line on a Lotus 1-2-3 spreadsheet. The procedure follows the same pattern as our manual display in Exhibit S16.7.

The total simulation on Lotus passed through 1,200 iterations; that is, 1,200 parts were finished by Ray. Simulation, as an analytic tool, has an advantage over quantitative methods in that it is a dynamic simulation whereas analytic methods show long-run average performance. As you can see in Exhibits S16.10 and S16.11, there is an unmistakable startup (or transient) phase. We could even raise some questions about the long-term operation of the line because it does not seem to have settled to a constant (steady state) value, even after the 1,200 items. Exhibit S16.10 shows 100 items that pass through the Bob and Ray two-stage system. Notice the wide variation in time for the first units completed. These figures are the average time that units take. It is a cumulative number; that is, the first unit takes the time generated by the random numbers. The average time for two units is the average time of the sum of the first and second units. The average time for three units is the average time for the sum of the first three units, and so on. This

E X H I B I T   S16.9   *Bob and Ray Two-Stage Assembly Line on Lotus 1-2-3*

		Bob				Ray						
Item	RN	Start Time	Perf. Time	Finish Time	Wait Time	RN	Start Time	Perf. Time	Finish Time	Wait Time	Average Time/Unit	Total Time	Average Time in System
1	93	0	70	70	0	0	70	10	80	70	80.0	80	80.0
2	52	70	50	120	0	44	120	50	170	40	85.0	100	90.0
3	15	120	30	150	20	72	170	60	230	0	76.7	110	96.7
4	64	170	50	220	10	35	230	40	270	0	67.5	100	97.5
5	86	230	60	290	0	2	290	10	300	20	60.0	70	92.0
6	20	290	40	330	0	82	330	70	400	30	66.7	110	95.0
7	83	330	60	390	10	31	400	40	440	0	62.9	110	97.1
8	89	400	60	460	0	13	460	20	480	20	60.0	80	95.0
9	69	460	50	510	0	53	510	50	560	30	62.2	100	95.6
10	41	510	50	560	0	48	560	50	610	0	61.0	100	96.0
11	32	560	40	600	10	13	610	20	630	0	57.3	70	93.6
12	1	610	10	620	10	67	630	60	690	0	57.5	80	92.5
13	11	630	30	660	30	91	690	70	760	0	58.5	130	95.4
14	2	690	10	700	60	76	760	60	820	0	58.6	130	97.9
15	11	760	30	790	30	41	820	40	860	0	57.3	100	98.0
16	55	820	50	870	0	34	870	40	910	10	56.9	90	97.5
17	18	870	30	900	10	28	910	30	940	0	55.3	70	95.9
18	39	910	40	950	0	53	950	50	1000	10	55.6	90	95.6
19	13	950	30	980	20	41	1000	40	1040	0	54.7	90	95.3
20	7	1000	20	1020	20	21	1040	30	1070	0	53.5	70	94.0
21	29	1040	40	1080	0	54	1080	50	1130	10	53.8	90	93.8
22	58	1080	50	1130	0	39	1130	40	1170	0	53.2	90	93.6
23	95	1130	70	1200	0	70	1200	60	1260	30	54.8	130	95.2
24	27	1200	40	1240	20	60	1260	50	1310	0	54.6	110	95.8
25	59	1260	50	1310	0	93	1310	80	1390	0	55.6	130	97.2
26	85	1310	60	1370	20	51	1390	50	1440	0	55.4	130	98.5
27	12	1390	30	1420	20	35	1440	40	1480	0	54.8	90	98.1
28	34	1440	40	1480	0	51	1480	50	1530	0	54.6	90	97.9
29	60	1480	50	1530	0	87	1530	70	1600	0	55.2	120	98.6
30	97	1530	80	1610	0	29	1610	30	1640	10	54.7	110	99.0

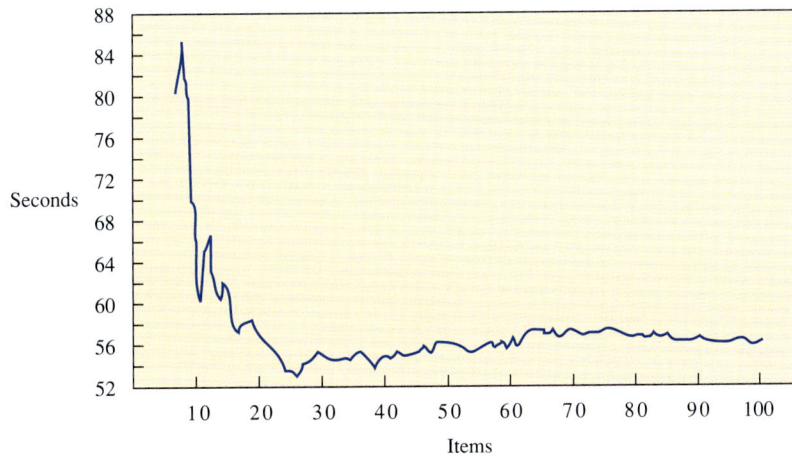

E X H I B I T   S16.10

Average Time per Unit of Output (Finish time/number of units)

E X H I B I T   S16.11

Average Time the Product Spends in the System

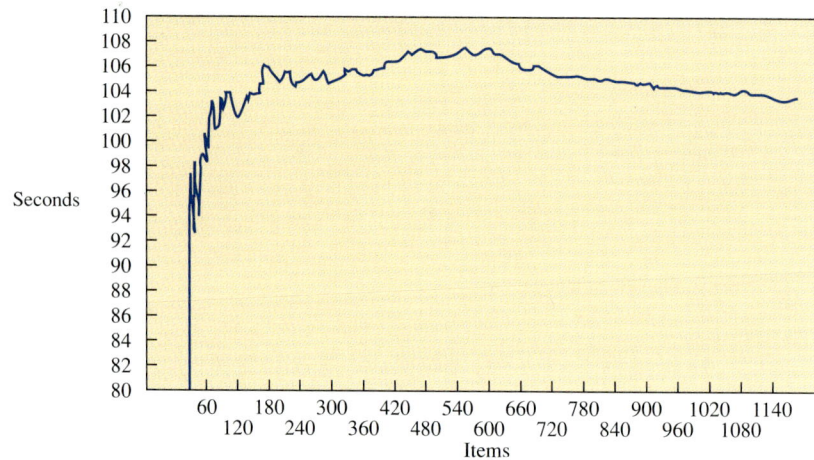

E X H I B I T   S16.12

Results of Simulating 1,200 Units Processed by Bob and Ray

	Bob	Ray	Unit
Utilization	0.81	0.85	
Average wait time	10.02	9.63	
Average performance time	46.48	46.88	
Average time per unit			57.65
Average time in system			103.38

display could have almost any starting shape, not necessarily what we have shown. It all depends on the stream of random numbers. What we can be sure of is that the times do oscillate for a while until they settle down as units are finished and smooth the average.

Exhibit S16.11 shows the average time that parts spend in the system. At the start, the display shows an increasing amount of time in the system. This can be expected because the system started empty and there are no interruptions for parts passing from Bob to Ray. Often parts enter the system and may have to wait between stages as work-in-process; this causes delays for subsequent parts and adds to the waiting time. As time goes on, however, stability should occur unless the capacity of the second stage is less than the first stage's. In our present case, we did not allow space between them. Therefore, if Bob finished first, he had to wait for Ray. If Ray finished first, he had to wait for Bob.

Exhibit S16.12 shows the results of simulating Bob and Ray completing 1,200 units of product. Compare these figures to those that we obtained simulating 10 items by hand. Not too bad, is it! The average performance time for Bob is shown as 46.48 seconds. This is close to the weighted average of what you would expect in the long run. For Bob it is (10 × 4 + 20 × 6 + 30 × 10 etc.)/100 = 45.9 seconds. Ray's expected time is (10 × 4 + 20 × 5 + 30 × 6 etc.)/50 = 46.4 seconds.

S16.5   SIMULATION PROGRAMS AND LANGUAGES

Simulation models can be classified as *continuous* or *discrete*. Continuous models are based on mathematical equations and therefore are continuous, with values for all points in time. In contrast, discrete simulation occurs only at specific points. For example, customers arriving at a bank teller's window would be discrete simulation. The simulation

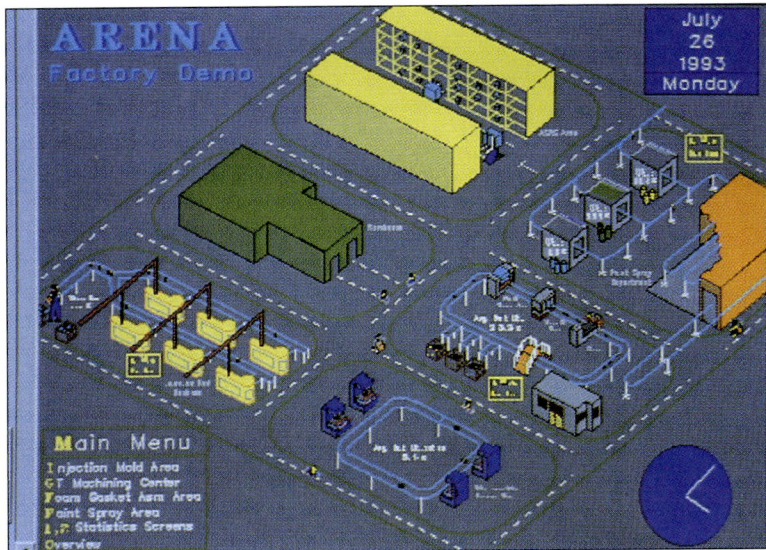

jumps from point to point; the arrival of a customer, the state of a service, the ending of service, the arrival of the next customer, and so on. Discrete simulation can also be triggered to run by units of time (daily, hourly, minute by minute). This is called *event simulation;* points in between either have no interest or cannot be computed because of the lack of some sort of mathematical relationships to link the succeeding events. Operations management applications almost exclusively use discrete (event) simulation.

Simulation programs also can be categorized as general-purpose and special-purpose. General-purpose software is really language that allows programmers to build their own models. Examples are SLAM II, SIMSCRIPT II.5, SIMAN, GPSS/H, GPSS/PC, PC-MODEL, and RESQ. Special-purpose software simulation programs are specially built to simulate specific applications, such as MAP/1, and SIMFACTORY. In a specialized simulation for manufacturing, for example, provisions in the model allow for specifying the number of work centers, their description, arrival rates, processing time, batch sizes, quantities of work in process, available resources including labor, sequences, and so on. Additionally, the program may allow the observer to watch the animated operation and see the quantities and flows throughout the system as the simulation is running. Data are collected, analyzed, and presented in a form most suitable for that type of application.

There are many software simulation programs available to use on computers, from micros to mainframes. How, then, do you choose a program from a long list?

The first step is to understand the different types of simulation. Then it becomes a matter of reviewing programs on the market to find one that fits your specific needs. (See the Breakthrough "Hospital Overcrowding Solutions Are Found with Simulation" on page 683 for a successful application of a commercial program.) Even if a program does exist, however, sometimes it's still easier to create a special-purpose one. It may be better suited and less troublesome to use.

As a last comment on simulation programs, do not rule out spreadsheets for simulation. As you noticed, we simulated Bob and Ray on a spreadsheet in the preceding section. Spreadsheets are becoming quite user-friendly and are adding many features, such as allowing random number generation and asking what-if questions. The simplicity in using a spreadsheet for simulation may well compensate for probably having to reduce the complexity of the problem somewhat in order to use the spreadsheet.

Hospital Overcrowding Solutions Are Found with Simulation

Thanks to increased life expectancy through improved health care coupled with shifting population demographics, hospitals everywhere are becoming increasingly overcrowded. Limited health care budgets are forcing hospitals to explore creative solutions. But creative solutions can be risky, so they need to be carefully evaluated. From the standpoint of cost, the earlier a solution can be evaluated and either accepted or rejected, the better.

Along these lines, the Outpatient Laboratory at Bay Medical Center was experiencing serious capacity constraints. Adding to their difficulties, a renovation designed to improve efficiency actually added to the overcrowding problem. In early 1992, Dave Nall, a Management Engineer for Bay Medical Center, ran a study to evaluate several alternatives and make recommendations designed at reducing bottlenecks and improving patient flow through the Outpatient Laboratory. The objective of this study was to develop and evaluate alternative ways of reducing overcrowding at the Outpatient Laboratory.

Solution

The key technology employed by Dave in conducting this analysis was computer simulation. Dave had used computer simulation numerous times in the past and had found that it was an efficient way to both gain insight into the problem as well as evaluate the solutions.

Through discussions with managers responsible for the Outpatient Laboratory, Dave built a network describing the patient's flow through the Laboratory as it was currently configured. Then, data were collected on the times required for patients to receive the various services they might need as well as the travel time between rooms where the service was provided. From this information, Dave constructed a Micro Saint computer simulation of the baseline Laboratory configuration.

Dave then modified the computer simulation and used it to study issues relating to three categories of solutions to Outpatient Laboratory overcrowding; 1) changing staff, including both medical and administrative staff, 2) utilizing another clinic as an overflow laboratory, and 3) possible redesign of the laboratory facility itself.

With respect to staffing, the computer simulation verified that the medical staff currently employed was indeed the optimal number. However, Dave found that the administrative staff, if anything, was overstaffed and that a staff reduction could take place with no appreciable reduction in patient service. Staffing was not the key

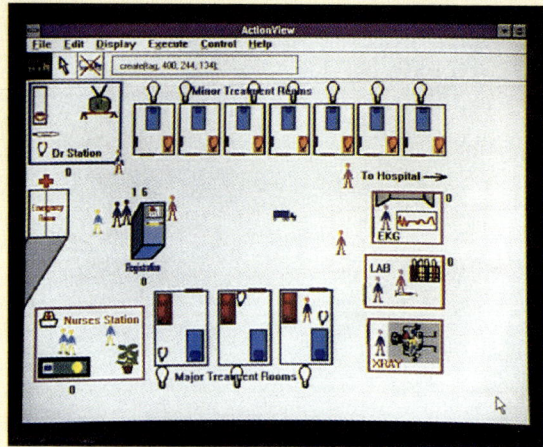

problem. With respect to the option of utilizing another laboratory as an overflow, there were significant opportunities for improving throughput if other patients could be enticed to use the another laboratory. While the simulation did not tell him how to get the patients to use an alternative laboratory, it did allow Dave to quantify the benefits of implementing policies that would increase alternative laboratory usage by 5%, 10%, etc. With respect to redesign of the existing outpatient laboratory, Dave determined that, with a relatively minor redesign of the facility and a procedural change, the laboratory would become significantly more productive. Increased productivity would, of course, lead to increased patient service.

Benefits

Individually, no one could have accurately guessed the impact of the different ways of addressing overcrowding at the Outpatient Laboratory at Bay Medical Center. Through the results of the simulation analysis and the insights gained, Dave was able to assess the relative merits of each alternative as well as predict their impact. With a small investment in Dave's time, Bay Medical Center was able to make informed decisions with an understanding of both costs and benefits. As a result, the right decisions were made, money was saved, and patients were better served.

Source: Micro Analysis and Design Simulation Software, Inc., Boulder, CO.

Simulation software takes a while to learn to use. Once a specific software is learned, the tendency is to stay with it for a long time so be careful when making the choice. Simulation software should

1. Be capable of being used interactively as well as allowing complete runs.
2. Be user-friendly and easy to understand.
3. Allow modules to be built and then connected. In this way models can be worked on separately without affecting the rest of the system.
4. Allow users to write and incorporate their own routines; no simulation program can provide for all needs.
5. Have building blocks that contain built-in commands (such as statistical analysis or decision rules of where to go next).
6. Have macro capability, such as the ability to develop machining cells.
7. Have material-flow capability. Operations involves the movement of material and people; the program should have the ability to model trucks, cranes, and conveyers, and so on.
8. Output standard statistics such as cycle times, utilizations, and wait times.
9. Allow a variety of data analysis alternatives for both input and output data.
10. Have animation capabilities to display graphically the product flow through the system.
11. Permit interactive debugging of the model so the user can trace flows through the model and more easily find errors.[6]

Desirable Features of Simulation Software

S16.6   ADVANTAGES AND DISADVANTAGES OF SIMULATION

The following is not intended as a comprehensive list of reasons why one should elect or not use simulation as a technique. Rather, we state some of the main points usually raised.

Advantages

1. Developing the model of a system often leads to a better understanding of the real system.
2. Time can be compressed in simulation; years of experience in the real system can be compressed into seconds or minutes.
3. Simulation does not disrupt ongoing activities of the real system.
4. Simulation is far more general than mathematical models and can be used where conditions are not suitable for standard mathematical analysis.
5. Simulation can be used as a game for training experience.
6. Simulation provides a more realistic replication of a system than mathematical analysis.
7. Simulation can be used to analyze transient conditions whereas mathematical techniques usually cannot.
8. Many standard packaged models, covering a wide range of topics, are available commercially.
9. Simulation answers what-if questions.

---

[6]S. Wali Haider and Jerry Banks, "Simulation Software Products for Analyzing Manufacturing Systems," *Industrial Engineering* 18, no. 7 (July 1986), pp. 98–103.

Disadvantages

1. While a great deal of time and effort may be spent to develop a model for simulation, there is no guarantee that the model will, in fact, provide good answers.

2. There is no way to prove that a simulation model's performance is completely reliable. Simulation involves numerous repetitions of sequences that are based on randomly generated occurrences. An apparently stable system can, with the right combination of events—however unlikely—explode.

3. Depending on the system to be simulated, building a simulation model can take anywhere from an hour to 100 worker years. Complicated systems can be very costly and take a long time.

4. Simulation may be less accurate than mathematical analysis because it is randomly based. If a given system can be represented by a mathematical model, it may be better to use than simulation.

5. A significant amount of computer time may be needed to run complex models.

6. The technique of simulation, while making progress, still lacks a standardized approach. Therefore, models of the same system built by different individuals may differ widely.

S16.7 CONCLUSION

We could make the statement that anything that can be done mathematically can be done with simulation. However, simulation is not always the best choice. Mathematical analysis, when appropriate to a specific problem, is usually faster and less expensive. Also, it is usually provable as far as the technique is concerned, and the only real question is whether the system is adequately represented by the mathematical model.

Simulation, however, has nothing fixed; there are no boundaries to building a model or making assumptions about the system. Expanding computer power and memory have pushed out the limits of what can be simulated. Further, the continued development of simulation languages and programs—both general-purpose programs (SIMAN, SLAM) and special-purpose (MAP/1, SIMFACTORY)—promises to make the entire process of creating simulation models much easier.

S16.8 SOLVED PROBLEMS

1. To use an old statistical example for simulation, if an urn contains 100 balls, of which 10 percent are green, 40 percent are red, and 50 percent are spotted, develop a simulation model of the process of drawing balls at random from the urn. Each time a ball is drawn and its color noted, it is replaced. Use the following random numbers as you desire.
   Simulate drawing 10 balls from the urn. Show which numbers you have used.

26768	66954	83125	08021
42613	17457	55503	36458
95457	03704	47019	05752
95276	56970	84828	05752

   SOLUTION
   Assign random numbers to the balls to correspond to the percentage present in the urn.

	Random Number
10 green balls	00–09
40 red balls	10–49
50 spotted balls	50–99

Many possible answers exist, depending on how the random numbers were assigned and which numbers were used for the list provided in the problem.

For the random number sequence above and using the first two numbers of those given, we obtain

RN	Color	RN	Color
26	Red	17	Red
42	Red	3	Green
95	Spotted	56	Spotted
95	Spotted	83	Spotted
66	Spotted	55	Spotted

For the 10 there were 1 green, 3 red, and 6 spotted balls—a good estimate based on a sample of only 10!

2. A rural clinic receives a delivery of fresh plasma once each week from a central blood bank. The supply varies according to demand from other clinics and hospitals in the region but ranges between four and nine pints of the most widely used blood type, type O. The number of patients per week requiring this blood varies from zero to four, and each patient may need from one to four pints. Given the following delivery quantities, patient distribution, and demand per patient, what would be the number of pints in excess or short for a six-week period? Use simulation to derive your answer. Consider that plasma is storable and there is currently none on hand.

Delivery Quantities		**Patient Distribution**		**Demand per Patient**	
Pints per Week	**Probability**	**Patients per Week Requiring Blood**	**Probability**	**Pints**	**Probability**
4	0.15	0	0.25	1	0.40
5	0.20	1	0.25	2	0.30
6	0.25	2	0.30	3	0.20
7	0.15	3	0.15	4	0.10
8	0.15	4	0.05		
9	0.10				

SOLUTION

Delivery			**Number of Patients**			**Patient Demand**		
Pints	**Probability**	**Random Number**	**Blood**	**Probability**	**Random Number**	**Pints**	**Probability**	**Random Number**
4	.15	00–14	0	.25	00–24	1	.40	00–39
5	.20	15–34	1	.25	25–49	2	.30	40–69
6	.25	35–59	2	.30	50–79	3	.20	70–89
7	.15	60–74	3	.15	80–94	4	.10	90–99
8	.15	75–89	4	.05	95–99			
9	.10	90–99						

Week No.	Beginning Inventory	Quantity Delivered		Total Blood on Hand	Patients Needing Blood		Quantity Needed			Number of Pints Remaining
		RN	Pints		RN	Patients	Patient	RN	Pints	
1	0	74	7	7	85	3	First	21	6	1
							Second	06	5	1
							Third	71	2	3
2	2	31	5	7	28	1		96	3	4
3	3	02	4	7	72	2	First	12	6	1
							Second	67	4	2
4	4	53	6	10	44	1		23	9	1
5	9	16	5	14	16	0			14	
6	14	40	6	20	83	3	First	65	18	2
							Second	34	17	1
							Third	82	14	3
7	14									

At the end of six weeks, there were 14 pints on hand.

S16.9   REVIEW AND DISCUSSION QUESTIONS

1. Why is simulation often called a technique of last resort?
2. What roles does statistical hypothesis testing play in simulation?
3. What determines whether a simulation model is valid?
4. Must you use a computer to get good information from a simulation? Explain.
5. What methods are used to increment time in a simulation model? How do they work?
6. What are the pros and cons of starting a simulation with the system empty? With the system in equilibrium?
7. Distinguish between known mathematical distribution and empirical distributions. What information is needed to simulate using a known mathematical distribution?
8. What is the importance of run length in simulation? Is a run of 100 observations twice as valid as a run of 50? Explain.

S16.10   PROBLEMS

See IM.

1. CLASSROOM SIMULATION: FISH FORWARDERS
This is a competitive exercise designed to test players' skills at setting inventory ordering rules over a 10-week planning horizon. Maximum profit at the end determines the winner.

Fish Forwarders supplies fresh shrimp to a variety of customers in the New Orleans area. It places orders for cases of shrimp from fleet representatives at the beginning of each week to meet a demand from its customers at the middle of the week. Shrimp are subsequently delivered to Fish Forwarders and then, at the end of the week, to its customers.

Both the supply of shrimp and the demand for shrimp are uncertain. The supply may vary as much as ±10 percent from the amount ordered, and by contract, Fish Forwarders must purchase this supply. The probability associated with this variation is −10 percent, 30 percent of the time; 0 percent, 50 percent of the time; and +10 percent, 20 percent of the time. Weekly demand for shrimp is normally distributed with a mean of 800 cases and standard deviation of 100 cases.

A case of shrimp costs Fish Forwarders $30 and sells for $50. Any shrimp not sold at the end of the week are sold to a cat-food company at $4 per case. Fish Forwarders may, if it

E X H I B I T S16.13 *Simulation Worksheet*

(1)	(2)	(3)		(4)		(5)	(6)	(7)	(8)		(9)
		Orders placed		Orders received		Available (regular and flash-frozen)	Demand (800 + 100Z)	Sales (minimum of demand or available)	Excess		Shortages
Week	Flash-frozen inventory	Regular	Flash-frozen	Regular	Flash-frozen				Regular	Flash	
1											
2											
3											
4											
5											
6											
7		MARDI GRAS				*					
8											
9											
10											
Total											

*Flash-frozen only.

chooses, order the shrimp flash-frozen by the supplier at dockside, but this raises the cost of a case by $4 and, hence, costs Fish Forwarders $34 per case. Flash-freezing enables Fish Forwarders to maintain an inventory of shrimp, but it costs $2 per case per week to store the shrimp at a local icehouse. The customers are indifferent to whether they get regular or flash-frozen shrimp. Fish Forwarders figures that its shortage cost is equal to its markup; that is, each case demanded but not available costs the company $50 − $30 or $20.

Procedure for play. The game requires that each week a decision be made as to how many cases to order of regular shrimp and flash-frozen shrimp. The number ordered may be any amount. The instructor plays the role of referee and supplies the random numbers. The steps in playing the game are as follows:

a. Decide on the order amount of regular shrimp or flash-frozen shrimp and enter the figures in column 3 of the worksheet. (See Exhibit S16.13.) Assume that there is no opening inventory of flash-frozen shrimp.

b. Determine the amount that arrives and enter it under "Orders received." To accomplish this, the referee draws a random number from a uniform random number table (such as that in Appendix B) and finds its associated level of variation from the following random number intervals: 00 to 29 = −10 percent, 30 to 79 = 0 percent, and 80 to 99 = +10 percent. If the random number is, say, 13, the amount of variation will be −10 percent. Thus if you decide to order 1,000 regular cases of shrimp and 100 flash-frozen cases, the amount you would actually receive would be 1,000 − 0.10(1,000), or 900 regular cases, and 100 − 0.10(100), or 90 flash-frozen cases. (Note that the variation is the same for both regular and flash-frozen shrimp.) These amounts are then entered in column 4.

c. Add the amount of flash-frozen shrimp in inventory (if any) to the quantity of regular and flash-frozen shrimp just received and enter this amount in column 5. This would be 990, using the figures provided earlier.

d. Determine the demand for shrimp. To accomplish this, the referee draws a random normal deviate value from Exhibit S16.4 and enters it into the equation at the top of column 6. Thus if the deviate value is −1.76, demand for the week is 800 + 100(−1.76), or 624.

E X H I B I T S16.14

Profit from Fish Forwarders' Operations

Revenue from sales ($50 × Col. 7)	$ _____	
Revenue from salvage ($4 × Col. 8 reg.)	$ _____	
Total revenue		$ _____
Cost of regular purchases ($30 × Col. 4 reg.)	$ _____	
Cost of flash-frozen purchases ($34 × Col. 4 flash)	$ _____	
Cost of holding flash-frozen shrimp ($2 × Col. 8 flash)	$ _____	
Cost of shortages ($20 × Col. 9)	$ _____	
Total cost		$ _____
Profit		$ _____

e. Determine the amount sold. This will be the lesser of the amount demanded (column 6) and the amount available (column 5). Thus, if a player has received 990 and demand is 624, the quantity entered will be 624 (with 990 − 624, or 366 left over).

f. Determine the excess. The amount of excess is simply that quantity remaining after demand for a given week is filled. Always assume that regular shrimp are sold before the flash-frozen. Thus if we use the 366 figure obtained in *(e)*, the excess would include all the original 90 cases of flash-frozen shrimp.

g. Determine shortages. This is simply the amount of unsatisfied demand each period, and it occurs only when demand is greater than sales. (Since all customers use the shrimp within the week in which they are delivered, back orders are not relevant.) The amount of shortages (in cases of shrimp) is entered in column 9.

Profit determination. Exhibit S16.14 is provided for determining the profit achieved at the end of play. The values to be entered in the table are obtained by summing the relevant columns of Exhibit S16.13 and making the calculations.

Assignment. Simulate operations for a total of 10 weeks. It is suggested that a 10-minute break be taken at the end of Week 5 and the players attempt to evaluate how they may improve their performance. They might also wish to plan an ordering strategy for the week of Mardi Gras, when no shrimp will be supplied.

2. The manager of a small post office is concerned that her growing township is overloading the one-window service being offered. She obtains sample data on 100 individuals who arrive for service:

Time between Arrivals (minutes)	Frequency	Service Time (minutes)	Frequency
1	8	1.0	12
2	35	1.5	21
3	34	2.0	36
4	17	2.5	19
5	6	3.0	7
	100	3.5	5
			100

Using the following random number sequence, simulate six arrivals; estimate the average customer waiting time and the average idle time for clerks.

RN: 08, 74, 24, 34, 45, 86, 31, 32, 45, 21, 10, 67, 60, 17, 60, 87, 74, 96

3. Thomas Magnus, a private investigator, has been contacted by a potential client in Kamalo, Molokai. The call came just in time because Magnus is down to his last $10. Employment,

however, is conditional on Magnus meeting the client at Kamalo within eight hours. Magnus, presently at the Masters' residence in Kipahulu, Maui, has three alternative ways to get to Kamalo. Magnus may

a. Drive to the native village of Honokahua and take an outrigger to Kamalo.

b. Drive to Honokahua and swim the 10 miles across Pailolo Channel to Kamalo.

c. Drive to Hana and ask his friend T. C. to fly him by helicopter to Kamalo.

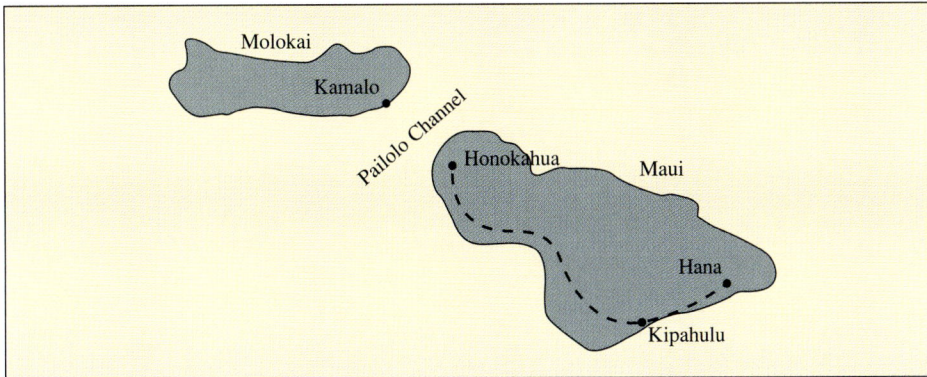

If option *a* is chosen, driving times to Honokahua are given to Distribution 1. Once at Honokahua, Magnus must negotiate with the friendly Tai natives. Negotiations always include a few Mai Tais, so if Magnus begins to negotiate, swimming becomes impossible. Negotiations center on how much each of the three outrigger crew members will be paid. Negotiation time, crew pay, and outrigger travel time are Distributions 3, 4, and 5, respectively. You may assume each crew member is paid the same amount. If crew pay totals more than $10, Magnus is out of luck—trip time may then be taken to be infinity.

If option *b* is chosen, driving times to Honokahua and swimming times are given in Distributions 1 and 6.

If option *c* is chosen, driving times to Hana are given in Distribution 2. T. C., however, is at the airport only 10 percent of the time. If T. C. is not at the airport, Magnus will wait for him to arrive. Magnus's waiting time is given by Distribution 8. T. C. may refuse to fly for the $10 Magnus has available; Magnus puts the probability of T. C. refusing to fly for $10 at 30 percent. You may assume negotiation time is zero. If T. C. refuses, Magnus will drive to Honokahua via Kipahula and swim to Kamalo. Helicopter flying times are given in Distribution 7.

Simulate each of the three alternative transportation plans *twice* and, based on your simulation results, calculate the average trip time for each plan. Use the following random numbers in the order they appear; do not skip any random numbers.

RN: 7, 3, 0, 4, 0, 5, 3, 5, 6, 1, 6, 6, 4, 8, 4, 9, 0, 7, 7, 1, 7, 0, 6, 8, 8, 7, 9, 0, 1, 2, 9, 7, 3, 2, 3, 8, 6, 0, 6, 0, 5, 9, 7, 9, 6, 4, 7, 2, 8, 7, 8, 1, 7, 0, 5

Distribution 1: Time to drive from Kipahulu to Honokahua (hours)

Time	Probability	RN
1	.2	0–1
1.5	.6	2–7
2	.2	8–9

Distribution 2: Time to drive from Kipahulu to Hana and vice versa (hours)

Time	Probability	RN
.5	.2	0–1
1	.7	2–8
1.5	.1	9

Distribution 3: Negotiation time (hours)

Time	Probability	RN
1	.2	0–1
1.5	.3	2–4
2	.3	5–7
2.5	.2	8–9

Distribution 4: Outrigger pay per crew member

Pay	Probability	RN
$2	.3	0–2
3	.3	3–5
4	.4	6–9

Distribution 5: Outrigger travel time from Honokahua to Kamalo (hours)

Time	Probability	RN
3	.1	0
4	.5	1–5
5	.4	6–9

Distribution 6: Time to swim from Honokahua to Kamalo (hours)

Time	Probability	RN
5	.2	0–1
6	.6	2–7
7	.2	8–9

Distribution 7: Time to fly from Hana to Kamalo (hours)

Time	Probability	RN
1	.1	0
1.5	.7	1–7
2	.2	8–9

Distribution 8: Magnus's waiting time at airport (hours)

Time	Probability	RN
1	.1	0
2	.2	1–2
3	.4	3–6
4	.3	7–9

4. A bank of machines in a manufacturing shop breaks down according to the following interarrival-time distribution. The time it takes one repairperson to complete the repair of a machine is given in the service-time distribution:

Interarrival Time (hours)	P(X)	RN		Service Time (hours)	P(X)	RN
.5	.30	0–29		.5	.25	0–24
1.0	.22	30–51		1.0	.20	25–44
1.5	.16	52–67		2.0	.25	45–69
2.0	.10	68–77		3.0	.15	70–84
3.0	.14	78–91		4.0	.10	85–94
4.0	.08	92–99		5.0	.05	95–99
	1.00				1.00	

Simulate the breakdown of five machines. Calculate the average machine downtime using two repairpersons and the following random number sequence. (Both repairpersons cannot work on the same machine.)

RN: 30, 81, 02, 91, 51, 08, 28, 44, 86, 84, 29, 08, 37, 34, 99

5. Jennifer Jones owns a small candy store she operates herself. A study was made observing the time between customers coming into the store, and the time that Ms. Jones took to serve them. The following data were collected from 100 customers observed:

Interarrival Time (minutes)	Number of Observations	Service Time (minutes)	Number of Observations
1	5	1	10
2	10	2	15
3	10	3	15
4	15	4	20
5	15	5	15
6	20	6	10
7	10	7	8
8	8	8	4
9	5	9	2
10	2	10	1

Simulate the system (all of the arrivals and services) until 10 customers pass through the system and are serviced by Ms. Jones.

How long does the average customer spend in the system? Use Appendix B to obtain random numbers.

6. A professional football coach has six running backs on his squad. He wants to evaluate how injuries might affect his stock of running backs. A minor injury causes a player to be removed from the game and miss only the next game. A major injury puts the player out of action for the rest of the season. The probability of a major injury in a game is 0.05. There is at most one major injury per game. The probability distribution of minor injuries per game is

Number of Injuries	Probability
0	.2
1	.5
2	.22
3	.05
4	.025
5	.005
	1.000

Injuries seem to happen in a completely random manner, with no discernible pattern over the season. A season is 10 games.

Using the following random numbers, simulate the fluctuations in the coach's stock of running backs over the season. Assume that he hires no additional running backs during the season.

RN: 044, 392, 898, 615, 986, 959, 558, 353, 577, 866, 305, 813, 024, 189, 878, 023, 285, 442, 862, 848, 060, 131, 963, 874, 805, 105, 452

7. At Tucson Mills, minor breakdowns of machines occur frequently. The occurrence of breakdowns and the service time to fix the machines are randomly distributed. Management is concerned with minimizing the cost of breakdowns. The cost per hour for the machines to be down is $40. The cost of service repairpersons is $12 per hour. A preliminary study has produced the following data on times between successive breakdowns and their service times:

Relative frequency of breakdowns

Time between breakdowns (in minutes)	4	5	6	7	8	9
Relative frequency	.10	.30	.25	.20	.10	.05

Relative frequency of service times

Service time (in minutes)	4	5	6	7	8	9
Relative frequency	.10	.40	.20	.15	.10	.05

Perform a simulation of 30 breakdowns under two conditions: with one service repairperson and with two service repairpersons.

Use the following random number sequence to determine time between breakdowns:

RN: 85, 16, 65, 76, 93, 99, 65, 70, 58, 44, 02, 85, 01, 97, 63, 52, 53, 11, 62, 28, 84, 82, 27, 20, 39, 70, 26, 21, 41, 81

Use the following random number sequence to determine service times:

RN: 68, 26, 85, 11, 16, 26, 95, 67, 97, 73, 75, 64, 26, 45, 01, 87, 20, 01, 19, 36, 69, 89, 81, 81, 02, 05, 10, 51, 24, 36

a. Using the results of the simulations, calculate

(1) The total idle time for the service repairpersons under each condition.

(2) The total delay caused by waiting for a service repairperson to begin working on a breakdown.

b. Determine the lowest-cost approach.

8. Jethro's service station has one gasoline pump. Because everyone in Kornfield County drives big cars, there is room at the station for only three cars, including the car at the pump. Cars arriving when there are already three cars at the station drive on to another station. Use the following probability distributions to simulate the arrival of four cars to Jethro's station:

Interarrival Time (minutes)	P(X)	RN		Service Time (minutes)	P(X)	RN
10	.40	0–39		5	.45	0–44
20	.35	40–74		10	.30	45–74
30	.20	75–94		15	.20	75–94
40	.05	95–99		20	.05	95–99

Calculate the average time cars spend at the station using the following random number sequence:

RN: 99, 00, 73, 09, 38, 53, 72, 91

9. You have been hired as a consultant by a supermarket chain to provide an answer to the basic question: How many items per customer should be permitted in the fast checkout line? This is no trivial question for the chain's management; your findings will be the basis for corporate policy for all 2,000 stores. The vice president of operations has given you one month to do the study and two assistants to help you gather the data.

In starting this study, you decide to avoid queuing theory as the tool for analysis (because of your concern about the reliability of its assumptions) and instead opt for simulation. Given the following data, explain in detail how you would go about your analysis stating (1) the criteria you would use in making your recommendation, (2) what additional data you would need to set up your simulation, (3) how you would gather the preliminary data, (4) how you would set up the problem for simulation, and (5) which factors would affect the applicability of your findings to all of the stores.

Store locations:	The United States and Canada
Hours of operation:	16 per day
Average store size:	9 checkout stands including fast checkout
Available checkers:	7 to 10 (Some engage in stocking activities when not at checkout stand.)

S16.11   SELECTED BIBLIOGRAPHY

Conway, R., W-L. Maxwell, J.D. McClain, and S.L. Worona. *XCELL & Factory Modeling System Release 4.0.* 3rd ed. San Francisco: Scientific Press, 1990.

Haider, S. Wali, and Jerry Banks. "Simulation Software Products for Analyzing Manufacturing Systems." *Industrial Engineering* 18, no. 7 (July 1986), pp. 98–103.

MicroAnalysis and Design Software Inc., "Hospital Overcrowding Solutions are Found with Simulation," *Industrial Engineering,* December 1993, p. 557.

Law, Averill M., and W. David Kelton. *Simulation Modeling and Analysis.* 2d ed. New York: McGraw-Hill, 1991.

Payne, James A. *Introduction to Simulation.* New York: McGraw-Hill, 1982.

Solomon, Susan L. *Simulation of Waiting Lines.* Englewood Cliffs, NJ: Prentice Hall, 1983.

Swedish, Julian. "Simulation Brings Productivity Enhancements to the Social Security Administration." *Industrial Engineering.* (May 1993), pp. 28–30.

Woolsey, G. "Whatever Happened to Simple Simulation? A Question and Answer." *Interfaces* 9, no. 4 (August 1979), pp. 9–11.

Chapter

17

Materials Management and Purchasing

CHAPTER OUTLINE

KEY TERMS

Purchasing

Procurement Process

Supply Management

Materials Management

Logistics

Value Density

Value Chain

Strategic Partnership

World Class Purchasing

Just-in-Time Purchasing

Single-Source Supplier

Qualified Supplier

Quick Response (QR)

Efficient Consumer Response (ECR)

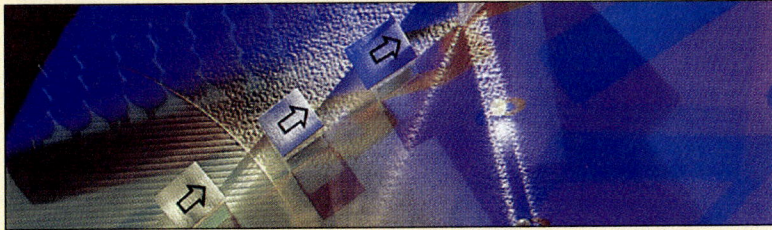

Barbara Serdar sells lots of men's suits at Macy's in the cavernous Mall of America near Minneapolis. But the trim 5-foot-2 clerk says she can hardly find anything in the store—or the mall, for that matter—that fits her. "By the time I get to the rack, they're all gone."

Sorry, Ms. Serdar, but the slim pickings in size 4 reflect the strategy retailers are using these days to improve profits in this sluggish economy.

In good times retailers use a sort of bell curve of sizes with the greatest number of items in the midrange. For an estimated 35 to 40 percent of women, that means sizes 6, 8, and 10. For men it's waist sizes 30 to 36 inches. In tough times, retailers snip away at the ends of the spectrum—women's sizes 4 and 14, for example.

While shrinking sizes may be a wise inventory control move, many retailers are passing up sales. The leading cause for a lost sale, say experts, is failure to carry the right sizes. The giant Gap Inc. chain, for example, carries nothing shorter than a 30-inch inseam in its popular men's khaki pants. Bergdorf Goodman, the New York fashion emporium, recognizes that similar inventory cuts have hurt business.

Not all retailers are trimming down in the sizing game. Nordstrom Inc. stores still carry 61 different sizes of men's shirts, though only 24 sizes are needed to cover the normal size range. Levi Strauss & Co. has made a wide range of size offerings a cornerstone of its successful strategy in pushing its Dockers men's pants. These companies, though, are the exception.

Our opening vignette presents the problem in deciding how many sizes a retail clothing store should carry. What is not mentioned is the variety of styles, colors, and patterns it should carry for each size. Currently, retailers tend to carry a larger variety of limited sizes—but should they carry a narrower variety in a wider range of sizes?

Some interesting questions could be asked about available products in general. Do we really need more than 100 different automobiles, each of which has annual changes? Do we need 100 different pasta sauces or 100 different shampoos? From a resource utilization and efficiency standpoint, the fewer the better. Manufacturers have always preferred long runs of fewer product types.

Such marketing decisions make purchasing and materials management a large problem. As the variety of products increases, the problems of forecasting, purchasing, stocking, and distribution increase exponentially. While demand for an entire product line is forecastable with some accuracy, individual item demands vary widely. The more items in the product line, the more difficult is the forecasting, purchasing, and distribution.

In manufacturing, purchased items account for 60 to 70 percent of the cost of goods sold. Many recent changes in purchasing, materials handling, and distribution systems have been brought on by

1. Competitive pressures from foreign firms.
2. Elevation of product quality to a very high level of importance.
3. International marketing and international purchasing.
4. Trends toward choosing sole-source suppliers for long-term relationships.
5. Rapid changes in product varieties and ranges making speed of delivery to the market essential.
6. Shortening of product life cycles, necessitating knowledge and control of inventories in the various pipelines.
7. Adoption of just-in-time production, which has changed the supplier relationships and also focused on reducing inventories.
8. Trends in the legal system holding manufacturers liable for product failures even though causes may be outside the production system itself.

In this chapter we discuss the purchasing and materials management functions, problems in global purchasing, quality issues, strategic issues, just-in-time purchasing, and electronic information flow.

17.1 DEFINITIONS

To begin, we need some definitions:

Purchasing. The department that traditionally acquires materials and services from outside suppliers.

Procurement process. The process of designing, specifying, sourcing, ordering, and disposing of materials, services, and equipment.

Supply management. A new process responsible for the design, development, optimization, and management of both the internal and external components of the organization's supply system. At a strategic level, this includes taking advantage of supply opportunities maintaining relationships with suppliers, and stressing continuous improvement.[1]

Materials management. Defined by the American Production and Inventory Control Society (APICS) as

The grouping of management functions supporting the complete cycle of material flow, from the purchase and internal control of production materials to the planning and control of work-in-process to the warehousing, shipping and distribution of the finished product.[2]

Logistics. A term often used interchangeably with *materials management.* APICS has defined *logistics* in two contexts:

In an industrial context, logistics refers to the art and science of obtaining and distributing materials and product. In a military sense (where it has greater usage), its meaning can also include the movement of personnel.[3]

In this text we favor using the term *materials management.* This emphasizes the importance of the materials management function, which extends from the purchase of materials from vendors through the system and out to delivery to customers. Interestingly, firms differ in how they group these functions under a single materials management manager. Some firms, for example, may leave transportation outside of the materials management activities.

Purchasing manager. An individual working for any private, public, or nonprofit organization who performs and/or has primary responsibility for the procurement of materials, equipment, or services for that organization. The size of the purchasing manager's department may range from one person to several thousand. The commodities may be purchased either for the use of the organization, for the manufacture or development of other materials, or for resale to other organizations or the general public.

To perform this function, the purchasing manager will engage in, or else will have direct responsibility for some or all of the following functions: reviewing procurement requests; soliciting and evaluating proposals; analyzing current and potential suppliers; conducting negotiations; executing, implementing, and administering contracts; developing forecasts and procurement strategies; supervising and/or monitoring the flow and storage of materials; and developing working relationships with suppliers and with other departments within the organization.

The purchasing manager has or shares responsibility for the administrative aspects of the purchasing department, and usually performs personnel functions such as hiring, training, and supervising other purchasing personnel.[4]

World class purchasing. A subjective phrase describing the quality of a buying or selling organization in all relevant areas, including supply management, cost and

---

[1]David N. Burt and Michael F. Doyle, *The American Keiretsu: A Strategic Weapon for Global Competitiveness* (Homewood, IL: Business One Irwin, 1993), p. 6.

[2]APICS Dictionary, 6th ed. (Falls Church, VA: American Production and Inventory Control Society, 1987). p. 29.

[3]Ibid. p. 26.

[4]Eugene W. Muller, *Job Analysis Identifying the Task of Purchasing* (Tempe, AZ: Center for Advanced Purchasing Studies/National Association of Purchasing Management, 1992), p. 66.

quality management, and order and invoice purchasing. Due to the tendency of world-class organizations to improve continuously, the term world class is an ever-moving target.[5]

17.2   MATERIALS MANAGEMENT IN MANUFACTURING

Materials management has become so important in the order fulfillment process that the functions it encompasses have increased and its hierarchical position in the organization has been raised. This section covers organizational placement of materials handling and some aspects of inventory control, such as materials movement systems and value density.

Organizational Placement of Materials Management

There is wide divergence of opinion about many aspects of materials management: where the function should be placed, what its responsibilities are, and whether it should be centralized or decentralized. While the final choice must always relate to the needs of the specific firm in question, the high cost of materials probably will support the current trend, which is to equate the materials management function with the other main functions of the organization. Such placement ensures executive-level attention to materials and gives the materials manager enough clout to be effective. A partial organization chart reflects this placement in Exhibit 17.1. Note the peculiar positioning of production planning and control. This area is crucial to manufacturing. As such, it may be assigned organizationally to materials management, but functionally to manufacturing, and physically located in the manufacturing area.

Production planning and control is responsible for the entire manufacturing system. It schedules jobs by date, routes them through the varied resources to do the work, decides on the inventory levels, and determines process batch and transfer batch sizes. In other words, production planning and control sees that the manufacturing job gets done. This is why it is located within Manufacturing so that personnel can closely observe the production system and respond appropriately.

E X H I B I T 17.1

Organization Chart Showing Materials Management Functions

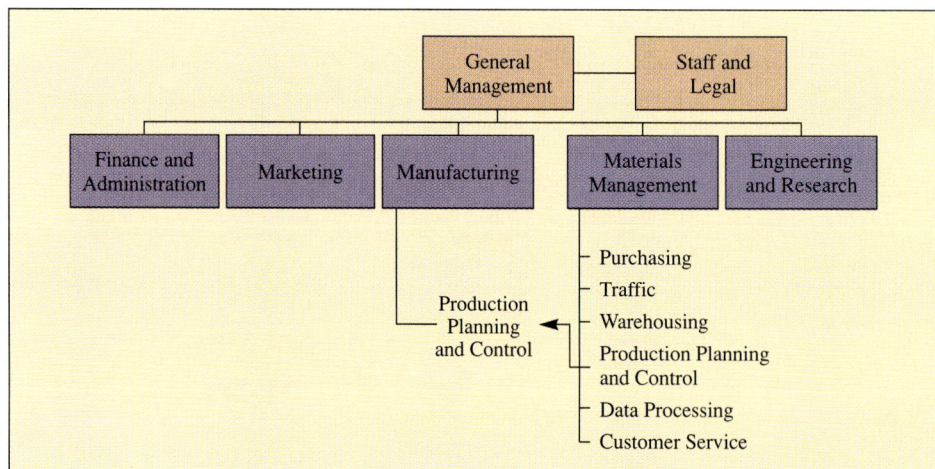

----

[5]David N. Burt, op cit., p. 7.

Different organizational structures and the placement of purchasing and materials management are possible depending on the purpose and the potential impact.

Product Development   Mendez and Pearson present some ideas for a new product team where purchasing and materials management play an important supporting role.[6] Mendez and Pearson state that purchasing and material management's key contributions are in the acquisition of suppliers that provide a continuous supply of materials, components, and services in accordance with quality and relevant performance measures; analysis and evaluation of make-or-buy decisions and the development of strategic alliances and partnerships; development of proposals for alternative materials; determination and timing of supplier involvement; purchase of tooling and equipment; and provision of insights into the competitive supply environment. As discussed in Chapter 3, suppliers are also critical team members who assist through initial product design suggestions, technological contributions, and quality ensurance considerations, all of which contribute to efficient manufacturability and minimization of the design-to-market cycle.[7]

Materials Handling Systems

The demand for large automated storage systems has been decreasing for the past few years, primarily for two reasons: (1) the trend toward reducing the quantities of inventories stored and (2) the trend toward just-in-time systems, which reduces work in process. This has, however, increased the need for smaller and more flexible systems that can be disassembled and moved easily.

Even though the trend toward just-in-time systems has lessened demand for large-scale automated storage systems, demand for finished-goods warehousing systems has held constant. At the same time, new types of materials handling and storage systems have been developed.

John Hill describes some of the techniques:

1. Unit-load automatic storage and retrieval systems (AS/RS). Major developments in this area include computer simulation programs that test various rules for the handling materials to try to improve productivity. Also, older systems are being upgraded to enable automatic identification of items and interfacing with automatic guided vehicles (AGV).

2. Miniloads, microloads, and tote stackers. With the trend toward maintaining small inventories, control of parts and kits is critical. Users of these devices are the automotive, airline, and electronics industries.

3. Carousels. Vertical and horizontal carousels move the inventory storage system to the worker. Carousels have high potential because of their very low maintenance costs—as low as 0.1 percent of the original cost annually. Carousels are easily installed or, if need be, disassembled and moved to new locations.

4. Flow racks and paperless picking. When workers pick items in conventional warehouses for orders, the potential for error is high. To increase productivity and reduce errors, some companies have assigned workers to specific inventory areas and have sent information about orders directly to them, perhaps via a CRT screen. The worker collects the needed items in the work area and presses a button to send the order on to the next inventory location, where more items

---

[6]Eduardo G. Mendez and John N. Pearson, "Purchasing's Role in Product Development: The Case for Time-Based Strategies," *International Journal of Purchasing and Materials Management*, Winter 1994, pp. 3–12.

[7]Ibid., p. 7.

are added. Results have shown error reductions of 90 percent or more, and up to 50 percent reduction in the average time to assemble the order.[8]

Demand for the materials handling systems and controls just described is expected to increase rapidly. Use of automatic guided vehicles is growing at 30 percent per year, partly because of the ease of installation. They are also being used as transporting devices to move material from one workstation to the next.

Value Density (Value per Unit of Weight)

A common and important decision in purchasing is whether an item should be shipped by air or by ground transportation. While it may seem oversimplified, the value of an item per pound of weight—**value density**—is an important measure when deciding where items should be stocked geographically and how they should be shipped. In a classic Harvard case study, the Sorenson Research Company must decide whether to stock inventory for shipment at major warehouses, minor warehouses, or garage warehouses, and whether to ship by ground or air carrier.[9] Analysis shows that the time saved by shipping by air can be justified if the shipping cost is appropriate. The decision involves a trade-off: the savings of reduced transit time versus the higher cost to ship. Obviously, the solution involves a combination of methods.

We can approach the problem by examining a specific situation. Consider, for example, the cost of shipping from Boston to Tucson. Assume that the inventory cost is 30 percent per year of the product value (which includes cost of capital, insurance, decrease in warehouse costs, etc.), that regular UPS shipments take eight days, and that we are considering second-day air service with Federal Express. We can set up a comparison table as in Exhibit 17.2.

The problem then becomes comparing the additional cost of transportation to the savings of six days. Logically we can make the general statement that expensive items can

---

[8]John M. Hill, "Changing Profile of Material Handling System," parts 1 and 2, *Industrial Engineering* 18, no. 11 (November 1986), pp. 68–73, and 18, no. 12 (December 1986), pp. 26–29.

[9]W. Earl Sasser et al., *Cases in Operations Management* (Homewood, IL: Richard D. Irwin, 1982). pp. 314–31.

E X H I B I T 17.2   *Sorenson Research Company Shipping Cost Comparison*

Shipping Weight (pounds)	United Parcel Service (8 days to deliver)	Federal Express (2 days to deliver)	Cost Savings with UPS	Break-Even Product Value	Break-Even Product Value (per pound)
1	$1.91	$11.50	$ 9.59	$1,944.64	$1,944.68
2	2.37	12.50	10.13	2,054.14	1,027.07
3	2.78	13.50	10.72	2,173.78	724.59
4	3.20	14.50	11.30	2,291.39	572.85
5	3.54	15.50	11.96	2,425.22	485.04
6	3.88	16.50	12.62	2,559.06	426.51
7	4.28	17.50	13.22	2,680.72	382.96
8	4.70	18.50	13.80	2,798.33	349.79
9	5.12	19.50	14.38	2,915.94	323.99
10	5.53	20.50	14.97	3,035.58	303.56

be sent by air from the factory warehouse, while lower-value items can be stocked at lower-level warehouses or shipped by a less expensive method.

$$\text{Regular shipment costs} - \text{Air shipping cost} = \text{Shipping cost savings}$$

At break-even, the cost savings is equal to inventory carrying cost.

$$\text{Cost savings} = \text{Inventory carrying cost} = \frac{\text{Item value} \times 0.30 \times 6 \text{ days}}{365 \text{ days per year}}$$

Solving for item value,

$$\text{Item value} = \frac{365 \times \text{Cost savings}}{0.30 \times 6}$$

The different cost savings in the fourth column of Exhibit 17.2 are substituted into the item value equation for each shipping weight. This gives the product value in the fifth column. Dividing by the package weight gives the breakeven product value per pound in the last column. The exhibit indicates that any item whose value is greater than that amount should be sent by air. For example, a five-pound shipment of integrated circuits whose average value is $500 per pound should be shipped by Federal Express.

17.3   PURCHASING

Concerning the control of costs, purchasing is by far the most important area in the firm because two-thirds of the cost of goods sold are purchased items. We say elsewhere that design has the major impact on costs. But that is true only when the design, manufacturing, and purchasing relationships are not run correctly. It is purchasing's responsibility to know what is out there. Purchasing needs to know materials, performance, availability, and suppliers. It needs to know (as it should know) which features of purchased products are cosmetic and which features are functional. This directs its department to search for sources that support requirements.

In this section we discuss value-based purchasing, the purchasing organization, the firm as its own internal supplier, the issue of single sourcing versus multiple sourcing, long-term manufacturer–supplier relationships, and some specific issues in just-in-time purchasing.

E X H I B I T 17.3
The Value Chain Concept

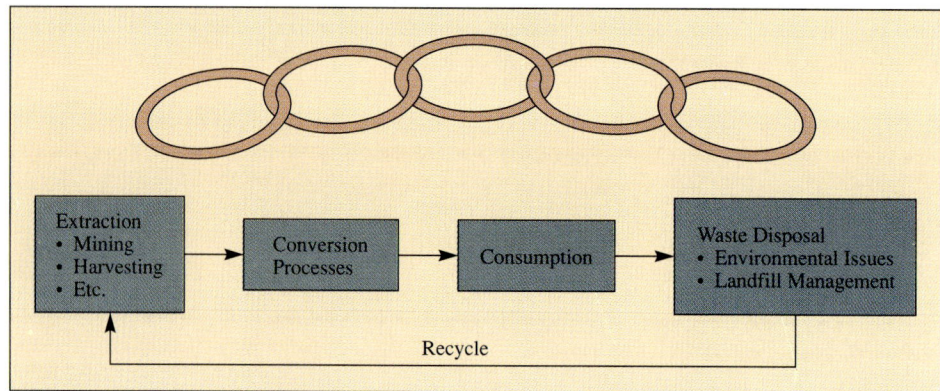

Source: David N. Burt and Michael F. Doyal, *The American Keiretsu: A Strategic Weapon for Global Competitiveness* (Homewood, IL: Business One Irwin, 1993), p. 9.

Value-Based Purchasing

In a **value chain** system, each link must add value. This value chain concept can be applied to many situations. Exhibit 17.3, for example, shows the complete cycle from earth and back to earth. Raw materials are extracted from earth via mining, agriculture, and other means; they are processed through some production method; they are then consumed such as by a customer; and they are disposed of (either recycled or stored as waste).

The value chain applied to an organization represents the organization as a series of links in a chain. The firm is in the center with its internal links. Upstream links involve the firm's suppliers; the firm's customers lie downstream. Value chain management identifies the interactions between each link in the chain and the links' roles in improving value. When applied to purchasing, the value chain concept attempts to create value through purchasing decisions, rather than focusing on cost savings through vendor selection and contract negotiations. In one case value may be added by improving product quality, in another case by faster response between links; in still another, it may be through better sourcing, inventory control, or higher-quality materials. Burt and Doyle give an example to illustrate a value chain using truck tires:

> Several years ago, the Japanese decided to manufacture truck tires for domestic use. Large Japanese tire manufacturers sent representatives to America to see how truck tires were designed and manufactured. They found that America produced an 8-ply bias-belted tire for truck applications, which was 12-ply rated and would carry 5,000 pounds. These tires could be recapped an average of one time. The Japanese decided to specify 14-ply truck tires for their domestic use. Obviously, 14-ply tires are far more expensive to produce than 8-ply tires, so why would otherwise intelligent engineers overdesign/specify truck tires to such an extent? The answer contains an example of the value-chain strategic thinking that is becoming so critical. The Japanese run their domestic tires until the tread is gone; then they sell the tire shells for around $75 to tire recappers in America. Fourteen-ply tire shells are in high demand as recaps. These tires can be recapped three or four times before they are sent into America's landfills.[10]

---

[10]Burt and Doyle, *American Keiretsu,* pp. 8–9.

Eugene Muller conducted a survey that updates a previous study by Harold Fearon.[11,12] Muller's survey differs significantly from Fearon's since that survey studied 297 large firms, whereas Muller's survey covered 1,541 persons employed in firms with a wide spectrum of sizes in eight sectors: manufacturing (U.S.), U.S. government/prime contractor, state/local government, institutional (primarily education and hospitals), service (primarily utilities, transportation, communication, insurance, banking), retail (wholesale, retail-resale, retail-nonresale), food (primarily food manufacturers, restaurants, and food distributors), and manufacturing (Europe). The survey was sent to randomly selected members of the National Association of Purchasing Managers.

The Purchasing Organization

The purposes of the survey were to compare purchasing managers' roles in various public and private sectors, and to update their duties. Here are some personal characteristics of the 1,541 respondents:

Gender	*Percentage*
Male	74.7%
Female	26.3

Job Title	**Percentage**
Manager/Director	58.8%
Senior Buyer	23.3
Intermediate Buyer	12
Executive/VP	4
Junior Buyer	1.9

Education	**Percentage**
Bachelors degree	47.7%
Some college	30.4
Master's degree	14.4
High School	5.9
Law degree	.8
Doctorate	.5
Some high school	.3

Number of personnel in respondents organization
Mean 28   Range 1-3,000

Number of personnel supervised by the respondent
Mean 6.1   Range 0-326

Years in present position
Mean 5.2   Range 1-40

Years with present employer
Mean 10.7   Range 1-65

Years in purchasing
Mean 13.3   Range 1-44

As a result of the survey, a list of 69 tasks were developed along with a description of the knowledge areas required by each task. Here is a summary of the areas where purchasing managers were heavily involved; examples of the tasks are shown in parentheses:

- Procurement requests (review requests according to needs, budget, and vendor sources).
- Solicitation and evaluation of proposals (request quote).
- Supplier analysis (evaluate suppliers).
- Negotiation process (prepare strategies and negotiate product prices, delivery, etc.).
- Contract execution, implementation, and administration (prepare and follow contracts through).
- Forecasting and strategies (develop forecasts and purchasing strategies).

---

[11]Muller, *Job Analysis*, pp. 1–68.
[12]Harold E. Fearon, "Organizational Relationships in Purchasing," *Journal of Purchasing and Materials Management*, Winter 1988, pp. 5–10.

- Material flows (supervise and route incoming materials).
- Considerations for enhancing purchasing performance (find new sources of supply, make changes in policy, implement an MRP system).
- External and internal relationships (develop relationships with suppliers and other firms and agencies).
- Administrative aspects of the Purchasing Department (develop goals, budgets).
- Personnel issues (conduct hiring, supervision, evaluation).

Only about half of the respondents were involved with inventory management issues (such as organizing and storing materials, and reviewing inventory).

The Firm as a Supplier

As cartoon character Pogo might have said, "We have found our supplier, and it is us." Manufacturing firms usually view themselves as buyers; that is, they purchase components, parts, and materials, and then they produce products and services. But who buys the components, parts, products, and services the firm produces? Manufacturing firms rarely sell directly to the ultimate consumer; some buyers are manufacturing firms that buy products and services and incorporate them into their own output. Other buyers are wholesalers, retailers, and distribution firms who buy the products and then distribute them further down the chain toward the ultimate consumers.

What difference does it make whether the firm acts as the buyer from suppliers or a supplier to other buyers? Buyers talk about such things as schedules, lot sizes, costs, lead times, and just-in-time delivery. We often take this as a given while finding suppliers who comply with our demands. As a supplier, however, the shoe is on the other foot. Lot-size schedules sent to us by our customers may not fit our MRP schedules; the just-in-time deliveries that we demand from our vendors may not be compatible with our job-shop production.

Randy Myer has made some interesting points concerning the need to understand the customer, to be able to evaluate the customer's costs, and even to decide whether the customer is worth keeping.[13] He reminds us that the balance of power in some areas is changing from the supplier to the buyer. In the retail business for example, average net return is 1 percent of sales. Suppliers average 4 percent net return! In the United Kingdom, the reverse is true in food retailing; retailers average 4 percent and suppliers 1 percent.

Myer suggests that firms should evaluate customers similarly to how they calculate their own return on assets. Companies can measure the marketing, selling, and product development costs as well as asset investments in inventory and receivables that they can attribute to each customer. Further actions may then be indicated; these range from promoting greater efforts to further develop high-return customers to severing relationships with other customers.

Exhibit 17.4 shows interesting findings by a package goods company: Profitability is not a function of customer size; rather, profitability is a function of customer growth rate, though negatively. Fast-growing companies take advantage of their suppliers in pressuring for cost reductions, taking full advantage of return allowances, or demanding just-in-time deliveries, payment schedules, and so on. The result of this effort to evaluate customers is better understanding of the customer, of the customer's needs, of where lines should be drawn, and of what deviations are possible.

---

[13]Randy Myer, "Suppliers–Manage Your Customers," *Harvard Business Review,* November–December 1989, pp. 160–68.

As a packaged-goods company found, profitability is usually not a function of customer size

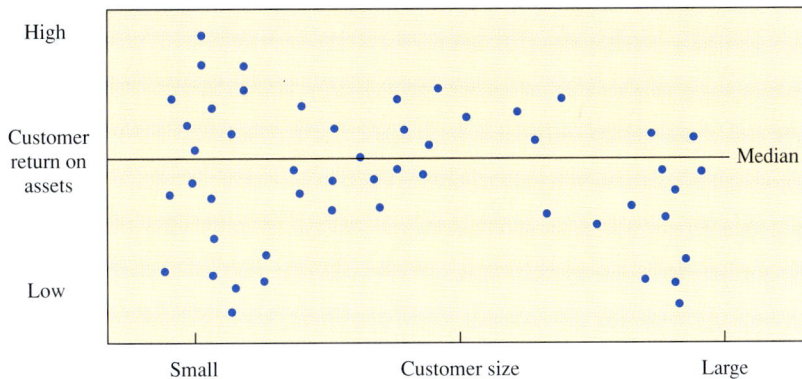

... but a function of customer growth rate

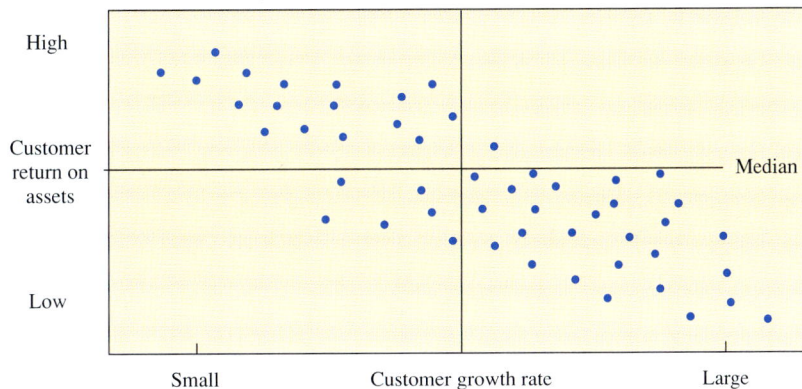

Note: Each dot represents one customer.

Source: Randy Myer, "Suppliers—Manage Your Customers," *Harvard Business Review,* November–December, 1989 p. 165.

Value Analysis

An approach widely used by purchasing departments is value analysis (VA). The basic idea is to compare the function performed by a purchased item with its cost in an attempt to find a lower-cost alternative. Exhibit 17.5 summarizes this approach. We must stress, though, that cost is only one issue in the broad scheme of things. Other factors that we discuss later include quality, delivery performance, technical knowledge, and compatibility.

Partnership Relationships: Buyer–Supplier

A **strategic partnership** between a buying firm and a supplying firm is defined as a continuing relationship involving a commitment over an extended time period, an exchange of information, and acknowledgment of the risks and rewards of the relationship.

In addition to cost, quality, and delivery reliability, supplier selection criteria includes factors such as management compatibility, goal congruence, and strategic direction of the supplier firm. Exhibit 17.6 shows supplier selection models currently in use. The first model used by Texas Instruments weights the suppliers according to Texas Instruments' benchmarks. The second one, used by IBM, is a mathematical model that looks only at cost-based factors. The objective of the IBM model is to minimize costs.

E X H I B I T 17.5

The Value Analysis Approach: Comparing Function with Cost

I. How to get started in value analysis: VA is proving a valuable operation in many companies. It is a means of reducing costs without impairing product quality. All you need to do to apply this technique is use a little initiative and extra effort in performing your duties.

II. Select a relatively high-cost or high-volume–purchased item to value analyze. This can be a part, material, or service. Select an item you believe is costing more than it should.

III. Find out completely how the item is used and what is expected of it—its *function*.

IV. Ask questions:
  1. Does its use contribute value?
  2. Is its cost proportionate to its usefulness?
  3. Can basic and secondary functions be separated?
  4. Have functional requirements changed over time?
  5. Does it need all its features?
  6. Is there anything better for the intended use?
  7. Are the original specs realistic under today's conditions?
  8. Can the item be eliminated?
  9. If the item is not standard, can a standard item be used?
  10. If it is a standard item, does it completely fit your application or is it a misfit?
  11. Does the item have greater capacity than required?
  12. Is there a similar item in inventory that could be used?
  13. Can the weight be reduced?
  14. Have new materials or designs been developed that would alter performance of the product?
  15. Are closer tolerances specified than are necessary?
  16. Is unnecessary machining performed on the item?
  17. Are unnecessary fine finishes specified?
  18. Is commercial quality specified?
  19. Can you make the item cheaper yourself?
  20. If you are making it now, can you buy it for less?
  21. Is the item properly classified for shipping purposes?
  22. Can cost of packaging be reduced?
  23. Are you asking your suppliers for suggestions to reduce cost?
  24. Do material, reasonable labor, overhead, and profit total its cost?
  25. Will another dependable supplier provide it for less?
  26. Is anyone buying it for less?

V. Now:
  1. Where practical, get samples of the proposed item(s).
  2. Select the best possibilities and propose changes.

VI. That's all: A thorough study is almost certain to uncover many potential savings!

Source: Michael R. Leenders and Harold E. Fearon, *Purchasing and Materials Management,* 10th ed. (Homewood, IL.: Richard D. Irwin, 1993), p. 516.

All of the models try (1) to make the supplier selection process more objective and (2) to quantify the criteria. While these measures are qualitative, the firms need to develop some sort of scale or weighting system for each factor. The important point here is that the buyer–vendor partnership can be a very long one and therefore should be evaluated carefully.[14]

What to Look for When Choosing a Supplier to Form a Partnership   Exhibit 17.7 shows four major areas of importance. First is financial issues—both firms are concerned with the financial conditions of their potential partners. Second is organizational culture and strategy. This is difficult to evaluate; much is gut feeling and personality fits among the individuals in each firm. Third is technology issues. The buying firm is looking for a supplier who has high technological capability and the ability to help in designing the

---

[14]Lisa M. Ellram, "The Supplier Selection-Decision in Strategic Partnerships," *Journal of Purchasing and Materials Management,* Fall 1990, pp. 8–14.

Study	Model
Models Currently in Use	
Gregory (1986)	Matrix model that weights supplier selection factors based on predetermined, written benchmarks (Texas Instruments)
Bender et al. (1985)	Mixed integer-linear programming model (IBM) generated by a user-friendly artificial intelligence interface
Other Models	
Timmerman (1986)	1. Categorical approach that rates suppliers on a number of equally weighted factors.
	2. Cost ratio method that quantifies all internal costs associated with conducting business with a supplier as a percentage of the supplier's costs, and adds these into that supplier's cost in supplier evaluation.
	3. Linear averaging approach that rates suppliers on a number of factors that are weighted by their importance.
Soukup (1987)	Payoff matrix to require purchasing to evaluate potential supplier's performance under a variety of scenarios.
Thompson (1990)	Modified weighted point approach that rates suppliers on a number of factors, weighted by importance, and then evaluates supplier performance under alternative scenarios by using a Monte Carlo simulation technique.

Source: Lisa M. Ellram, "The Supplier Selection-Decision in Strategic Partnerships," *Journal of Purchasing and Materials Management*, Fall 1990, p. 10.

Financial Issues
1. Economic performance
2. Financial stability

Organizational Culture and Strategy Issues
1. Feeling of trust
2. Management attitude/outlook for the future
3. Strategic fit
4. Top management compatibility
5. Compatibility across levels and functions of buyer and supplier firms
6. Supplier's organizational structure and personnel

Technology Issues
1. Assessment of current manufacturing facilities/capabilities
2. Assessment of future manufacturing capabilities
3. Supplier's design capabilities
4. Supplier's speed in development

Other Factors
1. Safety record of the supplier
2. Business references
3. Supplier's customer base

Source: Lisa M. Ellram, "The Supplier Selection-Decision in Strategic Partnerships," *Journal of Purchasing and Materials Management*, Fall 1990, p. 12.

buying firm's new products. The fourth area includes miscellaneous factors affecting business practices and performance.

Just-in-time purchasing is a major element of just-in-time (JIT) systems, discussed in Chapter 6. The basic idea behind just-in-time purchasing is to establish agreements with vendors to deliver small quantities of materials just in time for production. This can mean daily, twice-daily, and sometimes hourly deliveries of purchased items. This approach contrasts with the traditional approach of bulk buying items that are delivered far in advance of production. The critical elements of JIT purchasing are

Just-in-Time Purchasing

- Reduced lot sizes.
- Frequent and reliable delivery schedules.
- Reduced and highly reliable lead times.
- Consistently high quality levels for purchased materials.

Each of these elements constitutes a major benefit to the purchasing firm, not the least of which is shortening the procurement cycle.

The ultimate objectives should be a single reliable source for each item and the consolidation of several items from each supplier. The result is far fewer suppliers in total. U.S. companies that have implemented JIT purchasing through fewer suppliers have obtained the following benefits:

1. Consistent quality. Involving suppliers during the early stages of product design can consistently provide high-quality products.
2. Savings on resources. Minimum investment and resources, such as buyer's time, travel, and engineering are needed when using a limited number of suppliers.
3. Lower costs. The overall volume of items purchased is higher, which eventually leads to lower costs.
4. Special attention. The suppliers are more inclined to pay special attention to the buyer's needs, since the buyer represents a large account.
5. Saving on tooling. Buyers often provide tools to their suppliers. Concentrating on only one supplier therefore saves a great deal of tooling costs.
6. The establishment of long-term relationships with suppliers encourages loyalty and reduces the risk of an interrupted supply of parts to the buyer plant; this may be the most important benefit of all.

The most critical demands placed on the purchasing department to make JIT work are (1) reducing the number of suppliers and (2) locating suppliers who are nearby. (See Exhibit 17.8.) The strategy of single sourcing is to purchase all parts of a given kind from a single vendor. Nearby suppliers are obviously necessary to allow frequent, piece-by-piece delivery. How well purchasing handles these demands depends on the relationship the firm establishes with its suppliers. Suppliers should be seen as "outside partners" who can contribute to the long-run welfare of the buying firm instead of being seen as outside adversaries.[15]

JIT as an operating concept is a hot topic these days, but we must be careful not to become so captivated by the glamorous JIT single-source philosophy that we overlook the many occasions when multiple sourcing is justified. It is often advantageous to have suppliers compete for a firm's business. In addition to possible lower prices, interviewing and dealing with several vendors can give the buyer a lot of technical knowledge about the product—in many cases much more than from dealing with only one vendor. Also, many materials, parts, and suppliers are critical to a firm's continued operation, and any shutdown by a vendor—due to some sort of labor dispute or calamity such as a major fire or accident, for example—can significantly hurt. The U.S. Dept. of Defense must purchase military and critical supplies from more than one source. This is done, obviously, to reduce the risk of an enemy destroying the source of supply.

---

[15]Chan K. Hahn, Peter A. Pinto, and Daniel J. Bragg, " 'Just-in-Time' Production and Purchasing," *Journal of Purchasing and Materials Management*, Fall 1983, p. 10.

E X H I B I T 17.8
Characteristics of JIT Purchasing

Suppliers
Few suppliers
Nearby suppliers
Repeat business with same suppliers
Active use of analysis to enable desirable suppliers to become/stay price competitive
Clusters of remote suppliers
Competitive bidding mostly limited to new part numbers
Buyer plant resists vertical integration and subsequent wipeout of supplier business
Suppliers are encouraged to extend JIT buying to *their* suppliers

Quantities
Steady output rate (a desirable prerequisite)
Frequent deliveries in small lot quantities
Long-term contract agreements
Minimal release paperwork
Deliver quantities variable from release to release but fixed for whole contract term
Little or no permissible overage or underage of receipts
Suppliers encouraged to package in exact quantities
Suppliers encouraged to reduce their production lot sizes (or store unreleased material)

Quality
Minimal product specifications imposed on supplier
Help suppliers to meet quality requirements
Close relationships between buyers' and suppliers' quality ensurance people
Suppliers encouraged to use process control charts instead of lot sampling inspection

Shipping
Scheduling of inbound freight
Gain control by use of company-owned or contract shipping, contract warehousing, and trailers for freight consolidation/storage where possible instead of using common carriers

Source: Richard J. Schonberger and James P. Gilbert, "Just-in-Time Purchasing: A Challenge for U.S. Industry," *California Management Review,* Fall 1983, p. 58.

JIT Buyer–Supplier Relationship   A firm operating on a just-in-time basis requires that suppliers deliver very high-quality products frequently at a reasonable cost. As we discussed earlier, ideal conditions suggest selecting a few high-quality suppliers with excellent design capabilities and a record of meeting delivery schedules. Thus, this long-term arrangement becomes a partnership.

Which factors are of concern for the just-in-time supplier? Critics of JIT state that just-in-time works for the buyer that sets up the JIT schedule but does not work for the supplier that must follow that schedule. This hypothesis suggests that the supplier simply delivers JIT and produces internally according to an unrelated schedule. The net result is a transfer of inventory carrying responsibilities from buyer back to supplier. In a study of 27 firms in the auto industry, Charles O'Neal found mixed answers on this issue.[16] Twenty-two percent of the respondents perceive their suppliers to have higher inventories as a result of JIT, 30 percent about the same, and 48 percent lower. As their JIT programs continue, however, 82 percent of respondents expect their suppliers' inventories to be lower within the next five years.

In another study of 20 firms, Paul Dion, Peter Banting, and Loretta M. Hasey indicate that JIT leads to buyer's benefits of lower prices, better quality, improved service, and a reduced number of suppliers.[17] These findings are not unique to JIT environments; rather they are the result of the general trend toward preferred suppliers, single sourcing, and

---

[16]Charles O'Neal, "The Buyer–Seller Linkage in a Just-in-Time Environment," *Journal of Purchasing and Materials Management,* 25th anniversary issue, 1989, pp. 34–40.
[17]Paul A. Dion, Peter M. Banting, and Loretta M. Hassey, "The Impact of JIT in Industrial Marketers," *Industrial Marketing Management* 19, 1990. pp. 41–46.

E X H I B I T 17.9

Characteristics of JIT Manufacturers' Environments (Demand pattern versus key competitive pressure)

	Certain Demand	Uncertain Demand
Low-Cost Pressures	A	B
Delivery Pressures	C	D

Source: Reprinted with permission from the publisher; the National Association of Purchasing Management, Inc. Caron H. St. John and Kirk C. Heriot, "Small Suppliers and JIT Purchasing," *International Journal of Purchasing and Materials Management,* Winter 1994, p. 13.

long-term buyer–supplier partnerships. This study did find a problem of coordinating the buyer's JIT delivery with the suppliers' production schedules. One possible cause was suppliers' commitments to other buyers.

Just-in-time deliveries to General Motors, Ford, and Chrysler auto plants have inventory delivered hourly in some areas compared to monthly before JIT. Some Chrysler assembly plants have well over 100 turns per year. A decade ago, GM kept three months' supply of sheet steel on hand. Today, GM keeps three days' supply. Examples of the frequency of deliveries in the auto industry include

Struts arrive every four hours at Buick City.

Seats arrive every hour from a Lear Sigler plant.

Seats arrive in the exact assembly line sequence at Chrysler's Sterling Heights, Michigan; Dodge City, Montana; and St. Louis, Missouri, assembly plants.

Seats and tires arrive every hour at Honda's Marysville, Ohio, plant.

Diesel engines, axles, wheels, and tires arrive in the assembly line sequence at the Dodge plant in Warren, Michigan.

Adhering to such tight delivery schedules has caused many suppliers to locate close to the buyers' plants—within 10 to 20 miles. Such moves are not absolutely necessary though. With the good roads we have in the United States and with dependable transportation, a stable schedule is more important to the supplier than the location.

Small Suppliers and JIT Purchasing

Should a large firm buy from a small firm? Should a small firm make commitments to supply product to large firms? St. John and Heriot present a simple 2 × 2 model to discuss the advantages and disadvantages for buyers and small suppliers for the four cases in the 2 × 2 matrix.[18]

Exhibit 17.9 shows the simple matrix representing manufacturers using JIT methods under different possible conditions. Along the horizontal dimension the demand is either

[18]Caron H. St. John and Kirk C. Heriot, "Small Suppliers and JIT Purchasing," *International Journal of Purchasing and Materials Management,* Winter 1994, pp. 11–16.

certain or uncertain. The choices along the vertical dimension are the two competitive pressures faced by this JIT manufacturer. One pressure is for low-cost production; the other is for delivery performance such as meeting due dates, rescheduling, and changing volume.

Where does the small supplier fit into this matrix? Quadrant A, (the JIT buyer faces certain demand at low prices), presents a difficult situation for the small supplier. To compete with large suppliers, a small supplier must be able to focus operations on a narrow product line and greatly reduce costs. Otherwise, the large supplier definitely has the advantage.

Quadrant B, (the JIT buyer has uncertain demand at low prices), gives the advantage to the small supplier through flexibility and the ability to reschedule as needed by the buyer. Large suppliers are committed to use their resources efficiently for a variety of products: they also tend to have firmer non-negotiable schedules.

In Quadrant C, the JIT buyer faces certain demand with the need for delivery performance. This is the worst quadrant for small suppliers. Whereas the smaller supplier has more flexibility, the larger supplier may have a better history of delivery performance when due dates are known as in this case.

In Quadrant D, the JIT buyer faces uncertain demand and pressure for delivery performance. JIT manufacturers face changing due dates and volumes. The supplier will likely respond by producing goods as soon as the order is received and holding the inventory until the manufacturer needs it. If the small supplier has a narrow product line, the supplier may be able to link its production schedule to that of its buyer. That would be ideal for the buyer, especially if the small supplier is nearby. The danger in this situation is the tendency for the supplier to become a captive to the buyer along with all the disadvantages (pressure to continue to reduce costs, chance of being bought out by the JIT buyer, chance that the JIT buyer will set up its own production facility, etc.).

The small supplier must understand the rewards and risks when entering a relationship with a large buyer. Here is a summary analysis of each of the four quadrants in Exhibit 17.9.

Environment A   JIT manufacturer experiences certain demand and low-cost competitive pressure. Buyers require quality and on-time delivery, with lowest prices winning orders.

Implications for JIT buyers   Identify small, local suppliers with low overhead from limited product lines and customer base.

Opportunities for small suppliers   Focus on low total product costs. Exploit low overhead from narrow product line, limited customer base, and restricted design capabilities. Locate near customers to exploit low transportation costs.

Threats   Large competitors may achieve cost benefits from economies of scale, automation, or learning curve effects, thus closing off opportunities for small suppliers in this area.

Environment B   JIT manufacturer experiences uncertain demand and low-cost competitive pressure. JIT buyers require quality, and award orders based on schedule flexibility at attractive prices.

Implications for JIT buyers   Identify small local suppliers with simplified processes and product lines, low overhead costs, and flexible-scheduled direct workforce. Negotiate pricing based on volume over time.

Opportunities for small suppliers   Focus on maintaining schedule flexibility at low cost. Simplify products and processes to reduce lead times, number of component parts, and scheduling complexity. Maintain a very limited line of end items. Move to JIT processing with some raw material stocks. Exploit low overhead from narrow product line and limited marketing activity. Locate near customers to ensure cost-effective, fast delivery. Make use of part-time employees who may be flexible-scheduled rather than working overtime. Negotiate pricing based on volume over time.

Threats   Whiplash effect as size and timing of orders fluctuates may cause the small firm to hold idle labor, idle equipment, and excess work-in-process inventories to buffer against uncertainty. Those options will raise costs.

Environment C   JIT manufacturer experiences certain demand and delivery pressure. Buyers require reasonable prices and good quality, but award orders based on uniqueness of product or service, or on strength of supplier's reputation.

Implications for JIT buyers   Align with small suppliers that provide unique products or strong service.

Opportunities for small suppliers   The key opportunity in this environment is to offer a unique product or service. A small, standard product supplier competing directly with a large supplier may win the order if marketing efforts are extraordinary.

Threat   Marginally lower prices and schedule flexibility from suppliers will not have value.

Environment D   JIT manufacturer experiences uncertain demand and delivery pressure. Buyers require reasonable prices and high quality, but award orders based on absolute due date performance in the face of changing size and timing of order.

Implications for JIT buyers   Pay small local suppliers a price premium to support flexible delivery. Link production systems.

Implications for small suppliers   Focus on absolute due date performance in the face of changing size and timing of orders. Hold some work-in-process or end-item inventories to support flexible delivery to JIT customer. Hold excess capacity and consider linking schedules and inventory records to customer's production scheduling. Offset these expensive investments in flexibility through negotiated price premiums. Locate near customers where possible.

Threat   Small suppliers must avoid complete dominance by JIT customer and threat of backward integration.[19]

---

[19]Ibid., pp. 15–16. Reprinted with permission from the publisher, the National Association of Purchasing Management, Inc.

Historically, the objective of purchasing and materials management has always been to have two or more suppliers. The thinking was that competition would drive down price and reduce the risk of supplies being cut off. JIT production, with its critical need for quality, and the new worldwide emphasis on quality products, is changing the buyer–supplier relationship.

Multiple Suppliers versus Few Suppliers

In the early 1980s, U.S. auto manufacturers accepted materials, parts, and components with 1 to 3 percent defect rates. That amounts to 10,000 to 30,000 defects per million incoming parts! This defect rate is no longer acceptable.

Xerox Corporation lost half of its worldwide market share in copiers from 1976 to 1982. Xerox had over 5,000 suppliers and spent 80 percent of manufacturing cost on purchased materials. To try to turn the company around, Xerox reduced its suppliers to just 400 and trained them in statistical process control, total quality control, and just-in-time manufacturing. As a result, product costs were greatly reduced, reject rates were reduced by 93 percent, and production lead time was reduced from 52 weeks to 18 weeks.

Working closely with fewer suppliers has many rewards. General Electric Company, for instance, publicizes the names of its best suppliers and awards them better contracts. GE's Appliance Division invites its 100 best suppliers to its annual Supplier Appreciation Day.

To compete effectively in world markets, a firm must have high-quality suppliers with acceptable costs and timely delivery. Chief purchasing officers (CPOs) should compile lists of approved suppliers and then create supplier development programs to improve suppliers' technical ability, quality, delivery, and cost. More than 70 percent of the companies in one survey had approved buyer lists.[20]

The Western view is that single sourcing is a high risk for the buyer. Japan's single-sourcing tradition, however, may not be one of successful long-term sharing. It appears that the power is in the hands of the big buyers. John Ramsay states that power is so unbalanced in Japan's supplier network that suppliers are more like off-site workshops of the buyer.[21] The advantage to the buyer is that during economic down periods, the subcontracted work can be brought back into the buyer's plant. The buyer's firm can maintain stable employment while the supplier has a feast-or-famine existence.

In an attempt to improve their suppliers' quality, each year Pitney Bowes (PB) sends its purchasing personnel and quality engineers to visit vendors. They take along video cameras to tape operations on each supplier's shop floor. Back at PB, design and manufacturing engineers examine the tapes to learn which equipment the supplier uses and the line operator's performance in running that equipment. They also use the videos as excuses to talk with the supplier's workers to ascertain their attitude toward quality. As a result of these visits, some suppliers were removed from the vendor list. Suppliers are also brought to PB. During vendor days suppliers see PB's operation and obtain a better understanding of their participation in PB's production process. Suppliers are also taught statistical process control if necessary. PB has found that suppliers make useful suggestions on materials, design, and so on.

Texas Instruments perceived quality as being so important that it instituted a 13-step certification program. Results proved the program to be very good.

Ford Motor Company issues long-term (three-to-five–year) contracts to vendors. Practically every part is single sourced. Suppliers become involved during the design phase.

---

[20]Richard E. Plank and Valerie Kijewski, "The Use of Approved Supplier Lists," *International Journal of Purchasing and Materials Management,* Spring 1991, pp. 37–41.

[21]John Ramsay, "The Myth of the Cooperative Single Source," *Journal of Purchasing and Materials Management,* Winter 1990, pp. 2–5.

Simultaneous engineering means that the design of a part depends on how it is to be made; that is, the process to be used to make a product influences its design. Early involvement of the supplier is important because suppliers are experts in their areas. They certainly know more about their processes than Ford so their knowledge influences Ford's designs.

One other interesting note on Ford's supplier relationship. In Chapter 11 on job design, we discussed learning curves. We stated that continuous production improves performance. Since Ford's long-term contracts allow the effects of learning to really take hold and be significant, Ford attached clauses to reduce prices each year. This cost reduction was recognized to be a side benefit of the relationship and should be shared by Ford as well.

Single-Source Supplier Qualification

Choosing a company to be the **single-source supplier** to a manufacturer is an important procedure because buyer–supplier relationships can last for years. In Chapter 5 on total quality management, we discussed ISO 9000 certification at various levels, including independent outside certifiers. However, a firm can qualify a buyer itself. Qualifying a supplier is a team effort directed by the buyer. Members of the team include purchasing, quality assurance, design engineering, manufacturing engineering, operations, accounting, and industrial engineering. The buyer's team examines various areas of a supplier's operation. Richard Newman lists seven measures teams can use to evaluate a potential supplier:

1. *Equipment capability.* Can the supplier's equipment produce the product required by the buyer at the appropriate quality level? A process capability index (PCI) is a useful measurement. PCI is normally defined as the absolute design tolerance of the *machine or process,* divided by six standard deviations of the machine or process actual performance. (At a PCI = 1, this includes 99.7 percent of the total output, which is ± 3 standard deviations.)

   $$PCI = \text{Absolute design tolerance}/6\ \sigma$$

   In today's competitive market three defects per 1,000 would be unacceptable in most products where these parts are installed. This is handled by making specifications for the part narrower than the application specifications where the part will be used. This is C_{pk}, sometimes referred to as CPK, which we discussed in Supplement 5 on quality control methods.

2. *Quality assurance.* The supplier's quality control procedures are examined to determine.
   a. Where and whether incoming inspection takes place.
   b. The use of statistical process control by the supplier's sources.
   c. The supplier's use of statistical process control.
   d. Work-in-process inspection methods.
   e. Measurement devices and calibration.
   f. Procedures for handling rejected raw materials.
   g. Final inspection and packaging procedures.
   h. Packaging, inspecting, and testing procedures.

   Because quality begins at the supplier, equipment and process and quality control are essential.

3. *Financial capability.* This measure is the risk of doing business, especially over the long term. Typical measures are
   a. Clout ratio (Buyer's annual order value/Supplier's sales).
   b. Current ratio (Current assets/Current liabilities).
   c. Quick ratio [(Current assets − Inventory)/Current liabilities].

    d. Inventory turnover (Sales/Inventory).

    e. Collection period (Receivables/Sales per day).

    These measures indicate the financial health of the firm; the clout ratio indicates the potential value of the buyer to the supplier.

4. *Cost structure.* A firm must know the supplier's cost structure if a long-term relationship is to be considered. This includes materials, direct labor, overhead, sales and administrative costs, and profits as well. The buyer should know that costs are reasonable and what the future costs might be. Profits or costs that are too low, for example, would create future problems.

5. *Supplier value analysis effort.* Because the buyer–supplier relationship is intended to be ongoing, the buyer should expect improvements in the supplier and should participate in value analysis programs. Value analysis means that the supplier must

    a. Understand the need for all product specifications.

    b. Know which specifications are critical to performance.

    c. Know which specifications are cosmetic.

    The potential supplier's past history in value analysis programs should be examined as to the type of projects attempted, degree of success, and so forth.

6. *Production scheduling.* The supplier's methods for production scheduling and control can affect how the buyer's orders fit into the system. Existing capacities, methods of expediting, and follow-up procedures are important issues. Also, since production schedules are shared so that both buyer and seller can plan, compatibility of scheduling techniques is desirable.

7. *Contract performance.* How is performance by the supplier to be measured? While these evaluations need to be specified, they should not become a burden in the form of bulky reports. Ideally, contract performance should be on an exception basis, with only the variations creating attention.

    Qualifying a supplier can be time-consuming and expensive. However, the intent is to have a long-term, mutually beneficial relationship wherein the costs and time have been well spent.

    Purchasing managers believe they are on the right track in evaluating suppliers. James Morgan and Susan Zimmerman conducted the survey in Exhibit 17.10. They discovered the traits buyers look for in suppliers and the approaches buyers use to select new suppliers. As Exhibit 17.10 shows, the major method, at 50 percent, was to do a technical evaluation of the supplier and then award a small amount of business as a performance test. Another survey, depicted in Exhibit 17.11, showed that quality was the most important characteristic of a supplier's performance. Delivery performance was second.

    Purchasing professionals prefer having a small number of **qualified suppliers** because

1. Supplier development is costly.

2. The objective is a closer working relationship.

3. Fewer suppliers can be rewarded with substantial business.

17.4   GLOBAL SOURCING

We are at the beginning of a major change in the global economy. Great opportunities are developing because of the collapse of communism in the Eastern Bloc, the restructuring of countries such as Hungary and Czechoslovakia (now split into Slovakia and the Czech Republic), plus new markets in Turkey, India, South Africa, and so on. Already

E X H I B I T 17.10
Selecting and Testing Prospective New Suppliers

Traits Buyers Check First in Scanning New Suppliers

1. Quality capability
2. Technical competence
3. Process control
4. Pricing/cost factors
5. Financial stability
6. Engineering/manufacturing support
7. Management
8. Delivery
9. Service record
10. Training programs
11. Plant location

Percentage	Buyers' Approaches to Choosing a New Supplier
50%	Perform a technical evaluation and then give the potential supplier a limited amount of business to test out performance in a production situation.
25	Add the potential supplier to bid lists and make a technical evaluation after bids come in.
20	Add the potentially hot supplier to request-for-bid lists once a technical evaluation is made.
18	Perform a technical evaluation as soon as a potentially good supplier is spotted—without a specific job in mind.
6	Use all of the above approaches at one time or another.
1	Use an established rating system to measure the new prospect.

Note: Percentages do not add up to 100 percent because of use of multiple approaches.

Source: James P. Morgan, and Susan Zimmerman, "Status Report: Building World-Class Supplier Relationships," *Purchasing*, August 16, 1990, pp. 62–65.

we are seeing results of agreements such as NAFTA (North American Free Trade Agreement) and promising rewards if GATT (General Agreement on Tariffs and Trade) is passed. Though opening very slowly, China is a huge market and may someday be a worthwhile trading partner.

Purchasing in the International Marketplace

There are a number of terms used interchangeably: *global purchasing, global sourcing, foreign sourcing, international sourcing, multinational sourcing,* and a variety of combinations of these.

Originally, purchasing on an international basis was an attempt to reduce production costs in the face of competition—primarily foreign competition. Global sourcing has now gone well beyond cost reduction motives to strategic ones to look at product availability, technology, and delivery lead times as well as labor availability and quality.

From a purchasing standpoint, what prompts firms to enter foreign markets? In a survey of 149 firms, Birou and Fawcett found that the two main reasons why firms begin purchasing globally were a lower price and accessibility to products unavailable in the United States. Exhibit 17.12 shows their complete list of responses. We usually think that the United States is superior in technology and product quality, but note items 4 and 5 in the exhibit: advanced technology and higher-quality products available from foreign sources.

Global sourcing is a standard procedure for over half of all firms with annual sales of more than $10 million. What stands out in the list of purchased items is the small percentage of companies that purchase services. Exhibit 17.13 shows that while foreign purchases of materials, parts, and equipment range from 69 percent to 81 percent, only 16 percent of the companies surveyed purchased foreign services.

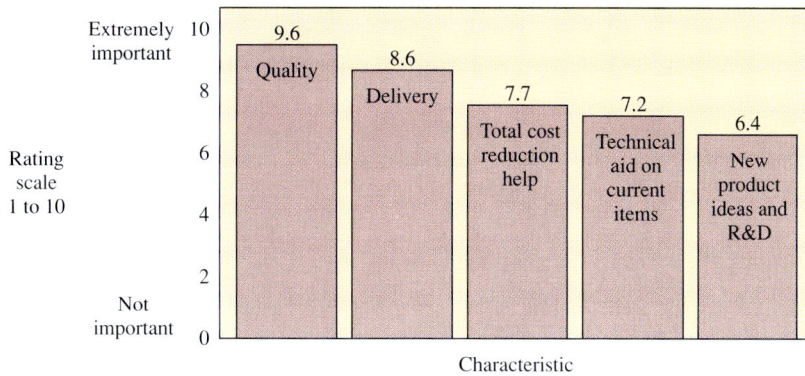

E X H I B I T 17.11
Important Issues in Supplier Performance

Source: Somerby Dowst, "Quality Suppliers: The Search Goes On," *Purchasing,* January 28, 1988, pp. 94A4–12.

E X H I B I T 17.12
Reasons for Beginning to Source Internationally

Rationale for International Sourcing	Percentage of Firms
1. Lower price available from foreign sources	74% of firms
2. Availability of foreign products that are not available domestically	49
3. Firm's worldwide operation and attitude	28
4. Advanced technology available from foreign sources	26
5. Higher-quality products available from foreign sources	25
6. Intensification of global competition	19
7. To help develop a foreign presence (precursor to global production or marketing)	17
8. To fulfill countertrade or local content requirements	17
9. Better delivery or service available from foreign sources	8

Source: Reprinted with permission from the publisher, the National Association of Purchasing Management, Inc. Laura M. Birou and Stanley E. Fawcett, "International Purchasing: Benefits, Requirements, and Challenges," *International Journal of Purchasing and Materials Management,* Spring 1993, p. 34.

Typically, evaluating foreign suppliers is more difficult and increased costs are relevant. Exhibit 17.13 shows cost elements for foreign sourcing. Naturally, most of these costs differ from domestic costs because of the expenses of dealing with foreign suppliers and exchange rates.

International sourcing is a competitive weapon if used correctly. International sourcing usually requires stable production, simpler designs, reduced numbers of components, and manufactured subassemblies as well as increased quality. It also promotes greater cooperation among manufacturing, marketing, and purchasing personnel.

In Chapter 5 on total quality management, we discussed certification of suppliers to ensure their performance in all aspects such as quality and delivery performance.

Exhibit 17.14 shows the top 26 of the 100 largest purchasing departments in the United States in 1990. The purchases are in total dollars both domestic and foreign. Also shown are purchases as a percentage of sales revenue and purchases as a percentage of product cost.

In total, the top 100 purchasing departments spent almost $.5 trillion on purchased goods and services.[22] A good deal of these purchases will likely shift to foreign purchases. What is expected to compensate are increased foreign sales of our domestically produced goods. So, while we may purchase more internationally, we are expected to sell more internationally too.

---

[22]Ernest Raia, "Purchasing's Top 100," *Purchasing,* November 22, 1990, pp. 51–55.

E X H I B I T   17.13

Foreign Sourcing Practices (Items purchased abroad)

Type of Purchases	Percentage of Respondents That Partially Source Abroad
Materials	76%
Machinery and equipment	69
Component parts	81
Services	16

Cost Elements to Evaluate
1. Unit price
2. Export taxes
3. International transportation costs
4. Insurance and tariffs
5. Brokerage costs
6. Letter of credit
7. Cost of money
8. Inland (domestic and foreign) freight cost
9. Risk of obsolescence
10. Cost of rejects
11. Damage in transit
12. Inventory holding costs
13. Technical support
14. Employee travel costs

Source: Joseph R. Carter and Ram Narasimhan, "Purchasing in the International Marketplace: Implications for Operations," *Journal of Purchasing and Materials Management,* Summer 1990, pp. 6, 8.

Of the 10 companies listing product cost in the last column of Exhibit 17.14, purchasing accounts for an average of 64.4 percent of product cost.

In the global market, service industries need logistic support as well as manufacturing industries whether it is sourcing (information or a hamburger), location (physical distribution of products or services), or monitoring flows of material, people, information, and ideas.

For international materials management, the specific organizational form is less important than having a clear, explicit assignment of responsibility and authority. Also important is the firm's reward structure; the firm's objectives must be clearly specified and appropriately rewarded. Otherwise, individuals may establish their own objectives, such as minimizing the cost of purchasing and transportation. While important, cost minimization should not be the sought-after goal. The ultimate goal is to choose suppliers who can become strategic partners that participate from the beginning of the product design stage.

Geographic Areas for Sourcing

Two-thirds of the imports of the United States come from 12 countries:

1. Japan	7. United Kingdom
2. Canada	8. France
3. Mexico	9. China
4. Germany	10. Italy
5. Taiwan	11. Hong Kong
6. South Korea	12. Singapore

Numbers 2 and 3 are our adjoining countries: Canada and Mexico. Note that half the list is in Asia and one-third is in Europe. The North American Free Trade Agreement passed in 1993 will further encourage trade among the United States, Canada, and Mexico.

For international purchasing throughout the world, there is a wide variety of production capabilities, labor costs, material costs, product quality, and reliability for delivery schedules. The best performing countries have political stability, a well-developed infra-

Company	$ Spent by Purchasing (millions)	Expenditures as a Percentage of Sales	Expenditures as a Percentage of Product Cost
General Motors	$50,566	50%	60%
Ford	50,000	60	68
Chrysler	21,864	63	70
IBM	20,000	32	—
General Electric	18,500	34	—
AT&T	10,600	29	—
Du Pont	10,000	28	60
GTE	9,264	53	—
United Technologies	9,000	46	—
Boeing	8,200	41	—
Caterpillar	7,000	61	—
Xerox	7,000	40	—
Exxon	6,900	8	—
ITT	5,900	29	40
International Paper	5,800	51	—
Goodyear Tire	5,800	53	—
Union Carbide	5,600	64	75
Dow Chemical	5,400	31	60
Westinghouse	5,400	42	85
Allied-Signal	5,400	45	—
General Dynamics	5,380	54	—
Mobil	5,300	10	—
Tenneco	5,220	37	—
Shell Oil	5,064	26	—
Lockheed	5,000	51	60
Digital Equipment	4,400	34	66

E X H I B I T 17.14

The 26 Largest Purchasing Departments in the United States

Source: Ernest Raia, "Purchasing's Top 100," *Purchasing,* November 22, 1990, p. 52.

structure (transportation, communication, energy, finance system), and a high-quality urban workforce. For more detailed information on the pros and cons of purchasing in various global markets, see the reading "Buying in the Common Global Economy" at the end of this chapter.

Deciding to examine the possibilities of international sourcing is just the first small step in the process of developing foreign suppliers. There are several ways to start.

Locating International Suppliers

1. *Trade shows.* This allows a firm to see the type of work that companies do, to pick up literature and business cards, and to discuss whether they do special orders.
2. *Personal contacts.* These contacts may be through acquaintances at other firms, friends overseas, other buyers, acquaintances through professional associations, and advice from the firm's other suppliers.
3. *Trade boards and foreign consulates.* Many of these have the prime function of developing sales opportunities for their countries.
4. *An intermediary hired to search out suppliers.* The best intermediaries specialize in specific countries and know all of those nations' firms and their capabilities

very well. In this way, an intermediary can be given a prototype or plans and come back with price quotes in a surprisingly short time.

International Distribution

How does a firm begin to develop foreign sources? We have just discussed how a potential supplier may have been identified through trade shows, personal contacts, or foreign consulates. Knowing the potential suppliers still does not answer the many questions of a firm that is new to global purchasing: How does one buy from a foreign source; what pitfalls are there? Exhibit 17.15 shows both primary sources (firms that manufac-

E X H I B I T 17.15   *Forms of International Distribution Channels*

Source Intermediaries or "Middlemen"	Advantages	Disadvantages
Distributors Buy and resell goods. Accept orders and payment. Assume warranty responsibility. May offer customer training.	Handle cultural, commercial, and technical problems. If delivery in United States, payment in dollars, standard terms. Simple handling of product defects.	Among the most costly sources; buyer pays both manufacturer's and distributor's profit and overhead. Probably foreign currency, L/C terms. (Letter of credit)
Manufacturer's Representatives Accept orders on behalf of a source; receive commission for the service. May provide technical and commercial support.	Handle cultural, commercial, and technical problems. Generally less expensive to use than a distributor.	Payment in foreign currency. L/C terms if a foreign rep. company. Bears no warranty liability; little use in dealing with defects.
Brokers Bring together parties to a transaction for a fee. Services vary widely.	Least expensive intermediary. Wide range of services possible. May have wide contacts in the industry. Most willing to negotiate.	Least responsible for source or product performance, warranty. Probably little technical support. Foreign currency, L/C terms probable.
Trading Companies Broad scope of activities from brokering, representation, distribution, program management.	Worldwide contacts, broadest scope of sources. Experience and capability. Few cultural or language problems.	Generally a costly alternative. Most prefer to trade in existing markets or to make a market for new product, not to deal in isolated inquiries. Because of their scale, most buyers have little leverage.
Primary Sources		
Large Multinationals The majority of international business. May prefer new customers to buy through distribution or U.S. subsidiaries, which cannot be considered an offshore source.	Undisputed capability; possible benefits of economies of scale. Good support, training, warranty performance. Few cultural or language impediments.	Because of scale, few buyers have negotiating leverage. No benefit in purchases through U.S. subsidiary.
Midsize Manufacturers The vast majority of source opportunities. Public or private. Most already exporting. May have a U.S. presence in a liaison office.	Low costs at acceptable levels of risk. Opportunities for close, long-term relationships.	Some cultural and language barriers to overcome. Foreign currency, letter of credit.
Small Specialty Firms Usually individually or privately owned. Limited capability; usually one process or service.	Lowest cost. Probably most personalized, attentive service.	Most likely to present cultural and language problems. Buyer responsible for freight, duty of transaction. Foreign currency, letter of credit.
Captives Wholly owned subsidiaries or subcontractors controlled by larger firms through investment or predatory purchasing.	If accessible, may be very inexpensive and accustomed to quality, on-time performance.	Normally unwilling or precluded from accepting direct orders. Extra cost if accessed through the dominant company.

Source: Thomas K. Hickman and William M. Hickman, Jr., *Global Purchasing: How to Buy Goods and Services in Foreign Markets* (Homewood, IL: Business One Irwin, 1992), pp. 58–59.

ture the products or produce the services) and intermediaries (middlemen who stand between the seller and the buyer). Unless a firm is quite experienced in direct purchases, dealing through an intermediary may be a good way to start in the international market. We will briefly comment on each of these sources.

A *distributor* usually carries a stock of a manufacturer's goods and has exclusive sales territorial rights. In underdeveloped countries these rights can vary widely. A *manufacturer's representative* does not carry a stock of goods but is a salesperson paid on commission. Generally, manufacturer's representatives have exclusive rights either to a territory or to a class of potential customers. A *broker's* primary purpose is to bring potential buyers and suppliers together, though many other supplementary services may be offered as well. *Trading companies* provide a wide variety of services—even financial and marketing if needed. They can also find technical help if needed by the buyer or supplier.

The *primary sources* are the actual manufacturers. If a firm has the experience in international purchasing, it is best to deal directly with the primary source rather than through an intermediary. Not only will it likely be cheaper, but chances of miscommunication are less when dealing directly. Of the primary sources (large multinationals, midsize manufacturers, small specialty firms, and captive firms), the small specialty firms are usually the best choice. The communication problems and the transactions and shipment are the areas that could become problems when dealing with small companies. Once a relationship is developed, it should be quite satisfactory.

17.5   ELECTRONIC INFORMATION FLOW

A supply chain links all of the stages together from raw materials through production to the consumer. While many operating systems (such as MRP-type systems) push the product out to the user, others pull it through (such as JIT systems where product is produced as needed). In all cases, however, the frequency and speed of communicating information through the chain has a great effect on inventory levels, efficiencies, costs, and so on. An area that is growing rapidly to try to speed up this communication is electronic information flow. This section reviews applications in the retail industry, such as department stores and supermarkets.

There are a number of application areas and several systems that have been developed: electronic data interchange (EDI), quick response (QR) and efficient consumer response (ECR). In all cases these mnemonics refer to the communication throughout a supply or distribution pipeline. This is a paperless communication between retailers and vendors. For several years prior to this, there already has been some improvement in communication through the use of open computer systems using UNIX or UNIX-type software, but EDI, QR, and ECR go far beyond that.

Quick response (QR) programs have grown rapidly. A survey by Deloitte and Touch shows that 68 percent of retailers have either implemented or plan to implement QR within two years.[23] Quick response is based on bar code scanning and EDI. Its intent is to create a just-in-time replenishment system between vendors and retailers.

Quick Response (QR)

Virtually all medium and large stores use *Universal Product Code (UPC)* bar code scanning. *Point-of-sale (POS)* scanning at the register also uses *price-look-up (PLU)*, as reported by 90 percent of the respondents.

---

[23]"Quick Response Grows," *Chain Store Age Executive,* May 1993, pp. 158–59.

Trucks Keep Inventories Rolling Past Warehouses to Production Lines

It seems warehouses have grown wheels.

Called "rolling inventories," trucks have become the place of choice for just-in-time stockpiles. Eighteen-wheelers pull up to factory loading docks to deliver parts that go almost immediately onto production lines, by-passing the warehouses.

"Companies now precisely plan their need of inventory so that [intermediate] warehouses aren't needed," says Don Schneider, president of trucking concern Schneider National Inc. and a member of the Chicago Federal Reserve Bank.

To be sure, just-in-time inventory methods aren't new. But as more companies come around to this approach, trucks and railcars have begun to function as warehouses for many producers—adding yet another anomaly to the economic recovery.

The construction of warehouse square footage tumbled nearly 18 percent in 1992 and 9 percent in 1993, even as the economy gained momentum and space in stores and shopping centers grew 6 percent and 12 percent, respectively.

For trucking companies, the trend means new business, but also more demanding customers. Many trucking companies say that in recent years, they've come under increasing pressure to deliver parts within a small window of time. "There are sometimes less than 10-minute lag times," says Larry Mulkey, president of Ryder Dedicated Logistics Inc., a Miami unit of transportation-services company Ryder Systems Inc.

Such use of trucks enables businesses to cut space costs, freeing up capital for investments such as equipment or new employees. "The back room decreases in size because you don't need it to store stockpiles and that means you have more floor space for selling," Mr. Mulkey says.

But a heavy reliance on trucks to keep inventories low isn't without its risks. The General Motors Corp., Toyota Motor Co. joint venture in Fremont, California, once had to shut down its production line because a just-in-time delivery truck broke down on the highway.

Ken Simonson, chief economist of the American Trucking Associations, says trucking for just-in-time orders generally works better in uncongested regions of the country.

But trucking companies have come a long way in eliminating delivery glitches. Mr. Schneider of Schneider National boasts that not one load was late because of the icy, wintry weather that hit much of the nation recently.

Technology enables trucking companies and their clients to track a load's progress from minute to minute. If a problem comes up, another truck can be dispatched immediately to pick up the load. Trucks also have become more reliable mechanically.

Source: Lucinda Harper, "Trucks Keep Inventories Rolling past Warehouses to Production Lines," *The Wall Street Journal,* February 7, 1994, p. A7A. Reprinted by permission of the Wall Street Journal © 1994 Dow Jones & Co., Inc. All rights reserved worldwide.

Efficient Consumer Response (ECR)

Efficient Consumer Response is a variation of QR and EDI adopted by the supermarket industry as a business strategy where distributors, suppliers, and grocers work closely together to bring products to consumers. They can use bar code and EDI. Savings will come from reduced supply chain costs and reduced inventory.

A study by Kurt Salmon Associates estimates a potential savings of more than $30 billion.[24] In the dry grocery segment this could cut supply-chain inventory from 104 days to 61 days. In another study by McKinsey estimates were that dry grocery consumer prices could be reduced an average of 10.8 percent through industrywide adoption of ECR.[25]

Without ECR, manufacturers push products on the markets by offering low prices on large quantities: A few times a year the manufacturer offers the grocer a low price on a large quantity of product. This is forward buying. The manufacturer then works with the supermarket to offer coupons and incentives to entice customers to buy the product dur-

---

[24]James Aaron Cooke, "The $30 Billion Promise," *Traffic Management,* December 1993, pp. 57–61.
[25]David B. Jenkins, "Jenkins Leads EDI Effort," *Chain Store Age Executive,* March 1993, p. 147.

ing a promotion. Products not sold during the promotion are stored in inventory to carry that supermarket until the next manufacturer's promotional deal.

ECR focuses on the customers to drive the system, not the manufacturers' deals. Customers pull goods through the store and through the pipeline by their purchases. This permits less inventory throughout the system.

Cooke cites a study that estimated that distributors purchase 80 percent of their merchandise during manufacturers' sales or "deals." They may buy four times per year and fill up their warehouses. Until the industry frees itself from this addiction to deal buying, all the great replenishment techniques will be worthless.[26] Most experts predict that the grocery industry will implement ECR philosophy by the year 2000. All companies are preparing for it.

Wal-Mart has won awards for its Satellite Network, first installed in 1987. This network supports data, voice, and video and allows real-time sales and inventory information.

Wal-Mart's Information System

Wal-Mart's electronic data interchange, installed in 1990, issues electronic purchase orders and receives invoices from virtually all of Wal-Mart's vendors.

Wal-Mart's Retail Link, first installed in 1991, allows vendors to directly access in real-time *point-of-sale (POS)* data. This allows vendors to create better forecasts and better inventory management. The POS data come directly from store cash registers so they reflect activity in real time. E-mail capability is also included for corresponding within the supply system concerning scheduling, payments, and so on. Retail Link also includes the spreadsheet Microsoft Excel for Windows so the spreadsheet data can be accessed throughout the system.

Using Retail Link and point-of-sale data, arrangements have been made with some large suppliers to make their own decisions about Wal-Mart's purchases from them. They directly access point-of-sale data and create their own purchase orders. Wal-Mart is attempting to implement EDI internationally, but little progress has been made so far.[27]

17.6 CONCLUSION

In manufacturing, two-thirds of the costs of manufactured goods are purchased materials. Because of this the purchasing function and materials management systems have taken on high profiles and are being placed at high organizational levels.

In this chapter we have tried to show the many things that have changed in the area of purchasing and materials management. Vendors from around the world not only compete through their own marketing efforts but also are aggressively searched out by buyers looking for low-cost, reliable sources.

The materials management problem is being shifted to a large extent to the seller. Purchasing contracts are now tied to delivery schedules for the seller. We covered a number of issues in JIT purchasing and delivery. The entry of electronic information flow has even further shifted the buyer's materials management to the vendor by allowing direct access to point-of-sales data and giving responsibility for forecasting and delivery of the vendor's product as needed. Such relationships tend to be long-term and make the selection of vendors even more important.

---

[26]Cooke, "$30 Billion," pp. 57–61.
[27]"Going beyond EDI: Wal-Mart Cited for Vendor Links," *Chain Store Age Executive*, March 1993, pp. 150–51.

17.7   REVIEW AND DISCUSSION QUESTIONS

1. Give pro and con arguments for carrying a wide range versus a small range of sizes as noted in the opening vignette.

2. What recent changes have caused materials management and purchasing to become much more important?

3. We used an example of a value chain using truck tires. Can you give other examples and describe the linkages and the logic for them?

4. Using data from the text, give a simple profile of a purchasing manager and his/her job.

5. How are potential suppliers qualified by a firm?

6. Which characteristics of a supplier are most important to the buyer?

7. What is meant by a *strategic partnership* between a buyer and a supplier?

8. JIT suppliers have additional pressures that other suppliers do not have. What are they?

9. Small suppliers don't stand a chance competing against large suppliers for orders requiring JIT delivery. True or false? Comment.

10. With so much productive capacity and room for expansion in the United States, why would a company choose to purchase items from a foreign firm? Discuss the pros and cons.

11. What are the trade-offs in single-source versus multiple-source purchasing?

12. Which skills and training are most important for a purchasing agent?

13. Currently you are using multiple suppliers for each purchased item. How would you go about choosing one of them to be your long-term sole source?

14. As a supplier, which factors would you consider about a buyer (your potential customer) to be important in setting up a long-term relationship?

15. If a firm decides to consider international sourcing, how would they go about finding foreign firms that could supply them?

16. In electronic information flow, briefly define EDI, quick response (QR), efficient consumer response (ECR), and point of sale (POS). How have these helped industry?

17. "JIT purchasing is nothing more than a ploy to have vendors take over the burden of carrying inventory." Comment.

18. Distinguish between push and pull distribution systems. Give pros and cons of each.

19. For the value density example in Exhibit 17.2, what would the effect be if a competing firm offers you a similar service for 10 percent less than Federal Express's rates?

C A S E

1 7 . 8   C A S E
Thomas Manufacturing Company

"Delivery of our 412 casting is critical. We can't just stop production for this casting every time you have a minor pattern problem," said Mr. Litt, engineer for Thomas Manufacturing.

"I'm not interested in running rejects," answered Mr. James of A&B Foundry. "I cannot overextend my time on these castings when the other jobs are waiting."

"If you can't cast them properly and on time, I'll just have to take our pattern to another foundry that can," retorted Mr. Litt.

"Go ahead! It's all yours. I have other jobs with fewer headaches," replied Mr. James.

Mr. Litt returned to Thomas Manufacturing with the 412 casting pattern. (A pattern is used in making molds in which the gray iron is formed. After cooling, the mold is broken off, leaving the desired casting.) He remembered that Mr. Dunn, vice president of manufacturing for Thomas (see Exhibit C17.1), had obtained a quote on his casting from Dawson, another gray iron foundry, several months before. It seemed that Dawson had the necessary capabilities to handle this casting.

To Mr. Litt's surprise, Mr. Dunn was not entirely happy to find the 412 pattern back in the plant. Mr. Dunn contacted personnel at Dawson Foundry, who said that they could not

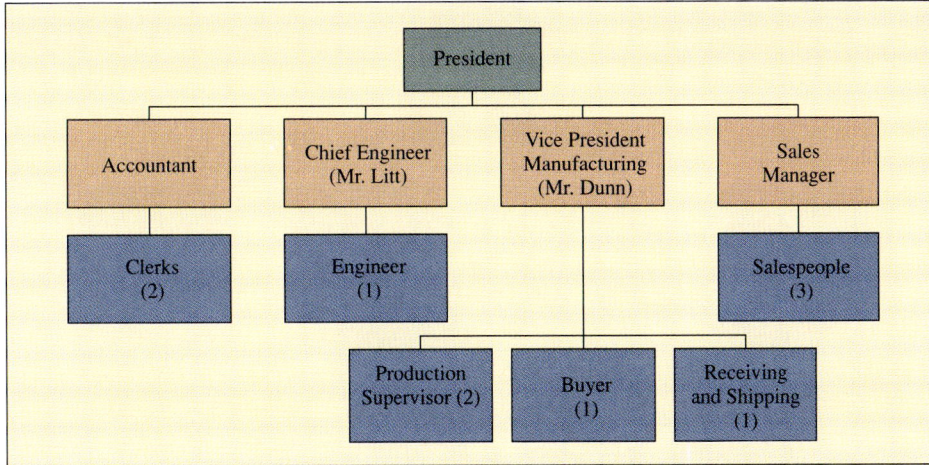

EXHIBIT C17.1

Organization Chart of Thomas Manufacturing Company

accept the job because of a major facilities conversion that would take six months. Locating another supplier would be difficult. Most foundries would undertake complex casting only if a number of orders for simple casting were placed at the same time.

Mr. Dunn knew that gray iron foundry capacity was tight. In general, foundries were specializing or closing down. Mr. Dunn had gathered some data on the gray iron industry located within a 500-mile radius of his plant (see Exhibit C17.2), which highlighted the problems his company was facing. There were three gray iron foundries within 60 miles of Thomas Manufacturing. Thomas had dealt with one foundry until it suffered a 12-month strike. Thomas then moved most of its casting needs to A&B Foundry, but Mr. Dunn had given the occasional order to Dawson and requested quotes quite regularly from them. In the past four years all had gone well with A&B Foundry. Mr. Dunn had planned to share his business with both foundries. A&B was comparable to Dawson on price and had done an excellent job until now.

A telephone call back to A&B Foundry indicated to Mr. Dunn that Mr. James was adamant in his refusal to take the pattern back.

The 412 Casting

Thomas Manufacturing Company was a portable generator manufacturer with sales above the $6 million level. Thomas employed approximately 160 people in a fairly modern plant. Many of its small portable generators were sold to clients all over North America.

The 412 casting was part of the most popular middle-of-the-line generator. The casting weighed 70 pounds and cost approximately $60; its pattern was worth $8,000. A run normally consisted of 100 castings, and Thomas usually received 100 castings every month. The 412 represented about 15 percent of Thomas's casting needs.

Normal lead time was at least eight weeks. When the supply problem arose, Thomas held six weeks' inventory.

Mr. Litt, an expert in pattern work, explained that the pattern was tricky, but once the difficulties were ironed out and the job set up, a hand molder could pour 50 castings in two days without any problems.

EXHIBIT C17.2

Foundry Data for Area within a 500-Mile Radius of the Thomas Plant

A. Shipments of Manufactured Goods

Gray Iron (commercial castings)	Quantity	Value
Previous year	280,000 tons	$65,000,000
Current year	243,000 tons	$54,000,000

B. Number of Establishments

									Current Year
140	133	131	134	137	134	134	128	126	116

10-Year History

Questions

1. What alternatives are open to Mr. Dunn to prevent disruption of his company's most popular generator?

2. Was it appropriate for Mr. Litt to repossess the 412 pattern?

3. From the data given, does it appear that the Thomas Company has any leverage in dealing with the foundries?

Source: M. R. Leenders, H. E. Fearon, and W. B. England, *Purchasing and Materials Management,* 7th ed. (Homewood, IL: Richard D. Irwin, 1980), pp. 50–53.

· C A S E

17.9 CASE
Ohio Tool Company (Vendor Selection)

The Ohio Tool Company designed a new machine, which it considered to be superior to anything else of its type on the market. Estimated sales were about $200,000 per year. The principal advantage of this machine over competition was a unique cam arrangement enabling the operator to adjust the unit quickly.

To achieve the advantages offered by the design, the cam—of which two were required per unit—had to be manufactured to very close tolerances. (See the accompanying sketch). Because of the difficulty of machining the several eccentric surfaces and the need for an integral locating key in the center bore, the part could not readily be made from solid bar stock.

Possible methods of manufacture rapidly narrowed down to some type of casting. The materials under consideration were aluminum, zinc, and iron. Aluminum and iron sand castings were excluded because the close tolerances on the finished part would require precise, very difficult secondary maching operations. Aluminum and zinc die castings could not be used because draft or taper on the cam surfaces that is necessary in order to remove the part from the die, would also necessitate secondary machining operations to render the surfaces true again.

Another possibility for producing the part seemed to be through powder metallurgy, a process by which finely divided metal particles (in this case powdered iron) were formed to the desired shape by means of high pressure in a metal die, and then "sintered" at high temperature to form a solid metal piece. The Ohio Tool Company located three possible powdered-metal sources and sent parts drawings to each.

Supplier A, located about 1,000 miles away, was one of the leaders in the powder metallurgy field. The Ohio Tool Company had purchased parts for another product from this supplier within the past year, and the supplier had failed to deliver on the agreed schedule. After many delivery promises via long-distance telephone and after a special trip to the plant by the purchasing manager, the parts arrived three months late. During this delay all other parts for the project had to be set aside and some workers laid off. In addition, the delay caused the Ohio Tool Company considerable loss of face with its customers because the product had been announced to the trade.

Supplier A submitted this quotation:

5,000 pieces	$0.146 each	Die cost—$1,968
10,000 pieces	$0.145 each	Delivery—Approximately 10 weeks, depending on
20,000 pieces	$0.144 each	the production schedule at the time order is entered.

The quotation did not include incoming freight cost of $0.012 each. Further, it was based on furnishing a cam with a slight projection on one of the surfaces, which would require a machining operation by the Ohio Tool Company at an estimated cost of $0.05 each.

Supplier B, located 300 miles away, was a relative newcomer to the powdered-metal field. The manager of the shop had been with this firm only a short time but had gained his experience from one of the old-line companies. The Ohio Tool Company's experience with this company had been very satisfactory. It had undertaken the job at the same costs as Supplier A and had produced satisfactory parts in record time.

In reply to the request for a quotation, Supplier B suggested that, since it could not manufacture to specified tolerances, they be relaxed on several dimensions. However, the engineering department at Ohio Tool insisted that the critical function of this cam necessitated the tolerances as originally specified. When this information was passed along to Supplier B, it asked to be excused from quoting.

A third supplier, with whom the Ohio Tool Company had had no previous dealings, was asked to quote on the part. Supplier C was a subsidiary of one of the large automotive concerns and had an excellent technical reputation. It was understood, however, that the parent company was considering introducing several powdered-metal parts on its line of automobiles. The quotation of Supplier C was

5,000 pieces	$0.186 each	Die cost—$890
10,000 pieces	$0.185 each	Delivery—10 weeks
20,000 pieces	$0.183 each	

Supplier C was located 900 miles from the Ohio Tool Company plant, and incoming freight would cost $0.012 per unit. The drawing accompanying the quotation indicated a projection on one of the cam surfaces, which would have to be machined by the Ohio Tool Company for the proper functioning of the part. Although special machining techniques would be required in this case, the Ohio Tool Company estimator felt the company could machine off the projection for about $0.06 each in quantities of 5,000 or more.

Because of the past performance record of Supplier B, the purchasing manager decided that he should make an effort to obtain a quotation. He made a personal visit to the plant to discuss the problem, and learned that the plant could hold the tolerances on the center hole closer than the engineering department required, making the cumulative tolerances on the outside diameter of the cam surfaces almost within the tolerance specified. The engineering department agreed to change the drawing accordingly and grant additional latitude on the cam surfaces. On this basis, Supplier B entered the following quotation:

5,000 pieces	$0.50 each	Die cost—$1,350
10,000 pieces	$0.40 each	Delivery—10 to 12 weeks
20,000 pieces	$0.32 each	
50,000 pieces	$0.275 each	

Freight in amounted to $0.005 each. The quotation was based on a part in exact accordance with the drawing, since the cost of secondary operations had been included in the quotation and would be performed by the supplier. By the time this quotation was received, manufacture of other parts of the product was ensured and final assembly was scheduled for 12 weeks from that date.

Upon reviewing all the quotations, the relatively high cost of Supplier B was readily apparent. The purchasing manager decided to call Supplier B and ask him to review his costs again. The quotation was revised:

| 5,000 pieces | $0.45 |
| 10,000 pieces | $0.37 |

No change in 20,000 and 50,000 price

Questions

1. Which vendor would you select for the job? Why?
2. Should a purchasing agent enter into negotiations with one vendor after bids from competitors have been examined?
3. With reference to Question 2, prepare a policy statement that would guide the future actions of the purchasing department.

READING

*Buying in the Common Global Economy**

The several generations who have lived under the socialist economics of communist rule will be reluctant to abandon the lifelong security the system offered. The emerging democracies will probably perpetuate social security. In the context of developing opportunities for sourcing in Eastern Europe, such programs will mean higher costs from a variety of taxes. Individuals will be taxed at a greater rate, adding to labor costs, and products will be taxed, probably in the form of value-added taxes (VAT) already common in Western Europe. Although the basic wages of Eastern Europe will mean initially low labor costs, the costs of rebuilding these ravaged economies while maintaining a large degree of individual security point to rapidly rising costs later in the decade.

The redevelopment of East Germany's economy will be unique because of reunification. Heavy investment will be needed to restore the East German infrastructure, for ex-

ample, for health care, pollution control, and for numerous other problems. Wages will be under pressure in West Germany as immigration from the East pushes up unemployment or jobs move into the lower-wage areas of East Germany.

These pressures may manifest themselves in sporadic displays of social unrest. Nevertheless, Germany is probably better poised to implement its own restoration than any of its neighbors. Although the economic pressures will be intense, both populations have waited too long for reunification to let it fail. Exports and investment will be encouraged to secure the capital needed to fund redevelopment. The pressure on wages and the availability of a large, well-educated, and highly motivated work force will ensure success. The offshore buyer will be able to source a wide variety of quality, high-technology products.

*Edited from Thomas K. Hickman and William M. Hickman, Jr. *Global Purchasing: How to Buy Goods and Services in Foreign Markets*, Homewood, IL: Business One Irwin, 1992, pp. 14–29.

Three major factors will dominate the development of the other Eastern European nations during the 1990s: (1) their pre-war economic and political relationships; (2) their current economic condition; and (3) the political and economic naiveté of both their governments and people. All three will tend to slow any expansion of the European Economic Community (EEC) to include the Eastern Europeans.

Some degree of suspicion toward Germany will lead Poland, Slovakia, and the Czech Republic to approach any involvement with the EEC slowly, especially since German reun<ification will probably lead it to a dominant role in the EEC. Since the EEC is so highly politicized, most of the Eastern European countries will, initially, be rather reluctant in approaching relations with it.

The tremendous need for capital will be the strongest factor slowing relationships with the EEC. Most of the Eastern European countries will want to avoid a close relationship with the EEC to ensure that the United States and Japan, the largest potential investor nations, perceive that they will receive equal status with the other nations of Europe. At most, they will probably seek the sort of association Turkey enjoys with the Community.

Czechoslovakia, the third largest industrial nation in Europe before the war and the one with the highest standard of living in the Eastern bloc, will progress most rapidly. (In 1993 the country split into Slovakia and the Czech Republic.) For the offshore buyer, this will not only mean that sources can be developed there more quickly, but that costs will increase more rapidly as well. Poland and Hungary will follow, at first with products such as are now available from the Newly Industrialized Countries (NICs) of the Far East. The progress of growth will mimic that of the Far East, with the lesser-developed countries following in the footsteps of the more advanced ones. Development in Bulgaria and Romania will be delayed by the ethnic rivalry that has long characterized the area.

The Soviet Union

The development of the USSR as a potential source will proceed along a far different path than that of Eastern Europe. Although their economies have clearly been devastated by 40 years of misrule, most had burgeoning industrial economies before the war, their economic development had generally paralleled that of Western Europe, and they had been developing skilled industrial workers and management. Eastern Europe's role within the Soviet bloc has largely been the transformation of Russian and other Soviet Republics' raw material into finished products.

Russia, the easternmost nation in Europe, greatly lagged behind the rest of Europe in industrializing. The massive spending of the Soviet Union in its defense industries has done little to prepare Russia to compete equally with the rest of the industrialized world.

The Soviet economy will change. Whether Yeltsin will accomplish restructuring the economy or whether change is forced on some successor is almost immaterial unless, of course, the change is violent. Even so, glasnost, perestroika, and the events and successes of Eastern Europe ensure some measure of market freedom. Major opportunities will be found in the Republics that remain in the Union, whatever form it may take, and stay within the purview of historical Russia.

Foreign ownership will probably not play much of a role in the development of this economy. Russian nationalism will dominate Russian politics. The process will therefore be much slower than the economic development of Eastern Europe.

Sourcing opportunities in Russia will therefore be found in situations that support the growth of industry, not merely the purchase of labor. Purchases that involve capital formation will be welcome. Supplying technology, tools, or know-how will generally be a key to developing a source. The Soviet Union wants investment, technology, and help in developing management skills, not aid. Even if aid is needed to help the country through some miserable winters, sourcing strategies should focus on providing technology and skills.

It may even be possible to develop a long-term partnership based on near-obsolete technology. Many companies have moved obsolete tools into lesser-developed countries, especially as automated assembly techniques were developed to offset rising labor costs. The Volkswagen Beetle, which continued in South America long after its disappearance in the United States, is probably the best-known example. Rather than having to retool an entire factory for automation and retrain its workers for a new technology, laying off many of them as a result, near-obsolete tooling may be a welcome path to development.

Moves toward a free market economy in the Soviet Union, even one that is allowed to develop more slowly, also could allow the Soviet Union to take advantage of its geographic proximity to both Eastern Europe and the Far East as a source of raw materials and commodity foods. Although somewhat colder than the Great Plains of the United States, the steppes of Russia could readily supplant them as a source of winter wheat if farmed the same way. The tiaga, a forested tier stretching across Russia between the steppes and the tundra, offers immense timber reserves for both markets as well. By the end of the 1990s, the United States may encounter considerable competition in the timber and grain markets of the Far East and Europe.

The Far East

The relative positions of the player nations in the Far East will remain constant through the 1990s, although the technological level of each will continue to grow.

Japan will remain at the forefront in exports and technology. *Technology-added* will begin to supplant *value-added* as the main component in export value as Japan's research investments and patents grow into mature products. Whether directly, in the form of licenses, or as a component cost for products available only from Japan, technology will represent a significant part of Japan's exports. Japan will be the only source for some products at the leading edge in electronics, optics, machine tools, and ceramics and will continue to dominate the markets of high-volume, process-intensive commodities such as computer memories. Japan's products will be available almost exclusively through subsidiary companies outside Japan or through the many large trading companies.

Korea, Taiwan, Hong Kong, and Singapore will displace Japan in many markets it now dominates. They will master the current technologies and produce at lower cost than Japan's rising wages will permit; Taiwan and Korea because they still lag far behind Japan in income, Hong Kong by producing in China. Singapore, in particular, will also focus increasingly on technology. It is already offering itself as an alternative to Hong Kong to well-educated Chinese reluctant to risk contact with China.

All of these will also continue to cascade their work and technology into other countries of Asia. Malaysia, Indonesia, Thailand, and the Philippines have been providing low-cost manufacturing labor, often building products from kits of material shipped in from another country, for many years. More recently, substantial investment has been made to produce a wide range of products as their manufacturing cost rose in the more highly industrialized countries. These include electronic components, wire and cable, and molded plastics as well as more complex assemblies.

All of these countries share much of the profile of a good source location. They have literacy rates near or above 90 percent. Except for the Philippines, all have concentrated urban populations. All have large university populations and are expected to continue strong emphasis on education.

From a sourcing viewpoint, perceived political stability is about the only factor that distinguishes these nations from one other. Despite the apparent fragility of government in the Philippines since Marcos, there has been a stable government there for many years, albeit one nobody seemed to be pleased with. Nevertheless, business flourished and few people want to reverse this process. The problems in the Philippines stem largely from the lack of infrastructure development; too much of the nation's wealth was siphoned off into corruption and graft. The greatest threats have come from the conservative elements, those who feel the government is not moving fast enough to correct the restraints on growth.

Much the same situation should occur in Indonesia where, under Sukarno and Suharto, almost four decades of stability have been enforced in much the same way Marcos did it in the Philippines. The more recent economic improvements in Indonesia, however, have been made with Suharto's support and actually represent a change in direction from the graft, corruption, and closed borders associated with the country. Expect continued progress in business and economic conditions, especially if there is an orderly change in government after Suharto. Even if there is not, a strong like-

lihood exists that, as in the Philippines, any new government will recognize the need for continuity in the business and industrial sectors of the economy.

The Association of South Eastern Asian Nations (ASEAN) will continue to grow in strength and importance. Singapore, Malaysia and Indonesia have already begun a trilateral association which includes Singapore; Johor, the Malaysian Sultanate just across the causeway from Singapore; and Batam, an Indonesian island easily accessible from Singapore by ferry. All of ASEAN plans to form an economic community similar to the EEC within the next fifteen years.

Throughout the Far East, many of the factors that characterized Japan's industrial development will be present as well, notably (1) strong efforts to improve national infrastructure, (2) increasing emphasis on intellectual and technological strength, and (3) occasional nontariff barriers to protect and perpetuate growth. There will be some attempts to limit wage growth, but few will be successful because the national traits that supported this phenomenon in Japan are rarely found elsewhere. Job-hopping for increased pay has become so common in Singapore that businesspeople are only half-joking when they ask, "How many of your workers came back from lunch today?" The funding for development must therefore come through taxation. Combined wage growth, increased taxes, and the currency appreciation that accompanies success will lead to continual price increases throughout the 1990s.

A search for further sourcing opportunities elsewhere in Asia should consider the common denominators of the countries just discussed: (1) a low-cost, concentrated labor pool; (2) a growing emphasis on education, infrastructure development, and other adjuncts to industrialization; and (3) the political stability needed to focus on long-term goals. In addition, they will all have the most important ingredient common to all the nations that have succeeded: aggressive businesspeople hungry for success.

A few other countries in the region offer most of these qualities. India has been a fairly stable democracy for many years, has a growing student population, and is recovering some of the many young Indians educated abroad, eager to capitalize on India's prospects. There is a huge, very low-wage labor pool, and the Indian government will lend up to 85 percent to Indians willing to employ workers in export-directed ventures.

Sri Lanka had sustained an economic program similar to those of other developing countries in Asia for some years before it was interrupted by the Tamil insurgency. Given a return to stability, sourcing prospects for labor-intensive products will be good there. Pakistan, assuming some relief from the pressures of supporting neighboring Afghanistan, may be in a position similar to that of India.

Products that could be reliably sourced in this last group of countries will probably fall into two narrow categories: (1) simple assemblies or fabrications having a high, repetitive labor content and minimal plant, tool, or manufacturing fixtures or (2) products from a manufacturer who has made significant plant investment and will subcontract assembly. Procurement will be a lengthy process, involving detailed instructions and training, extensive communications, and many unforeseen obstacles. Expect lengthy delays, poor initial quality, and irregular performance. Not surprisingly, these problems were exactly what early investors experienced and are just now being overcome in Thailand and Malaysia. To reap the same rewards, a prospective buyer must be prepared to encounter the same problems.

China

China compares very poorly with the other nations of Asia under all of the criteria identified for potential success. Its infrastructure is in miserable condition. Few roads are paved, there are few trucks to use them, and "central planning" uses the trucks inefficiently. Rail traffic is limited to routes between major cities, largely the legacy of the European railroads of the last century. Air traffic is poorly coordinated; tickets often must be purchased at each stage of a domestic journey and reservations are unreliable. Communication is difficult; telephone and telex facilities are frequently available only in community centers, not at places of business. At present, the country lacks enough capacity to make enough copper wire for its own power and communications requirements this century. From a sourcing standpoint, the difficulty of communicating orders, specifications, and changes and of moving people or material makes most other alternatives preferable to China.

China's literacy rate is low and several factors will tend to retard its improvement. The mere task of training enough teachers, especially to work in rural areas, will take far more than the years remaining in this decade. The difficulty of finding, training, and keeping skilled workers will make sourcing very difficult.

The political climate does not enhance the prospects for business. Heading a business-related organization is less desirable than holding a political position near power. Corruption in politics is rampant and, therefore, so is the financial reward of being in politics. Among the few prerequisites of managing a business is the potential for graft. To keep everyone employed, three to five times as many employees are assigned to a position as are actually needed for the task, effectively multiplying by three to five the cost to perform it.

Nevertheless, the patient buyer will find sourcing opportunities in China. Taiwanese firms are already complaining about their inability to compete with the mainland's low labor costs; the mainland has now replaced Taiwan as the United States' largest shoe supplier because its wages are only about a fourth of Taiwan's. Buyers who will have successful relationships in the next decade will have begun those relationships in the 1990s, both discovering the problems described above and learning how to deal with them. Firms who plan to start marketing there in the 1990s, hoping to reap the benefits of a tremendous market in the

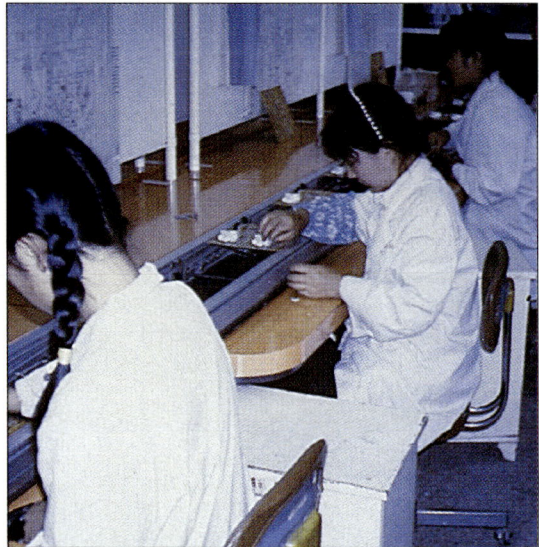

This worker-paced assembly line in Kumming, People's Republic of China produces computer subassemblies, but it is shut down 50 percent of the time due to lack of materials caused by the poor transportation system in the country.

future, should plan to source there as well. Given China's meager foreign reserves, some quid pro quo will be expected of those hoping to sell to China.

The areas of opportunity are already becoming evident. Guangdong province, sometimes facetiously called Northern Hong Kong, does virtually all of the electronics subcontracting for Hong Kong firms. Shanghai is currently the world's largest producer of single-sided printed circuit boards and has reasonably efficient capacity for double- and some multilayer boards as well. Beijing is constructing extensive industrial parks near the city with plans to ensure both equipment and a trained work force. Moreover, it is focusing on developing high-tech, export-oriented firms.

Little local material, technology, or skill can be assumed. The buyer must plan to provide kits for assembly if anything more than the simplest components or commodity materials are required. A need for exhaustive training should be anticipated, not only for the production staff but for supervisory, technical, and quality positions as well.

Buyers in China should recognize that the country is still intensely regional and that ventures that rely on participation from many different locations could be severely disrupted during a period of unrest. Guangdong, Shanghai, and Beijing, for example, all promote themselves independently, much as different cities in the U.S. do. Instability at the national level of China, however, would very likely disrupt communications, transportation and financial transactions between its regions and cities. A failure at the national level could be even more severe and see the nation deteriorate into the sort of factional feuding that has generally characterized dynastic changes in China. Given the failure of Communism in Eastern Europe and the Soviet Union, and the disintegration that followed it, such a change in China is not unthinkable.

In March 1994, President Clinton separated human rights issues from trade issues and renewed the Most Favored Nation Trade Status (MFN) with China.

Australia and New Zealand

The other two countries in this region of the world that meet all of the requirements for success are Australia and New Zealand. They haven't been addressed so far only because they don't fit in the pattern of development outlined for the rest of Asia.

Australia and New Zealand are both in the anomalous position of finding themselves associated with the Western nations because of their English-speaking heritage but competing with the nations of the Far East because of their geography. The cultural relationship of Australia and New Zealand with other English-speaking countries has long dominated their business relationships. Nevertheless, both find themselves in the position of commodity sources for the Far East, exporting ore, timber, wool, and foodstuffs.

A history of strong unions and labor governments has led both countries to the highest labor rates and lowest productivity in Asia. Recognizing their deteriorating competitive positions and dependence on agriculture and raw materials export, both Australia and New Zealand have begun extensive economic reforms. During the 1980s, taxes were cut, and price, wage, and currency controls were relaxed.

The offshore buyer will find both countries easy places to do business because neither language nor culture presents any obstacles. Unemployment is high, especially in New Zealand, so wages will probably remain stable, especially when compared to the rest of Asia. High wage costs may be offset by lower material costs and the benefits of a well-developed infrastructure.

Latin America

Latin America should offer rich opportunities for American sourcing operations during the 1990s. One simple reason is that it is easier to do business there than in Europe or Asia, where proximity favors the local buyers. The mere fact that the United States is eight or nine time zones away slows communications with both Europe and Asia but is not a factor in sourcing in Latin America.

At the same time, the following factors will combine to create a more favorable environment for procurement in Latin America:

1. Pressures to solve the massive debt problems of the Latin countries will result in structural changes in many of the debtor nations. Some of these will facilitate sourcing.
2. The Western Hemisphere will address the growing regional economic spheres in Europe and the Far East with cooperative measures intended to maintain

balance. Many of these will foster sourcing activity in Latin America.

The impetus to accelerate economic cooperation in the hemisphere is twofold: the miserable state of most Latin American economies and the need to counteract the competitive effects of the EEC's open trade.

The countries' individual attempts to correct their problems have been ineffectual. Regular, often violent, changes in government occur under slogans for reform, but few structural improvements result. Latin America continues to have a tremendous gulf between its poor and its wealthy. Many currencies are not convertible, and foreign exchange is often severely restricted. Much of the massive debt service is met by selling natural resources: Mexico's oil, Brazil's forests.

Much of the workforce is neither well educated nor urban. Central planning is too often focused on maintaining entrenched power, not solving problems; and the supporting bureaucrats are more often in patronage than career positions. The debt crises of most of the countries overshadow any long-term view of the problems.

Development in the Far East and Europe will provide a strong impetus for a coordinated approach to Latin America's problems. It will become increasingly apparent during the 1990s that the new, loosely knit economic spheres in Europe and the Far East will have significantly altered the patterns of world trade. Both of these economic communities will include rich, highly industrialized nations and nations with cheap labor, desire for growth, and close access to stable supplies for raw materials. In addition, because of the massive pent-up demand of Eastern Europe and the increasing affluence of the Asian nations, both regions will generate tremendous internal consumer demand during the decade.

Sourcing in both areas will more and more frequently reflect competition for production capacity as the United States loses its preeminence as the world's consumer. Fewer products will be tailored exclusively for the U.S. market, and many will bear the extra cost of features or requirements needed to market in Europe or the Far East. Among the added costs, for example, will be those of obtaining and maintaining regulatory agency approvals. In addition to Underwriters' Laboratories (UL) or Federal Communications Commission (FCC) approvals, more suppliers will also seek VDE or TUV (Germany) and JIS or VCCI (Japan) agency approvals to facilitate selling outside the United States.

American business has long been frustrated by inadequate protection of intellectual property rights, restrictive foreign exchange policies, and the difficulty of repatriating profits. From a national viewpoint, policies that support and enhance the development of a middle class will be seen as necessary for economic growth. Some sort of debt relief would add an extra incentive to participate while trade credits, development loans, and other devices would encourage growth.

The likely participants in such a process are those countries that are both carrying large debt or have already developed significant industry: Brazil, Venezuela, and, possibly, Argentina, Chile, and Costa Rica. A broader view of Latin American development would recognize these countries as foci to cascade development to other nations. This structure clearly indicates that, although the initiative is ostensibly hemispheric, the United States will reward nations individually for progress toward U.S. goals.

The United States, Canada, and Mexico have essentially opened their borders to trade through passage of the North America Free Trade Agreement (NAFTA). As labor costs continue to rise in the Far East and the Eastern European countries develop, an early start sourcing in Latin America may prove to be a wise decision.

Summary

Countries that have the best potential to offer stable and reliable sources of supply generally share three characteristics: a high degree of political stability; a well-developed infrastructure; and a well-educated, urban work force.

The progress of economic development follows a pattern of cascading industrialization as developed nations continually seek lower labor-cost markets. The pattern is clearly evident in Asia, where the United States and Japan first moved production to Taiwan, Hong Kong, Korea, and Singapore. Each of these countries has since begun to farm out its own labor-intensive industry, to Thailand, Malaysia, and Indonesia, for example. Cascading technology will follow in the same course.

The decade will see increasing polarization of super-regional trade agreements. Free trade within the European Economic Community serves to inhibit imports from anywhere else without being blatantly protectionist. In response, the United States, Canada, and Mexico have already reached a free trade agreement. Latin American will be encouraged to participate. The developed nations of Asia, already somewhat protectionist, will avoid overt measures to inhibit imports but will probably begin to react to the EEC and Western Hemisphere communities.

17.10   SELECTED BIBLIOGRAPHY

Bales, William A, and Harold F. Fearon, *CEO's/President's Perception and Expectations of the Purchasing Function.* Tempe, AZ: Center for Advanced Purchasing Studies, 1993.

Birou, Laura M., and Stanley E. Fawcett. "International Purchasing: Benefits, Requirements, and Challenges." *International Journal of Purchasing and Materials Management,* Spring 1993, pp. 28–37.

Bradley, Peter. "A Glimpse of Logistics of the Future." *Purchasing,* March 21, 1991, pp. 50–55.

Burt, David N, and Michael F. Doyle. *The American Keiretsu: A Strategic Weapon for Global Competitiveness.* Homewood, IL: Business One Irwin, 1993.

Cali, James F. *TQM for Purchasing Management.* New York: McGraw-Hill, 1993.

Dumond, Ellen J. "Moving Toward Value-Based Purchasing." *International Journal of Purchasing and Materials Management,* Spring 1994, pp. 3–8.

Fearon, Harold E., Donald W. Dobler, and Kenneth H. Killen. *The Purchasing Handbook,* 5th ed. New York: McGraw-Hill, 1993.

Graw, LeRoy H. *Cost/Price Analysis: Tools to Improve Profit Margins.* New York: Van Nostrand Reinhold, 1994.

Graw, LeRoy H., and Diedre M. Maples. *Service Purchasing: What Every Buyer Should Know.* New York: Van Nostrand Reinhold, 1994.

Guinipero, Larry C. "Motivating and Monitoring JIT Supplier Performance," *Journal of Purchasing and Materials Management,* Summer 1990, pp. 19–24.

Hahn, Chan K., Charles A. Watts, and Kee Young Kim. "The Supplier Development Program." *Journal of Purchasing and Materials Management,* Spring 1990, pp. 2–7.

Hickman, Thomas K., and William M. Hickman, Jr. *Global Purchasing: How to Buy Goods and Services in Foreign Markets.* Homewood, IL: Business One Irwin, 1992.

Hough, Harry E., and James M. Ashley. *Handbook of Buying and Purchasing Management.* Englewood Cliffs, NJ: Prentice-Hall, 1992.

Hutchins, Greg. *Purchasing Strategies for Total Quality: A Guide to Achieving Continuous Improvement.* Homewood, IL: Business One Irwin, 1992.

Lyons, Thomas F., A. Richard Krachenberg, and John W. Henke, Jr. "Mixed Motive Marriages: What's Next for Buyer Supplier Relations?" *Sloan Management Review,* Spring 1990, pp. 29–36.

Mikulski, Florian A. *"Managing Your Vendors: The Business of Buying Technology.* Englewood Cliffs, NJ: Prentice-Hall, 1993.

Morgan, James P., and Susan Zimmerman. "Building World-Class Supplier Relationships." *Purchasing,* August 16, 1990, pp. 62–65.

Morris, Jonathan, and Rob Imrie. *Transforming Buyer–Supplier Relations.* London: Macmillan Academic and Professional, 1992.

Muller, Eugene W. *Job Analysis: Identifying The Tasks of Purchasing.* Tempe, AZ: Center for Advanced Purchasing Studies, 1992.

Newman, Richard G. *Supplier Price Analysis: A Guide for Purchasing, Accounting, and Financial Analysis.* New York: Quorum Books, 1992.

Plank, Richard E., and Valerie Kijewski. "The Use of Approved Supplier Lists." *International Journal of Purchasing and Materials Management,* Spring 1991, pp. 3–41.

Raia, Ernest. "Purchasing's Top 100." *Purchasing,* November 22, 1990, pp. 51–55.

St. John, Caron H., and Kirk Heriot. "International Journal of Purchasing and Materials Management, Winter 1994, pp. 13–16.

St. John, Caron H., and Scott T. Young. "The Strategic Consistency between Purchasing and Production." *International Journal of Purchasing and Materials Management,* Spring 1991, pp. 15–20.

Sako, Mari. *Prices, Quality, and Trust: Inter-Firm Relations in Britain and Japan.* Cambridge, England: Cambridge University Press, 1992.

Schorr, John E. *Purchasing in the 21st Century.* Essex Junction, VT: Oliver Wight Publications, 1992.

VI

IMPROVING THE SYSTEM

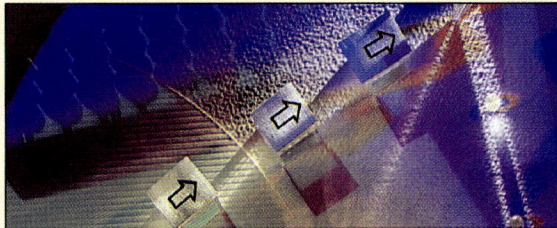

"If it ain't broke, don't fix it" is a questionable maxim in the business world of today. If a company isn't improving its production systems, its managers aren't doing their jobs. In this section we describe two major approaches to improvement—one focusing on change, business process reengineering, and the other focusing on the next generation of production planning concepts, synchronous manufacturing.

Section VI concludes with a consulting report that applies several of the book's key concepts to manufacturing strategy.

Chapter

18

Business Process Reengineering

CHAPTER OUTLINE

KEY TERMS

Reengineering

Operational Processes

Management Processes

Vision Statement

Process Redesign

Information Technology

Continuous Improvement

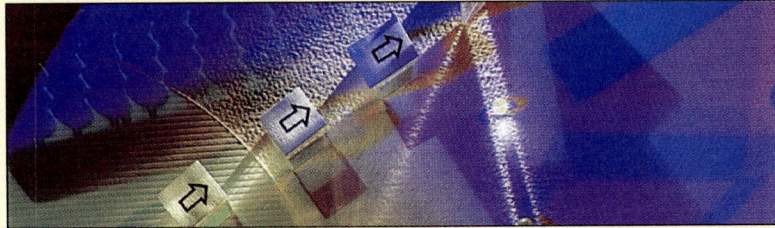

"It was a gut feeling I had," recalls Joe Colwin. "We were profitable, but not as profitable as I knew we should be." He was talking about Mid-States Aluminum Corp., a 30-year-old manufacturer of customized aluminum extrusions that he bought in 1984. Located in Fond du Lac, Wisconsin, the company has increased its sales 20 percent a year since 1984—a cumulative leap of some 500 percent. But the bottom line was not increasing at anywhere near that rate.

Colwin could not understand it. He had invested heavily in workforce training, new equipment, and total quality management. Yet the bottom line remained flat. "My gut said that our 'soft costs' were eating up money that should have gone to profits," Colwin says. These costs are created by processes and tasks that often involve redundant signoffs and duplicated work—steps that produce no customer value and for which customers are not willing to pay.

Reengineering has proceeded incrementally at Mid-States since 1991, when Colwin became convinced that his company was "sick." For example, it was applied to the critical routine of producing job estimates and quotes. Analysis showed that sales personnel spent $156,526 each year to prepare estimates and quotes for customers. But only 8 percent of these quotes were converted into actual orders. A significant amount of effort and money was being spent in activity that generated no revenue. Mid-States is now redesigning its estimating process so that accurate and consistent information generated by different departments can be funneled into a single, reliable source for people creating quotes. The company has also started to produce less complex price quotes tailored to help customers make quicker decisions. Moreover, these quotes are being prepared by clerical staff, allowing sales personnel to spend more of their time selling.

"We have more focus on the customer by more people . . . the whole company is getting closer to the customer," Colwin says.

Source: Ronald E. Yates, "The New Fix for Corporate America's Organizational Ills? Reengineering," *Chicago Tribune,* October 17, 1993. Copyrighted Chicago Tribune Company. All rights reserved. Used with permission.

Change is the only constant in today's business environment. In fact, the 90s have developed into the decade of radical change as businesses in the United States and around the world begin to realize that they are "entering the twenty-first century with companies designed during the nineteenth century to work well in the twentieth."[1] Organizations are now addressing the need to remain or become competitive through dramatic improvements in quality, costs, time-to-market, and customer service. They are doing this by attempting to reinvent themselves by organizing work around processes. The "de-Adam-Smithizing" of business has begun. The focus is shifting away from functional silos toward a holistic view of organizations. Such change is being made through process and organizational innovation as well as through creative application of information technology.

In this chapter we discuss business process reengineering, a management concept that many consider to be the essence of the next business revolution.

18.1   THE NATURE OF BUSINESS PROCESS REENGINEERING

Michael Hammer, the management expert who heads the reengineering movement, defines **reengineering** as "the fundamental rethinking and radical redesign of business processes to achieve dramatic improvements in critical, contemporary measures of performance, such as cost, quality, service, and speed."[2]

The focal point is the process. Another expert in the area, Thomas Davenport, divides processes into those that are operationally oriented (essentially, those related to the product and customer), and management oriented (those that deal with obtaining and coordinating resources). (See Exhibit 18.1.)

The concept of reengineering has been around for nearly two decades and was implemented in a piecemeal fashion in organizations. Production organizations have been in the vanguard without knowing it. They have undertaken reengineering by implementing concurrent engineering, lean production, cellular manufacturing, group technology, and pull-type production systems. These represent fundamental rethinking of the manufacturing process. Manufacturers generally made significant improvements in their internal operations during the 1980s. But excellence in manufacturing has not always translated to superior sustainable results in the marketplace. More recently, the focus appears to have shifted out of the manufacturing process to other interfunctional and interorganizational and customer-based processes. The 1992 Manufacturing Futures Survey reports similar views held by manufacturing executives.[3] Rapid advances in information technology and its applications have been a major enabler of business process reengineering in services.

But translating reengineering concepts into reality is predictably difficult because of the technological and cultural changes that it entails. A survey of top-level managers at 200 companies found that 40 percent of manufacturing executives and 80 percent of service executives knew that change will be needed. However, only 23 percent of the manufacturing and 50 percent of the service executives were confident that their firms know how to manage change.[4]

The greater awareness among service executives may be attributed to the fact that the significance of information is at the forefront in an otherwise intangible service environ-

---

[1]Michael Hammer and James Champy, *Reengineering the Corporation: A Manifesto for Business Revolution* (New York: Harper Business, 1993), p. 30.

[2]Ibid., p. 32.

[3]Jay S. Kim and Jeffrey G. Miller, "Building the Value Factory: A Progress Report for U.S. Manufacturing" (Boston: Boston University Manufacturing Roundtable Research Report, 1992).

[4]Julia King, "Reengineering Repercussions," *Computerworld* 27, no. 26 (June 28, 1993), p. 149.

E X H I B I T 18.1
*Typical Business
Processes in
Manufacturing Firms*

Operational	Management
Product development	Performance monitoring
Customer acquisition	Information management
Customer requirements identification	Asset management
Manufacturing	Human resource management
Integrated logistics	Planning and resource allocation
Order management	
Postsales service	

Reprinted by permission of Harvard Business School Press from *Process Innovation: Reengineering Work Through Information Technology* by Thomas H. Davenport. Boston: 1993, p. 8. Copyright 1993 by the President and Fellows of Harvard College.

ment. It is also extremely difficult to consider product innovation in services without considering the related reengineered process. Many manufacturing companies, on the other hand, have already reengineered some of their processes. This could explain manufacturing executives' lower *perceived* need to change, but quality products manufactured more quickly due to process improvements do not serve the customer when they remain in the warehouse awaiting order clarification or customer credit checks. As stated earlier, the very concept of manufacturing as a function needs revision. The survey also indicates the executives' consistent lack of confidence in their firms' ability to manage the necessary changes.

Global interest in business process reengineering is growing rapidly. Though Japanese companies do not typically use the term *reengineering* to describe radical process change, a recent survey suggests that they are very interested in developing new processes using information technology. The survey also found that Japanese firms rated developing new processes as a higher priority than their American and European counterparts.[5] In Korea and Singapore one of the authors spoke with several banks that are planning reengineering initiatives.

18.2 PRINCIPLES OF REENGINEERING

Reengineering is about achieving a significant improvement in processes so that contemporary customer requirements of quality, speed, innovation, customization, and service are met. This entails seven new rules of doing work proposed by Hammer relating to who does the work, where and when it is done, and information gathering and integration.[6]

Rule 1. Organize around outcomes, not tasks Several specialized tasks previously performed by different people should be combined into a single job. This could be performed by an individual "case worker" or by a "case team." The new job created should involve all the steps in a process that creates a well-defined outcome. Organizing around outcomes eliminates the need for handoffs, resulting in greater speed, productivity, and customer responsiveness. It also provides a single knowledgeable point of contact for the customer. GTE's "front-end technician" position described in the sidebar on the following page illustrates this principle.

---

[5]"Factories of the Future." Executive Summary of the 1990 International Manufacturing Futures Survey (Boston: Boston University, 1991).

[6]Michael Hammer, "Reengineer Work: Don't Automate, Obliterate," *Harvard Business Review* 90, no. 4 (July–August 1990), pp. 104–12.

The New GTE: Dreaming and Doing

S

"Reengineering is new, and it has to be done," asserts mangement guru Peter F. Drucker. Reengineering is for real. Done well, it delivers extraordinary gains in speed, productivity, and profitability. Reengineers start from the future and work backward, as if unconstrained by existing methods, people, or departments. In effect they ask, "If we were a new company, how would we run this place?" Then, with a meat axe and sandpaper, they make the company conform to their vision.

The same kind of reengineering has been underway at Stamford, Connecticut–based GTE Corp., the communications company that last year chalked up $2,099 billion in revenues—four-fifths from its telephone operations. Confronted by smaller, more nimble competitors, GTE has used several pilot reengineering programs to get closer to its customers. Marketing executives determined that customers wanted "one-stop shopping"—one telephone number that they can dial to solve any problem.

When it analyzed its customer service division, GTE found that a customer's problems were solved only once every 200 calls while the customer was still on the phone. By creating specially trained "front-end technicians" who have testing and switching equipment at the same desk where they take customers' calls, customers' problems were solved quickly, usually with "one stop." Now GTE is in the process of linking sales and billing to repair via a menu of touchtone options that will let customers connect to any service they wish. The first step was to "grow" GTE operators' jobs. That was done when they were given software that allows them to access corporate databases that were once off-limits so they can now deal with just about any customer problem. Pilot implementation projects have so far shown a 20 to 30 percent increase in productivity.

GTE's rewired customer-contact process displays most of the salient traits of reengineering. It is occurring in a dramatically altered competitive landscape; it is a major change, with big results; it cuts across departmental lines; it requires hefty investment in training and information technology; and layoffs result. Says Michael Hammer, reengineering's John the Baptist, "To succeed at reengineering, you have to be a visionary, a motivator, and a leg breaker."

GTE's specially trained "front-end technicians" help solve customer problems.

Source: Excerpted from Thomas A. Stewart, "Reengineering: The Hot New Managing Tool," *Fortune,* August 23, 1993, pp. 41–42; and Ronald E. Yates, "The New Fix for Corporate America's Organizational Ills? Reengineering," *Chicago Tribune,* October 17, 1993.

Rule 2. Have those who use the output of the process perform the process In other words, work should be carried out where it is makes the most sense to do it. This results in people closest to the process actually performing the work, which shifts work across traditional intra- and interorganizational boundaries. For instance, employees can make some of their own purchases without going through purchasing, customers can perform simple repairs themselves, and suppliers can be asked to manage parts inventory. Relocating work in this fashion eliminates the need to coordinate the performers and users of a process.

Rule 3. Merge information-processing work into the real work that produces the information This means that people who collect information should also be responsible for processing it. It minimizes the need for another group to reconcile and process that information, and greatly reduces errors by cutting the number of external contact points for a process. A typical accounts payable department that reconciles purchase orders, receiving notices, and supplier invoices is a case in point. Eliminating the need for invoices by processing orders and receiving information on-line, makes much work done in the traditional accounts payable function unnecessary.

Rule 4. Treat geographically dispersed resources as though they were centralized Information technology now makes the concept of hybrid centralized/decentralized operations a reality. It facilitates the parallel processing of work by separate organizational units that perform the same job, while improving the company's overall control. For instance, centralized databases and telecommunication networks now allow companies to link with separate units or individual field personnel, providing them with economies of scale while maintaining their individual flexibility and responsiveness to customers.

Rule 5. Link parallel activities instead of integrating their results The concept of only integrating the outcomes of parallel activities that must eventually come together is the primary cause for rework, high costs, and delays in the final outcome of the overall process. Such parallel activities should be linked continually and coordinated during the process. Concurrent engineering exemplifies this principle.

Rule 6. Put the decision point where the work is performed, and build control into the process Decision making should be made part of the work performed. This is possible today with a more educated and knowledgeable workforce plus decision-aiding technology. Controls are now made part of the process. The vertical compression that results produces flatter, more responsive organizations.

Rule 7. Capture information once—at the source Information should be collected and captured in the company's on-line information system only once—at the source where it was created. This approach avoids erroneous data entries and costly reentries.

The principles of business process reengineering just enumerated are based on a common platform of the innovative use of information technology. But creating a new process requires more than a creative application of information technology. A deeper understanding of the reasons behind current practices is required. (See Exhibit 18.2.) In addition, no two companies can undertake reengineering in identical ways. But the principles just discussed provide some essential guidelines for reengineering efforts.

Steps Manufacturers Take When Reorganizing

Outsourcing one or more operations	31%
Eliminating a product line	34%
Reducing the number of suppliers	34%
Reducing the number of production workers	41%
Flatting the layers of management	56%
Organizing operations by customer or product line	60%
Investing in automated equipment	76%
Significantly improving process flow in factory	87%

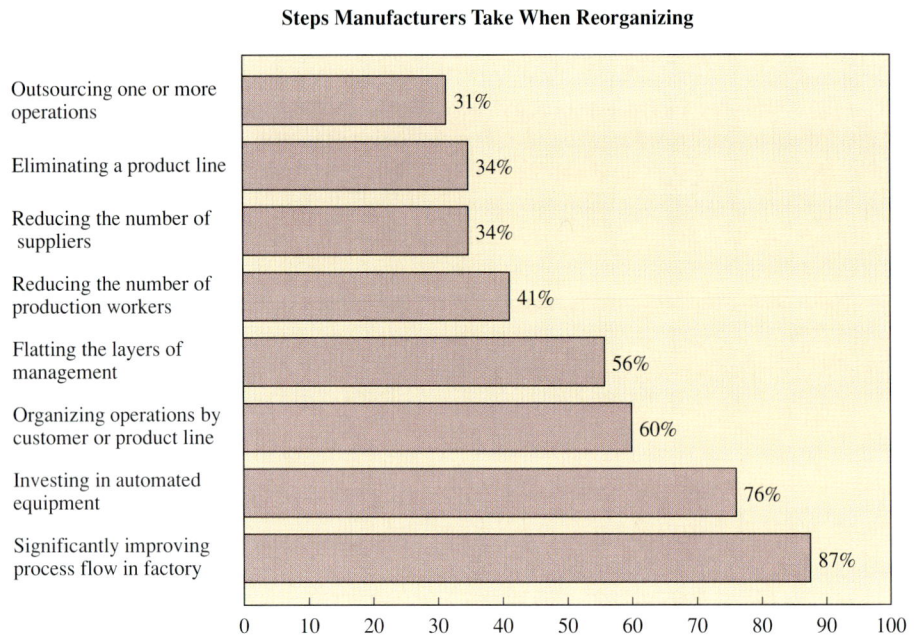

Source: Grant Thorton Survey of American Manufacturers Annual Report, p. 23. © 1993 Grant Thorton.

18.3   THE REENGINEERING PROCESS

Process reengineering requires innovation. See the above graph for examples of what manufacturers are doing. But that does not eliminate the need for a disciplined approach to the effort. Here is a six-step approach for process reengineering:

Step 1. State a case for action.

Step 2. Identify the process for reengineering.

Step 3. Evaluate enablers of reengineering.

Step 4. Understand the current process.

Step 5. Create a new process design.

Step 6. Implement the reengineered process.

Step 1. State a Case for Action

The need for change should be effectively communicated to company employees through educational and communication campaigns. Two key messages should be articulated: (1) a need for action ("Here is where we are as a company, and this is why we can't stay here.") and (2) a vision statement ("This is what we as a company need to become.").[7]

The objectives for reengineering must be in the form of a qualitative and quantitative **vision statement.** These objectives can include goals for cost reduction, time-to-market, quality and customer satisfaction levels, and financial indicators. The objectives can be used to measure progress and to constantly spur ongoing action. The vision statement presented by Federal Express in its infancy is a classic example: "We will deliver the package by 10:30 the next morning." This statement provided measurable operational objectives that redefined an industry.

---

[7]Hammer and Champy, *Reengineering the Corporation,* p. 149.

E X H I B I T 18.2
Reengineering Is Not

- Business fix of the month. It is not about "fixing," but rebuilding.
- Downsizing. But layoffs do result in most cases.
- Reorganizing or flattening organizations. But organizations do become flatter as a result of process improvements.
- Automation. It is about using information systems creatively.
- Total quality management. But the two approaches to change do share some common themes.

Source: Table Based on Michael Hammer and James Champy, *Reengineering the Corporation,* (New York: Harper Business, 1993), pp. 47–49. Copyright 1993 by Michael Hammer and James Champy. Reprinted by permission of HarperCollins Publishers, Inc.

The company's leader is responsible for communicating these important messages, first to senior management and then to the rest of the firm. This represents the first step in communication, an activity that must be continued consistently over the duration of the reengineering project. A senior management steering committee that includes the top executive typically champions the change process, sets goals, assigns resources, and expedites progress. Redesign and implementation are typically the responsibility of a cross-functional process evaluation team.

Step 2. Identify the Process for Reengineering

All major processes in an organization should be initially identified. However, not all major processes should be reengineered at the same time. The following questions define the criteria for selecting processes for reengineering:

Which processes are currently most problematic?

Which processes are critical to accomplishing company strategy and have the greatest impact on the company's customer?

Which processes are most likely to be successfully redesigned?

What is the project scope, and what are the costs involved?

What is the strength of the reengineering team, and the commitment of process owners and sponsors?

Can continuous improvement deliver the required improvements?

Is the process antiquated or is the technology used outdated?

Responses to these questions can be weighted in accordance with the company's need for improvement. The selected process should have a manageable reengineering project scope with well-defined process boundaries. Though all processes in organizations are interrelated, the limits of the current change effort must be identified.

Step 3. Evaluate Enablers of Reengineering

Information technology and human/organizational issues act as enablers of the reengineering process. Technology evaluation has now become a core competency required of all companies. Companies should develop the ability to evaluate current and emerging information technology, and identify creative applications to redesign their existing processes. Exhibit 18.3 (page 744) identifies categories in which information technology supports process reengineering. The breakthrough box, "Mellon Trust Reengineers Workflow Management System for 401(k) Plan," demonstrates the importance of information technology to BPR.

The current organizational culture should also be evaluated in light of the impending change to be brought about by reengineering. Participative and customer-oriented cultures that have evolved from the quality revolution of the 1980s provide a suitable environment for further change. Yet the magnitude of change created by process redesign makes the management of change a necessity. Issues of measurement and compensation,

Mellon Trust Reengineers Workflow Management System for 401(k) Plan

Fraught with change, the defined-contribution business presents opportunities only for those financial institutions that can meet the challenge of radically escalated customer expectations. Mellon Bank Corp.'s Master Trust Services is meeting this challenge by transforming the way it conducts business, using sophisticated technology to reengineer its information systems and workflow management.

Valuing 401(k) plans daily requires the latest in record-keeping and voice-response technology, which helps provide plan participants with 24-hour access to up-to-date investment information. With this data, participants can make informed decisions, tracking their holdings and transferring funds should their investment objectives require it.

Previously, the Mellon Trust defined-contribution department operated on a defined-benefit philosophy, revolving around monthly processing. But even with the monthly lead time, the operational components of cash management, reconciling Mellon record keeping with client payroll, and working in an automated manner with outside fund managers presented challenges to outmoded technology and workflow management. Up to 50 percent of a trust employee's time had been consumed by nonvalue-added activities, such as typing, photocopying and coordinating information that is not universally disseminated.

With this old system, trust employees were forced to concentrate on the process rather than the customer. Up to six copies of a document had to be produced and distributed between several different floors in two separate buildings. This constant passing of data back and forth not only took up valuable time, but created a propensity for potential errors. And these procedures were also less responsive.

Mellon Trust's workflow management system

Enlisting the expertise of an outside consultant enabled Mellon Trust to verify its BPR concepts as sound and determine that the concepts were economically feasible, says Barber. The consultant also developed a demonstration system for Mellon employees "like a little lab room," Barber adds. This system simulation was not only an excellent tool for orienting employees but for marketing as well. Potential clients were shown the system to exhibit Mellon's dedication to improving service quality.

Mellon describes the new workflow management system as an "intelligent" system that automatically, electronically manages and coordinates information associated with each step of the 401(k) process and each related department. Based on architecture consisting of an image server, PC workstations and local area networks (LAN), the system uses digital imaging to capture and display on workstations images of physical documents such as letters, forms and faxes. The system allows processing to be done at individual workstations while providing access to multiple mainframe systems and databases, and it is designed to facilitate report management by replacing paper or microfiche reports with computerized output to laser disk.

With this new system, each department captures and stores incoming client faxes directly into the system via fax modem. Documents received through the mail will be scanned into the system manually. A plan administrator reviews each image at his or her workstation to determine what action the account requires, entering the appropriate process codes and related information. The system then creates an electronic file "folder" and routes it to the appropriate departments via the LAN for further processing. The system audits each electronic file folder, and if any information is missing or incorrect, the system allows the plan administrator to write a brief note that is either automatically faxed back to the client or input into an automatic "call back" reminder. Once one activity in the service process is complete, the person re-

---

career paths, work enrichment, and new skills training should be addressed. The appropriate design of these factors will have significant impact on the successful implementation of the reengineered process.

Step 4. Understand the Current Process

The current process must be diagnosed as a means to understand it and its underlying assumptions. Broad performance parameters of existing processes must be determined. Process evaluation techniques from quality management such as flow charts, fishbone diagrams, and quality function deployment can be used. There is no need to document and analyze the current process in detail since the goal is not to fix the process, but to

sponsible for the next step sees it queued on his or her workstation along with processing instructions. Each workstation automatically interfaces with all mainframe processing systems so that it eliminates the effort of logging-on and accessing multiple systems, as well as the need to constantly re-enter data such as account name and number.

The Company expects this new system to yield benefits in four areas:

Quality—The new system should:

- reduce errors due to a lack of information;
- immediately detect processing difficulties;
- facilitate employee training in how to avoid errors;
- eliminate re-entry of data into multiple systems;
- automatically track and report service quality measures;
- build in work rules and error detection; and
- decrease risks associated with missed steps or misinterpretations of data.

Service—The new system should:

- easily accommodate customized service requests;
- produce accurate client status reports instantaneously;
- make management reports customized, more timely and more accurate;
- foster teamwork and client interaction;
- provide on-line responses to customer inquiries without delay;
- archive all documents and back-up notes in an electronic file folder; and
- automatically log all service inquiries.

Speed—The new system should:

- eliminate delays due to missing reminders or lack of follow-up;
- reduce work cycles with parallel processing;

- enable easier, quicker reallocation of staff resources to avoid backlogs;
- keep routine work flowing by eliminating time-consuming meetings and memos;
- implement revisions to processing requirements; and
- eliminate delays due to manual copying, logging and retrieving of files.

Control—The new system should:

- help enforce standard procedures:
- ensure that work files are accurate and up-to-date via a common workflow database;
- improve accountability by clearly defining which person is responsible for every step;
- automatically generate operating statistics for management review;
- automatically generate reminders and system checks;
- electronically create and seal audit trails; and
- guard against inadvertent or unwanted system disruptions through security control.

From transactions to relationships

The new workflow management system will be rolled out over the next nine months. In this period, the BPR team will reclassify jobs and train staff on the new operating environment, as well as bring new clients onto the new system.

Once the new system is in place, employees will receive technical training. Barber estimates that a telephone rep might need a week or two of training; client services people might require two to four half-day sessions. Even though the system has a user-friendly, icon-driven, Windows-like environment, it will require "a significant amount of training, even for casual users," Barber says. "You can have the best system in the world, but the people have to know how to use it to its potential."

Source: Reprinted from *Industrial Engineering Magazine*, May 1994. Copyright 1994, Institute of Industrial Engineers, 25 Technology Park/Atlanta, Norcross, Georgia 30092.

create a new one. Observation and participation in the actual process, as opposed to data collection and interviewing, are extremely valuable approaches that may be used to understand processes. However, the process must not be overstudied and reengineers should move quickly on to redesign.

Process redesign requires beginning with a clean sheet of paper. The creative nature of innovation makes it nonalgorithmic and nonroutine. Reengineers should suspend current rules, procedures, and values so as to create new process designs. They also need to utilize the principles of reengineering that have been discerned. However, with an increasing

Step 5. Create a New Process Design

E X H I B I T 18.3

The Impact of Information Technology on Process Innovation

Impact	Explanation
Automational	Eliminating human labor from a process
Informational	Capturing process information for purposes of understanding
Sequential	Changing process sequence or enabling parallelism
Tracking	Closely monitoring process status and objects
Analytical	Improving analysis of information and decision making
Geographical	Coordinating processes across distances
Integrative	Coordination between tasks and processes
Intellectual	Capturing and distributing intellectual assets
Disintermediating	Eliminating intermediaries from a process

Source: Reprinted by permission of Harvard Business School Press from *Process Innovation Reengineering Work Through Information Technology* by Thomas H. Davenport. Boston: 1993, p. 51. Copyright 1993 by The President and Fellows of Harvard College.

E X H I B I T 18.4

Elements of Success and Failure in Reengineering

Keys to Success

1. Set an aggressive reengineering performance target.

2. Commit 20 to 50 percent of the chief executive's time to the project.

3. Conduct a comprehensive review of customer needs, economic leverage points, and market trends.

4. Assign an additional senior executive to be responsible for implementation.

5. Conduct a comprehensive pilot of the new design.

Traps for Failure

1. Assign average performers to the reengineering project.

2. Measure only the plan, and not the actual process implemented.

3. Settle for the status quo, rather than pursue radical change.

4. Overlook communication, rather than implement an ongoing communications program.

Source: Reprinted by permission of Harvard Business Review. An excerpt from "How to Make Reengineering Really Work," by Gene Hall, Jim Rosenthal, and Judy Wade, November/December 1993, pp. 128-129. Copyright 1993 by the President and Fellows of Harvard College; all rights reserved.

ing number of successful cases of reengineering being publicized, benchmarking can also be used as a basis for idea creation. Section 18.4 discusses some important methods and tools applied in the process redesign phase of reengineering.

Step 6. Implement the Reengineered Process

Leadership is critical, not just to the implementation process, but to the entire reengineering effort. The extent of change necessitates the direct and continued engagement on the part of the senior executive and the senior management steering committee. Process engineering teams are typically responsible for implementing the new designs. However, support and buy-in from line managers are crucial to success because implementation changes accountabilities of line managers while expecting them to deliver on the improvements. Training employees in additional skills needed to perform in the new environment is also essential. The reengineered process design forms the basis for a pilot project that is followed by phased introduction. Postimplementation assessment is usually made in relation to the objectives defined at the beginning of the reengineering project.

Though reengineering success stories are being widely publicized today, 50 to 70 percent of all reengineering efforts fail. (Exhibit 18.4 presents elements of success and failure.) Even those organizations that greatly improve individual processes, in itself a success, may fail to translate these outcomes into company success. To be considered truly successful, reengineering should have a long-term impact on the firm's bottom line. (See "Aetna Insurance Reinvents Its Business Processes.") Essentially, reengineering efforts

Aetna Life and Casualty is the largest investor-owned financial services company in the United States. Headquartered in Hartford, Connecticut, it is organized around 16 strategic business units and employs over 42,000 people. By the mid-1980s the company had become a large, self-satisfied behemoth out of touch with its environment, customers, and competition. This resulted in slow growth, sagging productivity, and slipping financial performance. In 1990, Aetna's president, Ron Compton, challenged the business unit heads to break the cycle of mediocre performance and urged them to reinvent the way they did business. He stressed the need to reengineer business processes and procedures and to get key people involved in the revitalization effort. A corporate reengineering group was formed to act as internal consultants to the business units.

The steps in a typical reengineering effort at Aetna consist of

- Top-level executives sponsoring and funding a reengineering project.
- Forming an interdisciplinary management team.
- Identifying customers of the business products and services.
- Clarifying customers' critical needs and expectations.
- Identifying the core business processes that link different departments and connect the company with customers.
- Streamlining work processes between departments and enhancing products and services delivered to customers.
- Improving measures for monitoring core work processes.
- Benchmarking performance measures on core processes with the "best in class" competition.

Most reengineering projects at Aetna dealt with cumbersome systems for filling out forms and following procedures. Many of Aetna's processes were slow and definitely not "customer-friendly." As a result of reengineering, Aetna closed down its 120 local offices and replaced them with 22 full-service centers open 24 hours a day. Customers can now direct dial one of these centers for complete service. Aetna's Property and Casualty unit's sales and operating performances have already improved due to these changes.

Hurricane Andrew provided a rigorous test for the new process. Five thousand claims were received in a very short time, but most customers rated their service excellent. Aetna has now carried out over 10 major reengineering projects, with each averaging a $10 million payback on invested capital.

Source: Excerpted from Tim R. V. Davis, "Reengineering in Action," *Planning Review* 22, no. 4 (July–August 1993), pp. 49–54.

should be across the business unit and deep enough to impact the organization's various dimensions.[8]

18.4   PROCESS REDESIGN TECHNIQUES AND TOOLS

Inductive Thinking   This involves recognizing potential solutions, and then seeking and recognizing obvious or latent problems that may be solved. This approach is required in the creative application of information technology to reengineer processes. For instance, the use of teleconferencing is not to eliminate business travel entirely, but to be able to get more individuals working together.

---

[8]Gene Hall, Jim Rosenthal, and Judy Wade, "How to Make Reengineering Really Work," *Harvard Business Review* 93, no. 6 (November–December 1993), pp. 119–131.

Flowcharting   Though mentioned in Step 4 of the preceding section, flow charts or blueprints are the fundamental tool when initiating BPR. The flow chart may be the only tool that is used in 100 percent of the applications of BPR. They can be simple—such as boxes and arrows placed on a huge roll of brown paper that is then rolled out along a wall. (This was used by consultants studying BellSouth telephone company to help categorize initially 81 processes into the 13 most important "process streams" of the business.[9]) Or flow charts can be sophisticated proprietary charting software packages.

Creative Process Redesign   Applying the principles of reengineering discussed in Section 18.2 is an approach to creative process redesign. Questioning the assumptions that underlie current business practices leads to new methods. Many successes in process reengineering relate to procurement. These have arisen because of challenging long-held beliefs. Eliminating the rule that the supplier is a business adversary has led to sharing operational information to improve the combined performance of both supplier and buyer. The need for invoices as a prerequisite for payment has been altered. Reengineered firms now pay on receipt of goods, thus eliminating the need for invoices.

Process Benchmarking   Benchmarking is usually considered a continuous improvement tool. But it can also be used to gain information regarding a company's relative position in key business processes and core competencies. During the initial stages of a reengineering program, benchmarking can help create an industry context for the goals being set. Benchmarking will also provide a firm with examples of best practices in terms of new processes and the approach to their implementation. Benchmarking's value is not just to imitate another company's processes. Practitioners report that benchmarking's most important value in the reengineering process is that a team's imagination is stimulated when it sees creative solutions implemented by the companies being benchmarked. In some cases there may be no external standard for comparison.

Simulation   Discrete-event computer simulation and animation can be very useful in understanding processes. This is similar to simulation applications in process-flow situations in manufacturing or services operations. The simulations could be used to visualize and evaluate the redesigned processes. This can be accomplished even before the pilot project stage, providing reengineers with an appropriate tool for evaluating new processes.

Reengineering Software   There is adequate software available to help draw detailed process maps, and software tools for understanding existing processes and designing new ones are being developed on the basis of the U.S. Dept. of Defense process design methodology called Integrated Definition (IDEF). Texas Instruments' Business Design Facility and Meta Software's Design/IDEF are two such tools that facilitate modeling and evaluation of business processes.[10] The availability of such software tools and methodologies aids the redesign phase of process reengineering. The ultimate exercise, however, is an overall migration plan to move the organization from the current state to a

[9]Connie Brittain, "Reengineering Complements BellSouth's Major Business Strategies," *Industrial Engineering*, February 1994, pp. 34–36.
[10]"The Role of IT in Business Reengineering," *I/S Analyzer* 31, no. 8 (August 1993), pp. 11–14.

vastly improved future state. Reengineering software tools should be utilized within this framework.[11]

18.5   REENGINEERING AND CONTINUOUS IMPROVEMENT

The quality management movement has highlighted the significance of business processes and the need for their continuous improvement. It has also made organizations more customer-focused. The concepts of teamwork, worker participation and empowerment, cross-functionality, process analysis and measurement, supplier involvement, and benchmarking are significant contributions of quality management. In addition, the need for a "total" view of the organization has been reemphasized by quality management in an era of extensive functionalization of business. Quality management has also influenced company culture and values by exposing organizations to the need for change. The environment created by implementing quality management principles for over a decade provides an excellent basis for business process reengineering.

Quality management has emphasized continuous and incremental improvement of processes that are in control. Reengineering, on the other hand, is about radical discontinuous change through process innovation. Though reengineering and continuous improvement have some similarities, there are also significant differences between them. (See Exhibit 18.5 on the following page.)

The dissimilarities that have been identified may create an impression that reengineering is outside the realm of quality management. But quality gurus such as Deming and Juran have considered innovation and breakthroughs in processes as an essential part of quality management. This requires us to understand the relationship between reengineering and continuous improvement so that we may develop an integrated framework for operational change.

18.6   INTEGRATING REENGINEERING AND PROCESS IMPROVEMENT

Organizations must develop a framework for placing reengineering activity in the context of other change initiatives they may undertake. It should not be considered the once and for all "big fix." Integration will help keep the different change initiatives' expectations, methods, and results distinct from each other, thereby minimizing the confusion and cynicism that usually result from undertaking an assortment of management initiatives. Four approaches to integrating process improvement and reengineering activities in organizations are discussed next.[12]

Sequencing Change Initiatives   This approach suggests cycling through process stabilization, process reengineering, and continuous improvement. The disadvantage for such an initiative is that it may take at least five years to go through one cycle of change, which would be longer than many organizational learning cycles and product life cycles. Though this approach is discussed to a greater extent in management literature, the technique appears to be least valuable in practice.

---

[11]The University of Southern California School of Business Atrium Laboratory has developed a variety of computer tools to assist executives in reengineering business processes.

[12]Thomas H. Davenport, "Need Radical Innovation and Continuous Improvement? Integrate Process Reengineering and TQM," *Planning Review,* May–June 1993, pp. 6–12.

E X H I B I T 18.5

Reengineering versus Continuous Improvement

	Reengineering	**Continuous Improvement**
Similarities		
Basis of analysis	Processes	Processes
Performance measurement	Rigorous	Rigorous
Organizational change	Significant	Significant
Behavioral change	Significant	Significant
Time investment	Substantial	Substantial
Differences		
Level of change	Radical	Incremental
Starting point	Clean slate	Existing process
Participation	Top-down	Bottom-up
Typical scope	Broad, cross-functional	Narrow, within functions
Risk	High	Moderate
Primary enabler	Information technology	Statistical control
Type of change	Cultural and structural	Cultural

Reprinted by permission of Harvard Business School Press from *Process Innovation: Reengineering Work Through Information Technology* by Thomas H. Davenport. Boston: 1993, p. 11. Copyright 1993 by the President and Fellows of Harvard College.

Creating a Portfolio of Process Change Programs   This method involves the categorization of all processes and subprocesses in an organization on the basis of the type of change necessary. Criteria for selecting processes for reengineering could include relevance to strategy, current performance levels, capability of sponsor, available investment, and history of change. Many leading companies in process reengineering are adopting this approach to integration.

Limiting the Scope of Work Design   In this approach, high-level processes are designed by the reengineering teams responsible. But employees who perform the jobs design the detail work processes involved within the specifications decided by the reengineering team. This is an attempt to combine the participative nature of continuous improvement with the top-down approach common to process reengineering.

Undertaking Improvement through Innovation   This approach combines short-term improvement methods and long-term reengineering in the same process change effort. Improvement methods such as value analysis can be used to obtain quick benefits which are then invested in the longer-term reengineering effort. The improvement projects may also be a means to move the current process forward to a stage where radical process change is possible.

The different approaches to process change are complementary. Organizations need to determine how and when they need to apply the appropriate methods to their different processes. While it is important to have an integrated approach to operational change, it is far more important to effect that change.

18.7   CONCLUSION

Although we have presented reengineering in a positive light, it is not a panacea. Like any other management approach, how you apply it makes a difference.[13] Nevertheless, we believe that reengineering will eventually affect most organizations. The revolution

---

[13]An example of misapplication is Greyhound Lines, Inc., poorly designed and implemented Trips reservation system that according to *The Wall Street Journal* (October 20, 1994, pp. A1, A10) still can't assure a passenger a seat on a given bus.

in computer technology, that is a central feature of reengineering virtually guarantees this happening.

Operations management resides at the very heart of reengineering. The entire text has been devoted to understanding and managing processes by which goods and services are created. Reengineering involves integrating all of the operations concepts to come up with a new, more intelligent way of running the organization.

18.8 REVIEW AND DISCUSSION QUESTIONS

1. Think about the registration process at your university. Develop a flow chart to understand it. How would you radically redesign this process?

2. Have you driven any car lately? Try not to think of the insurance claims settlement process while you drive! How would you reengineer your insurance company's claims process?

3. Identify the typical processes in manufacturing firms. Discuss how the new product development process interacts with the traditional functions in the firm.

4. An order management process is at the heart of a company's operations. It begins with the customer placing an order with the company and continues through to the customer's receipt of that order and the firm's receipt of payment. Draw a flowchart describing this process. Identify organizational and information technology enablers that would help you innovate the order management process.

5. Sketch a typical materials procurement process that exists in functional organizations. Using reengineering principles, challenge the status quo and redesign this process.

6. An equipment manufacturer has the following steps in its order entry process:

   a. Sales representative takes order and faxes to Order Entry.
   b. Enter order into system (10 percent unclear or incorrect).
   c. Check stock availability (15 percent of orders not in stock).
   d. Perform customer credit check. (Ten percent of orders have credit issues.)
   e. Send bill of materials to warehouse.

   The order-receipt to warehouse cycle time is typically 48 hours, 80 percent of the orders are handled without error, and order handling costs are 6 percent of order revenue. Should you reengineer this process, or is continuous improvement the appropriate approach? If you choose to reengineer, how would you go about it?

CASE

18.9 CASE
A California Auto Club Reengineers Customer Service

For the 3 million members who count on its services, the California State Automobile Association (CSAA) often seems like a trusted member of the family.

Yet CSAA is no mom-and-pop operation. Were it a publicly traded corporation, CSAA, with its $3.2 billion in assets, would rank on the *Fortune* 500 list of America's largest diversified financial companies. Its 5,700 employees operate in a network of 72 district offices throughout its membership territory in Northern California and Nevada. CSAA's diversified operations range from tour books and emergency road services to airline ticketing, auto and home-owners insurance, and travelers checks.

Two years ago CSAA embarked on a long-term reengineering effort. From an operations center on the 23rd floor of its San Francisco headquarters, teams of employees have been putting every business process under a microscope. They are seeking ways to make operations better and more efficient, while rekindling the close relationship with members that had been CSAA's trademark.

"It was obvious that the old ways of doing business wouldn't work in the future, and that we needed to make some fundamental changes," says Gregory A. Smith, vice president and general manager of insurance operations. The goals are to improve customer service threefold; to reduce baseline expenses by as much as 20 percent; and to enrich jobs and enhance career growth for employees. For the daily transactions that are the bread and butter of the organization, the targeted process time reductions are also ambitious:

two days to renew an automobile policy instead of 25; two days for a new homeowners policy instead of 21; seven minutes for hotel reservations instead of 13.

A Reengineered Job

Through its reengineering effort, CSAA has designed a new system for serving customers centering around a new position called "member service consultant." The people serving in this job will be capable of handling 80 percent of a member's needs, from renting a car to making an insurance claim. Specialists will field the remaining calls or visits that require additional expertise.

Supporting the service consultant will be a new information system that links data that currently resides in three separate systems. This technology will enable a service consultant to respond to most members on the spot.

Business reengineering at CSAA is very much a work in progress, with pilot programs and tests scheduled for rollout through 1993. Before the reengineering effort was launched in February 1991, however, a preliminary phase was designed to find "quick hits"—immediate, tangible steps to streamline operations.

Three Quickies

One quick hit was to authorize field offices to give insured members a proof of coverage form that previously had to be routed through CSAA headquarters. Another streamlining step was to expand the expiration time for membership cards to two years instead of one, resulting in savings of about $500,000. Average turnaround time for processing new business applications was reduced from six days to three days; and the proportion of new auto policies that had to be "reworked" (processed more than once) dropped from 50 percent to 16 percent. In total, the quick hits resulted in estimated savings of nearly $4 million.

A Comprehensive Survey

Four employee teams, reflecting the range of CSAA's operations—sales and underwriting, claims, service delivery (representing the main functional areas)—were formed along with a strategic marketing team to focus on broader issues. These teams undertook the most comprehensive survey of CSAA members and employees in the organization's history. Members were asked about CSAA services and products in focus groups and during visits to district offices. Employees were asked a range of questions about their work including, "What would you do if you were president of CSAA for a day?"

The surveys showed remarkable coherence between the issues cited by members and employees. Most of the frustrations for both groups concerned the highly segmented way that CSAA's services were provided. A member visiting a typical office had to go to one window for an insurance claim, another for a road map, and still others for registra-

tion renewals, travelers checks, and additional services. As James P. Molinelli, executive vice president described it, "That's not service—that's a pinball effect." If a member phoned in for help, the CSAA staffer answering questions about underwriting couldn't handle a question about travel or claims, and had to refer callers to another phone number.

Telephone Gridlock

The whole issue of telephone service emerged as a headache for members and employees alike. Members spoke of confusing recorded messages and long waiting periods in limbo while on hold. By one estimate, up to 30 percent of callers were hanging up before being helped. Rather than battle the telephone log jam, some members were making personal visits to district offices for their transactions. However, increasing personnel at the offices was not only expensive, it didn't solve the long-term problem.

Furthermore, members and employees alike said that CSAA's activities had become so varied that it was difficult to understand the range of services. For example, many holders of automobile insurance policies said they were unaware that CSAA also offered homeowners insurance.

In addition to the internal issues, the reengineering effort also had to address an operating environment that was increasingly difficult and complex. New competition is entering every arena of CSAA's business, from car manufacturers offering their own emergency road services to companies providing computer systems that let travelers book airline flights from their homes.

Get Crazy

The reengineering teams are tackling these and other issues in a series of meetings that the service-delivery team describes as "Get Smart—Get Crazy—Get Serious—Get Going."

"The ground rules for the meetings were—no hidden agendas, be open and honest, and have a sense of urgency," says Phyllis M. Love, manager of mail and records processing, who serves on the teams. "At meetings there's a lot of back and forth, negotiation, and compromise."

The central issue that emerged was the fragmented way that CSAA services were dispensed—insurance underwriting here, travel services there. The member service consultant was a key innovation, but making it work required intensive cross-training for employees on the range of CSAA services, and a computer system that would pull all the vital information together and make it readily available. In the fall of 1991, three employees from field offices went to headquarters for an intensive, three-week cross-training program. They also helped design, develop, and test a prototype system that would support the new service consultant.

The acid test for the new business model came when the group began acting out scenarios simulating work in the CSAA office of the future. "Members" played by employees would interact with an employee playing the role of the service consultant. Needed modifications in the business model were identified, and within two months simulations were being conducted for senior CSAA management.

Meanwhile, the teams adhered to a policy of "communicate, communicate, communicate" to the entire CSAA workforce. Workshops and meetings in the field, posters and newsletters, and a series of videotapes called *New Directions* explained the rationale for the program, and helped prepare the workforce for the transition.

Sell with Scenarios

The powerful new information system will liberate the service consultants from a paper-intensive, error-prone work environment. On-screen prompts will announce changes in regulations and procedures, replacing stacks of thumbtacked memos that now fill up bulletin boards. The system will also allow the running of rapid "what-if" scenarios for a member who wants to know, for example, how changing the deductible will affect her insurance premium.

The reengineering effort is now being carried forward by five interdisciplinary teams whose focus includes workforce retraining, reward and performance measurement, and information technology.

"We're trying to create a learning environment for the future, for all levels of employees from clerical to management," says John Clark, a regional claims manager who has served on two reengineering teams.

A One Stop Shop

There's a "back to the future" aspect to the reengineering effort. "In the past, when district offices were smaller, a member could walk in and talk to anybody on the staff about any problem. Everyone in the office had to know something about everything, and members could get complete service with just one stop," says James P. Molinelli, executive vice president. Now, CSAA's best practices of the past are about to re-emerge with a distinctly contemporary look.

Questions

1. Describe the customer service process at CSAA and discuss the different phases of the reengineering effort.

2. Discuss process enablers' role developing the new design.

Source: Reprinted from Robert S. Buday, "Reengineering One Firm's Product Development and Another's Service Delivery," *Planning Review,* March-April 1993, pp. 17–19. Reprinted with permission from The Planning Forum, the International Society for Strategic Management and Planning.

18.10 SELECTED BIBLIOGRAPHY

Davenport, Thomas H. *Process Innovation: Reengineering Work through Information Technology.* Boston: Harvard Business School Press, 1993.

Davenport, Thomas H., and James E. Short. "The New Industrial Engineering: Information Technology and Business Process Redesign." *Sloan Management Review* 31, no. 4 (Summer 1990), pp. 11–27.

Davidson, William H. "Beyond Re-Engineering: The Three Phases of Business Transformation." *IBM Systems Journal* 32, no. 1 (1993) pp. 65–79.

Hall, Gene, Jim Rosenthal, and Judy Wade. "How to Make Reengineering Really Work." *Harvard Business Review* 93, no. 6 (November–December 1993), pp. 119–31.

Hammer, Michael. "Reengineering Work: Don't Automate, Obliterate." *Harvard Business Review* 90, no. 4 (July–August 1990), pp. 104–112.

Hammer, Michael, and James Champy. *Reengineering the Corporation: A Manifesto for Business Revolution.* New York: Harper Business, 1993.

Heygate, Richard, and Gresh Brebach. "Corporate Reengineering." *The McKinsey Quarterly,* Spring 1991, pp. 44–55.

Pine II, B. Joseph. *Mass Customization: The New Frontier in Business Competition.* Boston: Harvard Business School Press, 1992.

Reengineering Handbook. Indianapolis: AT&T Quality Steering Committee, February 1992.

Chapter

19

Synchronous Manufacturing

CHAPTER OUTLINE

KEY TERMS

Synchronous Manufacturing
Hockey-Stick Phenomenon
Throughput
Inventory
Operating Expense
Productivity
Unbalanced Capacity
Bottleneck, Nonbottleneck

Capacity-Constrained Resource (CCR)
Drum, Buffer, Rope
Time Buffer
Process and Transfer Batch
Dollar Days
Backward/Forward Scheduling
VAT Classification

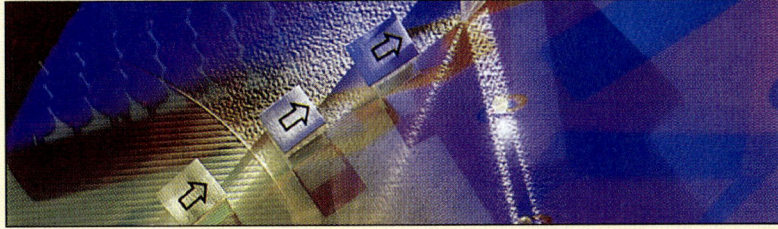

SCENE: Alex Rogo is the plant manager at the Barrington Plant of UniWare, a Division of UniCo. He has had a lot of trouble with his plant in keeping schedules, reducing inventory, improving quality, and cutting costs, among other problems. Bill Peach, division vice president, just visited him and gave him three months to improve, or else the plant will be closed.

Alex's son, Dave's Boy Scout troop is taking a 20-mile overnight hike (10 miles to Devil's Gulch where they will camp for the night, returning the following morning). Alex had been coaxed by his wife and son to accompany the troop. They are now on the hike and way behind schedule. The line of scouts is spread way out with the fastest kids in front; Herbie, the slowest, lags way behind in the rear. Alex is trying to figure out how he can make the Boy Scouts stay together and move faster.

Up front, you've got Andy, who wants to set a speed record. And here you are stuck behind Fat Herbie, the slowest kid in the woods. After an hour, the kid in front—if he's really moving at three miles per hour—is going to be two miles ahead—which means you're going to have to run two miles to catch up with him.

Alex is thinking, "If this were my plant, Peach wouldn't even give me three months. I'd already be on the street by now. The demand was for us to cover 10 miles in five hours, and we've only done half of that. Inventory is racing out of sight. The carrying costs on that inventory would be rising. We'd be ruining the company."

"Okay," I say. "Everybody join hands."

They all look at each other.

"Come on! Just do it!" I tell them. "And don't let go."

Then I take Herbie by the hand and, as if I'm dragging a chain, I go up the trail, snaking past the entire line. Hand in hand, the rest of the troop follows. I pass Andy and keep walking. When I'm twice the distance of the line-up, I stop. What I've done is turn the entire troop around so that the boys have exactly the opposite order they had before.

753

"Now listen up!" I say. "This is the order you're going to stay in until we reach where we're going. Understood? Nobody passes anybody.

"The idea of this hike is not to see who can get there the fastest. The idea is to get there together. We're not a bunch of individuals out here. We're a team."

So we start off again. And it works. No kidding. Everybody stays together behind Herbie. I've gone to the back of the line so I can keep tabs, and I keep waiting for the gaps to appear, but they don't.

"Mr. Rogo, can't we put somebody faster up front?" asks a kid ahead of me.

"Listen, if you guys want to go faster, then you have to figure out a way to let Herbie go faster," I tell them.

One of the kids in the rear says, "Hey, Herbie, what have you got in your pack?"

Herbie stops and turns around. I tell him to come to the back of the line and take off his pack. As he does, I take the pack from him—and nearly drop it.

"Herbie, this thing weighs a ton," I say. "What have you got in here?"

"Nothing much," says Herbie.

I open it up and reach in. Out comes a six-pack of soda. Next are some cans of spaghetti. Then come a box of candy bars, a jar of pickles, and two cans of tuna fish. Beneath a rain coat and rubber boots and a bag of tent stakes, I pull out a large iron skillet.

"Herbie, look, you've done a great job of lugging this stuff so far. But we have to make you able to move faster," I say. "If we take some of the load off you, you'll be able to do a better job at the front of the line."

Herbie finally seems to understand.

Again we start walking. But this time, Herbie can really move. Relieved of most of the weight in his pack, it's as if he's walking on air. We're flying now, doing twice the speed as a troop that we did before. And we still stay together. Inventory is down. Throughput is up.

Dave and I share the same tent that night. We're lying inside it, both of us tired. Dave is quiet for a while. Then he speaks up.

He says, "You know, Dad, I was really proud of you today."

"You were? How come?"

"The way you figured out what was going on and kept everyone together, and put Herbie in front."

"Thanks," I tell him. "Actually, I learned a lot of things today."

"You did?"

"Yeah, stuff that I think is going to help me straighten out the plant," I say.

"Really? Like what?"

"Are you sure you want to hear about it?"

"Sure I am," he claims.

This is the beginning of Alex's successful turnaround of his plant—applying simple principles to the plant's operation.

Source: Eliyahu M. Goldratt and Jeff Cox, *The Goal: A Process of Ongoing Improvement,* 2d rev. ed. (Great Barrington, MA: North River Press, 1992), pp. 114–18.

The story of Herbie is an analogy to the problems facing plant manager Alex Rogo and comes from a best selling novel *The Goal* by Dr. Eli Goldratt.[1] Around 1980, Goldratt started arguing that manufacturers were not doing a good job in scheduling and in controlling their resources and inventories. To try to solve this problem Goldratt developed software that scheduled jobs through manufacturing processes, taking into account limited facilities, machines, personnel, tools, materials, and any other constraints that would affect a firm's ability to adhere to a schedule. This was called *Optimized Production Technology (OPT)*. The schedules were feasible and accurate, and could be run on a computer in a fraction of the time that an MRP system took. This was because the scheduling logic was based on the separation of bottleneck and nonbottleneck operations. After approximately 100 large firms had installed this software, Goldratt and Robert Fox went on to promote the logic of the approach rather than the software. Goldratt has since developed his "Theory of Constraints" (TOC) and, in fact, is no longer associated with the software company.

We believe in the logic of Goldratt's approach to manufacturing and his focus: dealing with constraints. Therefore, we are devoting this chapter to Goldratt's teachings and applications. To correctly treat the topic, we decided to approach it in the same way that Goldratt did; that is, first defining some basic issues about firms—purposes, goals, performance measurements, and then dealing with scheduling, providing buffer inventories, the influences of quality, the interactions with marketing, and accounting.

In this chapter we discuss synchronous production. **Synchronous manufacturing** refers to the entire production process working together in harmony to achieve the goals of the firm. Synchronous manufacturing logic attempts to coordinate all resources so that they work together and are in harmony or are "synchronized." In such a synchronous state, emphasis is on the total system performance, not on localized performance measures such as labor or machine utilization.

19.1   HOCKEY-STICK PHENOMENON

Just about every company faces a problem called the **hockey-stick phenomenon**—rushing to meet quotas at the end of the time period. If the time period is a month, then this is an end-of-the-month-syndrome; if the period is a quarter, it is an end-of-the-quarter syndrome. (See Exhibit 19.1). It is called a hockey stick because it looks like a hockey stick—with a relatively flat bottom and a long, rapid rise like a handle. The reason that this is a problem is primarily because of the chaos that occurs at the end of the month. The system never runs smoothly; everyone works under pressure during the early flat part of the cycle as well as during the end of the cycle. The cause of the problem is that two sets of measurements are being employed: At the beginning of the period, cost accounting *efficiency* measurements are used. These are local measurements. This encourages minimizing setups through large batches. As the end of the month approaches, however, pressure mounts to meet a different set of measurements, one that relates to financial *performance*. They are stated in terms such as dollars of output shipped. On the financial statements these measurements are expressed as net profit, return on investment, and cash flow. As soon as the end of the month passes (with its daily overtime, weekend work, constant expediting, and frequent setups aimed toward getting the product out), pressure decreases and everyone again looks at the cost accounting measurements of standards and utilization—and so the cycle repeats.

---

[1] Most of this chapter is based on the writings and teachings of Dr. Eliyahu M. Goldratt and Robert E. Fox; the bibliography at the end of this chapter includes their publications. One of the authors of this text was a participant in several of their week-long seminars and courses. We thank Dr. Goldratt for his permission to freely use his concepts, definitions, and other material.

E X H I B I T 19.1
Hockey-Stick Phenomenon (The end-of-the-period rush)

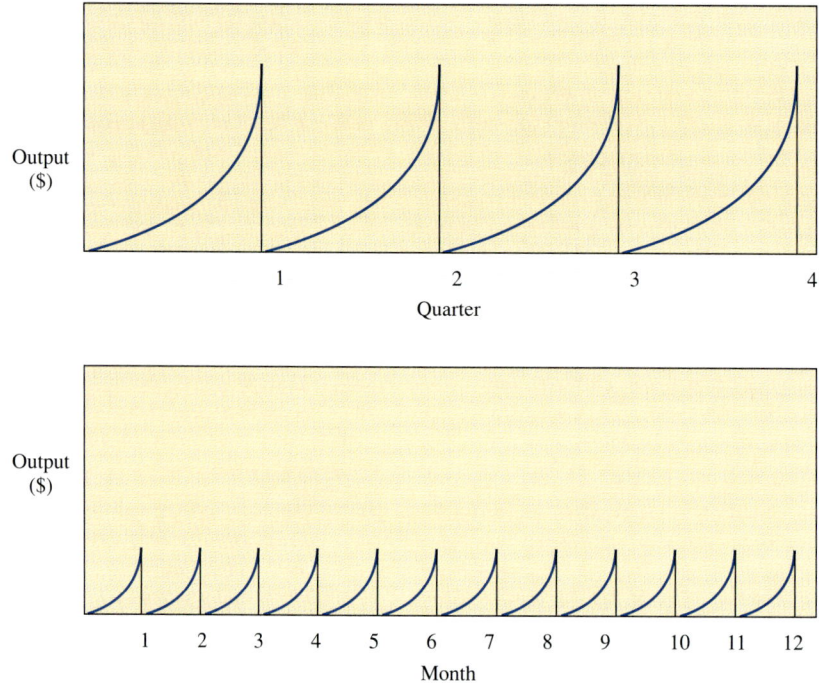

To emphasize the value of techniques such as synchronous manufacturing, Goldratt tells two stories of what can happen. One is about a firm that did not need the third shift because of a slump in the market. The workers were highly skilled and, because the company expected the market to rebound in three months, it decided to keep the workers. With a weekly payroll of $25,000, the company allocated $300,000 to carry the workers for three months, within which time they expected renewed market demand. To the surprise of management, however, these workers consumed $400,000 worth of inventory during the first week and another $400,000 during the second week so the workers were laid off. There was so much pressure to keep the workers busy that they were not allowed to just be idle (nor would the workers feel right just sitting around waiting). Two months later market demand increased, but not for the products that the workers had been producing.

The second story is about a plant whose demand went down because the overall market had deteriorated. Because the company was having cash flow problems, it decided to cut expenses. Noticing that the setup workers were the highest paid in the plant, management decided to double all the batch sizes (which meant only half the setups were needed) and lay off half the setup workers. The result put the plant out of business! With double batch sizes, the increase in work in process drained all the company's cash so that it could no longer operate.

19.2   GOAL OF THE FIRM

Although many people disagree with him, Goldratt has a very straightforward idea of the goal of a firm:

THE GOAL OF A FIRM IS TO MAKE MONEY.

Goldratt argues that while an organization may have many purposes—providing jobs, consuming raw materials, increasing sales, increasing share of the market, developing technology, or producing high-quality products—these do not guarantee long-term survival of the firm. They are means to achieve the goal, not the goal itself. If the firm makes money—and only then—it will prosper. When a firm has money, then it can place more emphasis on other objectives.

19.3 PERFORMANCE MEASUREMENTS

To adequately measure a firm's performance, two sets of measurements must be used: one from the financial point of view and the other from the operations point of view.

We have three measures of the firm's ability to make money:

Financial Measurements

1. *Net profit*—an absolute measurement in dollars
2. *Return on investment*—a relative measure based on investment.
3. *Cash flow*—a survival measurement.

All three measurements must be used together. For example, a *net profit* of $10 million is important as one measurement, but it has no real meaning until we know how much investment it took to generate that $10 million. If the investment was $100 million, this is a 10 percent *return on investment. Cash flow* is important since cash is necessary to pay bills for day-to-day operations; without cash, a firm can go bankrupt even though it is very sound in normal accounting terms. A firm can have a high profit and a high return on investment, but can still be short on cash if, for example, profit is invested in new equipment or tied up in inventory.

Operational Measurements

Financial measurements work well at the higher level, but they cannot be used at the operational level. We need another set of measurements that will give us guidance:

1. **Throughput**—the rate at which money is generated by the system through sales.
2. **Inventory**—all the money that the system has invested in purchasing things it intends to sell.
3. **Operating expenses**—all the money that the system spends to turn inventory into throughput.

Throughput is specifically defined as goods *sold*. An inventory of finished goods is not throughput, but inventory. Actual sales must occur. It is specifically defined this way to prevent the system from continuing to produce under the illusion that the goods *might* be sold. Such action simply increases costs, builds inventory, and consumes cash. Inventory that is carried (whether work in process or finished goods) is valued only at the cost of the materials it contains. Labor cost and machine hours are ignored. (In traditional accounting terms, money spent is called *value added.*)

While this is often an arguable point, using only the raw material cost is a conservative view. When using the value-added method (which includes all costs of production), inventory is inflated and presents some serious income and balance sheet problems. Consider, for example, work-in-process or finished-goods inventory that has become obsolete, or for which a contract was canceled. It is a difficult management decision to declare large amounts of inventory as scrap since it is often carried on the books as assets even though it may really have no value. Using just raw-materials cost also avoids the problem of determining which costs are direct and which are indirect.

E X H I B I T 19.2
Operational Goal

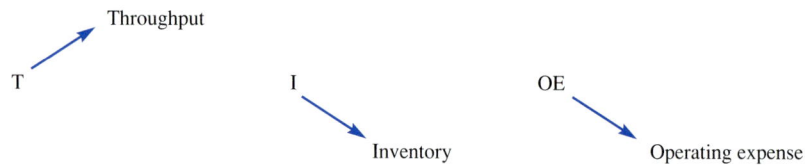

The operational goal of a firm is to increase throughput while reducing inventory and operating expense.

Operating expenses include production costs (such as direct labor, indirect labor, inventory carrying costs, equipment depreciation, and materials and supplies used in production) and administrative costs. The key difference here is that there is no need to separate direct and indirect labor.

As shown in Exhibit 19.2, the objective of a firm is to treat all three measurements simultaneously and continually; this achieves the goal of making money.

From an operations standpoint, the goal of the firm is to

Increase throughput while simultaneously reducing inventory and reducing operating expense.

Productivity

Typically, **productivity** is measured in terms of output per labor hour. However, this measurement does not ensure that the firm will make money (for example, when extra output is not sold but accumulates as inventory). To test whether productivity has increased, we should ask these questions: Has the action taken increased throughput? Has it decreased inventory? Has it decreased operational expense? This leads us to a new definition:

Productivity is all the actions that bring a company closer to its goals.

19.4   UNBALANCED CAPACITY

Historically (and still typically in most firms), manufacturers have tried to balance capacity across a sequence of processes in an attempt to match capacity with market demand. However, this is the wrong thing to do—**unbalanced capacity** is better. The vignette at the beginning of this chapter is an example of unbalanced capacity. Some Boy Scouts were fast walkers while Herbie was very slow. The challenge is to use this difference advantageously.

Consider a simple process line with several stations, for example. Once the output rate of the line has been established, production people try to make the capacities of all stations the same. This is done by adjusting machines or equipment used, workloads, skill and type of labor assigned, tools used, overtime budgeted, and so on.

In synchronous manufacturing thinking, however, making all capacities the same is viewed as a bad decision. Such a balance would be possible only if the output times of all stations were constant or had a very narrow distribution. A normal variation in output times causes downstream stations to have idle time when upstream stations take longer to process. Conversely, when upstream stations process in a shorter time, inventory builds up between the stations. The effect of the statistical variation is cumulative. The only way that this variation can be smoothed is by increasing work in process to absorb the variation (a bad choice since we should be trying to reduce work in process), or increasing capacities downstream to be able to make up for the longer upstream times. The rule here is that capacities within the process sequence should not be balanced to the same

E X H I B I T 19.3 *Processing and Completion Times, Process A to Process B*

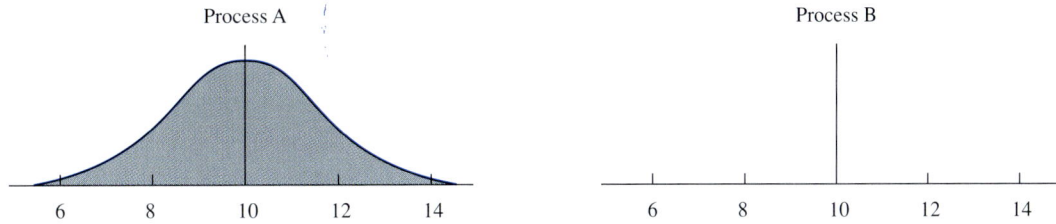

Process A

Process B

Item Number	Start Time	Processing Time	Finish Time
1	0 hrs	14 hrs	14 hrs
2	14	12	26
3	26	10	36
4	36	8	44
5	44	6	50
		Average = 10 hours	

Item Number	Start Time	Processing Time	Finish Time
1	14 hrs	10 hrs	24 hrs
2	26	10	36
3	36	10	46
4	46	10	56
5	56	10	66
		Average = 10 hours	

Here the flow is from Process A to Process B. Process A has a mean of 10 hours and a standard deviation of 2 hours; Process B has a constant 10-hour processing time.

E X H I B I T 19.4 *Processing and Completion Times Process B to Process A*

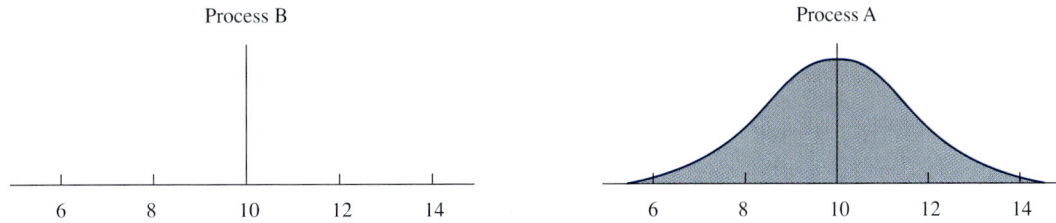

Process B

Process A

Item Number	Start Time	Processing Time	Finish Time
1	0 hrs	10 hrs	10 hrs
2	10	10	20
3	20	10	30
4	30	10	40
5	40	10	50
		Average = 10 hours	

Item Number	Start Time	Processing Time	Finish Time
1	10 hrs	6 hrs	16 hrs
2	20	8	28
3	30	10	40
4	40	12	52
5	52	14	66
		Average = 10 hours	

This is similar to Exhibit 19.3. However, the processing sequence has been reversed as well as the order of Process A's times.

levels. Rather, attempts should be made to balance the flow of product through the system. When flow is balanced, capacities are unbalanced. This idea is further explained in the next section.

Dependent Events and Statistical Fluctuations

The term dependent events refers to a process sequence. If a process flows from A to B to C to D, and each process must be completed before passing on to the next step, then B, C, and D are dependent events. The ability to do the next process is dependent on the preceding one.

Statistical fluctuation refers to the normal variation about a mean or average. When statistical fluctuations occur in a dependent sequence without any inventory between workstations, there is no opportunity to achieve the average output. When one process takes longer than the average, the next process cannot make up the time. We follow through an example of this to show what could happen.

Suppose that we wanted to process five items that could come from the two distributions in Exhibit 19.3. The processing sequence is from A to B with no space for inventory in between. Process A has a mean of 10 hours and a standard deviation of 2 hours. This means that we would expect 95.5 percent of the processing time to be between 6 hours and 14 hours (plus or minus 2 sigma). Process B has a constant processing time of 10 hours.

We see that the last item was completed in 66 hours, for an average of 13.2 hours per item, although the expected time of completion was 60, for an average of 12 hours per item (taking into account the waiting time for the first unit by Process B).

Suppose we reverse the process—B feeds A. To illustrate the possible delays, we also reverse A's performance times. (See Exhibit 19.4). Again, the completion time of the last item is greater than the average (13.2 hours rather than 12 hours). Process A and Process B have the same average performance time of 10 hours, and yet performance is late. In neither case could we achieve the expected output average rate. Why? Because the time lost when the second process is idle cannot be made up.

This example is intended to challenge the theory that capacities should be balanced to an average time. *Rather than balancing capacities, the flow of product through the system should be balanced.*

19.5 BOTTLENECKS, NONBOTTLENECKS, AND CAPACITY-CONSTRAINED RESOURCES

A **bottleneck** is defined as any resource whose capacity is less than the demand placed upon it. A bottleneck is a constraint within the system that limits throughput. It is that point in the manufacturing process where flow thins to a narrow stream. A bottleneck may be a machine, scarce or highly skilled labor, or a specialized tool. Observations in industry have shown that most plants have very few bottleneck operations, usually just several.

If there is no bottleneck, then excess capacity exists and the system should be changed to create a bottleneck (such as more setups or reduced capacity), which we will discuss later.

Capacity is defined as the available time for production. This excludes maintenance and other downtime. A **nonbottleneck** is a resource whose capacity is greater than the demand placed on it. A nonbottleneck, therefore, should not be working constantly since it can produce more than is needed. A nonbottleneck contains idle time.

A **capacity-constrained resource (CCR)** is one whose utilization is close to capacity and could be a bottleneck if it is not scheduled carefully. For example, a CCR may be receiving work in a job-shop environment from several sources. If these sources schedule their flow in a way that causes occasional idle time for the CCR in excess of its unused capacity time, the CCR becomes a bottleneck. This can happen if batch sizes are changed or if one of the upstream operations is not working for some reason and does not feed enough work to the CCR.

19.6 BASIC MANUFACTURING BUILDING BLOCKS

All manufacturing processes and flows can be simplified to four basic configurations, as shown in Exhibit 19.5. In Exhibit 19.5A, product that flows through Process X feeds into Process Y. In section B, Y is feeding X. In section C, Process X and Process Y are creating subassemblies, which are then combined, say to feed the market demand. In section D, Process X and Process Y are independent of each other and are supplying their own

E X H I B I T 19.5   *The Basic Building Blocks of Manufacturing Derived by Grouping Process Flows*

Description	Basic Building Blocks Simplified by Grouping Nonbottlenecks	Original Representation
A. Bottleneck feeding nonbottleneck	X ⟶ Y ⟶ Market	X → A → B → C → D → Market (Y grouping A–D)
B. Nonbottleneck feeding bottleneck	Y ⟶ X ⟶ Market	A → B → C → D → X → Market (Y grouping A–D)
C. Output of bottleneck and nonbottleneck assembled into a product	X, Y → Final Assembly → Market	X → Final Assembly → Market; Y (A → B → C → D)
D. Bottleneck and nonbottleneck have independent markets for their output	X → Market; Y → Market	A → B → C → D → X → Market (Y); → Market

X is a bottleneck.
Y is a nonbottleneck (has excess capacity).

markets. The last column in the exhibit shows possible sequences of nonbottleneck resources, which can be grouped and displayed as Y to simplify the representation.

The value in using these basic building blocks is that a production process can be greatly simplified for analysis and control. Rather than track and schedule all of the steps in a production sequence through nonbottleneck operations, for example, attention can be placed at the beginning and end points of the building block groupings.

19.7   METHODS FOR CONTROL IN SYNCHRONOUS MANUFACTURING

Using the four basic building blocks in manufacturing described in Exhibit 19.5, Exhibit 19.6 shows how bottlenecks and nonbottleneck resources should be managed. Assume that Resource X has a market demand of 200 units of product per month and Resource Y has a market demand of 150 units per month, regardless of the building block configuration. Assume also that both X and Y have 200 hours per month available. To help understand our example, assume that each unit of product passing through X takes one hour of processing time and each unit passing through Y takes 45 minutes. With the available times, 200 hours of Resource X can produce 200 units of product and 200 hours of Resource Y can produce 267 units of product. Let's consider each of the four building blocks.

In Exhibit 19.6A, the flow of product is in a dependent sequence, that is, it must pass through both Resource X (Machine X) and Resource Y (Machine Y). Resource X is the bottleneck since it has a capacity of 200 units whereas Y has a capacity of 267 units. Resource Y can be used only 75 percent of the time since it is starved for work. (X is not feeding it enough to allow it to work longer.) In this case, no extra product is produced.

Section B of the exhibit is the reverse of Section A: A nonbottleneck is feeding a bottleneck. Since X can be put through only 200 units, we must be careful not to produce more than 200 on Y, or inventory will build up as work in process.

E X H I B I T 19.6

Product Flow through the Four Basic Building Blocks

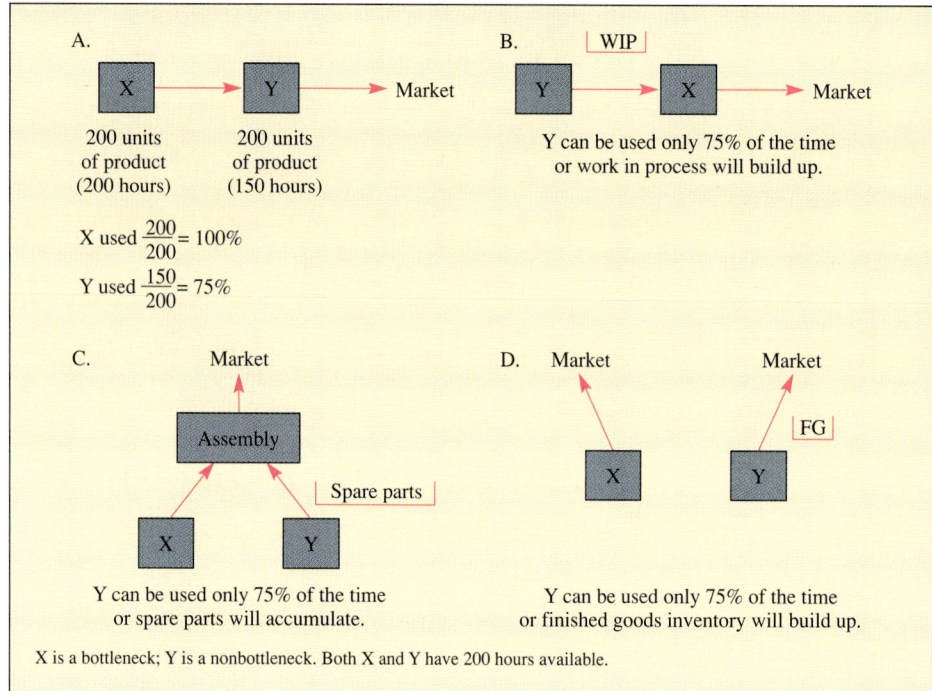

A.

X → Y → Market

200 units
of product
(200 hours)

200 units
of product
(150 hours)

X used $\frac{200}{200} = 100\%$

Y used $\frac{150}{200} = 75\%$

B. WIP

Y → X → Market

Y can be used only 75% of the time
or work in process will build up.

C.   Market

Assembly

Spare parts

X   Y

Y can be used only 75% of the time
or spare parts will accumulate.

D.   Market   Market

FG

X   Y

Y can be used only 75% of the time
or finished goods inventory will build up.

X is a bottleneck; Y is a nonbottleneck. Both X and Y have 200 hours available.

Section C of the exhibit shows that the outputs from X (a bottleneck) and Y (a nonbottleneck) are assembled into a product. As a nonbottleneck, Y has more capacity than X so it can be used only 75 percent of the time; otherwise spare parts accumulate.

In Section D, market demands for X and Y are 200 units of each. Since 200 units from Y corresponds to only 75 percent of its capacity, Y can be used only 75 percent of the time or finished-goods inventory will accumulate. The situations we have just discussed are important because current industry practice considers the percentage of resource utilization as one of the measures of performance. Such practice encourages the overuse of nonbottleneck resources, resulting in excess inventories.

Time Components

The following various kinds of time make up production cycle time:

1. *Setup time*—the time that a part spends waiting for a resource to be set up to work on this same part.
2. *Process time*—the time that the part is being processed.
3. *Queue time*—the time that a part waits for a resource while the resource is busy with something else.
4. *Wait time*—the time that a part waits not for a resource but for another part so that they can be assembled together.
5. *Idle time*—the unused time; that is, the cycle time less the sum of the setup time, processing time, queue time, and wait time.

For a part waiting to go through a bottleneck, queue time is the greatest. As we discuss later in this chapter, this is because the bottleneck has a fairly large amount of work to do in front of it (to make sure that is always working). For a nonbottleneck, wait time is the greatest. The part is just sitting there waiting for the arrival of other parts so that an assembly can take place.

Schedulers are tempted to save setup times. Supposing the batch sizes are doubled to save half the setup times. Then, with a double batch size, all of the other times (processing time, queue time, and wait time) increase twofold. Because these times are doubled while saving only half of the setup time, the net result is that the work in process is approximately doubled as is the investment in inventory.

There are two ways to find the bottleneck (or bottlenecks) in a system. One is to run a capacity resource profile; the other is to use our knowledge of the particular plant, look at the system in operation, and talk with supervisors and workers.   **Finding the Bottleneck**

A capacity resource profile is obtained by looking at the loads placed on each resource by the products that are scheduled through them. In running a capacity profile, we assume that the data are reasonably accurate, although not necessarily perfect. As an example, consider that products have been routed through resources M1 through M5. Suppose our first computation of the resource loads on each resource caused by these products shows the following:

M1   130 percent of capacity
M2   120 percent of capacity
M3   105 percent of capacity
M4   95 percent of capacity
M5   85 percent of capacity

For this first analysis, we can disregard any resources at lower percentages since they are nonbottlenecks and should not be a problem. With the list in hand, we should physically go to the facility and check all five operations. Note that M1, M2, and M3 are overloaded, that is, scheduled above their capacities. We would expect to see large quantities of inventory in front of M1. If this is not the case, errors must exist somewhere—perhaps in the bill of materials or in the routing sheets. Let's say that our observations and discussions with shop personnel showed that there were errors in M1, M2, M3, and M4. We tracked them down, made the appropriate corrections, and ran the capacity profile again:

M2   115 percent of capacity
M1   110 percent of capacity
M3   105 percent of capacity
M4   90 percent of capacity
M5   85 percent of capacity

M1, M2, and M3 are still showing a lack of sufficient capacity, but M2 is the most serious. If we now have confidence in our numbers, we use M2 as our bottleneck.

If the data contain too many errors to do a reliable data analysis, it may not be worth spending time (it could be months) making all the corrections. Instead, it would be quicker to use our knowledge about the VAT classification scheme (covered later in this chapter) to give us guidance. Defining the plant as V, A, or T helps direct us to where the bottlenecks would most likely be. To find a bottleneck, use the VAT scheme and then go and look and listen. From talking with workers and supervisors in the plant, we would expect to hear comments such as "We're always waiting for parts from the NC machine" or "They're feeding me more work than I can possibly do and I can't keep up." These are clues to be followed.

Saving Time on Bottleneck and Nonbottleneck Resources

Recall that a bottleneck is a resource whose capacity is less than the demand placed on it. Since we focus on bottlenecks as restricting *throughput* (defined as *sales*), a bottleneck's capacity is less than the market demand. There are a number of ways we can save time on a bottleneck (better tooling, higher-quality labor, larger batch sizes, reducing setup times, and so forth), but how valuable is this extra time? Very, very valuable!

An hour saved at the bottleneck adds an extra hour to the entire production system.

How about time saved on a nonbottleneck resource?

An hour saved at a nonbottleneck is a mirage and only adds an hour to its idle time.

Because a nonbottleneck has more capacity than the system needs for its current throughput, it already contains idle time. Implementing any measures to save more time does not increase throughput but only serves to increase its idle time.

Avoiding Changing a Nonbottleneck into a Bottleneck

When nonbottleneck resources are scheduled with larger batch sizes, this action could create a bottleneck that we certainly would want to avoid. Consider the case in Exhibit 19.7, where Y_1, Y_2, and Y_3 are nonbottleneck resources. Y_1 currently produces Part A, which is routed to Y_3, and Part B is routed to Y_2. To produce Part A, Y_1 has a 200-minute setup time and a processing time of 1 minute per part. Part A is currently produced in batches of 500 units. To produce Part B, Y_1 has a setup time of 150 minutes and 2 minutes' processing time per part. Part B is currently produced in batches of 200 units.

Since setup time is 200 minutes for Y_1 on Part A, both worker and supervisor mistakenly believe that more production can be gained if fewer setups are made. Let's assume that batch size is increased to 1,500 units and see what happens. The illusion is that we have saved 400 minutes of setup. (Instead of three setups taking 600 minutes to produce three batches of 500 units each, there is just one setup with a 1,500-unit batch.)

The problem is that the 400 minutes saved serves no purpose, but this delay did interfere with the production of Part B since Y_1 produces Part B for Y_2. The sequence before any changes were made was Part A (700 minutes), Part B (550 minutes), Part A (700 minutes), Part B (550 minutes), and so on. Now, however, when the Part A batch is increased to 1,500 units (1,700 minutes), Y_2 and Y_3 could well be starved for work and have to wait more time than they have available (30 percent idle time for Y_2 and 20

EXHIBIT 19.7
Nonbottleneck Resources

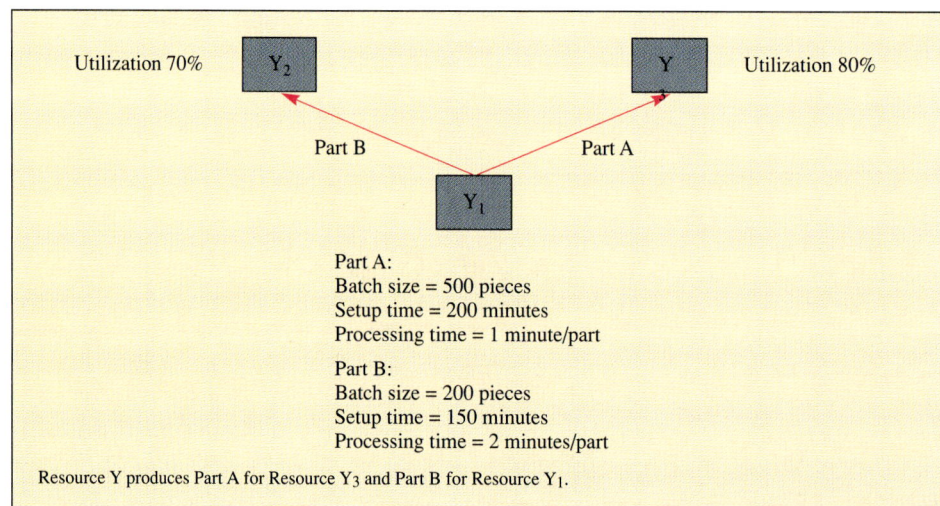

Part A:
Batch size = 500 pieces
Setup time = 200 minutes
Processing time = 1 minute/part

Part B:
Batch size = 200 pieces
Setup time = 150 minutes
Processing time = 2 minutes/part

Resource Y produces Part A for Resource Y_3 and Part B for Resource Y_1.

percent for Y_3). The new sequence would be Part A (1,700 minutes), Part B (1,350 minutes), and so on. Such an extended wait for Y_2 and Y_3 could be disruptive. Y_2 and Y_3 could become temporary bottlenecks and lose throughput for the system.

Every production system needs some control point or points to control the flow of product through the system. If the system contains a bottleneck, the bottleneck is the best place for control. This control point is called the **drum,** for it strikes the beat that the rest of the system (or those parts that it influences) uses to function. Recall that a *bottleneck* is defined as a resource that does not have the capacity to meet demand. Therefore, a bottleneck is working all the time and one reason for using it as a control point is to make sure that the operations upstream do not overproduce and build up excess work-in-process inventory that the bottleneck cannot handle.

Drum, Buffer, Rope

If there is no bottleneck, the next best place to set the drum would be a capacity-constrained resource (CCR). A capacity-constrained resource, remember, is one that is operating near capacity, but on the average has adequate capability as long as it is not incorrectly scheduled (for example, with too many setups, causing it to run short of capacity, or producing too large a lot size, thereby starving downstream operations).

If neither a bottleneck nor a CCR is present, the control point can be designated anywhere. The best position would generally be at some divergent point where the output of the resource is used in several downstream operations.

Dealing with the bottleneck is most critical, and our discussion focuses on ensuring that the bottleneck always has work to do. Exhibit 19.8 shows a simple linear flow A through G. Suppose that Resource D, which is a machine center, is a bottleneck. This means that the capacities are greater both upstream and downstream from it. If this sequence is not controlled, we would expect to see a large amount of inventory in front of work center D and very little anywhere else. There would be little finished-goods inventory because (by the definition of the term *bottleneck*) all the product produced would be taken by the market.

There are two things that we must do with this bottleneck:

1. Keep a **buffer** inventory in front of it to make sure that it always has something to work on. Because it is a bottleneck, its output determines the throughput of the system.
2. Communicate back upstream to A what D has produced so that A provides only that amount. This keeps inventory from building up. This communication is called the **rope.** It can be formal (such as a schedule) or informal (such as daily discussion).

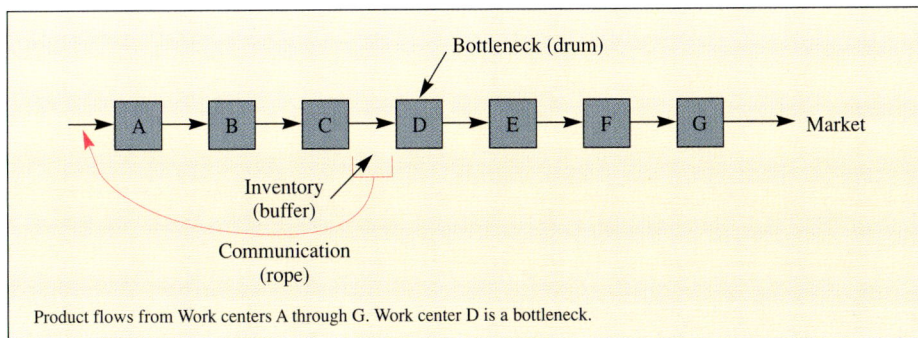

E X H I B I T 19.8
Linear Flow of Product with a Bottleneck

Bottleneck (drum)

A → B → C → D → E → F → G → Market

Inventory (buffer)

Communication (rope)

Product flows from Work centers A through G. Work center D is a bottleneck.

E X H I B I T   19.9

Capacity Profile of Work Center D (Showing assigned Jobs A through P over a period of four 24-hour days)

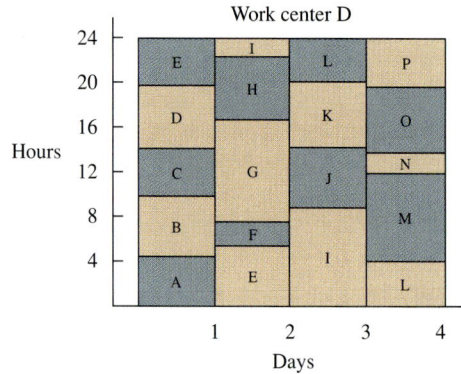

E X H I B I T   19.10

Linear Flow of Product with a Capacity-Constrained Resource

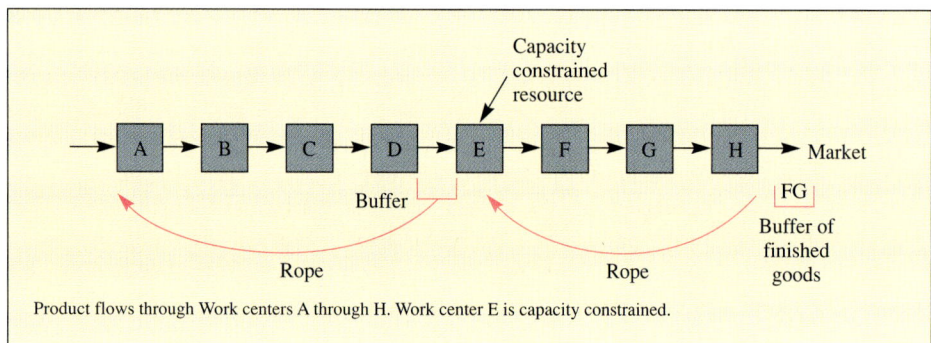

Product flows through Work centers A through H. Work center E is capacity constrained.

The buffer inventory in front of a bottleneck operation is a **time buffer.** We want to make sure that work center D always has work to do, and it does not matter which of the scheduled products are worked on. We might, for example, provide 96 hours of inventory in the buffer as shown in the sequence A through H in Exhibit 19.9. Jobs A through about half of E are scheduled during the 24 hours of Day 1; Jobs E through a portion of Job I are scheduled during the second 24-hour day; Jobs I through part of L are scheduled during the third 24-hour day; and Jobs L through P are scheduled during the fourth 24-hour day, for a total of 96 hours. This means that through normal variation, or if something happens upstream and the output has been temporarily stalled, D can work for another 96 hours protecting the throughput. (The 96 hours of work, incidentally, includes setups and processing times contained in the job sheets, which usually are based on engineering standard times.)

We might ask, How large should the time buffer be? The answer: As large as it needs to be to ensure that the bottleneck continues to work. By examining the variation of each operation, we can make a guess. Theoretically the size of the buffer can be computed statistically by examining past performance data, or the sequence can be simulated. In any event, precision is not critical. We could start with an estimate of the time buffer as one-fourth of the total lead time of the system. Say the sequence A to G in our example (Exhibit 19.8) took a total of 16 days. We could start with a buffer of four days in front of D. If during the next few days or weeks the buffer runs out, we need to increase the buffer size. We do this by releasing extra material to the first operation, A. On the other hand, if we find that our buffer never drops below three days, we might want to hold back releases to A and reduce the time buffer to three days. Experience is the best determination of the final buffer size.

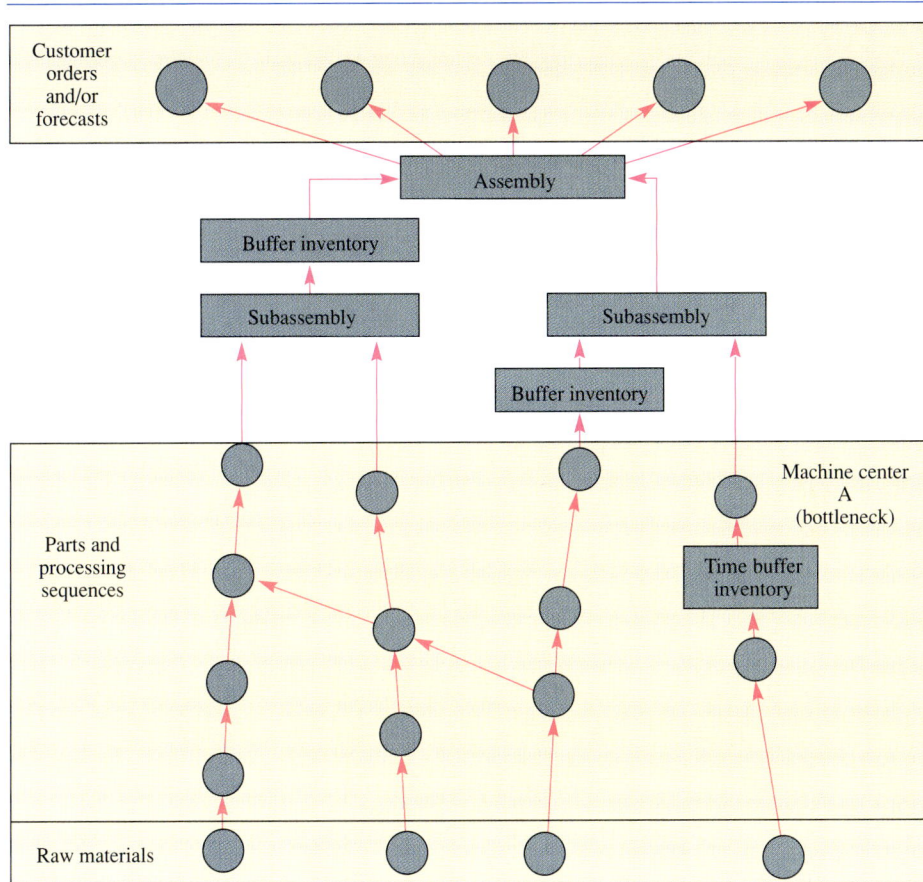

Product flows from raw materials through processing to the market. Inventory buffers protect throughput.

If the drum is not a bottleneck but a CCR (and thus it can have a small amount of idle time), we might want to create two buffer inventories—one in front of the CCR and the second at the end as finished goods. (See Exhibit 19.10.) The finished-goods inventory protects the market, and the time buffer in front of the CCR protects throughput. For this CCR case, the market cannot take all that we can produce so we want to ensure that finished goods are available when the market does decide to purchase.

We need two ropes in this case: (1) a rope communicating from finished-goods inventory back to the drum to increase or decrease output and (2) a rope from the drum back to the material release point, specifying how much material is needed.

Exhibit 19.11 is a more detailed network flow showing one bottleneck. Inventory is provided not only in front of that bottleneck but also after the nonbottleneck assembly to which it is assembled. This ensures that the flow of product after it leaves the bottleneck is not slowed down by having to wait.

Importance of Quality

An MRP system allows for rejects by building a larger batch than actually needed. A JIT system cannot tolerate poor quality since JIT success is based on a balanced capacity. A defective part or component can cause a JIT system to shut down, thereby losing throughput of the total system. Synchronous manufacturing, however, has excess capacity throughout the system, except for the bottleneck. If a bad part is produced upstream of the bottleneck, the result is that there is a loss of material only. Because of the excess capacity, there is still time to do another operation to replace the one just scrapped. For the bottleneck, however, extra time does not exist so there should be a quality control inspection just prior to the bottleneck to ensure that the bottleneck works only on good product. Also, there needs to be assurance downstream from the bottleneck that the passing product is not scrapped—that would mean lost throughput.

Batch Sizes

In an assembly line, what is the batch size? Some would say, "one" because one unit is moved at a time; others would say "infinity" since the line continues to produce the same item. Both answers are correct, but they differ in their point of view. The first answer, "one," in an assembly line focuses on the *part* transferred one unit at a time. The second focuses on the *process*. From the point of view of the resource, the process batch is infinity since it is continuing to run the same units. Thus, in an assembly line, we have a **process batch** of infinity (or all the units until we change to another process setup) and a **transfer batch** of one unit.

Setup costs and carrying costs were treated in depth in Chapter 14 ("Inventory Systems for Independent Demand"). In the present context, setup costs relate to the process batch and carrying costs relate to the transfer batch.

A process batch is of a size large enough or small enough to be processed in a particular length of time. From the point of view of a resource, two times are involved: setup time and processing run time (ignoring downtime for maintenance or repair). Larger process batch sizes require fewer setups and therefore can generate more processing time and more output. For bottleneck resources, larger batch sizes are desirable. For nonbottleneck resources, smaller process batch sizes are desirable (by using up the existing idle time), thereby reducing work-in-process inventory.

Transfer batches refer to the movement of part of the process batch. Rather than wait for the entire batch to be finished, work that has been completed by that operation can be moved to the next downstream workstation so that it can begin working on that batch. A transfer batch can be equal to a process batch but it cannot be larger.[2]

The advantage of using transfer batches that are smaller than the process batch quantity is that the total production is shorter so the amount of work in process is smaller. Exhibit 19.12 shows a situation where the total production lead time was reduced from 2,100 to 1,310 minutes by using a transfer batch size of 100 rather than 1,000, and reducing the process batch sizes of Operation 2.

How to Determine Process Batch and Transfer Batch Sizes

Logic would suggest that the master production schedule (however it was developed) be analyzed as to its effect on various work centers. In an MRP system, this means that the master production schedule should be run through the MRP and the CRP (capacity requirements planning program) to generate a detailed load on each work center. Srikanth states that from his experience there are too many errors in the manufacturing database to do this.[3] He suggests using the alternative procedures of first identifying the type of plant (V, A, or T, described later in this chapter) to suggest the probable CCRs and bottlenecks. There should be only

---

[2]It would not be logical to have a transfer batch larger than the process batch. This could only occur if a completed process batch was held until sometime later when a second batch was processed. If this later time was acceptable in the beginning, then both jobs should be combined and processed together at the later time.

[3]Mokshagundam L. Srikanth, "The Drum–Buffer–Rope System of Material Control" (New Haven, CT: Spectrum Management Group, 1987), pp. 25–37.

E X H I B I T 19.12   *Effect of Changing the Process Batch Sizes on Production Lead Time for a Job Order of 1,000 Units*

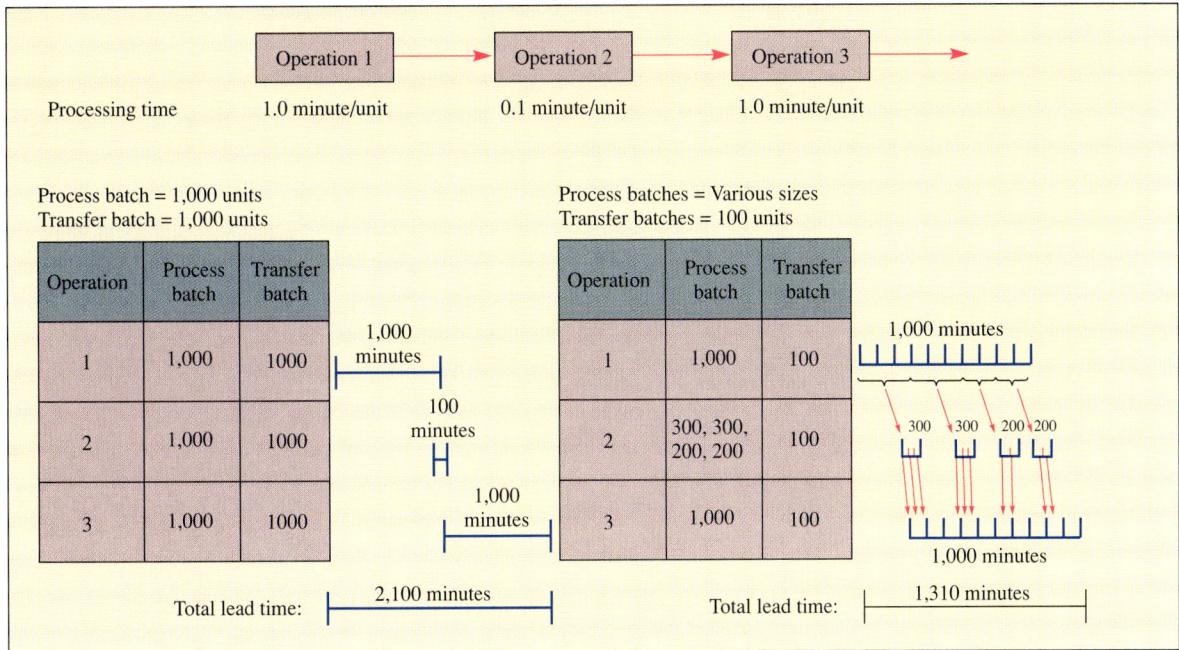

one (or a few), and they should be reviewed by managers so that they understand which re-sources are actually controlling their plant. These resources set the drumbeat.

Rather than try to adjust the master production schedule to change resource loads, it is more practical to control the flow at each bottleneck or CCR to bring the capacities in line. The process batch sizes and transfer batch sizes are changed after comparing past performances in meeting due dates.

Smaller transfer batches give lower work-in-process inventory but faster product flow (and consequently shorter lead time). More material handling is required, however. Larger transfer batches give longer lead times and higher inventories, but there is less material handling. Therefore, the transfer batch size is determined by a trade-off of production lead times, inventory reduction benefits, and costs of material movement.

When trying to control the flow at CCRs and bottlenecks, there are four possible situations:

1. A bottleneck (no idle time) with no setup required when changing from one product to another.
2. A bottleneck with setup times required to change from one product to another.
3. A capacity-constrained resource (CCR with a small amount of idle time) with no setup required to change from one product to another.
4. A CCR with setup time required when changing from one product to another.

In the first case, a bottleneck with no setup time to change products, jobs should be processed in the order of the schedule so that delivery is on time. Without setups, only the sequence is important. In the second case when setups are required, larger batch sizes combine separate similar jobs in the sequence. This means reaching ahead into future time periods. Some jobs will therefore be done early. Since this is a bottleneck resource, larger batches save setups and thereby increase throughput. (The setup time saved is used for processing.) The larger process batches may cause the early scheduled jobs to be late. Therefore, frequent small-sized transfer batches are necessary to try to shorten the lead time.

Situations 3 and 4 include a CCR without a setup and a CCR with setup time requirements. Handling the CCR would be similar to handling a nonbottleneck, though more carefully. That is, a CCR has some idle time. It would be appropriate here to cut the size of some of the process batches so that there can be more frequent changes of product. This would decrease lead time and jobs would be more likely to be done on time. In a make-to-stock situation cutting process batch sizes has a much more profound effect than increasing the number of transfer batches. This is because the resulting product mix is much greater, leading to reduced WIP and production lead time.

How to Treat Inventory and Where to Charge Inventory Costs

The traditional view of inventory is that its only negative impact on a firm's performance is its carrying cost. We realize now inventory's negative impact also comes from lengthening lead times and creating problems with engineering changes. (When an engineering change on a product comes through, which is frequent, product still within the production system often must be modified to include the changes. Therefore, less work in process reduces the number of engineering changes to be made.)

Fox and Goldratt propose to treat inventory as a loan given to the manufacturing unit. The value of the loan is based only on the purchased items that are part of the inventory. As we stated earlier, inventory is treated in this chapter as material cost only, and without any accounting-type value added from production. If inventory is carried as a loan to manufacturing, we need a way to measure how long the loan is carried. One measurement is dollar days.

Dollar Days   A useful performance measurement is the concept of **dollar days,** a measurement of the value of inventory and the time it stays within an area. To use this measure, we could simply multiply the total value of inventory by the number of days inventory spends within a department.

Suppose Department X carries an average inventory of $40,000, and, on the average, the inventory stays within the department five days. In dollar days then, Department X is charged with $40,000 times five days or $200,000 dollar days of inventory. At this point we cannot say the $200,000 is high or low, but it does show where the inventory is located. Management can then see where it should focus attention and determine acceptable levels. Techniques can be instituted to try to reduce the number of dollar days while being careful that such a measure does not become a local objective (i.e., minimizing dollar days) and hurt the global objectives (such as increasing ROI, cash flow, and net profit).

Dollar days could be beneficial in a variety of ways. Consider the current practice of using efficiencies or equipment utilization as a performance measurement. To get high utilizations, large amounts of inventory are held to keep everything working. However, high inventories would result in a high number of dollar days, which would discourage high levels of work in process. Dollar day measurements could also be used in other areas:

- Marketing, to discourage holding large amounts of finished-goods inventory. The net result would be to encourage sale of finished products.
- Purchasing, to discourage placing large purchase orders that on the surface appear to take advantage of quantity discounts. This would encourage just-in-time purchasing.

• Manufacturing, to discourage large work in process and producing earlier than needed. This would promote rapid flow of material within the plant.

19.8 COMPARING SYNCHRONOUS MANUFACTURING TO MRP AND JIT

MRP uses **backward scheduling** after having been fed a master production schedule. MRP schedules production through a bill of materials explosion in a backward manner—working backward in time from the desired completion date. As a secondary procedure, MRP, through its capacity resource planning module, develops capacity utilization profiles of work centers. When work centers are overloaded, either the master production schedule must be adjusted or enough slack capacity must be left unscheduled in the system so that work can be smoothed at the local level (by work center supervisors or the workers themselves). Trying to smooth capacity using MRP is so difficult and would require so many computer runs that capacity overloads and underloads are best left to local decisions, such as at the machine centers. An MRP schedule becomes invalid just days after it was created.

The synchronous manufacturing approach uses **forward scheduling** because it focuses on the critical resources. These are scheduled forward in time, ensuring that loads placed on them are within capacity. The noncritical (or nonbottleneck) resources are then scheduled to support the critical resources. (This can be done backward to minimize the length of time inventories are held.) This procedure ensures a feasible schedule. To help reduce lead time and work in process, in synchronous manufacturing the process batch size and transfer batch size are varied—a procedure that MRP is not able to do. (We say more on this later.)

Comparing JIT to synchronous manufacturing, JIT does an excellent job in reducing lead times and work in process, but it has several drawbacks:

1. JIT is limited to repetitive manufacturing.
2. JIT requires a stable production level (usually about a month long).
3. JIT does not allow very much flexibility in the products produced. (Products must be similar with a limited number of options.)
4. JIT still requires work in process when used with kanban so that there is "something to pull." This means that completed work must be stored on the downstream side of each workstation to be pulled by the next workstation.
5. Vendors need to be located nearby because the system depends on smaller, more frequent deliveries.

Since synchronous manufacturing uses a schedule to assign work to each workstation, there is no need for more work in process other than that being worked on. The exception is for inventory specifically placed in front of a bottleneck to ensure continual work, or at specific points downstream from a bottleneck to ensure flow of product.

Concerning continual improvements on the system, JIT is a trial-and-error procedure applied to a real system. In synchronous manufacturing, the system can be programmed and simulated on a computer since the schedules are realistic (can be accomplished) and computer run time is short.

19.9 VAT CLASSIFICATION OF FIRMS

All manufacturing firms can be classified into one or a combination of three types designated V, A, and T, depending on the products and processes. Exhibit 19.13 shows

---

E X H I B I T 19.13   *VAT Classification of Firms*

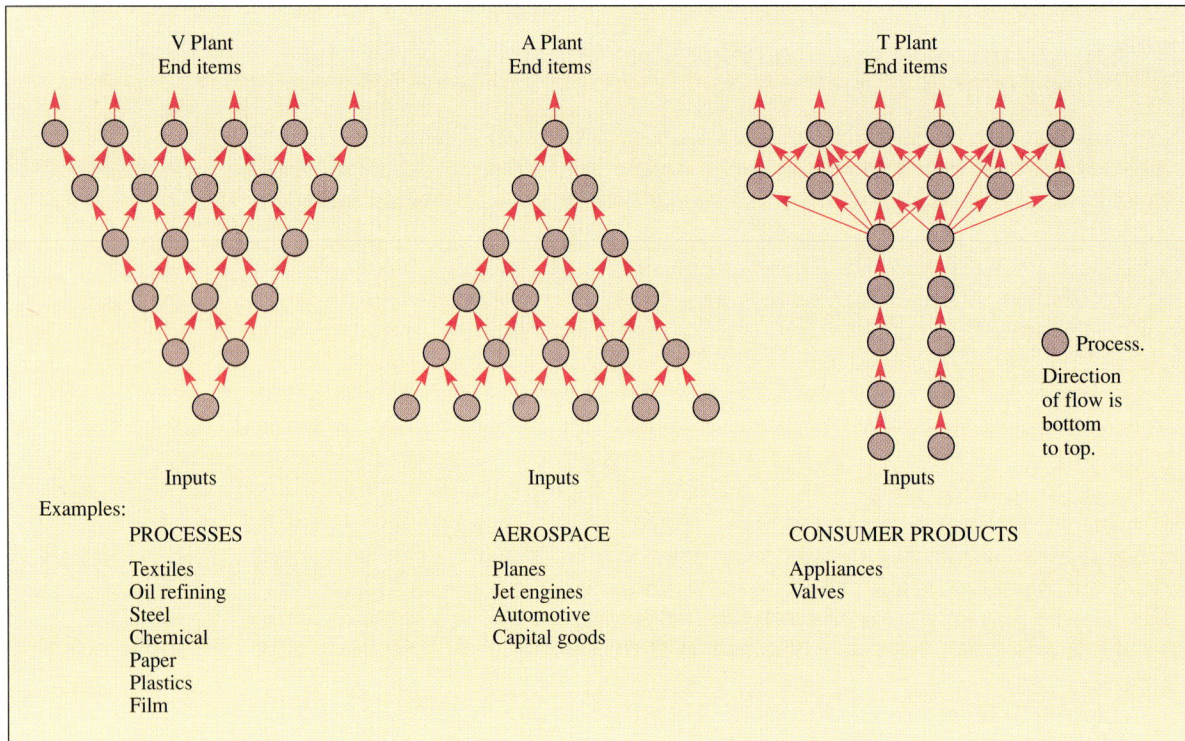

V Plant
End items

A Plant
End items

T Plant
End items

Process.
Direction
of flow is
bottom
to top.

Inputs

Inputs

Inputs

Examples:

PROCESSES	AEROSPACE	CONSUMER PRODUCTS
Textiles	Planes	Appliances
Oil refining	Jet engines	Valves
Steel	Automotive	
Chemical	Capital goods	
Paper		
Plastics		
Film		

all three types. The reason for using the **VAT classification** is obvious when we note the actual appearance of the product flow through the system. In a "V" plant, there are few raw materials and they are transformed through a relatively standard process into a much larger number of end products. Consider a steel plant, for example: A few raw materials are converted into a large number of types of sheet steel, beams, rods, wire, and so forth.

An "A" plant is the opposite. In an "A" plant many raw materials, components, and parts are converted into few end products. Examples in aerospace would be making jet engines, airplanes, and missiles. In a "T" plant, the final product is assembled in many different ways out of similar parts and components. There are two stages in the production process: First, the basic parts and components are manufactured in a relatively straightforward way (the lower portion of the T) and are stored. Second, assembly takes place, combining these common parts into the many possible options to create the final product.

"V" Plant

Exhibit 19.14 shows the characteristics of a "V" plant. Problems that occur in a "V" plant show up as poor customer service, poor delivery, and high inventories of finished goods. The basic cause is generally a zealous effort to achieve high utilization levels, which instigates overly large process batch sizes.

"A" Plant

Exhibit 19.15 shows the characteristics of an "A" plant. In an "A" plant, management areas of concern are low equipment utilization, high unplanned overtime, parts shortages, and lack of control of the production process. When the flow is controlled correctly, there is a better utilization of resources, overtime is reduced or eliminated, and inventory levels are greatly decreased.

Characteristics

- There are a large number of end items, compared to the number of raw materials.
- Products use essentially the same sequence and processes.
- Equipment is generally capital-intensive and specialized.
- There are a limited number of routings.
- Generally, each part crosses a resource only once.
- It tends to produce a large number of parts in a small amount of time.
- The total available space in the facility may be the only limit to inventory accumulation.
- Significant process changes require substantial resource investment.

Perceived Problems

- Finished-goods inventories are too large.
- Customer service/delivery is poor.
- Manufacturing managers complain that demand is constantly changing.
- Marketing managers complain that manufacturing is slow to respond.
- Interdepartmental conflicts are common.
- Production lead time becomes unpredictable.

Inventory Levels

If there is a bottleneck:

- Large inventory (usually of wrong items) exists in front of the bottleneck. This inventory is caused by misallocation and overproduction prior to the bottleneck.
- Beyond the bottleneck there are small queues since there is excess capacity.
- Management tends to blame this wrong inventory on changing demand.
- The firm is unable to respond to the market because of large inventory.
- Finished-goods inventories of the wrong products accumulate.

If there is no bottleneck:

- There are large finished-goods inventories of the wrong products.

Causes

- Batch sizes are too large because the plant is capital-intensive and the setup times are large.
- To achieve high levels of utilization, material is released to production too early.
- Supervisors are measured on utilizations of labor and equipment.
- Jobs are combined for larger batches, and product families are grouped together.
- Considerable expediting is done at the bottleneck.

Correct Course of Action

- Reduce batch size.
- Reduce production lead times. This improves forecast accuracy and the ability to react to changes in demand.
- Increase customer service with
  - Reliable promise dates.
  - Reduced production lead times.
- Reduce production costs by
  - Selling more product.
  - Reducing inventory.
  - Focusing on quality improvements.

"T" Plant

The main characteristic of a "T" plant is that the parts and components are common to many end items. The assembly of end products in a "T" plant is a combinational problem, with customers placing orders for different colors, features, or sizes, thus creating many possibilities. The lead time, as far as the customer is concerned, is the height of the cross bar of the T. This means that a customer's order is assembled from the standard parts and components that are stocked. Typically, management erroneously perceives the problem as a need for better forecasting, improved inventory control in warehouses, and reduced unit cost by controlling overtime and setups and by introducing automation and

E X H I B I T 19.15

"A" Plant

Characteristics

- Assembly feature is dominant.
- Machines tend to be general-purpose rather than specialized.
- Assembly time tends to be long.
- Resources are shared within and across routings.
- Resource efficiencies are less than 100 percent, but there is still overtime.
- Large completed-parts inventory exists, but severe shortages exist for other parts.
- Process time typically is less than production lead time.
- Wandering bottlenecks occur.
- Fabrication complains that demand is changing, leading to plant chaos and poor vendor performance.
- Operating expenses (particularly unplanned overtime) is a sore point.
- Problem parts are most likely not common to many assemblies.
- Relatively few parts cross the bottleneck (capacity constraint).
- Lack of control is voiced as the key problem.
- Assembly complains of shortages and mismatches.
- Production is designated early in the process (the opposite of a "V" plant).
- People perceive the problem as a lack of parts.
- Routings can vary widely; one part may require 50 operations, while another for the same assembly may require only a few.
- The same machine may be used several times on the same part during its routing.
- Parts are unique to specific end items (unlike a "V" or "T" plant); jet engine blades, for example, are only for particular engines.
- There is little opportunity for misallocation of parts because they are peculiar to end items.

Conventional Tactics for Corrective Action

Reduce unit cost by

- Strict control of overtime. (Management perceives abuse of overtime; restriction of use aggravates problem.)
- Automation of processes. (This makes matters worse since flexibility is lost through the automation.)
- Better planning of labor needs. (The illusion is that there are too many workers.)

Improve control by

- Integrated production system. (The problem here is that different parts of the plant operate differently so a single system is unlikely to satisfy all needs.)

Actual Causes

Too-large batch sizes and too-early release of material causing

- Moving bottlenecks.
- Low utilizations.
- Frequent use of overtime.
- All parts needed for assembly not being there at the same time; assembly operations constantly being short the parts needed to assemble the product.
- Frequent expediting to rush through missing parts.

Solution

- Reduce batch size.
- Use drum–buffer–rope for control.

---

simplified designs. Exhibit 19.16 summarizes "T" plant characteristics. The correct approach using synchronous manufacturing is to improve due-date delivery performance and to reduce operating expenses by

1. Controlling the flow through the fabrication portion of the process.
2. Reducing batch sizes to eliminate the wavelike motion.
3. Stopping the "stealing" of parts and components at assembly.

E X H I B I T 19.16

"T" Plant

Characteristics
- Two distinctive processes and flows:
  - Fabrication.
  - Assembly.
- Due-date performance is very poor; there is a split between very early and very late (e.g., 40 percent early, 20 percent on time, 40 percent late).
- Overtime and expediting in fabrication are random and frequent.
- A very high degree of commonality of parts is dominant.
- The assignment of parts (even subassemblies) to orders occurs very late in the process.
- Fabrication is done in huge batches.
- There is a large amount of inventory at common stocking level between fabrication and assembly.

Causes of Problems
- Improvement in due-date performance is attempted by heavy reliance on inventory of both finished and semifinished goods, and in volume and variety.
- The drive to attain efficiencies and dollars shipped
  - Undermines assembly activity objectives of due-date performance and assemble-to-order.
  - Undermines fabrication activity objective of purchase and fabricate to forecast.
  - Causes intentional misallocation of parts and cannibalization at assembly and subassembly areas.

Core Problem
- Due-date performance is bad and management cannot seem to do anything about it.

Solution
- Reduce batch sizes in fabrication.
- Use drum–buffer–rope in fabrication to control flow.
- Stop the "stealing" of parts and components in assembly.

The vertical part of the T is the fabrication process which needs to be controlled using smaller batches. These parts are then stored below the crossbar. Final assembly is done in the crossbar.

Stealing parts is caused by the pressure from each supervisor in the assembly process to maintain high utilizations. When supervisors and workers are caught up on orders that are currently due, or when they cannot assemble a product because parts are missing, they reach ahead and assemble products for future orders. The result is that some other products in the assembly area are short those items and therefore late.

In conclusion, the VAT classification can lead us quickly and directly to the source of the problem. Exhibit 19.17 summarizes plant characteristics and perceived problems. In a "V" plant, we would look for large inventories. In an "A" plant, we would expect to find moving bottlenecks. In a "T" plant, we would suspect that people are stealing parts to build ahead.

19.10 RELATIONSHIP WITH OTHER FUNCTIONAL AREAS

The production system must work closely with the other functional areas to achieve the best operating system. This section briefly discusses accounting and marketing—areas where conflicts can occur—and where cooperation and joint planning should occur.

Accounting's Influence on Equipment Investment Decisions

Sometimes we are led into making decisions to suit the measurement system rather than to follow the firm's goals. Consider the following example: Suppose that two old machines are currently being used to produce a product. The processing time for each is 20 minutes per part and, since each has the capacity of three parts per hour, they have the combined capacity of six per hour, which exactly meets the market demand of six parts

E X H I B I T 19.17
Summary of VAT Plant Characteristics and Perceived Problems

	Summary	
"V" Plant	Capital-intensive Highly mechanized Dedicated Inflexible Specialization within the flow process	
"A" Plant	Less capital-intensive Versatile Flexible machines Can work at different levels of product flow	

"T" Plant	Has fabrication and assembly areas
	Fabrication:
	    Short routing
	    Versatile machines
	Assembly area:
	    Assembly is the predominant activity.
	    Assembly lead time (days) is short.	

Management-Perceived Problems

"V" Plant	Cost is the focus.
"A" Plant	There is a need for control (constantly expediting, overtime, material availability, no idea of problem, wandering bottleneck).
"T" Plant	Due-date performance is usually bad, but management cannot seem to change it.

per hour. Suppose that engineering finds a new machine that produces parts in 12 minutes rather than 20. However, the capacity of this one machine is only five per hour, which does not meet the market demand. Logic would seem to dictate that the supervisor should use an old machine to make up the lacking one unit per hour. However, the system does not allow this. The standard has been changed from the 20 minutes each to 12 minutes each and performance would look very bad on paper because the variance would be 67 percent high $[20 - 12)/12]$ for units made on the old machines. The supervisor, therefore, would work the new machine on overtime.

Problems in Cost Accounting Measurements   Cost accounting is used for performance measurement, cost determinations, investment justification, and inventory valuation. Two sets of accounting performance measurements are used for evaluation: (1) global measurements, which are financial statements, showing net profit, return on investment, and cash flow (with which we agree), and (2) local cost accounting measurements showing efficiencies (as variances from standard) or utilization rate (hours worked/hours present).

From the cost accounting (local measurement) viewpoint, then, performance has traditionally been based on cost and full utilization. This logic forces supervisors to activate their workers all the time, which leads to excessive inventory. The cost accounting measurement system can also instigate other problems. For example, attempting to use the idle time to increase utilization can create a bottleneck, as we discussed earlier in this chapter. Any measurement system should support the objectives of the firm and not stand in the way. Fortunately, the cost accounting measurement philosophy is changing.

Bringing Together Marketing and Production

Marketing and production should communicate and conduct their activities in close harmony. In practice, however, they act very independently. There are many reasons for this. The difficulties range from differences in personalities and cultures to unlike systems of merits and rewards in the two functions. Marketing people are judged on the growth of the company in terms of sales, market share, and new products entered. Marketing is sales-oriented. Manufacturing people are evaluated on cost and utilization. Therefore, marketing wants a variety of products to increase the company's position while manufacturing is trying to reduce cost.

Data used for evaluating marketing and manufacturing are also quite different. Marketing data are "soft" (qualitative); manufacturing data are "hard" (quantitative). The orientation and experiences of marketing and production people also differ. Those in marketing management have likely come up through sales and a close association with customers. Top manufacturing managers have likely progressed through production operations and therefore have plant performance as a top objective.

Cultural differences can also be important in contrasting marketing and manufacturing personnel. Top managers in each can live quite differently since they have different motivations, goals, and hobbies as well. Marketing people tend to have a greater ego drive and are more outgoing. Manufacturing personnel tend to be more meticulous and perhaps more introverted (at least less extroverted than their marketing counterpart).

The solution to coping with these differences is to develop an equitable set of measurements to evaluate performance in each area, and to promote strong lines of communications so that they both contribute to reaching the firm's goals.

We now present two examples to show that different objectives and measurement criteria can lead to the wrong decisions. These examples also show that, even though you may have all the data required, you still may not be able to solve the problem—unless you know how!

E X A M P L E 19.1 / *What to Produce?* In this first example, three products (A, B, and C) are sold in the market at $50, $75, and $60 per unit, respectively. The market will take all that can be supplied.

Three work centers (X, Y, and Z) process the three products as shown in Exhibit 19.18. Processing times for each work center are also shown. Note that each work center works on all three products. Raw materials, parts, and components are added at each work center to produce each product. The per unit cost of these materials is shown as RM.

Which product or products should be produced?

S O L U T I O N Three different objectives could exist that lead to different conclusions:

1. Maximize sales revenue since marketing personnel are paid commission based on total revenue.
2. Maximize per unit gross profit.
3. Maximize total gross profit.

In this example we use gross profit as selling price less materials. We could also include other expenses such as operating expenses, but we left them out for simplicity. (We include operating expenses in our next example.)

Objective 1: Maximize sales commission. The decision is simple. Sell only B at $75 per unit, and none of A and C.

Objective 2: Maximize per unit gross profit.

(1) Product	(2) Selling Price	(3) Raw Material Cost	(4) Gross Profit per Unit (2) − (3)
A	$50	$20	$30
B	$75	$60	$15
C	$60	$40	$20

EXHIBIT 19.18

Prices and Production Requirements for Three Products and Three Work Centers

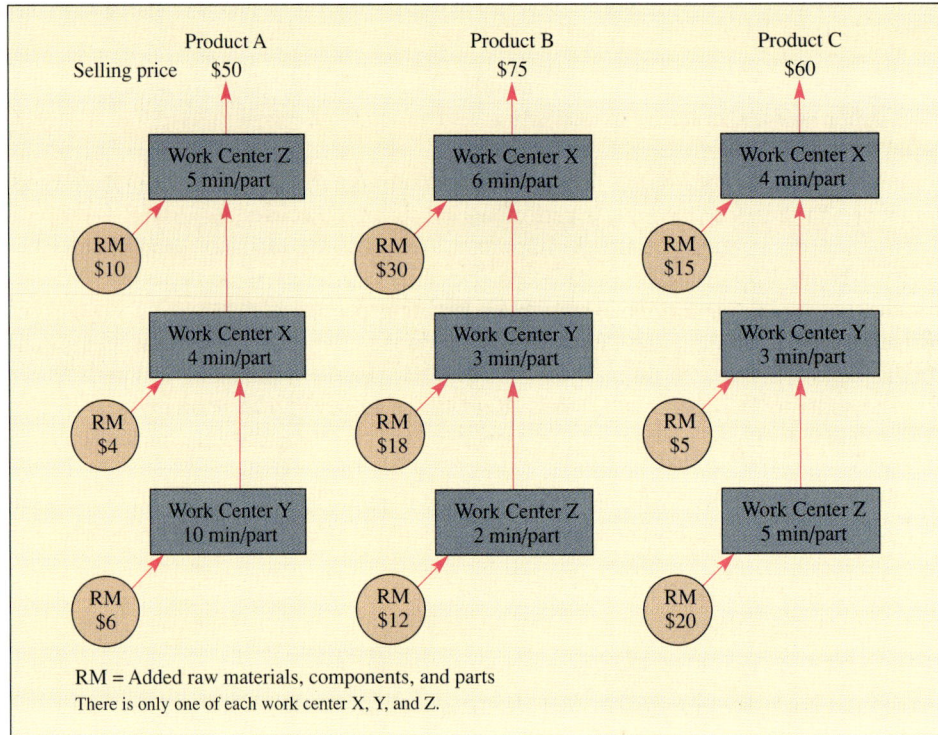

RM = Added raw materials, components, and parts
There is only one of each work center X, Y, and Z.

The decision would be to sell only product A, which has a $30 per unit gross profit.

Objective 3: Maximize total gross profit. We can solve this problem by finding either total gross profit for the period or the rate at which profit is generated. We use rate to solve the problem both because it is easier and because it is a more appropriate measure. We use profit per hour as rate.

Note that each product has a different work center which limits its output. The rate at which the product is made is then based on this bottleneck work center.

(1)	(2)	(3)	(4)	(5)	(6)	(7)	(8)
Product	Limiting Work Center	Processing Time per Unit (minutes)	Product Output Rate (per hour)	Selling Price	Raw Material Cost	Profit per Unit	Profit per Hour (4) × (7)
A	Y	10	6	$50	$20	$30	$180
B	X	6	10	75	60	15	150
C	Z	5	12	60	40	20	240

From our calculations, Product C provides the highest profit of $240 per hour. Note that we get three different answers:

1. We choose B to maximize commission.
2. We choose A to maximize profit per unit.
3. We choose C to maximize total profit.

Choosing Product C is obviously the correct answer for the firm.

In this example, all work centers were required for each product and each product had a different work center as a constraint. We did this to simplify the problem and to

E X H I B I T 19.19   *Production Requirements and Selling Price for Four Products*

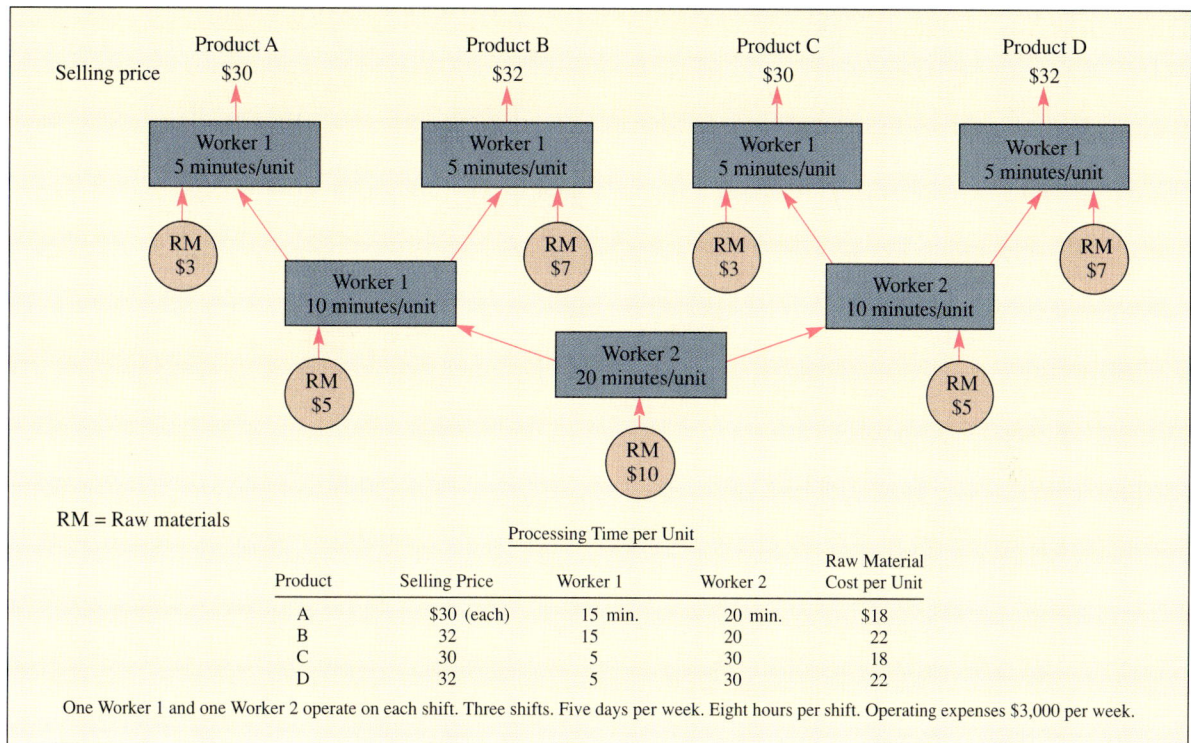

Product	Selling Price	Worker 1	Worker 2	Raw Material Cost per Unit
A	$30 (each)	15 min.	20 min.	$18
B	32	15	20	22
C	30	5	30	18
D	32	5	30	22

One Worker 1 and one Worker 2 operate on each shift. Three shifts. Five days per week. Eight hours per shift. Operating expenses $3,000 per week.

ensure that only one product would surface as the answer. If there were more work centers or the same work center constraint in different products, the problem could still easily be solved using linear programming (as in the Supplement to Chapter 8). ■

E X A M P L E 19.2 / *How Much to Produce?*   In this example, shown in Exhibit 19.19, there are two workers producing four products. The plant works three shifts. The market demand is unlimited and takes all the products that the workers can produce. The only stipulation is that the ratio of products sold cannot exceed 10 to 1 between the maximum sold of any one product and the minimum of another. For example, if the maximum number sold of any one of the products is 100 units, the minimum of any other cannot be fewer than 10 units. Workers 1 and 2, on each shift, are not cross-trained and can only work on their own operations. The time and raw material (RM) costs are shown in the exhibit, and a summary of the costs and times involved is on the lower portion of the exhibit. Weekly operating expenses are $3,000.

What quantities of A, B, C, and D should be produced?

S O L U T I O N   As in the previous example, there are three answers to this question, depending on each of the following objectives:

1. Maximizing commission for sales personnel.
2. Maximizing per unit gross profit.
3. Maximizing the utilization of the bottleneck resource (leading to maximum gross profit).

Objective 1: Maximizing sales commission on sales revenue. Sales personnel prefer to sell B and D (selling price $32) rather than A and C (selling price $30). Weekly operating expenses are $3,000.

The ratio of units sold will be: 1A : 10B : 1C : 10D.

Worker 2 on each shift is the bottleneck and therefore determines the output.[4]

$$5 \text{ days per week} \times 3 \text{ shifts} \times 8 \text{ hours} \times 60 \text{ minutes} = \frac{7{,}200 \text{ minutes per}}{\text{week available}}$$

Worker 2 spends these times on each unit:

A   20 minutes   C   30 minutes
B   20 minutes   D   30 minutes

The ratio of output units is 1 : 10 : 1 : 10. Therefore

$$1x(20) + 10x(20) + 1x(30) + 10x(30) = 7{,}200$$
$$550x = 7{,}200$$
$$x = 13.09$$

Therefore the numbers of units produced is

A = 13
B = 131
C = 13
D = 131

Gross profit per week (selling price less raw material less weekly expenses) is

$$13(30 - 18) + 131(32 - 22) + 13(30 - 18) + 131(32 - 22) - 3{,}000$$
$$= 156 + 1{,}310 + 156 + 1{,}310 - 3{,}000$$
$$= (\$68) \text{ loss.}$$

Objective 2: Maximizing per unit gross profit.

	Gross Profit	=	Selling Price	−	Raw Material Cost
A	12	=	30	−	18
B	10	=	32	−	22
C	12	=	30	−	18
D	10	=	32	−	22

A and C have the maximum gross profit so the ratio will be 10 : 1 : 10 : 1 for A, B, C, and D. Worker 2 is the constraint and has

$$5 \text{ days} \times 3 \text{ shifts} \times 8 \text{ hours} \times 60 \text{ minutes} = \frac{7{,}200 \text{ minutes available}}{\text{per week}}$$

As before, A and B take 20 minutes, while C and D take 30 minutes. Thus

$$10x(20) + 1x(20) + 10x(30) + 1x(30) = 7{,}200$$
$$550x = 7{,}200$$
$$x = 13$$

_____
[4]Note that if this truly is a bottleneck with an unlimited market demand, this should be a seven-day-per-week operation, not just a five-day workweek.

Therefore the numbers of units produced is

A = 131
B = 13
C = 131
D = 13

Gross profit (selling price less raw materials less $3,000 weekly expense) is

$$131(30 - 18) + 13(32 - 22) + 131(30 - 18) + 13(32 - 22) - 3,000$$
$$= 1,572 + 130 + 1,572 + 130 - 3,000$$
$$= \$404 \text{ profit}$$

Objective 3: Maximizing the use of the bottleneck resource, Worker 2. For every hour Worker 2 works, the following number of products and gross profit result

(1)	(2)	(3)	(4)	(5)	(6)
Product	Production Time	Units Produced per Hour	Selling Price Each	Raw Material Cost per Unit	Gross Profit per Hour (3) × [(4) − (5)]
A	20 minutes	3	$30	$18	$36
B	20	3	32	22	30
C	30	2	30	18	24
D	30	2	32	22	20

Product A generates the greatest gross profit per hour of Worker 2 time so the ratio is 10 : 1 : 1 : 1 for A, B, C, and D.

Available time for Worker 2 is the same as before:

3 shifts × 5 days × 8 hours × 60 minutes = 7,200 minutes

Worker 2 should produce 10 A's for every 1B, 1C, and 1D. Worker 2's average production rate is

$$10x(20) + 1x(20) + 1x(30) + 1x(30) = 7,200$$
$$280x = 7,200$$
$$x = 25.7$$

Therefore the number of units that should be produced is

A = 257
B = 25.7
C = 25.7
D = 25.7

Gross profit (price less raw materials less $3,000 weekly expenses) is

$$257(30 - 18) + 25.7(32 - 22) + 25.7(30 - 18) + 25.7(32 - 22) - 3,000$$
$$= 3,084 + 257 + 308.4 + 257 - 3,000$$
$$= \$906.40$$

The Trane Company

The Trane Company is a large industrial organization headquartered in LaCrosse, Wisconsin. The Trane Company's Commercial Systems factory in Macon, Georgia, produces the company's line of large self-contained air conditioner units for buildings. In 1987 the self-contained unit production was transferred from a sister factory to the Macon plant. The plant was originally configured in 1988 as a balanced assembly line to accept the self-contained unit production. The Macon factory operates on an eight-hour-per-day, five-days-per-week basis. Total plant employment is about 150 employees. There are about 90 direct-labor employees. All permanent Macon employees are salaried. Temporary employees are hired on a daily basis from a local employment agency. The number of temporary employees varies with the production rate from 0 to 25 percent of the permanent direct-labor employees. At the time of this writing, about 20 percent of the 90 direct-labor employees were temporaries. The factory had 1990 sales of about $25 million and was profitable under generally accepted accounting standards criteria.

The production planning and control system used at the Macon factory is a combination of MRP, JIT, and TOC.* An MRP system was purchased in early 1989. The software package is identified as CONTROL produced by Cincom, Inc. The decision to purchase the MRP software was based on a survey of factor user requirements that compared several different MRP systems. The MRP system consists of several generic modules linked by customized interfaces. Currently, the Macon factory uses the master production scheduling module, the MRP calculation module, the accounting module, and the bill-of-materials module. A separate purchasing system was selected and implemented together with the MRP system in 1989. The shop-floor control module that was available as part of the CONTROL software package was not implemented. The factory's decision not to implement the shop-floor control module was based on the desire to use TOC and JIT methods. Management believes that the MRP system provided a framework for the TOC and JIT methods.

The company employed an outside consultant in 1988 to improve aspects of the production process using the JIT approach. The Macon factory uses a leveled master production schedule, production schedule linearity, scheduled preventive maintenance, multiskilled employees, and plant layout revisions to accommodate JIT. Kanban triggers are also used for replenishing subassemblies into the final assembly area. Suppliers use triggering methods to replenish hardware and other purchased finished components. The factory is organized into five work teams, called cells, and all cell supervisors have been trained on JIT methods. Production decisions, such as the scheduling of overtime, are made by consensus of the cell employees.

The factory implemented TOC in 1989. The performance measurement aspects of throughput, inventory, and operating expense are used for internal management decisions. The shop floor is controlled by the drum–buffer–rope and buffer management methods. Management has been trained in the use of TOC techniques and the underlying performance measurement methods. The OPT software is not used at the factory. The bottleneck operation was identified and a "constraint" buffer was used as well as a "space" buffer after the bottleneck operation.

Inventory management is a shared responsibility between the cell supervisors and support employees. Manufacturing lead time is two to five days. Raw material is 70 percent of the total inventory and has a current turnover of about six times per year. Work-in-process inventory is about 10 percent of the total inventory investment and has a turnover of 100 times per year. Finished goods are about 20 percent of the total inventory and have a turnover of about 10 times per year. Factory management has 1992 turnover targets for raw material inventory of 12 times per year, work-in-process inventory at 250 times per year, and finished goods at 15 times per year.

*TOC (Theory of Constraints). See Exhibit 19.21 pg 785.

In summary, using three different objectives to decide how many of each product to make gave us three different results:

1. Maximizing sales commission resulted in a $68 loss.
2. Maximizing gross profit gave us a profit of $404.

When first begun, the balanced assembly line used the kanban pull system and produced an average of three units per day. When drum–buffer–rope and buffer management techniques were implemented, the assembly line average increased to six units per day with the same workforce. Management attributes the increase in productivity to TOC and believes that the dramatic reduction in lead time significantly contributes to the competitiveness of its product lines in the marketplace.

New Product Introduction

In 1991, The Trane Company was faced with a decision concerning whether to introduce two new products into the marketplace. The first product was a refrigerant cleaning service unit that measured approximately $5 \times 4 \times 3$ feet. The second product was a refrigerant evacuation unit that was smaller than the cleaning service unit. The company could have built the units in a factory in Pennsylvania. However, traditional cost-accounting–based calculations indicated that the expected price of the products would not be sufficient to generate a profit at that factory. The company then had to consider the abandonment of the two product lines. The self-contained air conditioner units assembled at the Macon factory measure about $7 \times 5 \times 10$ feet. Because of the much larger size, the Macon factory was not initially considered for the assembly of the two new product lines. The Macon factory undertook its own implementation study based on the TOC performance measurement methods. As a result of the study both products were assigned to be manufactured at the Macon factory and the product lines were introduced into the market in 1992. Traditional cost accounting valuation methods led the company to abandon two product lines that have proved to be profitable under TOC calculation.

The Macon factory determined that enough space had been made available through the use of TOC and JIT methods in what had been the finished stores area that both product lines could be assembled in the factory. Further, since neither of the product lines used the existing self-contained unit assembly line, the bottleneck opera-

tion would not be jeopardized by the introduction of the two products. Since factory space already existed, there would be no capital outlay except for the required assembly tools, considered an addition to operating expenses. Under TOC costing, only raw material costs are included in the inventory figure for each. All labor and overheads are part of operating expense and are controlled at the factory level rather than being assigned to a specific product. Therefore the expected selling price of both product lines exceeded the raw material inventory cost for the product lines. Operating expense at the plant level was determined to increase less than the total amount of throughput for each product line. The net profit from each product line was equal to total throughput minus the additional operating expense. Return on investment in the new product lines equalled the net profit from the new product lines divided by the added investment needed to support the new product lines. Therefore the Macon factory readily accepted the introduction of the two product lines while other factories could not justify the introduction using traditional cost accounting methods.

Two Accounting Systems

The Macon factory uses a dual accounting system. External reports are generated by the accounting module of the MRP system. The external reports are sent to Trane headquarters using traditional accounting methods (allocation of overheads is based on direct-labor hours). The factory is measured on profit-and-loss calculations based on standard accounting practices. Internal factory management reports use TOC methods based on throughput, inventory, and operating-expense calculations. To a degree the decision made by Trane headquarters to assign the two product lines to Macon indicates an acceptance of TOC calculations even though traditional performance measures are used in the formal external reporting system.

Source: M. S. Spencer, "Economic Theory, Cost Accounting, and Theory of Constraints: An Examination of Relationships and Problems," *International Journal of Production Research* 32, no. 2 (1994), pp. 304–7.

3. Maximizing the use of the capacity-constrained worker gave us the best profit, $906.40. ∎

Both examples demonstrate that production and marketing need to interact. Marketing should sell the most profitable use of available capacity. However, to plan capacity, production needs to know from marketing what products could be sold.

E X H I B I T 19.20

*Goldratt's Rules
of Production
Scheduling*

1. Do not balance capacity—balance the flow.
2. The level of utilization of a nonbottleneck resource is not determined by its own potential but by some other constraint in the system.
3. Utilization and activation of a resource are not the same.
4. An hour lost at a bottleneck is an hour lost for the entire system.
5. An hour saved at a nonbottleneck is a mirage.
6. Bottlenecks govern both throughput and inventory in the system.
7. Transfer batch may not and many times should not be equal to the process batch.
8. A process batch should be variable both along its route and in time.
9. Priorities can be set only by examining the system's constraints. Lead time is a derivative of the schedule.

19.11 CONCLUSION

The measurement system within a firm should encourage the increase of net profits, return on investment, and cash flow. The firm can accomplish this if, at the operations level, it rewards performance based on the amount of throughput, inventory, and operating expense created. This is essential for a firm's success.

To control throughput, inventory, and operating expense, the system must be analyzed to find bottlenecks and capacity-constrained resources. Only then can the company proceed to define a drum for control, buffers to ensure throughput, and ropes for communicating the correct information to the correct locations, while minimizing work in process everywhere else. Without this focus, problems are not correctly diagnosed and solution procedures are impossible.

Goldratt defines nine rules (Exhibit 19.20) to help guide the logic of an operating system and to identify the important points. These are basic to any operating system and originally were called the Nine Rules of OPT.

The underlying philosophy presented in this chapter—the vital importance of concentrating on system limitations imposed by capacity-constrained resources—has led Goldratt to broaden his view of the importance of system limitations and to develop his five-step "general theory of constraints."[5] (See Exhibit 19.21.)

While the terms *bottleneck* and *constraint* can mean essentially the same thing, Goldratt uses *constraint* in the broadest sense meaning anything that limits the performance of a system and slows or prevents it from continuing to move toward its goal.

This general theory of constraints directs companies to find what is stopping them from moving toward their goals and finding ways to get around this limitation. If, in a manufacturing environment, the limitation is insufficient capacity, then ways to break the constraint might be overtime, specialized tools, supporting equipment, exceptionally skilled workers, subcontracting, redesigning product or process, alternate routings, and so on. Point 5 (Exhibit 19.21) warns against letting biases in thinking prevent the search for further exploitation of constraints. For example, if a search and exploitation of a constraint has been conducted under the limitation of cost, make sure that this cost measure is not carried into the next search. Start clean each time.

One last comment in summary of this chapter: The firm should operate as a synchronized system, with all parts in harmony and supporting each other. Marketing, finance, production, and engineering (as well as all the other functional staff and administrative entities) are all necessary parts of the system and are all seeking to achieve the common goals of the firm.

---

[5]Eliyahu M. Goldratt, *The General Theory of Constraints* (New Haven, CT: Abraham Y. Goldratt Institute, 1989).

1. Identify the system constraints. (No improvement is possible unless the constraint or weakest link is found.)
2. Decide how to exploit the system constraints. (Make the constraints as effective as possible.)
3. Subordinate everything else to that decision. (Align every other part of the system to support the constraints even if this reduces the efficiency of nonconstraint resources.)
4. Elevate the system constraints. (If output is still inadequate, acquire more of this resource so it no longer is a constraint.)
5. If, in the previous steps, the constraints have been broken, go back to Step 1, but do not let inertia become the system constraint. (After this constraint problem is solved, go back to the beginning and start over. This is a continuous process of improvement: identifying constraints, breaking them, and then identifying the new ones that result.)

E X H I B I T 19.21
Goldratt's Theory
of Constraints

19.12 SOLVED PROBLEM

Here is the process flow for Products A, B, and C. Products A, B, and C sell for $20, $25, and $30, respectively. There is only one Resource X and one Resource Y which are used to produce A, B, and C for the numbers of minutes stated on the diagram. Raw materials are needed at the process steps as shown, with the costs in dollars per unit of raw material. (One unit is used for each product.)

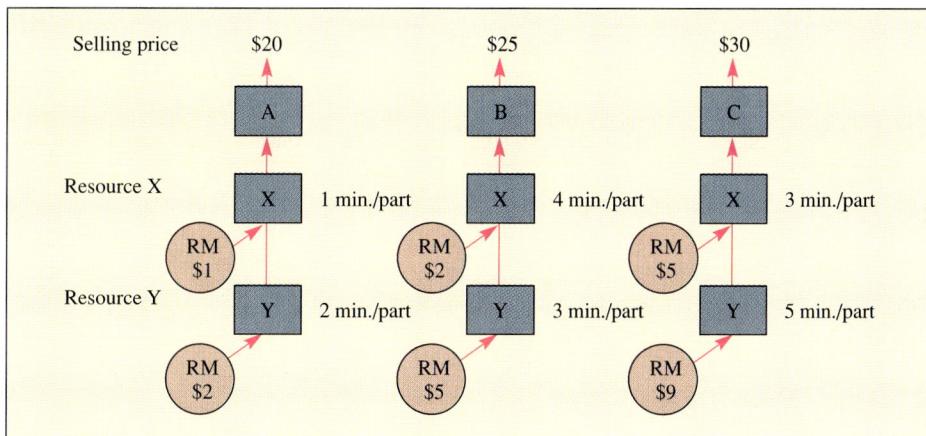

The market will take all that you can produce.

a. Which product would you produce to maximize gross margin per unit?

b. If sales personnel are paid on commission, which product or products would they sell and how many would they sell?

c. Which and how many product or products should you produce to maximize gross profit for a one-week period?

d. From (c), how much gross profit would there be for the week?

Solution

a. Maximizing gross margin per unit

	Gross Margin	=	Selling Price	−	Raw Material Cost
A	17	=	20	−	3
B	18	=	25	−	7
C	16	=	30	−	14

Product B will be produced.

b. Maximizing sales commission, they would sell the highest-priced product C (unless they knew the market and capacity limitations). If we assume the market will take all that we can make, then we would work 7 days/week, 24 hours/day.

Y is the constraint in producing C. The number of C we can make in a week is

$$C = \frac{8 \text{ hours/day} \times 7 \text{ days/week} \times 60 \text{ minutes/hour}}{5 \text{ minutes/part}} = 672 \text{ units}$$

c. To maximize profit, we need to compare profits per hour for each product.

(1) Product	(2) Constraint Resource	(3) Production Time on Resource	(4) Number of Units Output per Hour	(5) Selling Price ($)	(6) RM Cost ($)	(7) Gross Profit per Hour (4) × (5 − 6)
A	Y	2	30	20	3	$510
B	X	4	15	25	7	270
C	Y	5	12	30	14	192

If the constraining resource were the same for all three products, our problem would be solved and the answer would be to produce just A, and as many as possible. However, X is the constraint for B so the answer could be a combination of A and B. To test this we can see that the value of each hour of Y while producing B is

$$\frac{60 \text{ minutes/hour}}{3 \text{ minutes/unit}} \times (\$25 - 7) = \$360/\text{hour}$$

Since this is less than the $510 per hour producing A, we would produce only A. The number of units of A produced during the week is

$$\frac{60 \text{ minutes/hour} \times 24 \text{ hours/day} \times 7 \text{ days/week}}{2 \text{ minutes/unit}} = 5,040$$

d. Gross profit for the week is 5,040 × $17 = $85,680.

Solved using profit per hour: $510 × 24 × 7 = $85,680.

19.13 REVIEW AND DISCUSSION QUESTIONS

1. State the global performance measurements and operational performance measurements and briefly define each of them. How do these differ from traditional accounting measurements?
2. Discuss process batch and transfer batches. How might you determine what the sizes should be?
3. Compare and contrast JIT, MRP, and synchronized manufacturing, stating their main features such as where each is or might be used, amounts of raw materials and work-in-process inventories, production lead times and cycle times, and methods for control.
4. Compare and contrast VAT-type plants bringing in such points as where they are best applied, the main features of each (such as product flow and equipment type), major problems of each, likely source of the problems, and likely solutions to the problems.
5. Compare the importance and relevance of quality control in JIT, MRP, and synchronous manufacturing.
6. Discuss what is meant by forward loading and backward loading.
7. Define and explain the cause or causes of a moving bottleneck.

8. Explain how a nonbottleneck can become a bottleneck.

9. What are the functions of inventory in MRP, JIT, and synchronous manufacturing scheduling?

10. Define process batch and transfer batch and their meaning in each of these applications: MRP, JIT, and bottleneck or constrained resource logic.

11. Discuss how a production system is scheduled using MRP logic, JIT logic, and synchronous manufacturing logic.

12. Discuss the concept of "drum–buffer–rope."

13. From the standpoint of the scheduling process, how are resource limitations treated in an MRP application and how are they treated in a synchronous manufacturing application?

14. What are operations people's primary complaints against the accounting procedures used in most firms? Explain how such procedures can cause poor decisions for the total company.

15. Most manufacturing firms try to balance capacity for their production sequences. Some believe that this is an invalid strategy. Explain why balancing capacity does not work.

16. Transfer batches and process batches many times may not and should not be equal. Discuss.

19.14 PROBLEMS

1. For the four basic configurations that follow, assume that the market is demanding product that must be processed by both Resource X and Resource Y for Cases I, II, and III. For Case IV, both resources supply separate, but dependent markets; that is, the number of units of output from both X and Y must be equal.

   Plans are being made to produce a product that requires 40 minutes for each unit on Resource X and 30 minutes on Resource Y. Assume that there is only one unit of each of these resources, and that market demand is 1,400 units per month.

   How would you schedule X and Y? What would happen otherwise in each case?

2. On p. 788 are the process flow sequences for three products: A, B, and C. There are two bottleneck operations—on the first leg and fourth leg—marked with an X. Boxes represent processes, which may be either machine or manual. Suggest the location of the drum, buffer, and ropes.

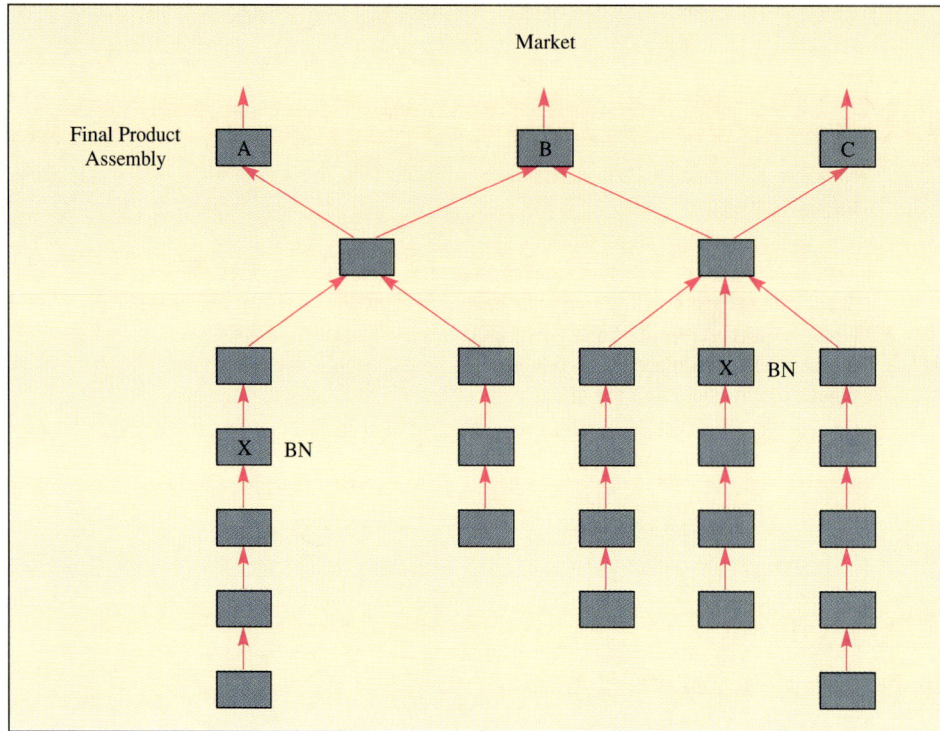

3. The accompanying figure shows a production network model with the parts and processing sequences. State clearly on the figure (1) where you would place inventory; (2) where you would perform inspection, and (3) where you would emphasize high-quality output. (Note: Operations may be shown either as rectangles in Problem 2 or as circles in Problem 3.)

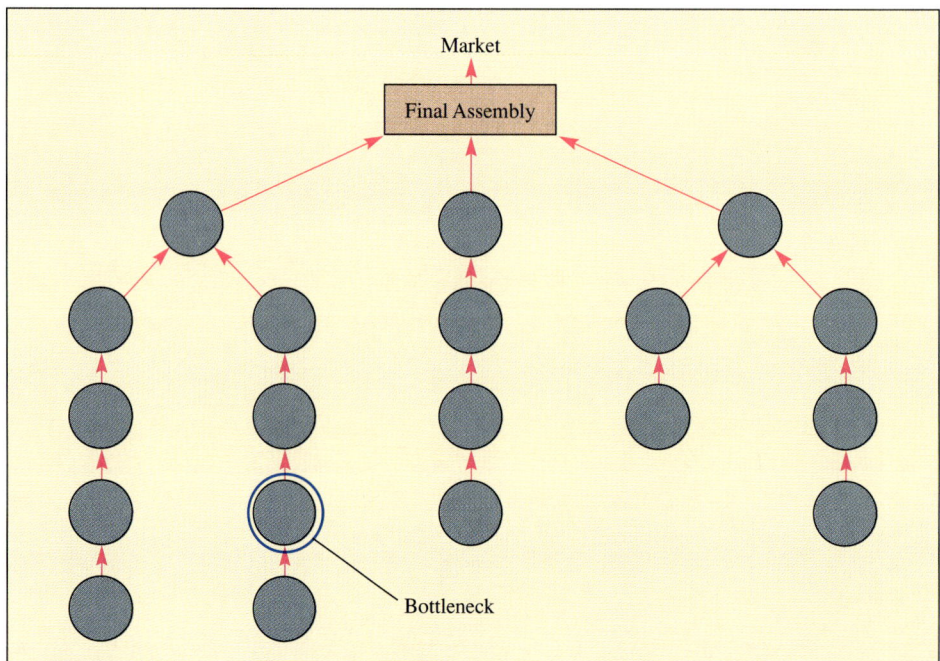

4. The following production flow shows Parts E, I, and N, Subassembly O, and final assembly for Product P.

   A to B to C to D to E
   F to G to H to I
   J to K to L to M to N
   E and I to O
   N and O to P

   B involves a bottleneck operation, and M involves a CCR.
   a. Draw out the process flow.
   b. Where would you locate buffer inventories?
   c. Where would you place inspection points?
   d. Where would you stress the importance of quality production?

5. Here are average process cycle times for several work centers. State which are bottlenecks, nonbottlenecks, and capacity–constrained resources.

Processing time	Setup time

Processing time	Setup	Idle

Processing time	Setup	Idle

Processing time	Setup	Idle

Processing time	Setup	Idle

6. The following diagram shows the flow process, raw material costs, and machine processing time for three products: A, B, and C. There are three machines (W, X, and Y) used in the production of these products; the times shown are in required minutes of production per unit. Raw material costs are shown in cost per unit of product. The market will take all that can be produced.

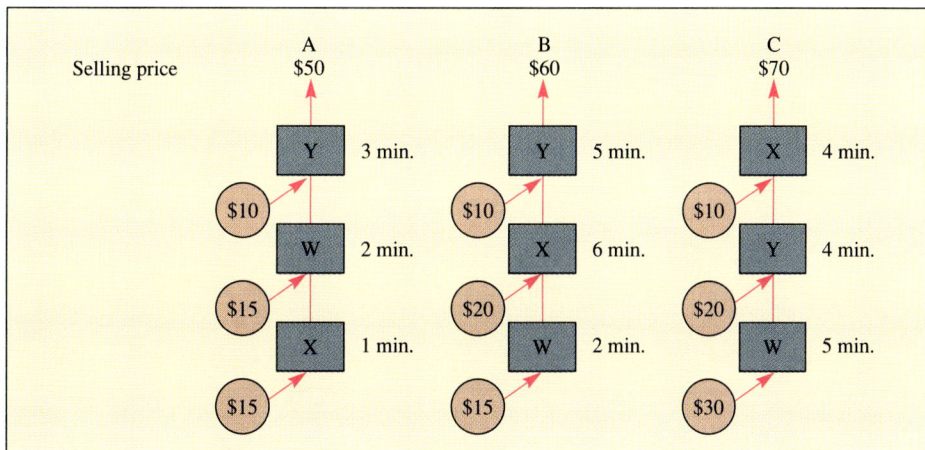

    a. Assuming that sales personnel are paid on a commission basis, which product should they sell?

    b. On the basis of maximizing gross profit per unit, which product should be sold?

    c. To maximize total profit for the firm, which product should be sold?

7. Willard Lock Company is losing market share because of horrendous due date performance and long delivery lead times. The company's inventory level is high and includes a good deal of finished goods that do not match the short-term orders. Material control analysis shows that purchasing has ordered on time, the vendors have delivered on time, and the scrap/rework rates have been as expected. However, the buildable mix of components and subassemblies does not generally match the short-term and past-due requirements at final assembly. End-of-month expediting and overtime is the rule, even though there is idle time early in the month. Overall efficiency figures are around 70 percent for the month. These figures are regarded as too low.

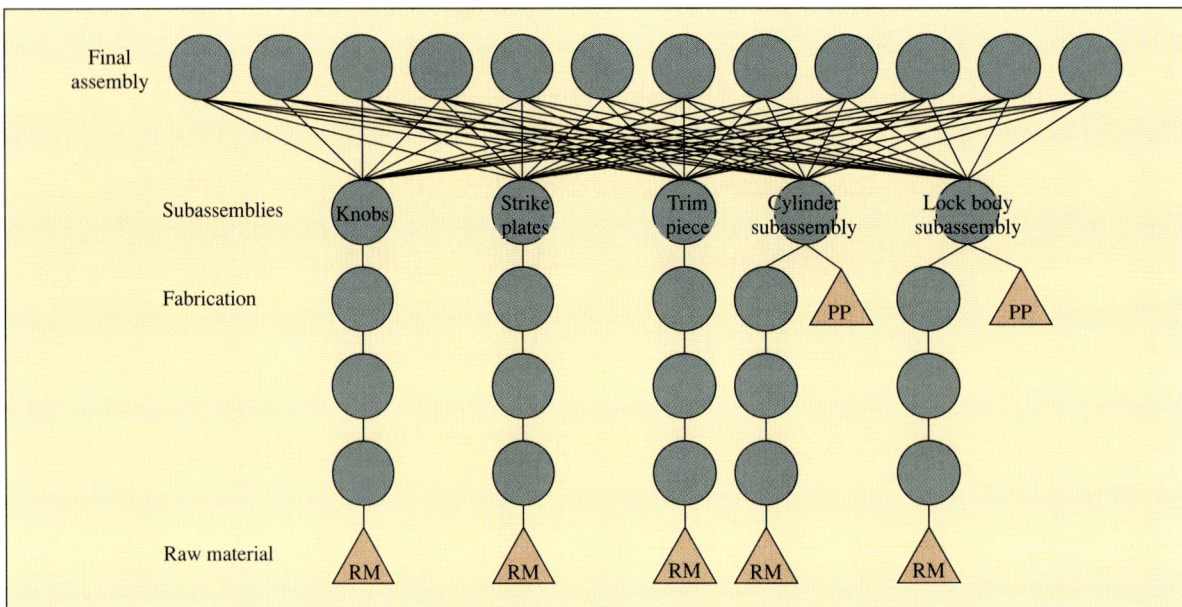

You have just been hired as a consultant and must come up with recommendations. Help the firm understand its problems. Specifically state some actions that it should take.

8. The M–N plant manufactures two different products: M and N. Selling prices and weekly market demands are shown in the diagram on p. 791. Each product uses raw materials with costs as shown. The plant has three different machines: A, B, and C. Each performs different tasks and can work on only one unit of material at a time.

Process times for each task are shown in the diagram. Each machine is available 2,400 minutes per week. There are no "Murphys" (major opportunities for the system to foul up). Setup and transfer times are zero. Demand is constant.

Operating expenses (including labor) total a constant $12,000 per week. Raw materials are not included in weekly operating expense.

    a. Where is the constraint in this plant?

    b. What product mix provides the highest profit?

    c. What is the maximum weekly net profit this plant can earn?

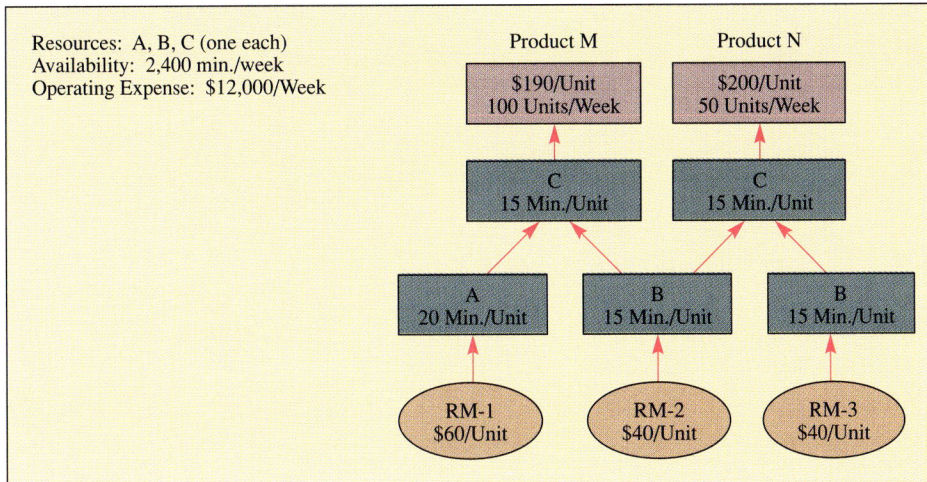

19.15   SELECTED BIBLIOGRAPHY

Aggarwal, S. "MRP, JIT, OPT, FMS?" *Harvard Business Review,* September-October 1985, pp. 8–16.

Fox, Robert E. "MRP, Kanban, or OPT—What's Best?" *Inventories and Production,* July-August, 1982.

———. "OPT: An Answer for America, Leapfrogging the Japanese, Part IV." *Inventories and Production* 3, no. 24 (March-April 1983).

———. "OPT vs. MRP: Thoughtware vs. Software." *Inventories and Production* 3, no. 6 (November-December 1983).

———. "OPT(imizing) JIT, Leapfrogging the Japanese." *APICS, Conference Proceedings* (Falls Church, VA: APICS, 1983), pp. 556–65.

Gardiner, Stanley C., and John H. Blackstone, Jr. "The 'Theory of Constraints' and the Make-or-Buy Decision." *International Journal of Purchasing and Materials Management* 27, no. 3 (Summer 1991), pp. 38–43.

Goldratt, Eliyahu M. "Computerized Shop Floor Scheduling." *International Journal of Production Research* 26, no. 3 (1988), pp. 443–55.

———. "Cost Accounting: The Number One Enemy of Productivity," *APICS, Conference Proceedings* (Falls Church, VA: APICS, 1983), pp. 433–35.

———. *The Haystack Syndrome: Sifting Information Out of the Data Ocean.* Croton-on-Hudson, NY: North River Press, 1990.

———. "What Is This Thing Called the Theory of Constraints and How Should It Be Implemented." Croton-on-Hudson, NY: North River Press, 1990.

———. "100% Data Accuracy—Need or Myth?" *APICS, Conference Proceedings* (Falls Church, VA: APICS, 1982), pp. 64–66.

———. "Late Night Discussions" Column. *Industry Week.* A variety of topics were covered during 1991–92.

Goldratt, Eliyahu M., and Jeff Cox. *The Goal: Excellence in Manufacturing.* 2d rev. ed. Croton-on-Hudson, NY: North River Press, 1992.

Goldratt, Eliyahu M., and Robert E. Fox. *The Race for a Competitive Edge.* Milford, CT: Creative Output, 1986.

Kaplan, Robert S. "Yesterday's Accounting Undermines Production." *Harvard Business Review,* July-August 1984, pp. 95–102.

Neely, A. D., and M. D. Byrne. "A Simulation Study of Bottleneck Scheduling." *International Journal of Production Economics* 26, no. 1–3 (1992), pp. 187–92.

Plossl, George W. "Managing by the Numbers—But Which Numbers." *APICS, Conference Proceedings* (Falls Church, VA: APICS, 1987), pp. 499–503.

Spencer, M. S. "Economic Theory, Cost Accounting, and Theory of Constraints: An Examination of Relationships and Problems." *International Journal of Production Research* 32, no. 2 (1994), pp. 299–308.

Srikanth, Mokshagundam L., and Harold E. Cavallaro, Jr. *Regaining Competitiveness: Putting the Goal to Work.* New Haven, CT: Spectrum, 1987.

Umble, M. Michael, and M. L. Srikanth. *Synchronous Manufacturing: Principles for World Class Excellence.* Cincinnati: Southwestern, 1990.

Vollmann, Thomas E. "OPT as an Enhancement to MRP II." *Production and Inventory Management,* 2d quarter 1986, pp. 38–47.

Weston, F. C., Jr. "Functional Goals Are Often in Conflict with Each Other." *Industrial Engineering* 23, no. 11 (November 1991), pp. 25–29.

Epilogue

■

How the Pros Do It

EPILOGUE OUTLINE

As a final service to our readers, we have included the following operations strategy consulting report prepared by the MAC Consulting Group. This report (originally published in *MAC Classics* in September 1987) shows how professionals go about developing an operations strategy for a client. As well as being a model of a well-constructed report, it illustrates an advanced application and synthesis of a number of important concepts covered throughout this book. In reviewing this report, do not get too entangled with the details. Rather, think about (1) the structure and process followed by the MAC team and (2) the report's benefits to management.[1]

---

[1] In 1991, the MAC Group became Gemini Consulting.

In February, the COO (chief operating officer) of a leading major appliance manufacturing company asked the MAC Group to help develop an "operations strategy for the 1990s." We won this assignment against strong competition, including two consulting firms that had previously carried out major operations assignments for our client. Our value-added proposal was judged the "most strategic" by the client.

Ultimately, we were able to demonstrate to our client's satisfaction that we were capable of closely integrating operations strategy with business and marketing strategies. To do so, over the course of four months, we developed a number of industry scenarios for the future, described the driving forces underlying each scenario, and developed hypotheses about the industry's competitive structure, product-market characteristics, and manufacturing technology. Together with the client, we developed a new mission and strategy that will make operations a key source of competitive advantages for the company for the next 10 to 15 years.

E.1   COMPARATIVE INDUSTRY APPROACH

One of the first discoveries we made in examining this industry was how similar it is to the automotive industry. Major appliances are relatively big-ticket consumer durable products. While somewhat less complex than automobiles, the design, engineering, and manufacturing procedures and technologies of such appliances are almost identical to those of automobiles. One difference is that the major appliance industry evolution appears to lag the automotive industry by about 10 to 15 years. As we started working with our client, we learned that company executives actually watched auto industry developments very closely for signs of how their own industry would evolve.

This similarity to the auto industry was helpful in two ways. First, we were able to draw on the extensive knowledge about the auto industry possessed by the team members (and other MAC Group consultants) from the outset to develop the analytical plan and hypotheses for this assignment. In some instances, we were actually able to apply lessons learned from the automotive industry directly to our client's situation. Second, our client found it helpful to use the auto industry as a reference when discussing strategic options and new ideas.

E.2   FRAMEWORK FOR IDENTIFYING FUTURE OPERATIONS MISSION

Our preliminary industry analyses carried out during proposal development clearly showed the major appliance industry was undergoing profound structural changes, beginning in the early 1980s. Initial discussions with key client managers confirmed this fact. We used the following analytical framework for identifying future operations capabilities. (See Exhibit E.1.)

E X H I B I T E.1

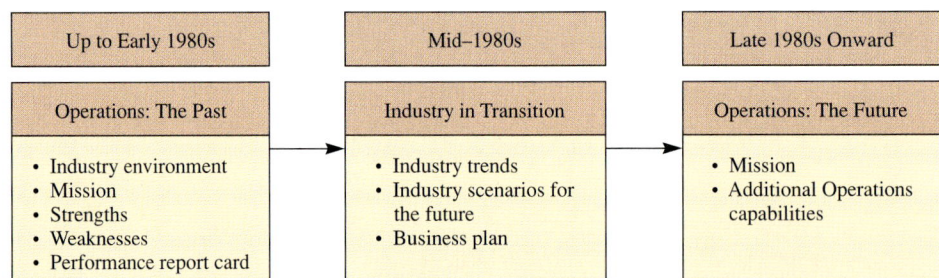

Up until the early 1980s, the U.S. major appliance market was relatively stable. Our client had a clearly defined and widely understood operations mission that was consistent with the marketplace's needs. To evaluate our client's efforts to achieve this mission, we divided the whole operations function into eight policy areas for analysis:

Past Operations

1. Plant (focus, size, and location).
2. Product design.
3. Process systems and technology.
4. Capacity.
5. Vertical integration (make–buy).
6. Quality.
7. MIS.
8. Organization.

It was apparent that our client had performed extremely well overall in achieving its stated mission. By focusing on the eight policy areas, we were able to pinpoint specific operations strengths and weaknesses. We compared our client's performance with its peers in the U.S. market, as well as with "world-class" standards from related industries such as automobiles and copiers. For example, our client was very pleased with the 300 percent improvement the company had achieved in inventory turnover—an outstanding achievement by industry standards. However, world-class standards for inventory turnover exceeded our client's by 200 percent. Our client was shocked to find out how much more the company could improve its performance.

We developed a performance report card (Exhibit E.2) to reveal how our client compared with the U.S. major appliance industry and with world-class standards. Our report card spurred the client to stretch its vision of short-term cost reduction. As the inventory turnover example showed, our client had the potential to "slash" its cost if it were to implement the appropriate performance-improvement programs. Many companies in other industries had shown the way, achieving short-term cost improvements of up to 20 percent by focusing on world-class standards.

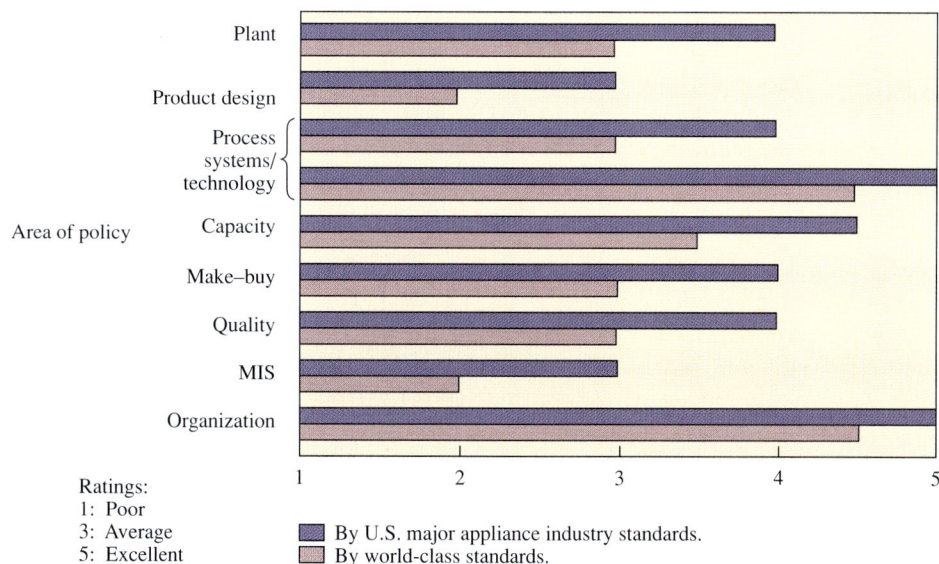

E X H I B I T E.2

Ratings:
1: Poor
3: Average
5: Excellent

By U.S. major appliance industry standards.
By world-class standards.

E X H I B I T E.3

EXHIBIT E.3

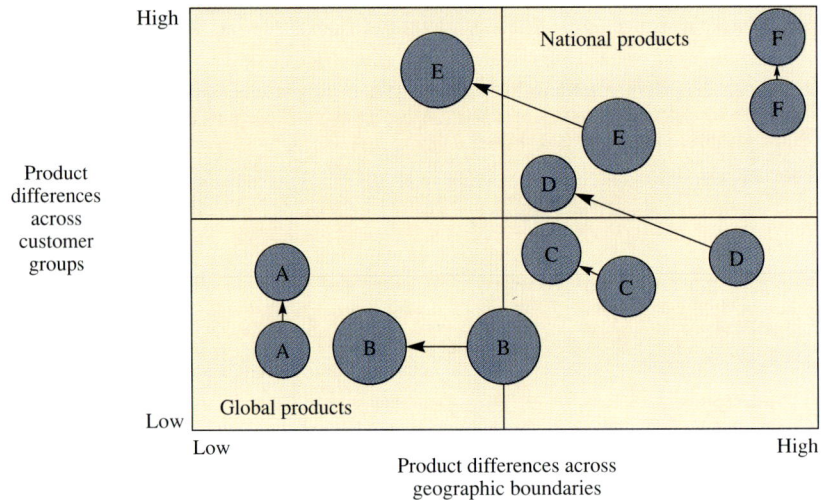

Industry in Transition

To determine the client's long-term operations mission, our team first developed a number of possible industry scenarios for the future. We then analyzed industry trends: major changes in the competitive environment, product market, and manufacturing systems and technology.

Again, the auto industry proved a good source of ideas for industry scenarios. Over the last two decades, experts have formulated numerous scenarios for the auto industry, ranging from an industry dominated by a handful of megaplayers, selling "world cars" made in giant plants that are located in low-cost areas, to an industry with many small players competing in niche markets. From our analysis of this and other related industries, we identified three likely scenarios for the major appliance industries: global oligopoly, global fragmentation, and national markets.

Analysis of market share trends, mergers/acquisitions, and capital investments pointed to more competition on a global basis. However, the data also showed that the trends differed between marketing/sales, product development, and manufacturing. In fact, we found it useful to examine the trends in even greater detail (e.g., in manufacturing to distinguish between large components and small components, and between subassembly and final assembly).

To better understand product trends, we analyzed the different major appliance products in terms of product differences across customer groups and across geographic boundaries. Exhibit E.3 showed that there are many different categories of products. Those in the lower left quadrant are "standardized global" products, with relatively little product differentiation by customer groups or geographic locations. At the other extreme, on the upper right, are the "highly differentiated national" products. These vary greatly, depending on the target customer groups. They are also very specific to each region, culture, and level of economic development.

We surveyed the technology used in manufacturing, and learned that "hard" (inflexible) automation was widely used, driven by traditional principles of scale economies from high-volume production and maximizing batch sizes. Manual processes were the main source of flexibility, to cope with product variation. However, we noticed that advanced manufacturing technology already in use in similar industries could readily be applied in the major appliance industry—indeed, some companies have begun installing such technology, albeit on a small scale. This was significant because the advanced tech-

Manufacturing Activities Chart   **E X H I B I T E.4**

	Products	A	B	C	D	E		F		G	
						I	II	I	II	I	II
Components	Presses and metal fabrication	—	—	—	—	—	—	—	—	—	—
	Plastics										
	Injection molding	—	—	—	—	—		—	—	—	—
	Extrusion							—			
	Thermal forming							—			
	Finishing										
	Porcelain		—	—		—	—		—		—
	Powder cost		—	—		—					
	Dip	—	—	—		—	—	—	—	—	—
	Miscellaneous processes										
	Welding and soldering			—		—	—	—	—	—	—
	Wire bending			—							
	Foaming							—	—		—
	Machining		—								
Assembly	Sub assembly	—		—		—	—	—	—	—	—
	Final assembly	—	—	—	—	—	—	—	—	—	—

nology is suitable for producing small lot sizes rapidly, with low work-in-process inventory and very high quality.

Once we had developed a list of possible industry scenarios and analyzed industry trends, we and our client then evaluated these two sets of information together to arrive at a view of the way the industry would evolve.

Our team then reviewed the long-term business plan of the client and found it to be consistent with the industry scenario that we believed was most likely. Successful implementation of the business plan, however, necessitated a major change in our client's operations strategy. We therefore set about developing a new mission that would ensure that the client's operations remained a key competitive weapon.

Future Operations

E.3 BUSINESS AND MANUFACTURING ECONOMICS

A key activity, before we started developing strategic options, was gaining a greater understanding of the client's business and manufacturing economics. We charted manufacturing activities (see Exhibit E.4) and conducted detailed cost analyses of the client's different product lines, using costed bills of materials.

Our analysis indicated two distinct manufacturing activities, each with unique features and management needs—both of which were managed exactly the same way. (See Exhibit E.5.)

Our cost analysis also showed that direct labor constituted only a small fraction of total manufacturing costs. The appliance manufacturing cost structure resembled that of high-tech industries more than traditional metal fabrication industries, in fact.

We next tried to understand the impact of economies of scale in this business. Rather than approaching this problem theoretically, we decided to use actual performance data to help answer this question. Fixed factory burden and production volume for three ma-

E X H I B I T E.5

Components	Assembly
• Highly automated	• Labor intensive
• High burden content relative to direct labor	• Utilizes a large proportion of direct labor going into product
• Total component burden exceeds assembly burden	• Cost of labor and burden are comparable
• High scale economies	• Low scale economies

jor product lines were plotted against time, and indicated three distinct factory burden behaviors over time. (See Exhibit E.6.)

Product A continued to realize scale economies—total factory burden growing slower than volume, and factory burden per unit decreasing. Product B appeared to have just reached the onset of diseconomies of scale. Product C certainly suffered from severe diseconomies of scale, with total factory burden increasing much faster than volume!

Plotting factory burden per unit against volume was even more enlightening. (See Exhibit E.7.)

A perfect U-shape scale economies/diseconomies curve resulted. For management, the curve illustrated that—for current manufacturing technology and management approach— the minimum efficient scale for plants producing Products A, B, and C was between X and Y units per year. It also showed that the plant for Product C was probably much too big.

We plotted other performance parameters: units produced per dollar of property, plant and equipment used, growth of sales, general and administrative expenses versus volume, and field service incidence over time. These charts further demonstrated that the client had not leveraged its fixed costs as volume increased. In other words, the company's fixed costs had become variable!

Our analysis of sales by SKU revealed the classic 80–20 phenomenon—80 percent of the sales came from 20 percent of the SKUs. For example, a single SKU (out of a total

E X H I B I T E.6   *Volume and Burden Trends*

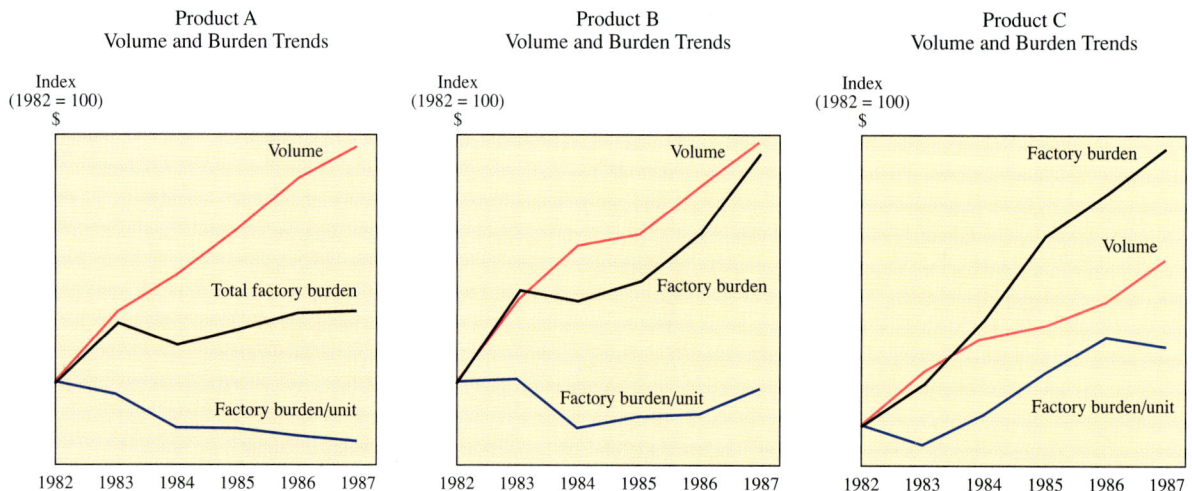

Product A
Volume and Burden Trends

Product B
Volume and Burden Trends

Product C
Volume and Burden Trends

Scale Curve

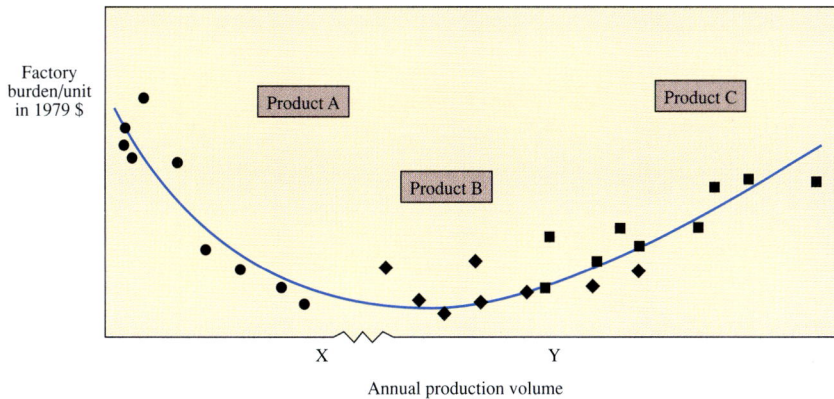

of 200 plus) accounted for about 15 percent of total sales for one of the products. This suggested that focusing plants by volume could be very cost-effective.

E.4 FOUR OPERATIONS POLICY AREAS

Four of the operations policy areas that the team examined were

1. Manufacturing technology.
2. Plant architecture.
3. Concept-to-production organization and process.
4. Manufacturing performance.

To illustrate the analytics used and work conducted by the team, specific examples from each policy area will be discussed in detail in the next four sections.

Manufacturing Technology

One manufacturing technology factor we addressed was flexible automation. Due to product proliferation, the number of SKUs was continuing to increase. Flexible automation is one approach to solving the product proliferation problem. We decided to use a case study of an existing similar plant to illustrate flexible automation. We chose IBM's Austin, Texas, plant, a fully automated assembly plant for personal computers. Our case example convinced the client that automated flexible assembly technology was available, and was not merely "pie-in-the-sky" technology.

Following the case study, we developed a "first-cut" design of a flexible assembly plant for Product A. (See Exhibit E.8 for a schematic.)

However, to be more convincing, we thought it necessary to carry out some engineering design to provide the broad outlines of the systems, equipment, performance, and costs. As examples, we defined the number of production cells, how many robots and what type, number of tasks and cycle time per task, and even general principles by which the product should be designed.

We selected a stringent set of performance specifications to illustrate the potential of this technology:

• Capacity of 150,000 units/year. (Current plants are many times larger.)
• Efficient lot size of one.

EXHIBIT E.8

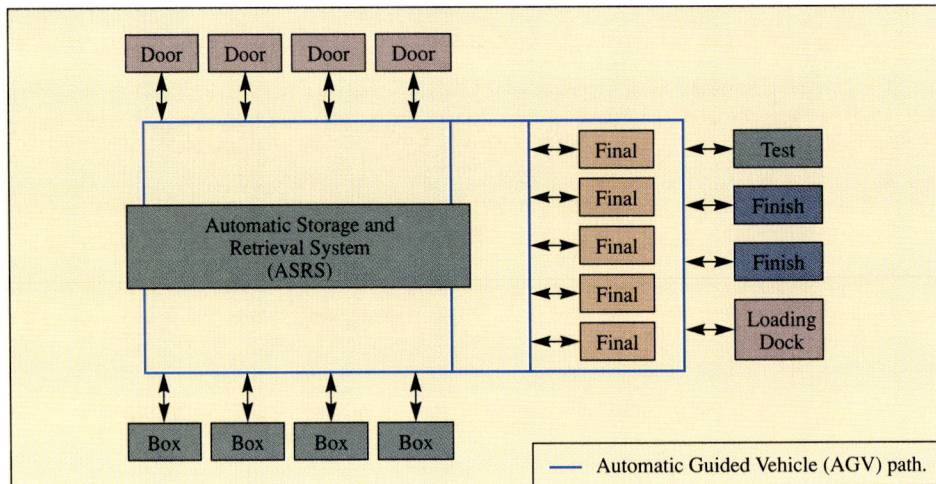

Automatic Guided Vehicle (AGV) path.

- Fully automated assembly, material handling, and control systems.
- Minimal incoming, WIP, and outgoing inventory.

Despite the exacting performance specifications and considerably smaller scale, our estimated unit cost (considering people and depreciation only) was comparable to the projected cost for a new high-volume plant.

Besides cost, the flexible automation approach offered other competitive advantages: low scale, high quality, small increments for capital expansion, short production cycle time, volume flexibility (change production by shutting a cell rather than a whole line), and faster new-product introduction. (Process engineering for new products is mainly software.)

Plant Architecture

Two of the most critical issues in plant architecture are how big should a plant be, and how to focus the plant. Fortunately, at the time of our assignment, our client was considering ways to expand production capacity for a major product line. We therefore were able to use this as a real-life case study on plant architecture decisions. While our client had been following our activities with extreme interest throughout the project, top management displayed even greater interest in this part of the assignment, primarily because we were analyzing issues surrounding a realtime strategic decision.

The first set of options was either to expand an existing plant or to build a new facility. Conventional economies of scale calculations would show expansion as being far cheaper and hence desirable, because the plant could leverage off the existing fixed burden, thus decreasing fixed burden per unit. However, our earlier analysis had shown that unit fixed burden for that specific plant was increasing with volume. Using the actual burden curve and 10-year project cash flow analysis, we were able to show that building a new facility had a net present value of +$24 million versus −$70 million for expansion.

Moreover, we were able to demonstrate that the NPV could be further improved by (1) focusing the existing and new facility on high- and low-volume products respectively and (2) using flexible assembly technology at the new facility to handle the low-volume products. We did this by estimating the impact of these two options on direct labor productivity, quality, and factory burden.

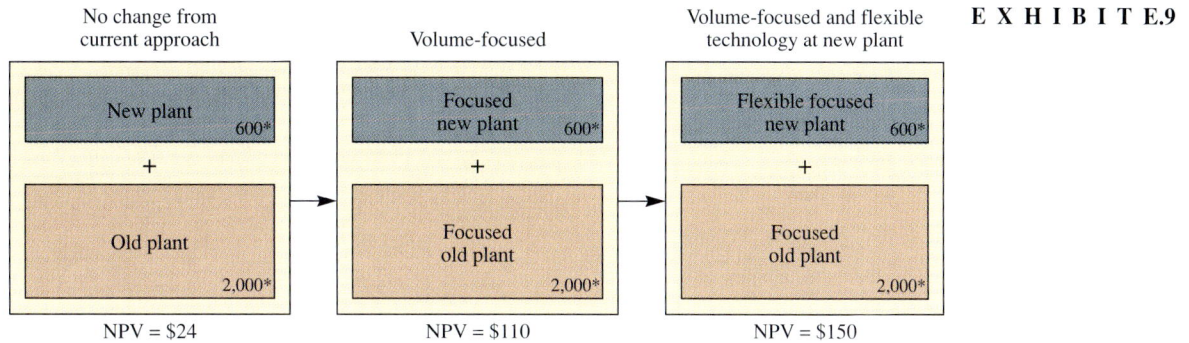

Over and above a favorable NPV analysis, we could also point out the strategic considerations favoring a new plant: more focus by market segment, better position for further expansion of new facility, less risk of losing total production capacity due to plant shutdown, and higher quality through more focus.

To develop the target plant architecture, we integrated our findings from manufacturing technology, plant size/focus, business and manufacturing economics, and customer distributions. Presenting the architecture visually created a much bigger impact than written description would have. Exhibit E.10 charts one of the options considered. In this option, all the facilities would be located close to all others to facilitate sharing of common components, effective communication, and quick transfer of expertise and technologies from plant to plant, and between the tech center and plants, and to help build a strong supplier base around the cluster.

E X H I B I T E.10

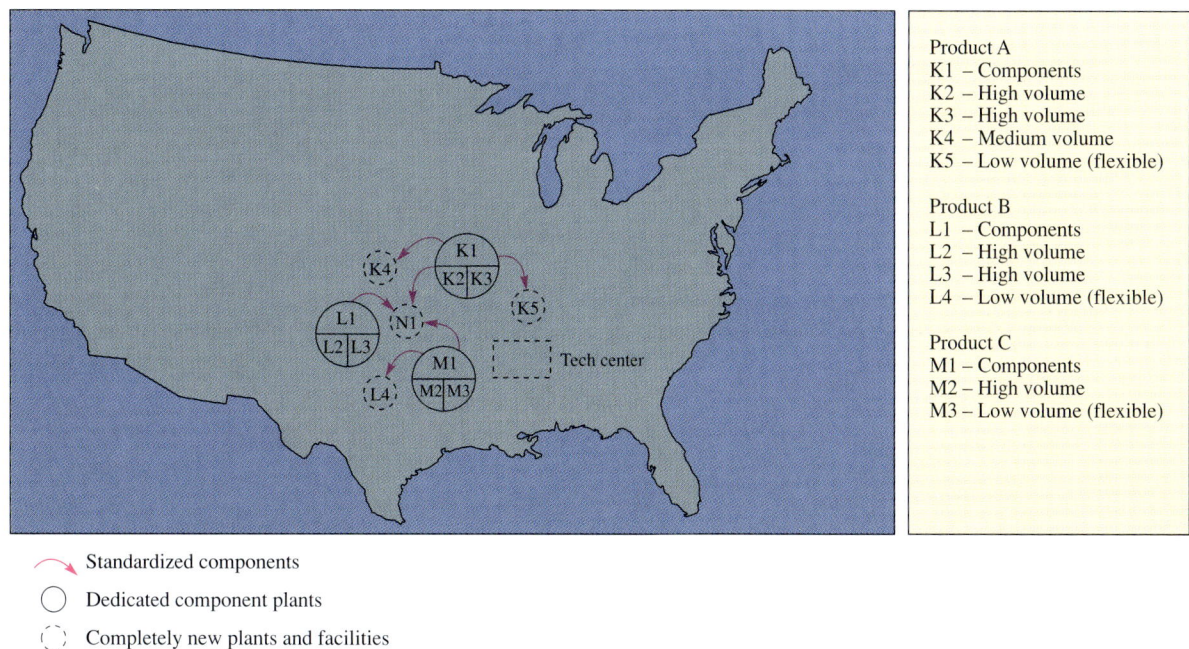

E X H I B I T E.11

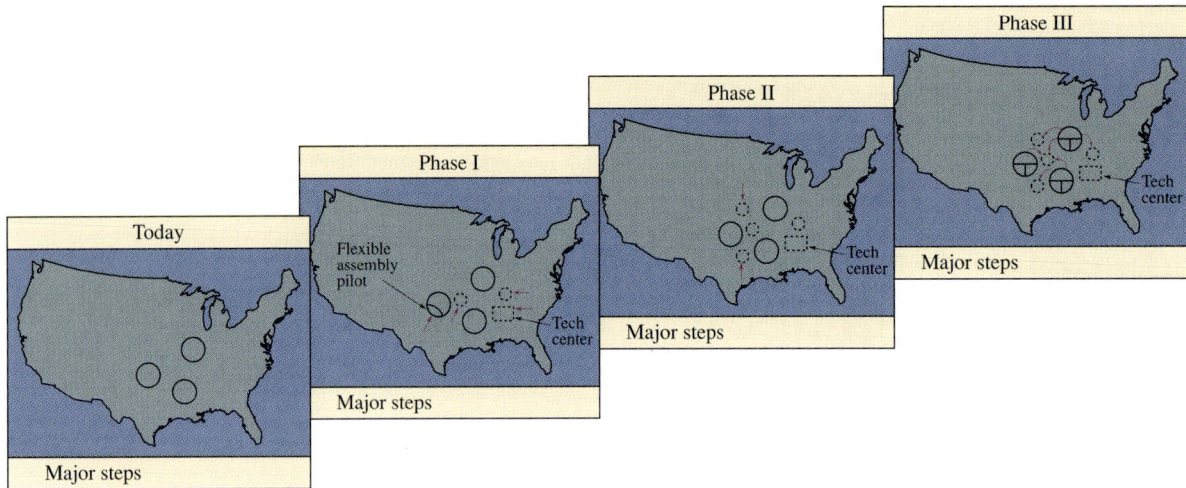

Exhibit E.11 shows how the transition plan for such an option would look. It also describes major actions by phases. We found that our phase-by-phase transition plan really helped the client get a good feel for the various plant architecture options. By following the action steps (e.g., in year *x*, close Plant A and move component manufacturing to Plant B and assembly to Plant C), the alternative concepts seemed to gain much quicker acceptance.

Concept-to-Production Organization and Process

We made extensive use of data and findings from ongoing research work by Harvard Professor Kim Clark to develop the recommendations on the concept-to-production process. Companies that succeed in new-product development generally use some or all of the following approaches:

- Overlapping (parallel) project phases with continuous dialogue between upstream and downstream phases.
- Early conflict identification and low-level conflict resolution.
- Integrated project team organization structure.
- Application of just-in-time principles to the product development process.

Our client seemed to be surprised that successful companies (mostly Japanese) have development lead time averaging 3½ years versus a little over 5 years for the less successful ones (mostly U.S. and European). Besides requiring a longer lead time, less successful companies use four times as much engineering effort per project.

In developing the concept-to-production organization, we focused on two primary dimensions:

- Functions involved in concept-to-production (primarily):
    Product planning.
    Product engineering.
    Process engineering.

		Time Frame		
		Short Term	Medium Term	Long Term

F u n c t i o n	Product Planning	• Customer feedback:
		  – End users.
		  – Dealers.
			• Specifications for new products.
			
			• Product positioning.
			
			• Marketing plans.
				• Market competitive trends.
				
				• Product concepts.
				
				• Product strategy.

	Product Engineering	• Product enhancements and extensions.
		
		• Design changes in response to:
		  – Process feedback.
		  – Customer feedback.
			• New product design:
			  – New generation.
			  – Major redesign.
				• Concept study.
				
				• Technology base (e.g., electronics, sensors, materials).

	Process Engineering	• Process changes in response to product enhancements and extensions. • Ongoing process improvements. • Operational problems.	• Design and installation of processes for new products. • Major redesign of existing processes.	• Concept study. • Technology base (e.g., robotics, inspection).

- Time frame of activities:
  Short term (0 to 2 years, operational/current product issues).
  Medium term (1 to 5 years, new products).
  Long term (more than four years, strategic/positioning issues).

We then defined the tasks/activities for each function-time frame. (See Exhibit E.12.)

Based on the findings on concept-to-production process and the tasks for each function-time frame cell discussed above, we then developed general guidelines for organizing the activities in each time frame. Lastly, we developed our recommendations for the concept-to-production organization. (See Exhibit E.13.)

While it appears that manufacturing performance is a short-term operational issue, it has been shown time and time again that long-term restructuring of manufacturing cannot be properly implemented unless processes are in control, a quality-driven organization is in place, and manufacturing tasks are rationalized. In addition, improving manufacturing performance can significantly improve short-term profitability and generate funds to implement the long-term restructuring.

Manufacturing Performance: Quality and Complexity

The stakes were very high. Using one division alone, we identified cost saving potential exceeding $100 million per year! Such savings would be realized by implementing five programs:

- Improve manufacturing process control.
- Rationalize supplier base and improve vendor performance.
- Review product lines to rationalize product models and weed out "unnecessary" SKUs.

	Short Term	Medium Term	Long Term
Overall	• Division based.	• Project team.	• Centralized by function.
Product Planning	Sales / Product A / Product B / • • •	• Project team: New-generation products	Marketing planning
Product Engineering	Product engineering / Product A / Product B / • • •	• Heavyweight project manager: Addition to existing product family.	Advanced product development / Product research
Process Engineering	Manufacturing engineering / Plant I / Plant II / • • •		Advanced process development / Process research

- Improve production scheduling and inventory management.
- Refine product designs to increase use of standard parts and ease of manufacturing.

E.5 CONCLUSION

We presented our final recommendations to our client in June. They were well received by the operations staff and by executive officers from all functions in the company. Our client is currently preparing plans for a phased implementation of our recommendations.

E.6 REVIEW AND DISCUSSION QUESTIONS

1. What is the "comparative industry approach"? What factors would you use to select a comparative industry?
2. What concepts and issues from the text are in fact addressed in the report?
3. What action plan would you suggest to the client company to implement the MAC Group's recommendations? Specifically, where would you start? How would you measure success?

Appendixes

■

OUTLINE

Financial Analysis in Production and Operations Management

In this appendix we review basic concepts and tools of financial analysis for OM. These include the types of cost (fixed, variable, sunk, opportunity, avoidable), risk and expected value, and depreciation (straight line, sum-of-the-years'-digits, declining balance, double-declining balance, and depreciation-by-use). We also discuss activity-based costing. Our focus is on capital investment decisions.

CONCEPTS AND DEFINITIONS

We will begin this appendix with some basic definitions.

Fixed Costs

A fixed cost is any expense that remains constant regardless of the level of output. Although no cost is truly fixed, many types of expense are virtually fixed over a wide range of output. Examples are rent, property taxes, most types of depreciation, insurance payments, and salaries of top management.

Variable Costs

Variable costs are expenses that fluctuate directly with changes in the level of output. For example, each additional unit of sheet steel produced by USX requires a specific amount of material and labor. The incremental cost of this additional material and labor can be isolated and assigned to each unit of sheet steel produced. Many overhead expenses are also variable since utility bills, maintenance expense, and so forth vary with the production level.

Exhibit A.1 illustrates the fixed and variable cost components of total cost. Note that total cost increases at the same rate as variable costs because fixed costs are constant.

Sunk Costs

Sunk costs are past expenses or investments that have no salvage value and therefore should not be taken into account in considering investment alternatives. Sunk costs could also be current costs that are essentially fixed, such as rent on a building. For example, suppose an ice cream manufacturing firm occupies a rented building and is considering making sherbet in the same building. If the company enters sherbet production, its cost

---

E X H I B I T A.1

Fixed and Variable Cost Components of Total Cost

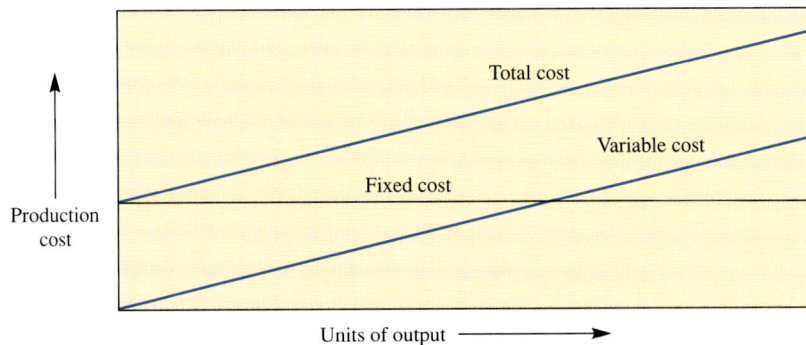

accountant will assign some of the rental expense to the sherbet operation. However, the building rent remains unchanged and therefore is not a relevant expense to be considered in making the decision. The rent is *sunk;* that is, it continues to exist and does not change in amount regardless of the decision.

Opportunity Costs

Opportunity cost is the benefit *forgone,* or advantage *lost,* that results from choosing one action over the *best-known alternative* course of action.

Suppose a firm has $100,000 to invest, and two alternatives of comparable risk present themselves, each requiring a $100,000 investment. Investment A will net $25,000; Investment B will net $23,000. Investment A is clearly the better choice, with a $25,000 net return. If the decision is made to invest in B instead of A, the opportunity cost of B then is $2,000, which is the benefit forgone.

Avoidable Costs

Avoidable costs include any expense that is *not* incurred if an investment is made but that *must* be incurred if the investment is *not* made. Suppose a company owns a metal lathe that is not in working condition but is needed for the firm's operations. Since the lathe must be repaired or replaced, the repair costs are avoidable if a new lathe is purchased. Avoidable costs reduce the cost of a new investment because they are not incurred if the investment is made. Avoidable costs are an example of how it is possible to "save" money by spending money.

Risk and Expected Value

Risk is inherent in any investment because the future can never be predicted with absolute certainty. To deal with this uncertainty, mathematical techniques such as expected value can help. Expected value is the expected outcome multiplied by the probability of its occurrence. Recall that in the preceding example the expected outcome of Alternative A was $25,000 and B, $23,000. Suppose the probability of A's actual outcome is 80 percent while B's probability is 90 percent. The expected values of the alternatives are determined as follows:

$$\begin{matrix} \text{Expected} \\ \text{outcome} \end{matrix} \times \begin{matrix} \text{Probability that actual} \\ \text{outcome will be the} \\ \text{expected outcome} \end{matrix} = \begin{matrix} \text{Expected} \\ \text{value} \end{matrix}$$

Investment A: $25,000 \times 0.80 = $20,000

Investment B: $23,000 \times 0.90 = $20,700

Investment B is now seen to be the better choice, with a net advantage over A of $700.

Economic Life and Obsolescence

When a firm invests in an income-producing asset, the productive life of the asset is estimated. For accounting purposes, the asset is depreciated over this period. It is assumed that the asset will perform its function during this time and then be considered obsolete or worn out, and replacement will be required. This view of asset life rarely coincides with reality.

Assume that a machine expected to have a productive life of 10 years is purchased. If at any time during the ensuing 10 years a new machine is developed that can perform the same task more efficiently or economically, the old machine has become obsolete. Whether or not it is "worn out" is irrelevant.

The *economic life* of a machine is the period over which it provides the best method for performing its task. When a superior method is developed, the machine has become obsolete. Thus the stated *book value* of a machine can be a meaningless figure.

Depreciation

Depreciation is a method for allocating costs of capital equipment. The value of any capital asset—buildings, machinery, and so forth—decreases as its useful life is expended. *Amortization* and *depreciation* are often used interchangeably. Through convention, however, *depreciation* refers to the allocation of cost due to the physical or functional deterioration of *tangible* (physical) assets, such as buildings or equipment, while *amortization* refers to the allocation of cost over the useful life of *intangible* assets, such as patents, leases, franchises, and goodwill.

Depreciation procedures may not reflect an asset's true value at any point in its life because obsolescence may at any time cause a large difference between true value and book value. Also, since depreciation rates significantly affect taxes, a firm may choose a particular method from the several alternatives with more consideration for its effect on taxes than its ability to make the book value of an asset reflect the true resale value.

Next we describe five commonly used methods of depreciation.

Straight-Line Method   Under this method, an asset's value is reduced in uniform annual amounts over its estimated useful life. The general formula is

$$\text{Annual amount to be depreciated} = \frac{\text{Cost} - \text{Salvage value}}{\text{Estimated useful life}}$$

A machine costing $10,000, with an estimated salvage value of $0 and an estimated life of 10 years, would be depreciated at the rate of $1,000 per year for each of the 10 years. If its estimated salvage value at the end of the 10 years is $1,000, the annual depreciation charge is

$$\frac{\$10,000 - \$1,000}{10} = \$900$$

Sum-of-the-Years'-Digits (SYD) Method   The purpose of the SYD method is to reduce the book value of an asset rapidly in early years and at a lower rate in the later years of its life.

Suppose that the estimated useful life is five years. The numbers add up to 15: $1 + 2 + 3 + 4 + 5 = 15$. Therefore, we depreciate the asset by $5 \div 15$ after the first year, $4 \div 15$ after the second year, and so on, down to $1 \div 15$ in the last year.

Declining-Balance Method   This method also achieves an accelerated depreciation. The asset's value is decreased by reducing its book value by a constant percentage each year. The percentage rate selected is often the one that just reduces book value to salvage value at the end of the asset's estimated life. In any case, the asset should never be reduced below estimated salvage value. Use of the declining-balance method and allowable rates are controlled by Internal Revenue Service regulations. As a simplified illustration, the preceding example is used in the next table with an arbitrarily selected rate of 40 percent. Note that depreciation is based on full cost, *not* cost minus salvage value.

Year	Depreciation Rate	Beginning Book Value	Depreciation Charge	Accumulated Depreciation	Ending Book Value
1	0.40	$17,000	$6,800	$ 6,800	$10,200
2	0.40	10,200	4,080	10,880	6,120
3	0.40	6,120	2,448	13,328	3,672
4	0.40	3,672	1,469	14,797	2,203
5		2,203	203	15,000	2,000

In the fifth year, reducing book value by 40 percent would have caused it to drop below salvage value. Consequently, the asset was depreciated by only $203, which decreased book value to salvage value.

Double-Declining-Balance Method   Again, for tax advantages, the double-declining-balance method offers higher depreciation early in the life span. This method uses a percentage twice the straight line for the life span of the item but applies this rate to the undepreciated original cost. The method is the same as the declining-balance method, but the term *double-declining balance* means double the straight-line rate. Thus equipment with a 10-year life span would have a straight-line depreciation rate of 10 percent per year and a double-declining-balance rate (applied to the undepreciated amount) of 20 percent per year.

Depreciation-by-Use Method   The purpose of this method is to depreciate a capital investment in proportion to its use. It is applicable, for example, to a machine that performs the same operation many times. The life of the machine is not estimated in years but rather in the total number of operations it may reasonably be expected to perform before wearing out. Suppose that a metal-stamping press has an estimated life of 1 million stamps and costs $100,000. The charge for depreciation per stamp is then $100,000 ÷ 1,000,000 or $0.10. Assuming a $0 salvage value, the depreciation charges are as shown in the accompanying table.

Year	Total Yearly Stamps	Cost per Stamp	Yearly Depreciation Charge	Accumulated Depreciation	Ending Book Value
1	150,000	0.10	$15,000	$ 15,000	$85,000
2	300,000	0.10	30,000	45,000	55,000
3	200,000	0.10	20,000	65,000	35,000
4	200,000	0.10	20,000	85,000	15,000
5	100,000	0.10	10,000	95,000	5,000
6	50,000	0.10	5,000	100,000	0

The depreciation-by-use method is an attempt to gear depreciation charges to actual use and thereby coordinate expense charges with productive output more accurately. Also, since a machine's resale value is related to its remaining productive life, it is hoped that book value will approximate resale value. The danger, of course, is that technological improvements will render the machine obsolete, in which case book value will not reflect true value.

ACTIVITY-BASED COSTING

To know how much it costs to make a certain product or deliver a service, some method of allocating overhead costs to production activities must be applied. The traditional approach is to allocate overhead costs to products on the basis of direct labor dollars or hours. By dividing the total estimated overhead costs by total budgeted direct labor hours, an overhead rate can be established. The problem with this approach is that direct labor as a percentage of total costs has fallen dramatically over the past decade. For example, introduction of advanced manufacturing technology and other productivity improvements has driven direct labor to as low as 7 to 10 percent of total manufacturing costs in many

E X H I B I T A.2

Traditional and Activity-Based Costing

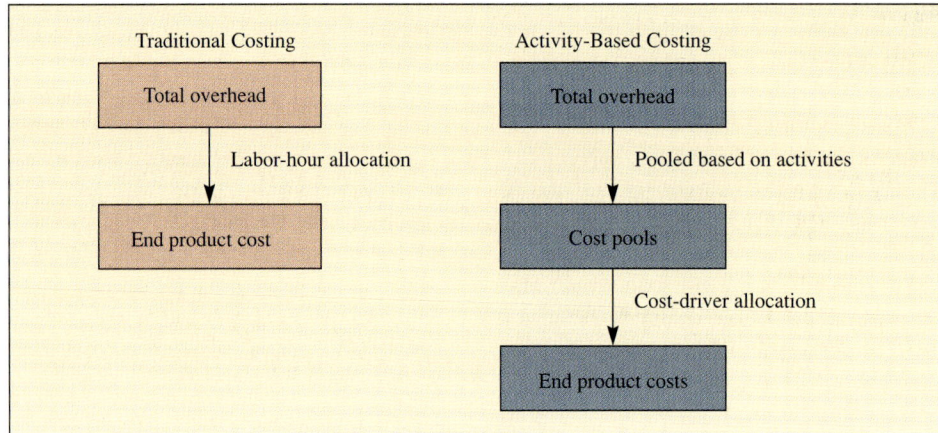

industries. As a result, overhead rates of 600 percent or even 1,000 percent are found in some highly automated plants.[1]

This traditional accounting practice of allocating overhead to direct labor can lead to questionable investment decisions; for example, automated processes may be chosen over labor-intensive processes based on a comparison of projected costs. Unfortunately, overhead does not disappear when the equipment is installed and overall costs may actually be lower with the labor-intensive process. It can also lead to wasted effort since an inordinate amount of time is spent tracking direct labor hours. For example, one plant spent 65 percent of computer costs tracking information about direct labor transactions even though direct labor accounted for only 4 percent of total production costs.[2]

Activity-based costing techniques have been developed to alleviate these problems by refining the overhead allocation process to more directly reflect actual proportions of overhead consumed by the production activity. Causal factors, known as cost drivers, are identified and used as the means for allocating overhead. These factors might include machine hours, beds occupied, computer time, flight hours, or miles driven. The accuracy of overhead allocation, of course, depends on the selection of appropriate cost drivers.

Activity-based costing involves a two-stage allocation process with the first stage assigning overhead costs to cost activity pools. These pools represent activities such as performing machine setups, issuing purchase orders, and inspecting parts. In the second stage, costs are assigned from these pools to activities based on the number or amount of pool-related activity required in their completion. Exhibit A.2 shows a comparison of traditional cost accounting and activity-based costing.

Consider the example of activity-based costing in Exhibit A.3. Two products, A and B, are produced using the same number of labor hours. Applying traditional costing, identical overhead costs would be charged to each product. By applying activity-based costing, traceable costs are assigned to specific activities. Because each product required a different amount of transactions, different overhead amounts are allocated to these products from the pools.

---

[1]Matthew J. Libertore, *Selection and Evaluation of Advanced Manufacturing Technologies* (New York: Springer-Verlag, 1990), pp. 231–56.

[2]Thomas Johnson and Robert Kaplan, *Relevance Lost: The Rise and Fall of Management Accounting* (Boston: Harvard Business School Press, 1987), p. 188.

Basic Data

Activity	Traceable Costs	Events of Transactions		
		Total	**Product A**	**Product B**
Machine setups	$230,000	5,000	3,000	2,000
Quality inspections	160,000	8,000	5,000	3,000
Production orders	81,000	600	200	400
Machine-hours worked	314,000	40,000	12,000	28,000
Material receipts	90,000	750	150	600
	$875,000			

Overhead Rates by Activity

Activity	*(a)* Traceable Costs	*(b)* Total Events or Transactions	*(a) ÷ (b)* Rate per Event or Transaction
Machine setups	$230,000	5,000	$46/setup
Quality inspections	160,000	8,000	$20/inspection
Production orders	81,000	600	$135/order
Machine-hours worked	314,000	40,000	$7.85/hour
Material receipts	90,000	750	$120/receipt

Overhead Cost per Unit of Product

	Product A		Product B	
	Events or Transactions	**Amount**	**Events or Transactions**	**Amount**
Machine setups, at $46/setup	3,000	$138,000	2,000	$ 92,000
Quality inspections, at $20/inspection	5,000	100,000	3,000	60,000
Production orders, at $135/order	200	27,000	400	54,000
Machine-hours worked, at $7.85/hour	12,000	94,200	28,000	219,800
Material receipts, at $120/receipt	150	18,000	600	72,000
Total overhead cost assigned *(a)*		$377,200		$497,800
Number of units produced *(b)*		5,000		20,000
Overhead cost per unit, *(a) ÷ (b)*		$75.44		$24.89

Source: Ray Garrison, *Managerial Accounting*, 6th ed. (Homewood, IL: Richard D. Irwin, 1991), p. 94.

As stated earlier, activity-based costing overcomes the problem of cost distortion by creating a cost pool for each activity or transaction that can be identified as a cost driver, and by assigning overhead cost to products or jobs on a basis of the number of separate activities required for their completion. Thus, in the previous situation, the low-volume product would be assigned the bulk of the costs for machine setup, purchase orders, and quality inspections, thereby showing it to have high unit costs compared to the other product.

Finally, activity-based costing is sometimes referred to as *transactions costing*. This transactions focus gives rise to another major advantage over other costing methods; that is, that it improves the traceability of overhead costs and thus results in more accurate *unit* cost data for management.

THE EFFECTS OF TAXES

Tax rates and the methods of applying them occasionally change. When analysts evaluate investment proposals, tax considerations often prove to be the deciding factor since depreciation expenses directly affect taxable income and therefore profit. The ability to write off depreciation in early years provides an added source of funds for investment. Before 1986, firms could employ an *investment tax credit,* which allowed a direct reduction in tax liability. But tax laws change so it is crucial to stay on top of current tax laws and try to predict future changes that may affect current investments and accounting procedures.

For example, a one-time investment of $1,000 at 14 percent allowed to compound for 65 years could be worth $5 million. However, that 14 percent is a *nominal rate,* and nominal rates do not reflect buying power; real rates do. Real rates—that which remains after adjusting for inflation—are historically about 3 to 5 percent. If the rate of return remains 14 percent for 65 years, future inflation will erode 90 percent of the $5 million buying power!

The general formula for compound value is

$$V_n = P_1(1 + i)^n$$

where

V = Value at the end of a specific year

n = Length of the compounding period

P_1 = Principal, or value at the beginning of a specific year

i = Interest rate

and the subscript represents the length of the compounding period.

For example, the compound value of $10 earning 10 percent interest after three years is $13.31. It is derived as follows:

$$\begin{aligned} V_3 &= P_1(1 + i)^3 \\ &= \$10(1 + 0.10)^3 \\ &= \$10(1.331) = \$13.31 \end{aligned}$$

CHOOSING AMONG SPECIFIC INVESTMENT PROPOSALS

The capital investment decision has become highly rationalized, as evidenced by the variety of techniques available for its solution. In contrast to pricing or marketing decisions, the capital investment decision can usually be made with a higher degree of confidence because the variables affecting the decision are relatively well known and can be quantified with fair accuracy.

Investment decisions may be grouped into six general categories:

1. Purchase of new equipment or facilities.
2. Replacement of existing equipment or facilities.
3. Make-or-buy decisions.
4. Lease-or-buy decisions.
5. Temporary shutdowns or plant-abandonment decisions.
6. Addition or elimination of a product or product line.

Investment decisions are made with regard to the *lowest acceptable rate of return* on investment. As a starting point, the lowest acceptable rate of return may be considered to be the cost of investment capital needed to underwrite the expenditure. Certainly an investment will not be made if it does not return at least the cost of capital.

Investments are generally ranked according to the return they yield in excess of their cost of capital. In this way a business with only limited investment funds can select investment alternatives that yield the highest *net* returns. (*Net return* is the earnings an investment yields after gross earnings have been reduced by the cost of the funds used to finance the investment.) In general, investments should not be made unless the return in funds exceeds the *marginal* cost of investment capital. (*Marginal cost* is the incremental cost of each new acquisition of funds from outside sources.)

INTEREST RATE EFFECTS

There are two basic ways to account for the effects of interest accumulation. One is to compute the total amount created over the time period into the future as the *compound value*. The other is to remove the interest rate effect over time by reducing all future sums to present-day dollars, or the *present value*.

Compound Value of a Single Amount

Albert Einstein was quoted as saying that compound interest is the eighth wonder of the world. After reviewing this section showing compound interest's dramatic growth effects over a long time, you might wish to propose a new government regulation: On the birth of a child, the parents must put, say, $1,000 into a retirement fund for that child at age 65. This might reduce the pressure on Social Security and other state and federal pension plans. While inflation would decrease the value significantly (as we showed in the previous section), there would still be a lot left over. At 14 percent interest, our $1,000 would increase to $500,000 after subtracting the $4.5 million for inflation. That is still a 500-fold increase. (Many mutual funds today have long-term performances in excess of 14 percent per year.)

Most calculators make such computation easy. However, many people still refer to tables for compound values. Using Appendix G, Table G.1 (compound sum of $1), for example, we see that the value of $1 at 10 percent interest after three years is $1.331. Multiplying this figure by $10 gives $13.31, as computed previously.

Compound Value of an Annuity

An *annuity* is the receipt of a constant sum each year for a specified number of years. Usually an annuity is received at the end of a period and does not earn interest during that period. Therefore, an annuity of $10 for three years would bring in $10 at the end of the first year (allowing the $10 to earn interest if invested for the remaining two years), $10 at the end of the second year (allowing the $10 to earn interest for the remaining one year), and $10 at the end of the third year (with no time to earn interest). If the annuity receipts were placed in a bank savings account at 5 percent interest, the total or compound value of the $10 at 5 percent for the three years would be

Year	Receipt at End of Year	Compound Interest Factor $(1 + i)^n$	Value at End of Third Year
1	$10.00 ×	$(1 + 0.05)^2 =$	$11.02
2	10.00 ×	$(1 + 0.05)^1 =$	10.50
3	10.00 ×	$(1 + 0.05)^0 =$	10.00
			$31.52

The general formula for finding the compound value of an annuity is

$$S_n = R[(1 + i)^{n-1} + (1 + i)^{n-2} + \ldots + (1 + i)^1 + 1]$$

where

S_n = Compound value of an annuity

R = Periodic receipts in dollars

n = Length of the annuity in years

Applying this formula to the preceding example, we get

$$S_n = R[(1 + i)^2 + (1 + i) + 1]$$
$$= \$10[(1 + 0.05)^2 + (1 + 0.05) + 1] = \$31.52$$

In Appendix G, Table G.2 lists the compound value factor of $1 for 5 percent after three years as 3.152. Multiplying this factor by $10 yields $31.52.

In a fashion similar to our previous retirement investment example, consider the beneficial effects of investing $2,000 each year, just starting at the age of 21. Assume investments in AAA-rated bonds are available today yielding 9 percent. From Table G.2 in Appendix G, after 30 years (at age 51) the investment is worth 136.3 times $2,000 or $272,600. Fourteen years later (at age 65) this would be worth $963,044 (using a hand calculator, since the table only goes up to 30 years, and assuming the $2,000 is a deposited at the end of each year)! But what 21-year-old thinks about retirement?

Present Value of a Future Single Payment

Compound values are used to determine future value after a specific period has elapsed; present value (PV) procedures accomplish just the reverse. They are used to determine the current value of a sum or stream of receipts expected to be received in the future. Most investment decision techniques use present value concepts rather than compound values. Since decisions affecting the future are made in the present, it is better to convert future returns into their present value at the time the decision is being made. In this way, investment alternatives are placed in better perspective in terms of current dollars.

An example makes this more apparent. If a rich uncle offers to make you a gift of $100 today or $250 after 10 years, which should you choose? You must determine whether the $250 in 10 years will be worth more than the $100 now. Suppose that you base your decision on the rate of inflation in the economy and believe that inflation averages 10 percent per year. By deflating the $250, you can compare its relative purchasing power with $100 received today. Procedurally, this is accomplished by solving the compound formula for the present sum, P, where V is the future amount of $250 in 10 years at 10 percent. The compound value formula is

$$V = P(1 + i)^n$$

Dividing both sides by $(1 + i)^n$ gives

$$P = \frac{V}{(1 + I)^n}$$

$$= \frac{250}{(1 + 0.10)^{10}} = \$96.39$$

This shows that, at a 10 percent inflation rate, $250 in 10 years will be worth $96.39 today. The rational choice, then, is to take the $100 now.

The use of tables is also standard practice in solving present value problems. With reference to Appendix G, Table G.3, the present value factor for $1 received 10 years hence is 0.386. Multiplying this factor by $250 yields $96.50.

The present value of an annuity is the value of an annual amount to be received over a future period expressed in terms of the present. To find the value of an annuity of $100 for three years at 10 percent, find the factor in the present value table that applies to 10 percent in *each* of the three years in which the amount is received and multiply each receipt by this factor. Then sum the resulting figures. Remember that annuities are usually received at the end of each period.

Present Value of an Annuity

Year	Amount Received at End of Year	Present Value Factor at 10%	Present Value
1	$100 ×	0.909 =	$ 90.90
2	100 ×	0.826 =	82.60
3	100 ×	0.751 =	75.10
Total receipts	$300	Total present value =	$248.60

The general formula used to derive the present value of an annuity is

$$A_n = R\left[\frac{1}{(1+i)} + \frac{1}{(1+i)^2} + \ldots + \frac{1}{(1+i)^n}\right]$$

where

A_n = Present value of an annuity of n years

R = Periodic receipts

n = Length of the annuity in years

Applying the formula to the preceding example gives

$$A_n = \$100\left[\frac{1}{(1+0.10)} + \frac{1}{(1+0.10)^2} + \frac{1}{(1+0.10)^3}\right]$$
$$= \$100\,(2.487) = \$248.70$$

In Appendix G, Table G.4 contains present values of an annuity for varying maturities. The present value factor for an annuity of $1 for three years at 10 percent (from Appendix G, Table G.4) is 2.487. Since our sum is $100 rather than $1, we multiply this factor by $100 to arrive at $248.70.

When the stream of future receipts is uneven, the present value of each annual receipt must be calculated. The present values of the receipts for all years are then summed to arrive at total present value. This process can sometimes be tedious, but it is unavoidable.

The term *discounted cash flow (DCF)* refers to total stream of payments that an asset will generate in the future discounted to the present time. This is simply present value analysis that includes all flows: single payments, annuities, and all others.

Discounted Cash Flow (DCF)

METHODS OF RANKING INVESTMENTS

The net present value method is commonly used in business. With this method, decisions are based on the amount by which the present value of a projected income stream exceeds the cost of an investment.

Net Present Value

A firm is considering two alternative investments. The first costs $30,000 and the second, $50,000. The expected yearly cash income streams are shown in the next table.

	Cash Inflow	
Year	Alternative A	Alternative B
1	$10,000	$15,000
2	10,000	15,000
3	10,000	15,000
4	10,000	15,000
5	10,000	15,000

To choose between Alternatives A and B, find which has the highest net present value. Assume an 8 percent cost of capital.

Alternative A

3.993 (PV factor) × $10,000 = $39,930
Less cost of investment   = 30,000
Net present value   = $ 9,930

Alternative B

3.993 (PV factor) × $15,000 = $59,895
Less cost of investment   = 50,000
Net present value   = $ 9,895

Investment A is the better alternative. Its net present value exceeds Investment B's by $35 ($9,930 − $9,895 = $35).

Payback Period

The payback method ranks investments according to the time required for each investment to return earnings equal to the cost of the investment. The rationale is that the sooner the investment capital can be recovered, the sooner it can be reinvested in new revenue-producing projects. Thus, supposedly, a firm will be able to get the most benefit from its available investment funds.

Consider two alternatives requiring a $1,000 investment each. The first will earn $200 per year for six years; the second will earn $300 per year for the first three years and $100 per year for the next three years.

If the first alternative is selected, the initial investment of $1,000 will be recovered at the end of the fifth year. The income produced by the second alternative will total $1,000 after only four years. The second alternative will permit reinvestment of the full $1,000 in new revenue-producing projects one year sooner than the first.

Though the payback method is declining in popularity as the sole measure in investment decisions, it is still frequently used in conjunction with other methods to indicate the time commitment of funds. The major problems with payback are that it does not consider income beyond the payback period and it ignores the time value of money. A method that ignores the time value of money must be considered questionable.

Internal Rate of Return

The internal rate of return may be defined as the interest rate that equates the present value of an income stream with the cost of an investment. There is no procedure or formula that may be used directly to compute the internal rate of return—it must be found by interpolation or iterative calculation.

Suppose we wish to find the internal rate of return for an investment costing $12,000 that will yield a cash inflow of $4,000 per year for four years. We see that the present value factor sought is

$$\frac{\$12,000}{\$4,000} = 3.000$$

and we seek the interest rate that will provide this factor over a four-year period. The interest rate must lie between 12 and 14 percent because 3.000 lies between 3.037 and 2.914 (in the fourth row of Appendix G, Table G.4). Linear interpolation between these values, according to the equation

$$I = 12 + (14 - 12)\frac{(3.037 - 3.000)}{(3.037 - 2.914)}$$
$$= 12 + 0.602 = 12.602\%$$

gives a good approximation to the actual internal rate of return.

When the income stream is discounted at 12.6 percent, the resulting present value closely approximates the cost of investment. Thus the internal rate of return for this investment is 12.6 percent. The cost of capital can be compared with the internal rate of return to determine the net rate of return on the investment. If, in this example, the cost of capital were 8 percent, the net rate of return on the investment would be 4.6 percent.

The net present value and internal rate of return methods involve procedures that are essentially the same. They differ in that the net present value method enables investment alternatives to be compared in terms of the dollar value in excess of cost, whereas the internal rate of return method permits comparison of rates of return on alternative investments. Moreover, the internal rate of return method occasionally encounters problems in calculation, as multiple rates frequently appear in the computation.

Ranking Investments with Uneven Lives

When proposed investments have the same life expectancy, comparison among them, using the preceding methods, will give a reasonable picture of their relative value. When lives are unequal, however, there is the question of how to relate the two different time periods. Should replacements be considered the same as the original? Should productivity for the shorter-term unit that will be replaced earlier be considered to have higher productivity? How should the cost of future units be estimated?

No estimate dealing with investments unforeseen at the time of decision can be expected to reflect a high degree of accuracy. Still, the problem must be dealt with, and some assumptions must be made in order to determine a ranking.

SAMPLE PROBLEMS: INVESTMENT DECISIONS

E X A M P L E   A.1 / *An Expansion Decision*   William J. Wilson Ceramic Products, Inc., leases plant facilities in which firebrick is manufactured. Because of rising demand, Wilson could increase sales by investing in new equipment to expand output. The selling price of $10 per brick will remain unchanged if output and sales increase. Based on engineering and cost estimates, the accounting department provides management with the following cost estimates based on an annual increased output of 100,000 bricks.

Cost of new equipment having an expected life of five years	$500,000
Equipment installation cost	20,000
Expected salvage value	0
New operation's share of annual lease expense	40,000
Annual increase in utility expenses	40,000
Annual increase in labor costs	160,000
Annual additional cost for raw materials	400,000

The sum-of-the-years'-digits method of depreciation will be used, and taxes are paid at a rate of 40 percent. Wilson's policy is not to invest capital in projects earning less than a 20 percent rate of return. Should the proposed expansion be undertaken?

SOLUTION   Compute cost of investment:

Acquisition cost of equipment	$500,000
Equipment installation costs	20,000
Total cost of investment	$520,000

Determine yearly cash flows throughout the life of the investment.

The lease expense is a sunk cost. It will be incurred whether or not the investment is made and is therefore irrelevant to the decision and should be disregarded. Annual production expenses to be considered are utility, labor, and raw materials. These total $600,000 per year.

Annual sales revenue is $10 \times 100,000$ units of output, which totals $1,000,000. Yearly income before depreciation and taxes is thus $1,000,000 gross revenue, less $600,000 expenses, or $400,000.

Next, determine the depreciation charges to be deducted from the $400,000 income each year using the SYD method (sum-of-years' digits $= 1 + 2 + 3 + 4 + 5 = 15$):

Year	Proportion of $500,000 to Be Depreciated	Depreciation Charge
1	5/15 $\times$ $500,000	= $166,667
2	4/15 $\times$ 500,000	= 133,333
3	3/15 $\times$ 500,000	= 100,000
4	2/15 $\times$ 500,000	= 66,667
5	1/15 $\times$ 500,000	= 33,333
	Accumulated depreciation	$500,000

Find each year's cash flow when taxes are 40 percent. Cash flow for only the first year is illustrated:

Earnings before depreciation and taxes		$400,000
Deduct: Taxes at 40%	$160,000	
Add: Tax benefit of depreciation expense (0.4 $\times$ 166,667)	66,667	93,333
Cash flow (1st year)		$306,667

Determine present value of the cash flow. Since Wilson demands at least a 20 percent rate of return on investments, multiply the cash flows by the 20 percent present value factor for each year. The factor for each respective year must be used because the cash flows are not an annuity.

S O L U T I O N   Find total cost incurred if the part were manufactured:

Additional fixed costs	$ 50,000
Additional labor costs	125,000
Raw materials cost	600,000
Additional overhead costs = 0.12 × $500,000	60,000
Total cost to manufacturer	$835,000

Find the cost per unit to manufacture:

$$\frac{\$835,000}{100,000} = \$8.35 \text{ per unit}$$

Triple X should continue to buy the part. Manufacturing costs exceed the present cost to purchase by $0.10 per unit.   ■

SELECTED BIBLIOGRAPHY

Brigham, Eugene F. *Fundamentals of Financial Management.* New York: Dryden Press, 1986.

Gitman, Lawrence J. *Principles of Managerial Finance.* 4th ed. New York: Harper & Row, 1985.

Gup, Benton E. *Principles of Financial Management,* 2d ed. New York: John Wiley & Sons, 1987.

Hodder, James E., and Henry E. Riggs. "Pitfalls in Evaluating Risky Projects." *Harvard Business Review,* January–February 1985, pp. 128–35.

Pringle, John J., and Robert S. Harris. *Essentials of Managerial Finance.* Glenview, IL: Scott, Foresman, 1984.

Soloman, Eyra, and John J. Pringle. *An Introduction to Financial Management.* Santa Monica, CA: Goodyear, 1980.

Van Horne, James C. *Financial Management and Policy.* 7th ed. Englewood Cliffs, NJ: Prentice Hall, 1986.

———. *Fundamentals of Financial Management.* 6th ed. Englewood Cliffs, NJ: Prentice Hall, 1986.

Welsch, Glenn A., and Robert N. Anthony. *Fundamentals of Financial Accounting.* Homewood, IL: Richard D. Irwin, 1984.

Appendix B

Uniformly Distributed Random Digits

56970	10799	52098	04184	54967	72938	50834	23777	08392
83125	85077	60490	44369	66130	72936	69848	59973	08144
55503	21383	02464	26141	68779	66388	75242	82690	74099
47019	06683	33203	29603	54553	25971	69573	83854	24715
84828	61152	79526	29554	84580	37859	28504	61980	34997
08021	31331	79227	05748	51276	57143	31926	00915	45821
36458	28285	30424	98420	72925	40729	22337	48293	86847
05752	96045	36847	87729	81679	59126	59437	33225	31280
26768	02513	58454	56958	20575	76746	40878	06846	32828
42613	72456	43030	58085	06766	60227	96414	32671	45587
95457	12176	65482	25596	02678	54592	63607	82096	21913
95276	67524	63564	95958	39750	64379	46059	51666	10433
66954	53574	64776	92345	95110	59448	77249	54044	67942
17457	44151	14113	02462	02798	54977	48340	66738	60184
03704	23322	83214	59337	01695	60666	97410	55064	17427
21538	16997	33210	60337	27976	70661	08250	69509	60264
57178	16730	08310	70348	11317	71623	55510	64750	87759
31048	40058	94953	55866	96283	40620	52087	80817	74533
69799	83300	16498	80733	96422	58078	99643	39847	96884
90595	65017	59231	17772	67831	33317	00520	90401	41700
33570	34761	08039	78784	09977	29398	93896	78227	90110
15340	82760	57477	13898	48431	72936	78160	87240	52710
64079	07733	36512	56186	99098	48850	72527	08486	10951
63491	84886	67118	62063	74958	20946	28147	39338	32109
92003	76568	41034	28260	79708	00770	88643	21188	01850

Normally Distributed Random Digits

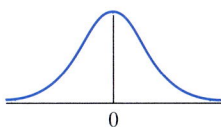

An entry in the table is the value z from a normal distribution with a mean of 0 and a standard deviation of 1.

1.98677	1.23481	−.28360	.99217	−.87919	−.21600
−.59341	1.54221	−.65806	1.08372	1.68560	1.14899
.11340	.19126	−.65084	.12188	.02338	−.61545
.89783	−.54929	−.03663	−1.89506	.15158	−.20061
−.50790	1.14463	1.30917	1.26528	.09459	.16423
−1.63968	−.63248	.21482	−1.16241	−.60015	−.55233
1.14081	−.29988	−.48053	−1.21397	−.34391	−1.84881
−.43354	−.32855	.67115	.52289	−1.42796	−.14181
.05707	.35331	.20470	.01847	1.71086	−1.44738
.77153	.72576	−.29833	.26139	1.25845	−.35468
−1.38286	.04406	−.75499	.61068	.61903	−.96845
1.60166	−1.66161	.70886	−.20302	−.28373	2.07219
−.48781	.02629	−.34306	2.00746	−1.12059	.07943
−1.10632	1.18250	−.60065	.09737	.63297	1.00659
.77000	−.87214	−.63584	−.39546	−.72776	.45594
−.56882	−.23153	−2.03852	−.28101	.30384	−.14246
.27721	−.04776	.11740	−.17211	1.63483	1.34221
−.40251	−.31052	−1.04834	−.23243	−1.52224	.85903
1.27086	−.93166	−.03766	1.21016	.13451	.81941
1.14464	.56176	.89824	1.54670	1.48411	.14422
.04172	1.49672	−.15490	.77084	−.29064	2.87643
−.36795	1.22318	−1.05084	−1.05409	.82052	.09670
1.94110	1.00826	−.85411	−1.31341	−1.85921	.74578
.14946	−2.75470	−.10830	1.02845	.69291	−.78579

Appendix D

Areas of the Standard Normal Distribution

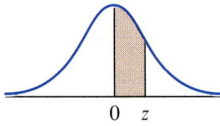

An entry in the table is the proportion under the entire curve which is between $z = 0$ and a positive value of z. Areas for negative values of z are obtained by symmetry.

z	.00	.01	.02	.03	.04	.05	.06	.07	.08	.09
0.0	.0000	.0040	.0080	.0120	.0160	.0199	.0239	.0279	.0319	.0359
0.1	.0398	.0438	.0478	.0517	.0557	.0596	.0636	.0675	.0714	.0753
0.2	.0793	.0832	.0871	.0910	.0948	.0987	.1026	.1064	.1103	.1141
0.3	.1179	.1217	.1255	.1293	.1331	.1368	.1406	.1443	.1480	.1517
0.4	.1554	.1591	.1628	.1664	.1700	.1736	.1772	.1808	.1844	.1879
0.5	.1915	.1950	.1985	.2019	.2054	.2088	.2123	.2157	.2190	.2224
0.6	.2257	.2291	.2324	.2357	.2389	.2422	.2454	.2486	.2517	.2549
0.7	.2580	.2611	.2642	.2673	.2703	.2734	.2764	.2794	.2823	.2852
0.8	.2881	.2910	.2939	.2967	.2995	.3023	.3051	.3078	.3106	.3133
0.9	.3159	.3186	.3212	.3238	.3264	.3289	.3315	.3340	.3365	.3389
1.0	.3413	.3438	.3461	.3485	.3508	.3531	.3554	.3577	.3599	.3621
1.1	.3643	.3665	.3686	.3708	.3729	.3749	.3770	.3790	.3810	.3830
1.2	.3849	.3869	.3888	.3907	.3925	.3944	.3962	.3980	.3997	.4015
1.3	.4032	.4049	.4066	.4082	.4099	.4115	.4131	.4147	.4162	.4177
1.4	.4192	.4207	.4222	.4236	.4251	.4265	.4279	.4292	.4306	.4319
1.5	.4332	.4345	.4357	.4370	.4382	.4394	.4406	.4418	.4429	.4441
1.6	.4452	.4463	.4474	.4484	.4495	.4505	.4515	.4525	.4535	.4545
1.7	.4554	.4564	.4573	.4582	.4591	.4599	.4608	.4616	.4625	.4633
1.8	.4641	.4649	.4656	.4664	.4671	.4678	.4686	.4693	.4699	.4706
1.9	.4713	.4719	.4726	.4732	.4738	.4744	.4750	.4756	.4761	.4767
2.0	.4772	.4778	.4783	.4788	.4793	.4798	.4803	.4808	.4812	.4817
2.1	.4821	.4826	.4830	.4834	.4838	.4842	.4846	.4850	.4854	.4857
2.2	.4861	.4864	.4868	.4871	.4875	.4878	.4881	.4884	.4887	.4890
2.3	.4893	.4896	.4898	.4901	.4904	.4906	.4909	.4911	.4913	.4916
2.4	.4918	.4920	.4922	.4925	.4927	.4929	.4931	.4932	.4934	.4936
2.5	.4938	.4940	.4941	.4943	.4945	.4946	.4948	.4949	.4951	.4952
2.6	.4953	.4955	.4956	.4957	.4959	.4960	.4961	.4962	.4963	.4964
2.7	.4965	.4966	.4967	.4968	.4969	.4970	.4971	.4972	.4973	.4974
2.8	.4974	.4975	.4976	.4977	.4977	.4978	.4979	.4979	.4980	.4981
2.9	.4981	.4982	.4982	.4983	.4984	.4984	.4985	.4985	.4986	.4986
3.0	.4987	.4987	.4987	.4988	.4988	.4989	.4989	.4989	.4990	.4990

Source: Paul G. Hoel, *Elementary Stastistics* (New York: John Wiley & Sons, 1960), p. 240.

Appendix E

Areas of the Cumulative Standard Normal Distribution

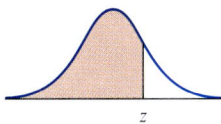

An entry in the table is the proportion under the curve cumulated from the negative tail.

z	$G(z)$	z	$G(z)$	z	$G(z)$
−4.00	0.00003	−1.30	0.09680	1.40	0.91924
−3.95	0.00004	−1.25	0.10565	1.45	0.92647
−3.90	0.00005	−1.20	0.11507	1.50	0.93319
−3.85	0.00006	−1.15	0.12507	1.55	0.93943
−3.80	0.00007	−1.10	0.13567	1.60	0.94520
−3.75	0.00009	−1.05	0.14686	1.65	0.95053
−3.70	0.00011	−1.00	0.15866	1.70	0.95543
−3.65	0.00013	−0.95	0.17106	1.75	0.95994
−3.60	0.00016	−0.90	0.18406	1.80	0.96407
−3.55	0.00019	−0.85	0.19766	1.85	0.96784
−3.50	0.00023	−0.80	0.21186	1.90	0.97128
−3.45	0.00028	−0.75	0.22663	1.95	0.97441
−3.40	0.00034	−0.70	0.24196	2.00	0.97725
−3.35	0.00040	−0.65	0.25785	2.05	0.97982
−3.30	0.00048	−0.60	0.27425	2.10	0.98214
−3.25	0.00058	−0.55	0.29116	2.15	0.98422
−3.20	0.00069	−0.50	0.30854	2.20	0.98610
−3.15	0.00082	−0.45	0.32636	2.25	0.98778
−3.10	0.00097	−0.40	0.34458	2.30	0.98928
−3.05	0.00114	−0.35	0.36317	2.35	0.99061
−3.00	0.00135	−0.30	0.38209	2.40	0.99180
−2.95	0.00159	−0.25	0.40129	2.45	0.99286
−2.90	0.00187	−0.20	0.42074	2.50	0.99379
−2.85	0.00219	−0.15	0.44038	2.55	0.99461
−2.80	0.00256	−0.10	0.46017	2.60	0.99534
−2.75	0.00298	−0.05	0.48006	2.65	0.99598
−2.70	0.00347	0.00	0.50000	2.70	0.99653
−2.65	0.00402	0.05	0.51994	2.75	0.99702
−2.60	0.00466	0.10	0.53983	2.80	0.99744
−2.55	0.00539	0.15	0.55962	2.85	0.99781
−2.50	0.00621	0.20	0.57926	2.90	0.99813
−2.45	0.00714	0.25	0.59871	2.95	0.99841
−2.40	0.00820	0.30	0.61791	3.00	0.99865
−2.35	0.00939	0.35	0.63683	3.05	0.99886
−2.30	0.01072	0.40	0.65542	3.10	0.99903
−2.25	0.01222	0.45	0.67364	3.15	0.99918
−2.20	0.01390	0.50	0.69146	3.20	0.99931
−2.15	0.01578	0.55	0.70884	3.25	0.99942
−2.10	0.01786	0.60	0.72575	3.30	0.99952
−2.05	0.02018	0.65	0.74215	3.35	0.99960
−2.00	0.02275	0.70	0.75804	3.40	0.99966
−1.95	0.02559	0.75	0.77337	3.45	0.99972
−1.90	0.02872	0.80	0.78814	3.50	0.99977
−1.85	0.03216	0.85	0.80234	3.55	0.99981
−1.80	0.03593	0.90	0.81594	3.60	0.99984
−1.75	0.04006	0.95	0.82894	3.65	0.99987
−1.70	0.04457	1.00	0.84134	3.70	0.99989
−1.65	0.04947	1.05	0.85314	3.75	0.99991
−1.60	0.05480	1.10	0.86433	3.80	0.99993
−1.55	0.06057	1.15	0.87493	3.85	0.99994
−1.50	0.06681	1.20	0.88493	3.90	0.99995
−1.45	0.07353	1.25	0.89435	3.95	0.99996
−1.40	0.08076	1.30	0.90320	4.00	0.99997
−1.35	0.08851	1.35	0.91149		

Source: Bernard Ostle, *Statistics in Research*, 2d ed. (Ames: Iowa State University Press, 1967).

Appendix F

Negative Exponential Distribution: Values of e^{-x}

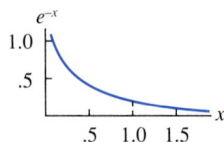

x	e^{-x} (value)	x	e^{-x} (value)	x	e^{-x} (value)	x	e^{-x} (value)
0.00	1.00000	0.50	0.60653	1.00	0.36788	1.50	0.22313
0.01	0.99005	0.51	.60050	1.01	.36422	1.51	.22091
0.02	.98020	0.52	.59452	1.02	.36060	1.52	.21871
0.03	.97045	0.53	.58860	1.03	.35701	1.53	.21654
0.04	.96079	0.54	.58275	1.04	.35345	1.54	.21438
0.05	.95123	0.55	.57695	1.05	.34994	1.55	.21225
0.06	.94176	0.56	.57121	1.06	.34646	1.56	.21014
0.07	.93239	0.57	.56553	1.07	.34301	1.57	.20805
0.08	.92312	0.58	.55990	1.08	.33960	1.58	.20598
0.09	.91393	0.59	.55433	1.09	.33622	1.59	.20393
0.10	.90484	0.60	.54881	1.10	.33287	1.60	.20190
0.11	.89583	0.61	.54335	1.11	.32956	1.61	.19989
0.12	.88692	0.62	.53794	1.12	.32628	1.62	.19790
0.13	.87809	0.63	.53259	1.13	.32303	1.63	.19593
0.14	.86936	0.64	.52729	1.14	.31982	1.64	.19398
0.15	.86071	0.65	.52205	1.15	.31664	1.65	.19205
0.16	.87514	0.66	.51685	1.16	.31349	1.66	.19014
0.17	.84366	0.67	.51171	1.17	.31037	1.67	.18825
0.18	.83527	0.68	.50662	1.18	.30728	1.68	.18637
0.19	.82696	0.69	.50158	1.19	.30422	1.69	.18452
0.20	.81873	0.70	.49659	1.20	.30119	1.70	.18268
0.21	.81058	0.71	.49164	1.21	.29820	1.71	.18087
0.22	.80252	0.72	.48675	1.22	.29523	1.72	.17907
0.23	.79453	0.73	.48191	1.23	.29229	1.73	.17728
0.24	.78663	0.74	.47711	1.24	.28938	1.74	.17552
0.25	.77880	0.75	.47237	1.25	.28650	1.75	.17377
0.26	.77105	0.76	.46767	1.26	.28365	1.76	.17204
0.27	.76338	0.77	.46301	1.27	.28083	1.77	.17033
0.28	.75578	0.78	.45841	1.28	.27804	1.78	.16864
0.29	.74826	0.79	.45384	1.29	.27527	1.79	.16696
0.30	.74082	0.80	.44933	1.30	.27253	1.80	.16530
0.31	.73345	0.81	.44486	1.31	.26982	1.81	.16365
0.32	.72615	0.82	.44043	1.32	.26714	1.82	.16203
0.33	.71892	0.83	.43605	1.33	.26448	1.83	.16041
0.34	.71177	0.84	.43171	1.34	.26185	1.84	.15882
0.35	.70469	0.85	.42741	1.35	.25924	1.85	.15724
0.36	.69768	0.86	.42316	1.36	.25666	1.86	.15567
0.37	.69073	0.87	.41895	1.37	.25411	1.87	.15412
0.38	.68386	0.88	.41478	1.38	.25158	1.88	.15259
0.39	.67706	0.89	.41066	1.39	.24908	1.89	.15107
0.40	.67032	0.90	.40657	1.40	.24660	1.90	.14957
0.41	.66365	0.91	.40252	1.41	.24414	1.91	.14808
0.42	.65705	0.92	.39852	1.42	.24171	1.92	.14661
0.43	.65051	0.93	.39455	1.43	.23931	1.93	.14515
0.44	.64404	0.94	.39063	1.44	.23693	1.94	.14370
0.45	.63763	0.95	.38674	1.45	.23457	1.95	.14227
0.46	.63128	0.96	.38289	1.46	.23224	1.96	.14086
0.47	.62500	0.97	.37908	1.47	.22993	1.97	.13946
0.48	.61878	0.98	.37531	1.48	.22764	1.98	.13807
0.49	.61263	0.99	.37158	1.49	.22537	1.99	.13670
0.50	.60653	1.00	.36788	1.50	.22313	2.00	.13534

Interest Tables

T A B L E G . 1 Compound Sum of $1

Year	1%	2%	3%	4%	5%	6%	7%	8%	9%
1	1.010	1.020	1.030	1.040	1.050	1.060	1.070	1.080	1.090
2	1.020	1.040	1.061	1.082	1.102	1.124	1.145	1.166	1.188
3	1.030	1.061	1.093	1.125	1.158	1.191	1.225	1.260	1.295
4	1.041	1.082	1.126	1.170	1.216	1.262	1.311	1.360	1.412
5	1.051	1.104	1.159	1.217	1.276	1.338	1.403	1.469	1.539
6	1.062	1.126	1.194	1.265	1.340	1.419	1.501	1.587	1.677
7	1.072	1.149	1.230	1.316	1.407	1.504	1.606	1.714	1.828
8	1.083	1.172	1.267	1.369	1.477	1.594	1.718	1.851	1.993
9	1.094	1.195	1.305	1.423	1.551	1.689	1.838	1.999	2.172
10	1.105	1.219	1.344	1.480	1.629	1.791	1.967	2.159	2.367
11	1.116	1.243	1.384	1.539	1.710	1.898	2.105	2.332	2.580
12	1.127	1.268	1.426	1.601	1.796	2.012	2.252	2.518	2.813
13	1.138	1.294	1.469	1.665	1.886	2.133	2.410	2.720	3.066
14	1.149	1.319	1.513	1.732	1.980	2.261	2.579	2.937	3.342
15	1.161	1.346	1.558	1.801	2.079	2.397	2.759	3.172	3.642
16	1.173	1.373	1.605	1.873	2.183	2.540	2.952	3.426	3.970
17	1.184	1.400	1.653	1.948	2.292	2.693	3.159	3.700	4.328
18	1.196	1.428	1.702	2.026	2.407	2.854	3.380	3.996	4.717
19	1.208	1.457	1.754	2.107	2.527	3.026	3.617	4.316	5.142
20	1.220	1.486	1.806	2.191	2.653	3.207	3.870	4.661	5.604
25	1.282	1.641	2.094	2.666	3.386	4.292	5.427	6.848	8.623
30	1.348	1.811	2.427	3.243	4.322	5.743	7.612	10.063	13.268

Year	10%	12%	14%	15%	16%	18%	20%	24%	28%
1	1.100	1.120	1.140	1.150	1.160	1.180	1.200	1.240	1.280
2	1.210	1.254	1.300	1.322	1.346	1.392	1.440	1.538	1.638
3	1.331	1.405	1.482	1.521	1.561	1.643	1.728	1.907	2.067
4	1.464	1.574	1.689	1.749	1.811	1.939	2.074	2.364	2.684
5	1.611	1.762	1.925	2.011	2.100	2.288	2.488	2.932	3.436
6	1.772	1.974	2.195	2.313	2.436	2.700	2.986	3.635	4.398
7	1.949	2.211	2.502	2.660	2.826	3.185	3.583	4.508	5.629
8	2.144	2.476	2.853	3.059	3.278	3.759	4.300	5.590	7.206
9	2.358	2.773	3.252	3.518	3.803	4.435	5.160	6.931	9.223
10	2.594	3.106	3.707	4.046	4.411	5.234	6.192	8.594	11.806
11	2.853	3.479	4.226	4.652	5.117	6.176	7.430	10.657	15.112
12	3.138	3.896	4.818	5.350	5.936	7.288	8.916	13.215	19.343
13	3.452	4.363	5.492	6.153	6.886	8.599	10.699	16.386	24.759
14	3.797	4.887	6.261	7.076	7.988	10.147	12.839	20.319	31.691
15	4.177	5.474	7.138	8.137	9.266	11.974	15.407	25.196	40.565
16	4.595	6.130	8.137	9.358	10.748	14.129	18.488	31.243	51.923
17	5.054	6.866	9.276	10.761	12.468	16.672	22.186	38.741	66.461
18	5.560	7.690	10.575	12.375	14.463	19.673	26.623	48.039	85.071
19	6.116	8.613	12.056	14.232	16.777	23.214	31.948	59.568	108.89
20	6.728	9.646	13.743	16.367	19.461	27.393	38.338	73.864	139.38
25	10.835	17.000	26.462	32.919	40.874	62.669	95.396	216.542	478.90
30	17.449	29.960	50.950	66.212	85.850	143.371	237.376	634.820	1645.5

T A B L E   G . 2   Sum of an Annuity of $1 for N Years

Year	1%	2%	3%	4%	5%	6%	7%	8%
1	1.000	1.000	1.000	1.000	1.000	1.000	1.000	1.000
2	2.010	2.020	2.030	2.040	2.050	2.060	2.070	2.080
3	2.030	3.060	3.091	3.122	3.152	3.184	3.215	3.246
4	4.060	4.122	4.184	4.246	4.310	4.375	4.440	4.506
5	5.101	5.204	5.309	5.416	5.526	5.637	5.751	5.867
6	6.152	6.308	6.468	6.633	6.802	6.975	7.153	7.336
7	7.214	7.434	7.662	7.898	8.142	8.394	8.654	8.923
8	8.286	8.583	8.892	9.214	9.549	9.897	10.260	10.637
9	9.369	9.755	10.159	10.583	11.027	11.491	11.978	12.488
10	10.462	10.950	11.464	12.006	12.578	13.181	13.816	14.487
11	11.567	12.169	12.808	13.486	14.207	14.972	15.784	16.645
12	12.683	13.412	14.192	15.026	15.917	16.870	17.888	18.977
13	13.809	14.680	15.618	16.627	17.713	18.882	20.141	21.495
14	14.947	15.974	17.086	18.292	19.599	21.051	22.550	24.215
15	16.097	17.293	18.599	20.024	21.579	23.276	25.129	27.152
16	17.258	18.639	20.157	21.825	23.657	25.673	27.888	30.324
17	18.430	20.012	21.762	23.698	25.840	28.213	30.840	33.750
18	19.615	21.412	23.414	25.645	28.132	30.906	33.999	37.450
19	20.811	22.841	25.117	27.671	30.539	33.760	37.379	41.446
20	22.019	24.297	26.870	29.778	33.066	36.786	40.995	45.762
25	28.243	32.030	36.459	41.646	47.727	54.865	63.249	73.106
30	34.785	40.568	47.575	56.085	66.439	79.058	94.461	113.283

Year	9%	10%	12%	14%	16%	18%	20%	24%
1	1.000	1.000	1.000	1.000	1.000	1.000	1.000	1.000
2	2.090	2.100	2.120	2.140	2.160	2.180	2.200	2.240
3	3.278	3.310	3.374	3.440	3.506	3.572	3.640	3.778
4	4.573	4.641	4.770	4.921	5.066	5.215	5.368	5.684
5	5.985	6.105	6.353	6.610	6.877	7.154	7.442	8.048
6	7.523	7.716	8.115	8.536	8.977	9.442	9.930	10.980
7	9.200	9.487	10.089	10.730	11.414	12.142	12.916	14.615
8	11.028	11.436	12.300	13.233	14.240	15.327	16.499	19.123
9	13.021	13.579	14.776	16.085	17.518	19.086	20.799	24.712
10	15.193	15.937	17.549	19.337	21.321	23.521	25.959	31.643
11	17.560	18.531	20.655	23.044	25.733	28.755	32.150	40.238
12	20.141	21.384	24.133	27.271	30.850	34.931	39.580	50.985
13	22.953	24.523	28.029	32.089	36.786	42.219	48.497	64.110
14	26.019	27.975	32.393	37.581	43.672	50.818	59.196	80.496
15	29.361	31.772	37.280	43.842	51.660	60.965	72.035	100.815
16	33.003	35.950	42.753	50.980	60.925	72.939	87.442	126.011
17	36.974	40.545	48.884	59.118	71.673	87.068	105.931	157.253
18	41.301	45.599	55.750	68.394	84.141	103.740	128.117	195.994
19	46.018	51.159	63.440	78.969	98.603	123.414	154.740	244.033
20	51.160	57.275	72.052	91.025	115.380	146.628	186.688	303.601
25	84.701	93.347	133.334	181.871	249.214	342.603	471.981	898.092
30	136.308	164.494	241.333	356.787	530.312	790.948	1181.882	2640.916

T A B L E   G . 3   Present Value of $1

Year	1%	2%	3%	4%	5%	6%	7%	8%	9%	10%	12%	14%	15%
1	.990	.980	.971	.962	.952	.943	.935	.926	.917	.909	.893	.877	.870
2	.980	.961	.943	.925	.907	.890	.873	.857	.842	.826	.797	.769	.756
3	.971	.942	.915	.889	.864	.840	.816	.794	.772	.751	.712	.675	.658
4	.961	.924	.889	.855	.823	.792	.763	.735	.708	.683	.636	.592	.572
5	.951	.906	.863	.822	.784	.747	.713	.681	.650	.621	.567	.519	.497
6	.942	.888	.838	.790	.746	.705	.666	.630	.596	.564	.507	.456	.432
7	.933	.871	.813	.760	.711	.665	.623	.583	.547	.513	.452	.400	.376
8	.923	.853	.789	.731	.677	.627	.582	.540	.502	.467	.404	.351	.327
9	.914	.837	.766	.703	.645	.592	.544	.500	.460	.424	.361	.308	.284
10	.905	.820	.744	.676	.614	.558	.508	.463	.422	.386	.322	.270	.247
11	.896	.804	.722	.650	.585	.527	.475	.429	.388	.350	.287	.237	.215
12	.887	.788	.701	.625	.557	.497	.444	.397	.356	.319	.257	.208	.187
13	.879	.773	.681	.601	.530	.469	.415	.368	.326	.290	.229	.182	.163
14	.870	.758	.661	.577	.505	.442	.388	.340	.299	.263	.205	.160	.141
15	.861	.743	.642	.555	.481	.417	.362	.315	.275	.239	.183	.140	.123
16	.853	.728	.623	.534	.458	.394	.339	.292	.252	.218	.163	.123	.107
17	.844	.714	.605	.513	.436	.371	.317	.270	.231	.198	.146	.108	.093
18	.836	.700	.587	.494	.416	.350	.296	.250	.212	.180	.130	.095	.081
19	.828	.686	.570	.475	.396	.331	.276	.232	.194	.164	.116	.083	.070
20	.820	.673	.554	.456	.377	.312	.258	.215	.178	.149	.104	.073	.061
25	.780	.610	.478	.375	.295	.233	.184	.146	.116	.092	.059	.038	.030
30	.742	.552	.412	.308	.231	.174	.131	.099	.075	.057	.033	.020	.015

Year	16%	18%	20%	24%	28%	32%	36%	40%	50%	60%	70%	80%	90%
1	.862	.847	.833	.806	.781	.758	.735	.714	.667	.625	.588	.556	.526
2	.743	.718	.694	.650	.610	.574	.541	.510	.444	.391	.346	.309	.277
3	.641	.609	.579	.524	.477	.435	.398	.364	.296	.244	.204	.171	.146
4	.552	.516	.482	.423	.373	.329	.292	.260	.198	.153	.120	.095	.077
5	.476	.437	.402	.341	.291	.250	.215	.186	.132	.095	.070	.053	.040
6	.410	.370	.335	.275	.227	.189	.158	.133	.088	.060	.041	.029	.021
7	.354	.314	.279	.222	.178	.143	.116	.095	.059	.037	.024	.016	.011
8	.305	.266	.233	.179	.139	.108	.085	.068	.039	.023	.014	.009	.006
9	.263	.226	.194	.144	.108	.082	.063	.048	.026	.015	.008	.005	.003
10	.227	.191	.162	.116	.085	.062	.046	.035	.017	.009	.005	.003	.002
11	.195	.162	.135	.094	.066	.047	.034	.025	.012	.006	.003	.002	.001
12	.168	.137	.112	.076	.052	.036	.025	.018	.008	.004	.002	.001	.001
13	.145	.116	.093	.061	.040	.027	.018	.013	.005	.002	.001	.001	.000
14	.125	.099	.078	.049	.032	.021	.014	.009	.003	.001	.001	.000	.000
15	.108	.084	.065	.040	.025	.016	.010	.006	.002	.001	.000	.000	.000
16	.093	.071	.054	.032	.019	.012	.007	.005	.002	.001	.000	.000	
17	.080	.060	.045	.026	.015	.009	.005	.003	.001	.000	.000		
18	.069	.051	.038	.021	.012	.007	.004	.002	.001	.000	.000		
19	.060	.043	.031	.017	.009	.005	.003	.002	.000	.000			
20	.051	.037	.026	.014	.007	.004	.002	.001	.000	.000			
25	.024	.016	.010	.005	.002	.001	.000	.000					
30	.012	.007	.004	.002	.001	.000	.000						

TABLE G.4 Present Value of an Annuity of $1

Year	1%	2%	3%	4%	5%	6%	7%	8%	9%	10%
1	0.990	0.980	0.971	0.962	0.952	0.943	0.935	0.926	0.917	0.909
2	1.970	1.942	1.913	1.886	1.859	1.833	1.808	1.783	1.759	1.736
3	2.941	2.884	2.829	2.775	2.723	2.673	2.624	2.577	2.531	2.487
4	3.902	3.808	3.717	3.630	3.546	3.465	3.387	3.312	3.240	3.170
5	4.853	4.713	4.580	4.452	4.329	4.212	4.100	3.993	3.890	3.791
6	5.795	5.601	5.417	5.242	5.076	4.917	4.766	4.623	4.486	4.355
7	6.728	6.472	6.230	6.002	5.786	5.582	5.389	5.206	5.033	4.868
8	7.652	7.325	7.020	6.733	6.463	6.210	6.971	5.747	5.535	5.335
9	8.566	8.162	7.786	7.435	7.108	6.802	6.515	6.247	5.985	5.759
10	9.471	8.983	8.530	8.111	7.722	7.360	7.024	6.710	6.418	6.145
11	10.368	9.787	9.253	8.760	8.306	7.887	7.449	7.139	6.805	6.495
12	11.255	10.575	9.954	9.385	8.863	8.384	7.943	7.536	7.161	6.814
13	12.134	11.348	10.635	9.986	9.394	8.853	8.358	7.904	7.487	7.103
14	13.004	12.106	11.296	10.563	9.899	9.295	8.745	8.244	7.786	7.367
15	13.865	12.849	11.938	11.118	10.380	9.712	9.108	8.559	8.060	7.606
16	14.718	13.578	12.561	11.652	10.838	10.106	9.447	8.851	8.312	7.824
17	15.562	14.292	13.166	12.166	11.274	10.477	9.763	9.122	8.544	8.022
18	16.398	14.992	13.754	12.659	11.690	10.828	10.059	9.372	8.756	8.201
19	17.226	15.678	14.324	13.134	12.085	11.158	10.336	9.604	8.950	8.365
20	18.046	16.351	14.877	13.590	12.462	11.470	10.594	9.818	9.128	8.514
25	22.023	19.523	17.413	15.622	14.094	12.783	11.654	10.675	9.823	9.077
30	25.808	22.397	19.600	17.292	15.373	13.765	12.409	11.258	10.274	9.427

Year	12%	14%	16%	18%	20%	24%	28%	32%	36%
1	0.893	0.877	0.862	0.847	0.833	0.806	0.781	0.758	0.735
2	1.690	1.647	1.605	1.566	1.528	1.457	1.392	1.332	1.276
3	2.402	2.322	2.246	2.174	2.106	1.981	1.868	1.766	1.674
4	3.037	2.914	2.798	2.690	2.589	2.404	2.241	2.096	1.966
5	3.605	3.433	3.274	3.127	2.991	2.745	2.532	2.345	2.181
6	4.111	3.889	3.685	3.498	3.326	3.020	2.759	2.534	2.339
7	4.564	4.288	4.039	3.812	3.605	3.242	2.937	2.678	2.455
8	4.968	4.639	4.344	4.078	3.837	3.421	3.076	2.786	2.540
9	5.328	4.946	4.607	4.303	4.031	3.566	3.184	2.868	2.603
10	5.650	5.216	4.833	4.494	4.193	3.682	3.269	2.930	2.650
11	5.988	5.453	5.029	4.656	4.327	3.776	3.335	2.978	2.683
12	6.194	5.660	5.197	4.793	4.439	3.851	3.387	3.013	2.708
13	6.424	5.842	5.342	4.910	4.533	3.912	3.427	3.040	2.727
14	6.628	6.002	5.468	5.008	4.611	3.962	3.459	3.061	2.740
15	6.811	6.142	5.575	5.092	4.675	4.001	3.483	3.076	2.750
16	6.974	6.265	5.669	5.162	4.730	4.033	3.503	3.088	2.758
17	7.120	6.373	5.749	5.222	4.775	4.059	3.518	3.097	2.763
18	7.250	6.467	5.818	5.273	4.812	4.080	3.529	3.104	2.767
19	7.366	6.550	5.877	5.316	4.844	4.097	3.539	3.109	2.770
20	7.469	6.623	5.929	5.353	4.870	4.110	3.546	3.113	2.772
25	7.843	6.873	6.097	5.467	4.948	4.147	3.564	3.122	2.776
30	8.055	7.003	6.177	5.517	4.979	4.160	3.569	3.124	2.778

Appendix H

Answers to Selected Problems

Supplement 4

1. $\bar{t}_s = 4.125$ minutes
   $\bar{n}_l = 4.05$ cars
   $\bar{n}_s = 4.95$ cars

5. *a.* $L = .22$ waiting.
   b. $W = .466$ hours
   c. $D = .362$

9. *a.* 5 trucks.
   b. 20 minutes.
   c. 83.3%.
   d. 482.

13. *a.* 9.167 minutes.
    b. 9.091 people.
    c. 0.7513.
    d. 0.9091; 90.9% of the time.
    e. 4.167 minutes.

17. *a.* 4.167 people
    b. 1 hour.
    c. $1 - .422 = .578$.

Supplement 5

1. *a.* Not inspecting cost = $20/hr. Cost to
   inspect = $9/hr.
   Therefore, inspect.
   b. $.18 each.
   c. $.22 per unit.

5. Yes, inspecting is cheaper.

9. *a.* $n = 31.3$ (Round sample size n up).
   b. Random sample 32; reject if more than 8 are
   defective.

13. *a.* $2.73 per unit.
    b. Loss per unit will increase.
    c. $1.54 per unit

Chapter 7

3. *a.* February 84
   March 86
   April 90
   May 88
   June 84
   b. MAD = 15.

7.

Quarter	Forecast
9	232
10	281
11	239
12	231

11. *a.* April to September = 130, 150, 160, 170,
    160, 150
    b. April to September = 136, 146, 150, 159,
    153, 146
    c. Exponential smoothing performed better.

15. MAD = 104
    TS = 3.1
    Model is acceptable, but could be better.

19. *a.* MAD = 90
    TS = -1.67
    b. Model okay since tracking is -1.67.

23. *a.* 358.
    b. 325.
    c. $F_{\text{two months ago}} = 440$.
    $F_{\text{last month}} = 422$.
    $F_{\text{this month}} = 403$.

Chapter 8

3. No. Must consider demand in fourth year.

Supplement 8

1. Optimum combination is B = 10 and A = 15.

5. *a.*

	D	E	F	G
A	0	0	25	25
B	40	0	0	0
C	10	60	0	5
Total Cost = $1,000				

9. *a.* $x = 60$, $Y = 0$,
   $Z = 90$; $S_1 = 0$.
   $S_2 = 0$, $S_3 = 40$
   b.

	Would you buy?	At what price?	How many?
S_1	Yes	<2	15
S_2	Yes	<3	45
S_3	Yes	<0	∞

	Would you sell?	At what price?	How many?
S_1	Yes	>2	30
S_2	Yes	>3	20
S_3	Yes	>0	40

Chapter 9

1. $C_x = 176.7$
   $C_Y = 241.5$

Chapter 10

3. *a.* 27 seconds.
   b. 6 stations.
   c. 91.4%
   d. Work 45 minutes per day overtime.

7. *b.* 90 seconds.
   c. 4.55.
   d. 5 stations.
   e. 91%.
   f. Reduce cycle time to 85 seconds and work 17.6 minutes overtime.

Chapter 11

3. *a.* 1.35 minutes.
   b. 1.51 minutes.
   c. ST = 1.53 minutes. The worker would not make the bonus.

7. *a.* NT = .9286 min./part.
   b. ST = 1.0679 min./part.
   c. Daily output = 449.50.
      Day's wages = $44.49.

11. LR Labor, 80%
    LR Parts, 90%
    Labor = 11,556 hours
    Parts = $330,876.

15. 4,710 hours

19. *a.* 3rd = 35.1 hrs.
    b. Average = 7.9 hrs. each; well worth it.

Chapter 12

3. *b.* A-C-F-G-I and A-D-F-G-I
   c. C: 2 weeks;
      D: 2 weeks;
      G: 2 weeks.
   d. Three paths: A-B-E-I; A-C-F-G-I; and A-D-F-G-I; 14 weeks.

6. *a.* Critical path is A-E-G-C-D.
   b. 26 weeks.
   c. No difference in completion date.

Chapter 13

3. Total cost = $413,600.

6. 1. Ending inventory = safety stock.
   2. Inventory cost includes forecast and safety stock.

3. Shortage cost is only based on the forecast.
   Total cost = $413,750.

Chapter 14

3. $q = 179.148$

7. *a.* $Q = 1,225$
      $R = 824$.
   b. $q = 390 -$ Inventory on hand.

11. *a.* $Q = 89.44$
    b. $223.61
    c. $223.61

17. ~624

21. 7,500 blades

25. 208 boxes

29. 5,000 pounds

Chapter 15

3.

8. Least total cost method: Order 250 units in period one for periods 1-8;
   Least unit cost method: Order 450 units in period one for periods 1-9.

11. *c.* .A
    .B(2)
    .E(4)
    .F(3)
    .C(3)
    .D(3)
    .H(2)
    .E(5)
    .G(2)
    .D(1)

   d.

level 0	100 units of A
level 1	200 units of B
	300 units of C
level 2	600 units of F
	600 units of H
	1000 units of D
level 3	3800 units of E
	1200 units of G

Chapter 16

3. Job order 5, 6, 7, 3, 1, 2, 4

7. Critical ratio schedule: 5, 3, 2, 4, 1
   Earliest due date, job priority: 2, 5, 3, 4, 1.
   Shortest priority time (including delay time): 2, 1, 4, 3, 5.

Supplement 16

2. Average customer waiting time = ⅙ min.
Average teller idle time = ⁴⁄₆ min.

7. *a.*

		Condition 1	Condition 2
	1)	Idle 18 min	76 + 134 = 120 min.
	2)	Delay 87 min.	0 min.

b.

	Condition 1	Condition 2
Cost of repairman	$ 38.80	$ 77.20
Cost of machine down	175.33	117.33
	$214.13	$194.53

Chapter 19

1. Case I:
   X used = 9333.3 hours
   Y used = 700 hours

Case II:
   Y = 700 hrs.
   X = 933.3 hrs.
Case III:
   X = 933.3 hrs.
   Y = 700 hrs.
Case IV:
   X = 933.3 hrs.
   Y = 700 hrs.
Otherwise:
Case I: no problem.
Case II: Excess WIP.
Case III: Excess spare parts.
Case IV: Excess finished goods.

8. *a.* Machine B is the constraint.
   b. 100 product M, as many N as possible.
   c. $600

Name Index

Subject Index

PHOTO CREDITS

CHAPTER 1 *p. 6,* Courtesy Ben & Jerry's Homemade, Inc.; *p. 11,* Photo courtesy of Hewlett-Packard Company; *p. 17,* Louis Psihoyos/Matrix International, Inc.

CHAPTER 2 *p. 26,* Courtesy Federal Express; *p. 33,* Courtesy Citicorp; *p. 45,* Reprinted with permission of Compaq Computer Corporation. All Rights Reserved.

CHAPTER 3 *p. 54, 55,* Business Week, December 3, 1990, p. 135; *p. 61,* Courtesy the Boeing Company; *p. 62,* Courtesy Miller Brewing Company; *p. 72–73,* Ed Kashi © 1994.

SUPPLEMENT 3 *p. 80,* Courtesy McDonald's Corporation; *p. 82,* Courtesy Xerox Corporation; *p. 84,* Courtesy Ford Motor Company; *p. 94,* Courtesy Federal Express; *p. 98,* Courtesy Motorola.

CHAPTER 4 *p. 110,* Courtesy Marriott corporation; *p. 116,* Tass/Sovfoto; *p. 120,* Richard Chase.

SUPPLEMENT 4 *p. 139,* David Ball/Tony Stone Images.

CHAPTER 5 *p. 165,* Photograph courtesy of the National Institute of Standards & Technology, Office of Quality Programs, Gaithersburg, Maryland, 20899. Photograph by Steuben; *p. 172,* Courtesy Westinghouse Electric Corporation; *p. 172,* Courtesy Milliken & Company, Inc., *p. 186,* Mark Davis.

SUPPLEMENT 5 *p. 212,* Courtesy Hershey Foods Corporation; *p. 221,* Courtesy Motorola.

CHAPTER 6 *p. 239,* Courtesy Saturn Corporation; *p. 244,* Courtesy Bernard Welding Equipment Company; *p. 244,* Courtesy McDonnell-Douglas; *p. 253,* Courtesy Ryder System, Inc.

CHAPTER 7 *p. 264,* Donna Cox, Robert Patterson/NCSA, University of Illinois.

CHAPTER 8 *p. 323,* Courtesy Xerox Corporation; *p. 338,* Courtesy Shouldice Hospital.

CHAPTER 9 *p. 376,* Courtesy Archer Daniels Midland Company; *p. 377,* Courtesy Toys "R" Us, Inc.

CHAPTER 10 *p. 406,* Courtesy Cimtechnologies Corporation; *p. 410,* Photo courtesy of Hewlett-Packard Company; *p. 418–419,* Courtesy Bachman Design Group.

CHAPTER 11 *p. 437,* Courtesy Ford Motor Company; *p. 468,* Courtesy the University of Chicago.

CHAPTER 12 *p. 490,* Courtesy the Boeing Company.

CHAPTER 13 *p. 517,* Courtesy Kawasaki Motors Manufacturing Corp., U.S.A.

CHAPTER 14 *p. 547,* Courtesy Bernard Welding Equipment Company; *p. 548,* Courtesy Navistar International Transportation Corp.; *p. 573,* Photo courtesy of Hewlett-Packard Company.

CHAPTER 15 *p. 595,* Photo courtesy Allen-Bradley, a Rockwell International Company.

CHAPTER 16 *p. 636,* Courtesy Bernard Welding Equipment Company.

SUPPLEMENT 16 *p. 681,* Courtesy Systems Modeling Corporation; *p. 683,* Courtesy Micro Analysis & Design Simulation Software, Inc.

CHAPTER 17 *p. 700,* Reprinted with permission of Compaq Computer Corporation. All Rights Reserved; *p. 730,* Mark Davis.

CHAPTER 18 *p. 738,* Courtesy GTE Corporation.